HANDBOOK
OF
CRIMINOLOGY

Contributors

Stuart Adams, *American University*
M. Cherif Bassiouni, *DePaul University*
William J. Chambliss, *University of California, Santa Barbara*
John P. Clark, *University of Minnesota*
Charles W. Dean, *University of Hartford*
Robert M. Emerson, *University of California, Los Angeles*
LaMar T. Empey, *University of Southern California*
Franco Ferracuti, *University of Rome*
John H. Gagnon, *State University of New York, Stony Brook*
Gilbert Geis, *University of California, Irvine*
Daniel Glaser, *University of Southern California*
William H. Hewitt, *Mansfield State College*
James A. Inciardi, *University of Miami*
John Irwin, *San Francisco State University*
John M. McKee, *Rehabilitation Research Foundation*
Hans W. Mattick, *University of Illinois, Chicago Circle*
Michael A. Milan, *Rehabilitation Research Foundation*
H. G. Moeller, *East Carolina University*
Donald J. Newman, *State University of New York, Albany*
Graeme Newman, *State University of New York, Albany*
Lloyd E. Ohlin, *Harvard University*
Vincent O'Leary, *State University of New York, Albany*
Brian Parker, *California State University, Sacramento*
Llad Phillips, *University of California, Santa Barbara*
David J. Pittman, *Washington University*
Albert J. Reiss, Jr., *Yale University*
N. Dickon Reppucci, *Yale University*
Loren H. Roth, *National Institute of Mental Health*
Clarence Schrag, *University of Washington*
Robert B. Seidman, *University of Wisconsin*
Saleem A. Shah, *National Institute of Mental Health*
James F. Short, Jr., *Washington State University*
Richard E. Sykes, *University of Minnesota*
Jackson Toby, *Rutgers University*
Harold L. Votey, Jr., *University of California, Santa Barbara*
John A. Wallace, *Office of Probation, New York City*
Billy L. Wayson, *U.S. Bureau of Prisons*

HV 6028
. G5
1974

HANDBOOK
OF
CRIMINOLOGY

Edited by
Daniel Glaser
University of Southern California

Rand McNally College Publishing Company · Chicago

RAND McNALLY HANDBOOK SERIES

INDIANA
PURDUE
LIBRARY
OCT 26 1977
FORT WAYNE

WITHDRAWN

Handbook of Personality Theory and Research
Edgar F. Borgatta and William W. Lambert, Eds.

Handbook of Marriage and the Family
Harold T. Christensen, Ed.

Handbook of Criminology
Daniel Glaser, Ed.

Handbook of Socialization Theory and Research
David A. Goslin, Ed.

Handbook of Social and Cultural Anthropology
John J. Honigmann, Ed.

Handbook of Organizations
James G. March, Ed.

Handbook of Communication
Ithiel de Sola Pool, Wilbur Schramm,
Frederick W. Frey, Nathan Maccoby,
and Edwin B. Parker, Eds.

Handbook on the Study of Social Problems
Erwin O. Smigel, Ed.

Second Handbook of Research on Teaching
Robert M. W. Travers, Ed.

Current printing (last digit)
15 14 13 12 11 10 9 8 7 6 5 4 3 2 1

Copyright © 1974 by Rand McNally College Publishing Company
All rights reserved
Printed in U.S.A.
Library of Congress Catalog Card Number 74–241

Preface

The objective of this book is to present the most comprehensive and authoritative statement possible on all aspects of criminology. Such a goal, of course, is never fully attained, but the striving for it accounts for this book's features. A wide range of topics and points of view are represented in diverse styles by many authors, but all are concerned with basic principles and with scientific evidence.

Most of the contributors to this volume became criminologists after academic specialization in sociology, but psychology, law, and medicine each have several representatives, and there also is some reflection of other disciplines. Most of the writers are university professors, but several are administrators of criminal justice agencies, an appreciable proportion have had careers in both of these occupations, and a few are employed purely in research. One is an ex-prisoner now a professor and spokesman for the offender's view. It is presumed that such a mixture makes this book both practical and theoretically sophisticated.

While these writings are sometimes quite technical, all chapters are believed to be comprehensible to the nonspecialist. Introductions to the major sections are designed to orient readers to the concerns of the separate chapters.

I am grateful to the chapter authors, from whom I learned much, and to my wife, Pearl, for assistance in the many tasks which this publication required.

Daniel Glaser

Acknowledgments

Acknowledgment is made to the following for their kind permission to reprint material from copyrighted sources:

Chapter 1

The Macmillan Company for Emile Durkheim, *The Division of Labor in Society*, translated by George Simpson, Copyright 1947, The Free Press; the University of Pennsylvania Law Review and Fred B. Rothman & Company for Caleb Foote, "Vagrancy-type Law and Its Administration," *University of Pennsylvania Law Review* 104: 603–650 (1956), © 1956 by the University of Pennsylvania Law Review; The Bobbs-Merrill Company, Inc. for Jerome Hall, *Theft, Law and Society*, second edition, copyright 1935 and 1952, by The Bobbs-Merrill Company, Inc., reprinted by permission, all rights reserved; The Society for the Study of Social Problems for Pamela A. Roby, "Politics and Criminal Law: Revision of the New York State Penal Law on Prostitution," *Social Problems*, Vol. 17, No. 1, 1969.

Chapter 2

Holt, Rinehart and Winston, Inc., for Marshall B. Clinard and Richard Quinney, *Criminal Behavior Systems*, second edition, 1973.

Chapter 4

American Journal of Medicine and Dr. Paul D. MacLean, "Contrasting Functions of Limbic and Neocortical Systems of the Brain and Their Relevance to Psychophysiological Aspects of Medicine," *American Journal of Medicine*, Vol. 25(1958), p. 615; Associated Book Publishers (International) Ltd. for M. E. Wolfgang and F. Ferracuti, *The Subculture of Violence*, 1967, Methuen & Co. Ltd, publishers.

Chapter 5

Institute of Human Relations Press for Marvin Wolfgang, *Crime and Race*, copyright the American Jewish Committee 1964, all rights reserved; Associated Book Publishers Ltd. for M. E. Wolfgang and F. Ferracuti, *The Subculture of Violence*, 1967, Methuen & Co. Ltd., publishers.

Chapter 8

Prentice-Hall, Inc. for *Nader: The People's Lawyer*, by Robert F. Buckhorn, © 1972 by Robert F. Buckhorn, reprinted with permission of the publisher; The Macmillan Company for Mary O. Cameron, *The Booster and the Snitch*, Copyright 1964 The Free Press of Glencoe, a Division of The Macmillan Co., Inc.; Sweet & Maxwell Ltd. for A. E. Cox, "Shoplifting," *Criminal Law Review 1968*, p. 425; Los Angeles Times for "Morganthau Deplores Attitudes on Crime," by Robert Dallos, *Los Angeles Times*, June 27, 1969; Holt, Rinehart and Winston, Inc. for Gilbert Geis, "The Heavy Electrical Equipment Antitrust Cases of 1961," in M. B. Clinard and R. Quinney, *Criminal Behavior Systems*, 1967, and E. H. Sutherland, *White Collar Crime*, 1949.

Chapter 9

The Macmillan Company for Howard S. Becker, *Outsiders: Studies in the Sociology of Deviance*, Copyright © 1963 The Free Press, a Division of Macmillan Publishing Co., Inc.; Holt, Rinehart and Winston, Inc. for Marshall B. Clinard and Richard Quinney, *Criminal Behavior Systems*, second edition, 1973; Reader's Digest for "The Big Business of Hijacking," by Bill Surface, *Reader's Digest*, January, 1968.

Chapter 10

The Associated Press for Ann Blackman, "Street Gangs Go Conservative," *Spokane Daily Chronicle*, November 22, 1971; Rand McNally & Company for Ralph H. Turner, "Collective Behavior," in Robert E. L. Faris (ed.), *Handbook of Modern Sociology*, © 1964 by Rand McNally & Co., p. 390; The Society for the Study of Social Problems for Harold Finestone, "Cats, Kicks, and Color," *Social Problems*, Vol. 5, No. 1, 1957, and Harold W. Pfautz, "Near-Group Theory and Collective Behavior: A Critical Reformulation," *Social Problems*, Vol. 9, No. 2, 1961; Holt, Rinehart and Winston, Inc. for *The Vice Lords: Warriors of the Streets*, by R. L. Keiser, 1969; Harper & Row, Publishers, Inc. for A. M. Lee (ed.), *New Outline of Principles of Sociology*, third edition, © 1969 Barnes & Noble; Harcourt Brace Jovanovich, Inc. for "Crime and Juvenile Delinquency," by A. K. Cohen and J. F. Short, Jr., in *Contemporary Social Problems*, third edition, by Robert K. Merton and Robert Nisbet, 1971; The American Academy of Political and Social Science for H. L. Neiburg, "Agnostics—Rituals of Conflict," *The Annals*, September, 1970; Harper & Row for S. Kobrin and H. Finestone, "Drug Addiction among Young Persons in Chicago," in James F. Short, Jr., (ed.), *Gang Delinquency and Delinquent Subcultures*, 1968; The University of Chicago Press for J. F. Short, Jr. and F. L. Strodtbeck, *Group Process and Gang Delinquency*, © 1965 The University of Chicago; The Macmillan Company for "Fashion," by Herbert Blumer in *The International Encyclopedia of the Social Sciences*, vol. 5, and "Collective Behavior," by Kurt Lang and Gladys E. Lang, in *The International Encyclopedia of the Social Sciences*, vol. 2, David L. Sills, Editor-in-Chief, Copyright 1968 by Crowell-Collier and Macmillan, Inc.

Chapter 14

Charles C Thomas, Publisher for M. Cherif Bassiouni, *Criminal Law and Its Processes*, 1969, courtesy of Charles C Thomas; The Foundation Press, Inc. for Harold J. Berman, *The Nature and Functions of Law*, 1958; Harvard University Press for Harold J. Berman, *Soviet Criminal Law and Procedure: The RSFSR Codes*, 1966; Harvard Law Review for Note, "Developments in the Law: Confessions," *Harvard Law Review* 79 (March):935, copyright 1966 by The Harvard Law Review Association.

Chapter 17

Harvard Law Review for Thurman Arnold, "Professor Hart's Theology," *Harvard Law Review* 73(May):1298, copyright 1960 by The Harvard Law Review Association; Wisconsin Law Review for Lawrence Friedman, "On Legalistic Reasoning—A Footnote to Weber," *Wisconsin Law Review* 1966(Winter):148; George Allen & Unwin Ltd. and Viking Press for *The State in Theory and Practice*, by Harold J. Laski, copyright 1935 by Harold J. Laski, copyright © renewed 1963 by Frida Laski, reprinted by permission of The Viking Press, Inc.; Wayne State University Press for "The Justices of the Supreme Court: A Collective Portrait," by J. A. Schmidhauser, *Midwest Journal of Political Science* 3(1), 1959, © 1959 by Wayne State University Press, reprinted by permission.

Chapter 19

The Macmillan Company for Howard S. Becker, *Outsiders: Studies in the Sociology of Deviance*, Copyright © 1963, The Free Press, a Division of Macmillan Publishing Co., Inc., and Robert K. Merton, *Social Theory and Social Structure*, revised edition, © Copyright The Free Press 1957.

Chapter 20

Pergamon Publishing Company for Daniel G. Brown, "Behavior Analysis and Intervention in Counseling and Psychotherapy," in H. C. Rickard (ed.), *Behavioral Intervention in Human Problems*, © 1971 Pergamon Press, Inc.

Chapter 23

Lexington Books, D. C. Heath and Company for *Halfway Houses: Community-Centered Correction and Treatment*, by Oliver J. Keller, Jr. and Benedict S. Alper (Lexington, Mass.: Lexington Books, D. C. Heath and Company, 1970).

Chapter 27

Northwestern University School of Law for Francis A. Allen, "Criminal Justice, Legal Values and the Rehabilitative Ideal," *Journal of Criminal Law, Criminology and Police Science* Vol. 50, No. 3 (Sept.–Oct.), 1959; American Correctional Association for "Declaration of Principles of the American Correctional Association" in the 1970 edition of the *Manual of Correctional Standards*.

Chapter 31

The Macmillan Company for Howard S. Becker, *Outsiders: Studies in the Sociology of Deviance*, Copyright © 1963 The Free Press, a Division of Macmillan Publishing Co., Inc.; International Association of Chiefs of Police, Inc. for Robert M. Carter and G. Thomas Gitchoff, "An Alternative to Youthful Mass Disorder," *The Police Chief*, July, 1970; The Society for the Study of Social Problems for Kai T. Erikson, "Notes on the Sociology of Deviants," *Social Problems*, Vol. 9, No. 4, 1962; Sage Publications, Inc. for Jack P. Gibbs, "Conceptions of Deviant Behavior: The Old and the New," *Pacific Sociological Review*, Vol. 9, No. 2 (Spring 1966), pp. 9–14, by permission of the publisher; The University of Chicago Press for J. F. Short, Jr. and F. L. Strodtbeck, *Group Process and Gang Delinquency*, © 1965 The University of Chicago.

Table of Contents

PART I

EXPLANATIONS FOR CRIME AND DELINQUENCY: THEORY AND EVIDENCE

Introduction—Part I

The first requirements for coping with crime are an awareness of its dimensions and an understanding of its causes. These are highly related concerns, for crime is far from a homogeneous phenomenon, and, therefore, any explanations for it must account for its variations.

This explanatory task begins with the question addressed by our opening chapter: How and why do specific kinds of behavior come to be defined as crime? Sociologist of law William J. Chambliss reviews a variety of alternative causal theories and tests them by tracing emergence or change in Anglo-American statutes on such diverse offenses as vagrancy, theft, narcotics, prostitution, and organization of a trust in restraint of trade. Chambliss finds intergroup conflicts in all legal change, with the outcome of these conflicts determined by one or more factors, such as economic power, expansionist orientations of enforcement bureaucracies, and mobilization of bias by established status groups against the flaunting of their standards of morality. No single explanation accounts for the outcome of all such conflicts, but economic elites have most consistently had a predominant influence.

Our second chapter, by the editor, points out that the way in which offenses or offenders are classified depends upon the classifier's purpose, and discusses some approaches to three objectives in classification: adjudication, enumeration, and explanation. It deals first with the ascription of responsibility on the basis of age, sanity, and intelligence, the confounding of these matters in practice, and the adjudicative codification of crime. Enumeration is seen as dependent on whether a crime elicits complaints from victims, disturbs an audience, or occurs in private transactions, and these aspects also strongly affect the possibility of an offense being effectively controlled by the state. The dependence of scientific explanation on both idealized and empirical typologies, and on interaction between them, is stressed. While several resulting explanatory classifications are summarized, the tendency of science to progress from typologies to dimensions is pointed out, and is illustrated by the individual-collective, instrumental-expressive, and career-situational explanatory dimensions of crime.

In Chapter 3, sociologist Jackson Toby finds three main pathologies of socialization explain the motivation of people to engage in behavior that most of their society considers wrong. The first is ineffectiveness of socializing agents—most commonly of parents in transmitting their norms to their own children. Toby lists research findings on requirements for effective socialization, then considers the second pathology, inappropriate socialization, that is, the transmission of deviant standards of right and wrong. This, he argues, usually involves the third pathology of motivation, ambivalence. Elucidating a theory of the sociologist Talcott Parsons, Toby points out the tendency to cope with inconsistent normative standards by special efforts at justifying and compulsively expressing one standard rather than its opposite. Theory and research are cited on ambivalence as a source of rebelliousness. Despite these three pathologies of socialization which make for deviant *motivation*, deviant *behavior* does

3

not necessarily occur. This depends on the effectiveness of the social control of deviance by the family, the peer group, the school, the job and the administration of justice.

A common error pointed out by psychologist Saleem A. Shah and psychiatrist Loren H. Roth in Chapter 4 is to assume that biological and psychophysiological factors in criminality contradict rather than interact with sociocultural causal processes. A large variety of disorders of the nervous system are described and explained in their chapter, with evidence that these disorders foster irritability, rage, and other emotional and cognitive features that may be associated with law-violating behavior, especially with some of the most unstructured and puzzling types of assaultive acts. Since such acts do not usually follow these nervous system conditions, it is evident that crimes reflect an interaction of psychophysiological states with social learning and reinforcement experiences and opportunities in individual life histories, and that a full explanation must interrelate all of these factors.

The crimes which probably disturb the public most, assaultive offenses, are differentiated and interpreted in Chapter 5 by the Italian physician and psychologist Franco Ferracuti and the Australian psychologist and sociologist Graeme Newman. After reviewing the problems of assessing trends in total rates, they summarize the more adequate information on statistical correlates of assault with age, sex, urbanization, socioeconomic status, ethnicity, and region of the offenders, as well as with various attributes and behaviors of the victims. They classify explanations for these crimes as barrier, inevitability, bad influence, and culture theories, which cut across scientific fields such as biology, psychoanalysis, and sociology. The gross statistical distribution of assaultive offenses seems best accounted for by their subculture of violence explanation, but a need for further research to qualify this explanation is indicated in order to understand variations within the large statistical categories.

In discussing drugs, addiction, and crime in Chapter 6, medical sociologist David J. Pittman differentiates addiction, habituation, dependence, and abuse. He presents historical and biological analyses of the use of the "problem drugs": alcohol, cannabis (marijuana and hashish), opiates, cocaine, amphetamines, hallucinogens, and barbiturates. The relationship of each to crime is then discussed, as well as the leading approaches to reducing the extent to which their use constitutes a social problem.

In Chapter 7, sociologist John Gagnon reviews the relationship of deviance theory and criminology in the history of sociology, and their bearing on the study of sexual conduct and crime, as an introduction to his chapter. He then analyzes in detail the process of conventional sexual development in American society, the way in which the legal process attaches criminal labels to a small fraction of sexual acts and actors, and the relationship of these phenomena to life-cycle stages and to social structure. Both social causation and the effects of legal response are dealt with in separate discussions of the collective sexual alternatives of pornography, homosexuality, and prostitution, as well as the individual types of sexual offense which involve force, children, or incest.

Avocational crimes are distinguished by sociologist Gilbert Geis in Chapter 8 as offenses by persons who do not regard themselves as criminals, derive most of their income or status from noncriminal activities, and are deterrable by the prospect of being publicly labeled as criminals. He reviews intensively the analysis of white-collar crime in criminology, and alerts us to the prospects of its rapid expansion as concern with consumer fraud grows in the wake of what he calls "the Nader phenomenon." A variety of detailed research findings on nonprofessional shoplifting are summarized, including the predominance of women among known perpetrators, discriminatory enforcement of laws against it, and public reactions when observing it. Finally, some needs for further research on avocational crime are pointed out.

Perhaps the most comprehensive of available analyses of vocational crime is provided in Chapter 9 by sociologist James A. Inciardi. Historic trends in professional crimes of stealth—pocket-picking, shoplifting, burglary, forgery, counterfeiting, sneak-thieving and confidence games—and the social relationships and occupational norms they engender are described and explained. A similarly intensive account is provided for professional "heavy" crimes, which involve actual or threatened violence, from the outlawry and piracy of former eras to today's armed robbery and hijacking. This is followed by a distinctive analysis of organized crime in the United States, differentiating fact from fancy on its historic linkage with organizations in Italy, and its current ramifications. Finally, some of the features of our society and of criminal careers are pointed out to account for the viability of all major types of vocational crime.

While the chapters summarized thus far account mainly for relatively stable features and correlates of crime, sociologist James F. Short, Jr., in the final chapter in this part, is concerned with the dynamics of unstructured situations in which delinquency and crime arise without clear guides for conduct. He provides extensive illustrative case data and cogent explanatory theory on deviant fads and fashions in the criminogenic interaction of street-corner society, on the struggles for status in boys' gangs, on the dynamics of riotous outbreaks, and on the spread of criminal behavior patterns. We are left with a sense that one gets closer to the actual process of interaction in ostensibly "spontaneous" group offenses by means of collective behavior theory and case studies; these provide what philosophers of science have called "a context of discovery," which complements the "context of validation" in more abstract theory and statistics.

CHAPTER 1

The State, the Law, and the Definition of Behavior as Criminal or Delinquent

William J. Chambliss

University of California, Santa Barbara

It was fashionable, a few years back, to speak of crime and delinquency as though these were characteristics possessed by some people but not by others. In the heyday of such thinking, the search was on for physical, biological, or psychological traits and social experiences which led people to become "criminal" or "delinquent".[1] There is still a recognized need to look for characteristics and experiences of people which lead them to live lives different from those of their neighbors—whether the difference is in commitment to criminality, Catholicism, or cooking.

It is now generally recognized, however, that the starting point for the systematic study of crime is *not* to ask why some people become criminal while others do not, but to ask first why is it that some acts get defined as criminal while others do not. Criminology begins, then, with the sociology of law: the study of the institutions which create, interpret, and enforce the rules that tolerate and encourage one set of behaviors while prohibiting and discouraging another.

The creation of laws that define behavior as criminal or delinquent begins with the legislative enactment of a statute or a court decision that stipulates penal sanctions for the commission or omission of an act. But the process of defining only begins at this point; it ends with the enforcement of the rules created by the legislature or courts and includes the decisions of police to look for deviant acts in certain places and not in others, prosecutors' decisions to prosecute certain cases and not others, and courts, prison officials, and parole boards' decisions to interpret and enforce the laws in certain

I am deeply indebted to Richard Appelbaum, W. G. O. Carson, Donald Cressey, Daniel Glaser, Milton Mankoff, David Mechanic, and Robert Seidman for insightful criticisms and suggestions on an earlier version of this chapter. Their generosity and intelligence have been responsible for whatever value this chapter has but for none of its shortcomings.

1. See, for example, Cohen (1955), Merton (1957), Miller (1958), and Cloward and Ohlin (1960). Donald Cressey has pointed out that an earlier generation of criminologists, particularly Sutherland (1924), Sellin (1938), and Tannenbaum (1938), were less likely to ignore the importance of the criminal lawmaking process; see Cressey (1968) and Sutherland and Cressey (1970).

ways. In this process it is convenient and useful to differentiate *rule-creation* from *rule-enforcement* agencies. In societies with a centralized government, the principal rule-creating agencies are the legislatures and the appellate courts. The principal rule-enforcement agencies are the police, prosecuting attorneys, courts, and prisons. Obviously a complete discussion of the role of these various agencies is not justified in this introduction. (For a fuller treatment see Chambliss, 1969; Quinney, 1970; Chambliss & Seidman, 1971; Schwartz & Skolnick, 1971.) We shall, therefore, narrow our sights to concentrate on the rule-creating functions of the state, leaving for other chapters the role of rule-enforcement agencies.

MODELS OF RULE CREATION

Theories of the origin of criminal law parallel rather closely general theories of society. The chief division is between those who see the state as being controlled by and reflecting the interests of particular social classes and those who see the state as responding to the views of the general 'public. The Marxian view that "in every era the ruling ideas are the ideas of the ruling class" anchors one end of this theoretical debate and the natural-law view that the state is merely the reflection and translation of the *volksgeist* anchors the other. In between are a host of lower-level (i.e., less general) theories that see the criminal law as reflecting the organized efforts of "moral entrepreneurs" (Becker, 1963), bureaucratic interests (Chambliss, 1969; Hetzler, 1971), and downwardly mobile social classes (Gusfield, 1963) on the one hand, or that see the law as reflecting "perceived social needs" (Hall, 1952), the "public interest" (Auerbach et al., 1961) and "moral indignation" (Ranulf, 1933) on the other. We shall look at each of these theoretical models and see the degree to which extant empirical data on the creation of criminal law is compatible with the models.

In the end, we will conclude that none of the more prominent theories can account for the creation of all criminal law. It is, nevertheless, clear from the research evidence that some models come closer to providing a general explanation than do others. The paradigm that is most compatible with the facts is one that recognizes the critical role played by social conflict in the generation of criminal law. The conflicts may be manifested in violent confrontations between social classes or more genteelly in the form of institutionalized dispute-settling procedures. Regardless of the form the conflict takes, in the end it is the existence of the structurally induced conflicts between groups in the society that determines the form and content of the criminal law. Of course, not all groups or social classes are equally potent and those which control the economic resources of the society will influence the shape of the law more profoundly and more permanently than will any other group or class. Nonetheless, there are limits to the power of a "ruling class" or "ruling elite" to determine the law's content. These limits are set in the course of history as the society moves through those struggles which result from its particular organizational structure.

THE CREATION OF CRIMINAL LAW AND ECONOMIC ELITES

Research into the origins of criminal laws substantiates quite clearly the important role played in their creation by those classes that control the economic resources of the society. Whether looked at in terms of *consequences*—that is, the effect the laws have after passage—or the *dynamics* of the lawmaking process, the results are very much the same: those social classes who control the resources of the society are more likely to have their interests represented by the state through the criminal law than are any and all other social groups. First, we shall look at those instances where the definition of behavior as criminal or delinquent has arisen as a result of *direct involvement* on the part of economic elites in the rule-creation process.

A number of historical, cross-cultural, and contemporary studies of criminal law creation have shown how criminal laws are consciously and explicitly enacted to serve the interests of those who control the economic resources. Nowhere is this more clearly illustrated than in laws used to coerce an otherwise unwilling labor force into providing that labor which is the basis for the economic structure of the society. England's colonial policies in Africa are illustrative.

THE CREATION OF CRIMINAL LAW AND ECONOMIC INTERESTS

When England began colonizing Africa one of the first and last problems faced was to establish procedures by which the colonies could be made economically profitable. Being a nation of laws, it was not surprising to find legal institutions at the forefront of the struggle. The history of colonial law, which is only now being written, is replete with the open involvement of white elites in the creation of criminal laws designed to serve their economic interests. Indeed, it is not off the mark to say that the entire history of colonial criminal law legislation is that of a dominant social class defining as criminal those acts which it served their economic interests to so define. The corollary of this is that colonial law did *not* usually define as criminal those acts which, although offensive to the Englishman's "notions of justice, equity and good conscience," were not offensive to his economic interests.[2]

The East African "poll tax" and "registration" laws are instructive in this regard. East Africa had a settler economy. Whites moved in and established large plantations for raising tea, coffee, and sisal for export and sale abroad. Such an economic system depended upon the ready availability of masses of cheap labor. There were, however, few incentives for the Africans to leave their villages and work arduously on the white-man's farms. Criminal laws were created which guaranteed the settlers a constant source of cheap labor (Seidman, 1971). Sir Harry Johnston noted:

> Given abundance of cheap labour, the financial security of the Protectorate is established. . . . All that needs to be done is for the Administration to act as friends of both sides, and introduce the native labourer to the European capitalist. A gentle insistence that the native should contribute his fair share to the revenue of the country by paying his tax is all that is necessary on our part to ensure his taking a share in life's labour which no human being should avoid (Johnston, 1895:96).

A similar view is also expressed by the governor of Kenya:

> We consider that taxation is the only possible method of compelling the native to leave his Reserve for the purpose of seeking work . . . it is on this (taxation) that the supply of labour and the price of labour depends. To raise the rate of wages would not increase but would diminish the supply of labour. A rise in the rate of wages would enable the hut or poll tax of a family, sub-tribe, or tribe to be earned by fewer external workers (Sir Percy Girovard, as quoted in Lees, 1924:186).

---

2. Note, for example, the toleration of a complete lack of due process within tribes as long as the tribe worked and contributed to the colonial regime; see Clairmonte (1969) and Seidman (1971).

To effect the Africans' compliance with this system of forced labor, criminal law sanctions of fines, imprisonment, and corporal punishment were imposed on people who failed to pay their taxes.

Even with this incentive to ensure that the African take "a share of life's labour which no human being should avoid," the settler's labor problems were not solved, for:

> Labourers who deserted as soon as they had earned enough to pay their taxes were no use to the settlers. To meet their (the settlers') demands, the government in 1919 put into effect a native registration ordinance which compelled all Africans over the age of sixteen to register by giving a set of fingerprint impressions, which were then forwarded to a central fingerprint bureau. By this method, nearly all deserters could be traced and returned to their employers if they broke a contract. Fines (up to $75.00) and imprisonment (up to 90 days) were imposed for a host of minor labour offenses. Another form of compulsion took shape in vagrancy laws which operated against Africans who left the reserves without becoming wage earners (Aaronovitch & Aaronovitch, 1947:99–100).[3]

The colonial setting was, of course, a unique one but the general character of the criminal law and the definition of behavior as deviant that it illustrates is not at all atypical. The development of vagrancy laws in England and the United States is also a history of defining certain acts as criminal in order to serve the interests of the ruling class. Again we find this explicitly articulated in the statutes themselves. In 1274 a prevagrancy statute was passed whose primary goal was to protect the church, which was at this time a mainstay of the ruling class, from the impoverished seeking shelter:

> Because that abbies and houses of religion have been overcharged and sore grieved, by the report of great men and other, so that their goods have not been sufficient for themselves, whereby they have been greatly hindered and impoverished, that they cannot maintain themselves, nor such charity as they have been accustomed to do; it is provided, that none shall come to eat or lodge in any house of religion, or any other's foundation than of his own, at the costs of the house, unless he be required by the governor of the home before his coming hither (3 Ed. 1 c. 1).

Even more to the point was the history of the vagrancy statutes from 1349 onward, a history of legislative enactment and innovation designed to provide labor for the established economic elites of the society. Of considerable importance in the analysis that follows is to note that as the economic resources of the society change (from feudal agrarianism to commerce and trade), the content and focus of the criminal law changes.

In 1349 the first vagrancy statute was passed and the wording of this statute made its intention quite clear:

> Because that many valiant beggars, as long as they may live of begging, do refuse to labour, giving themselves to idleness and vice, and sometimes to theft and other abominations; it is ordained, that none upon pain of imprisonment shall, under the colour of pity or alms, give any thing to such which may labour, or presume to favour them towards their desires; so that thereby they may be compelled to labour for their necessary living.

It was further provided by this statute that:

> every man and woman, of what condition he be, free or bond, able in body, and within the age of threescore years, not living in merchandise nor exercising any craft, nor having

---

3. For a discussion of a similar use of criminal law in Guatemala, see Appelbaum (1966).

of his own whereon to live, nor proper land whereon to occupy himself, and not serving any other, if he in convenient service (his estate considered) be required to serve, shall be bounded to serve him which shall him require. . . . And if any refuse, he shall on conviction by two true men, . . . be committed to gaol till he find surety to serve.

And if any workman or servant, of what estate or condition he be, retained in any man's service, do depart from the said service without reasonable cause or license, before the term agreed on, he shall have pain of imprisonment (23 Ed. 3).

There was also in this statute the stipulation that the workers should receive a standard wage. In 1351 this statute was strengthened by the stipulation:

And none shall go out of the town where he dwelled in winter, to serve the summer, if he may serve in the same town [25 Ed. 3 (1351)].

By statute [34 Ed. 3 (1360)] the punishment for these acts became imprisonment for fifteen days and if they "do not justify themselves by the end of that time, to be sent to gaol till they do."

The prime mover for the creation of these laws was the Black Death, which struck England about 1348. Among the many disastrous consequences of the plague on the social structure was the fact that it decimated the labor force. It is estimated that by the time the pestilence had run its course at least 50 percent of the population of England had died from the plague. This decimation of the labor force would necessitate rather drastic innovations in any society but its impact was heightened in England where, at this time, the economy was highly dependent upon a ready supply of cheap labor.

Even before the pestilence, the availability of an adequate supply of cheap labor was becoming a problem for the feudal landowners. The Crusades and various wars had made money necessary to the lords and, as a result, the lords frequently agreed to sell the serfs their freedom in order to obtain the needed funds. The serfs, for their part, sought to escape from serfdom (by "fair means" or "foul") because the larger towns, which were becoming commercial and trade centers during this period, could offer the serf greater personal freedom as well as a higher standard of living.

By the middle of the 14th century the outward uniformity of the manorial system had become in practice considerably varied . . . for the peasant had begun to drift to the towns and it was unlikely that the old village life in its unpleasant aspects should not be resented. Moreover the constant wars against France and Scotland were fought mainly with mercenaries after Henry III's time and most villages contributed to the new armies. The bolder serfs either joined the armies or fled to the towns, and even in the villages the free men who held by villein tenure were as eager to commute their services as the serfs were to escape. Only the amount of "free" labor available enabled the lord to work his demesne in many places (Bradshaw, 1915:54).

And he says regarding the effect of the Black Death:

in 1348 the Black Death reached England and the vast mortality that ensued destroyed that reserve of labour which alone had made the manorial system even nominally possible (p. 54).

The immediate result of these events was, of course, no surprise: wages for the "free" man rose considerably and this increased, on the one hand, the landowner's problems and, on the other hand, the plight of the unfree tenant. For although wages increased for the personally free laborers, it, of course, did not necessarily add to the standard of living of the serf; if anything it made his position worse because the landowner would be hard pressed to pay for the personally free labor which he needed and would thus find it more and more difficult to maintain the standard of living for the serf which he had heretofore supplied. Thus the serf had no alternative but flight if he chose to better his position. Furthermore, flight generally meant both freedom and better conditions, since the possibility of work in the new weaving industry was great and the chance of being caught small (Bradshaw, 1915:57).

It was under these conditions that we find the first vagrancy statutes emerging. There is little question but that these statutes were designed for one express purpose: to force laborers (whether personally free or unfree) to accept employment at a low wage in order to insure the landowner an adequate supply of labor at a price he could afford to pay. Caleb Foote concurs with this interpretation when he notes that the anti-migratory policy behind vagrancy legislation began

> as an essential complement of the wage stabilization legislation which accompanied the breakup of feudalism and the depopulation caused by the Black Death. By the Statutes of Labourers in 1349–1351, every able-bodied person without other means of support was required to work for wages fixed at the level preceding the Black Death; it was unlawful to accept more, or to refuse an offer to work, or to flee from one county to another to avoid offers of work or to seek higher wages, or to give alms to able-bodied beggars who refused to work (Foote, 1956:615).

In short, as Foote says in another place, this was an "attempt to make the vagrancy statutes a substitute for serfdom" (p. 615). This same conclusion is equally apparent from the wording of the statute, where it is stated:

> Because great part of the people, and especially of workmen and servants, late died in pestilence; many seeing the necessity of masters, and great scarcity of servants, will not serve without excessive wages, and some rather willing to beg in idleness than by labour to get their living: it is ordained, that every man and woman, of what condition he be, free or bond, able in body and within the age of three-score years, not living in merchandise, (etc.) be required to serve. . . .

The innovation in the law was a direct result of the aforementioned changes in the social setting. The law was clearly and consciously designed to serve the interests of the ruling class of feudal landlords at the expense of the serfs or working classes. The vagrancy laws were designed to alleviate a condition defined by the lawmakers as undesirable. The solution was to attempt to force a reversal, as it were, of a social process which was well under way; that is, to curtail mobility of laborers in such a way that labor would not become a commodity for which the landowners would have to compete.

A SHIFT IN FOCAL CONCERN

Following the squelching of the Peasants' Revolt in 1381, the services of the serfs to the lord "tended to become less and less exacted, although in certain forms they lingered on till the seventeenth century. . . . By the sixteenth century few knew that there were any bondmen in England . . . and in 1575 Queen Elizabeth listened to the prayers of almost the last serfs in England . . . and granted them manumission" (Bradshaw, 1915: 61).

In view of this change we would expect corresponding changes in the vagrancy laws. Beginning with the lessening of punishment in the statute of 1503, we find these changes. However, instead of remaining dormant (or becoming more so) or being negated altogether, the vagrancy statutes experienced a shift in focal concern. With this shift the statutes served a new and equally important function for the ruling class of England. The first statute that indicates this change was adopted in 1530 [22 H. 8. c. 12 (1530)]. It stated:

> If any person, being whole and mighty in body, and able to labour, be taken in begging, or be vagrant and can give no reckoning how he lawfully gets his living . . . and all other idle persons going about, some of them using divers and subtil crafty and unlawful games and plays, and some of them feigning themselves to have knowledge of . . . crafty sciences . . . shall be punished as provided.

What is most significant about this statute is the shift from an earlier concern with laborers to a concern with *criminal* activities. To be sure, the stipulation of persons "being whole and mighty in body, and able to labour, be taken in begging, or be vagrant" sounds very much like the concerns of the earlier statutes. Some important differences are apparent, however, when the rest of the statute includes those who "can give no reckoning how he lawfully gets his living"; "some of them using divers and subtil crafty and unlawful games and plays." This is the first statute which specifically focuses upon these kinds of criteria for adjudging someone a vagrant.

It is significant that in this statute the severity of punishment is increased so as to be greater not only than that provided by the 1503 statute but the punishment is more severe than that which had been provided by *any* of the pre-1503 statutes as well. For someone who is merely idle and gives no reckoning of how he makes his living the offender shall be:

> had to the next market town, or other place where they [the constables] shall think most convenient, and there to be tied to the end of a cart naked, and to be beaten with whips throughout the same market town or other place, till his body be bloody by reason of such whipping" [22 H. 8. c. 12 (1530)].

But, for those who use "divers and subtil crafty and unlawful games and plays," etc., the punishment is "whipping at two days together in manner aforesaid." For the second offense, such persons are:

> scourged two days, and the third day to be put upon the pillory from nine of the clock till eleven before noon of the same day and to have one of his ears cut off [22 H. 8. c. 12 (1530)].

And if he offend the third time "to have like punishment with whipping, standing on the pillory and to have his other ear cut off."

This statute (1) makes a distinction between types of offenders and applies the more severe punishment to those who are clearly engaged in "criminal" activities, (2) mentions a specific concern with categories of "unlawful" behavior, and (3) applies a type of punishment (cutting off the ear) which is generally reserved for offenders who are defined as likely to be fairly serious criminals.

Only five years later we find for the first time that the punishment of death is applied to the crime of vagrancy. We also note a change in terminology in the statute:

> . . . and if any ruffians . . . after having been once apprehended . . . shall wander, loiter, or idle use themselves and play the vagabonds . . . shall be eftsoons not only whipped

again, but shall have the gristle of his right ear clean cut off. And if he shall again offend, he shall be committed to gaol till the next sessions; and being there convicted upon indictment, he shall have judgment to suffer pains and execution of death, as a felon, as an enemy of the commonwealth [27 H. 8. c. 25 (1535)].

It is significant that the statute now makes persons who repeat the crime of vagrancy felons. During this period then, the focal concern of the vagrancy statutes becomes a concern for the control of felons and is no longer primarily concerned with the movement of laborers.

These statutory changes were a direct response to changes taking place in England's social structure during this period. We have already pointed out that feudalism was decaying rapidly. Concomitant with the breakup of feudalism was an increased emphasis upon commerce and trade. The commercial emphasis in England at the turn of the sixteenth century is of particular importance in the development of vagrancy laws. With commercialism came considerable traffic bearing valuable goods. Where there were 169 important merchants in the middle of the fourteenth century, there were 3,000 merchants engaged in foreign trade alone at the beginning of the sixteenth century (Hall, 1952:21). England became highly dependent upon commerce for its economic surplus. Italians conducted a great deal of the commerce of England during this early period and were held in low repute by the populace. They were subject to attacks by citizens and, more important, were frequently robbed of their goods while transporting them. "The general insecurity of the times made any transportation hazardous. The special risks to which the alien merchant was subjected gave rise to the royal practice of issuing formally executed covenants of safe conduct through the realm" (Hall, 1952:23).

Such a situation not only called for the enforcement of existing laws but also called for the creation of new laws which would facilitate the control of persons preying upon merchants transporting goods. The vagrancy statutes were revived in order to fulfill just such a purpose. Persons who had committed no serious felony but who were suspected of being capable of doing so could be apprehended and incapacitated through the application of vagrancy laws once these laws were refocused so as to include "any ruffians . . . [who] shall wander, loiter, or idle use themselves and play the vagabonds" [H. 8. c. 25 (1535)].

The new focal concern is continued in 1 Ed. 6. c. 3 (1547) and in fact is made more general so as to include:

Whoever man or woman, being not lame, impotent, or so aged or diseased that he or she cannot work, not having whereon to live, shall be lurking in any house, or loitering or idle wandering by the highway side, or in streets, cities, towns, or villages, not applying themselves to some honest labour, and so continuing for three days; or running away from their work; every such person shall be taken for a vagabond. And . . . upon conviction of two witnesses . . . the same loiterer [shall] be marked with a hot iron in the breast with the letter V, and adjudged him to the person bringing him, to be his slave for two years.

Should the vagabond run away, upon conviction, he was to be branded by a hot iron with the letter S on the forehead and to be thenceforth declared a slave forever. And in 1571 there is modification of the punishment to be inflicted, whereby the offender is to be "branded on the chest with the letter V" (for vagabond). And, if he is convicted the second time, the brand is to be made on the forehead. It is worth noting here that this method of punishment, which first appeared in 1530 and is repeated here with somewhat more force, is also an indication of a change in the type of person to whom the law is intended to apply. For it is likely that nothing so permanent as branding would be applied to someone who was wandering but looking for work, or at worst merely idle and not particularly dangerous per se. On the other hand, it could well be applied to someone who was likely to be engaged in other criminal activities in connection with being "vagrant."

By 1571 in the statute of 14 E. 1. c. 5 the shift in focal concern is fully developed:

> All rogues, vagabonds, and sturdy beggars shall . . . be committed to the common gaol . . . he shall be grievously whipped, and burnt thro the gristle of the right ear with a hot iron of the compass of an inch about. . . . And for the second offense, he shall be adjudged a felon, unless some person will take him for two years in to his service. And for the third offense, he shall be adjudged guilty of felony without benefit of clergy.

And there is included a long list of persons who fall within the statute:

> proctors, procurators, idle persons going about using subtil, crafty and unlawful games or plays; and some of them feigning themselves to have knowledge of . . . absurd sciences . . . and all fencers, bearwards, common players in interludes, and minstrels . . . all jugglers, pedlars, tinkers, petty chapmen . . . and all counterfeiters of licenses, passports and users of the same.

The major significance of this statute is that it includes all the previously defined offenders and adds some more. Significantly, those added are more clearly criminal types, counterfeiters, for example. It is also significant that there is the following qualification of this statute: "Provided also, that this act shall not extend to cookers, or harvest folks, that travel for harvest work, corn or hay."

The emphasis upon the criminalistic aspect of vagrants continues in chapter 17 of the same statute:

> Whereas divers *licentious* persons wander up and down in all parts of the realm, to countenance their *wicked behavior;* and do continually assemble themselves armed in the highways, and elsewhere in troops, *to the great terror* of her majesty's true subjects, the *impeachment of her laws,* and the disturbance of the peace and tranquility of the realm; and whereas many outrages are daily committed by these dissolute persons, and more are likely to ensue if speedy remedy be not provided (italics added).

With minor variations (e.g., offering a reward for the capture of a vagrant) the statutes remain essentially of this nature until 1743. In 1743 there was once more an expansion of the types of persons included such that

> all persons going about as patent gatherers, or gatherers of alms, under pretense of loss by fire or other casualty; or going about as collectors for prisons, gaols, or hospitals; all persons playing or betting at any unlawful games; and all persons who run away and leave their wives or children . . . all persons wandering abroad, and lodging in ale-houses, barns, out-houses, or in the open air, not giving good account of themselves,

were types of offenders added to those already included.

In sum, the foregoing analysis of the vagrancy laws demonstrates that these laws were a legislative innovation which reflected the socially perceived necessity of providing an abundance of cheap labor to England's ruling class of landowners during a period when serfdom was breaking down and when the pool of available labor was depleted. With the eventual breakup of feudalism the need for such laws disappeared and the increased dependence of the economy upon commerce and trade rendered the former use of the vagrancy statutes irrelevant. As a result, for a substantial period the vagrancy statutes were dormant, undergoing only minor changes and, presumably, being applied infrequently. Finally, the vagrancy laws were subjected to considerable alteration through a shift in the focal concern of the statutes. Whereas in their inception the laws focused upon the "idle" and "those refusing to labor," after the turn of the sixteenth century the emphasis came to be upon "rogues," "vagabonds," and others who were suspected of being engaged in criminal activities. During this period the focus was particularly upon "roadmen" who preyed upon citizens who transported goods from one place to another. The increased importance of commerce to England during this period brought forth laws to protect persons engaged in this enterprise and the vagrancy statutes provided one source for such protection by refocusing the acts to be included under these statutes.

The more recent history of the vagrancy statutes has continued to repeat the same basic process. During times of harvest in states where agriculture is big business, vagrancy statutes are enforced as a means of providing cheap labor (Spradley, 1970). Conversely, during periods of recession when there is an overabundance of cheap labor, these same statutes are used to restrict the mobility of the unemployed [*Edwards* v. *California*, 314 U.S. 160 (1941)].

These historical data are essential if we are to comprehend the rule-creation process but they cannot tell us what the process is today. Presumably the role of the ruling class in the creation of criminal laws could have changed substantially in recent years. The available evidence suggests that this has not happened. Indeed, what evidence there is suggests that *even those laws that appear to be contrary to the interests of those who control the economic resources were in fact created to help them increase their profits.*

Since the 1900s there has been a heady growth in America of criminal laws ostensibly designed to curb the excesses of private enterprise. The Sherman antitrust laws, pure food and drug laws, restrictions on the use of "unfair competition," and the like have emerged as a whole new area of criminal law. On the surface it would appear that these laws represent strong evidence that under certain circumstances criminal laws are passed that are purposely and explicitly contrary to the interests of the most powerful economic sectors of the society. Closer examination reveals, however, that even laws that are, on the surface, inimical to the interests of those who control the resources of the society, are laws that, in fact, were promoted and shaped by those very same groups as a means of enhancing and improving their control over the means of production.

Gabriel Kolko has provided historical analysis of the emergence of laws regulating the railroad and meat-packing industries that demonstrates quite clearly that in these areas the laws were, in fact, promoted and shaped by the largest companies in these fields in an effort to control competition from smaller companies and to insure better markets for the large companies' products (Kolko, 1963, 1965).

In the latter part of the nineteenth century the railroad industry was in a state of chaos created by intense competition and national economic crises. In June, 1877 a general strike of railroad workers surprised and incapacitated the industry. One consequence of the strike was to establish the role that the state would have in conflicts between workers and industry:

> Out of the crisis came a working view of the role of the state in industrial society which was consistently applied during the next three decades: if for some reason the power of various key business interests was endangered, even for causes of their own making, the state was to intervene to preserve their dominant position (Kolko, 1965:12).

The fact that this principle emerged from the strike was doubtless no surprise to the railroad owners. They had, after all, become established and powerful largely through the cooperation of the state in the early years of their development (Hurst, 1950, 1956). The strike, however, underlined for them the value to be had from stronger cooperation with the federal bureaucracy.

Thus began a movement within the railroad industry itself to seek federal regulation. Previous efforts at pooling by competitive railroads had been largely a failure and the industry had remained intensely competitive.

Profits were low for many companies and bankruptcies not uncommon. Eventually the major railroad companies came to realize that federal regulation which would establish uniform prices at a level guaranteeing profits to the industry was an acceptable and desirable solution. It was, in effect, the use of criminal law legislation to benefit the larger, established railroads to the disadvantage of the smaller ones. Price and policy regulation by the federal government reduced competition and thus eliminated the possibility that a small company might take business away from a larger one. Although widely touted as antimonopoly legislation, the establishment of the Interstate Commerce Commission and enactment of the statutes controlling railroad activities were essentially moves to encourage monopolies within the railroad industry.

The history of criminal law legislation geared ostensibly to regulate the unsanitary practices of the meat-packing industry shows the same underlying motivation. The large meat-packing firms were suffering financially in competition with smaller firms which were able to undersell them. The entire industry engaged in incredibly unsanitary processing practices that resulted in widespread illness. The larger firms were also being hurt by the fact that the often unhealthy meat sold abroad was reducing the demand in Europe for American meat products. A solution to both problems for the large corporations was legislation creating government inspection of meat processing. This would, of course, raise the cost of producing the meat but for the large firms the increased cost would be minimal as it could be spread over a large output. For the small firms, however, the increased cost would destroy their competitive advantage. Simultaneously, meat-inspection laws would improve the health qualities and thereby enable American manufacturers to compete favorably for European markets. Realizing this led the large meat-packers to lobby for federal regulations to control the industry. The government responded to these pressures by passing laws making it a crime to produce meat under unsanitary conditions. The legislation thus aided the large meat-packers in their competition with smaller firms. Upton Sinclair, who inadvertently popularized the unsanitary conditions in the meat-packing industry (he was mainly concerned with working conditions when he wrote in 1904 but it was sanitation that became the issue), accurately described both the reason for passing and the effects of the meat-packing regulations:

> The Federal inspection of meat was, historically, established at the packer's request; . . . it is maintained and paid for by the people of the United States for the benefit of the packers; . . . men wearing the blue uniforms and brass buttons of the United States service are employed for the purpose of certifying to the nations of the civilized world that all the diseased and tainted meat which happens to come into existence in the United States of America is carefully sifted out and consumed by the American people (Sinclair, 1906:3).

During the legislative debates establishing federal inspection of meat, the large meat-packers were consulted and helped draw up the bills. Samuel H. Cowan, the lawyer for the National Livestock Association, was asked to write a bill acceptable to the packers, which he did. When President Roosevelt criticized the bill, Senator Wadsworth responded: "I told you on Wednesday night when I submitted the bill to you, that the packers insisted before our committee on having a rigid inspection law passed. Their life depends on it. They placed no obstacle in our way" (Kolko, 1963: 106).

When the bill was finally passed and the head of the Department of Agriculture announced to a gathering of the large meat-packers his department's intention to enforce the new laws strictly and rigidly, he was greeted with a round of applause from the industry. For the new laws would, as George Perkins wrote to J. P. Morgan, "be of very great advantage . . . as it will practically give [the meat-packers] a government certificate for their goods" (Kolko, 1963:106).

Economic interests also become involved in criminal law legislation in order to protect themselves against laws that would interfere with their profits. This process was illustrated and an important set of general principles concerning criminal definitions illuminated by the passage in the United States of The Comprehensive Drug Abuse, Prevention and Control Act of 1970.[4] This statute was designed to control the distribution and use of "dangerous drugs" and included the controversial provision that law enforcement agents could enter private dwellings without knocking in order to search and investigate for the presence of dangerous drugs. In the course of legislative hearings it became apparent that legislation designed to control the use and distribution of drugs in the United States was circumscribed by the fact that legislators would *not* endorse legislation inimical to the interests of the pharmaceutical industry even in the face of overwhelming evidence that the industry was responsible for much of the widespread use of drugs. The drug problem was carefully defined and publicized by the drug industry and legislators as a problem involving "freaky youth" and lower-class slum dwellers despite substantial evidence indicating that the dangers of drug use were by no means limited to these classes of persons.

The Comprehensive Drug Abuse, Prevention and Control Act was a bill introduced to the Congress by President Nixon with, predictably, the strong support of two of his major law enforcement officers: Attorney General John Mitchell and the director of the Bureau of Narcotics and Dangerous Drugs, John Ingersoll.

The bill, as drafted by the Nixon administration with consultation from representatives of the drug industry, was tantamount to providing heretofore unheard of powers to the law-enforcement bureaucracies of the state and federal governments in the enforcement of laws controlling the distribution and possession of "drugs." Significantly, however, the drugs that received the greatest emphasis were those that were either imported or produced easily by individuals: heroin, marijuana, and LSD being the principal examples. Drugs which were produced by pharmaceutical manufacturers, even though they were generally sold illegally, were left virtually uncontrolled in the bill. This came about not by accident but through the concerted efforts of the pharmaceutical industry to see that their economic interests were protected.

The issue, so far as the pharmacists were concerned, centered on the manufacture of amphetamines, metaphetamines (referred to as "speed") and two drugs closely related to these: Librium and Valium.

In a series of testimonies and hearings before various congressional committees and on the floor of the two houses the following facts were brought to light:

Each year in the United States the pharmaceutical industry produces between *eight and ten billion* amphetamine pills. These pills are consumed mainly by the white,

---

4. This section is based on Graham (1971). For a discussion of economic interests in the legislation of laws controlling safety standards in factories and pollution, see Carson (1971).

middle-class American—the housewife, the businessman, students, physicians, and athletes. According to testimony by representatives from the medical profession and the National Institute of Mental Health, many of the consumers of these pills have become psychologically dependent upon them. Furthermore, two of the drugs—Librium and Valium—are, according to testimony before the Congress, likely to lead to extreme depression and suicide. Dr. Stanley Cohen of the National Institute of Mental Health testified that prolonged use of these drugs was common and that it could result in malnutrition, prolonged psychotic states, heart irregularities, convulsions, hepatitis, and sustained brain damage (House Hearings, Feb., 1970:606, 607, 610).

The Bureau of Narcotics and Dangerous Drugs provided the Congress with a report that pinpointed two drugs, Valium and Librium, as being involved in 36 suicides and 750 attempted suicides.

Dr. John D. Griffith of the Vanderbilt Medical School stated: "amphetamine addiction is more widespread, more incapacitating, more dangerous and socially disrupting than narcotic addiction." He further testified that "making these drugs available for obesity and depression has proved to be quite harmful to the public" (House Hearings, Feb., 1970:616, 618).

The Director of Student Health Services at the University of Utah testified:

> Amphetamines provide one of the major ironies of the whole field of drug abuse. We continue to insist that they are good drugs when used under medical supervision, but their greatest use turns out to be frivolous, illegal and highly destructive to the user (House Hearings, Feb., 1970:636, 641).

These protestations of danger to the public and inherent problems of addiction, suicide, and the like may or may not be accurate. They are, in any event, no more questionable than the evidence provided on the horrors and dangers of other drugs such as LSD, marijuana, and heroin, which are not part of the profit system of the pharmaceutical companies.

The failure of Congress or the state bureaucracies concerned with "crime" to include these drugs in the same category as the more widely publicized ones did not result from their presentation of any evidence contradicting the findings mentioned above. It resulted simply from a willingness or a desire to ignore evidence that would have forced the passage of a law inimical to the interests of the drug industry.

That the drug industry profits greatly from the current freedom to manufacture and distribute these drugs is also clearly documented in the hearings. Hoffman-La-Roche Laboratories, producers of Valium and Librium, earned a profit in one year of over $4 million on these two drugs alone (Graham, 1971).

Most of the eight billion pills were sold legally through prescriptions provided by doctors. Many, however, were produced by these firms and diverted into the illegal market. The Bureau of Narcotics and Dangerous Drugs estimated that between 75 and 90 percent of the amphetamines on the illegal market had been produced legally by American drug companies. Some of these pills get into the illegal market through forged prescriptions, theft, and fraud. But the drug industry is clearly a willing and cooperative victim of some of these practices. Narcotics bureau officers reported that it was possible to simply write drug companies using fake addresses and stationery and obtain massive quantities of the drugs. One agent reported obtaining twenty-five thousand pills by sending a letter to a drug company and signing his name as a medical doctor. The prescriptions on amphetamines and related drugs also invite misuse in that it is possible to write the prescription for an indefinite supply enabling the prescription holder to return to the drugstore at will to have the prescription refilled.

Expert testimony was also forthcoming that the real medical needs of the society could be met by, at most, the production of only a few thousand (instead of eight or ten billion) pills a year. Dr. John Griffith of Vanderbilt University Medical School testified that "a few thousand tablets would supply the whole medical needs of the country" (House Hearings, Feb., 1970:458).

There was even considerable evidence presented that the amphetamines were of almost no medical use whatsoever, irrespective of the dangers that inhered in their widespread distribution. Congressman Claude Pepper of Florida reported that his Select Committee on Crime had, in the fall of 1969, distributed questionnaires to medical deans and health organizations throughout the United States. Of fifty-three responses received by his committee only one suggested that the drug had any use whatsoever and this one suggested that its use was limited to "early stages of a diet program." A representative from the National Institute of Mental Health (Dr. Stanley Cohen) estimated that 99 percent of the prescriptions were supposedly for dietary purposes. Obesity thus becomes a legitimate excuse to get high on speed.

The testimony and reports of medical experts were not, of course, the only side presented at the congressional hearings. At every stage in the history of the bill the pharmaceutical interests were well represented. The Director of the Bureau of Narcotics and Dangerous Drugs admitted, under questioning, that representatives from the drug industry had been involved in drafting the bill for the administration.

During the congressional hearings the drug-industry lobbyists testified, as did leading industry figures. The testimony invariably emphasized the danger of "speed freaks" but denied that the industry had any responsibility for such things. Further, the industry apologists stressed the medicinal value of amphetamines: a value largely contradicted by independent testimony. Finally, the industry spokesmen insisted that present controls were adequate and that government intervention would violate the freedom of the industry necessary for it to serve the public interest.

In the end all testimony and facts contrary to the drug-industry's view were simply swept under the rug. The pharmaceutical companies employed lobbyists, the national pharmaceutical associations sent representatives, and the Congress passed the bill without controlling the manufacture and distribution of any of the drugs from which the drug industry profits. In this way Congress avoided two problems: on the one hand, it did not provide legislation that would have angered the drug industry. On the other hand, they did pass a law which made it possible to arrest, prosecute, and convict more readily those powerless members of society who engage in the taking of drugs, the profits of which did not go to the established industries. There is no way to interpret this legislation as a completely sincere attempt to do something about drug abuse; it is, in consequence and by design, an example of how the laws reflect the interests of those in power at the expense (both financial and psychological) of those who lack the economic, and therefore the political, power to influence the legislative process. The Comprehensive Drug Abuse, Prevention and Control Act of 1970, which was strongly supported by President Nixon and Attorney General Mitchell as an important piece of ammunition in the arsenal against crime, was, in effect, an important piece of ammunition in the arsenal of the drug industry to reduce competition from unorganized entrepreneurs.

THE MOBILIZATION OF BIAS

Thus far we have dealt only with laws where there was a conscious effort by lawmakers (legislatures and appellate courts) to protect the interests of the economic elites of the society. Important as this is as a source of definition of behavior as criminal or delinquent, it leaves out a whole world of criminal law information which reflects the interests of economic elites *not* consciously but nonetheless effectively. The key to understanding this aspect of criminal law creation is Schattschneider's concept "the mobilization of bias."[5]

> All forms of political organization have a bias in favor of the exploitation of some kinds of conflict and the suppression of others because organization is the mobilization of bias (Schattschneider, 1960:71).

The criminal law creation process organizes into it the views of those classes who control the economic resources as a result of the entire matrix of recruitment, socialization, and situational pressures upon those who create the laws. Legislatures, appellate court judges, and committee members are drawn largely from upper-class members of society; legal advice comes disproportionately from law firms whose principal clients are the major industrial and financial corporations of the country; interest groups are organized to define problems and influence lawmakers in the interests of those who have the resources to finance and support the existence of specialists in the rule-creation process.

Furthermore, "some issues are organized into politics while others are organized out" (Schattschneider, 1960:71). The mobilization of bias also includes the fact that much of what takes place in the creation of rules is "non-decision-making." For example, neither legislature nor appellate court in the United States would consider the question of whether it is criminal for a motion picture magnate to spend $20 thousand on a birthday party for his daughter while people are starving a few blocks from the night club he rented for the occasion, or whether it should be a crime for the wife of the Attorney General of the United States to have 200 pairs of shoes while people in the Appalachian Mountains cannot afford shoes to send their children to school. It is simply assumed as part of the prevailing definition of reality that such an issue is "beyond the pale" of lawmaking institutions.

In the end, the mobilization of bias accounts for the emergence and focus of much of the criminal law in ways that are compatible with the dominant economic interests of the society. Even the structure of the criminal law process is influenced by the structural bias inherent in the operation and functioning of the law in a class-structured society. Take, for example, the emergence of the adversary process—one of the cornerstones of Anglo-American law frequently viewed as a fundamental feature insuring that the criminal law process will be unbiased and provide equal treatment to all regardless of their social or economic position. In fact, this process emerged and was maintained precisely because it provided a means of perpetuating the inequality that was so fundamental to the society in which it emerged.

The principle of the adversary process as a key part of criminal procedure emerged in England during the period from 1300 to 1600.[6] Among the early tribal groups of England, criminal disputes were handled by kinship groups; "trial" was a matter of accomplishing some reconciliation between the offending parties. "Guilt" was not at issue: only the maintenance of group harmony was of consequence (Chambliss & Seidman, 1971:28–36).

---

5. This concept was first suggested by Schattschneider (1960). See also Bachrach and Baratz (1962, 1970).

6. I am indebted to Robert Seidman for this analysis, which appeared in Chambliss and Seidman (1971).

Before the fourteenth century, criminals were apprehended primarily by devices rooted in the *gemeinschaft* character of English rural life. The arrest of persons not yet indicted was a responsibility of the community. In the thirteenth century, for example, a *vill*—the smallest administrative "governmental" unit of the country—might be liable for failure to arrest those who had committed homicide; or, if the vill could not pay, the *hundred*—the next larger unit—was liable. As these older institutions decayed between the fourteenth and early sixteenth centuries, the law came to rely on the individual action of the citizen:

> Just as in the older law, all these rules [of pleading and of trial] must be put in motion and strictly obeyed by the parties at their own risk so now the parties must put in motion the machinery (Holdsworth, 1924a:598).

The modern state gradually took shape in England between the twelfth and sixteenth centuries. It was constructed on the ashes of feudalism and resulted from the bloody conflicts that raged between the Crown and barons, led by the Tudor monarchs, Henry VII, Henry VIII, and Elizabeth I. The Crown was supported by the ruling oligarchies of the towns and especially by the ruling elite of London. The victory of the Crown was thus a victory for the London elites.

Following the emergence of the state in this period there was a long period of instability and constant danger to its existence. There was no standing army and no police force. That the state through its control of the legal system supported the progressive weighting of the scales of justice in favor of the prosecution was not surprising.

The list of limitations on the ability of the accused to protect himself during the period between the sixteenth and mid-eighteenth centuries makes long and—to our values—painful reading. To insure that the jurors felt the weight of the evidence, witnesses were allowed to be called by the Crown, but not by the defense; the defendant, unsworn, had to reply to the evidence against him as best he could from memory. In *Throckmorton*'s case [1 St. Tr. 869 (1554)], a trial for high treason, for example, a witness referred to some statements made by a man called Arnold. Throckmorton, seeing a friend, Fitz Williams, in the audience, called upon him to be sworn as a witness to rebut the testimony. One of the commissioners trying the case said: "Go your ways, Fitz Williams, the court hath nothing to do with you. Peradventure you would not be so ready in a good cause" [1 St. Tr. 885 (1554)]. Statutes were enacted in 1589 and 1607 allowing witnesses for the defense, but, illogically enough, prohibiting their being sworn.

Statutes were passed making it more difficult for accused persons to get bail. In the absence of bail, an accused person remained incarcerated before trial, making it more difficult for him to prepare his case [31 Eliz. c. 4 (1588)]. Inquisitorial proceedings against suspects were permitted by justices of the peace, the Privy Council, or the judges [4 James 1 c. 1 sec. 6 (1606)].

> The magistrates interpreted their power widely. They actively got up the case against the prisoner, not only by questioning him and the witnesses against him, but also by searching for evidence against him. . . . These examinations were conducted secretly, and the evidence was communicated to the prosecutor and the judge, but not to the prisoner (Holdsworth, 1924b:91).

In addition, the Council used torture and incarceration to extract confessions, and in important cases simply disregarded what procedural rules there were.

Even that hallowed palladium of English liberty, the jury, did not remain immune from tampering. After Throckmorton had defended himself so brilliantly that the jury acquitted him, they were committed to prison for their verdict. Four submitted and apologized, but eight were haled before the Star Chamber some six months and more after the trial. They were discharged only after payment of £250 in fines (three, who were not worth so much, were fined £60). The foreman forfeited £2,000. This rigor was fatal to Sir John Throckmorton, who was found guilty and therefore was executed upon the same evidence on which his brother had been acquitted.

In charges of felony and treason the defendant was at first not allowed to have counsel. Indeed, he was not even permitted a copy of the statute under which he was being tried. Slowly, counsel were admitted to argue points of law for the accused. Not until the latter part of the eighteenth century was defense counsel permitted to cross-examine witnesses, and it was 1836 before defense counsel was permitted to address the jury (Williams, 1963:7–8).

The judges did not regard themselves as impartial arbiters between the individual and the state; their commitment to their royal masters was, more frequently than not, made quite clear. In the *Elwes* case [2 St. Tr. 936 (1554)], for example, Lord Coke, the presiding judge, cross-examined the accused closely, and finally produced against him a statement made by a man named Franklin. The statement had been made privately and not even upon oath before Coke himself, at five o'clock in the morning, before the court sat (Stephen, 1883:332).

The conduct of prosecutors was similarly open in its bias. The great Lord Coke himself, acting as prosecutor of Sir Walter Raleigh, abused the latter unmercifully before the jury:

Lord Coke: Thou art the most vile and execrable traitor that ever lived.

Raleigh: You speak indiscreetly, barbarously and uncivilly.

Lord Coke: I want words sufficient to express thy viperous treasons.

Raleigh: I think you want words, indeed, for you have spoken one thing half a dozen times.

Lord Coke: Thou are an odious fellow. Thy name is hateful to all the realm of England for thy pride.

Raleigh: It will go hard to prove a measuring case between you and me, Mr. Attorney.

Lord Coke: Well, I will now make it appear that there never lived a viler viper upon the face of the earth than thou (Stephen, 1883:333).

The judges' feeling that they were part of the governing arm is perhaps nowhere made clearer than in Raleigh's case. The accused insisted on the right to call as witness, Cobham, who had confessed to treason implicating Raleigh, but who had retracted his confession. Justice Warburton said:

I marvel, Sir Walter, that you, being of such experience and wit, should stand on this point: for so many horse stealers may escape, if they may not be condemned without witnesses (Stephen, 1883:334–35).

The unflagging support which the towns had given the Tudors withered shortly after the defeat of the Spanish Armada, and the feudal landowner's last hope for power in England. Almost immediately, the townsmen began to oppose the new Tudor aristocracy, an opposition that broke into open rebellion under Cromwell. The weighted scales in criminal trials did not reach a better balance during this period, but remained largely as before.

Following the "Glorious Revolution" in 1688, however, a relatively long period of tranquility in British government ensued, which was the century and a half during which the aristocratic constitution held sway. Active threat of revolution disappeared. The aristocracy were firmly in control of the government without significant challenge. The machinery of justice in the countryside centered around the justice of the peace, almost invariably a member of the landed gentry, who acted both as local administrator and as magistrate. The initiation of criminal prosecutions, in this relatively calm epoch, fell more and more on primate persons. The notion of the independence of the judiciary, first clearly identified as a significant political fact in 1688, was more easily entrenched as political stability became less closely entwined with the criminal process.

Then the introduction of commerce and trade brought into existence the new entrepreneurial class which ultimately was to force the aristocrats to share the reins of power. The emerging class of merchants and financiers were greatly helped by the intellectual revolution that was taking place all over Europe. In criminal law, the most important consequence of this revolution was the developing notion of *nullum crimen sine lege* and *nulla poena sine lege*—no crime without a law and no punishment without a law. The concept of *nulla poena* embodied the emerging capitalist classes' need for clarity, on which their entire economic enterprise rested. The law was a means of limiting the powers of the aristocratic government, which excluded them and used its powers indiscriminately through the courts to put down their organizations.

The adversary system was, for the capitalists, a device by which rational and sensible decisions in the legal order could be made, in which the prosecutor's suspicions could be challenged, and in which the state could be compelled to submit suspicions to verification. The individualistic nature of the adversary process was conducive to these ends; and it was congenial with the new capitalist class just as in the economic realm they relied on individual enterprise: "Every man must fend for himself."

The result of the mobilization of bias in favor of the emerging elite was a system of litigation in which formal differentiation on the basis of birth, wealth, or position was abolished. The rhetoric was that all men were equal before the law. In an old saw, the law was magnificently impartial: both rich and poor would be arrested for sleeping under bridges. In fact, the adversary system provided only a paper equality. Without affirmative aid to the poor or ignorant, the protections of the adversary system were limited to protection of the emergent capitalist class from discriminatory treatment by the old aristocracy. In a non-decision-making mobilization of bias, the new laws conveniently failed to provide real access to the benefits of the adversary process for the workers or the poor.

The private prosecution of offenses was one of the advantages of the criminal law system for the new ruling groups in England. The costs of prosecution were, at first, borne by the private prosecutor entirely. By 1861, however, as a result of almost a century of piecemeal legislation, the private prosecutor obtained the right to recover, after conviction, the costs of the prosecution, which in England included not merely relatively trivial court costs, but counsel fees as well. Conversely, in case of an acquittal, the prosecutor had to pay the costs incurred by the accused. Even as amended in 1861, the law still obviously favored the wealthy for they could better take the risk of losing the prosecution than could the working class or the poor.

Private prosecution, moreover, met the needs of the new industrial elites another way. By making the enforcement of criminal law, like the enforcement of the civil law, a matter of litigation between private parties, the state as represented by the judge became a mere arbiter between private interests. The state was made to appear as providing a neutral framework within which conflict and struggle could take place according to rules, thus ensuring that private initiative would be allowed the fullest play. As James Fitzjames Stephen, L.J., said in his spirited defense of nineteenth-century English criminal procedure:

> No stronger or more effectual guarantee can be provided for the due observance of the law of the land, by all persons under all circumstances, than is given by the power, conceded by the English system, of testing the legality of any conduct of which he disapproves, either on private or public grounds, by a criminal prosecution. Many such prosecutions, both in our days and in earlier times, have given legal vent to feelings in every way entitled to respect, and have decided peaceably, and in an authentic manner, many questions of great constitutional importance (Stephen, 1883:496).

These reforms in criminal procedure were not easily won. The statute of 1836, which finally gave the accused person full right to the counsel, for example, was strongly opposed by twelve of the fifteen judges; Justice Park even threatened to resign if the bill were passed. (He reconsidered after the enactment [Williams, 1963:8].) But in time the elements of what in this country we call due process became entrenched in English law.

The adversary system was thus an ideal arrangement which met the demands of the new masters of industry and commerce. They demanded and, in time, achieved a system of litigation that at once gave them a defense against the old aristocratic government and guaranteed their advantage over all lower classes.

In the United States, the Bill of Rights was framed while this great sea of change was under way in English criminal procedure. The Founding Fathers, having just rebelled against precisely the same aristocratic government against which the new English industrialist class was still struggling, demanded legal-rational legitimacy. They wrote into the new Constitution most of the significant reforms that were still being incubated in England: due process of law, the independence of the judiciary, the right to a jury, *habeas corpus*, the right to counsel, the right to summon witnesses in defense, the right to bail, indictment by grand jury, the privilege against self-incrimination. In short, due process ensured the institution of the adversary system and resolved a major conflict between competing elites without redistributing power or privilege to the lower classes. Significantly, all this came about in England and the United States through the mobilization of bias in the criminal law-making process as the perspective and needs of those who control societies' economic resources get translated into law.

THE LAW OF THEFT AND THE MOBILIZATION OF BIAS

The heart of a capitalist economic system is the protection of private property which is, by definition, the cornerstone upon which capitalist economies function.[7] It is not surprising, then, to find that the criminal law reflects this basic concern. Of particular interest to understanding the creation of legal rules is that during feudal times, when landowners were the undisputed masters of the economic resources of the society, laws concerning theft were largely unsophisticated, unsubtle, and narrowly defined. It was

---

7. This section draws heavily upon Hall (1952), but does not come to the same theoretical conclusion he does.

only with the advent of commerce and trade in Europe that the laws of theft that hold sway in contemporary capitalistic societies took their present form. Only as the feudal landowners lost control over the resources of the society and, therefore, over the law-making machinery did laws of theft emerge to protect the interests of the developing economic elites. This process took place largely through mobilization of bias and was effected through a series of decisions rendered by the appellate courts in England.

A turning point in the law of theft came in the *Carrier* case, which was decided in England in 1473:

> The facts are simple enough: the defendant was hired to carry certain bales to Southampton. Instead of fulfilling his obligation, he carried the goods to another place, broke open the bales and took the contents. He was apprehended and charged with felony (Hall, 1952:4).

At the time that the defendant was arrested and tried with a felony there was no law in England that made it a crime for anyone to convert to their own use goods which they came by legally. There had been an earlier rule applicable to servants but this had subsequently been disallowed prior to the *Carrier* case. Yet despite this lack of prevailing common law or legislative enactment a tribunal of the most learned judges in England decided against the defendant and found him guilty of larceny. By so doing they essentially established a new law and one which was central to the well-being of the emergent class of capitalist traders and industrialists.

There was, of course, great debate at the time of the decision, first among the judges making the decisions, then among legal scholars. There was no possibility that the new law could be justified logically but it was possible for the judges to create legal fictions that justified the decision. In this way the interests of the new upper class were protected, not through their direct involvement in law creation but through the "perceived need" of the judges sitting on the highest courts of the time. The "perceived need," of course, represented the mobilization of a bias which favored the interests of the dominant economic class.

Following the *Carrier* case in 1473, the law of theft expanded and developed throughout the sixteenth, seventeenth, and eighteenth centuries with the decisions in the eighteenth century playing the major role. "Larceny by servant" became established in the sixteenth century and over time the courts continuously interpreted cases so as to expand at every turn the legal definition of "possession of the master" to include even instances where the master had never seen the goods, so long as the servant placed goods received by him in a receptacle of his master. The courts also broadened the interpretation of "servant" to include cashiers, clerks, and persons hired to transport goods from place to place.

The law was, however, not always construed in ways consistent with the interests of the now dominant business class. In 1799, in the case of *King* v. *Joseph Bazeley*, the court found a bank clerk who had taken a hundred pounds and pocketed the money without putting it into the possession of the bank, even so far as placing it in a drawer and later withdrawing it, "not guilty." The former stretching of the law of theft had apparently reached its limit and would have required too great an innovation even in an area of law where innovation by judges had been the characteristic trend for the preceding three hundred years. Shortly after the *Bazeley* case, in the same year, the first embezzlement statute [39 Geo. III c. 85 (1799)] was passed thus absolving the appellate courts of the necessity for creating embezzlement laws.

In time, through legislative enactment and appellate court decisions, the law of theft was extended to include protection for the property owners against "larceny by trick," as well as all forms of converting property of others to personal use without the express consent and legal agreement of the original owner. It also became a crime for a third party to receive stolen property, thus adding one more thread to the ever-tightening web of protection for property owners. In 1692 it was enacted that:

> And forasmuch as thieves and robbers are much encouraged to commit such offenses, because a great number of persons make it their trade and business to deal in the buying of stolen goods; be it therefore enacted by the authority aforesaid, that if any person or persons shall buy or receive any goods or chattel that shall be feloniously taken or stolen from any other person, knowing the same to be stolen, he or they shall be taken and deemed an accessary or accessaries to such felony after the fact, and shall incur the same punishment, as an accessary or accessaries to the felony after the felony committed (3 and 4 W. and M. c. 9, IV).

BUREAUCRACIES AS A SOURCE OF CRIMINAL LAW

The argument and the data presented thus far have all been to the effect that those classes that control a society's economic resources also determine the content and form of the criminal law: the definition of what is criminal or delinquent. That this is so can scarcely be denied but it is not the whole story. First, there are groups other than economic elites capable of influencing and determining criminal laws. Second, conflicts which inhere in the structure of society also bring about changes in the prevailing definitions of crime.

Among nonelite groups that are a source of definitions of behavior as criminal or delinquent, none is more important in modern society than the bureaucracies that carry out the work of the state. Government bureaucracies may, in the last analysis, be controlled by those who influence the society's economic resources (see Chambliss, 1971), but they also have a life and a force of their own which increasingly influence what is defined as criminal or delinquent. The power of established bureaucracies to influence society's definition of behavior as deviant has been superbly documented in Foucault's study of *Madness and Civilization* (1965).

Prior to the fifteenth and sixteenth centuries there had been established in Europe, mostly in France and England, many leprosariums—as many as 200 in France alone. In the late fifteenth and early sixteenth centuries these leprosariums became emptied, probably due to the end of the Crusades, which apparently fostered the spread of leprosy. These hospitals and their administrative machinery stood unused or were in danger of becoming unused. By various royal decrees, obviously affected by the economic conditions of the times (the unemployed group swelled with returning Crusaders), these institutions began to house a whole host of misfits—beggars, criminals, insane and diseased persons—who were not needed or could not be used in the labor force. What is significant is the tendency of the bureaucracies that formerly dealt with lepers to be perpetuated by becoming institutions for housing the criminal, sick, insane, and vagrant.

During the Middle Ages madness was considered a touch of the divinity. One might be odd behaviorally but he was viewed as existing on some other plane of being. The madman was more the fool, the jester, perhaps the genius. Fools were sometimes put on ships, left to drift from port to port, only to be pushed out to sea again after a certain town had looked and been reminded of foolishness. Hence the name "Ship of Fools" ("Navarre Schift"). In the literature one finds madness as a voyage—another country. There is no element of depravity. And from a voyage of exile one may return "home."

The sense of moral degeneracy or depravity in the individual does not attach itself to the concept of madness until *after* the emergence from confinement. It seems very clear that the institution itself shaped the concept of madness. The confinement was a brutalizing experience. Boredom and abominable conditions led to illness and pain. Even those who did not become sick physically became less than coherent after years of chains and damp walls. Madness was not seen as a medical problem, rather the insane were viewed as beasts, forfeiting their humanity by their behavior. But again the "touch of the divine" hung on from the Middle Ages, except now it was not a touch of genius, of eccentric inspiration, but the touch of doom, of "falling from grace," of falling from humanity into bestiality—a God-given, inscrutable weakness in character.

The point of interest here is that for economic reasons, but in no small measure solely for the purpose of using an established bureaucratic structure, a whole host of "social problems" were created by the state. The bureaucracy thus created the laws and the law created the public view of the act.

Since the precedent was established in Europe, the role of bureaucracies in the creation of criminal laws has steadily increased in influence. Today the most important bureaucratic sources of new law are the law-enforcement bureaucracies themselves.

The fact that law-enforcement bureaucracies have become an important source of criminal law creation is quite ironic. It is akin to relying on General Motors as the prime source of laws setting automotive safety standards. Often, the treatment of representatives of law-enforcement bureaucracies by legislatures and judges assumes that by virtue of the bureaucracies' special role in society they necessarily possess a special expertise. A host of evidence suggests just the opposite: that by virtue of their special role, they have an especially biased view that would make objective testimony impossible. In general, law-enforcement agencies' concern with criminal law creation (either in legislatures or courts) leads to the emergence of laws which contribute to the smooth functioning of the law-enforcement bureaucracy irrespective of whether or not the laws are in the interest of society at large. Take, for example, the history of drug laws in the United States.

In no area of criminal law legislation have the law-enforcement agencies been more active than in the area of drug control. In the earlier discussions of the Comprehensive Drug Abuse, Prevention and Control Act of 1970 I pointed out how the Department of Justice and the Bureau of Narcotics and Dangerous Drugs participated in drafting this legislation and then in guiding it through the committees and houses of Congress. The influence of law-enforcement bureaucracies was apparent in both what they did and did not do. On the one hand, they were instrumental in defining the drug problem as primarily a problem of "freaks" and "criminal types," thus clearly focusing the scope of the law on the lower class and the youth groups taking drugs. The information which these agencies had on the relationship between the legal manufacture of drugs and the illegal drug market was only produced when demanded by congressmen. The law-enforcement agencies, in short, acted in the interests of the drug manufacturers both in the content of the proposed legislation and in the information supplied to the law-makers. Such a stance was good bureaucratic strategy in that it reduced the likelihood of opposition to the bill from a powerful lobby. Furthermore, it did *not* make the law enforcers responsible for enforcing laws against the will of strong economic interests. At the same time the bill did provide greater license for law enforcers to arrest and prosecute those classes and groups who could be processed with relative freedom from bureaucratic strain (Chambliss, 1969). The 1970 drug law is not unique: indeed, it is no exaggeration to say that the entire set of rules governing the enforcement of anti-drug laws has derived more from regulations of the law-enforcement bureaucracies than from legislators or appellate-court decisions (Lindesmith, 1965).

It was largely due to the efforts of the Federal Narcotics Bureau (later renamed the Bureau of Narcotics and Dangerous Drugs) that in 1937 the Marihuana Tax Act was passed:

> Prior to 1937 Mr. Anslinger (then the director of the Federal Bureau of Narcotics) and the Bureau of Narcotics had spearheaded a propaganda campaign against marihuana on the ground that it produced an immense amount of violent crime such as rape, mayhem, and murder, and that many traffic accidents could be attributed to it (Lindesmith, 1965:230).

The campaign and the propaganda were spearheaded by and paid for with funds from the Bureau that would have the responsibility for the enforcement of the law. The bill was passed with little discussion in Congress. The congressmen apparently assumed that the Bureau of Narcotics was the ultimate authority on such matters and did not see it as necessary or wise to call for outside testimony. This was a classic case of an organization being in a position to expand its domain vastly and to legitimize its need for greater resources by controlling the information available to the lawmakers.

The Narcotics Bureau had also created public support for antimarijuana legislation by feeding magazines and newspapers stories on the dangers of marijuana. Becker's comparison (1963) of the number of articles dealing with marijuana for the years preceding and following the 1937 Congress reveals the emergence of media interest in a previously dormant issue. That this media interest was fanned by the Narcotics Bureau is evidenced by the fact that the articles contained cases supplied by the Bureau as well as "data" distributed by Bureau personnel (Becker, 1963).

The lawmaking function of the bureaucracy was extended as well to the state level. Through the production and distribution of information and through personal influence the Bureau of Narcotics activated state and municipal law-enforcement agencies and obtained passage of antimarijuana laws duplicating the federal laws in most of the states.

The laws governing the use of opiates in the United States show a similar pattern. In the U.S. prior to 1914 addicts could and did readily obtain drugs from pharmacies, physicians, and even mail-order houses. In 1914 the Harrison Act was passed as a revenue measure, and was designed "to make the entire process of drug distribution within the country a matter of record" (Lindesmith, 1965). The act did not make it a crime to be an addict or to take drugs. However, the administrative orders of the Federal Narcotics Bureau and the Bureau's careful selection of court cases in effect translated the Harrison Act into a law that punished drug addicts for their addiction (Lindesmith, 1965). The Federal Narcotics Bureau also through administrative practices—even in the face of laws contradicting these practices—pursued a policy of arresting and prosecuting selected medical doctors who provided drugs for addicts. These practices were effective in creating a law by administrative practice which was never created by legislature or appellate court (Lindesmith, 1965). In the end, the policies and propaganda of the Narcotics Bureau also created public support for its policies where none existed originally (Becker, 1963; Duster, 1970).

An analysis of juvenile-court legislation in California has also shown the power of law-enforcement bureaucracies in creating law (Lemert, 1970). Lemert's analysis of the emergence and functioning of the California Youth Authority makes clear how bureaucratic needs may determine the shape of law:

> the pressing need for a budget to support the C.Y.A.'s Division of Institutions has meant that where the choice has had to be made beween upgrading juvenile court operation through new legislation and maintaining dominant organizational interests, the latter

has prevailed. . . . The need to support and administer existing institutions, as well as construct new ones, soon established budgetary priority for the Division of Institutions, and came to occupy the largest share of time, energies, and attention of administrators and staff. Recruitment practices, in-training programs, and job assignments tended to preserve a custodial pattern of action within the Division of Institutions, despite the California Youth Authority's informal dedication and official allegiance to the purposes of individualized treatment (Lemert, 1970:56, 52).

It is likely that these cases do little more than expose the more visible examples of bureaucratic involvement in the creation of laws. The general rule of law creation that emerges is that bureaucracies will use their resources, power, and influence to obtain passage and suppression of laws that represent the interests of the bureaucracies themselves. The "public interest" or the long-range goals of law are largely irrelevant or at least are only secondary to the interests of the bureaucracies in running and expanding trouble-free organizations.

PUBLIC INDIGNATION

Part of the mythology that surrounds the law is the view that new laws are created as a result of a change in the values of "the people." This perspective, which is often espoused by social scientists as well as lawyers, sees an assumed "value-consensus" of the community as the root of all law. As we have seen from the data presented, such a view scarcely does justice to the realities of legislation. There is, nevertheless, a substantial body of data which indicates that public views on morality *do* affect legislation especially those views of segments of the public which get representation by groups of moral entrepreneurs: that is, groups organized to influence lawmaking and enforcement according to their view of morality.

Some of the earliest systematic work on the issue of public indignation and criminal law legislation was done by the Danish sociologist Svend Ranulf in the two classical studies, *The Jealousy of the Gods* (1933) and *Moral Indignation and Middle Class Psychology* (1938). Ranulf shows by careful historical analysis that in both Greece and Europe the "disinterested tendency to punish" for moral breeches emerges with the development of a lower-middle class. Ranulf's explanation for this phenomenon is that moral indignation stems from a basic tendency of the lower-middle class to envy the position of the more affluent classes. This psychological interpretation is not particularly enlightening but, as Ranulf notes, accepting the historical sequence of events does not necessitate the acceptance of his explanation.

More recently Troy Duster (1970) and Joseph Gusfield (1963) have contributed to the study of the role of public indignation with their studies of drug laws and prohibition, respectively.

Duster's study is largely devoted to a refutation of the cliché that we "cannot legislate morality"; or in the words of William Graham Sumner, stateways cannot make folkways. Duster shows quite clearly how the passage of the antidrug law in 1914 (the Harrison Act) combined with the propagandizing and bureaucratic efforts of federal law-enforcement agencies led eventually to widespread acceptance among the middle classes of the idea that drug use was immoral, sinful, and dangerous.

Further evidence of the role of moral entrepreneurs as a force creating changes in the criminal law is provided by Joseph Gusfield's study (1963) of the emergence of prohibition laws. Gusfield argues persuasively that the moving force behind the emergence of prohibition laws was an organized effort by those segments of the middle class who saw their economic and social position being threatened by changing economic forces. It was essentially the decline of the importance of small-town society with its middle-class, rural background that created a constituency desirous of asserting its importance through law. This threatened, downwardly mobile class managed to bring sufficient political pressure that laws were passed to placate them (Sinclair, 1964).

The effects of public indignation on the emergence and shape of the criminal law are also provided by an examination of the role of groups organized to protect the "public interest." In the United States much of the law governing criminal procedure has been written and rewritten by groups of moral entrepreneurs, especially the American Civil Liberties Union and the National Association for the Advancement of Colored People (Chambliss & Seidman, 1971). The ACLU has been particularly active in criminal law cases where their concern has been with police procedures. In a series of landmark decisions of the U.S. Supreme Court, the ACLU provided funds and legal counsel which virtually rewrote the laws governing police behavior. These moral entrepreneurs, although protecting the rights of the lower classes, are themselves composed of middle-class members of the community and are supported by financial contributions from that same middle class.

It is not the case, however, that the moral indignation of the middle classes is any guarantee that criminal laws will be passed. In general it appears that middle-class indignation is most likely to culminate in the creation of new law when the indignation coalesces into a working organization with specific roles and financial backing.

Middle-class organizations are, for the most part, unable to combat or counteract the forces of the classes who control the economic resources of the society. As we saw earlier in the history of criminal law legislation, the economic elites' interests are protected by their ability to directly influence legislation and by their mobilization of bias which flows from their position in the society. During the discussion of the Drug Abuse, Prevention and Control Act of 1970, for example, the interests of the law-enforcement bureaucracies and the drug industry were so fully represented that the moral indignation of the middle class, which was ostensibly the basis for the passage of the law, was simply an excuse used to legitimize a law which was first and foremost a reflection of the wishes of more powerful interests.

The groups of moral entrepreneurs who represent the indignation of at least some segment of the middle class fare best when they engage less-potent forces than the economic elites. In particular, their effect on criminal law legislation is likely to be most noticeable where they engage the law-enforcement bureaucracies or only small businesses.

Such was the case in a recent debate in New York over revision of the laws concerning prostitution (Roby, 1969). The issue arose over Article 230 (one of approximately 520 sections) of the 1965 New York State Penal Law. Sections 230.00, 230.05, and 230.10 of the code provide:

§ 230.00   Prostitution
A person is guilty of prostitution when such person engages or agrees or offers to engage in sexual conduct with another person in return for a fee.
Prostitution is a violation. L. 1965, c. 1030, eff. Sept. 1, 1967.

§ 230.05   Patronizing a prostitute
A person is guilty of patronizing a prostitute when:
1. Pursuant to a prior understanding, he pays a fee to another person as compensation for such person or a third person having engaged in sexual conduct with him; or
2. He pays or agrees to pay a fee to another person pursuant to an understanding that in return therefor such person or a third person will engage in sexual conduct with him; or

3. He solicits or requests another person to engage in sexual conduct with him in return for a fee.

Patronizing a prostitute is a violation. L. 1965, c. 1030, eff. Sept. 1, 1967.

§ 230.10   Prostitution and patronizing a prostitute; no defense

In any prosecution for prostitution or patronizing a prostitute, the sex of the two parties or prospective parties to the sexual conduct engaged in, contemplated, or solicited is immaterial, and it is no defense that:

1. Such persons were of the same sex; or

2. The person who received, agreed to receive or solicited a fee was a male and the person who paid or agreed or offered to pay such fee was a female. L. 1965, c. 1030, eff. Sept. 1, 1967.

At the time this revised code was proposed prostitution was subject to a penalty of up to three years in a reformatory or a year in jail. Further, prostitution was, until 1960, defined by court decisions as an act commitable only by a female. In 1960, by court decision, homosexuality was incorporated under the umbrella of the statute (Roby, 1969:87).

The new code on prostitution made two significant changes: first, it included as a violation patronizing a prostitute and, second, it greatly reduced the penalty for prostitution by making the act a "violation" rather than a crime. The maximum sentence for a violation is fifteen days rather than a year in jail.

In 1961 the governor of New York appointed a commission to recommend needed revisions of the Penal Law and the Code of Criminal Procedure. The commission staff relied heavily on the advice of Chief Justice John M. Murtagh, a judge nationally known for his concern with criminal procedures in dealing with prostitution. The commission members also relied on Great Britain's *Wolfenden Report* (1963), the model penal codes of the American Bar Association, and procedures in other states.

After four years of work the commission held "public hearings" on the proposed penal code revision. "The public" was probably unaware of the event but some special interest groups were not. Of the 520 articles only the one dealing with prostitution was revised as a result of these hearings. The major change wrought was the addition of "patronizing a prostitute" as a violation, something which was *not* included in the commission's original proposed code. The major proponent for including "patronizing" was the American Social Health Association, which argued that the only way to control the spread of disease effectively was by punishing the patron. The Association's view was buttressed by arguments from Dorris Clarke, attorney and retired chief probation officer of the New York City Magistrates Court. Further support came from testimony of an independent doctor who argued that since both customer and prostitute were guilty, both should be punished.

Combating this position were Judge Murtagh and a few spokesmen for the police who argued that the police needed to have the confidence of customers in order to get testimony against prostitutes.

The opposition was, at this point, no match in number or organization and thus the patron clause was written into the law.

On the eve of the new law becoming effective the police relaxed their enforcement policies. Subsequently a rumor circulated that there was an influx of prostitutes into the city. The source of the rumor is not clear but:

New York politicians, businessmen, and the police may have begun to talk about an influx of prostitutes and the need for a "cleanup" because they were dissatisfied with the law becoming "soft" on prostitutes (Roby, 1969:94).

During this time police department representatives began telling newsmen of increases in prostitution.

The commission that had drafted the new law denied these allegations. In any event, in August, 1967 midtown businessmen and the New York Hotel Association, along with politicians and government officials, pressured the police to get rid of the prostitutes in the area of Times Square.

Approximately two weeks before the new law was to become effective the police made a series of raids around Times Square and arrested suspected prostitutes by the score! On August 20 alone 121 were arrested on Times Square. Between August and September 23, 1,300 arrests were made. Most of those that *followed* the date when the new law became effective (September 1) were for loitering or disorderly conduct.

The New York Civil Liberties Union, the Legal Aid Society, and a New York judge all made vociferous protests over the mass arrest of persons for disorderly conduct and loitering when it was obvious, even to the police, that these charges would not stand up in court. The NYCLU reported on September 22, 1967:

> In a press release, the New York Civil Liberties Union protested police practices in the "Times Square cleanup campaign." The NYCLU reported, "Literally hundreds of women have been arrested and charged with disorderly conduct during the summer months, and the situation still continues." ". . . There is a conspiracy on the part of the police to deprive these women of their civil rights by arresting them on insubstantial charges." ". . . Women are being arrested in a dragnet and charged with disorderly conduct and loitering in order to raise the number of arrests." ". . . Many innocent girls are undoubtedly being caught in the net and the entire practice is an outrageous perversion of the judicial process. Furthermore, women who refuse to submit to the unlawful practices of the police have been manhandled."
>
> The Union reported Judge Basel saying, "I don't doubt that most of them are prostitutes, but it is a violation of the civil liberties of these girls. Even streetwalkers are entitled to their Constitutional rights. The District Attorney moved in all these cases to have the charges thrown out, but in every case the girls were arrested after it was too late for night court, so they were kept over night with no substantial charges pending against them" (Roby, 1969:95).

The police roundup continued. From September 23 to September 30 another 1,100 arrests were made. These arrests brought the total from August 20 to September 30 to 2,400; this total was only 200 less arrests in six weeks than had been reported during the preceding six months. Significantly, only 61 percent of the arrests for violation of the prostitution ordinance involved the arrest of patrons despite the fact that the only legal basis for arresting prostitutes was for a policeman to observe a patron offering and a prostitute accepting a fee.

Thus began a campaign by the police department, in cooperation with the hotel association and businessmen in the area, to change those parts of the new penal code that liberalized the prostitution laws. In September, 1967 the police department prefiled amendments to be considered by the 1968 legislature. These amendments, in effect, would have given the police almost complete discretion in the arrest of suspected prostitutes; they would have returned prostitution to the status of a crime, thus increasing the penalties, and these amendments would have effectively enabled the police to avoid the application of the law to patrons without formally changing this part of the penal code.

The mayor of New York City created a committee to look into the new law and the problem of prostitution. The committee in the end recommended that prostitution be reclassified a crime instead of its present status as a "violation" (thereby the penalty would have increased from fifteen days to one year in jail). But the committee did *not* recommend adopting any of the other changes advocated by the police and the hotel association. When this proposal was presented before the state legislature, it went to a Senate committee which voted *against* sending the bill back to the Senate: thus the law was kept as passed in 1967 for another year. In the end, the welfare, civil liberties, and bar association interests dominated over the interests of the police and the businessmen with respect to the severity of the sanctions and the criteria for making an arrest. The police and businessmen held sway over enforcement policies but this did *not* culminate in any immediate change in the law.

The New York Bar Association, NYCLU, and Legal Aid Society, along with some prominent public figures, proved to be more potent forces in shaping the formal law than did the police and the hotel owners association.

The analysis of the New York controversy over prostitution makes this point. For the most part the controversy over the new law was limited to different groups of moral entrepreneurs from the middle class: civil liberties and welfare groups on the one side, police and small businessmen on the other. The issue was largely irrelevant to the economic elites of the state or even to the bulk of the city population, and as a result, they were apathetic. To the extent that the upper classes were represented at all in the debate, the new legislation was tacitly supported, judging from the support given by the bar associations and commissions in their suggested revisions. This case also illustrates how police, prosecutorial, and judicial discretion can subvert the law. The 1965 revision made patrons, who doubtless represented the entire spectrum of social classes, equally culpable. The police, however, through selective enforcement, rendered this aspect of the law virtually meaningless and forced reconsideration by the lawmakers.

MODELS OF LAW CREATION

Until recently the prevailing view in modern social thought—both legal and social science—has centered on one or more of the following propositions:

1. The law represents the value-consensus of the society.
2. The law represents those values and perspectives which are fundamental to social order.
3. The law represents those values and perspectives which it is in the public interest to protect.
4. The state as represented in the legal system is value-neutral.
5. In pluralistic societies the law represents the interests of the society at large by mediating between competing interest groups.

Among sociologists the work of Emile Durkheim is the outstanding example of the systematic analysis of law from this perspective. It is, therefore, worth spending some time appraising Durkheim's thesis as put forth in *The Division of Labor in Society* (1893). My concern here will not be to point out contradictions, inconsistencies, or tautologies in Durkheim's work but only to explore how closely Durkheim's thesis fits with extant empirical data.

Durkheim stated his central thesis quite clearly: for an act to be a crime that is punishable by law, it must be (1) universally offensive to the collective conscience of the people, (2) strongly opposed, and (3) a clear and precise form of behavior. In his words:

> the only common characteristic of crimes is that they consist . . . in acts universally disapproved of by members of each society . . . crime shocks sentiments which, for a given social system, are found in all healthy consciences (1893:73).

> The collective sentiments to which crime corresponds must, therefore, singularize themselves from others by some distinctive property; they must have a certain average in-

tensity. Not only are they engraven in all consciences, but they are strongly engraven (p. 77).

The wayward son, however, and even the most hardened egotist are not treated as criminals. It is not sufficient, then, that the sentiments be strong; they must be precise (p. 79).

An act is criminal when it offends strong and defined states of the collective conscience (p. 80).

Those acts, to offend the common conscience, need not relate ". . . to vital interests of society nor to a minimum of justice" (1893:81). Durkheim argues that a single murder may have less dire social consequences than the failure of the stock market, yet the former is a crime for the reasons stated and the latter is not.

Durkheim distinguishes two types of law: Restitutive and Repressive. Restitutive law "is not expiatory, but consists of a simple *return to state*" (1893:111). Repressive law is one which "in any degree whatever, invokes against its author the characteristic reaction which we term punishment" (p. 70). Restitutive laws, or as he sometimes says, "co-operative laws with restitutive sanctions" (p. 129), are laws that invoke rule enforcement but which (a) do not reflect the collective conscience (they reflect only the opinions of *some* of the members of society), and (b) do not reflect sentiments that are strongly felt. Therefore, these laws do *not* invoke penal sanctions but only rule enforcement. The more specialized the functions of law, the less the laws represent the common conscience. As a result, they cannot then offend the common conscience since they are in fact marginal and not common to all. Thus expiatory responses are likely. "The rules which determine them cannot have the superior force, the transcendent authority which, when offended, demands expiation" (1893:127).

There is very little evidence in the studies of the process by which laws are created that would support Durkheim's thesis. It is obvious that, contrary to Durkheim's expectations, industrial societies have tended to pass more and more repressive laws (Kadish, 1967) and that these laws have reflected special interests to a greater extent than they reflect the feelings of "all healthy consciences." Indeed, the reverse is closer to the mark: the collective conscience is largely irrelevant to the creation of laws. What relationship there is tends to be a consequence rather than a cause of new laws.

A view closely related to Durkheim's has also held considerable influence. This is the often-expressed belief that criminal law represents an attempt to control acts which it is in the "public interest" to control. Auerbach et al. attempted a listing of minimal elements of "the public interest":

a) It is in the "public interest" that our nation be free from outside dictation in determining its destiny; that it have the power of self-determination. . . .

b) It is in the public interest to preserve the legitimated institutions through which conflicts in our society are adjusted and peaceful change effected, no matter how distasteful particular decisions reached by these institutions may be to particular groups in our society. In other words, the preservation of democracy—government with the freely given consent of the governed—is in the public interest.

c) It is in the public interest that no group in our society should become so powerful that it can submerge the claims of all other groups.

d) It is in the public interest that all claims made by individuals and groups in our society should at least be heard and considered by the law-making authorities. This proposition, which calls for recognition of the freedom to speak and to associate with others in pursuit of group interests, is a fundamental assumption of the democratic order.

e) It is in the public interest that every individual enjoy a minimum decent life and that the degree of inequality in the opportunities open to individuals be lessened (1961:661).

A variety of arguments suggest that this statement of a national public interest is invalid. Even assuming that there were a value-consensus on these propositions, the range of questions that come before lawmaking agencies and the state is largely outside their scope. Such a view is not a very useful or interesting guide to the study of lawmaking, for very few questions coming before lawmakers actually touch on any of these generalized objectives. Rather, they tend to be much narrower: What should the penalty be for prostitution? Should the patron be punished? Does the law of theft include "breaking bale and carrying away"? Are amphetamines to be included as dangerous drugs? Should students engaged in disruption in state universities automatically be expelled upon conviction? The usual questions coming before lawmaking authorities only rarely touch on the large questions suggested by any list of supposed "public interests."

Second, even if one were to accept these statements of "the public interest," the actual questions coming before lawmakers that even touch on these objectives are never very simple. Whether or not the United States ought to simply turn itself over to a foreign power, for example, is a question that has never come and doubtless never will come before any legislature. Rather, the question is always partial and problematic: Is joining the United Nations, and the surrender of sovereignty *pro tanto*, for example, too serious an invasion of the "public interest" in independence? If "freedom to speak" is "a fundamental assumption of the democratic order," then it can be argued that no private individual or corporation ought to control newspapers, television, or other institutions of the mass media, which instead should be equally available to all without regard to their financial resources. That would require government control of the mass media, which might well be regarded as the negation of free speech. While, no doubt, it is in the public interest that every individual should enjoy the minimum essentials of a decent life, exactly how much is a "minimum"? Is it in the public interest to reduce the size of "big business" in order to keep that group from attaining too much power, even if it can be shown that large economic units are more efficient than smaller ones? And if one decides to reduce the size of "big business," what is to be the standard of acceptable maximum size?

Third, is it true that even this list of "the minimal elements of the public interest" would be unanimously accepted? It is notable for omitting any reference to minimum protection for property. Many members of the propertied classes, at least in the American society, would insist that such a guarantee is an essential component of the "public interest." The list omits any statement that equality of treatment before the law regardless of race or color is a necessary ingredient of "the public interest"; white racists would hardly complain of this omission but others surely would.

Fourth, what a majority conceives of as "the public interest" at any period in history is not a constant. Not so long ago a majority of the lawmakers believed that it was in the public interest to prevent any citizen from buying alcoholic beverages. Not very long before that, in the long view of history, no doubt a majority believed that it was in the public interest to burn wretched old women at the stake as witches. How can one be sure that today's perception of "the public interest" is not merely an evanescent reflection of the value-sets of the majority?

Finally, consider the second of the propositions put forward, the broadest and most overarching of all: "It is in the public interest to preserve the legitimated institutions through which conflicts in society are adjusted and peaceful change effected." So long as real poverty exists, it seems clear that the fifth assertion of "the public interest," i.e., "that every individual enjoy a minimum decent life," is sharply in conflict with the second. Which of these interests is to be overriding? The repeated phenomenon of urban rioting in the ghettos of America suggests that there is no value-consensus on the relative weight to be given to any of these propositions which purport to define "the public interest."

The reason why this or any other set of claimed "public interest" elements, a commonly held *summum bonum*, can never adequately describe the actual state of affairs can be explained philosophically as well as empirically. John Dewey (1938) has argued that a distinction must be made between *that which is prized* and the *process of valuation*. No doubt we all have general, culturally acquired objectives, i.e., things which are prized. In any specific instance, however, how we define these general-ized goals depends on a complex process of considering objective constraints, relative costs and benefits, and the valuation of alternative means. In this process of valuation, our generalized objectives are necessarily modified and changed as they become con-crete and definite—i.e., in Dewey's language, as they become ends-in-view. Whatever the relative cultural agreement on general, broad prizings, there is never any complete agreement on any specific end in view.

The particular norms prescribed by law always are specific. They always command the role-occupant to act in specific ways. It is always a statement, not of generalized prizings, but of a specific end in view. It is the result of a process of valuation. On that valuation there is never complete agreement, for there is no complete agreement on the relative weightings to be given the various prizings held in different strata of the society, nor on the relative valuation to be given to different means.

In short, every assertion that a specific law should have a certain content must necessarily reflect the process of valuation of its proponents, and by the same token, it will be opposed to the processes of valuation of its opponents. The nature of law as a normative system, commanding what ought to be done, necessitates that it will favor one group as against another. The proof, whatever academic model-builders may say, lies in the fact that there is some opposition to *every* proposed new rule, whether or not the lawmakers themselves are unanimous. Even a declaration of war in the face of armed attack is never supported by the *entire* population.

That the law necessarily advances the values of some groups in society and opposes others reflects the fact that in any complex, modern society there is no value-consensus that is relevant to the law. That is so because of the very nature of the different "webs of life" that exist. It is a function of society itself.

For many of the same reasons, the view that the state is a value-neutral agent which weighs competing interests and distributes the available resources equitably is equally untenable. There are, indeed, competing interests but the competitors enter the arena with vastly different resources and, therefore, much different chances of suc-cess (Reich, 1964; Domhoff, 1970). The state, rather than being value-neutral, is, in fact, an agent of the side which controls the production and distribution of the soci-ety's available resources. The criminal law is then first and foremost a reflection of the interests and ideologies of the governing class—whether that class is private indus-try or state bureaucracy. Only secondarily, and even then only in minor ways, does the criminal law reflect the value-consensus, the public interest, or the sifting and weighing of competing interests.

A model more consistent with the realities of legal change must take into account differences in power which stem largely from differences in control over the economic resources of the society. More importantly, an adequate model to account for the defini-tion of behavior as criminal or delinquent must recognize that in societies with social class divisions there is inevitably conflict between social classes and it is this class conflict which is the moving force for legal changes. Actions of the ruling class or representatives thereof as well as the machinations of moral entrepreneurs and the mobilization of bias all reflect attempts by various social classes to have their own interests and ideologies implemented by the state through the legal system.[8] It is, of course, true that the conflicts that are the basis of legal changes are not fought by equals. Thus those who control the economic and political resources of the society will inevitably see their interests and ideologies more often represented in the law than will others.

There are, of course, issues that are of only minor consequence to the established economic and political relations in the society. Such issues may be described by the pluralist perspective that sees different interest groups of more or less equal power arguing in the value-neutral arena of state bureaucracies. It seems clear that such instances are rare, and, in fact, even when the issue is the wording of prostitution laws or the changes in juvenile court laws there are differences in power between groups and these differences will usually determine the outcome of the struggle.

SUMMARY AND CONCLUSION

From the Black Death in feudal England where the vagrancy laws emerged and were shaped, through the Star Chamber in the fifteenth century where judges defined the law of theft in order to protect the interests of the ruling classes, to the legislatures of New York and California and the appellate courts of the United States lies a vast array of criminal laws that have been created, contradicted, reformulated, and allowed to die. Constructing a general theory that can account for such a wide range of events is no simple task. It is not surprising that such efforts often fall short of their goal.

Looking only at the two most general models of rule creation: the "value-consensus" and the "ruling class" models and pitting them against the extant empirical data leave little doubt but that both fall short of the mark. The value-consensus model which suggests that community consensus is the moving force behind the definition of behavior as criminal and delinquent finds little support in the systematic study of the development of criminal law. The ruling class model falls short as an adequate explanation to the extent that it posits a monolithic ruling class which sits in jurisdiction over a passive mass of people and passes laws reflecting only the interests of those who rule.

On the other hand, the importance of the ruling class in determining the shape of the criminal law cannot be gainsaid—whether that influence is through direct involvement in the law-creating process or merely through the mobilization of bias. Nor, for that matter, can the influence of "public opinion" (especially as this is organized around moral entrepreneurs) be ignored as a source of criminal law. Thus both general models contain some valuable truths to which must be added the important role played by bureaucracies, vested interest groups, and even individuals acting virtually alone (Lewis, 1966).

An alternative model compatible with the data is best described as a conflict theory of legal change. The starting point for this theory is the recognition that modern, industrialized society is composed of numerous social classes and interest groups who

---

8. Most broadly conceived, each of these sources of law may be summarized under the concept of "interest groups" (Quinney, 1970). But such a general concept does little more than provide an umbrella under which to put these various social processes. Further, the notion of "interest groups" often leads to the erroneous implication that competition for control of or influence over the state is a battle between equals where social class differences are largely irrelevant. It seems analytically wiser to deal with all the sources of criminal law creation and to see them as stemming from basic conflicts within the society.

compete for the favors of the state. The stratification of society into social classes where there are substantial (and at times vast) differences in wealth, power, and prestige inevitably leads to conflict between the extant classes. It is in the course of working through and living with these inherent conflicts that the law takes its particular content and form. It is out of the conflicts generated by social class divisions that the definition of some acts as criminal or delinquent emerges.

So long as class conflicts are latent, those who sit at the top of the political and economic structure of the society can manipulate the criminal laws to suit their own purposes. But when class conflict breaks into open rebellion, as it often does in such societies (Rubenstein, 1970), then the state must enact legislation and the courts reinterpret laws in ways that are perceived as solutions to the conflict. During times of manifest class conflict, legislatures and courts will simultaneously create criminal laws that provide greater control over those groups who are engaged in acts disruptive to the status quo and laws which appear to alleviate the conditions which are seen as giving rise to the social conflicts.

In between crises or perhaps as an adjunct to the legislative-judicial innovations taking place because of them, bureaucracies can mobilize and moral entrepreneurs organize to plead their case before the lawmaking bodies. Without the changes in economic structure that accompanied England's transition from feudalism to capitalism the laws of theft and vagrancy (to mention only two) would not have taken the form they did, just as the Supreme Court decisions and legislative enactments of the 1960s that effectively refocused substantial areas of the criminal law would not have taken place without the riots, rebellions, and overt social conflicts which characterized that historical period in America.

Crime is a political phenomenon. What gets defined as criminal or delinquent behavior is the result of a political process within which rules are formed which prohibit or require people to behave in certain ways. It is this process which must be understood as it bears on the definition of behavior as criminal if we are to proceed to the study of criminal *behavior*. Thus to ask "why is it that some acts get defined as criminal while others do not" is the starting point for all systematic study of crime and criminal behavior. Nothing is inherently criminal, it is only the response that makes it so. If we are to explain crime, we must first explain the social forces that cause some acts to be defined as criminal while other acts are not.

REFERENCES

Aaronovitch, S., and K. Aaronovitch.
   1947   Crisis in Kenya. London: Lawrence & Withorp.

Appelbaum, Richard P.
   1966   "Seasonal migration in San Ildefonso: its causes and its consequences." Public and International Affairs 4(Spring):117–159.

Auerbach, D., K. Garrison, W. Hurst, and S. Mermin.
   1961   The Legal Process: An Introduction to Decision-Making by Judicial, Legislative, Executive, and Administrative Agencies. San Francisco: Chandler.

Bachrach, Peter, and Morton Baratz.
   1962   "Two faces of power." American Political Science Review 51(December): 947–952.

   1970   Power and Poverty: Theory and Practice. New York: Oxford University Press.

Becker, Howard.
    1963   Outsiders: Studies in the Sociology of Deviance. New York: Free Press of Glencoe.

Bradshaw, F.
    1915   A Social History of England. London: University of London Press.

Carson, W. G. O.
    1971   "The sociology of crime and the emergence of criminal laws." Paper presented at the British Sociological Association, London, April.

Chambliss, William J.
    1964   "A sociological analysis of the law of vagrancy." Social Problems 11(Summer):67–77.
    1967   "Types of deviance and the effectiveness of legal sanction." Wisconsin Law Review 1967(Summer):703–723.
    1969   Crime and the Legal Process. New York: McGraw-Hill.
    1971   "Vice, corruption, bureaucracy and power." Wisconsin Law Review 1971 (December):1150–1173.

Chambliss, William J., and Robert B. Seidman.
    1971   Law, Order and Power. Reading, Mass.: Addison-Wesley.

Clairmonte, Paul.
    1969   "Nigeria under colonial rule." Ibadan, Nigeria: Behavioral Science Research Institute, University of Ibadan (mimeographed).

Cloward, Richard A., and Lloyd E. Ohlin.
    1960   Delinquency and Opportunity: A Theory of Delinquent Gangs. New York: Free Press of Glencoe.

Cohen, Albert K.
    1955   Delinquent Boys. Glencoe, Ill.: Free Press.

Cressey, Donald R.
    1968   "Culture conflict, differential association, and normative conflict." Pp. 43–54 in Marvin Wolfgang (ed.), Crime and Culture: Essays in Honor of Thorsten Sellin. New York: Wiley.

Deutscher, Irwin.
    1955   "The petty offender." Federal Probation 19(June):609–617.

Dewey, John.
    1938   Logic: The Theory of Inquiry. New York: Holt.

Domhoff, G. William.
    1970   The Higher Circles. New York: Random House.

Durkheim, Emile.
    1893   The Division of Labor in Society. Translation by George Simpson. Glencoe, Ill.: Free Press (1947 edition).

Duster, Troy.
    1970   The Legislation of Morality: Law, Drugs and Moral Judgment. New York: Free Press.

Foote, Caleb.
    1956   "Vagrancy-type law and its administration." University of Pennsylvania Law Review 104:603–650.

Foucault, Michael.
    1965   Madness and Civilization: A History of Insanity in the Age of Reason. New York: Pantheon Books.

Friedman, Lawrence, and Stewart Macaulay.
  1969   Law and the Behavioral Sciences. Indianapolis: Bobbs-Merrill.
Glaser, Daniel.
  1971   "Criminology and public policy." American Sociologist 6:30–37.
Graham, James M.
  1971   Profits At All Costs: Amphetamine Politics on Capitol Hill. Ann Arbor:
          University of Michigan (mimeographed).
Gusfield, Joseph R.
  1963   Symbolic Crusade: Status Politics and the American Temperance Move-
          ment. Urbana: University of Illinois Press.
Halisbury, Earl of.
  1912   The Laws of England. Bell Yard, Temple Bar, London: Butterworth & Co.
Hall, Jerome.
  1952   Theft, Law, and Society. Revised Edition. Indianapolis: Bobbs-Merrill.
Hetzler, Antoinette.
  1971   "The law: a study of administrators as mediators of legal change." Ph.D.
          dissertation, University of California at Santa Barbara.
Holdsworth, Sir William.
  1924a   A History of English Law, vol. 3. Boston: Little, Brown.
  1924b   A History of English Law, vol. 5. Boston: Little, Brown.
Hurst, J. Willard.
  1950   The Growth of American Law: The Law Makers. Boston: Little, Brown.
  1956   Law and Conditions of Freedom. Madison: University of Wisconsin Press.
Jeffery, C. Ray.
  1957   "The development of crime in early English society." Journal of Criminal
          Law, Criminology and Police Science 47(March–April):647–666.
Johnston, Sir Harry.
  1895   Trade and General Conditions Report. Nyasaland.
Kadish, Sanford H.
  1967   "The crisis of overcriminalization." Annals of the American Academy of
          Political and Social Science 374(November):157–170.
Kolko, Gabriel.
  1963   The Triumph of Conservatism. New York: Free Press of Glencoe.
  1965   Railroads and Regulations. Princeton: Princeton University Press.
Lees, Norman.
  1924   Kenya. London: Leonard & Virginia Woolf.
Lemert, Edwin M.
  1967a   Human Deviance, Social Problems and Social Control. Englewood Cliffs,
          N.J.: Prentice-Hall.
  1967b   "Legislating change in the juvenile court." Wisconsin Law Review 1967
          (Spring):421–448.
  1970   Social Action and Legal Change: Revolution within the Juvenile Court.
          Chicago: Aldine.
Lenski, Gerhard.
  1966   Power and Privilege. New York: McGraw-Hill.
Lewis, Anthony.
  1966   Gideon's Trumpet. New York: Vintage Books.

Lindesmith, Alfred R.
  1965   The Addict and the Law. Bloomington: Indiana University Press.
  1968   Addiction and Opiates. Chicago: Aldine.

Merton, Robert K.
  1957   "Social structure and anomie." Chap. 4 in Robert K. Merton, Social Theory and Social Structure. Glencoe, Ill.: Free Press.

Miller, Walter B.
  1958   "Lower class culture as a generating milieu of gang delinquency." Journal of Social Issues 14(3):5–19.

Quinney, Richard.
  1970   The Social Reality of Crime. New York: Little, Brown.

Ranulf, Svend.
  1933   The Jealousy of the Gods, vols. 1, 2. London: Williams & Northgate Ltd.
  1938   Moral Indignation and Middle Class Psychology. Copenhagen: Levin & Monksgard.

Reich, Charles A.
  1964   "The new property." Yale Law Journal 73(April):733–787.

Roby, Pamela A.
  1969   "Politics and criminal law: revision of the New York state penal law on prostitution." Social Problems 17(Summer):83–109.

Rubenstein, Richard E.
  1970   Rebels in Eden. Boston: Little, Brown.

Schattschneider, E. E.
  1960   The Semi-Sovereign People: A Realist's View of Democracy in America. New York: Holt, Rinehart & Winston.

Schwartz, Richard, and Jerome Skolnick.
  1971   Society and the Legal Order. New York: Basic Books.

Seidman, Robert B.
  1971   Law and Development. Madison: University of Wisconsin (mimeographed).

Sellin, Thorsten.
  1938   Culture Conflict and Crime. New York: Social Science Research Council Bulletin 41.

Sinclair, Andrew.
  1964   Era of Excess: A Social History of the Prohibition Movement. New York: Harper & Row.

Sinclair, Upton.
  1906   The Jungle. Cambridge, Mass.: Bentley Roberts, Inc.

Spradley, James P.
  1970   You Owe Yourself a Drunk. New York: Little, Brown.

Stephen, J. F.
  1883   A History of the Criminal Law of England, vol. 1. London: Macmillan.

Sutherland, Edwin H.
  1924   Criminology. Philadelphia: Lippincott.

Sutherland, Edwin H., and Donald R. Cressey.
  1970   Criminology. Eighth Edition. Philadelphia: Lippincott.

Tannenbaum, Frank.
  1938   Crime and the Community. New York: Columbia University Press.

Walker, Nigel.
   1968   Crime and Insanity in England. 2 volumes. Edinburgh: Edinburgh University Press.
Williams, Glanville L.
   1963   The Proof of Guilt: A Study of English Criminal Trial. London: Stevens.
Wolfenden Report.
   1963   Report of the Committee on Homosexual Offenses and Prostitution. New York: Stein & Day.

CHAPTER 2

The Classification of Offenses and Offenders

Daniel Glaser

University of Southern California

How do we know when an act is a crime? How do we distinguish one crime or criminal from another? Answers to these questions depend on the purposes of those who make such designations and on the preconceptions which they bring to this task. Concern here will be with some consequences of three broad objectives in the classification of offenses and offenders: *adjudication, enumeration,* and *explanation.* It should be stressed, however, that many prevailing classification systems are multipurpose, and their categories may not be mutually exclusive. Furthermore, some differentiations made for one objective, such as enumeration, may have very important implications for other purposes, such as correction or control. Yet one must also conclude that in both criminological research and the administration of justice all classifications prove somewhat deficient in accomplishing their aims. This inadequacy is caused by complexities, ambiguities, and inconsistencies in human behavior as well as in the language for describing human behavior.

The principal aspects of classification that will concern us are:

I Adjudicative Classification
  A. By responsibility
     1. Based on age (nonage, juvenile delinquent, youthful offender, or criminal)
     2. Based on sanity (insane or sane; the quasi insane)
     3. Based on intelligence
     4. Blurring of classifications in practice
  B. By mental competence at time of trial
  C. By maximum severity of permissible punishment (misdemeanor or felony; infamous or noninfamous)
  D. By specific offense charged: crime codifications
II Enumerative Classification
  A. Offenses eliciting complaints from victims (predations and criminal negligence)
  B. Offenses disturbing audiences (illegal performances)
  C. Offenses in private transactions (illegal sale, possession, or consumption)
III Explanatory Classification
  A. Idealized and empirical typologies

    B. Explanatory dimensions
       1. Individual or collective
       2. Instrumental or expressive
       3. Career commitment or situational

ADJUDICATIVE CLASSIFICATION

Crime is any act lawfully punishable by the state. It is a legal classification of behavior made by judges or juries in ruling on specific cases. Our concern here will be with four kinds of differentiation made by the courts: (a) on criminal responsibility; (b) on competence to stand trial; (c) on maximum severity of punishment that is permissible; and (d) on specific charges that must be proved if the accused is to be convicted.

    The first two of the above four distinctions involve classification of offenders, while the last two are classification of offenses, but any criminal conviction tends to stamp a permanent label on the person convicted. Being found guilty of burglary makes one a "burglar" forever, conviction for a forgery tags one a "forger," and similarly for all categories of offenses. Such long-term stigma, frequently with consequences unanticipated by the court, characterizes all of the adjudicative classifications to be discussed here.

A. Classification by Responsibility

A basic premise of most criminal law is that conviction for a crime requires evidence of *mens rea*, or intent to commit the crime, in addition to proof that the accused committed it. Intent is not directly involved in crimes of negligence, but in these offenses a conviction requires demonstration that the accused failed to take reasonable precautions against unintended consequences in certain matters for which he was responsible (as in recklessly homicidal automobile driving). Thus, in both crimes of intent and crimes of negligence the accused must be proved responsible for the offenses charged.

    The concern of the criminal law with responsibility reflects its objectives of retribution and deterrence. Both of these aims imply that an offender is blameworthy because he knowingly chooses to do wrong or neglects to do right. Deterrence presumes the accused to be a reasoning person who would not wish to commit a crime if he expected it to bring him unpleasant consequences. The objective in deterrence is to make the unpleasantness of the state's punishment exceed the pleasure that a potential offender may expect from the crime. This is the essence of "classical" criminal law theory (see Phillipson, 1923); since the late eighteenth and early nineteenth centuries, it has had a tremendous influence, despite later evidence that some crimes of passion or of addiction are not appreciably deterred by penalties, and despite increasing accent on rehabilitation as the purpose guiding state decisions on offenders. Indeed, classical views of responsibility are not radically different from those expressed much earlier. The sixteenth and seventeenth century English-law commentators Henry de Bracton and Sir Edward Coke stressed deterrence, citing similar views from as far back as Justinian of ancient Rome. Coke asserted that "the punishment of a man who is deprived of reason and understanding cannot be an example to others. No felony . . . can be committed without a felonious intent and purpose" (quoted in Platt & Diamond, 1965:359).

    Classification of criminals by their responsibility would appear to be a matter of deciding whether or not they are criminals, and hence an inappropriate concern in a chapter on methods of distinguishing among offenders. Some violators of criminal law are differentiated from others on the grounds that they are only partially responsible, however, and those whose responsibility is contested form several different borderline categories. Three factors creating these marginal groups will be considered: age, sanity, and intelligence.

1. Age and Criminal Responsibility

If a child only a few years old damages valuable property or finds a loaded gun and wounds or kills someone, the child usually is not regarded by the law as a criminal. This exclusion involves the ancient principle of *nonage*, which meant in old British Common Law that a person less than 7 years old could not be held responsible for any crime. The child was deemed too undeveloped mentally to be capable of understanding the criminal nature of his actions. Subsequently the age limit of nonage, also referred to as infancy, was raised in many jurisdictions, and today it is most often 12 years. Even when nonage was fixed at 7 years, the determination of criminal responsibility on the basis of age was left to the discretion of the court for persons between 7 and 14 years old (Platt & Diamond, 1966; Bassiouni, 1969:86–87).

Starting at the end of the nineteenth century and spreading rapidly in the early twentieth century, a second concept, that of *juvenile delinquency,* modified the law's view of responsibility when a crime is committed by a young person. This development grew out of the notion that during adolescence, the transitional age range between childhood and adulthood, persons are only partially responsible for their behavior.

If a child or adolescent is not responsible for offenses he commits, who is? The philosophy underlying emergence of the juvenile court places responsibility in the parents; if the parents are absent or incapable of adequately exercising responsibility for their child's behavior, the court assigns this burden to the state. The concept of *parens patriae,* or the state as parent, gives government the authority to declare any child found delinquent a ward of the state until he reaches the age when he is legally an adult, or until the state deems that the parents or guardians are capable of assuming parental responsibility satisfactorily.

Accordingly, *juvenile delinquency* refers both to any behavior by a person under a legally specified age which would be considered a crime if he were above that age, and to a large variety of other behavior deemed conducive to crime. The latter has been specified by statutes to include truancy from school or home, disobedience or disrespect for parents or teachers, being out at late hours, loitering, smoking, cursing, and many other acts. Persistence in disobedient behavior, usually called *incorrigibility* in the law, is the usual basis for declaring a young person delinquent even if he or she has committed no act that could be called a crime if done at an older age. After a certain birthday specified by law, usually 18, youths may curse their parents and teachers or leave home without being subject to arrest and confinement for it; before this birthday they risk incarceration by such acts.

The age range of juvenile delinquency is specified as "under 18" in about two-thirds of the United States, with most of the remaining jurisdictions having a lower age limit but a few having a higher one. The concept of nonage has little utility where the definition of delinquency applies to all accused persons below the delinquency age limit. In about four out of five states, however, some persons below the juvenile delinquency age limit but above the nonage limit may be regarded as criminally responsible as though adults, if the court deems their criminality is exceptional for their age. In most states this treatment of juvenile offenders as adults is at the discretion of the court, and occurs only when the juveniles' offenses are unusually serious or persistent. In a few states the delinquency category is inapplicable for certain serious criminal charges, such as murder (American Law Institute, 1957:7–13).

In a few states of the United States, and in several other nations, still another classification of offenders by age may be made in the criminal courts to differentiate degree of responsibility. The U.S. federal courts, for example, have the option of declaring that an accused person 18 to 21 years old is neither a juvenile nor an adult, but rather a "youthful offender." In New York state such persons could be adjudged "wayward minors," and several other jurisdictions have similar distinctions intermediate between juvenile and adult status. These classifications permit courts to impose a more flexible type of correctional-institution sentence than is authorized for adult offenders. Sometimes such sentences are served in special facilities, such as the Borstals in Britain.

While the distinction of juvenile delinquency from adult criminality has important consequences for judicial and correctional administration, it has little relevance to the causal analysis of behavior; the operation of causal factors does not change abruptly at an age prescribed by statute or by judicial decision. That is why the distinction of delinquency from adult crime is not important in explaining offenses but is essential to description of practice in the administration of justice.

2. Sanity and Criminal Responsibility

As indicated in our introduction to the concept of responsibility in the criminal law, if a person of any age seems to have no clear idea of what he is doing when he commits a crime, or no control over his doing it, it is difficult to hold him answerable for his crime. *Insanity* is a legal concept that refers to this type of diminished responsibility.

The problem of specifying with precision what constitutes insanity, as a defense against criminal charges, reached a major bench mark in the history of Anglo-American law in the *M'Naghten* case of 1843. M'Naghten, who killed the British prime minister's secretary through mistaking him for the prime minister, was acquitted on grounds that his delusions of persecution by his intended victim constituted insanity. So great was the public outcry at M'Naghten's escape from capital punishment that an inquiry of the court was made by the House of Lords, resulting in a formal statement that acquittal on grounds of insanity requires proof that "at the time of the committing of the act, the party accused was labouring under such a defect of reason, from disease of the mind, as not to know the nature and quality of the act he was doing; or if he did know it, that he did not know he was doing what was wrong" (Goldstein, 1967:45). These *M'Naghten* rules, sometimes called the "Right or Wrong Test," simply summarize principles long prevalent in both British and Continental law (Walker, 1968). The rules have been continually criticized by psychiatrists and have been replaced or supplemented in some jurisdictions, but they still govern determination of insanity in most courts of English-speaking countries.

The first widespread supplement to *M'Naghten* was the "irresistible impulse" rule. This asserts that even if an accused knows the difference between right and wrong and knows that what he is doing is wrong, he can be held not guilty by reason of insanity if his mind was incapable of resisting the impulse to commit the wrong act. This has been called "the control test" by A. S. Goldstein (1967:chap. 5), who points out that it is very diversely formulated and interpreted, so that it may be viewed both as applicable only to criminal acts initiated very suddenly (on "impulse"), and to acts reflecting the offender's inability to control long-term and deep-seated neuroses or psychoses.

The major landmark in American law on the insanity defense is the *Durham* decision of 1954, in which Judge David L. Bazelon of the Court of Appeals for the District of Columbia asserted that "an accused is not criminally responsible if his unlawful act was the product of mental disease or defect" [*Durham* v. *U.S.*, 214 F. 2d 862, 874 (D.C. Cir., 1954)]. This broad "product rule" was hailed by psychiatrists as deferral to their judgment that personalities and their mental ailments are too complex to permit diagnosis simply by the "right or wrong" or the "irresistible impulse" tests. The *Durham* judgment was resisted by lawyers, however, as too vague, as potentially an escape from punishment for most offenders, and as presuming more precision and consensus in psychiatric diagnosis than actually exists. It has thus far been adopted in only a few state and federal jurisdictions.

More widely adopted is a compromise between the *M'Naghten* and *Durham* formulations, issued by the American Law Institute in 1955 in a draft of its Model Penal Code. The ALI rule asserts: "A person is not responsible for criminal conduct if at the time of such conduct as a result of mental disease or defect he lacks substantial capacity either to appreciate the criminality of his conduct or to conform his conduct to the requirements of the law." It further stipulates that "the terms 'mental disease or defect' do not include an abnormality manifested only by repeated criminal or otherwise antisocial conduct" (American Law Institute, 1961:4). This statement encompasses all prior rules in a single formulation, and in modern language. Thus it connotes both emotion and cognition by replacing "know" with "appreciate" in restating the *M'Naghten* rule. It also refers to self-control ("capacity . . . to conform one's conduct") to imply the irresistible impulse rule. Finally, it includes the *Durham* phrase "mental disease or defect," but in ruling out the assumption that criminal behavior alone can be considered evidence of mental illness, it tries to prevent commitment to mental hospitals of persons resembling in behavior typical prison inmates more than typical mental-hospital patients. There is growing psychiatric as well as bar association support for this ALI formulation.

All rules and directions have thus far not greatly diminished the problems of criminal courts in determining for whom the defense of insanity is justified. Two major factors account for this failure. In the first place, persons most readily and unambiguously deemed psychotic when arrested never get to criminal court; they are referred by police and prosecutors directly to mental-hospital commitment hearings, and if found psychotic are not charged with crimes. Thus the courts receive only the most ambiguous cases. Secondly, the symptoms differentiating most psychotics from nonpsychotics are not manifested continuously and consistently. Most people diagnosed psychotic because of their delusions of persecution, their extremely manic or depressive states, or their hallucinations, function with no revelation of these symptoms most of the time; conversely, many people considered nonpsychotic exhibit these symptoms occasionally. As A. S. Goldstein observes:

> . . . Mental disease tends to represent an impairment of function or constriction of forces which exist in all of us. These forces may be set onto an abnormal course by a virtually infinite variety of pressures and situations. . . . For example, when does the person who "daydreams" a great deal become "schizoid"? At what point does the "schizoid" become a schizophrenic? And what is the difference between a daydream and a hallucination . . . ? (1967:35).

In general, the defense of insanity is likely to be employed only in cases with serious charges, and only where the mental state of the accused is most uncertain.

Perhaps because of these difficulties of diagnosis, whether a court employs the *M'Naghten* or the *Durham* instructions apparently makes little long-run difference in the proportion of cases found not guilty by reason of insanity. In 1954, the year of the *Durham* decision in the District of Columbia, only two-tenths of 1 percent of the District's terminated criminal cases were found not guilty by reason of insanity. In the years that followed the District's adoption of the *Durham* rule, mental disease or defect was claimed more frequently as a defense, and not guilty by reason of insanity was increasingly a directed verdict from the bench. Therefore, the proportion of cases terminated on this ground increased, reaching a peak of 5.1 percent in 1962. This proportion then declined, however, leveling at around 2 percent. The decline apparently occurred largely because the mental hospital staff psychiatrists, who advise this court, became less eager to apply *Durham* freely when offenders found insane proved to be more culturally than psychotically deviant and so much more intractable than the typical mental patient that they posed serious problems for hospital management, and they received little treatment when hospitalized (Arens, 1967, 1969).

Even the 2 percent of District of Columbia criminal cases now terminated as not guilty by reason of insanity represents a tenfold increase from pre-*Durham* days, but similar increases have occurred in most courts without the *Durham* rule. One could argue that this increase, both in the District and elsewhere, was not so much due to the *Durham* instructions as to the greater legal attention to mental defects aroused in part by the *Durham* controversy. Indeed, the entire nation experienced a growth of concern with mental ailments during the third quarter of the twentieth century.

Evidence that the *Durham* formulation does not greatly affect the success of an insanity defense is provided by experiments in which thirty simulated juries were drawn from regular venire lists and paid to hear and rule on a tape-recording of the *Durham* case (Simon, 1967:chap. 3). Ten juries were given the *M'Naghten* instructions, ten the *Durham* instructions, and ten a "no rule" instruction consisting only of: "If you believe the defendant was insane at the time he committed the act of which he is accused, then you must find the defendant not guilty by reason of insanity." Six of the latter juries, without insanity defined for them, acquitted on grounds of insanity, as compared with seven of the ten with *M'Naghten* instructions, and only four of the ten with *Durham* instructions. Three of the *Durham* juries were "hung," compared with only one in each of the other two groups of ten. The remaining juries in each group found the accused guilty. When the jurors in the above experiment were asked individually to recall what their judgments had been before they deliberated collectively as a jury, 76 percent of those with the "no rule" instructions, 59 percent of those with the *M'Naghten* rules, and 65 percent of those with the *Durham* instructions reported that their initial conclusion had been not guilty by reason of insanity (Simon, 1967: chap. 3).

When three larger sets of simulated juries were given an incest case with the three types of instruction, the *M'Naghten*-instructed jurors were distinctly the most reluctant to hold the accused not guilty by reason of insanity, but the proportions of each finding were almost identical for the *Durham* and the "no rule" instructed jurors (Simon, 1967:chap. 3). Again A. S. Goldstein provides us with an apt conclusion:

> So long as we do not know what really "causes" crime, the insanity defense will have to be framed in a way which permits juries to express the feelings of the community. . . . [We] shall have to be content with . . . a loosely framed guide for a process

in which particular cases are reconciled with the hard-to-state purposes of the substantive law. Those purposes are, in turn, fixed by bodies which are authorized, through
political processes, to speak for society (1967:91).

Additional evidence of the ambiguity and inconsistency of distinctions between
the criminal and the insane is provided indirectly by follow-ups of those released to the
community after being found not guilty by reason of insanity and committed to a
mental hospital. In a three-year follow-up of Missouri cases, Morrow and Peterson
(1966) found that 43 percent were reconfined, 37 percent for criminal offenses and 6
percent for purely psychiatric symptoms. Half of those committing new offenses were
given criminal-court sentences, hence were not considered insane this time. There is
increasingly dramatic evidence of the unreliability of mental-hospital diagnosis (cf.
Rosenhan, 1973).

A growing reaction to the problems of ruling on sanity is to propose complete
abolition of the insanity defense. As Norval Morris (1968) illustrates from his investigations in Illinois, being judged criminally insane tends to create for the accused a
double stigma, as both bad and mad, instead of one stigma replacing the other. Morris
and most of the critics of the insanity defense whose arguments he summarizes recommend that the court first determine only whether or not the accused committed the
crime, regardless of his mental state at the time of the offense. These critics state or
imply that the court should investigate the mental state of an alleged offender only after
he is proved guilty of the offense charged, in determining how dangerous he is to others,
and how to make him less dangerous. Several of those whom Morris summarizes even
call for elimination of *mens rea*—the concern with criminal intent—in arriving at a
verdict on whether or not the accused committed the crime (see also Morris & Hawkins,
1969:chap. 7).

The insanity plea would seem irrelevant if differences between mental-hospital
and correctional systems disappeared. Such a convergence would occur if both systems
provided:

1. involuntary confinement only by court order and only for those adjudicated
   dangerous;
2. reduction of custodial restrictions for these confinees on the basis of administrative judgment as to their diminished dangerousness;
3. legal limits on the duration of any custodial restriction without a new adjudication;
4. for most cases, reduction of restrictions on a conditional basis before the maximum authorized period of custody;
5. rehabilitation services (e.g., education or psychotherapy) to those involuntarily
   confined only if they desire it, that is, making treatment voluntary;
6. almost every kind of treatment service presumed to serve individual rehabilitative needs;
7. rewards for participation in treatment programs more on the basis of clear
   evidence that such a reward system reduces postrelease dangerousness than
   just on evidence that it better adapts the inmate to institutional life.

There is much evidence that the types of convergence described above are developing, but two important additional questions that should be addressed in assessing the
desirability of insanity pleas are: (1) whether the social consequences of criminal and
mental-hospital commitments are similar, in terms of rejection or acceptance by friends,
relatives, employers, and others; (2) whether there are deterrent effects on unknown
potential offenders which result from imprisonment but not from mental-hospital con-

finement of known lawbreakers. One might reasonably speculate that differences in stigma would disappear, and that the general deterrent effects of confinement following an offense would not be altered, if convergence of mental-hospital and correctional systems occurred and the insanity plea were abolished. Much research is needed on variations in stigma and in deterrent effects, however, for such arguments to be made with great confidence.

Abolition of the insanity defense would certainly not eliminate the public's unusual concern with that 1 or 2 percent of felony cases in which sanity is now a major issue. These are most frequently crimes of violence which appear to have either deviant sexual motivation or incomprehensible motives, rather than the more customary incentives of rage, profit, or fear. Such cases in recent years, for example, include California's "Manson family," Boston's "Strangler" and Chicago's Speck. Although they are a small part of the crime total, cases of this type receive disproportionate mass media coverage and thereby distort the public's conception of crime risks and criminals. That psychiatrists differ markedly in assessing the sanity of such offenders is highlighted at the trials in which psychiatrists for each side are subjected to examination and cross-examination. Avoidance of such "battles of the experts" by Massachusetts' *Briggs* law or by laws in other states that refer contested cases to a board of psychiatrists who present a single report for both sides in the case only serves to mask or suppress, rather than to eliminate, the ambiguity of the responsibility question. These psychiatrically controversial offenders can appropriately be singled out as quasi-insane, regardless of ultimate court decisions on their sanity, for they pose distinct problems for both the courts and public policy because of the attention they receive (Glaser, 1972:59–62). Most of them may also pose unique problems for causal analysis and treatment, when compared to more ordinary types of offenders.

3. Intelligence and Criminal Responsibility

The preceding discussion dealt with responsibility from the standpoint of mental disease. This has received much attention in criminal law and criminology, perhaps because the insanity defense is used almost exclusively in prominent offenses, especially murder. Much less conspicuous and hardly studied, but perhaps involved in a larger number of cases of delinquency and minor crimes, is the questioning of responsibility on the basis of low intelligence rather than of insanity.

Estimates of the proportion of the United States population that is mentally retarded generally run from 2 to 3 percent, and comparable estimates are made in European countries. Variation in estimates results from difficulties in standardizing the definition and measurement of this condition. This reflects the fact that a large proportion of persons singled out for labeling as retarded, especially those called "educable retarded" (identified as approximately I.Q. 50 to 70, and formerly called "morons"), as well as some of those called "trainable retarded" (identified as approximately I.Q. 25 to 50, and formerly called "imbeciles"), are distinguished from the general population more by cultural traits and social processes than by biological differences alone (Farber, 1968:chap. 3). Sociocultural factors in the subject or in his environment have less effect, relative to biological factors, in determining the self-sufficiency of the "untrainable mentally retarded" (I.Q. under 25, and formerly called "idiots").

Only about 4 percent of the estimated mentally retarded in the United States are confined in institutions (Farber, 1968:187). Nevertheless, the total confined is nearly two hundred thousand, or about the same as the number of inmates in state and federal prisons. Another half-million mentally retarded, or about 10 percent of the estimated total, are enrolled in special classes for the retarded in local schools. Many of this approximately 14 percent of the total retarded, especially that one-fourth of the institutional population considered educable, appear to differ from the remaining 86 percent of the mentally retarded not so much in being less intelligent as in being more deviant in their conduct or in lacking aid from family or others in the free community. It has been repeatedly asserted by researchers at institutions for the retarded with whom I have spoken that deviancy of conduct especially characterizes many of the juvenile inmates of these establishments; it is inferred that they are confined more because of delinquency and dependency than because of stupidity. Apparently officials, being human, frequently make the most expedient decisions in dealing with other humans, even when such decisions are not consistent by legal norms or by other relevant criteria.

4. Blurring of Responsibility Classifications in Practice

That age, mental health, and low intelligence are highly inconsistent influences in determining whether an alleged offender is classified by government agencies as delinquent, criminal, mentally diseased, or mentally deficient is indicated not only by personal impressions, such as those cited above, but also by several systematic studies. These still are quite limited in scope and precision, but they suggest some dimensions and causes of the overlapping characteristics and histories of those committed to mental-health agencies and those placed under the control of correctional officials.

In one of the few systematic empirical studies of delinquency among persons hospitalized for mental disease or defect, Miller and Kenney (1966) investigated 247 patients, comprising all those 12 to 19 years old admitted to a Nebraska state psychiatric facility in a three-year period ending in mid-1964. The official reasons for referral specified a need for psychiatric evaluation or treatment, but inquiry revealed that 71 percent were referred because of complaints of antisocial conduct, about half of these involving conflict with the law. The latter were sent to the hospital predominantly by courts, prosecutors, police, or social agencies, with the request, essentially, that this problem child be taken out of the community. Ten percent were diagnosed as having personality disorders, rather than being psychotic, psychoneurotic, or brain-damaged. Those law violators diagnosed as personality disorders were adjudged by the staff as the least disturbed of the adolescent inmates, the most puzzled over the reasons for their admission, and the least responsive to inpatient treatment. This contrasted with those committed on the initiative of physicians or family seeking help in coping with clear-cut disabilities, who were diagnosed most often as having psychotic disorders.

In the above study sample, recommendations for transfer to outpatient treatment were made for 82 percent of those referred because of antisocial conduct and for 79 percent of those referred only because of disabilities. This recommendation was carried out in the community for only 68 percent of the antisocial cases, but for 90 percent of the disability cases. A follow-up six months after conclusion of the sampling period found that about half the antisocial patients were under some type of supervision in the community, about a fourth had been discharged from supervision, and about 15 percent were in institutions, one-third of these in state training schools. Treatment information was not available on the remaining 10 percent. These proportions were about the same whether or not the recommendations for outpatient mental-health care had been followed. Contrastingly, none of the disability cases were in state training schools, but 24 percent were in state hospitals as compared with only 3 percent of the antisocial cases.

Levine (1970) took a systematic sample of 100 cases from the population of a state hospital in the 1960s and found, on examining their files, that crimes were described in the behavior leading to admission to the hospital for 71 of them. Of the 154 separate crimes reported in these files, 24 were felonies and 130 were misdemeanors. These offenses included 2 first degree murders, 6 aggravated assaults, 4 statutory rapes, and 30 simple assaults. Levine then took a random selection of 100 admissions during 1955, a decade earlier, but located files for only 84 and found that of these, 24 had died while in the hospital. For the remaining 60 he identified crimes described in the files as leading to the hospital admission, and asked a local county attorney to indicate the jail or prison term that would normally be imposed for such offense. He also tabulated the duration of their hospitalization. The months of potential criminal incarceration and of actual hospital confinement for these 60 patients yielded two highly skewed statistical distributions, but transforming the number of months to logarithms normalized the distributions somewhat and yielded a correlation of 0.22 between them. For schizophrenic patients considered separately, the correlation was 0.51. In terms of duration of denial of liberty, the consequences of criminal and mental illness commitments for these patients would not have been extremely different.

Blankenship and Martin (1972) compared 1964–66 first admission 14- and 15-year-old boys in a correctional institution with first admissions of the same age in a mental-health institution. These two state facilities served the same set of Southern California counties. The more intense the delinquency record, as measured by reported offenses per month in the period of freedom following the first offense, and the more grave they were on a scale of offense severity, the more probable was confinement in the correctional rather than the mental institution. Nevertheless, considerable overlap was found in the delinquency records of inmates at the two establishments.

In a questionnaire study of 106 policemen from 48 Illinois cities, Blankenship (1968) found that the officers all reported classifying as mentally ill rather than criminal some of the offenders whom they had arrested. Their responses indicated that police classification of a juvenile as mentally ill was evoked primarily by sexual deviance, unrestrained or unfocused aggression, or inability to respond appropriately to the officer and the situation.

Systematic study of the actual decision-making process in police and court offices might indicate that factors other than the behavior of the accused also influence whether an alleged offender is sent to a mental or to a correctional institution. Impressions I have had, supported by conversations with psychiatrists, psychologists, and sociologists who have worked or visited extensively in these two types of institutions, indicate that, for less serious offenses especially, the institution to which an offender is sent is determined partly by: (1) which is administratively easier for the prosecutor, and in nonmetropolitan counties, which involves the shorter trip for the sheriff; (2) preferences of the offender's parents, where the offender is a juvenile; (3) preferences of complainants, especially against juveniles, against the aged, and, regardless of age, against women, as there often is more guilt-feeling from sending such persons to correctional confinement than from sending them to a state hospital (though the latter may result in longer and less rehabilitative confinement); (4) social status of the alleged offenders, with those of lower status in the community more likely than others to receive a correctional rather than a mental-health commitment, and correctional sentences unlikely if the family of the accused promises treatment at a private psychiatric facility. These four impressions merit more rigorous empirical investigation.

B. Mental Competence

Classification of offenders by their presumed responsibility is frequently confused with the adjudicative classification of offenders by their competence to stand trial. Whether or not a person was responsible at the time of the offense, the law bars his criminal prosecution if at the time of trial he suffers from mental or physical disease or defect that prevents him from understanding the nature and purpose of the legal proceedings against him, assisting in his defense, or in the case of a death penalty, understanding the nature and purpose of this penalty. Claims to incompetence have the effect of motions for continuance; they usually are made in pretrial proceedings. If these claims are on mental grounds and are upheld, they usually result in the commitment of the accused to a mental institution until deemed competent, at which time a trial may occur. They are not a defense against criminal charges in a trial but a bar to holding a trial, or even to pretrial pleading.

McGarry (1971) reports that prior to 1960 most men sent from the criminal courts of Massachusetts to the state hospital at Bridgewater because they were deemed incompetent to stand trial were kept there so long that they left the hospital by death rather than by return to court. In 1963 he and his associates examined 219 such patients and found 148 to be incompetent and 71 competent. About half of those found competent had been confined less than two years, while the average period of hospitalization of those found incompetent was 14.9 years. McGarry observes:

> The long terms of hospitalization for those found to be incompetent . . . compared with the relatively short terms of those found to be competent . . . more than suggest that most had been competent for trial early in their hospitalization and that a return for trial at that time would likely have spared them decades of hopeless and regressive institutionalization (1971:1183; see also, McGarry, 1969).

Subsequent to their 1963 examination by McGarry's group, the 71 found competent had the following experiences:

Charges dropped:

15	had criminal charges dropped while in the hospital. (In some cases charges were dropped years *prior to the time of McGarry's examination, but the hospital had never been notified that charges were dropped.*)
9	had charges dropped *after McGarry's findings* on their competence were sent to the courts.
24	Total never prosecuted for charges that led to their hospitalization (included 4 originally charged with murder).

Tried in court:

14	found not guilty by reason of insanity at the time of the offense (included 12 alleged murderers, but some were subsequently released from the hospital as having regained sanity).
14	sentenced to prison (of whom 8 were released within the next six years).
19	sentenced to jail or probation.
47	Total receiving trials.
71	Grand Total

In 1969 McGarry attempted to trace the careers of the 71 patients in the approximately six years since he found them competent. He learned that 50 had been released to the community during this period, for a total of 159 man-years, or an average of more than three years each. Twenty-four of the 50 had been arrested during their post-hospital freedom, but only 5 for felonies, a rearrest rate (erroneously labelled "recidivism") less than that of felons paroled from the state prison. McGarry and his associates at Harvard have developed a screening instrument to facilitate rapid determination of competency to stand trial (Lipsitt et al., 1971). State and federal court decisions, beginning in 1972–73, limited the permissible duration of confinement for incompetence without referral back to court.

C. Classification by Maximum Permissible Punishment

The efforts that government agencies make to investigate crimes, and the cost of providing high-salaried legal experts and clerical staff to assure fair and competent hearings and assessment of charges, obviously cannot be of equal magnitude for all offenses, from the most trivial to the most grave. The processing of one contested murder case frequently requires expenditures of hundreds of thousands of dollars for salaries and facilities, including costs of both prosecution and defense, as well as costs of court administration. Clearly the public would not routinely countenance similar expenditures for contested minor cases, such as thefts of items worth less than five dollars, although an exhaustive police investigation and a full hearing of possible evidence and argument for both sides could conceivably be as necessary for proof beyond a reasonable doubt in many of these minor offenses as in some murder cases.

A number of adjudicative classifications of offenses are designed to fix upper and lower limits to the expense and quality of the state's reaction to a specific crime. The underlying principle appears to be that the state's investment should vary in some proportion to the maximum deprivation of liberty it might impose if the accused should be found guilty. The most pervasive of these classifications in Anglo-American law is the Common Law separation of felonies from misdemeanors.

This distinction dates back to medieval years, when felonies were described as *mala in se* because they were regarded as evil in themselves, as crimes by natural law, and as mortal sins, hence warranting capital punishment. Misdemeanors were *mala prohibita* or evil only because prohibited by man, and hence not justifying the death penalty. Regarding modern usage of these terms Tappan observed:

> . . . Many people criticize the classification of crimes into the felony and misdemeanor categories on the ground that there is no meaningful dividing line between the two and that, very commonly, conduct that in one state would be a felony is a misdemeanor elsewhere and vice versa. Absurdities appear frequently where a crime is divided into grades, part of which are felonies, part misdemeanors (1960:19n).

The current implications of this distinction for government action begin at the police level. Police usually are authorized to arrest a person without a warrant whenever they have "reasonable cause" to believe that he has committed a felony, whereas they can arrest for a misdemeanor only when it is committed "in their presence." The exact meaning of these specifications, however, is often in dispute (on debated issues, see LaFave, 1965:chaps. 11, 12).

As far as court procedure is concerned, Walker asserts:

> The older distinction between felonies and misdemeanours is now of much less importance than that between indictable and non-indictable offences. . . . There are

certain procedural differences at trial, and convicted felons suffer from additional disabilities, such as disqualification for ecclesiastical office, which must inconvenience only a minority (1965:14n).

While these remarks were applied to Britain, they fit much of the United States also, although in many jurisdictions the prosecutor's filing of an "information" with the court has replaced the indictment procedure of accusation for all or most felonies, and it is even more widely used for misdemeanors. Among the many alternatives in judicial resources and defendant rights that frequently vary with the offense charged, and depend upon the maximum penalty authorized for the offense, are: whether or not the trial requires a judge who is a lawyer, whether the presence of counsel for the defense and prosecution is required, whether an exact transcript of proceedings is kept, whether the defendant has a right to a preliminary hearing, and whether he has the right to a twelve-man jury or to any jury. These assorted details and their exact relationship to classifications of offenses differ considerably from one jurisdiction to another.

In a majority of the states of the United States felonies are punishable by confinement in a state prison, usually for a term of more than one year, while misdemeanors are punishable by confinement for not more than one year in a county or municipal jail (or, in some states, in a state farm or other state institution for misdemeanants). These refer only to the maximum permissible confinement penalties; lesser confinement, probation, or fines are also permissible, as well as suspended sentences.

Diverse additional classifications of offenses are also made on the basis of maximum penalty, with corresponding differences in police and court procedures and in the rights of the defendant. Wherever capital punishment has been statutorily permissible, whether or not it was actually imposed, some procedures and rights usually have been applicable only to persons charged or convicted of capital offenses. For example, in several states classification as a juvenile delinquent and processing in juvenile court is not permissible for a person of juvenile age but above nonage if a capital offense is charged. Many states also divide their lesser offenses into several categories (such as misdemeanors, infractions, violations), with different police and court procedures, different courts, and different maximum penalties for each. Perhaps the most frequent modification of the felony-misdemeanor dichotomy is the division of one or both of these into several grades (e.g., felony of the first degree, felony of the second degree, etc.), with different penalties and sometimes variations in procedures or in court jurisdiction for each grade. In some states the felony and misdemeanor terminology has been dropped, but then other labels are employed for analogous classifications of offenses based on the maximum permissible penalty, and prescribing accordingly the procedure for investigation and trial.

Another interesting classification of crimes by their maximum penalty is the designation of some offenses as *infamous,* which meant in older English "without fame" and implies—in today's language—"with bad reputation." In Common Law this was, essentially, a prescription of the stigma that an offense should attach to the offender for the rest of his life. For example, it formerly meant that the offender's testimony or oath would no longer be acceptable in any legal proceedings. With extension of the franchise it referred to offenses for which the convicted person would forever forfeit the right to vote or to hold public office. Today it still has these implications, sometimes called "civil death," plus a variety of others, such as denial of the right to be licensed according to one's qualifications for various trades or professions.

In many jurisdictions all felonies automatically are infamous crimes, but traditionally this designation is applied only to the most serious felonies.

D. Classification by Specific Charges

In a sense the court's decision as to whether a person is guilty or not guilty is a classification of individuals, but our concern here is with the subsequent classifications made of those found guilty.

The most pervasive and essential of these is the specification of offenses of which a person is found guilty. Because this is at once the classification most familiar to readers yet the most variable in exact terminology from one jurisdiction to the next, only its broad outlines and implications will be discussed here, rather than all of the distinct labels for separate offenses and the definitions for each.

Theoretically, the major functions of specification of charges in court operations are: to direct the prosecutor (and through him, the grand jury, where it is involved) on what facts must be proved to convict the accused; to inform the defendant and his counsel of the allegations they must try to disprove; to instruct the judge on his jurisdiction in the case; to define for the judge (and through him, for the trial jury where it is involved) the type of evidence needed to establish guilt; to specify permissible sentences; to establish some details of procedural rights (e.g., bail and appeal). In practice, however, 70 to 95 percent of felony cases—varying by jurisdiction—are resolved not by trial but by pretrial bargaining over the charges to which the defendant will plead guilty.

In plea bargaining, the prosecutor's objective in specifying charges often is to create the possibility of his changing the accusation to somewhat lesser charges that the public would consider tolerable (for details, see Sudnow, 1965; Newman, 1966; Carney & Fuller, 1969; Miller, 1969). Police and prosecutors customarily "overcharge" suspects, that is, they initially make accusations more severe than those they can prove or than those carrying penalties with which they believe the public would be satisfied. Not only does this permit reduction of charges to be made later by the prosecution in exchange for a plea of guilty, but initial bail tends to be determined according to a fixed scale based on the offenses charged, with higher bail for more severe charges. "Overcharging" thus enriches bail bondsmen, who in turn are contributors to prosecutor's, judge's, and sheriff's campaign funds.

The function of charge specification for the defense counsel in plea bargaining is to permit him to be of some service even to clients who, he is certain, are guilty (Sudnow, 1965; Blumberg, 1967:chap. 5). By obtaining the reduction in bail and the lesser penalty that go with a reduction in charge, the lawyer benefits his client even if he does not obtain an acquittal. His conscience is thus served with respect to both earning his fees and protecting society from criminals. The plea bargaining usually is achieved, however, by delay and distortion of proceedings that make our courts, as agencies for the accurate and efficient determination of guilt or innocence, gross failures by comparison with those of many other countries.

Specification of charges is most rationally achieved in the criminal law by codification. Most states, however, codify only one or two times per century and in the interim, amend their criminal law by a haphazard patchwork of separate statutes imposing penalties for specific behaviors. Specifications prevailing in the United States are illustrated by a draft for California prepared by the state's Joint Legislative Committee for Revision of the Penal Code (1971). The most important distinction is that made between offenses against the person and offenses against property. Additional major categories include: offenses against sexual morality, public decency, and the family; offenses against the administration of government (e.g., bribery); offenses against public order (e.g., disrupting a meeting); offenses involving weapons; offenses against public welfare; and offenses involving sports corruption and gambling.

Two distinct styles of offense specification are illustrated by the draft California code cited above, and by the Illinois Criminal Code of 1961. The California document leaves largely unchanged that state's ostensible policy of giving the courts little discretion in fixing penalties, for it distinguishes by statute several forms of each offense and prescribes a specific penalty for each. Thus six types of offenses involving death are differentiated: murder of the first degree, murder of the second degree, manslaughter, culpable homicide (by negligence), vehicular homicide, and assisting suicide. Illinois distinguishes four types of offense involving death: murder, voluntary manslaughter, involuntary manslaughter (or reckless homicide), and the archaic "concealing death of a bastard," but gives the court much latitude in deciding on a sentence. In California the basic distinction between degrees of murder is that first degree now involves killing that is "deliberate and premeditated" (language which the proposed revision replaces by "pursuant to a plan"), while second degree involves simply killing "with intent to kill." In Illinois there is only one degree of murder and it covers killing either with intent to kill, with intent to "do great bodily harm," "with knowledge that one's acts will cause death," or with knowledge that one's acts "create a strong probability of death or great bodily harm." Once a person is convicted of a specific degree of murder in California the judge or jury must impose only the specific minimum and maximum penalty prescribed by law (with the choice formerly only between death or life imprisonment for first degree murder, but the death option currently ruled unconstitutional by the California and federal Supreme Courts). In Illinois a conviction for murder leaves the judge or jury with the task of choosing a minimum sentence of imprisonment that cannot be less than fourteen years but can be any higher figure, and a maximum sentence that can be any term exceeding the minimum sentence or life imprisonment or (until the federal decision) death.

As was pointed out long ago by Ohlin and Remington (1958), plea bargaining largely eliminates the intended effects on court sentencing discretion of these two styles in the specification of offenses. When the code makes many distinctions, bargaining is used to change the offense specified, such as the prosecutor's obtaining judicial concurrence in reducing murder charges from first to second degree or to manslaughter, thus changing the sentence that is mandatory. When there are fewer distinctions in the offense that can be charged, as in Illinois, bargaining is more often over the prosecutor's recommendations on sentencing, and the bargaining more frequently involves the judge informally in off-the-record tripartite negotiation with prosecution and defense (McIntyre, 1968). Alteration of the charges from the time of arrest to the time of conviction, as a result of bargaining processes, makes enumeration of offenses by official statistics on arrests or convictions especially difficult. This procedure impedes efforts to assess crime statistically, and analysis of these difficulties may illuminate several other problems in public policy on crime and delinquency control or prevention.

ENUMERATIVE CLASSIFICATION

That it is necesary to distinguish among crimes in order to count them meaningfully is readily evident. How does one count gambling offenses? By each throw of the dice, by each monetary transaction, or by each session? And what if it is a 24-hour operation with shifting customers that never closes? How does one count units of public drunkenness for persons intoxicated every day on skid row streets? What are the separate offenses if embezzlement or extortion involve years of regular money transfers? Finally, how does one add all these offenses with murders, rapes, and other crimes to determine a community's total crime rate?

The first step in bringing order to such a task is to separate offenses which pose different types of enumerative problems not only in defining their units, but in procurement of data on their occurrence. "Optimum procedures for measuring the prevalence of crime . . . depend on whether the crime creates a death, a complaining victim, a satisfied customer, an annoyed audience or a dangerous condition" (Glaser, 1967:104). These distinctions for purposes of crime measurement are closely linked to problems of crime control, so analysis of enumeration problems and their solution may also reveal optimum strategies for combating crime.

A. Offenses Eliciting Complaints from Victims

The most useful basis for differentiating crimes is by whether or not they usually result in someone complaining that they or their friends or relatives have been victimized. This distinction aids both measurement and control. Deliberately victimizing crimes may appropriately be called *predations,* as contrasted with acts of unintentional victimization which comprise *crimes of negligence.*

Predations are the acts most widely and consistently regarded as crime. They include offenses against persons—the "crimes of violence"—such as murder, assault, and rape—and offenses against property—such as theft, burglary, and forgery. Robbery—taking someone else's property by force or threat of force—is a crime against both person and property, but usually is classified with crimes against persons.

The most accurate, widely available statistics on the extent of crime in any community, region, or society generally are on predations known to the police. These acts are reported to police simply because the victims or their friends or relatives desire police assistance; while a request for police assistance does not occur in every predation, in no other category of offenses are such requests made so consistently. Therefore, no other major group of crimes can be counted as readily as predations.

The FBI rectricts its tabulation of crime rates to seven forms of predation, the so-called Index Offenses: "non-negligent homicide, robbery, non-statutory rape, aggravated assault, burglary, auto theft, other theft over $50." "These crimes were selected . . . ," it points out, "because, as a group, they represent the most common local crime problem" and they "are those considered to be most consistently reported to police" (F.B.I., 1972:5). Nevertheless, there is great variation in the proportion of these predations that are reported to the police, in addition to some variation in the thoroughness with which the police record them, and each of these types of offense poses unique problems for enumeration.

Homicides usually are known to both police and public-health authorities, since the latter must collect a physician's report on the cause of each death. A comparison of police and health statistics on homicide, therefore, is an effective way of checking on the completeness of each. Because of the gravity of death, both police and public-health officials usually are informed whenever a death appears to result from homicide, discrepancies between the statistics which each compiles are slight, and the differences between them result mainly from uncertainties that probably will always exist in some cases in determining the cause of death.

Statistics on assault are necessarily much less complete than actual assaultive behavior for many reasons. First, a large proportion of physical attacks occurs among friends and relatives who are reluctant to refer each other to the police. Second, it is often difficult for the police to decide who started a fight, hence who were the attackers and who the attacked. Third, many people find it humiliating to report being the victim of an assault if they were the losers in the struggle, and unnecessary if they were the winners. Fourth, legal terms for assault vary somewhat vaguely and inconsistently to indicate seriousness; it is simply called "assault" when it is regarded as a misdemeanor, but there are diverse terms, such as "aggravated assault," when it is regarded as a felony, especially when it results in severe bodily injury or endangers someone's life. In court proceedings classification of an act as any kind of assault is often arbitrary; in the course of plea bargaining charges are often reduced to simpler assault or to disorderly conduct in exchange for a plea of guilty, especially when the complainant's anger diminishes and he declines to press charges.

Rape is likewise grossly underreported because it is a humiliating experience to the victim; it frequently is committed by someone whom the victim knows and has willingly accompanied, and reporting it simply adds additional shame. In most states sexual intercourse with a girl under 16 years of age is statutory rape even if the female participates eagerly—indeed, even if she seduces her partner—but most such behavior is not reported to the police because neither participant regards herself or himself as unwillingly victimized, and they keep it secret from those who might report it.

The only crimes against persons, other than murder, on which statistics are fairly complete are holdups of business firms, particularly banks. Most other robberies also are reported to the police, but some are unreported because the victim knows the offender, the amount involved is small, the victim is not confident that the police will be effective, or he is uncomfortable in dealing with police. Crimes against property also are underreported for these reasons, and because small thefts frequently are not noticed by the victim, especially if committed against a store or other business operation. Pilfering by employees and shoplifting are simply counted as part of the stock "shrinkage" estimated periodically after inventories. The major category of theft on which data are fairly accurate is auto theft; police usually are informed of this offense because of the value of automobiles, the fact that they are insured, and the fact that the owner may be held responsible for accidents committed in his vehicle by the thief.

The above observations on completeness of reporting for various types of predation, and on reasons for underreporting, stem mainly from victim survey research pioneered by the President's Commission on Law Enforcement and Administration of Justice (1967a). By asking representative samples of a community's adult population whether in the past year or other period anyone in their household was the victim of predations, each described separately to facilitate recollection, one can obtain an estimate of the predation rate independent of police tabulations on crimes reported to them. By asking those in the sample who report being victimized whether they informed the police when these crimes occurred—and, if not, why not—one obtains estimates on the distribution of underreporting in official crime statistics, in addition to evidence on the reasons for failure to report crimes to the police. While the survey data also are presumably incomplete, their collection independent of police data makes them a valuable supplement to official statistics; they provide an estimate of the multiplier needed to be applied to police statistics to obtain more valid conclusions on crime rates (e.g., multiply official rates by 1.3).

The President's Commission study (1967a:21) found that FBI statistics on rape in the United States during 1965 were only about one-fourth as high as those obtained by asking a cross-section of the United States population whether anyone in their household had suffered rape in the past year. Probably this survey's data were also incomplete. On grand theft and aggravated assault the FBI rates were only about half the survey rates, and on burglary and robbery they were about two-thirds the survey rates. Their survey indicated that FBI figures were only about one-third complete for burglary from individuals, but were practically complete for burglaries from business and other organizations. The national sample for this survey was presumed representative, but was somewhat small for such specific crime estimation. Other surveys were sponsored by the commission in a few high crime-rate metropolitan neighborhoods. These indicated that police information on offense rates was much less complete for these neighborhoods than for the nation as a whole (President's Commission, 1967b:17–19).

These victim surveys indicate an incompleteness in official crime statistics which implies that a large part of the annual crime increase announced by the FBI throughout the 1960s and early 1970s was only an increase in the percentage of crimes reported to police and in the completeness of their recording of crime reports. During the years of alleged rapid crime-rate increase there was a marked growth in the sale of insurance policies covering theft, and hence requiring reporting of theft losses to the police in order to collect insurance. There was also a rapid growth in the professionalization of police forces. Both of these trends could have made reporting and recording of predations appreciably more complete, and thus could have created an illusion on the extent of increase in actual crime rates. There probably was a decline in the multiplier needed to change FBI crime rates to actual rates, at the same time that actual rates may have increased somewhat.

From the foregoing one could reasonably conclude that the value of survey data for assessing and guiding police and other crime-control agencies is so obvious that all major metropolitan police forces and the federal government should have instituted victim survey research soon after its potential was demonstrated by the President's Commission. Inertia in criminal justice agencies is such, however, that this type of relatively inexpensive scientific guidance of policy has been developed very slowly, despite hundreds of millions of dollars spent on "law-enforcement assistance."

The FBI's Index Offenses do not include forgery, embezzlement, counterfeiting, confidence games, and other types of fraud not because they are unimportant predations, but because they are difficult for the police to know about very fully, and because they are often difficult to count even when much detail on them is known. While police agencies tabulate statistics on the complaints they receive about these crimes of deception, and they record and report to the FBI their volume of arrests on these charges, many frauds are never even detected by their victims. Furthermore, much fraud that is discovered results in complaints not to the police, but instead, to various regulatory agencies with fraud-investigation functions, such as the Food and Drug Administration and the Internal Revenue Service. A large portion of the offenses these agencies investigate, however, comes to their attention not through victim complaints, but through the efforts of their own staff to discover fraud.

Americans who believe themselves to have been defrauded tend to be more concerned with obtaining restitution than with participating in prosecution, for in our courts these two pursuits are largely independent endeavors and are exceptionally time-consuming. Contrastingly, in much of Europe and elsewhere prosecution of criminal charges of fraud or negligence must usually be initiated by the victim in a single judicial process that may result in court orders for both punishment of the offender and his restitution of losses to the victim. Statistics on the volume of fraud in a country clearly depend greatly on the government's investigative resources, and on its education of the public to detect and report fraud, regardless of the actual volume of fraud that occurs. Therefore, these are offenses on which only the crudest estimates of frequency are now possible, and for which any statements on trends or distribution must usually be considered extremely speculative.

Several other types of predation also pose distinctive technical problems beyond routine police enumerative capacities. One example, arson, is classified by Inciardi (1970) into five types of motive: revenge, excitement, insurance fraud, vandalism, and to cover up another crime. All of these must be distinguished from fires due to accidents, noncriminal negligence, or natural causes. This classification task is assigned primarily to fire departments. They are aided by insurance company investigators. Therefore, police tabulations on arson usually apply only to the complaints filed and arrests made when there is evidence as to the perpetrators.

Negligence offenses resemble predations in their clear victimization of innocent persons, but differ in that no harm is intended by the offender. Carelessness in operation of a motor vehicle is the act most frequently designated a crime of negligence, and it may be prosecuted as a crime even if no victimization occurs—as in reckless driving—in order to prevent injury to anyone. Since negligence prosecuted before it creates any victims is known by the police only to the extent that they look for it, figures on the volume of such offenses are determined by the frequency of police patrol independent of the amount of criminally negligent behavior. In the long run, however, if police patrol and prosecution have deterrent effects, the public's illegal carelessness would decline as the frequency of patrol increased. That efficient law enforcement by police and courts clearly deter drunken driving has conclusively been demonstrated in experience with the breathalyzer (Ross et al., 1970), and may well occur with other types of offenses not readily hidden from the police.

Criminal negligence in manufacture and construction is a growing concern of the law. It may be prosecuted on the basis of health or safety inspections, usually by agencies other than the police. When these types of negligence are criminal, they tend to be brought into court only after they result in injury, and then most frequently in civil suits for restitution initiated by the victims rather than in state prosecution on criminal charges.

Fraud, arson, and negligence offenses illustrate the ongoing historic process whereby more and more kinds of private damage, or torts, are designated as criminal. This trend makes action against their perpetrators a concern of the state rather than just an interest of the victim. All types of predation and crimes of negligence were once torts. The law's conception of murder, robbery, and theft as crimes rather than torts first occurred only when the elite were victims, and gradually was extended to the rest of the citizenry.

Offenses eliciting victimization complaints appear to be the only types of behavior for which definition as crime has been cumulative and seems nearly irreversible. Perhaps this is so because they are the only offenses that involve clear interference with the liberties and opportunities of other persons. This increase in the definition of victimizing acts as crime seems to reflect what Parsons (1971) has pointed out are three interrelated trends in the evolution of modern societies, highly persistent trends if viewed over appreciable periods of history: (1) progressive differentiation of institutions, organizations, and roles into more diverse forms, each with specialized functions, so that the components of society become increasingly interdependent; (2) inclusion of larger percentages of the population in both determining their government (extension of the franchise) and benefiting from it (growth of government welfare concerns); (3) shift of public values from concern with the morality of very specific features of behavior—dress, speech, amusement, for example—to concern only with more general values, such as honesty, responsibility, and consideration for others.

The three trends in societal evolution described above seem to be an inevitable result of technological development, and they may be irreversible trends because technological innovation is cumulative. If these observations are correct, offenses eliciting victimization complaints (predations and crimes of negligence) may ultimately be the only kinds of behavior that are designated as criminal.

B. Offenses Disturbing Audiences

Marginal to offenses evoking complaints from victims are acts that become crimes because they are distasteful to onlookers, rather than clearly victimizing anyone. An example is indecent exposure. One may be nude in private as much as one desires, but if someone in a public place can see it, nakedness becomes a crime.

A less readily classifiable offense is disorderly conduct, often called "disturbing the peace." It may include fighting, and thus overlaps assault. It may include blocking pedestrian or vehicular traffic, or simply disturbing someone by being noisy. Here persons are victimized, so these acts may be either predations or crimes of negligence, depending on whether or not the disturber intended to make others uncomfortable. Being noisy is not an offense, however, if no one is disturbed; when none object, one may legally yell or play music as loudly and as long as one desires.

Public intoxication is another crime determined by the audience; being drunk in private is perfectly legal as long as one does not disturb the peace or commit other offenses. Traditionally the initial complainants in public intoxication arrests usually were the police. Most of these arrests were made by police patrols in the skid row areas of our major cities where lonely and improvident alcoholics tend to congregate. These arrests diminished during the late 1960s and the 1970s, as they were futile in reducing the alcoholism of such persons, court processing and jailing were expensive, and there were complaints that such arrests were carried out in a mechanical quota-filling fashion. Many cities shifted from jailing drunks to transporting them to detoxification centers, if they came voluntarily. There the inebriates may sober up, receive medical attention, and be recruited by Alcoholics Anonymous or other treatment agencies. This procedure proved cheaper for the cities and more effective in reducing public drunkenness than did criminal prosecution.

In all these acts which are crimes because they disturb audiences, acts which I have also called "illegal performance" crimes (Glaser, 1972), police officers must decide on the street whether to treat the behavior as a crime, view it as a symptom of illness requiring mental-health care, or simply placate any complainants and disregard the offending behavior. Increasingly, treating it as a crime becomes only a last resort. The authority to make an arrest if the offender does not cooperate in these negotiations, however, augments the police officer's success at peacemaking (Bittner, 1967), although it also gives him a discretion than can readily be abused. Special training programs for the police emphasize human-relations skills, particularly in de-escalating domestic quarrels, which in many suburban and other predominantly residential areas is the most frequent complaint received by the police. Extensive research has been aimed at enhancing the effectiveness of such training (see, for example, Toch, 1969; Bard, 1970).

The foregoing discussion implies various difficulties in obtaining precise statistics on the frequency of the kinds of behavior that are criminal if they offend an audience. One can tabulate the number of complaints for these acts which the police receive, or the number of arrests they make, but because of great variation in police exercise of discretion in reacting to such behavior, the results of these tabulations will be determined much more by police policy than by illegal public activity. In addition, society's trend to generality in its values, discussed in the preceding section, steadily reduces the range of behavior which offends audiences. This ongoing historic process is illustrated by the fact that only a few decades ago complaints occurred and men were routinely arrested if they were bare-chested at beaches or other public places, and there was no doubt as to the criminality of females attired at public places in garb like the bikinis and hot pants fashionable today. Illegal performance is clearly a declining kind of crime not because of any decrease in the behavior considered offensive at any given time, but because of changes in public conceptions of that behavior.

C. Offenses in Private Transactions

From the standpoint of enumeration problems, the remaining major category in this classification consists of behavior which is criminal even though all parties involved participate willingly, none complain, and the activity is not in public view. They are often called "consensual" or "victimless" crimes. These are acts of illegal consumption or sales, such as prostitution, homosexual offenses, illegal narcotics use, and illegal gambling. In the case of drugs, even possession can constitute a crime. The enumeration difficulty for such offenses comes mainly from the fact that only a minute fraction of these activities evoke complaints; the police can only learn about them through entrapment, infiltration, eavesdropping, wiretapping, or the use of monetary or other, sometimes questionable, incentives to obtain informants. These problems in enumeration clearly mirror difficulties in police and judicial control, especially if the illegal activities are easily hidden, yet widely supported or at least tolerated by the public.

There is a long history of failure to enforce the laws against offenses in private transactions, and frequent corruption of the police or the judiciary is associated with them. Police activity deters visibility of these crimes, but people who wish to pursue them in private usually have no difficulty in doing so. If the demand for an illegal substance or service is inelastic, supplying it will be especially profitable when it is scarce. If the substance or service also is readily concealed and is available through many alternative channels, police success in closing one source only raises the price and expands the market for other suppliers. For these reasons, government claims to success in suppressing narcotics, gambling, prostitution, and homosexuality have been valid only briefly, if at all. Frequently government suppression efforts, particularly in gambling and drugs, have simply shifted the illegal business from less resourceful amateur and small operators to the most highly professional and ruthless criminal organizations. These groups maneuver supply channels nationally and internationally, discover and exploit chinks in government incorruptibility, promote increased patronage for their enterprises, and reinvest their earnings from these pursuits in legitimate business fields which they corrupt (Cressey, 1969).

Some offenses in private transactions are rapidly diminishing through no longer being defined as crimes. Abortion is an example. When no longer prohibited it can be regulated, that is, defined as criminal only if done with unqualified personnel or unapproved facilities. Other private transactions are being redefined as criminal only if they offend an audience. This is now the case with homosexuality. In Illinois in

1961 it ceased to be a crime if it involved only consenting adults acting in private. The 1970s saw similar redefinition elsewhere either by statute or by law-enforcement practice. Methadone maintenance for addicts, as well as public lotteries and state-operated off-track gambling are additional examples of crime elimination by defining as legal what once was declared criminal.

Movements for further legalization of drug use, gambling, and other private-transaction crimes seem to be gaining support. This change comes partly from our growing generality of values, which expands tolerance for private vices. It also results partly from realization by legislators that repeal of these prohibitions reduces the profits of organized crime, reduces predations by addicts, reduces the corruptibility of law-enforcement agencies, and probably increases support for these agencies by focusing their efforts on the predations and crimes of negligence for which the public more consistently desires police action.

EXPLANATORY CLASSIFICATION

The first step in trying to understand complex and diverse phenomena is to describe them, and thereby, to classify their variations. Classification is the primary concern in what F. S. C. Northrop (1947) has called the "natural history" stage of science, which precedes the preoccupation of science with abstract explanatory theory. Thus, systematic description and classification of plants and animals preceded—and laid the foundation for—the explanation of biological variation by the theory of evolution and by modern genetics theory.

Explanation, nevertheless, has a feedback effect upon classification. Description at any given time focuses on those aspects which prior explanations suggest are important; as Kuhn (1962) points out, aspects that are inexplicable from the stand-point of established theory tend to be overlooked. Yet, when persistent problems of explanation finally evoke a revision of theory, or what Kuhn calls a "scientific revolution," attention is paid to previously overlooked aspects of a set of phenomena, and they may then be classified differently.

Any extensive effort at comprehensive enumerative classification, by highlighting the diversity of behavior comprising crime, clearly implies that no single explanation can account for all offenses and offenders. Therefore, the first step in explanation should be to designate those criminal phenomena which one proposes to explain. Two strategies prevail in such efforts, to identify types and to abstract dimensions, but these two methods may be interacting aspects of a single knowledge-building process. Furthermore, in typing alone there are two interacting approaches, each of which may make a separate contribution to the discernment of dimensions.

A. Idealized and Empirical Typologies

Classification of people, to sharpen social-science theory regarding them, can be viewed as using but one of two alternative methods at any particular time. One method is conceptual and the other observational, but pursuit of either implies that the other has been dealt with previously. If the observation is subjective and open-ended, however, rather than a set of formal and objective operations, the conceptual and observational activities may be difficult to distinguish in practice, even though they are analytically distinct. It is only the formal observational methods that we shall designate here as empirical, using the term in a narrower sense for this discussion than it normally receives.

The conceptual procedure in developing explanatory classification is best exemplified by the "ideal type" methodology of Max Weber (1949:89–104). He would have us formulate an extreme or "pure" view of each separate type of person in a society during a particular period in order to understand what is distinctive and most relevant for explanation purposes in the many real persons of a particular group. No actual member of this group need precisely fit such an idealized conception. For example, the ideal types of bureaucrat, capitalist, or Calvinist described by Weber are not presumed to be identical with all persons labeled by these terms; the types are mental constructs of a theorist as he tries to conceptualize the most characteristic thinking of each group of people he is typing, and thereby to provide a meaningful explanation for their behavior, although actual members of such groups may each deviate somewhat from the ideal type.

The ideal-type method of Weber is a subjective analog to the more objectively formulated procedures of physicists when they try to explain mechanical phenomena by postulating perfect vacuums and frictionless surfaces, although the real world always has imperfect vacuums and friction which must be taken into account for absolutely precise and comprehensive explanations of particular physical events. As Lopreato and Alston (1970) point out, Weber's method is a special case of the strategy of idealization involved in all theory construction. We explain complex events by conceiving of them as simpler than they are, and therefore, we frequently must qualify our theoretical explanations to account for particular historical events which differ in some details from the theoretical category by which we type them.

The alternative to this idealization approach is to apply a standardized observation or measurement procedure in order to sort all persons in a particular sample or population into distinct categories. Such empirical typing is illustrated by statistical factor and cluster analysis of questionnaire or test items. In these analyses rigorous statistical procedures are employed to identify the sets of questions for which responses vary most independently from responses to other items, or to group the people whose answers to certain questions or problems are most similar to those of other people in their group and most different from the responses of other persons. Often such surprising combinations of questions or of people are shown by these statistical procedures to share common characteristics that names must be coined to label what seems distinctive about each group.

Winch (1947) called these two broad approaches to explanatory classification "heuristic" and "empirical." The heuristic or idealized typology is based upon reflection over prior observations, whether these observations were highly systematic or diffuse, precise or vague. Usually diffuse impressions are the observations most conducive to creative typing. Each category of an idealized type is often derived from thinking about only a few cases which a particular causal theory seems to explain most dramatically; the cases that are thought of as a separate type epitomize such a conceived causal process more adequately than other cases.

An idealized view of all people in each category as having a distinct set of characteristics facilitates simple generalizations about complex populations. Therefore, idealized typing occurs not just in science but also in everyday life; social types and stereotypes are forms of idealized explanatory classification (for fuller discussion, see Glaser & Stratton, 1961). A distinctive feature of idealized typologies is that their creators seek to *illustrate* the typology rather than to *demonstrate* its range of applicability to actual cases. The utility of empirical typing tends to be more specifically demonstrated. This contrast has been evident repeatedly in criminology.

Among pioneers in idealized typing of criminals were the nineteenth-century criminal anthropologists, notably Lombroso. He inferred that prisoners who had what he considered atavistic physical features were "born criminals," and others he differentiated as "insane criminals," "criminals by passion," and "occasional criminals." He *illustrated* dramatically the "born criminals" by searching prison populations for them. Goring, however, investigated whether Lombroso's distinctions could be *demonstrated*, for he applied them to all cases in a representative sample of English convicts, as well as to samples of nonprison populations—soldiers, hospital patients, university students. What this revealed could never have been discovered by Lombroso's procedure; the physical features that Lombroso postulated were evidence of born criminality occurred in about the same proportion for each of these groups of adults that Goring studied. Therefore, Goring's research largely discredited Lombroso's explanatory theory (Vold, 1958:50–59; Schafer, 1969:124–28, 185–86).

A distinctively sociological method of typing criminals was proposed by Edwin H. Sutherland through his concept of "behavior systems in crime." He identified these systems by three features: (1) Each is an integrated unit of "individual acts, codes, traditions, *esprit de corps*, social relationships among the direct participants, and indirect participations of many other persons. It is thus essentially a group way of life" (Sutherland & Cressey, 1970:280). In short, he identifies each system as involving a distinct network of intrasystem communication, and a consequent subculture. Therefore, he asserts (2) that it "is not unique to any particular individuals" (p. 280). The systems which Sutherland describes illustrate what Durkheim (1895) called "social facts," for each system exists independently of any of the individuals who participate in it, each survives as participants come and go, yet each creates behavioral constraints on its participants. Furthermore, (3) those who share a criminal behavior system form a self-conscious group; there is a "feeling of identification of those who participate in it" (Sutherland & Cressey, 1970:280).

Sutherland illustrated the behavior system of professional theft primarily from the life story of one thief. On the basis of a limited number of cases selected in a haphazard manner, he also described circus grifting and kidnapping as behavior systems. Although Sutherland presented no complete typology and provided only gross speculations as to the number and distribution of persons in each system, confidence that each system he described is empirically a somewhat distinct sociocultural type is gained by the consistency and tone of authenticity in his reports from a few informants, or even by confidence inspired by one informant.

Any such Sutherlandian account of behavior systems in crime embodies knowledge acquired by the techniques of social anthropology. Indeed, it is often more difficult for the criminologist to learn details of the lives of his subjects than it is for an anthropologist to learn intricacies of preliterate tribal life, for the criminologist is studying behavior that is covert because its disclosure might result in arrest and punishment. Furthermore, while distinct subcultures develop among isolated delinquent and criminal groups, acculturation repeatedly occurs among them from the members of different groups being thrown together in correctional institutions, if not in the community. A certain amount of idealization is therefore involved in treating any criminal behavior system as a fully discrete and homogeneous category. For example, informants will differ somewhat in defining the boundaries of their system, that is, in specifying whom it includes and who is marginal to it or excluded.

Clinard and Quinney (1973) in one of the most thorough studies of the literature on what they call "criminal behavior systems," distinguish nine categories: violent personal crime, occasional property crime, occupational crime, political crime, public order crime, conventional crime, corporate crime, organized crime, professional crime.

They indicate that these distinctions reflect five considerations: (1) The responses of lawmaking, enforcement, and adjudication agencies to various interest groups. (2) The proportion of the criminal's total career that is involved in his or her crimes (low on violent personal and occasional property crime; high on organized and professional crime). (3) The extent of group support for the crime (low on violent personal and occasional property crime; high on political, conventional, corporate, organized, and professional crime). (4) Correspondence between the criminal behavior and legitimate behavior (low on violent personal and occasional property crime; high on occupational and corporate crime, which is illustrated by "white-collar" offenses). (5) Intensity of societal reaction to the crime (high on violent personal, political, and conventional crime; low on occupational crime). It is evident that these categories differ from Sutherland's behavior systems even by definition, in that not all involve a feeling of group identity among those who participate in a particular type of offense. Indeed, some of their types (such as occupational and corporate crime) include persons extremely diverse in the extent to which they share a criminal subculture. As the authors remark, "typologies differ according to the purposes they are to serve (Clinard & Quinney, 1973:14); their typology serves well the task of summarizing what are currently the most criminologically interesting aspects of the vast available information and inference on illegal behavior.

Perhaps the most purely empirical procedure in classification of criminals into types is that of Roebuck (1967). He procured the criminal record sheets for a random sample of 400 black inmates of the District of Columbia prison at Lorton, Virginia and classified them by whether they had been arrested for one, two, three, or more different types of legal charges. By adopting arbitrary classification rules for ambiguous cases (essentially, ignoring small or not-recent deviations from the predominant patterns in long careers), he sorted all 400 into thirteen types, which are presented below, each followed by the number of cases in his sample from each type.

    A. One type of legal charge offenders: narcotics (50); robbery (32); gambling (16); burglary (15); sex offenses (15); fraud (10); auto theft (8); forgery and counterfeiting (4).

    B. Double legal charge offenders: larceny and burglary (64); drunkenness and assault (40).

    C. Triple legal charge offenders: drunkenness, assault, and robbery (43).

    D. Mixed pattern ("Jack-of-all-trades offender"): (71).

    E. No pattern (offenses not indicated, but all were heroin addicts): (32).

The generality of Roebuck's findings on the relative frequency of these types of arrest record would be enhanced, of course, if his method were also applied to samples from other locations and not restricted to a particular ethnic group. Its explanatory value, however, was the result of his going beyond the legal charge data to interview offenders in each category, essentially in an anthropological manner, to determine if they shared a distinctive subculture and life-history pattern. For some groups, such as the "numbers racket" gamblers, his effort to differentiate subcultures resulted in a contribution to the ethnography of American crime. For others, Roebuck discovered an impressive degree of similarity in life histories. For example, almost all the black armed robbers combined in their experiences early conflict at home with participation in adolescent street life where violence provided the main source of reputation and self-concept. Implicit here is a "differential identification" causal theory (Glaser, 1956). His other groups, such as the sex offenders, were more diverse. At any rate, Roebuck's procedures of formulating and objectively applying empirical classification rules resulted in his distinguishing several categories of offenders for whose criminality further investigation and a more idealized approach produced well-grounded explanations.

This complementarity of empirical and idealized typing was also demonstrated by Gibbons (1965, 1968). His operations reversed the procedure which Roebuck employed, however, for he utilized an idealistic approach first and undertook a systematic empirical check later. Initially he endeavored to identify separate roles in offenses, and to relate these to variations in the backgrounds of those who committed them, in order to differentiate types of what he called "role careers." Applying this approach to available literature on offenders and to his personal observations, he described the following varieties of role careers:

A. *Property offenders:* professional thief, professional "heavy" criminal, semi-professional criminal, amateur shoplifter, naive check forger, automobile thief "joyrider," property offender "one-time loser."

B. *"Respectable citizen" criminals:* white-collar criminal, embezzler, professional "fringe" violator.

C. *Murderers and assaultists:* personal offender "one-time loser," psychopathic assaultist.

D. *Sexual deviant criminals:* statutory rapist, aggressive rapist, violent sex offender, nonviolent sex offender, incest offender, male homosexual.

E. *Other criminals:* organized criminal, opiate addict, "skid row" alcoholic.

The above list, derived from Gibbons's 1968 book, differs slightly from that of his 1965 book, and both are among the most comprehensive and well-grounded of typologies in criminological literature, but neither was presented as exhaustive; they simply encompass the varieties Gibbons sought to describe and explain in these particular publications. His justifiable premise is ". . . that progress in explaining lawbreaking . . . or in correcting . . . [it] . . . demands that the heterogeneous assortment of criminal roles be sorted out into homogeneous patterns for study" (1968:v).

Application of the Gibbons typologies to a cross-section of criminals soon reveals that most cases differ in some conspicuous features from any category in the typology. This impression was confirmed when Hartjen and Gibbons (1969), aided by the staff of a California probation office, tried to classify 655 probationers by Gibbons's 1965 typology. They found not only that they had to add two types, "alcoholic delinquent" and "marijuana hippie," but also that slightly over half the sample (343 of 655) did not fit any of the types. Three persons employed in the typing agreed completely on the appropriate type designation for only 145 cases, and agreed that 243 did not fit any of the types. For the remaining 167 cases typed there was agreement by only two of the three judges, but for the 100 additional cases not typed, no agreement occurred in typing by any pair of the judges. There is simply too enormous an amount of variation in delinquency, crime, and life style in America for a relatively specific set of type descriptions to fit all cases well.

Explanatory classifications presented thus far differentiate offenders rather than offenses, but the act of committing a single offense may be regarded as one stage in a criminal career, and the only stage if there is no recidivism. Cressey's study of embezzlers (1953) is unique in criminology for its concern with redefining a particular offense in order to explain it more satisfactorily than would be possible with legal classifications. He defined embezzlement as the violation of trust by a person who prior to the offense had a career which clearly established him as trustworthy. By this definition he included in his sample some persons convicted of forgery or confidence games rather than embezzlement, but he excluded professional confidence men charged with embezzlement, for their crimes did not occur during a career of distinct trustworthiness. Cressey's embezzlers, therefore, were such persons as long-respected bank employees, reputable real estate brokers, and elected public officials, for it was only with persons of these social attributes that all three of the embezzlement determinants in his explanation were always present before the offense: (1) they had a financial problem that their social status and relationships led them to perceive as unshareable, for its disclosure would destroy the reputation of trustworthiness on which their positions depended; (2) they then conceived the embezzlement scheme as a way of solving this problem; (3) they committed the crime only after they had developed a rationalization by which they could interpret the embezzlement as compatible with a view of themselves as moral and noncriminal.

Cressey's procedure in theory-building is known as "analytic induction." It consists, essentially, of: (1) defining a phenomenon and formulating an explanation for it; (2) searching for instances of the phenomenon that the explanation does not fit; (3) wherever such a negative instance is found, either reformulating the explanation or redefining the phenomena that are explained, or both, so the explanation is applied only to those things to which it is applicable and it fits all such cases (for a fuller description and some classical references, see Denzin, 1970:194–201, 218).

Analytic induction is, thus, the progressive refinement of an idealized explanatory classification on the basis of empirical testing. It is useful in that it makes both explanations and classifications more appropriately qualified. It has both contributions and limitations as a method of theory and classification development that will be briefly indicated.

Analytic induction ultimately produces a deductive system, and in this sense its explanation follows logically rather than empirically from the definitions of the phenomena to be explained. Thus, to fit all cases, Lindesmith (1938) had to: (a) define opiate addiction as existing only when the opiate users know that the drugs they are taking cause withdrawal symptoms and that these symptoms are relieved only by taking more opiates; (b) define withdrawal symptoms as fearful experiences following cessation of opiate use. He then explained the persistent drug-taking in opiate addiction as caused by a fear of withdrawal symptoms in persons who know that opiates prevent these symptoms.

Deduction is involved in all explanations, but all explanations also are based on inductions which classify those aspects of reality with which the explanation is concerned. Such induction always involves idealization when dealing with complex natural phenomena, for the definitions must pay attention to fewer of the variations and dimensions of the phenomena denoted than are actually discerned, and the application of these definitions to reality is always somewhat unreliable. Two kinds of questions, one on validity and one on utility, should be addressed to an analytic induction theory of human behavior. The validity question is whether the aspects of reality that the theory implies are sequential and actually are observable in this sequential relationship. The utility question is whether the theory deals with aspects of the phenomena that interest and puzzle us.

Analytic induction theories frequently become so limited in their concerns and qualified in their formulations that they neglect what are generally regarded as important aspects of the phenomena they are presumed to explain. Lindesmith's theory (1938) explains the desperation of the opiate addict's search for a continuous supply of drugs; when promulgated this theory was especially useful because it more adequately explained this desperation than did the then-competing purely chemical or mystical explanations for what might be called the "drug-fiend syndrome." This theory does not explain initial opiate use, however, and this is especially problematic today, when most users begin in nonmedical settings. It also does not explain the long-prevalent high frequency of relapse to opiate use years after withdrawal symptoms have disappeared (notably, after long incarceration in a prison or hospital). Finally, it does not explain the dramatic changes historically in the age, ethnic, and other social correlates of opiate use. (For a fuller discussion, see Glaser et al., 1971.)

While those who have developed analytic induction theories of behavior have presented them as empirically demonstrated, reporting conscientious but unsuccessful searches for negative cases, one may reasonably contend that, like other idealized formulations, their theories are only illustrated. This criticism arises because the theorists made their observations only in terms of retrospectively reported subjective experiences, and because they know in advance what phenomena they should impute to their subjects in order to validate their theory. One may reasonably contend, for example, that a more adequate test of the empirical utility of Cressey's theory of embezzlement (1953) requires independent classification of cases by several investigators not committed to the theory, their use of standardized and reliability-tested investigatory procedures, and their studying both alleged embezzlers and similarly situated persons who did not embezzle. After determining that all of the subjects had at a previous time established themselves as trustworthy, the investigators would have to establish whether the subjects had ever, after attaining their position of trust, experienced the three alleged determinants of embezzlement. A cross-tabulation would then reveal whether all the embezzlers and only the embezzlers had experienced the three determinants. This sort of investigation, of course, would never yield absolutely reliable data (e.g., some of the presumed nonembezzlers may be undetected embezzlers, but any approximation of this procedure yielding a marked statistical association in the final cross-tabulation would be impressive support for Cressey's theory. Furthermore, an in-depth analysis of the negative cases from such a study (those who embezzled without all three determinants or who had all three but did not embezzle, or subjects who had only some of the determinants who were either embezzlers or nonembezzlers), could greatly enhance the considerable contribution to our understanding of embezzlement which Cressey's study provides.

There clearly is a need for alternation and interaction between analytic induction or other idealizing approaches to explanatory classification on the one hand, and empirical measurement of the fit of actual cases to sets of presumably relevant categories, on the other hand. This mixture is what Bailey (1973) distinguishes as "classical" typing. Experience thus far suggests that more of this type of interaction would reveal that idealized typing is a way of discovering salient dimensions while empirical typing is an often serendipitous way of validating them. Empirical checks disclose fictions in typologies and a reality that is multidimensional, but fictions also are manifest in every verbal or mathematical representation of multidimensionality, except for those which are too vague to be useful. For these and other reasons that will be discussed in closing this chapter, there is utility in both typological and dimensional approaches to explanatory classification.

B. Explanatory Dimensions

When a "pure" type of criminal is conceived in an idealized typology, the theorist usually appears to be thinking about the extreme of a separate dimension on which there are all degrees of variation. For most dimensions the distribution of cases probably falls in a bell-shaped curve, with the majority in the middle range and fewer at the extremes. Thus a vocational criminal is one who derives all of his income from crime and an avocational or amateur offender is one who never pursues crime for a living. But these extreme types define a dimension of *vocationalism in crime* along which the careers of adult criminals are distributed, with most having some mixture of legitimate and illegitimate income.

Numerous dimensions have been suggested by the typologies already cited. These include assaultiveness, sexual motivation, drug dependency, professionalism, social status, deceptiveness, and many others. Several of these constructs are variables which apply to a degree to almost all crimes and criminals. Most are discussed elsewhere in this book. Therefore, the balance of this chapter will be concerned with three dimensions of presumed causation in crime, applicable to a large variety of offenses, and on which criminologists have had intense disagreement. These three dimensions are labeled here in terms of their contrasting extremes, but separate crimes may involve mixtures of these opposites rather than either extreme exclusively. The three are:

(1) *Individuation:* whether crime causation is seen as *within an individual* offender or is ascribed to a *group* of persons of which he was a member or by which he was affected.

(2) *Emotionality:* whether the crime is of *instrumental* motivation, serving only as a means of obtaining some other objective, or is *expressive,* in being pursued for the emotional satisfaction of committing it, as an end in itself.

(3) *Commitment:* whether the crime is pursued as part of a *career* to which the individual is committed, or is primarily *situational* in origin at the time and place of its occurrence.

All three of these dimensions appear in explanations for most crimes, but each of the three may well be a pseudodimension, in that it actually consists of two or more independent variables. Nevertheless, every one of these ostensible dimensions has frequently been the basis of intense but moot argument about the causes of delinquency and crime.

1. Individualistic versus Group-Oriented Explanations

Police and courts almost always have the task of assessing guilt for each suspect separately. If questions of criminal intent or of legal responsibility are raised, they usually are questions about the individual psychology of each separate alleged offender. Durations of confinement and correctional programs are determined mainly by what are perceived as the personal characteristics of each convicted person. Therefore, officials in criminal justice agencies most frequently ascribe crime to the personality of the individual criminal, and when puzzled as to the causation of an offense they consult psychiatrists or psychologists.

Legislators and commentators on societal problems generally see crime as a collective matter. They are concerned with higher or lower crime rates, and explain them by referring to the characteristics of groups or to the conditions of a community. If they turn to science for evidence or inference on this, they employ sociology or economics, rather than psychology, more regularly than do the criminal justice agencies involved in case decisions.

Resembling the legendary blind men who each felt a different part of the elephant and, therefore, described it differently, psychologists and sociologists often offer radically contrasting classifications and explanations for crime. Clinical psychologists or psychiatrists usually are consulted by courts or correctional agencies only on those offenders whom officials regard as differing from most criminals in emotionality. Many prominent psychiatric and psychoanalytic explanations, consequently, are derived from atypical samples of offenders. This may explain their ascription of delinquency and crime primarily to instinctual emotions in all of us which the offenders do not learn to control (e.g., Aichhorn's psychoanalytic classic of 1925, with its introduction by Freud, and Friedlander's 1947 work).

Sociologists focus instead on the collective characteristics of crimes or criminals. For example, they correlate crime occurrence or the attributes of arrestees or convicts with neighborhood traits, societal conditions, or group affiliations. Their numerous and extensive interpretations of these data have been laconically summarized by Hirschi (1969) as explanations in terms of conformity to a *deviant culture* or of resort to delinquency to relieve *strain* from a discrepancy between actual and expected social conditions. In either case, in contrast to the psychological theorists, the sociologists viewed crime as a collective phenomenon. Indeed, they demonstrated that most reported initial delinquency was undertaken by two or more juveniles acting together rather than as lone offenders (Eynon & Reckless, 1961), and that delinquents feel more committed to peers than do nondelinquents (Erickson & Empey, 1965). Their most influential general explanation for crime ascribed it to differential association with sources of criminal rather than anticriminal learning, stressing such aspects or consequences of associations as intimacy, intensity, priority, identification, and reinforcement (Glaser, 1956; Burgess & Akers, 1968; Sutherland & Cressey, 1970:chap. 4).

Like the blind men and the elephant, psychologists and sociologists can both be valid in their contrasting views of delinquents and criminals. Each may be explaining different aspects of offenses and offenders, and both could be in error if they claim that their explanations are complete and sufficient. Social relationships necessarily are a major factor in any individual's learning at every stage in life. Therefore, even if a person commits crimes completely alone, social experiences have helped shape the moral values, emotional reaction tendencies, rationalizations, habits, and techniques involved in his or her crimes. Conversely, the regularities of behavior, feeling, and ideation that distinguish what we label as personality tend to make an individual's behavior somewhat unique at all stages in life. Therefore, even when a person commits crimes only in collaboration with others, personality has affected each individual's opportunities to participate in such group activity, and the manner in which he performs criminal roles in a collective enterprise.

Despite such fusion of personal and social factors in all crime, efforts have been made to differentiate offenses and offenders by their separate social and personality causation. An early form was to conceive of these two causal influences as in a zero-sum relationship, with each contributing a percentage of all causation, so that one crime might be 80 percent caused by personality and 20 percent by social factors, another might be 50-50, and so forth (Lindesmith & Dunham, 1941). This is of limited utility, however, if—as we suggested—personality patterns are largely caused by social experiences and social experiences reflect personality. Indeed, any causal explanation for human conduct is a purely verbal representation of relationships between antecedents and consequences in a more complex actual world. In these representations the concepts employed cannot be applied or measured with precision, yet they are useful if they reduce our puzzlement, and one explanation may be accepted as more valid than alternative explanations if it consistently leads us to more accurate prediction of behavior.

Perusal of psychological literature on delinquency soon conveys the impression that every psychological test ever developed has been applied to the differentiation of delinquents or criminals from presumed nonoffenders. In a classic survey of 113 such studies in the first half of the twentieth century Schuessler and Cressey (1950) concluded that only 42 percent of these efforts successfully distinguished the law-abiding from the lawbreaking subjects in terms of personality measures. They found that the various studies yielded such inconsistent results, however, with the same test frequently showing opposite relationships in different studies, that they concluded that no association had been demonstrated between criminality and any personality trait measured.

The Waldo and Dinitz (1967) survey of 94 studies published between 1950 and 1965 found that 81 percent discriminated significantly between delinquents or criminals and presumed nonoffenders, including 91 percent of the studies using objective tests, 75 percent of those using performance tests, and 63 percent of those using projective tests. The most marked and consistent findings were from two objective measures, the Psychopathic Deviate (Pd) scale of the Minnesota Multiphasic Personality Inventory and the Socialization (So) scale of the California Personality Inventory, but these scales consist largely of inquiries about the prior delinquency or criminality of the subjects. Furthermore, while the differences between means for the groups compared were often statistically significant, they were never extremely great in magnitude; there was much dispersion about the mean in each group and hence great overlap of the offenders and nonoffenders in all traits measured. The authors concluded, essentially, that personality can neither be justifiably dismissed nor unquestioningly assumed to be an independent causal variable in criminality.

The most sophisticated studies suggest that there is a complex interaction among sociocultural influences, personality variations within culturally homogeneous groups, and delinquent or criminal behavior. Conger and Miller (1966) found that the relationship of personality ratings to delinquent behavior varied with age, social class, ethnicity, and intelligence. Hindelang (1971) found that the relationship of extroversion and neuroticism scores to admitted delinquency depended upon the kind of delinquency, and that relationships to neuroticism were curvilinear (the moderately neurotic were more delinquent than those least or most neurotic). These and other studies suggest that individual personality characteristics affect success and failure in both legitimate and illegitimate pursuits, but they do this diversely in different social and cultural settings. Furthermore, for explanation and for treatment or control, both sociocultural and personality differences among offenders may be more important than those between offenders and nonoffenders.

2. Crime as Instrumental or Expressive

One distinction affecting the way crimes can be explained contrasts offenses pursued mainly for what they yield (e.g., money, automobiles, or other property) with offenses that directly express emotion (e.g., assaults in anger or lust). By this criterion property predations may be presumed to be *instrumental,* in that they are a means of obtaining satisfaction from the products of crime rather than from the criminal acts themselves. Crimes against persons more often appear to be *expressive,* as direct attempts at emotional gratification, and therefore, as ends in themselves.

The above impressions on the instrumental or emotional factors in different crimes fit common sense, but frequently are questioned by specialists. Their challenges are important, for whether criminality is viewed as rational or passionate may greatly affect policies for reducing crime. If a thief commits crimes because he is more successful in obtaining income in this manner than by legitimate employment, reformation efforts may focus on teaching him a trade and getting him a job. Conversely, if the act of theft fills a deep-seated emotional need, providing an alternative source of income will not make the thief law-abiding.

Emotions are private experiences. They cannot be directly observed by another person, but are imputed from behavior and utterances. People may conceal their emotions from others, however, and according to psychoanalytic theory, even from themselves. Or, when someone shows passions openly and intensely, the clinical psychologist may infer that this behavior is actually determined by unconscious feelings, often the opposite of those manifested; the visible passions are viewed as a reaction-formation or some other defense mechanism to repress contrasting feelings that are latent in the unconscious. There are extensive and often persuasive case analyses on such themes in the psychoanalytic literature on crime and delinquency (e.g., Eissler, 1949), but that these are speculative explanations is implicit in the very concept of the unconscious, which is the foundation of psychoanalytic theory.

Presumably such emotional dynamics are involved in all or most crime and in much other behavior, but psychiatrists, psychoanalysts, and clinical psychologists are consulted primarily on offenders whose characters puzzle police, court, or correctional officials. Search for atypical or unconscious expressive components predominates in efforts to explain offenses that "make no sense" as instrumental acts (e.g., when an affluent person shoplifts petty items) or that seem motivated by much more than the familiar emotions of assaultive crimes (e.g., "senseless" killings, rape of a very old woman or a small child, vicious assault on an invalid).

It is appropriate that we probe deeper and speculate more freely as to causation in cases that are puzzling. Pride of accomplishment usually is an emotion involved in any successful completion of a risky venture, in any show of skill, or even in being lucky. Opportunities for such pride are provided by much delinquency and crime, which may explain how avidly they are pursued. As Goffman (1967) points out, people everywhere are attracted to somewhat risky undertakings not for the sake of these actions, but to demonstrate their character to themselves and to others. People uncertain about their own qualities or about how they are regarded by others frequently initiate behavior involving some risk of a disappointing response if they perceive it as also a chance for them to demonstrate their worth. This occurs in much threatening, bullying, insulting, bluffing, challenging, flirting, or "showing off." Those who behave in these ways gamble for a gratifying response while risking a humiliating outcome. They try to limit their risks to what Goffman calls "practical gambles," but the intensity of their satisfaction with success is often determined by the severity of the risk they took to obtain it.

Because adolescents and youth are so preoccupied with establishing what kinds of persons they are, and because they frequently experience a sense of failure and desperation in this endeavor, they are especially attracted by the risk-taking in delinquency and crime. Stealing, fighting, drug use, and other crimes by juveniles and young adults, particularly those pursued in a group setting (e.g., participation in gang rapes), can usually be understood only if the need to demonstrate ability to meet challenges is taken into account. As Werthman (1967) has vividly shown, much delinquency is what Goffman (1967) calls a "character game"; it is interaction among peers for the sake of demonstrating adultlike independence, and one of the most effective ways for a juvenile to show this is by successfully defying adults.

Crime may be committed mainly because it is an available chance to perform, a stage on which to show oneself, for those who desperately seek such opportunities. These expressive aspects cannot wisely be overlooked; even in offenses that appear to be instrumental activity pursued in an unemotional way, money or property may motivate behavior not just as a means of getting something else, but as symbols of accomplishment competing with alternative influences on self-conception. The instrumental-expressive classification is not an either-or disjunction among offenses, but perhaps two somewhat independent and continuous variables. They are explanatory dimensions especially relevant to sentencing and correctional policy, for if delinquents and criminals are to be reformed they must be attracted to legitimate pursuits that offer more appealing and enduring self-concept enhancement than their illegal behavior provides.

3. Career Commitment versus Situational Explanations

There is a recurrent divergence in explanations for crime analogous to the continual dilemma of sentence determination in criminal law: should one focus on the offense or emphasize the offender? Did the misdeed result only from the dynamics of a situation or was it a manifestation of commitment to a career of crime?

Situational offenses are well exemplified by most murders, for a majority of these most serious of crimes appear to develop in the course of a gradually escalating argument between relatives or acquaintances. That the situation often determines who is murdered and who is the murderer is indicated by findings that in 25 to 38 percent of homicides the victim delivered the first blow in the altercation which culminated in his death (Hepburn & Voss, 1970).

Career commitment offenses are best illustrated by the predations of professional thieves. As Inciardi vividly shows in his chapter in this book, such people feel committed to engaging in crime not only because it is their sole source of income and because they have pride in their skill, they often have relationships with dealers in stolen goods, lawyers, and associates with whom their success at theft is a major source of mutual obligation, personal warmth, esteem, and respect. As Becker (1960) points out, commitment to an occupational career or to other aspects of a way of life depends largely on how much people value the impressions they believe their patterns of living have made on others, in addition to its tangible rewards and the investment of time and wealth that has gone into achieving it.

Most of the criminals and ex-criminals who can be traced in large numbers, those subjected to correctional custody or supervision for predations, have personal histories suggesting neither commitment to a career in crime nor purely chance situational determinants in their offenses. From large-sample follow-ups of federal prisoners it seemed evident that the careers of most traced a "zigzag path" from noncriminal to criminal pursuits and back again (Glaser, 1969:chap. 17). Success seemed to evoke repetition and persistence, whether in legitimate or illegal undertakings, and created an increasing degree of commitment, while acute failure in either fostered a shift to alternative pursuits, but often in an incompetent manner conducive to more failure and a reversal again. Situational factors seem to influence reversals when commitment is marginal; people change their way of life when things "are not going well" and a tempting opportunity to change develops.

Three crimes—burglary, grand theft, and auto theft—account for over 86 percent of the predatory felonies known to the police in the United States among the seven types—the so-called Index Crimes—for which tabulations are made nationally (F.B.I., 1972:6). A majority of the arrestees for these three crimes are under 18 years of age, over two-thirds are under 21, and over three-fourths are under 30. For robbery, the next most frequent Index Crime, a majority of arrestees are under 21, over three-fourths are under 25, and nearly nine-tenths are under 30 (1972:122–23). Clearly, instrumental property crime is most often a young person's preoccupation, as far as can be determined from arrest data. It is pursued by people at an age when career commitments are not yet firm.

As Short and Strodtbeck (1965:chap. 11) conclude from extensive research, youthful offenders tend to balance immediate certainty of status loss among peers if they fail to maintain their delinquent or criminal life style with a remote chance of penalties. In terms of alternative risks for them, their offenses in group situations are not so irrational and shortsighted as they appear to outsiders. These researchers also show that delinquents do not differ much from nondelinquents in highly valuing jobs; they simply differ in their willingness to accept crime as an alternative means for gratifying economic desires when satisfactory jobs are not available (Short & Strodtbeck, 1965:chap. 3). Extreme unemployment rates persistently prevail among youth, especially among those out of school, unskilled, and from economically deprived homes. In the light of these findings, it is both understandable that such youth contribute so disproportionately to the property predation rate, and also, that they usually reform at some point when they have had more successful experience in legitimate employment, with social relationships that increase their commitment to it.

The observations presented here suggest that situational and career commitment explanations for any single offense are meaningless unless considered simultaneously. While situational temptations or pressures can be conceived which would greatly affect almost anyone's prospects of engaging in crime, the actual reactions of people to specific situations appear to be determined by their career commitments. Those committed to demonstrating their manliness to themselves and to their friends who have been socialized in a subculture which indicates when this must be done by violence will react to a situational rebuff or insult differently from persons with other commitments and other cultural emphases. Indeed, persons committed to making a living by crime, to risking arrest in order to demonstrate their manliness, or to capitalizing on their femininity illegally will seek out conducive situations. Most people seem to have some marginality in their commitment to avoid illegal behavior; they usually conform to the law, but in some circumstances they will commit an offense, whether it is speeding, cheating on their income tax, or assault. The most influential explanatory variable in all crime usually appears to be commitment to obeying or to avoiding the law, but the situation is always a partially independent and separate causal complex.

Though in science one moves from idealized typologies to continuous dimensions, abandoning the initial heuristic types, if diversity in official reactions to persons classified as delinquent or criminal is to be justified, the offenders must be differentiated into types. Thus people eventually must categorize again for policy purposes, on some empirical basis, perhaps guided by the scientifically discerned dimensions deemed relevant to policy. Only if they then systematically and rigorously test the prognostic inferences underlying their policy classifications, however, will they achieve greater justice, humanity, and safety in coping with crime.

REFERENCES

Aichhorn, August.
  1925   Wayward Youth. English Edition, 1935. New York: Viking.
American Law Institute (A.L.I.)
  1957   Model Penal Code, Tentative Draft No. 7. Philadelphia: American Law Institute.
  1961   Model Penal Code, Proposed Final Draft No. 1. Philadelphia: American Law Institute.

Arens, Richard.
 1967   "The Durham Rule in action: judicial psychiatry and psychiatric justice."
         Law and Society Review 1(June):41–80.
 1969   Make Mad the Guilty. Springfield, Ill.: Thomas.

Bailey, Kenneth D.
 1973   "Monothetic and polythetic typologies and their relation to conceptualiza-
         tion, measurement and scaling." American Sociological Review 38(Febru-
         ary):18–33.

Bard, Morton.
 1970   Training Police as Specialists in Family Crisis Intervention. Washington:
         U.S. Government Printing Office.

Bassiouni, M. Cherif.
 1969   Criminal Law and its Processes. Springfield, Ill.: Thomas.

Becker, Howard S.
 1960   "Notes on the concept of commitment." American Journal of Sociology
         66(July):32–40.

Bittner, Egon.
 1967   "The police on skid row: a study of peace-keeping." American Sociological
         Review 32(October):699–715.

Blankenship, Ralph L.
 1968   "Police response to signs of mental disturbance among juvenile offenders."
         M.A. dissertation, University of Illinois.

Blankenship, Ralph L., and George H. Martin.
 1972   "Some factors related to differential labeling of juvenile offenders" (un-
         published).

Blumberg, Abraham.
 1967   Criminal Justice. Chicago: Quadrangle Books.

Burgess, R. L., and R. L. Akers.
 1968   "A differential association-reinforcement theory of criminal behavior."
         Social Problems 14(Fall):128–147.

Carney, Francis J., and Ann L. Fuller.
 1969   "A study of plea bargaining in murder cases in Massachusetts." Suffolk
         University Law Review 3(Spring):292–307.

Clinard, Marshall B., and Richard Quinney.
 1973   Criminal Behavior Systems. Second Edition. New York: Holt, Rinehart &
         Winston.

Conger, John J., and Wilber C. Miller.
 1966   Personality, Social Class and Delinquency. New York: Wiley.

Cressey, Donald R.
 1953   Other People's Money. Glencoe, Ill.: Free Press.
 1969   Theft of a Nation. New York: Harper & Row.

Denzin, Norman K.
 1970   The Research Act. Chicago: Aldine.

Durkheim, Emile.
 1895   The Rules of Sociological Method. Eighth Edition. Translated and edited
         by Sarah A. Solovay and John H. Mueller. Edited by G. E. G. Catlin.
         Glencoe, Ill.: Free Press (1950 edition).

Eissler, R. K. (ed.)
    1949   Searchlights on Delinquency. New York: International Universities Press.
Erickson, Maynard L., and LaMar T. Empey.
    1965   "Class position, peers and delinquency." Sociology and Social Research 49(April):268–282.
Eynon, Thomas G., and Walter C. Reckless.
    1961   "Companionship at delinquency onset." British Journal of Criminology (October):162–170.
Farber, Bernard.
    1968   Mental Retardation: Its Social Context and Social Consequences. Boston: Houghton Mifflin.
Federal Bureau of Investigation (F.B.I.)
    1972   Crime in the United States: Uniform Crime Reports—1971. Washington: U.S. Government Printing Office.
Friedlander, Kate.
    1947   Psychoanalytic Approach to Juvenile Delinquency. New York: International Universities Press.
Gibbons, Don C.
    1965   Changing the Lawbreaker. Englewood Cliffs, N.J.: Prentice-Hall.
    1968   Society, Crime and Criminal Careers. Englewood Cliffs, N.J.: Prentice-Hall.
Glaser, Daniel.
    1956   "Criminality theories and behavioral images." American Journal of Sociology 61(March):433–444.
    1962   "Prediction tables as accounting devices for judges and parole boards." Crime and Delinquency 8(July):239–258.
    1964   The Effectiveness of a Prison and Parole System. Indianapolis: Bobbs-Merrill.
    1967   "National goals and indicators for the reduction of crime and delinquency." Annals of the American Academy of Political and Social Science 371(May): 104–126.
    1969   The Effectiveness of a Prison and Parole System. Abridged Edition. Indianapolis: Bobbs-Merrill.
    1972   Adult Crime and Social Policy. Englewood Cliffs, N.J.: Prentice-Hall.
Glaser, Daniel, Bernard Lander, and William Abbott.
    1971   "Opiate addicted and non-addicted siblings in a slum area." Social Problems 18(Spring):510–521.
Glaser, Daniel, and John R. Stratton.
    1961   "Measuring inmate change in prison," in Donald R. Cressey (ed.), The Prison. New York: Holt, Rinehart & Winston.
Goffman, Erving.
    1967   "Where the action is," in E. Goffman, Interaction Ritual. Garden City, N.Y: Doubleday Anchor Books.
Goldstein, Abraham S.
    1967   The Insanity Defense. New Haven: Yale University Press.
Hartjen, Clayton A., and Don C. Gibbons.
    1969   "An empirical investigation of a criminal typology." Sociology and Social Research 54(October): 56–62.

Hepburn, John, and Harwin L. Voss.
1970   "Patterns of criminal homicide: a comparison of Chicago and Philadelphia." Criminology 8(May):21–45.

Hindelang, Michael J.
1971   "Extroversion, neuroticism and self-reported delinquent involvement." Journal of Research in Crime and Delinquency 8(January):23–31.

Hirschi, Travis.
1969   Causes of Delinquency. Berkeley: University of California Press.

Inciardi, James A.
1970   "The adult firesetter: a typology." Criminology (August):145–155.

Joint Legislative Committee for Revision of the Penal Code.
1971   The Criminal Code. Los Angeles: State of California.

Kuhn, Thomas S.
1962   The Structure of Scientific Revolutions. Chicago: University of Chicago Press.

LaFave, Wayne R.
1965   Arrest. Boston: Little, Brown.

Levine, David.
1970   "Criminal behavior and mental institutionalization." Journal of Clinical Psychology 26(July):279–284.

Lindesmith, Alfred R.
1938   "A sociological theory of drug addiction." American Journal of Sociology 43(January):593–613.

Lindesmith, A. R., and H. W. Dunham.
1941   "Some principles of criminal typology." Social Forces 19(March):307–314.

Lipsitt, Paul D., David Lelos, and A. Louis McGarry.
1971   "Competency for trial: a screening instrument." American Journal of Psychiatry 128(July):105–109.

Lopreato, Joseph, and Letitia Alston.
1970   "Ideal types and idealization." American Sociological Review 35(February):88–96.

McGarry, A. Louis.
1969   "Demonstration and research in competency for trial and mental illness: review and preview." Boston University Law Review 49(Winter):46–61.
1971   "The fate of psychotic offenders returned for trial." American Journal of Psychiatry 127(March):1181–1184.

McIntyre, Donald M.
1968   "A study of judicial dominance of the charging process." Journal of Criminal Law, Criminology and Police Science 59(December):463–490.

Miller, Frank W.
1969   Prosecution. Boston: Little, Brown.

Miller, Robert R., and Emmet Kenney.
1966   "Adolescent delinquency and the myth of hospital treatment." Crime and Delinquency 12(January):38–48.

Morris, Norval.
1968   "Psychiatry and the dangerous criminal." Southern California Law Review 41:514–547.

Morris, Norval, and Gordon Hawkins.
  1969   The Honest Politician's Guide to Crime Control. Chicago: University of
          Chicago Press.

Morrow, William R., and Donald B. Peterson.
  1966   "Follow-up of discharged psychiatric offenders: 'not guilty by reason of in-
          sanity' and 'criminal sexual psychopaths.' " Journal of Criminal Law, Crim-
          inology and Police Science 57(March) :31–34.

Newman, Donald J.
  1966   Conviction: The Determination of Guilt or Innocence Without Trial. Bos-
          ton: Little, Brown.

Northrop, F. S. C.
  1947   The Logic of the Sciences and the Humanities. New York: Macmillan.

Ohlin, Lloyd E., and Frank J. Remington.
  1958   "Sentencing structure: its effect upon systems for the administration of crim-
          inal justice." Law and Contemporary Problems 23(Summer) :495–507.

Parsons, Talcott.
  1971   The System of Modern Societies. Englewood Cliffs, N.J.: Prentice-Hall.

Phillipson, Coleman.
  1923   Three Criminal Law Reformers: Beccaria, Bentham, Romilly. London: Dent.

Platt, Anthony Michael, and Bernard L. Diamond.
  1965   "The origins and development of the 'wild beast' concept of mental illness
          and its relation to theories of criminal responsibility." Journal of the His-
          tory of the Behavioral Sciences 1(October) :355–367.
  1966   "The origins of the 'right and wrong' test of criminal responsibility and its
          subsequent development in the United States: an historical survey." Cali-
          fornia Law Review 54(August) :1227–1260.

President's Commission on Law Enforcement and Administration of Justice.
  1967a   The Challenge of Crime in a Free Society. Washington, D.C.: U.S. Govern-
          ment Printing Office.
  1967b   Task Force Report: Crime and its Impact—An Assessment. Washington,
          D.C.: U.S. Government Printing Office.

Roebuck, Julian B.
  1967   Criminal Typology. Springfield, Ill.: Thomas.

Rosenhan, D. L.
  1973   "On being sane in insane places." Science 179(January 19) :250–258.

Ross, H. Laurence, Donald T. Campbell, and Gene V. Glass.
  1970   "Determining the social effects of a legal reform: the British "Breathalyzer"
          crackdown of 1967." American Behavioral Scientist 13(March/April) :
          495–509.

Schafer, Stephen.
  1969   Theories in Criminology. New York: Random House.

Schuessler, Karl F., and Donald R. Cressey.
  1950   "Personality characteristics of criminals." American Journal of Sociology
          55(March) :476–484.

Short, James F., Jr., and Fred L. Strodtbeck.
  1965   Group Process and Gang Delinquency. Chicago: University of Chicago
          Press.

Simon, Rita James.
    1967   The Jury and the Defense of Insanity. Boston: Little, Brown.

Sudnow, David.
    1965   "Normal crimes: sociological features of the penal code in a public defender's office." Social Problems 12(Winter):255–276.

Sutherland, E. H., and D. R. Cressey.
    1970   Criminology. Eighth Edition. Philadelphia: Lippincott.

Tappan, Paul W.
    1960   Crime, Justice and Correction. New York: McGraw-Hill.

Toch, Hans H.
    1969   Violent Men. Chicago: Aldine.

Vold, George B.
    1958   Theoretical Criminology. New York: Oxford.

Waldo, Gordon P., and Simon Dinitz.
    1967   "Personality attributes of the criminal: an analysis of research studies, 1950–65." Journal of Research in Crime and Delinquency 4(July):185–202.

Walker, Nigel.
    1965   Crime and Punishment in Britain. Edinburgh: Edinburgh University Press.
    1968   Crime and Insanity in England. Vol. 1: The Historical Perspective. Edinburgh: Edinburgh University Press.

Weber, Max.
    1949   The Methodology of the Social Sciences. Translation by E. A. Shils and H. A. Finch. Glencoe, Ill.: Free Press.

Werthman, Carl.
    1967   "The function of social definitions in the development of criminal careers," Appendix J of President's Commission on Law Enforcement and Administration of Justice, Task Force Report: Juvenile Delinquency and Youth Crime. Washington, D.C.: U.S. Government Printing Office.

Winch, Robert F.
    1947   "Heuristic and empirical typologies: a job for factor analysis." American Sociological Review 12(February):68–75.

CHAPTER 3

The Socialization and Control of Deviant Motivation

Jackson Toby

Rutgers University

Crimes, the phenomena criminologists try to explain, are defined in the course of a political process (Glaser, 1971:30–31). When student members of the New Left level criticism at bourgeois America by claiming that Angela Davis was a political prisoner, criminologists may surprise them by conceding even more. Since crimes are acts defined by a political process and adjudicated and punished by the state, *all* prison inmates are political prisoners: rapists, burglars, murderers, pickpockets. The legislators and judges who enact and interpret the criminal law are not a random sample of the population. Women, children, ethnic minorities, and the poor are underrepresented in lawmaking roles. However hard legislators and judges *try* to speak for the entire society, they cannot help paying more attention to some views of what is right and wrong than to others. This means in practice that they codify a limited and often parochial morality in the criminal law. Laws against abortions drawn up by predominantly male state legislators are quite different from what female legislators might have enacted. For a similar reason, laws prohibiting the sale of alcoholic beverages to those under 21 may change now that 18 year olds have the franchise in the United States.

Conceding that all prisoners are political prisoners might imply that prisoners are prisoners, whether in the United States or in the Soviet Union or in South Africa, and therefore that criminologists from these countries have much in common. Indeed, this issue was an embarrassment at the fourth United Nations Congress on the Prevention of Crime and the Treatment of Offenders in Stockholm in August, 1965. The head of the South African delegation was the then minister of justice, Balthazar J. Vorster, who is now the South African prime minister. Mr. Vorster's reputation for jailing and harassing opponents of *apartheid* had preceded him to Stockholm, and the Swedish press thundered against him nearly every day. The Congress's headquarters was picketed by Swedes urging condemnation of South Africa in general and her minister of justice in particular. One intellectual issue for criminologists at the Congress was the basis upon which the state defines punishable behavior. By reference to which values of what segment of the society is a prohibition legitimated? Legality is not enough. One kind of crime exists when the legitimating values are widely shared so that even prisoners regard their punishment as appropriate, another when prisoners feel morally superior to their captors (as with the opponents of *apartheid* in South

African prisons). To put the same point another way, *crime* has nothing to do with morality; crime is any behavior the state is organized to punish. But criminology, if it is to make sense as a behavioral science, must consider crime in the context of tendencies toward value-consensus in the society; the probability of an individual violating a criminal law differs depending on whether or not he and his reference groups are morally committed to the law in question.

To what extent is there normative consensus about the reprehensibility of specific crimes in various types of societies? Is value-pluralism more likely than value-consensus in heterogeneous and changing cultures? Thus, in the United States, there is no clear consensus that marijuana smoking is *wrong* despite punitive laws against its sale or use in most jurisdictions. Instead, American society is polarized into a large group, probably a majority, who consider marijuana use wrong and a smaller group (but a substantial proportion of adolescents and young adults) who consider pot harmless and are *indignant* at societal interference. In situations like this, the sociological concepts of the criminologist are unsuited to the problem of explaining the motivations behind the crime. It is the opposition of the collective conscience that draws together otherwise dissimilar statutory crimes and makes them amenable to sociological study. In the absence of this common opposition, motivations of a thousand kinds can explain why people wish to drive an automobile at eighty miles an hour, beat up an enemy, or take something without paying for it. In short, the intellectual tools of the criminologist are better suited for explaining crimes supported by a value-consensus of the population, that is, for explaining crimes that are also deviance, such as violent rape or premeditated murder. Deviance consists of the purposive defiance or evasion of a normative consensus. Not all deviant behavior is criminal; the state does not prohibit body odor despite the American horror of people who smell. On the other hand, not all crimes constitute deviance; many statutory offenses, e.g., patent infringement and drunken driving, arouse neither guilt in the offender nor community indignation (Sutherland, 1949; Ross, 1960–61).

THE GENESIS OF DEVIANT MOTIVATION

If criminology should limit its explanatory efforts to accounting for consensual crimes (rather than all statutory crimes) the task is more precisely defined. But this is a sensible agenda for criminology only if consensual crimes constitute a substantial proportion of total crime. And this is unlikely if, as some sociologists believe, value-conflict is more pervasive in social systems than value-agreement (Quinney, 1970:16–18). Even among sociologists who assume that consensus exists about what is deviance in *small* social systems, many think that this consensus is not characteristic of pluralistic, changing industrial societies. I shall not attempt to address these questions, which are partly empirical and partly conceptual. Depending on the level of abstractness with which values are defined, consensus appears more pervasive or less so. I shall assume that sufficient consensus exists about what deviant behavior is so that consensual crimes are worthy of explanation. How are consensual crimes to be explained? Some criminological theories imply that the full explanation of deviant *behavior* lies in the identification of deviant *motivation*. The problem then becomes: How does deviant motivation develop in a society in which consensus exists about right and wrong? Three types of answers are given to this question, all deriving deviant motivation from pathologies of socialization.

Inadequate Socialization

The first type of explanation of socialization failure attributes it to deficiencies in the interactional process between socializing agents and socializees—most commonly between parents and their own children (Bredemeier & Stephenson, 1962:126–28). The parent does not want the child to steal, but parental rejection or neglect or overprotection creates conditions under which the child does not internalize the parent's norms. Indeed, some parents fail so miserably to capitalize on the sensitivity of the child to parental desires that they create in their children a need to do precisely the opposite of what parents want them to do. Whereas most children strengthen their tendencies to conform to the wishes of other people as a result of family socialization, some children become alienated from norm givers; they are predisposed to defy not only their parents but others who attempt to teach them existing values (Parsons, 1951: 233–34).

Under what conditions do parental efforts at socialization fail to produce internalization? One reason why it is so difficult to specify these conditions with any assurance is that the biological variability of human organisms generates variability of results in addition to the variability contributed by different styles of socialization. Another reason is that the family is not a closed system; other influences impinge on the child besides those of his parents. Still, enough research has accumulated to codify the conditions conducive to internalization of the values and norms taught by socializing agents, at least tentatively (Toby: 1971:109–10):

1. *Clear definition of the appropriate norms.* Unless the child knows precisely what behavior his socializers expect of him, he will have difficulty modifying his previous behavior pattern. Suppose, for example, that the father of a boy has a more aggressive conception of the male role than the mother. These inconsistent expectations of the parents make it difficult for the boy to discipline childish impulses in the interest of conforming to "the male role."

2. *Solidarity between the person being socialized and the socializing agent.* Unless the child feels accepted by his family, he will not value membership in the family and will have no great incentive to conform to the demands family members impose upon him.

3. *A permissive attitude on the part of socializing agents toward a limited amount of regressive behavior.* Unless the child is permitted some missteps (and some backward steps) as he moves toward mature behavior, he will be afraid to try out the new behavior expected by his parents. The child who stutters is usually a child who was not permitted to speak unfluently in the course of speech training (Lemert, 1951:143–64). Talcott Parsons has an intriguing hypothesis about parental permissiveness (Parsons & Bales, 1955:78–80). He suggests that both parents, in tandem, are important to successful socialization: one tends to be permissive and the other demands increasingly mature behavior. Parsons believes that this division of parental labor is more effective than one in which parents are equally responsible for pressure and permissiveness. The female parent is usually the permissive one in Western societies, but Parsons regards it as less important which parent is permissive than that there be role differentiation between the parents.

4. *An emotionally controlled reaction on the part of socializing agents toward rebellious behavior.* A common reaction of children toward parental demands is counterattack. The child challenges parental authority by a rebellious tantrum, by refusing to obey, or by conspicuous disregard of the request. It is tempting for the

parent, especially an insecure parent, to meet the challenge by a temper tantrum of his own. However, socialization of the child will occur more quickly if the parent preserves his "cool"—pressing his demands firmly but refusing to reciprocate the child's hostility.

5. *Rewards for learning the role and an absence of reward for failing to learn it.* The child must feel that his efforts to learn what his parents expect him to learn have paid off. This does not mean he must receive candy or money or toys. The most important reward available to parents (or to any socializing agent) is a relational reward, that is, a favorable attitude.

Presumably, children whose socialization experiences in the family do not fulfill these conditions develop personality structures that fail to include the values and norms that their parents tried to transmit. Such children may be described as having neurotic, psychotic, or psychopathic personalities; their personalities may indeed be malintegrated. From the point of view of the criminologist, however, their most interesting characteristic is lack of motivation to conform to the consensual order. In describing them as being "inadequately" socialized, we are speaking of inadequacy only by the criterion of functioning within that order.

Inappropriate Socialization

The second type of explanation of socialization pathology attributes it to socialization within a subsystem of the society so that the individual learns values and norms inappropriate for functioning within the larger society (Bredemeier & Stephenson, 1962:126–28). The family unit itself can be a source of inappropriate socialization in a large society differentiated into social classes, ethnic groups, regions, and urban and rural communities. Insofar as these subgroups merely place slightly different emphases on what are common values, the amount of inappropriate socialization arising from these variations is small. But differences in emphasis shade off into differences in kind; hence some families, purposively or unwittingly, transmit a deviant culture.

In the criminological literature *family* sources of inappropriate socialization are less often considered than the *neighborhood* and the *peer group* (Thrasher, 1927: Shaw & McKay, 1942). Particularly in discussions of adolescent delinquency in the slums of large cities, the task becomes one of identifying a deviant *culture*, such as that of delinquent gangs (Cohen, 1955; Cloward & Ohlin, 1960). Explaining deviant *behavior* on the part of youngsters exposed to such influences is treated as not problematical. As Hirschi pointed out,

> cultural deviance theory assumes that cultures, not persons, are deviant. It assumes that in living up to the demands of his own culture, the person automatically comes into conflict with the law (1969:229).

A difficulty with theories of deviant subcultures is that those exposed to them are also exposed to conforming subsystems. As Matza put it, the subculture of delinquency is manned by children.

> Children have a curious way of being influenced by the society of elders which frequently includes parents, almost all of whom, whatever their own proclivities, are united in their denunciation of delinquent deeds (1964:37).

In short, deviant subcultures are not as autonomous as the culture of an isolated preliterate society described by an anthropologist. That is why the explanation of delinquency by anthropologist Walter Miller (1958) as a simple expression of cultural preoccupations with toughness, smartness, and excitement leaves something out. What is left out is the superordinate culture from which the subculture is a departure and which has implications for child socialization. If problems of adequacy of socialization arise in families whose values are essentially compatible with those of the larger society, more frequent problems of socialization can be expected within deviant subcultures because deviant subcultures are attempting to socialize in the face of competition. In short, deviant subcultures, far from producing deviants automatically, can be expected to produce persons with equivocal and perhaps ambivalent motivation.

Ambivalent Socialization

Talcott Parsons has provided a consistent exposition of a third source of deviant motivation: ambivalence (1951: chap. 7). According to Parsons, the delinquent gang member has internalized as a result of previous socialization in the family and the school values incompatible with theft and assault. If the gang encourages him to steal, this deviant norm conflicts with a value pointing in a law-abiding direction. How does he resolve the inner conflict? He resolves it by expressing either side of the ambivalent motivational structure, but whichever he does, he does it compulsively—in order to overcome the opposite motivational tendency in his psyche. If he steals, he not only takes things that do not belong to him; he protests that he is only getting back what others have illegitimately taken from him. If he *doesn't* steal, he regards those who steal as punks who ought to be severely punished.

Ambivalent socialization can arise from a sequence of socialization in the family followed by further socialization to incompatible norms in the peer group. A large proportion of gang delinquents presumably follow this pattern. Ambivalent socialization can also arise from inadequate socialization in the family or in other primary groups. Take the matter of sexual identity. Suppose as a result of socializing experiences with his mother and father a boy develops unconscious doubts as to whether his sexual preferences lie with members of the opposite sex or with members of his own sex. One motivational outcome might be to attempt to prove his heterosexuality by a succession of female conquests and, perhaps simultaneously, by expressing a loathing for "queers." The other possibility is to express compulsively the homosexual element in his personality by idealizing homosexual love and by saying that females "turn my stomach."

Parsons does not specify in detail how ambivalence is generated. He does not, for example, distinguish inadequate from inappropriate socialization in producing ambivalence. Instead he speaks of "strain," defined as psychological distress arising from the failure of significant others to live up to what the individual feels are legitimate expectations (1951:252). Fortunately, the concept of strain, although vague on the causal side, is clearer when it comes to deviant effects. Strain theories of deviance are not new; the new element that Parsons contributed was his insistence that strain leads to ambivalence. Thus, Robert Merton developed a strain theory of deviance by arguing that inferior statuses are more vulnerable than élite statuses to the temptation to violate societal rules (1938). Stinchcombe's study of high-school rebellion draws on the tradition of strain theories of deviance (1964). Stinchcombe maintains—and supports his claim with survey data—that those high-school students who do not see the relevance of high-school studies for their adult lives are more likely to defy the authority of teachers than students who perceive high school as leading to a desirable future. Given his knowledge of the meaning of various courses of study in American culture, Stinchcombe infers that students in the college course have better "articulation" of the present with the future than students whose curriculum choice is ambiguous. Not surprisingly, Stinchcombe predicts that students with poor articulation feel alienated and more likely to rebel. He also predicts that boys from middle-class families whose curriculum choice is ambiguous will be *more* rebellious than working-class boys with equally poor articulation, and the data bear him out (1964:83). In Parsons's terms, such boys are under greater strain; they are disappointed in the school's response to them. Their greater rebellion can be understood as a response to an initially greater commitment to school success.

In short, strain theories like Merton's and Stinchcombe's supplement the Parsonian theory of motivational ambivalence. Such theories offer an explanation of the pressures leading to ambivalence. They can be interpreted in a socialization frame of reference to explain how previously internalized values can be partially undermined. The rebels in the school studied by Stinchcombe did not entirely lose their respect for teachers and for education; but a succession of disappointing experiences at school created a dilemma for them. They had either to think of themselves as inadequate students in a just system or as conscripted soldiers in an unworthy cause. Some of them, some of the time, chose the latter alternative, thus accounting for negativistic attitudes and rebellious behavior. Stinchcombe was careful to distinguish attitudes ("expressive alienation") from behavior ("rebellion"). And he pointed out that his articulation theory was designed to account only for the emergence of expressive alienation. Whether that alienation would be expressed in rebellious behavior depended on additional considerations. He recognized that some rebellious behavior occurred as a result of situational pressures on youngsters who were *not* alienated. Conversely, some alienated youngsters did *not* act out their attitudes in behavior, perhaps because they did not have opportunities to do so without severe sanctions, perhaps because they were too timid, or for any number of other reasons. Like Stinchcombe, Parsons is careful to distinguish between deviant motivation and deviant behavior; he does not equate the two. In fact, Parsons spends considerable energy discussing conditions under which deviant motivation will eventuate in deviant behavior (1951:283–97) as well as conditions under which social control mechanisms successfully contain deviant motivation (1951:297–321).

THE SOCIAL CONTROL OF DEVIANT MOTIVATION

Another way of putting the distinction between deviant motivation and deviant behavior is to point out that personality systems and social systems contribute separately to deviant behavior. In the course of socialization, personality structures are formed that vary in the need to defy the collective conscience. These personalities with their varying needs become committed to a plurality of interactive systems—families, peer groups, educational organizations, work organizations, neighborhoods—which act with greater or lesser effectiveness to arrest deviant tendencies before they become well established in the behavioral repertoire of the individual. Thus, it is conceivable that a personality with strong deviant tendencies will participate in interactive systems that inhibit the expression of these tendencies or make expression prohibitively costly. Under these conditions, they do not get expressed in behavior, or perhaps the positive side of the ambivalence gets expressed and the positive side seems more like superconformity than deviance. Similarly, a personality with only weak tendencies toward deviance might participate in interactive systems in which such tendencies are encouraged rather than inhibited—with the outcome that weak tendencies are acted out.

The foregoing theoretical discussion sounds as though the contributions of personality and social system to deviant behavior are virtually independent. But do not personality and social systems contain a common value element? Values and norms internalized in personalities through the process of socialization are simultaneously institutionalized in social systems. And is it not likely that individuals exposed to socialization that fails to inculcate central societal values successfully are also the individuals whose social participations are not likely to check deviant tendencies? The notion of social stratification hypothesizes such an interrelationship between socialization and social control. Those fairly low in the hierarchy of stratification are presumed less likely to internalize societal values and less likely to find themselves subject to the formal and informal controls of interactive systems. In short, the theory of social stratification provides a basis for expecting more deviance on lower than on higher levels of the system of social stratification.

In the field of criminology, empirical studies of the incidence of crime on different social-class levels have produced equivocal results. Studies based on official records, e.g., arrests, show disproportionate criminality in the lower classes (Shaw & McKay, 1942; Reiss & Rhodes, 1961; Shannon, 1963). Studies based on self-reported crime show negligible social class differences in rates (Nye, 1958; Christie et al., 1965; Hirschi, 1969). A reasonable inference from these data is that the correlation between socialization processes and social-control processes is weak. Modern societies are sufficiently pluralistic that the system of social stratification is not tightly integrated; the personality tendencies to deviance produced by socialization are not consistently reinforced by social-control processes. On the other hand, it is implausible that these tendencies are *reversed* by social-control processes. Reversal would require a negative relationship between socialization and social control, and a negative correlation belies the universal tendency for differentiated levels of reward and opportunity to exist in a society. This reasoning leads to the conclusion that tendencies to deviance produced by socialization are necessarily somewhat reinforced by processes of social control, a formulation not compatible with data from the self-report studies of criminality. Unless some logical error has been made in the theory, the apparent lack of relationship between social class and criminality in the self-report studies must be an artifact of the research procedures used in gathering the data.

This challenge to the results of the self-report studies does not imply that the true relationship is necessarily very strong. In a pluralistic society, it may well be weak. Furthermore, errors of measurement may further reduce the strength of the true relationship. The theory only predicts that social-system participation will not, *on the average,* reverse the direction of family socialization but rather reinforce it. There are many social-system contexts in which deviant personality tendencies can be extirpated or reinforced. We shall discuss four prominent ones in the remainder of this chapter: the family, the peer group, the educational-occupational system, and the formal control system of the larger society.

The Family Control System

Although the family is the context in which socialization of the child begins, socialization in the family does not end with adolescence; it persists as long as the child interacts with parents and siblings. Social control, like socialization, is a process within a social system tending to produce conforming behavior. The difference between them is that socialization is directed largely at the *personality* of the role player; it seeks to motivate him to want to do what the rules of the interactive system require him to do. Social control is directed more at the *behavior* of the role player; it pressures him to conform regardless of his motivational inclinations (Bredemeier & Stephenson, 1962: 146).[1] Obviously, this distinction is an analytical one. In concrete interactions between parents and children both aspects are present simultaneously. Neither the parents nor the children would be able to distinguish the two aspects readily. Nevertheless, it is a useful distinction for the sociologist because it calls attention to the prudential aspects of family life that continue whether or not personality change occurs. Thus, Hirschi asked 4,077 students entering public junior and senior high schools of the city of Richmond, California, the following questions: "Does your mother know whom you are with when you are away from home?" and "Does your mother know where you are when you are away from home?" (1969:88–89). Boys who answered "usually" to both questions were much more likely than boys who answered "never" to say that they had *not* committed one of a variety of delinquent acts. Presumably, the psychological presence of the mothers inhibited delinquency even among youngsters whose personalities permitted criminal behavior. Hirschi could not disentangle the effects of socialization from the effects of social control. Those boys who felt the psychological presence of their mothers when outside of the home were probably boys whose personalities were more likely to contain conventional values. However, the relationship found between replies to the two questions and self-reported delinquency was stronger than the relationship usually reported between personality variables and delinquency (Schuessler & Cressey, 1950).

Some youngsters do not have to account to their parents for their comings and goings. Their parents do not supervise their recreational activities, enforce a regular bedtime, or inquire about their homework (Nye, 1958:92–101). There is food in the refrigerator for them to take when they are hungry, but the family does not usually sit down to eat a meal together. They do not watch television with their parents, go to the weddings of relatives with them, or on family outings (Nye, 1958:102–9). They are not expected to do chores around the house on any regular basis, partly because their parents do not insist on such contributions. It is a life free of restraint, but it is also a life without guidance, as Durkheim would have put it (Parsons, 1968). This type of situation is often called "family disorganization" in the sociological literature, and studies have established a relationship between weak family controls and delinquency (Rodman & Grams, 1967:188–221). Studies have also shown that these weak family controls are more likely in low-income families and families of ethnic minorities than in middle-class families (Lewis, 1965). To sum up: it seems likely that over and above the indirect effect of the family on crime through generating variability in deviant personality tendencies, the family of orientation has a direct effect on delinquency by controlling some youngsters more effectively than others. Some families supervise their children more extensively than others. Additional evidence for this conclusion emerges from a study of the differential impact of family disorganization on preadolescents compared to adolescents and on girls compared with boys (Toby, 1957b). It was found that a broken home was more likely to operate as a delinquency-producing factor in the categories of youngsters where family control is normally strong, namely, preadolescents and girls. The smallest difference in delinquency rates was between adolescent boys from broken homes and adolescent boys from intact homes, presumably because parental supervision of adolescent boys is weak even in intact homes.

---

1. In emphasizing the behavioral rather than the motivational aspect of social control, I recognize that I am giving the opposite emphasis from that of Parsons (1951:297–321). For the purpose of understanding criminal motivation and behavior, which are my concerns in this chapter, a behavioral emphasis simplifies the discussion. For a broader analysis of deviance, which would include mental illness, preoccupation with behavioral control might not be tenable.

The Peer-Group Control System

The adolescent peer group has a bad press. The sociological literature tends to treat the family as a bulwark against delinquency and the peer group as antisocial (Thrasher, 1927). This ready equation of peer group with antisocial behavior is partly the result of a sampling bias: studies of peer groups tends to be made in slum communities rather than in stable middle-class neighborhoods. The best-known study of "street-corner society" was conducted during the latter part of the Great Depression in an Italian ghetto (Whyte, 1955). Employment opportunities for young men were scarce, and consequently adolescent irresponsibility was prolonged into the 20s. Even under these unusual conditions, deviant behavior was not the main concern of the peer group, as it seems to be in other studies (Shaw, 1931). Another sociological source of the bad reputation of the adolescent peer group is the inference from studies of high-school cultures that the peer group is anti-intellectual (Coleman, 1961).

Theoretical analysis suggests that the values of the peer group must be somewhat congruent with the values of the families and the neighborhoods in which the peer group is located. And, as a matter of fact, a large number of youngsters confirm this point by enrolling in peer-group organizations under adult sponsorship and influence: boys' clubs, settlement house youth groups, 4-H clubs, church youth groups, and the extracurricular clubs at high school and college. What is usually being referred to in discussions of "peer groups" is a special kind of peer group: groups that develop spontaneously in the neighborhood and that lack adult sponsorship or control. These autonomous groups come into being, exist for several years as vehicles for expressing the interests of particular cliques of adolescents, and then disintegrate. Since they are not usually age-graded and do not have a stable identity, their interests are somewhat unpredictable. They are more likely to tolerate stealing, drunkenness, or assaultive behavior than members of groups structurally attached to adults whose responsibilities in the larger society make them sympathetic interpreters of conventional values and conduct norms. Even autonomous power groups, however, vary in their stance toward deviance; only the most extreme street-corner groups require blatantly deviant behavior of members.

In the face of the bad reputation of the peer group, Hirschi's discovery (1969) of a negative relationship between peer-group attachment and delinquency was not only unexpected; it should have been startling. For Hirschi found that the closer the attachment to peers the less likely the boy was to be delinquent. This finding was replicated in his data several times with different indices. Boys who said they would like to be the kind of person that their best friends are "in most ways" were less likely to report delinquent acts than boys who responded "not at all" (1969:146). Boys who said they respected their best friends' opinions about the important things in life "completely" were less likely to report delinquent acts than those who responded "not at all" (p. 147). It might be inferred from these data that a nondelinquent peer group can bring social pressure to bear on members to prevent delinquent behavior. This is part of the story. A sizeable minority of boys in the sample reported that they would feel worse over the reaction of their friends than over the reaction of their parents if they should be caught stealing. Presumably these were nondelinquent friends. But the influence of nondelinquent friends is not the complete explanation. Hirschi examined the cases of boys who reported that one or more of their friends had been picked up by the police. Among these boys, all of whom had a somewhat delinquent peer group, those who said that they wanted to be like their best friends "in most ways" were *least* likely to report engaging in delinquent behavior (pp. 151–52). Hirschi's explanation for this apparent paradox was that solidarity with peers tended to produce, not imitation, but behavior that would result in approval. Except for the most extreme gang delinquents, peer groups held conventional standards and disapproved of delinquent behavior.

> Attachment to peers does not foster alienation from cónventional persons and institutions; it if anything fosters commitment to them. There is no foundation for the belief that the delinquent gang is an intensely solidary group comprising "the most fit and able youngsters in their community." On the contrary, those committing delinquent acts are not likely to think much of each other; distrust and suspicion, not intense solidarity, are the foundations of the delinquent gang (Hirschi, 1969:154).

The Hirschi study addressed a related question, one basic to an assessment of the role of the peer group in delinquency. Why *do* boys gravitate toward delinquent friends? Is it a matter of chance exposure to delinquent associations, as the theory of differential association (Sutherland & Cressey, 1970:71–93) seems to imply? Or are there characteristics possessed by youngsters that predispose them to delinquent associations so that, even within a high-delinquency neighborhood, some are vulnerable to influence from delinquents and others are not? Reckless and his colleagues, Dinitz and Scarpitti, have demonstrated that "good boys" exist in high-delinquency neighborhoods; they hypothesize that these boys are insulated from delinquent peers by self-concepts incompatible with delinquent behavior (Dinitz et al., 1962:515–17). They attribute the favorable concept of self to inner strength derived from socialization. Other sociologists have suggested that the inner strength comes, at least in part, from better prospects for educational and occupational success (Cohen, 1955; Cloward & Ohlin, 1960; Toby & Toby, 1961; Stinchcombe, 1964). These prospects give some adolescents a greater stake in conformity than others (Toby, 1957a:12–17). Hirschi asked several questions in his survey that enabled him to rate respondents in terms of their differential stake in conformity (1969:158). Hirschi was able to show that a low stake in conformity made the commission of delinquent acts more likely; a low stake in conformity was also associated with having delinquent friends. But the delinquency of companions and the stake in conformity were *independently* related to the commission of delinquent acts (1969:156); delinquency of companions was not solely an intervening variable linking the stake in conformity to delinquent behavior. From these data Hirschi inferred that stake in conformity is causally prior to delinquent associations. Or, to put it another way, boys with a low stake in conformity are more likely to be delinquent than boys with a higher stake in conformity. In addition, they are more likely to acquire delinquent friends who reinforce the tendency to delinquency derived from their initial low stake in conformity—"birds of a feather flock together" (Glueck & Glueck, 1950:164).

The Educational-Occupational Control System

In the previous section on the peer-group control system, the concept of differential stake in conformity was introduced to explain why some boys are more likely than others to gravitate toward delinquents. It was also pointed out in passing that low stake in conformity tends to produce delinquent behavior apart from its indirect effect through delinquent companions. School failure of one kind or another (retardation, low intelligence-test scores, low grades, truancy, early school leaving) has long been known to correlate with delinquency (Toby, 1957c). The question has been one of establishing the causal order (Hirschi & Selvin, 1967:52–72). Does a commitment to a delinquent life-style crowd out conventional academic interests? Or does academic incompetence, however it is caused, reduce the stake in conformity? Hirschi is able to demonstrate that the latter interpretation of the causal order is more plausible.

> The causal chain runs from academic incompetence to poor school performance to disliking of school to rejection of the school's authority to the commission of delinquent acts. All statistical relations relevant to this causal chain have been presented, and all are in fact consistent with it (1969:132).

The less a youngster cares about the rewards the school allocates or the goals it urges him to aspire to, the less capable it is of guiding his behavior. Attachment makes him accessible to control. Alienation frees him to do what he wishes, whether teachers approve or not.

Precisely the same argument applies to the occupational system. The higher are occupational aspirations, the lower is the delinquency rate—even if the youngster's *expectations* are less high than his *aspirations* (Hirschi, 1969:182–83). The perceived cost of delinquency is greater if the youngster feels that a high status may be in jeopardy. However, current success and bright future prospects tend to go together. We should not overestimate the controlling effect of the *distant* future; the controlling effect of *current* involvements are probably more significant for most youngsters (Hirschi, 1969:185–86). How does this line of reasoning fit the known facts about Negro-white differentials in criminality? Rather well. Black youngsters are less likely to achieve academic success in school than white youngsters and less likely to aspire to and expect high occupational status. Since a higher proportion of them have a low stake in conformity, the higher incidence of deviant behavior is easy to understand. Hirschi found that the higher rate of official delinquency among Negro boys (as compared with whites) could be largely accounted for in his data by lower average verbal aptitude scores of black youngsters (1969:79–80). The same reasoning interpreted the lower delinquency rate of second-generation Jewish boys as compared with second-generation Italian boys nearly a half century ago as a concomitant of better status prospects (Toby, 1958:542–50).

The Formal Control System

Because modern societies are so differentiated, the social control of deviant motivation takes place not in one integrated context but in many: in the family, the peer group, the educational system, the occupational system, and a variety of voluntary associations. One of the problems of social control in a complex society is this lack of integration. An individual can have a role in one group which attempts to control his behavior in one direction and a role in another group which attempts to control his behavior in an incompatible direction (Toby, 1952). Social control would thus be unpredictable in the individual case, depending on the groups in which he happened to have roles, unless politically organized society took ultimate responsibility for social control. That is exactly what happens. Official agencies of law enforcement provide a societal standard of legitimate control. Sociologists speak of some controls as "informal" to contrast them with "formal" controls, such as those exercised by the police, the courts, and the prisons. Punishment is usually discussed in the formal context (Toby, 1964; Andenaes, 1966; Zimring, 1971). The formal-informal distinction is an artificial one and confuses the discussion of social control. Rewards and punishments are central to social control and are administered in all groups that attempt to influence the behavior of members.

What then is the rationale of singling out bureaucratic and political contexts in discussions of punishment? One possible rationale is that relational rewards and punishments (approval and disapproval) are less important in these contexts, and power and force more important. Thus, the types of rewards and punishments utilized by different agencies of control may differ. It is possible that formal sanctions are less effective in influencing behavior than the more personal responses found in face-to-face groups. Nevertheless, the possibility of formal sanctions sometimes deters some persons from expressing deviant tendencies compatible with their personality structures. Thus, one study has shown that enforcement of fines for illegal parking decreased the amount of illegal parking (Chambliss, 1966). Another study showed that the 1967 highway safety act enacted in Great Britain dramatically reduced highway casualties from October to December, 1967, compared with the same period in 1966 (Andenaes, 1971:546–53). The act established a new offense, driving with a blood alcohol level of .08 percent, and the British government launched an extensive publicity campaign two weeks prior to the effective date of the new law (October 9, 1967) to make Britons aware that a drunken driver automatically loses his driver's license for one year and may also be fined and imprisoned for four months. Although the reduction in casualties did not continue as it began, the overall reduction in casualties for the first year was 10 percent (compared with the previous year). This represented 1,152 fewer fatalities, 11,177 fewer seriously injured, and 28,130 fewer slightly injured (Andenaes, 1971:550). In short, coercive control exerted by the state through the threat of negative sanctions is sometimes effective. One reason why its effectiveness is underestimated is that an increase in sanctions may be marginally effective or not effective at all if sanctions are already severe. Thus, the *increase* of the penalty for murder from life imprisonment to execution may not increase the deterrent effect. But the *reduction* of the penalty to a $5 fine might *increase* the murder rate considerably.

Relational rewards and punishments are probably less important in impersonal bureaucratic or political contexts than in informal groups. Approval and disapproval are major controls in the family and the peer group; coercive sanctions are largely symbolic of positive or negative attitudes in these contexts. Nonetheless, formal sanctions do not wholly lack a relational dimension. The threat of impersonal negative sanctions serves to expose the reputational vulnerability of the potential offender. His reputational rewards in the community—high status in the stratification system—are placed in jeopardy by arrests and convictions in much the same way that educational and occupational prospects are jeopardized by delinquency.

CONCLUSION

Figure 1 attempts to sum up the argument of this chapter. Socialization experiences structure motivation so that most personalities offer major impediments to most forms of deviant behavior. Given the sociocultural heterogeneity of modern societies and the resulting unlikelihood of uniform socialization, however, virtually every form of deviance is permitted by *some* personalities. This means that deviant *motivation* is endemic and that the elimination of such motivation is not a promising basis for limiting deviant *behavior*. Deviant behavior is more likely to be minimized by social control mechanisms: by placing people in interactive contexts where they become motivated *not* to express whatever personality tendencies toward deviance that they have. *Informal* social control may well be the most effective type of control, but the size and heterogeneity of urban industrial societies guarantee that some deviant behavior will occur

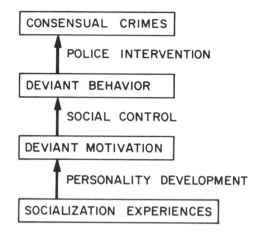

FIGURE 1. Explaining consensual crimes.

despite informal control. Some of this deviant behavior is defined by the collective leadership of the society as intolerable; laws are passed prohibiting it; and police and courts attempt to enforce such laws.

Deviant behavior that *formal* agencies of social control attempt to reduce is what this chapter calls consensual crimes. A high level of consensual criminality is probably inevitable in urban industrial societies under modern conditions of social organiza-tion—unless, of course, the society is so concerned with reducing criminality that it is willing to place its citizenry under totalitarian police supervision. Democratic countries recognize that such a price is too high. One implication of this recognition is an accept-ance of criminality as a cost of living in a free society. Another implication is that, short of adopting totalitarian controls, some types of effort to control deviance by invoking the criminal sanction will be ineffective, as, for example, with the illegal consumption offenses (Glaser, 1971:32). Furthermore, it is possible that, by taking vigorous punitive measures against a form of deviant behavior, a bad situation can be made even worse. This may have happened with programs to control drug addiction in the United States. Where does this leave us? It suggests that modern societies must learn to live with higher levels of criminality than they would prefer to have because the cost of reducing criminality appreciably is unacceptable.

REFERENCES

Andenaes, Johannes.
    1966   "The general preventive effects of punishment." University of Pennsylvania Law Review 114(May):949–983.
    1971   "Deterrence and specific offenses." University of Chicago Law Review 38 (Spring):537–553.
Bredemeier, Harry C., and Richard M. Stephenson.
    1962   The Analysis of Social Systems. New York: Holt, Rinehart & Winston.
Chambliss, William J.
    1966   "The deterrent influence of punishment." Crime and Delinquency 12(Janu-ary):70–75.

Christie, Nils, Johannes Andenaes, and Sigurd Skirbekk.
    1965   "A study of self-reported crime." Scandinavian Studies in Criminology
            1:86–116.
Cloward, Richard A., and Lloyd E. Ohlin.
    1960   Delinquency and Opportunity: A Theory of Delinquent Gangs. New York:
            Free Press of Glencoe.
Cohen, Albert K.
    1955   Delinquent Boys: The Culture of the Gang. Glencoe, Ill.: Free Press.
Coleman, James S.
    1961   The Adolescent Society. New York: Free Press of Glencoe.
Dinitz, Simon, Frank R. Scarpitti, and Walter C. Reckless.
    1962   "Delinquency vulnerability: a cross group and longitudinal analysis."
            American Sociological Review 27(August):515–517.
Glaser, Daniel.
    1971   "Criminology and public policy." American Sociologist 6(June):30–37.
Glueck, Eleanor, and Sheldon Glueck.
    1950   Unraveling Juvenile Delinquency. New York: Commonwealth Fund.
Hirschi, Travis.
    1969   Causes of Delinquency. Berkeley: University of California Press.
Hirschi, Travis, and Hanan C. Selvin.
    1967   Delinquency Research: An Appraisal of Analytic Methods. New York:
            Free Press.
Lewis, Hylan.
    1965   "Child rearing among low-income families." Pp. 342–353 in Louis A. Fer-
            man, Joyce L. Kornbluh, and Alan Haber (eds.), Poverty in America: A
            Book of Readings. Ann Arbor: University of Michigan Press.
Lemert, Edwin M.
    1951   Social Pathology. New York: McGraw-Hill.
Matza, David.
    1964   Delinquency and Drift. New York: Wiley.
Merton, Robert K.
    1938   "Social structure and anomie." American Sociological Review 3(October):
            672–682.
Miller, Walter B.
    1958   "Lower class culture as a generating milieu of gang delinquency." Journal
            of Social Issues 14:5–19.
Nye, F. Ivan.
    1958   Family Relationships and Delinquent Behavior. New York: Wiley.
Parsons, Talcott.
    1951   The Social System. Glencoe, Ill.: Free Press.
    1968   "Emile Durkheim." Pp. 311–320 in David L. Sills (ed.), International En-
            cyclopedia of the Social Sciences, vol. 4. New York: Macmillan.
Parsons, Talcott, and Robert F. Bales.
    1955   Family, Socialization and Interaction Process. Glencoe, Ill.: Free Press.
Quinney, Richard.
    1970   The Social Reality of Crime. Boston: Little, Brown.

Reiss, Albert J., Jr., and Albert L. Rhodes.
    1961   "The distribution of juvenile delinquency in the social class structure."
            American Sociological Review 26(October):720–732.

Rodman, Hyman, and Paul Grams.
    1967   "Juvenile delinquency and the family: a review and discussion." Pp. 188–
            221 in President's Commission on Law Enforcement and Administration
            of Justice, Task Force Report: Juvenile Delinquency and Youth Crime.
            Washington, D.C.: U.S. Government Printing Office.

Ross, H. Laurence.
    1960   "Traffic law violation: a folk crime." Social Problems 8(Winter):236–237.
    –61

Schuessler, Karl F., and Donald R. Cressey.
    1950   "Personality characteristics of criminals." American Journal of Sociology
            55(March):476–484.

Shannon, Lyle W.
    1963   "Types and patterns of delinquency referral in a middle-sized city." British
            Journal of Criminology 4(July):24–36.

Shaw, Clifford R.
    1931   Natural History of a Delinquent Career. Chicago: University of Chicago
            Press.

Shaw, Clifford R., and Henry D. McKay.
    1942   Juvenile Delinquency and Urban Areas. Chicago: University of Chicago
            Press.

Stinchcombe, Arthur L.
    1964   Rebellion in a High School. Chicago: Quadrangle Books.

Sutherland, Edwin H.
    1949   White Collar Crime. New York: Holt, Rinehart & Winston.

Sutherland, Edwin H., and Donald R. Cressey.
    1970   Criminology. Eighth Edition. Philadelphia: Lippincott.

Thrasher, Frederic M.
    1927   The Gang. Chicago: University of Chicago Press.

Toby, Jackson.
    1952   "Some variables in role conflict analysis." Social Forces 30(March):323–
            327.
    1957a   "Social disorganization and stake in conformity: complementary factors
            in the predatory behavior of young hoodlums." Journal of Criminal Law,
            Criminology and Police Science 48(May–June):12–17.
    1957b   "The differential impact of family disorganization." American Sociological
            Review 22(October):505–512.
    1957c   "Orientation to education as a factor in the school maladjustment of lower-
            class children." Social Forces 35(March):259–266.
    1958   "Hoodlum or businessman: an American dilemma." Pp. 542–550 in Mar-
            shall Sklare (ed.), The Jews: Social Patterns of an American Group. Glen-
            coe, Ill.: Free Press.
    1964   "Is punishment necessary?" Journal of Criminal Law, Criminology and
            Police Science 55(September):332–337.
    1967   "Affluence and adolescent crime." Pp. 132–144 in President's Commission
            on Law Enforcement and Administration of Justice, Task Force Report:

Juvenile Delinquency and Youth Crime. Washington, D.C.: U.S. Government Printing Office.

1971   Contemporary Society: An Introduction to Sociology. Second Edition. New York: Wiley.

Toby, Jackson, and Marcia L. Toby.
1961   Low School Status as a Predisposing Factor in Subcultural Delinquency. Cooperative research project of United States Office of Education and Rutgers University (mimeographed).

Whyte, William Foote.
1955   Street Corner Society: The Social Structure of an Italian Slum. Second Edition. Chicago: University of Chicago Press.

Zimring, Franklin E.
1971   Perspectives on Deterrence. Public Health Service Publication 2056. Washington, D.C.: U.S. Government Printing Office.

CHAPTER 4

Biological and Psychophysiological Factors in Criminality

Saleem A. Shah and Loren H. Roth

National Institute of Mental Health

Discussions of the relationship between biological factors and criminality have had a rather long but, perhaps, not too distinguished history. Criminology texts in the United States rather typically devote a chapter or section to such historical developments and generally focus on the poorly conceptualized and somewhat naive (by current scientific standards) notions of scholars such as Dugdale (1877), Lombroso (1911), Goddard (1913), and Hooton (1939). Such earlier and simplistic statements regarding the biological contributions to crime and delinquency have been criticized repeatedly, and very rightfully, and rejected by each generation of criminology texts (see, for example, Reckless, 1967; Johnson, 1968; Sutherland & Cressey, 1970).

Recent advances in the biological sciences have led to a veritable explosion of knowledge concerning the variety of biological factors influencing human behavior. Advances in experimental behavior genetics, human population genetics, the biochemistry of the nervous system, experimental and clinical endocrinology and neurophysiology, and many related developments now permit more sophisticated understanding of the complexities of nature-nurture interactions as they influence the growth, development, and functioning of the human organism (see, for example, Meade & Parkes, 1965; Clemente & Lindsley, 1967; Spuhler, 1967; Glass, 1968; Garattini & Sigg, 1969; McClearn, 1969; Handler, 1970; Walzer, 1970).

Despite the proliferation of relevant literature, it is quite evident that in recent decades the role of biological influences on behavior has been given relatively little attention in the sociological and criminological literature (Eckland, 1967; Means, 1967; Bressler, 1968). For example, the text by Sutherland and Cressey (1970) devotes less than one-half page of its more than 600 pages to the rather provocative subject of the relatively high proportion of electroencephalographic (EEG) abnormalities among certain subgroups in the offender population. By contrast, in their discussion of the subculture of violence, Wolfgang and Ferracuti (1967) provide a fairly thorough discussion of this subject along with various other biological factors. However, these authors assert that even when cases of conduct disorder are shown to have a high incidence of EEG abnormalities "the relationship *is never invariable or total*" (p. 198, emphasis added). Wolfgang and Ferracuti also conclude that, because "inner characteristics do not *by themselves* explain aggressive behavior" (emphasis added), one is led back to the external social environment to find the "causative key" to aggression (p. 143).

The implication is given by Wolfgang and Ferracuti that biological contributions are expected to provide "invariable or total" explanations "by themselves" in order for criminologists to give them serious consideration. The obvious fact is, however, that if we used similar criteria for accepting the importance of sociological and psychological factors, we would undoubtedly have to dismiss most of these variables since they also rarely—if ever—demonstrate *invariable* relationships with, nor do they provide *total explanations* for, complex phenomena, such as aggression and crime.

The above examples notwithstanding, it must be added that Wolfgang and Ferracuti, in their comprehensive review of the relevant literature pertaining to violence, do urge interdisciplinary and integrated approaches to the study of such phenomena. We point out the styles of expression used by these authors in reference to biological factors in order to suggest that an implicit "either/or" view—one which tends to pit biological variables *against* environmental variables—seems to be indicated even in the thinking of these very sophisticated criminologists.

Various other instances of somewhat dichotomized thinking about biological influences on behavior are readily found in the criminological literature. For example, Johnson (1968) discusses biological variables, along with psychological and psychiatric approaches, in Chapter 7 titled, "Earlier and Individualistic Theories." This sociologist states that "biological or genetic explanations assume that the criminal is structurally different than the noncriminal" (p. 159). While such assumptions were indeed made by some of the earlier students of criminal biology, this statement scarcely constitutes an accurate reflection of thinking during the past several decades. Johnson also suggests that the "individualistic" approaches are similar "in that all hold crime to be the result of some individual maladjustment and, consequently, inevitable" (p. 159). We characterize this statement as also being inaccurate and as reflecting a rather dated and poor understanding of the complexities involved in the continuous interactions between organismic and environmental variables influencing behavior.

There is an understandable tendency on the part of scientists and scholars to view, conceptualize, study, and attempt to understand various phenomena from the perspective of their own discipline. Thus, in studying deviant behavior, social and behavioral scientists typically tend to emphasize social, psychological, and environmental variables to the relative neglect of biological factors. Similarly, we shall point out instances in which biological scientists have tended to make claims and assertions that cannot be supported by available evidence. In a sense, then, this chapter is an attempt to correct what we perceive as an imbalance in the field of criminology.

We wish to emphasize that no direct or one-to-one causal relationship between biological variables and law-violating behavior is being postulated here. Neither do we wish to assert, nor even to imply, that biological variables by themselves provide a very complete explanation for the complexities of human behavior. We do assert, however, that an understanding of biological determinants is essential in order to obtain a more complete and better understanding of behavior so as to develop more adequate theories and explanations of human behavior—regardless of whether the behavior is defined as antisocial and criminal, or as prosocial.

A PERSPECTIVE ON THE NATURE-NURTURE CONTROVERSY

Despite rather impressive developments in recent years in the field of behavior genetics, there is a reluctance in the social and behavioral sciences to accept the influence of genetic variables on behavior. It would appear that, in addition to muted continuations of the nature-nurture controversy and various theoretical and disciplinary biases, there may well be also some ideological factors underlying this situation. For example, Pastore (1949) found that sociopolitical preferences among a group of twenty-four psychologists, sociologists, and biologists tended to distinguish "environmentalists" from "hereditarians." Among the twelve persons classified as "liberals or radicals," eleven were "environmentalists," while among the twelve "conservatives," eleven were "hereditarians." It is somewhat disconcerting that the scientific study of important issues can be distorted in many instances by one's ideological preferences and biases.

It would be fair to say that, by and large, some modified version of John Locke's (1959) *tabula rasa* notion is entertained by most social and behavioral scientists. It should be pointed out, however, that Locke did *not* claim that all people are born alike at birth. Rather, he maintained that there are no inborn ideas and that experience is of paramount importance in affecting mental development. In psychology, one of the strongest environmentalist orientations was provided by John B. Watson (1924) and his espousal of what is sometimes referred to as "radical behaviorism."

Sociology also has demonstrated considerable reluctance to accept genetic contributions to the understanding of human behavior. Indeed, the resistance in sociology seems much greater than that in psychology. Means (1967) has discussed the neglect of biological influences in sociology and notes that the rule in sociology seems to have been to attack biological determinism and thus "liberate" sociology from any dependence on biological factors. This trend might in some ways relate to Durkheim's (1895) principle that the determining causes of "social facts" should be sought among preceding social facts and not in the states of the individual. Eckland (1967) notes that there appears to have been a vested interest in sociology for establishing a strong environmentalist approach to the study of human behavior. He goes on to suggest that the sociological reaction against biological contributions appears to have been determined by exaggerated and even misguided *biologism* and its manifestations in Social Darwinism. Similarly, Bressler (1968) suggests that sociological aversion to social biology is based on more than a simple rejection of faulty evidence. Rather, such aversion seems supported by a lingering suspicion that biological explanations of social behavior may end with predatory ethics, such as demonstrated by the early eugenicists, Social Darwinism, and the Third Reich. Moreover, in further reference to such ideological antipathy, social biology may also be viewed by social scientists as offering a presumptive threat to the empirical foundations of welfare liberalism.

It is unfortunate that residual features of the old nature-nurture controversy impede the free exchange of ideas and concepts among various disciplines. McClearn (1969) notes that among social scientists there often appears to be an implicit, if not even explicit, feeling that any points conceded to biological factors reduce in some way the importance of environmental factors. This dichotomous and zero-sum approach to behavorial determination is as unwarranted as it is widespread. The facts of the matter are that the variables and processes constituting the domain of the biological scientist are in *continuous interaction* with those of the social and behavioral scientists. Shah (1972) has noted some of the reasons why biological and genetic factors in human behavior are not readily accepted by many social and behavioral scientists.

DEFINITION OF SOME KEY TERMS AND CONCEPTS

When we use the term *criminality* in this chapter, we are referring to a range of socially deviant behaviors, which officially have been defined as and which could be labeled and handled as crimes. The official labeling of behavior as *criminal* relates not only to the deviant act by an individual, but also to the societal response processes whereby the act is officially defined and labeled (Shah, 1969). Our concern here is with those socially deviant and antisocial acts which violate legal norms, even though the bulk of such behavior does not come to official attention and thus may not be officially labeled (see, e.g., Williams & Gold, 1972).

More specifically, we shall be concerned in this chapter with the relationship of a variety of organism-related variables that are of importance in understanding certain forms of poorly regulated behaviors; these behaviors violate social and legal norms and have a high probability of being officially labeled as "delinquent" or "criminal." It is our contention that biological variables do indeed influence behavior in varying degrees. Thus, it is neither surprising nor shocking to point out that such variables also play a role in determining certain classes of behavior that have a high probability of being labeled as "criminal." While social and environmental influences would generally account for a large proportion of the variance, biological factors also need to be considered.

By *biological* we refer to a broad range of processes and conditions that typically are considered as *belonging to* or as *characteristic of* the organism, rather than its *present* environment. There are a number of terms, which tend to get lumped together in common discourse as referring to biological or "non-environmental" influences; these terms need to be distinguished.

The predictable parental contributions are referred to as *hereditary*. As indicated in Figure 1, all that is *innate*, i.e., in the genes, need not be inherited, because there are possible mutations between parent and child. Thus, a person's *genotype* (the genetic contribution of an organism) includes both hereditary and innate contributions. What is *congenital*, i.e., present at birth, need not be innate, since post-genetic effects may occur while the organism is developing in the womb. And, when reference is made to the *constitution*, it is generally understood to refer to the relatively constant physiological composition and biological makeup of the organism. The constitution may, however, undergo changes in the process of development or as a function of accident, for example, brain injury or disease (Cattell, 1966).

By *psychophysiological* we mean certain quantifiable indices of nervous system functioning (generally, the autonomic nervous system) which have traditionally been related, at least partially, to emotional response factors (Cannon, 1929). Factors such as galvanic skin response, heart rate, other measures of attention and arousal, and biochemical responses (e.g., the effects of epinephrine and norepinephrine) are included. These factors are also biological variables but differ generally from some of those mentioned previously in that the psychophysiological variables have been susceptible to experimental manipulation in human populations. Observations about genotype and phenotype in humans depend more on natural observations and inferences.

By and large, scientists no longer talk in terms of heredity *or* environment, nor do they think of organism-related variables as *opposed to*, or *versus*, environmental influences. However, as we have noted earlier, discipline-oriented education, narrow specialization, and conceptual and ideological preferences do enable scientists to greatly emphasize or to underplay—sometimes even to completely ignore—the influence of particular sets of variables affecting human behavior.

Modern geneticists have pointed out that a nature-nurture dichotomy is clearly untenable, incorrect, and meaningless. The subject has to be discussed in terms of the continuous and complex interactions between an organism and its environment, and the relative contributions of both sets of variables in determining the behavior of the

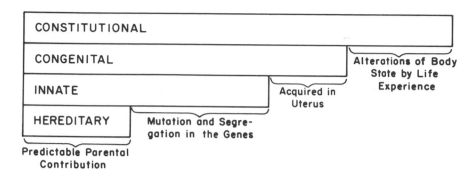

FIGURE 1. Definitions of contributions to personality commonly considered "non-environmental." After Cattell, 1966:34.

organism. *Genotype* refers to the totality of factors that make up the genetic complement of an organism. *Phenotype* refers to the totality of that which can be observed or inferred, physically or chemically, about the organism. It is axiomatic that the phenotype cannot be inherited. Rather, it develops as a function of interactions between the genotype and the environment. Environmental influences must be considered in the broadest sense to include all events following conception that produce changes in the organism. All traits, characteristics, and phenotypic features are determined, therefore, by the genotype and the sequence of environments with which the genotype interacts. As Dobzhansky (1962) has expressed it, "There is no organism without a genotype and no genotype can exist outside a spatio-temporal continuum, an environment" (p. 42).

It is important to emphasize that what is inherited is not a particular trait or characteristic, but the way in which the development of the organism responds to its environment. Since there are an infinite number of environments, a single genotype might be associated with an infinite number of phenotypes. Stated differently, the genotype determines the reactions and the responses of the developing, or aging, organism to the environment. The genotype, in essence, determines the norm of reaction or, as Gottesman (1966) has described it, a *reaction range*. In order to conceptualize the contributions of heredity to a trait such as intelligence, for example, we may think of heredity as fixing a *reaction range*. Within this framework, a genotype may be viewed as determining an indefinite, but nevertheless circumscribed, assortment or range of phenotypes. Each phenotype would be expected to correspond to one of the possible environmental regimes to which the genotype could be exposed (Gottesman, 1966).

With few possible exceptions, there do not appear to be any genes for behavior. Rather, most genes (or more accurately, combinations of multiple genes) contribute to determining the range of potential for a particular trait in a given individual, while the past and present environments determine the actual state of that individual within that range (Fuller & Thompson, 1960; Davis, 1970). At a molecular level the explanation for this is now clearer. Gene structure determines protein structure, but the regulatory mechanisms for gene action respond to stimuli from the environment, thus determining the amount of protein actually made (Davis, 1970). Moreover, genes operate at the molecular level of organization, and the pathway from gene to behavior is mediated through the successively complex intermediaries of enzymes, hormones, and neurons (Fuller & Thompson, 1960).

To further emphasize the importance of nature-nurture interactions in the determination of traits and characteristics of an organism, some examples may be cited.

1. It has been demonstrated that aggressive behavior can be evoked in free-ranging monkeys by stimulation of implanted intracerebral electrodes. However, such stimulation produces differing results depending upon the hierarchical structure of the monkey colony. Monkeys exhibit aggressive behavior with this stimulation when a submissive monkey is present as a target, but such responses are inhibited (despite the brain stimulation) in the presence of a dominant animal (Delgado, 1969).

2. In humans, low birth weight and subsequent lowered intelligence tend to show an association. However, the research by Drillien (1970) indicates that low birth weight and lowered I.Q. tend to be linked only in the case of environmentally disadvantaged groups. Children growing up in more favorable circumstances seem able to make up for a poor start in life.

3. Among children with centrencephalic epilepsy (a specific type of abnormality noted on the EEG), 37 percent of their siblings had a similar abnormality but only 13 percent have a history of convulsions. The potentiality for a seizure disorder (inherited in this case) does not mean that the individual will inevitably or necessarily have one; some other factors are also needed to produce a "clinical case" (Metrakos & Metrakos, 1961).

Further, a number of studies suggest that temperamental traits, such as extraversion and introversion (Eysenck, 1964), dominance, assertion, activity, and neuroticism (Vandenberg, 1960), depression and psychopathic deviation (Gottesman, 1963), and certain cognitive styles (Witkin et al., 1954; Witkin et al., 1962) demonstrate a heritable component.

The above examples and related studies provide ample evidence that the human infant is not merely a passive recipient of environmental stimuli and provisions. Rather, the infant organizes experiences in ways that are peculiar to it as a function of the continuous interactions between nature and nurture. Such studies also point to the importance of early experiences in shaping later responses. Early experiences are not only integrated along a psychological dimension, but are also incorporated in developing neural structures (see, for example, Conner & Levine, 1969; Schulte, 1971).

A CONCEPTUAL FRAMEWORK FOR VIEWING ORGANISM-ENVIRONMENT INTERACTIONS IN REFERENCE TO CRIMINAL BEHAVIOR

It should be quite evident by now that we are not talking about an either/or nor about an all-or-none type of biological influence upon human behavior. We begin with the conceptualization that behavior has to be understood as involving interactions between an organism and a particular environment. When we refer to organismic variables, we include here psychological, physiological, biochemical, genetic, and the related biological factors that endow the organism with certain response capabilities and predispositions, and a central nervous system apparatus with a potential for vastly differentiated responses to environmental inputs. Our concern in this chapter will be with the organism-related variables defined earlier as relating to the biological and psychophysiological factors, rather than the psychological.

Within the conceptual framework outlined above we cannot, of course, separate or parcel out the biological from the various social and environmental factors. Indeed, such dichotomous thinking, whether it be "tilted" towards social and environmental or toward biological variables, makes little conceptual, logical, or practical sense. Rather, tendencies toward the dichotomous modes of thinking would serve simply to limit, obstruct, and hinder a broad, multidisciplinary approach to understanding human behavior in its natural complexities.

We wish also to make very explicit that there is no particular category of criminal behavior, not even in the case of episodic violence, which is specially determined by biological factors. We do not assert any direct or one-to-one causal relationship between biological factors and criminal acts. We view organism-related and environmental variables as jointly determining behavior.

We shall also report on observations that have been made in selected populations where it is difficult to ascertain whether the variables of interest pertain to the labeling process itself, the behavior that has been labeled, or the likelihood of a certain administrative disposition, such as probation or parole, or release or retention in prison. If, for example, we were to find an increased frequency of persons with epilepsy in penal institutions (an example of *point prevalence data*), it may mean that such persons are at high risk for engaging in acts defined as crimes, that they are more often caught or incarcerated for the crimes they do commit, or that they are less likely to be paroled. On the other hand, such data may imply, at a minimum, that individuals with epilepsy (and especially those from the lower social class) are at an adaptive disadvantage in society *as it is presently constituted;* that is, they may have a higher risk for being officially labeled and handled as criminals than are law-violators without epilepsy.

SOME HISTORICAL BACKGROUND

Concern with the individual causes of criminal behavior, whether related to biological or psychological factors, has a long history. Since this history is typically summarized in criminological texts and related publications (see, for example, Radzinowicz, 1966), we shall provide here only a brief and selective summary of some of the earlier concerns with biological and constitutional factors in criminality.

While Cesare Lombroso could be considered as the first person to undertake a systematic effort to study biological factors in criminal behavior, several previous approaches to such lines of inquiry must also be noted. There were, for example, the physiognomists, such as J. K. Lavater; the phrenologists like Franz Joseph Gall and Johann K. Spurzheim, who attempted a type of craniology with their study of certain bumps on the head that were believed to reflect the structure of underlying brain lobes. Related to these efforts were the notions of "degeneracy" propounded by Morel, and the work of early alienists, such as J. C. Pritchard and H. Maudsley, who were concerned with moral insanity (Radzinowicz, 1966).

In the United States, Dugdale (1877) did a detailed genealogical study of the Jukes family covering some 1,200 persons and spanning almost an entire century. An extensive history of "pauperism, prostitution, exhaustion, disease, fornication and illegitimacy" was documented. Although this study is often cited as having suggested evidence for the hereditary nature of crime, a close reading of the original text is rather illuminating. Only 76 of the 709 individuals traced had evidence of criminal histories, and Dugdale directly states that "environment is the ultimate controlling factor in determining careers" (p. 66).

In 1876, Lombroso's first edition of *L'uomo Delinquente* was published. It contained his original doctrine of evolutionary atavism; that is, the characteristics of primitive men and of inferior animals periodically reappeared in certain individuals. Lombroso had noticed certain atavistic features in the skull of a famous brigand and connected these characteristics with criminal types. He pointed out several "stigmata of degeneration," such as certain characteristics of the head and skull, lobeless ears, large and protruding jaws, low foreheads, small or receding chins, and facial asymmetries. Eventually, this early criminal anthropologist studied several thousand criminals and modified his theories, although notions of stigmata and biologic inferiority were retained (Lombroso, 1911).

The claims by Lombroso were not based on studies of control populations against which the "stigmata of degeneration" could be compared. These claims lost much of their appeal when Enrico Ferri (one of Lombroso's students) found that 63 percent of Italian soldiers also showed some of the stigmata of degeneration (Montagu, 1941). Similarly, using careful anthropometric measurements, Goring (1913:369) examined more than 3,000 English criminals, along with students and sailors serving as controls, and concluded that the results simply did not confirm Lombroso's assertions pertaining to criminal anthropology.

Another well-known genealogical study relevant to our concerns was conducted in the United States by Goddard (1913), the research director of a training school in New Jersey for "feebleminded" boys and girls. Investigating the family history of one of his wards, Deborah Kallikak, Goddard discovered that she was the offspring of a brief union between a Revolutionary War soldier and a feebleminded girl. Eventually a pedigree of 484 descendants of this union, of whom 143 were feebleminded and several were illegitimate, alcoholic, and prostitutes, was developed. The same soldier later married a Quaker girl and fathered a long line of upstanding citizens. These findings impressed Goddard very much and he concluded that "bad stock" was the cause of feeblemindedness and that such persons should not be permitted to reproduce. As a result of related intelligence testing of delinquent children, of whom a sizeable proportion were found to be feebleminded, Goddard was led to attach an association between feeblemindedness and crime and delinquency. Interestingly, a surprising fact omitted in most discussions of this study was the finding that *only three* of the Kallikak family (a total of 484) were "criminals" (Goddard, 1913).

One of the most extreme statements of the hereditarian position was provided by Hooton (1939), who published comparative anthropological studies of several thousands of prisoners, along with some nonoffenders and insane persons serving as controls. One hundred and seven measurements were made and various statistical comparisons analyzed. The findings led Hooton to conclude that external appearance and behavior were "bound together in an indissoluble organic association" and that the primary cause of crime was biological inferiority (p. 6). Hooton's methods, selection of controls, and his conclusions have been severely criticized (see, e.g., Montagu, 1941; Vold, 1958).

The work of two other groups needs to be mentioned. Sheldon et al. (1940) and Sheldon and Stevens (1942), extending the observations of Kretschmer, differentiated three human somatotypes (body types): *endomorphic* (soft, round, and fat); *mesomorphic* (bony, muscular, and athletic); and *ectomorphic* (tall, thin, and fragile). Sheldon was of the opinion that these somatotypes had temperamental correlates. He also explored this relationship in a study of 200 delinquent youth and found them to be predominantly mesomorphic (Sheldon, 1949). This work has been paralleled by the investigations of Eleanor and Sheldon Glueck (1956), who reported that 60.1 percent of 500 delinquent youth were mesomorphic as compared with only 30.7 percent mesomorphs in a nondelinquent control group matched for age, sex, and socioeconomic class. The temperamental correlations with mesomorphy noted by these investigators pertain to such characteristics as social assertiveness, less-inhibited motor responses, and less submissiveness to authority. The Gluecks attempted a greater differentiation in their study as compared with the work of Sheldon. The Gluecks found, for example, that delinquency was more likely in mesomorphs who also manifested other temperamental traits atypical of the usual mesomorphic constellation (1956). These studies have been subjected to criticism on a number of methodological and conceptual grounds (see, for example, Sutherland & Cressey, 1970).

Several more recent studies tend to give some substance to the observations of Sheldon and the Gluecks and there are continuing reports on the relationship of physical constitution and temperament (see, for example, Gibbens, 1963; Eysenck, 1964; Cortes and Gatti, 1972). A report by Sheard (1971) reveals interesting differential effects of psychoactive drugs according to body type. For example, mesomorphic aggressive prisoners have been found to show a better treatment response to lithium carbonate than do ectomorphs.

The meaning of these somatotype observations is, of course, still far from clear. It would be fair to say that the meaning and relationship of somatotype to classes of behavior likely to be defined as delinquent and criminal are still somewhat open issues.

From a historical perspective it should also be noted that each biologic theory shows some congruence with the predispositions and technologies of its era. Contemporaries of Dugdale and Lombroso, for example, were committed to the view that dementia praecox (schizophrenia) would reveal an underlying neuropathology (Kolb, 1968). Also, brain localization in the investigation of disorders of speech and understanding had received impetus from the work of Broca, Wernicke, and Liepmann (Geschwind, 1965). Within such a milieu it appears understandable why similar works in the field of criminology, at face value, seemed reasonable. Second, until recently, biological contributions to criminology in many instances have tended to be intertwined with various eugenic concerns. The data presented in some of the reports also appear to have provided the authors an opportunity to express opinions about the necessity for and the means by which the race might be bettered. Such improvement was, of course, also in harmony with the views of the Social Darwinists (Hofstadter, 1955). Third, most of these studies quite appropriately have been criticized for the absence of or the inadequate nature of their control groups, and the logic of their conclusions.

THE RANGE OF BIOLOGICAL CONTRIBUTIONS TO CRIMINAL BEHAVIOR

Prior to discussing specific biological variables having direct and more indirect relevance to criminality, there are some general issues which need to be given attention.

Generalizability of Findings from Animal Research

References have already been made to research on subhuman animal species to illustrate certain basic points and principles. There are, of course, rather obvious reasons why most of the experimental work on the neurological substrates of behavior has used subhuman species. Such research simply could not be done on human subjects. However, as a result of clinical work with humans suffering from brain tumors, head injuries, and the like, many aspects of the knowledge derived from animal research have been compared with the functioning of the human brain.

McClearn (1969) warns that it is possible to make two kinds of mistakes in interpreting animal research. One mistake would be to accept uncritically evidence from one species as descriptive of some process or function in another species. Indeed, there is considerable research evidence showing species-specific differences; for example, with respect to aggressive behavior between one particular breed of mice and another, and between mice and rats (see, e.g., Denenberg et al., 1968; Denenberg & Zarrow, 1970). The second mistake that can be made is to deny that *any* generalizability can be sought reasonably. Both kinds of mistakes are made and often can be attributed to biological naivete. The first mistake follows from a failure to appreciate the *variations* described; the second mistake arises from a failure to appreciate the *theme.*

The weight of the available evidence on the neurophysiological bases for aggressive behavior seems to indicate that man, for all his encephalization (i.e., the increased role of the cerebral cortex in exerting a regulative function on bodily processes and emotion), has not escaped from the biological determinants of aggressive behavior. Man, too, has brain circuits that, when activated, result in an increased tendency toward destructive behavior (Moyer, 1969). Thus, even though there is a wider range of modulation and differentiation of behavior in man, as well as numerous complexities in the triggering and controlling of such biological capacities, these basic capabilities are present, nevertheless.

In summary, the general attitude taken toward data obtained from subhuman animals is to regard it as suggestive. One should be neither too eager to apply the data unaltered to man nor to deny any relevance of the data to human processes. In many cases the accumulation of data from a variety of sources will provide a general scheme in which human processes become understandable. In other cases, after research efforts have clarified processes at one phyletic level, hypotheses will be suggested that can be tested directly on man.

Biological Variables of Interest

Our concern here is with a wide range of possible biologic contributions to classes of behavior reflecting poor modulation and control; these behaviors have a high probability of violating criminal laws. We do not assert the view that biological variables are involved in some "either/or" (present or absent) fashion. Nor do we view biological variables as having any total or invariable determining influences on the behaviors of concern to us in this chapter.

There are undoubtedly a few cases where it could be argued that the biological variables involved appeared to have been both necessary and sufficient to produce types of behavior which violated criminal laws. For example, there have been a number of reports of personality changes and manifestations of psychiatric disorders and aggressive behaviors in persons with central nervous system tumors and other brain pathology (e.g., Zeman & King, 1958; Fenton & Udwin, 1965; Malamud, 1967). Similarly, there have been a number of reports of various forms of sexual deviation (e.g., exhibitionism, fetishism, and transvestism) associated with brain dysfunctioning (Hunter et al., 1963; Walinder, 1965; Kolarsky et al., 1967; Epstein, 1969; Blumer, 1970). However, in most instances we could only begin to question the relative contribution of biological factors in their interactions with the psychological, social, and situational determinants of the particular behavior.

Biological variables *more directly related* to criminal behavior include:
1. Tumors and atrophic or other destructive or inflammatory processes of the limbic system, which result in marked behavioral abnormality.
2. The continuum of cases beginning with frank and clinically apparent epileptic seizures, and extending from these *ictal* events (i.e., behaviors occurring during

a seizure) to post-ictal confusion or automatisms, inter-ictal (between seizures) outbursts or episodic behaviors, electroencephalogram abnormalities themselves (with or without a history of seizure disorders), the controversial subject of certain peculiarities exhibited by temporal lobe epileptics, and episodic behavior disorders with no other evidence of seizures.

3. Endocrine abnormalities, especially those where levels of testosterone (the "male" hormone) or progesterone and estrogen ("female" hormones) appear to be correlated with behavior, and hypoglycemic disorders.

Our discussion of biological variables *more indirectly related* to criminal behavior will cover:

1. Perinatal birth complications shown to have a strong socioeconomic class correlation, a correlation which seems to parallel that of the distribution of officially labeled criminality and delinquency.
2. Minimal brain dysfunction in children and adolescents, especially as this relates to EEG and other neurological abnormalities, hyperkinesis, reading disorders, and related behavioral characteristics that tend to increase the probability of future identification of such individuals as delinquent.
3. Genetic research pertaining to possible heritable components in personality and psychopathic disorders.
4. The possible relationship between certain chromosomal abnormalities (47,XYY and 47,XXY, or Klinefelter's syndrome) and antisocial, aggressive, or other behaviors likely to be labeled criminal.
5. More recent studies on the association between physique, temperament, and behavior.
6. Various psychophysiological variables related to conditioning and with psychopathic disorders.

NEUROANATOMY AND PHYSIOLOGY OF THE LIMBIC SYSTEM

Certain portions of the central nervous system, especially the limbic areas of the brain, have considerable importance in the regulation and control of emotional, aggressive, sexual, and other behaviors. We would like to describe briefly the neuroanatomy, role, and functions of these structures.[1]

A portion of the brain, present in all species of mammals, and upon the functional integrity of which vegetative behaviors (as well as the elaboration of certain "affects," e.g., rage and fear) depend, has been delimited during the past forty years by the experimental work and writings of Bard (1928), Cannon (1929), Papez (1937), MacLean (1949, 1952), Wasman and Flynn (1962) and many others. MacLean (1952) has designated this collection of structures as the "limbic system." Alternative names for the limbic system are "visceral" or "emotional brain."

Limbic areas of the brain are shown in the shaded section of Figure 2, which indicates the position of these structures in the medial surface of the brain hemispheres and their extension into the midline brain structures. The limbic system includes portions of the thalamus and hypothalamus, upper parts of the brain stem, and the other structures lying in a C-shaped arrangement outlining or bordering (the Latin word *limbus* means *border*) the inner surfaces of the cerebral hemispheres: the cingulum,

---

1. Readers interested in further information should see, for a general review: MacLean, 1968; Boelkins and Heiser, 1970; Mark and Ervin, 1970; for a review of neuroanatomical and behavioral correlates: Kaada, 1967; Moyer, 1968; Pribram, 1969; Black, 1970; Smythies, 1970.

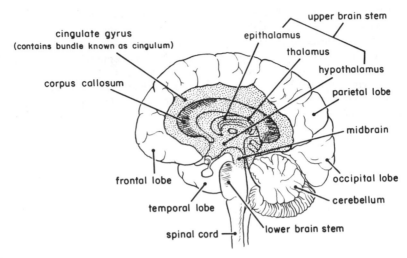

FIGURE 2. Limbic areas of the brain. From Mark and Ervin, 1970:20.

hippocampus, and hippocampal gyrus. Also included are nuclear masses within the temporal lobe (the amygdala), portions of the frontal lobes (septal nucleii, medial and orbital cortex), as well as other portions of the temporal cortex.

Figure 3 provides a schematic representation of the major anatomical features, nodal points, and some of the connecting pathways involving the limbic system. It forms a loop, the so-called Papez circuit. The non-olfactory pathways are virtually non-existent in reptiles, become progressively larger in the evolution of the primates, and reach their culmination in man (MacLean, 1970). The manner in which these structures have become functionally associated is beyond the scope of this discussion. Our purpose here is simply to describe the more important features of the limbic system to make our subsequent discussion more meaningful.

In humans there has been a tremendous elaboration of the cortical mantle surrounding the limbic structures, a fact which undoubtedly accounts for much of man's uniqueness in contrast to the lower animals. Geschwind (1968) points out that learning in subhuman primates is much more dependent on limbic associations than it is for humans. For example, human beings are uniquely able to associate words with visual or tactile impressions and to use and understand symbols. Nevertheless, based particularly on studies of the effects of various diseases affecting the limbic structures, it is apparent that man has not lost his dependence on the limbic system for the expression of emotional behavior (Aird, 1968; Epstein, 1969; Sweet et al., 1969; Blumer, 1970; Currier et al., 1971).

Some major points to be remembered about the limbic system are:

1. Under normal conditions limbic activity is well integrated with inhibitory portions of the brain, i.e., with the inhibitory cortex (Kaada, 1967; Lindsley, 1967). Among the limbic structures certain portions are inhibitory (i.e., the medial septum), while others appear to contain both excitatory and inhibitory structures in close proximity. For example, both the amygdala and hippocampus contain different areas that can inhibit or promote aggression in experimental animals (Egger & Flynn, 1963; Siegel & Flynn, 1968). Stimulation of the amygdala in humans can lead to fear (the most frequently aroused affect), rage, or even direct attack (Stevens et al., 1969; Mark & Ervin, 1970).

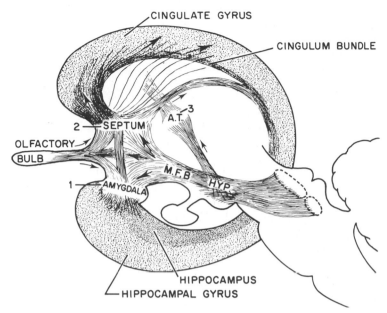

FIGURE 3. A schematic representation of the major anatomical features of the limbic system. From MacLean, 1958:615.

2. The connections of these portions of the brain with each other are extensive and at least two (Livingston, 1969) or three (MacLean, 1968) functionally affiliated major pathways or subdivisions have been identified thus far.

3. Major pathways, with their cortical inputs, connect with the hypothalamus and the brain stem. They probably affect both autonomic and endocrine outflow tracts and mediate the expression of a broad range of emotional and vegetative behavior, for example, pleasurable activities, fear, anger, sexual gratification, and eating. Moreover, the limbic system makes intimate connections with portions of the brain stem (the reticular activating system). This area is now known to be essential for the arousal and alerting functions of the entire organism (Lindsley, 1970).

4. Although certain portions of the hypothalamic nucleii have rather extensive connections with other parts of the brain, there is no area of the limbic system that functions autonomously or directs all of the other brain areas.

5. The meeting of the various connecting pathways within the hypothalamus is also of interest because it is this area of the brain, rather than the pituitary, which is functionally the true "master gland" of the endocrine system (Krieger, 1971). Pituitary outflow is under the direct control of the hypothalamus through various feedback loops with peripheral hormone systems. Moreover, certain activities of the limbic system are either synergistic with or require the presence of circulating hormones in order to function normally. For example, the frequency of fighting in castrated male animals in standardized situations is subnormal but it returns to normal when androgens are given to the animals (Conner & Levine, 1969). Extensive data also link levels of neurohumors in the brain (norepinephrine and its metabolites) to aggression (e.g., Rothballer, 1967; Reiss, 1972).

6. These considerations and much experimental data have led to various theories of limbic system functioning and the relationships among these structures. Smythies

(1970) states that the entire limbic system may function to select the appropriate behavior to any given set of stimuli, for example, various environmental inputs. There is no simple one-to-one correspondence between structure and functions. What is elicited from the limbic system changes with behavioral settings; similarly, different symptom constellations are seen more often at one age than at another (Serafetinides, 1970).

The information about the limbic system summarized thus far, albeit in rather simplified form, is relatively noncontroversial. Since human beings have built-in mechanisms for efficiently integrating and directing the expression of aggressive behavior, difficulties arise if one argues that such mechanisms ought to be viewed as instinct. Lorenz (1967) argued that man has within him an "aggressive drive" which must be expressed periodically or sublimated. There are many problems with such a view. The experimental data clearly show the importance of the environment and experience in affecting the nature of the responses; also, alternative views are plausible and have been stated rather elegantly by Montagu (1968) and Scott (1970).

Furthermore, Moyer (1968) has summarized the physiological evidence pointing to the fact that aggression is *not* a unitary concept. Rather, there are different kinds of aggression just as there are different kinds of consummatory behaviors. Thus, any attempt to find a single physiological basis for aggression might well lead to confusing and contradictory results. A given type of experimental manipulation may well facilitate one kind of aggression, suppress another, and have no effect whatsoever on a third. Moyer (1968) has proposed eight kinds of aggression based primarily on the stimulus situations which elicit them: *Predatory aggression, inter-male aggression, fear-induced aggression, irritable aggression, territorial defense, maternal aggression, instrumental aggression,* and *sex-related aggression.* (This classification is derived from and pertains to a variety of subhuman animal species.)

In order to better understand the importance of the limbic system in aggressive and sexual responses in humans, it is useful to consider the behavioral effects of disease and injury to the central nervous system. It is important to note that limbic structures and certain portions of the cerebral cortex have a high sensitivity to anoxia, hypoglycemia, and other physiological insults (Glaser, 1967). The encephalitic disorders frequently have a limbic localization; similarly, the antecedents of temporal lobe epilepsy rather frequently are believed to involve brain damage at birth (in some instances due to anoxia) (Aird et al., 1967).

Malfunction of the nervous system is generally expressed in two ways: *negative* symptoms (or hypofunctions) and *positive* symptoms (or release of functions). These two general effects interact so the damaged nervous system usually exhibits delay or slowness of functions, as well as irritability or fluctuations in functions. In other words, a loss of modulation of function occurs and the normal balance between facilitation and inhibition is disturbed (Holmes, 1960; Belmont & Handler, 1971). It is not surprising, therefore, that there are some rather convincing cases in humans where tumors or atrophic or other irritable lesions in portions of the limbic system have evidently led to assaults, murder, and other types of abnormal and explosive behaviors resulting from "misfires" in the system (see, e.g., Davis, 1959; Podolsky, 1962; Malamud, 1967; Freemon & Nevis, 1969; Sweet et al., 1969).

Evidence for the importance of limbic structures in modulating and influencing emotional and aggressive behaviors is also provided by the results of selected neurosurgical procedures performed over the last ten years (see, e.g., Narabayashi et al., 1963; Heimburger et al., 1966; Sano, 1966; Mark & Ervin, 1970; Sano et al., 1970;

Vaernet & Madsen, 1970). The great majority of these procedures have been performed in severely disabled persons with refractory forms of epilepsy or in cases of brain disease accompanied by aggressive behavior. These surgical interventions typically involve focal destruction of small areas of the limbic structures, for example, parts of the fornix or the upper midbrain, but more usually portions of the amygdala or the posterior hypothalamus. Changes following surgery include a decrease in aggressive and destructive behavior, a diminution of rage and anger, and a generally "calming" effect (Narabayashi et al., 1963; Heimburger et al., 1966; Sano et al., 1970). While these changes generally occur without other unacceptable changes in intellectual or social functioning, decreases in spontaneity and other similar effects have also been noted. Although these extreme therapeutic procedures have been justified in light of the very serious and refractory behavioral abnormalities presented, we emphasize that rather critical ethical and public-policy questions are clearly involved and need to be considered carefully. We cite these studies simply to provide additional evidence concerning the important role of the limbic system in the mediation of emotional behavior associated with aggression and violence.

Another important concept is necessary for understanding limbic system functioning: the concept of *threshold*. Human aggression, for example, is not a simple on-off function. We are all capable of rather extreme violence given sufficient and appropriate provocation. Thus, it is not unreasonable to suppose that disturbances in the normal functioning of the limbic system might alter thresholds of response; this would lead to an increased readiness of the neurons within these structures to respond to normally sub-threshold stimuli. Various cases of persons showing seizure disorders and other behavioral problems following head injuries have been described. For example, Gloor (1967:119–120) reports the case of a man who began to have seizures and manifested a variety of other behavioral symptoms within six months after injury to the right frontal region of the head. The seizures were preceded or followed by outbursts of temper and threats of violence. Frequent rage episodes, apparently unrelated to any manifestations of seizure and provoked by the most trifling stimuli, were also quite common.

Among the limbic structures, the amygdala and hippocampus have the lowest thresholds for the initiation of electric seizure discharges of any structure in the brain (Kaada, 1967). Seizure activity in the limbic system, once begun, tends to propagate along limbic pathways (Walker, 1970). It is this feature of the limbic system that very likely accounts for the wide range of affective behaviors elicited from it, e.g., anger, fear, rage, autonomic and sexual responses, and aspects of psychotic behavior, such as hallucination and depersonalization.

BIOLOGICAL VARIABLES MORE DIRECTLY RELATED TO CRIMINAL BEHAVIOR

The cases and illustrations in the following discussion represent somewhat extreme and relatively infrequent events. Remember, however, that the influence of biological variables *cannot* be conceptualized in terms of an "either/or" (absent or present) fashion. The more extreme cases of behavior and organic pathology come to attention more readily and, thus, are available for study precisely because of the glaring nature of the symptoms manifested. Our basic purpose is to point out that, given the notion of a continuum of biological influences upon behavior, less severe cases of limbic system dysfunctioning, for example, could also have various effects upon behavior even though in attenuated and less-obvious fashion. Thus, throughout the following discussion, bear in mind the notion of a continuous range of biological influences, as well as the interaction of these variables with environmental influences.

Tumors and Related Structural Disorders of the Limbic System

Structural disorders of the limbic system demonstrate that the propensities of the human organism can be altered by focal brain disease (e.g., the threshold for response). The precise location of such damage to the central nervous system makes a difference. A typical case will illustrate this point.

A 20-year-old girl complained over the period of a year of frequent urination and increased thirst and desire to eat. Medical examinations revealed *diabetes insipidus*, a special type of diabetes which is different from *diabetes mellitus* (sugar diabetes). A hypothalamic tumor was diagnosed but could not be located during an operation. Over the next year and a half, the patient underwent extreme behavior changes which included unprovoked laughing, crying, and rage. She would hit and attempt to bite her examiners, but would later express regret for her unprovoked aggressiveness. A second operation showed an untreatable tumor. Over the next three months she deteriorated further and eventually died. An autopsy revealed a hypothalamic tumor (Reeves & Plum, 1969). Other similar cases have been described in the literature (see, e.g., Zeman & King, 1958; Malamud, 1967; Sweet et al., 1969).

Especially remarkable about these cases is that sometimes for several years abnormal behavior preceded any other suggestion of central nervous system abnormality, such as seizures, confusion, or gait irregularities. These abnormalities eventually provided clues to the diagnosis; however, some diagnoses were never suspected until revealed at autopsy. Examples of assaults, attempted assaults, sexual assaults, and burglary are included in the reported literature (see, e.g., Malamud, 1967). Some of the cases are not as clear-cut as the one described above; other psychological and social factors (e.g., disturbed family background) undoubtedly also contributed to the behavioral manifestations. What makes the brain pathology convincing in certain of these cases, as probably both *necessary* and *sufficient* to have produced the disturbed behaviors, is the normal history prior to the appearance of the tumor. Also, it is known that this particular pattern of pathology fits rather well with what is known about limbic system functioning and dysfunctioning; for example, clinical cases with increased aggressiveness have been associated with septal area tumors (Zeman & King, 1958).

Another example of the very direct contribution of brain disease to behaviors that could be labeled criminal or delinquent is the encephalitic disorders. As is now well known, many children exhibited psychopathic and behavior disorders as a consequence of the encephalitic epidemics during the 1920s. Among the survivors who had mental indicators during the acute illness, 53.6 percent continued to show mental problems after recovery. In the 3 to 10 age group, destructiveness, impulsivity, firesetting, and abnormal sexual behavior were observed; such behaviors occurred among children who were previously normal (Brill, 1959). These children, like the tumor patient described above, would also express remorse about their behavioral outbursts. More recently Himmelhoch et al. (1970) have described some cases of sub-acute encephalitis with aggressive behavior; here also the neuropathology appears to have affected the limbic areas.

Since the base rates for these disorders are rather low, the prevalence of such disorders among delinquent and criminal populations would also be very low.

The Continuum of Epilepsy-Related Disorders

Few disorders are as intriguing and as unclear as epilepsy, a condition known since antiquity. Epileptic seizures are states produced by an abnormal excessive neuronal discharge within the central nervous system (Penfield & Jasper, 1954:20); another definition states that epilepsy "is a paroxysmal cerebral dysrhythmia" (Gibbs et al., 1937). A great many factors may cause epileptic seizures: trauma to the brain, tumors, and metabolic conditions. However, in about two-thirds to three-fourths of the cases, the cause of the seizures is unknown. It is known that there is a heritable component in some instances (Metrakos & Metrakos, 1961).

Epileptic seizures may be divided into three main types:

1. *Grand mal* seizures are typically manifested by generalized and observable fits during which consciousness is lost and the person has amnesia for what happened during the seizure or *ictus*. The seizure is usually followed by a period of drowsiness and confusion.

2. *Petit mal* (or centrencephalic) seizures are characterized by lapses of consciousness without significant motor activity or falling. The person may continue to do automatically what he had been doing when the seizure began. Prolonged periods of automatic behavior are described as "petit mal status."

3. Psychomotor (or temporal lobe) epilepsy is the most frequent form of the disorder in adults and has a variety of features including greater predominance of subjective experiences (fear, anxiety, and visual imagery), and automatic behavior (fumbling, lip-smacking, and postural changes) (Ward et al., 1969; Tucker & Pincus, 1973). While some memory for the seizure is retained, it is nearly always incomplete; there may also be complete amnesia.

The reporting of epilepsy presents some problems. For example, the diagnosis may focus on the electroencephalographic abnormalities which usually accompany the clinical state; or, more commonly, the diagnosis may be based on the clinical picture itself. Neither solution alone is satisfactory, since not all persons with clinical epilepsy have an abnormal EEG (as these tracings are usually obtained); nor do all persons with the typical EEG abnormality manifest the clinical disorder (Brain & Walton, 1969). Carelessness about this point has led to an unfortunate homogenizing of the epilepsy literature relevant to criminology, a confusion only recently being sorted out (Monroe, 1970).

It is best, therefore, to think of a continuum of epilepsy-related disorders, namely, *ictal disturbances* (clinical seizures), *inter-ictal* (i.e., between seizures) *disturbances*, and *EEG abnormalities*.

Ictal Disturbances. Our concern here is with particular behaviors (e.g., assaults and fire-setting) associated with ictal events, which may be labeled officially as crimes. It is possible that such acts may have occurred at the time of the seizure or shortly thereafter (within minutes to several hours). Such offenses are often reported with the characteristic statement that they seemed "driven," "mechanical," or "unmotivated." Often, such ictal disturbances involve automatic behavior, usually with later partial or complete amnesia; such behavior may also be associated with periods of confusion, the so-called twilight states. Examples of such disordered behavior, with reasonable documentation, have been reported by Davidson (1947) and Gunn and Fenton (1971).

However, despite the importance of the phenomenon when it occurs, very few cases of criminal acts committed during ictal disturbances can be cited. It seems that the association between epileptic seizures (in their classical description) and behaviors likely to be labeled criminal appears to have been overstated in the past. Consciously directed activity during or just after the seizure is unlikely, and the aggressiveness that has been noted may be related typically to the patient's confused efforts to fight off attempts to restrain him (Lorentz de Haas, 1963; Monroe, 1970; Rodin, 1973).

Recent misunderstanding of the relationship of epilepsy to criminal behavior partly appears to have followed from the findings of greater prevalence of electro-encephalographic abnormalities among repetitively assaultive offenders and psychopaths. Such findings have been interpreted to imply that the criminal behavior occurred during a clinical seizure. For example, the report by Hill and Pond (1952) is often cited. In their investigation Hill and Pond found 18 epileptics among 105 murderers: 9 by clinical criteria, 3 by EEG criteria, and 6 by both. However, these authors also noted that there was no evidence that any of the 18 persons had suffered a seizure at the time of the crime. Gunn and Fenton (1971) reviewed the histories of 158 epileptic prisoners and 29 hospitalized epileptic prisoners and found only 3 or 4 who possibly had committed crimes during their seizures (automatic behavior). This lack of association between classical epileptic seizures and crime is further supported by data from several large studies of patients with epilepsy of various types (Alstrom, 1950; Lennox & Lennox, 1960:969–73; Lorentz de Haas, 1963; Livingston, 1964).

Nevertheless, there is evidence that suggests an association between certain types of epilepsy and behaviors likely to be labeled criminal. In part, the evidence represents advances in technology which allow better assessment of precisely what epilepsy is or is not. In this discussion we view epilepsy as a *paroxysmal cerebral dysrhythmia*.

The following recent events are noteworthy:

1. There are indications that surface brain-wave recordings (the standard type) are a poor reflection of what is occurring in the depths of the brain, especially in limbic areas. Spiking in limbic structures (as the amygdala and hippocampus) can occur with no reflection in the surface of the brain but it may be associated with irrational or aggressive behavior (Mark & Ervin, 1970; Monroe, 1970). These observations have opened the possibility that some behavior disorders (including aggressive behaviors) may be related, at least in part, to previously unrecognized subcortical epilepsy.

2. Monroe (1970) has reported that EEG activation procedures using alpha chloralose (a drug which increases the excitability of the central nervous system) produce differing effects in the electroencephalogram; the number of false negatives is reduced without significantly increasing the false positives. These activated EEG tracings correlate with the patient's history of major aggression, or history of episodic behavior wth impulsivity. It is obvious that more sensitive assessment procedures are needed to distinguish abnormal neuronal firings accompanying or producing the behavior.

The above observations also raise the question whether behaviors of epileptic patients previously considered to be inter-ictal (i.e., between seizures) may, in fact, be manifestations of continuing seizure discharges. The behavior itself seems to be one clue that seizures are occurring, even though sophisticated methodology is required to make a proper diagnosis. The usual distinctions between ictus and inter-ictus are becoming obscured. Monroe (1970) has also observed that some patients have prolonged ictal periods (lasting more than twenty-four hours) with abnormal brain spiking, and accompanied by outbursts of crying and violence.

A recent series of 130 patients studied at the Massachusetts General Hospital supported these observations (Bach-y-Rita et al., 1971). These patients came to the emergency ward with complaints of extreme impulsivity, fears of loss of control, breaks in consciousness, and extreme episodic violence. Fifty percent of these patients had histories of criminal arrest. Ten percent of the group were found to have previously undiagnosed temporal lobe epilepsy as evidenced by temporal lobe spikes. Clinically one group showed seizurelike patterns; and still other cases displayed symptoms of pathological intoxication. It is important to note, however, that these and other studies (e.g., Maletzky, 1973) are as yet uncontrolled. The frequency of amygdala spiking in normals, for example, is as yet unknown. In related studies it has been found that prisoners with epilepsy are no more criminally violent than those without epilepsy, though they may be more impulsive (Gunn & Bonn, 1971).

Inter-Ictal Disturbances. There is evidence that in temporal lobe cases (psychomotor epilepsy), inter-ictal hostility and aggressive outbursts may be found in one-fourth to one-third of selected cases (Glaser, 1967; Ounsted, 1969; Taylor, 1969; Serafetinides, 1970). Glaser describes stubbornness, school difficulties, hyperactivity, and a variety of behavior disorders in children with limbic epilepsy; Epstein (1969) and Kolarsky et al. (1967) present cases of sexual deviation that appear to be related to temporal lobe damage.

It needs to be stressed, however, that these are selected cases and that there are other controlled studies that tend to dispute these findings (e.g., Stevens, 1966; Mignone et al., 1970; Rodin, 1973). The problem here may be considered in terms of an epidemiologic as opposed to a clinical approach to the phenomenon. It seems undisputed that certain temporal lobe cases are aggressive, difficult to manage, and that they display behavior disorders. However, it could not be said, therefore, that temporal lobe disease is usually associated with such behavior.

These findings illustrate a second important point about certain forms of epilepsy, namely, the relationship between abnormal behavior and epilepsy is strongest when there is good historical evidence for brain damage *in addition* to the clinical picture of a seizure disorder. Ounsted (1969) reports a study in which children with temporal lobe epilepsy (most with other types of seizures as well) were followed for an average of ten years. When there was a clear history of cerebral insult (e.g., trauma, infection, convulsive hypoxia), 38 to 49 percent of these children showed "catastrophic rages"; in the absence of such a history, but still with a mixed seizure disorder, the risk of "catastrophic rages" decreased to 21 percent. A small number of children with pure temporal lobe seizures showed no rages at all, however.

The link between the epileptic condition and forms of behavior likely to be labeled criminal thus appears to be somewhat indirect. This association is not mediated by the clinical seizures; rather, both appear to be related to a third condition, a malfunction of the brain that possibly affects learning, mood, and the modulation of behavior.

The EEG and Behavior. Another approach to epilepsy-related disorders has been to conduct electroencephalographic examinations of various populations exhibiting disturbed behavior. There is an immense literature on this subject. Among the various groups studied have been persons who have committed violent crimes, "motiveless" criminals, imprisoned psychopaths, and clinic children displaying disturbed conduct, e.g., stealing, temper tantrums, and impulsive disorders (see, e.g., Stafford-Clark & Taylor, 1949; Davis, 1959; Knott, 1965; Stevens et al., 1968; Williams, 1969). The results of these studies are not very clear and there have been some contradictory findings.

Studies of offenders (usually incarcerated criminals) have rather consistently shown excessive proportions of EEG abnormalities: 40 to 50 percent of the offenders as compared to the 10 to 15 percent abnormalities expected in the general population. When more selected groups of criminals have been studied, the rates of abnormalities, at times, have been even higher, as in the case of motiveless murderers, psychiatrically disturbed murderers, or the recurrently violent (Hill & Pond, 1952; Sayed et al., 1969; British Medical Journal, 1970).

For example, Williams (1969) randomly sampled 333 subjects from among the 1,250 persons who had been referred to him for EEG study. Subjects who had demonstrated a pattern of habitual violence manifested EEG abnormalities about 3 *times* as high (65 percent) as those who had committed a single act of major violence (24 percent). When Williams removed from the total sample all cases of possible organic brain damage, ascertained on clinical grounds, the differences in rates of abnormal EEGs in the two groups was further accentuated. The habitually violent group now showed a 5-*times* higher incidence of abnormalities compared to those with a single violent offense.

In a rather comprehensive review of the subject, Ellingson (1955) provides the following overall percentages of abnormal EEGs in various groups: normals: about 15 percent; neurotic disorders: about 15 percent; schizophrenia: about 20 to 30 percent; behavior disorders of children and psychopathic disorders: about 50 percent. A similar and somewhat parallel series of EEG abnormalities can be constructed for the following groups: high-school children described as free from behavior and learning problems: 5 percent (cited in Gross, 1971:86); healthy pilots: 7 percent (Bennett, 1967); inadequate psychopaths: 32 percent; and aggressive psychopaths: 65 percent (British Medical Journal, 1970).

A rather interesting study by Lennox-Buchthal et al. (1960) revealed that the rate of crashes due to pilot error among Air Force pilots was 3 times higher (22 percent versus 7 percent) in pilots with "marked and paroxysmally abnormal" EEGs, than in those with "normal or slightly abnormal" EEGs. While there was no direct way of relating the possibility of impaired consciousness to the crashes, there is other evidence (Powell, 1956) which relates a paroxysmal EEG as one of the several factors associated with loss of consciousness during flight.

These findings suggest a general rather than any specific association between EEG findings and disturbed behavior. The EEG abnormalities may correlate with some as yet poorly understood altered neurological functioning which may increase the likelihood of erratic behaviors in the populations studied (criminal, psychiatric, non-patient), and/or with the probability of a person's behavior being labeled as criminal or mentally disturbed (Cohen et al., 1970).

A great diversity of results in the aforementioned studies (see Knott, 1965), however, points rather clearly to the variabilities in EEG techniques, the definitions of criminal behavior, possible variations in the interpretation of the obtained EEG patterns, and the correction or the lack of such correction of the data for age. Moreover, the use of proper control groups and the obvious need to utilize double-blind techniques in evaluating the EEG tracings from the study subjects and the control groups are essential research procedures, if such findings are to have more meaning and significance.

Some General Considerations Concerning Epilepsy and Criminality. There are very few studies which have quantified the features of epileptic seizures, inter-ictal behavior, or EEG abnormalities in a prospective manner. Hence, the risk that these disorders pose for particular behavior problems and their relationship with the prognosis for severe behavior disorders remain essentially unknown.

Some promising developments do appear to be in sight. For example, Monroe (1970) has found his activated EEGs to be of greater usefulness than the usual EEG procedures in distinguishing between patients who manifested episodic and serious aggressive behavior versus those who did not.

Another important, but as yet incompletely understood, subject pertains to the relationship of epilepsy (or related EEG changes) to various intoxicants. A strong association between alcohol intake and violent crimes has often been described (e.g., Mulvihill et al., 1969), and cerebral physiology presumably plays some role. Usually the intoxication phenomenon is attributed to the cortical depressant effects of alcohol, as well as to the disturbing effects on the overall balance of excitation and inhibition within the nervous system. More popularly, although rather loosely, it is stated that "the superego is soluble in alcohol!"

More focal neurophysiologic mechanisms may be involved, and there is recent evidence indicating that limbic structures are sensitive to the effects of alcohol (Mark & Ervin, 1970). For example, a syndrome of *pathological intoxication* has been described in which only a few drinks serve to unleash epileptoid behavior, for example, explosive aggression and later amnesia (Marinacci, 1963; Bach-y-Rita et al., 1970; Skelton, 1970; Bach-y-Rita et al., 1971). These reports tend to implicate frontal and temporal lobe EEG changes in the occurrence of this syndrome, although the findings have been inconsistent. A nature-nurture interaction is again illustrated since the environmental setting and social context of the drinking seems to be a critical factor. When the alcohol effects are tested in the laboratory without the usual social context of the drinking situation, these disordered behaviors and EEG changes are *not* always elicited in these individuals even though clinical drunkenness is readily produced (Bach-y-Rita et al., 1970).

There are also a certain number of epileptics who appear to deteriorate over time for as yet poorly understood reasons; the deterioration is reflected by lowered I.Q.s and the appearance of mental disorders (Rodin, 1968; Bagley, 1971). In this group there is somewhat better epidemiologic evidence for an increased probability of behaviors likely to be labeled criminal. Alstrom (1950), for example, reports significantly higher incidence of criminality in a group of "mentally changed" epileptics in comparison to a control group; most of these cases involved property offenses. There were no "heinous" crimes committed.

Despite our commitment to the concept of nature-nurture interactions, there are very few studies which have systematically investigated such interactions with reference to epilepsy-related disorders. Ounsted (1969), Taylor (1969), and Bagley (1971) have emphasized the contributions of lower social-class status, learning, and poor family background to the production of the overall behavioral picture. Among patients seen at an epilepsy clinic, Rodin (1973) found that early behavioral history and diffuse organic signs, but not psychomotor epilepsy, were associated with aggression. Grunberg and Pond (1957) found that the incidence of disturbed family background was much higher in epileptic children with behavior disorders than in those without these disorders.

It would not be too much of an overstatement to suggest the possibility that the assessment of many characteristics (whether these pertain to social, psychological, or biological factors) in a population of incarcerated offenders will doubtless reveal relatively high proportions of disability or abnormality, in view of the extreme selectivity of such groups. Thus, it may often be a matter of the investigator's background and disciplinary bias as to which set of factors he decides to regard as most important (Roth et al., 1972).

The Influence of Endocrine Hormones

This section will consider some of the better-documented relationships between peripheral hormones and behaviors of interest in criminology. We have chosen to focus our interest mainly on the hormones of sexual reproduction, since the data on other hormones (especially those of the adrenal glands in their interaction with adrenalin-like compounds) indicate at present a more indirect or nonspecific contribution to the behaviors of our concern.[2]

Hormones are secreted by the glands of the body; for example, the pituitary gland, adrenals, gonads, pancreas, and thyroid. These internal secretions control, and are themselves controlled, by certain anatomical features of the body; these hormones affect the threshold for various types of responses and have extensive feedback loops with the central nervous system (Rothballer, 1967; Krieger, 1971).

The relationship of endocrinology and behavior is providing some very interesting and elegant pieces of research in complex nature-nurture interactions. For example, considerable experimental work has demonstrated that, among subhuman animals, males are generally more aggressive than females and this greater aggressivity is dependent on androgen (the male hormone). Likewise, castration experiments with subsequent replacement of appropriate hormones also indicate that androgen has a facilitative influence on various sorts of within-species aggression in male animals. Furthermore, in most animals, gonadectomy essentially eliminates sexual activity, while replacement of appropriate sex hormones restores such behavior. This is less true, though, for primates (Goy, 1964; Gray, 1971).

There is also extensive literature indicating that the effects of sex hormones are conditioned by other factors. For example, in several species, alterations in the amount of testosterone do not appear to raise animals from a lower level in the behavioral hierarchy to a higher one (Grunt & Young, 1952). Moreover, antecedent social experience also plays a major role in the sexual behavior of the adult animal; thus, failure to learn the appropriate social or sex role by infant monkeys was found to result in manifestations of abnormal behavior as adults (Harlow & Harlow, 1970).

Considerable evidence has developed showing that the presence of androgen during early fetal development is essential for the normal development of the hypothalamic neural structures associated with male behavior in later life. If androgen is present during certain critical stages in fetal life, the hypothalamus is organized in a male fashion regardless of the chromosome or genetic sex of the animal. If androgen is missing before this critical period of morphological development of external sex organs, a female is produced. In accordance with these principles, laboratory experiments with animals (Conner & Levine, 1969) have shown that neonatally castrated rats show femalelike patterns of aggressive behavior in experimental situations; these patterns are not significantly affected by male hormones since the hypothalamus has been organized in a female fashion. Also, genetically female monkeys exposed to androgen *in utero* exhibit male patterns in prepubertal behaviors; that is, they initiate rough play, assert dominance, and mount females in sex play (Money, 1968:38). Human females exposed to excess androgen prenatally (as a result of an enzymatic

---

2. For further information pertinent to hormones, see Michael, 1968; Norris and Lloyd, 1971; Money and Ehrhardt, 1972; and to drugs, see Rothballer, 1967; Valzelli, 1967.

defect called the *adrenogenital syndrome*) exhibit an excess of "tomboyism," preference for masculine-associated toys, and increased energy expenditure (Money, 1968).

These studies illustrate the following principles: (1) neural structures and their feedback loops related to endocrine hormones are anatomically shaped at an early age as either masculine or feminine types; (2) this shaping seems to affect in subtle ways the probability of certain sexual and assertive patterns of behavior occurring later in life; and (3) these resultant behaviors are further influenced by the "hormonal milieu" of the organism in its current environment.

We wish to stress, however, that in human beings there is convincing evidence that all of the above considerations are not nearly as important as factors of early social environment and experiences. Nothing contributes so strongly to human gender identity as the assigned sex of rearing. By 3 years of age, gender identity (the realization "I am a boy" or "I am a girl") is strongly fixed, regardless of the variability of physical genitalia that may be present in some of the intersex disorders (Hampson & Ferrier, 1968). This is best illustrated by the report of Money et al. (1955) of hermaphrodites (sexually ambiguous individuals) with the same chromosomal diagnosis being successfully assigned to a different sex of rearing.

What seems most clear in endocrine-related disorders is that beginning with heredity, each link in the chain contributes its own quota of influence to all the links before it; no link appears to be supreme (Money, 1969).

How does all this relate to criminology? The points of relevance are:

1. In free-ranging monkeys, animals either high in dominance rank or showing more frequent aggressive behavior tend to have higher plasma testosterone concentrations (Rose et al., 1971). In human males the behavioral traits of dominance, aggression, psychometric manifestations of hostility and aggressive feelings, and homosexuality are being related presently to levels of circulating testosterone or rates of testosterone production (Kolodny et al., 1971; Persky et al., 1971). For example, Kolodny et al. report lower levels of plasma testosterone (about halfway between normal male and normal female levels) in a group of exclusively homosexual males; sperm-count measurements also correlated with degree of homosexuality. These authors stress, however, that the above correlations may be relevant to only a small proportion of homosexuals.

2. Administration of estrogen to sexually active men generally leads to rapid decrease of sexual drive and potency (Norris & Lloyd, 1971). However, it is not clear whether this effect is primarily on central nervous system areas regulating such behaviors or whether it primarily influences testicular production of male hormones. Similar results are also reported when progesterone compounds are administered to men. (Progesterone, a compound in oral contraceptives, is a hormone that is important in females for preparing and maintaining the womb.) These observations have led to the use of estrogen and progesterone in the management of sex offenders (Golla & Hodge, 1949; Money, 1968); however, carefully controlled studies on this subject are presently lacking insofar as we can ascertain.

3. It needs to be emphasized that there is no evidence at present that administration of testosterone to above-normal levels in males leads to heightened sexuality (Norris & Lloyd, 1971); in other words there are no endocrine data which presently support a super-male concept. The administration of testosterone to an androgen-deficient male does restore sexual drive and potency, or a feeling of well-being; in other males, heightened or pathological drive has not been related to androgen levels, though this is not yet well researched. Furthermore, the associations of testosterone levels with homosexuality noted above are cross-sectional observations. This means that

only an association, not a cause-and-effect relationship, has thus far been demonstrated. It is possible that the pattern of homosexuality may itself lead to lowered testosterone levels. For example, it has been noted that low testosterone levels in impotent men have returned to normal following successful psychotherapy (Lloyd, 1968).

4. A most recent study in this area (Kreuz & Rose, 1972) failed to show a difference in testosterone levels between institutionally and noninstitutionally violent male prisoners; however, testosterone levels were related to a prisoner's positive history of violent crime during adolescence.

The Premenstrual Syndromes and Some Behavioral Correlates. It is clinically well known that fluctuations of mood in women frequently occur in association with the menstrual cycle. Indeed, *premenstrual tension*, as this phenomenon has been called, seems to be the most common of minor endocrine disorders. It has been estimated that about 25 percent of all women suffer in moderate or severe degrees from this syndrome, and that possibly as many as 40 percent of all women experience some degree of distress during the premenstrual and menstrual periods (Greene & Dalton, 1953; Coppen & Kessel, 1963; Dalton, 1964; Mandell & Mandell, 1967; Hamburg et al., 1968; Wetzel et al., 1971).

The symptoms more commonly experienced, although in markedly varying degrees, include: tension and nervousness, irritability, fatigue and exhaustion, headaches, depressed moods, abdominal bloating and pain, muscle stiffness and cramps, various autonomic reactions (such as dizziness, cold sweats, and nausea), and other symptoms (see, e.g., Moos, 1969). Studies have also indicated that there is no single or uniform aspect to the premenstrual or menstrual syndrome; rather, a variety of subtypes have been indicated by factor analytic studies (Moos, 1969).

The various symptoms associated with the premenstrual and menstrual periods appear to be related to the imbalance between estrogen and progesterone levels; in particular, to the deficiency of progesterone during the premenstrual period. An interesting common feature of premenstrual distress and postpartum psychiatric disorders is that both occur at a time when circulating progesterone is at a very low level.

The importance of premenstrual and menstrual symptomatology is appearing in a new light with the increasing accumulation of evidence that a large proportion of suicides or suicide attempts, admissions for psychiatric illness or acute medical and surgical reasons, as well as involvement in criminal acts by women appear to occur during these periods. For example, Dalton (1964) found that the four premenstrual and four menstrual days accounted for 45 percent of the sick calls by female industrial employees, 45 percent of acute psychiatric admissions, 49 percent of acute surgical and medical admissions, and 52 percent of emergency accident admissions. Also, it was during these eight days that 49 percent of women prisoners had committed their crimes.

Morton et al. (1953) studied 249 volunteer prisoners at a state penal farm and found that 51 percent of the prison population suffered from premenstrual tensions. In a more detailed study of 58 women who had committed crimes of violence (murder, manslaughter, and assaults), it was found that 62 percent of this group had committed their crimes during the premenstrual period, and another 17 percent had committed their crimes during the menstrual period. It is rather significant that *79 percent* of these crimes had occurred during the premenstrual and menstrual periods.

Similarly, Dalton (1961) studied 386 newly convicted prisoners and found that of those who were menstruating regularly (74 percent), nearly half (49 percent) committed their crimes during the premenstrual and menstrual periods. Assuming an equal distribution across the menstrual cycle, only two-sevenths (or 29 percent) of all crimes would be expected during this eight-day period. The probability of obtaining the actual distribution (49 percent) by chance would be less than one in a thousand.

Dalton (1961) also studied 94 regularly menstruating prisoners who had received reports for rule-violating behavior, and discovered that 51 (or 54 percent) had been disorderly during their premenstrual or menstrual periods. Among the 54 prisoners who had been reported only once, the misbehavior was associated with menstruation in 43 percent of the cases. However, among the 40 women who had been reported for misconduct more than once, 70 percent of the incidents were associated with menstruation.

The relationship between the premenstrual and menstrual syndrome and low levels of circulating progesterone is further confirmed by the finding of Greene and Dalton (1953) that treatment with a progestogen was almost invariably successful.

These studies suggest a highly significant relationship between certain periods of the menstrual cycle and emotional and behavioral distress, especially for women with certain subtypes of premenstrual and menstrual symptoms. It would appear that, for a number of women, hormonal changes resulting in irritability, tension, nervousness, and related symptoms markedly increase the probability of committing crimes. However, during these periods women law-violators could be more likely to be detected, since slower reaction time, lethargy, and fatigue are also experienced by many women at these times. Nevertheless, premenstrual and menstrual symptoms resulting in tension and irritability could facilitate crimes of violence.

It must be emphasized, however, that endocrinological factors contribute to deviant behaviors in conjunction with other factors; it is not suggested that the endocrine imbalance by itself determines these behaviors. Indeed, Coppen and Kessel (1963) found that women who complained of irritability during premenstrual and menstrual periods were more likely to be irritable at other times too. These investigators concluded that premenstrual and menstrual symptoms were an exacerbation of certain personality traits.

The Hypoglycemic Disorders. Low blood sugar (hypoglycemia) has been known for a long time to cause impaired central nervous system functioning. This peculiar sensitivity of the brain to the lack of blood sugar stems from the fact that the brain is the only organ that obtains its energy from combustion of carbohydrates alone; other organs (such as the liver, the kidneys, and the heart) can oxidize carbohydrates and fat. Thus, when deprived of blood sugar, the brain has no alternate food supply, its metabolism slows down, and cerebral functions are impaired (Himwich, 1952).

Hypoglycemia is usually, though not always, related to *diabetes mellitus* (sugar diabetes), or to the treatment of this condition with insulin. Spontaneous hypoglycemia may also be found in *susceptible persons* and episodes may be induced by factors such as: starvation (especially lack of carbohydrates), muscular overexertion, diarrhea and vomiting, lactation, and sometimes menstruation.

Hypoglycemic symptoms include tremors of the hands, staggering gait, blurred speech, weakness of concentration, confusion, and irritation; if blood sugar levels drop even lower, there may be various psychotic manifestations, convulsions, and eventually, stupor and coma. Typically, there is amnesia following such episodes. During the hypoglycemic episodes explosive personality changes may take place and such behavioral patterns, in many instances, may initiate psychiatric care (Bleicher, 1970).

Various hypoglycemia-associated criminal acts, such as "motiveless murder," assaults, sexual offenses, and other law violations have been reported (see, e.g., Wilder,

1940, 1947; Podolsky, 1964). Since some of the symptoms of hypoglycemia resemble drunkenness (e.g., staggering gait, blurred speech, and confusion), persons with such problems, at times, may be handled as drunks.

Despite the many references in the literature associating hypoglycemia with criminal behavior, the supporting data are rather poor. By and large, documentation is of an anecdotal nature, and there is a lack of careful recent studies. While we are unable to estimate the degree to which hypoglycemic disorders may involve persons in trouble with the law, the base rates would probably be rather low; interestingly, these rates have never been systematically measured. However, in view of the symptoms of the hypoglycemic condition, it is possible that law-violating and aggressive behaviors have an increased probability of occurring during these episodes.

The Effects of Epinephrine and Norepinephrine. Epinephrine and norepinephrine, catecholamines, are also known as adrenalin and noradrenalin. They require brief mention here because they have been studied rather extensively in a variety of psychiatric disorders, and because they have been found to play an important role in the mediation of hostility, anger, rage, and aggressive disorders (Gerard, 1959; Kety, 1970; Reiss, 1972).

In 1955 some important research was presented relating "anger directed outwards" by humans to the secretion of norepinephrine, and "anger directed inwards" to the secretion of epinephrine (Funkenstein, 1955). The complexity of analysis in this area was further demonstrated by Schachter and Singer (1962) when they showed that the administration of epinephrine could lead to different emotional states (anger or euphoria) depending upon the social setting and the expectancy or set of the individual.

The literature on this topic has proliferated and indicates the importance of both peripheral and central biogenic amines (compounds that are related to adrenalin and noradrenalin) as neurotransmitters, i.e., as responsible for the transmission of electrical impulses within the nervous system. For example, epinephrine has been shown to increase cerebral metabolism, to produce anxiety in humans, to stimulate the neurons directly, and also to lower their thresholds to stimulation by nerve impulses (Gerard, 1959).

Of more direct interest and relevance to criminology is the recently summarized information that amphetamines act on the nervous system by affecting neurotransmitters, in part by causing release of norepinephrine (Stein & Wise, 1970). Such observations make more rational, and provide a theoretical underpinning for, the reports of assault and murder associated with amphetamine abuse (Ellinwood, 1971). Also of interest is Sheard's (1971) observations concerning the efficacy of lithium carbonate in the treatment of aggressive prisoners; although the exact mechanism of the action of the drug is unknown, lithium seems to affect the adrenalin-like neurotransmitters.

BIOLOGICAL VARIABLES MORE INDIRECTLY RELATED
TO CRIMINAL BEHAVIOR

Some Correlates and Effects of Perinatal Pathology

In 1912 there was a catastrophic event: the Titanic hit an iceberg and went down with more than 1,500 of its passengers and crew. Among the women who were traveling in first-class accommodations, 4 out of a total of 143 were lost; of the 93 women traveling in second class, 15 were lost; and, of the 179 women traveling third class, 81 were lost (Antonovsky, 1967:31). Thus, although death is the final lot of all living things, as the above incident illustrated, the timing and manner of death is related in many respects to a person's social position and class.

The same appears to be true for certain other indices of health and disability that have relevance for criminology. We shall indicate how a variety of class-linked social and environmental factors influence the biological integrity of individuals, and how the interaction of organismic and environmental variables affects a person's adaptive capabilities in society.

Because of the variability of the available data in this area, for purposes of our discussion, we shall equate socioeconomic class with income, type of occupation, or white and nonwhite status. This will facilitate our discussion, because all of these variables are presently correlated with socioeconomic indices to a large extent.

Several sets of data require consideration.

Prenatal Care. The President's Panel on Mental Retardation (1962) noted that half of all births at city hospitals in the District of Columbia in 1961 were to mothers who had received no prenatal care. Similarly, the report of the Joint Commission on Mental Health of Children (1969) estimated that approximately one million infants would be born that year to women who had received no medical care during their pregnancies, or no adequate obstetrical care for delivery. Toxemias of pregnancy, a dangerous form of maternal high blood pressure, have also been found to be strongly associated with social class: 3 percent in high-income groups and 15 percent in low-income groups (President's Panel on Mental Retardation, 1962).

Infant Mortality. The National Center for Health Statistics reports the death rate within the first year of life for all infants born alive in 1965 was about 40 deaths per thousand for nonwhites, and 22 deaths per thousand for whites (Richmond & Weinberger, 1970:28).

Prematurity. Two separate indices are used to evaluate prematurity: birth weight and length of gestation. Using official statistics for 1965, we learn that 13.8 percent of nonwhite infants had a birth weight of 2,500 grams or less, as compared with 7.2 percent for whites. If data for nonwhites are considered separately, it becomes evident that these figures are mainly correlated with socioeconomic class rather than with race. For example, a Nashville study stratified a nonwhite group socioeconomically and grouped the women on a ten-point scale according to level of family income and education. The frequency of birth weights below 2,500 grams increased from a low of 5.3 percent in the *most fortunate group* to a high of 23.3 percent in the *poorest* group (Birch, 1971:147).

Preterm births in 1967 occurred at the rate of 10.9 percent for nonwhites and 5.8 percent for whites. Moreover, for infants with low birth weights (i.e., 2,500 grams or less), infant mortality has been reported to be 17 times higher than that for heavier infants (Chase & Byrnes, 1970).

Several studies have indicated that not only are premature children at greater risk for intellectual impairment, but such children have been found rather consistently to be more subject to personality disorders than children of higher birth weight (Birch, 1971). For example, Pasamanick and Knobloch (1966), in their study in Baltimore, found histories of prematurity 3 times as often in white children with behavior disorders and $3\frac{1}{2}$ times as often among Negro children, as among their respective controls. Among the behavior-disordered children studied, the highest association of complications of the prenatal period was found in children in both racial groups described as hyperactive, confused, and disorganized.

Still other studies have indicated that among the poor, the risk for central nervous system damage is not confined to the intrauterine period. The early development period is also critical in the process of growth and maturation since supportive cells of the human brain continue to divide until about 8 to 10 months of age in the cerebellum, cerebrum, and the brain stem (Winick, 1970). Therefore, postnatal events can help to repair or may further exacerbate disadvantages that may have been present at birth (Drillien, 1970; Birch, 1971; Wender, 1971).

Prenatal variables are often associated with postnatal events that are class-linked; hence postnatal factors constitute further possible handicaps. Such postnatal events include infant malnutrition (Birch, 1971; Montagu, 1972); lead poisoning, which in subtler forms may be associated with depressed I.Q., poor school performance, and hyperactivity (Lin-Fu, 1970; David et al., 1972); the battered-child syndrome, also found to be associated with low birth weight (Gil, 1970; Klein & Stern, 1971); and maternal deprivation (Wortis & Freedman, 1968). It has also been noted that by age 3 children from disadvantaged families manifest diminished performance (Richmond & Weinberger, 1970). The possible relationship of this diminished performance to both prenatal and postnatal variables is being studied.

All of the above data support the contention that the population with a high incidence of organic and organic-like syndromes also shows high perinatal mortality rates (Gruenberg, 1964).

The literature in these areas appears to support Pasamanick and Knobloch's (1960, 1966) hypothesis of a "continuum of reproductive casualty." At one end of this continuum are abortion, stillbirths, and neonatal deaths, and at various points along the continuum are gradients of neurological dysfunctions interacting with the environment to produce a variety of deviant behaviors, including childhood psychoses, mental deficiency, and childhood behavior disorders.

In addition to the more general public health data pertaining to a variety of morbidity indices, there have also been a number of studies which have attempted to relate central nervous system dysfunctioning to perinatal and birth complications.

For example, Pasamanick and Knobloch (1966) studied the birth histories of more than 9,000 children, secured from schools, clinics, and institutions, showing various abnormalities and compared them with the birth histories of matched controls. Complications of pregnancy and premature births were found with significantly greater frequency where the children had cerebral palsy, epilepsy, behavior disorders, mental deficiency, or reading disabilities. The incidence of these abnormalities was also higher among nonwhites.

Mednick (1970) and his associates have been engaged in an intensive longitudinal study of 207 "normally functioning" children at high risk for becoming schizophrenic, since they were born to chronic and severely schizophrenic mothers. Detailed studies of the 20 youngsters who have come to psychiatric attention thus far provide two very interesting findings: (1) these youngsters manifest more impulsive behavior disorders (along with delinquent acts) than they do schizophrenia; and (2) the impulsive and behavior-disorder characteristics were strongly associated with earlier and well-documented histories of the mothers' pregnancy and birth complications.

These 20 youngsters (the Sick Group) were compared with a Well Group (children of schizophrenic mothers who have not yet manifested any problems), and a Control Group (carefully matched children born to normal mothers). The investigators found that the mothers of fully 70 percent of the Sick Group had suffered one or more pregnancy and birth complications (PBC), as contrasted with 15 percent incidence in the Well Group, and 33 percent in the Controls.

To complete our discussion, we would like also to point to some negative findings. For example, Pasamanick and Knobloch (1966) also studied delinquent adolescents in Columbus, Ohio, and found no association between delinquency and prematurity or mother's complications of pregnancy. Similarly, Jonsson (1967) found that the incidence of birth complications for the mothers of 100 delinquent boys was no higher than in a population of nondelinquent controls. There was, however, an excess of both low- and high-birth-weight boys in the delinquents. McNeil et al. (1970) found that the frequency of prematurity in a sample of aggressive youngsters with behavior disorders was not as high as that in a group of socially withdrawn youngsters, also with behavior problems. The level of birth complications did not distinguish between subgroups of the behaviorally disturbed. The Kauai pregnancy study, a ten-year follow-up of children who suffered perinatal stress, found no correlation between aggressiveness of the children and severity of the perinatal stress (Werner et al., 1968).

What are the implications of the above sets of data for problems of concern to criminology? It is, of course, well known that the offender population (those who have been officially labeled as criminals, and especially those who are incarcerated) is drawn largely from groups with the highest epidemiological risk for prenatal and postnatal deleterious influences (President's Commission, 1967b). It seems possible that the overall adaptability and neurological functioning of offender populations may be diminished in comparison with less-selective populations, partly on the basis of the aforementioned associations.[3]

We do *not* wish to imply that many behaviors likely to be officially labeled as crimes are the product of neurological difficulties. We are suggesting that individuals belonging to population groups at greater risk for perinatal and birth complications and resultant neurological dysfunctioning, who are further exposed to unfavorable social environments during their lives, in general, would be expected to display higher rates of deviant behaviors likely to lead to criminal labeling.

Clearly, one has to consider the many ways in which biological variables interact differentially with environmental variables. For example, Drillien (1964) found that children whose mothers had severe pregnancy and birth complications were much more likely to develop behavior difficulties in cases where interpersonal relationships in the family were badly disturbed.

Minimal Brain Dysfunction

A related set of behaviors exhibited by some children and adolescents has been described as the Minimal Brain Dysfunction (MBD) syndrome, previously known as Minimal Brain Damage (Pincus & Glaser, 1966; Wender, 1971). Use of the term Minimal Brain Dysfunction (MBD) indicates that these children are, generally, of around average intelligence and manifest certain learning or behavioral disabilities, which are associated with central nervous system dysfunctioning. The central nervous system dysfunctions include various combinations of impairment in perception, conceptualization, language, attention span, memory, and impulse or motor control (Clements, 1966). A more flexible definition is offered by Pincus and Glaser (1966) who suggest that MBD is merely a label for certain kinds of aberrant behavior.

---

3. For further information relating neurological functioning to criminal offenses and sociopathy, see Small, 1966; Hertzig and Birch, 1968.

The behaviors of interest may vary somewhat as a function of the age of the child at the time of the medical diagnosis. More specifically, in two- to four-year olds the major manifestations are destructiveness, demanding and strong-willed behaviors, and difficulty with discipline. During nursery and early elementary-school years, the behaviors involve short attention span, low frustration tolerance, temper tantrums, and hyperactivity. Beginning about the third grade, reading disorders and learning problems are evidenced, along with behavior problems, such as stealing, lying, and fire-setting. During adolescence, the behaviors of concern involve academic underachievement, and negativistic and antisocial behaviors (Wender, 1971).

While this list is fairly comprehensive for the behaviors of interest, we wish to stress that not all of these behaviors necessarily occur in any single child, nor do the behavioral sequences have to follow in the order described. Indeed, for some children, there may not be any discernible sequence. For example, a child may show hyperactivity without presenting any of the other symptoms.

Among the features that serve to interrelate the above sets of behavioral manifestations are the findings that in a proportion of these cases the behaviors are, at least partly, organically determined; also that these youngsters, in most cases (about two-thirds), show a favorable response to treatment with amphetamines and other stimulant drugs (Wender, 1971; O'Malley & Eisenberg, 1973).

Neuropathology may underlie some cases of such childhood behavior disorders (Ingram, 1956; Glaser, 1967; Aird, 1968; Towbin, 1971). An excess of "soft" neurological signs (i.e., abnormal neurological findings which fail to provide accurate localization for a nervous system lesion) have been noted in about 50 percent of MBD cases (Wikler et al., 1970; Wender, 1971). While nervous system pathology could be present in many of the various cases described above, it is also possible that the behavioral phenomena and altered physiology in MBD may represent developmental lags, or may be maturational or time-limited in nature, i.e., something many of the children may outgrow. "Harder" neurological signs have also been observed in some cases (e.g., Twitchell, 1971; Myklebust, 1973).

Likewise, EEG abnormalities sometimes have been found to accompany the behaviors associated with MBD, but, as we have pointed out earlier in this chapter, the exact meaning of such abnormalities is poorly understood. Nevertheless, the usual improvement that results from use of stimulant drugs and the lack of improvement with other drugs or with psychological forms of treatment alone suggests the possibility that some sort of abnormal physiology may well underlie at least some of the MBD cases.

The foregoing discussion makes it evident that grouping the range of behavioral problems under the term Minimum Brain Dysfunction does not clarify this rather complicated area. It might also be stressed that the primary diagnosis of the disorder is actually *behavioral*, rather than one based on neurological signs. Among the limitations of the concept of MBD is the lack of consistent findings of neurological abnormalities; at least 50 percent of the cases do not display abnormal neurology (Wender, 1971). Moreover, there is no consistent picture nor understanding as to the etiology of these disorders. Wender has reviewed the most prominent and likely etiological hypotheses, namely, brain damage, polygenic inheritance (genetic transmission via a combination of genes), perinatal determinants, and psychogenic, as well as simply extreme placement on a normal distribution curve. Some support seems to be available for all the foregoing etiological hypotheses, along with additional contributions from poor home environments.[4]

---

4. For a recent review of this complex topic, see Walzer and Wolff, 1973.

Since poor school performance is perhaps the most outstanding correlate of this syndrome, it is not difficult to postulate a chain of events proceeding from poor learning and leading to dropping out of school, and later delinquent identification. This progression, which has been noted by numerous psychological and sociological studies of delinquency (e.g., President's Commission, 1967a), seems especially important in the case of individuals belonging to economically disadvantaged groups. Related to this hypothesis, Denhoff (1965) has reported that 53 percent of 109 school dropouts and delinquents showed organic features which were judged to contribute to their academic failure. Mulligan (1972) reaches similar conclusions in a more recent article.

Several longitudinal follow-up studies have been done in this area in recent years (e.g., Menkes et al., 1967; Mendelson et al., 1971; Weiss et al., 1971). These studies have revealed what others have suspected but have not been able to document: that some of the youngsters manifesting behavior disorders *do not grow out of them*. The classic work by Robins (1966) also documents the persistence of behavior disorders and antisocial conduct well into adult life.

Finally, we again point out a useful generality concerning the current state of biology and criminality: no matter how helpful certain biological variables seem to be in thinking about the genesis or treatment of certain behaviors, biology taken alone is of relatively poor prognostic value. Indeed, in most instances, the biological indices will probably be inferior to the various behaviors themselves as future predictors. For example, Stevens et al. (1968) reported that adverse family environment led all other predisposing factors in differentiating between behavior-problem children and controls, despite the finding of 47 percent abnormal EEGs in the problem youngsters. Antisocial behavior in hyperactive children in later years is associated with disturbed family background and an earlier history of high aggression rating (Weiss et al., 1971).

Thus, various biological difficulties, behavior disorders, and antisocial conduct may be associated with the Minimal Brain Dysfunction syndrome, and the recommended treatment of these MBD-related problems is at least partly biological.

Genetics and Crime

There are several types of studies that fall under the heading of behavior genetics. The essential question is: Do genetic factors predispose some individuals toward disruptive, aggressive, or other insufficiently regulated behaviors, and which patterns of behavior are likely to be defined and handled as criminal?

Although the emphasis in this section is ultimately on behavior, we wish to reiterate that typically what is inherited is *not* a particular form of behavior (be it aggressive, antisocial, or altruistic), but certain genetically determined structures that influence behavior as a result of interactions with the environment. The genetic contributions are mediated through enzymatic, hormonal, or other structural pathways of the nervous system.

Various methods are used for assessing the *heritability* of a trait, i.e., the relative contribution of genetic and environmental causes. For example, comparisons have been made between identical (one-egg or monozygotic) and fraternal (two-egg or dizygotic) twins. The logic for the comparison, stated very simply, is: since monozygotic twins have identical genotypes (barring mutations), any dissimilarity between members of the pair must be due to environmental influences, whether intrauterine or postnatal. Fraternal twins differ genetically but have a number of environmental similarities, e.g., birth rank and maternal age. When both types of twins are studied, the effect of different environments on the same genotype or the expression of different genotypes under very similar environments can be evaluated. Thus, with respect to any given genetically determined trait, there should be greater similarity between identical than fraternal twins. If both members of a twin pair develop the same phenotypic characteristic being studied, they are called *concordant* for that trait or characteristic. If the phenotypic characteristics are different, the members of the twin pair are designated *discordant* for that trait. Thus, if the concordance rate for identical twins is significantly greater, it could be inferred that the trait has some genetic loading. In so doing, however, the assumption is made that the environmental differences are the same for identical and fraternal twins. Such an assumption may or may not be tenable and should be independently assessed with respect to the trait being studied (Rosenthal, 1970).

Although twin studies are useful, they are liable to certain kinds of error. For example, the investigator may not have accurate information concerning the zygosity of the twins, i.e., whether in fact they are identical or same-sex fraternal. There are also difficulties, and possible biases, in the classification of the phenotypic behavior of concern, as whether the person is accurately diagnosed as a schizophrenic or alcoholic. This problem is especially noteworthy in the field of criminology since criminal convictions are not a very reliable index of criminal behavior and reflect only a small proportion of all law-violating behaviors.

Because of these problems with twin studies, more recent research has taken advantage of adoption by focusing on individuals who were separated from their biological parents soon after birth and were raised by non-relatives. First, the behavior of interest is specified (e.g., schizophrenia or criminality). Next, the families (biological or adoptive) of the *index cases* (i.e., one of the individuals who possesses the trait under study) are compared with the families (biological or adoptive) of the control cases (i.e., the adopted children who have not manifested the behavior of concern) (Rosenthal, 1970). This approach allows a well-controlled analysis which seeks to parcel out hereditary and environmental contributions.

Twin Studies: Old and New. Lange (1931) conducted the first fairly systematic genetic study of criminal behavior in 1929. He was so impressed by his findings that he entitled his report "Crime as Destiny." Among his thirteen pairs of identical twins, ten were concordant for penal confinement, while fifteen of the seventeen fraternal pairs were discordant, i.e., one of the pair had remained clear of trouble with the law.

Although these results appear striking, they are subject to most of the weaknesses of twin studies. Subsequent studies, which have been somewhat better in their design, have had less striking results. For example, a study done by Kranz in 1936 obtained 66 percent concordance for the presence of criminal records among identical twins and 54 percent concordance among fraternal twins (Rosenthal, 1970:232). The insignificant difference between identical and fraternal twins and the relatively high concordance rate among the fraternal pairs indicate the predominant role of social and environmental factors in explaining the phenotypic characteristic, viz., criminal behavior that came to official attention.

These and several related studies have been summarized by Christiansen (1968) to show that 66.7 percent of all the identical twins studied were concordant for some sort of officially labeled criminal behavior, as compared with 30.4 percent concordance among fraternal twins. Despite the two-to-one ratio of concordance for identical over fraternal twins, the results must be regarded as inconclusive because of various methodological problems, and also because none of the earlier studies was based upon a complete and unselected sample of twins. For example, when one begins a study with known criminals (or known schizophrenics), there is the possibility that concordant cases might be located more easily and that the investigator might also be biased in the classification of borderline cases of the trait among siblings.

Christiansen's own study (1968) is somewhat different. He ascertained the criminal histories of *all twins*, about 6,000 pairs, born in the Danish islands between 1880 and 1910, where both twins had survived until at least age 15. The excellent record-keeping system in Denmark made such a study quite feasible. Results are provided for 218 same-sex twin pairs where at least one member had manifested some evidence of criminal behavior (as indicated by the Central Police Register and/or by local penal registers). For males, 35.8 percent of the identical twins were concordant for criminal conduct as compared to 12.3 percent concordance among fraternal twins. For females, the concordance rates for criminal behavior were 21.4 percent among identical twins and 4.3 percent among fraternal twins.

Christiansen's results indicate that somewhat lower concordance rates are obtained when an unselected sample of twins is studied. However, it is noteworthy that Christiansen's data indicate that given a criminal who is a twin, the identical twin is about $2\frac{1}{2}$ times as likely to be involved with the law as compared to a fraternal twin. While some methodological issues remain to be clarified in this study, we would suggest that the data support the hypothesis that at least some of the variance is accounted for by genetic contributions.

Before completing our discussion of twin studies, we would like also to note several studies that have demonstrated a certain concordance for various personality and temperamental traits, e.g., depression, psychopathy, and introversion-extraversion (Eysenck, 1956, 1964; Vandenberg, 1960; Gottesman, 1963).

Adoption Studies. One of the ways in which the interacting effects of genetic and environmental factors can be separated is to study individuals who have been reared apart from biological relatives, and to compare the prevalence of mental disorder among the biological and adoptive relatives of the *index case.*

A very interesting and methodologically sophisticated study of psychopathy has recently been reported by Schulsinger (1972). He defined *psychopathy* as a consistent pattern of impulse-ridden or acting-out behavior lasting beyond the age of 19 years; further diagnostic criteria and distinctions were also developed. Other types of psychiatric complications and disorders were specifically excluded from the category of *psychopathy;* for example, schizoid-type psychopaths, character neuroses, and cases where acting-out behavior was present along with psychotic or borderline-psychotic disorders. Three raters diagnosed each case and there was 82 percent overall agreement among the raters regarding the presence or absence of psychopathy.

Using these criteria, 57 psychopathic *index cases* were selected from 507 adoptees with known mental disorders. A careful case-by-case matching was then done for variables of age, sex, age at transfer to adoptive homes, and social class of adoptive parents. In about every case it was possible to find an almost perfectly matched non-psychopathic adopted control.

Mental illness among the relatives was ascertained through a careful search of the central register of psychiatric hospital admissions and the archives of all psychiatric institutions in Denmark. All the available case record materials were reviewed and classified by Schulsinger on a "blind" basis. In view of some variations in the quality of the case materials as a function of the institution, it was decided to operate with a *spectrum* of personality disorders in which psychopathy was the "nuclear" disease. The *psychopathic spectrum* included cases of psychopathy, character deviations, hysterical character disorders, individuals with problems of alcoholism, drug abuse, and criminality, as well as those classified as "probable psychopaths."

Schulsinger found that, of the 305 biological relatives of the *index cases,* 44 (14.4 percent) suffered from *psychopathic spectrum* disorders, while only 19 (or 6.7 percent) of the 285 biological relatives of the control cases suffered from such disorders. Among the adoptive relatives, 7.6 percent of the 131 *index case* relatives and 5.3 percent of the 133 control relatives suffered from such disorders. In other words, psychopaths who had been separated from their biological parents soon after birth were a little more than twice as likely to have biological relatives with similar or closely related psychiatric disorders than were the non-psychopaths.

A further strength of Schulsinger's study is his ability to check on the relative importance of certain environmental factors in the etiology of personality disorders, namely, central nervous system involvement as a result of birth complications and early infantile deprivation. Schulsinger checked the relevance of these factors by using mid-wife reports (for birth complications), and by using number of environmental shifts and length of institutionalization during early childhood as indices of early infantile deprivation. No significant differences were found among the index and control cases.

The design of this study provides a demonstration of possible genetic factors in the etiology of psychopathy. Clearly, this does not mean, nor does it even imply, that various environmental factors are thereby excluded. However, the data do indicate that the prevalence of psychopathy and related disorders among adoptive parents (suggesting a psychological and social-learning etiology) can be excluded as an important factor in the cases studied.

Chromosomal Abnormalities and Criminal Behavior

Chromosomes are microscopic structures present in all cell nuclei which carry the basic genetic material, *genes.* Human beings typically have 46 chromosomes, of which 44 are body-forming autosomes and 2 are sex-determining chromosomes. Thus, the typical male chromosomal complement is 46,XY and the typical female complement is 46,XX. Sometimes, however, an individual may possess more or less than the normal chromosome complement, usually due to the process of nondisjunction, i.e., improper separation of the chromosomes during meiotic cell division. The chromosomal abnormalities, which have been the subject of much study in reference to disordered behavior among males, are the 47,XXY complement (also known as *Klinefelter's syndrome*) and the 47,XYY complement.[5]

Consistent with our use of the terms defined earlier in this chapter, chromosomal disorders are *innate* or *congenital,* but not necessarily hereditary. The errors in cell division occur in the development of particular fertilized eggs; other brothers and sisters of the affected individual need not and usually are not affected by these anomalies (47,XXY and 47,XYY).

The 47,XYY Chromosomal Anomaly. During the past five or six years, there has been considerable scientific (as well as public) interest in the relationship between certain chromosomal abnormalities and behavioral and psychiatric disorders. Although the 47,XYY anomaly was first noted by Sandberg et al. in 1961, and although this and other chromosomal abnormalities have been the subject of study in genetics laboratories for several years, the topic was drawn into newspaper headlines largely as a result of speculation linking the presence of an extra Y chromosome in

---

5. For more information about the fundamentals of genetics and chromosomal abnormalities, see Court Brown, 1968; Carter, 1969; McKusick, 1969; Ferguson-Smith, 1970; German, 1970.

males with criminal and violent behavior (see, e.g., Casey et al., 1966; Forssman & Hambert, 1967; Nielsen, 1968; Telfer, 1968). Among the so-called super-males reported in the news media to have the XYY anomaly was Richard Speck, the convicted killer of eight Chicago nurses. However, subsequent reports indicated that Speck was *not* an XYY male.[6]

Since the 47,XYY anomaly has received considerable attention in the scientific and professional literature, we shall restrict this discussion to some of the more salient considerations.[7]

✓ Several of the earlier reports on 47,XYY males had noted that such individuals were rather tall and had histories of criminal and aggressive behavior. These observations led to numerous surveys among tall males in institutions for the mentally subnormal and mentally ill, for delinquents and criminals, as well as for mentally disordered offenders. The number of persons found to have the extra Y chromosome markedly exceeded the prevalence rate estimated for this anomaly in the general population (National Institute of Mental Health, 1970).

Despite the biased nature of the populations surveyed and many other conceptual and methodological complications in most of the earlier studies (see, e.g., Kessler & Moos, 1970; National Institute of Mental Health, 1970; Shah, 1972), some investigators concluded that the extra Y chromosome in some manner predisposed such males to engage in antisocial and violent behavior. One writer, for example, stated that it seemed "reasonable to suggest that [the] antisocial behavior is due to the extra Y chromosome" (Price & Whatmore, 1967). Another investigator questioned why men commit crimes of violence and then offered the answer, "For some, the urge to violence may be inborn—may be traced to something called the Y chromosome" (Telfer, 1968).

There have been numerous reports of rather high prevalence rates for the XYY chromosome complement among a variety of institutionalized populations, especially in the case of law-violators who also display mental disorders (e.g., Casey et al., 1966; Jacobs et al., 1968).

Data from many of these studies have been summarized and discussed in the NIMH report (1970), as well as by Kessler and Moos (1970), Baker (1972), and Owen (1972). In Table 1 we provide the major findings of the prevalence studies which

TABLE 1

PREVALENCE RATES FOR 47,XYY SUBJECTS IN VARIOUS INSTITUTIONS

Type of Institution	No Height Selection		Height Selection	
	Number	Percent	Number	Percent
Ordinary Prisons	3,001	0.467	2,835	1.20
Special Institutions	1,482	2.23	1,159	5.61
(Mental retardation—penal)	330	1.52	134	3.73
(Mental illness—penal)	531	1.51	371	2.97
(Security hospitals)	621	3.22	654	7.49
Psychiatric Hospitals	1,328	0.226	771	1.56

Newborn and general adult population rate estimated as 1:700 or 0.143%.
Source: Adapted from Baker, 1972:57.

---

6. Chicago Tribune, November 26, 1968, 1A:16. See also Engel, 1972.

7. Further information on the 47,XYY anomaly may be found in Kessler and Moos, 1970; National Institute of Mental Health, 1970; Baker, 1972; Owen, 1972; Borgaonkar and Shah, 1974.

have been reviewed most recently by Baker. Compared to the newborn and estimated general adult population rate of one XYY case in 700 males (Ratcliffe et al., 1970), the rates for unselected cases in the penal and special institutional groups is higher. Moreover, when tall males are selectively screened, there is almost invariably a higher prevalence rate for the 47,XYY anomaly. Of especial interest is the fact that the prevalence rate for XYY cases in security hospitals (for mentally disordered offenders) is more than *20 times* greater than that estimated for the general population.

The increased frequency of XYY cases among institutionalized delinquents and offenders may relate to the possibility that tall law-violators may be more vulnerable to social responses leading to decisions to incarcerate. If this hypothesis is correct, we should expect to find an elevated height distribution among the institutionalized populations. While large-scale and systematic studies on this question are presently lacking, at least two studies have failed to find an increased distribution of tall males among confined delinquents (Hook & Kim, 1971; Borgaonkar et al., 1972); one study did find an increased distribution of tall males (Witkin, 1972).

Some recent surveys of institutionalized groups conducted without any selection for height have obtained lower prevalence rates for the XYY and the XXY anomalies in penal populations. For example, Jacobs et al. (1971) screened 909 males in penal institutions and found only a single 47,XYY case; similarly, out of 1,119 boys examined in approved schools, 4 were found to be XYY. Given the frequency of one XYY male in 700 male births (Ratcliffe et al., 1970), the prevalence noted was not significantly different from that in the newborn and estimated general adult population. Similarly, the finding of two 47,XYY cases in a population of 510 men from penal institutions who were 178 cm. or more in height was also not much higher than the expected prevalence rate for that height in that general population, a rate of approximately 1 in 210 adult males (Jacobs et al., 1971). As these authors note, these penal surveys provide no evidence of an association between the XYY and XXY chromosome abnormalities and criminal behavior. However, Jacobs et al. do note that a *twentyfold* increase in 47,XYY males is indicated for mentally disordered males confined in security hospitals.

Similarly, Baker et al. (1970) indicate that they did not find the difference in prevalence of chromosome errors between penal and non-penal populations to be significant (at the .05 level) when subjects of all heights and all chromosomal categories were compared. Interestingly, some of the investigators whose earlier studies and reports led to some of the premature speculations about the XYY anomaly in recent years have urged more cautious conclusions (e.g., Jacobs et al., 1971). Similarly, other investigators have pointed out that individuals with the 47,XYY karyotype may have been unfairly stigmatized by being described as typically aggressive and violent (Clark et al., 1970).

While there have been numerous reports suggesting a fairly definite "47,XYY syndrome," the considerable variations in the cases discovered (including persons with average or even superior intelligence, as well as those without any history of trouble with the law) make it evident that no such consistent *syndrome* seems to exist in fact. Based upon his review of almost one-hundred cases Hienz (1969) describes four types of clinical pictures associated with the XYY anomaly. In all cases there was overgrowth manifested by increased height; the other variations related to intelligence, the presence of somatic or genital anomalies, and criminal or antisocial behavior. Since most of the cases studied by Hienz were derived from screening of institutional populations, when more cases of "normal" and well-functioning XYY individuals are located through surveys of the general population, the obtained heterogeneity would be expected to increase further.

In his recent review, Owen (1972) provides a long list of behavioral descriptions derived from case reports of 47,XYY males. A very wide and heterogeneous collection of descriptive terms has been used ranging from diagnoses of schizophrenia and personality disorder, to descriptions of "impulsivity," "irresponsibility," "inferiority feelings," "placid and obedient," "pleasant and cooperative," and also "serious" and "hardworking." Since the bulk of the cases reported in the literature have come from various institutionalized populations, it is hardly surprising that descriptions of psychiatric pathology and behavior problems have been abundant.

In view of the studies indicating an incidence rate of about 1:700 among newborn males,[8] and since there is no evidence that such individuals have any increased mortality compared to 46,XY males, it is obvious that literally thousands of males with such karyotypes must be present in the general population. For example, Jacobs et al. (1971) estimate that there are approximately 2,500 men with this anomaly in Scotland; only a small fraction of these have been located in the various institutions that have been screened for chromosomal anomalies.

We must conclude, therefore, that despite the fact that certain chromosomal abnormalities can and, indeed, do affect physical and mental functioning in various ways, and even though there have been numerous reported cases of incarcerated criminals with the XYY karyotype, there is no firm evidence at the present time that establishes a cause-and-effect relationship between this chromosome anomaly and criminal and aggressive behavior. However, a strong association has been indicated between the 47,XYY cases and mental and behavioral disorders by the *twentyfold* increased prevalence of such cases in security hospitals for mentally disordered offenders.

There are also a few studies (e.g., Nielsen, 1970; Tsuboi, 1970) that indicate that XYY offenders coming from disharmonious and broken homes tend to have histories of earlier and more frequent troubles with the law. Thus, the behavioral manifestations of the abnormal karyotype must be understood in reference to the particular environments which also influence the growth and development of the individual.

The 47,XXY Chromosomal Abnormality. The general picture of the 47,XXY male is more homogeneous (compared to the XYY cases) since this condition constitutes a well-studied clinical entity even independent of a laboratory diagnosis of the extra X chromosome. Indeed, the entity—commonly referred to as Klinefelter's syndrome (47,XXY)—was recognized for some time prior to the existence of the technology allowing for its laboratory diagnosis (Klinefelter et al., 1942). The Klinefelter cases typically present a normal developmental picture during infancy and childhood, but around puberty the anomaly becomes evident: these males show hypogonadism (soft and small testes), in many cases they develop gynecomastia (i.e., increased breast tissue, like that of an adolescent girl), diminished facial hair, and a female pattern of pubic hair distribution; they tend to be tall and thin with long legs and arms, and in practically all cases these males are sterile (Becker et al., 1966; Swanson & Stipes, 1969). Some impairment of intelligence (I.Q.s between 75 and 90) is common but is not invariable (Forssman, 1970). Androgen levels (testosterone) may also be normal, but usually are somewhat reduced; in about one-third of the cases sexual drive is reported to be decreased (Swanson & Stipes, 1969). A frequent phenotypic characteristic of these males is their increased stature, although they tend on the average to not be as tall as the 47,XYY males (Baker et al., 1970). The general

---

8. More recent data reviewed by Borgaonkar and Shah (1974) suggest that the incidence rate for the general population may be as low as one XYY case in 1,500 to 3,000 males.

estimated incidence of this chromosomal anomaly is about 1 in 700 newborn male births (Ratcliffe et al., 1970).

In addition to the aforementioned physical characteristics, it is the opinion of most investigators that these males are at greater risk for a variety of mental disorders, especially disturbances in the sexual area, e.g., homosexuality, transsexualism, pedophilia, and other sexual aberrations (Mosier et al., 1960; Baker & Stoller, 1968).

There have been numerous reports of an increased prevalence of Klinefelter males in institutions for the retarded and mental hospitals, as well as some penal populations (e.g., Forssman & Hambert, 1963; Nielsen & Fischer, 1965). While the newborn incidence and general population prevalence rates for Klinefelter males are estimated to be about 1 in 700 (Ratcliffe et al., 1970), in surveys of institutional populations, rates of 1 percent and even higher have been obtained (e.g., Nielsen & Fischer, 1965). A variety of diagnosable mental disorders have been reported among Klinefelter males; "immature" sexual practices and sex offenses against children also have been noted (e.g., Mosier et al., 1960; Swanson & Stipes, 1969; Nielson, 1970). However, it is impossible to say what proportion of unselected Klinefelter males exhibit these deviant characteristics; we suspect it would very likely not be as high as has been reported on the basis of the studies of institutionalized populations.

The interaction of organismic and environmental variables is again noted since Klinefelter males coming from disharmonious and disturbed family backgrounds tend to have higher rates for trouble with the law than such persons coming from more stable family backgrounds (e.g., Nielsen, 1970).

The specific links between the extra X chromosome and behavior likely to be labeled criminal are speculative at this point. Possible relationships of this disorder to focal hypothalamic endocrine pathology (as discussed earlier in this chapter) will be of future research interest. In the main, the various speculations which have been made in the literature remain simply that. For example, Hambert (1966) believes that the chromosomal unbalance in cells of the nervous system tends to lead to cerebral dysfunction; this dysfunction, in turn, expresses itself in a wide range of behavioral disorders.

However, many of the variables currently being explored are of a more psychological and social interest, such as uncertain gender identity, confusion and concern about the feminine physique (slim build with enlarged breast areas), and sparse facial hair distribution (Swanson & Stipes, 1969). Some investigators have been studying the EEG abnormalities, while others have been concerned with variations in endocrine (testosterone) levels and have even attempted treatment along these dimensions (e.g., Myhre et al., 1970). It is possible that the mental subnormality, social liabilities, and decreased overall social functioning, when coupled with probable psychological conflict and stress pertaining to their masculine identity, may well explain much of the behavior of the Klinefelter males. Such developmental stress may cause some individuals to withdraw, while others may act out sexually or aggressively in efforts to prove their masculinity.

The greater consistency of reports about the 47,XXY males does suggest more strongly than the literature on the 47,XYY cases that there is some relationship between the 47,XXY abnormality, a greater likelihood of behavioral disorders, and a criminal or antisocial label. As this brief review indicates, not all Klinefelter males are at risk for social, mental, and legal difficulties; in cases where behavior disorders do result, it seems that the chromosomal abnormality acts in conjunction with other factors (such as family background) to combine to determine the ultimate appearance of a case of disordered behavior.

In conclusion, then, we would suggest that the numerous reports in the literature, which tend to assert some kind of a direct and causal relationship between these types of chromosomal abnormalities (the 47,XYY and the 47,XXY) and criminal behavior, in many instances have gone beyond the conclusions that could reasonably be drawn from presently available data. While strong associations are clearly indicated when there is, for example, a *twentyfold* increase of XYY cases in security hospitals over the general population prevalence rates, the precise nature of the causal relationships remains to be established. However, such evidence does *not* merit peremptory dismissal as environmentally oriented scientists may feel inclined to do at times. Also, it seems quite possible that the phenotypic variations present in Klinefelter males may increase their vulnerability to certain behavioral and sexual problems.

It would certainly be a violation of the conceptual framework discussed earlier in this chapter, as well as of scientific thinking generally, to assume that aberrations of gross chromosomal structure would result exclusively, or even generally, in a very specific type of behavior: antisocial or criminal conduct. However, if there are anatomical, biochemical, or neurophysiological systems which depend upon specific genes, then it is possible that some nonspecific alterations of behavior may be produced. For example, greater height and size, hyperactivity, and aggressiveness could, in interactions with particular environmental influences, facilitate patterns of behavior socialized into athletics, sports, aggressive business, and other careers; such characteristics could also become channeled into patterns of behavior that may have a high probability of being socially defined as criminal.

Physique, Constitution, and Behavior

We have already alluded to some of the earlier attempts to relate constitutional factors to temperament and behavior, as well as to delinquent and criminal behavior more specifically. Here we shall summarize briefly a number of interesting and rather consistent findings from a variety of studies pertaining to the relationship of physique, temperament, and behavior. To place the interpretation of these findings within a broader frame of reference, we shall first discuss some of the hypothesized mechanisms through which the above relationship might be mediated and explained.

Some Possible Mediating Mechanisms. The studies to be discussed indicate a consistent pattern of relationship between certain aspects of physique and constitution, and certain characteristics of temperament and behavior. These patterns merit closer attention despite the fact that the available evidence concerning the association between physique and criminality, though very suggestive, requires more carefully designed replications.

However, critical questions remain concerning the specification of the pathways or mechanisms whereby these associations between physical and behavioral components might be verified. Lindzey (1967) suggests five possible and discriminable means for predicting these associations.

1. A common experiential or environmental class of events may have a characteristic influence upon personality or behavior and, at the same time, have a regular and detectable effect upon physique. Some research on the relationship between obesity and parent-child relations (e.g., maternal overprotectiveness), as well as other studies, have been cited by Lindzey as a basis for this hypothesis.

2. There is the inevitable observation that behavior is directly limited or facilitated to various degrees by physical characteristics. Thus, size and other physical

attributes of an individual have an obvious relationship to skills in athletics and sports, just as tonal discrimination is related to musical achievements. Dimensions of height, weight, and strength, along with other physical attributes, place rather direct general limits upon the responses the individual can hope to make adaptively in a given environmental setting.

3. Directly related to the preceding point, there are some fairly clear consequences of a particular set of physical attributes, even though they are indirect. For example, within our society, an individual who is well above average in size, strength, and coordination will tend to be recruited fairly early in life into competitive athletics; such experiences will also have an influence in terms of various social responses, which will further shape social roles and behaviors. It is very possible that two types of social selection may help to account for the higher proportion of mesomorphic individuals involved in officially defined delinquent and criminal behavior. First, the male, adolescent peer group may tend to provide peer-group reinforcement to "tough and masculine" boys and function to recruit them into delinquent activities. Such social reinforcement would be especially competitive with rewards for success in schools in high-delinquency areas where youth are more likely to be "on their own" due to familial and crowded housing circumstances. Second, differential responses to mesomorphic deviants by key decision-makers in the juvenile and criminal justice agencies may help to funnel a higher proportion of such individuals into the social control systems.

4. Within each society, various physical characteristics tend to have a social stimulus value, which tends to increase the likelihood of certain types of social responses. For example, to the extent that a given society holds some common expectations of the "fat man," the "redhead," the person with a "receding chin," and the "muscularly built male," it is likely that persons who fit these categories (whether the categories are stereotyped or not) will be exposed to a somewhat different set of environmental responses and social learning experiences.

5. We come, finally, to the mechanism that is probably most objectionable to many American social and behavioral scientists: joint biological determinants of both physique and behavior. This type of association could be produced by a set of physiological processes that demonstrably influence both constitution and behavior. Endocrine functioning could provide a possible example of such a physiological process. Or, the link might relate to a common set of genetic determinants, even though we do not have sufficient information at present concerning the exact processes by which genetic variations are translated into morphological and behavioral variations. Lindzey (1967) cites a number of studies which indicate that genetic variation makes a significant contribution to morphological variables. Given this observation, it seems reasonable to anticipate that a gene (or genes) that influences variations in morphology may have multiple effects, some of which may be manifested behaviorally. If we were to take examples from human genetic abnormalities, there are numerous instances of conditions that, under the normal range of environmental variation, are controlled by genetic factors and include *both* physical and behavioral deviations. For example, *Down's syndrome* (or mongolism), now known to be related to a translocation associated with the 21st chromosome, leads to a variety of rather clear-cut physical and behavioral consequences. Or, to take a more relevant, and as yet still not fully understood entity, we may consider the case of *Klinefelter's syndrome* (47,XXY) discussed previously. We have already indicated the several physical anomalies that led to the identification of this clinical entity long before the precise nature of the chromosomal variation had been discovered. Although more needs to be

learned about this syndrome, it seems possible that the genetic effects on the hormonal system which lead to hypogonadism and gynecomastia in Klinefelter males may also have certain behavioral effects.

Some Somatotype Studies. Several methods have been used for describing and measuring physique. Perhaps the best known is Sheldon's method (Sheldon et al., 1940; Sheldon & Stevens, 1942) of measuring the components of *endomorphy*, *mesomorphy*, and *ectomorphy*, with ratings for each dimension derived from a standardized set of photographs by means of a complex rating procedure. Parnell (1958) has devised another method in which he measures variables comparable to those of Sheldon but which are labeled *fat, muscularity*, and *linearity*. Parnell's rating system uses a thirteen-point (instead of Sheldon's seven-point) scale, proceeding from one to seven by half points.

In Sheldon's method an extreme endomorph (soft, round, and fat) would receive a score of 7–1–1; the extreme mesomorph (muscular, athletic, and bony) would receive a rating of 1–7–1; and the extreme ectomorph (tall, thin, and fragile) would receive a rating of 1–1–7. Sheldon (1949) found that the mean somatotype of 200 white, male, college students was 3.2–3.8–3.4, while the mean somatotype of 200 delinquents was: 3.5–4.6–2.7. The mean somatotype of serious delinquents, referred to as "criminals" by Sheldon, was: 3.4–5.4–1.8 (Cortes & Gatti, 1972:14).

Glueck and Glueck (1956) also reported on somatotype comparisons between their 500 persistent delinquents and 500 nondelinquents. Among the delinquents, mesomorphy was again found to be the most dominant component. They found that 60.1 percent of the delinquents were mesomorphic as compared with only 30.7 percent mesomorphy in the nondelinquents. However, as noted by several critics, there were many methodological problems in this somatotyping study, not the least of which was the unreliable aspect of the measurement procedures used.

Cortes and Gatti (1972) studied 100 delinquent and 100 nondelinquent boys and 20 incarcerated criminals. Their criterion of delinquency and criminality consisted of official adjudication. The nondelinquents were seniors from a private high school in the Boston area in the same age range (16.5 to 18.5 years) as the delinquent youngsters; none of the nondelinquents had any record of delinquency. The selection of the delinquents was *not* made by the researchers; rather, they asked the institutional authorities and probation officers for boys within the selected age range. All of the 220 subjects, however, were somatotyped by Cortes, a procedure which could have introduced a source of bias in the ratings. The mean somatotype of the nondelinquent boys was 3.9–3.5–3.5, while that of the delinquents was 3.5–4.4–3.1; the mean somatotype of the 20 adult criminals was 2.8–5.4–3.1.

There is an interesting and noteworthy consistency in the findings of Sheldon (1949), the Gluecks (Glueck & Glueck, 1956), and Cortes and Gatti (1972) in regard to the increased proportion of mesomorphy and ectomorphy among delinquents as compared with the nondelinquent groups also studied. In Sheldon's study 64.5 percent of the delinquents were mesomorphic and 7.0 percent were ectomorphic; the Gluecks found 60.1 percent mesomorphic and 14.4 percent ectomorphic; and Cortes and Gatti found 57.0 percent of the delinquents to be mesomorphic and 16.0 percent to be ectomorphic.

While all these studies could be criticized for certain methodological weaknesses, such as the selection and matching of delinquent and nondelinquent subjects and the possibilities of introducing bias in the rating procedures, the consistent relationship between mesomorphic physique and officially defined delinquent and criminal status is certainly noteworthy. Similar findings were also obtained by Gibbens (1963) in a study of delinquent English boys. A study by Epps and Parnell (1952) is of particular interest; they studied girls in England and found that, when compared with female college students, the delinquent females were shorter and heavier in build and more muscular.

While the major concern in this chapter is with criminality, a broader issue concerns the more general relationship or association between physique and personality or temperament. Two other studies are worth mentioning in this regard, especially since these researchers managed to minimize, more successfully than others, the possibilities of data or experimenter bias.

Child (1950) studied 414 male undergraduate college students. The students were routinely somatotyped as freshmen; later, as sophomores, they were asked to complete a questionnaire that consisted of multiple-choice questions concerning their own feelings and behavior. Each item was designed to measure some aspect of behavior that, on the basis of Sheldon's study (Sheldon & Stevens, 1942) of temperament, was believed to be related to one or more dimensions of physique. A total of ninety-four predictions were made, *in advance* of any data analysis, concerning associations between self-ratings and somatotype ratings; these predictions were reflections of what Sheldon had previously reported in his studies of physique and temperament. More than three-fourths (77 percent) of the predictions in regard to the direction of the relationship between physical components and self-ratings were confirmed; more than one-fifth of the predictions were confirmed at the .05 level, while only one of the findings that reversed the prediction was significant at this level.

A related study was done by Walker (1963) using 125 male and female nursery-school children as subjects. The somatotype measures were based upon ratings made *independently* by three different judges; their ratings were then combined and averaged. Each of the children was also rated from one to seven for sixty-four specific behavioral items by two of five judges; none of these judges were involved in the ratings of physique, and at least two of them were ignorant of the purpose of the study. The individual score for each item was again derived by averaging the judges' ratings. These items had been selected for their pertinence to Sheldon's findings (Sheldon & Stevens, 1942), and a total of 292 specific predictions were made *in advance* and tested separately for the male and female subjects. Altogether, 73 percent of the predictions were confirmed in direction and 21 percent were confirmed at or below the .05 level of significance; only 3 percent of the predictions were disconfirmed at the .05 level.

We wish to emphasize, however, that the findings of an association between certain constitutional components and temperament and behavior, of course, do *not* allow any causal inferences to be drawn.

Some Related Research. There is also evidence from closely related areas demonstrating a rather clear relationship between the variables of constitution and those of temperament and behavior. There has been considerable research pointing to the individuality of infants and children at very early stages of their development. In fact, several studies indicate that the individuality of children and their first signs of autonomy in infancy are heavily determined by their constitutional conditions and dispositions. For example, Walters (1965) was able to demonstrate that fetal movements during the seventh month were correlated significantly with postnatal motor and adaptive scores on the Gesell Development Schedules at 12, 24, and 36 weeks of age. Similarly, Lipton et al. (1961) were able to differentiate newborn infants according to cardiac-rate responses. These authors suggest that such physiological responses very likely form major links in the chain that leads to characteristic emotional manifestations in later years. Bridger (1961) was able to distinguish four groups of infants according to their ability to habituate and discriminate through their sensory apparatus. Some babies respond to most stimuli and habituate to them quickly; others respond to most stimuli but do not habituate or habituate slowly; still other babies respond to few stimuli but habituate quickly when they do respond; a fourth group of babies respond to few stimuli and do not habituate.

Thomas et al. (1963) conducted an extensive longitudinal study on temperamental patterns during the first two years of life. These investigators used nine categories for assessing individuality: activity level, rhythmicity, approach or withdrawal to new objects or situations, adaptability (responses to new or altered situations), threshold and intensity of responsiveness, quality of mood, distractibility, attention span, and persistence. It was found that initially identifiable characteristics of reactivity were persistent features of the child's behavior throughout the first two years of life. As an illustration of this finding, these investigators note that, other things being equal, children with clear-cut patterns of rhythmicity in elimination were more readily toilet trained than were children in whom evacuation of bowels occurred irregularly and with no temporal patterning. In addition to the major attention that has traditionally been given in psychology to the effects on the child of the parents' responses, these investigators suggest that the child's primary reaction pattern may well tend to influence the parents' immediate and persistent reactions to him.

These studies of infants point out that the issue of the relationship between constitution, temperament, and behavior is not limited simply to the relatively few studies that have concerned themselves with delinquent and criminal behavior. We would suggest that delinquency and criminality need to be viewed and understood within the broader framework of the relationships between constitution, physique, and particular patterns of behavior—regardless of whether the behavioral patterns are officially defined as delinquent or criminal.

Consistent with our conceptual framework, we again emphasize the importance of viewing genotype and environmental interactions as *jointly* determining various aspects of the phenotype. However, we note that the statements of some sociologists suggest a poor understanding and/or appreciation of the basic developments in modern genetics and biology. For example, Clinard writes "If . . . body type were associated with certain deviations, control would have to be achieved through selective eugenic breeding and sterilization" (1968:198).

Such statements by some of the leading criminologists in the field reflect an unfortunate state of affairs in the level of understanding of basic biological facts, and about the ways in which organismic and environmental variables influence the phenotype.

In summary, we have attempted to place the issue of the relationship between physique and criminal behavior within a broader perspective. A variety of evidence has been cited indicating a relationship between components of constitution and physique and those of temperament and behavior. Although we believe the available evidence regarding physique and criminality is not as convincing as it could be, in view of the methodological problems inherent in some of the studies cited above, we do feel that it would be inappropriate to dismiss out-of-hand findings which are both consistent and quite suggestive. Hopefully, this discussion will make it evident that the topic merits closer and more careful attention from criminologists than it has received in the past.

Psychophysiology and Criminology

The *autonomic nervous system* innervates the involuntary musculature of the internal organs and glands, and also determines the tone of the blood vessels. It contains two parts: (1) the *sympathetic nervous system* is dominant during periods of emotional arousal and stress (e.g., during anger, anxiety, and fear); it mediates the physiological concomitants of these states, such as fast heart rate, sweating, and changes in galvanic skin response (i.e., the resistance of the skin to an electric current); and (2) the *parasympathetic nervous system* is dominant during more quiescent and relaxed bodily states and during vegetative states, e.g., digestion of food. In contrast to the effects of the sympathetic system, the parasympathetic system builds up and conserves the body's store of energy, e.g., slowing of the heart, reduction of blood pressure, and diversion of blood to the digestive tract. However, the sympathetic and parasympathetic systems are not always opposed to each other; there are instances in which the parasympathetic system is also active during emotional states. Although the entire autonomic nervous system is structurally considered part of the peripheral nervous system, autonomic effects may be produced by central (i.e., cortical) stimulation. Also, Neal Miller (1969) has demonstrated that the autonomic nervous system, although traditionally considered "involuntary," is capable of both classical (Pavlovian) as well as instrumental (operant) conditioning.

Much of the research to be discussed here pertains to psychopathy or psychopathic personality. While there continues to be much dispute in psychiatric and psychological circles concerning the precise characteristics of this diagnostic category, the most frequently employed criteria for recognizing this disorder still appear to be those listed by Cleckley (1955:380–81): (1) superficial charm and good intelligence; (2) absence of delusions and other psychotic signs; (3) absence of "nervousness" and other psychoneurotic features; (4) unreliability; (5) untruthfulness and insincerity; (6) lack of remorse or shame; (7) inadequately motivated antisocial behavior; (8) poor judgment and failure to learn from experience; (9) pathological egocentricity and incapacity for love; (10) general poverty in major emotional reactions; (11) specific lack of insight; (12) unresponsiveness to general interpersonal relationships; (13) fantastic and uninviting behavior, sometimes provoked by alcohol; (14) suicide rarely carried out; (15) sex life impersonal and poorly integrated; and (16) failure to follow any life plan.

While these criteria are admittedly very general and, in varying degrees, they could apply to a variety of poorly socialized individuals, the accumulation of the several characteristics as well as their degree, do tend to discriminate individuals described as psychopaths or sociopaths from a broader range of persons with other personality disorders. The psychophysiological research to be discussed has attempted to elucidate the physiological substrates of these personality and behavioral characteristics.

Eysenck's studies (1964) with the Maudsley Personality Inventory have led to the delineation of two independent axes along which personality characteristics may be placed: the introversion-extraversion dimension, and the stable-unstable (or neuroticism) dimension. He has reviewed evidence that certain prisoners and psychopathic groups are more likely to be extraverts (i.e., outgoing, active, sociable and impulsive) than introverts (individuals inclined to be quiet, passive, and somewhat unsociable). Eysenck has also reviewed various experiments which show that extraverts condition more poorly than introverts. These aspects of conditionability are related, Eysenck points out, to aspects of anxiety, fear, and conscience development. The thrust of Eysenck's position, to simplify a very involved discussion, is that extraverts (especially those with features of "instability") condition poorly to socializing experiences and thus are at greater risk for psychopathy and other forms of socially deviant behavior. In brief, Eysenck suggests that there is a constitutional predisposition to psychopathy.

Some landmark research on psychopathy and conditionability was done by Lykken (1955, 1957); this work has led to a considerable volume of subsequent research aimed at further clarification and elucidation of the original findings. In brief, Lykken found that nonimprisoned "normals" displayed a ready ability in avoidance-learning situations, where errors resulted in administration of a shock. In contrast, psychopaths or sociopaths (the terms generally are used synonymously) manifested very poor avoidance learning; these subjects received about as many shocks at the end of the learning experiment as during the first few trials. A group of non-sociopathic prisoners was intermediate between the extreme groups (the nonimprisoned normals and the confined sociopaths); the non-sociopathic prisoners displayed better avoidance learning than the sociopaths, but did not perform as well as the normals.

Lykken's research has been replicated by Schachter and Latane (1964) in a very elegant series of experiments; similar work has also been done by many other investigators. The essential findings by Lykken, as well as those derived from Schachter and Latane's replication, are very clear: normals and sociopaths are equally capable of learning positively reinforced tasks (rewarded learning); however, on avoidance learning (which, presumably, is mediated by anxiety), the two groups differ sharply—normals learn very well, but sociopaths learn very poorly. Schachter and Latane (1964) carried this work further. Prison psychologists and case workers were provided Cleckley's description (1955) of sociopaths and were asked to nominate prisoners who fit the description closely, as well as prisoners who did not. Using a blind experimental design with alternating placebo, these investigators were able to show that while sociopaths did not improve their avoidance learning at all when injected with a placebo, they were able to learn dramatically well when injected with adrenalin (a sympathomimetic drug). In contrast, normals appeared to be adversely affected by adrenalin and did not learn well at all under this condition. Thus, there appears to be a marked interaction between degree of sociopathy and the effects of sympathetic arousal on avoidance-learning ability.

Schachter and Latane (1964) cite various studies indicating the greater autonomic reactivity of sociopaths. It has also been suggested, and verified by experimental research, that subjects who improved their avoidance learning in response to adrenalin will tend to manifest sociopathic behavior. It would appear, then, that failure to learn shock avoidance on Lykken's apparatus may provide an analog for the real-life situation of sociopaths, in that these individuals seem unable to profit from social experiences and appear less able to avoid behaviors likely to result in punishing consequences. Schachter and Latane's studies revealed that reactivity to adrenalin was, in fact, a better predictor of avoidance-learning ability than any single one or even any combination of Cleckley's criteria (1955) of psychopathy. This remarkable relationship (significant at approximately the .005 level) most certainly indicates that adrenalin sensitivity is involved in the sociopathic complex.

While these experimental findings are fairly clear, indeed even dramatic, their interpretation is not such a simple matter. Schachter and Latane (1964) suggest that sociopaths are individuals characterized by marked autonomic reactivity and who, over the course of their development, have not learned to apply emotional labels to their states of arousal. This interpretation by Schachter and Latane indicates that sociopathy may be derived from the physiological condition of autonomic hyper-reactivity, rather than that the autonomic hyper-reactivity is derived from a series of assumptions about the cognitive and psychodynamic world of sociopaths. (In other research, Schachter [1964] and Schachter and Singer [1962] have demonstrated that sympathetic arousal is not necessarily associated with an emotional state; cognitive and situational factors determine whether or not a state of physiological arousal will be labeled as an emotion.)

In some related studies Schachter and Wheeler (1962) tried to test the notion that fear and anxiety may provide an inhibiting effect on antisocial impulses. In an experimental study of cheating, they used chlorpromazine (because of its sympathetic depressant effects) to reduce fear. It was found that 30.3 percent of all chlorpromazine subjects cheated as compared with only 19.7 percent of subjects on placebo. The results were even more marked when the data were analyzed for chlorpromazine subjects on whom the drug had clear effects (as measured by indices such as dryness of the mouth, stuffiness of the nose, and pulse changes). Some 40 percent of the subjects on whom the drug worked had cheated, as compared with about 20 percent of subjects on placebo. This difference was significant by chi-square analysis at the .02 level of confidence.

Given the presumed emotional flatness of the sociopaths, these autonomic characteristics should dampen both the restraints against committing criminal acts, as well as the intensity of impulses to commit such acts. Quite obviously, however, criminal behavior is not motivated only by factors of emotion or passion, but also because of acquisitiveness and factors of economic or other gain. Thus, one might anticipate different patterns of crime for normals and sociopaths. Generally speaking, suggest Schachter and Latane (1964), sociopaths should be involved in predominantly "cool" crimes such as burglary, forgery, con games, and the like; normals should tend more often to be involved in activities such as assaults, sex crimes, and manslaughter. Based upon an analysis of the criminal subjects in their study, Schachter and Latane found that only 40 percent of the forty-five sociopaths, as compared to 69 percent of the thirty-five normals, had committed a crime at any point in their criminal careers that by any stretch of legal categorization might include elements of passion, e.g., assault, manslaughter, or rape. This finding was obtained despite the fact that the sociopaths averaged almost twice as many crimes as did the normals. On the whole sociopaths were chronic burglars and con men.

We wish to emphasize that the extension of the experimental findings by Schachter and Latane (1964) to comparisons of the actual criminal patterns of sociopaths and normals involves all the questions and complexities of the particular samples studied, as well as the unreliability of the entire criminal justice response to criminal behavior. What should be focused upon especially, however, is the rather clear-cut finding that certain physiological components do seem to discriminate sociopaths from normals, and that these physiological factors have been rather precisely related in laboratory experiments to the sociopaths' demonstrated inability to learn under conditions of punishment avoidance.

As interesting as the findings of Schachter and Latane (1964) are, it must be noted that other related research has pointed to the great complexities of delineating the relationships between psychological and physiological components, as well as to some of the conceptual problems which definitely remain to be clarified.

Hare (1970) has summarized the mass of work done in these areas, including his own research. He reports some findings which appear to contradict, in some ways, the work of Schachter and Latane. Contrary to the findings of Schachter and Latane and others, Hare indicates that on many measures of autonomic reactivity the response of psychopaths is diminished compared to normals. That is, the normal state of sociopaths is one of hypo-arousal, and they show less anxiety than do normals. Hare summarizes many other lines of evidence suggesting that a fundamental defect in sociopathy is one of diminished responsiveness to environmental stimuli. Like Eysenck (1956, 1964), Hare also relates this defect to subsequent poor learning, specifically, an inability to acquire conditioned fear responses.

While some of Hare's findings do appear to contradict those of Schachter and Latane, our own assessment of this rather complicated data leads us to believe that the problem relates more to interpretation of the obtained findings than to basic contradiction in the salient features of the findings reported earlier in this section. Certainly, concepts such as hypo- and hyper-arousal and hypo- and hyper-reactivity, which are used by all workers in this field, require further clarification and empirical support before their full meaning and implications will become clear. Also, as with the endocrine data presented earlier in this chapter, data obtained from cross-sectional studies must be cautiously interpreted in reference to cause-and-effect relationships.

However, there are certain findings which remain consistent across clinical as well as experimental studies:

1. Psychiatrists and other clinicians for many years have identified a class of persons characterized by emotional flatness and chronic misbehavior as psychopaths or sociopaths. Lykken, Schachter and Latane, Hare, and many others have experimentally verified the relatively "anxiety-free" nature of sociopaths.

2. The body of experimental studies has demonstrated fairly consistently that a variety of emotional states, including fear and anxiety, can be influenced through the manipulation of sympathetic nervous system activation.

3. The experiment with chlorpromazine and its effect on cheating suggests that even a weak sympathetic depressant can facilitate at least some mild forms of "antisocial" behavior.

4. Almost all of this research has pointed to the ability of sociopaths to learn as well as normals under conditions of positive reinforcement, and also to their marked *inability* to learn under conditions of pain avoidance.

In the light of these findings, it seems evident that the chronic misbehavior of sociopaths and their generally poor response to efforts to change such behavior patterns are *not* simply a function of socialization experiences, and subcultural and related factors. At least for the class of persons described as sociopaths, there is presumably a constitutional (physiological) component that interacts with certain environmental variables to generate sociopathic and related patterns of behavior. Moreover, the physiological characteristics particularly manifested by sociopaths are not distributed in an all-or-none fashion. As indicated by Lykken's (1955) group of non-sociopathic prisoners, who placed between the sociopaths and nonimprisoned normals on avoidance learning, these characteristics appear to have wider distribution.

Since sociopaths seem to learn quite well under conditions of positive reinforcement but very poorly in avoidance situations, the considerable advances in the experimental analysis of behavior and related behavior-modification technology appear to hold much relevance for more effective procedures for socializing and treating such persons.

BIOLOGICALLY ORIENTED (MEDICAL) ASPECTS OF PREVENTION AND TREATMENT

As indicated in our conceptual framework, it is not possible to go directly from biological variables of the kinds described to patterns of behavior socially defined as delinquent and criminal. There is no medical treatment for armed robbery, murder, assault, larceny, nor, in fact, for any other *crime*. To make such a claim would violate logic as well as our conceptual scheme. In discussing biologically oriented approaches to the prevention and treatment of delinquency and crime, we focus on behaviors and related problems that are amenable to medical intervention and remediation.

Some Considerations Pertaining to Prevention

In addressing the very broad issue of crime prevention, we will discuss first the public health concepts and strategies of primary, secondary, and tertiary prevention (Caplan, 1964). The use of these public health concepts is not designed to suggest, nor even to imply, that problems of delinquency and crime need to be viewed and handled within a medical framework. Rather, in view of the many differing notions of *prevention* in the criminological literature, we wish to use the public health concepts to illustrate various levels, targets, and stages of preventive intervention, as well as to point to the logic for these approaches.

Primary prevention refers to the most fundamental aspect of preventive medicine: prevention of the development of a disorder. For example, in infectious diseases this effort would involve immunization, public sanitation, and related measures. In problems of delinquency and crime, primary prevention efforts would be directed generally towards criminogenic aspects of the sociocultural environment, as well as at especially vulnerable population groups. In a very real sense, these efforts seek to get at more basic causes of the problem, they require relatively large expenditures, and they may often entail major improvements in social systems and institutions concerned with the delivery of essential services, especially to population groups "at risk." Primary prevention efforts also involve major sociopolitical considerations, assessments of priorities, and decisions pertaining to broad public policy.

Secondary prevention refers essentially to early case finding as a way of decreasing future and more serious morbidity. The medical examples here would pertain to the screening of population groups for tuberculosis, heart disease, and related problems. In the concerns of this chapter, such preventive efforts would involve attention to individuals and groups manifesting early signs of behavioral and social problems, which are logically and empirically related to increased risks of subsequent delinquency and crime. For example, secondary prevention efforts could be directed toward youngsters who have begun to manifest serious learning and behavior problems in the classroom and who display patterns of aggressive and violent behavior. Such early behaviors may be especially worthy of attention when they involve youngsters from more socially disadvantaged population groups. However, given the possibilities of stigmatizing labels, self-fulfilling prophesies, and related problems of accurate predictions, as well as the effectiveness of preventive interventions, a sound empirical approach—rather than one based primarily upon ideological zeal—is very essential. Interventions also need to be directed at those aspects of the social environment that seem to evoke and facilitate deviant behaviors. Various policy and programmatic decisions also have to be made concerning the precise points at which secondary prevention efforts should be initiated, the resources needed for such interventions, and consideration of costs and benefits.

Tertiary prevention involves the adequate treatment of existing cases of a disorder or problem so as to prevent further relapses or deterioration. In our particular areas of concern, these efforts pertain essentially to reducing recidivism among adjudicated and convicted offenders.

Although it is difficult to estimate the amounts (or even the general proportions) of societal resources allocated to these types of delinquency and crime-prevention efforts, it is our impression that the greatest attention and the largest proportion of resources are devoted to tertiary prevention, i.e., efforts to deal with the problems after they have become quite obvious.

We shall now discuss the relevance and implications of these biological variables to various strategies of delinquency and crime prevention.

Primary Prevention. For at least four of the various biological disorders or anomalies we have discussed in this chapter (epilepsy, endocrine-related problems, perinatal pathology, minimal brain dysfunction, and possibly chromosomal disorders), primary prevention lies, at least partly, in the provision of adequate nutrition and prenatal and postnatal care to the most vulnerable mothers and infants. This involves population groups that are most disadvantaged from a socioeconomic standpoint.

Specifically, in our previous discussion dealing with the correlates and effects of perinatal pathology, studies have demonstrated rather consistently the relationship of prematurity and complications of pregnancy to a variety of disorders, e.g., cerebral palsy, epilepsy, mental deficiency, behavior disorders, and learning difficulties (see, e.g., Pasamanick & Knobloch, 1966). Epilepsy may be associated with brain damage, which can be sustained during intrauterine life and delivery; thus, adequate care of mothers and infants seems obviously important in the prevention of future morbidity (Taylor & Bower, 1971). Brain damage sustained at birth provides at least one possible explanation for the syndrome of minimal brain dysfunction, retardation, and childhood behavior disorders. Robinson and Puck (1967) have reported evidence that chromosome disorders appear to be associated with depressed socioeconomic status, even though the nature or mechanism for such a relationship is not presently known.

Moreover, toxemias of pregnancy, placental disorders, and prematurity, as well as most nonspecific acute and chronic infections, are all heavily aggregated in the lowest socioeconomic groups in our population. Infants born in these groups, therefore, are not only at greatest risk prenatally, but the risks continue postnatally in terms of continued disadvantages pertaining to nutrition, general physical and medical care, and availability of remedial resources (Knobloch & Pasamanick, 1966; Pasamanick & Knobloch, 1966; Birch, 1971). Needless to say, the socioeconomically depressed and disadvantaged groups contribute very heavily to almost all indices of social morbidity including the phenomena of delinquency and crime as indicated by official statistics.

There is, however, some promising recent evidence that the effects of very low birth weight may be remedied if proper intensive care and treatment are available for such infants (Rawlings et al., 1971). There is also experimental evidence (Tompkins & Wiehl, 1954) indicating the beneficial effects of dietary supplements in reducing toxemias and the incidence of premature births. The highest incidence of severe or moderate toxemias occurs in patients who are 15 percent or more underweight at the start of pregnancy. This study showed that patients who received *both* protein and vitamin supplements had an incidence of toxemias of 0.6 percent, and all these cases were mild. The group with no dietary supplements had an incidence of toxemias almost 8 times greater, 4.7 percent; while those who had *either* protein or vitamin supplements had a toxemia incidence of 2.2 percent.

It seems evident, therefore, that national resources allocated for prenatal and perinatal care among the most disadvantaged societal groups may well offer one of the best ways to minimize a variety of future handicaps among children whose socioeconomic and ethnic circumstances alone make them more vulnerable to future delinquent and criminal labels.

To the extent that prematurity and complications of pregnancy have been shown to be etiologically related to a variety of behavior disorders and learning difficulties (see, e.g., Knobloch & Pasamanick, 1966), and to the extent that these patterns of behavior appear logically to increase the risk of delinquent and criminal labels, these primary prevention efforts bear a fairly clear relationship to the problems of our concern in this chapter.

Secondary Prevention. In this category of preventive efforts for purposes of illustration, we shall discuss minimal brain dysfunction, and shall allude briefly to the Klinefelter cases (47,XXY) to indicate some future possibilities. The beneficial effects of the stimulant type of drugs in the treatment of minimal brain dysfunction has been noted previously. We must stress again, however, that the organic underpinnings of this disorder are presently unclear. Moreover, we do *not* equate minimal brain dysfunction or hyperkinesis with organic brain damage. It has also been pointed out that there is no single type of hyperactive child (Fish, 1971). Nevertheless, drug treatment with the amphetamines for carefully diagnosed cases does appear indicated in some children with behavior problems associated with hyperactivity, poor concentration, poor attention, and related behavior problems (Bazell, 1971). These types of drugs also have been found to be beneficial in the treatment of learning disorders associated with the aforementioned problems (Conners et al., 1969).

The available evidence is not strong enough to allow the recommendation of broad screening programs to detect and medically treat cases of this behavioral syndrome. However, it is our opinion that children with a clear, medically established diagnosis of minimal brain dysfunction, or with symptoms suggesting such a diagnosis, do require early evaluation and appropriate treatment. These behavioral problems (hyperactivity, irritability, restlessness, etc.) could easily be further complicated and compounded as a function of social interactions with teachers and peers, and the child could be propelled into roles and behaviors that would increase the likelihood of labeling as a delinquent. In contrast, successful management of this disorder in grade school, along with appropriate psychological and educational assistance, might help to prevent scholastic problems, dropping out of school, and related behavior problems.

The *Klinefelter syndrome* cases provide an interesting example where hormone therapy appears to hold some promise as a way of preventing some of the psychopathological features that accompany this condition. Myhre et al. (1970) describe the results of testosterone treatment of five Klinefelter males over a seven-month period and report that the men became more assertive, more alert, and that they demonstrated an increase in goal-directed behavior and better work performance. The subjects also developed an apparent increase in muscle mass and a more masculine body contour. The investigators note that testosterone therapy for incomplete masculinization or for feminization may be more appropriate for Klinefelter males during adolescence, rather than in the pre- or postadolescent periods.

Tertiary Prevention. This type of intervention needs special diagnostic studies to ascertain the presence of the episodic dyscontrol syndrome in offenders with histories of recurrent and easily elicited violent behavior. Appropriate pharmacological treatment could be provided then in conjunction with various other treatment and rehabilitative programs (see, e.g., Monroe, 1970; Bach-y-Rita et al., 1971).

Some Biologically Oriented Approaches to Treatment

Another way of addressing the relevant medical issues concerning the treatment of delinquents and offenders is to conceptualize a continuum of behaviors, ranging from fairly global to quite specific, which may be affected by therapeutic drugs.

Aggressive, Episodic, and Related Behavior Disorders. Eisenberg et al. (1963) performed a controlled double-blind study using dextroamphetamine with delinquent boys who had been judged to be the most troublesome in their cottages. The behaviors of the boys before, during, and after drug treatment were rated by means of a forty-three item symptom scale covering a wide range of personal and social behaviors. A positive drug effect was demonstrated with improved functioning for the youths receiving amphetamine. It may be noted that similar observations have been made for at least thirty years (e.g., Korey, 1944), although not on the basis of carefully controlled studies.

There have been numerous reports indicating the usefulness of anticonvulsant drugs for the treatment of certain episodic (epileptoid) behavior disorders accompanied by aggressive behavior (e.g., Monroe, 1970). It appears that anticonvulsants (with or without one of the minor tranquilizers such as Librium) hold some value for treating aggressive prison inmates (e.g., Turner, 1969). The favorable effects of Dilantin (diphenylhydantoin) on irritability, explosiveness, and aggressive behavior in selected prison inmates have also been described by Resnick (1967).

However, this literature is simply not clear enough at this point to allow any definitive statements. Although several glowing reports have appeared, we note particularly the lack of significant results when carefully controlled double-blind studies have been conducted (e.g., Lefkowitz, 1969; Looker & Conners, 1970; Conners et al., 1971). As things stand now, the treating physician needs to consider the usefulness of Dilantin and related drugs on a case by case basis; some of the reports do indicate very obvious and marked improvements achieved with these drugs.

Sheard (1971) has reported on the effectiveness of lithium carbonate for prison inmates with histories of aggressive and assaultive behavior. A single-blind experimental design with alternating placebo was used (i.e., the patients did not know when they were on the drug and when on placebo). Results were measured on the basis of ratings of aggressiveness done independently by prison staff by counting the number of violations of prison rules and related behavior problems. A good response to lithium was revealed, especially for inmates of mesomorphic constitution and for those who found their own aggressiveness to be a source of tension and anxiety.

Other cases of aggressive and psychotic behaviors in penal institutions are related to these considerations. In cases of psychosis, with or without accompanying violence, a number of drugs are available which offer useful therapeutic effects. Among the major tranquilizers, Haldol (Haloperidol) has been found effective in the treatment and management of chronically assaultive and psychotic inmates who were unresponsive to phenothiazine-type drugs (Darling, 1971). Haldol has also been found to be effective in controlled studies with psychiatric outpatients and children hospitalized for various types of behavior disorders (Barker & Fraser, 1968; Cunningham et al., 1968). In the outpatient treatment and management of persons who threaten violence and who have histories of such behavior, Valium and drugs like Thorazine have been found to be useful agents (Lion et al., 1968).

Sexual Disorders. It is in the area of sexual disorders that we probably find the closest equivalence between certain behaviors and the likelihood of receiving a criminal label. A variety of drugs are now available which can influence sexual response and behavior.

Golla and Hodge (1949) reviewed earlier literature and noted that sexual drive and desire (libido) may be reduced in males by the administration of estrogen (female hormone) compounds. These authors reported thirteen cases in which libido was decreased after administration of estrogen to persons complaining of "an uncontrollable sexual urge" that had led to trouble. In a more recent report Norris and Lloyd (1971) note that administration of estrogens to sexually active men leads to rapid loss of sexual drive and potency. Money (1970) and other workers at Johns Hopkins University are investigating the effectiveness of Provera (a progestational compound with antiandrogen effects) with sexual offenders.

A more recent report by Cooper et al. (1972) describes the results of anti-androgen therapy (using cyproterone acetate) in three cases of hypersexuality accompanied by compulsive and aggressive sexual behavior. One of the cases, for example, involved a 40-year-old man who had made a number of sexual assaults upon his 15-year-old daughter, and had manifested various other forms of sexually deviant behavior. In all cases there was considerable erotic arousal and compulsive sexual fantasies, along with poorly controlled behavioral manifestations of such urges. Administration of the drug resulted in reductions in erotic fantasies, sexual urges, and related sexual behaviors in all cases. In addition to the sexual inhibitory effects, the drug also had an unmistakable general tranquilizing action. Three weeks after stopping the drug, sexual responsiveness had returned to pretrial levels, along with increases in levels of plasma testosterone. Thus, the effects of the drug are not only quick, but they are readily reversible with no side effects or toxic manifestations noted. Moreover, there were no signs of feminization (an advantage over estrogen), and both clinical and endocrine effects were completely reversible after eight weeks.

Pharmacological treatment in certain cases (e.g., assaultive and violent individuals and those convicted for sexual crimes) has possible advantages where very long penal sentences are typically provided. Similarly, in twenty-eight states there are special laws pertaining to "sexual psychopaths" (and similarly designated sexual and other dangerous offenders) which provide for their *indeterminate* confinement (Brakel & Rock, 1971).

With further advances in therapeutic methods, appropriate outpatient treatment and handling of such offenders could offer an alternative to long-term confinement in penal and related institutions. Moreover, while the endocrine agents used with sex offenders do not have lasting effects after the drug is discontinued, their treatment could be accompanied with other forms of behavioral therapy designed to bring about better discrimination and control in the expression of sexual urges without running afoul of the law.

We do wish to emphasize, however, that prior to the use of these treatment modalities further research is needed to ascertain the consequences (after- and side effects) of long-term use of such drugs, as well as to obtain more precise information about their effectiveness based upon carefully controlled experimental studies. Since incarceration, especially for long-term and indeterminate periods, reflects a very stringent and even deleterious form of social control, the possibilities for community-based treatment could offer a socially acceptable, as well as a more humanitarian, approach to the treatment and handling of such offenders. Use of these drugs in legal settings, however, would clearly require very careful monitoring in order to guard against possible misuse of such therapeutic procedures.

SUMMARY AND CONCLUSIONS

We have attempted in the foregoing review and discussion to point to a variety of biological variables which have relevance and importance for a more complete understanding of delinquent and criminal behavior. Our objective has not been to emphasize the organismic factors in opposition to social and environmental variables, nor to pit nature against nurture in a continuation of an outmoded debate on an incorrectly posed issue. Rather, since the phenotypic characteristics of an organism are the result of continuous interactions between the genotype and the environments to which the genotype is exposed, we have emphasized that more adequate information about organismic variables is necessary for a better understanding of human behavior—including socially deviant behavior.

Among the biological variables that we have discussed are: disorders of the limbic portions of the brain; the continuum of epilepsy-related disorders; endocrine-related problems; perinatal pathology and its strong association with socioeconomic class; minimal brain dysfunction; some suggested genetic factors; sex-chromosome disorders; more recent studies of physique, temperament, and behavior; and some constitutional and psychophysiological factors.

We have tried to maintain an objective stance in our delineation of the biological data presented; conflicting and contradictory evidence has also been discussed in the interest of providing an accurate and complete picture. The major purpose of this chapter was to bring to the attention of criminologists recent developments in the biological sciences, which typically are not presented in appropriate detail and perspective in most criminological writings.

The basic issue here is not one of asking if certain biological factors are absolutely deterministic of certain delinquent or criminal behaviors. The material presented in this chapter certainly does not indicate any inevitable or absolute relationship of biological variables with deviant behaviors. Rather, given certain behavioral sequences, we need to be concerned about the biological variables that should be considered as part of a more comprehensive system of explanation. Our basic point in this chapter has been to suggest that in problems of crime and delinquency, much evidence indicates that biological factors should be considered in any adequate scientific explanation.

The very social groups which account for high rates of officially recorded delinquency and crime are also markedly overrepresented in the "continuum of reproductive casualties." Certain prenatal, perinatal, and postnatal factors (complications of pregnancy, prematurity, and malnutrition) are associated with a variety of neurological and related disorders in the child. These problems are exacerbated by postnatal social experiences which add further stress to the affected youngsters from the aforementioned population groups, and make them more vulnerable to a variety of difficulties in adapting to existing societal situations.

Official statistics also point to the much heavier involvement of young males (especially nonwhites) in delinquent and criminal behavior. In fact, considerable reference has been made in the literature to the concepts of shared values, conduct norms, sex-role expectations, and social-class variations as they differentially influence the male's concern with "toughness," "heart," "rep," and related preoccupation with *maschismo.*

Important as these social factors unquestionably are, the role of endocrine hormones (testosterone levels) in sexual differentiation, as well as with the behavioral characteristics of assertiveness and aggression, is also noteworthy. It is clear, however, that the biological influences interact with social variables and are generally considerably shaped and modified by the social experiences.

At various points in this chapter, we have noted the rather strong disciplinary and ideological biases which seem to be reflected in the alacrity with which sociologists and criminologists dismiss biologically based notions regarding human behavior, including deviant behavior. Such sociological antipathy for biogenic factors has also been noted by several other commentators (e.g., Eckland, 1967; Means, 1967; Bressler, 1968). The usual biogenic explanations and related ameliorative proposals appear to be either ignored or introduced in a polemical context to discount their importance.

Bressler (1968) has suggested that some of the sociological resistance to social biology may be related to the ideology of welfare liberalism, which claims the loyalty of most sociologists. These ideological commitments and certain historical examples of exaggerated *biologism* appear to have colored sociological views about genetics and biology. Regrettably, many sociologists do not seem to realize that to point out that part of the variance for a trait is genetically determined *does not* imply the absence of environmental influences upon such characteristics. In a very real sense, every characteristic of an organism is both genetic and environmental in origin. While the genotype determines the potentialities of an organism, the environment determines to what degree and which of these potentialities will be realized during the course of development.

Quite understandably, the conceptual, theoretical, and methodological orientations of scientists in various disciplines tend to determine, and even to constrain, the questions that are likely to be asked, and the manner in which answers are to be obtained, as well as explained. Problems of delinquency and crime require much more attention than could possibly be provided by any one or two disciplines. These behaviors, like all human behavior, are determined by a very large and heterogeneous array of biological, social, psychological, and other factors. Any claim or suggestion by a particular discipline to have discovered a single cause or even a set of causes underlying all this complexity would be presumptuous and, indeed, would offend scientific credibility. Hence, collaborative and multidisciplinary efforts need to be facilitated diligently. Moreover, the basic scientific value of open-mindedness, in our view, needs to be further reinforced and supported by greater exposure to and information about closely related disciplines if better integrated knowledge and understanding are to be achieved in the life sciences.

REFERENCES

Aird, R. B.
   1968   "Clinical syndromes of the limbic system." International Journal of Neurology 6:340–352.

Aird, R. B., A. M. Venturini, and P. M. Spielman.
   1967   "Antecedents of temporal lobe epilepsy." Archives of Neurology 16:67–73.

Alstrom, C. A.
   1950   "A study of epilepsy in its clinical, social, and genetic aspects." Acta Psychiatrica et Neurologica. Supplement 63:1–284.

Antonovsky, A.
   1967   "Social class, life expectancy, and overall mortality." Milbank Memorial Fund Quarterly 45(2) Part 1:31–73.

Bach-y-Rita, G., J. R. Lion, C. E. Climent, and F. R. Ervin.
   1971   "Episodic dyscontrol: a study of 130 violent patients." American Journal of Psychiatry 127:1473–1478.

Bach-y-Rita, G., J. R. Lion, and F. R. Ervin.
   1970   "Pathological intoxication: clinical and electroencephalographic studies." American Journal of Psychiatry 127:698–703.

Bagley, C.
    1971   The Social Psychology of the Epileptic Child. Coral Gables, Fla.: University
            of Miami Press.

Baker, D.
    1972   "Chromosome errors and antisocial behavior." CRC Critical Reviews in
            Clinical Laboratory Sciences 3:41–101.

Baker, D., M. A. Telfer, C. E. Richardson, and G. R. Clark.
    1970   "Chromosome errors in men with antisocial behavior. Comparison of se-
            lected men with 'Klinefelter's syndrome' and XYY chromosome pattern."
            Journal of the American Medical Association 214:869–878.

Baker, H. J., and R. J. Stoller.
    1968   "Sexual psychopathology in the hypogonadal male." Archives of General
            Psychiatry 18:631–634.

Bard, P.
    1928   "A diencephalic mechanism for the expression of rage with special reference
            to the sympathetic nervous system." American Journal of Physiology 84:
            490–515.

Barker, P., and I. A. Fraser.
    1968   "A controlled trial of haloperidol in children." British Journal of Psychiatry
            114:855–857.

Bazell, R. J.
    1971   "Panel sanctions amphetamines for hyperkinetic children." Science 171:
            1223.

Becker, K. L., D. L. Hoffman, A. Albert, L. O. Underdahl, and H. L. Mason.
    1966   "Klinefelter's syndrome, clinical and laboratory findings in 50 patients."
            Archives of Internal Medicine 118:314–321.

Belmont, I., and A. Handler.
    1971   "Delayed information processing and judgement of temporal order follow-
            ing cerebral damage." Journal of Nervous and Mental Disease 152:353–361.

Bennett, D. R.
    1967   "Control electroencephalographic study of flying personnel." International
            Psychiatry Clinics 4(1):23–35.

Birch, H. G.
    1971   "Functional effects of fetal malnutrition." Hospital Practice 6(3):134–148.

Black, P. (ed.)
    1970   Physiological Correlates of Emotion. New York: Academic Press.

Bleicher, S. J.
    1970   "Hypoglycemia," in M. Ellenberg and H. Rifkin (eds.), Diabetes Mellitus,
            Theory and Practice. New York: McGraw-Hill.

Blumer, D.
    1970   "Changes of sexual behavior related to temporal lobe disorders in man."
            Journal of Sex Research 6:173–180.

Boelkins, R. C., and J. F. Heiser.
    1970   "Biological bases of aggression," in D. N. Daniels, M. F. Gilula, and F. M.
            Ochberg (eds.), Violence and the Struggle for Existence. Boston: Little,
            Brown.

Borgaonkar, D. S., and S. A. Shah.
  1974   "The XYY chromosome male—or syndrome?" in A. A. Steinberg and A. G. Bearn (eds.), Progress in Medical Genetics, vol. 10. New York: Grune & Stratton (in press).

Borgaonkar, D. S., W. M. Unger, S. M. Moore, and T. A. Crofton.
  1972   "47,XYY syndrome, height, and institutionalization of juvenile delinquents." British Journal of Psychiatry 120:549–550.

Brain, W. R., and J. N. Walton.
  1969   Brain's Diseases of the Nervous System. London: Oxford University Press.

Brakel, S. J., and R. S. Rock (eds.)
  1971   The Mentally Disabled and the Law. Revised Edition. Chicago: University of Chicago Press.

Bressler, M.
  1968   "Sociology, biology, and ideology," in D. Glass (ed.), Genetics. New York: Rockefeller University Press.

Bridger, W. H.
  1961   "Sensory habituation and discrimination in the human neonate." American Journal of Psychiatry 117:991–996.

Brill, H.
  1959   "Postencephalitic psychiatric conditions," in S. Arieti (ed.), American Handbook of Psychiatry, vol. 2. New York: Basic Books.

British Medical Journal.
  1970   "Violent crime and the EEG." 2:193.

Cannon, W. B.
  1929   Bodily Changes in Pain, Hunger, Fear and Rage. College Park, Md.: McGrath Pub. (1970 edition).

Caplan, G.
  1964   Principles of Preventive Psychiatry. New York: Basic Books.

Carter, C. O.
  1969   An ABC of Medical Genetics. Boston: Little, Brown.

Casey, M. D., L. J. Segall, D. R. K. Street, and C. E. Blank.
  1966   "Sex chromosome abnormalities in two state hospitals for patients requiring special security." Nature 209:641–642.

Cattell, R. B.
  1966   The Scientific Analysis of Personality. Chicago: Aldine.

Chase, H. F., and M. E. Byrnes.
  1970   "Trends in 'prematurity': United States, 1950–1967." American Journal of Public Health 60:1967–1983.

Child, I.
  1950   "The relationship of somatype to self-ratings on Sheldon's temperamental traits." Journal of Personality 18:440–453.

Christiansen, K. O.
  1968   "Threshold of tolerance in various population groups illustrated by results from the Danish criminologic twin study," in A. V. S. de Reuck and R. Porter (eds.), The Mentally Abnormal Offender. Boston: Little, Brown.

Clark, G. R., M. A. Telfer, D. Baker, and M. Rosen.
  1970   "Sex chromosomes, crime, and psychosis." American Journal of Psychiatry 126:1659–1663.

Cleckley, H.
   1955   The Mask of Sanity. Third Edition. St. Louis: Mosby.

Clemente, C. D., and D. B. Lindsley (eds.)
   1967   Brain Function. Aggression and Defense: Neural Mechanisms and Social
           Patterns, vol. 5. Berkeley: University of California Press.

Clements, S. D.
   1966   Minimal Brain Dysfunction in Children. Terminology and Identification,
           phase one of a three-phase project. National Institute of Neurological Dis-
           eases and Blindness. Monograph 3, U.S. Public Health Service. 1415. Wash-
           ington, D.C.: U.S. Government Printing Office.

Clinard, M. B.
   1968   Sociology of Deviant Behavior. Third Edition. New York: Holt, Rinehart &
           Winston.

Cohen, M., D. F. Klein, and F. Struve.
   1970   "Relationship between electroencephalographic and sociometric variables
           among psychiatric patients." American Journal of Psychiatry 127:97–101.

Conner, R. L., and S. Levine.
   1969   "Hormonal influences on aggressive behavior," in S. Garattini and E. B.
           Sigg (eds.), Aggressive Behaviour. New York: Wiley.

Conners, C. K., R. Kramer, G. H. Rothschild, L. Schwartz, and A. Stone.
   1971   "Treatment of young delinquent boys with diphenylhydantoin sodium and
           methyphenidate." Archives of General Psychiatry 24:156–160.

Conners, C. K., G. Rothschild, L. Eisenberg, L. S. Schwartz, and E. Robinson.
   1969   "Dextroamphetamine sulfate in children with learning disorders, effects on
           perception, learning and achievement." Archives of General Psychiatry 21:
           182–190.

Cooper, A. J., A. A. A. Ismail, A. L. Phanjoo, and D. L. Love.
   1972   "Antiandrogen (cyproterone acetate) therapy in deviant hypersexuality."
           British Journal of Psychiatry 120:59–63.

Coppen, A., and N. Kessel.
   1963   "Menstruation and personality." British Journal of Psychiatry 109:711–
           721.

Cortes, J. B., and F. M. Gatti.
   1972   Delinquency and Crime: A Biopsychosocial Approach. New York: Seminar
           Press.

Court Brown, W. M.
   1968   "Males with an XYY sex chromosome complement." Journal of Medical
           Genetics 5:341–359.

Cunningham, M. A., V. Pillai, and W. J. Blachford Rogers.
   1968   "Haloperidol in the treatment of children with severe behavior disorders."
           British Journal of Psychiatry 114:845–854.

Currier, R. D., S. C. Little, J. F. Suess, and O. J. Andy.
   1971   "Sexual seizures." Archives of Neurology 25:260–264.

Dalton, K.
   1961   "Menstruation and crime." British Medical Journal 2:1752–1753.
   1964   The Premenstrual Syndrome. Springfield, Ill.: Thomas.

Darling, H. F.
1971   "Haloperidol in 60 criminal psychotics." Diseases of the Nervous System 32:31–34.

David, O., J. Clark, and K. Voeller.
1972   "Lead and hyperactivity," Lancet 2:900–903.

Davidson, G. A.
1947   "Psychomotor epilepsy." Canadian Medical Journal 56:410–414.

Davis, B. D.
1970   "Prospects for genetic intervention in man." Science 170:1279–1283.

Davis, E.
1959   "Explosive or episodic behavior disorders in children as epileptic equivalents." Medical Journal of Australia 2:474–481.

Delgado, J. M. R.
1969   "Offensive-defensive behavior in free monkeys and chimpanzees induced by radio stimulation of the brain," in S. Garattini and E. B. Sigg (eds.), Aggressive Behaviour. New York: Wiley.

Denenberg, V. H., R. E. Paschke, and M. X. Zarrow.
1968   "Killing of mice by rats prevented by early interaction between the two species." Psychonomic Science 11:39.

Denenberg, V. H., and M. X. Zarrow.
1970   "Rat pax." Psychology Today 3:45–47, 66–67.

Denhoff, E.
1965   "Bridges to burn and build, a presidential address." Developmental Medicine and Child Neurology 7:3–8.

Dobzhansky, T.
1962   Mankind Evolving: The Evolution of the Human Species. New Haven: Yale University Press.

Drillien, C. M.
1964   The Growth and Development of the Prematurely Born Infant. Baltimore: Williams & Wilkins.
1970   "The small-for-date infant: etiology and progress." Pediatric Clinics of North America 17:9–24.

Dugdale, R. L.
1877   The Jukes—A Study of Crime, Pauperism, Disease, and Heredity. New York: G. P. Putnam and Sons.

Durkheim, E.
1895   The Rules of Sociological Method. Translated by George Simpson. New York: Free Press of Glencoe (1964 edition).

Eckland, B. K.
1967   "Genetics and sociology: a reconsideration." American Sociological Review 32:173–194.

Egger, M. D., and J. P. Flynn.
1963   "Effects of electrical stimulation of the amygdala on hypothalamically elicited attack behavior in cats." Journal of Neurophysiology 26:705–720.

Eisenberg, L., R. Lachman, P. A. Molling, A. Lockner, J. D. Mizelle, and C. K. Conners.
1963   "A psychopharmacologic experiment in a training school for delinquent boys, methods, problems, findings." American Journal of Orthopsychiatry 33:431–447.

Ellingson, R. J.
   1955   "The incidence of E.E.G. abnormality among patients with mental disorders of apparently non-organic origin: a critical review." American Journal of Psychiatry 111:263–275.

Ellinwood, E. H.
   1971   "Assault and homicide associated with amphetamine abuse." American Journal of Psychiatry 127:1170–1175.

Engel, E.
   1972   "Guest editorial: the making of an XYY." American Journal of Mental Deficiency 77:123–127.

Epps, P., and R. W. Parnell.
   1952   "Physique and temperament of women delinquents compared with women undergraduates." British Journal of Medical Psychology 25:249–255.

Epstein, A. W.
   1969   "Disordered human sexual behavior associated with temporal lobe dysfunction." Medical Aspects of Human Sexuality 3(2):62–68.

Eysenck, H. J.
   1956   "The inheritance of extraversion-introversion." Acta Psychologica 12:95–110.
   1964   Crime and Personality. Boston: Houghton Mifflin.

Fenton, G. W., and E. L. Udwin.
   1965   "Homicide, temporal lobe epilepsy, and depression, a case report." British Journal of Psychiatry 111:304–306.

Ferguson-Smith, M. A.
   1970   "Chromosomal abnormalities II: sex chromosome defects." Hospital Practice 5(4):88–100.

Fish, B.
   1971   "Treating hyperactive children." Journal of the American Medical Association 218:1427.

Forssman, H.
   1970   "The mental implications of sex chromosome aberrations." British Journal of Psychiatry 117:353–363.

Forssman, H., and G. Hambert.
   1963   "Incidence of Klinefelter's syndrome among mental patients." Lancet 1:1327.
   1967   "Chromosomes and antisocial behavior." Excerpta Criminologica 7:113–117.

Freemon, F. R., and A. H. Nevis.
   1969   "Temporal lobe sexual seizures." Neurology 19:87–90.

Fuller, J. L., and W. R. Thompson.
   1960   Behavior Genetics. New York: Wiley.

Funkenstein, D. H.
   1955   "The physiology of fear and anger." Scientific American 192(May):74–80.

Garattini, S., and E. B. Sigg (eds.)
   1969   Aggressive Behaviour. New York: Wiley.

Gerard, R. W.
   1959   "Neurophysiology: brain and behavior," in S. Arieti (ed.), American Handbook of Psychiatry, vol. 2. New York: Basic Books.

German, J.
1970   "Studying human chromosomes today." American Scientist 58:182–201.
Geschwind, N.
1965   "Disconnexion syndromes in animals and man, I." Brain 88:237–294.
1968   "Neurological functions of language," in H. R. Myklebust (ed.), Progress in Learning Disabilities, vol. 1. New York: Grune & Stratton.
Gibbens, T. C. N.
1963   Psychiatric Study of Borstal Lads. London: Oxford University Press.
Gibbs, F. A., E. L. Gibbs, and W. G. Lennox.
1937   "Epilepsy: a paroxysmal cerebral dysrhythmia." Brain 60:377–388.
Gil, D. G.
1970   Violence Against Children. Cambridge: Harvard University Press.
Glaser, G.
1967   "Limbic epilepsy in childhood." Journal of Nervous and Mental Disease 144:391–397.
Glass, D. C. (ed.)
1968   Genetics: Proceedings of a Conference under the Auspices of the Russell Sage Foundation, the Social Science Research Council and the Rockefeller University. New York: Rockefeller University Press.
Gloor, P.
1967   "Discussion." Pp. 116–124 in C. D. Clemente and D. B. Lindsley (eds.), Brain Function. Aggression and Defense, vol. 5. Berkeley: University of California Press.
Glueck, S., and E. Glueck.
1956   Physique and Delinquency. New York: Harper & Bros.
Goddard, H. H.
1913   The Kallikak Family, A Study in the Heredity of Feeble Mindedness. New York: Macmillan.
Golla, F. L., and R. S. Hodge.
1949   "Hormone treatment of the sexual offender." Lancet 256:1006–1007.
Goring, C.
1913   The English Convict. London: H.M. Stationery Office.
Gottesman, I. I.
1963   "Heritability of personality: a demonstration." Psychological Monographs 77, Whole No. 572:1–21.
1966   "Genetic variance in adaptive personality traits." Journal of Child Psychology and Psychiatry 7:199–208.
Goy, R. W.
1964   "Reproduction behavior in mammals," in C. W. Lloyd (ed.), Human Reproduction and Sexual Behavior. Philadelphia: Lea & Febiger.
Gray, J. A.
1971   "Sex differences in emotional behaviour in mammals, including man: endocrine bases." Acta Psychologica 35:29–46.
Greene, R., and K. Dalton.
1953   "The premenstrual syndrome." British Medical Journal 1:1007–1014.
Gross, M.
1971   "Violence associated with organic brain disease," in J. Fawcett (ed.), Dynamics of Violence. Chicago: American Medical Association.

Gruenberg, E. M.
1964   "Some epidemiological aspects of congenital brain damage," in H. G. Birch (ed.), Brain Damage in Children, The Biologic and Social Aspects. Baltimore: Williams & Wilkins.

Grunberg, F., and D. A. Pond.
1957   "Conduct disorders in epileptic children." Journal of Neurology, Neurosurgery and Psychiatry 20:65–68.

Grunt, J. A., and W. C. Young.
1952   "Differential reactivity of individuals and the response of the guinea pig to testosterone proprionate." Endocrinology 51:237–248.

Gunn, J., and J. Bonn.
1971   "Criminality and violence in epileptic prisoners." British Journal of Psychiatry 118:337–343.

Gunn, J., and G. Fenton.
1971   "Epilepsy, automatism, and crime." Lancet 1:1173–1176.

Hambert, G.
1966   "Males with positive sex chromatin. An epidemiologic investigation followed by psychiatric study of 75 cases." Thesis Akademiforlaget Goteburg.

Hamburg, D. A., R. H. Moos, and I. D. Yalom.
1968   "Studies of distress in the menstrual cycle and the postpartum period," in R. P. Michael (ed.), Endocrinology and Human Behavior. New York: Oxford University Press.

Hampson, J. L., and P. Ferrier.
1968   "Intersexuality." Medical Aspects of Human Sexuality 2(3):45–51.

Handler, P. (ed.)
1970   Biology and the Future of Man. New York: Oxford University Press.

Hare, R. D.
1970   Psychopathy: Theory and Research. New York: Wiley.

Harlow, H. F., and M. K. Harlow.
1970   "Developmental aspects of emotional behavior," in P. Black (ed.), Physiological Correlates of Emotion. New York: Academic Press.

Heimburger, R. F., C. C. Whitlock, and J. E. Kalsbeck.
1966   "Stereotaxic amygdalotomy for epilepsy with aggressive behavior." Journal of the American Medical Association 198:741–745.

Hertzig, M. E., and H. G. Birch.
1968   "Neurologic organization in psychiatrically disturbed adolescents, a comparative consideration of sex differences." Archives of General Psychiatry 19:528–537.

Hienz, H. A.
1969   "YY-syndrome forms." Lancet 1:155–156.

Hill, D., and D. A. Pond.
1952   "Reflections on one hundred capital cases submitted to electroencephalography." Journal of Mental Science 98:23–43.

Himmelhoch, J., J. Pincus, G. Tucker, and T. Detre.
1970   "Sub-acute encephalitis: behavioural and neurological aspects." British Journal of Psychiatry 116:531–538.

Himwich, H. E.
  1952   "Effect of shock therapies on the brain," in Biology of Mental Health and Disease. Report of the 27th Annual Conference of the Milbank Fund. New York: Hoeker.

Hofstadter, R.
  1955   Social Darwinism in American Thought. Boston: Beacon Press.

Holmes, G.
  1960   Introduction to Clinical Neurology. Edinburgh: E & S Livingston Ltd.

Hook, E. B., and D. S. Kim.
  1971   "Height and antisocial behavior in XY and XYY boys." Science 172:284–286.

Hooton, E. A.
  1939   Crime and the Mind. Cambridge: Harvard University Press.

Hunter, R., L. Valentine, and W. H. McMenemy.
  1963   "Temporal lobe epilepsy supervening of longstanding transvestism and fetishism." Epilepsia 4:60–65.

Ingram, T.
  1956   "A characteristic form of overactive behavior in brain damaged children." Journal of Mental Science 102:550–558.

Jacobs, P. A., W. H. Price, W. M. Court Brown, R. P. Brittain, and P. B. Whatmore.
  1968   "Chromosome studies on men in a maximum security hospital." Annals of Human Genetics 31:339–358.

Jacobs, P. A., W. H. Price, S. Richmond, and R. A. W. Ratcliff.
  1971   "Chromosome surveys in penal institutions and approved schools." Journal of Medical Genetics 8:49–58.

Joint Commission on Mental Health of Children.
  1969   Crisis in Child Mental Health: Challenge for the 1970's. New York: Harper & Row.

Johnson, E. H.
  1968   Crime, Correction, and Society. Revised Edition. Homewood, Ill.: Dorsey Press.

Jonsson, G.
  1967   "Delinquent boys, their parents and grandparents." Acta Psychiatrica Scandinavica 43(Supplement 195):1–264.

Kaada, B.
  1967   "Brain mechanisms related to aggressive behavior," in C. D. Clemente and D. B. Lindsley (eds.), Brain Function. Aggression and Defense, vol. 5. Berkeley: University of California Press.

Kessler, S., and R. H. Moos.
  1970   "The XYY karyotype and criminality: a review." Journal of Psychiatric Research 7:153–170.

Kety, S. S.
  1970   "Neurochemical aspects of emotional behavior," in P. Black (ed.), Physiological Correlates of Emotion. New York: Academic Press.

Klein, M., and L. Stern.
  1971   "Low birth weight and the battered child syndrome." American Journal of Diseases of Children 122:15–18.

Klinefelter, H. F., E. C. Reifenstein, and F. Albright.
1942   "Syndrome characterized by gynecomastia, aspermatogenesis without A-Leydigism and increased excretion of follicle stimulating hormone." Journal of Clinical Endocrinology 2:615–627.

Knobloch, H., and B. Pasamanick.
1966   "Prospective studies on the epidemiology of reproductive casualty: methods, findings and some implications." Merrill-Palmer Quarterly of Behavior and Development 12:27–43.

Knott, J. R.
1965   "Electroencephalograms in psychopathic personality and in murderers," in W. P. Wilson (ed.), Applications of Electroencephalography in Psychiatry. Durham, N.C.: Duke University Press.

Kolarsky, A., K. Freund, J. Machek, and O. Polak.
1967   "Male sexual deviation, association with early temporal lobe damage." Archives of General Psychiatry 17:735–743.

Kolb, L. C.
1968   Noyes' Modern Clinical Psychiatry. Philadelphia: W. B. Saunders.

Kolodny, R. C., W. H. Masters, J. Hendryx, and G. Toro.
1971   "Plasma testosterone and semen changes in male homosexuals." New England Journal of Medicine 285:1170–1174.

Korey, S. R.
1944   "The effects of benzedrine sulfate on the behavior of psychopathic and neurotic juvenile delinquents." Psychiatric Quarterly 18:127–137.

Kreuz, L. E., and R. M. Rose.
1972   "Assessment of aggressive behavior and plasma testosterone in a young criminal population." Psychosomatic Medicine 34:321–332.

Krieger, D.
1971   "The hypothalamus and neuroendocrinology." Hospital Practice 6(9):87–99.

Lange, J.
1931   Crime as Destiny. Translated by C. Haldane. London: George Allen & Unwin.

Lefkowitz, M. M.
1969   "Effects of diphenylhydantoin on disruptive behavior, study of male delinquents." Archives of General Psychiatry 20:643–651.

Lennox, W. G., and M. A. Lennox.
1960   Epilepsy and Related Disorders, vol. 2. Boston: Little, Brown.

Lennox-Buchthal, M., F. Buchthal, and P. Rosenfalck.
1960   "Correlation of electroencephalographic findings with crash rate of military jet pilots." Epilepsia 1:366–372.

Lindsley, D. B.
1967   "Discussion." Pp. 72–91 in C. D. Clemente and D. B. Lindsley (eds.), Brain Function. Aggression and Defense, vol. 5. Berkeley: University of California Press.

1970   "The role of non-specific reticulo-thalamo-cortical systems in emotion," in P. Black (ed.), Physiological Correlates of Emotion. New York: Academic Press.

Lindzey, G.
    1967   "Behavior and morphological variation," in J. N. Spuhler (ed.), Genetic
            Diversity and Human Behavior. Chicago: Aldine.
Lin-Fu, J. S.
    1970   Lead Poisoning in Children. U.S. Public Health Service Publication No.
            2108. Washington, D.C.: U.S. Government Printing Office.
Lion, J. R., G. Bach-y-Rita, and F. R. Ervin.
    1968   "The self referred violent patient." Journal of the American Medical Asso-
            ciation 205:503–505.
Lipton, E. L., A. Steinschneider, and J. B. Richmond.
    1961   "Autonomic functioning in the neonate." Psychosomatic Medicine 23:472–
            484.
Livingston, K. E.
    1969   "The frontal lobes revisited, the case for a second look." Archives of Neu-
            rology 20:90–95.
Livingston, S.
    1964   "Epilepsy and murder." Journal of the American Medical Association 188:
            172.
Lloyd, C. W.
    1968   "The influence of hormones on human sexual behavior," in E. B. Astwood
            and C. E. Cassidy (eds.), Clinical Endocrinology, vol. 2. New York: Grune.
Locke, John.
    1959   An Essay Concerning Human Understanding. Collated and annotated by
            A. C. Fraser. 2 volumes. New York: Dover.
Lombroso, C.
    1911   Crime, its Causes and Remedies. Translated by H. P. Horton. Boston: Little,
            Brown.
Looker, A., and C. K. Conners.
    1970   "Diphenylhydantoin in children with severe temper tantrums." Archives of
            General Psychiatry 23:80–89.
Lorentz de Haas, A.M.
    1963   "Epilepsy and criminality." British Journal of Criminology 3:248–256.
Lorenz, K.
    1967   On Aggression. New York: Bantam Books.
Lykken, D. T.
    1955   "A study of anxiety in the sociopathic personality." Ph.D. dissertation, Uni-
            versity of Minnesota.
    1957   "A study of anxiety in the sociopathic personality." Journal of Abnormal
            and Social Psychology 55:6–10.
MacLean, P. D.
    1949   "Psychosomatic disease and the 'visceral brain,' recent developments bear-
            ing on the Papez theory of emotion." Psychosomatic Medicine 11:338–353.
    1952   "Some psychiatric implications of physiological studies on fronto-temporal
            portion of limbic system (visceral brain)." Electroencephalography and
            Clinical Neurophysiology 4:407–418.
    1958   "Contrasting functions of limbic and neocortical systems of the brain and
            their relevance to psychophysical aspects of medicine." American Journal of
            Medicine 25:611–626.

1968   "Alternative neural pathways to violence," in L. Ng (ed.), Alternatives to Violence. New York: Time-Life Books.

1970   "The limbic brain in relation to the psychoses." Pp. 129–146 in P. Black (ed.), Physiological Correlates of Emotion. New York: Academic Press.

McClearn, G. E.
1969   "Biological bases of social behavior with special reference to violent behavior." Pp. 979–1017 in D. J. Mulvihill, M. M. Tumin, and L. A. Curtis, Crimes of Violence, vol. 13. Washington, D.C.: U.S. Government Printing Office.

McKusick, V. A.
1969   Human Genetics. Second Edition. Englewood Cliffs, N.J.: Prentice-Hall.

McNeil, T. F., R. Wiegerink, and J. E. Dozier.
1970   "Pregnancy and birth complications in the births of seriously, moderately, and mildly behaviorally disturbed children." Journal of Nervous and Mental Disease 151:24–34.

Malamud, N.
1967   "Psychiatric disorder with intracranial tumors of limbic system." Archives of Neurology 17:113–123.

Maletzky, B. M.
1973   "The episodic dyscontrol syndrome." Diseases of the Nervous System 34:178–185.

Mandell, A. J., and M. P. Mandell.
1967   "Suicide and the menstrual cycle." Journal of the American Medical Association 200:792–793.

Marinacci, A. A.
1963   "A special type of temporal lobe (psychomotor) seizures following ingestion of alcohol." Bulletin of Los Angeles Neurological Society 28:241–250.

Mark, V. H., and F. R. Ervin.
1970   Violence and the Brain. New York: Harper & Row.

Meade, J. E., and A. S. Parkes (eds.)
1965   Biological Aspects of Social Problems. New York: Plenum Press.

Means, R. L.
1967   "Sociology, biology, and the analysis of social problems." Social Problems 15:200–212.

Mednick, S. A.
1970   "Breakdown in individuals at high risk for schizophrenia: possible predispositional perinatal factors." Mental Hygiene 54:50–63.

Mendelson, W., N. Johnson, and M. A. Stewart.
1971   "Hyperactive children as teenagers: a follow-up study." Journal of Nervous and Mental Disease 153:273–279.

Menkes, M. M., J. S. Rowe, and J. H. Menkes.
1967   "A twenty five year follow-up study on the hyperkinetic child with minimal brain dysfunction." Pediatrics 39:393–399.

Metrakos, K., and J. D. Metrakos.
1961   "Genetics of convulsive disorders. II. Genetic and electroencephalographic studies in centrencephalic epilepsy." Neurology 11:471–483.

Michael, R. P. (ed.)
1968   Endocrinology and Human Behavior. New York: Oxford University Press.

Mignone, R. J., E. F. Donnelly, and D. Sadowsky.
1970   "Psychological and neurological comparisons of psychomotor and non-psychomotor epileptic patients." Epilepsia 11:345–359.

Miller, N. E.
1969   "Psychosomatic effects of specific types of training." Annals of New York Academy of Science 159:1025–1040.

Money, J.
1968   "Influence of hormones on psychosexual differentiation." Medical Aspects of Human Sexuality 2(11):32–42.
1969   "Fatherhood behavior and gender identity." Medical Aspects of Human Sexuality 3(9):67–80.
1970   "Use of an androgen depleting hormone in the treatment of male sex offenders." Journal of Sex Research 6:165–172.

Money, J., and A. A. Ehrhardt.
1972   Man and Woman, Boy and Girl. Baltimore: Johns Hopkins Press.

Money, J., J. G. Hampson, and J. L. Hampson.
1955   "An examination of some basic sexual concepts: the evidence of human hermaphroditism." Bulletin of Johns Hopkins Hospital 97:301–319.

Monroe, R. R.
1970   Episodic Behavioral Disorders, A Psychodynamic and Neurophysiologic Analysis. Cambridge: Harvard University Press.

Montagu, M. F. A.
1941   "The biologist looks at crime." Annals of the American Academy of Political and Social Science 217:46–57.
1968   Man and Aggression. New York: Oxford University Press.
1972   "Sociogenic brain damage." American Anthropologist 74:1045–1061.

Moos, R.
1969   "Typology of menstrual cycle symptoms." American Journal of Obstetrics and Gynecology 103:390–402.

Morton, J. H., H. Additon, R. G. Addison, L. Hunt, and J. J. Sullivan.
1953   "A clinical study of premenstrual tension." American Journal of Obstetrics and Gynecology 65:1182–1191.

Mosier, H. D., L. W. Scott, and H. F. Dingman.
1960   "Sexually deviant behavior in Klinefelter's syndrome." Journal of Pediatrics 57:479–483.

Moyer, K. E.
1968   "Kinds of aggression and their physiological basis." Communications in Behavioral Biology 2:65–87.
1969   "A preliminary model of aggressive behavior," in J. P. Scott and B. E. Eleftheriou (eds.), The Physiology of Fighting and Defeat. Chicago: University of Chicago Press.

Mulligan, W.
1972   "Dyslexia, specific learning disability and delinquency." Juvenile Justice 23:20–25.

Mulvihill, D. J., M. M. Tumin, and L. A. Curtis.
  1969   Crimes of Violence, vols. 11, 12, 13. Staff Report to National Commission on
          the Causes and Prevention of Violence. Washington, D.C.: U.S. Government
          Printing Office.
Myhre, S. A., R. H. A. Ruvalcaba, H. R. Johnson, H. C. Thuline, and V. C. Kelley.
  1970   "The effects of testosterone treatment in Klinefelter's syndrome." Journal of
          Pediatrics 76:267–276.
Myklebust, H. R.
  1973   "Identification and diagnosis of children with learning disabilities: an inter-
          disciplinary study of criteria." Seminars in Psychiatry 5:55–77.
Narabayashi, H., T. Nagao, Y. Saito, M. Yoshida, and M. Nagahata.
  1963   "Stereotaxic amygdalotomy for behavior disorders." Archives of Neurology
          9:1–16.
National Institute of Mental Health.
  1970   Report on the XYY Chromosomal Abnormality. Washington, D.C.: U.S.
          Government Printing Office.
Nielsen, J.
  1968   "The XYY syndrome in a mental hospital." British Journal of Criminology
          8:186–203.
  1970   "Criminality among patients with Klinefelter's syndrome and the XYY syn-
          drome." British Journal of Psychiatry 117:365–369.
Nielsen, J., and M. Fischer.
  1965   "Sex-chromatin and sex chromosome abnormalities in male hypogonadal
          mental patients." British Journal of Psychiatry 111:641–647.
Norris, R. V., and C. W. Lloyd.
  1971   "Psychosexual effects of hormone therapy." Medical Aspects of Human
          Sexuality 5(9):129–146.
O'Malley, J. E., and L. Eisenberg.
  1973   "The hyperkinetic syndrome." Seminars in Psychiatry 5:95–103.
Ounsted, C.
  1969   "Aggression and epilepsy rage in children with temporal lobe epilepsy."
          Journal of Psychosomatic Research 13:237–242.
Owen, D. R.
  1972   "The 47,XYY male: a review." Psychological Bulletin 78:209–233.
Papez, J. W.
  1937   "A proposed mechanism of emotion." Archives of Neurology and Psychia-
          try 38:725–743.
Parnell, R. W.
  1958   Behavior and Physique: An Introduction to Practical and Applied Soma-
          tometry. London: Arnold.
Pasamanick, B., and H. Knobloch.
  1960   "Brain damage and reproductive casualty." American Journal of Orthopsy-
          chiatry 30:298–305.
  1966   "Retrospective studies on the epidemiology of reproductive casualty: old and
          new." Merrill-Palmer Quarterly of Behavior and Development 12:1–26.
Pastore, N.
  1949   The Nature-Nurture Controversy. New York: King's Crown.

Penfield, W., and H. H. Jasper.
    1954   Epilepsy and the Functional Anatomy of the Human Brain. Boston: Little,
            Brown.
Persky, H., K. D. Smith, and G. K. Basu.
    1971   "Relation of psychological measures of aggression and hostility to testoster-
            one production in man." Psychosomatic Medicine 33:265–277.
Pincus, J. H., and G. H. Glaser.
    1966   "The syndrome of 'minimal brain damage' in childhood." New England
            Journal of Medicine 275:27–35.
Podolsky, E.
    1962   "The epileptic murderer." Medico-Legal Journal 30:176–179.
    1964   "The chemistry of murder." Pakistan Medical Journal 15:9–14.
Powell, T. J.
    1956   "Episodic unconsciousness in pilots during flight." Journal of Aviation
            Medicine 27:301–316.
President's Commission on Law Enforcement and Administration of Justice.
    1967a   Task Force Report: Juvenile Delinquency and Youth Crime. Washington,
            D.C.: U.S. Government Printing Office.
    1967b   The Challenge of Crime in a Free Society. Washington, D.C.: U.S. Govern-
            ment Printing Office.
President's Panel on Mental Retardation.
    1962   A Proposed Program for National Action to Combat Mental Retardation.
            Washington, D.C.: U.S. Government Printing Office.
Pribram, K. H.
    1969   "Neural servosystems and the structure of personality." Journal of Nervous
            and Mental Disease 149:30–39.
Price, W. H., and P. B. Whatmore.
    1967   "Criminal behavior and the XYY male." Nature 213:815.
Radzinowicz, L.
    1966   Ideology and Crime. New York: Columbia University Press.
Ratcliffe, S. G., A. L. Stewart, M. M. Melville, P. A. Jacobs, and A. J. Keay.
    1970   "Chromosome studies on 3500 newborn male infants." Lancet 1:121–122.
Rawlings, G., E. O. R. Reynolds, A. Stewart, and L. B. Strang.
    1971   "Changing prognosis for infants of very low birth weight." Lancet 1:516–
            519.
Reckless, W. C.
    1967   The Crime Problem. Fourth Edition. New York: Appleton-Century-Crofts.
Reeves, A. G., and F. Plum.
    1969   "Hyperphagia, rage, and dementia accompanying a ventromedial hypothal-
            amic neoplasm." Archives of Neurology 20:616–624.
Reiss, D. J.
    1972   "The relationship between brain norepinephrine and aggressive behavior."
            Research Publications of the Association for Research in Nervous and Men-
            tal Disease 50:266–296.
Resnick, O.
    1967   "The psychoactive properties of diphenylhydantoin: experiences with

prisoners and juvenile delinquents." International Journal of Neuropsychiatry (Supplement 2) 3:S30–S48.

Richmond, J. B., and H. L. Weinberger.
1970   "Program implications of new knowledge regarding the physical, intellectual, and emotional growth and development and unmet needs of children and youth." American Journal of Public Health 60(Supplement):23–67.

Robins, L. N.
1966   Deviant Children Grown Up. Baltimore: Williams & Wilkins.

Robinson, A., and T. T. Puck.
1967   "Studies on chromosomal nondisjunction in man. II." American Journal of Human Genetics 19:112–129.

Rodin, E. A.
1968   The Prognosis of Patients with Epilepsy. Springfield, Ill.: Thomas.
1973   "Psychomotor epilepsy and aggressive behavior." Archives of General Psychiatry 28:210–213.

Rose, R. M., J. W. Holaday, and I. S. Bernstein.
1971   "Plasma testosterone, dominance rank and aggressive behavior in male rhesus monkeys." Nature 231:366–368.

Rosenthal, D.
1970   Genetic Theory and Abnormal Behavior. New York: McGraw-Hill.

Roth, L. H., A. M. Rollins, and F. R. Ervin.
1972   "Violent and non-violent prisoners: a comparison. #1." Paper presented at meetings of the American Psychiatric Association, Dallas (unpublished).

Rothballer, A.
1967   "Aggression, defense and neurohumors," in C. D. Clemente and D. B. Lindsley (eds.), Brain Function. Aggression and Defense, vol. 5. Berkeley: University of California Press.

Sandberg, A. A., G. F. Koepf, T. Ishiara, and T. S. Hauschka.
1961   "An XYY human male." Lancet 2:488–489.

Sano, K.
1966   "Sedative stereoencephalotomy: fornicotomy, upper mesencephalic reticulotomy, and posterior-medial hypothalamotomy," in T. Tokizane and J. P. Schade (eds.), Progress in Brain Research, vol. 21. Amsterdam: Elsevier Pub. Co.

Sano, K., Y. Mayanagi, H. Sekino, M. Ogashiwa, and B. Ishijima.
1970   "Results of stimulation and destruction of the posterior hypothalamus in man." Journal of Neurosurgery 33:689–707.

Sayed, Z. A., S. A. Lewis, and R. P. Brittain.
1969   "An electroencephalographic and psychiatric study of thirty-two insane murderers." British Journal of Psychiatry 115:1115–1124.

Schachter, S.
1964   "The interaction of cognitive and physiological determinants of emotional state," in L. Berkowitz (ed.), Advances in Experimental Social Psychology, vol. 1. New York: Academic Press.

Schachter, S., and B. Latane.
1964   "Crime, cognition, and the autonomic nervous system," in D. Levine (ed.), Nebraska Symposium on Motivation. Lincoln: University of Nebraska Press.

Schachter, S., and J. E. Singer.
  1962   "Cognitive, social and physiological determinants of emotional state." Psychological Review 69:379–399.

Schachter, S., and L. Wheeler.
  1962   "Epinephrine, chlorpromazine, and amusement." Journal of Abnormal and Social Psychology 65:121–128.

Schulsinger, F.
  1972   "Psychopathy: heredity and environment." International Journal of Mental Health 1:190–206.

Schulte, F. J.
  1971   "Current concepts in minimal brain dysfunction." Journal of the American Medical Association 217:1237–1238.

Scott, J. P.
  1970   "Biology and human aggression." American Journal of Orthopsychiatry 40:568–576.

Serafetinides, E. A.
  1970   "Psychiatric aspects of temporal lobe epilepsy," in E. Niedermeyer (ed.), Modern Problems of Pharmacopsychiatry. Epilepsy, Recent Views on Theory, Diagnosis and Therapy of Epilepsy, vol. 4. New York: S. Karger.

Shah, S. A.
  1969   "Crime and mental illness: some problems in defining and labelling deviant behavior." Mental Hygiene 53:21–33.
  1972   "Recent developments in human genetics and their implications for problems of social deviance," in D. Bergsma (ed.), Advances in Human Genetics and Their Impact on Society. Birth Defects, Original Article Series 8(4): 42–82.

Sheard, M. H.
  1971   "Effect of lithium on human aggression." Nature 230:113–114.

Sheldon, W. H.
  1949   Varieties of Delinquent Youth. New York: Harper & Bros.

Sheldon, W. H., and S. S. Stevens.
  1942   The Varieties of Temperament. New York: Harper.

Sheldon, W. H., S. S. Stevens, and W. B. Tucker.
  1940   The Varieties of Human Physique. New York: Harper.

Siegel, A., and J. P. Flynn.
  1968   "Differential effects of electrical stimulation and lesions of the hippocampus and adjacent regions upon attack behavior of cats." Brain Research 7:252–267.

Skelton, W. D.
  1970   "Alcohol, violent behavior and the electroencephalogram." Southern Medical Journal 63:465–466.

Small, J. G.
  1966   "The organic dimension of crime." Archives of General Psychiatry 15:82–89.

Smythies, J. R.
  1970   Brain Mechanisms and Behavior. New York: Academic Press.

Spuhler, J. N. (ed.)
1967   Genetic Diversity and Human Behavior. Chicago: Aldine.

Stafford-Clark, D., and F. H. Taylor.
1949   "Clinical and electroencephalographic studies of prisoners charged with murder." Journal of Neurology, Neurosurgery and Psychiatry 12:325–330.

Stein, L., and C. D. Wise.
1970   "Behavioral pharmacology of central stimulants," in W. G. Clark and J. del Giudice (eds.), Principles of Psychopharmacology. New York: Academic Press.

Stevens, J. R.
1966   "Psychiatric implications of psychomotor epilepsy." Archives of General Psychiatry 14:461–471.

Stevens, J. R., V. H. Mark, F. R. Ervin, P. Pacheco, and K. Suematsu.
1969   "Deep temporal stimulation in man, long latency, long lasting psychological changes." Archives of Neurology 21:157–169.

Stevens, J. R., K. Sachdev, and V. Milstein.
1968   "Behavior disorders of childhood and the electroencephalogram." Archives of Neurology 18:160–177.

Sutherland, E. H., and D. R. Cressey.
1970   Criminology. Eighth Edition. Philadelphia: Lippincott.

Swanson, D. W., and A. H. Stipes.
1969   "Psychiatric aspects of Klinefelter's syndrome." American Journal of Psychiatry 126:814–822.

Sweet, W. H., F. R. Ervin, and V. H. Mark.
1969   "The relationship of violent behavior to focal cerebral disease," in S. Garattini and E. B. Sigg (eds.), Aggressive Behaviour. New York: Wiley.

Taylor, D. C.
1969   "Aggression and epilepsy." Journal of Psychosomatic Research 13:229–236.

Taylor, D. C., and B. D. Bower.
1971   "Prevention in epileptic disorders." Lancet 2:1136–1138.

Telfer, M. A.
1968   "Are some criminals born that way?" Think 34(Nov.–Dec.):24–28.

Thomas, A., S. Chess, H. G. Birch, M. Hertzig, and S. Korn.
1963   Behavioral Individuality in Early Childhood. New York: New York University Press.

Tompkins, W. T., and D. G. Wiehl.
1954   "Maternal and newborn nutrition studies at Philadelphia Lying-in Hospital." Maternal Studies II. Prematurity and Maternal Nutrition in the Promotion of Maternal and Newborn Health. New York: Milbank Memorial Fund.

Towbin, A.
1971   "Organic causes of minimal brain dysfunction—perinatal origin of minimal cerebral lesions." Journal of the American Medical Association 217:1207–1214.

Tsuboi, T.
1970   "Crimino-biologic study of patients with the XYY syndrome and Klinefelter's syndrome." Humangenetik 10:68–84.

Tucker, G. J., and J. H. Pincus.
    1973   Behavioral Neurology. New York: Oxford University Press.

Turner, W. J.
    1969   "Anticonvulsive agents in the treatment of aggression," in S. Garattini and
            E. B. Sigg (eds.), Aggressive Behaviour. New York: Wiley.

Twitchell, T.
    1971   "A behavioral syndrome." Science 174:135–136.

Vaernet, K., and A. Madsen.
    1970   "Stereotaxic amygdalotomy and baso-frontal tractotomy in psychotics with
            aggressive behavior." Journal of Neurology, Neurosurgery and Psychiatry
            33:858–863.

Valzelli, L.
    1967   "Drugs and aggressiveness." Advances in Pharmacology 5:79–108.

Vandenberg, S. G.
    1960   "Hereditary factors in normal personality traits (as measured by inven-
            tories)," in J. Wortis (ed.), Recent Advances in Biological Psychiatry.
            New York: Grune & Stratton.

Vold, G.
    1958   Theoretical Criminology. New York: Oxford University Press.

Walinder, J.
    1965   "Transvestism: definition and evidence in favor of occasional derivation
            from cerebral dysfunction." International Journal of Neuropsychiatry 1:
            567–573.

Walker, A. E.
    1970   "The propagation of the epileptic discharges," in E. Niedermeyer (ed.),
            Modern Problems of Pharmacopsychiatry. Epilepsy, Recent Views on The-
            ory, Diagnosis and Therapy of Epilepsy, vol. 4. New York: S. Karger.

Walker, R. N.
    1963   "Body build and behavior in young children: II. Body build and parents'
            ratings." Child Development 34:1–23.

Walters, C. E.
    1965   "The prediction of postnatal development from fetal activity." Child Devel-
            opment 36:801–808.

Walzer, S.
    1970   Behavior Genetics. Seminars in Psychiatry 2(February): whole.

Walzer, S., and P. H. Wolff (eds.)
    1973   Minimal Cerebral Dysfunction in Children. Seminars in Psychiatry 5(Feb-
            ruary): whole.

Ward, A. A., H. H. Jasper, and A. Pope.
    1969   "Clinical and experimental challenges of the epilepsies," in H. H. Jasper et
            al. (eds.), Basic Mechanisms of the Epilepsies. Boston: Little, Brown.

Wasman, M., and J. P. Flynn.
    1962   "Directed attack elicited from hypothalamus." Archives of Neurology 6:
            220–227.

Watson, J. B.
    1924   Behaviorism. New York: Norton (1930 edition).

Weiss, G., K. Minde, J. S. Werry, V. Douglas, and E. Nemeth.
    1971   "Studies on the hyperactive child. VIII. Five year follow up." Archives of
            General Psychiatry 24:409–414.

Wender, P. H.
    1971   Minimal Brain Dysfunction in Children. New York: Wiley.

Werner, E., J. M. Bierman, F. E. French, K. Simonian, A. Connor, R. S. Smith, and
            M. Campbell.
    1968   "Reproductive and environmental casualties: a report on the 10 year follow-
            up of the children of the Kauai pregnancy study." Pediatrics 42:112–127.

Wetzel, R. D., T. Reich, and J. N. McClure.
    1971   "Phase of the menstrual cycle and self-referrals to a suicide prevention serv-
            ice." British Journal of Psychiatry 119:523–524.

Wikler, A., J. F. Dixon, and J. B. Parker.
    1970   "Brain function in problem children and controls: psychometric neurologic
            and electroencephalographic comparisons." American Journal of Psychiatry
            127:634–645.

Wilder, J.
    1940   "Problems of criminal psychology related to hypoglycemic states." Journal
            of Criminal Psychopathology 1:219–320.
    1947   "Sugar metabolism in its relation to criminology," in R. M. Lindner and
            R. V. Seliger (eds.), Handbook of Correctional Psychology. New York:
            Philosophical Library.

Williams, D.
    1969   "Neural factors related to habitual aggression, consideration of differences
            between those habitual aggressives and others who have committed crimes
            of violence." Brain 92:503–520.

Williams, J. R., and M. Gold.
    1972   "From delinquent behavior to official delinquency." Social Problems 20:
            209–229.

Winick, M.
    1970   "Cellular growth in intrauterine malnutrition." Pediatric Clinics of North
            America 17:69–78.

Witkin, H. A.
    1972   The XYY Syndrome. Summary Progress Report to National Institute of
            Mental Health, Grant MH 17653 (unpublished).

Witkin, H. A., R. B. Dyk, H. F. Faterson, D. R. Goodenough, and S. A. Karp.
    1962   Psychological Differentiation. New York: Wiley.

Witkin, H. A., H. B. Lewis, M. Hertzman, K. Machover, P. B. Meissner, and S. Wapner.
    1954   Personality through Perception. New York: Harper.

Wolfgang, M. E., and F. Ferracuti.
    1967   The Subculture of Violence. London: Tavistock.

Wortis, H., and A. Freedman.
    1968   "The contribution of social environment to the development of premature
            children." American Journal of Orthopsychiatry 35:57–68.

Zeman, W., and F. A. King.
    1958   "Tumors of the septum pellucidum and adjacent structures, with abnormal
            affective behavior: an anterior midline syndrome." Journal of Nervous and
            Mental Disease 127:490–502.

CHAPTER 5

Assaultive Offenses

Franco Ferracuti and Graeme Newman

University of Rome and *State University of New York, Albany*

"Crimes of Violence," the staff report to the National Commission on the Causes and Prevention of Violence by Mulvihill, Tumin, and Curtis (1969) defines crimes of violence as "the use or threatened use of force to secure one's own end against the will of another that results or can result in the destruction or harm of person or property or in the deprivation of individual freedom" (1969:4). This is a very broad definition of crimes of violence, and the writers of that report made it quite explicit that they considered forceful acts against property, whether a person was directly concerned as a victim or not, to be crimes of violence.

The scope of this chapter is confined to assaultive offenses, which we define as the use of or threat of use of force on a victim by an offender. We shall not deal with acts which are directed primarily towards property, where the victim may suffer indirectly from the damage of his property, and will confine ourselves to acts that come more closely within the shorter Oxford Dictionary definition of the word *assault*: "To make a violent hostile attack by physical means upon; to commit an assault upon the person of." For an offense to be considered assaultive, therefore, it must be one in which the victim is made to suffer directly at the hands of the offender.

Since 1959, the FBI has defined crimes of violence, for the purpose of the construction of a national index, as the offenses of murder, forcible rape, robbery, and aggravated assault (F.B.I., 1970). Mulvihill et al. (1969), however, with their broader definition of violence, include such acts as criminal homicide, forcible rape, robbery, aggravated assault, suicide, violent auto fatalities, child abuses, other sex offenses, other assaults, disorderly conduct, burglary, arson, vandalism, individual violent acts related to gangs, and individual violent acts related to organized crime.

Applying our definition of assaultive behaviour to this list, only the acts of suicide, burglary, arson, and vandalism would be excluded. There are two difficult problems here. First, the notion of intent is of central importance in deciding whether an act that results in violent injury to the victim is criminal or not. For example, violent deaths resulting from auto accidents are seen as "accidents" or "unintentional killings," and often no clear "blame" is attached to any party as far as the criminal law is concerned. It is becoming increasingly apparent, however, that the motor car can be as dangerous an implement of violence as a gun. Certainly many more deaths result from use of the motor car than from a gun (Mulvihill et al., 1969:7). A brief outline of the legal definitions of homicide demonstrates this difficulty.

Homicide is the killing of one human being by another. The legal categories are:

1. *Excusable homicide* is intentional killing where no blame attaches.

2. *Justifiable homicide* is intentional killing sanctioned by law, such as killing a person in legitimate self-defense.

3. *Murder* is defined by common law as the unlawful killing of a human being with malice aforethought, deliberation, and murderous intent. There are various categories or degrees of murder which depend upon the degree of premeditation and intent.

4. *Voluntary manslaughter* is the killing of another person without premeditation, malice, or murderous intent and this is sometimes referred to as *nonnegligent manslaughter*.

The various states of the U.S. vary somewhat in their definitions of these categories, and some have additional categories, such as *felony-murder*, when a person participates in a felony which results in someone being killed (not necessarily by him), or *vehicular homicide*. The term *homicide* refers to all the above categories. In the U.S. criminal homicide is used to refer only to murder and nonnegligent manslaughter mainly because this is the distinction used by the FBI (1970). This difference is often not recognized by laymen, and can cause considerable confusion in interpreting crime statistics (Inbau & Sowle, 1960).

The second problem, especially concerning assault, is that most legal definitions refer to the use of or *threat* of the use of force on another person. This means that the seriousness or "criminality" of an assaultive act cannot always be assessed by the injury done to the victim, for although the victim may be menaced with a gun, if he hands over the money or does not call for the police, he may not be actually physically injured, though, of course, he may suffer fright and shock. The legal problem, therefore, is to decide what constitutes a threat. To some extent this problem can be circumvented by attending to the subjective aspects of the offender's behaviour, such as his malicious intent and so on. But data on the offender's behaviour may be missing or unreliable. One solution is to identify the threat in terms of the implement of force which is used as a threat. Thus, many crimes are considered to be more serious if they are committed with the use of a firearm or other dangerous weapon, and even, in many cases, imitations of such weapons. It can be seen, however, that very often, especially in the case of "other assaults," the extent to which such threatening behaviour will become defined as criminal will depend largely upon whether an onlooker or the victim decides to involve the police. Certainly it will have a great deal to do with the relationship between the victim and the offender, with which we shall deal shortly.

One would expect that *aggravated assault* would be more easily definable. It is defined by the FBI (1970) as assault with intent to kill or for the purpose of inflicting severe bodily injury, usually with a weapon or any other means likely to produce serious bodily harm. It excludes the lesser forms of assault, such as assault and battery, and fighting. But as Mulvihill et al. (1969:11) point out, the distinction between these acts, especially between criminal homicide and aggravated assault may depend to a very large extent not so much on the state of mind of the offender, but upon such factors as the speed of the ambulance, competence of the surgeon, or area of the body where the weapon strikes. Other FBI definitions of assaultive offenses are:

1. *Forcible rape* includes carnal knowledge of a female forcibly and against her will, and assaults to rape, regardless of the victim's age. It excludes statutory rape, where no force is employed but the victim is below the age of consent.

2. *Robbery* is the stealing or taking of anything of value from a person by force or by creating fear. It includes strong-arm robbery, stick-ups, armed robbery, assault to rob, and attempt to rob.

3. *Child abuse,* sometimes popularly known as the *"battered-child syndrome,"*

is particularly difficult to define, mainly because many cases of child abuse may result from parental neglect which may not mean intentional abuse or assault upon the child. Gil and Noble consider that child abuse is the "non-accidental attack or physical injury, including criminal as well as fatal injury, inflicted upon children by persons caring for them" (1967:3). Moreover, an additional problem is that it is difficult to draw the line between what is legally permissible parental discipline, which may involve physical punishment, and the point where the punishment may be considered abusive. The reporting of such crimes is often limited to their accidental discovery by an attending physician or by nurses, and it is highly uneven.

METHODS OF MEASURING ASSAULTIVE CRIME

The Administrative Base of Crime Statistics

The problems of collecting and interpreting crime statistics have been reported over and again in the literature, especially in relation to the shortcomings of the FBI's *Uniform Crime Reports* (Wolfgang, 1963; Lejins, 1966; Robinson, 1966). Mulvihill et al. (1969:16–42) report these criticisms, which we may summarize here for convenience:

1. The data are not comparable over time because early reporting, in the 1930s, was not representative (only 400 agencies participated as against 8,500 today).

2. The legal definitions of crimes vary according to each state; in an effort to improve these statistics, the FBI changed the definitions of some of the index crimes in 1958, thus making comparisons before and after that date difficult.

3. The perennial problem of the "dark number" of crime is "without doubt the greatest constraint on the validity of statistics in the United States or any other country" (Mulvihill et al., 1968:18). The dark number refers to the gap between crime reported to the police (the FBI measure) and that which actually occurs. Some offenses have a very low reportability because they are either never discovered by the police or are concealed by the victim. Of violent crimes, forcible rape has been found to have a very low reportability (President's Commission, 1967a:18). In comparison, however, criminal homicide is one of the most highly visible crimes, and has both a high reporting and clearance rate (Wolfgang & Ferracuti, 1967:258). The recent victimization studies conducted by Ennis (1967) in Chicago, Biderman et al. (1967) in Washington, D.C., and Reiss (1967) in Michigan have demonstrated the enormous differences which may exist in the reportability of the FBI's Index Crimes. Table 1

TABLE 1
CRIME RATES OBTAINED BY THE ENNIS
SURVEY OF VICTIM REPORTS OF CRIMES
COMPARED TO RATES REPORTED BY
POLICE TO THE FBI
(per hundred thousand population)

	Ennis Survey (1965-66)	FBI Rate (1965)
Criminal homicide	3.0	5.1
Forcible rape	42.5	11.6
Robbery	94.0	61.4
Aggravated assault	218.3	106.4

Source: Mulvihill et al., 1969:20.

displays the differences in crime rates in violent crimes, as surveyed by Ennis, in comparison to the rates reported by the FBI. Criminal homicide is the only crime which comes anywhere near the FBI rate. It is for this reason that, when we compare rates for assaultive offenses according to the usual sociological variables such as age, sex, and race, we shall rely more upon homicide statistics than any other.

4. Police misclassification in recording crimes occurs, especially with aggravated assault and forcible rape (President's Commission on Crime in D.C., 1966:49; Chappell & Singer, 1973:19).

5. Other criticisms are that more refined classifications are needed; multiple events should be given consideration.

Research Approaches

Research surveys of assaultive crimes have varied considerably in the type of statistics they have used. Although police statistics have been the most popular in the United States (such as the studies by Harlan, 1950; and by Wolfgang, 1958), others have used court convictions or prisoner populations (Gillin, 1946). Of course the rates will vary according to the different criteria used. The methodology used in these studies has usually been more detailed analysis of available administrative statistics · for a particular city or police district. In 1964 Sellin and Wolfgang developed a special method for reanalyzing police records in an effort to overcome the offender-offense dichotomy and to introduce into the construction of a crime index an assessment of the seriousness of the different crimes. The question of seriousness had long been a source of controversy over the FBI's selection of crimes for its index. Because the Sellin-Wolfgang method has been given prominence now in two national reports (President's Commission, 1967a; Mulvihill et al., 1969), and by the Council of Europe (1970) in relation to the construction of internationally comparable crime indexes, we should describe it briefly here in relation to assaultive offenses.

First, the Sellin-Wolfgang approach avoids the problem of whether to count offenses or offenders by using the act or event as the pivotal concept, since an offense may be composed of many acts, each varying in seriousness. The seriousness of an act was conceived of in strictly objective terms (in the legal sense of that word), as to whether injury, theft, or damage resulted from the act. Next, by using one of the many psychophysical scaling methods, they selected sections of the public which they defined as representative of middle-class opinion, and asked them to rate the comparative seriousness of a wide range of criminal acts. In this way they hoped to arrive at a general assessment of how important or serious various crimes were in terms of the broad values of society. Their results were supportive of their hypothesis of additivity of the score values, which allowed for interesting quantitative comparisons of the crimes. Table 2 displays the comparative scores of seriousness for a selection of the assaultive offenses used in the Sellin-Wolfgang study. Because of the additivity assumption, it may be concluded that a single and simple crime resulting in death is 26 times more serious than a simple minor assault, $2\frac{1}{2}$ times as serious as rape, and so on.

It should be noted, however, that the disregard of the "subjective" or psychological elements of a criminal act so central in any legal discussion concerning comparative seriousness of crimes, leaves open the question as to just what the term *seriousness*, as measured by Sellin and Wolfgang (1964), means, and may widen the gap between sociological and legal conceptions of crime. Furthermore, some criticisms of the methodology in the Sellin-Wolfgang study have appeared. The European criticism is that the approach simply adumbrates the already lopsided U.S. preoccupation with police statistics (Rose, 1970:34–51), and in America, Erickson (1970: 145–46) argues that Sellin and Wolfgang arbitrarily discarded 77 percent of the original 10 percent random sample which they had selected for their study from the files of the Philadelphia Police Department. Thus, he argues that the index is of limited scope. These criticisms sharply conflict with actual trends in research, for Mulvihill et al. (1969) note at least ten replicas of the Sellin-Wolfgang scaling of seriousness, a number of which are being conducted in other countries as well as the United States.

In summary, it may be said that although the research index tends to be more detailed and based upon criminological theory rather than administrative facilities, the extent to which it is generally applicable to an assessment of the amount of violent crime in a society or nation awaits further study. In the meantime, although the criticisms made of the FBI Crime Reports are very serious ones, we should note, as did Beattie and Kenney (1966) after their exhaustive analysis of earlier crime reports, that these *Uniform Crime Reports* do, in fact, represent the only available nationwide information on crime statistics in the United States. We shall in the following discussion of the extent of assaultive crime try to present a blend of both administrative and research statistics.

PHENOMENOLOGICAL PATTERNING OF ASSAULTIVE CRIME

General Trends and Levels

Having accepted the fact of the unreliability of crime statistics, it is wise to proceed with caution. It is apparent that most types of crime (with the possible exception of forcible rape) have increased over the past twenty years (Mulvihill et al., 1969:55). Beattie and Kenney (1966) analyzed FBI statistics for the 1948–57 period and found that while the increase for assaultive crimes was only 4 percent for that period, for property crimes it was 46 percent. However, criminal homicide showed a 23 percent *decrease* for that period. In 1958, as we have noted, the FBI introduced changes in their reporting system. The combined rate for the three major property crimes (burglary, larceny over $50, and auto theft) increased by 127.3 percent from 1958 to

TABLE 2

MAGNITUDE ESTIMATION SCORES OF SERIOUSNESS
FOR SELECTED ASSAULTIVE OFFENSES

	Score
Simple criminal homicide	26
Assaultive offenses	
Where victim is hospitalized	7
Where victim is treated and discharged	4
Victim mildly wounded, doesn't require professional care	1
Basic score for sexual intercourse by force	10
If the victim is intimidated by a weapon	12

Adapted from Sellin and Wolfgang, 1964: 274–318.

1968, while the rate for the four major violent crimes (criminal homicide, forcible rape, robbery, and aggravated assault) increased 99.6 percent (Mulvihill et al., 1969: 54–57). Reporting overall percent increases can, however, be misleading without also reporting total volume of offenses. For example, the 47.8 percent increase reported for criminal homicide for 1958–68 sounds enormous, but, in fact, it represents an increase from only 4.6 to 6.8 crimes per hundred thousand population. On the other hand, a 79.6 percent increase for aggravated assault represents an increase in volume of from 78.8 to 141.3 crimes per hundred thousand population. A similar increase is reported for robbery. Mulvihill et al. (1969) state, however, that conclusions concerning the extent of increase in forcible rape cannot be made because of the poor reportability of this crime. The question of how "serious" the comparative increases are for society may depend to a large extent upon the values which the society places upon each type of crime.

Before discussing the significance of the variations in incidence of violent crimes, it is necessary to consider the main sociological variables which have been found to be related to assaultive crimes. These are age, sex, race, and urbanization.

Age and Sex

That assaultive crimes, such as homicide, are predominantly crimes of young males from their late teens to their early 30s, is now well established (Hoffman, 1925:23; Brearley, 1932:78–79; De Porte & Parkhurst, 1935:57; Dublin & Bunzel, 1935:128; Cassidy, 1941:297; Banay, 1943:110; Kilpatrick, 1943:396; Von Hentig, 1947:115; Pollak, 1950:156; Royal Commission, 1953:308–9; Henry & Short, 1954:88–89; Wolfgang, 1958; Bensing & Schroeder, 1960; Palmer, 1960; Gibson & Klein, 1961:24–27; Morris & Blom-Cooper, 1961; McClintock, 1963:45–46; Pittman & Handy, 1964; Siciliano, 1965:723). The data on age are based on arrest statistics because age is not usually available for reported crime. Mulvihill et al. analyzed the FBI data for forcible rape arrests, robbery arrests, and aggravated assault arrests and although the patterning of offenders by age was quite similar to the homicide statistics, there was a much clearer tendency for the 15–17-year-old age group to approach the 18–24 rate, with both groups showing a marked increase since 1965 in assaultive offenses (1969:84–85). McClintock also found this tendency toward an increase in assaultive behaviour in these age groups in England and Wales (1963:56–57). For forcible rape, on the basis of both administrative and research statistics, probably about two-thirds of all such offenses are committed by males under the age of 25 (Svalastoga, 1962; Amir, 1967; Hayman et al., 1968; F.B.I., 1969), although a recent study of rape in New York found a somewhat older offender group, with at least half above 25 (Chappell & Singer, 1973).

The validity of these findings is, of course, questionable for it may be argued that police may tend to arrest young people more than older. While younger persons may be more prone to commit forcible rapes and other assaultive offenses, it is questionable if this holds true also for criminal homicide.

Wolfgang (1967:284) notes that every study of homicide has found a low rate of female homicide as compared to the male rate. Verkko (1951:51–57) suggested that there was a greater stability in female homicide, because it retained a standard volume even when the overall homicide rate was high or low. This instability notion is also supported by the study of forty-eight societies by Bacon et al. (1963) where women's criminal aggression was not found to be especially greater in societies where their role was more assertive and more responsible for economic activity.

Mulvihill, Tumin and Curtis concluded that for the 1958–67 period, "it is safe to infer that the true level of violent crime is still disproportionately weighted towards male offenders" (1969:86). They were unable to draw any conclusions as to whether the increase in violent crime involved a greater or lesser percentage increase in female crime compared to that of the male. It was suggested, however, that the types of assaultive offenses which females were more likely to commit were those of the more "intimate" type, such as murder, rather than street crimes, such as robbery.

Popular Interpretations of the Age-Sex Relationships. The most popular explanation of the high youthful male rate of violent crime has been summed up by Wolfgang and Ferracuti (1967:259–60) in terms of predominant values of the masculine ideal, physical prowess, toughness, and so on (see also Miller et al., 1961). The middle-aged need not display their manliness through physical oppression—they have more money, power, and opportunity to assert themselves and manipulate others in business competition and large bureaucracies, and, besides, they are less physically equipped to do so. Obviously this loose generalization has limited value for it is quite possible that certain groups or aggregations of people in a society will prize their own set of aggression-related values and their own accepted ways of displaying aggression regardless of age. A look at social-class distribution of assaultive crime will, in fact, show this to be the case.

Urbanization and Social Class: Regional Variations

It is well known that people with certain common interests and attributes, such as money, middle- or lower-class values, similar upbringing, and religion, tend to live in common areas either in the city, the suburbs, and even broad regions of the U.S. If this hypothesis is correct, we should expect these groups to display differing rates in assaultive crime.

Urbanization. Many classic studies in criminology have identified the "urban crisis" in one form or another, such as the crowded slum of the inner city, the run-down industrial areas, the shifting populations which live in these areas, and the lack of recreational facilities, as being related to many forms of crime (Shaw & McKay, 1942; Morris, 1958).

A strong relationship exists between urbanization and the assaultive crime of homicide. The middle classes usually live in the suburbs of American cities, and the rate there is considerably lower than the large city rate. It is, however, the size of the city itself which is the dominant factor in criminal homicide. Mulvihill et al. (1969:64) report a very similar pattern for the other three violent crimes of forcible rape, robbery, and aggravated assault.

Regional Comparisons. Mulvihill et al. attempted regional comparisons upon the basis of FBI data and also of the National Opinion Research Center victimization studies (Ennis, 1967). However, they cautioned that because the bulk of crime in the U.S. is in the large cities, regional comparisons become only comparisons of the large cities in these regions. Nevertheless, the report concludes that the "true criminal homicide rate is highest in the South," that the "true forcible rape rate is higher in the West," and that robbery is significantly lower in the South (Mulvihill et al., 1969:80). Both the Mulvihill et al. and the Ennis data were too conflicting to allow conclusions concerning aggravated assault.

It is worth noting at this point that, because of this clear relationship between age, urbanization, and assaultive crime, shifts in the age structure of the population and in regional habitation may explain a not too small proportion of the increase in assaultive crime in recent years. Mulvihill et al. (1969:60–61) calculate that at least 12 percent of the increase from 1950 to 1965 can be explained by shifts in age structure alone, while 17 percent may be explained by the increases in urban populations.

Social Class. The relationship between low socioeconomic class and high rate of assaultive crime has been affirmed in many studies and many countries: in Italy: Morselli (1879) and Ferri (1895:710–12); in the United States: from Brearley (1932:43–45) and Wolfgang (1958), to Bensing and Schroeder (1960:119–57); in Denmark: Svalastoga (1956); in Finland: Verkko (1951:145–62); in England: McClintock (1963:133–36) and Morris and Blom-Cooper (1963); in India and Ceylon: Strauss and Strauss (1953), Bloch (1960), Jayewardene (1960, 1963, 1964), Driver (1961), and Wood (1961a, 1961b); in Mexico: Bustamante and Bravo (1957), and Alzaga (1967); and in South Africa: Lamont (1961).

Although most crimes in general (with the exception of white-collar crimes) are attributed to the lower socioeconomic classes, there is evidence to suggest less difference between the classes (Svalastoga, 1962; Pittman & Handy, 1964; Pokorny, 1965a, 1965b). The evidence against this conclusion is provided by the anonymous self-report studies of Christie et al. (1965) and Elmhorn (1965) where subjects of all social classes tended to report that they had committed a wide range of acts which could be considered as potentially criminal behaviour, but where no great differences among the social classes were apparent (see also Hardt & Bodine, 1965). The implication here is that the rates may be the same for all classes, but that the police and criminal justice system in general tends to concentrate selectively more upon the lower classes. However, Wolfgang and Ferracuti (1967:261) argued that people are very unlikely to report a homicide which they have committed, though they may "boast" about other crimes. Furthermore, these self-report studies do not include homicide in their questionnaires. A more recent self-report study (using interviews) by Gold (1966) on undetected delinquent behaviour affirmed the inverse relationship between social class and criminality for boys. This is not to say, of course, that upper- and middle-class homicides do not occur. But, when they do occur, they are most often characterized by major psychopathology of the offender, or are a planned, "rational," premeditated murder where the offender has been able to justify to himself the performance of the deed. This is in contrast to the outbursts of aggression resulting from trivial altercations which are typical of the lower-class homicidal offender. This pattern was found in a very high proportion of the cases studied by Wolfgang (1958) over a five-year period. Wolfgang found that 90–95 percent of criminal homicide offenders of both races were from the blue-collar, low socioeconomic class (1958:37). A higher involvement of the lower socioeconomic class in other types of assaultive crime is also very likely. In Philadelphia, Amir (1965:153) found 90 percent of forcible rape offenders, and Normandeau (1968:186) found 92–97 percent of robbery offenders to be lower class. Pittman and Handy (1964) found the lower class to predominate in assaultive crime in St. Louis, and the President's Commission on Crime in the District of Columbia (1966:131–32) found approximately 40 percent of violent crime offenders of both races to be unemployed and many others in unskilled occupations. The victim-offender survey in Mulvihill et al. (1969:chap. 5) also displays similar findings.

So far, we have referred to the lower social-class involvement without distinguishing between black and white races where the studies provided such a breakdown. It is commonplace to note that those who make up the larger proportion of the lower income groups of America are blacks. When it has been possible, however, to hold race constant, the differences between upper and lower class still hold. It is clear that to be black *and* lower class makes for a very high likelihood of involvement in assaultive crime (Wolfgang et al., 1972). This is our next important variable.

Race

Let us first deal with the question as to whether there really is a higher rate of assaultive crime for blacks as against whites. Although, since 1964 (the first year the FBI began to break down arrest statistics by race), administrative statistics have shown considerably higher rates for blacks as against whites, the validity of these statistics has been questioned on the grounds that the police are more likely to seek out and arrest blacks than whites. Keeping to our cautious use of crime statistics, Table 3 displays the striking difference in criminal homicide rates between races, based upon FBI data. The cohort study by Wolfgang et al. (1972) on a birth cohort of 2,902 nonwhite and 7,043 white youths provides an interesting check on the FBI's statistics, especially as the research nature of the study allowed a more rigorous collection and definition of offenses. Table 3 displays the striking similarity in the findings. Arrest statistics in regard to race can be extremely misleading. As Wolfgang (1964:51) points out, arrests in any year represent only 30 percent of all index crimes recorded. Garfinkel (1949) found that substantially fewer indictments were made in North Carolina when whites killed blacks than when blacks killed whites. Myrdal (1944) found that over the period 1920–32 out of 497 blacks killed by white persons in the South, 54 percent were slain by police officers. Other studies reporting similar discrimination are summarized by Wolfgang (1964). But regarding these problems, Mulvihill et al. (1969:94) still conclude: "in spite of the weaknesses of the data, it is difficult to believe that the much higher arrest levels are due only to reporting errors or biases." Furthermore they suggest that the rate of criminal homicide, and possibly robbery, for 1964–67 has been increasing faster for blacks than for whites, though conclusions cannot be reached for aggravated assault and forcible rape.

Homicide is the second leading cause of death among black men 15–25 years old, and the third among all men 25–44. Furthermore, it is well established that homi-

TABLE 3

RELATIONSHIP OF BLACK TO WHITE ARREST RATES
FOR FOUR TYPES OF ASSAULTIVE CRIME
(10–17-year-old age group)

| | Number of Times Black Rate Higher than White | |
Offense	FBI (1958–67)	Wolfgang et al. (1955–63)
Criminal homicide	17	Insufficient data
Forcible rape	12	13
Robbery	20	20
Aggravated assault	8	10

Sources: Federal Bureau of Investigation, *Crime in the United States: Uniform Crime Reports,* 1958 through 1967; Wolfgang et al., 1972.

cide and probably assaultive crimes are basically intragroup crimes that occur between people who have frequent contact with each other. Garfinkel (1949) determined that only 9 percent of the homicides he studied during 1930–40 were interracial, and other studies since then have found lesser proportions: Harlan (1950), 3 percent; Wolfgang (1958), 6 percent; Pittman and Handy (1964), 4 percent; and Meyers (reported in Wolfgang, 1964), 3 percent. Similar interrace patterning was reported by Mulvihill et al. (1969:299–300) for aggravated assault and forcible rape. The exception, however, was armed robbery where 4 percent of offenses were interracial and where blacks robbing whites was the typical pattern.

One need hardly point out that it cannot be concluded from all the data presented above that blacks are intrinsically, or biologically, or in some way "by nature," more violent. As Wolfgang has eloquently stated:

> . . . if a careful, detached scholar knew nothing about crime rates but was aware of the social, economic and political disparities between Whites and Negroes in the United States, and if this diligent researcher had prior knowledge of the historical status of the American Negro, what would be the most plausible hypothesis our scholar could make about the crime rate of Negroes? Even this small amount of relevant knowledge would justify the expectation that Negroes would be found to have a higher crime rate than Whites (1964:31).

It is, furthermore, methodologically unsound to assume that one can compare crime rates for blacks and whites of the same socioeconomic status. Such a procedure grossly oversimplifies the situation of the blacks. The case is eloquently stated by Shaw and McKay:

> The important fact about rates of delinquency for Negro boys is that they, too, vary by type or area. They are higher than the rates for white boys, but it cannnot be said that they are higher than rates for white boys in comparable areas, since it is impossible to reproduce in white communities the circumstances under which Negro children live. Even if it were possible to parallel the low economic status and the inadequacy of institutions in the white community, it would not be possible to reproduce the effects of segregation and the barriers to upward mobility. These combine to create for the Negro child a type of social world in which the higher rates of delinquency are not unintelligible (1949:617).

Mulvihill et al. (1969:133–34) also list other works which consider this problem in detail.

Relationship Between Offender and Victim

We have already touched upon the notion of the intragroup nature of assaultive crime in that blacks kill blacks, whites kill whites. For criminal homicide it is also the case that predominantly males kill males, women kill women, or relatives and persons over 25 kill persons of the same age category (Wolfgang, 1958; McClintock, 1963; Voss & Hepburn, 1968; Mulvihill et al., 1969:209). Where cross-sex homicides occur, it is most commonly a laborer killing his wife (Mulvihill et al., 1969:244). Wolfgang (1958) found that 37 percent of the homicides he studied issued from trivial altercations, 13 percent from domestic quarrels, and another 11 percent from jealousy. A similar pattern was also found by Voss and Hepburn (1968) in Chicago, by Pokorny (1965a, 1965b) in Houston, and by Bensing and Schroeder (1960) in Cleveland.

Similar victim patterns are reported for aggravated assault, though with a higher proportion of female/male assaults (Mulvihill et al., 1969:209). Apart from the obvious male against female, no clear pattern for rape was reported. The leading offender-victim combination for armed robbery was black males 18–23 robbing white males 26 and over.

The Wolfgang study (1958) also found that 25 percent of the homicides occurred between family members. Similarly, the Voss and Hepburn study (1968) in Chicago found 42 percent of homicides to be between friends or relatives, the President's Commission on Crime in the District of Columbia (1966) found 27 percent of homicides to be between spouses, and Pokorny (1965a, 1965b) reported that only 1 percent of criminal homicides occurred between strangers, while 50 percent were between relatives and close friends.

The victim survey data analyzed by Mulvihill et al. (1969) shows a somewhat lower rate. However, it is clear from Table 4 that criminal homicide is the most intimate of violent crimes (Goode, 1969) and that forcible rape and armed robbery are more commonly perpetrated upon strangers.

The Family and Assaultive Crime

As we have seen, a considerable proportion of assaultive crime occurs between members of the family or intimate primary group. A number of types of assaultive crime—some rare, but others not so rare—occur within this setting.

Spouse Killings. The FBI's reports for 1969 (1970) revealed that over one-half of the 25 percent of criminal homicides occurring within the family involved spouse killings. Of this, 54 percent were wife killings, 46 percent were husband killings. Similar findings were reported by Wolfgang (1958), where he found that husbands were more likely to be killed in the kitchen with a butcher knife, and wives were more likely to be slain in the bedroom. Psychiatric research suggests that the act of wife killing is not motivated by mental disease, but primarily by aggression resulting from frustration of dependency needs or from excessive jealousy (Cormier, 1962; Perdue, 1966).

Parent Killings. Iskrant and Joliet (1968) report that parent killings amount to only 6 percent of family killings, and that they are virtually always carried out by the son. Matricide appears to occur more frequently than patricide (McKnight et al., 1966). Wertham (1941) found that most mother killers had been excessively attached

TABLE 4
PERCENT OF CRIMINAL HOMICIDES IN SEVENTEEN CITIES
ACCORDING TO VICTIM-OFFENDER RELATIONSHIP
AND TYPE OF ASSAULTIVE CRIME, 1967

	Criminal homicide	Aggravated assault	Forcible rape	Armed robbery
Primary group (i.e., family and close friends)	33.7	20.6	10.2	1.0
Nonprimary	45.4	55.0	85.7	90.8
Not known	20.9	24.3	4.1	8.2

Adapted from Mulvihill et al., 1969:217.

to their mothers since early childhood, and appeared as well-behaved children until the time of the murder (see also Mcgargee, 1967). The killing was often instigated by a trivial circumstance though the son had commonly fought against the impulse to kill his mother for some time. Concealment of the deed was usually lacking and the murderer usually made a full, voluntary confession. However, it should be noted that children who kill are rare (Wolfgang, 1967:4). There are approximately 700 parent killings a year in the United States and about one-third of the victims of children who kill are members of the immediate family (Shah & Weber, 1968:217). The study by McNeil (1966) suggests that when children kill, it is most often the natural outcome of sudden violence using whatever weapon is closest at hand, although Wolfgang and Ferracuti (1967:260) claim that these rare cases are usually caused by individual pathologies, such as brain damage, or clear-cut mental disturbance. Bender (1934) and Podolsky (1965) have tried to delineate "dangerous symptoms" of children who may kill, but these have been based upon extremely small samples. Furthermore, although Bender keeps to the more traditional clinically definable pathologies, such as organic brain damage or abnormal EEG, Podolsky goes as far as suggesting that the model child's extreme goodness may be a warning sign (1965:99).

Infanticide, Child Killing and Child Abuse. Infanticide is usually distinguished from child murder because the killing may result more from a philosophical belief or an argued humanitarian viewpoint than from some overt psychosis as has been found more commonly with studies of murderers of children (Mathesen, 1941; McDermaid & Winkler, 1955; Chapman, 1959; Kingler, 1959; Holzer, 1961; West, 1966). Although the majority of murderers are mostly the mothers of the victim, no research has been conducted to investigate the extent to which medical practitioners may perpetrate infanticide on humanitarian grounds. Where psychopathology has been found, it is characterized as "child-centered obsessional depression," where the parent suffers from a feeling of inability to care for the child, or a depressive state with suicidal tendencies.

Myers (1967) studied eighty-three cases of homicide in which adolescents were victims, and found that sixty of these were killed by a parent or close relative, and where slayings were by mothers (the vast majority), there was evidence of overt psychosis. This finding is supported by a number of previous studies (Morton, 1934; Smith, 1960; Adelson, 1961; Gatti, 1963).

However, there is a growing body of literature which suggests that child killings may result from "widespread aggressive primitive behaviour" on the part of some parents (Wolfgang & Ferracuti, 1967:208), and a survey by Gil reported in Mulvihill et al. (1969:108), using a representative sample, found that 58.3 percent of the respondents thought that "almost anybody could at some time injure a child in his care."

Unfortunately, it is extremely difficult to establish the extent of child abuse because of the poor reportability of the crime. One parent usually protects the other. The victims tend to be mostly under 3 years old and often the physician fails to report such cases, even though all states in the U.S. now have mandatory reporting laws (Polansky & Polansky, 1967). Before this legislation, Jeter (1963) studied 377 thousand public child-welfare service cases for 1961, and found that child abuse or neglect were the most important presenting problems. It was estimated that approximately 183 thousand children were involved in neglect, abuse, or exploitation on any one day in the U.S. Subsequently, Zalba (1966) has estimated that 200 to 250 thousand children in the U.S. need protective services each year and of these 30 thousand need protection against serious physical abuse. Gil and Noble (1967) found that 3 percent of a national sample of adults over 21 reported having knowledge of an incident of child abuse during the preceding year. This seemed far too high, and Gil (1968) conducted a further study of officially reported child abuse in forty U.S. cities and countries, and found 6 thousand cases of child abuse. After reviewing much of this evidence, Mulvihill et al. conclude: "Six thousand reported cases of physical abuse per year in a nation of 200 million, in spite of under reporting, do not constitute a major social problem at least in relative terms, tragic as every single incident may be" (1969:109).

As with child killings, the majority of child abuse cases are the result of parental aggression rather than aggression of strangers, baby-sitters, or even other close relatives (De Francis, 1963). Little objective research is available concerning the family characteristics relating to the now popularly termed "battered child" syndrome (Ferracuti et al., 1966). The studies of both De Francis (1963) and Elmer (1967) suggest that at least two-thirds or more were intact families at the time of the aggressive acts. The average age of the mother was 26, and of the father 30 (De Francis, 1963). The families were not transient, were self-supporting, though they tended to be isolated from community activities. Both Elmer (1967) and Gil (1968) found a definite over-representation of lower socioeconomic families, and there is the likelihood that the "hard core" family, characterized by apathy, unemployment, drunkenness, and prostitution, vacillating parental attitudes, or remorseful overprotectiveness and emotional explosiveness, is related to some types of child abuse (Young, 1964; Howells, 1966).

INTERPRETATIONS OF THE DATA

Although it has been possible to present data on the different variables as though they were separate aspects of assaultive crime, their interpretation or explanation in terms of the theories we have at our disposal cannot be attempted in such a piecemeal fashion because all such variables as age, sex, class, race, and urbanization are basically constructs, and often are not independent or exhaustive categories. Each category presupposes a large set of socially prescribed values or characteristics which, when imposed upon data, are to some extent stereotypical (Herzog [1970] summarizes this problem and has an extensive bibliography). This applies equally to a category like sex, which, although biologically definable, carries with it a large number of socially prescribed values, and to other categories, such as social class, which is not definable biologically and certainly quite difficult to define in social terms. Age as a variable also is misleading when we consider that young people develop at very different rates, both physically and mentally. Care should be taken, therefore, in making blanket statements concerning the relationship between any of these variables and assaultive behaviour—especially in relation to individual behaviour. We shall, therefore, break with the earlier format, and in the following pages present brief outlines of the main ideas which may be used to explain variations and occurrence of assaultive behaviour.

It is worthwhile to note that the most recent theories—both in psychology and sociology—that have been used to explain violent behaviour have most often been developed in relation to somewhat less specific aspects of behaviour, such as deviance or crime in general and, in fact, normal behaviour. The reason for this is the gradual decline over the past ten to fifteen years of the idea that criminals are in some way intrinsically (either physically or psychologically) different from other people. Minor exceptions to this are the latest chromosome theories (Fox, 1970). But, generally speaking, the most favored theories over the past ten years have been those which leaned toward the propositions that (a) all behaviour is learned, (b) what is criminal or deviant depends upon who is doing the defining, and (c) thus a criminal may be any (normal) person to whom the label has been attached. There are, of course, exceptions to each step of these propositions, but they fairly accurately represent the current criminological scene. In presenting the basic concepts to explain the variables of assaultive behaviour, we shall also break with the usual procedure of dividing them into the levels of biology, psychology, and sociology, and shall instead present ideas which can be said to extend across one or more levels of analysis. We choose this method because we affirm the necessity of retaining an integrated conceptualization of violent behaviour (Wolfgang & Ferracuti, 1967), and, with the limited space available, this may be the most efficacious way of maintaining integration.

It is, of course, clear that we shall be heavily involved in *ex post facto* explanations of crime data. This is regrettable but unavoidable when one considers that the data presented in the first section has been collected largely for administrative reasons rather than to test specific causal hypotheses. The best that can be done, therefore, is to try to merge theories that derive from different levels of analysis into each other, and thus hope to cover a broad sweep of causally related factors.

Barrier Theories

Since Freud's idea of the damming up of the libido, various theories have evolved which have adopted this idea as a model in one form or another. The most well-known sociological counterpart has been Merton's theory (1968) of deviance and anomie, and its offshoot, opportunity theory. Simply stated, Merton's theory was that society is structured in such a way that people must pursue a common goal (in America: success as measured by financial resources). Unfortunately, not all have access to the means of obtaining this goal, so broad societal adaptations result. Open rebellion occurs as one of these adaptations when both the means and the goal are rejected. As Merton says, "When the institutional system is regarded as the barrier to the satisfaction of legitimized goals, the stage is set for rebellion as an adaptive response" (Merton, 1968:210). Merton insisted that such adaptations were societal in nature, so he saw this aspect of his theory as explaining the rise of revolutions and other types of group violence. Nevertheless, it is clear that the model underlying this theory is one in which man is depicted as striving for something he cannot get because there is a barrier in his way. Why should it be specifically *rebellion* that is the modal response to this "sociological bind"? Without the added assumption that such a situation does something to a person so he acts out, or erupts forth, the Mertonian theory cannot answer this question. But when the theory is stated in this form, it can be seen that it resembles quite closely the frustration-aggression hypothesis, which has been a classic model in psychology since the work of Dollard et al. (1939).

Despite the large amount of research that has been conducted in this area, especially in more recent times by psychologists such as Berkowitz (1962), the frustration-aggression hypothesis remains questionable. The scope of this chapter does not permit us to go into the complex relationships between frustration and aggression, except to say that, in relation to the Mertonian model, the only conclusion that can be safely drawn from the psychological research is that it is not clear that aggression necessarily follows frustration (Wolfgang & Ferracuti, 1967:143–46). The difficulty of specifying the causal relationship between frustration and aggression at the laboratory level makes it quite understandable that efforts made in criminology to apply this hypothesis directly to the study of homicides (Henry & Short, 1954; Palmer, 1960) have produced equivocal results, which can be easily interpreted according to other theories (Reckless, 1961:138–40). The McCary study (1949) fails to support the Henry and

Short claim that Southern Negro groups were more extrapunitively aggressive because they were more frustrated. Yet it must surely be clear today that blacks as a group are more frustrated. And it is apparent that their rates of assaultive behaviour especially among themselves *are* very high. However, one would have thought that, because Merton (1968) uses the word "rebellion," it is implied that the direction of aggression would be toward those who were successful, in this case blacks against whites. This is not the case according to the data we have presented. The Mertonian model, therefore, does not easily explain race differences in "assaultive" behaviour.

With this model it might be possible to explain sex differences if we assume that it is the role of men in a traditional capitalist society to achieve success (as measured by money) while women stay at home. Thus, we would expect men to encounter more barriers to success, become more frustrated, and subsequently more aggressive. On the other hand, the arguments of the women's liberation movement are that women suffer the greatest barrier of all, being relegated to a "housewife only" role, resulting in the stereotype of the frustrated housewife. However, the rate of assaultive behaviour of females is extremely low compared to males, and although housewives, when they are criminally violent, tend to attack their husbands, it is likely that this is related to a complex of interpersonal factors as well as, or even more than, the wife's frustration from being kept from the monetary goal of success.

As far as age differences are concerned, Merton's model (1968) bears a close similarity to the popular explanation which we summarized during our presentation of the data: that adults have more opportunity to assert themselves and manipulate others so there are less barriers to their success. For younger people, there is a world dominated by the rules of the older generation with which they must conform to succeed. Youths who have not learned these rules (essentially middle-class rules as Cohen [1955] argues) will be unable to achieve their goals and frustration and aggression may result. Once again, however, it is clear from the data presented that much youthful aggression is not directed against those who are succeeding (and thus it cannot be truly called a rebellion) but against each other. We may conclude that the Mertonian model fits only tenuously into this patterning of assaultive crime.

Who could be said to be more frustrated according to the Mertonian model? The psychological implications of the Mertonian scheme are that those who are denied the means to attain their goal will be frustrated, and if success, as measured by money, is the dominant goal, it must mean that the lower classes (the unsuccessful by this standard) will be frustrated or more frustrated, and thus more aggressive. The Cloward and Ohlin (1960) extension of the theory suggests that there are higher rates of violence by lower than by upper classes, and that the lower classes are oriented toward the success goals of the middle class. And a further broad assumption of this barrier model is that some element of the human personality, either an instinct or a learned drive of aggression, erupts when man's dominant desires are thwarted. This leads us to the next two explanatory models: the bad influence theory, and the idea that aggression is an unavoidable or inevitable part of human existence.

Theories of Inevitability

The most basic and probably the oldest theory of aggression is the idea that man is aggressive by nature, that there is within every man a born instinct of aggression.

An important distinction has been made in the psychological literature which should be borne in mind when considering the various sociological theories related to the inevitability of aggression. There are two broad types of aggression: one which assumes an aggressive drive that is reinforced by inflicting pain on the victim (Dollard et al., 1939) ; the other is instrumental aggression, where aggressive responses are reinforced in the same way as those that follow any instrumental response (Buss, 1961). These responses represent distinct divergences in the conception of aggression for the former assumes a basic, if not innate, or at least deeply embedded, aggressive drive, while the latter clearly places aggression on the level of every other type of social learning.

It is apparent that the first type is more related to the frustration-aggression concept, and thus may underlie the Mertonian scheme. This is not surprising when we consider that the Mertonian model had its starting point in Durkheim's theory (1897) of anomie, in which man was seen as potentially irrational and requiring exterior controls and constraints. The second type of aggression is more related to the "bad company" theories which we shall discuss next.

We should realize that the work of Dollard et al. (1939) and Sears (1943), while adopting the learning theory model of Hull (1943), was essentially translating the Freudian views on the instinct of aggression into hypotheses which could be tested in the laboratory. While the tendency of learning theorists since that time has been to argue that a basic instinct of aggression does not exist, their work, nevertheless, supported the idea that some driving force called aggression developed in humans, and that this aggressive behaviour could be elicited by certain identifiable stimuli. While Freud placed heavy emphasis upon the innate quality of the instincts of sex and aggression, later learning theorists and neo-Freudians have emphasized the very large part which social experience plays in the development of the instinct of aggression.

The Freudian idea of this reservoir of aggression existing inside man has also played an important role in catharsis theories, which, in typical psychoanalytical fashion, point to the importance of social institutions which allow "letting off steam." Thus, it is argued that the watching of violence may be cathartic (Berkowitz, 1962), as may partaking in rough and violent sports. Such a view assumes that aggression "dams up" inside a person and needs to be released every now and again. It also means that contact with violent others may not necessarily lead to a person becoming violent. It is important to note the distinction here between learning and performance: bad company theories, as we shall see shortly, may provide the foundations for the learning of aggressive responses, but not necessarily for their performance.

The "inevitability" theory, on the other hand, suggests that aggressive acts will be performed because of the internal drive for aggression. If we were to draw a link to the barrier theories here, we might posit that settings which allowed more opportunity to release aggression would be less frustrating and more cathartic. Thus, middle classes should be more aggressive because there is supposedly more attempt to inhibit aggressive responses. As this idea is not supported by the data, the aggressive drive theory can only be supported if we further argue that middle classes have more chance for "displacement" of aggression in legitimate ways, and thus have lower rates of assaultive crime. Thus, the Cloward and Ohlin (1960) formulation concerning differential opportunity would become one in which there was differential opportunity to displace aggression by legitimate or illegitimate means.

By far the strongest thrust toward the idea of the inevitability of aggression has come more recently from the revival of instinct theories in the work of the ethologists. Eibl-Eibesfeldt (1961) begins with the observation that fighting between members of the same species is almost universal since species members must compete for food, nesting places, and so on. Yet both he and Tinbergen (1968) point out that this aggressive behaviour in animals is highly ritualized and rarely leads to death or serious injuries as it does in humans. In the face of arguments and research of learning theorists against the idea of an innate aggressive drive, Konrad Lorenz (1966) has insisted that an aggressive instinct exists though he does say that it is modifiable, and the way that it manifests itself may depend considerably upon predominant societal and cultural norms. Further, Lorenz points to what may be called "releasing" mechanisms, where certain types of situations will automatically release aggressive behaviour. Thus, if we adopt the "territorial imperative" (Ardrey, 1963), we find that many animal species will defend their territory or nest with great zeal if it is threatened. The idea resulting from this is to ascribe the high urban rates of assaultive crime, especially gang-related violence, to an instinct for defense of territory. This whole string of explanatory hypotheses depends almost entirely upon research evidence collected from the study of animal behaviour, and thus its transposition into the human setting has often been questioned (Scott, 1958).

The fact remains, it must be stated, that if we accept solely the idea of an aggression instinct, which cannot be modified, there is no way of explaining the differential rates of assaultive behaviour between different societal groups except to make the dead-end hypothesis that certain groups of people are innately more aggressive than others. Such a view has formed the basis for the stereotypical prejudices about blacks and other minority groups in America and elsewhere. The implication of this view is that no matter whether we call it instinct, drive, or habit, we must assume modifiability, or call a halt to social research. Furthermore, the term *innate* is extremely misleading. The popular use of the word implies that people inherit traits in isolation from their culture. The fact is that innateness, or heredity, both biological and social, are closely tied to the cultural and social history of the group. A long history of extremely impoverished and disturbed social and physical conditions may result in the gradual destruction of the people, and thus affect each subsequent generation. It is clear, therefore, that we must look toward the culture of the particular group to understand why its pattern of behaviour is different from other groups in society.

Bad Influence Theories

In essence, all of the subculture theories of delinquency are variations of this theme, and most build upon the differential association theory of Sutherland (Sutherland & Cressey, 1970). These theories explicitly assume that violent persons learn their violent responses from other violent persons. The Cloward and Ohlin theory (1960) is a sophisticated reformulation of this idea into Merton's language (1968). The means to success may be either legitimate or illegitimate, depending, one presumes, upon whom one knows or is influenced by. Short and Strodtbeck (1965), for example, theorize that delinquents may not be oriented toward the values of the middle class, but are oriented to the values of their gang and directed to achieving status within that set of values. If assaultive behaviour is valued highly by the gang, then that behaviour will be indulged in as a means to achieve status. From this theoretical shift, the orientation toward goals is given lesser importance, and the role of learning and the transmission of values related to violence is asserted more strongly. The Wolfgang and Ferracuti (1967) subculture theory of violence, which will be discussed below, is a logical extension of this theoretical perspective.

Much of the research in social psychology in this area has centered upon the process of learning aggressive behaviour, especially upon the role of models of aggression and the conditions under which one will learn aggressive responses from such models. The work of Bandura and Walters (1959, 1963), Trasler (1962), and Eysenck (1964) has attempted to account for the differential imitation and learning of aggression. Of relevance to this chapter, we may extract two important conclusions from the research: (1) The majority of learning theory models posit a positive or accumulative aspect of conditioning in which a person develops new models of behaviour as a result of positive (or reinforcing) experiences with role models. Thus, if a child is brought up in a setting in which violence is *valued* as a way of life, he will probably learn violent responses. (2) The majority of learning theory models also posit a negative or inhibiting aspect to the conditioning process, so persons brought up in a setting where they are not taught to inhibit their aggressive impulses may become impulsively aggressive (Wolfgang & Ferracuti, 1967:149).

The data on assaultive crime certainly demonstrate prevalence of the former type of aggressive behaviour for, as we have seen, the majority of assaultive crime is of an "intragroup" nature, and much more frequent in some groups than in others. Furthermore, Bandura and Walters (1959, 1963) point out that the differential learning of aggression may depend very much upon the overall personality development of the child, which, in turn, depends strongly upon the social environment—the values to be internalized and the models available. Thus, the fact that entirely different sets of values are favored for boys as against girls (such as manliness or toughness) would suggest that this differential process may be related to the wide difference in assaultive behaviour between the sexes. Indeed, by this hypothesis we should expect that the whole process would be self-perpetuating in that aggressive male adults may be models for their sons, who in turn become aggressive models for their sons. There is considerable evidence in the literature that this process occurs in fact (Sears, 1943; Bandura & Walters, 1959; Lovaas, 1961; see Wolfgang & Ferracuti, 1967:177 for bibliography), and furthermore that strong identification with the father is unnecessary: the aggressive father, regardless of the nature of his relationship with the child, is sufficient to elicit imitating responses from the child (A. Freud, 1937; Bandura & Huston, 1961).

The theory stated in this form, however, does not seem to explain the age differences in assaultive crime, for we should expect that the adults, if they are models for aggression, would have just as high rates as juveniles, in fact they might even be higher if juveniles were still learning from them. Thus, some proposition concerning the changes in aggressive behaviour in relation to personality development and maturity would seem more appropriate here. This social-learning model is unable as yet to take into account the complex psychological adjustments and compensations which may take place over time. But taking the perspective as it stands, it is apparent that it could well explain the differences in race and social-class rates of violence. It is obvious that in cultures in which there are more aggressive models for children to imitate and in cultures which value violence more than others higher rates of assaultive behaviour should result. There is abundant evidence in the literature which links patterns of child rearing, race, and social class with the learning of aggression (Sears, 1943; Davis & Havighurst, 1946; Bossard, 1948; McArthur, 1955; White, 1955; Brim, 1957; Gold, 1958; Montague & Epps, 1958; Kohlberg, 1959; Kohn, 1963; Kriesberg, 1963; Leggett, 1963; Rodman, 1963; Minturn & Lambert, 1964; Roger, 1964).

Considered in relation to this evidence, it is reasonable to posit that bad influence theories may explain a considerable part of the differential violence rates for race and social class.

Culture Theories

In many ways, culture theories of violence embrace all aspects of the theories which we have briefly described above. The emphasis, however, is upon the differential patterning of conditioning and social learning, external constraints, values and norms, attitudes and life styles, and orientations toward the values of one's own culture or those of another. However, Wolfgang and Ferracuti (1967) suggest that over and above this differential patterning is the homogeneity of the cultural group, the closeness of physical and social contact, the common acquiescence to norms and values. As they point out:

> Homicide is most prevalent, or the highest rates of homicide occur, among a relatively homogeneous sub-cultural group in any large urban community. Similar prevalent rates can be found in some rural areas. The value system of this group, we are contending, constitutes a sub-culture of violence. From a psychological viewpoint, we might hypothesize that the greater the degree of integration of the individual into this sub-culture, the higher the probability that his behaviour will be violent in a variety of situations. From the sociological side, there should be a direct relationship between rates of homicide and the extent to which the sub-culture of violence represents a cluster of values around the theme of violence (1967:152).

At the intracultural level, we can see that the data support this theory in that there are considerable differences in assaultive crime among various groups in society which adhere to different sets of values, and that much assaultive crime occurs within groups, rather than across groups. Further evidence may come from the study of cultural groups with the highest rates of homicide, with a view to studying the value system of the subculture, ". . . the importance of human life in the scale of values, the kinds of expected reaction to certain types of stimuli, and the general personality of the sub-cultural actors" (Wolfgang & Ferracuti, 1967:153). When one notes that a considerable amount of criminal homicide occurs as a result of trivial altercations between persons closely related to each other, one can see that even the smallest details of the way people expect each other to act may be important to the understanding of violent crime (see Wolfgang, 1958:188–89).

Apart from the "subcultural" differences in rates of assaultive crime, evidence for the cultural perspective also comes from cross-cultural comparisons of assaultive behaviour. The evidence is of two types: (1) from international crime statistics, and (2) descriptive data concerning codes of violence in usually small, isolated communities.

First, let us consider the international comparison of rates of assaultive crime. We should begin with the usual warning: as we noted at the beginning of this chapter, the interpretation of crime statistics is somewhat chancy. When we do it internationally, the difficulties are multiplied many times. Different countries have widely varying laws and definitions of crime, quite different court and police systems, differing traditions and values as to what is considered criminal or violent, different administrative procedures for collecting crime statistics. Because of this, in considering international differences, we shall keep to criminal homicide as being the statistic with the least recording and reporting error. We will note some differences for other crimes only for interest.

Mulvihill et al. (1969:118–27) report international crime statistics for the period 1955 to 1966 which clearly show that the United States maintains a criminal homicide rate approximately twice that of many other industrialized countries. However, if we consider rate of *increase* over these ten years, a somewhat different picture emerges in which the U.S. rate, although in the group of countries showing high increases, nevertheless has only increased at half Norway's rate, about the same as Germany and Denmark, but double that of England and Wales (Mulvihill et al., 1969:120).

Table 5, which includes many other countries besides industrialized Western countries, indicates that there are a number of countries which have considerably higher rates than the U.S. Out of the sixty-nine countries represented, nineteen display higher rates than the U.S. for criminal homicide, and eighteen for robbery. The rates for Burma, Ethiopia, Pakistan, British Guyana, Congo, and Thailand are extremely high. There seems to be a generally high rate for developing nations. Large cultural groups differ considerably in the amount of assaultive crime as measured by criminal homicide, and this seems to be unrelated to the political or economic structure of the society, since countries similar to the U.S. in this regard have lower rates, yet some countries widely different from the U.S. have higher and some lower rates. It is, there-

TABLE 5
OFFENDERS DETECTED BY POLICE FOR
MURDER OR ROBBERY,
VARIOUS COUNTRIES, 1966
(rates per hundred thousand population)

Country	Murder	Robbery
Aden	2.0	35.0
Antilles (Neth.) (1965)	13.4	303.8
Argentina	3.09	24.03
Australia (1965)	2.04	54.46
Austria	2.0	238.0
Bermuda	8.0	496.0
British Guyana	14.1	24.6
British Solomons	1.43	14.78
British West Indies	8.9	not rep.
Brunei (1965)	—	7.0
Burma	86.1	417.5
Canada	1.9	15.6
Ceylon	12.21	38.82
China, Republic of	12.39	121.744
Congo (Brazzaville)	27.7	8.2
Cyprus	5.27	47.61
Denmark	.2	58.9
England and Wales	.34	105.2
Ethiopia	25.74	21.52
Fiji	1.0	30.0
Finland	1.8	140.8
France	2.58	41.83
Germany, Fed. Rep. (incl. West Berlin)	3.0	141.2
Ghana	.48	1.05
Greece (1965)	.7	not rep.
Hong Kong	1.13	16.98
India	2.7	9.0
Indonesia	.19	20.28
Iran	.7	3.0
Ireland, Republic of	.4	100.7
Israel	2.9	359.7
Italy	3.58	100.28

fore, more likely that it is the complex interplay of values, norms, and life styles that permit the use of violence, rather than gross economic or political factors, although, of course, these variables are undoubtedly interrelated. The popular view that violence is an American way of life gains considerable support from this analysis.

A number of accounts of cultural groups with value systems strongly supporting the use of violence are available.

Violencia Colombiana. For the period from 1938 to 1956 there were extremely high increases in homicides in Colombia related to a kind of undeclared civil war, or "epidemic disorder" (Caplow, 1963), between the two main political parties. As of 1960 the homicide rate per hundred thousand for Colombia was 33.8 compared to 14.6 in 1938, and in several districts the rate was nearly twice as high as the official rate. Homicide has been the leading form of death for the 15–44-year age group, and the forms of killing, especially in the guerrilla operations, have taken an extremely sadistic form. Killing has become an everyday, public event, and a whole set of new words has

TABLE 5—Continued

Country	Murder	Robbery
Ivory Coast	2.2	19.9
Jamaica	4.6	159.4
Japan	2.3	3.84
Korea, Republic of	1.41	92.2
Kuwait	7.55	29.39
Libya	11.2	37.1
Luxembourg	8.92	94.46
Madagascar	2.8	15.4
Malawi	2.2	55.3
Malaysia	.5	1.9
Monaco	—	17.6
Morocco	1.0	15.6
Netherlands	3.0	119.4
Nigeria	1.6	5.9
Northern Ireland	.35	82.7
Norway	.19	74.47
Pakistan	20.77	28.24
Peru	7.9	21.46
Philippines	19.05	11.53
Portugal	2.2	3.0
Scotland	1.88	233.58
Senegal	6.1	36.1
Sierra Leone	1.36	13.36
Singapore	.88	10.5
Spain	.54	24.59
Surinam	3.0	54.0
Sweden	.3	61.6
Syria	6.0	11.0
Thailand	21.2	21.48
Trinidad	19.0	51.0
Tunisia	2.54	16.3
Uganda	14.4	60.1
United Arab Republic	7.6	.8
U.S.A.	5.6	78.3
Zambia	1.2	1.6

Source: INTERPOL, *International Crime Statistics*, 1965–66.

arisen to describe the various methods of mutilation, naming of guerrilla leaders, and plans for extermination. In fact, leaders often become idealized figures. Obviously, political aspects have been related to this problem, but it is difficult to avoid the suggestion that the gradual absorption into the culture of values idealizing and approving of violence as a style of life may have contributed to the seemingly senseless spiraling of violence over the eighteen-year period. As Wolfgang and Ferracuti observe: "Moreover, most guerrilla leaders today appear to be sons of parents killed in the *violencia*. Thus, the general appearance and expectation of brutality reinforce the acceptance of violence as a chief value" (1967:279), and indoctrination of children about methods of killing is widely practiced. (See Wolfgang & Ferracuti, 1967:275–79, and p. 325 for extensive bibliography.)

Sardinia, Barbaricino Code. Pigliaru (1970) has studied the use of violence, especially vendetta homicides, which are regulated by a set of norms and codes. Although today this vendetta code is less common, the work by Ferracuti, Lazzari, and Wolfgang (1970) attempted to show that there should be psychological differences between homicidal offenders from the subcultural setting of Sardinia and those from the "larger culture" of Italy. Briefly, the hypothesis was that those from the subculture, because they have internalized the value systems favoring violence, should display less guilt. Some support was found for this hypothesis.

Mexico. Mexico exhibits a generally high homicide rate, with rural and coastal areas displaying much higher rates. In these areas, Mexican social analysts have asserted that physically aggressive forms of behaviour "constitute positive values of the particular ethics of some social groups" (Alzaga, 1967:327). In some areas there is evidence for a fatalistic expectation of violence or death. In the village of Acan, in the Tarascan area of Mexico, political controversies and the vendetta have led to the use of violence as the normal means of settling differences (Friedrich, 1964). Homicide is not as sadistic as it is in Colombia, but is carried out uncensured provided it conforms to the socially accepted patterns of vendetta. There is strong pressure for men to demonstrate their "valor" in situations which are defined as warranting violence. It seems that violence emerged at the beginning of this century during the agrarian revolution, and has never been abandoned as an accepted means of achieving political success.

Albania. Crisafulli and Di Tullio (1942) reported the especially high rate of homicide in Albanian soldiers, and emphasized the importance of the *besa* (pacification of blood), which was a vendetta tradition transmitted from generation to generation in the Albanian mountain regions.

Albanova, Italy. Wolfgang and Ferracuti (1967) report that this small community of thirty thousand has had the highest rate of violent crimes in Europe. Outbreaks of violence appear to be spontaneous, preceded by offenses that in nearby areas would be solved peacefully or go unnoticed. But the value system requires that the Albanese must kill to redeem an offense. This means, as in Sardinia, that one should react to an offense with a more serious, more damaging offense.

Cross-Cultural Process

Although the cultures of violence we have described in the foregoing section are in relatively isolated communities, there is a special aspect of culture theories of violence

in which an exchange process occurs when two (or more) cultures exist in some specified relationship to each other. There are many variations of this theme. There may be
culture conflict (Sellin, 1938) where the norms of two different cultures conflict as
occurs during periods of immigration. There may be subcultures (e.g., Cohen, 1955)
that arise either in opposition to or in defiance of the dominant or parent culture
(Wolfgang & Ferracuti, 1967:95).

The scope of this chapter does not permit us to go into details of these culture
theories, but we would like to focus upon a specific aspect which has been neglected
in criminological writing on violence: the nature of the exchange process between the
dominant culture and the subculture. We take as our model here the works of Fanon
(1963, 1967) who focused upon the Manichaean aspects of this relationship. Fanon
pointed to the intrinsic black-white morality involved in the colonial attitude of the
"native," in that the "white settler" was only able to define himself as "good" by defining the native as "evil." Thus, the settler treats the native as something less than
human, with the result that violence *across* culture groups is exhibited (i.e., whites kill
blacks rather than whites kill whites). On the other hand, the natives, having been
taught for many generations that this is what they are (i.e., evil), and because the
white culture so completely dominates the society, are unable to conceive of themselves
in any other way except in the white image.

Evidence for this kind of self-image held by the American Negro is presented by
Coles (1967). Thus, the black man's ideal is to become white, which of course is
clearly an impossible desire. The result, therefore, is hatred of his own image and, because his brother's image is the same, he hates him, too. Thus, blacks kill blacks
because of this distorted self-hatred. Lorenz (1966) argues that although people are
instinctively aggressive, it is, nevertheless, difficult to assault anyone with whom one
has an intimate relationship. But even leaving aside the Freudian notion that love is
invariably accompanied by hate, it is easy to see that in the Manichaean situation of
the Negro, his intimate relationships are distorted by his hatred of himself and those
around him who remind him of himself. This conception of the psychological plight
of the black man could help to explain the highly intragroup nature of Negro violence
in the U.S.

CONCLUSIONS

In the light of these small culture studies, of the differential patterning of violent crime
among cultures and segments of cultures, and of the evidence for the highly intragroup,
socially intimate nature of much violent crime, it seems reasonable to accept as one
all-inclusive perspective the idea of cultures of violence. As a way of summarizing the
main paradigms of this hypothesis, Wolfgang and Ferracuti postulate the following
concerning the nature of subcultures of violence:

1. No subculture can be totally different from or totally in conflict with the society
of which it is a part.

2. To establish the existence of a subculture of violence does not require that the
actors sharing in these basic value elements should express violence in all situations.

3. The potential resort or willingness to resort to violence in a variety of situations
emphasizes the penetrating and diffusive character of this culture theme.

4. The subcultural ethos of violence may be shared by all ages in a sub-society,
but this ethos is most prominent in a limited age group, ranging from late adolescence to
middle age.

5. The counter-norm is nonviolence.

6. The development of favorable attitudes toward, and the use of, violence in a subculture usually involve learned behaviour and a process of differential learning, association, or identification.

7. The use of violence in a subculture is not necessarily viewed as illicit conduct and the users therefore do not have to deal with feelings of guilt about their aggression (1967:159–61).

Obviously, further testing and, perhaps, qualification of the culture theories are needed, and equally obviously, alternative theories need to be tested. Revision of the theory undoubtedly will emerge from the interdisciplinary research efforts under way in several parts of the world.

REFERENCES

Adelson, L.
  1961   "Slaughter of the innocents. A study of forty-six homicides in which the victims were children." New England Journal of Medicine 264(26):1345–1349.

Alzaga, J. M. V.
  1967   "Epidemiology of homicide in Mexico, D.F." Reported in M. E. Wolfgang and F. Ferracuti, The Subculture of Violence. London: Methuen.

Amir, M.
  1965   "Patterns in forcible rape." Ph.D. dissertation, University of Pennsylvania.
  1967   "Victim precipitated forcible rape." Journal of Criminal Law, Criminology and Police Science 58:493–502.

Ardrey, R.
  1963   African Genesis. New York: Atheneum.

Bacon, M. K., I. L. Child, and H. Barry, III.
  1963   "A cross-cultural study of correlates of crime." Journal of Abnormal and Social Psychology 4:291–300.

Banay, R. S.
  1943   "A study of 22 men convicted of murder in the first degree." Journal of Criminal Law and Criminology 34(July):106–111.

Bandura, A., and A. C. Huston.
  1961   "Identification as a process of incidental learning." Journal of Abnormal and Social Psychology 63:311–318.

Bandura, A., and R. H. Walters.
  1959   Adolescent Aggression. New York: Ronald Press.
  1963   Social Learning and Personality Development. New York: Holt, Rinehart & Winston.

Beattie, R. H., and J. P. Kenney.
  1966   "Aggressive crimes." Annals of the American Academy of Political and Social Science 364:73–85.

Bender, L.
  1934   "Psychiatric mechanisms in child murderers." Journal of Nervous and Mental Disease 80:32–47.

Bensing, R. C., and O. J. Schroeder.
  1969   Homicide in an Urban Community. Springfield, Ill.: Thomas.

Berkowitz, L.
   1962   Aggression: A Social Psychological Analysis. New York: McGraw-Hill.
Biderman, A. D., L. A. Johnson, J. McIntyre, and A. W. Weir.
   1967   Field Surveys 1: Report on a Pilot Study in the District of Columbia on
           Victimization and Attitudes toward Law Enforcement. Report of research
           study submitted to the President's Commission on Law Enforcement and
           Administration of Justice. Washington, D.C.: U.S. Government Printing
           Office.
Bloch, H.
   1960   "Research report on homicide, attempted homicide and crimes of violence."
           Colombo: Ceylon Police Report.
Bossard, J. H. S.
   1948   The Sociology of Child Development. New York: Harper & Bros.
Brearley, H. C.
   1932   Homicide in the United States. Chapel Hill: University of North Carolina
           Press.
Brim, O. G.
   1957   "Parent-child relations as a social system: I. Parent and child roles." Child
           Development 28:342–364.
Buss, A. H.
   1961   The Psychology of Aggression. New York: Wiley.
Bustamante, M. E., and M. A. Bravo B.
   1957   "Epidemiologia del homicidio en México." Higiene 9:21–23.
Caplow, T.
   1963   "La violencia." Columbia University Forum (Winter):45–46.
Cassidy, J. H.
   1941   "Personality study of 200 murderers." Journal of Criminal Psychopathol-
           ogy 2:296–304.
Chapman, A. H.
   1959   "Obsession of infanticide." Archives of General Psychiatry 1:12–16.
Chappell, D., and S. Singer.
   1973   "Rape in New York City: a study of material in the police files and its mean-
           ing." Research report, School of Criminal Justice, State University of New
           York at Albany (unpublished).
Christie, N., J. Andenaes, and S. Skirbekk.
   1965   "A study of self-reported crime." Pp. 86–116 in Scandinavian Studies in
           Criminology, vol. 1. London: Tavistock.
Cloward, R. A., and L. E. Ohlin.
   1960   Delinquency and Opportunity. New York: Free Press of Glencoe.
Cohen, A. K.
   1955   Delinquent Boys. Glencoe, Ill.: Free Press.
Coles, R.
   1967   Children of Crisis: A Study of Courage and Fear. Boston: Little, Brown.
Cormier, B. M.
   1962   "Psychodynamics of homicide committed in a marital relationship." Cor-
           rective Psychiatry and Journal of Social Therapy 8:187–194.
The Council of Europe.
   1970   Indexes of Crime. Strasbourg.

Crisafulli, A., and B. Di Tullio.
   1942   Aspetti della Criminalità Militarc nel Settore Albanese. Tirana: Tipografia
          Militare.
Davis, A., and R. J. Havighurst.
   1946   "Racial class and color difference in child rearing." American Sociological
          Review 11:698–710.
De Francis, V.
   1963   "Child abuse. Preview of a nation-wide survey." Paper presented at an
          associate group meeting jointly sponsored by the Children's Division of the
          American Humane Society, the American Public Welfare Association, and
          the Child Welfare League of America at the National Conference on Social
          Welfare, Cleveland, May.
De Porte, J. V., and E. Parkhurst.
   1935   "Homicide in New York state. A statistical study of the victims and crimi-
          nals in 37 counties in 1921–30." Human Biology 7:47–73.
Dollard, J., L. W. Doob, N. E. Miller, O. H. Mowrer, R. R. Sears, C. S. Ford, C. I.
          Hovland, and R. T. Sollenberger.
   1939   Frustration and Aggression. New Haven: Yale University Press.
Driver, E. D.
   1961   "Interaction and criminal homicide in India." Social Forces 40:153–158.
Dublin, L. I., and B. Bunzel.
   1935   "Thou shalt not kill: a study of homicide in the United States." Survey
          Graphic 24(March):127–131.
Durkheim, E.
   1897   Suicide. Translation by John A. Spaulding and George Simpson. Glencoe,
          Ill.: Free Press (1951 edition).
Eibl-Eibesfeldt, I.
   1961   "The fighting behavior of animals." Scientific American 205(December):
          34, 112–116.
Elmer, E.
   1967   Children in Jeopardy. Pittsburgh: University of Pittsburgh Press.
Elmhorn, K.
   1965   "Study in self-reported delinquency among school children in Stockholm."
          Pp. 117–146 in Scandinavian Studies in Criminology, vol. 1. London: Tavi-
          stock.
Ennis, P. H.
   1967   Field Surveys 2: Criminal Victimization in the United States; Report of a
          National Survey. Report of research study submitted to the President's
          Commission on Law Enforcement and Administration of Justice. Washing-
          ton, D.C.: U.S. Government Printing Office.
Erickson, M. L.
   1970   Review—Delinquency: Selected Studies, by T. Sellin and M. Wolfgang.
          American Sociological Review 35:1115–1116.
Eysenck, H. J.
   1964   Crime and Personality. Boston: Houghton Mifflin.
Fanon, F.
   1963   The Wretched of the Earth. New York: Grove Press.
   1967   Black Skin, White Masks. New York: Grove Press.

Federal Bureau of Investigation (F.B.I.)
   1969   Crime in the United States: Uniform Crime Reports—1968. Washington, D.C.: U.S. Government Printing Office.
   1970   Crime in the United States: Uniform Crime Reports—1969. Washington, D.C.: U.S. Government Printing Office.

Ferracuti, F., M. Fontanesi, G. Legramente, and E. Zilli.
   1966   "La sindrome del bambino maltrattato. Rassegna della letteratura ed esemplificazione clinica." Quaderni di Criminologia Clinica 1:55–80.

Ferracuti, F., R. Lazzari, and M. E. Wolfgang.
   1970   Violence in Sardinia. Rome: Bulzoni.

Ferri, E.
   1895   L'Omicidio. Torino: Fratelli Bocca.

Fox, R.
   1970   The Extra Y Chromosome and Deviant Behavior. Toronto: Center of Criminology, University of Toronto.

Freud, Anna.
   1937   The Ego and the Mechanisms of Defence. London: Hogarth.

Friedrich, P.
   1964   "El homicidio politico en Acan." Revista de Ceincias Sociales 8(1):27–51.

Garfinkel, H.
   1949   "Research note on inter- and intra-racial homicides." Social Forces 27:369–381.

Gatti, R.
   1963   "L'Omicidio del fanciullo." Minerva Medico-Legale 5:134–141.

Gibson, E., and S. Klein.
   1961   Murder. London: H.M. Stationery Office.

Gil, D. G.
   1968   "Nation-wide survey of legally reported physical abuse of children." Brandeis University, Papers in Social Welfare, 15.

Gil, D. G., and J. H. Noble.
   1967   "Public knowledge, attitudes, and opinions about physical child abuse in the United States." Brandeis University, Papers in Social Welfare, 14(September).

Gillin, J. L.
   1946   The Wisconsin Prisoner. Madison: University of Wisconsin Press.

Gold, M.
   1958   "Suicide, homicide and the socialization of aggression." American Journal of Sociology 63(May):651–661.
   1966   "Undetected delinquent behavior." Journal of Research in Crime and Delinquency 13(January):27–46.

Goode, W. J.
   1969   "Violence between intimates," in D. J. Mulvihill, M. M. Tumin, and L. A. Curtis, Crimes of Violence, vol. 13. Washington, D.C.: U.S. Government Printing Office.

Hardt, R. H., and G. E. Bodine.
   1965   Development of Self-Report Instruments in Delinquency Research. Syracuse, N.Y.: Syracuse University Youth Development Center.

Harlan, H.
  1950　"Five hundred homicides." Journal of Criminal Law and Criminology 40:
       736–752.

Hayman, C., W. Stewart, F. Lewis, and M. Grant.
  1968　"Sexual assault on women and children in the District of Columbia." Pub-
       lic Health Reports 83(December):1021–1028.

Henry, A. F., and J. F. Short, Jr.
  1954　Suicide and Homicide. Glencoe, Ill.: Free Press.

Herzog, E.
  1970　"Social stereotypes and social research." Journal of Social Issues 26(3):
       109–125.

Hoffman, F. L.
  1925　The Homicide Problem. Newark, N.J.: Prudential Press.

Holzer, R.
  1961　"Ein Beitrag zum mütterlichen Kindesmord." Deutsche Zeitschrift für die
       gesamte gerichtliche Medizin 51(1):1–6.

Howells, J. G.
  1966　"The psychopathogenesis of hard-core families." American Journal of Psy-
       chiatry 22:1159–1164.

Hull, C. L.
  1943　Principles of Behavior: An Introduction to Behavior Theory. New York:
       Appleton-Crofts.

Inbau, F. E., and C. R. Sowle.
  1960　Criminal Justice: Cases and Comments. Brooklyn: Foundation Press.

Iskrant, A. P., and P. U. Joliet.
  1968　Accidents and Homicide. Cambridge: Harvard University Press.

Jayewardene, C. H. S.
  1960　"Criminal homicide: a study in culture conflict." Ph.D. dissertation, Uni-
       versity of Pennsylvania.
  1963　"Criminal cultures and subcultures." Probation and Child Care Journal
       2(June):1–5.
  1964　"Criminal homicide in Ceylon." Probation and Child Care Journal 3(Janu-
       ary):15–30.

Jeter, H. R.
  1963　Children, Problems, and Services in Child Welfare Programs. Children's
       Bureau Publication N. 403. Washington, D.C.: U.S. Department of Health,
       Education and Welfare.

Kilpatrick, J. J.
  1943　"Murder in the Deep South." Survey Graphic 32(October): 395–397.

Kingler, H. M.
  1959　"Zum problem der kindersmörderin." Kriminalistik 13(5):192–194.

Kohlberg, L.
  1959　"Status as perspective on society: an interpretation of class differences in
       children's moral judgements." Paper presented at the Society for Research
       in Child Development Symposium on Moral Process, Bethesda, Maryland,
       March 21.

Kohn, M. L.
  1963   "Social class and parent-child relationships: an interpretation." American
          Journal of Sociology 68:471–480.

Kriesberg, L.
  1963   "The relationship between socio-economic rank and behavior." Social
          Problems 10:334–353.

Lamont, A. M.
  1961   "Forensic psychiatric practice in South African mental hospital." South
          Africa Medical Journal 35(40):833–837.

Leggett, J. C.
  1963   "Uprootedness and working-class consciousness." American Journal of So-
          ciology 68:682–692.

Lejins, P.
  1966   "Uniform crime reports." Michigan Law Review 64(April):1011–1030.

Lorenz, K.
  1966   On Aggression. New York: Harcourt Brace.

Lovaas, O. I.
  1961   "Effect of exposure to symbolic aggression on aggressive behavior." Child
          Development 32:37–44.

McArthur, C.
  1955   "Personality differences between middle and upper classes." Journal of Ab-
          normal and Social Psychology 50:247–274.

McCary, J. L.
  1949   "Ethnic and cultural reactions to frustration." Journal of Personality 18(3):
          321–326.

McClintock, F. H.
  1963   Crimes of Violence. London: Macmillan.

McDermaid, G., and E. Winkler.
  1955   "Psychopathology of infanticide." Journal of Clinical and Experimental
          Psychopathology and Quarterly Review of Psychiatry and Neurology 16:22–
          41.

McKnight, C. K., J. W. Mohr, R. E. Quinsey, and J. Erochko.
  1966   "Matricide and mental illness." Canadian Psychiatric Association Journal
          11:99–106.

McNeil, E. B.
  1966   "Violence and human development." Annals of the American Academy of
          Political and Social Science 364:149–157.

Matheson, J. C. M.
  1941   "Infanticide." Medical Legal Review 9:135–152.

Megargee, E. I.
  1967   "Matricide, patricide, and the dynamics of aggression." Paper presented at
          the American Psychological Association Meetings, Washington, D.C. (mim-
          eographed).

Merton, R. K.
  1968   Social Theory and Social Structure. Third Edition. New York: Free Press.

Miller, W. B., H. Geertz, and H. S. G. Cutter.
  1961   "Aggression in a boys' street corner group." Psychiatry 24:283–298.

Minturn, L., and W. W. Lambert.
    1964   Mothers of Six Cultures, especially pp. 136–162, "Aggression training: mother-directed aggression." New York: Wiley.

Montague, J. B., and E. G. Epps.
    1958   "Attitudes toward social mobility as revealed by samples of Negro and white boys." Pacific Sociological Review 1:81–84.

Morris, T.
    1958   The Criminal Area. London: Routledge & Kegan Paul.

Morris, T., and L. Blom-Cooper.
    1961   "Murder in microcosm." The Observer (London) :3–26.
    1963   A Calendar of Murder. London: Michael Joseph.

Morselli, E.
    1879   Il Suicidio. Milano: Dumolard.

Morton, J. H.
    1934   "Female homicides." Journal of Mental Science 80:64–74.

Mulvihill, D. J., M. M. Tumin, and L. A. Curtis.
    1969   Crimes of Violence, vol. 11. Staff Report to National Commission on the Causes and Prevention of Violence. Washington, D.C.: U.S. Government Printing Office.

Myers, S. A.
    1967   "The child player." Archives of General Psychiatry 17:211–213.

Myrdal, G.
    1944   An American Dilemma. New York: Harper & Row.

Normandeau, A.
    1968   "Patterns and trends in robbery." Ph.D. dissertation, University of Pennsylvania.

Palmer, S.
    1960   A Study of Murder. New York: Crowell.

Perdue, W. C.
    1966   "A preliminary investigation into uxoricide." Diseases of the Nervous System 27:808–811.

Pigliaru, A.
    1970   Il Banditismo in Sardegna: La Vendetta Barbaricina. Milano: Guiffrè.

Pittman, D. J., and W. Handy.
    1964   "Patterns in criminal aggravated assault." Journal of Criminal Law, Criminology and Police Science 55:462–470.

Podolsky, E.
    1965   "Children who kill." General Practitioner 31:98–102.

Pokorny, A. D.
    1965a   "A comparison of homicides in two cities." Journal of Criminal Law, Criminology and Police Science 56:478–487.
    1965b   "Human violence—a comparison of homicide, aggravated assault, suicide and attempted suicide." Journal of Crminal Law, Criminology and Police Science 56:488–497.

Polansky, N. A., and N. F. Polansky.
    1967   "The current status of child abuse and child neglect in this country." Paper prepared for the Joint Commission on the Mental Health of Children.

Pollak, O.
1950   The Criminality of Women. Philadelphia: University of Pennsylvania Press.

President's Commission on Crime in the District of Columbia.
1966   Report of the President's Commission on Crime in the District of Columbia. Washington, D.C.: U.S. Government Printing Office.

President's Commission on Law Enforcement and Administration of Justice.
1967a   Task Force Report: Science and Technology. Washington, D.C.: U.S. Government Printing Office.
1967b   Task Force Report: Crime and Its Impact: An Assessment. Washington, D.C.: U.S. Government Printing Office.

Reckless, W.
1961   The Crime Problem. Third Edition. New York: Appleton-Century-Crofts.

Reiss, A. J., Jr.
1967   "Measurement of the nature and amount of crime." Section 1 in Field Surveys 3: Studies in Crime and Law Enforcement in Major Metropolitan Areas, vol. 1. Report of research study submitted to President's Commission on Law Enforcement and Administration of Justice. Washington, D.C.: U.S. Government Printing Office.

Robinson, S. M.
1966   "A critical view of the uniform crime reports." Michigan Law Review 64(April):1031–1054.

Rodman, H.
1963   "The lower-class value stretch." Social Forces 42:205–215.

Roger, C. R.
1964   "Toward a modern approach to values: the valuing process in the mature person." Journal of Abnormal and Social Psychology 68:160–167.

Rose, G. N. G.
1970   "The merits of an index of crime of the kind devised by Sellin and Wolfgang." In Council of Europe, Indexes of Crime. Strasbourg.

Royal Commission on Capital Punishment.
1953   1949–1953 Report. London: H.M. Stationery Office.

Scott, J. P.
1958   Aggression. Chicago: University of Chicago Press.

Sears, R. R.
1943   Survey of Objective Studies of Psychoanalytic Concepts. New York: Social Science Research Council Bulletin 51.

Sellin, T.
1938   Culture Conflict and Crime. New York: Social Science Research Council Bulletin 41.

Sellin, T., and M. E. Wolfgang.
1964   The Measurement of Delinquency. New York: Wiley.

Shah, S., and G. Weber.
1968   "The problem of individual violence." Report submitted to National Commission on the Causes and Prevention of Violence (unpublished).

Shaw, C., and H. D. McKay.
1942   Juvenile Delinquency and Urban Areas. Chicago: University of Chicago Press.
1949   "Rejoinder." American Sociological Review 14(October):617.

Short, J. F., Jr., and F. L. Strodtbeck.
    1965   Group Process and Gang Delinquency. Chicago: University of Chicago
            Press.
Siciliano, S.
    1965   L'Omicidio—Studio su un'Indagine Criminologica Compiuta in Danimarca.
            Padova: Cedam.
Smith, G. B.
    1960   "Murder of infants by parents in situations of stress." Journal of Social
            Therapy 6(1):9–17.
Strauss, J. H., and M. A. Strauss.
    1953   "Suicide, homicide and social structure in Ceylon." American Journal of
            Sociology 58:461–469.
Sutherland, E., and D. R. Cressey.
    1970   Criminology. Eighth Edition. New York: Lippincott.
Svalastoga, K.
    1956   "Homicide and social contact in Denmark." American Journal of Sociology
            62:37–41.
    1962   "Rape and social structure." Pacific Sociological Review 5:48–53.
Tinbergen, N.
    1968   "On war and peace in animals and man." Science 160:1411–1418.
Trasler, G.
    1962   The Explanation of Criminality. London: Routledge & Kegan Paul.
Verkko, V.
    1951   Homicides and Suicides in Finland and Their Dependence on National Char-
            acter. Copenhagen: Gads Forlag.
Von Hentig, H.
    1947   Crime: Causes and Conditions. New York: McGraw-Hill.
Voss, Harwin L., and John R. Hepburn.
    1968   "Patterns in criminal homicide in Chicago." Journal of Criminal Law, Crim-
            inology and Police Science 59:499–508.
Wertham, F.
    1941   Dark Legends: A Study in Murder. New York: Duell, Sloan & Pearce.
West, D. J.
    1966   Murder Followed by Suicide. Cambridge: Harvard University Press.
White, C. R.
    1955   "Social class differences in the use of leisure." American Journal of Soci-
            ology 61:145–151.
Wolfgang, M. E.
    1958   Patterns in Criminal Homicide. Philadelphia: University of Pennsylvania
            Press.
    1963   "Uniform crime reports: a critical appraisal." University of Pennsylvania
            Law Review 3(April):708–738.
    1964   Crime and Race. 1964 edition. New York: Institute of Human Relations
            Press.
    1967   Studies in Homicide. New York: Harper & Row.
Wolfgang, M. E., and F. Ferracuti.
    1967   The Subculture of Violence. London: Methuen.

Wolfgang, M. E., R. M. Figlio, and T. Sellin.
   1972   Delinquency in a Birth Cohort. Chicago: University of Chicago Press.
Wood, A. L.
   1961a   "Crime and aggression in changing Ceylon." Transactions of the American
            Philosophical Society, New Series, 51:part 8(December).
   1961b   "A socio-structural analysis of murder, suicide, and economic crime in Cey-
            lon." American Sociological Review 26(October):744–753.
Young, L.
   1964   Wednesday's Children. New York: McGraw-Hill.
Zalba, S. R.
   1966   "The abused child: I. A survey of the problem." Social Work 11:3–16.

CHAPTER 6

Drugs, Addiction, and Crime

David J. Pittman

Washington University

Man's relationship to drugs is a long one, antedating recorded history. Drugs have been used for religious, medicinal, hedonistic, and social purposes. Cultural and legal attitudes towards drugs vary. For example, a drug, such as alcohol, may be highly exalted by one society (e.g., France) and at the same time prohibited by another (e.g., Kuwait), or, another drug, such as cannabis, may be widely used by one segment of a community and severely frowned upon by another part of it. Furthermore, over time a community's attitude toward a drug may reverse itself; opiates were legally accepted in the United States prior to World War I and were legally prohibited, except under strict regulation, after that time. The current drug problem in the United States (whether it be among the returning military personnel from Vietnam or the civilian population) and other countries is not a new phenomenon, although it is more complex than previously.

The increased complexity of the drug problem is related to the tremendous scientific advances in the field of pharmacology over the last thirty years. Society today has at its disposal drugs that cover the whole spectrum of human behavior. Besides the "contraceptive pill" we have others to sedate us when we are nervous, excite us when we are dull, slim us when we are fat, fatten us when we are thin, awaken us when we are sleepy, put us to sleep when we are awake, cure us when we are sick, and make us sick when we are well. Thus, on one hand, drugs can enhance our ability to function more effectively but, on the other side, they can carry our minds out of the realm of reality into loneliness, despair, and hopelessness.

In discussing such an emotionally charged area as drugs, it is imperative to maintain a rational perspective. Miracle drugs of the antibiotic family (such as penicillin), steroids, insulin, and others have brought a revolution to the treatment of many of mankind's illnesses. Thus, drugs in a generic sense have achieved widespread acceptance in all countries, whether obtained by prescription or "over-the-counter." The mass media in Western society is filled with advertisements of chemical agents which will remedy many of our problems—whether they be body odor, headache, bad breath, or digestive upset. Yet any drug or chemical agent can be misused with negative consequences to the individual and society. Fortunately, there are few drugs out of the thousands available which are consistently misused by any significant portion of the population.

DRUG TERMINOLOGY

Much confusion surrounds the scientific and social terminology used in reference to drugs. The first problem centers on the question, "What is addiction?" Authorities disagree as to what actually constitutes addiction, and as a result, which drugs are addictive. One noted pharmacologist has stated:

> The true status of our knowledge regarding drug addiction is now as it has always been, i.e., a mystery. Much is known of the pharmacology of these agents but the exact mechanisms of addiction, and even analgesia, continue to be elusive (Sherrod, 1966:453).

One reason addiction continues to puzzle scientists is the multifaceted character of the phenomenon. Addiction to drugs (of which alcohol is one) is typically the result of many interacting factors. It is not just the effect of the drug on the person, but the social-psychological state of the individual is crucial, i.e., how he reacts to the drug in his particular environment.

Since there are many different addictive drugs and many factors influence a person's becoming addicted, it is difficult to discover any direct cause-effect relationship for addiction. Thus, it is not sufficient to state that the reason a person is addicted is that he took excessive amounts of a certain drug. One must also consider the drug in question, the laws regarding it, the society's attitude toward the chemical agent (which is not always reflected in the laws), the individual's attitude toward it, and the physical and psychological makeup of the individual. Stated differently, knowledge of the drug per se is necessary for understanding addiction, but it is not sufficient for a full comprehension of the pathology (Glatt et al., 1967:2).

In drug research four terms frequently appear which have relevance for this chapter: *addiction, habituation, dependence,* and *abuse.* These terms are not, unfortunately, mutually exclusive and there are frequent disagreements about their precise meaning.

Addiction

There are three properties that a drug must have before it is considered addictive: it must produce tolerance, an abstinence (withdrawal) syndrome, and craving (Glatt et al., 1967:3). Tolerance means that the drug must be taken in progressively larger doses in order to achieve the desired result. Simplified, tolerance develops as follows: if a person begins to take daily one grain of drug A, he finds that at the end of several weeks the drug no longer affects him in the same manner. He then increases his dosage to two grains daily. Then, after a month or so, the person again realizes that drug A no longer produces the desired effect. He therefore increases his daily dosage to three grains, and so on.

If the person is suddenly prevented from taking any more of drug A, he experiences an abstinence syndrome. These symptoms vary from one drug to another and depend on the amount of drugs being taken. The abstinence syndrome is characterized by physical symptoms, such as stomach cramps, diarrhea, and irritability.

The person taking drug A will develop a craving for the drug that is due not only to the physical effects which the drug has on his body but also to the fact that he fears the abstinence syndrome. Too, he may develop a psychological craving which is not fully understood. Typically, many addicts who have been successfully withdrawn from a drug develop a strong desire to begin taking the drug again. This is one of several reasons why the relapse rate after treatment for addicts is extremely high.

Habituation

There are many habit-forming agents which some people use, such as coffee, tea, and tobacco. Also some drugs are habit-forming. Simply stated, all addictive drugs are habit-forming, but not all habit-forming drugs are addictive in the pharmacological sense. Habituation is primarily psychological as a physical abstinence syndrome does not develop when the agent is suddenly withdrawn from the individual. There are, however, habit-forming drugs, such as certain amphetamines, where tolerance does develop but there is no abstinence syndrome. In short, habituation may consist of tolerance and craving (primarily psychological) but it is never followed by an abstinence syndrome.

Dependence

In 1964 the World Health Organization (W.H.O., 1964) released a report from its expert committee on drugs which combined the terms *addiction* and *habituation* under one term—*dependence*. This committee felt that the scientific literature reflected much confusion between addiction and habituation, and as a result, the classification of a drug as addictive or habit-forming was difficult. The WHO Committee suggested each drug should be described by its particular type of dependence, e.g., "drug dependence of the alcohol type." Thus the substitution of the word *dependence* for both addiction and habituation is an attempt to clarify drug terminology. Despite their suggestion of using dependence, widespread use of addiction and habituation continues and will be used in this chapter's discussion.

Abuse or Misuse

Almost all drugs that have been produced for medical and/or scientific use as well as beverage alcohol have their consumption controlled by legal statutes. People who use drugs illegally and/or for some purpose other than that for which the drug was commonly designed or in a manner other than prescribed by the physician are said to be abusing the drug. Generally speaking, people who are dependent on drugs are also abusing them. However, there are some people who take drugs but never become dependent upon them. In summary, persons who use drugs for other than the generally accepted reasons or who take them illegally but are not dependent on them are classified as drug abusers or misusers.

PROBLEM DRUGS

Those drugs which are most related to the crime problem in Western society may be divided into six categories: (1) ethyl alcohol; (2) cannabis; (3) opiates, synthetic opiates, and cocaine; (4) amphetamines; (5) hallucinogens; and (6) barbituates.

Ethyl Alcohol

Although there are numerous types of alcohol, ethyl alcohol is the one of concern in this chapter for it is the type that is consumed by humans. Alcohol is made by small organisms that are found almost everywhere. How these tiny organisms make alcohol has been succinctly stated by Chafetz:

> No grape or grain or other attractive flower makes alcohol. Rather these fruits of the soil are devoured by the yeast, or ferment germ, and the germ then evacuates alcohol as its waste product (1965:37).

Pharmacologically alcohol depresses the central nervous system. It has its most serious effect on the human brain. The intensity of alcohol's effect on the human is directly related to its concentration in the blood and brain tissue. Alcohol begins to impair the brain's ability to function at the 0.05 percent level, i.e., 0.05 grams of alcohol per 100 cc. of blood.

Alcohol is the most widely used drug in Western society and numerically it is the most abused drug by population in the United States, despite the mass media's attention to marijuana or heroin. A recently completed study of American drinking habits (Cahalan et al., 1969) based on a national probability sample of the population aged 21 or older obtained a wealth of information on drinking practices and attitudes in terms of such sociological variables as age, sex, race, religion, ethnicity, income, etc. These researchers, by utilizing a Q-F-V index (for quantity, frequency, and variability) of drinking have classified the American population into five groups of drinkers: (1) "abstainers" (32 percent of the sample) who report that they drank less than once a year; (2) "infrequent drinkers" (15 percent) who drank less than once a month; (3) "light drinkers" (28 percent) who drank at least once a month but only in small quantities; (4) "moderate drinkers" (13 percent) who drank several times a month, usually no more than three or four drinks per occasion; and (5) "heavy drinkers" (12 percent) who drank almost every day, frequently consuming five or more drinks per occasion. This latter group probably includes most of the estimated nine million Americans who are considered alcoholics or problem drinkers by health officials.

Cannabis

Marijuana, charas, hemp, hashish, bhang, pot, tea, and weed are just a few of the terms used throughout the world to describe products of the female plant *Cannabis sativa* or Indian hemp (Glatt et al., 1967:5–7). Cannabis has been used for medicinal, social, and pleasurable purposes for thousands of years, rivaling opium in its history. It was popular with Indian philosophers and was widely used by Arabs at the time of the Crusades.

The plant's popularity has not diminished in the Middle East and India; currently cannabis is enjoying wide acceptance in Western countries despite national and international efforts to suppress its use. Also, cannabis's approbation in Western society is entirely the result of nonmedical purposes, for it is no longer used as a medicine.

Cannabis is commonly called pot, marijuana, charge, weed, hashish or hash, and grass. It is almost always smoked in the form of a cigarette, which is referred to as a smoke, joint, or reefer. Occasionally, cannabis is smoked with opium; this mixture is termed charas. Cannabis varies greatly in its potency which correlates with the growing conditions to which the plant is subjected. The best grade of cannabis is grown in semiarid regions. There is regular cannabis, which consists of the pulverized leaves and stems of the plant. Then there is the more powerful type, which is made up largely of dried resin from the flower of the plant; this type of cannabis is hash or hashish.

The effect cannabis has on individuals varies greatly. This variance can partly be explained by the different grades of cannabis. However, it has also been suggested that persons learn what to expect from the drug before they actually take it (Becker, 1953). Thus, if someone is advised that pot will help him appreciate the "true" meaning of a painting, the painting will take on new and exciting dimensions for the pot smoker. How much the pharmacology of the drug has to do with the experience is difficult to discern. Still there are several general effects that cannabis appears to have on most persons. Users talk of the drug's euphoric qualities which give them a sense of well-being, light-headedness, and pleasant experiences in perceiving things.

Cannabis is not physically addictive. Although habituation has been reported in the Middle East, it is not very common to find someone habituated to the drug in Western countries. Users frequently compare it favorably to alcohol, saying it is less dangerous, results in a better form of intoxication, and does not have the unpleasant aftereffects frequently associated with alcohol. Those who advocate legalization of cannabis compare it to a social drug like alcohol, only not as harmful as the latter, they state. Yet, cannabis is illegal. It has been accused of leading persons to using dangerous drugs, such as heroin. True, some persons who take cannabis later become dependent upon other drugs; however, many users of cannabis never progress to taking dangerous drugs. In short, it is incorrect to state that there exists a direct causal relationship between taking cannabis and addictive drugs.

As a result of the illegality of cannabis, persons who use it frequently associate with others illicitly taking other drugs, and vice versa. The cannabis smoker may frequently come into contact with other drug users, and because of this he is more likely to become dependent upon some other drug than is someone from the general public under such circumstances. This would not be due to any inherent properties of cannabis; rather, the dependence would be the result of the social milieu associated with cannabis (which is caused in no small part by its illegality) and the sociopsychological makeup of the individual.

Opiates, Synthetic Opiates, and Cocaine

For over four thousand years man has cultivated opium poppies in Asia for opium, which has been eaten, smoked, and drunk in solutions (Glatt et al., 1967:8–9). Although nowadays opium use is not found often, it is sometimes used for smoking. More important today are the opiates derived from opium. Three of the best-known ones are morphine, heroin, and codeine. Besides opiates, there have been many synthetic opiates developed, such as methadone and pethidine. Medically these drugs have proved valuable, especially as analgesics. They depress the central nervous system and, by so doing, make the person unaware of his pain. They also have a mild euphoric effect which gives the individual a feeling of complacent well-being.

All opiates and synthetic opiates are pharmacologically addictive. Persons becoming dependent do not suffer serious symptoms directly from the drugs. They frequently become constipated and are drowsy. The most serious effects are indirectly associated with the drug in that addicts typically become totally preoccupied with it and lose interest in sex, work, food, and clothes. This disinterest, of course, has a negative effect on their health in that they frequently develop infections from unsterile injections (practically all addicts inject their drugs intramuscularly or intravenously). These drugs have a cross-tolerance so that one opiate can be substituted for another.

Cocaine is not an opiate, nor is it pharmacologically addictive. It is included in this section because it is frequently taken in combination with the opiates in Great Britain and other countries.

Cocaine is derived from the coca plant. South American Indians have chewed coca leaves throughout their recorded history for their stimulating effect. Cocaine is more powerful than coca, but opiate addicts use it primarily for the same reasons as the Indians. Opiates sedate the person and make him listless; cocaine counteracts the depressing effect of opiates and gives the users more "life." Also, cocaine offers a bigger "kick" or "buzz" (although fleeting) as a result of its being a relatively powerful stimulant.

Individuals can develop a cocaine habit and a tolerance for the drug. There is, however, no physical abstinence syndrome.

Amphetamines

Amphetamine or benzedrine was developed during the late 1920s (Glatt et al., 1967:7). Since then, many other "amphetamines" have been developed; chemical derivatives of benzedrine such as dexedrine, methedrine, Durophet, and the amphetamine-like product Preludin. These drugs stimulate the central nervous system and are widely used medically to combat fatigue, depression, and obesity. Amphetamines, besides stimulating the indivdual, also produce euphoria to a limited extent and, in general, give the user a sense of well-being. The public frequently refers to these drugs as "pep pills" or "speed."

Amphetamines are habit-forming; in the past most cases of dependence were found among middle-aged housewives who frequently had the drug prescribed to them by doctors in connection with weight reduction. More recently, amphetamine dependence is seen among teen-agers who obtained the drug illegally in order to stay awake over weekends. Some youth use it as an alternative to alcohol, i.e., as a means to facilitate social interaction. Undoubtedly the majority of youth who use amphetamines are only misusers and never become dependent upon the substance. For those who do become dependent, many exhibit the following symptoms: impairment of psychomotor function, insomnia, anorexia, paranoia, general restlessness, psychosocial deterioration, and a very unpleasant withdrawal ("come down") syndrome of depression.

Besides amphetamines, there are also amphetamine-barbiturate combinations. The most popular is Drinamyl. This drug has more or less the same effect as a pure amphetamine, but the barbiturate element tends to keep the user from becoming too restless and excited; also the effect of the drug does not wear off as abruptly as an amphetamine when the dosage is discontinued.

Hallucinogens

The three principal drugs in this group are mescaline, psilocybin, and lysergic acid diethylamide (LSD 25 or LSD). These drugs are also designated as phantastica, psychedelic, and psychotomimetic drugs (Glatt et al., 1967:9-11). The variety of descriptive terms indicates the numerous attitudes toward these drugs and our limited knowledge of them. Hallucinogenic, of course, means producing hallucinations, yet there is some doubt about whether the drugs produce hallucinations or simply distort perception. To correct this confusion, some experts prefer giving these drugs the equally uncertain term *phantastica*, which means falling somewhere between hallucinations and illusions. An even more obscure term, at least for persons who have not taken the drug, is *psychedelic*. This term (mind-opening or mind-manifesting) refers to that quality of these drugs which allows the person to expand his "consciousness." The psychedelic experience or "trip" allows the user to become "aware of things he did not know existed" and to remember his very early childhood. Last is the term *psychotomimetic* (mimic psychosis).

The above terms have been brought about by the researchers' inability to discover exactly how this group of drugs (which we have called "hallucinogens") acts on the brain. As a result, the scientists have described the drug by its manifestations, i.e., how people overtly react to it.

Unfortunately, people react in different ways that are related not only to the amount and frequency of dosage, but to environmental variables. For example, individuals who initially take a hallucinogen under the direction of a "guide" (a person who has experience with the drug) are led and guided throughout their "trip." The guide tells the initiate what to expect, how to react, and, on the whole, assists him throughout his drug experience. As a result, the journey will vary from one guide to another. Also, persons who take hallucinogens on their own will experience different effects depending in part on their surroundings and personality. To a lesser extent, the above analysis holds true for the other drugs we have discussed but, as we shall now document, hallucinogens are extremely powerful and affect users in a way that can justly be called bizarre.

LSD, psilocybin, and mescaline all have similar effects, although LSD is, by far, the most powerful of the three. It is a synthetic drug discovered in 1943. Although realizing this was a most unusual and powerful drug, scientists were at somewhat of a loss to find a use for LSD. Contrastingly, Indians had been using psilocybin (found in certain Mexican mushrooms) and mescaline (found in the peyote cactus indigenous to the southwestern part of the United States and northern Mexico) for centuries, mainly in religious ceremonies. (Psilocybin and mescaline can now be produced synthetically.) Soon these hallucinogens were being used in clinical experiments and as a therapeutic aid. It has been reported to have been used for treating psychiatric diseases, alcoholism, and rehabilitating criminals. The common factor in all these therapies seems to be that the patients "gain a greater insight of themselves and the world," and thus may be better equipped to cope with their problems. Critics point out that these studies never "prove" that hallucinogens are beneficial—that the researchers never develop rigid control experiments which would truly test the efficacy of the drug.

Today what is creating great concern in Western society is the illicit use of hallucinogens. It is one thing to give an hallucinogen in a clinical setting, quite another to take the drug in a layman's apartment. These powerful drugs alter the mind of the user in some manner which produces strange, sometimes beautiful, at other times horrible, hallucinations or illusions. In most cases, users suffer few aftereffects, nor do they become pharmacologically addicted. But more serious are the tragic consequences sometimes produced through the illicit use of these drugs to engender a hallucinogen "trip." People have attempted to fly out of windows and stop trains or cars under the influence of these drugs. It may be that the drug was not the cause of the accidents; it is possible that the persons were mentally unbalanced before taking the drug, or perhaps the drug acted as a catalyst by exaggerating some minor psychological defect. Until we know more about these drugs, their use should be confined to experimental clinics. Unfortunately, this is impossible, for there is already a black market for them.

Barbiturates

Derived from barbituric acid, barbiturates were first developed in the latter part of the nineteenth century and became popular in the early 1900s (Glatt et al., 1967:7–8). This drug acts on the central nervous system by calming and, if used in sufficient strength, sedating the individual. Thus, these pills are sometimes referred to as "sleepers." Typically, barbiturates are prescribed for insomnia and nervousness, and to a lesser degree are used as an anesthetic. Some common barbiturates are Nembutal, Amytal, and

Seconal. Unfortunately, they are pharmacologically addictive if taken excessively over a period of time.

Before 1960, barbiturate dependence was typically a condition of middle-aged persons, especially females, and some alcoholics. It should be emphasized that alcohol and barbiturates are a dangerous combination since both are depressants and used together can even lead to accidental death. More recently, barbiturate dependence has been noted among youngsters, though they usually employ barbiturates in combination with other drugs. Occasionally a doctor prescribes a barbiturate to someone using cocaine or amphetamines. The latter two excite and activate a person to such a degree that relaxing and sleeping are difficult; therefore, barbiturates are used to combat these symptoms of agitation. Some of the symptoms of a barbiturate-dependence state are the inability to coordinate voluntary body movements, to control emotions, and to think normally. Barbiturates have a cross-tolerance, i.e., one barbiturate can be substituted for another.

DRUGS AND CRIMINALITY

Although we have previously noted that alcohol is a drug, it is our contention that the combination of drug and alcohol abuse under the same general heading of addiction or dependency is so broad that it would hamper an understanding of their relationships to criminality. This position is based on the legal status of drugs and alcohol in Western societies. The purchase and consumption of beverage alcohol is legal, although there may be restrictions on the age of the purchaser and the locale and time for buying and consuming alcohol. Despite experiments with Prohibition in certain Western countries after World War I, the consensus is that the purchasing and consuming of alcoholic beverages by the *average* individual carries with it no great threat of addiction. More specifically, it is estimated that in the United States only one in every twelve drinkers (around 8 to 9 percent) will develop alcoholism. In most European countries, with the possible exception of France, the rate of alcohol addicts among drinkers is even lower than for the United States.

The legal situation with reference to drugs is quite different. For all practical purposes, the obtaining of drugs is surrounded by strict proscriptions. The individual must obtain a medical prescription for the drug or seek his supply from illicit sources—generally the black market. In short, the ingestion of drugs orally or intravenously by an individual is surrounded not only by strict legal norms but by cultural taboos. There are few situations in Western society that allow free and unhindered access to drugs. There appears to be general awareness that opiate (especially heroin) addicts through time prefer to inject the agent intravenously. The process of becoming "hooked" on heroin requires little time—a few weeks or months. This stands in strong contrast to the long sequence of years involved in becoming alcohol addicts; furthermore, clinically it is known that many individuals ingest large quantities of alcohol over many years without becoming alcohol addicts.

Furthermore, the most widely held position is that drug addiction and alcoholism are diseases. To a certain extent, the courts and legislative bodies are beginning to accept this idea for it is not illegal to be a drug addict or alcoholic. Rather, behaviors associated with these conditions are illegal; for the drug addict, it is the illegal procurement, possession, and use of illegal drugs, and for the alcoholic it is public intoxication. As we will discuss later, there is a movement to repeal public intoxication laws as they relate to chronic alcoholics.

Currently there is concern over whether a person can be arrested for behavior which is a manifestation of a disease. It is felt that such individuals lack *mens rea* or criminal intent, and that ". . . any disease which deprives the individual of capacity to control his conduct will excuse conduct which would otherwise be condemned" [*Easter* v. *District of Columbia* 361 F.2d 50 (D.C. Cir. 1966) (*en banc*) rev'g 209 A.2d 625 (D.C. Ct. App. 1965)]. It is on this foundation that decriminalization of the behavior of drug addicts and chronic alcoholics is being constructed.

For purposes of this chapter we shall discuss separately the relationship of alcohol addiction and other drug addiction to criminality.

ALCOHOLISM AND CRIMINALITY

Public Intoxication

There are specific criminal categories that are intimately related to the use of alcoholic beverages. Most clearly involved are violations of public intoxication statutes and closely related charges of disorderly conduct, vagrancy, trespassing and peace disturbance, liquor law violations, and driving under the influence of alcoholic beverages, i.e., while intoxicated. In terms of magnitude the most frequent violation of criminal statutes in the United States is for public drunkenness.

Historically in North America and Europe, public drunkenness has been defined as a criminal violation in almost every legal jurisdiction. Laws exist on state and municipal levels prohibiting public drunkenness. Although disorderliness is a prerequisite for arrest under some laws, the homeless skid-row inebriates face repeated arrest for disorderly and nondisorderly drunkenness.

Chronic drunkenness offenders are a group of excessive drinkers who may or may not be alcoholics, but whose drinking has involved them in difficulties with the police, the courts, and the penal institutions. They are a group for whom the penal sanctions of the society have failed along with existent community resources for rehabilitation. Although some of these men (very seldom women) are confirmed alcoholics, others are individuals whose present use of alcohol is preliminary to confirmed alcoholism; and others are nonaddicted excessive drinkers who will never become alcoholics.

Magnitude of the Problem

The more intense the enforcement of laws, the greater the effect they have on the deviancy. For the public intoxication offender, the enforcement is indeed intense. The President's Commission on Law Enforcement and Administration of Justice in its final report stated:

> Two million arrests in 1965—one of every three arrests in America—were for the offense of public drunkenness. The great volume of these arrests places an extremely heavy load on the operations of the criminal justice system. It burdens police, clogs lower criminal courts and crowds penal institutions throughout the United States (President's Commission, 1967:233).

There are, however, variations from city to city in how severely the drunkenness statutes are enforced by the police. At one extreme are the practices in Atlanta and Washington, D.C., where enforcement procedures are very strict: in Atlanta, in 1965, of a total of 92,965 arrests, 52.5 percent were for drunkenness; while in Washington, D.C., the corresponding figure for 86,464 arrests was 51.8 percent for drunkenness. At the permissive end is St. Louis, where the police are more tolerant and have a sociomedical orientation to alcoholism: there, in 1965, of all arrests (44,701), 5.5 percent were for drunkenness (President's Commission, 1967:234). The change from a punitive to a sociomedical orientation toward chronic drunkenness offenders in St. Louis will be discussed in greater detail later in this chapter.

In 1970, the FBI reported 1,512,672 arrests for public drunkenness by 5,270 agencies that encompassed a population of 151,604,000 (F.B.I., 1971). This figure accounted for approximately 23 percent of the total arrests for all offenses and is more than the number of arrests for index crime offenses. If alcohol-related offenses (driving under the influence of alcohol, disorderly conduct, liquor-law violations, and vagrancy) were added to this percentage, it would constitute around 43 percent of all reported arrests in the United States in 1970 (F.B.I., 1971).

A large number of these actions involve the repeated arrest of the same men. To illustrate, let us take the case of Portland, Oregon, for 1963; in this year there were eleven thousand law violations involving drunkenness or the effects of drinking, but only around two thousand different persons accounted for these arrests (Wippel, 1964).

Persons arrested and held for prosecution for public drunkenness are almost never represented by counsel and almost always found guilty. In 1969 reports to the FBI from 2,640 cities representing a population of 66,155,000 showed that 86.2 percent of all persons charged with public drunkenness were found guilty (F.B.I., 1970). This suggests that offenders whose violations are alcohol-related frequently find themselves incarcerated. Indeed, there is strong evidence that chronic inebriates constitute one of the largest groupings of individuals incarcerated in short-term correctional institutions. Alcohol-related offenses accounted for 35 percent of the incarcerations in the St. Louis City Workhouse for the period 1957–59. Benz (1964) completed a study of the penal population in the Monroe County (Rochester, New York) Jail, which showed that alcoholic offenders accounted for 62.5 percent of the prisoners and 73.1 percent of the total commitments in the year 1962.

Social policies directed against a particular deviancy affect some group members differently than others, resulting in a corresponding effect on the larger public. It has also previously been suggested that the very nature of public intoxication or drunkenness excludes most middle-class and upper-class alcoholics and excessive drinkers who typically drink in private or semiprivate surroundings. American sociocultural values and legal statutes do not condemn individuals for excessive drinking as long as they do not bother other persons. Thus, public drunkenness laws affect mainly the lower class who drink in public and, in effect, are class laws. There is also evidence which tentatively suggests that, within the lower class, some persons feel the brunt of the law more than others (Pittman & Gordon, 1958; Benz, 1964).

Recent Court Decisions

Two major legal decisions in 1966 affecting the public intoxication offender in the United States were rendered. First the United States Court of Appeals for the Fourth Circuit in Richmond in January, 1966, found in favor of the appellant, Joe B. Driver of North Carolina, who had been arrested more than two hundred times for public intoxication. In a unanimous decision, Judge Bryan stated for the court:

> The upshot of our decision is that the State cannot stamp an unpretending chronic alcoholic as a criminal if his drunken public display is involuntary as a result of disease. However, nothing we have said precludes appropriate detention of him for treat-

ment and rehabilitation so long as he is not marked a criminal [*Driver* v. *Hinnant* 356 F.2d 761 (4th Cir. 1966)].

In the same vein in March, 1966, the United States Court of Appeals for the District of Columbia in its unanimous ruling in favor of the appellant, DeWitt Easter, who was contesting his conviction for public intoxication on the grounds that he was a chronic alcoholic, stated: "Chronic alcoholism is a defense to the charge of public intoxication and therefore is not a crime" [*Easter* v. *District of Columbia* 361 F.2d 50 (D.C. Cir. 1966)].

In 1967, the Supreme Court of the United States was asked to rule, in *Powell* v. *Texas* [392 U.S. 514 (1968)], on the constitutionality of the use of a public intoxication statute in cases involving chronic alcoholics. It was the contention of medical, legal, and other professional groups supporting Powell that chronic alcoholism was a positive defense to the charge of public intoxication, and that these individuals should not be incarcerated but should receive medical and social treatment. In June, 1968, the Supreme Court, in a narrow five-to-four decision, held that a chronic alcoholic could be convicted under a state law against public drunkenness. The majority decision was by four members of the Court who joined in one opinion and by a fifth justice whose opinion agreed with the result reached by them but who took a narrower position in doing so. However, this decision did not negate the lower-court decisions, given the absence of a clear-cut majority of five justices agreeing in one decision. Thus local and state laws (which have been enacted subsequent to the *Powell* decision) that allow chronic alcoholism as a valid defense to public intoxication criminal charges are constitutional.

It should be underscored that these court cases deal only with the chronic alcoholic and one manifestation of his disease—public intoxication. This is illustrated in the following excerpt from the legal brief filed on behalf of DeWitt Easter by his attorneys. It states:

> There is no quarrel here with the principle of the Harris case that Section 25-128 of the D.C. Code [public intoxication statute] may be used to punish the normal individual who goes on a "binge" from time to time, or the common drunkard whose intoxication results from indolence but not from addiction. Such persons could, if they wished, control their drinking, and therefore are criminally responsible for their actions. Nor does Appellant [Easter] argue that a chronic alcoholic who drives a car, or commits murder, is *ipso facto* not guilty. A finding that a chronic alcoholic has no capacity to avoid appearing in public in an intoxicated condition is *not* a finding that a chronic alcoholic may with impunity commit murder . . . that is an entirely different question of criminal responsibility . . . [*Easter* v. *District of Columbia* 209 A.2d (D.C. Ct. App. 1965):11–12].

Thus the *mens rea* approach is aimed at helping only the chronic alcoholic, and does not encompass all chronic drunkenness offenders nor cope with the great range of alcohol-related offenses, such as vagrancy, common assault, and disorderly conduct.

The President's Commission on Law Enforcement and Administration of Justice

The President's Commission on Law Enforcement and Administration of Justice, commonly known as the Crime Commission, was appointed by President Johnson in 1965 to study crime problems and made its report in 1967. One chapter of the

Commission's report, dealing with alcoholism and drunkenness offenses, made significant recommendations concerning this problem which are expected to be enacted into law.

The Commission recommended:

> 1. Drunkenness should not in itself be a criminal offense. Disorderly and other criminal conduct accompanied by drunkenness should remain punishable as separate crimes. The implementation of this recommendation requires the development of adequate civil detoxification procedures.
> 2. Communities should establish detoxification units as part of comprehensive treatment programs.
> 3. Communities should coordinate and extend aftercare resources, including supportive residential housing.
> 4. Research by private and governmental agencies into alcoholism, the problems of alcoholics, and methods of treatment should be expanded. . . . Consideration should be given to providing further legislation on the Federal level for the promotion of the necessary coordinated treatment programs (President's Commission, 1967:256–57).

The recommendation that drunkenness in itself should no longer be a crime is a major breakthrough in establishing a redefinition of the chronic drunkenness offender as a sick instead of a criminal individual. The seeds of this concept of alcoholism as an illness were sown over the last twenty-five years in Europe and the United States and have gradually grown to the point of the widespread acceptance of alcoholism as a disease on both continents.

Innovations in Handling Public Intoxicants

Bold approaches to handling the problem of public drunkenness within a sociomedical context first occurred interestingly enough in Eastern Europe—namely, Czechoslovakia and Poland—with the establishment of "sobering-up stations" or detoxification centers. These stations instead of jails were used to process drunkenness cases.

Sobering-up stations have become an integral part of the network of alcoholism services in Poland and Czechoslovakia. For example, in Warsaw any person found drunk on the street or lying in a doorway is taken by police to the sobering-up station. The Warsaw station is a 150-bed facility on the grounds of the State Sanatorium for Mental Disorders, and is one of the twenty-two such sobering-up stations in the country established under the Anti-Alcoholism Act of 1959 to handle "drunk-on-street" cases. The Warsaw facility in 1967 had approximately 25,000 admissions; thus the public drunkenness offender in Poland is originally handled in a sociomedical facility instead of a jail.

Basically, the Warsaw sobering-up station routine for an intoxication case is as follows: The intoxicated person is registered by a clerk at the station, undressed, examined by a physician or intern, given a shot of vitamins or other medication, given a shower, and put to bed for eight to twenty-four hours. These stations provide for treatment of acute alcoholism and early case detection of alcoholics.

In Czechoslovakia, patients from the sobering-up station are referred to lectures on alcoholism and its effects (called "Sunday Schools" since the lectures are held on Sunday). Generally when the individual appears a second or third time at the sobering-up station, a full scale medical and social evaluation begins and a plan for therapeutic intervention is worked out, involving voluntary approaches at first. If the patient does not proceed with voluntary treatment, then compulsory treatment is begun.

The first detoxification center to open in North America for persons detained by the police for public intoxication was in St. Louis in November, 1966, sponsored by that city's Metropolitan Police Department in cooperation with St. Mary's Infirmary and the Social Science Institute, Washington University, under a grant from the Office of Law Enforcement Assistance of the U.S. Department of Justice, supplemented by local and state funds.

The elements for social change in St. Louis were found in the emphasis the city's power structure—government, police, civic leaders, and social agencies—placed on the rehabilitation of the alcoholics. Much educational work with these groups and the area's mass media had prepared the community to accept the idea that public drunkenness offenders were sick individuals who needed sociomedical care instead of a fine or jail terms. For example, in 1962 and 1963 many key St. Louis personnel visited the Alcoholism Treatment and Research Center and held many informal conferences with staff members (Pittman, 1967a).

As a result of these conferences and further studies, the St. Louis Board of Police Commissioners in 1963 instituted a major policy change in reference to intoxicated persons on the street. The St. Louis Metropolitan Police Department made it mandatory for all individuals "picked up" from St. Louis streets to be taken to the emergency rooms of one of the two city hospitals for physical examination. This meant that routine physical evaluation was provided all alcoholics processed by the police; if these individuals were in need of medical care, they were to be hospitalized instead of being jailed. If medical care were deemed unnecessary, the intoxicated person was "held until sober"—not more than twenty hours—and released to the community.

St. Louis was one of the few American cities in which this innovation in the handling of the public intoxication case occurred. It squarely placed the locus of responsibility for the alcoholic in the treatment sphere and was in keeping with modern practices toward the publicly intoxicated person in a number of European countries. However, the Board of Police Commissioners was dissatisfied that large numbers of alcoholics were not admitted to the hospitals for medical care. At times more than 90 percent of the "examined" public intoxicants were returned by the physicians to the police for processing.

Thus, the Metropolitan Police Department of St. Louis was one of the few agencies to apply for a grant for the operation of a detoxification center when such centers became eligible for support under the Law Enforcement Assistance Act of 1965. The Detoxification and Diagnostic Evaluation Center in St. Louis (originally at St. Mary's Infirmary, and in December, 1968, permanently transferred to the St. Louis State Hospital) is a thirty-bed unit with 24-hour medical and nursing coverage, a total of forty full- and part-time employees and an annual budget of approximately $325,000. The goals of the Center are:

1. To remove chronic inebriates to a sociomedical locus of responsibility which will markedly reduce police processing.
2. To remove chronic inebriates from the city courts and jails.
3. To provide sociomedical treatment for them.
4. To begin their rehabilitation.
5. To refer them to an agency for further rehabilitation, with the goal that they will return to society as productive persons.

The Detoxification Center is the first systematic attempt in North America to provide treatment for the alcoholic at the moment the police intervene in the process. The Center works as follows:

1. A police officer brings the "intoxicated" person to the reception room.
2. Center personnel complete a medical examination of the patient.
3. The patient is showered, given clean clothing, and assigned a bed.
4. Special nursing care and diets are provided.
5. Therapeutic activities—films, group meetings, discussions, and lectures—are provided.
6. Each patient is counseled individually.
7. The patient, when necessary, is referred to other social, health, and governmental services for further help.
8. The average length of stay is seven to ten days.

The St. Louis Center in over the first four years of its operation has become a model for the United States. A follow-up evaluation study, conducted by the Social Science Institute (Weber, 1970) of 200 consecutive patients treated at the Center, who elected to stay for the full treatment period of normally seven days and who resided in or near the St. Louis metropolitan area for approximately three months prior to admission, showed results which far surpassed the expectations of police and treatment personnel. Approximately 20 percent of the chronic inebriates were abstinent when reinterviewed in the community three months after discharge from the Center, 56 percent were gainfully employed, and 31 percent had shown marked improvement in their drinking patterns. Based on Weber's study, Table 1 shows how the patients fared in the areas evaluated. These results were achieved with a group that had been considered helpless and hopeless by most observers. But we must always remember that no group is ever hopeless unless our expectations define it as such.

From its opening on November 18, 1966, to September 30, 1970, the St. Louis Detoxification and Diagnostic Evaluation Center has handled 4,405 admissions. The patient profile statistically is as follows: sex: male, 94 percent, female, 6 percent; race: white, 82 percent, black, 18 percent; marital status: single, 21 percent, separated, widowed, or divorced, 65 percent, married, 13 percent, and unknown, 1 percent; occupational skills: unskilled, 53 percent, semiskilled, 22 percent, elderly or disabled, 19 percent, and unknown, 6 percent. The median age of the patients is 48 years.

As stated previously, alcoholism is a chronic progressive illness; therefore relapses are to be expected. However, 46 percent of the over 4,000 patients have been admitted only once. The remaining 54 percent have had two or more admissions. The treatment

TABLE 1
EVALUATION OF 200 PATIENTS FOLLOWED UP THREE MONTHS AFTER DISCHARGE FROM THE ST. LOUIS DETOXIFICATION AND DIAGNOSTIC EVALUATION CENTER

	Markedly Improved	Remained Same	Deteriorated	Unable to Rate
Drinking	51%	46%	3%	0
Employment	25%	66%	5%	4
Income	16%	72%	8%	4
Health	56%	35%	9%	0
Housing	14%	83%	3%	0

Based on Weber, 1970:18.

facility is unlocked, although previous to the Center's opening, these same people would have been jailed for public intoxication; only 10 percent have left against medical advice.

Given the success of the Detoxification Center in St. Louis, the public was extremely receptive to legal changes in the public intoxication ordinance. In Missouri, public drunkenness is governed by local laws; in October, 1967, the St. Louis Board of Aldermen unanimously passed a new ordinance governing public intoxication without any court pressure being needed. It was sponsored by then-Alderman Joseph Roddy, who had been active in creating a more enlightened community climate for rehabilitating alcoholics in Missouri. The essence of St. Louis's new ordinance is that chronic alcoholism is a positive defense to a charge of public intoxication. However, few cases of public intoxication involving chronic alcoholics find their way to the municipal court any more, as they are given medical and social treatment at the Detoxification Center.

These innovations in the care of chronic drunkenness offenders in St. Louis and in Missouri are indicative of changes occurring throughout the United States. As examples, the North Carolina General Assembly in 1967, Maryland in 1968, North Dakota in 1969, and Florida in 1971 revised their public intoxication statutes to provide that chronic alcoholism was a disease and, thereby, a positive defense to the charge of public intoxication. We can expect other states and municipalities, at a quickening pace, to revise and liberalize their public intoxication statutes.

The provision of adequate emergency care facilities for public alcoholics is now accelerating both in the United States and Europe. In New York City the Vera Institute of Justice established in 1967 a demonstration alcoholism treatment project known as the Manhattan Bowery Project (Morgan & Goldfarb, 1968) for skid-row indigent individuals. The operation is composed of three parts: (1) a street rescue team composed of a civilian medical person and a plainclothes policeman, who attempt to persuade the indigent drunkenness cases to voluntarily enter the treatment facility; (2) a detoxification center to provide emergency medical care for approximately five days; and (3) placement or referral to an aftercare facility. As has been the case with the St. Louis Center, the Bowery Project found that these chronic alcoholics have been extremely responsive to treatment and some are beginning to show progress in coping with their chronic debilitating disease of alcoholism. Similar results are being shown by the detoxification centers in Des Moines, Iowa, Washington, D.C., Kansas City, Houston, Orlando, Seattle, etc.

In 1963, the Swedish Parliament ordered the creation of a Governmental Commission to study the "criminalization of drunkenness and the methods of care and treatment of acutely intoxicated persons." As Pittman and Gordon did in their study, *Revolving Door* (1958), the Swedish Commission rejected the traditional policy in their country of arresting and punishing the acutely intoxicated individual. Following the lead of Poland and Czechoslovakia, the Swedish Commission recommended that special medical stations or detoxification centers be established in the major cities of the country. The Commission tested the practicability of the detoxification centers in the two cities and stated, "The detoxification clinic concept is not only fully workable, but it also creates entirely new premises for an active and socio-medical treatment of drunks."

It should also be noted that the British government has proposed that the public intoxication offender be removed from the criminal process, and that he be treated as a medical and social-welfare case.

But the tragedy is that implementation of new medical and social philosophy in reference to alcoholism with new programs has been so difficult to obtain, and that individuals are still being jailed for exhibiting the symptoms of chronic alcoholism, i.e., repeated public intoxication.

However, as this chapter demonstrates, major advances in handling the problem of chronic drunkenness offenders are taking place in Poland, Czechoslovakia, in St. Louis and Missouri, in New York City, and Sweden. These changes, based on legislative action and the creation of detoxification facilities and supportive social-welfare services, demonstrate what governmental agencies can accomplish when they are willing to take action on this major sociomedical problem. The ultimate goal of all governmental bodies in reference to this problem should be the complete removal of chronic alcoholics, whose only offense is public intoxication, from the jail cells and drunk tanks of the world to sociomedical treatment facilities.

Crime and Alcohol Use

Two major research approaches have characterized the investigation of the relationship of crime and alcohol use. First, what is the drinking behavior of the individual when he commits a crime? Second, what is the correlation between long-standing alcohol abuse and criminality.

In determining the drinking status of the individual at the commission of the crime, two research techniques have been used. Illustrative of one approach is Marvin E. Wolfgang's (1958) study of homicides committed in Philadelphia in 1948–52, composed of 588 victims (cases) and 621 offenders. He reports that "either or both the victim and offender had been drinking immediately prior to the slaying in nearly two-thirds of the cases" (p. 322).

A second, more accurate research technique is to analyze the blood or urine of the individual for alcohol content immediately after the commission of the crime. Illustrative of this approach is the program in Columbus, Ohio, where urine analysis for alcohol concentration was completed in a study by Shupe (1954:661) on "882 persons picked up during or immediately after the commission of a felony" during the period March, 1951, to March, 1955. Shupe states:

> The figures show that crimes of physical violence are associated with intoxicated persons. Cuttings (11 to 1 under the influence of alcohol), the carrying of concealed weapons (8 to 1 under the influence of alcohol) are definitely crimes of alcohol influence, even crimes of true intoxication (1954:663).

Thus, the closest relationship between intoxication and criminal behavior (except for public intoxication) has been established for criminal categories involving assaultive behavior. This relationship is especially high for lower-lower-class blacks and whites. More than likely, aggression in these groups is weakly controlled and the drinking of alcoholic beverages serves as a triggering mechanism for the external release of aggression. There are certain types of key situations located in lower-class life in which alcohol is a major factor in assaultive behavior. A frequent locale is the lower-class tavern which is an important social institution for this class. Assaultive episodes are precipitated during the drinking situation by quarrels that center around defaming personal honor, threats to masculinity, and questions about one's birth legitimacy. Personal quarrels between husband and wife, especially after the husband's drinking, frequently result in assaultive episodes in the lower-lower-class family.

Shupe's conclusion that 64 percent of his sample of 882 individuals were "under the influence of alcohol to such an extent that their inhibitions were reduced" (1954: 664) is of major significance to American criminologists. Excessive drinking of alcoholic beverages is an important fact in the commission of crimes.

The Department of Transportation (DOT) as well as the general public are very concerned about reducing the high loss of life on the nation's highways. A major campaign has been mounted by the DOT in conjunction with state and municipal authorities to remove intoxicated drivers from the roads and to rehabilitate them since approximately 50 percent of the fatal highway crashes in the United States involve a highly intoxicated driver. This can be confirmed by spot studies by scientists throughout this country. For example, of the first forty-three individuals killed in motor vehicle accidents in St. Louis County, Missouri, in 1966, thirty had alcohol-blood levels of 0.15 or higher, which is indicative of heavy intoxication. *The New York Times,* March 13, 1966, reported that in San Antonio in the last nine years 61 percent of the drivers and pedestrians killed had been intoxicated. The blood alcohol levels were 0.15 or higher. The research of Selzer (Selzer & Weiss, 1965) in Michigan confirms that a sizable proportion, 40 percent of those drivers responsible for fatal motor-vehicle accidents, can be diagnosed as alcoholics.

Between 40 and 50 percent of those incarcerated in penal institutions for felonies in the United States have a drinking problem. The most systematic study of a prison population is one completed by a team of Washington University psychiatrists, headed by Sam Guze (Guze et al., 1962), who examined psychiatrically a series of 223 consecutive criminals, including probationers, parolees, and "flat-timers" at the Missouri State Penitentiary at Jefferson City. Although 48 percent of the sample were diagnosed as having no psychiatric disorder, 43 percent were diagnosed as alcoholics, the largest percentage by far in any psychiatric category.

Another relationship between intoxication and criminality is found in the factors associated with continuation of a criminal career. Previous criminological studies have indicated that the major variable correlated with dropout from criminal activity is increasing age.

A recent study at the Institute of Criminology at the University of Copenhagen, Denmark, however, indicates that dropout from criminal activity is correlated with increasing age, unless the individual has an alcoholic problem. If he has an alcoholic problem, there is a strong tendency for the individual to maintain his criminal pattern in the middle years of life. Furthermore, as Pittman and Gordon (1958) have noted in *Revolving Door,* there is a tendency for certain criminals, who earlier in their criminal careers were involved in complex forms of crime, to become petty criminals with alcoholic complications in their middle and later years. These kinds of criminals may be referred to as double failures since earlier in life they used crime as a vehicle for social mobility, achievement, and success but failed to make the grade in high-level criminal activity. These are the men who do not become successful criminals. In later life they experience a second failure by being unsuccessful, petty criminals and frequently use a retreatist form of adaptation—chronic drunkenness.

OTHER DRUGS AND CRIMINALITY

Historical Overview of Narcotics Control in the United States

The present system of narcotics control in the United States dates back to the Harrison Act of 1914 which was originally intended as a revenue law for taxing narcotics. Prior to the passage of this law, Americans could buy narcotics from the local pharmacy. People were frequently unaware of their addiction but marveled at the euphoric power of certain brands of patent medicines. To what extent drug addiction constituted a problem in the United States in the early 1900s is uncertain, but it is estimated that there were at least two hundred thousand addicts at that time.

Beginning shortly after World War I under the provisions of the Harrison Act, the police and courts, especially at the federal level, began a vigorous campaign of suppressing the use of narcotic drugs. Various federal court decisions made it difficult for physicians to prescribe for and treat narcotics addicts (Duster, 1970). As a result, by the late 1920s, the United States had an extensive underworld trafficking in narcotics. The underworld traffic in drugs in the United States developed in the following sequential manner:

1. There existed a large number of individuals using drugs.
2. Another group of individuals for various reasons viewed the consumption of these drugs as undesirable, and this group placed sanctions on the consumers and attempted to stop trafficking in those drugs.
3. The market for these drugs still existed, but legal sources were nonexistent.
4. A third group of individuals sold the drugs through illegal channels for large profits. This would be a typical prototype for an underworld marketing process and was repeated during the American prohibition on alcoholic beverages (1920–33).

Thus the negative social policy of repression in the United States resulted in the following consequences: (1) a thriving illicit traffic in drugs; (2) a significant amount of addict crime, mainly of the property type to obtain money to purchase drugs; and (3) a subculture of drug addicts, particularly among youth, which perpetuates itself since addicts and suppliers gather together in a protective response against society's agents of control.

America's rigid policy toward addicts resulted in certain states (for example, California and Missouri) passing laws making it a criminal offense to be a drug addict. These laws, however, were declared unconstitutional by the United States Supreme Court decision in *Robinson* v. *California* [370 U.S. 660, 666–667 (1962)], which ruled that drug addiction in and of itself was not a criminal offense. Further symptomatic of the country's hysteria about drugs was the enactment by legislatures of some states (such as Louisiana) of the optional death penalty for pushers convicted of selling drugs to underage persons.

There is no doubt that the control policies followed by the United States Bureau of Narcotics and the various state agencies reinforced an image, especially during the early 1950s, of a dope-fiend menace in American society. The characterization of the drug addict as a perverse and degenerate individual prone to committing violent crimes and engaging in sexual orgies was frequently found in the popular literature.

Drug Usage Patterns in the United States

There have been noticeable changes in the drug addict population in the United States and to a lesser extent in Western Europe since the end of World War II. Prior to this time, most drug addicts were middle-aged and older persons from the middle and upper economic classes of society. Many of those individuals were either from the medical and allied professions or were "therapeutic" addicts—those who became addicted to drugs originally during the course of illness, such as cancer patients.

The pattern of drug usage began to change drastically after World War II. Glaser and O'Leary (1966) have written that six new trends characterize drug usage in America. These are:

1. Increased drug usage by young persons, especially those under 21 years of age. Particularly popular among the young are marijuana and, to a lesser extent, methedrine (speed) and LSD.
2. Increased drug usage by individuals of lower economic status.
3. Concentration of drug usage among minority groups, especially Negroes in the worst slums of New York and Chicago, by Puerto Ricans in New York slums, and by Negroes, Mexican-Americans, and lower-income whites in the Southwest and California.
4. Concentration of drug addiction in the larger American cities.
5. Association of drug addiction with other types of criminality. Many drug addicts have criminal and juvenile records prior to becoming addicts.
6. Increased usage of new drugs, such as LSD and amphetamines.

There are indications that this pattern of changed drug usage in the United States is the forerunner of the one that has spread to Great Britain and to a lesser extent to Western Europe. But to maintain perspective, it should be noted that in the broad historical sense drugs are a relatively recent phenomenon in Western society. In the United States, for example, the method of using a hypodermic syringe for intravenously injecting morphine was not known until just prior to the American Civil War. Despite the almost hysterical emphasis by the mass media on drug addiction in the United States, Canada, and Great Britain, the problem is numerically small in comparison to alcoholism. More specifically, estimates of drug addicts range from two hundred to three hundred thousand in the United States in comparison to nine million alcoholics.

Magnitude of Problem

The period from 1965 to 1970 has shown an astronomical explosion in the number of arrests in the United States for drug-law violations. In 1970, 3,381 agencies with a population of 122,233,000 reported 293,971 arrests on narcotic-drug law violations in comparison to 43,550 in these same jurisdictions in 1965. This was an increase of 675 percent in the five-year period (F.B.I., 1971).

Although the FBI *Uniform Crime Reports* do not specify which drug is unlawfully possessed, sold, or used, there is little question that most of these violations involve the nonnarcotic drug, cannabis. For example, violations of the California statutes governing marijuana use account for 35 percent of the felony arrests in Los Angeles County and more than 25 percent of the felony arrests in that state (Kwitney, 1971).

Generally speaking, most legislative bodies have reached the conclusion that the penalties attached to violation of the marijuana statutes are too severe. Thus, simple possession of cannabis in many states has been reduced from a felony to a misdemeanor. These legal changes, of course, do not satisfy those who favor the complete elimination of these statutes and the placing of marijuana under controls similar to those of alcoholic beverages.

A number of the drug arrests do involve "hard" drugs, such as heroin and synthetic opiates. Heroin addiction is commonly linked to crimes such as larceny, burglary, robbery, and prostitution as it requires large sums of money to support the narcotics habit. One reporter (Kwitney, 1971) has estimated that a hard-core heroin addict has to steal $25,000 in cash or $100,000 in goods yearly to support his habit, given the prices on the black market. Heroin addiction, confined in the 1950s and the first half of the 1960s to the ghettos and slums of the major American cities of New

York, Chicago, and Los Angeles, has diffused somewhat to other cities and more affluent areas such as the suburbs.

Decriminalization of Drug Addiction and Its Treatment

Beginning with the landmark *Robinson* case in 1962 in which the Supreme Court ruled that drug addiction in and of itself was not a crime, a sociomedical orientation towards drug addiction has gathered momentum in the United States. This position is based on the assumption that drug addiction is an illness and the drug addict is a sick person who requires treatment not incarceration. This position is slowly being implemented in state and federal laws concerning drug addiction and the provision of public funds for the rehabilitation of drug abusers.

A major problem still exists in the social policy arena in that laws try to distinguish between those who, on one hand, produce and sell illegal drugs or who violate rules governing legal drugs which are abused, and, on the other hand, those individuals who are drug abusers (including addicts). In some cases, especially with heroin, those who illegally sell the drug (pushers) are also addicts themselves. Thus, the distinction between the seller and abuser of drugs is not a precise one which can be promulgated in law.

The current modern treatment orientation toward drug addiction started with the founding of Synanon in California in 1958 by Charles (Chuck) Dederich, who had worked through a drinking problem himself. Synanon is a community of former drug addicts, many of whom have criminal records. Founded by Dederich with a $33 unemployment check, it has spread to many communities in the United States, although its growth has not been as spectacular as that of Alcoholics Anonymous. Volkman and Cressey (1963) have studied the internal dynamics of Synanon and have attempted to explain how the principles of the organization aid many drug addicts to become nonusers of drugs. Basically, the only admission requirement is the person's *"expressed willingness* to submit one's self to a group that hates drug addiction" (Volkman & Cressey, 1963:132). While at Synanon the addict must not take drugs and is positively rewarded by the group for staying off drugs and displaying antidrug attitudes. Synanon operates through small evening meetings of six to ten people, which emphasize anticriminal and antidrug norms, as well as emotional adjustments. Synanon, like Alcoholics Anonymous, makes no claim that it cures people; it seeks to help a man "stay away" from drugs as A.A. helps the individual to "stay away" from alcohol (Yablonsky, 1965).

Synanon, as A.A., is voluntary; no one is committed by the court to them or are the organizations under state supervision. However, given the increased recognition of the drug problem, state authorities perhaps following the lead of the federal government with its original drug treatment hospitals at Lexington, Kentucky, and Fort Worth, Texas, have established in the last decade an increasing number of facilities for voluntary and involuntary treatment of drug abusers. The California Rehabilitation Center (CRC), a state-operated institution, was among the first to be established to handle a criminal addict population, and has been researched by the sociologist Troy Duster (1970), who points up many of the crucial problems in such rehabilitation facilities. Paramount in Duster's logic is that the drug addict sees himself as morally different and inferior to the nonaddicted members of the society; in short, the addict has incorporated society's negative attitudes to addiction and addicts into his own identity. The identity makes any rehabilitation program almost doomed to failure because of the society's attitudes.

Emerging from the ghettos of large cities such as St. Louis and Chicago have been self-help organizations for narcotics addicts. Typical of these is the Narcotics Service Council (NASCO) in St. Louis founded by a charismatic leader, Don Mitchell, himself a recovered black addict, who first began to help other black addicts. Mitchell enlisted the aid of law-enforcement officers, political officials, and the local business community leadership in helping his organization. NASCO in its treatment program, unlike Synanon, enlists the aid of professional personnel, e.g., sociologists, psychologists, and psychiatrists, to work in conjunction with the recovered addicts. Its goal, through its residential treatment facility and outpatient group therapy sessions, is to aid individuals not only to become drug-free but antidrug in their personal orientation. Mitchell's group strongly believes in the dictum that drug addiction was triggered by the community environment, and therefore the rehabilitation program must be community-based. Every effort is made to return the addict to gainful employment, as it is believed that this creates self-respect and self-reliance again in the addict.

In recent years great emphasis has been placed on methadone maintenance therapy which was pioneered by Dole and Nyswander (1966, 1968). Methadone is a synthetic opiate which is used as a substitute for heroin; unlike heroin it does not give the addicts a "high," but it does satisfy the craving for heroin and blocks the euphoric effects of heroin (Gillespie, 1970). It should be remembered that methadone is an addictive drug and this form of treatment is only a partial answer to the addict's problems. Its advocates, however, point out that the most important first step is to get the patient into a productive role in the community rather than just being drug-free. Methadone, usually given to the patient in orange juice, allows the addict to obtain employment and ideally removes him from his all-consuming quest for heroin on the black market.

In a recent study conducted by Connor and Kremen (1971) at the Greenwich House Counseling Center in New York, which provides treatment for addicts through methadone maintenance therapy, these members concluded that their sample of drug abusers expected more results from their treatment than was actually obtained. Although the patients no longer used heroin, problems of loneliness, moodiness, poor self-image, and conflict in sexual identification remained. Thus, from this study and clinical observations it is evident that a drug-treatment program for heroin addicts requires not only methadone but also adjunctive therapies such as counseling, vocational rehabilitation, group and individual psychotherapy, etc.

Most communities are currently in a state of flux in terms of the organizational structure that will be responsible for the drug problem. In February, 1970, the United Community Funds and Councils of America (UCFCA) held a one-day workshop on the drug problem with special emphasis on what planning activities in the drug field were occurring, to discuss pending legislation, governmental and private plans, and available resources. The UCFCA Conference found that different agencies view the problem in different ways. Part of their statement is interesting, for it reflects the state of confusion in reference to what groups are responsible for what part of the drug problem. Their conference summary in part states:

> . . . the law enforcer sees drug abuse as a crime; to the doctor, it is an illness; the psychiatrist looks for the need for effective preventive education. This leads to a fragmented approach, which is compounded by the growing numbers of local agencies initiating independent programs; effort is wasted, and existing community resources are not used to the fullest possible extent.
>
> Part of the problem lies in the difficulty of estimating its dimensions, and in the controversy that rages around the effects of different chemical compounds. There is no

doubt, however, that drug abuse is moving down with respect to age and up in the social scale; it is a school problem in many affluent suburbs.

Representatives of the federal government at the workshop emphasized the need for research; little is known about the nature of many narcotics, the results of their continued use or abuse, or the underlying causes of addiction. Nor is sufficient information available on the recidivism rate of the various treatment modalities to permit the prediction that any given method will be effective in a given specific case (*Washington Bulletin*, 1970:1–2).

The conference summary is perhaps a pessimistic note on which to conclude this chapter's section on drug abuse and criminality, but it represents a valid statement of current community sentiments. In conclusion, however, one would expect that the decade of the 1970s will see an acceleration in the trend to decriminalize those aspects of behavior which are symptoms of alcoholism and drug addiction.

REFERENCES

Becker, Howard.
  1953   "Becoming a marihuana user." American Journal of Sociology 59:235–242.

Benz, Elizabeth.
  1964   Man on the Periphery. Rochester, N.Y.: Rochester Bureau of Municipal Research, Inc.

Cahalan, Don, Ira H. Cisin, and Helen M. Crossley.
  1969   American Drinking Practices: A National Study of Drinking Behavior and Attitudes. New Brunswick, N.J.: Rutgers Center of Alcohol Studies.

Chafetz, M. E.
  1965   Liquor: The Servant of Man. Boston: Little, Brown.

Connor, Thomas, and Eleanor Kremen.
  1971   "Methadone maintenance—is it enough?" British Journal of Addiction 66:53–70.

Dole, Vincent P., and Marie E. Nyswander.
  1966   "Rehabilitation of heroin addicts after blockade with methadone." New York State Journal of Medicine 66:2011–2017.
  1968   "Methadone maintenance and its implications for theories of narcotic addiction," in A. Wikler (ed.), The Addictive States. Baltimore: William & Wilkins.

Duster, Troy.
  1970   The Legislation of Morality. New York: Free Press.

Federal Bureau of Investigation (F.B.I.)
  1970   Crime in the United States: Uniform Crime Reports—1969. Washington, D.C.: U.S. Government Printing Office.
  1971   Crime in the United States: Uniform Crime Reports—1970. Washington, D.C.: U.S. Government Printing Office.

Gillespie, Duff G. (ed.)
  1970   Drug Abuse and Law Enforcement. St. Louis: Social Science Institute, Washington University.

Gillespie, D. G., M. C. Glatt, D. R. Hills, and D. J. Pittman.
  1967   "Drug dependence and abuse in England." British Journal of Addiction
          62:155–170.

Glaser, D., and V. O'Leary.
  1966   The Control and Treatment of Narcotic Use. U.S. Department of Health,
          Education and Welfare, Parole Series, J.D. 5004. Washington, D.C.: U.S.
          Government Printing Office.

Glatt, M. D., D. J. Pittman, D. G. Gillespie, and D. R. Hills.
  1967   The Drug Scene in Great Britain: Journey Into Loneliness. London: Edward
          Arnold, Ltd.

Guze, Samuel B., Vincent B. Tuason, Paul D. Gatfield, Mark A. Stuart, and Bruce
          Picken.
  1962   "Psychiatric illness and crime with particular reference to alcoholism: a
          study of 223 criminals." Journal of Nervous and Mental Disease 134:512–
          513.

Hutt, Peter Barton.
  1967   "The legal control of alcoholism towards a public health concept." Pp. 124–
          128 in David J. Pittman (ed.), Alcoholism. New York: Harper & Row.

Kwitney, Jonathan.
  1971   "Policing morality." Wall Street Journal August 25:1, 9.

Morgan, Robert, and Charles Goldfarb.
  1968   "Report on the Manhattan Bowery project." January 31 (mimeographed).

Pittman, David J.
  1964   "Homeless men." Transaction 1(January):15–16.
  1967a   "Public intoxication and the alcoholic offender in American society." Pp.
          7–28 in President's Commission on Law Enforcement and Administration of
          Justice, Task Force Report: Drunkenness. Washington, D.C.: U.S. Govern-
          ment Printing Office.
  1967b   "The rush to combine: sociological dissimilarities between drug addiction
          and alcoholism." British Journal of Addiction 62:373–343.
  1968   "New approaches to the chronic drunkenness offenders." State Government
          41:164–170.
  1970   "Jamming the revolving door: new approaches to the public drunkenness
          offenders." Pp. 263–276 in Elizabeth W. Post (ed.), World Dialogue on
          Alcohol and Drug Dependence. Boston: Beacon Press.

Pittman, David J., and Duff G. Gillespie.
  1967   "Social policy as deviancy reinforcement: the case of the public intoxication
          offender." Pp. 106–124 in David J. Pittman (ed.), Alcoholism. New York:
          Harper & Row.

Pittman, David J., and C. Wayne Gordon.
  1958   Revolving Door: A Study of the Chronic Police Case Inebriate. Glencoe, Ill.:
          Free Press.

Pittman, David J., and Muriel W. Sterne.
  1965   Alcoholism: Community Agency Attitudes and Their Impact on Treatment
          Services. U.S. Department of Health, Education and Welfare, PHS Publi-
          cation No. 1273. Washington, D.C.: U.S. Government Printing Office.

President's Commission on Law Enforcement and Administration of Justice.
1967   The Challenge of Crime in a Free Society. Washington, D.C.: U.S. Government Printing Office.

Selzer, Melvin L., and Sue Weiss.
1965   "Alcoholism and fatal traffic accidents—a study in futility." Municipal Court Review 5:15–20.

Sherrod, J. M.
1966   "The pharmacology and physiology of drug addiction." Illinois Medical Journal 130:453.

Shupe, Lloyd M.
1954   "Alcohol and crime: a study of the urine alcohol concentration found in 882 persons arrested during or immediately after the commission of a felony." Journal of Criminal Law, Criminology and Police Science 44: 661–664.

Volkman, Rita, and Donald R. Cressey.
1963   "Differential association and the rehabilitation of drug addicts." American Journal of Sociology 69:129–142.

Washington Bulletin.
1970   Conference of United Community Funds and Councils of America Workshop, February 21 (July 13).

Weber, James.
1970   "Final evaluation report," in The St. Louis Detoxification and Diagnostic Evaluation Center. Law Enforcement Assistance Administration, U.S. Department of Justice Grant #284 (S. 093). Washington, D.C.: U.S. Government Printing Office.

Wippel, R. R.
1964   Personal communication from Portland, Oregon.

Wolfgang, Marvin E.
1958   Patterns of Criminal Homicide. Philadelphia: University of Pennsylvania Press.

World Health Organization (W.H.O.)
1964   WHO Expert Committee on Addiction Producing Drugs. World Health Organization Technical Report Series No. 273.

Yablonsky, Lewis.
1965   The Tunnel Back: Synanon. New York: Macmillan.

CHAPTER 7

Sexual Conduct and Crime

John H. Gagnon

State University of New York, Stony Brook

CRIMINOLOGY, DEVIANCE AND SEXUAL CONDUCT

Since the publication of the last major conventional criminological works on the sex offender, there has been a profound decline in the number of research reports and studies that have taken as their primary focus the intersect between the criminal law and sexual behavior. A retrospective look suggests that even the volume *Sex Offenders* (Gebhard et al., 1965) was a late manifestation of this type of research since it and most of the other large-scale general empirical studies of sex offenders (Abrahamsen, 1950; Karpman, 1954; Glueck, 1956; Radzinowicz, 1957) were conceived, though published some years later, in the intellectual and scientific climate of the late 1940s and early 1950s. This decline in the volume of research activity has been neither a consequence of a decline in an interest in sexuality in the society (for the opposite is suggested by the increased frequency of open discussion of sexual matters and representations of sexual behavior in the media), nor a consequence of a decreased interest in things criminal and illegal (for the opposite is suggested by the current passion for law, order, and safe streets). It seems rather to be a result of changes that have occurred in what are conceived to be the central problems of the field of criminology as well as the rapid changes in the level of public attention given to all aspects of sexuality. These have submerged an older, more prepossessing interest in sexual crime.

On the level of the sociology of criminology the emergence of the category "deviant behavior" as a more general label than "criminal behavior" for nonconforming social activity has deeply impacted the field of criminology. This relabeling has expanded the focus of research attention to persons committing crimes who remain uncaught, to the parallels between deviant and conforming or criminal and noncriminal behavior, to the role of conventional institutions in the development and maintenance of nonconforming behavior, and to the existence of subcultures that serve to support alternative moral careers. Such a reconceptualization of at least some aspects of crim-

Based in part on research supported by USPHS grants MH 12535 and HD 02257 from the National Institute of Mental Health and HD 4156 from the National Institute of Child Health and Human Development, and the Graduate School of the State University of New York at Stony Brook.

inal behavior into a subclass of deviancy has called attention to unsolved empirical and conceptual problems in the practice of criminological research.

It is apparent that few of the ideas of present-day students of deviance are missing from the sociocriminological works of the Chicago tradition beginning in the middle 1920s. Indeed, most of the works of modern deviance researchers take as their focal concerns conceptions that were central to the criminological work of Burgess, McKay, and Shaw from the late 1920s to the early 1940s. The normality of delinquent behavior in neighborhoods which appeared disorganized to the middle-class view, the psychological conventionality of criminal careers, and the belief that courts confirmed juveniles into delinquent life-styles by selective labeling were the bread-and-butter ideas of this tradition in criminology. For these themes to take root and begin to reshape the day-to-day practice of criminology (both sociological and nonsociological), however, required a change in the society surrounding criminology. For example, Lindesmith's early research on the organization and character of opiate addiction which focused on the interaction of social-psychological processes (what is now called labeling) with the character of drug-enforcement practices have only begun to have serious academic, nonacademic, and public-policy implications after major changes have occurred in the way in which drug-taking behavior has been experienced and distributed in the society (Lindesmith, 1938, 1968).

This movement toward the reconceptualization of nonconforming behavior as being the product of social conditions was deeply embedded in the sociological tradition in criminology, but influential studies of the criminal, sexual and otherwise, were frequently the concern of psychologists, psychiatrists, and physicians who saw the origins of criminal behavior largely in individual attributes and explainable through individual differences. Even though these views represented a shift from the point of view that crime was the result of a vicious nature or a faulty moral education, they still focused their attention on defects in the individual—defects that involved feeblemindedness, hormonal imbalances, psychopathy, body types, and, more recently, defective chromosomes.[1] As these theories were abandoned as general theories of criminogenesis, in the face of data from control groups, they were appropriated to explain the behavior of the sex offender since, at that time, there were not bodies of control data which identified general patterns of sexual behavior in the population. During this period in the history of criminology (and, in part, it remains so today), violations of sexual codes were explained by the general public through moral rather than social or psychological categories.

The success of deviance theory outside of sociology as an acceptable explanatory model for behavior is largely the result of general educational changes that have made the society more amenable to psychological and sociological explanations for behavior (whether they are correct or not). Thus, the recent "sociologizing" and "psychologizing" of large portions of the population have made plausible the argument that homosexuality should be decriminalized—and, more radically, that it might be a sexual alternative to heterosexuality. As a form of deviance, homosexuality is released from either moral or psychological opprobrium. However, changes in the conception of sexual criminality are very recent, since the study of sexual offenses was even more nar-

---

1. A review of the contest between socially and individually based theories (either biological or psychological) can be found in any standard sociological criminology text. It might be argued that a large portion of the energy of sociological criminology prior to 1950 was spent debunking these particularistic theories of criminality and criminogenesis (see, for example, the works of Edwin Sutherland, 1956).

rowly circumscribed by societal limitations in its procedures and empirical content than was the study of other forms of criminal behavior.

It has been historically possible to argue that nonsexual criminal and noncriminal behavior might share some of the same motivational content—boys do well in sports because they want to be liked by their peers and boys steal cars because they want to be liked by their peers. Alternatively, criminality might be defined at least in part by societal prejudices or structural inequality—the internalization of a desire for success can lead to criminal behavior if persons are not given access to means for success. Yet it seemed impossible to grant this overlap of motives or of social structure in the study or discussion of sexual criminality.

The exclusion of the sexual from the rest of social life, which has marked most of the American experience until the very recent past, was the primary force shaping the way that we understood not only nearly all aspects of the behavior of the sexual criminal, but noncriminal sexuality as well. Because sexuality was excluded from normal social and scientific discourse, the study of sexuality in both its conventional and unconventional modes became deeply distorted. Prior to the late 1930s it was extremely difficult to study any form of sexual activity in the society except that of the neurotic, the psychotic, or the criminal (for a review of research, see Kinsey et al., 1948; Kinsey et al., 1953). The study of sex crimes then possessed the same weaknesses as all Lombrosian criminologies: in the absence of a body of knowledge about the origins of noncriminal sexual behavior, one could not determine the origins of criminal sexual behavior. In the absence of some knowledge about the distributions of various forms of sexual conduct in the society, it is impossible to determine whether the population who had been captured are representative of the population at large.

In the period prior to the early 1950s, conventional members of the society lived in a state of deep collective ignorance about sex and made assumptions about their own behavior and about the behavior of others based on limited dyadic interactions or on conversations that were rooted in collective sexual fantasies. In these circumstances it is not surprising that theoretical assertions about the origin and development of sexual activity were both primitive and defective. The most sophisticated extant theory was, of course, that of psychoanalysis, but except for a rather narrow population of intellectuals, it had limited acceptance. Indeed, its ultimate acceptability to large segments of the population was in some degree a function of the fact that it shared many of the same defects as folk wisdom about the sources and origins of sexual behavior (Gagnon & Simon, 1973). The critical underlying belief in both the folklore and Freud was that sexual behavior was the result of the existence of a powerful, biologically based drive which required expression in some fashion. While this powerful drive was largely limited to men, it was possible for at least some abnormal women to exhibit some of the same kinds of compulsive need for sexual activity. The management of this powerful drive was based on the mechanisms of repression, inhibition, and legal sanction. The drive was to be repressed in childhood and adolescence by the processes of moral injunction and protection from vice and bad examples and in adulthood by the imposition of appropriate criminal sanctions. The drive model also dominated most sophisticated theoretical sociological thinking as well, so that the functional sociologist could agree with the local police chief that prostitutes might be a necessary evil in order to protect good girls from seduction or rape (Davis, 1971).

Within this societal context the study of sexual criminality was limited to those who had been caught, more often limited to those who had been convicted and confined, and the representation of the sexual offender to the public was largely screened through a media image of violence and seduction with the ultimate excitement found in a report of the rape murder of a child by a previously convicted sex offender on parole. In this sociocultural circumstance the newspaper report of the sex crime could fascinate and even thrill a population living in a state of sexual ignorance and tension. For a society that believed in the potency of sexuality as a drive, but whose members existed in a state of sexual irrelation to others, the sex offender became the personification of the human beast whose actions could be symbolically consumed as were other dramatic eruptions (fires, earthquakes, wars) by conventional social life.

Publication of the two Kinsey studies in 1948 and 1953 marked the landmark dates that can be set for changes in the societal response to sexuality. It is apparent that the publication of these two volumes was at once symptom and cause and that there was significant societal preparation required for the support of a complex scientific enterprise such as the Kinsey research. The project required from 1938 to 1953 the support of a major university, funding from a major foundation, the willingness of subjects to talk, however selected, and the willingness of a major medical publisher to take a serious publishing risk. Even with all of this the reception of these volumes caused a violent societal furor and an impact on the level of public consciousness (though of a shorter duration) comparable to the reception of Darwin's *Origin of the Species*. While the general scientific impact, at least at the level of generating new research, was relatively minimal, the Kinsey reports were a device through which the society was confronted with a version of its own sexuality. The words orgasm, premarital coitus, sexual outlet, homosexuality, and mouth genital contact burst from the closet into the society. Those people who had not read the book were educated by the press and magazine reports. The significance of the two books in formulating the conditions under which sexual knowledge came to American society cannot be underestimated.

The impact of the two volumes on the study of sexual criminality was also profound, but in a very complex way. Critical to the study of sexual crime was the evidence from the Kinsey reports, severely attacked on sampling grounds to be sure, that vast numbers of persons in the United States were violating criminal statutes in their sexual conduct every day. The Kinsey figures were widely quoted: 37 percent of males had ever had a homosexual experience, perhaps 4 percent of the adult male and 1 to 3 percent of the adult female population were exclusively homosexual, 69 percent of the males had ever gone to a prostitute, half of the women had had premarital coitus, anywhere from 70 to 90 percent of the males had done so as well, and mouth genital contact was practiced by about half of men and women in marriage. Depending on the jurisdiction all of these acts were forms of criminal behavior and, indeed, as Kinsey obsessively points out, nearly all sexual acts except coitus in marriage and solitary masturbation were then defined as criminal acts. There was an immediate recognition of the difficulty that these figures created, especially for those forms of sexual criminality which had either close to or majority levels of the population performing them. It was very difficult to conceive what meaning prior studies of adulterers, fornicators, or those charged with heterosexual mouth genital contact could have and doubts began to emerge about studies of other less common forms of behavior as well. At the same time, however, the Kinsey data threw little light on those sex offenses whose commission involved victims, such as rape, incest, exhibitionism, window peeping, child molestation, and other offenses involving the age of consent. It was these kinds of offenses that engaged the attention of the criminologist during and after the Second World War—still attending to arrested and convicted offenders.

This criminological research on sex offenders was characterized by two major themes: the attempt to develop some homogeneity of offender types and a search for sexual and nonsexual factors in the individual life histories that had some predictive power in terms of the offense behavior. Methodologically this research largely dealt with statistical life histories. Types were created, largely drawn from the categories that are created by the criminal law or some deriviation from them, and records of individuals were collected together under one or another rubric. The life history data focused on what were conceived to be predisposing sexual experiences or nonsexual experiences that might have had impact on sexual development. These researchers were affected by the kinds of sexual questions that the Kinsey research used in its studies, but largely remained, except for modest psychoanalytic interpretations, atheoretical and without a systematic conceptual apparatus, either criminologically or in terms of general explanations of sexual conduct and development.

As the criminological study of the sex offender began to lose its impetus in the middle 1950s, a series of studies were made of male homosexuals and the communities in which some portion of male homosexuals live. These studies were largely sporadic, having their origins in either psychological studies which grew into community studies or in relatively accidental studies of individual homosexual communities (Leznoff & Westley, 1956; Achilles, 1967; Hooker, 1967). By the middle of the 1960s a number of homosexual communities had been studied, at least one community (San Francisco) had been the object of relatively continuous research interest for nearly a decade and these communities had been used as sampling points for the collection of data on both male and female homosexuals. The intellectual roots of most of these studies (some psychological studies excepted) resided in research on deviant behavior with a major concern for the processes by which unconventional life-styles emerge and are maintained. The informing imagery of this tradition took its roots from the Chicago tradition in the study of conventional and unconventional occupations in the city. Hence, the descriptive language of the deviance tradition, when it is not infused with the language of the theatre, is derived from the language of careers and occupational categories (Goffman, 1959; Becker, 1963).

The study of sexual criminality has been largely submerged in the study of sexual deviance over the last ten years, just as the former media reporting of the activities of the sexual criminal has been submerged in reports about pornography, wife swapping, homosexuality, and the sexual revolution among the young. The media representation of the sexual life of the society may still be skewed, but it is not nearly repressed to the degree that it was prior to Kinsey. Indeed, if there are systematic patterns of distortion, they may be in the direction of representing greater levels of sexual activity than there are in fact. However, the study of sexual deviance has, for the most part, not concerned itself with the study of that body of acts that has dominated the concern of the criminologist except for the study of homosexuality and prostitution. Offenses involving children, violence, incest, and problems of public order have not been central to the study of deviance theorists.

Both conventional criminology and students of sexual conduct as deviance have been concerned with relatively circumscribed areas of sexual behavior which were selected because they represent accessible data sources that were appropriate to the problem-finding aspects of their conceptual and theoretical interests. Concern with sexual behavior as criminal and sexual actors as members of a criminal class quickly leads the researcher to that domain of action defined by the criminal legal process. This process itself is rarely of interest; attention is paid only to the collection of individuals who have been brought together at various levels of the process and defined thereby as incumbents of the role "sex offender." These agencies are then used as the sampling procedures through which researchable populations are collected from the general population. In contrast, deviance theorists have looked at those activities which more informal collecting agencies identify and label in addition to the criminal legal process. The net is spread far wider, but since the persons of interest need somehow to have been previously labeled as "deviant," the collectivity to which they belong becomes both of interest in itself and of interest as a sampling point for the gathering of cases. If there is no collectivity (exhibitionists, for instance, have no collectivity), then the collection of cases is frustrated. Further, the deviance orientation commonly tends to exclude an interest in the conventional processes of socialization since it is commonly concerned with the field of action within which deviant activity is maintained. This creates considerable difficulty for studying the relation between deviant and nondeviant behavior and shares some of the difficulties of conventional criminology in that the individual cases studied are the outcome of a selection process the character of which cannot be inferred from individuals after they are selected.

The limitations of these two perspectives for the study of unconventional sexual conduct derives only in part from the problem of sampling of cases, though this is a serious and problematic issue. Problems of inference even in what are conceived to be nonstatistical studies as well as the meaning of many types of statistical operations calculated on nonsampled populations represent grave difficulties for either the criminologist or student of deviance. However, an equally difficult issue is that both the criminologist and the student of sexual conduct as deviance commonly operate in the absence of even a descriptive theory of sexual development and are unable to relate the behavior in which they are interested to conventional processes of development which represent the background for unconventional sexual expressions.

To the degree that the offender or deviant takes his motivations from conventional development or from a subcultural or class variant of it, to the degree that he shares motivations learned in that process, or to the degree that his behavior is the interactive product of conforming and nonconforming elements in his life-style, the understanding of behavior as either deviant or criminal is dependent on a descriptive model of conventional development. What is required is a model of sexual development that comprehends the complex interrelation between the sequential processes of socialization into sexual roles, the development of variants or alternatives to the conventional outcome of that socialization process (some of which are defined as deviant, others which are defined as criminal), the interactional situation of participants in such sexual activities, and the existence of a criminal legal process that selects persons from both conventional and deviant socialization patterns to make up the category of captured "sex offenders" and legitimate victims.

THE PROCESS OF CONVENTIONAL SEXUAL DEVELOPMENT

Central to our understanding of the relation between sexual behavior and crime is the availability of a minimum descriptive model of psychosexual development which does not show the defects of simple or complex drive reduction biological models. Such a model provides a set of ways of understanding the relation between conventional sexual development, sexual deviance, and sexual crime.

In a number of other places Gagnon, with his colleague, William Simon, have outlined in relative detail a learning and cognitively based model as an alternative explanation for both the individual's existential experience of sexuality and the role of sexuality in the larger sociocultural process (Simon & Gagnon, 1969; Gagnon & Simon, 1973). In this model the sexual is seen not as a drive to be precariously controlled by the individual, his culture, and the surrounding social organization, but as a learned capacity. The model argues that learning is involved down to the level of identifying the internal sensations that are appropriate to sexual response. The range of processes to be learned includes one's own internal bodily states, the appropriate anatomic parts on the self and others to respond to or to stimulate, what other persons are sexually appropriate (by gender, age, familial status, socioeconomic class, race, canons of beauty), situations in which to be aroused, unaroused, to lubricate, and to have orgasm, and, in addition, an organizing and sequencing system to put all of this together. Connecting these elements to the society and collective experience are the extrasexual meanings and metaphors which provide the sexual act with such emotions as passion and constraint, fear and attraction, love and hate, purity and corruption, affirmation and transgression.

It is clear that this assembly of processes, values, techniques, and cognitive strategies is not learned all at once; however, the usual Freudian model of psychosexual development, which takes as its basic organizing metaphor the organs and orifices of the body being progressively eroticized, is faulty whether or not it is attached to the drive model of sexuality. Most of the elements of the ultimate sexual scenario (and there are a number of such scenarios in most societies) are learned in nonsexual situations and then combined with sexual elements later in life. The Freudian attribution of sexuality to the early years of life, in the sense that adults experience sexuality, is an error, though many forms of attachment, moral commitments, and items of gender identity are formed early in life. The socially defined period of childhood is remarkable in American and most Western societies for its lack of sexually motivated behavior in most social-class situations. There is some sex *play*, some victimization of children by sex offenders, some prepubertal masturbation, but little that conforms to both the objective criteria and subjective experience of adults in sexual activity. The significant learning that relates to sexuality that occurs prior to puberty in this society is nonsexual in character. A substrate of nonsexual learning is formed composed of a collection of cultural style elements that are part of a loosely formed gender package (gender differences in aggression, proaction, cleanliness, obedience, conformity), a set of values attached to the body, and the internalization of moral values attached to parental figures. None of these is sexual in character and it only obscures the issue to discern beneath them a mysteriously wise nature working out its wiles through the processes of the object choice and the like.

During early puberty overt sexual behavior develops rapidly among most males, commonly masturbatory activity that has basic social-class variation. Concurrently or later, depending again on class, there is the first direct contact with heterosexuality. Among females there seems a continuation of that commitment to romance, love, and marriage which predates menarche, and the appearance of the menses is rarely linked to the sexual except by anxious adults. What is important for both genders is that there is the emergence during this period of a commitment to certain protosexual experiences and the beginning of an integration of nonsexual training and certain activities that seem to be sexual to adults. Further, it is with this change in the outward appearance of the bodies of these young people that they begin, at least tentatively, to be treated by adults as sexual creatures and also begin to see each other in protosexual roles.

In middle and late adolescence, these vague patterns are assembled into the conventional processes of dating and mating. The movement is from a period dominated by *homosocial* values into a period where there is competition between values based on relations with persons of the same gender to a life in which *heterosocial* values are either significant or dominant. It is apparent that commitments to heterosociality and homosociality are not dependent on or necessarily correlated with commitments to heterosexuality and homosexuality. Heterosexual and homosexual acts may occur in various kinds of environments in which the significant referent for the behavior is not the person with whom the act is occurring. Thus, adolescent boys have intercourse for the purposes of validation of their masculinity among other males; similarly, acts of homosexual prostitution occur among young males who are acting out the needs of a homosocial peer group (Reiss, 1961). In societies (or subcultures) where male-male relations are highly valued (high homosocial) and females are viewed only as cooks, mothers, and sex objects, male-male nonsexual relations commonly dominate the societies' interpersonal systems and define the meaning and value of heterosexuality.

This period between 14 and 20 (the end is variable) is when young people begin to act out and practice the conventional scripts which organize the physiological, psychological, and social elements of conventional sexual responses. Young people with what are defined as deviant or protodeviant feelings or adaptations often find this period extremely confusing, since there is no clear-cut set of definitions of how and in what way their behaviors differ from the behavior of the normal young (Dank, 1971: 182). Both deviant and conventional sexual careers are shaped and organized during this period, but the former are often delayed in their ultimate organization. Commonly, most young people reach the end of adolescence with an organized set of sexual activities and performances and, depending on class and other factors, have practiced a certain number of the basic sexual physical acts and emotional expressions that go with them.

The end of adolescence is usually conventional marriage for most young people—the sexual culmination of which is usually more extensive premarital sexual experimentation limited to a small number of persons who have been defined as appropriate marital partners. Sexual patterns during the rest of the life cycle are largely defined by distinctions between the married and unmarried state. The availability of sexual partners during specific moments in the life cycle is most often determined by whether one is or is not married to the person with whom one is having sex. The concatenation of sexual exclusivity, romantic attachment, childbearing, and a lifetime together shapes the character and meaning of nearly every sexual performance that occurs after the average age when marriage is likely for most people in the society. Even homosexuals have their status as single persons and their lack of children as their primary public identifying marks during this period of their life rather than their sexual object choice.

During the middle portion of the life cycle the bulk of heterosexuals who have married heterosexuals have sex primarily with their marital partners, with differing levels of sexual variation in the specific physical activities that are performed depending on class, education, and religion (Kinsey et al., 1948; Kinsey et al., 1953). There is a steady decline in sexual activity between spouses in the late 30s and early 40s with a major drop in the middle 50s for large portions of the population. Most of this decline is attributable to nonbiological factors, especially up to age 55, in both genders. Boredom, declining physical beauty, alternative social interests, all easily erode the significance of sexual activity as a major organizing element in the lives of the majority of persons. There is some extramarital coitus, more for men than for women, but few in the population have the endurance, logistical skills, and income necessary to carry on major affairs and a marriage at the same time. The steady decline in frequency of coitus is differential by social class as are the differences in extramarital coitus and variations in types of sexual activity. This decline in sexual activity can be interrupted by divorce and other separations, and there is reversion to the nonmarried pattern during these periods for most, followed by a drift back into marriage. Divorce in later years and widowhood are rarely accompanied by major resurgences in sexual behavior.

It is not a concern of this chapter to develop a general and universal stage model of psychological development in the tradition of Erikson since these models are generally faulty, becoming time-bound and reified. Such models fail to draw our attention to modal processes by becoming objects of study in themselves. The point of the descriptive process offered here is to delineate periods in the life cycle during which certain events commonly take place in this culture. It should be noted clearly here that these periods are not seen as *necessary*, either within or across cultures, nor *necessary* in some psychodynamic sense. They are roughly what has happened between the 1930s and 1970s in a complex Western society, largely to its white working- and middle-class populations and in large measure to those persons of most ethnic and racial minorities who are attached to these modal schemes of development or who have not been entirely alienated from them. There can be vast reversals and changes in the design of human sexuality from the feelings it evokes to the kinds of things that are appropriate to or included in its performance elements. The age and moment when specific behaviors can be introduced, performed, and lived with vary enormously, so that any biological fixity in the sequence of behavior is most likely to occur in infancy and very little after that.

Table 1, which presents the sequencing of conventional sexual development, is primarily of heuristic value for examining the connections between deviance, criminality, and conventional development. Persons are selected as participants in deviant conduct or to be actors in what are defined as criminal acts from various points in this cycle. The meaning of their deviancy or criminality is largely drawn from their place in this sequential collection of socializing agents, institutions, and programs. Hence the meaning of heterosexuality for two 14 year olds who are having intercourse and who are discovered by their parents or arrested by the police emerges from their stage in sexual socialization. Their motivations for the act, and the consequences of discovery or arrest must be understood in terms of where they are in the developmental process and many times where their discoverers or arrestors are in that same process. Equally true of the two 14-year-old males who are having sex together is that the meaning of their homosexuality arises from a specific point in the life cycle, and its significance as crime or deviance is embedded in both that life-cycle moment and the local culture (or in complex societies, in a subculture). Thus, the interaction of fathers and daughters in incest will be meaningful not in terms of some abstract violation of the incest taboo, but as a consequence of the character of the family in which they live and the ages of the two participants. This is similarly true of the child who is the victim of sexual offense, since the meaning of the offense for the child is drawn from his or her available intellectual and emotional resources for organizing experience. *The gender identity–sexual identity–family formation–reproduction pattern* in this society is the central informing process for sexual life; deviance and criminality draw much of their meaning from its existence.

This table contains a set of stages with flexible age boundaries, social components that are significant in either sexual or nonsexual learning during them, and a rough suggestion of what is being learned or assembled. The word *assembly* is used quite deliberately. It was selected to indicate the collage-like, constructed, put-together, indeed, artificial character of human development, and to oppose an imagery of the natural flowering of an organic process.

This rough outline of a sexual career is the most common heterosexual pattern available in the United States society and, even with the introduction of divorce and

TABLE 1

A HEURISTIC CONCEPTION OF CONVENTIONAL STAGES IN SEXUAL DEVELOPMENT

1. *Stage and Ages*   Infancy (Ages: 0–2½ to 3)
   Significant Agents   Mother to Family
   Assemblies   Formation of base for conventional gender identity package.

2. *Stage and Ages*   Childhood (Ages: 3–11)
   Significant Agents   Family to Peers, increasing Media
   Assemblies   Consolidation of conventional gender identity package; modesty-shame learning; nonsexually motivated "sex" play; learning of sex words without content; learning of sex activities without naming; learning of general moral categories; mass media through commercials and programming content reinforcing conventional gender, sex, and family roles; media also preparing for participation in youth culture.

3. *Stage and Ages*   Early adolescence (Ages: 11–15)
   Significant Agents   Family, Same-sex Peers, Media
   Assemblies   First societal identification as a conventional sexual performer; first overt physical sexual activity with self or others; development of sexual fantasy materials; beginnings of male/female divergence in overt sexual activity; application of gender package to sexual acts; application of moral values to emergent sexual behavior; privatization of sexual activities; same-sex peers reinforce homosocial values; family begins to lose moral control; media reinforces conventional adult content of gender roles; media attaches consumer practices to gender success; basic attachment to youth culture formed.

4. *Stage and Ages*   Later adolescence (Ages: 15–18)
   Significant Agents   Same-sex Peers, Cross-sex Peers increasing, Media, Family reducing
   Assemblies   Increased practice of integrating of sexual acts with nonsexual social relations; movement to heterosocial values; increased frequency of sexual activity; declining family controls; continuing media reinforcement of sexual-gender roles and consumer and youth-culture values; sexual experience with wider range of peers; common completion of sexual fantasy content; consolidation of gender differences in sexual roles and activity; good girl/bad girl—maternal/erotic distinctions completed.

5. *Stage and Ages*   Early adulthood (Ages: 18–23)
   Significant Agents   Same-sex and Cross-sex Peers, Media, Minimum Family of Origin
   Assemblies   Mate selection, narrowing of mate choice; increased amount of sexual practice; commitment to love by male, sex by female; linkage of passion to love; dyadic regressions; insulation from family judgment and peer judgment; increasing pressure to marry; relief from same-sex competition by stabilization of cross-sex contacts; legitimization of sexual activity by peers and romantic code; media reinforces youth-culture values of romance and virtues of marriage; experience with falling in and out of love; termination of protected school/student statuses.

6. *Stage and Ages*   Final mate selection—Early marriage (Ages: 20–27)
   Significant Agents   Fiancee(s), Spouse, Same-sex Peers, Family of Origin increases
   Assemblies   Regularizes and legitimizes sexual activity; stable rates of sex activity; variation in kinds of sexual behavior; children born in most cases; increasing sexual anxiety about children; family values reinforced by children and family of origin; declining eroticism, increased maternalism; culmination of purchasing/consumer values in wedding gifts or buying new products; routinization of sexual behavior; decreased contact with cross-sex peers unless they are married; interaction in multiple dyads; sexual activities restricted by pregnancy, children, work.

TABLE 1—Continued

7. *Stage and Ages* *Significant Agents* *Assemblies*	Middle marriage (Ages: 28–45) Spouse, Same-sex Peers, Family of Origin, Married Peers Declining sexual activity in marriage; some extramarital sexual experimentation; maturing children; conflict of erotic with maternal; emergence of sexual dissatisfactions; increase in occupational commitments; declines in physical energy and physical beauty; fantasy competition by youth culture; continual multiple dyadic interactions and insulation from cross-sex peers; marriage moving to nonsexual basis for stability and continuity.
8. *Stage and Ages* *Significant Agents* *Assemblies*	Post–young children (Ages: 45+) Spouse, Same-sex Peers, Married Peers Further decline in sexual activity; some extramarital sexual experimentation; substitution of nonsexual commitments other than children as basis of marriage; further decline in physical strength and beauty; further desexualization of gender identity; movement out of public sexual arena.

widowhood, the cycle does not vary except in small and minor ways. Similar modal career patterns with greater or lesser variability could be described for some of those sexual minorities who operate with alternative sexual patterns in the society. Indeed, this conventional heterosexual process is the modal sexual career that all alternative patterns must confront. The man who desires large numbers of females, the homosexual man or woman, and the sexually active woman must live with the reality of this pattern, its values, and its links to the past and the future in a day-to-day way. This assembly designates the availability of sexual partners, their ages, their incomes, their point in the economic process, their time commitments, all of which shape their sexual careers far more than the minor influences of sexual desire. If these contentions are correct, then sexual deviances and crimes will be largely defined by the ways in which sexuality is learned and is integrated into social life.

CONVENTIONAL DEVELOPMENT, DEVIANCE, AND CRIME

From this description of the conventional developmental sequence, it is apparent that there are many occasions for various kinds of errors to occur in performance and for a variety of reasons. These arise in part because learning is extended over a long period of time, because the final script requires the correct assembly and timing of elements learned under differing conditions, and because the conventional heterosexual script, which is one end point of all of the assembled subelements, is heavily masked and hidden from the learners as they learn. Even while various subtasks are being learned (such as modesty training in both genders or arousal by males to various items of female apparel), the connection of these subelements to a sequence of sexual arousal as part of the act of intercourse or even a knowledge that that act exists may not be available to the learner. Most persons in the society ultimately learn some minimally acceptable version of the sexual script that is appropriate to heterosexual relations in marriage and the sexual component itself is often submerged in the marriage as the result of the increasing significance of childbearing and rearing as well as occupational and leisure goals.

These conditions of conventional development contain the origins of the kinds of unconventional or deviant patterns that are available to members of the society. Since the outcome state of the learning process contains a certain number of constraints in terms of modes of approach to sexual access, the legal conditions of sexual access, the gender of the object of sexual interest, the age of the object, the relationship to the object, and the sites of the performance, a substantial variety of unconventional alternatives are evident and under appropriate conditions such alternatives can emerge into what are called deviant careers or alternative life-styles. From the point of view of the conventional actor, these alternatives have very different statuses or significance and the degree of deviance that any one of them expresses will vary widely. Thus, mouth genital contact in heterosexual marriage may be marginally deviant and require certain kinds of value neutralization to perform, but a single act of homosexual behavior may involve severe anxiety. The present hierarchy of opprobrium is not inherent in the exclusions involved in the conventional script and which of the violations of the prescriptions of the conventional script are most vigorously condemned do not arise from the script itself, but from other values given to sexual actors from other situations (hence, male homosexuality is more condemned than female homosexuality; the variation in gender choice is the same in both cases, but not the sanction).

What is most obvious about those aspects of sexual conduct that are conceived to be deviant behavior is the differential levels of social organization that are involved in their expression. Thus, a substantial number of deviant sexual activities are primarily associated with and performed by persons who are conventional in nearly all aspects of their life, including the sexual. These behaviors are either involved in facilitating conventional sexual activity before marriage (premarital coitus with companions), reinforcing of conventional male-gender roles (coitus with prostitutes or with "bad" girls), increasing sexual bonding in marriage (variation in sexual positions or nongenital sexual play) or linked to problems associated with marriage stability (extramarital coitus). This is what has been called in another location "normal" sexual deviance because it is either involved in the development of conventional sexual scripts or because it is performed by largely conventional actors whose behavior does not involve them in what Lemert has described as secondary forms of deviance (Lemert, 1967; Simon & Gagnon, 1968).

Those forms of sexual conduct that have the most visible collective or subcultural aspects are male and female homosexuality, pornography, and female prostitution. Clearly such sexual activities express those aspects of behavior which are amenable to the kinds of questions and deliver the kinds of answers that are most comfortable to sociological perspectives on deviance. They illustrate vividly the processes by which persons enter into a deviant adaptation and the conditions of that adaptation that maintain them in it. It is apparent that homosexuality in its community dimension and prostitution conceived as career and life adaptation manifest subcultural or bounded characteristics. The sociological interests in these forms of behavior have been concerned with the internal community characteristics of these behaviors, avoiding the externalities; they have not been interested in the origins (in early developmental terms) of these activities and in how such homosexual conduct shares common content, styles, and motivations with conventional heterosexual development.

The domain of sexual conduct involving traditional individual sex offenders has not been well treated in deviance theory and is still dealt with largely through conventional criminological models. These are behaviors that involve force (normally all heterosexual), disparities in age (both heterosexual and homosexual if the object is very young), violations of close relationships by blood or marriage, and violations of public order (exhibitionism and voyeurism). These behaviors, both in their origins and in their maintenance, seem largely intractable or inexplicable from the point of view of deviance theory. Since the behavior, in most cases, seems not to require a deviant collectivity in order for it to manifest or maintain itself, explanations that are based in patterns of differential association, deviant learning, or subcultural elements are inadequate to deal with them. This lack of a visible and immediate social dimension for the behavior has largely left it to the concern of individual abnormal psychology.

As has been noted before, the bulk of sexual conduct in this society is still defined as criminal by the law, except for those jurisdictions that have revised their criminal codes over the last few years. Thus, nearly all of the behaviors that are considered to be deviant—including all extramarital sexual intercourse and many other intra- and extramarital sexual activities—are in many, if not most, state jurisdictions and in those appropriate federal jurisdictions against the criminal law. This has not meant, as with some other forms of behavior, that the majority of these sexual offenses have been, in the past, or are, at the present time, seriously pursued by the police. Indeed, the profile of the law has been sufficiently low in some areas that persons who have committed criminal sexual acts and been arrested did not know that they had committed a crime. As has been noted before, the content and methods of sexual socialization are such that many factors which affect the performance of sexual acts are not made known to sexual actors. This is especially true with regard to information about the law and other normative elements that need to be learned outside of informal contexts.

The activity of what has been called the "traditional criminal legal process" with reference to sexual behavior intersects both the processes of normal sexual socialization as well as those activities that are conceived to be sexually deviant, but the impact of this process is differential, seriously impinging on various kinds of behavior, hovering like an ominous menace with reference to others, and remaining nearly irrelevant with reference to still others. The traditional criminal process affects behavior on two levels. It is at one level a sampling agency, that is, by its reputation, activities, beliefs, and normal operating procedures, it collects from the population of sexual actors those who will be arrested as sexual offenders and from the population of sexual acts those that will be defined as sexual offenses. These two sampling procedures are related (offenses and offenders), but only in very complex ways which differ depending on the kind of offense involved. Conventionally, there is an indication that an offense has occurred prior to the attachment of an offender to it, but offenders can confess to offenses that the police do not know about (as well as to those that they have not committed in order to be cooperative), and offenders can be caught in the midst of behavior so the act and the actor are defined as offense and offender at a single instant.

While for certain purposes the institutional processes of the police, prosecution, courts, jails, and prisons can be considered a monolithic system, it must be noted that they differ in their conduct toward various kinds of offenses, offenders, and victims and, therefore, the collection of individuals and acts that are represented from the moment of report of a crime to the collection of acts attributed to a collection of persons in prison includes or excludes persons for all kinds of reasons that have nothing to do with the etiology of the offense or significant behavioral commonalities of other sorts. Losses occur within each institutional setting and must be considered as a basic confounding variable in any discussion of the "sexual offender." This skewed collection process in the traditional criminal legal system has been relatively well known for many years and has been a covert dictum in criminological inquiry. However, in few studies of offenders is consideration given to the way in which our understanding of the relationship between acts, actors, motivation, and etiology is shaped by the processes of selection. This has been particularly true of sexual offenders in conventional criminological studies where the pool of individuals gathered for study has been largely the consequence of the collecting procedures of the criminal legal system. These collections of individuals may be selected for reasons that are irrelevant to a concern for the sources of the behavior or even for a concern with something called criminality. The decision to assume that sexual offenders who are captured are some special pool of individuals defined by some set of attributes other than the fact that they have been caught commonly rests on unproved assumptions about the collection procedures involved.

If the traditional criminal legal system operated only to gather individuals who had been accused of some sexual offense and passively processed them, we might be able to determine both the sexual and nonsexual bases for the skewed collection and make some inferences about at least a limited portion of the population. However, evidence has existed in the past and is being accumulated today which indicates that far from being a passive instrument for separating the sheep from the goats, the criminal legal system actively works to shape and change an individual's self-conception by processes of identity stripping, rites of degradation, labeling, and the imposition and normalization of motives. Research, primarily on juveniles and on mental patients, suggests that social processing institutions have an active role in labeling persons as deviant, as a consequence of interaction both with others (often more experienced) going through the same process, and with members of the processing agency (Scheff, 1966). As a result alternative vocabularies of motives for explaining their own behavior are learned by individuals as they are handled by the agency.

In large measure, person-processing agencies are concerned with completing their tasks with as little difficulty as possible, and operate to smooth edges off those persons who do not appear to agency staff to match the attributes that are appropriate for the commission of certain kinds of crimes (Sudnow, 1965). Those who work at various levels within the criminal legal system possess theories of motivation and an imagery of the normal sexual criminal which, in part, derives from the society's folklore about sexual motivations and behavior as well as from a skewed experience of dealing only with those who fall afoul of the policing system. To the end of making their own system work, they actively promote such versions of reality and to a greater or lesser extent impose these versions of the sexual offender on those persons who come into their hands (and, through the media, on the society at large). To some degree offenders either share these versions of the world or are converted to them by the activities and persuasiveness of the criminal legal system. While the separate units of the criminal legal system are somewhat interlocked, there are significant differences in the motivational theories of various units largely because of the variation in social-class backgrounds of participants in these units. While the individual policeman may well be horrified by a sex offender's behavior, the judge whose experience is more contaminated by a psychiatric-world view may take a very different stance toward specific kinds of sex offenders brought before him.

The criminal legal system, as a sampling agency as well as by creatively shaping the behavior of those it selects, intersects both the processes of normal development and those who vary from this process. This system, however, although very active with captured sex offenders, assumes a passive and reactive posture to the existence of the unreported sexual act. Very few sexual crimes are detected by the police as part of a systematic campaign to find everyone who has committed such an act. This posture is consonant with nearly all that we know about the activity of police agencies—they wait until someone calls instances or suspicions of instances of criminal events to their attention. The fact that this is normal procedure for the police makes the distinction between crimes with and crimes without victims of major significance for the area of sexual conduct. Most of the sexual offenses that were considered in the rubric "normal deviance," as well as those that are characterized by some collective social dimension, are offenses without victims. Thus, mouth genital contact between consenting persons, either homosexual or heterosexual, for pay or for pleasure, is a victimless crime in that there is no complainant to come to the police and assert that he or she was the victim of such an act. This is especially true of those acts that we have described as normal deviance. Their discovery is commonly accidental or emerges out of other offenses or crimes associated with them which have no sexual content or motivation. The pursuit by the police of offenses surrounding pornography, homosexuality, and prostitution possesses some of the same aspects. Since there is no ready victim, the activity of the police is largely responsive to moral entrepreneurs, elections, departmental shake-ups, or particular interests of department members in suppressing or taxing vice. Police activity with reference to all of these behaviors is sporadic and is concerned with maintaining the appearance of public order and the boundaries between conventional and unconventional sexual expressions.

Those offenses that have been the concern of conventional criminology have largely been those for which there are specifiable victims and the victims have either reported the existence of an offense or both the existence of an offense and an offender. These cases have largely been offenses against children and minors, incest, offenses involving force and violence, and offenses that are disruptive of public order. The dilemma for the criminologist is that differential reporting by victims of offenses further compounds the inefficient procedures of the criminal legal system as a case-collection or social-bookkeeping agency. Thus, each offense tends to emerge out of specific social contexts and the victim must be prepared to take on the onus of having been involved in a sexual offense.

As is evident from the normal processes of sexual socialization, the willingness of an individual to take on the task of convincing a police agency that he or she has been victimized is sharply reduced when victimization may involve status degradation for the victim, discussion of intimate events with uncaring and often suspicious outsiders, and a very high risk that the offender will not be apprehended (Gagnon, 1965). What is apparent is that victims or those who act for them (in the case of a child) are involved in negotiating new statuses by presenting information and other evidence that sexual events took place. The victim status is not conferred automatically, and the victim must leap many hurdles involved in the criminal legal process along with the offender and suffer many of the same experiences, for the elements of the system attempt to impose on both the status of a "normal" sex offense victim to match the status of the "normal" criminal sex offender. Very often this "normal" status means conforming to the conventional sexual morality of the local police by maintaining the image of a "good" sexual reputation, so that reporting a crime "successfully" may require denials of participation in the acts which led up to it.

The process of differential reporting and victim status negotiation adds still another complication to the case-collecting functions of the criminal legal process, skewing the character of the victim population, and the count of offenses, as well as the pool of individuals from which the police can then collect people to be named as sex offenders. Figure 1 shows the procedure through which our knowledge of sex offenses and offenders is screened. The differential character of this procedure for each offense category must be considered in determining what we *can* know about various kinds of sexual

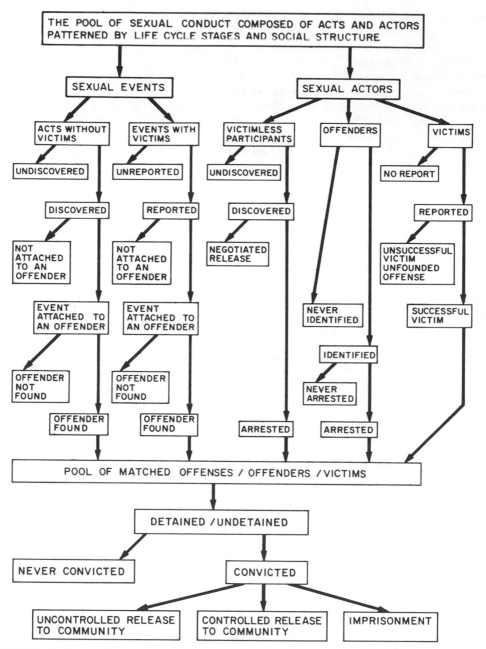

FIGURE 1. A flow diagram of the processing of sexual events and sexual actors as they intersect the criminal legal process.

offenses and the kinds of questions appropriate to ask of sets of data and individuals that are gathered together at any point in the process. Any discussion of individual offense types must then take this process as its frame and determine what can be known from information gathered at any point in the process or the degree to which institutional data gathered for institutional purposes is meaningful for the kinds of questions that need to be asked.[2]

OFFENSE BEHAVIOR EMERGING FROM CONVENTIONAL SOCIOSEXUAL PROCESSES

Since the criminal statutes with reference to sexual behavior cast such a wide net, most of the activities participated in by young people prior to marriage, as well as variations in sexual activity during marriage and extramarital coitus, are vulnerable in many jurisdictions to criminal sanction. It is apparent, however, that very few people who engage in premarital coitus with a consenting companion (representing close to half of all females and a large majority of males) are ever caught up in the toils of the criminal law as a result of the behavior itself. This same situation exists for those who engage in mouth genital conduct prior to or during marriage, though the rates for this behavior approach half of all married couples and larger proportions for middle- and upper-class segments of the population. Indeed, such behavior is encouraged by marriage manuals of various religious persuasions as a legitimate form of sexual foreplay. Extramarital coitus or coitus between marriages for those widowed and divorced is relatively common (one-fourth of women had extramarital coitus, about half of men; coitus between marriages commonly involves most men and women in preparation for another marriage).

The bulk of these acts remain undiscovered and, indeed, unpursued by the police. One of the few pools of cases studied of what were called heterosexual voluntary offenses against adults and minors was included in the volume *Sex Offenders* (Gebhard et al., 1965). This study is based on a collection of convicted and imprisoned offenders

---

2. The gathering of cases for research reports based on the collection of data and reporting procedures of the criminal legal process contains other problematic aspects in addition to having a skewed relation to the population of actors who are performing acts in the community and influencing either modestly or profoundly the self-conception of those who fall into its hands. Those studies which use the compiled case records of police departments, probation offices, parole agents, and prisons' records of any sort face the difficulty that these records are themselves gathered for an institutional purpose and that the institutional purpose is likely to distort data or conceal them from view. Inmates being interviewed for parole have their future in their hands and they are competing against previously compiled dossiers of wrongdoing. The content of such an interview used for research purposes must take into account that the record is a residue and condensate of human interaction that was purposive within the system of alternatives that was available for the persons involved. This same kind of caution applies to police records of reports of offenders (they *are* trying to convict them), statements or reports of statements by victims, running records of juvenile contacts with probation officers in juvenile courts, as well as records created at any point in time that are to be included in an institutionalized procedure for managing people.

These same problems emerge with the study of offenders at various points of their participation in the criminal legal system. Interviews with offenders recently caught or in jail or prison draw much of their ambient value from the context in which one finds the prisoner. Thus, the offender as a "criminal" close to the site of the crime, at times with a victim present, shapes the policeman's criminology as surely as does the sociologist's contact with the offender as a "prisoner" far removed from the site of the crime and in an institutional context that enhances displays of passivity and subordinate behavior. The image of the criminal as underdog derives much of its power from this situation, but this condition is often only marginally related to the criminal in the context of the crime. The dilemma of the criminologist is that it is extremely difficult to sort out the differences in reporting and the way in which reports differ when they are gathered in these varying circumstances. What can and cannot be studied at the various points and with various collections of individuals is, at present, still quite obscure.

that had been screened through the entire legal process, including incarceration; the offenders themselves were interviewed between the early 1940s and the early 1950s.

Apparently, from this study and from other more impressionistic sources, offenders who are arrested or imprisoned for these kinds of offenses are commonly: (a) those who have accidental failures in nonsexual aspects of normal sexual interaction (e.g., a woman out of jealousy accuses her husband of adultery, a woman who is having difficulties with a man accuses him of forcing her to commit fellatio); (b) those whose sexual lives are unconventional but who attract the attention of police or other moral entrepreneurs for nonsexual reasons; (c) those whose sexual activities are discovered by the police in the course of other duties (e.g., a burglary investigation or police intervention at a disorderly party reveals an adulterous relationship). In many of the cases nonsexual violations of commonly respected standards of personal conduct are policed through the invocation of sex laws. This was a common use of the fornication statutes prior to the 1950s as unwanted persons in small towns and rural locales were "floated out of the community" by sex-offense convictions. This same kind of harassing use of the sex statutes can occur with commune or hippie groups who settle in what are otherwise conventional and often conservative rural communities.

While such arrests do occur among adults, juveniles are often more vulnerable to these kinds of interventions. First, sexual socialization is not nearly complete for the adolescent and errors in judgment by either males or females can lead to police involvement. Second, because the sexuality of adolescents is commonly denied, their sexual experimentation that has to take place in less private settings, and their displays of intimacy (that would be ignored if performed by adults) attract police attention. Thus, intercourse or heavy petting occurring in a "lover's lane" or in places where there is a likelihood of discovery by either the police or parents exposes both adolescent males and females to the risk of arrest. Accidental discovery of this sort can result in criminal sanctions, though parents are often loath to report their own children and juvenile courts commonly give probation to these kinds of offenses. A considerably greater risk is run in those cases in which the girl is underage and the offense can be construed as statutory rape. Discovery in these circumstances can interrupt what is normal courtship behavior in many communities, or parents can invoke the criminal sanctions to break up relationships of which they do not approve. It is unclear how often the age of consent statutes are used, though it is possible to estimate that it is more likely in rural and small towns where the criminal law is used to maintain the local moral order and conservative sexual standards for adolescents (Reiss, 1960).

Except for women prostitutes, juvenile females represent nearly the only population of female sex offenders in the United States. Evidence from juvenile court records suggests that large numbers of females who are brought before the courts appear there as a consequence of some attributed or actual sexual activity. The girl who is labeled incorrigible, uncontrollable, or a runaway is commonly the girl who is involved in sexual activity with which the parents cannot cope or who is associated with males who are themselves involved in delinquent or criminal behavior. In these cases the juvenile courts are used to police the sexual mores of what are conceived to be promiscuous girls. It is clear that the case-collection procedures used by the police and juvenile courts are class biased and actually focus only on those sexually active female adolescents whose behavior troubles their parents, the local community, or the police. As a consequence of the way in which they are handled and of the labeling of their behavior that occurs in police and court settings, these girls become vulnerable to either disorderly marital and familial lives beginning in early adulthood, or are more vulnerable to recruitment into lives of prostitution. To some degree, these girls are par-

ticipating in what are relatively normal developmental processes, though
activities are carried on in circumstances that make them more likely
volved with enforcement agencies. Here recruitment to deviance and crimin...
emerges from the intersect of policing and conventional sexual development.

There are other ways in which such girls can come to the attention of law-enforcement agencies and these are related to the by-products of sexual behavior. Thus, the
girl who gets pregnant (under current normal conditions the use of contraceptives is
not a part of the routine adolescent sexual script) finds herself identified as an unwed
mother or can participate in a criminal act if the abortion she procures is illegal. Even
when the abortions are legal, there are special problems associated with being an
adolescent that require that the pregnancy be made known to parents. This means that
the teenager must disclose her experienced sexual status to her parents and medical
personnel and negotiate the degree of stigma she will have. The surviving abortion
laws and ignorance tend to increase the number of unwed mothers and develop a subset
of deviant careers associated with by-products of sexual activity (Rains, 1971). The
negotiation of sexually stigmatized identities in adolescence creates circumstances in
which accusations of more serious offenses can emerge. Thus, the young woman who
is discovered in coitus, who comes in too late, or who becomes pregnant can negotiate
purity by accusing the male of rape. Because of the ambiguous moral status of sexual
activity among adolescents, the activity can be seen as a normal part of mating and
mate selection in later adolescence, but is an error for younger adolescents. In these
situations contests occur about the moral character of the youthful participants,
contests that involve parents, law-enforcement agencies, and adolescents in largely
futile struggles to assign blame and culpability. Commonly, the solution to the problem
is resolved to the advantage of the persons of highest social status or of those who
previously had the better moral reputation.

The last major area of normal deviance that comes to the attention of law-enforcement officials is that of extramarital coitus which is conventionally controlled by the
adultery statutes. The lack of interest shown by the police in this form of activity is
demonstrated by the New York situation at the time that adultery was the only grounds
for divorce in that state. The New York City Police Department made no arrests of
the very large number of self-confessed adulterers who were processed by the New
York divorce courts. For a time it appeared that there would be some police activity
related to those couples who had become involved in wife swapping, swinging, or group
sex, but there is no evidence that the police have developed any extensive concern with
this kind of offense behavior. The participants are often vulnerable through letters
written between them and some charges of obscenity have been made as a result of the
interstate transport of erotic materials between members of swinging groups and over
the text of some of the letters or handbooks that have been exchanged. However, with
the general weakening of the obscenity statutes, there has been a decline in these kinds
of arrests as well. Extramarital coitus as well as coitus that occurs between marriages
among adults are forms of behavior which seem, when conducted with the very minimum of care, rarely to attract the attention of the police. While there may be some
charges that arise out of carelessness, spite, and other reasons in rural and small town
jurisdictions, these laws are largely dead letters, except for the rare and exceptional
case.

Much the same kind of argument can be made for arrests that arise from mouth
genital and other noncoital contacts between consenting adults. These are rarely
prosecuted and rarely come to the attention of policing agencies. A number of recent
cases have involved older men and young women in relatively ambiguous circumstances

and the charges appeared to arise from problems of the management of stigma on the part of the females. There are circumstances under which wives sometimes complain of being forced to commit mouth genital contact by their husbands, but these charges are commonly made in some attempt to use the local law-enforcement agents to control other aspects of the husband's behavior. When the offender is sentenced, such families are often, to their surprise, left without a breadwinner, since the charges carry serious penalties.

The collection of persons who fall into the hands of the traditional criminal legal process, whose acts have been related to normal sexual development or activities, is the consequence of completely adventitious processes commonly linked to mismanagement of both sexual and nonsexual aspects of life. The application of criminal sanctions to the sexual aspects of their conduct often represents the use of the most expeditious available legal device. It has much in common with the use of loitering or disorderly conduct charges when no other charge is easily available. In this case, the law is like a land mine, exploding under the feet of the unwary, not only sexually, but socially. Probably those most seriously affected by this situation are adolescents whose peculiar status in the society promotes sexual experimentation as part of normal sexual development, but rarely provides guidelines for its performance or protection against the consequences of errors in judgment. The adolescent, by virtue of his or her age status, is made vulnerable to criminal sanctions for behavior that, if performed at a slightly older age, would be seen as part of normal dating behavior. Young women are at greater risk than young men, since their behavior is defined as immoral and promiscuous and they tend to be gathered into a subset of the incorrigible and wayward.

Practically nothing can be learned about sexual behavior or sexual deviance by studying this subset of cases, especially among adults, since the processes of gathering are nearly independent of the original intentions of the legal prescriptions. It is also probably not very useful to generalize from this subset of young women to any larger group of adolescents in the society. They are selected out largely because of errors in judgment, and their sexual behavior probably does not differ from many other young women who, by virtue of good luck or social station, manage to avoid becoming labeled incorrigible, getting pregnant, or contracting a venereal disease.

COLLECTIVE FORMS OF SEXUAL ALTERNATIVES

Homosexuality of both men and women, male and female prostitution, and pornography are those forms of sexual conduct in the society that suffer from police attention on a more or less sporadic basis. Changing societal conditions of the late 1960s and the 1970s have begun a process of liberalization of statutes which has been moving a substantial body of these kinds of offenses outside the orbit of criminal law, even though the legal changes have not improved public attitudes toward the homosexual or the pornographer.

Pornography

This liberalizing drift can be observed in the case of pornography where both the courts and study commissions have undercut the behavior of law-enforcement officials acting as morality police and censors. During the 1950s there were endless campaigns against pornography on the newsstands and in movies (girlie magazines—including *Playboy*, soft-cover books, and films were frequently, if unsystematically, censored), postal and customs control of pornographic materials, and community campaigns against smut. The situation of the late 1960s and early 1970s, however, has shown a dramatic shift in the openness of the society toward depictions of the sexual act as well as nudity (Commission on Obscenity and Pornography, 1971). As has been noted, this has been largely the work of the courts, but there has been a substantial drop in the activity level of the police as well. At the present time, it is possible to argue that there are now available the widest possible range of adult-audience films with explicit depictions of sexual activity, books that describe unequivocally and in four-letter words the widest range of sexual activity, and, with slightly more difficulty, materials that through drawings, photos, and films explicitly depict all forms of sexual activity. These materials are not available in small towns or in parts of middle America, but they are nearly universally available in large cities, and X-rated films are widely accessible nearly everywhere in the country.

Prior to the 1950s, police, on their own and in coordination with certain moral entrepreneurs, saw to it that newsstands, bookstores, movie theaters, and arcades were kept relatively clear of erotic materials. Such policing involved arrests of either purveyors, bookstore owners, or movie projectionists, and largely served as a taxing measure which kept the appearance of public order. At the same time, through more adventitious processes, the police also arrested individuals whom they found with erotic photos or books in their cars and charged them with the possession of pornography. Through raids for other reasons, they also collected additional pornographic materials and offenders. Few of these cases came to court, most being settled by the confiscation of the pornographic materials, except when large amounts were seized or when there was a commercial operation in hand. There is substantial evidence that many of these arrests were settled through bribery, especially when the discovery was private and did not involve an outside moral agent. As the general level of sexual openness has increased in the society, fewer and fewer moral crusades have occurred in communities and fewer police have involved themselves in arresting those engaged in the vending of sexually explicit materials.

These enforcement forays into the world of pornography failed in large measure to identify either those who used pornography, the use to which they put it, or the dimensions of pornography sales as an economic enterprise. From more recent studies conducted outside the orbit of law-enforcement agencies, it is apparent that relatively large numbers of young males see pornography at least on a sporadic basis without any serious outcome for either their sexual or nonsexual behaviors. Other uses of pornography, outside of adolescent male contexts, occur in private consumption of books and photographs by males, normally middle class in their social origins, by male voluntary groups such as college fraternities, social organizations of working-class and lower-middle-class males, and the consumption of directly sexual or marginally sexual movies or arcade materials for both middle-class males and for young males of all classes (Gagnon & Simon, 1967a). The evidence is that such materials are largely supplemental to conventional fantasies or supportive of conventional masculinity needs of males. The historical reason given for this police attention to the problem of pornography was that exposure to explicitly sexual materials perverted the young and aroused unnatural sexual desires that resulted in sex crimes. Since pornography represented the visible surface of the sexual problem in the society, its incidence and availability were seen as direct correlates of both change in sexual values and the direct incitement of sexual crimes. The underlying theoretical posture was that in the presence of arousing sexual stimuli, the sexual beast that was assumed to be inside of each individual was going to be aroused, released, or at least corrupted.

Given the extensive patterns in use of pornography, the steadily increasing explicitness of the sexual backdrop of daily life, and a correlative lack of increase in the rate of sexual offenses over the last decade, the expectation that police behavior controlling pornography indirectly controlled sex offenses seems to have been based on a false premise. This contention cannot be tested in the U.S., given the generally uneven quality of the evidence, but research in Denmark, which has made a national change in the availability of sexual material, suggests that a complex series of outcomes marks any change in the availability of sexual materials to the general populace (Kutchinsky, 1972). By carefully examining over time changes in attitudes toward sex offenses by citizens and the police, checking official reports, and interviewing citizens about the rate of victimization they had experienced, it was possible to argue that certain kinds of offenses actually declined (voyeurism and offenses against children), certain offenses declined because victims reduced their reports (women were not as disturbed by exhibitionists), there were reductions in some offenses seemingly unrelated to the availability of pornography (indecent approaches to adult women declined due to changes of reporting frequency), and in still other kinds of offenses, there was no change at all (rape and other related serious crimes against adult women). What Kutchinsky's research suggests is that there is complex interaction between sex offense behavior and the use of pornography when it is available on a general basis.

It is clear that different kinds of consequences will result from the increased permissiveness of United States society, though some of the results may parallel the Danish experience. Unfortunately, the increasing sexual liberalization has not come as a result of a legislative confrontation with the issues that resulted in statutory changes, but through the discretionary power of the courts influencing police and the prosecutor's behavior. Since there is a reduced likelihood of conviction, there has been a reduction in police activity with the intent to convict. At the same time there is still the risk of corruption and differential enforcement since material considered pornographic could still be seized and purveyors arrested under local statutes. The process of decriminalization through reduced enforcement involves serious risks since any police action continues to stigmatize the behavior and the police retain the right (if not the intent) to subject it to legal sanctions. What this method of decriminalization usually results in is the use of the dead letter statute for new and/or political purposes.

Homosexuality

The current relation between homosexuality and the criminal legal process is extremely unstable. Beginning with the publication of *Sexual Behavior in the Human Male* (Kinsey et al., 1948) with its figure of 37 percent of the males in the society ever having had a single homosexual contact, there has been a growing discontent with the criminal status of homosexual activity, both male and female. This discontent has expressed itself in a number of ways: first, through the work of criminologists whose studies of the homosexual suggested that public stereotypes were incorrect and that the homosexual was not a dangerous seducer of youth; second, through the work of social scientists studying the homosexual community and determining the existence of similarities and relations between homosexual and heterosexual life-styles; and finally, through the work of legal reformers whose concern was with the corrupting influence on law-enforcement agencies of having to enforce what were conceived as moral regulations on persons who were committing what came to be defined as crimes without victims. Paralleling this shift in the nonhomosexual world, there were demands for change from the homosexual community itself, beginning with informational self-help organizations in the 1950s that changed to more militant and confrontational styles in the late 1960s and early 1970s. There developed an alliance between many researchers on homosexuality and the homosexual community in their common interest in the decriminalization of homosexuality. This process began in Illinois in 1961 when homosexual contacts between adults in private became noncriminal as part of a general revision of the criminal code. Since 1961 in four other states decriminalization has occurred on an ad hoc basis.

Even with this shift toward decriminalization in some states, there is still a continuation of conventional police practices in other jurisdictions and from some reports a continued harassment of the homosexual in those states where the private act is not against the law. Changes in this section of the statute (acts in private) offer only the mildest form of reform since the largest proportion of homosexual offenders are arrested in public or quasi-public situations in which they are looking for sexual partners, e.g., in the confines of a homosexual bar or meeting place, or as the result of a sexual contact with a slightly underage male. It is not uncommon in these cases for the police to use *agent provocateurs* to elicit a homosexual approach before the arrest is made, but this practice varies over time in the same jurisdiction and from jurisdiction to jurisdiction.

The police response to the existence of homosexuality in any community is commonly confined nearly exclusively to male homosexuals, since the style of life of female homosexuals largely keeps them outside of the orbit of police activity (Simon & Gagnon, 1967). The female homosexual rarely gets involved in disputes in public; there are crimes of passion that have been linked to female homosexual relationships, but these are perhaps as rare as crimes of passion always are. Even in the public manifestations of female homosexuality there is a sedateness and calm that is disturbed only by the presence of heterosexual males who find the lesbian a problem for their masculinity. In addition, for those young women who are attracted to women when they are adolescents, there is rarely an overt situation which would bring their preferences to the attention of the police. Women with a basic preference for other women rarely fall afoul of the police and when they do so it is largely in connection with other kinds of behavior that are defined as criminal.

The response of the criminal legal process to male homosexuality normally emerges from about five circumstances:

1. The police operate at the margins of the homosexual community and keep its more overt aspects invisible to the conventional community. This involves the policing of public toilets that are frequented by homosexuals, sporadic raids on homosexual bars, beaches, and parks, and the harassment of street hustling or outrageous behavior in public places.

2. Law-enforcement agencies use the information from persons arrested in the above circumstances to arrest other persons who might be implicated and exploit the results of household searches that discover letters, photographs, and other materials that may implicate other homosexuals.

3. Anti-homosexual crusades can be set off by a sudden community discovery of homosexuals in their midst. Such crusades begin when relatively innocent communities discover the homosexual "menace" and a concerted effort is made to put the homosexual community under surveillance. These attempts can be community- or institutionwide (e.g., universities, government agencies, towns, etc.). Such homosexual hunts usually collapse when the extent of the behavior is discovered or when a child or relative of a major figure in the community is caught in the net.

4. Another source of police involvement with the homosexual community is through criminal offenses that are associated with homosexuality. There are two dimen-

sions involved here; one arises because of preferences for sexual partners among homosexual males (that may, in part, be derived from the legal status of homosexuality), and the other is the vulnerability of the homosexual to criminals because of the social and legal status of homosexuality. One of the characteristics of male homosexuals is that substantial numbers of them have well-developed preferences for males who give the appearance of excessive masculinity, or young males who appear new to the homosexual marketplace, or for a different male in nearly every sexual encounter. Whether these particular preferences are rooted in the stigmatized status of the homosexual is unclear since these same preferences (the desire for cosmetically erotic females, younger females, or for many different females) on the part of heterosexual males are generally only ambivalently disapproved, if at all. As a result of this situation, there has developed in the larger cities and in some smaller communities specific locations in which such males can be found either for affection or for pay. Many of these young men are recruited from delinquent or quasi-delinquent communities and the homosexual can be victimized either through theft or blackmail by these young men. Other homosexuals who present themselves as heterosexual to the conventional world or who are heterosexually married are often driven to the use of these males or these locations in order to find sexual contacts. As a result there is a heightened level of vulnerability for these males since they are both less able and less experienced in operating in these circumstances, and because they are concealing a conventional family structure as well. Such males are easily blackmailed by either their homosexual partners or by the police if they are arrested in the most marginally suspicious circumstances. The legal status of homosexuality makes the homosexual vulnerable to victimization and makes a law-enforcement response to that victimization, even if well intended, extremely difficult. Homicides, robberies, and assaults that arise out of homosexual relationships are concealed or badly investigated because the victim is unable to establish a sense of trust in the police. If the homosexual has been involved in what is considered to be a sexual crime, there is a minimal likelihood that he will report being robbed during a criminal act. Further, there is no guarantee to the victim that there will not be further reprisals against him or his friends.

5. The smallest proportion of police activity results from reactions to public reports of specific criminal offenses which involve homosexual activity. While the policing of the public manifestations of homosexuality may be elicited by complaints from well-placed moral entrepreneurs, reports of single homosexual offenses come mainly from parents charging that their children or young adolescents have had a homosexual contact with an adult (for example, the proverbial Boy Scout master, or they have been picked up by a homosexual while hitchhiking). These situations are quite different from paragraph 4 and involve the intersection of homosexual adults with younger people; from the legal point of view, they involve criminal and victim in the way that adult homosexual contacts do not.

These responses of the police intersect with the conventional pattern of the development of an extensive homosexual commitment or life-style as well as with fragmentary or sporadic homosexual activity. It is apparent that a sexual preference for males rather than females or even having a joint preference for males and females is expressive of a multiplicity of etiologies or causes and a multiplicity of present motivations. This is true of heterosexuality as well, but its preferred status in the society submerges the complexity of its origins and gives it a semblance of cohesiveness and order that is commonly denied unconventional sexual expressions. As a consequence, there exists in the society as wide a (and, perhaps, a wider) variety of sexual styles among homosexuals as among heterosexuals, or rather, homosexual acts are integrated into other life elements in a larger variety of ways.

The conventional homosexual career contains a number of periods of time during which the homosexual is particularly vulnerable to the police. Young homosexual males can be arrested if they enter into places of usual homosexual congregation since they are vulnerable both as adolescents and as homosexuals. Since most homosexual congregating places are those that serve liquor and there is only now emerging recreational locations for the younger homosexual, the bars serve as risky points of entry for them (Hooker, 1967). These younger males are attractive to older males since they are new faces on the scene, but these relationships are dangerous since the young male may live at home or setting up a cohabitation may result in legal trouble for both males. Congruent with entry into public homosexual life-styles, there is a period during which a large number of homosexual males affirm their new-found and released sexuality through large amounts of sexual activity (Dank, 1971). These males often embark on an endless search for new sexual partners in highly vulnerable locations (bars, baths, parks) with a low degree of discrimination about the characteristics of their partners or the situation in which they find themselves. Both their naivete and their desire combine to put them at considerable risk. Most males pass through this phase, but some retain a strong commitment to sexual adventure and these males often find themselves in legal or other trouble because of the places and ways in which they seek sexual activity. During periods of sexual monogamy many homosexual males are less vulnerable, but at the breakup of relationships there is sometimes either a burst of sexual activity or a search for another partner which increases risk (Hoffman, 1968).

A substantial amount of involvement with the law can also be a consequence of homosexual activity by males who are not living the conventional homosexual lifestyle, but who venture into homosexual contacts in other ways. Some of these are males who maintain conventional heterosexual lives but have homosexual activity as part of a preference or out of some form of stress or anxiety. Such males appear in the regular recreational locations of the homosexual community or frequent the more public locations for homosexual contact where the promise of anonymous sex is available. In these latter locations relatively elaborate and complex interactional relationships are developed to promote a hurried and tense sexual contact. As a recent study shows (Humphreys, 1970), the stigmatized status of homosexuality in general and the difficulties of integrating it into an otherwise conventional life-style promotes sexual contacts under conditions of relative sexual and personal degradation and at high risk to the participants. These sites are both collecting points for homosexuals who are simply looking for additional partners and those members of the community with largely conventional identities. A police action in these locations results in a mixed bag of persons without either a current homogeneity of life-style or a historical homogeneity of reasons for their homosexual involvement.

Homosexual contacts by adults with adolescents or children present an extremely mixed picture. Some contacts with adolescent males can result from normal mistakes about the age of consent (a 16 year old really looks 18), but there are a minority of persons who have strong attachments to males around the age of puberty. The existence of homosexual photo magazines for young boys, some of them prepubescent, indicates at least a fantasy interest in boys and nubile adolescents in some proportion of the male homosexual population. It is doubtful whether this fantasy activity is converted to overt activity in any large measure. Studies of homosexual offenses against adolescents and young children are relatively rare, but Gebhard et al. (1965) included such groups classified by age of the victim. This research suggests that the contacts with children are largely substitutive of contacts with slightly older boys (normally around 12 and over), but that there is a certain amount of generalized pedophilia, regardless of gender, represented in a few of these offenses. While this particular group of offenders was more homosexually experienced than other offender groups (other than those who had offended homosexually against adults), they offered a substantial picture of heterosexual activity as well. In some cases this heterosexuality also included a pedophilic interest in female children.

These contacts with younger males also result from a homosexual interest concealed inside of other adult-child roles (teacher, older friend, guide). The legal categorization masks as many differences in motivation and development among offenders as it exposes. One can estimate that a larger number of these kinds of offense occur than are reported, with young males not telling their parents about transient homosexual contacts or approaches. The impact of these offenses on conventional sexual development is currently unclear since most of the studies of child victimization are of females. A substantial number of homosexuals report in adulthood that they had a homosexual experience with an older male (perhaps only an older adolescent) early in life which would indicate that there is some significance at least for those males who have other predisposing experiences. Studies of adolescent male sex offenders, however, report that few males continued their offense behavior into adulthood, indicating a low level of predictability from adolescent to adult experiences. A review of the Kinsey data (Kinsey et al., 1948) on the homosexual experience of college-going males suggests that about 25 percent of all college-entering males (about 80 percent of those having homosexual experiences) have their homosexual experiences mostly sporadically and prior to age 18, and 5 to 7 percent of all such males (about 20 percent of those with homosexual experience) have homosexual experience thereafter (Gagnon & Simon, 1967b). It is possible to suggest that only a minority of males who have homosexual experiences in adolescence continue homosexual activity into adulthood.

It is presently estimated that about 3 to 4 percent of adult males are largely or exclusively homosexual. If these males are having homosexual experiences on an average of 2 times per week, it is apparent that there are some two to three million homosexual acts committed per week in the U.S. Clearly the criminal legal process intersects this activity only on the most sporadic basis, existing as a trap for the unwary, the foolish, the unlucky, and the uninitiated. The continuing thrust toward decriminalization will obviously remove a substantial number of potential sex offenders from the legal roles. If homosexual groups achieve their goals (the nonstigmatization of homosexual preferences), there will surely be a reduction in the age of consent parallel to that for heterosexuality. It is presently quite unclear what impact this decriminalization will have in the lives of the heterosexuals who have sporadic homosexual experiences or those homosexuals who pick up partners in public locations. For this group, the easy location of appropriate sexual partners might well have to wait for the creation of social institutions other than bars, baths, and the like for the approach to sexual partners, or a basic change in heterosexual relations, such that these kinds of institutions become available for the heterosexual who is seeking impersonal sex as well. The ultimate removal of homosexuality as a contributing or significant factor in criminal statistics or involvement in the criminal legal process depends as much on the destigmatizing of the behavior as it does on decriminalization. At the point of destigmatization criminal offenses against homosexuals can be reported to the police, men may have families and homosexual outlets, and homosexual meeting places will be more generally open. What impact this will have on the social organization of homosexual life as it is presently constituted is unknown.

Prostitution

In some ways the prostitution of females partly parallels some elements of male homosexuality since it offers the heterosexual male an opportunity for impersonal sexuality. Contact with the prostitute, however differentiated by class, context, or ritual elements, contains the implicit assumption that the two participants in the sexual act are going to remain strangers to each other. The transfer of dollars furthers this contractual status of the act and symbolically serves to replace the normal erotic buildup which is necessary for many males in conventional heterosexual contacts (Gagnon, 1968).

Prostitution (other than the adventitious arrests of the sexually active adolescent girl) is the only seriously pursued sexual crime committed by women in the United States. It is illegal in forty-nine states and legal only in narrow circumstances in one. While it is clearly recognized that the act of prostitution requires an entire stage of actors, a cast largely defined by its illegal status, only the prostitute is regularly treated as a criminal. Thus, the customer, the steerer, the bellboy, the taxicab driver, the hotel and motel owner, the property trustee, all stand outside of the legal situation. The only male who is arrested is the pimp and this rarely occurs since he is a primary conduit through which licit and illicit funds are funneled to the police, lawyers, and bondsmen who are employed in the legal criminal process and who directly or indirectly tax the prostitute. Many of these men could be said to be living off the earnings of prostitutes.

American society has vacillated considerably in its treatment of the prostitute over the last fifty years, especially since the large-scale repression of the 1920s, and changes in sexual mores and social structure have led to a general decline in the frequency with which males go to prostitutes before, during, or after marriage (Holmes, 1972). It appears from the limited data available that the incidence of prostitute contacts has not changed, only the frequency (Kinsey et al., 1948). At the same time the site of prostitution has changed from the brothel where it was neatly bounded by the police to the street, the tavern, and the telephone, where control, at least in its older forms, is far more difficult. This has been compounded by the existence of a slightly freer sexual situation in which the distinction between good women and bad women on sexual grounds is far more problematic especially in those situations where a public place is used to make heterosexual contacts (Roebuck & Spray, 1967).

Prostitution at the present time is a relatively stable activity (in terms of numbers and acts) in the society and probably grows more or less visible as police activity increases or decreases. Vigorous enforcement, long sentences, and a policy of sequestration will reduce both visibility and the presence of prostitutes. The increased visibility of prostitutes in cities like New York and San Francisco is, in part, due to the changes in the climate of former ghetto bright-lights areas where white customers are now less likely to go. The sudden efflorescence of prostitutes in midtown Manhattan is a function of the women going where the men are rather than the men going into the less visible areas of the city. It is perhaps this sudden emergence of the prostitute into the central city that results in reports of increased prostitute-client violence. Formerly the prostitute maintained her occupation in marginal areas where there was no contempt expressed for her status. Now when her trade must be plied in the midst of conventional others, both rejecting males (formerly the males who were accosted were all interested or they would not have been in that section of the city) and hostile conventional females, there is a greater potential for aggression and violence. At the same time it is best not to overestimate this increase since there was considerable rolling and robbery of clients when men went to prostitutes in less public areas. The other major change has been the increased recruitment of prostitutes from minority ethnic groups (a historical practice, but they were mostly white ethnics in the past) and the increased use of hard drugs. This latter change is a critical phenomenon in the large cities of the United States and also accounts for the increased levels of aggression among those who have not earned enough during the work day to handle the cost of the drug habit.

Our response to the prostitute is still locked into nineteenth-century forms and legal proscriptions. The police are active at the margins of the behavior seeking to reduce its public aspects while retaining its availability for the customers. In part the police also are involved in increasing the safety of the customer since the activity takes place in a quasi-criminal atmosphere. There are grave difficulties in this since the customer is involved in a criminal act (much the same as the homosexual) and is loath to admit that he has been robbed or assaulted in the course of a purchased (and, therefore, degraded) sexual encounter. In addition, customers often have conventional identities to protect which reduces their willingness to testify or bring complaints.

The dilemma for the prostitute is that it is nearly impossible, even for the call girl, to avoid living at least part of her life inside the "life" of prostitution if only to have emotional and psychological support for selling what is societally regarded as a nonpurchasable item (Jackman et al., 1963; Bryan, 1965). The existence of this burden of guilt is practically intolerable for younger women and movement into a life where most social contacts are with those who also share this world is often impossible to avoid. By participating in this life, women are exposed to the more delinquent and criminal components of the society (Hirschi, 1962).

Since the acquisition of the new customers requires the prostitute to be entangled in a network of referrals, even a prostitute of the most cautious sort will come to the attention of law-enforcement people or organized crime if she is involved in prostitution in given areas of the country. Even when arrests do not result, criminalization often does. This is especially true in those communities where prostitution is a leisure or vacation service. In these cases control over free-enterprise prostitution is complete and all women must work inside a known criminal network. The police will often arrest these women in order to give them a record or in order to intimidate them for sexual purposes.

While the call girl or the woman who manages her prostitution in nonpublic ways can operate outside the control of the police, this would seem to be quite rare. In the case of street, bar, or other public prostitutes, it is likely that nearly all will fall afoul of the police at some point in their career, if only as a token arrest as part of the drive to reduce prostitution or because the police generally tend to arrest all new girls in order to stigmatize them. Such arrests tend to be the normal lot of the street or bar hustler since she is constantly exposed to community regard.

Recruitment into prostitution is predominantly of women from minorities, poverty groups, or as a result of involvement with juvenile authorities. There is also some movement into prostitution from the quasi-erotic occupations in which women are partial commodities (entertainment, modeling, stripping) and the transition to making money for another commodity activity can easily result in an atmosphere of relative sexual permissiveness (Salutin, 1973). These occupations are also vulnerable to economic fluctuation (in periods of depression models can easily become prostitutes) and the majority of females are recruited to them for having erotic physical attributes that are not necessarily connected with skilled money management. Indeed, there are pressures against economic prudence: first, in the socialization of the "sexy" appearing female (she is early given presents and gifts), and second, in her guilt over receiving filthy lucre (she divests herself of it). Finally, they share with prostitution a life-style that is out of synchronization with conventional female adjustments in the society in terms of daily as well as life-cycle experiences.

INDIVIDUAL SEXUAL OFFENSES

As has been noted before, the sexual offenses that have been of greatest interest to criminologists are those that have involved force and violence (normally heterosexual crimes against victims of all ages which have been construed under the rape, assault, child molestation, or murder statutes), heterosexual behavior that is criminal only if committed by adults with minors and children (usually limited to offenses against those 13 and under), heterosexual behavior between relatives, and offenses against the public order.

These sex offenses normally involve victims, but the victims' response to the offense is not simple nor do similarly named offenses arise out of necessarily similar circumstances. The bulk of these offenses are called to the attention of the police through complaints. Rarely are sex offenders arrested during the commission of the act by the normal routines of police surveillance. Cases can be found in which the police in their normal activity come upon offenders in the commission of the offense (largely involved in assault, offenses against children, or public indecency), but these are extremely rare. The police are thus required to demonstrate their own reputation in the community as a decent and reliable agency before victims are willing to expose themselves to the police process.

Offenses Involving Force and Violence

Excluding offenses against children which involve violence, there is a large number of crimes in which force is used by a male in order to gain some sort of sexual access to a female. Probably the most satisfactory distinction in these cases is between those offenses that occur between persons who previously knew each other and those that occur between total strangers. The existence of a relationship, no matter how primitive, between a man and a woman tends to be a central variable in the differential reporting of the offense, and the degree to which the offense itself is perceived as an outgrowth of a conventional sexual relationship or of what, for want of a better word, can be called a problem of impulse control or management. Here we should not focus on the faulty control of a mystical drive, but rather the outcome of confused learning that may not have anything directly to do with sexual expression.

Probably the largest proportion of sexual contacts that involve force, violence, or threat are those in what appears (at least to males) to be a conventional sexual encounter that has gone wrong (Gebhard et al., 1965). Clearly the development and organization of a sexual relationship that begins between two strangers depends on the ability of the two persons to share similar expectations about the specific outcome of their interactions, or at least to submit to a parallel set of meta-rules about how the expectations can be changed. Sexual relationships themselves are fraught with ambiguity since it is a rare set of persons who can sequence communication in such a way that the man's desire and the woman's desire are directly coordinated. In the conventional social script the woman is more doubtful and often has the view that she would like to get to know the male somewhat better, while the male tends to press for a more rapid movement from social to sexual interaction. Since much of this interaction is nonverbal, when the exact point of female consent occurs is reasonably tricky to determine and even the woman participant may be unsure herself about when she decided to have or not to have intercourse on any specific occasion. Thus, it is always problematic for a woman if she wishes to identify the relationship as containing excessive force, for it depends upon the degree to which her own sticking point occurred after the male assumed that she had said yes.

It is likely that a majority of unreported sexual relationships containing what the woman would describe as an excessive amount of force are those in which the partners know each other, but are in the early stages of a relationship. Further, they tend to arise in situations where the classification of a woman as good or bad is defined by where the couple meets or by the woman's social accessibility independent of conventional family contacts. Thus, the set of values that define what is an appropriate relationship between men and women and the permissible limits of sexual behavior become the framework outside of which aggressive sexual encounters can occur.

Consequently, there are a substantial number of rape reports arising out of adolescent dating situations, out of quasi-conventional contacts in bars, pickups on the street, or in other dating situations in which the expectations of the two partners have gone awry (Amir, 1971). The degree to which the characteristics of reported offenses represent the acts which occur in the community is unclear. They surely do not represent the acts, but the way in which they vary is extremely difficult to predict in the absence of evidence. The study by Kirkpatrick and Kanin (1957) outlines cases of aggression on a college campus. This study suggests that there is a great deal of aggressive behavior occurring under what are conventional circumstances and few of the events are reported to the police. This is especially true when the situation is largely conventional and when the two partners are persons who have known each other. In these situations the woman is morally disarmed unless she can show major physical injury since she is working against the problem of being a credible victim. Not only do the police have standards for an appropriate offender with all of the motivational apparatus that that involves, but they also have standards for victims. To the degree that the woman is known to the man, has had sex with him before, has a bad reputation, seems nonhysterical and uninjured, she ceases to be a victim and becomes a woman who failed to "come across" in the situation, someone who was a tease and deserved what she got. Further, if the situation involved problematic elements beyond the degradation involved in rape (the victim is married, going to be married, or is underage and her parents don't know), there is a further tendency not to report the offense.

From the only national study of victimization, it is apparent that the rape rate per one hundred thousand is quadrupled when sample data are compared with the FBI's *Uniform Crime Reports* (Ennis, 1967). Thus, the number of rapes reported, when someone in a household was interviewed about their own and other members' victim experiences, in 1965–66 generated a rate of 42.5 rapes per one hundred thousand per year in contrast to the 11.6 per one hundred thousand in the *Uniform Crime Reports*. Even this former figure is clearly an underestimate since there are two factors operating to reduce the reports. First, different respondents in any household do not know what happened to others in the household (mothers may not know about daughters, husbands about wives, etc.), and second, there is still reticence in reporting rapes even if they occurred to other persons in the household. This would indicate that the 42.5 per one hundred thousand should be multiplied by a still larger factor.

There are a substantial proportion of these kinds of events that lie under the surface of conventional heterosexual relationships, especially during the premarital period and at all social levels. In these situations males seeking sexual adventure (as they are trained to do) interact with young females who have a fundamental misapprehension of males' attitudes toward sexuality. These general societywide attitudes are exacerbated in those subcultures where a basic distinction is made between good girls and bad girls, and the latter is often the victim of sexual assault because of local codes about the sexual accessibility of such females. Having the appellation "bad," they give up the protections normally given to women who are marriageable. In these situations such girls are vulnerable to group rape situations which grow out of the masculinity values of the male youth culture in certain ethnic areas.

Two forms of rape, the "gang bang" and the group rape, by young males are variants of rape situations which arise in part out of the "normal" value structure of social relations in certain social levels. The gang bang is a sexual contact by a group of males with a single woman, either for pay or voluntarily. These events often occur under ambiguous circumstances growing out of existing all-male social groupings in which group sexual intercourse provides a common validation of sexual prowess and shared male values (a parallel is the all-male group watching a stag movie). Some proportion of these events involve force and violence, others verge into it because the males refuse to pay for the sex afterwards. In some few cases the entire arrangement involves an unwilling woman or the woman becomes unwilling during the act as the number of males increases. It is nearly impossible to secure arrests and convictions in these cases unless there is a clear-cut status distinction between the woman and the men and it must be explicit that the woman was not previously involved with them. These events grow increasingly rare as the supporting social structure of male-male groups erodes and now occur primarily in male gang or military subgroups. What is important is not the frequency of the activity, but the degree to which it grows not out of individual pathology, but out of a variation in normal gender socialization.

Events that are qualitatively similar to the gang bang are group rapes in which two or more males have intercourse with a female against her will. In these situations a group of adolescent males in the course of all-male activities rape women who appear to be sufficiently erotically degraded or who provoke their hostility through ignoring them. Thus, rapes in lovers' lanes or of prostitutes involve women who have their sexual status marked as vulnerable to such attacks. Other women who have higher status than the males provoke such assaults by treating such males with contempt. Both being too good or too bad places a woman at some risk in terms of these male values.

Of the very large pool of events that involves excessive force and violence, the ones that are easiest to report are those in which the woman is the victim of an act committed by a stranger with whom she has had no prior social interaction. In this case her victim status is relatively pure, but at the same time the probability of successful legal action is relatively poor. In those cases in which the male is a stranger and the interaction is short and violent, the problems of identification are problematic. When the victim is known to the offender, his arrest is assured. The question is which of the potential variant versions of the reality of the social interaction can be supported. Women are more likely to report the kinds of offenses that involve strangers than those that involve men known to them, but there are substantial constraints against reporting either. The sense of personal degradation, the problem of reputation, and the normal problems of being handled by inept medical and police agencies often prevent a woman from reporting.

At the present time we know very little about the male offender who, outside of any social interaction, initiates a forcible sexual contact with a woman to whom he is a stranger (there are some males who have picked a victim who know of the woman

ut her being aware of him). It is apparent that the male is proceeding with
a sort of social script which legitimates the normative violation at least at that
ant. Gebhard et al. (1965) contains the best descriptions of that subclass of males
who are involved in these kinds of sexual encounters. While the categories depart
from normal psychological or etiological classification systems, they seem to relate to
the elements of behavior that characterize the nonsexual conduct of these men. The
authors identify a series of subclasses among sex offenses involving force, the most
common of which were men whose sexual contacts with women regularly included
threat or violence (about one-third of this study's cases) combined with a history
of generalized violence. The expression of violence emerges as the central theme in
these males' behavior, perhaps indicating that they well represent a subclass of men
who are committed to violence rather than to sex. The second largest class was the
amoral delinquent, that is, males whose general life-styles involved aggressive self-
seeking (though the authors' "egocentric hedonism" seems too abstract a description);
their approach to sexuality is the same as their approach to other desires (this pattern
characterized many of those offenders against consenting adolescent females). The
third group were those males whose judgment seems to be blunted by alcohol and
drunkenness or whose sensibilities and ability to cope with sexual situations are distorted. A last group were those men whose behavior was termed explosive, that is,
there was nothing in the accessible history of the individual to predict any behaviors
of this kind (he is not a "normal" rapist); in these cases the male seems unable to
interpret the appropriate signs of assent and, captivated by his own internal states,
uses force.

What is most interesting about the categories developed by Gebhard et al. (1965)
is that they involve the management of sexual behavior in the context of other forms
of behavior. The sexual act is shaped by the existence of other factors, general
aggressivity, a heedless hedonistic life-style, the confusions of alcohol, and the problems of sexual repression. In consequence, it is very difficult to settle on a series of
categories that exhaustively describe the offender, indicating that relatively disparate
kinds of males are collected by the legal criminal process, but not altogether randomly
since the more criminal will appear more often, as will those who have a general
predisposition to violence. What is required to understand them is a knowledge of
the way in which the conventional sexual script which exists for males seeking sexual
activity contains elements that contribute to these crimes. Aggression, drinking, and
sexual ignorance are involved in many sexual encounters in this society, but only in
some of them is excessive force used, and few of these ultimately become the basis
of the charge of or conviction for rape.

Offenses Against Children and Young Adolescents

The social margin between childhood and adolescence is complex in Western societies
and is made more difficult by the intermediate status of adolescence between childhood
and adulthood. A substantial amount of exploratory sexual activity occurs between
young people of the same age during adolescence, sometimes resulting in criminal involvement, but more often serving as the learning and testing period for behaviors that
will characterize their adult status (Reiss, 1960). Variations in biological growth
contribute to the confusions of this period with a wide variety of developmental
moments or stages between 10 and 16. There are girls of 12 who have adult secondary

sexual characteristics and girls of 16 who look childlike. Often it is the former who are more vulnerable to early sexual experience, either as the result of peer inter-action or sexual approaches by slightly older males. Some of these offenses that involve a confusion about age may, in fact, be legitimate in motivation, but contravene standards about the age of sexual partners.

The bulk of offenses against children are against either males or females who clearly are underage and who were selected because they are children. Many of these cases appear to be substitutive, that is, no adults were available, or the male feels sexually inadequate with adult females. Offenders against children represent the most complicated sex offense behavior from nearly any analytic point of view. Indeed, as with most variant sexual expressions that do not have obvious collective or social structural aspects, there is a substantial amount of idiosyncratic behavior. Contact with children can be expressive of a long range of motives that are largely nonsexual, though the sexual motive itself becomes the central concern of policing agencies. A search for affection, or for unjudged relationships, or senility are all aspects of sexual contacts between adults and children which are not expressions of "perversions of sexual development," but rather the integration of sexual acts with motives and desires that vary only slightly from conventional script elements. One factor that has led to confusion in dealing with the sex offender has been the focus on the sexual element in the offense and avoidance of other aspects of behavior which are nonsexual, of which the sexual offense is expressive.

The pool of offenders and the pool of victims who fall afoul of the law are complexly selected from a pool of interacting persons who make up those males and children having sexual contacts. There is a wide range of kinds of contacts that are sub-sumed under the rubric sex offenses against children, contacts that range from a casual touching and nongenital petting to actual coitus in the case of females and extensive homosexual contacts in the case of males (Gagnon, 1965). In terms of duration, they range from the most fleeting contacts to relationships that have great emotional depth lasting over a number of years. The character of the relationship between the child and the adult interacts in a complex fashion with the nature of the relationship between the child and his parents.

In the case of adult-child offenses, the collection process for offenses is two step —children report to their parents, their parents report to the police. At both of these points there is a loss in reporting, but for differing reasons. The child does not report the event to the parents depending in some measure on the degree that he or she is implicated in the offense—has he enjoyed it? does he or she feel complicity?— and to the degree that the child is free to talk to its parents about sex behavior. It is clear from the study of victims and from the study of normal socialization that chil-dren do not interpret the offense behavior of adults in the same way that adults do (Gagnon, 1965). From discussions of psychosocial development, what is perceived to be sexual by adults is perceived by children as unpleasant or immodest or is anxiety-provoking, so the child's description of the event, both in objective and motivational terms, is vastly different from that of the adult's. This disparateness is greater the younger the child, for while the young child may know that something is happening, he or she is often not sure what. It is this sense of discomfort that the child reports to par-ents who convert the ambiguous report into a sexual offense. Prior parental responses to other kinds of ambiguous events will condition the child's capacities to report others to them. These reports will be offered in proportion to the extent that lines of com-munication to parents are open, the event occurred with a stranger, the event was frightening, and it leaves the child feeling unimplicated in its causation. Implication in causation is often very difficult for the child to construe; he or she may assume a guilty sense because it occurred while the child was in a forbidden place, or because the child was doing something else that it was warned against.

Parents must decide whether or not they wish to expose their child to the police and the courts, an experience that they know will be unpleasant for the child. There are no data available on this decision process, but the parent is probably guided by principles both similar to and different from those of the child. If the child is unimplicated and the offense was frightening, the parent might well report it, but counterbalancing this tendency is the parents' knowledge that the possibility of arrest and conviction is relatively poor. Perhaps the crucial element in reporting is the use of the police to protect the safety of children from persons who are in the proximate environment of the child (janitors, shopkeepers, casually known neighbors) who are implicated by the child in such offenses. Strangers are commonly not apprehended even if reported (except for those males who may commit many such offenses), and there are constraints against reporting when the child is closely involved with the adult. It is the in-between cases—acquaintances and casual friends—who are most likely to be arrested, since both parents and children more easily report them and the police can more easily arrest them. These processes seem to be the critical elements of the representation of any offender in the pool of persons who are arrested and incarcerated for offenses against children.

In the Gebhard et al. (1965) study, this resultant group of offenders against children largely comprised males who presented no gross pathologies, but who were officially diagnosed as pedophiles, sociosexually underdeveloped, or amoral delinquents, while others carried certain relatively more obvious complications, such as alcoholism, psychosis, and senile deterioration. While there is a certain primitive air to these categories, they do have a more certain character than those which operate at a greater distance from the offense activity itself. However, at no point do the categories offered have any deeper significance than organizing what appear to be qualitatively similar individuals around some salient attribute, in these cases a presenting problem or symptom. What appears in nearly all of the studies is the disparateness of the offenders and the essentially ad hoc character of the organizing themes or explanations for their behavior. This is in part due to the fact that the legal criminal process collects persons at various points in their sexual and psychological careers even with reference to the offense behavior. There are serious problems about the representativeness of the motivational characteristics of the offender population, and about one's ability to combine in a single category the senile deteriorate and adolescent defective, since their similarity lies only in the object of the offense.

The best judgment that one can currently make on the state of our knowledge of the offender against children is little better than the theories generated by the law-enforcement agencies. The behavior appears idiosyncratic though there are subgroups of offenders who have at least marginal similarities, but there is no connection between the larger nonsexual class of events or categories to which they belong and the sex offense behavior itself. Of the many alcoholics, only some molest children. The question remains, why these? What we appear to have is the intersect of a number of behavioral modes of action (drinking, a sense of sexual arousal, an available child, and no resistance to a sexual performance) and what remains difficult to explain is the way in which the lack of resistance to a sexual object like a child is integrated into other social scripts.

There is some evidence that there is rarely any significant consequence of this interaction for the child in terms of later experience and adjustment (Gagnon, 1965). This is true of children who do and do not tell their parents, though often among the latter there is some considerable fright engendered by parental actions. The child rarely interprets the act in the terms that the adult intends except in those cases where the relationship is extended and the child is close to puberty. Often even the experience of orgasm is not perceived as sexual by the child. The most common reactions involve a sense of uneasiness, fright, and sometimes horror; the most difficult results for children are from offenses which involve aggression and coercion.

It is difficult to determine the proportion of men who commit these acts without incurring any criminal sanctions. There are records of men with extensive histories of sexual contact with children, and many such men appear in prisons having been finally identified after a long series of offenses. There are still others who probably have developed sufficient interpersonal skills with children that they remain unapprehended. There is a constant tension here between the benefits of experience and the dangers of continued involvement for the offender. The stranger who commits a single impulsive act has a low risk because he is largely unidentifiable, especially if he does not offend again, but he has a high risk because the act is often unplanned, clouded by alcohol, or inept. The experienced and "compulsive" child molester possesses greater skill in managing the interaction, but as in all criminality, "The hounds may make many mistakes, but the fox only one."

Clearly these factors affect the pool of studiable persons who are collected at various points in the criminal legal process, but either at the level of kinds of offenders (as described, say, by Gebhard et al., 1965) or in terms of more abstract categories (as in psychoanalytic studies), it is unclear how the collection of offenders and victims compares with the total population in the general pool of sexual activity between adults and children.

Incest Offenses

Perhaps more than any other sex offender, an understanding of the incest offender and his victim requires a larger reading of the context of action in which they operate, and, indeed, the distribution of offenses that violate the incest taboo is an indicant of the character of the socialization processes of the society and the vulnerabilities of family organization (Weinberg, 1955). Clearly the two largest groups of incest pairs are father-daughter (or stepfather-stepdaughter) and brother-sister. The frequency of the latter seems to decline with removal from isolated rural areas where there are few outside social and sexual opportunities and a deteriorated family structure. Because of cultural differences, brother-sister incest is rarely studied and little speculation can be made about it. It is the former offense about which the most is known and it is central to our considerations here.

Apparently, the congeries of individual and collective circumstances required for incest to occur in this culture are relatively rare. This constellation, as we presently understand it from our pool of reported cases, requires a mother who is withdrawn from the family situation as wife and caretaker, a father who is commonly a failure in nonfamilial situations, and the availability of daughters. This is the incest pattern as seen by the juvenile and criminal courts, a pattern that can persist over a series of daughters, only coming to light by accident through a daughter trying to get out of the situation or as a result of a last daughter leaving the home.

Studies of families, offenders, and victims show this pattern of familial deformation inside of which the incest offense occurs. The problem remains that many families are disordered in similar or near-similar ways. Why did incest occur in this one? The combination of an unemployed male, drinking, with an absent wife and an available daughter is conducive but not causative. The particularity of the incest offense itself may ultimately appear to be one of many outcomes of the disordered family, in which this offense is but one alternative symptom.

It is reasonable to speculate that a substantial number of incest cases never come to the attention of the police because the family breaks up or the offense behavior terminates due to changes in family organization before the police learn of the behavior. Also, in multiple daughter families there is evidence that a series of older daughters are often involved in incest prior to a younger daughter. In these cases the number of victims is large, but the offender is apprehended only for the youngest daughter. Another factor is the daughter's willingness to exhibit other symptoms that stigmatize her in other ways (running away) and exposing her father in situations where the mother is a covert accomplice of the offense behavior.

It is possible that in this category of offenses the fit between the captured population and the noncaptured population may be very good, even though the former is selected relatively adventitiously from the pool of actors involved in incest. If the incest offenses are more often drawn from disordered family structures (incest can be, but is more than rarely, the outcome of a planned family process regardless of images drawn from pornographic literature) residing in relative poverty, there is a collective and familial similarity that reduces the idiosyncrasy of individual behavior. Often this behavior has a dynamic character, offenders, victims, and families changing in response to external societal processes and exigencies of the individual life cycle. The disordered image of the incest offender found in conventional criminological literature probably results from a simple cross-sectional view of the offense and viewing the offender independently of the family context in which the offense behavior occurred.

CONCLUSION

Any attempt to reorder our understanding of the relation between criminal law and sexual conduct during this period of rapid social change must, of necessity, be speculative. Speculative not in the sense of being anti-empirical, but speculative in the sense that most of the data are not available, the data that have been collected are deeply flawed, and the conceptual process that would properly select the appropriate data is only beginning to emerge. Largely it has been the processes of social change that have exposed the weaknesses of many of our criminological beliefs rather than a serious consideration of the ideas within academe. Hence (as we have noted) the limited quality of our thought about drug use has been challenged more by the changing patterns of use in the society than by academic postures, however valuable they might have been as responses to those changes.

The study of the relation between sexual conduct and crime requires a much greater level of sophistication on the part of all behavioral scientists. This is true because of our increasing commitment to a more comprehensive view of sexual conduct in the society and to the ways in which conventional and unconventional sexual conduct are intersected by the criminal legal process. Further, this involves an understanding of conventional psychosexual development as it appears within any specific cultural matrix and the way in which this conventional pattern produces variant or unconventional choices. At the same time the variant and unconventional responses must be seen as having an organized or cultural dimension and as existing in some tension with the conventional patterns themselves. Finally, the activity and behaviors of the policing functions of the culture (here writ large to include all persons involved in the policing of behavior) with reference to sexuality must be viewed as a process that cross-cuts conventional and unconventional life patterns to produce the specific techniques that cultures create with a view to controlling behavior. Clearly the current evidence for the understanding of any one of these aspects of social life is severely limited, but it seems critical that all of these aspects be taken into account in the understanding of any set of behavior that exists at the intersects.

Considerations of conventional sexual development, alternative sexual patterns, and the policing system allow a richer and more complex view of what are legitimate data and begin to offer a critical perspective on the data that already exist. Such evidence also suggests the degree to which any set of outcomes for the individual is embedded in a culture which has specific historical characteristics, and that changes in any of the processes (normal development, alternative development, and the policing structure) will change the character of the outcomes. For instance, the particular status of the homosexual preference in United States society depends on the pattern of conventional socialization and the routes into a homosexual preference, the stigmatized status of the homosexual, the existence of homosexual communities, and the character of the policing functions with reference to the homosexual. Changes in any of these elements will have very different impacts on the outcomes for individuals, and it is important to note that changes can occur in different processes without concomitant changes in the others. Thus, it is very difficult to predict in any sure fashion the kind of outcomes for the society or for various individuals that might result from changes in any of the various processes. This does not mean that change should not be proposed or even advocated, but sure predictions of outcomes are extremely risky.

The trends that are apparent, which might affect one or all of the processes, are the increasingly sexual character of the societal backdrop (in terms of pornography and free sexual expression), the more slowly emerging decriminalization of sexual behavior, the existence of libertarian groups either with specific sexual-change goals (gay liberation) or groups with gender-change goals (the equal-rights amendment), as well as other changes in what are now conceived as being the nonsexual spheres of life (changes in levels of achievement orientation, bureaucratization of larger sectors of the society, and various "greening" movements). All taken together it is apparent that large sections of behavior will be removed from the orbit of the official policing agencies while, at the same time, alternative control or management procedures do not exist. Indeed, it is now proper to question whether or not control *as an idea* in the organization of societies is not a limited perspective on the way in which people manage their own lives.

Given the limited amount of information available, it is likely that most decisions will be made in the absence of adequate knowledge and, in part, both our discovery of new ways of observing the world around us and the changes in that world are part and parcel of the same processes. Perhaps the research response may well have only historical implications since the rates of change seem to occur faster than research projects can be completed. In the study of sexual conduct, we have come to the point where a purely criminological response is in itself a measure of inadequacy.

REFERENCES

Abrahamsen, David.
　1950　Report on Study of 102 Sex Offenders at Sing Sing Prison. Utica, N.Y.: State Hospitals Press (March).

Achilles, Nancy.
　1967　"The development of the homosexual bar as an institution." Pp. 228–244 in J. H. Gagnon and W. Simon (eds.), Sexual Deviance. New York: Harper & Row.

Amir, Menachem.
　1971　Patterns of Forcible Rape. Chicago: University of Chicago Press.

Becker, Howard.
　1963　Outsiders. New York: Free Press of Glencoe.

Bryan, James.
　1965　"Apprenticeships in prostitution." Social Problems 12(Winter):278–297.

Commission on Obscenity and Pornography.
　1971　Technical Reports. Vols. 1–7. Washington, D.C.: U.S. Government Printing Office.

Dank, Barry M.
　1971　"Coming out in the gay world." Psychiatry 34(May):180–197.

Davis, Kingsley.
　1971　"Sexual behavior." Pp. 313–360 in R. K. Merton and R. Nisbet, Contemporary Social Problems. New York: Harcourt Brace Jovanovich.

Ennis, Philip H.
　1967　Field Surveys 2: Criminal Victimization in the United States; Report of a National Survey. Report of research study submitted to the President's Commission on Law Enforcement and Administration of Justice. Washington, D.C.: U.S. Government Printing Office.

Gagnon, John H.
　1965　"Female child victims of sex offenses." Social Problems 2(Fall):176–192.
　1968　"Prostitution." Pp. 592–598 in The International Encyclopedia of the Social Sciences, vol. 12. Second Edition. New York: Macmillan.

Gagnon, John H., and William Simon.
　1967a　"Pornography: raging menace or paper tiger." Trans-action 4(July–August):41–48.
　1967b　"The sociological perspective on homosexuality." The Dublin Review (Summer):96–114.
　1973　Sexual Conduct: The Social Sources of Human Sexuality. Chicago: Aldine.

Gebhard, P. H., J. H. Gagnon, W. P. Pomeroy, and C. V. Christenson.
　1965　Sex Offenders: An Analysis of Types. New York: Harper & Row.

Glueck, Bernard C.
　1956　Final Report, Research Project for the Study and Treatment of Persons Convicted of Crimes Involving Sexual Aberrations. June, 1952 to June, 1955. Albany: New York State Department of Hygiene.

Goffman, Erving.
　1959　The Presentation of Self in Everyday Life. Garden City, N.Y.: Doubleday-Anchor.

Hirschi, Travis.
   1962   "The professional prostitute." Berkeley Journal of Sociology 7(Spring):
           33–50.
Hoffman, Martin.
   1968   The Gay World. New York: Basic Books.
Holmes, Kay Ann.
   1972   "Reflections by gaslight: prostitution in another time." Issues in Criminol-
           ogy 7(Winter):83–101.
Hooker, Evelyn.
   1967   "The homosexual community." Pp. 167–184 in J. H. Gagnon and W. Simon
           (eds.), Sexual Deviance. New York: Harper & Row.
Humphreys, Laud.
   1970   Tearoom Trade: Impersonal Sex in Public Places. London: Duckworth.
Jackman, N. R., R. O'Toole, and G. Geis.
   1963   "The self-image of the prostitute." Sociological Quarterly 4(April):150–
           161.
Karpman, Benjamin.
   1954   The Sexual Offender and His Offenses: Etiology, Pathology, Psycho-
           dynamics and Treatment. New York: Julian.
Kinsey, Alfred C., Wardell B. Pomeroy, and Clyde E. Martin.
   1948   Sexual Behavior in the Human Male. Philadelphia: Saunders.
Kinsey, Alfred C., Wardell B. Pomeroy, Clyde E. Martin, and Paul H. Gebhard.
   1953   Sexual Behavior in the Human Female. Philadelphia: Saunders.
Kirkpatrick, Clifford, and Eugene Kanin.
   1957   "Male sex aggression on a university campus." American Sociological Re-
           view 22(February):52–58.
Kutchinsky, Berl.
   1972   Pornography and Sex Crimes in Denmark: Early Research Findings. Lon-
           don: Martin Robertson.
Lemert, Edwin.
   1967   Human Deviance, Social Problems and Social Control. New York: Prentice-
           Hall.
Leznoff, Maurice, and William A. Westley.
   1956   "The homosexual community." Social Problems 3(April):257–263.
Lindesmith, Alfred R.
   1938   "A sociological theory of drug addiction." American Journal of Sociology
           43(January):593–613.
   1968   Addiction and Opiates. Chicago: Aldine.
Radzinowicz, Leon.
   1957   Sexual Offenses: A Report of the Cambridge Department of Criminal Sci-
           ence. London: Macmillan.
Rains, Prudence M.
   1971   Becoming an Unwed Mother. Chicago: Aldine-Atherton.
Reiss, Albert J., Jr.
   1960   "Sex offenses: the marginal status of the adolescent." Law and Contempo-
           rary Problems 25(2):309–333.

1961   "The social integration of queers and peers." Social Problems 9(Fall):102–120.

Roebuck, Julian, and S. Lee Spray.
1967   "The cocktail lounge: a study of heterosexual relations in a public organization." American Journal of Sociology 72(January):388–395.

Salutin, Marylin.
1973   "Stripper morality," in J. H. Gagnon and W. Simon (eds.), The Sexual Scene. Second Edition. New York: Dutton.

Scheff, Thomas.
1966   Being Mentally Ill: A Sociological Theory. Chicago: Aldine.

Simon, William, and John H. Gagnon.
1967   "The lesbians: a preliminary overview," in J. H. Gagnon and W. Simon (eds.), Sexual Deviance. New York: Harper & Row.
1968   "Sexual deviance and the contemporary American scene." Annals of the American Academy of Political and Social Science 375(March):106–122.
1969   "On psychosexual development," in D. A. Goslin (ed.), Handbook of Socialization Theory and Research. Chicago: Rand McNally.

Sudnow, David.
1965   "Normal crimes." Social Problems 12(Winter):255–276.

Sutherland, E. H.
1956   The Sutherland Papers. Albert Cohen, Alfred Lindesmith, and Karl Schuessler (eds.). Bloomington: Indiana University Press.

Weinberg, S. Kirson.
1955   Incest Behavior. New York: Citadel.

CHAPTER **8**

Avocational Crime

Gilbert Geis

University of California, Irvine

The term *avocational crime* is defined here by a triumvirate of interlocking conditions: (1) the crime is committed by a person who does not think of himself as a criminal; (2) the crime is committed by a person whose major source of income or status is in activities other than crime; and (3) the crime is deterrable by the prospect of publicly labeling the offender as a criminal. This term refers primarily to offenses against property, especially to offenses such as the two types which receive primary attention in this chapter, shoplifting and that rather inexact category which in American studies of criminal behavior has come to be labeled "white-collar crime." Crimes committed against the person which fall into the "avocational" category tend to be indirect; that is, they usually involve negligence or inadvertence. The novelist F. Scott Fitzgerald has, in a different context, portrayed the attitudes involved in such crimes well: "They were careless people. . . . They smashed up things and creatures and retreated back into their money or their vast carelessness, or whatever it was that kept them together, and let other people clean up the mess they had made" (1953:136).

Self-Image

The distinction in terms of self-image between avocational criminals and their more traditional lawbreaking sisters and brethren was pointed out by Sutherland in regard to businessmen who violate regulatory laws carrying criminal penalties. "They think of themselves as honest men, not as criminals, whereas professional thieves, when they speak honestly, admit that they are thieves," Sutherland (1956:95–96) observed. A professional thief offers support for Sutherland's thesis. An interrogator asks: "If you were to describe yourself in one word, would the description invariably be 'a criminal'?" The response is: "Yes, definitely. That's what I am. I never think of myself in any other way" (Parker & Allerton, 1962:65).

The statement of a vice-president of General Electric, just convicted of criminal violation of the Sherman Antitrust Act, indicates contrariwise how avocational criminals view themselves: "All of you know that next Monday, in Philadelphia, I will start serving a thirty-day jail term, along with six other *businessmen* for conduct which has been *interpreted* as being in conflict with the *complex* antitrust laws" (italics added; *New York Times*, Feb. 25, 1961). It is the possibility of settling upon an alternative description of self—a businessman instead of a thief—and the adroitness in derogating the statute—as complex and arguable rather than a self-evident criminal law—that allows the avocational offender to sidestep introjection of the obloquy attached to the acts of traditional kinds of offenders. The roots of such processes are visible in the response of a senior partner of J. P. Morgan to questions from a congressional committee investigating the crimes of Richard Whitney, a former president of the New York Stock Exchange:

> Sure, but you use the word stealing. It never occurred to me that Richard Whitney was a thief. What occurred to me was that he had gotten into a terrible jam, and had made improper and unlawful use of securities; that his brother was proposing to try and make good his default. . . . It made me ill almost that all the time he could have been deceiving his wife and community. Well, it was just—inconceivable (Brooks, 1970: 285).

Perhaps the point is best made by noting that two members of the Attorney General's National Committee to Study the Antitrust Laws strongly opposed the inclusion of criminal penalties in the antitrust statutes. They supported their position in the following manner:

> Of all the great industries that contributed most to the winning of the war there is hardly one that has not been branded by either indictment or injunction suit as violators of this criminal statute.
> Our enemies do not fail to take advantage of that strange anomaly, in their never-ending charges that we are a nation of criminal monopolists (1955:353).

Imagine anyone suggesting that armed robbery and burglary ought to stop being crimes because their prosecution is giving the United States a bad reputation abroad.

Illustrations of the enabling self-image of avocational offenders abound in criminological literature, but there are few studies of any sophistication tracing the sources of these self-images or systematically investigating consequences of reinforcement or impairment of the offender's view of himself. It can be argued that a strong self-image as a law-abiding and decent citizen allows the offender to suffer through assaults on that viewpoint and to emerge ready to perform comfortably in roles that the defining elements of the society wish for him. Certainly, much of the thrust toward keeping criminal offenders out of prison is built upon the achievement of such a goal. It can also be argued, of course, that failure to penetrate the caul of self-righteousness of the avocational offender permits him to continue his criminal career, unhampered by the mediating influence of guilt and anxiety.

An important factor in sustaining the self-image of the avocational lawbreaker is likely to be the absence of moral indignation regarding his behavior among his peers, as well as the access these peers have to centers of power and publicity. Sutherland pointed out that the mass media themselves are industries, and, therefore, that they tend to be sympathetic to the cause of businessmen who have run afoul of the criminal law. "Public opinion in regard to picking pockets would not be well organized if most of the information regarding the crime came to the public directly from the pickpockets themselves," he observed (1949:50). Note, for instance, the following comments by friends and neighbors following the conviction of a Westinghouse executive in the heavy electrical-equipment industry conspiracy case. The executive had been reelected vice-president of the United Fund Organization in his town on the day he was sentenced to jail. Said one friend: "I think that the only thing John could be guilty of is doing his job with the same conscientious attitude with which he goes about everything he undertakes." The man's wife was reported in the national press to have "endured the situation with fortitude" and to be "fulfilling her customary civic and social engagements" (United Press International, Feb. 16, 1961).

For traditional kinds of offenders, similar processes are at work, of course. The pickpocket loses little prestige among his peers when he is arrested, except in terms of the presumed absence of adequate skill or luck that led to his downfall. It is forceful reiteration by entrenched persons which leads him to regard himself as a "criminal" rather than as, say, a Robin Hood who has taken ill-gotten wealth from the rich and undeserving and, ultimately, redistributed it among the poor and God-favored. As the definition of "crime" becomes more politicized in the United States (see Schwendinger & Schwendinger, 1970), however, traditional kinds of offenders may be enabled to view themselves in the same manner as avocational criminals. Rape of a white woman by a black man (Cleaver, 1968), for instance, could reasonably and perhaps convincingly be regarded as retaliation for prior humiliation, much as some shoplifters maintain their self-esteem by pointing out that it is only the large and well-insured stores from which they steal (Smigel, 1956).

Studies that scale the heinousness of specific offenses in terms of public opinion, in the manner of the work done by Sellin and Wolfgang (1964), and then determine the consequences of such definitions on the self-image of particular kinds of offenders might contribute to a better understanding of the dynamics of avocational offending and its consequences. Changes over time in social definitions and the implications of such changes could also fruitfully be explored. Kadish (1963), for instance, has suggested that many avocational offenses currently are viewed with "moral neutrality," and that this view makes demands for stringent enforcement of the relevant statutes and harsh punishment of their violators both incongruous and unfeasible. The situation could be altered, Kadish suggests, by "inculcating the sentiment of moral disapproval in the community" regarding those acts the propagandist thinks deserving of tougher treatment. Stricter enforcement and vivid mass media portrayal of the "horror" of such offenses could contribute, of course, to growing moral disapproval. The difficulty arises in changing public opinion and law-enforcement practices independently, so that both can escalate congruently against behaviors which are deemed socially destructive. A further difficulty lies in predicting the full costs and consequences of such a course once it is set.

Source of Income

The self-image component of avocational crime is closely related to the second definitional element, that concerned with the fact that avocational criminals derive most of their income and prestige from legal behavior. This immeasurably aids them in continuing to see themselves as respectable and honorable folk. The matter does not concern only the proportional amount of time devoted to law-abiding and criminal activity, however, but also involves those aspects of a person's being and behavior which come to define all of him. A man who commits armed robbery offenses, and who also spends much of his time as a factory worker, sandpapering furniture, will be defined most fundamentally as an "armed robber." A streetwalking prostitute who devotes most of her nonworking hours to seeing to it that her children are well raised will be called a "whore," not a "mother." Conversely, a man who violates tie-in agreement laws or who carries on outlawed insider transactions will be defined as a "businessman" or as a "stockbroker," and a woman from Oak Park with four children who steals regularly at Marshall Field's will be identified as a "suburban housewife." The anomalous and seemingly discordant nature of the legal and illegal activities may be regarded in part as the reason for the varied identifications. Suburban housewives who shoplift (and are caught at it) are relatively rare. But this hardly stands up logically; furniture sandpaperers who are armed robbers are not very common either.

The fundamental phenomenon at work appears to be an extension of the American tendency to believe that "evil causes evil." Crime is "bad"; high prestige in the corporate hierarchy is "good." It is incongruous, surprising, and interesting when good things are associated with bad things, when Richard Cory (but not Joe Heroin-addict) commits suicide. The juxtaposition is newsworthy, a matter of human interest. Witness, for example, the difficulties Americans have had in rearranging their etiological thinking to incorporate the fact that quiet, withdrawn individuals—Lee Harvey Oswald, Sirhan Sirhan, James Earl Ray, and Arthur Bremer—are the major assassins of contemporary times (Rensberger, 1972). A striking illustration of this theme is found in Winick's (1961) pre-facto investigation of the traits that college students believed would mark New York's "Mad Bomber" when he was caught. Responses concentrated on a variety of intense social and psychological aberrations. Few persons thought that the Bomber would prove to be nothing more exceptional than an old man with a grudge against the gas company.

Ralph Nader has elegantly made the point that traditional offenders no less than avocational offenders devote most of their time and talents to pursuits other than crime. Nader had been castigating the automobile industry for acts which he believed constituted criminal negligence. He was interrupted by Senator Stevens of Alaska, who maintained that Nader was not giving adequate credit to American industry for its many "outstanding achievements." "Do you give credit to a burglar," Nader asked rhetorically, "because he doesn't burglarize 99 percent of the time?" (*Los Angeles Times,* May 11, 1971).

This is not to say that the distinction between avocational and vocational crime in terms of the source of income and prestige of perpetrators is totally spurious. Corporate officials have a high status in our society; furniture sandpaperers do not. Suburban housewives are considered creditable persons when they tend faithfully to their household chores. When corporate officials steal, the extra income generally supplements what nonetheless is a high, legally earned salary. When suburban housewives steal, the value of what they take is generally less than the funds available to them out of the family's income.

Veblen (1899) supplies an important key to the distinction between the avocational and the traditional criminal. The avocational criminal is engaged in "conspicuous consumption," pursuing an activity that by general social standards is superfluous and even redundant, and therefore admirable by its very wastefulness. For a doctor to steal an extra $10,000 a year through illegal fee-splitting, when his lawful annual income is already $80,000, seems to many people more awesome than woesome. Avocational criminal acts that do not even provide financial reward for their perpetrators appear almost altruistic, dazzling by their very selflessness and needlessness. The electrical-equipment conspirators, for instance, attempted to define themselves to the public (and to the sentencing judge) as persons fundamentally most interested in maintaining stable prices, because such prices would allow employees who might otherwise have to be fired to retain their jobs. The clandestine nature of the price-fixing arrangements, and the obvious sense of wrongdoing associated with them tended, however, to undercut the force of these rationalizations, and allowed the judge to offer an alternative explanation:

> They were torn between conscience and an approved corporate policy, with the rewarding objectives of promotion, comfortable security, and large salaries. They were the organization, or company, man; the conformist who goes along with his superiors and finds balm for his conscience in additional comforts and security of his place in the corporate setup (Geis, 1967:146).

Nonetheless, the conspirators apparently suffered little loss of social standing. Typical was the General Electric executive who went from his brief term in jail to the vice-presidency (and soon thereafter to the presidency) of another firm at an annual salary of about $75,000.

Americans, most of whom are fundamentally Marxists (in the sense of their ubiquitous belief that man is basically an economic creature, and that all men have their price), find it difficult to condemn the well-to-do criminal who yearns for an even greater share of that which is available. The déclassé criminal, however, is a competitor and a threat, and to allow him a noncriminal definition is to grant legitimacy to roles (pool hustler, factory worker, welfare case) that might undercut the status of the defining agent, and particularly might raise the etiological specter slumbering in the idea that evil (that is, crime) is caused by good, bad, and indifferent circumstances. To strip the avocational criminal of his legitimated status also would serve to endanger the hoped-for immutability of the defining agent's own position.

The Issue of Deterrence

It is considered axiomatic that criminal justice sanctions have particular success when they are brought to bear upon avocational criminals. It is not that the self-image of the avocational criminal suffers dramatically, nor that he loses status and income, but rather it is a matter of "relative deprivation." The deprivation of the avocational criminal, once he is apprehended, is unexpected, uncommon, awkward, and inconvenient. It necessitates a reconciliation between common-sense definitions of his behavior and his rationalizations for it, a process generally unnecessary for the traditional offender, who finds no great discrepancy between what is happening and what he had anticipated: "Blackmen born in the U.S. and fortunate enough to live past the age of eighteen are conditioned to accept the inevitability of prison" (Jackson, 1970:9). Perhaps the most telling insight into this process comes from a study of the German concentration camp survivors (Luchterhand, 1952), which found that Communist prisoners, prepared for their fate, survived relatively well in captivity, while Jews, concerned with making sense of their condition, suffered extraordinary stress and disorganization.

Statements suggesting the efficacy of criminal justice sanctions against avocational offenders are commonplace. An early, colorful thesis is that of Ross (Herling, 1962:289), who believed that the "brake of prison walls" represented the best approach to controlling "criminaloid" business and professional men—the "slippery wheels" of the society. In part, the presumed impact of sanctions rests on the fact that continuing success in the upperworld is dependent upon at least a facade of respectability. A former head of the Federal Trade Commission, seeking more effective regulation, thought he had located the point of maximum leverage: "The Achilles heel of the advertising profession," he said, "is that you worship at the altar of the positive image" (*New York Times*, Feb. 10, 1966).

A recent case illustrates this point. Merrill Lynch, a brokerage house, had been accused of passing along "insider" information to favored stockholders about heavy losses by the Douglas Aircraft Company. Tipped off, these customers sold 190,000 shares of Douglas stock a few days before public announcement of the company's financial situation, avoiding losses and/or reaping profits of $4.5 million. At the same time that it was telling its big institutional investors to unload the Douglas stock, Merrill Lynch was peddling the tainted merchandise to some of its smaller clients. Called before the Securities and Exchange Commission, Merrill Lynch immediately filed an order asking that the Commission "be restrained from engaging further in publicity activities concerning the issue in the proceedings" (*Wall Street Journal,* Sept. 24, 1968). "There was a good deal of sympathy for Merrill Lynch from its rival member firms on the New York Stock Exchange," a newspaper reported. Sources were quoted as saying: "We think this is bad for all of us in the securities industry in terms of our public image. After all, this thing happened to the firm that is the pillar of morality" (*New York Times,* Dec. 1, 1968).

The issue has been summed up by Llewellyn in the following terms:

> A great deal of confused thinking has been done on the deterrent effect of severe punishments. They may be futile in dealing with the professional criminal. They may be footless in preventing crimes of passion. But when the question is one of urging the great well-meaning public into conduct which happens to be slightly inconvenient, severe punishments in the offing are capable of effect (1962:403–4).

Then, Llewellyn adds, most importantly: "The effect may come at too high a price; that is another matter" (p. 404).

Concerning avocational offenders who violate the income tax laws, James Bennett, a former head of the federal Bureau of Prisons, has noted: "The doctrine of deterrence, while it hasn't worked very well for some types of crime and offenders, has had a most benign effect on those who do not like to pay taxes" (1955:537). The best statement by far on the subject is that of Cameron in regard to avocational shoplifters:

> Again and again store people explain to pilferers that they are under arrest as thieves, that they will, in the normal course of events, be taken in a police van to jail, held in jail until bond is raised, and tried in court before a judge and sentenced. Interrogation procedures at the store are directed specifically and consciously toward breaking down any illusion that the shoplifter may possess that his behavior is merely regarded as "naughty" or "bad." . . . It becomes increasingly clear to the pilferer that he is considered a thief and is in imminent danger of being hauled into court and publicly exhibited as such. This realization is often accompanied by dramatic changes in attitudes and by severe emotional disturbance (1964:160–62).

A critical issue in regard to deterrence of avocational offenders concerns the need to reconcile two divergent lines of reasoning in criminological thinking and writing. The first insists that there are too many crimes, and that many acts performed by powerless individuals are being defined as criminal so that lower-class persons can be kept in their place. Such reasoning suggests that the criminal law (like the psychiatric ethos [Szasz, 1963]) is often a weapon of the entrenched, used arbitrarily to punish behavior threatening to the status hegemony. To ameliorate this situation, the argument goes, there ought to be, at a minimum, a decriminalization of victimless crimes, such as prostitution and gambling (Schur, 1965; Geis, 1972). Also, there ought to be milder responses to offenses most commonly performed by persons who have less than a fair share of what the society has to offer. Prison sentences and other forms of harsh retaliation, it is said, only further alienate and brutalize traditional kinds of offenders.

In regard to avocational offenders, the reasoning has tended to take an almost diametrically opposed form. Since such offenders tend to be notably responsive to criminal sanctions—they are said to become more conforming rather than more alienated after imprisonment—such sanctions ought to be employed more often. Protagonists of this view cite the responses of the General Electrical executives to a congressional committee:

> "They would never get me to do it again. . . . I would starve before I would do it again," one conspirator said. Another . . . was asked: "Suppose your superior tells you to resume the meetings, will they be resumed?" "No, sir," he answered with feeling. "I would leave the company rather than participate in the meetings again" (Geis, 1973: 195).

It is argued, in this respect, that "crime in the suites" is massively underpunished, while "crime in the streets" is viciously overpunished, both in terms of fairness and in regard to the usefulness of the punishment.

Some justification for tougher responses to avocational crime may be found in the fact that the consequences of such behavior can be said to be more deleterious than those ensuing from traditional offenses. Durkheim (1895) has argued that traditional crime tends to cement a society by providing object lessons to the well-behaved about the consequences of aberrance. Avocational crime, on the other hand, is said to dent severely the social fabric by creating distrust and encouraging rationalizations for deviance. On the former point, the report of the President's Commission on Law Enforcement and Administration of Justice maintained that "white-collar crime affects the whole moral climate of our society. Derelictions by corporations and their managers, who usually occupy leadership positions in their communities, establish an example which tends to erode the moral base of the law" (1967a:104). In regard to rationalizations by traditional offenders said to have their source in avocational crime, the following hypothesis has been put forward:

> If the affluent flagrantly disregard the law, the poor and the deprived will follow their leadership. If the indigent who is brought into the police station rightly believes that the affluent are going unpunished for their crimes, then we have not only failed to achieve our goal of equal justice, but we have also created the conditions that breed further disrespect for the law (Dallos, 1969).

This issue has not been confronted with much sophistication in criminological literature, and has been ignored in experimental research. The tendency has been for the criminologist to manifest a compassionate concern with the fate of the traditional offender (though condemning his behavior), and to demonstrate a rather fiery, almost biblical anger against the depredations of the avocational offender, especially when the latter is located in the business and professional classes.

Definitional Summary

Each of the three components of the definition of avocational crime—the self-image of the offender, the sources of his income and status, and his deterrability—pinpoints what seem to be relevant and differentiating characteristics of a separable kind of criminal activity. Such distinctions between avocational and other kinds of crime, however, also test skills in conceptual and semantic discrimination. Political criminals, for instance, may meet some of the avocational crime criteria, but they are apt to remain undeterrable. Indeed, they are often greatly encouraged by public unmasking and recrimination. Murder—to take another offense—varies in a number of respects from avocational crime, while sharing some of its attributes. Murderers most usually agree with the defining agents that the act is not a decent sort of thing, and they tend to be inclined (though this has not yet been adequately studied) to find exculpatory explanations for their behavior, insisting that it was a response to undue provocation or to similar kinds of situational imperatives. These explanations seem to be more intensely held than those of the avocational criminal, perhaps because murder involves such heavy condemnation. In this sense—though again the evidence for clear judgment is not yet available—murder is probably much less deterrable than avocational crime through the process of public labeling.

Classifying offenders in terms of the three specified criteria is, of course, but one manner in which avocational violators of the criminal law can be approached. The classificatory system chosen, it should be recognized, focuses attention on certain facets of the behavior and forecloses examination of others. More importantly, it tends to insist upon particular kinds of value conclusions. Emphasis on the deterrability of avocational crimes, as a defined characteristic, almost inevitably suggests social policies which can be undertaken to reduce the number of such offenses. If another classificatory scheme were employed—one, say, that concentrated on the consequences of acts, whether criminal or noncriminal, then the policy implications would be quite different. In that case, the implication might well be that there ought to be consistency in the application of criminal justice sanctions, and that harmful acts ought to be equivalently outlawed. Thus, when Nader asks college students: "Do you know that you can be arrested for urinating in the street, but industry is free to pollute the nation's rivers and lakes?" (Buckhorn, 1972:160), the organizing principle employed runs directly to the value conclusion sought.

Frames of reference and values, of course, are neither self-evidently correct nor self-evidently erroneous. But, as we shall note below in regard to Sutherland's work on white-collar crime, such commitments can be deceptive if they are unduly camouflaged or presented for other than what they are. Science demands objectivity and honesty in handling materials; ideological sophistication demands self-awareness and forthcomingness in regard to the subject discussed and the approach employed. The definition of avocational crime in such terms should be seen as based upon, among other things, a belief in the doctrine of *noblesse oblige*, that those who have the most of what society has to offer owe a greater obligation than the dispossessed to refrain from hurting and exploiting others. It has elements of vengeance embedded in it, implicit in the suggestion that the destruction of the self-image of avocational offenders as honest and decent citizens is a useful social enterprise. Most fundamentally, however, the ideological thesis is that society ought to outlaw acts which can, with logic, be shown directly to hurt and deprive innocent people—armed robbery, pollution, burglary, insider transactions, false advertising, rape. Ultimately, the costs and benefits of diverse approaches to such questions need to be considered in terms of eddying effects and countervailing consequences. It has been suggested, for example, that employee theft ought to be allowed to proceed discreetly, on the ground that it contributes to employee morale and that attempts to control it are more expensive than the loss of merchandise. Criminology, at the moment, is far from having at hand solid experimental data in regard to such policy matters, and has only barely begun to look at the skeletons in its ideological closet.

WHITE-COLLAR CRIME

Very few pieces of research have been published on white-collar crime during the past two decades; perhaps an average of one original investigation annually, plus an occasional reiteration or reinterpretation of previous work and theory. The absence of cumulative, block-building work on white-collar crime is obvious from any bibliographic search (Tompkins, 1967; Geis, 1968). This deficiency exists despite the movement in criminology toward social concern, and the obvious muckraking potentialities in exploring white-collar crime.

Reasons for the sparse amount of writing on white-collar crime are manifold. For one thing, etiological explanation, an enterprise accorded high status in sociological work, is inordinately difficult in regard to white-collar crime. Standard kinds of correlative research (involving variables such as age, socioeconomic background, and race) are obviously inappropriate for understanding white-collar offenders and offenses. Psychopathy and/or an inability to defer gratification do not provide much insight into antitrust violations and the pollution of navigable waters. Labeling theory, concentrating on the social processes which lead to the criminalization of certain kinds of behavior and to the consequences of such processes, seems singularly awkward when brought to bear upon white-collar crime. White-collar offenders often are labeled. A General Electric official, for instance, complained that he was exposed to "relentless publicity" (*New York Times*, Mar. 17, 1961), and he said that the newspapers "never laid off for a second. They have used some terms which I don't think are necessary— they don't use the term 'price fixing.' It's always 'price rigging' or trying to make it as sensational as possible" (Geis, 1967:149). But the labeling seems to produce results not in keeping with the dire consequences alleged for it when it is brought to bear upon vocational offenders.

In addition, detailed information regarding white-collar crime is notably difficult to come by. Sociologists, who dominate academic criminology, tend to have some additional training in psychology or anthropology, but to be unacquainted with economic theory and research. Corporate board rooms are generally impervious to first-hand observation; even the Mafia (or whatever that group is) seems to abide more by the spirit of the Freedom of Information Act than does the corporate world. Nobody is tapping the telephones at General Motors, and making the transcripts available to a prurient public. Dossiers on business executives (unlike those on organized criminals) were not made available to staff members of the President's Commission on Law Enforcement and Administration of Justice, and apparently neither the FBI nor the CIA, much less the President's Office for Consumer Affairs, is using undercover agents to infiltrate the Chrysler Corporation or Alcoa to discover what alleged conspiracies are being hatched against the public interest. Organized criminals themselves are sensitive to the discrimination. When Salvatore Bonano, believed to be a leading figure in organized crime, was sentenced, his attorney delivered the following plea for leniency:

> It [Bonano's criminal act] does not speak of the sort of activity where the public screams for protection, Your Honor. I think that in the vernacular the defendant stands before you convicted of having committed a white-collar crime, Your Honor. I most respectfully . . . suggest to the court that he should be sentenced in conformity with people who have been convicted of white-collar crimes, and not be sentenced on the basis of his being Salvatore Bonano (Talese, 1971:479).

What information on white-collar crime becomes available to sociologists from congressional investigations or court cases tends to be fragmentary and rather unresponsive to fine points of criminological theorizing. Corporations often plead *nolo contendere* to criminal charges, a luxury unavailable to robbers and burglars. Such pleas muzzle attempts to accumulate trial information, always a rich data source. Those few white-collar criminals sentenced to correctional facilities tend to be long gone from their cells before the sociological researcher, questionnaire poised, locates them. White-collar criminals too, especially those from the corporate world, are quite as skillful and adept as researchers, so that they can sidestep adroitly the kinds of invidious inquiries that often mark studies of vocational criminals. Further, white-collar criminals can appear forbidding when cocooned in their executive suites, protected from criminologists by condescending secretaries. I was told, for instance, that the corporation officials convicted in the heavy electrical-equipment conspiracy were removed from probation status early because the probation officers complained that it was demeaning for them to have to sit long hours in plush waiting rooms to see their clients in order to determine if they had obeyed the rules since last they had been visited.

White-Collar Crime Ideologically

Not too long ago, but before the "sexual revolution" in the United States, the then–theater critic of the *New York Times* (Kauffmann, 1966) pointed out that social taboos against homosexuality were producing a curious result in the Broadway theater. Large numbers of homosexuals were employed in theater jobs, he noted, and they often would insert gay language, homosexual motifs, and similar kinds of in-group innuendo into plays which on the surface were concerned with heterosexual themes. Audiences at times were confused; often they laughed for the wrong reasons at the wrong times. The joke they thought they understood often was really on them. It was a sly bit of revenge on the part of homosexuals for the censorship and discrimination they suffered. Also, of course, it was a nasty kind of retaliation, subverting and exploiting not only the condemners but also their more innocent theater-going companions.

Much the same kind of subterfuge pervaded the earliest studies of white-collar crime. Such work began in 1939, with the celebrated presidential address on white-collar crime by Edwin H. Sutherland (1940) to the American Sociological Society. Sutherland is the only criminologist ever selected to head the sociological group. In his speech, and later in *White Collar Crime* (1949), Sutherland maintained that his primary—indeed, his only—interest lay in theoretical issues. By the second sentence of the speech, he had begun to establish his ground cover:

> This paper . . . is a comparison of crime in the upper, or white-collar class . . . and crime in the lower class. . . . This comparison is made for the purpose of developing theories of criminal behavior, not for the purpose of muckraking or of reforming anything except criminology (Sutherland, 1940:1).

These statements are patently disingenuous. Sutherland felt an obligation to be "scientific"—this was where sociology was at. His statement was much like the disclaimers of eighteenth-century satirists faced with ostracism and excommunication were their heresies to become manifest.

Very few studies have been done attempting to relate the background of criminologists, such as Sutherland, to their world views and published papers. In part, such biographical probes have not been undertaken because academics tend to live relatively unexciting and uninteresting lives; in part, too, because criminology itself has never been a high-status enterprise, even within the sociological realm, much less in terms of intellectual work in general.

Many of the gaps in the "sociology of knowledge" regarding Sutherland's work on white-collar crime, however, have recently been filled in a doctoral dissertation by Snodgrass (1972). Sutherland, Snodgrass found, was raised in Grand Island, Nebraska, where his father, an ordained Baptist minister, was professor of economics at Grand Island College, a small, conservative school from which Sutherland received his bachelor's degree. Sutherland's background, Snodgrass writes, "was mobile, deeply religious, and intellectual" (1972:221). His father was an austere fundamentalist. In his academic career, Sutherland "for the most part went quietly about researching and offering his tentative explanations, but he could get mad. His repugnance for the crimes of business was restrained for twenty-five years or more until it welled up in him and *White Collar Crime* erupted with a vengeance" (p. 228). But, says Snodgrass, "Sutherland was no radical. . . . Given his agrarian roots, midwestern origins, provincial affiliations, urban resentments, economic education, and Baptist upbringing, he resembled much more the old-time prophet" (p. 229). Sutherland, in short, was not interested in reforms such as the rearrangement of wealth or the restructuring of social classes, but rather in the apprehension of all criminals, regardless of their position in the society.

Definitionally, the concept of white-collar crime has always been something of a mess. This is probably because Sutherland, who gave birth to the concept, had no particular concern with its theoretical integrity. Sutherland was pushing his theory of "differential association," an aggregation of theorems of highly unequal power about human learning which attempts to explain not only white-collar crime, but all criminal behavior. Since the same theory can embrace confidence games, abortion, rape, car theft, embezzling, and antitrust violations with equal hospitality, it mattered little whether any of these phenomena were differentiated from any others with any precision (Geis, 1962). In addition, by keeping his definition loose, Sutherland could put under his microscope a large variety of those business behaviors which he found so offensive.

An early Sutherland definition was that white-collar crime could be defined "approximately" as a "crime committed by a person of respectability and high social status in the course of his occupation" (1949:9). This designation, however, contains a number of problems. Consider, for example, the crimes of two corporate managers, one respected, the other not (say the second is a former organized-crime boss, now gone righteous, but still far from country-club material). Both might commit the same offense in the course of their occupation—perhaps a social security law violation. One of the violators would presumably satisfy Sutherland regarding his credentials as a bona fide white-collar criminal. The second, lacking respectability, would not. Thus, it is neither the act nor the particular statute which has been violated that is the reference point for classification, but rather the social position of the actor.

Nor is Sutherland any more helpful in other elaborations on the definition of white-collar crime. One such attempt appears in an early footnote in his monograph in which he observes that "the term 'white-collar' is used here to refer principally to business managers and executives, in the sense in which it was used by a president of General Motors who wrote *An Autobiography of a White Collar Worker*" (1949:9). But only a year before, Sutherland had said: "The term white-collar is used in the sense in which it was used by President Sloan of General Motors, who wrote a book entitled *The Autobiography of a White Collar Worker*. The term is used more generally to refer to the wage-earning class which wears good clothes at work, such as clerks in stores" (1956:79). Perhaps the matter of Sutherland's indifference to careful definition is best epitomized by the fact that, though he was an unusually meticulous scholar, he missed the title of the source of his definition, which was A. P. Sloan's *Adventures of a White-Collar Man* (1941).

Indeed, Sutherland's most exhaustive discussion of the definitional labyrinths involved in his concept of white-collar crime seems like a parody of pedantic obscurantism:

> Perhaps it should be repeated that "white-collar" (upper) and "lower" classes merely designate persons of high- and low-socioeconomic status. Income and amount of money involved in the crime are not the sole criteria. Many persons of "low" socioeconomic status are "white-collar" criminals in the sense that they are well-dressed, well-educated, and have high incomes; but "white-collar" as used in this paper means "respected," "socially accepted and approved," "looked up to." Some people in this class may not be well-dressed or well-educated or have high incomes, although the "upper" classes usually exceed the "lower" classes in these respects, as well as in social status (1940:44).

The semantic waters have been so muddied by Sutherland that today it seems wisest to move upstream rather than to attempt a purification project. The difficulty of such a move lies in the fact that the term "white-collar crime" and the spirit it represents were magnetic enough to draw the concept deeply into criminological and popular thought. The foreign literature nicely illustrates the appeal of Sutherland's formulation, with direct translation of the phrase "white-collar crime" into *crime en col blanc* (Normandeau, 1965; Kellens, 1968; Pinatel, 1970), *criminalitá in colletti bianchi* (Loschiavo, 1963); *weisse-kragen-kriminalität* (Binder, 1962); and *el delito du cuello blanco* (Sutherland, 1969). In the Netherlands, a recent article sought to find "a good Dutch word" for white-collar crime, and suggested that the editors of the journal extend a prize for the best effort (Weringh, 1969). Mannheim's (1965) judgment is undoubtedly correct: If there were a Nobel Prize for criminology, Sutherland would have received it for his work on white-collar crime.

Notwithstanding, the need for definitional clarification is vital. The first step might be to delineate statutes which can reasonably be regarded as referring to "economic crime" or "occupational crime" or to "avocational acts," and to bring to an end concentration upon the class position of perpetrators. White-collar crimes can be committed by persons in all social classes. New York taxi drivers sometimes illegally keep their flags up when they are riding in the suburbs, which allows them to skim part of the fare without the likelihood of being detected. Truck drivers sometimes keep two sets of books, one for the Interstate Commerce Commission, the other for themselves, so that they can arrange their schedules to maximize the length of stopovers in attractive places. These behaviors are much like those of "upper class" and "respectable" law violators, both in their conception and in the official response to them, and they are among the kinds of events that need to be taken into account when criminology extends research into forms of lawbreaking other than that tabulated in FBI reports and that castigated as white-collar crime.

In Sutherland's Wake

The work on white-collar crime that has been published since Sutherland broke ground has tended to be idiosyncratic rather than systematic. A researcher gains access to certain materials—as Clinard (1952) did during his service with the Office of Price Administration in the second World War—or he settles upon a thesis or dissertation topic, in the manner that Hartung (1950), Newman (1957), and Quinney (1963) did, and investigates a very special field. Afterwards, his attention shifts elsewhere, perhaps because the pickings are easier. Certainly, the logistics of sociological publication discourage investigation into avocational white-collar crime, since such work does not readily lend itself to statistical analysis and hard-data reports. The white-collar crime researcher might write an article, then a book, and later perhaps a general overview of the theory and substantive content of work on white-collar crime. Then he moves along. A striking finding from an inventory of the literature on white-collar crime is that no more than two or three researchers have done more than half a handful of pieces on the subject.

It is not that there is a dearth of hypotheses to be investigated. Sutherland himself threw out hunches with almost profligate abandon. He hypothesized, for instance, that white-collar offenders are scornful of government officials and processes, that they share social and economic views held by the judges and prosecuting officials, that they are treated tenderly by the mass media, that the pleas of upper executives that they are unaware of lawbreaking beneath them are nothing more than alibis similar to those of vocational offenders. Other ideas worth pursuit appear like overripe fruit in the literature on white-collar crime: Cressey (1953) has suggested that embezzlers are motivated not by wine, women, and song, but by nonsharable problems, suitable rationalizations, and the cognitive connection between their difficulty and its possible resolution. The idea has never been tested elsewhere or replicated on embezzlers. Quinney (1963) suggests that the attitudes of professionals about their work might predict their behavior in regard to the legal constraints under which it is carried on. Lane (1953) has offered a number of ideas about the structure of companies and their tendency to violate the law. Aubert (1952) has suggested that researchers might profitably concentrate upon legislation and the public's interpretation of it when attempting to understand white-collar crime. Ball (1960) offers the idea that investigation of objective circumstances and subjective responses to such circumstances might be informative in regard to the emergence of offenses such as violations of rent-control laws.

In the long run, studies of the white-collar crime segment of avocational crime will have to be incorporated into the mainstream of behavioral science research, drawing intellectual nourishment from the diverse disciplines that enter into study of criminal behavior. In the short run, though, there is a pressing need for accumulation of case studies, for hypothesis testing, and for the kind of research that moves forward by careful, additive processes. The analogy of Lewis and Stewart is aptly chosen: "Private enterprise remains extraordinarily private. . . . We know more about the motives, habits, and most intimate arcana of primitive peoples in New Guinea . . . than we do of the denizens of executive suites in Unilever, Citroen, or General Electric" (1961: 111–12). It is ethnographies of white-collar and other forms of avocational crime that are, at the moment, so pressingly required to advance our understanding of these behaviors.

Areas of Insight

Elsewhere (Geis, 1974), I have noted areas which the study of white-collar crime enlightens. Among them, the following seem particularly noteworthy:

1. White-collar crime challenges the more banal kinds of explanations of criminal activity. To say that poverty "causes" crime, for instance, fails utterly to account for widespread lawbreaking by persons who are extraordinarily affluent.

2. White-collar crime indicates the distribution of power in our society. An examination of the statute books shows what kinds of occupational acts have come to be included within the criminal code and what go unproscribed. The enactment of laws curbing the activities of certain persons demonstrates that, at least for a moment, other persons with other interests had the power to prevail legislatively.

3. White-collar crime portrays the manner in which power is exercised in our society. A review of upperworld violations and the manner in which they are prosecuted and punished tells who is able to control what in American society and the extent to which such control is effective.

4. White-collar crime provides an indication of the degree of hypocrisy present in a society. Such hypocrisy may be seen as leverage by means of which the society may be forced toward congruence between its verbal commitments and its actual conduct, much as Myrdal (1944) insisted that the "dilemma" in the United States between conduct toward minorities and democratic values exerted incessant pressure toward a reconciliation along the lines of the values. In regard to white-collar crime, hypocrisy exists when fraud among the lower classes is viewed with distaste and punished, while upper-class deception is countenanced and defined as nothing more malevolent than "shrewd business practice."

5. White-collar crime illustrates changes in social and business life. Thus, the old-time grocer, weighing his merchandise by hand and dealing on a personal basis with his customers, probably had less inclination and less opportunity to defraud. Today's supermarkets, engaged essentially in the rental of shelf space to manufacturers, epitomize impersonality, with consequences for the emergence of a new form of crime, that involving consumer fraud.

6. White-collar crime furnishes material helpful for an understanding of changes in social values. Reviews of legislative enactments, for instance, show that an emerging "right to life" doctrine is being enunciated in the United States. Laws demanding that foods be uncontaminated and that pollution be controlled represent the outcome of an ethos insisting that man be accorded every reasonable opportunity to remain alive and healthy until cut down by uncontrollable forces. In the future, if support grows for enunciation of the right of each human being to achieve his full potential, new forms of white-collar crime will be legislated.

These postulates, as well as those noted earlier, constitute the kinds of general propositions that would emerge in greater detail, with additional refinements, or with negating counterstatements, were the investigation of white-collar crime to proceed at the same pace that exploration of many forms of vocational crime now takes.

The Nader Phenomenon

No discussion of white-collar crime would be complete without consideration of the work of Ralph Nader and his associates. Nader's efforts have intersected directly with those of the criminological establishment only once (1969), when he briefly reviewed the President's Commission work (1967b) in regard to the "few words on business crime" that were "tucked away in the ninth and final Task Force Report." Nader used the contents of the report as a springboard for one of his favorite themes: that there ought to be more, and more severe, criminal penalties for corporate offenders. In this instance, he criticized the work of a lobbyist for the automobile industry who had convinced Congress to remove criminal penalties from the auto safety legislation enacted in 1966.

There is a particularly interesting sentence in the Nader piece on the Crime Commission's effort: "Scratch the image of any industry and unsavory practices become visible" (1969:140). The Nader statement is strikingly similar to a much quoted observation of Sutherland: "White-collar criminality is found in every occupation, as can be discovered readily in casual conversation with a representative of an occupation by asking him, 'What crooked practices are found in your occupation?' " (1940:3). The parallel between Nader and Sutherland is, in fact, much more fundamental. Nader, like Sutherland, is strongly opposed to what he regards as the trend in the United States toward "corporate socialism," a condition in which important decisions about the welfare of the country are made secretly and together by corporate powers. Unlike Sutherland, however, Nader feels no obligation to surround his views with a theoretical cushion; indeed, he has been scornful of such efforts, as when he talks about "the leisure of the theory class" (McCarry, 1972:216). Nader's underlying philosophy is preeminently clear. Like Lord Acton, he believes that power tends to corrupt and absolute power to corrupt absolutely. The duty of the involved citizen for Nader is to see to it that a keen eye is kept upon government, business, and the professions, the major locales of power, so that they fulfill their public obligations.

Nader's work is instructive for criminologists. For one thing, it demonstrates the possibility of acquiring substantial data on government and business processes, if enough doggedness goes into the effort. It indicates, too, I think, how the locus and structure of academic criminology in the United States have often been responsible for the direction and tone of its work and conclusions. Note might be taken, for instance, that virtually all of the leading criminologists in the United States have been midwesterners located at the Big Ten land-grant universities—men such as Vold at Minnesota, Sutherland at Indiana, Gillin at Wisconsin, Taft at Illinois. Yet the centers of power in the United States are Washington, D.C., and New York City. Washington proper has no major university. In New York City, scholars at so prestigious an institution as Columbia University barely deign to work in the field of crime. Merton, for instance, has been publicly critical of what he saw in himself in the earlier part of his career as a "slum-encouraged provincialism of thinking that the primary subject-matter of sociology was centered on such peripheral problems of social life as divorce and juvenile delinquency" (1957:17).

Nader, working in Washington, has access to records, officials, agencies, and similar on-site sources of information about criminal activity of an avocational nature. The American criminologists who set the framework for the field more often than not had to be satisfied with studies of prisoners—penal institutions were in the hinterlands too—and with relating criminal behavior to such things as race, sex, age, and urban-rural locale.

Nader, like Sutherland, is a muckraker, with command of vibrant language and a drive toward drawing incessant parallels between traditional and avocational crime. "Smogging" is compared to "mugging," for instance, and "smogging" is said to have taken on the proportions of a "massive crime wave" which has been neglected by federal and state compilations on lawbreaking (Nader, 1970:viii). Typical of Nader's approach is the following juxtaposition of the response by official agencies to diverse behaviors:

> The Chicago Seven kept twelve lawyers busy in the Justice Department. I've yet to hear of *one* of Attorney General Mitchell's lawyers concerning himself with the Detroit Four. GM and Ford are criminals. This is serious enough to hand over to Vice President Agnew for action—but before he becomes interested we'll have to find polluters who wear beards and sandals (McCarry, 1972:306).

Particularly interesting also has been Nader's exploration of alternative sanctions to be employed against avocational offenders, given the fact that there is an obvious reluctance in the United States to employ the full force of the criminal law. Nader has recommended the suspension of corporate managers and board members from their jobs, temporary bans on corporate advertising because of deceptive practices, required publication of violations to inform consumers who have been harmed or deceived by culpable conduct, and imposition of environmental bankruptcy for a company continually contaminating its neighbors' environment (Nader, 1971:xviii).

He has also begun to advocate measures against violators similar to those reportedly used in China. Nader has been impressed, he notes, that the gap between people in China appears to have been lessened by programs such as that which insists that college professors take a month or more each year to help harvest the crops. Nader envisages such an approach, coerced in regard to corporate executives who commit crimes, as creating heightened empathy, much in the manner tried by the women of Leningrad, during the city's bombardment, who led a captured German pilot to an area where a mound of bodies lay and screamed at him: "Do you see what you did, you murderer? Do you see?" (Salisbury, 1969:445). As Nader puts the matter:

> One of the best solutions is to get people at the top of institutions to go through what their victims go through. The coal magnate should work a couple of weeks in the coal mine each year (McCarry, 1972:315).

Elsewhere, Nader has set forth a similar version of the proposal:

> I've always thought that it was a good idea for every head of an organization to spend two weeks on the line—for the president of the copper company to spend two weeks in the smelter; for the president of a coal mine to spend two weeks in the mines next to the rank and file. People at the top must find out what is going on rather than relying on a sanitized memo from a public relations man. If people learn by experience, there is hope of toning down some of the insensitivities of society (Buckhorn, 1972:297).

At the moment, these ideas remain in an embryonic state, but they have a high priority in Nader's thinking. For criminologists, they represent an unexplored area of investigation.

SHOPLIFTING

The character of published writings on avocational crime changes dramatically as the reviewer moves from the literature regarding white-collar offenses to that concerned with shoplifting. An important source of the distinction is that the latter crime has a specific legal definition. The elements of shoplifting, *Corpus Juris Secundum* notes, are generally "the willful taking of possession of goods offered for sale by a mercantile establishment without the knowledge or consent of the seller, with the intention of converting such goods to one's own use without having paid the purchase price" (1968, vol. 52a:406). The same source points out that in some jurisdictions a distinction is made between amateur and professional shoplifters so that the possession of shoplifting paraphernalia, such as a "booster box," constitutes sufficient evidence of the intent to commit the crime to support conviction.

This definitional exactness allows a relatively homogenized approach to the subject. Thus, the traits of apprehended shoplifters may be tabulated—a favorite criminological enterprise—and various ideas may be put forward to explain the disproportionate number of women, blacks, whites, young, disturbed, old, and men in the ranks of shoplifters taking different kinds of items from different kinds of stores at different times of the day and year (Arieff & Bowie, 1947; Gibbens & Prince, 1962; Robin, 1963; Cameron, 1964; Won & Yamamoto, 1968; Brady & Mitchell, 1971). Hypotheses may be checked: for example, research can be conducted bearing on the idea that shoplifting is a psychiatrically symbolic offense, demonstrated by the fact that women tend unduly to steal umbrellas, which are phallic symbols. The finding that women do indeed steal more umbrellas than other items equally represented in department stores, but that they do so only when it is raining outside (Rolph, 1966) suggests that at least the testable portion of the hypothesis is in error.

A prime difficulty with shoplifting studies concerns determination with a semblance of accuracy of the "dark figure" of the offense, that is, the number of episodes that occur in proportion to the number against which diverse kinds of official actions are taken. Sellin (1937) pointed out that there was a great deal more shoplifting handled unofficially in Philadelphia each year than the total of all recorded thefts in the city. But the important—and still untaken—next step is to measure and compare the apprehensions against the total number of acts taking place. A first move in this direction is the reported result by Management Safeguards, Inc., a consulting organization, that one in every fifteen shoppers observed closely in a variety of settings helped himself or herself to merchandise (*New York Times*, Dec. 21, 1970).

In part, research on shoplifting has avoided the issue of representativeness of its study populations by implying that shoplifting is rather uniformly committed and that apprehension, and particularly prosecution, represents the end process of discriminatory tactics that contribute to the labeling of disenfranchised persons as deviants. Robin (1963) has noted that among apprehended shoplifters, blacks and poor persons tended to be prosecuted more often than members of other groups who also had been caught. Recently, however, Cohen and Stark (n.d.) have reported, through the use of factor-analysis techniques, that the value of merchandise stolen and the presumed likelihood of the offender repeating the offense (based on the assumption that the unemployed are heavier risks) were more explanatory of discriminatory enforcement than race alone, though they grant that the prosecution rationale may itself camouflage initial feelings of hostility toward outgroup members. The same authors attempted to gain some insight into the differential apprehension rate by calculating the ethnic and sex mixes among the shoppers in the stores they investigated. This procedure, while an advance over more primitive methods which compare the ratio of apprehended shoplifters to that of groups they represent in the general population or in the immediate store area, still falls far short of a true delineation of the universe of shoplifters, particularly in terms of such things as the amount of time spent shopping, kinds of purchases made, store-selection patterns, and amounts spent.

Further approaches to the measurement of the extent of shoplifting designed to place apprehended violators into a more exact context might be had from calculations of the so-called "inventory shrinkage" of a store (Edwards, 1958), that is, of the difference between the amount that sale of goods ought to realize and the amount actually registered. In this way the sums taken by shoplifters, multiplied by the amounts they indicate they have stolen over a stipulated period of time, might begin to provide a sense of the hidden segment of the shoplifting iceberg. The difficulty here is that many stores do not differentiate between losses from sales, such as reduced prices on damaged merchandise, and losses from theft, and they cannot separate employee theft—said to be 75 percent of the total theft loss (President's Commission,

1967b)—from shoplifting. In addition, employees in some stores will appropriate merchandise for their own use and then make up the difference in sales figures by overcharging unwary customers for their legitimate purchases (Bennett, 1968).

The most pronounced ideological element in shoplifting studies, aside from attempts to demonstrate biased enforcement strategies, lies in efforts to relate the ethos of self-service salesmanship and advertising approaches to the level of shoplifting activity. An expression of this view is reported by Gibbens and Prince (1962) that a store in Engand sets out to achieve a certain level of shoplifting as a demonstration of the adequate lure of goods on display. If the shoplifting rate falls below the anticipated level, the store rearranges its shelves and counters, on the assumption that they are not offering sufficient temptation for impulse buying—and stealing.

It should be worthwhile to determine how public attitudes bear upon the introjection of self-image ingredients by the shoplifting offender. Longitudinal studies of the careers of shoplifters would be useful, and experimental situations in which different kinds of case dispositions, done randomly (presuming ethical objections can be met), were surveyed to determine the impacts of varying social responses to the criminal behavior. Given the inordinate amount of discretion now exercised in handling shoplifting, some regularization of procedures might prove particularly valuable for providing information not only on such matters as recidivism, but, rather more importantly, on the consequences for the total life pattern of the individuals involved. Like so much else in American life, the pettiness of amateur shoplifting—the trivial sums and banal items usually involved—make it a derogated enterprise when seen from above, and particularly when compared to the impressive performance and high rewards of many white-collar offenders. Note, for instance, the class-consciousness and condescension of the following observation, which was undoubtedly intended as nothing more than a good-natured and rather sympathetic account of the variety of persons who are caught shoplifting:

> They display all human emotions from the humor of the old Cockney lady stuffing sweaters into her bag under the keen eye of a store detective and who charmingly advises the store detective to help herself because if she doesn't take them someone else will, to the utter tragedy of a person such as a vicar's wife from a small country village who is tempted by the attractive things beyond the husband's stipend and who has to return to her village after her well-publicized conviction (Cox, 1968:425).

The apparent overrepresentation of women in shoplifting episodes—note the sex of both offenders in the anecdote above—merits more detailed attention. Cameron (1964) reports that 74 percent of the shoplifters in her study were women and Robin (1963) lists the total for his investigation at 60 percent. Given the generally low proportion of women found committing most traditional kinds of crime, exploration of the female shoplifting pattern should help in further explaining socialization patterns in the United States. The role played by the female shoplifter in domestic situations, her relationship to her husband, if she is married, the training of her own children— all of these represent unexplored facets of shoplifting behavior. In regard to heroin use by women, Chein et al. have offered the "simple hypothesis . . . that females are less likely than males to express their tension in ways that are detectably and flagrantly violative of the prevailing social codes" (1964:300). Researchers should be interested in determining if female shoplifting meets this test and, if so, why certain women rather than others choose it for their purposes.

An initial venture into assessing public behavior in regard to shoplifting is the recently reported work of Gelfand et al. (1973). The experimenters staged simulated shoplifting incidents in two large drug-variety stores, one in an upper-income, suburban area, and the second in a lower-income, central-city location. Their confederate—a 21-year-old coed who pretended to be shoplifting—varied her clothing between hippie, youth-culture dress and conventional clothing. The girl first attempted to attract a customer's attention by dropping a small article, rattling a package, or reaching for an item located very close to the shopper. The experimenters, who videotaped the proceedings from an observation window about fifteen feet above the floor of the stores, notified the girl by means of a radio hidden in her purse that the other customer was now aware of her. She then blatantly removed several items of merchandise and stuffed them into her purse. After the girl and the other customer had left the store, the experimenters interviewed the customers, including those who had and those who had not reported the girl to store authorities. Only 26 percent of the customers said that they had been aware of the girl taking goods; the remainder said that they were intent upon their own business and did not notice her. Of the 26 percent who reported observing her, 30 percent told store personnel about what they had witnessed. The girl's appearance did not prove to be related to whether she would be reported for her "crime," but she was more often reported by men, by higher socioeconomic-status shoppers, and by middle-aged compared with younger and aged individuals. Persons raised in rural environments reported the girl more often than those who had been brought up in large cities. One customer, the study deviant in terms of his response, accosted the girl, falsely claiming that he was a store detective, and said that he would have to detain her if she did not return what she had taken.

The findings might not be generalizable to another setting because of the heavy—80 percent—Mormon representation among the shoppers, but they provide an example for the kinds of experimental field investigations which have rarely been conducted by criminologists, who prefer to gather their data in other than simulated settings, with some gains, but with considerable loss of control over their variables—and notably so in regard to investigations of shoplifting.

The roster of presumed motivations for shoplifting is interesting in comparison to those sometimes alleged for white-collar crime. A newspaper account (*New York Times*, May 21, 1972), for instance, indicates that security personnel in the retail trade list the quest for thrills high among the reasons why youths steal from stores. Other summary explanations put forward for shoplifting were high prices, poor service, a philosophy favoring "rip offs" from the establishment and, in some instances, a failure by youngsters to appreciate that shoplifting can be penalized by criminal sanctions. An English commentator (Rolph, 1966) finds a rather different coterie of explanations for shoplifting: depression, resentment, keeping up appearances, meanness, escapism, and advertising pressures. Research to establish the accuracy and distribution of these possible impelling forces seems in order. Particularly interesting would be attempts to discover the meaning of shoplifting to the offender in terms of the satisfaction of his alleged drives to commit the act. A stricture by Sutherland (1956), included in his differential association theory, however, provides sound advice for all who seek to ascertain motivation for criminal behavior: Though criminal behavior is an expression of general needs and values, it is not explained by those general needs and values since noncriminal behavior is an expression of the same needs and values.

The simplest explanation of shoplifting would be that it occurs when an individual has learned to want something which he finds accessible, and which he believes he can acquire without too great a risk of suffering more discomfort either immediately or in the long run than the pleasure to be gained from possession of the item(s). This Benthamite, hedonistic wisdom, however, merely outlines after the fact what possibly led to the fact. Research is sorely needed in regard to the general views of shoplifters about the act and its meaning to them, as they understand it. Given the rather common occurrence of shoplifting, it might be desirable to gather information on a large sample of youngsters prior to any involvement in the behavior and then to ascertain if any items serve to differentiate the shoplifters from the nonshoplifters and those who are caught from those who are not.

As in so many other regards with criminological work, cross-cultural investigations of shoplifting need to be done to broaden the base of conclusions and theories. Compulsive, symbolic shoplifting, or kleptomania, also probably needs further exploration. My inclination has been to agree with those who believed that kleptomania was another of the many psychiatric fables (Neustatter, 1953; Cameron, 1964), destructible by the observation that alleged kleptomaniacs gain astonishing control over their impulse when they notice a store detective about. However, rather curiously, in the midst of writing this section of the chapter, I had a visit from a former student, asking that a letter reporting his class work be addressed to the Probation Department. He had twice been caught stealing in the neighborhood supermarket, had himself shrewdly enrolled in a group therapy program before the court made the suggestion, and now was seeking to understand what had happened to him. As he told it to me: "The second time they caught me I had some meat under my jacket, but I also had three packets of Kool-Aid. My wife, her kid, me—none of us like the damned stuff. We hate it, we never drink it."

CONCLUSION

Avocational crime is committed by persons who define themselves and who tend to be defined by the society as essentially law-abiding individuals. Their acts, as we have seen, violate a wide range of statutes, and their traits, aside from their defined participation in part-time criminal activity, run a gamut. The need in criminology, obviously, is to inject some further order into this highly variegated analytical category. Perhaps the best way to do so would be to concentrate upon the statutes involved, and to build investigations in terms of questions such as the following:

1. How and why was the statute enacted and for what purpose were criminal sanctions included in it?

2. What consequences does the statute seek to prevent?

3. What other behaviors which produce the same or similar consequences are not now outlawed and why is this so?

4. Who violates the statute, and how and why do these persons do what they do?

5. What are the consequences of their violation, in terms of official response?

6. What are the consequences in terms of the performance of the proscribed behavior, that is, what harm eventuates from the criminal act?

7. What ultimately seems to change over the short and long run for the person(s) involved in the crime, for others similarly situated, and for the social system?

Parallel questions will suggest themselves while the details of the investigation are falling into place. The need is for both hypothesis testing and detailed case studies of specific instances of avocational crimes by individuals acting alone and by individuals committing institutional-related offenses.

The best single historical study of a criminal law statute, which placed the development and enforcement of the law into a social context, is Jerome Hall's (1952) work on the law of theft. Mueller (1969) has rather glamorized Hall's achievement, which is substantial enough as it is, but he does provide a sense of the results that can be achieved by scholars who single-mindedly persist in digging at a criminological issue until it yields up its meaning:

> One man, working alone with little more than a good library, paper, a pencil and a 75-watt bulb, can shed more light on the inner workings, on the actual and supposed structure and content of the criminal law, and on the need for reform, than can a battery of research assistants working under the direction of a high-price research director sitting in a mahogany paneled office with indirect lighting. But the method Hall pioneered requires stamina, perseverance and ingenuity, characteristics hard to obtain except in an era of depression and unemployment (Mueller, 1969:177).

Mueller's own hypothesis—that stamina and perseverance flower most readily in nonaffluent periods—is but another of those intuitions that has a counterpart for research into avocational crime, where the question would be to determine the relationship between economic conditions and the increase or decrease in particular kinds of avocational crimes.

Perhaps most fundamentally the key investigative issue relates to the manner in which individuals introject and act upon views of legitimacy and the manner in which they come to perceive action possibilities, both in regard to outlawing of certain behaviors and in regard to the performance of certain acts which have certain meanings for them. Merton (1946) has put the matter in a quite common-sense way, reminiscent of the "noble lie" that Plato thought essential to knit the fabric of a social structure in which all would achieve subjective contentment by accepting unquestioningly the fiction that objective circumstances were reasonable. Merton offered the case of

> an elderly housewife with a small income and a limited grade school education, who reaffirms the legitimacy of present arrangements. "People with good heads deserve more. If my head isn't as good as another, why should I get the same as you? I didn't try hard enough for it. . . . How do people get rich? They're smarter than we are." (1946: 168–69)

Contentment with or passive acceptance of what are believed by others to be unjust social arrangements may, of course, be seen as a totally undesirable outcome, just as crime—avocational and vocational alike—may reasonably be viewed as a method to shake up a social system and move it more closely toward what are regarded as better conditions. Obviously, these are intricate kinds of issues, necessitating a blend, and yet a distinction between empirical and ideological matters. In criminology, growing self-awareness about the value implications implicit in research ought not to be allowed to turn sour and become nothing more than a marshaling of selected data to support a new set of overt beliefs that have replaced earlier, covert attachments.

REFERENCES

Arieff, A. J., and C. G. Bowie.
  1947   "Some psychiatric aspects of shoplifting." Journal of Clinical Psychopathology 8:565–576.

Attorney General's National Committee to Study the Antitrust Laws.
  1955   Report. Washington, D.C.: U.S. Government Printing Office.

Aubert, V.
1952   "White-collar crime and social structure." American Journal of Sociology 58:263–271.

Ball, H. V.
1960   "Social structure and rent-control violations." American Journal of Sociology 65:598–604.

Bennett, H. M.
1968   "Shoplifting in Midtown." Criminal Law Review August:413–425.

Bennett, J.
1955   "After sentence—what?" Journal of Criminal Law, Criminology and Police Science 45:537–540.

Binder, M.
1962   "Weisse-kragen-kriminalität." Kriminalistik (Hamburg) 16(June):251–255.

Brady, J. F., and J. G. Mitchell.
1971   "Shoplifting in Melbourne." Australian and New Zealand Journal of Criminology 4:154–162.

Brooks, J.
1970   Once in Golconda. New York: Harper Colophon.

Buckhorn, R. F.
1972   Nader, the People's Lawyer. Englewood Cliffs, N.J.: Prentice-Hall.

Cameron, M. O.
1964   The Booster and the Snitch: Department Store Shoplifting. New York: Free Press of Glencoe.

Chein, I., D. L. Gerard, R. S. Lee, and E. Rosenfeld.
1964   The Road to H, Narcotics, Delinquency, and Social Policy. New York: Basic Books.

Cleaver, E.
1968   Soul on Ice. New York: Dell.

Clinard, M. B.
1952   The Black Market. New York: Rinehart.

Cohen, L., and R. Stark.
n.d.   "Labeling theory and the five finger discount, an empirical test of shoplifting" (unpublished).

Cox, A. E.
1968   "Shoplifting." Criminal Law Review August:425–432.

Cressey, D. R.
1953   Other People's Money: A Study in the Social Psychology of Embezzlement. Glencoe, Ill.: Free Press.

Dallos, R.
1969   "Morgenthau deplores attitudes on crime." Los Angeles Times June 27.

Durkheim, E.
1895   The Rules of Sociological Method. Eighth Edition. Translated by Sarah A. Solovay and John H. Mueller. Edited by G. E. G. Catlin. Chicago: University of Chicago Press (1938 edition).

Edwards, L. E.
1958   Shoplifting and Shrinkage Protection for Stores. Springfield, Ill.: Thomas.
Fitzgerald, F. S.
1953   "The Great Gatsby," in Three Novels of F. Scott Fitzgerald. New York: Scribners.
Geis, G.
1962   "Toward a delineation of white-collar offenses." Sociological Inquiry 32: 159–171.
1967   "The heavy electrical equipment antitrust cases of 1961." Pp. 139–150 in M. B. Clinard and R. Quinney (eds.), Criminal Behavior Systems. New York: Holt, Rinehart & Winston.
1968   White-Collar Criminal: The Offender in Business and the Professions. New York: Atherton.
1972   Not the Law's Business: An Examination of Homosexuality, Abortion, Prostitution, Narcotics, and Gambling in the United States. Washington, D.C.: U.S. Government Printing Office.
1973   "Deterring corporate crime." Pp. 182–197 in R. Nader and M. Green (eds.), Corporate Power in America. New York: Grossman.
1974   "Occupational crime," in A. Blumberg (ed.), Current Perspectives on Criminal Behavior. New York: Random House.
Gelfand, D. M., D. P. Hartmann, P. Walder, and B. Page.
1973   "Who reports shoplifters?" Journal of Personality and Social Psychology 25(February):276–283.
Gibbens, T. C. N., and J. Prince.
1962   Shoplifting. London: Institute for the Study and Treatment of Delinquency.
Hall, J.
1952   Theft, Law, and Society. Second Edition. Indianapolis: Bobbs-Merrill.
Hartung, F. E.
1950   "White-collar offenses in the wholesale meat industry in Detroit." American Journal of Sociology 56:25–32.
Herling, J.
1962   The Great Price Conspiracy. Washington, D.C.: Luce.
Jackson, G.
1970   Soledad Brother. New York: Bantam Books.
Kadish, S. H.
1963   "Some observations on the use of criminal sanctions in the enforcement of economic legislation." University of Chicago Law Review 30:423–449.
Kauffmann, S.
1966   "Homosexual drama and its disguises." New York Times January 13(2):1.
Kellens, G.
1968   "Du 'crime en col blanc' au 'delit de chevalier.' " Annales de la Faculté de Droit de Liège 30:60–124.
Lane, R. E.
1953   "Why businessmen violate the law." Journal of Criminal Law, Criminology and Police Science 44:151–165.
Lewis, R., and R. Stewart.
1961   The Managers. New York: New American Library.

Llewellyn, K. N.
  1962   Jurisprudence. Chicago: University of Chicago Press.

Loschiavo, G. G.
  1963   "La mafia della lupara e quella dei 'coletti bianchi.' " La Giustizia Penale
          68:336–344.

Luchterhand, E.
  1952   "Prison behavior and social system in Nazi concentration camps." Ph.D.
          dissertation, University of Wisconsin.

McCarry, C.
  1972   Citizen Nader. New York: Saturday Review Press.

Mannheim, H.
  1965   Comparative Criminology. Boston: Houghton Mifflin.

Merton, R. K.
  1946   Mass Persuasion: The Social Psychology of a War Bond Drive. New York:
          Harper.
  1957   Social Theory and Social Structure. Glencoe, Ill.: Free Press.

Mueller, G. O. W.
  1969   Crime, Law and the Scholars. Seattle: University of Washington Press.

Myrdal, G.
  1944   An American Dilemma. New York: Harper.

Nader, R.
  1969   "Business crime." Pp. 138–140 in D. Sanford (ed.), Hot War on the Con-
          sumer. New York: Pitman.
  1970   "Foreword." Pp. vii–ix in J. Esposito, Vanishing Air. New York: Grossman.
  1971   "Introduction." Pp. xi–xix in M. Mintz and J. S. Cohen, America, Inc. New
          York: Dial.

Neustatter, W. L.
  1953   Psychological Disorder and Crime. London: Johnson.

Newman, D. J.
  1957   "Public attitudes toward a form of white collar crime." Social Problems
          4:228–232.

Normandeau, A.
  1965   "Les deviations en affaires et la 'crime en col blanc.' " Review of Interna-
          tional Criminal and Police Technology 19:247–258.

Parker, T., and R. Allerton.
  1962   The Courage of His Convictions. New York: Norton.

Pinatel, J.
  1970   "La criminalité dans les différents cercles sociaux." Revue de Science Crimi-
          nelle 25(July–September):677–684.

President's Commission on Law Enforcement and Administration of Justice.
  1967a   The Challenge of Crime in a Free Society. Washington, D.C.: U.S. Govern-
          ment Printing Office.
  1967b   Task Force Report: Crime and Its Impact: An Assessment. Washington,
          D.C.: U.S. Government Printing Office.

Quinney, R.
  1963   "Occupational structure and criminal behavior: prescription violations by
          retail pharmacists." Social Problems 11:179–185.

Rensberger, B.
   1972   "Bremer's way of life likened to 3 assassins." New York Times May 21.
Robin, G. D.
   1963   "Patterns of department store shoplifting." Crime and Delinquency 9:163–172.
Rolph, C. H.
   1966   "Dealing with shoplifters." New Statesman 72:14.
Salisbury, H. E.
   1969   The 900 Days; The Siege of Leningrad. New York: Avon.
Schur, E. M.
   1965   Crimes Without Victims. Englewood Cliffs, N.J.: Prentice-Hall.
Schwendinger, H., and J. Schwendinger.
   1970   "Defenders of order or guardians of human rights?" Issues in Criminology 5:123–157.
Sellin, T.
   1937   Research Memorandum on Crime in the Depression. New York: Social Science Research Council.
Sellin, T., and M. E. Wolfgang.
   1964   The Management of Delinquency. New York: Wiley.
Sloan, A. P.
   1941   Adventures of a White-Collar Man. New York: Doubleday.
Smigel, E. O.
   1956   "Public attitudes toward stealing in relation to the size of the victim organization." American Sociological Review 21:320–347.
Smigel, E. O., and J. E. Conklin.
   1972   "Norms and attitudes toward business-related crimes." Paper prepared for symposium on Studies of Public Experience, Knowledge, and Opinion of Crime and Justice, Bureau of Social Science Research, Washington, March 16–18.
Snodgrass, J.
   1972   "The American criminological tradition, portraits of the men and ideology in a discipline." Ph.D. dissertation, University of Pennsylvania.
Sutherland, E. H.
   1940   "White-collar criminality." American Sociological Review 5:1–12.
   1949   White Collar Crime. New York: Dryden.
   1956   The Sutherland Papers. A. Cohen, A. Lindesmith, and K. Schuessler (eds.). Bloomington: Indiana University Press.
   1969   El Delito du Cuello Blanco. Caracas: Editiones de la Bibliotheca.
Szasz, T. S.
   1963   Law, Liberty and Psychiatry. New York: Macmillan.
Talese, G.
   1971   Honor Thy Father. New York: World.
Tompkins, D. C.
   1967   White Collar Crime: A Bibliography. Berkeley: Institute of Government Studies, University of California.
Veblen, T.
   1899   The Theory of the Leisure Class. New York: Macmillan.

Weringh, J. van.
    1969   "White collar crime, een terreinverkenning." Nederlands Tijdschrift voor Criminologie 11:133–144.

Winick, C.
    1961   "How people perceived the 'Mad Bomber.'" Public Opinion Quarterly 25: 25–38.

Won, G., and G. Yamamoto.
    1968   "Social structure and deviant behavior: a study of shoplifting." Sociology and Social Research 53:44–55.

CHAPTER **9**

Vocational Crime

James A. Inciardi

University of Miami

Crime is one of the most ancient of human phenomena, and its manifestation at a vocational level has been known for many millennia. That crime was a "calling" as early as the pre-Christian era is suggested in the Old Testament. Abimelech, illegitimate son of Gideon, contracted professional killers for the disposal of his seventy legitimate brothers; the sons of Eli may have been the originators of extortion; and observations of prostitution as an occupational pursuit occurred perhaps even earlier than the recollections of Moses and the Chosen People. Later periods in archeological time gave further witness to crime as a vocation. Theft and prostitution as careers can be noted in the *Lives* of Plutarch and the *Annals* of Tacitus; the craft of the pickpocket appears in Petronius's *Satyricon*. And beyond the first thousand years after Christ, both history and literature vividly describe the existence of crime as a life-style (Hibbert, 1963). As such, crime is the vocation and career of the offender. It is undertaken as an occupation on a long-term and repetitive basis. As a "calling," vocational crime reflects a high degree of commitment; the offender becomes a "secondary deviant" (Lemert, 1967) and circumscribes his life organization with his criminal activity.

The observation and analysis of vocational crime have pervaded the evolutionary growth of the science of criminology. To Lombroso (1911:xxvi–xxvii, 419), for example, the career offenders were "criminaloids," a variety of "individuals who constitute the gradations between the born criminal and the honest man." Ferri (1896:13–25) also noted the peculiar nature of the career offender, but even prior to these first contributions to the "scientific" study of crime, Frégier's *Des Classes Dangereuses de la Population dans les Grandes Villes* and Buret's *De la Misère des Classes laborieuses en Angleterre et en France* explored the attitudes, habits, and ways of life of these "dangerous classes" and "criminal classes" (Radzinowicz, 1966:38–46). More recent analyses of vocational crime focus upon the offenders' occupational career pattern, emphasizing processes of initiation and maturation, life-style, social organization, isolation, and survival (see Sutherland, 1937; Cressey, 1969; Quinney, 1970:267–73; Clinard & Quinney, 1973:224–63). Within this framework, *vocational crime can be defined as offense behavior that is pursued as an occupational career for the purpose of obtaining a steady flow of income. The development of the criminal vocation begins with an initiation and socialization into the world of crime, attended by a maturation process involving the acquisition of the skills, knowledge, and associations appropriate for maintaining the desired occupation.*

This discussion of vocational crime is both historical and contemporary in framework, utilizing history not only to describe patterns from the past, but also as an analytical tool to link the past with the present, and, thereby, to explain contemporary data.

The types of vocational crime are threefold: (1) *professional crime;* (2) *professional "heavy" crime;* and (3) *organized crime.*

1. *Professional crime* refers to nonviolent forms of criminal occupation pursued with a high degree of skill, to maximize financial gain and minimize the possibility of apprehension. The more typical forms of professional crime include picking pockets, shoplifting, burglary, forgery and counterfeiting, extortion, sneak-thieving, and confidence games.

2. *Professional "heavy" crime* involves highly skilled offenses for monetary gain but employing elements of coercion and the use or threat of violence or of property damage. The specific crimes include armed robbery, hijacking, and sometimes burglary, arson, and kidnapping. They are completed with surprise and speed in order to diminish the risks of apprehension.

3. *Organized crime* designates business enterprises directed toward economic gain through illegal activities. It provides illegal goods and services through activities that include gambling, loan-sharking, commercialized vice, bootlegging, trafficking in narcotics, disposing of stolen merchandise, and infiltrating legitimate businesses.

PROFESSIONAL CRIME

A variety of conceptualization is apparent throughout criminological literature relative to the focus and meaning of professional crime, or more specifically, *professional theft.* Barnes and Teeters (1959:54–55), for example, employ the terms "habitual" and "true chronic" for a number of criminal types, including what has already been described as the "professional." Lindesmith and Dunham (1941) have constructed the "habitual situational" type as a residual category embracing a continuum from "situational" to "professional," and with Taft (1956:236–49) they have suggested that professional crime is organized crime, since some degree of structure and cooperation is necessary for its successful execution. Cavan (1962:96) and Caldwell (1965:132, 135), in an alternative direction, include professional "heavy" offenders with professional offenders. Yet the notions promulgated by Sutherland (1937:3) were specific, describing the professional thief as a nonviolent property offender who makes a regular business of stealing. But this conception was not Sutherland's creation. The label of "professional" seems to have its roots in the underworld, perhaps five hundred years ago (see Judges, 1930), and as a criminal label it has been continuously applied by self-styled professional criminals to other professionals in terms of criteria specified by ingroup members as the minimum requirements for admission to the profession (Quennell, n.d.; Irwin, 1909; Scott, 1916; Black, 1927; Ingram, 1930; Maurer, 1964; Jackson, 1969).

Professional Crime in History

The development of professional crime as a behavior system seems to have originated in the disintegration of the feudal order in Europe between 1350 and 1550. Its evolution was hastened by the mobility and economic changes which resulted from that disintegration.

The lower classes in Europe during the fifteenth century suffered increasing restlessness and misery when the decrease in population due to the Black Death a century earlier was alleviated and the urban population began to grow rapidly. As trade and commerce developed in seaports and interior cities, assuring landowners a ready market for foodstuffs, land became valuable and many peasants were forced from their land. The decreasing yield of soil, however, caused the institution of the three-field system, thus forcing additional serfs from those portions which had to remain fallow (Rusche & Kirchheimer, 1939:11). In England specifically, the economic changes during this period were closely associated with the rise of a rogue and vagabond class (Aydelotte, 1913:5).[1] Ownership of land became individual rather than communal. Serfs attempted to improve their conditions as peasantry by severing themselves from the soil and accepting wages, but this alternative led to a more intense state of destitution. As sheep farming steadily increased, the enclosure acts, which began in the twelfth century, more drastically affected the peasants, for their lands as well as waste lands suddenly became usable as pasture.

In Britain the feudal retainers, those hordes of peasants recruited into the armies of the feudal lords during the War of the Roses, also contributed to the growing class of landless, masterless, and penniless men. From 1485 to 1550 they were little more than ordinary marauders; many received no wages, and were forced to steal for a living (Aydelotte, 1913:12–13). The Church also played a role in the development of the vagabond classes by its institutionalized system of almsgiving. The clergy gave charity to anyone who approached their doors, and when this aid was discontinued during the Reformation, there was little to take its place. Furthermore, no provision had been made for the homeless monks, and they, too, were reduced to begging.

The wandering groups of vagabonds and masterless men who were unable to support themselves without land were joined by jugglers, minstrels, and gypsies. Their way of life in the countryside was abetted by hordes of rogues and vagabonds in the aftermath of the plague of 1349. Disruptions of relations between landowners and laborers also caused many peasants to become runaways (Jusserand, 1929:254–55). They were joined by those who had no desire to work (p. 141), and by robbers, poachers, and bandits, all of whom found a natural asylum in the forests where they began to build many of the cultural traditions that later shifted to the growing cities.

Knowledge of the Elizabethan professional criminals, who came from the country forests and highways to swell the criminal classes of London, Exeter, Norwich, and Bristol, comes from a collection of Tudor and early Stuart tracts, pamphlets, and ballads which described the life and times of these rogues and vagabonds, thieves and sharpers, cozeners and conny-catchers.[2] Conny-catching was originally Elizabethan slang for a particular method of cheating at cards, but it came to be used to describe any method of

---

1. England has been chosen for this analysis since this period has been highlighted in numerous historical and literary sources. Furthermore, the similarities of language and cultural traditions of these early English peoples with those of their American successors are factors that can be readily observed. Processes similar to British experiences have also been referenced in German history (see Lindesmith & Levin, 1937).

2. The majority of these pamphlets have been reprinted in Judges (1930) and Viles and Furnivall (1880). The historical reliability of the materials, furthermore, has been thoroughly investigated. Aydelotte (1913:76–78, 114–39) has indicated that the statements of the pamphleteers were confirmed by many sources in Elizabethan history and literature. Many of the early English laws were directed against the types of activity illustrated, and Elizabethan satires and plays dealing with contemporary life described the characters and tricks found in the pamphlets. Furthermore, collections of letters dating back to the late sixteenth century made numerous references to these thieves and rogues (Wright, 1838:18, 166, 245–51; Chandler, 1907).

swindling (Aydelotte, 1913:1). The *conny* was the victim of the swindle. The pamphlets give considerable evidence that the conny-catchers were a fraternity of thieves, a "gallant company of shifters" who lived by their wits and took pride in their work. Conny-catching was a full-time profession found predominantly in the city of London during the terms of court when numerous country men crowded into the city for business and pleasure. The thieves congregated in bowling alleys, dicing houses, brothels, ordinaries, and as Fennor pointed out, prisons.[3] The conny-catching *laws*, the methods or cheating tricks used by the thieves, were discussed under the following terms (Judges, 1930: 149–78):

1. *High law*—the art of highway robbery.
2. *Sacking law*—brothel keeping.
3. *Cheating law*—swindling with dice.
4. *Crossbiting law*—swindling and extortion by prostitutes.
5. *Conny-catching law*—swindling by card tricks.
6. *Versing law*—swindling with false gold.
7. *Figging law*—the art of the *cutpurse* (pickpocket).
8. *Bernard's law*—cheating a drunk with cards.
9. *Black art*—picking locks.
10. *Curbing law*—hooking from open windows.
11. *Vincent's law*—swindling at bowling games.
12. *Prigging law*—horse stealing.
13. *Lifting law*—shoplifting and general stealing.

The *laws* of cheating and thievery described by the pamphleteers have survived the passing centuries. Characteristic of both contemporary and Elizabethan professional criminals, figging law was descriptive of two types of pickpockets, the *nip* and the *foist*. The nip used a knife to secure the wallet or purse, thus obtaining the label of *cutpurse*, while the foist used his fingers. These pickpockets frequented the resorts, assemblies, plays, and fairs. Often a cohort would sing a ballad while the foists drifted among the gathering crowd. The *lift* was a shoplifter, but generally he did not confine his activities to shops and stores, operating wherever goods were available—the gaming houses, ordinaries, ale houses, and bowling alleys. He had agility and dexterity, as did the foists, and worked alone as well as in groups. Receivers of stolen goods were also within the network of Elizabethan lifts. These brokers purchased stolen merchandise at any time of day or night, and disposed of the goods not only in England, but also through arrangements with French and Dutch brokers (Aydelotte, 1913:164). Curbing law described the activities of the *hooker* or *curber*, varieties of Elizabethan burglars and housebreakers. The black art was the craft of the *lockpick*, a specialized thief who opened locks with precision instruments forged by smiths in Italy. Cheating law, versing law, Vincent's law, and conny-catching law referred to the multiplicity of swindles and confidence operations executed with the use of fraudulent dice, cards, or other objects.

Status levels existed among the Elizabethan thieves, in addition to an *esprit de corps*. Among pickpockets, for example, the foist commanded greater prestige than the nip, and there was a sharp demarcation between *city* nips and *country* nips. In the totality of rogues, vagabonds, thieves, and beggars of whom the pamphlets spoke, the city rogues and sharpers were of the highest order of vagrants. Similarly, crossbiting law—extortion by prostitutes in a manner not unlike nineteenth and twentieth century

---

3. William Fennor's *The Counter's Commonwealth*, for example, written in 1617 and reprinted in its entirety in Judges (1930:423–87), describes the author's arrest and experiences while in prison.

badger games—was described by Greene (1592) as "a public profession of shameless cozenage, mixed with incestuous whoredoms, as ill as was practiced in Gomorrah or Sodom."

Historical evidence suggests that numerous Elizabethan vagrants and sharpers had gravitated to specific sections of the cities. In pre-Tudor times, there were designated areas which, because of ecclesiastical franchises, claimed to be independent of the royal legal system (Judges, 1930:149–78). The King's writs did not penetrate these "bastard sanctuaries," and they rapidly became havens for debtors and criminals. This "right of franchise" began to collapse under the Reformation statutes of Henry VIII and the Parliament of Edward VI. But with the exception of the more heinous of felony offenders, the majority of the fugitives remained protected perhaps even beyond the early eighteenth-century reign of George I (Jusserand, 1929:173–74).

The criminal patterns characteristic of the Elizabethan rogues and vagabonds were not limited to British soil, for they were appearing in continental Europe as well (Chandler, 1907). Furthermore, changes in penal and correctional systems during the seventeenth and eighteenth centuries fostered introduction of this criminal behavior system to the New World. The late 1600s, for example, witnessed a growth in mass-produced goods as European towns expanded, and trade multiplied as the American colonies developed. The population failed to keep pace with the possibilities for employment, with England, France, and Germany ravaged by wars. As industrial potential grew, demand for laborers reached a crisis level, and all methods were used to expand their numbers. In addition to increases in the birth rate, child and prison labor were exploited. Convicts were used as galley slaves, placed in penal servitude at hard labor, and transported to America for colonization (Ives, 1914; Parsons, 1926:273–75; Rusche & Kirchheimer, 1939:24–60). Although Spain and Portugal had begun to tap the labor power of convicts as early as the fifteenth century by shipping them to colonies and military settlements, England was the first country to establish any systematic transportation of prisoners as a method of colonial expansion (Froude, 1864).

The Vagrancy Act of 1597 legalized deportation, and batches of dissolute persons were sporadically transported to Virginia from its founding in 1606. Between 1655 and 1699, at least 4,431 prisoners were transported, and through legal statutes in 1718 and 1720, transportation became the regular sentence for many types of thievery. The ship *Old Bailey*, for example, carried no less than 10,000 persons between 1717 and 1775 (Rusche & Kirchheimer, 1939:60), and between 1607 and 1775 some 30,000 convicts or one twenty-fifth of all immigrants coming to America during that period were landed almost exclusively in the Chesapeake area (Furnas, 1969:105). French criminals were transported to New Orleans from 1701 to 1722, and after the abolition of galley servitude caused a herding of criminals in Toulon and Marseilles, transportation was reestablished in 1791. Furthermore, German convicts during this period were shipped to North America as slaves (Rusche & Kirchheimer, 1939:123–25). Although the number of professional thieves among these transplanted groups has never been recorded, their influences were noted. As early as 1672, the records of the Suffolk County Court (Massachusetts) recognized that the "Art of Conny-catching" had arrived in the colonies (Clough, 1959:239). The social organization and occupational structure of professional criminality had become firmly established in England by the nineteenth century (Quennell, n.d.; Levin & Lindesmith, 1937; Moritz, 1965), and any examination of the growth of vice areas in the United States suggests the continuing influence of English and European professionals upon American criminality.[4]

---

4. Extensive reference materials offering testimony on these phenomena are noted in Inciardi, 1973:91–92.

The Categories of Professional Crime[5]

The categories of professional crime contemporary to the United States are, for the most part, centuries old, having been transmitted from one generation of criminals to another since the days of the Elizabethan rogues. Modifications in techniques, newer varieties of crime, and more efficient methods of committing old crimes, however, have indeed appeared concurrently with changes in technology and social conditions. An overview of the history of professional crime in Britain and America suggests, nevertheless, that the more common types of professional crime have tended to remain limited to the following areas:

1. Burglary
    Safe burglary
    House burglary
2. Sneak Theft
    Bank sneak theft
    House sneak theft
    Shoplifting
    Pennyweighting
    Pickpocketing
    Lush-working
3. Confidence Swindling
    The short con
    The big con
    Circus grifting
4. Forgery and Counterfeiting
5. Extortion

1. Burglary. *Safe burglary* was a rare phenomenon prior to the Civil War. During the 1860s, however, the federal government began circulating millions of "greenbacks" and securities "payable to the bearer," and by the close of that decade the breaking and entering of safes had become a major undertaking of the professional underworld (Hamilton, 1952:34). *Safe-blowers* were considered to be among the elite of this segment of the profession (Crapsey, 1872: 16–17; Clark & Eubank, 1927:36), but their techniques were rarely exercised without some assurance that the high risk would be rewarded. Safe doors were readily blown apart by powder and fuses positioned in precision-drilled holes. Safes were wrapped in wet blankets to muffle such explosions, and the initial entry to the banks was gained through keys produced from wax impressions. The safe-blowers of the 1870s maintained an extensive knowledge of explosives as well as the mechanical aspects of safe construction. Later they learned to *thrash out the soup* (extract nitro from sticks of dynamite). The use of explosives for opening safes was noted as early as 1853 (Clark & Eubank, 1927:36), but a sharp decline has been apparent since the turn of the century. In addition to the severe penal-

---

5. The source materials used for the analysis of professional crime in this chapter include an array of primary and secondary documents including autobiographies of criminals and police officers, recollections of thieves, journalists, victims, police, and other participant observers, and observational and research data secured from both professional and lay personnel. In addition, while employed by the New York State Division of Parole, I conducted many interviews that elicited numerous perspectives from twenty professional thieves as well as from a variety of police and community members who had contacts with such offenders. In addition to the published references which are cited throughout this work, additional source materials were consulted for background and supportive purposes (see Inciardi, 1973).

ties imposed for the use of nitroglycerine (Jackson, 1969:102), even the most skillful blasting techniques became outdated when the acetylene torch allowed thieves to rapidly cut through metal (Varna, 1957:110). *Combination-safe pickers* have also been among the safe burglars since the last century (Byrnes, 1895:11; Varna, 1957:110–11), and other enduring methods have included drilling, and *peeling* the metal with chisels (Jackson:1969).

The story of safe breaking features the industry's continued effort to produce a burglar-proof safe and the underworld's ability to keep pace with modern technology (see Sutherland, 1947:205–6), but such burglary, particularly from banks, began to decline at the beginning of this century with the inception of time locks and electric alarm systems. These left the trade open only to mechanical genius, and indeed, bank vaults became virtually impregnable. In 1962, for example, when the building located at 15 Broad Street in New York City was being prepared for demolition, the task of dismantling the 10' x 20' vault of the Morgan Guarantee Trust Company occupied two thousand man-hours of labor. The door to the vault alone weighed some forty tons.[6] Modern money fortresses are far too expensive for all but the largest firms, however, but the tens of thousands of smaller and older safes still in use allow experts in explosives, acetylene work, or straight lock-picking to pursue criminal careers (Martin, 1952; Varna, 1957; Jackson, 1969).

House burglary has been a persistent form of professional criminality since the days of Shakespeare's youth, and has undergone only minimal change during the past fifteen decades. As early as 1821, the London cracksman or professional housebreaker had already developed a notable reputation (Egan, 1905b:179), and by 1854 skeleton keys and jimmys of different types were in operation as major forms of burglars' tools in this country (Williams, 1959:41). Modern professional burglars rely less upon skeleton keys and other mechanical devices and more upon their own mechanical ability. The more lucrative burglaries have rarely been haphazard operations based on random selection of homes as potential targets. Many burglars are *tipped off* as to the location of homes with valuable contents and when the occupants will be away from their residences.[7]

2. Sneak Theft. The sneak thief has been referred to as "all that is determined, patient, plausible, scheming, thoroughly educated and able in roguery" (Crapsey, 1872;

---

6. Personal communication from acetylene torch operators who engineered the project (May 5, 1968).

7. There seems to be considerable corroboration on this point. A professional burglar, whom I interviewed shortly after his release from New York City's Rikers Island Penitentiary, indicated that while *working* in suburban Chicago during the early 1960s, information regarding household contents, as well as vacation schedules of residents, was provided by a cohort who operated a milk route for the local dairy. The victim of a Memorial Day weekend burglary suggested the possibility of *tipster* activity initiated by personnel in his employ who represented the only individuals knowledgeable of the nature and length of his planned trip. During this incident, the burglars had moved into his home, systematically removed three floors of valuables including money, jewelry, household appliances, clothing, and antiques, and evidence suggested that they had eaten and slept at the location for no less than a twenty-four hour period. Tipsters tend to be members of legitimate occupations who, through either conversational or observational contacts, have some access to homeowners' patterns of movement (Byrnes, 1895; Black, 1927:141; Martin, 1952:96; Genêt, 1964:58; Crookston, 1967:127–28; Jackson, 1969:121–22); and Shover's (1971) interviews with twenty-six tipsters indicated that more than half had legitimate occupations with such access, including bartenders, repairmen or deliverymen, and beauticians, or were employees of the victimized individuals.

15). As such, the sneak is an outlaw who does not, at the outset of his crime, proclaim his intentions by some work or act; he is a thief who has the ability to remain unnoticed, blending with his environment while stealing in the proximity of the awake and active victims. In a historical perspective, the *bank sneak* was considered the most skillful and the "highest possible criminal development" (p. 15). As a *bond robber* or *damper sneak*, he entered banking institutions with an appearance of respectability to engage in financial discussions within reach of an open safe. The theft would occur when the attention of bank personnel was diverted to some other situation; it often extracted large amounts of money and remained unnoticed for many hours. Bank sneak gangs were composed of a lookout, a conversationalist to distract the banker's attention, and a small-sized man who could "sneak" behind a counter and quickly gather cash or bonds (Campbell et al., 1892:673). They prowled the financial areas of large cities dressed as honest merchants or stockbrokers, always alert for an opportunity to steal. They often frequented the hotels and other haunts of the financial leaders to learn their interests and weaknesses, and whatever else might be useful in on-site distractional conversations.

Bank sneak-thieving was especially lucrative in New York during the post–Civil War reconstruction period, when banking institutions multiplied rapidly and most were concentrated in this city's financial district. Sneak thieves loitered in that area on a daily basis and cash-filled boxes disappeared from tellers' cages regularly and within the view of special detectives. In response to this situation, Thomas Byrnes, the city's chief of detectives during the 1880s and later chief of police, instituted a special patrol system in 1889 in the Wall Street area which virtually eliminated thefts by bank sneaks there (Byrnes, 1895:13). The new system involved a detective subsquad in the financial district with special patrols during business hours, and telephone connections between the Wall Street substation and the banks. Nevertheless, activities of bank sneak thieves persisted in this country up until World War II. Since then, however, banking institutions have increased security measures, and in contemporary banks with electronically controlled doors and cages, photoelectrically operated alarm systems, and closed-circuit television, such practices are almost impossible.

The procedures used by the bank sneak thief were also applied to stores, where they were referred to as *till-tapping*. As one of a group lured a proprietor from his store on one pretext or another, his confederates would enter from a rear door and remove whatever money was in the *till*, or cash register. Till-tapping continues to exist, although not necessarily under the same label. A shoplifter, paroled from Sing Sing prison in 1966, indicated to me that with the carelessness of shopkeepers regarding open cash registers, the profession continues to have a bright future:

> During the busy hours of the day and busy seasons of the year, you can always find an open register within the reach of the customer. Down here [the financial district of New York City], coffee shops are good targets at lunch hour. People are rushing in and out; the cashier wants to see that everyone pays; she looks to see if the chap leaving paid his check, and bang, you've got it. . . . Christmas is a good season too. Store cops are looking for shoplifters or just trying to keep order. They don't watch the registers. They don't watch the crooks who make a legitimate purchase to get near that money box. . . . One time I walked right into the cage in the refund department and counted out the money, no one even looked at me—it was a busy day.

Similarly, another professional reported to me:

> Taking cash from a till is the easiest kind of stealing. If you're alert and fast, you have a good income. I kept away from the big stores—too many people to watch. The busy

specialty shops on 34th Street or Nassau Street always have a lot of customers, a lot of confusion, and few employees. Liquor stores are not good though, the owner is there and it's his money, and he's more careful. Besides, he's suspicious to start with.

House sneaks employed methods considerably different from the more daring thefts from banks. The *bed-chamber sneak*, an ally of the early bank burglar, entered the homes of bank owners or officers as they slept, and made wax impressions of their keys. It was for this reason that safe-blowers had easy access to banking institutions, businesses, and stores. *Second-story sneaks* were similar to burglars in that they entered dwellings and removed various articles of value, but they were sneaks in that they accomplished their art while the buildings were occupied and while the inhabitants were awake. Little is known regarding the evolution of the house sneak or *porch-climber* of the nineteenth century. Contemporary literature does not refer to him specifically, yet many of his methods appear in the efforts of modern burglars. The status of the *second-story man* is less certain. The newer varieties of residential housing, including the small one- and two-family units and large apartment buildings, offer difficult settings for daytime prowling and entry. On the other hand, fire escapes have expanded the access to some living quarters. With respect to the existence of modern sneak thieves, an ex-pickpocket turned narcotic addict explained:

> I haven't heard the term "sneak thief" in a long time, maybe ten or twenty years. Most of the old timers have died off or are in jail. Many of 'em are dead. You still have them though, but they're called something else. Most of the good ones specialize. The guy that steals coats is a "coat thief"; or if he steals from butchers or the stock yards he's a "ham thief." I met one about five years ago at Rikers. He was a "hotel thief." He looked for open rooms and made a lot of hits, but it never amounted to anything.

Shoplifting, as a later development of Elizabethan lifting law, can also be regarded as a variety of sneak theft. Although the shoplifter has isolated his theft to specific locations and employs devices and techniques peculiar only to his own trade, the basic pattern of "theft by sneaking" is characteristic.

The history of shoplifting indicates only minor changes in operation over time. During the late 1800s, shoplifters were of two types, "the regular criminal professional and the kleptomaniac" (Byrnes, 1895:25). The professional practitioners usually worked in large groups or in pairs, and the more common method involved the distraction of the storekeeper with idle conversation by one thief while another filled his pockets with merchandise. Female shoplifters used the same procedure with the addition of large pockets under their dresses which were sustained by girdles about their waists (Crapsey, 1872:26). Farley (1876:56) noted that females of this type often specialized in the theft of expensive lace handkerchiefs. Sutherland (1937:48) reported two types of professional shoplifters: the *booster* and the *heel*. The booster contacted salesmen and stole from the articles displayed before him; the heel operated without the assistance of the salesman. Both types were daring and confident, and appeared in the uniform of the normal upstanding customer. Modern shoplifters have been divided into *boosters*, the professional commercial shoplifters, and *snitches*, the pilferers who steal for their own consumption (Cameron, 1964:39). The booster steals for profit while the snitch steals for use. Cameron indicated that boosters seem to gravitate toward New York City, preferring the large number of small stores (p. 42). This preserves their anonymity for greater lengths of time since in other major cities large stores protected by detectives who become familar with the well-known professionals seem to predominate. *Booster skirts* or *bloomers,* garments which are designed especially for holding stolen merchandise, have been common forms of concealment for more than a century, and were observed as early as the 1820s:

> The pregnancy was assumed, the better to evade suspicion; her under garments were completely lined with hooks, to which were suspended, in vast variety, articles of stolen property, including not only those of light weight, viz. handkerchiefs, shawls, stockings, etc., but several of less portable description, amongst which were two pieces of Irish linen. These articles had been conveyed through an aperture in her upper habiliment of sufficient dimensions to admit an easy access to the general repository. The ingenuity of this invention created much surprise, and as it greatly facilitated concealment and evaded detection, there is no doubt of its having frequently produced a rich harvest (Egan, 1905b:136).

There is no accurate index of the number of shoplifters in operation today. Cameron (1964:58) suggested that about 10 percent of those arrested in department stores are professionals, yet this figure reflects only a small segment of the thefts. Not all shoplifters are detected, and of those who are, many are not approached since management does not wish to run the risk of arresting a respectable customer. The value of goods taken from retailers annually has been estimated as ranging from $200 million to $3 billion, not including $5 million per day in losses from employee pilferage (Alexander & Moolman, 1969:10, 77; Hellman, 1970:34). Losses of supermarkets alone have been estimated as no less than $250 million (Reckless, 1967:165). These thefts, furthermore, can be attributed to four distinct groups: (1) the professional *boosters* and *heels;* (2) the amateur "pilferers" who steal for their own use; (3) store employees who steal for their own consumption; and (4) narcotic addicts who shoplift merchandise for resale as a means of supporting their drug habits.[8] As is indicated by one of my informants, a pickpocket and shoplifter retired due to old age and the onset of arthritis, several of these categories may overlap one another:

> Women always made better shoplifts. Their sex gives them the advantage. They have more places to hide the stuff and they can always dangle a bag between their legs. They also get more sympathy or holler louder if they're caught. . . . Lots of addicts are shoplifts, and lots of pros become addicts and shoplift. So many of the old timers have fallen that way.

Pennyweighting, which involves the substitution of spurious jewelry or gems for the genuine, is a highly sophisticated form of shoplifting requiring knowledge of precious stones. Chicago May, a prostitute and extortionist, indicated that the pennyweighter had to be familiar with the weight, size, and color of gems, have the ability to appraise them instantly, and carry a perfect mental image of the jewelry or stone (Sharpe, 1928:239). Pennyweighting has suffered a decline over the past three decades. Contemporary jewelers are extremely careful about leaving their goods unattended, and jewelers' exchanges are protected by security guards and closed-circuit television. As one informant indicated: "The pennyweighter went out with the end of the Depression, or at least there hasn't been any new ones since then. I guess it's because easy targets are few and far between nowadays, making the profession unprofitable."

---

8. A pilot study of self-reported criminal activities indicated that fifteen male addicts had committed this crime on 1,272 occasions over a four-year period, and fifteen female addicts admitted to 2,556 instances of shoplifting over a three-year period (Inciardi & Chambers, 1972).

Similarly, I conducted interviews during 1969 with forty-four independent jewelry shop operators on Manhattan's Fifth Avenue, Broadway, and Bowery; Brooklyn's Fifth Avenue, Flatbush Avenue, and Fulton Street; and Bronx's Fordham Road; as well as with twenty-seven jewelers in three "exchanges" in New York's diamond center. Of the seventy-one operators, only one had been victimized since they had been in business, or since World War II if they were established prior to 1950; three had employees who had been victimized on one occasion, although in two cases the employees were suspected and consequently fired; and seven had recollections of hearing about it during the period under study. The respondents attributed the scarcity of offenses to the difficulties in obtaining perfectly matched substitutes, the jewelers' personal precautions, and the presence of closed-circuit television, security guards, and locked display cases. Fifty-six jewelers or 81 percent of the sample had observed "suspicious characters" during the period, and attributed the lack of victimization in those cases to their own diligence.

Pickpocketing is a form of sneak theft, for as Maurer (1964:59) has pointed out it involves the successful robbery of money from a person without his cooperation or knowledge. Methods of picking pockets have remained unchanged perhaps for thousands of years, and reference to the practitioners of this profession, as noted earlier, can be found in literature dating back to the days of Nero. Elizabethan literature closely observed the nature of this trade, but except for slight modifications in technique made necessary by changing clothing fashions, the pickpocket of centuries ago differs little from his contemporary counterpart. Beyond minor changes in argot, past discussions of pickpocketing offer little variation from the depth analysis by Maurer (1964).[9] The process of pickpocketing includes: (1) the selection of victim, (2) the locating of the money on the victim's person, (3) the maneuvering of the victim into the proper position, (4) the act of theft, and (5) the passing of the stolen property. Pickpockets usually work in groups of two or more, each member playing a specific role in the total operation.

Professional pickpockets seek only those victims who appear to have money enough to make their theft worthwhile. The ability to select the proper victim (*mark*) is an occupational intuition and is based upon many years of experience. The money is then located on the victim's person by feeling his pockets (*fanning*). This operation is done by one mob member (*the tool*) while another (*the stall*) closely watches the victim's movements. This operation is not necessary if the location of the pocketbook or wallet (*the loot*) is known. The stall maneuvers the victim into the proper position, and the tool removes the wallet. The success of the operation is due to the distractions by the stall, the dexterity of the tool, and their combined teamwork. As a safety precaution, the tool usually passes the pocketbook or wallet to another mob member, for in the event that he is suspected he will be *clean* when approached by the victim or police. As soon as is possible, the stolen wallet is emptied of its contents and discarded.

Modern pickpockets seem to thrive in crowds, a situation not unlike the Elizabethan foists and nips who plundered the countrymen that filled the streets of London during the terms of court. The workshop and arena of theft is the city street, the railroad station, the bus depot, the amusement park, any places where there are people who are likely to have money. Yet as Maurer (1964:174) has pointed out, the pickpocket does not need a large crowd to work in. The experienced pickpocket can successfully operate in areas of sparse population, a situation which will catch the victim off his guard.

---

9. For references descriptive of pickpocketing over a one-hundred-year period, see Inciardi, 1973:112.

The profession of picking pockets has been able to survive generations and centuries, undergoing little change and alteration, and seemingly untouched by technological change. In spite of the use of checks, charge accounts, and credit cards, which reduce the need for carrying cash, people still carry valuables and currency on their person. Fashion tends periodically to alter the course of the profession, but rather than causing its enhancement or downfall, it merely influences the development or shifting of techniques. On the other hand, the profession has suffered a decline due to a lack of new recruits. Maurer (p. 171) estimated that in 1945 there were about five or six thousand *class cannons* (expert pickpockets) while that number was reduced to approximately one thousand by 1955. By 1965, according to one expert pickpocket from Times Square, the total number suffered even further reduction:

> Most of the ones left are old timers, and I say that there are probably no more than six or seven hundred in the whole country—if that much. There are plenty of amateurs, young ones, old ones, prostitutes, addicts, but they were never associated with the old time mobs. The kids are just not interested in it as a profession. Probably 'cause there's no money in it. And they're right.

Similarly, a member of the Pickpocket and Confidence Squad of the New York City Police Department indicated: "You see very few of the real experts these days. They have either quit, died, or are in jail, and they are rarely replaced."

Lush workers, known in this country since before the Civil War (Asbury, 1934: 149–50), are low-status pickpockets who prowl dark halls, alleys, parks, and public waiting rooms to steal from sleeping drunks or other sleepers. The lush worker is not usually a *professional* criminal. Muggers, prostitutes who steal from their customers, and the vagrants from other criminal enterprises are found among them. It has usually been undertaken by professionals only when they are in desperate need of money or working without the protection (and good graces) of a pickpocket mob. The common lush workers or *jackrollers* work alone, or in twos and threes in subways, railroad and bus terminals, in parks during the warm months, on the back streets of the waterfront, on skid rows, and in the amusement districts (Lewis, 1912:15; O'Connor, 1928:129; Asbury, 1934:149–50; Dressler, 1951:76). Campion (1957:34) noted specific techniques used by lush workers. One method involves two workers sitting at either side of a drunk in a subway or on a park bench, and unfolding a newspaper between them as if the three were reading it together. Shielded by the paper, the lush workers empty the victim's pockets and remove whatever jewelry he may have. A lush worker can also be a type of con man who approaches a potential victim in a bar, buys him drinks, and volunteers to take him home when he has had too much, robbing him somewhere along the way.

3. Confidence Games. *Swindling,* or *confidence games,* refers to any operations in which advantage is taken of the confidence placed by the victim in the swindler or confidence man. A swindle or confidence game is fraud: any misrepresentation by trickery or deceit, any false representation by word or conduct.

Activities of confidence swindlers have been known for centuries, perhaps even further removed in time than the efforts of the Elizabethan rogues. The varieties and types of this form of criminality are as numerous as social situations, for a con game can be undertaken in any situation where one individual may place trust in another. The confidence operator is a smooth, adroit talker, and has the ability to "size up" and manipulate people. Furthermore, he has a winning personality, is shrewd and agile, and is an excellent actor. The two classes of confidence games, the *big con* and the *short con*, are differentiated according to the amount of preparation needed and the quantity of benefits reaped. *Circus grifting* is a type of short con, but is best treated separately since its occupational setting is considerably different from other con games. All confidence operations, whether large or small, usually involve the following steps (see Maurer, 1940:17–18):

1. Locating and investigating the victim (*putting up the mark*);
2. Gaining the victim's confidence (*playing the con*);
3. Steering him to meet the insideman (*roping the mark*);
4. Showing the victim how he can make a large amount of money—most often dishonestly (*telling the tale*);
5. Allowing the victim to earn a profit (*the convincer*)—this is not always present in short con games;
6. Determining how much the victim will invest (*the breakdown*);
7. Sending the victim for his money (*putting him on the send*);
8. Fleecing him (*the touch*);
9. Getting rid of him (*the blowoff*);
10. Forestalling action by the law (*putting in the fix*).

The short con is designed to obtain whatever money the victim may have on his person at the time he is approached. It can be operated at almost any place, and in a short period of time. Virtually thousands of rackets of this type have been undertaken over the years, but most are variations on a few basic ideas. The success of the short-con racket depends upon a combination of four factors: (1) the existence of an opportunity, namely, a victim with money; (2) the easy, convincing manner of the confidence operator; (3) the gullibility of the victim; and (4) the victim's greed or desire to gain something dishonestly. It has been suggested by numerous writers that it is the intrinsic dishonesty of the victim that makes the confidence game possible. Maurer (1940:15) maintained that the success of a confidence scheme depended upon the "fundamental dishonesty" of the victim, or as Chic Conwell indicated, "it is impossible to beat an honest man in a confidence game" (Sutherland, 1937:69). All professional thieves seem to agree on this point, that the victim must have "larceny in his heart" before a swindle can be effected.

One of the more common rackets, called *ring falling* by John Awdeley in his *The Fraternity of Vagabonds* in 1552 (see Viles & Furnivall, 1880), was reported again by Egan (1905a: 358–59) in the early nineteenth century as *ring-dropping*. A variety of ring-dropping might involve a pair of female victims and two swindlers. One operator would engage in conversation with the ladies as they walked, and after a short period he would find a pair of earrings, a ring, or some other jewelry along their path. After informing them that they were entitled to half the value of the articles since they were in his presence when he found them, a second operator would appear, observe the goods, and declare that they were pure gold. The ensuing conversation would induce the women to provide money to the first operator for his share. When offered later to a jeweler, the women would learn that the jewelry was worthless. Another variation of this same idea exists now as the *pigeon drop* (Roebuck, 1967:194–95). This short con is similar to high-pressure salesmanship. After securing the victim, his gullibility is played upon by the manipulative abilities of the operator. And as many observers have indicated, con men are usually well dressed, exuding an air of real or fictitious prosperity, and their smooth flow of conversation is wonderfully soothing to the vanity of the proposed victim (Felstead, 1923; Varna, 1957).

The number of swindles would be difficult to calculate, yet in every arena of social activity, numerous varieties exist. In 1873, sixty-four different types of swindles were listed by Lening (1893:168), and some years later, MacDonald (1938) described no less than one hundred varieties. The more common short-con rackets include the selling of worthless articles which are allegedly stolen or of a high value but "discounted," the legitimate purchase of goods with worthless checks, and swindles with dice or cards. Descriptions and explanations of numerous short-con enterprises in all types of literature in the last few centuries indicate a fascination with the offense. Much of the anti-urban literature, which launched a hostile attack upon city life from 1850 through the turn of the century, explored every phase of swindling and confidence operations (Martin, 1868; Smith, 1868; Buel, 1891; Campbell et al., 1892). The work of Greiner (1904) is one of many illustrated guidebooks specifically designed as a warning to rural folk. It outlined more than two hundred and fifty swindles, the majority of which continue to exist.[10]

Big-con games involve greater preparation than the short con, and the profits reaped are larger. The big-con men are uppermost in the professional underworld, and appear to be businessmen of the highest caliber. Their rackets include stock and real estate swindles, fraudulent business deals, and securing money under false pretenses from wealthy people. The three major big-con games are *the rag, the wire,* and *the payoff,* all of which follow the basic framework of confidence swindling in general (see Norfleet, 1927; Smith, 1938; Maurer, 1940). Perhaps the most well known of the big con men was "Yellow Kid" Weil, who is said to have acquired about $8 million in various swindles (Brannon, 1948:389), and was a master at taking an everyday situation and turning it into a lucrative swindle.

Confidence men often dream about the rarely obtained "big one." It may be the fixed telegraph message which delays the results of a horse race thus enabling one to bet heavily on a "sure thing"; it may be a land swindle that causes thousands of acres of worthless desert to earn millions of dollars; or it may be a fraud that disposes of millions of shares of worthless stock. It is this confidence game that usually causes the professional to exit from the rackets, and the execution of any such elaborate scheme is possible only with the accumulated wealth of knowledge obtained as a long-term operator. Among the more unique examples was the perpetual motion machine of John Ernest Worrell Keely (Hynd, 1963:13–39). Keely, an ex-carnival pitchman, began a hoax in 1874 that reaped many fortunes and lasted for a quarter of a century. His nonexistent perpetual motion machine, "which would produce a force more powerful than steam and electricity," involved the financiers of many cities, the public of two continents, and the United States Secretary of War. Before his career ended, Keely had a 372-page volume written on his "discovery," over a million dollars in cash, a life of luxury for twenty-five years, and an international reputation.

The story of John Keely is an unusual one, but the methods of his operation were not. The basic ingredients of the con were at work, a complex of efforts which are still present in our social system. The practitioners of such operations may be less colorful than Keely, but the profits of many stock and land swindles often approach the size of his earnings.[11]

---

10. A number of other guidebooks of this type are listed in Inciardi, 1973:120.

11. I have interviewed a number of individuals at all occupational levels who have been victimized by contemporary stock swindles. One Brooklyn family, during the period 1958–63, turned over some $10,000 to one such operator. In 1962, twenty-four businessmen in Brooklyn's Red Hook section lost $40,000 through purchases of worthless bonds alleged to convey 15% annual interest. And my gullibility was exposed to a land swindle during 1963, which allegedly conveyed developed homesites upon payment of "minimal closing and engineering costs."

Circus grifting represents a behavior system in crime which is parallel to that of the confidence games, yet in a different setting. The circus grifter is a professional criminal who rarely interacts with any professionals other than his own kind—circus grifters or carnival sharpers, and pickpockets. Circus grifting consists of sure-thing gambling: *the shell game, the blower, the bucket game, the milk-bottle game, the nail game, slum skillo, the spindle,* and numerous other games of chance which are controlled by foot levers or assorted mechanical devices and the linguistic dexterity of the operators (Inciardi & Petersen, 1973).

Grifters are recruited from the ranks of confidence operators and are members of a cohesive group which has little contact with other professional thieves or even with the circus performers with whom they are traveling. A strong and extensive fraternity exists among these thieves since during the winter seasons, those from all circuses and carnivals gather in the same locality. In addition to the grifters and potential victims, dishonest circus managements and public officials are necessary for the existence of this behavior system (Sutherland & Cressey, 1970:287). Irwin (1909:51–52, 83–85) estimated that as much as 80 percent of circus profits prior to the turn of the century were derived from confidence outfits and crooked gambling games. Necessary for the successful operation of a dishonest circus or carnival operation was the *fixer.* In many organizations, the gamblers and con men pooled their daily returns and the fixer would draw 10 percent for payment to local officials when complaints were made. Of the remaining returns, 55 percent went back to the con men and 35 percent to the circus management.

Circus grifting existed in practically all circuses in 1880, in perhaps all except Ringling Brothers in 1900, and in all except the largest circuses in 1930 (Sutherland & Cressey, 1970:287). As late as 1949 there were over three hundred circuses and carnivals in the United States and Canada, and a large number of these contained many of the games in which grifting often occurs. The gambling centers, or *gaft joints,* employ numerous devices which prevent the victim from winning. In the milk-bottle game, which requires the knocking down of five wooden bottles set into a pyramid, the bottom bottles remain stationary, having been loaded with lead. The nail game requires the hammering of a nail into a log with one blow. Huge amounts are bet when the first nail, as a free enticement, readily enters the wood. The victim then receives defective nails which bend regardless of the manner in which they are struck. The bucket game finds the victim throwing baseballs into a bucket which is tilted towards him. If all three balls remain inside the bucket, he wins. The first ball usually enters, but a device is triggered that causes subsequent balls to bounce out. Race track wheels, chuck wheels, and variations of the common wheel of fortune are controlled by foot levers.

Other circus and carnival games include the use of dice or playing cards. *Cloth,* for example, involves a pair of dice and a sheet of green felt marked off in numbered squares. When the dice are thrown, the dealer counts the number of dots showing and compares them with the numbered squares. Certain squares are marked for prizes, others are marked "conditional"—meaning that the victim must double his bet, roll again, and win four times the usual prize should his number equal that of a winning square—and one square marked "lose." The victim is maneuvered into rolling "conditionals" until all his money is on the table and finally, by use of visual distraction, he finds that his last throw of the dice adds to *twenty-three,* the number of the square labeled "lose."

Many early circus grifters and carnival sharpers were proficient at gambling with cards, and deceived their victims with a host of gamblers' tricks both on and off the circus grounds. *Faro* was a popular gambling game employed in this capacity. It is one of the oldest gambling games played with cards, drawing its name from the picture of Pharaoh on the French playing cards imported to England during the seventeenth century (Morehcad et al., 1964:521). By the time of the Civil War it had become popular in this country, and in 1894 it was considered the national card game. In its use by sharpers and gamblers, the victim was given several opportunities to win. After the stakes of the game had been raised, a losing hand was dealt by operator manipulation.

Sutherland and Cressey (1970:288) have reported that circus grifting has been decreasing in recent years. Many circuses depend upon their prestige and reputation for continued success, leaving grifting to the smaller enterprise that can readily change its name as a protection from outraged communities. Maurer (1964:96), in his discussion of pickpockets who work at carnivals, indicated that the circus grift (as far as pickpocketing operations were concerned) was almost obsolete. Although the presence of circus grifting is said to be passing from the American scene, other evidence suggests that carnival sharpers are still operative. I have observed the milk-bottle game, the nail game, the bucket game, and *the doll game* (a variation of the milk-bottle game) in operation at carnivals and fairs in Suffolk County, New York; Dade County, Florida; Franklin County, Maine; at street fairs in lower Manhattan; and at Coney Island. Coney Island is not the amusement center it was prior to the repeal of Prohibition, but I located eight concession operators there in the late 1960s who have been rooted in the area since the 1930s. Virtually all of them readily spoke of the con games and tricks played on the unsuspecting tourist, yet only two admitted that such practices exist today. The local police precinct, however, still hears complaints of fraud. A patrolman indicated:

> During the summer, Coney Island is carnival time . . . it attracts everyone from the con man to the pickpocket. Some of the concession operators are dishonest, but most of them are straight and are here to earn a living. The con men float in with the tourists and aren't attached to the area, and they clear out after Labor Day.

Similarly, a bookmaker indicated:

> I used to travel with the shows, but now I just don't have the energy, but it wasn't so long ago either. In '64 I must have worked at fairs in five states [as an operator of games of chance similar to the bucket game] and the people are as eager and gullible as ever.

Although the carnival sharper as a professional criminal may be approaching extinction, many of the old timers still operate according to this informant. The opportunities certainly exist, since state, county, and youth fairs contract concession operators (rides and games of chance), providing a continuing and highly mobile arena for the practice of their profession. Furthermore, the recent observations by Lewis (1970) offer confirmation of the existence of grifters, sharpers, con men, and gaff joints in carnivals which travel throughout contemporary America.[12]

4. *Forgery and Counterfeiting.* *Forgery* and *counterfeiting* are types of fraud but are alternative to confidence operations since the thief is in a less face-to-face relationship with the victim. Furthermore, the victim is not involved with the forger for the purpose of winning, or earning money dishonestly. Forgery and counterfeiting are fraud in that the act of forging a name or note carries an intent to deceive. Legally,

---

12. For further information regarding dishonest practices related to the circus and carnival worlds, see Inciardi and Petersen, 1973.

these categories refer to the "making, altering, uttering, or possessing, with intent to defraud, anything false which is made to appear true," and bonds, stocks, checks, and currency are the items most often made or altered in the acts of forgery and counterfeiting (F.B.I., 1968:57). The nineteenth-century frauds of this nature involved the imitation of handwriting, duplication of corporation bonds and securities, printing of currency, and raising of the values of bank checks (Campbell et al., 1892:712). While forgers duped the operators of small businesses on countless occasions, the large banking institutions were the major targets.

Many of the early forgers had elaborate schemes, which brought them hundreds of thousands of dollars during their careers. Roger Benton, a master check forger in the early part of this century, operated simultaneously in different parts of the country (Ballou & Benton, 1936:250–52). In one scheme he set up a fictitious business in New Haven while his partner established himself in Pittsburgh. Four lawyers were contacted for the purpose of collecting an unpaid bill of $4,000 from an alleged client in Pittsburgh. The lawyers forwarded collection notices to Pittsburgh, where Benton's partner received them and answered that he had only $3,200 to send as full payment. Benton instructed the lawyers to demand certified checks that were easily forged by his partner. Upon receipt of the checks, the lawyers deposited them in their accounts, kept an agreed commission of $800 and gave Benton a check for the remaining $2,400. This operation, which took relatively little time to consummate, would net the pair a total of $9,600.

The counterfeiter or forger was not always a member of the professional underworld. The engraver who made false securities and bank notes operated in secrecy, and passed his bogus bills through agents. Sutherland (1937:77) reported that many a professional thief became involved in this complex of illegality by either purchasing and passing counterfeit money, robbing post offices of money orders and subsequently passing them in cities throughout the country, or forging travelers' checks acquired by pickpocketing. Members of counterfeit mobs have little contact with professional thieves, making their participation in the professional underworld difficult.

The early thieves effectively committed serious assaults upon banking institutions as a result of unsophisticated methods of detection and apprehension as well as the inferior quality of the materials being forged. As technological improvements were made in the production of inks, papers, protectographs and check writing machines, and in the processes of printing and engraving, those who were committed to forgery and counterfeiting as a profession found their occupation more risky. Lemert (1958) has suggested that the vulnerability of forgery as a profession has been heightened in recent years by the fact that the type of persons engaged in *passing* the worthless goods have included bar waitresses, unattached women, drug addicts, alcoholics, petty thieves, and transient unemployed thieves—types who might readily inform on one another if threatened with long-term incarceration. Furthermore, with the widespread use of personal checks, which are easily forged and passed, the habitual and systematic forger can operate as a lone wolf, unattached to other thieves. Such isolation inhibits the incorporation of the professional criminals' conceptions of conformity and deviance, and encourages an identification with the middle-class value system. One informant, paroled after a three-year incarceration for forgery, suggested that few "true" professionals exist today. His fifty years of professional forgery, with over eighty arrests in all parts of America, are indicative of a long and highly mobile career, with only a few years spent in prison:

I have been arrested over fifty times, almost always for forgery. And I think I'm one of a kind. There are few good forgers any more, and they don't work in mobs as they did fifty years ago. I've worked alone so long that I only see familiar faces on the T.V. set—and I don't even *know* those people.

Modern forgery is seemingly undertaken by solitary thieves with blank checks stolen from individuals or corporations (Gentry, 1966:225–42; Gartner, 1968:81–88; Jackson, 1969). Losses from such forgery, furthermore, have been of a greater magnitude than in the past. In 1966, for example, one estimate was placed at $800 million per year, or approximately $2 million per day or $1,500 per minute (Gentry, 1966:230). The American Bankers Association, in a more conservative frame of reference, indicated economic losses of $70 million for 1968, representing a 16 percent increase from the previous year (Gartner, 1968:82). What percentage of these figures encompasses the efforts of the professional forger is not known.

That the majority of modern forgers are of a "lone wolf" type does not necessarily suggest a decline in the numbers of professionals. Some of the more celebrated personalities in the annals of professional forgery had been "lone wolves" for all or part of their careers. Jackson's (1969) account of a professional forger and safe robber depicts similar situations in which solo operators would purchase counterfeit checks and identification from thieves who produce blank checks, secure legitimate personal checks from burglars, or set up dummy businesses with others for the purpose of having banks print official checks for them. Evidence does suggest, however, that some organized forgery groups may exist which are equipped with printing plants that prepare counterfeit checks with magnetically encoded account numbers that are able to pass computer inspection (Gartner, 1968:86).

Check-kiting is a swindle related to forgery that is directed against banks. This fraudulent operation involves the covering of bad checks with other bad checks. A professional bank swindler might open a series of checking accounts at scattered banks with deposits of $25. At Bank Z he cashes a $100 check drawn on Bank X, depositing $25 and pocketing $75. He then covers the Bank X check with a $250 check on Bank Y, depositing $125 and pocketing $125. This latter check on Bank Y is made good with a $500 check on Bank Z, with $300 deposited and $200 pocketed. Manipulations of this type have been executed by both individuals and organized groups of bank swindlers, with single operations accumulating thefts in excess of one-half million dollars (Gentry, 1966:240–41).

Double-pledging is similar to kiting, and is undertaken with false collateral on loans. The more common types involve selling a mortgage to several different banks, or securing loans based on fraudulent insurance policies (p. 241). Travelers checks provide an arena for the forger's operations, as well as the theft or illicit production of credit cards (Gentry, 1966:242–59; Gartner, 1968:103–4).

Counterfeiting is related to forgery in that it represents an alternative method of producing illegal tender. Although the most common form of counterfeiting involves the manufacture of false treasury notes, earlier methods also included the raising of legitimate $10 bills to $50 denominations (Wooldridge, 1901:334–37). Contemporary counterfeit operations range from solitary entrepreneurs who produce and distribute only a few bills at a time, to large organizations undertaking currency fraud running into millions of dollars. These large counterfeit organizations employ a variety of individuals: artists, engravers, draftsmen, and photographers who produce the currency, and professional thieves, hustlers, and pickpockets who pass the finished products. Such organizations may also include middlemen who make arrangements for the sale and distribution of large quantities of the false money. In addition to treasury notes, the larger counterfeiting gangs also manufacture and distribute passports, share scrip, visa stamps, legal agreements, documents of all types, travelers' checks, and sometimes paintings, sculpture, and china (Smith, 1944; Varna, 1957:158–77).[13] As an enterprise of the professional criminal, counterfeiting is usually limited to the hustling levels since the large operations require substantial investments for equipment and staffing. Furthermore, without sufficient financial backing, it has been difficult to induce essentially legitimate printers and engravers to prostitute their arts to counterfeit uses (Spenser, 1934:253; Smith, 1944; Varna, 1957).

5. *Extortion.* *Extortion* essentially refers to the securing of money or property from an individual by means of an illegal use of fear. Within the professional underworld, extortion, or *blackmail,* is usually perpetrated when a victim is accused of, or found engaged in, some illegal or immoral act. Such acts are more commonly of a sexual nature, and the victims are forced to pay for the silence of the extortionists. The common extortion rackets are the *shake* or *shakedown,* and the *badger* and *panel* games.

Extortion within the framework of illicit sexual acts appears in the writings of the Elizabethan pamphleteers as crossbiting law. As described by S.R. in his 1610 publication *Martin Markall, Beadle of Bridewell* (Judges, 1930:383–427), crossbiting was undertaken in the following manner:

> . . . Some base rogue . . . , that keepeth a whore as a friend, or marries one to be his maintainer, consents or constrains those creatures to yield the use of their bodies to other men, that so, taking them together, they may strip the lecher of all the money in his purse or that he can presently make (p. 418).

Although this form of solicitation has likely been associated with prostitution for thousands of years, its invention was attributed to one Laurence Crossbiter in the year 1491 (p. 418).

The Elizabethan crossbiter's pretense as the outraged husband of a whore represents the basis of the badger, panel, and shakedown rackets of nineteenth and twentieth century United States. The term *badger* seems to derive from the Anglo *badge* (see Grose, 1971), first referred to in 1725. A *badge* was "a malefactor burned in the hand," or a tormented person. With the meanings of "torment," "annoy," or "malign," the term *badger* then appeared in O'Keeffe's *Wild Oats* (published in 1798), and Dickens's *Pickwick Papers* and *Great Expectations* (published in 1836 and 1860). During the middle 1800s, *badger* had also become part of American underworld slang, referring to a *panel thief*—"a fellow who robs a man's pocket after he has been enticed into bed with a woman" (Matsell, 1859:9). The panel game as such was the basis of much of the professional criminals' extortion rackets. There were several variations of panel or badger games, usually involving the collective efforts of sneak thieves, prostitutes, and other types of criminals. In the typical situation, a female entices a man to her room, but while they engage in sexual relations, a wall panel slides open from which a thief enters to replace the money in the victim's wallet with paper, and then silently exits. After the theft has taken place, sounds are heard which the woman claims to be her husband. The victim quickly dresses and hastily leaves through a rear door, unaware that he has been robbed. Variations of this practice were known in most of the larger cities in the last century (Martin, 1868; Crapsey, 1872).

As early as 1848, a prostitute's room was known as a *panel-crib* (Judson, 1848),

---

13. In addition, a narcotic addict I knew regularly produced counterfeit physicians' prescription blanks which he sold on retail and wholesale bases.

perhaps from the fourteenth century *parnel* meaning prostitute, found in Langland's *The Vision of William Concerning Piers Plowman*. A panel-crib was also known as a *shakedown*, hence, the shakedown racket. And the meaning of this term seems to be rooted in the descriptive context of an impoverished resting place. Egan (1821:164) described a shakedown as a temporary substitute for a bed, "a two-penny layer of straw"; Mayhew (1861) used the term with reference to the poor mattresses in lodging houses, as did Dickens in his *Great Expectations*. In an alternative setting, a *shake* was also a whore (Farmer & Henley, 1970:151), or a theft from one's pocket (Grose, 1971). The twentieth-century badger games rarely use the sliding panel, but a "wronged husband" confronts the embracing couple, threatens to make the matter public, but suggests that money be paid in return for his silence (MacDonald, 1938:133–34). Although the use of the sliding panel seems to have disappeared, the panel man or sneak thief, known to some as *creeps*, may still sneak from under a bed, an adjoining room, closet, or even a large trunk (Sharpe, 1928:283).[14] Today's extortion rackets similar to the badger game often employ a photographer, who will "sell" his pictures of the compromising situation; and a contemporary analysis of prostitution by Winick and Kinsie (1971:27–28) notes current usage of creeps and panel houses.

Sutherland (1937:78) described two variations of the shake: the *muzzle* and the *income tax*. The muzzle allegedly began as a professional racket around 1909 at a poolroom near Broadway and West 43rd Street in New York City. The first operation involved waiting until two men would enter a nearby subway toilet. When they were interrupted and found in a compromising situation, money was demanded in lieu of a report to the police. Later applications involved impersonations of police officers, or the use of a *steerer* who played the role of a homosexual (p. 80). Evidence suggests that this practice continues.[15] By contrast, the *income tax* extortionist accuses the more hidden deviant of falsifying his income tax returns, and threatens exposure. This shakedown operator usually impersonates a revenue officer, and since many individuals do indeed submit incorrect returns, guilt is readily admitted and payment for the officer's silence is made (Sutherland, 1937:80). In other cases, the shakedown operator may examine a businessman's stock, often taking "evidence" of undeclared goods (perhaps uncut diamonds), leaving the merchant a receipt. The thief is never heard from again.

Diversification and Hustling. The forger or passer of forged materials, the burglar, the con man, and other members of the society of professional criminals may not necessarily spend their entire career following one form of thieving. The pickpocket is more apt to remain a pickpocket, but other professionals, even the confidence operator, may become involved in shoplifting, burglary, sneak-thieving, or even forms of extortion. Due to connections, opportunity, and social conditions they may take part in a multiplicity of offenses (Sutherland, 1937:42; Martin, 1952:13; Inciardi, 1973:142). Professional thieves have been forced to change their pursuits in this manner for several reasons. Bank burglaries, hijacking, and post-office robberies were highly visible

---

14. The panel man or *creep*, however, was not restricted to thieving in badger situations. On other occasions, he would be employed in a heated, smoke-filled room where alcohol was flowing freely and card-playing or other kinds of gambling were in operation. When a potential victim would remove his jacket due to the excessive heat, the panel man would sneak from his hiding and rob the contents of the unwatched clothing.

15. A young addict and *queer worker*, who supported his habit by submitting to homosexual advances for payment, indicated that extortion of homosexuals still exists in the Times Square area, but mostly by nonaddict, nonhomosexual teenagers. For an account of adolescent queer workers, see Reiss, 1964.

forms of theft, and the risks were too great if carried out on a regular basis.[16] Pick-pocketing, shoplifting, and sneak-thieving often had small returns. The high costs of the professionals' style of life, the costs for police protection and the *fix* made it neces-sary for them to take advantage of every criminal opportunity. In the course of one day, the accomplished professional thief might shoplift a coat from a department store, *beat* a store cashier for extra change by fast talking (the *hipe racket*, see MacDonald, 1938: 183–84), purchase merchandise with forged checks for later resale, and purchase and pass counterfeit money.

Many rackets cannot be pursued on a regular basis as a result of unstable oppor-tunities. These include *smashing*, the breaking of a jeweler's window and looting its contents (Dearden, 1925:82–83; Wensley, 1930:200), and *dragging*, a residual term descriptive of theft from cars, store robberies, and theft from pedestrians (Hapgood, 1903:92–100; Williamson, 1962:78). Until only recently, auto theft and auto stripping undertaken by professional criminals was usually a transitory operation (Dearden, 1925:102–3; Booth, 1929:194–95; Martin, 1952:115). Contemporary reports suggest, however, that such theft is now undertaken on a more regular basis and with highly efficient and organized planning (President's Commission, 1967c; Gartner, 1968:108–18).

Diversification and variation in criminal pursuits have often been referred to as *hustling:*

> . . . hustling means moving around the bars and being seen; it means asking "What's up?" It means "connecting" in the morning with two others who have a burglary set up for the evening, calling a man you know to see if he wants to buy ten stolen alpaca sweaters at $5 each, and scouting the streets for an easy victim. It means being versatile; passing checks, rolling a drunk, driving for a stickup, boosting a car, bur-glarizing a store. It is a planless kind of existence, but with a purpose—to make as much money as can be made each day, no holds barred (President's Commission, 1967a:97).

Although the hustlers usually include the rank and file thieves who never progressed into a specialized occupational pattern and who manifest a diminished attachment to underworld codes of conduct, many an expert grafter has resorted to such activities during various stages of his career (Hapgood, 1903; Spenser, 1934; Martin, 1952; MacKenzie, 1955; Jackson, 1969).

Peripheral yet associated with the professional underworld and the hustling way of life are the *hangers-on*. These individuals usually have a marketable talent or con-nection which enables them to work in concert with thieves. *Feelers-out*, for example, locate desirable places for undertaking thefts; *finger men*, like tipsters, frequent private parties or fashionable bars to learn the identity and residence of potential wealthy targets (Hapgood, 1903:110; Dressler, 1951:126–27). *Corner men* have a wide range of associations and an ability to remember faces. They are posted in front of establishments where illicit businesses are located or where thefts might be in progress for the purpose of detecting "suspicious" passersby (Phelan, 1953:175–86). Other hangers-on have included *steerers* for confidence men, *outside men* (lookouts), *kit carriers* and *toolmakers* for burglars, and *trailers* for panel workers. The majority of these individuals were not full-time thieves, but rather spent their days hanging around hotels and amusement districts, running messages, fetching taxis, and odd-

---

16. In the "ideal typical" sense, professional crime is limited to nonviolent categories of criminal behavior. On numerous occasions, however, there was some interaction among the differ-ent types of vocational criminals. This notion is discussed later.

jobbing. Others did regular work, but of the nature that brought them in contact with the professionals and their victims, such as cabdrivers, newspaper vendors, bartenders, or bellhops. The hangers-on who act as trailers for badger workers and pickpockets, and as finger men and steerers continue to be juxtaposed to the professional underworld. In the modern metropolis they can be found in the amusement centers running errands for both the legitimate and nonlegitimate members of the society. They represent "service personnel" for the professionals and organized rackets, and are rarely trusted. As one such personality indicated:

> I act in the capacity of a "go-between," for big-time thieves and small-time racketeers.
> . . . Many of my activities have included carrying drugs or stolen goods, pimping for
> pimps, watching for cops, and even working for cops.

Receivers of Stolen Goods. The *receivers* or *fences* represent a group of "businessmen" who operate in conjunction with thieves for the purpose of disposing of the stolen goods. They are not necessarily thieves or criminals, and rarely conceive of themselves as such. Rather, they are businessmen who have the opportunity and connections for the disposal of almost any item in any quantity.

Large-scale fencing operations seem to have evolved from the extraordinary criminal empire of Jonathan Wild. Wild worked in league with eighteenth-century highwaymen, pickpockets, housebreakers, and shoplifters. His profits from the disposal of stolen goods were so large that he purchased a sloop, the *Captain Roger Johnson*, with which he traded stolen jewelry, articles of plate, and banknotes with Holland and Flanders. Wild also organized different types of criminals into district groups, and received a percentage of their felonious earnings. When his career ended at the gallows in 1725, the business of dealing in stolen merchandise was emerging as a major enterprise of the London underworld (see Hayward, 1735:247–72; Hall, 1952:62–79; Pringle, 1963:88–100). By the mid-1800s receivers were established throughout London in a variety of types (Quennell, n.d.:305–10). *Dolly shops* were of the lowest order. As unlicensed pawnshops, they carried the clothing, tools, furniture, and books rejected by the licensed pawnbrokers. The dolly shops paid one-eighth the value of the articles delivered, and sold them to members of low-income groups. The *licensed pawnbrokers* were of the higher order, dealing in stolen jewelry and watches and paying one-fourth the market value to the thief. In addition, private individuals acted as receivers, and refiners accepted silver plate and other precious metals for melting down. Finally, the *lodging houses, beer shops,* and *coffee shops* frequented by thieves were used for bartering and trading contraband. Mayhew's analysis in 1862 found 2,843 locations for dealing in stolen merchandise (Quennell, n.d.:310).

Although Joseph Erich, who operated on New York City's Maiden Lane in 1855, was the first large-scale receiver in the United States (Crapsey, 1872:84), the most celebrated fence in the history of the nation was Fredericka ("Marm" or "Mother") Mandelbaum (Flynt, 1901:91; Asbury, 1927:214–18). Mother Mandelbaum owned a three-story building at 79 Clinton Street at the intersection of Rivington Street on New York's Lower East Side. In her elegantly decorated home, which occupied the two upper floors, she entertained police officials and politicians, as well as the most notorious criminals and professionals from two continents. On the main floor, she operated a small dry-goods store that fronted a huge clapboard extension in which the fruits of many of the thefts of the country's most successful bank and store burglars were held for storage and sale. In her early career she peddled stolen goods from house to house, but during the two decades following 1862, estimates of her dealings were as high as $10 million. On a yearly retainer of $5,000, the law firm of Howe and Hummell was able to protect her from arrest until 1884, when a reform movement had her indicted on charges of grand larceny and receiving stolen goods. She forfeited bail, however, fled to Canada, and spent the remainder of her life there. Considerable folklore exists regarding Mrs. Mandelbaum and she is mentioned in the autobiographies of many professional criminals.

Fencing operations are primary to the functioning of the professional criminal, and they are structurally organized on several levels. Although there are few fences who have operations approaching the magnitude of Mrs. Mandelbaum's, there are receivers who have connections for disposing of numerous types of merchandise on a regular basis. Many are "legitimate" businessmen who have a retail outlet for specific articles, and maintain regular contacts with thieves. Alternatively, some may fence their own merchandise—at bars, filling stations, and retail stores. As such, the buyer becomes the receiver, adapting to an immediate situation for the purpose of making easy money. And finally, stolen merchandise is sold in residential areas from door to door, and often readily accepted by the budget-conscious housewife (Inciardi, 1973:149).

The Interactional Setting of Professional Crime

A subculture is a normative system of a particular group that is essentially different from the dominant culture. It includes learned behaviors common to the group and characteristic ways of acting and thinking that, together, constitute a relatively cohesive cultural system (Mercer, 1958:34; Young & Mack, 1959:49). The professional underworld has a subculture. Its structure of norms, goals, career patterns, and style of life, and its consequent social organization are essentially different from those of the wider society within which it functions. In many respects, the subculture of the professional criminal is also a *contraculture*, for its normative system contrasts sharply with that of the dominant culture. The shared attitudes, values, rules, and codes are affected by the nature of the relationship between this segment of the underworld and those of the upperworld. The norms and behavior systems of the more accomplished thieves have been maintained in isolated settings since the Elizabethan period of English history. And isolation has been a functional necessity.

The offenses committed by professional thieves had long since been defined as deviant when the conny-catchers first appeared on the streets and in the taverns of London. The subcultural knit emerged from the thieves' reaction to official attempts at repression and control. As skillful practitioners of a criminal art form, the cozeners often worked in groups as a measure of efficiency and as a means of exchanging ideas and techniques. Since the members of these early groups engaged in similar types of crime, the ingroup association was further stabilized through their repeated appearances at the specialized locations where the victims could be found. As skills and techniques underwent revision and perfection, reaction from the vicitimized public emerged, resulting in the enactment of laws against conny-catching. But to defend against their common enemy, further solidarity of thieves became apparent as a system of graft developed which provided avenues of protection and defense (Aydelotte, 1913:104).

Professional criminality began to emerge as a way of life in America during the nineteenth century. Although there were some earlier reports of professionalized theft, its main growth was concurrent with urbanization. For in colonial America, there were few opportunities for any professional to practice his art and craft. The large urban center has represented his habitat and such areas of population density did not exist in pre-industrial America. In 1620, the colonial population was estimated at

2,302 persons; by 1650, the figure marginally exceeded 50,000; and not until 1750 was the population of the thirteen colonies above one million (U.S. Bureau of Census, 1960:756). It is the city that provides areas of subcultural diffusion and differential association; it is the city that provides the wealth and agglomeration of people necessary for making the profession of crime lucrative; it is the city that provides the anonymity within which the professional appears less visible.

The early colonies had no cities. They were comprised of a series of outposts with the few larger settlements failing to approach the size of the smaller cities of a century later. Furthermore, in many areas there were few cases of theft simply because there was little to steal. Colonists had small houses, few personal belongings, and only the necessities of clothing. In addition, if theft did indeed occur, the scarcity of roads and paths would have made escape difficult, and the limited population would have diminished the likelihood of any thief being successful in concealing his identity or selling the stolen goods (Semmes, 1938:41–49). Even within the small cities similar situations existed, and the more common forms of crime were the nocturnal disturbances of seamen on shore leave, civil disorder, illicit trade by pirates, and a limited amount of commercialized prostitution (Earle, 1915:233, 249; Bridenbaugh, 1955:68–70, 223–24, 379–84, 1965:258–60; Glaab & Brown, 1967:95).

By the nineteenth century, the growth of cities had become apparent; and accompanying the process of urbanization was the emergence of the vice area. Prostitution and commercialized vice had been present in all cities, but while America was under British rule and during the early days of the republic, its proportions never reached an advanced state. Small segregated vice areas were common in waterfront districts in which brothels, taverns, and saloons catered to seamen on leave. As successive wars plagued the colonies, hordes of prostitutes followed soldiers as they either occupied or were stationed in cities, but periodic raids upon the "ladies of ill-repute" prevented vice from overflowing into the city as a whole (Bridenbaugh, 1965:318).

It was not until the 1840s and later that criminal gangs, criminal districts, and vice areas became prevalent; *prerequisite to the establishment and growth of a professional criminal subculture was the positive influence of an already developed criminal culture and an active criminal class.* The history of urban America suggests that although increments in the density of general population and crime were likely associated with industrialization, trans-Atlantic migrations, and demographic shifts, the evolutionary path of the urban criminal district was usually guided by one or more specific, often unique and cataclysmic, factors. Whether the city was a great seaport or an interior change point, this notion held steadfast. In San Francisco it was the discovery of gold in 1848; in New Orleans it was piracy and the riverboat; in Chicago it was extremely rapid population growth combined with the city's role as focal point for the American railroad complex; and for the cities along the Mississippi it was the keelman from the river and wagoners heading west.[17] The growth of New York City's vice areas and criminal districts, spirited by the Revolutionary War and successive population movements, illustrates such an evolutionary process.

---

17. Standard works in urban history document these processes (see Inciardi, 1973). The growth of the *Barbary Coast* of San Francisco, in particular, is descriptive of a process that has been characteristic of many places where the sudden discovery of rare minerals attracted a focused population. As the news of the discovery of gold in California was heard throughout the world, for example, men in search of a fortune began to arrive in San Francisco from remote ports of call. In addition to miners, there were the operators whose designs were focused upon the bulging pockets of the more successful prospectors. A similar process emerged with the discovery of oil in Pithole, Pennsylvania (see Babcock, 1919; Asbury, 1942).

Although New York had maintained a share of crime and prostitution since the first settlement had grown into a city, the Revolutionary War was the initial stimulus and catalyst in developing its vice areas and criminal districts. Characteristic of every war, the presence of soldiers had attracted prostitutes, gamblers, and saloon keepers, and near present-day Washington Square a tent colony housing such individuals soon developed (Ellis, 1966:159). When the city was occupied by the British during the latter part of 1776, bands of English and German soldiers arrived, pushing the armed services population to 33,000. This not only encouraged an additional influx of prostitutes, but provided the setting for a functioning locus for black-marketeering, smuggling, and graft. The soldiers, furthermore, extended the spectrum of illicit activities: "The countryside for a radius of thirty miles became a no-man's land, wherein irregulars from both armies raided and plundered and burned and killed" (p. 172). These marauders used the city as a headquarters until New York was reoccupied by American troops in 1783. But the canvas town had become rooted in the soil and remained operative, even subsequent to the war's end.[18]

Upon this foundation were added the effects of population massing from both internal and external migrations. What Peterson (1958) called *flight from the land* offers a description of the effects of the Industrial Revolution upon the growth of the city. Farmers had been displaced from the soil when machinery reduced the productivity of their manual efforts while the rise of factories in the urban areas provided one of the few means for employment. In an alternative path, the European population, essentially agrarian, had expanded from 140 million in 1750 to 260 million in 1850 (Handlin, 1951:25). Such increases placed strains on the total family system which subsisted on the productivity of the land. As life expectancy increased and families grew larger, support from limited acreage was impossible, especially during years of famine (Handlin, 1951:7–36; Hansen, 1961). Faced with starvation, the European peasants sought hope in the New World. From 1819 to 1900, 19 million immigrants arrived in America (Taeuber & Taeuber, 1958:48–70): 644,000 British migrated between 1843 and 1890 and shortly before the end of the century there were 2 million Irish-born in the United States (Thomas, 1954:57). As these immigrants arrived in the New World, they became stranded in the port cities. The fatigue and hardships of the trans-Atlantic crossing and the exhaustion of funds prevented them from going any further (Handlin, 1951:60–63). A significant proportion immigrated through the port of New York, and since lower Manhattan's factories offered employment, many elected to remain. Pay was low, but the voyagers were anxious to avoid starvation and, consequently, they were forced to live on but a few dollars each week.

Unable to understand urban life, the newcomers had few choices open to them. With large and growing families and only minimal income, they crowded into the less-desirable sections of New York already vacated by a poor but more mobile aggregate. The confrontation with the new way of life, the separation and loneliness, the insecurity and uncertainty of employment, and the feelings of insignificance, crisis, and frustration amid such squalid conditions had their understandable effects:

> Almost resignedly, the immigrants witnessed in themselves a deterioration. All relationships became less binding, all behavior more dependent on individual whim. The result was a marked personal decline and a noticeable wavering of standards (Handlin, 1951: 155).

---

18. For a description of the criminal activities in New York City during the Revolutionary period, see Bartram (1888:27, 49, 162–63), and Wertenbaker (1948:158–71).

Gambling, drinking, and pauperism became apparent, and the atmosphere provided a keynote and attraction for criminals who were dispersed in other areas of the city and country. Although the immigrant was rarely a serious lawbreaker, his offspring was attentive to whatever might increase his standards of living. Membership in a gang provided a sense of belonging and a utilitarian base for obtaining money. Theft and violence were characteristic of the slum's gangs, while saloons, dance halls, and houses of prostitution were found in many of its tenements. "River gangs," in addition to robbery, murder, theft, and the disposal of stolen goods, shanghaied many sailors and citizens for long trips to the fever ports of the world (Asbury, 1934:150–52; O'Connor, 1958:25). Gambling and commercialized vice were made possible by dishonest city government, bribery, and police corruption. Promoters of untold illegal activities found refuge in the slum areas, which represented the habitats of the professional underworld in their purest form. Boss Tweed of nineteenth-century New York City allegedly cheated the city out of $30 million in cash and an additional $170 million in bribes and other types of graft; Richard Croker, who became perhaps the most powerful leader New York politics had ever known, accumulated some $7 million a year from police protection extended to every form of vice and crime. Tweed, Croker, and the other Tammany bosses held control of the city by dictating nominations, intimidating voters, bribing drifters and criminals to vote several times each, and naturalizing thousands of aliens with the understanding that they would vote as instructed. Under such dictatorships the leaders were able to maintain their bribery-based symbiotic relationship with the police and the areas of vice (see Werner, 1928; Steffens, 1931:231–38; Morris, 1951:215–33; Ellis, 1966:327–57; Richardson, 1970:214–83).

Although the periods of machine politics in New York and other cities extended protection to the centers of vice, a number of factors contributed to the development and refinement of a protective fraternity of professional criminals in America. Initially, the periods of city bossism were not indefinite, and a succession of reforms tended to render the Tweeds and Crokers ineffective (Glaab & Brown, 1967:201–27). Other cities were able to maintain governments which were not molested to the degree experienced by New York. Furthermore, special police efforts were directed against the professional underworld. Pinkerton's National Detective Agency, founded in 1850 and having unlimited power of arrest, extended private protection to the banks who were at the mercy of sneak thieves, burglars, and forgers (Pinkerton, 1880; Horan & Swiggett, 1951; Horan, 1969). That the Pinkertons were effective was well recognized by professional thieves (Clark & Eubank, 1927:80; Guerin, 1928:286–87), and pressure on bank thieves was so intense that more complex lines of communication had to be developed within the ranks of the underworld (Moore, 1893). Byrnes, as police chief of New York, attempted to rid his city of professional criminals in spite of his apparent acceptance of graft from the Tammany administration (Ellis, 1966:434, 437). While he was in command, the local and transient grafters took special care as to their operations and movements, consulted one another as to which police officers could be paid off, and tightened their own internal security system (Flynt, 1901:94; White, 1907:317). And as Guerin stated: "the minute he [Byrnes] got an idea you were crooked he would keep his men after you until he had you inside [jail]" (1928:60).

As a consequence of their attempts to keep social control at bay, the professional criminals of America developed a closely knit organization within a socially and psychologically isolated milieu. They associated with strangers only when it was a necessary part of their business activity (Sutherland, 1937:165–66).

The habitat of the professional criminal remains within the submerged regions of vice and crime, the amusement centers,[19] the "Rialto of the Half World" (Zorbaugh, 1929:105–26), or the rooming-house and skid-row districts. These areas are composed of gambling and taxi dance halls, rooming houses and cheap hotels, houses of prostitution, third-rate bars, poolrooms, second-hand stores and pawn shops, or theater, restaurant, and penny arcade complexes. Within the districts are the girls, the gaiety, and the excitement that attract the victims for the pickpocket and the confidence swindler. Every city has its *line*, its *tenderloin*, its *strip*. What is found in this quarter of the larger cities can also be had on a proportionate level in the smaller urban centers, the satellite cities, and the provincial county seats, as well as the roadhouses located beyond the limits of the cities and adjacent to the rural-urban fringe.

New York's Tenderloin, Five Points, Satan's Circus, and Hell's Kitchen have passed into history, but the sixteen square blocks of Times Square and segments of 6th and 8th Avenues, 23rd Street and 125th Street remain cloaked in the stigma of criminal subcultural infiltration. The professional criminals of past and present, and of Britain and America, usually gravitate to the vice area when arriving in any city: "I . . . took a room in Charles Square, Hoxton. . . . Hoxton in those days was a haunt of all types of criminals; it was to the London Underworld what Soho is today" (Allen, n.d.:57). In a comparative context, a parole officer assigned to the Times Square area of Manhattan during the late 1960s indicated:

> Every thief, pimp and whore seem to end up in this area . . . it's the toughest place to supervise a man, or just keep track of him. . . . Most of my case load is either young junkies or old time pickpockets and con men, and when they're paroled to a furnished room program in this area you know they're back at it again.

And similarly, a pickpocket I supervised as a parole officer stated: "I go to 42nd Street because any other home I never had. . . . The best of the profession are in and out, working or waiting to connect." Finally, a police officer on duty in this area during the same period reflected: "It's the ass-hole of the city. All you have to do is rub your fingers on any wall and ten thieves jump out."

Central to the habitat of the professional criminal is the *hangout*—the meeting place where thieves of all types congregate for leisure or making business arrangements. The hangout may be a pool room, a cafeteria or cabaret, but more regularly a bar or tavern where the activity is informal and unstructured allowing the practitioners and

---

19. The history of New York City's Coney Island tends to illustrate this point. Its career as an amusement center and seaside resort began in 1829. The earliest visitors to Coney Island were essentially aristocratic, since the half-day trip by ferry and stagecoach was at a substantial cost, and signatures on the hotel registers included Daniel Webster, Henry Clay, John C. Calhoun, Jenny Lind, P. T. Barnum, Herman Melville, and Sam Houston. When the area was made more accessible in 1847 with the initiation of trips to Coney Island Point aboard a small side-wheeler, a rougher element became apparent. Numerous groups found the Point attractive for outings that concentrated on heavy drinking and fighting, a situation which stimulated the visitation of gamblers and thieves. The effective establishment of this area as a criminal habitat occurred in 1875 when Michael Norton, a Tammany ward politician, purchased the Point and erected numerous shacks to serve as hotels, saloons, and pavilions. Among Norton's friends were pickpockets, prostitutes, panel-girls, and swindlers for whom he arranged excursions to his "Norton's Point." Commercialized prostitution was established at the Point during this period, and a continuing influx of professional criminals was concurrent with the later growth of entertainment pavilions, race tracks, prizefighting exhibitions, and games of chance (Pilat & Ranson, 1943; McCullough, 1957).

hustlers to interact (Allen, n.d.:61, 217–19; Sharpe, 1928:47; Sutherland, 1937:158–61). The Elizabethan hangouts were the *ordinaries*—the eating houses which served a set meal and where drinking and gambling were commonplace (Aydelotte, 1913: 79–80). Their later counterparts during the eighteenth and into the twentieth centuries were the *public houses* or roadhouses or bars, essentially similar but variously named in different places and at different times (Quennell, n.d.:76; Martin, 1868:363; Pottle, 1950; Maurer, 1964:23–24).

Professional criminals of the 1950s, 1960s, and early 1970s, including pickpockets, burglars, confidence operators, and shoplifters continue to congregate in hangouts with locus, nature, structure, and process essentially similar, and in many ways identical to that of previous centuries. A Brooklyn-born sneak thief and burglar with a criminal history spanning four decades reflected upon his 1967 scene (New York City):

> The bars along 48th and 49th [Streets] from 6th to 8th Avenues are to me what the golf and country clubs are to the execs. That's where we do *our* business, where we meet key people, and where we relax. Whenever you get in town you know where you need to go and each of us has our favorites.

Or more specifically, "they [hangouts] are the only places on Earth where I feel free to talk to my own kind."

A large segment of the professional criminal population is essentially a floating body and without any fixed abode (Best, 1930:221). This is functionally related to the nature and structure of the occupation. The territorial imperatives of the efficient pursuit of the criminal profession are the greater urban centers, the arteries and cross-roads of travel and commerce, and wherever else crowds and mobile wealth may converge. Pickpockets, confidence men, shoplifters, and other thieves who do not have the anonymity of the burglar must remain transient. They must operate among strangers in order to remain inconspicuous and, consequently, they cannot establish roots in any community or neighborhood where they will become known. Thus, the majority of professional criminals live in transient settings in the general vicinity of their hangouts. The more common residential entities are hotels and rooming houses (Hapgood, 1903:125; Sutherland, 1937:157; Martin, 1952:45).

Skid-row establishments, the *tourist hotels*, and cheap lodging houses or *flophouses*,[20] are residential haunts for many professional criminals during any low points in their careers. Numerous low-echelon pickpockets can be found at these resorts in most skid-row areas—on New York's Bowery and similar sections of Chicago and Seattle. One ex-pickpocket suggested that increasing numbers of his colleagues continue to gravitate to these areas since picking pockets is a dying profession and practitioners who are old and have lost their nerve and skill have no other places to stay. By contrast, a pickpocket of long duration stressed the idea that flophouses are frequented

---

20. *Tourist hotels* are usually on skid row but are not always part of it (Wallace, 1968: 32–34). They are used by policemen for *cooping* (resting or sleeping or avoiding the elements while on a tour of duty) and by prostitutes and their clients, procurers, and pimps. These hotels are the higher quality skid-row residences, and derive their name from *tourist*—a well-dressed hobo or tramp (Partridge, 1961b:736). The *flophouse* or cheap lodging house on skid row has changed little over nearly a century. It can be a room where guests sleep on the floor or in bare, wooden bunks (Anderson, 1923:30–31), or any hobo hotel (Stiff, 1930:205), and numerous sources have highlighted their use by criminals (Martin, 1868:345–46; Campbell et al., 1892:645–46; Riis, 1902: 154–74; Black, 1927; Sharpe, 1928).

only by local pickpockets and the destitute thieves who have become members of the lowest criminal classes and have visible ties with the *tramp* world. A skid-row hustler, flop-dweller, and old-time pickpocket who *worked* Canal Street in New York City agreed with this comment:

> For what I can see you have only the bums. . . . I've been drifting in and out and up and down . . . a little begging, a little stealing, and if I make a good score . . . I can leave and pull out of the hobo scene and maybe for good.

Within the arena of hangouts and residential settings of professional criminals, the majority of their associations and communications unfold. Interaction is indeed delineated by territorial referents, a phenomenon functionally emergent from the needs for safety, security, and cooperation. And from this socially and psychologically isolated milieu, their somewhat unique social organization developed and stabilized. Such "differential association" is characteristic of professional criminals.[21] The relative freedom of communication within the habitat rapidly transmits information on crimes, arrests, new techniques, and new rackets. Since the professionals are highly mobile and frequent underworld establishments in many cities, a national network of communication exists. The arrival of a thief in any town or city is often followed by a visit to the known hangouts. Every professional thief is a repository of information and these ceremonial visitations serve to define the parameters of this new environment (Sutherland, 1937:210). Since the forces of social control are the common enemy, transmitted knowledge on them becomes the collective property of the profession. Such mandates as "Baldy is a square cop . . . ," "keep clear of the 'downtown squad,' " or "the cops at Woody's have a thousand eyes" are dispatched from one thief to another and become the working knowledge of their society. This interchange is known to the representatives of law and order:

> Professional thieves are united against law enforcement officers, their common enemy. A booster landing in town will look up fellow workers to get the dope . . . what stores are hot, what the lowdown is on city hall, where the best scores can be taken off (Dressler, 1951:263).

Within the circuitry of this defense and informational system are carried messages and the shared events and knowledge of the professional underworld. As such, the criminal communication complex is a verbal analog of national mass-media, telegraph, and postal service, and has been symbolically called a *grapevine:*

> I knew of this but had no direct word from him. One night, though, the long tendrils of the underworld grapevine reached into my room with a message from him (Ballou & Benton, 1936:311).
>
> The word got around. The underworld grapevine is a wonderful thing. I began to be known as a "square cop" (Campion, 1957:91).

Thus, the grapevine is a loosely organized, yet a highly efficient arrangement for the verbal transmission of information over long and short distances, and represents the primary means of communication for the professional criminal population (Sharpe,

---

21. See materials noted in Inciardi, 1973:170.

1928; Cooper, 1937:97; Maurer, 1964:154; Jackson, 1969:180–81).[22] Its existence is a functional necessity for the survival of this criminal aggregate because thieves are vulnerable to the incriminating aspects of the written word. Furthermore, their high level of residential mobility and their pursuit of anonymity precludes their establishing any permanent mailing address.[23] This situation was described in a contemporary setting by a department-store shoplifter, pickpocket, and sneak thief who has been stealing professionally for more than three decades in major cities throughout the United States:

> I can't get along with standard ways of getting in touch. I haven't lived in a place with a phone listed in my name since maybe 1945 or sometime around there . . . I may be on the move, in jail, or something, and nobody can really send me anything . . . the only way I have is through "the other guys."

Of decisive importance to professional criminal communication patterns and systems of isolation and insulation is the verbal camouflage and symbolism of argot. Virtually all groups whose organization is devoted to specialized activities or purposes that are peripheral to the mainstream of society have a unique and artificial language. This language, or argot, expresses the specific behavioral orientations of the group. It is a mark of professional affiliation. More importantly, argot emerges among deviant and criminal groups as a reflection of their solidarity in defense against pressures. The common language tends to bind members into a strong fraternal order enabling them to protect themselves more effectively from the threats of the dominant culture and forces of social control; it emphasizes the attitudes and values of their subculture while downgrading those of the larger society or of competing subcultural groups (Sutherland, 1937:16–20; Maurer, 1940:269–74, 1964, 1967).[24]

The argot of the professional criminal reflects underworld isolation and ingroup solidarity, and provides shorthand referencing of technical processes. More importantly, it is used as a means of identification. A professional criminal is able to determine after only a few minutes of conversation with a stranger whether he is acquainted with the underworld, what rackets he has experience with, and whom he is acquainted with. The argot is not used to conceal meanings from the general public and add secrecy to a conversation. Rather, in places where others can overhear verbal exchanges, conventional English is substituted since the peculiarities of argot construction and usage would serve only to attract attention to the thieves. These func-

---

22. Dressler (1951:79) has testified to the existence of at least one variety of written communication, a *thieves' journal*, with articles like "How to Beat a Rap," "How to Stand Up Under the D.A.'s Questions," "The Easy Way to Do Time," and social notes like "Big Jake is Wintering in Joliet" and "Dropped in Chi."

23. Maurer (1964:25, 38, 153–54) has indicated that there is an additional need for verbal communication among pickpockets since a large majority received little formal education and illiteracy is common.

24. Argot also is a means of identifying activities and behavior patterns not normally communicated by more traditional language; it highlights the more critical aspects of subcultural processes and status distinctions, and symbolizes the more complex traits of group life and consciousness. The structural and functional aspects and specialized processes of argot have been highlighted among numerous subcultural groups including prison inmates (Clemmer, 1958), social and ethnic minorities (Strong, 1943; Baker, 1950), homosexuals (Cory & LeRoy, 1963), narcotic addicts (Maurer, 1936, 1938), as well as a variety of specialized criminal populations (Maurer, 1939, 1941, 1943, 1944, 1947).

tional roles of argot, furthermore, are generally shared throughout the professional underworld (see Sutherland, 1937; Maurer, 1940, 1964; Jackson, 1969).

Professional argot serves as a vehicle for the content of the subculture, especially the technology (Maurer, 1964:52). Linguistic constructions have been handed down from criminal to criminal and from generation to generation so that a portion of the language of contemporary professional criminals is centuries old, with numerous similarities to that of the Elizabethan underworld. The following terms highlight the longevity of professional criminal argot.[25]

Beef—A criminal charge; an arrest (Maurer, 1964:55,112,119; Jackson, 1969:55). Perhaps a rhyming variant of *thief*, a *beef* was, in Elizabethan cant, "a warning against," or "an incitement to pursue" a thief. Such usage appeared in 1796 (Grose, 1963, 1971), and has been in American criminal argot since circa 1900 (Flynt, 1899, 1901; Lewis, 1912; Casey & Casey, 1921; Black, 1927; Maurer, 1940, 1964). The most recent usage by Jackson (1969:55–56) includes *fade the beef*, meaning "deal with the arrest."

Duds—Clothes. *Duds*, from the fifteenth century English *dudde*, or cloth, persisted during the sixteenth and seventeenth centuries with its earliest appearance in Harmon's *Caveat* (in Judges, 1930:61–118). The term has been part of British and American criminal argot since the 1700s (see Judson, 1848; Matsell, 1859; Grose, 1963, 1971), but typically fell into general slang usage circa 1880 (Grose, 1963:132), where it has remained.

Fall—An arrest. It is likely that *fall* descended from *fall of the leaf*, an eighteenth-century British term for death on the gallows (see citations by Partridge, 1961b: 299). References to the term as an arrest have appeared throughout American underworld literature for nearly ten decades, with usage still contemporary (Horsley, 1887; Moore, 1893; Flynt, 1901; Hapgood, 1903; Number 1500, 1904; Lewis, 1912; Black, 1927; Guerin, 1928; Irwin, 1931; Sutherland, 1937; Martin, 1952; Jackson, 1969).

Mark—A victim; an easy victim. *Mark* has maintained its current meaning since the mid-1700s (see citations by Partridge, 1961b:431–32). American references span some eight decades (Pinkerton, 1886; London, 1907; Stiff, 1930; Sutherland, 1937; Maurer, 1940, 1964; Jackson, 1969).

Prat; Pratting—The hip pocket; to push gently by backing into a person; to maneuver into position (Sutherland, 1937:240; Maurer, 1964:64–74). *Prat*, used essentially by pickpockets, has had numerous and alternative references to the hind quarters since the days of the Elizabethan thieves. The earliest record of the term appears in Herman's *Caveat* (in Judges, 1930:61–118).

Yegg—A tramp thief found mainly along railroad lines and specializing in burglary and the robbery of poorly protected safes in country towns, or from railroad cars and freight houses (Irwin, 1931:197). *Yegg* seems to have originated in the United States circa 1880 but its proposed etymology is conflicting, with derivations attributed to the gypsies (Guerin, 1928:285–86), the Chinese-Americans (Black, 1927:172), and John Yegg, allegedly the first safe robber to use nitroglycerine

---

25. The etymological investigations have been based on three types of source materials: (a) word origin anthologies (Emery & Brewster, 1938; Partridge, 1959; Morris & Morris, 1962); (b) slang and argot dictionaries (Partridge, n.d.; 1961a; 1961b; Matsell, 1859; Irwin, 1931; Spindrift, 1932; Goldin et al., 1950; Wentworth & Flexner, 1960; Grose, 1963, 1971; Farmer & Henley, 1970); and (c) the human documents quoted throughout the chapter.

(Emery & Brewster, 1938:2238; Goldin et al., 1950:242; Wentworth & Flexner, 1960:591). The meaning of *yegg* has changed somewhat over time. Tramp and underworld sources refer to *yegg* or *yeggman* as defined above (Flynt, 1900, 1901; Kemp, 1922; Stiff, 1930), but others have suggested meanings of "safe blowers in general" and "bank robbers" (Scott, 1916:63–65; Guerin, 1928:285–86; Cooper, 1936:78, 108). The widening of this term seems to descend from writings of and about Allan Pinkerton (Pinkerton, 1880, 1886; Black, 1927:172; Horan & Swiggett, 1951; Horan, 1969). The term is now obsolete but did appear with frequency in *Dick Tracy* and other comic strips during the late 1940s.

An additional aspect of argot formation is the use of *monickers*, or nicknames. The majority of professional criminals abandon their family names and assume others which remain with them in the underworld throughout their lives. The monicker is usually a colorful designation, and, resembling the practices of primitive peoples, its acquisition may represent a commemoration of some personal characteristic, exploit, or former occupation, or it may designate a criminal's place of birth or some other location pertinent to his life history (Maurer, 1940:273–74, 1964:162; Goffman, 1963:59). The nicknames, such as "Yellow Kid," "Chicago May," "Sheenie Annie," "Little Kick," "Shoebox Miller," become the genuine names of professionals and they are referenced as such by both criminals and agents of law enforcement (Flynt, 1901; Hapgood, 1903; Lowrie, 1912, 1915; Felstead, 1923; Black, 1927; Guerin, 1928; Fabian, 1950, 1954; Campion, 1957; Varna, 1957). In this respect, one thief indicated to me:

> I've been called that name ["Crying Phil"] for the better part of twenty years. Some son-of-a-bitch cop in the 71st Precinct [N.Y.C.P.D.] called me that and it got on my yellow sheet [criminal history sheet]. . . . Since then, everyone called me that.

The verbal communication and face-to-face interaction within the aggregate habitats of professional criminals foster feelings of congeniality and a consensus among them (Sutherland, 1937:5–6, 39–42, 202–6; Jackson, 1969:155). This consensus survives in spite of many hostilities between them. Should a thief enter some location and observe that another in his fraternity is being watched by police, he will alert the latter regardless of any personal animosity which might exist. Such behavior is seemingly recognized as a functional prerequisite for survival. A sneak thief who regularly worked the hotel prowl at tourist and convention centers of major cities illustrated this consensual activity. He was advised by another thief that several Miami Beach hotels were waiting for his arrival and had instructed security personnel regarding his behavior and identity. The informer was not fond of this thief, but the behavior was "necessary" since the future might unfold a reverse situation and the favor could be returned.[26]

Since interaction and association take place predominantly within the subculture and fraternity, emergent friendships are usually restricted to members of the underworld. The thief has little opportunity to make friends of legitimate citizens for his associations with the dominant culture occur in a limited context. They may be either of a transitory-functional nature as in purchasing a car, ordering a meal, or riding a bus, or on a victim-offender basis with both precluding the possibility of lasting

---

26. In discussing this idea with a professional burglar, he commented that such congeniality was "strictly economic and not because of any love for one's fellow man."

association (Ballou & Benton, 1936; Martin, 1952; Jackson, 1969). Thieves may have friendly relations with their semilegitimate business acquaintances, such as lawyers, fixers, fences, politicians, and police, but the bonds are usually temporary or half-hearted since they have economic and occupational overtones. Furthermore, these citizens often fear the possibility of rumors connecting them with the underworld and, hence, confine their associations with thieves to impersonal and businesslike foundations. On the other hand, many thieves have friendships in the wider society which they contracted prior to their entrance into the underworld (Callahan, 1928; Booth, 1929; Smithson, 1930; Spenser, 1934, 1957; Sutherland, 1937; Martin, 1952; Jackson, 1969). The friends are rarely seen, however, and are not called upon for nefarious purposes since the nature of the relationships might be jeopardized. Thieves may contact their legitimate friends for some small favor, but these are few, short, and irregular. A practitioner of the short con who originated in Denver and was arrested, imprisoned, and paroled in the state of New York indicated to me:

> I had one straight friend, Bill A——. He was an accountant and his wife a dress-maker. . . . I'd pay them a visit every couple of years around Christmas, but never any more than that. He'd get nervous if I came by too often.

Lasting friendships among thieves are few since patterns of mobility and incarceration have disruptive influences. Yet long-term friendships sometimes occur in settings where several thieves work together for long periods with only short interruptions by jail. Relationships of this type have existed for considerable lengths of time, with some originating in boyhood (Hapgood, 1903; Booth, 1929; Martin, 1952).

Stealing as a Business

Professional crime, as a deviant "calling" or vocation, manifests many of the structural aspects that are characteristic of all occupational career patterns. Initially, its survival as a behavior system is dependent upon the recruiting of new members, but, unlike the professions and legitimate occupations, there are no formal organizations or mechanisms for the replenishment of personnel. Rather, recruitment into the ranks of the professional underworld can be formal or informal, directed or haphazard, and by design or chance and unstructured drift. At the same time, admission to the profession is indeed regulated since learning opportunities are controlled by its membership.

The socioeconomic and occupational backgrounds of professionals are many and varied. Sutherland (1937:21–24) has indicated that generally most started their occupational life in legitimate employment, and few had been amateur thieves and slum dwellers. As such, the more appropriate backgrounds for recruitment would include trade and service positions situated in proximity to the social universe of the professionals—waiters in saloons, bars, and beer gardens, cabdrivers, bellboys and hotel clerks, waitresses, and prostitutes. In addition, the pathways to the recruitment process tend to be more accessible to workers in parallel occupations:

> The etcher becomes a counterfeiter; the skilled worker or foreman of the lock company becomes a safecracker; the worker in a stockbroker's office gets into "hot" bonds (Reckless, 1967:287).

While these avenues of recruitment have provided substance to the community of professional criminals, some evidence suggests that the social and territorial bases for such career appointments remain unrestricted. Human documents indicate that these skilled thieves stem from all class levels; they may indeed shift from a legitimate occupation to a career in crime, while others graduate from petty to professional crime, or experience almost direct recruitment without the benefit of prior criminality or occupational experience. Characteristic of many of these individuals was a series of social and personal contingencies and opportunity structures that led to their differential association with professional thieves. Most were either the first or only child of their parental family; early environments were socially and/or religiously rigid and restrictive; daydreaming and a desire to "wander" and "see the world" approached universality; and employment at *street trades* (shining shoes, newspaper sales, etc.) and relationships with older *street-wise* children were characteristic of formative years.[27] In numerous other cases, recruits were reared in slum or working-class environments where the exposure to underworld phenomena was high (for example, see Guerin, 1928; Maurer, 1964).

Whatever way the initial exposure to the professional underworld may occur, entrance into the fraternity is preceded by periods of differential association and training. Thieves often become the individual's reference group, for he patterns his behavior after those he strives to emulate. Training is initiated through direct contact with professional thieves. During the apprenticeship, the full spectrum of skills, techniques, argot, codes—all of the intimate knowledge and common property of the profession—is handed down from the experienced thief to the novice (Sharpe, 1928: 33–78; Ingram, 1930:35, 40; Van Cise, 1936:268; Sutherland, 1937:14–15; Maurer, 1964:157–62; Jackson, 1969:73, 77, 83).

The prison setting represents one of the more active centers in recruitment and training of professional criminals. Both amateurs and veteran offenders often gain entrance into the underworld of more skillful criminal practitioners through institutionalized tutelage.[28] Even the seasoned professionals may become acquainted with new skills and rackets there, plus variations on more traditional operations, and contact with thieves outside their usual spheres of activity (see, for example, Spenser, 1934, 1957). Less significant in the recruitment and training of professional criminals are the *fagins* of years past, who ran schools with curricula for the generation of young and expert pickpockets and shoplifts (for example, Quennell, n.d.:188–89; Lewis, 1901:16; Wooldridge, 1901:198). Maurer (1964:157) has indicated that there are no such "schools," and any reports of little scholars and a slyly beaming old Fagin smack more of Dickens and sentimental journalism than reality in the world of the modern pickpocket. One experienced pickpocket indicated to Maurer: "I never had no such training. I never heard tell of a school for the whiz, and I never in all my life heard any cannon mention such a thing" (p. 157). And to this comment one of my pickpocket informants added: "Oh, I guess we've all heard of those things, with dummies and bells and other teaching aids and things, but that's T.V. stuff. . . . Nothing more."

With the exception of burglars, safe robbers, and other "thieves of the night," the outward appearance of professional criminals is crucial. Pickpockets, shoplifters, sneak thieves, and forgers, specifically, can never dress flashily or stand out in a crowd; they must go by unnoticed. The con man must identify with the clothing posture of his

---

27. These characteristics are manifest in various thieves' autobiographies; see Inciardi, 1973: 182–83.

28. This phenomenon has been highlighted, not only in contemporary studies of corrections and penology, but also in a variety of earlier human documents (see, for example, Harris, 1847; Hapgood, 1903; Wood, 1932).

victim. Thieves must have *grift sense* or *larceny sense*, that partly inherent, partly learned, psychological complex of intuitive powers that enables them to do the right thing at the most appropriate time (Campion, 1957:133; Maurer, 1964:25, 75, 159). "Larceny sense, it seems, is the ability to smell out good hauls, to sense the exact moment for the kill, and to know when it is wise to desist" (Dressler, 1951:255).

The acquisition of knowledge and skills, the mastering of techniques, the sharpening of grift sense, and the awakening consciousness of the dangers of stealing and need for caution and precaution represent a maturation process. In parallel with many legitimate occupational careers, the experienced thief undergoes professionalization in crime. Many pickpockets begin as *moll buzzers*, specializing in thefts from open handbags, as lush workers, or they steal purses from church pews, theater seats, and automobiles; they reach the top of their craft as *pants-pocket workers* (Quennel, n.d.: 189–90; Campion, 1957:54–55; Maurer, 1964). Professionalization in crime may also emerge as a thief works his way through numerous types of theft. Many professionals began as amateur thieves or hustlers, developed through shoplifting and moll-buzzing, and finally become highly specialized at predatory crimes that included precision theft, safe burglary, and short and big confidence operations (e.g., Hapgood, 1903; MacKenzie, 1955).

An alternative pattern in a thief's movement toward the positive end of the professionalization continuum is the manipulation of a *right grift* or *sure-thing graft*. Once a specific type of criminal endeavor gives the thief mobile wealth, verbal dexterity, and political attachment necessary for guaranteeing his absolute immunity from police interference, he tends to specialize in it (Flynt, 1900:64; Hapgood, 1903:125–27; Sutherland, 1937:117). In this respect, a shoplifter commented:

> I had a made-to-order arrangement with the store cops in half a dozen places, and everyone made out. I'd work and split the take on some later occasion. If some eager sales girl decided that I was a thief, which almost never happened, the cops would always be slow in answering calls to the department where they knew I was working.

To the trained professional thief, stealing is a business (Sutherland, 1937:140; Dressler, 1951:244; Martin, 1952:56). Like other commercial enterprises, theft involves the hard work of planning and execution. Business possibilities, conditions, returns, locations, opportunities, new methods—all the factors affecting the economic feasibility of theft are approached in the manner common to other business pursuits. Crucial in this respect is the ability to respond to opportunities as they present themselves during the course of a day's work (Allen, n.d.:187, 189; MacKenzie, 1955:93).

The thief, furthermore, is his own market-research analyst, carefully determining the most advantageous locations for specific types of stealing: moll buzzers work in shopping districts, shoplifters concentrate on department stores and specialty shops in central business districts, short-con operators frequent railroad stations and bank entrances. The usefulness of every location is dictated by the nature of the particular graft, by the size, type, and mobility of the population at hand, the presence of other thieves and police, the time of day, the season of the year, and the architectural, technological, and topographical arrangements of the chosen areas (Irwin, 1909; Anonymous, 1922; Sutherland, 1937:148–53; Maurer, 1964; Jackson, 1969).

Stealing to order is undertaken by a number of professional thieves (Haggart, 1821:38, 67–69; Spenser, 1934:265; Jackson, 1969:87). Although it was described by Sutherland (1937:146–48) as limited and highly vulnerable, several contemporary professional thieves have pointed to this variety of crime as one with a significant frequency. A number of my informants regularly secured specific merchandise at a predetermined price, while others maintained buyers' "want lists," which were filled as the desired items became available. In describing a highly organized operation of this kind, a burglar stated:

> I have sources for gettin' big appliances, my brother gets stereo equipment, another boy has a connection for coins, a third can get silverware and antiques . . . from a door knob to the Mona Lisa. . . . We act as brokers for each other and everybody makes out.

Stealing to order tends to be the most profitable form of property disposal since the alternative of *mapping goods* to a *fence* adds a middleman to most transactions. These *receivers* are of a variety of types, ranging from *buyers* who deal exclusively in stolen goods to legitimate retailers and wholesalers who have natural access routes for specific lines of merchandise (Allen, n.d.:132–35; Black, 1927:145, 283, 336; Ingram, 1930:156–70; Martin, 1952:104; Jackson, 1969:86–87). While some thieves increase their profit margin by stealing only currency, others peddle objects to legitimate business owners. Some forty interviews, which I undertook with a nonrandom selection of haberdashers in Brooklyn, New York during 1967, described the contemporary nature of this practice. Virtually all of these establishments had been offered bulk quantities of men's dry goods on at least one occasion during the twenty-four months prior to the interview. Furthermore, the majority of these "offerings" included expensive suits, coats, sweaters, and shirts, in gross lots and at prices below the normal wholesale values.

The earnings of professional criminals vary with the nature and frequency of their criminal acts, skills, opportunities, and expenses. It is generally agreed that their earnings are irregular (Flynt, 1901:150–58; Sutherland, 1937:142–45; Dressler, 1951: 246; Maurer, 1964:37). A thief may encounter a several thousand dollar *score* (theft), followed by weeks of only minimal accomplishment. Maurer (1964:38) estimated $15,000 as the annual upper limit for pickpockets, since wallets that may sometimes hold $100 or $1,000 more often contain only $20 or perhaps $2. Confidence operators, safe robbers, and forgers, on the other hand, have accomplished thefts of hundreds of thousands of dollars (Norfleet, 1927; Van Cise, 1936; Brannon, 1948; Gentry, 1966). Crucial in the determination of the thief's income, however, are the expenses incident to his profession. In addition to the discounted returns offered by the receivers of stolen merchandise, substantial portions of the professional criminals' earnings filter into the hands of *fixers* who arrange their immunity from arrest or prosecution.

The maintenance of any thief's business activity, economic mobility, and professional freedom and standing in the world of crime is largely dependent upon an ability to remain immune from incarceration. The *fixing* of arrests and court appearances is engineered through bribing victims, police, witnesses, bailiffs, court personnel, juries, prosecutors, and judges. During the last century, derailments of the criminal justice process could be readily "purchased" from high-level officials in city administrations and from local patrolmen situated in the urban vice areas (Colburn, 1880; Moore, 1893; Flynt, 1901; White, 1907). The evolution of case-fixing since then has been relatively static, with two types of procedures. Some professional criminals act in their own behalf, making monetary payoffs directly to their arresting officers. In the majority of cases, however, *professional fixers* are retained. These entrepreneurs of graft can be lawyers, business or political personalities, or private citizens having access to whatever level of the judicial system is deemed necessary for negotiation of a fix. Payoffs may range from several hundreds to several thousands of dollars (Sutherland, 1937:82–118; Maurer, 1964:130–37), and since professional thieves are arrested frequently (Sutherland, 1937:122; Dressler, 1951:243; see also Guerin, 1928; Sharpe, 1928; Jackson, 1969), fixing may severely curtail their new incomes.

A number of individual thieves and gangs of thieves maintain *fall dough* or *fall money*—funds set aside for the fixing of cases. Fall money is an underworld community chest. It is accumulated over varying lengths of time by allocating part or all of the proceeds of one or more thefts to an escrow status to be deployed as needed for case-fixing, for supporting the wife of an incarcerated thief, or for providing spending or gambling monies for an institutionalized mob member (Irwin, 1909:88; Sutherland, 1937:111; Dressler, 1951:83; Varna, 1957:117; Jackson, 1969:83). Yet this practice remains mainly an ideal. Only the most successful of thieves can maintain significant economic surpluses; a transiency exists among thieves and mobs that precludes any long-term security for escrow holdings. More typically, the high costs of case-fixing force thieves to sacrifice their total assets whenever their freedom falls in jeopardy.

Although data on the incidence and prevalence of case-fixing during the past decade are limited, the phenomenon continues at numerous levels in the criminal justice system. In addition to frequent reports in mass media (for example, *Time*, 1971:23), a survey of the New York City Bar Association suggests widespread case-fixing within the criminal courts through bribing judges, suborning perjured testimony, and "taking care" of jurors (Carlin, 1966:87), and the professional thief described by Jackson (1969:123–42) outlined the structure of the fix in a contemporary setting.

The nexus of theft, arrest, the fix, and earnings was variously described by my respondents:

> . . . it works almost all of the time. If you know the cop, it can end right there. If not, well, lots of other things can happen . . . your lawyer gets to the prosecutor, the jury, the bondsman, the judge, the guy making the complaint.

> Money can sometimes convince the man to drop the charge or keep missing the court dates. The money man [fixer] can set things up so you get bail and skip . . . he can also have the prosecutor and assistant D.A. reduce the charge so the burglary one [first degree] becomes fourth rate . . . maybe breaking and entering.

> When you know the right people and have good enough backing, you can set any case right. I know that right here in this fair city [New York], back in '64 the grand jury was fixed for $50,000, with half to the D.A.

> It all adds up to one thing—you get your freedom, or nearly so, but it costs you all you've got. One time it ran some $2,000 to set right a $300 beef.

All of the twenty professional criminals interviewed had employed the fix on a frequent basis, and collectively, their recorded arrest histories suggested the following ratios:

arrest:arraignment	100:83.3
arraignment:dismissal at arraignment	100:20
arraignment:indictment	100:12
arraignment:guilty plea	100:79
indictment:conviction	100:23.3
conviction:incarceration	100:66.7
arrest: felony conviction	100:5.8
arrest:commitment for one year or more	100:3.5

The expenses incident to case-fixing and the discounted returns acquired from the routine fencing of loot combine to place economic hardships on the rank and file of the professional underworld. Alternative sources of support are uncommon. Full- or part-time employment is rare. Few thieves seek legitimate work since scorn and ridicule would be anticipated from their peers. Furthermore, the search for employment is often futile since many fail to have trades or adequate references (Guerin, 1928:244; Sutherland, 1937:188). Rather, any sources of income beyond the domain of theft tend to be of a deviant order. Maurer (1964:36) indicated that some lower-echelon pickpockets may act as procurers and live off the wages of their women. The arrest histories of my respondents, in turn, reflect instances of bookmaking, procuring, and drug selling. In fact, of these twenty individuals, seven had received their current state penitentiary commitments on the basis of felonious sales of heroin to undercover and plainclothes police.

On the other hand, legitimate avenues for support occur with some frequency when the professional thief is placed within the structure of a parole setting. Initially, parole boards are difficult to fix, and the granting of parole tends to be delayed when a long history of arrests is indicated (Sutherland, 1937:188; Martin, 1952:171, 176; MacKenzie, 1955:232–33). Under such circumstances, violation of one's parole agreement invariably results in revocation and reconfinement with only fractional chances for re-parole. Thus, the thief considers two alternatives: he can abscond from parole supervision and continue to pursue his profession, or he can remain arrest-free and maintain stable residence and employment until his parole time is completed. The latter situation tends to be more common since outstanding parole-violation warrants typically eliminate the possibility of successfully fixing any subsequent arrests, and hence, impinge upon the long-term profitability of a career in crime.

Professional crime, as a business enterprise, reflects many of the structural, organizational, and procedural attributes characteristic of legitimate occupational categories. Many thieves, for example, may work alone, but the more typical operations are undertaken within a group orientation. The size and permanency of a group or *mob* varies according to the type of theft, the method of operation, and the set, setting, and general nature of the planned activity.[29] Professional crime, as a complex of both autonomous and interrelated systems of criminal activity, reflects a somewhat universal and permanent status hierarchy. Although pride in one's own criminal specialty has often resulted in alternative structuring of the pecking order of crime, some one hundred years of observations suggest a five-level class system: (1) bank burglars, bank sneak thieves, and *big-con* operators; (2) forgers and counterfeiters; (3) house and store burglars, *short-con* operators and pennyweighters; (4) hotel and house sneak thieves, shakedown workers, and shoplifters; (5) pickpockets and lush workers (see, for example, Quennell, n.d.; Crapsey, 1872; Hapgood, 1903; White, 1907:309; Scott, 1916:58–62; Ingram, 1930:123–25; Dressler, 1951:79–81, 247; Jackson, 1969: 156–59). Furthermore, more rigidly structured indicators of class position appear within specific categories of theft, most notably with pickpockets (Campion, 1957: 51–59; Varna, 1957:49; Maurer, 1964:163–64), and confidence men (Maurer, 1940; Brannon, 1948; Varna, 1957:16, 34).

Professional stealing incorporates a series of business maxims and rules. As fundamental principles functionally related to the safety of an individual or mob, they command universal compliance. The imperative "never grift on the way out" suggests

---

29. The organizational structure of the mob is discussed in detail in Sutherland (1937:27–42) and Maurer (1964), and similar perspectives appear throughout the autobiographies cited.

that a thief ought not be greedy and attempt to steal a multitude of items during the course of a single operation. Sutherland (1937:13–14) illustrates the pragmatic nature of this rule with the story of a department store shoplifting mob that had executed a several hundred dollar *score* (theft). Their arrest came as they left the premises, resulting from an observed theft of some nineteen-cent fingernail files taken from a counter near the store exit. Similarly, an experienced burglar recalled:

> I learned that rule the hard way. When I was twenty-one, I leaned across the counter of a grocery store and pulled a roll of bills out of this cigar box he had shoved down between two piles of empty sacks. I was really proud of myself and everything was cool. . . . But the bastard sees me taking an *Old Nick* [candy bar] . . . yelling and beefing he chases me down the street right into a corner of four cops.

The normative imperatives of the professional underworld also include a complex structure of ethical codes and mores. In their purest form, these might be stated as follows: (a) do not hold out money or property from fellow-criminals; (b) pay debts to other criminals as rapidly as possible; (c) members of a mob must deal honestly with one another; (d) mob members must not cut in on one another's operational roles; (e) mob members must endeavor to fix cases involving other members; and most importantly, (f) thieves must never inform the police as to the crimes of fellow thieves. As such, they represent the underworld *code* and the substance of the "honor among thieves."

This code of honor logically stems from the underworld's isolation, and from a solidarity that reflects centuries of conflict with the dominant culture and the forces of social control. But the solidarity is only transparent and the honor an elusive ideal, for it is generally agreed by both lawman and thief that infraction and violation more often than adherence typify the binding nature of the code.[30] Acceptance or rejection of the code of honor is determined by pragmatic considerations, for thieves relate to its prescriptions and proscriptions as it affects their life space. Professional criminals adhere to the code in order to maintain their position within the underworld. Dishonest dealings with a fellow thief may encourage ostracism by members of the underworld; failure to pay debts may eliminate any future credit; and failure to initiate a fix can be retaliated in kind.

Informing on other criminals, the most serious breach in the underworld, can result in scorn, avoidance, ostracism, loss of professional standing, physical abuse, and even death. On the other hand, violations of the rules and codes tend to appear when the benefits seemingly outweigh the costs, typically in an arrest situation when freedom is offered in exchange for information. Nevertheless, the rules often hold their adhesive quality through effective, yet informal, enforcement. This is most pronounced among high-status professionals who have greater need for communication with and cooperation from other members of their fraternity. As one short-con operator stipulated:

> . . . honor among thieves? Well—yes and no. You do have some old pros who might talk about honor, but they're so well heeled and well connected that they can afford to be honorable. But for most people it's a question of do unto others . . . you play by the rules because you may need a favor some day, or because the guy you skip on, or the guy you rap to the cops about—you never know where he'll turn up. Maybe

---

30. This is universally noted in the autobiographies of both criminals and lawmen; see references in Inciardi, 1973:202.

he's got something on you, or maybe he ends up as your cellmate, or he says bad things about you . . . you can't tell how these things could turn out.

Or similarly, from a burglar:

There is no honor among thieves. It's politics and just good sense plain and simple. If you want to stay in business . . . stay alive, you play the game and you don't cheat. If you have to pay your dues, then you pay your dues!

Professional Criminals' View of the World

The professional criminals' view of the world, their ethos, is a complex set of attitudes, values, ideals, and ideologies regarding their profession, themselves, their peers, the dominant culture, and life in general. Crucial to this ethos is the thief's conception of his occupation. He works at crime as a business, it is his living, and he is recognized and accepted by other members in his class as a "professional." "Professional" implies achievement in the art of stealing and a total commitment to a way of life. The professional criminal sees himself as separate and apart from the amateur thief, the violent criminal, and the sex offender (Hapgood, 1903:78, 271; Black, 1927:240–41; Sutherland, 1937:4–5; Maurer, 1964:10, 29–30, 130–31), and looks down upon nonmembers of his profession:

. . . the rest of them are on-again, off-again, hooligans, mulligans. . . . They're just not professional. I guess we frown on them as much as a doctor would a chiropractor. It's the same thing. A doctor, he's got a profession, and anything short of that, . . . is not enough (Jackson, 1969:144).

Professional criminals maintain an elaborate system of rationalizations which are employed to justify their own behavior. They redefine their actions as parallel to the dishonest practices of businessmen and law-enforcement personnel (Ballou & Benton, 1936:216; Sutherland, 1937:178–79; Martin, 1952:279; Campion, 1957:219–20). They devalue their victims, suggesting that they had "larceny in their hearts," were attempting to take advantage of the thief, or could easily absorb their losses (Sharpe, 1928:12; Sutherland, 1937:176–80; Brannon, 1948:173, 293; Martin, 1952:58). They romanticize their role as that of a modern Robin Hood who redistributes ill-gotten or ill-deserved wealth (Brannon, 1948). Such rationalizations combine to provide a psychological support system which enables them to view stealing simply as a business, and be unencumbered by any superego action (Sutherland, 1937:176–80; Dressler, 1951:77; Martin, 1952:279). Therefore, their victim becomes defined as no more than a means to an end, as a vehicle to be used without consideration (Sutherland, 1937: 174; Maurer, 1964:117, 173). But the victim is also a symbol, a representative of a culture which the thief does not understand and has rejected. In this capacity the victim is a *sucker* and is hated by some, disliked by many, and disenfranchised by all. It is for this reason that professional thieves, feeling superior to their victims, react in a negative and hostile manner to being robbed, as it places them, too, in the status and role of the sucker (Hapgood, 1903:78; Irwin, 1909:56; Sutherland, 1937:173–74).

Although the attitudinal complex of the professional criminal is unfortunate to the victim and society, the criminal justice system holds a less focused position. "Due-process" is not typically conceived in terms of "justice" or "injustice," but rather, as activities circumscribing arrest and disposition, as part of the "racket." Attitudes towards police, law enforcement, and case-fixing are somewhat cynical but less than currish: police are ignorant, but they are not enemies; arrests are to be avoided, but not feared; fixing of cases is a business practice; and confinement is an occupational hazard (Black, 1927:150; Sharpe, 1928:15; Sutherland, 1937:120–31; Martin, 1952: 244–45; MacKenzie, 1955:36, 200, 205; Maurer, 1964:195–97; Jackson, 1969:158).

Prison engenders a variety of reactions from professional criminals. Again, the large majority view incarceration as "part of the racket." They "do their time" as comfortably and quietly as possible. Others, when the sentence is excessively long, consider quitting the rackets. In general, thieves see no value in incarceration. Furthermore, they resist any rehabilitation efforts and return to the practice of their profession immediately after discharge (Sutherland, 1937; Dressler, 1951; Martin, 1952; Jackson, 1969). A New York pickpocket explained:

> This is my profession, and nothing else can pay my rent. What I mean is that ordinary jobs hold no future . . . I have no other trade . . . this is all I can do and as soon as my time is up I'll go back to the street.

The goals sought by the professional thief are money and expertise in one specific line of work. Failure and disgrace include inefficiency and poverty. Although proficiency and expertise rationally describe the general prerequisites for success, thieves evaluate the positive and negative events in their lives in terms of luck and circumstance. This tendency seems to pervade the lives of most professional offenders, and the belief in luck and circumstance as dictators of fate stimulates a faith in superstition and omen.[31] Some, however, have recognized their own exercises in self-deception:

> I played games with myself on more than one occasion. Sometimes I'd do something real stupid, and say it was because of Friday the 13th. Other times, when I was down, or tense, or just scared, I'd find some old wives' tale to blame it on.

Tension is prominent among professional thieves. Processes associated with the planning and execution of a crime, making a getaway, selling the proceeds of a theft, wondering if clues had been left behind, and avoiding the notice of victims and police, all combine to create momentary excitement and strain. Thieves readily admit that such tension culminates shortly after an operation has been completed, and easements are sought through a variety of pleasure-seeking activities. Subsequent behavior patterns involve extravagant spending on women, gambling, or general merriment (see, for example, Jackson, 1969:83, 113, 210). Pickpockets frequently resort to the use of narcotic drugs in their efforts to reduce tension and anxiety (Maurer, 1964:26, 34–35, 71), but drug use is not limited to the pickpocket, and has been the cause of many a thief's exit from the profession. Narcotic addicts as professional thieves are viewed as unreliable, and ultimately, scorn and ostracism initiate their gradual slippage from the favor and protection of the fraternity (Sharpe, 1928:13, 57, 157; Ingram, 1930:52–53, 78; Sutherland, 1937:160–62; Campion, 1957:156, 215; Jackson, 1969:71, 94, 105–9).

In addition to a dependence on drugs, "exit from the profession" is accomplished or forced through a number of alternative paths. Many die, become too old to steal successfully and retire to homes for the aged or to skid rows, or are expelled from the profession for serious violations of the underworld canons of ethics. Exit from the profession can result from a loss of protection, generally occurring through poor or unfortunate relations with fixers. Extremely long prison sentences, in turn, may often

---

31. See autobiographical references in Inciardi, 1973:207.

"shock" a thief into reform or incarcerate him until old age. In an alternative direction, a number of thieves have become fixers, moved into the ranks of organized crime, or transferred their economic pursuits to some legitimate occupation (Inciardi, 1973:208–10). Finally, physical disability has forced some from the profession (Lewis, 1970:30), while a select minority of the more talented members of the underworld have become writers. Although female thieves tend to follow similar patterns of career termination, several have also been known to marry individuals in legitimate occupations, thus isolating themselves from all prior underworld affiliations (Sutherland, 1937:25).[32]

Deterrence occupies only limited space among the exit routes of professional thieves. While many, in their autobiographies, address notions of reform suggesting that "crime does not pay" (for example, Black, 1927), professional criminals generally maintain that neither fear of arrest, fear of imprisonment, nor actual incarcerations tend to play significant roles in long-term career planning (for example, Lowrie, 1912:37, 300). Also:

> In the first place, the professional thief doesn't see the consequences the way you might. He may not think of arrest as "a possible." Or he may weigh the returns against what the payoff might cost. . . . Prison don't scare 'em, or me either. If the *bust* [arrest] does come through, the *joint* [prison] might not. If it does, your *bit* [prison term] is short. If it's long, it's tough shit and you just live with it! You don't cry about it—live with it! You stick it out as one of those things!

Among the retired thieves—the disabled, the outcast, the inept, and the demoralized—there are many who drift into skid-row subcultures. The history of professional crime suggests, furthermore, that some correspondence has existed between these two worlds for more than ninety years. There are also mid-twentieth-century indices of the derelict thief as an occupant of the urban pariah. The manager of the Clover Hotel on New York's Bowery commented to me that at least ten of his regular boarders, now "destitute and incurable alcoholics," were known to him during the 1940s and 1950s as expert pickpockets. Although several factors have combined to bring about a dispersion of skid-row areas (Wallace, 1968:24–25), a number of rooming houses and hotels in urban interstitial areas shelter almost exclusively the homeless man now supported by public assistance or veterans' pensions. In this respect, a caseworker indicated that Brooklyn's Times Plaza Hotel housed a portion of the Bowery migrants, and among twenty-three who had become wards of the city, thirteen had criminal records spanning some three decades: seven had been pickpockets, two had been shoplifters, two had been sneak thieves, and the remainder were of a more "rank-and-file" nature.

The Decline of Professional Crime

The history of professional crime suggests both static and dynamic qualities in its methodological perspectives, its social organization, and its occupational structure. It suggests conflict, change, modification, persistence, and stability as technological and

---

32. A number of somewhat unique patterns of occupational change have emerged over time. Hapgood (1903:260) suggested that some thieves became Pinkerton detectives, and in a more contemporary setting, a pickpocket and shoplifter reported a similar transference to me. This individual, through contacts made during a long period of confinement, was able to put his thirty years' experience to work as a *spotter* on the security team of a large department store. Another thief, a pickpocket turned addict, graduated from a residential drug-treatment facility and became a group therapist in a therapeutic community for narcotic addicts.

social alterations shifted to interface positions with the procedural mechanisms of successful theft. As such, the differential movements of science, technology, fad, and fashion encroached upon the productivity and security of numerous forms of theft, while enhancing that of others. As specific criminal pursuits passed into obscurity, came into being, changed, or endured, the essence of professional crime as a functional pattern and subcultural system remained relatively unchanged. History also suggests, however, that although this criminal behavior system has sustained itself for perhaps five centuries, much of the generic substance of the phenomenon in its classical form may be facing extinction.

No specific data are available as to the incidence and prevalence of professional theft during any period, yet documents from years past seemingly locate the more utopian period as spanning the eight decades between the Civil War and World War II. Estimates as to the size of the professional criminal population prior to this century ranged upward to in excess of one hundred thousand (Crapsey, 1872; Brace, 1880; Byrnes, 1895; Flynt, 1900), and during the initial decades of the 1900s numerous authors testified as to the continued prominence of the profession (see Van Cise, 1936; Sutherland, 1937). Alternatively, a collection of contemporary observers from the underworld and the upperworld describe the profession as all but depleted. Estimates of decline in the size of the fraternity of successful pickpockets from an almost limitless number in 1900 to no more than a thousand or two by the close of the 1960s have already been cited, and various subtle changes in a negative direction have been reported by other types of professional thieves and police specialists (Dearden, 1925; Mooney, 1935; Martin, 1952; Maurer, 1964:40, 130–32, 171–72; Jackson, 1969). The emergent series of factors and events combining to effect a decline in professional criminality during the twentieth century, and specifically since the 1940s, are suggestive of a process that has numerous theoretical and practical implications. These contrast with the conditions rendering less successful the attempts to repress professional theft during the many centuries following its primal appearance in Elizabethan England and its later growth in urban America.

The prevailing criminal justice structures of fifteenth-, sixteenth-, and seventeenth-century England often precluded the enforcement of legal statutes and the conviction of criminals, affording little, if any, burdens on the pursuit of crime as a profession (see Jusserand, 1929; Judges, 1930:xxv–lvii; George, 1965:5–15). Police systems were inadequate, inefficient, and often nonexistent; terrorizing of judges and juries or the ransoming of opponents was not uncommon; districts with ecclesiastical franchises offered sanctuary for the robber and thief. The harshness of many laws combined with failures in securing convictions thus loosened the deterrent effects of most criminal processing. Although death by hanging, penal servitude, or transportation reached high levels during some periods, the uncertainties of detection and adjudication extended little value to the meaning of justice or punishment in the minds of British thieves. Somewhat parallel circumstances characterized America's early urban centers. Metropolitan police systems were poorly organized, were manipulated by city bosses, and were ill equipped for the effective enforcement of law (Missouri Joint Committee, 1868; Costello, 1884; Flinn & Wilkie, 1887; Sprogle, 1887; Walling, 1887; Richardson, 1970). Perhaps among the more decisive factors extending security to the profession of theft was an almost total lack of formalized relations among the police organizations in the innumerable jurisdictions throughout the United States. Cooperative enforcement between district and state agencies was minimal, and in the absence of any structured interstate compacts and extradition procedures, the transient nature of the skillful thief made apprehension highly problematic.

The series of events that eroded the security and longevity of the criminal profession was haphazard and unintegrated, and evolved during the major part of a one-hundred-year period. Among the earlier inputs to this process was the establishment of a uniformed guard force in 1850 by Allan Pinkerton which later developed into the Pinkerton National Detective Agency (Horan & Swiggett, 1951:4–5). Similar to the Royal Canadian Mounted Police (see Phillips, 1954), the Pinkertons were a versatile law-enforcement body having an unlimited power of arrest and the ability to operate without the limitations normally imposed by jurisdictional boundaries. As a private organization, their services were contracted by business and community groups, and by large and small public police agencies; their efforts resulted not only in the arrest and conviction of many sneak thieves and burglars, but also in the complete loss of thieves' protection to operate in sectors of countless cities (Asbury, 1927, 1938, 1940; Horan & Swiggett, 1951; Hamilton, 1952; Horan, 1969). Concomitant with the growth of the Pinkerton Agency were designs for the formalization of police agency relations on a national basis, allowing for a more versatile interchange of criminal data and cooperative action (National Police Convention, 1871:30). By 1893, state and local police federations were organized into the International Association of Chiefs of Police, and with the aid of a national clearinghouse for criminal identification records, the new bureau's cooperative action began to impinge upon the almost unlimited security that was enjoyed by interstate fugitives (Smith, 1940:273).

During these same decades, advances in police technology increased probabilities in the detection and recognition of known criminals who, heretofore, had only to cope with imprecisions of identification by primitive photographic plates and personal observation. Initially, the impact of Alphonse Bertillon on this integrated frontier of crime and science has been well documented (Parsons, 1926:244; Smith, 1940:273; Rhodes, 1956; Thorwald, 1967:4–5; Richardson, 1970:263). Based on the notion that human beings differ in their anatomical dimensions, Bertillon's achievement in 1882 was a technical means whereby measurements of the head and body could be standardized to yield a characteristic formula for each individual. *Bertillonage* superseded the dependence on interrogation of witnesses or the intuition and cunning of detectives, and limited the thief's ability to hide behind different names, clothing, and style of hair and beard. The Bertillon system endured for some thirty years, but was ultimately replaced when fingerprinting became established as a totally infallible means of personal identification.[33]

Fingerprinting was slow in reaching maturity. Although its history suggests that even primitive man was conscious of the diversified ridges on the tips of his fingers, it was not until the 1880s that the use of fingerprints as a mechanism of personal identification was examined at a scientific level (Cooper, 1936:76–93; Hoover, 1938; Browne & Brock, 1953; Thorwald, 1967; F.B.I., 1970a). The installation of fingerprints as a formal means of criminal identification was initiated in 1891 by Juan Vucetich, an Argentinian police official. A decade later fingerprinting for criminal purposes appeared in England and Wales, and it started in the United States in 1903. The more formidable nature of fingerprinting became apparent with the formation of the Identification Division of the FBI in 1924 with a nucleus of 810,188 prints (F.B.I.,

---

33. The limitations of Bertillon measurements were illustrated with the case of Will West in 1903. Upon his arrival at the United States Penitentiary at Leavenworth, Kansas, West denied previous imprisonment at that institution yet his measurements and photograph matched those of a William West already recorded in prison files. The latter West's record also indicated the man to have already been incarcerated to serve a life sentence for murder, suggesting two men with the same names, Bertillon measurements, and photographs. Subsequently, the fingerprints of Will West and William West were impressed and compared, showing no resemblance in the patterns (Cooper, 1936:91–93; F.B.I., 1970a:6–7).

1970a:5). This division has operated in cooperation with police agencies on a national basis, and by October 1, 1971 its archives contained a total of 200,483,728 fingerprint files (Hoover, 1971).

The twentieth century witnessed many phenomena which, combined with the growth of police science, also suppressed the operative security of the professional thief. The growth of telecommunication media aided in the rapid notice of crime commission and the transmission of identification data. The evolution of urbanization into metropolitan sprawl, compounded by the increased use of auto and air travel, reduced the availability and usefulness of long train rides through desolate rural areas during periods of flight. The widespread use of stolen automobiles by thieves for long-distance transportation was reduced by insurance laws and the more effective recovery of vehicles. Strict passport systems almost totally eliminated international operations and intercontinental flight. Similarly, changes in national and local statutes also proved to be detrimental. Federal legislation increased the ecology of risk relative to bank thefts and interstate flight. The numerous habitual-offender laws levied life sentences on many career offenders (Guerin, 1928:287–88; Maurer, 1964:24; Jackson, 1969:231). In an alternate perspective, the series of reform movements that began during the 1890s combined with modern designs for urban redevelopment and renewal have brought about serious shrinkage or total elimination of the vice areas that provided so much interaction and isolation for the professional. And within this same context, changes within the organizational bureaucratic structuring of many police and court systems made the fixing of cases more difficult. Phenomena associated with addiction to narcotic drugs have affected the way of life and security of the professional. As noted earlier, many thieves, especially pickpockets, tended to embrace the use of opiate drugs, but enforcement of the drug laws resulted in long-term incarcerations for many. The physically dependent nature of the addict made him more prone to "cooperating" with law-enforcement officers in lieu of arrest. This resulted not only in the entrapment of fellow thieves but also in the pronouncement of the addict-thief's unreliability as a professional.

The convergence of this series of factors not only reduced the numbers of professional offenders, but in so doing weakened the stability of the profession as a long-term economic pursuit, thus creating significant shortages in the number of potential recruits. Yet the recent literature and interview and observational data do indeed testify to the continued existence of the *grift* (professional theft). Testimony already cited supports the notion of continued professionalized activity among pickpockets, shoplifters, confidence men, burglars, sneak thieves, circus grifters, and forgers, even if their proportion in the total population may be less than it once was. Professional thieves in their traditional characterizations were found by Roebuck (1967) among a random selection of offenders sentenced to the District of Columbia Reformatory during 1954 and 1955; Moolman's (1970:17–19) analysis of contemporary burglary prevention efforts reported the continued existence of the professional burglar or *pickman;* the field investigations undertaken by the President's Commission (1967c) uncovered an array of professional criminals in four of the nation's major cities; confidence operators approached the 1970s with many of the century-old frauds and con games (Waldman, 1969), as well as more modern innovations (Levinson, 1971).[34] Finally, as reflected by Federal Bank Robbery Statute violations reported to the FBI from 1946

---

34. The vacation fraud described by Levinson (1971) victimized several Brooklyn physicians whom I knew. The confidence operator, Bernard Eisenstadt, who managed to swindle thousands of dollars and avoid incarceration, was described as having manners and deployment patterns similar to those discussed in Sutherland (1937) and Maurer (1940).

to 1970, the summary statistics indicated in Table 1 suggest that although bank burglary *rates* may have declined during the twenty-five year period, the gross change involved a fivefold increase (Hoover, 1971).

Contemporary reports of professional theft, although indicative of survival in the
classical design of functional structure and in fraternal integration, present both fleeting and redefined images of this criminal behavior system. Participants and observers
offering comment seemingly depict the active entrepreneurs of a generation past, when
the dynamism of the profession provided economic and libertarian security for an
expanded complement of members. The newer practitioners of offense phenomena that
were characteristic of the more traditional thieves tend to lack the skills and interactional networks of their predecessors. Levinson's (1971) confidence operator resembled the isolated white-collar thief; Lemert's (1958) forgers maintained little or no
contact with an underworld; contemporary pickmen rarely possess the skill and expertise that was common among the earlier house and store burglars and second-story
men (Moolman, 1970:17–19); modern pickpockets, by contrast with the older *class
cannons*, make few attempts at well-organized operations (Maurer, 1964:40, 66, 69,
90); more and more the latter-day professional seems to forfeit any pursuit of focused
specialization in lieu of the less-skilled and more-haphazard "hustling" way of life
(President's Commission, 1967c). And within this more diverse arena of crime, diffu-

TABLE 1

BANK BURGLARIES REPORTED TO FBI UNDER
FEDERAL BANK ROBBERY AND INCIDENTAL CRIMES STATUTE

| Calendar Year | Total Reports* 100% | Bank Burglaries | | | |
		Number of Reports	% of All Reports	Percent Changes Annual	Cumulative
1946	203	99	49	–	–
1947	191	71	37	−45	−45
1948	212	85	40	+ 8	−18
1949	236	110	47	+18	− 4
1950	226	98	43	− 9	−12
1951	273	132	48	+12	− 2
1952	328	135	41	−15	−16
1953	418	154	37	−10	−24
1954	517	176	34	− 8	−31
1955	526	160	30	−12	−39
1956	450	131	29	− 3	−41
1957	491	171	35	+21	−29
1958	704	206	29	−17	−41
1959	782	244	31	+ 7	−37
1960	810	258	32	+ 3	−35
1961	955	298	31	− 3	−37
1962	1,250	352	28	−10	−43
1963	1,548	393	25	−11	−50
1964	1,668	416	25	0	−50
1965	1,749	395	23	− 8	−53
1966	1,871	551	29	+26	−41
1967	2,551	660	26	−10	−47
1968	2,658	642	24	− 8	−51
1969	2,663	681	26	+ 8	−47
1970	3,029	505	16	−38	−67

* Includes robberies and other larcenies.
Source: Hoover, 1971.

sion paths and new images are abundant, and definitions of what is *professional* incorporate the full spectrum of this wider hustling world. As such, "professional theft" will continue to atrophy until its more unique qualities become only references within the history of crime.

PROFESSIONAL "HEAVY" CRIME

Reflections on the general nature of professional "heavy" crime have tended to be limited and arbitrary. The specific criminal role patterns descriptive of this behavior system have seemingly eluded ordering into any concise theoretical structuring, and efforts in this direction have resulted only in residual designs. The parameters of professional "heavy" crime have been specified in numerous alternative conceptions of criminality in variable and overlapping contexts. This is reflected, for example, in the works of Clinard and Quinney (1973), Bloch and Geis (1970), Nahrendorf (1967), Gibbons (1965), and Gibbons and Garrity (1959). Although an ideal, typical, unitary concept for professional "heavy" crime is not attained here, a basis for application and use of the label, as well as an analysis of the subsumed orders of behavior, are offered.

As contrasted with the texture of professional theft, "heavy" crime employs the skillful and proficient use of coercion, force, and threat. Typically descriptive of armed robbery, organization and planning occur prior to the commission of offenses, and the elements of speed and surprise are introduced for reducing the risks of apprehension. The participating offenders are economically motivated and pursue their activities in an occupational or career frame of reference, with socialization into and professionalization within the world of crime normally occurring through a process of differential association. Organization and cooperation in the effective execution of crimes are restricted to a limited sphere of individuals. Although "lone wolf" operators are indigenous to the profession, the majority of efforts are group oriented.

Unlike the "professional" designation among thieves, the label "professional heavy" was not of ingroup origin. Rather, it emerged through the combined enterprises of the underworld and the upperworld. *Heavy* appears throughout both early and late professional criminal and hobo argots, referring to *that which is dangerous and risky or involves force or violence* (see Mayhew, 1861; Reitman, 1937; Sutherland, 1937). Since 1925, *heavy* has carried the connotation of "tough" in popular slang usage (Wentworth & Flexner, 1960:250); by 1930 the term had begun to fall into disuse within the underworld (see Partridge, 1961b:326–27). References to the "heavy" as a "professional" do not appear in criminals' human documents; by contrast, professional thieves viewed "heavy" behavior as that of the amateur (for example, Sutherland, 1937; Maurer, 1964:39). That "heavy" was a "professional" seemingly was conceived within the discipline of criminology, on the part of theorists who recognized the unique stature of the "professional thief," yet wished to highlight the expertise and occupational context of specific aggressive behaviors (for example, Gibbons, 1965:102). As such the term was analytical and differentiating to the extent that it delineated the full range of one diverse field.

A view toward the history of crime suggests that central to a conceptualization of professional "heavy" crime is the notion of *banditry*. In its purest form, banditry is the practice of marauding by organized or semiorganized groups. It emerges on the frontiers of society and is characteristic of segments of the outcast or oppressed. Methods are highly visible and pitiless, while goal orientations are occupational and economic. Banditry endures until such time as its effective arena is encroached upon by civilization, and is suppressed or dispersed when the advancing society can no longer contain it. The specific action patterns of banditry vary as does the essence of "frontier" or "civilization"; implicit in the closing of old frontiers is the emergence or expansion of newer ones.

The phenomena of banditry or professional "heavy" crime are manifest in piracy, in the grand manner of *Blackbeard* and *Henry Morgan*. Piracy was banditry on a maritime frontier. Spirited initially by the Spanish discovery of America in 1492, the West Indies became the frontier of Europe and remained so for some three hundred years. The buccaneers and pirates of the Caribbean were the counterparts of the notorious highwaymen of seventeenth- and eighteenth-century England, the desperados of the American West, the public enemies of the depression-ridden 1930s, and the billion-dollar cargo hijackers of the contemporary postindustrial era. Each had its own unique frontier, miscreant populations, and intruding civilization, yet common to all were corresponding patterns of social change which defined the context of their genesis, rise, and decline.

Piracy emerged in the Western Hemisphere in response to a congeries of natural and social events.[35] The voyages of Columbus provided Spain with an early start in courting the treasures of the New World, and ensuing territorial conquests gave that nation an almost total claim on the soil of the Americas, as well as the financial strength to construct the most powerful navy in Europe. France and England became allied against this domination, and the growing hostilities were further stimulated by a Spanish colonial policy which prohibited non-Spanish traders in Spanish America. Trade, with cargos often in excess of $100 million per ship, found its natural right of way through the Caribbean waters, made highly navigable by the Gulf Stream currents, prevailing winds, and sheltering islands of the West Indies. Yet this same interconnection of sea and segmented land was also naturally disposed for the nursery of piracy.

The topography of the West Indies was well suited for piracy. Located along the heavily traveled Gulf Stream routes, the islands provided landside strongholds in close proximity to the effective arena of the illicit aquatic ventures. The endless number of coves offered natural opportunities for ambush, and with only scattered habitation and development throughout the Indies, these marine bandits of the tropics could swiftly retreat to the security and sanctuary of unobserved seclusion.

The West Indies had become an entrenchment for the socially dispossessed during the seventeenth and eighteenth centuries (Woodbury, 1951:27–50). They were a collective repository for the transported convict and the social, political, economic, and spiritual displacements of Britain, France, and Spain (Rusche & Kirchheimer, 1939); they were a sanctuary for the runaway indenture and the unemployed "free willer" who had sold himself under an indenture agreement. The island of Tortuga off the coast of Haiti was well situated for the fugitive sailors from the wreck of *La Rochelle*, for groups of exiled French Calvinists already embittered by Spanish religious persecutions, and for the English, French, and Dutch sea tramps who had been denied entry to the Spanish colonies. Finally, the Treaty of Utrecht in 1713, which put an end to the War of the Spanish Succession, pushed throngs of vagrant sailors from the disbanded fighting fleets into the seaport towns of the Indies.

---

35. For a historical account of piracy in the Western Hemisphere, see Gosse (1924, 1932), and Means (1935).

The grand era of piracy began in 1714 when Capt. Henry Jennings and three hundred seamen descended upon the salvage crew of a grounded Spanish galleon, looting the vessel of some three hundred thousand *pieces of eight* (Woodbury, 1951: 51–69). News of the event proved inspirational to the social pariah and displaced mariner on the Caribbean waterfronts; ships were seized, manned, and turned pirate. The initial efforts of these seafaring robbers were focused on the highly loathed Spanish, but in time their armed plunder recognized few national differences.

The decline of piracy began with the march of civilization into the maritime frontier in the West Indies. The peace of Utrecht marked the onset of but a brief armistice, to be followed by almost uninterrupted warfare for the ensuing century. England, in conflict with France and Spain, fought for supremacy of the seas within a theater of operations encompassing the West Indies. The swells of vagrant seamen, which heretofore had manned the colors of the *Jolly Roger*, now dwindled as the Royal Navy employed inducements and press-gangs for stocking a growing need for crew. Individual pirate vessels represented only minimal opposition to the newer wartime fleets, and naval maneuvers were often subjoined with penetrating amphibious operations. With a final British victory in the West Indies, new legal codes and sanctions were generated to reduce the existing violence and corruption of the islands' drunken and brawling youth, thus making systematic colonization more attractive.

Thus, piracy was maintained only to the extent that the maritime frontier endured. As the nursery of the pirate, the West Indies had been the fountainhead of a phenomenon which vexed shipping not only in the Caribbean, but in the seas surrounding Africa, India, and the East as well (Gosse, 1932; Means, 1935; Woodbury, 1951). But as the source grew sterile and the frontier transformed, the demise of piracy came to pass in the waters of both hemispheres.[36]

... from Jesse James to John Dillinger

"Heavy" crime as it existed a century ago can be initially conceptualized in terms of a composite fabrication of natural and social events that generated a variety of temporally concurrent and operationally similar offense patterns. The outlaws of the American West—the organized groups of cattle thieves and rustlers, the bank bandits and robbers of train and stagecoach—although alternative and divergent in their particular foci, emerged from a common phenomenal nexus, were spirited by a shared ethos, and pursued parallel criminal career systems. They grew in part from discontinuity and rebellion in an expanding nation left torn and disorganized by a civil war,

---

36. Corresponding patterns of banditry and piracy characterized the evolution and disintegration of the land pirates of the Natchez Trace, the Hudson River, and numerous other inland waterways and harbors during eighteenth- and nineteenth-century America (see Martin, 1868; Coates, 1930; Richardson, 1970).

Similarly, the conceptual notions of banditry are descriptive of the era of English highwaymen which spanned the major portion of the seventeenth and eighteenth centuries. The structural nature of highway robbery was spirited and supported by a convergence of advances in the development of handguns, the existence of secluded country by-ways, and an excess of wealthy travelers on a frontier characterized by England's unique posture as the only country in the civilized world without a national police force. The highwayman and his frontier disappeared with the onset of interlocking banking systems, the building of the railroad, the enclosure of the wild country heaths, and the establishment of armed police patrols (see Hayward, 1735; Pringle, 1958, 1963).

and in part from the pioneer spirit of the frontier, which both attracted and engendered strength, self-sufficiency, and rugged individualism.[37]

The American frontier from the days of Sir Francis Drake and Daniel Boone was Elizabethan in its quality—simple, childlike, and savage. It was a land of wilderness, to be approached afoot, on horseback, in barges, or by wagon by only those most durable and violent, having a readiness for adventure. It was a land of riches where swift and easy fortunes were sought by turbulent populations of miners, and by the crude, lawless, and aggressive, and where written law lacked form and coloration.

The professional outlaws emerged from this complex of pioneer phenomena during the period following the surrender at Appomattox in 1865. Initially, many were Union and Confederate veterans who wandered the country in penniless vagabondage searching for excitement. Much of their drift was routed to the southwest when Congress opened millions of acres there for settlement and development. In these free lands were endless herds of cattle, left untended and unbounded during the war years. Much of this stock was also unbranded; proof of their ownership was notably impossible, and "possession was nine points of the law." Branding these *mavericks*[38] extended a natural opportunity for rapid economic security for the newly arrived homesteader, as it was deemed legitimate cow hunting (Raine, 1929:116–17; Adams, 1948:165–68; Kelly, 1958:357–69). But others claimed prior right to this public domain in Texas, Oklahoma, and Wyoming, which was staked by them decades before the war. Their relentless and violent persecution of the homesteader and small rancher made cattlemen in general the common enemy of many settlers, and the mavericking of random steers evolved into rustling as an organized business (Kelly, 1958:75–76; Drago, 1969: 156–57). To this new collective of frontier predators were added the miscreant soldiers of fortune—the thieves, prostitutes, and whiskey peddlers—who sought refuge in the territory west of Fort Smith, Arkansas. This seventy-four-thousand square miles of Indian country from Texas and Kansas to Colorado had "rights of sanctuary," for there was no court or formal law under which a fugitive could be extradited (Shirley, 1957).

To the profession of organized banditry and surpassing the efforts of the cattle thieves were added the robbers of stage, train, and bank. The first "regular" stagecoach service began during the autumn of 1849 in California (Hawgood, 1969:249), and became a recognized mode of travel soon after the first Concord coach was brought by clipper ship around the Horn to the streets of San Francisco in 1850 (Harlow, 1934:175–76). Although stage robbery began in 1852 (Loomis, 1968:142), its boldest exploits marked the major portion of the 1870s (Cook, 1882:155–64). It became a regular trade during that decade in California, Wyoming, Montana, and the Dakotas, made profitable by the gold dust and investors carried through the mountainous and secluded mining regions. Train robbery was also among the efforts of the frontier road agents, beginning on October 6, 1866 when John and Simeon Reno secured $13,000 from the safe aboard an Ohio & Mississippi Railway express car near Seymour, Indiana (Harlow, 1934:331–37; Holbrook, 1962:369–71). The Renos were seemingly the

---

37. It should be noted here that an industrious school of fiction has embroidered the history of the American outlaw with countless misconceptions, exaggerations, and outright falsehoods. The more reliable segments of this literature are noted in Adams's *Six Guns and Saddle Leather* (1969), which provides an annotated critique of some 2,500 contributions to Western Americana.

38. The term *maverick*, referring to any unbranded animal running loose in open range, descends from Colonel Maverick, a Texas rancher made wealthy by branding the unmarked occupants of the free lands (Hough, 1918:146–47; Williamson, 1930:177).

founders of this typically American institution, which was to endure for a half century. Following the Reno gang, train robbery began in Missouri and Nevada in 1870 and had its most notorious era during that decade.

Jesse Woodson James was among the more celebrated of the train pirates.[39] He was a product of the hardships and embitterment of the Civil War and the Kansas-Missouri border wars, and began his outlaw career in bank robbery with the aid of Cole, Jim, John, and Bob Younger. Jesse and his troupe first reached a national audience on July 21, 1873 with the holdup of a Chicago, Rock Island & Pacific train near Adair, Iowa. Their estimated $4,000 theft was decidedly small when contrasted with other efforts of the period, but the James-Younger technique of wrecking the train prior to its robbery represented a new and daring contribution to outlawry.

Few lines of demarcation separated the train robbers from the bank bandits of the post–Civil War decades, for the same individuals invariably pursued both avenues of theft. Yet, while organized posses of lawmen and townspeople actively pursued the bank predators, thus making their work risky, train robbery survived with only limited opposition. This resulted not only from the security extended by the seclusion of the country rail sidings, but from a widespread apathy toward the railroad industry as well. The 1830s had marked the initial building of railroad networks throughout the eastern United States with a total of 35,085 miles of track by 1865 (Hawgood, 1969: 234). At the close of the Civil War, however, only 3,272 track-miles traversed the whole of the trans-Mississippi West, and it was not until late in the Reconstruction Era that railroad transportation began to play a significant role in western expansion.

Bitterness and hatred for the railroads were landmarked in the late 1860s by the policies of the Southern Pacific (Block, 1959:9–12) combined with conflicts over the Kansas land grants in 1854–90 (Gates, 1966). The Southern Pacific had induced pioneer investment and development in areas proposed for routing, later disclaiming these settlers' legal title to their lands. It was also claimed that many railroads were bypassing prosperous communities as a penalty for not cooperating with them, and that federal land policies allowed many railroads to grab millions of acres, which they then sold at exorbitant prices. Political and advertising patronage enabled the railroads to engage in rate discrimination and monopolistic practices, and much of the Western public felt cheated in land deals, freight rates, and wildcat stocks and bonds. They worried little when others preyed on the railroads, so criminals in the tradition of Jesse and Frank James, the Younger brothers, and others operated with what, in retrospect, appears to have been comparative ease and safety. Indeed, many of them became celebrated heroes (Warner & King, 1940; Horan, 1949; Hungerford, 1949; Wellman, 1961; Holbrook, 1962:369–88; Drago, 1964, 1968).

Folklore often depicts the bandits of the American West as ribald, hysterical, and contorted humans in a playground of idle masculinity. Actually, rustlers and robbers were the functionaries of a highly developed vocation and business, made profitable by the skillful use of their natural and social environments. The successful planning and execution of their crimes were made secure by the manipulation of an intermountain topography of confusing ranges of high mountains, segmented by wide deserts, and creviced with inaccessible canyons. An intimate knowledge of the dim trails and widely spaced water holes that bridged a path of wilderness extending from Mexico to Canada permitted one to define the boundaries of an impregnable area.

---

39. Hundreds of volumes have been written describing the life and career of Jesse James, and the majority are characterized by errors and outright falsehoods. One of the few accurate accounts is the work of Settle (1966).

FIGURE 1. The outlaw trail, the Western cattle trails, and Western bandit country.

This domain was known as the *Outlaw Trail*, spanning five states and intersecting the borders of three nations (Figure 1). Positionally significant along the Trail was *Brown's Hole*, an inaccessible mountain-walled valley lying partially in the states of Utah, Colorado, and Wyoming. It offered unlimited security and sanctuary since any attempt to capture a fugitive or recover stolen stock from within its perimeter would require the unlikely cooperation of officers from three adjoining states. Brown's Hole was the headquarters for the major population of Utah and Wyoming cattle and horse thieves, including the legendary Butch Cassidy and the Wild Bunch. It had its own routine, social life, and codes of conduct, with permanent settlements where children grew into young men trained as expert rustlers, bank robbers, and stagecoach predators (Warner & King, 1940; Dunham & Dunham, 1947; Kelly, 1958).

To the north of Brown's Hole, the Outlaw Trail passed through the *Hole-in-the-Wall* en route to its uppermost point above the Little Rockies of Montana. Located in Johnson County, Wyoming, adjacent to vast and protected grazing lands, the Hole-in-the-Wall was also a lure for the territory's illicit cow hunters; and just west of Deadwood, South Dakota—the explosive boom town of the 1870s celebrated as a junction city for robbers, gamblers, and bounty hunters—it accepted such fugitive operatives as Jesse and Frank James and the Younger brothers (LeFors, 1953; Kelly, 1958; Huntington, 1959; Crawford, 1962).

South of Brown's Hole was situated the most isolated hideout in the West—*Robbers' Roost*. As a plateau based at the summit of the San Rafael Swell, it represented a natural rock fortress which endured from 1870 to 1895 (Warner & King, 1940; Dunham & Dunham, 1947; Kelly, 1958). Of similar arrangement and texture were other bandit sanctuaries as *Robbers Cave* in the San Boise Mountains of Oklahoma (Drago, 1964), *Jackson Hole* in Wyoming (Warner & King, 1940), the *Dakota Badlands* (Cook, 1882; Hawgood, 1969), the *Cookson Hills,* an outthrust of the Ozark Mountains in northeast Oklahoma (Wellman, 1961; Drago, 1964), and the *Osage Hills,* just west of the Cookson range (Wellman, 1961; Drago, 1964). These fail-safe asylums along the Outlaw Trail and its neighboring out-regions not only extended protection to the fleeting bandit and outlaw, but of greater impact, they provided the organized rustlers with positional access to those established cattle trails that reached northward from Texas to the railhead cow towns of the Great Plains (see Gard, 1954; Mercer, 1954; Drago, 1965).

Heavy crimes declined in the American West as social and technological changes brought civilization to the frontier. The outlaw era began with the close of the Civil War and endured for some five decades. Yet almost immediately after the onset of its more mature ventures during the 1870s, the phenomena that would serve to initiate its deterioration and ultimately limit its duration grew rapidly. The long cattle drives, for example, which permitted the rustler to raid slow-moving herds, diminished rapidly during the 1880s. The beef magnates of the previous decade had foreseen the end of free grazing on public lands and purchased the better pasture areas for later fencing (Gard, 1954: 206–12). Barbed wire, given additional yet reluctant support in an effort to contain the growing aggregates of sheep (Hawgood, 1969:338), ultimately blocked the efforts of drovers. Railroads were also piercing deeper into the Texas range lands with offers of better facilities and more favorable rates for stock shipment. By 1890, the old cattle trails had become almost totally abandoned (Gard, 1954:259–64; Drago, 1965:243–52). The stage robber was similarly driven to more opulent horizons when the discomforts of the stagecoach limited their usefulness (see, for example, Bunn, 1853:240), and the hazards of highway robbery forced many shippers to seek alternate methods of transport (Cook, 1882). Rail growth drained much of the profit from the stage industry during the 1870s and 1880s (Hawgood, 1969:234–72).

Patterns of evolutionary growth also occurred in the nation's criminal justice machinery and private law-enforcement bodies. In 1875, for example, a United States District Court was established at Fort Smith, Arkansas, and given jurisdiction and enforcement powers in that seventy-four-thousand square mile territory once regarded as a virtual sanctuary (Shirley, 1957). In addition, the Texas Rangers, first equipped by Stephen Austin in 1823 as a settler's protection against Indians and later organized as a corps of irregular fighters at the outbreak of the Texas Revolution in 1835, evolved into an effective thrust against outlaws subsequent to 1870 (Webb, 1935; Castleman, 1944). Stage and express lines, banks, and railroads were afforded protection by private organizations, such as the Rocky Mountain Detective Association (Cook, 1882), The Pinkerton National Detective Agency (Rowan, 1931; Horan, 1969) and Wells, Fargo & Company (Hungerford, 1949; Loomis, 1968; Lake, 1969). These public, private, and railroad-owned enforcement groups increased the risks and diminished the profits of train robbery. Baggage cars were equipped with stalls of fast horses and ramps for the immediate pursuit of bandits. Detectives and guards rode unobtrusively in coaches. Single locomotives were kept ready on sidings to speed alarms and transport posses. Substantial rewards were offered, and federal involvement extended investigations beyond the limitations of county and state boundaries. Technology joined the law-enforcement effort through more efficient avenues of communication and transportation, and forensic science made identification and apprehension less difficult.

The legal, economic, social, and technological changes that caused the decline of the outlaw raiders of the trans-Mississippi rail systems also defined the limits of bank robbery. Furthermore, all forms of Western barbarism were decidedly impacted by county and town vigilance committees, which represented quasi-public efforts to adapt self-government to the special conditions of the frontier. The *vigilante* (watchman) was first described in Victor Prudon's *Vigilantes des Los Angeles, 1836* (Bean, 1968:136–37), and received paramount attention in the historical pulp journalism which often glorified the vigilance committees of post–gold rush California (Williams, 1921). Similar attachments of self-appointed enforcement bodies emerged in frontier Montana, Idaho, Nevada, Nebraska, Wyoming, and North Dakota as localized efforts to limit the activities of rustlers, horse thieves, bank robbers, and road agents (see Dimsdale, 1866; Simpson, 1893; Homsher, 1960). Finally, the contoured frontier base of the professional bandit experienced additional transformation with the westward expansion of the more tangible constituents of civilization. America's urbanization gained momentum following the Civil War reaching farther inland with rival trading centers to serve each frontier outpost. Industrialization, exploitation of new resources, and transoceanic migrations created new settlements, competing cities, and metropolitan centers.

> . . . The bandits had been born of the wilderness: its thickets and swamps had been the background and its lonely trails the scene of all their operations. And now the wilderness itself was vanishing; the scene had shifted, and like actors on a vacant stage, they were left with no background for the consummation of their plotting (Coates, 1930:301).

With the beginning of a new century the West appeared conquered. Train robberies dropped from twenty-nine in 1900 to seven in 1905, and never increased significantly (Holbrook, 1962:386). And the Outlaw Trail had also disappeared—laid waste, barren, and eroded by the endless thousands of wooly sheep that tore at the roots of its landscape, devouring even the hoary sagebrush (Kelly, 1958:301–3). Only a limited number of the old-style Western bandits survived (Warner and King, 1940; Wellman, 1961:296–308; Shirley, 1965).

The more modern bandits of the twentieth-century depression era were the ideational descendants of the earlier outlaw breed. Theirs was a frontier of more social than natural components—public apathy and rapid social change. The crash of 1929 severed the national income, hundreds of banks collapsed, and thirteen million Americans were jobless; radicalism was prominent and endorsements for a Communist presidential candidate in 1932 were heard from Dos Passos, Dreiser, and other notable opinion-makers. Urban centers became so immense that local law enforcement grew unwieldy and inefficient, and areas of vice and corruption were unbounded. Finally, the changes in law, science, and community organization, which ultimately led to the demise of the rustler and robber of stage, bank, and train a few decades previous, permitted newer adaptations in criminality. Armed with machine guns, the new professional "heavies" re-created the frontier pattern of swift and rapid assault followed by an immediate and elusive retreat. Fast cars and intricate systems of highways replaced the bridled desert and canyon escape routes. Now, like commuters, the outlaws shuttled between distant cities or to adjoining states for sanctuary. Local police were helpless: they had few modern weapons; their patrol vehicles were old and often disabled; they were under-staffed and poorly paid, many times having to provide their own guns and transporta-tion. Police chiefs were frequently changed by new political administrations at the cost of morale and efficiency. County officials were equally held at bay, state police were little more than paper organizations, and federal authority was subject to the politics of local pressure and states' rights.

Such was the setting of the crime wave of the 1930s, with principals like John Dil-linger, Frank Nash, Wilbur Underhill, "Pretty Boy" Floyd, Bonnie Parker and Clyde Barrow, "Machine Gun" Kelly, Ma Barker, Alvin Karpis, and "Baby Face" Nelson (Kirkpatrick, 1934; Cooper, 1936, 1937; Hoover, 1938; Toland, 1963). Bank robbery was their primary objective, undertaken openly and insolently as in the days of the outlaw West. Organization characterized every detail, with all operations carefully planned and methods and routes for escape predetermined. Gangs were closely knit to insure loyalty and cohesion. Contacts were formalized in the vice areas and in under-world *cooling-off joints*, where criminal money could always find safety. The towns of Joplin, Missouri, St. Paul, Minnesota, and Hot Springs, Arkansas were popular; here one could always find the fences for stolen goods and money, the physicians who never reported gunshot wounds, the lawyers who knew how to evade the law, the police who could be bribed, the tailors who made clothes with concealed pistol pockets, the me-chanics who constructed bulletproof cars, and the *tipsters* and *markers* who advised which places to rob (Cooper, 1936; Hoover, 1938:65–68; Audett, 1954; Toland, 1963). Similarly organized were the kidnappers, many of whom were also meshed in the pro-fessional bank-robbery operations (Sullivan, 1932; Cooper, 1936; Hoover, 1938).

Yet this era of professional banditry was short lived. The criminals who had chosen organized bank robbery and kidnapping as a vocational pursuit endured for less than a decade, essentially as a result of the efforts of the Federal Bureau of Investiga-tion. This new force of special agents, trained in the use of rifles, pistols, shotguns, and submachine guns, had been developing since 1924. Each of its officers was also equipped with a knowledge of fingerprint identification, scientific crime detection, and the preser-vation of evidence at the scenes of crime. The effectiveness of this Bureau was demon-strated immediately following a series of national crime bills authored by U.S. Attorney General Homer S. Cummings, passed by Congress during May and June of 1934, and signed into law by President Franklin D. Roosevelt. Under the new legislation it became a federal offense to assault or cause the death of a federal officer, to rob a national bank, to flee across state boundaries to avoid prosecution or testifying in federal criminal cases, to transport stolen property valued at $5,000 or more across state lines, to use interstate communications in extortion attempts, and to carry hostages or kidnap vic-tims from one state to another. Furthermore, Bureau agents were authorized to carry weapons at all times and were given full police powers in all jurisdictions throughout the nation (Hoover, 1938; Cook, 1964; Turner, 1970). The effect was to provide the FBI with an authority and with methods not previously held by any enforcement body, thus preventing the professional robbers and kidnappers from their interstate flight into undisputed sanctuary. Within a few years the majority of the known outlaws and "public enemies" were apprehended (Corey, 1936; Wellman, 1961; Toland, 1963).

In retrospect, the professional "heavy" offenders and their prototypes from the early West were more than ideationally similar in activity and operation. Rather, the frontier outlaw was succeeded by the depression bandit, often forming a continuing criminal heritage and tradition handed down from generation to generation through a series of unbroken personal connections. Indeed, the elements of geographical proximity and social legacy were well suited for such a modern adaptation. John Dillinger, "Baby Face" Nelson, the Barker family, Alvin Karpis, "Machine Gun" Kelly, Bonnie Parker, and the Barrow brothers were fourth- and fifth-generation Americans. Many descended from the Ozarks and the Osage and Cookson Hills, as did Jesse and Frank James and the Younger brothers. And these areas, even with the onset of a new century, were not altogether a closed frontier. Oklahoma was a territory until 1907, and statehood was withheld from Arizona and New Mexico until 1912. The rugged hills west of Fort Smith, Arkansas, cut with narrow valleys, steep watercourses, picturesque bluffs, and natural caves, remained without paved roads as late as the 1930s and served as a rest and refuge depot for the outlaws of both periods (Wellman, 1961). The population, too, was of limited density, for urban growth had been slow in occupying these regions and metropolitan expansion was yet to come. The pioneer traditions similarly endured. Personal and community conflicts were handled arbitrarily by the permanent settlers, respect for Eastern legislators held little dominance, and contempt for subservience and obedience was characteristically strong.

It was within this setting that both generations of outlaws were first socialized into the underworld and escorted to maturity. Here the exploits of the thieves and rustlers of the Western mountains and plains remained current in the minds of the people. Jesse James, the Youngers, Billy the Kid, and the other more notorious agents of road and rail were not forgotten; as ancestral and legendary heroes, they were very much a part of the local folklore. Ma Barker, for example, reaching her twenty-first birthday in 1893, spent her youth and adolescence as a contemporary of the Dalton brothers, the Doolin gang, and the James-Younger troupe. Henry Starr was still to prey upon banks for some two decades when John Dillinger was born.

Characteristic of this lineal portrait was the historical connection between William Clarke Quantrill and Charles "Pretty Boy" Floyd. As suggested by Figure 2, theirs was a seventy-year line, beginning with a renegade gentry of the mid-nineteenth century. Quantrill was the cornerstone of an organized band of guerrillas which emerged from the Kansas-Missouri border wars and came into prominence during the Civil War. Jesse James and Cole Younger were among these outlaw raiders; John Shirley, an innkeeper from Carthage, Missouri and a Confederate sympathizer, always extended hospitality to the marauding group. And it was from Cole Younger and John Shirley that "Pretty Boy" Floyd's criminal heritage descended. Shirley was the father of Belle Starr, the notorious "bandit queen" who was the mistress of Cole Younger and alleged wife of Sam Starr, a Cherokee Indian. During her outlaw reign in the 1880s, Henry Starr was among her active followers, and his career extended into the twentieth century to merge finally with the efforts of Frank Nash and Al Spencer. Spencer, Nash, and Starr were outlaws of a transitional nature, and linked the past to the later operations of "Pretty Boy" Floyd. Floyd spent his youth in Oklahoma's celebrated Cookson Hills,

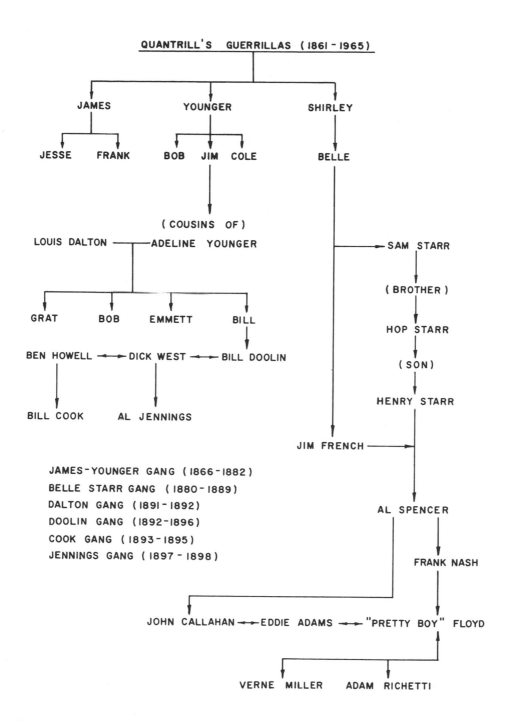

FIGURE 2. The Quantrill-Floyd criminal lineage. Based on Elliot (1892), Cooper (1936, 1937), Warner and King (1940), Rascoe (1941), Barker (1949), Wellman (1961), Toland (1963), Drago (1964, 1969), Shirley (1965), Settle (1966).

but his migration to Wichita, Kansas, in the early 1920s, introduced him to John Callahan, who schooled him in the dynamics of robbery and acquainted him with segments of his underworld affiliates. Callahan had been a fence for Al Spencer, and an associate of Frank Nash and Eddie Adams. And it was here that Adams and Nash became known to Floyd. Adams and Nash remained as Floyd's allies for the duration of his brief career, which endured for less than a decade.[40]

Contemporary "Heavy" Crime

The demise of the Western outlaw and the violent warfare between the FBI and the John Dillingers only altered the texture of professional "heavy" crime. Indeed, bank raids declined with the onset of federal involvement in the investigation and prosecution of such institutional robberies, reaching a low point of only 24 events during 1943. Yet by 1950, this figure had increased to 81, to 346 in 1959, and the decade of the 1960s reflected a further escalation of 409 percent (F.B.I., 1971:17). This dramatic increase, however, reflected more involvement of nonprofessional offenders. A comprehensive FBI review of 238 bank holdups which occurred during the summer months of 1964 indicated:

> Many of the violations . . . revealed that the robbers seldom made any well-defined plans as to their methods of operation or getaway. . . . One pair of armed robbers jumped from their car and dashed up to the doors of a bank only to find they were locked. Seven robbers were arrested inside by the bank guards or police officers who were summoned while the teller stalled. Twenty-four who attempted robberies were thwarted by bank employees who either refused to comply with their demands, screamed, or merely ducked behind their cages or calmly walked away. In one of these cases, the bandit fled when the teller fainted, and in another, the teller advised the would-be bandit that she was going to faint and he told her to go ahead, then calmly walked out (F.B.I., 1970c:289).

This unsophisticated character of bank robbery is also evident by high rates of clearance. Of the 332 offenders involved in the 238 cases surveyed by the FBI, 63 percent were apprehended. Furthermore, of those subjects regularly arrested by the FBI for bank robbery almost half have no prior records of any type or histories of only a minor nature (Bloch & Geis, 1970:290). Camp (1967) found that many bank robberies were precipitated by overdue installment payments.

On the other hand, the sources cited above and others concomitantly suggest that the skillful bank bandit has manifested some degree of survival (see Reynolds, 1953; Audett, 1954; Camp, 1967). Typical contemporary operations occur at branch banks in rural areas where escape is more likely, or where architectural designs have reduced the risk. The robbers, acting both alone and in concert with others, draw heavily upon the underworld's resources, using its network of information, its hideout systems, and its supply of experienced car thieves, drivers, and gunmen. Patience is demanded of the successful bank robber: the necessity of thorough observation of banking routines, the study of traffic conditions and road systems in and around the buildings to be raided, and later meetings with the handlers of stolen money. Such attributes were characteristic of the experienced bandits who flocked to Montreal during the 1960s, the No. 1 city in North America for bank robbery, where ninety-three cases occurred during

---

40. This discussion of the connection between Quantrill and Floyd is based primarily on the research undertaken by Wellman (1961).

1968 with only the limited rate of clearance by arrest of 25 percent. Their operations were described:

> Robbers work in teams . . . heavily armed. . . . Their planning is careful and their timing precise. Knowing that it takes police about three minutes to respond to an alarm, the robbers usually take no more than a minute to leap over the counters and clean out the cash drawers (Gartner, 1968:77–78).

The social organization and occupational techniques of the restricted field of professional bank robbery are reflected to a greater extent by those found in the wider spectrum of professional *armed robbery*. Professional "heavy" crime, as such, exists with more frequency in the area of store robbery and hijacking (Einstadter, 1969). The engineering of any operation or *job* is a group product arrived at through a process of interaction. The decided strategy determines the role of each gang member according to an assessment of individuals' strengths and weaknesses. Although there is some variation from group to group, the vast majority of professional robberies manifest the following characteristics of procedural contrivance: (a) there is a definite target that has assurances of a profitable outcome; (b) the target is fully studied several weeks in advance; (c) mock or practice trials are made; (d) timetables are established and escape routes charted; (e) there is a getaway car with a special driver; (f) there is a lookout man, and a gunman with an accomplice for inside operations; (g) there is a planned time, place, and method for the division of money (DeBaun, 1950; Roebuck & Cadwallader, 1961; Roebuck, 1967:106–17; Einstadter, 1969). In this respect Willie Sutton described the general preparations for robbing a bank:

> . . . I studied the habits of the employees and the guards and the cops on the beat. I learned the complete layout of a bank, and drew a plan. . . . I learned the location of every burglar alarm and safeguard. . . . I rehearsed my men thoroughly in their parts (Reynolds, 1953:19).

In contrast with the traditional professional thieves, such as safe burglars, pickpockets, or confidence operators, whose criminal pursuits require manual and/or verbal dexterity, only the *synthesizing* of an armed robbery demands talent; its *commission* does not (Einstadter, 1969:77). Skill is limited to style and amount of planning, and these determine the nature of the three levels of robbery tactics (p. 76):

1. *The Ambush*—little planning; participants attack an establishment in guerrilla fashion; randomness in selection of victim; high incidence of violence.
2. *The Selective Raid*—some planning; limited analysis of site conditions; tentative plan of approach.
3. *The Planned Operation*—well planned and well structured in every aspect; risks are held to a minimum.

Alternative to the more successful robberies perpetrated against banking institutions, precision hijacking and diamond theft fall within the arena of the *Planned Operation*, and reflect acute organization and substantial profit. During 1966, for example, hijacking in the United States claimed an estimated $120 million worth of merchandise from more than 10,000 trucks, with an increase to some $750 million in 1968, and $880 million in 1969 (Surface, 1968; Williams, 1970). Such expansions have seemingly occurred as a result of shippers preparing single-product cargos, thus alleviating the task of multi-item disposal operations on the part of thieves. Furthermore, more and more bargain-hunting consumers and financially pressed retailers and wholesalers continue to create black markets by seeking stolen items. Finally, the relative ease in stealing unguarded trucks or intercepting transport vehicles on poorly patroled high-ways carries a low-risk value when compared with other robbery operations (Gartner, 1968:119–22; Surface, 1968; Williams, 1970). And a high degree of professionalism is exhibited by the precision and efficiency of the predators—merchandise is stolen to order, specialized equipment is employed, and goods are cataloged. For example:

> Or look at a 16-man gang in Illinois . . . the hijackers used "consultants" to tip them on movements of valuable cargos; custom-built "work cars" equipped with police radios, racing engines and switches to turn off rear lights; and a "crash car" containing gunmen, instructed to "take out any heat" caused by police during any operation (Surface, 1968:116).

Diamond theft also reflects precision of operation and high profitability factors. Although robberies of this type occur with a limited frequency, they share a somewhat extensive history (see, for example, Stringer, 1923). Diamonds have always represented prized targets due to their small size and concentrated value. Furthermore, since only the diamond cutter who has divided a stone can ultimately identify it, these gems have the additional quality of being virtually untraceable. Data from the late 1960s indicate that major diamond robberies occur at a rate of five or six per year among more than four hundred salesmen who travel throughout the world carrying as much as $1 million in cargo on their person (Gartner, 1968: 152–55). Thieves work with patience, often staking out salesmen's homes and hiring assistants to monitor airport arrivals (p. 155).[41] In addition, a diamond setter and part-time carrier and salesman commented that merchants, unguarded and unarmed, often transport $25 thousand to $100 thousand worth of these precious stones on local trips within New York City's diamond center. Since only one robbery can net the potential holdup man a handsome annual income, his essential planning can assume a more longitudinal and systematic role than that characteristic of other lucrative crime planning (Frank, 1965). Yet due to the infrequency of these offense phenomena only a minimal understanding of the structure and process of diamond theft can be had, rendering generalizations limited and tentative.

Similarly unavailable are adequate data and theory on the professional arsonist. Comments have described the skilled *torch* who employs elaborate devices for setting fires on contract as a service for overinsured businessmen (see Bloch & Geis, 1970:296; Breslin, 1970). Yet the few studies of fire-setters have failed to locate such professionals in treatment or incarcerated populations (Lewis & Yarnell, 1951; Inciardi, 1970). Reports on these seemingly profit-motivated types describe them as amateur offenders and "pyromaniacs" (Battle & Weston, 1954; Lord, 1957). In general, the rational system of this multitude of career "heavies" dictates a conscious choice of offense targets where only agent-victims are present. The preference for banks, loan companies, supermarkets, groceries, liquor and drug stores, and gas stations delineates that any such victim is an amorphous mass and confrontations with employees become an impersonal matter

---

41. Prior knowledge of daily routines was seemingly associated with a robbery of more than five dozen diamonds during late 1969. The victim reported to me that a team of bandits entered his premises at a time when he usually had no customers, they indicated a knowledge of his personal history, and were aware of the extent of the valuables kept in his vault. He also reported that Providence, Rhode Island and Revere, Massachusetts are the major habitats of diamond thieves. Providence is a center for jewelry manufacturing and Revere is a resort-amusement suburb of Boston. This point was corroborated in 1972 by an insurance investigator and a private detective working in the Boston-Somerville-Revere-Lynn area of Massachusetts.

(Reynolds, 1953; Audett, 1954; Camp, 1967; Einstadter, 1969). In addition to this denial of the victim, rationalizations define the open face-to-face behavior as "not too dishonest." On a more pragmatic level, victims with no personal stake in the object to be robbed are preferred since the risks of resistance are reduced.

The typical career in professional "heavy" crime usually involves early experiences with a juvenile gang where techniques and rationalizations for the deviant behavior are gradually and continuously learned. Individuals move from petty offenses to auto theft, burglary, and robbery, and as young adults their experiences with police, courts, and reformatories add to their sophistication in criminality and to deviant self-conceptions. Positioned at the fringes of society, members of the "heavy" rackets view robbery as a mechanism to "get-rich-quick," to become socially mobile, and to start anew, rather than as a vocation or career. Yet with their placement in a life-style and operating social milieu having an ethos of "easy come, easy go," such offenders often fail to advance economically or translate gains into objects of conventional worth, thus locking themselves more firmly into their career.

As a final note, professional "heavy" offenders of the contemporary era are appearing in fewer and fewer numbers as the frontiers of their effective operational settings continue to recede. Bank robbery has been all but totally thwarted by integrated law-enforcement systems, by scientific advances in safeguard mechanisms, and by architecturally superior physical plants. Similar gains have not been extended to those alternative robbery target points—the drug and liquor stores, and gas stations—yet their lower cash yields require more repeated activities, thus increasing risk potentials and reducing professional involvement. As indicated in Table 2, this vulnerability became more apparent with the close of the 1960s. Initially, the total number of robbery offenses increased from 153,400 in 1966 to 348,400 in 1970. Similarly, the robbery rate per hundred thousand population more than doubled, from 78 to 171, while the percentage of these crimes cleared by arrest diminished from 32 percent in 1966 to 29 percent five years later. Yet the data also suggest that the relative amount of robbery changed little, from 5 percent of all index crime in 1966 to 6 percent by the close of the decade.

Growth in the risk-taking nature of robbery emerges at several levels of analysis. Arrest rates increased from 34 to 58 per hundred thousand population, an upward change of 71 percent over the five-year period; in cities with populations in excess of 250,000 the even greater increase of 77 percent emerged. Furthermore, this growth was not accompanied by corresponding changes in the relative amount of police personnel. The 15 percent expansion in enforcement officers, from 200 to 230 per hundred thousand population has been attended by decreases in the available force per thousand offenses (−50 percent), per thousand arrests (−32 percent), and per thousand arrests in cities of over 250,000 population (−31 percent). Thus, the incidence of robbery grew in both absolute number and rate, yet arrests increased at an even more spirited rate and with the enforcement body reduced relative to the upward changes in the general and offender populations. These data also reflect expanded involvement in robbery on the part of the inexperienced. While the increase has been gradual during the latter part of the decade—31 percent and 33 percent of the arrestees being under age 18 in 1966 and 1970, respectively—these figures represent 29 percent and 43 percent increases in that age-specific group since 1960 (F.B.I., 1967:112–13, 1971:122–24). Finally the data also indicate some sharp declines in the profitability of robbery beginning in 1970.

These preliminary indicators of some declines in the incidence or prevalence of professional heavy crime need not be predictive of its virtual elimination. For a backward glance at the full spectrum of the participant offenders suggests a pattern which has received favorable responses from segments of the social order over time, and which may be entering a new quadrant along a cyclical path. Historical testimony documents the genesis of professional "heavies" as emerging from the fringes of organized society into frontiers beset with few obstacles to a prosperous course of banditry. They persisted until the civilizations of law, technology, and growth circumscribed, enveloped, and finally conquered their natural environments. Yet, as killers, thieves, and oppressors, the more exhibitionistic varieties became America's folk heroes. Although less altruistic than myth might relate, they were challengers of an encroaching *lex loci*. Captain Kidd fought the hated Spanish fleets, the James-Younger gang battled the despised entrepreneurs of the railroads, Clyde Barrow provided a depression-stricken rural America with vicarious revenge against banks, and Willie Sutton three times escaped from a highly criticized correctional establishment. Furthermore, they robbed institutions, not people. Indeed, they were seen as modern Robin Hoods. An almost outworn pattern repeatedly pictured them as robbing the rich to give to the poor. Minor mythology has described them as men of action, fighting their way through regions often stagnant with despair or apathy, forfeiting their option to be free men,

TABLE 2

ROBBERY TREND ANALYSIS, 1966–70

Trend Characteristics	Calendar Year				
	1966	1967	1968	1969	1970
Total offenses[1,2]	153,400	202,100	261,700	297,600	348,400
Annual percent increase[3]	+14	+27	+30	+14	+17
Rate/100,000 population	78	102	131	147	171
Annual percent increase[3]	+13	+27	+28	+13	+16
Percent of total crime	5%	5%	6%	6%	6%
Offenses cleared by arrest:					
No.	49,100	60,600	70,700	80,400	101,000
Percent	32%	30%	27%	27%	29%
Rate/100,000 population	34	41	48	53	58
Rate/100,000 population (cities over 250,000 pop.)	77	95	113	124	136
Arrestees under age 18	31%	32%	33%	33%	33%
Arrestees under age 25	71%	73%	75%	77%	77%
Average bank loss	$3,986	$5,000	$5,200	$4,526	$4,166
Average victim loss	$ 256	$ 261	$ 269	$ 288	$ 235
Police/100,000 population	200	200	210	220	230
Police/1,000 offenses	2,600	1,700	1,600	1,500	1,300
Police/1,000 arrests	5,900	4,900	4,400	4,200	4,000
Police/1,000 arrests (cities 250,000+ pop.)	3,500	2,800	2,600	2,500	2,400

[1] Offense total based on all reporting agencies and estimates for unreported areas.
[2] Figures rounded to nearest 100s.
[3] Discrepancies in percent increases and rates relative to base data due to recurrent updating of base populations, number of reporting agencies and crime index totals by FBI.
Source: F.B.I., 1967:1, 12–15, 1968:1, 13–17, 115, 1969:1, 13–17, 110, 1970b:13–16, 40, 108, 1971:14–18, 42, 120.

pitting themselves against the harsh and hostile worlds of authority and orthodoxy. The era of the nomadic bandit of the frontier has now passed, and that of the free-lance robber-gunman has begun to fade. Yet this response to outlaw daring continues to be vital in public ideology. Charles Starkweather—the 1958 Nebraska teenage killer of no less than eleven humans—was the protagonist of the adolescent context of an era, and for a period was a teenage hero and idol (see *New York Times*, 1958: January 31, February 4, May 6). More recently, D. B. Cooper, the parachuting skyjacker who jumped from a commercial jet with a $200,000 ransom provided by the airline, became a folk-hero in a manner not unlike the phenomena of Jesse James, John Dillinger, and Robin Hood (Trotter, 1972).

ORGANIZED CRIME

Organized crime, syndicated crime, or *racketeering*[42] generally refers to any business operations structured for the purpose of economic gain through illegal activities (Sellin, 1963; Cressey, 1969). As such, it concentrates on the distribution of illegal goods and services—gambling, prostitution, *loan-sharking* (usury), illicit drugs—and is characterized by the following:

1. Hierarchical structure involving a system of specifically defined relationships with mutual obligations and privileges.

2. Monopolistic control or establishment of spheres of influence among different organizations and over geographic areas.

3. Dependence upon the potential use of force and violence to maintain internal discipline and restrain competition.

4. Maintenance of permanent immunity from interference from law enforcement and other agencies of government.

5. Large financial gains secured through specialization in one or more combinations of enterprises (Clinard & Quinney, 1973:225).

It is generally believed that organized crime involves a nationwide alliance of criminals that controls much of the gambling, loan-sharking, and narcotics traffic in the United States, combined with a monopolistic influence over a number of legitimate business operations and wholesale and retail firms (Cressey, 1969:x–xi). While there is some dispute as to how "organized" this complex of offense activity actually is, or to what extent a national or international crime cartel is or has been operative, crime on the large scale currently reported by criminologists and the general public did not exist prior to this century. Yet the history of urban America suggests that there were

---

42. A review of the literature descriptive of organized crime suggests that of the many hundreds of published manuscripts, only a limited few represent sources of empirical data. Primary in this respect have been the findings of governmentally sponsored hearings and investigations; for example, Illinois Association for Criminal Justice (1929), Turkus and Feder (1951), Peterson (1952, 1969), Special Crime Study Commission (1953), McClellan (1962), President's Commission (1967d), Kefauver (1968), Maas (1968), Messick (1969a), and New York State Temporary Commission (1970). In addition, a variety of patchwork analyses have utilized materials secured from government reports, newspaper commentaries, informers, court proceedings, and wire-tap data. The current interpretation has been based on these and similar sources combined with a variety of historical materials descriptive of urban social-problem phenomena. Finally, background data were obtained from morgues or archives of the following newspapers: *The New York Times, Chicago Times, Chicago Sun-Times, Chicago Tribune, Miami Herald, New York Herald Tribune, New York Journal American,* and *Brooklyn Eagle.* Some caution must be exercised in approaching many of the works on organized crime which tend to be of an impressionistic nature.

prototypes of syndicated crime beginning in the 1800s which maintained control of illegal activities in specific areas and manifested the general principles of organization. They developed from the generations of street gangs in New York, Chicago, New Orleans, and other ports of call that had been receiving the masses of destitute immigrants throughout the century. In New York, independent gangs had been growing since the 1830s, each with its own frontier and selective methods of soliciting tribute. Each gang battled for supremacy of an area, where possession meant new sites for saloons, gambling rooms, brothels, and the privilege of levying tribute against respectable merchants. Of a similar nature were the gangs in Chicago, and somewhat parallel circumstances resulting from the combined phenomena of immigration and massing of population, police graft, vice-district interests, and city bossism also existed in Washington, D.C., Boston, Philadelphia, Cleveland, St. Louis, New Orleans, and San Francisco.[43]

Included in pre-1920 crime organizations were the tongs, designed and implemented by the Chinese in the California gold fields during the early 1860s (see Bode, 1896; Irwin, 1908; Gong & Grant, 1930; Jue, 1951). While influential in mining areas and railroad construction camps, the Chinese tongs had their primary entrenchments in the "Chinatowns" of San Francisco and New York where they operated gambling resorts, dance halls, opium dens, and houses of prostitution, and exercised control over the Oriental slave trade. Each tong had an administrative power hierarchy, as well as professional warriors and assassins who acted as guards, collectors, enforcers, murderers, and infantrymen. These imposing bodies of hatchet men or *boo how doy* were trained in the art of fighting with hands, feet, guns, knives, and hatchets, and remained relatively unmolested by conventional law-enforcement groups due to the isolated cultural frontier in which they were active. As organizations contrived for the operation and defense of illegal Chinese interests, their history is marked by numerous and bloody *tong wars* which regularly defined the nature and boundaries of the vice region and power. In spite of their violent functioning, the tongs endured through the turn of the new century (Manion, 1924; Thrasher, 1927:208–12), and remain in loose confederations as entrepreneurs of contemporary Chinese gambling interests (Axthelm, 1971).

Prohibition and the Genesis of Organized Crime in America

From the multitude of neighborhood gangs that maintained control over a number of illicit operations in only limited territorial spheres, organized crime emerged as an expansion into more diverse areas of illegal activity and over wider geographical ranges with the onset of the Prohibition Era. This period in American history, initiated by the adoption of the Eighteenth Amendment in 1920, represented the final achievement of a process that had been slowly developing since the early days of the republic. The prohibition "movement" was an assertion of a rural Protestant mind against the urban culture that was emerging at the close of the nineteenth century. Doctrines of the earliest colonial settlers designated country and village life as good, while life in the city was "wicked" (Sinclair, 1964:1–11). This *agrarian myth* (Hofstadter, 1955: 24–25) tended to shape perceptions of reality and overt behavior. Anti-city feelings and commentary designated drinking and the liquor trade as key signatures of urban morality (see Child, 1843; Congregational Churches of Connecticut, 1875; Willard, 1883; Steffens, 1931:858–64). And these were diametrically opposed to the more rural

---

43. For extensive bibliographic references on this point, see Inciardi, 1973:275.

creeds of Methodism, Baptism, Presbyterianism, and Congregationalism with their emphasis on individual human toil and profound faith in the Bible.

This anti-urban movement was climaxed by the implementation of the national prohibition law, and with its onset in 1920, illegal liquor tradesmen rapidly appeared. The change from legal to illicit alcohol enterprise did not involve sudden designs, training, or initiation, for both juridicial and criminal phenomena had been prepared for immediate illegal adaptations. As early as 1857 thirteen states had already passed legislation prohibiting alcohol (Morison, 1965:516); Kansas, with a state prohibition law since the early 1880s, provided an apt training ground for bootleggers (Wellman, 1961: 311). The well-developed criminal gangs and criminal districts of the major urban centers were only too eager to revise the scope of their unlawful economic expertise. Given the inspiration and a context in which to operate, aggregates of central city gangsters more vigorously strived in their attempts to transcend the limitations of their disorganized immigrant and minority colonies through a grotesque parody of the Horatio Alger myth; they seized upon the opportunities provided by the new legislative mandate as a potentially fruitful path to status and wealth. The primitive kinds of racketeering that had been shared by neighborhood-limited city gangs were replaced by liquor syndication which was developed by graduates of these less sophisticated bands.

... from Johnny Torrio to Al Capone

The early 1920s witnessed consolidation among the broad fields of petty gangsterism within metropolitan America. The bioenergetics of both individual and semiorganized bands of amateur racketeers, burglars, horse-track thieves, and bank robbers shifted into new relationships. With efforts focused upon the illicit alcohol industry, these rapidly formulating trusts organized manufacturing arrangements, supply lines, and avenues for retail trade. Speakeasies became ubiquitous and varied in kind, ranging from the more marginal *clip joints, cab joints,* and *steer joints* found in cellars and back rooms, to the better-class brownstone resorts which operated under the guise of "private clubs" (Asbury, 1950; Morris, 1951:322–26; Still, 1956:275–76, 295–97; Allsop, 1968). To inebriated millions, they provided an assortment of bootleg alcohols, affectionately referred to as *coffin varnish, craw rot, rot gut, tarantula juice, sheep dip, panther piss,* and *belch* (Allsop, 1968:33–34). And for the manufacturers and distributors of the outlawed brew, bootleg patronage transformed alcohol into the nation's largest industry:

> in a single year of Prohibition, the United States consumed 200 million gallons of hard liquor, 684 million gallons of malt liquor and 118 million gallons of wine, and in that twelve months the income of professional bootleggers was assessed at 4,000 million dollars (p. 33).

Perhaps the beginnings of modern criminal syndication can be posted with Johnny Torrio's entrance into the liquor rackets some six months subsequent to enactment of the Volstead Act. Torrio's career experiences by 1908 included leadership of a New York waterfront gang, brothel operation, and *black-handing.* His more dynamic involvement in the distribution of illegal goods and services began in Chicago in 1909 at the invitation of "Diamond Jim" Colosimo, the pre-Prohibition boss of the Illinois underworld. Torrio organized the local vice industry and ultimately gained command

of the entire Chicago territory via his assassination of Colosimo in 1920. His development of a unified alcohol syndicate began with investments in numerous breweries.
Small bootleg gangs were then offered employment under his banner, with blackjacks
and brass knuckles utilized to disperse the reluctant few. By 1923, Torrio's empire
included partnerships in 8 breweries, the control of beer distribution to 12,000 speakeasies, and the direction of 100 gambling rooms and 50 houses of prostitution (Allsop,
1968; McPhaul, 1970; Messick, 1971; Sann, 1971b). While Torrio reigned firm in
Chicago, he laid the foundation for his colleagues' later acceptance of his suggestion
that a national syndicate could be effective. He had become acquainted with Frank
Costello and Joe Adonis in New York, Dinty Colbeck, chief of Egan's Rats of St. Louis,
Charley Binaggio of Kansas City, and Abe Bernstein, boss of Detroit's Purple Gang
(Lyle, 1960). He was allied with the six Genna brothers, from whom he regularly purchased whiskey, and with Charles Luciano ("Lucky" Luciano), the New York pimp
mogul (McPhaul, 1970). Within his organization were Al Capone—hired years previously by Torrio as a $35-a-week bouncer in his Four Deuces whorehouse—as well as
Charley and Rocco Fischette, Frank Nitti, and "Greasy Thumb" Jake Guzirk (Sullivan,
1929; Pasley, 1930; Kobler, 1971). Torrio was respected by his associates and was
known to extend help in emergencies. His reputation was further enhanced by his many
attempts to maintain peace within the underworld, as evidenced by his avoidance of
gangland combat with George "Bugs" Moran and Dion O'Banion of Chicago's North
Side organization (McPhaul, 1970).

Torrio's control of alcohol production and distribution, prostitution, and gambling
was temporarily interrupted in 1924 with his arrest and conviction for bootlegging.
From a prison cell, he abdicated to Al Capone, who later commanded a gross productivity estimated at $100 million in 1927 (Kobler, 1971; Sann, 1971a). Capone failed to
maintain the personal and organizational stature that was reflected by his predecessor.
His rivalry with the Moran-Aiello gang, culminated by the St. Valentine's Day Massacre
in 1929, not only brought the nation's interest to bear on his activities, but it similarly
created derision and contempt among underworld leaders. Capone's occupational course
in organized crime was ultimately brought to a close in 1931 with his eleven-year sentence for income-tax evasion.

The setting provided by the prohibition amendment not only defined the contours
of direction and growth for the Torrio-Capone operations, but in like manner it served
to place the career lines of numerous additional gangland figures into a focused perspective. For in 1920, criminals of a diverse nature converged upon the task of slaking
the nation's thirst: Frank Costello, graduate of an East Harlem gang and a prison term
for a weapons violation, developed a rum-running mechanism financed by gambler
Arnold Rothstein; Dutch Schultz, formerly a burglar, became, first, a beer truck driver
and, ultimately, a prominent speakeasy operator; Lucky Luciano, active in the sale of
drugs, moved to the newly formed bootlegging corps of Joe Masseria; and Dion
O'Banion, earlier a footpad and safe burglar, developed the illicit alcohol trades on
Chicago's North Side (Katcher, 1959; Tyler, 1962; McPhaul, 1970).

Efforts to enforce the Eighteenth Amendment were a total failure, costing the federal government some $375 million and an additional share in local appropriations of
$3 billion. By contrast, annual alcohol sales exceeded $3 billion and illicit saloons
quantitatively surpassed the number of legal barrooms of the pre-Prohibition Era.
Finally, the national economic distress of the 1930s amplified the death rattle of the
antiliquor law. The potentials for tax revenues and employment offered by a govern-
ment-sanctioned alcohol industry were opulent, and the Twenty-first Amendment
became the resting place for the misguided legislation (McAdoo, 1928; National Commission on Law Observance and Enforcement, 1931a, 1931b; Lyle, 1960).

. . . dalla Mafia alla Cosa Nostra

American syndicated crime, as Cressey (1969:34) has suggested, is a system based on a rational design for safety and profit. As such, smaller firms involved in the sale of illicit goods and services, in order for their supplies to meet demands, must expand operations through a division of labor that might include financiers, purchasing agents, transportation specialists, lawyers, accountants, and employee-training personnel. Furthermore, consolidation and integration of the separate divisions of labor and areas of expertise into a large-scale organization are required to maximize profits and minimize competition. This process necessitates rational decisions for peaceful coexistence (Cressey, 1969:35).

Data relative to the organizational dimensions of organized crime are of a limited nature, and as a result a number of diverse interpretations have emerged regarding the basic issues of size and control. At one extreme, Morris and Hawkins (1970) describe the alleged national organization as pure fantasy, while Cressey (1969) suggests a high degree of unity in both regional and national operations. Perhaps the organized underworld is of national scope, but bound by only a loose confederation. Only added data can provide an ultimate resolution of this issue. Yet, at present, some reconstruction and interpretation of the past can suggest alternative insights as to this organizational query. This is an important topic in the sociology of crime for several reasons. First, the majority of analyses of organized crime are founded on this dimensional note. Both popular and scholarly contributions permissively concede to the assertions of gargantuan size and complexity, and to the political, legislative, and economic implications which might logically flow therefrom. These typically describe the impact of organized crime in undermining the structure of free enterprise, in crippling the effectiveness of conventional law-enforcement machinery, and in making significant gains in an expanding number of other potential spheres. Accurate insights on behalf of the organizational nature and dimensions of the phenomena under study would place such analyses and conclusions into an appropriate perspective. Second, the functional arrangement and operations of organized crime are invariably framed in a conspiratorial context, with such terms bandied about as *Mafia, Cosa Nostra, Camorra,* and *L'Unione siciliana.* Not only have these referents been misused and misinterpreted, but in some cases their origins and pragmatic functions have never been correctly located. Valid data on these groups can suggest their position in the full complex of organized crime, and in turn, offer some considerations regarding the overall question of structure. Finally, in spite of the typical framing of organized crime in terms of an "organization," contemporary controlling efforts invariably focus upon "individuals." It might be recalled here that *professional crime* had evolved a functional structure that persisted until such time as changes in technology and law began to erode its foundations. Similarly, some insight as to the functional structure of organized crime might suggest directions for thwarting its efforts from an "organizational" rather than an "individual" level. No definitive and final proclamations are offered in this analysis, but some background materials are presented that can serve in the theoretical and empirical effort to understand the structure and process of the organized underworld of "syndicated" crime.

In describing the structural arrangement of organized crime in the United States, current testimony has indicated that:

1. there is a nationwide alliance of at least twenty-four tightly knit "families" of criminals;
2. the "members" of these "families" are Italians and Sicilians by birth or national origin;

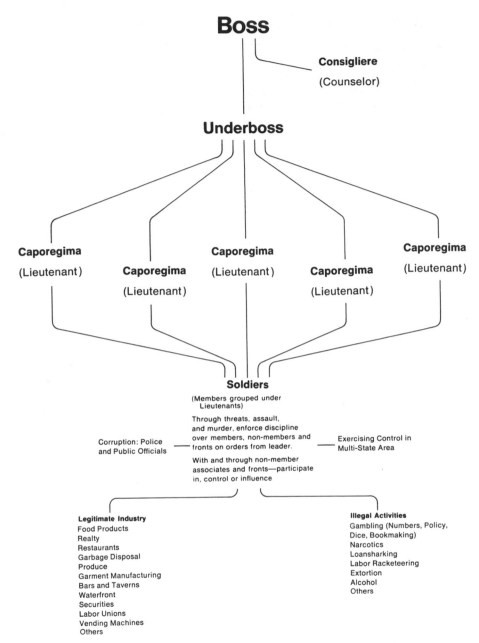

FIGURE 3. An organized crime family. From President's Commission, 1967d:9.

3. each "family" has a boss who directs the activities of its "members";
4. the "families" are linked together as members of *La Cosa Nostra*;
5. the leaders of the more powerful "families" combine as a "Commission" to direct the motions of *La Cosa Nostra*; and
6. "families" are linked to non-*Cosa Nostra* syndicates by an elaborate series of "treaties" and "understandings."

The materials descriptive of *La Cosa Nostra* have been culled from a myriad of reports from police observers, informants, wiretaps, and electronic "bugs." They suggest that the skeletal structure of the "families" and "Commission" of *La Cosa Nostra* came into being in 1931, as the major outgrowth of the "Castellammaresi War" (President's Commission, 1967d; Maas, 1968; Cressey, 1969, 1970; Salerno & Tompkins, 1969). Alternatively labeled as the "Masseria-Maranzano War," it was a fourteen-month struggle in 1930 and 1931 between Italian and Sicilian gangs in the U.S.A.; it was an armed conflict between the "Mustache Petes," or "Greasers," of the old-country *Mafia* who had operated the city gangs in a feudalistic context since before the turn of the twentieth century, and the groups of "Young Turks" who were determined in their efforts to structure the feudal "locals" into a more geographically expansive confederation. Giuseppe "Joe, the Boss" Masseria of New York, allied with many future mobsters of note—Luciano, Genovese, Costello, Terranova, Moretti, Adonis, Scalise, Anastasia, and Gambino—was representative of the old-world *Mafiosi*, and emerged from the 1920s as the most powerful single figure in Italian crime. In the manner of the clannish *Mafia*, Masseria was firm in the conviction that regional groups ought to dictate the subtleties of their own operations, and at the cost of anyone who might interfere. He maintained neither faith nor trust in "combinations" or "alliances" of criminal groups, nor did he find any cooperation with non-Italian individuals or organizations suitable. Masseria's bid for absolute supremacy of the Italian underworld instigated the Castellammaresi war. It began with his attempt to eliminate Salvatore Maranzano and other Castellammaresi powers (a contingent of men from in and around the Sicilian town of Castellammare del Golfo)—Joseph Bonnano and Joseph Profaci in Brooklyn, Buffalo's Stefano Magaddino, and Joseph Aiello in Chicago. The ensuing conflict involved leaders across the country. Those of the old-world Mafia, including Masseria and Maranzano, lost their lives.[44] The peace treaty in 1931 which brought an end to the war seemingly destroyed the concept of an absolute national or even regional ruler—the *Mafia*-styled "boss of bosses." In New York, a *"consigliere of six"* was instituted as an arbitration board and court, and similar local boards became operative in Chicago and Detroit.

The chief interpreters of those events which occurred before, during, and after the Castellammaresi war have framed their expository comments in terms of *Mafia, Camorra,* and *L'Unione siciliana.* Cressey (1969:29–53), Messick (1969a:16–22), and Salerno and Tompkins (1969:85–86) refer to a civil war within the *Mafia* between the more clannish old-world types and the Americanized younger members; Reid (1969: 24–28) and Maas (1968:85–112) note the traditional tensions that existed between Sicilians and Neapolitans—the *Mafia* and *Camorra;* and Turkus and Feder (1951:87), in an alternative context, view the treaty following the war as marking the end of the *Mafia* in the United States with *L'Unione siciliana* as its designated replacement. Given these diverse conceptions of a phenomenon that, historically, seemed crucial in determining the organizational structure and directionality of the Italian-American underworld, a digression into the nature and breadth of these "societies" appears warranted. And at an additional level of influence, the developmental effects of the Sicilian *Mafia,* the Neapolitan *Camorra,* the *Unione siciliana,* and to some degree, the *Black Hand* were not limited to the emergent contours of New World/Sicilian-Italian

---

44. The chronology of the Castellammaresi war has been reconstructed in the literature from a variety of sources, including press reports, police files, and the Valachi testimony (see Maas, 1968). For a more complete history of this conflict, see Cressey (1969), Kobler (1971), and Sann (1971a).

crime syndication. These segmented associational phenomena carried a concomitant impacted significance for the less culturally restricted and more comprehensive spectrum of organized criminal activity.

1. La mafia. Characteristic of all Sicilians has been a state of mind and philosophy of life that guided the historical evolution of their operating political and economic systems. It is a kind of primitive chivalry which engenders a cohesion among friends in their united offense against common enemies. As a prevailing moral code, it fosters a distrust for formal law and authority, subscribes to the defense of one's dignity, and requires the strictest silence in matters deemed secret. These cultural traits have existed for perhaps the past millennium and their strictures are unconditionally demanded regardless of pursuant costs (Barzini, 1964; Sciascia, 1966; Smith, 1969). Such an ideological climate was both initiated and spirited by the endless centuries of foreign conquest of Sicilian soil, for each successive invasion had been attended by rapacious governments and marauding bands of native *malviventi*. Within this setting of oppression and resentment, *La Mafia* developed and prospered, first appearing in 1282 with the outbreak of the Sicilian Vespers. Defense and revolution against French tyranny generated the energetic *compagnie d'armi*, a Sicilian peasant band which emphasized primitive justice. They defended the weak, punished the robber and transgressor, and fought to right the inhumanity of alien law. Yet over time, the once primordial and arcadian bands degenerated into outlawry and brutality through multilevel systems of extortion directed against both landowners and laborers (Franchetti & Sonnino, 1877; Barzini, 1964).

Chronicles of *La Mafia* have been both numerous and dogmatic, with a striking disagreement as to the specific root of the term in Sicilian history. Reid (1969:4–5), for example, locates the initial use of *Mafia* at the outbreak of the Sicilian Vespers on March 30, 1282, tracing it to the motto of the insurrection—"Morte Alla Francia Italia Anela! (Death to the French is Italy's cry)." Varna (1957:58) prefers the theory that *Mafia* was created in 1860 by Joseph Mazzini, a Sicilian gang leader. As such, Mazzini allegedly contracted the initials of his slogan which read, translated into English, "Mazzini authorizes theft, arson, and poisoning." And Talese (1971:189–90), returning to Easter Monday in 1282, relates the rape of a maiden on her wedding day and the anguished cries of her mother—"*ma fia, ma fia* (my daughter, my daughter)." These and similar explanations appear throughout recent literature but a scholarly analysis of the Italian language during these periods combined with an examination of Sicilian history suggests that they are all pure fiction. More laudable comments on the origins of *Mafia* from Italian historical and literary works link the root and meaning of the term to elements prevailing within the Sicilian culture. *Mafia* is seemingly of Sicilian-Arabic content, descending from the etyma *hafa*—to preserve, protect, and act as guardian; from *mo'hafi*—friend or companion; from *mo'hafah*—to defend; and from *mo'hafiat*—preservation, safety, power, integrity, strength, and a state which designates the remedy of damage and ill (DaAleppo & Calvaruso, 1910:226–29). That the Arabic *mo'hafiat* became *mafiat* by elision, and *mafia* by apocope, can be drawn from Pitre (1884, 1894, 1898, 1902), who described the latter as a dialect term common in pre-1860 Palermo. It expressed "beauty and excellence," united with notions of "superiority" and "bravery"; and in reference to *man* it meant something more: "the consciousness of being a man," "assurance of the mind," "boldness" but never "defiance," and "arrogance" but never "haughtiness." Thus, both Arabic-Sicilian linguistic referents and common *Palermitani* usages converged to generate *Mafia*'s polycentric meanings: protection against the arrogance of the powerful, remedy to any damage, sturdiness of body, strength and serenity of spirit, the best and most exquisite part of everything.

The first use of *Mafia* in a criminal context can be attributed to Giuseppe Rizzoto's dialect play *I Mafuisi della Vicaria* (Barzini, 1971:327), a presentation dedicated to "the handsome and daring men" of Palermo's local jail. Following its initial performance in 1863, *I Mafuisi* was an immediate success and remained popular for a number of years thereafter. The term *Mafiosi* was rapidly seized upon and has been commonly used by non-*Mafia* members ever since. Actual *Mafiosi* have never subscribed to this identifier. They prefer to note one another as *amici*—"friends," or "friends of friends" —and their organization as *Società onorata*—"the honored society," or "the society of friends."

The spirit and structure of the Sicilian *Società onorata* has changed little over the past century (see Pitre, 1894; Barzini, 1964, 1971). The first nucleus is the family, and unions of more powerful families are known as *cosche*. Numerous *cosche* pursuing similar activities often form an alliance called *consorteria* and all of the *consorterie* in Sicily form the *Società onorata* or *Mafia*. Numerous *Mafie* exist in Sicily, each specializing in exacting tribute from a variety of economic affairs—citrus groves, wholesale fruit, irrigation, etc. (Barzini, 1964, 1971). They establish order, provide protection, fix prices, and arrange contracts, each in a specific territory. Immunity from prosecution is supported by *l'omerta*, the Sicilian code of silence, and is reinforced by fear generated through death consignments extended for noncompliance with *società* demands. Yet the domain of the Sicilian *Mafia* is of a limited nature. The theory of an international conspiracy with headquarters in Sicily is neither probable nor possible. Established only in Western Sicily, the *società* fails to muster influence in Messina, or Cantania, less than two hundred kilometers east of Palermo (Dolci, 1959; Barzini, 1964, 1971). Its spirit and code are an oral tradition, developed and implemented as an adaptation to factors peculiar to the Sicilian social, legal, and economic complex. It is a fluid and incoherent association with only vague boundaries; as Barzini says:

> It is not a strictly organized association, with hierarchies, written statutes, headquarters, a ruling elite and an undisputed chief. It is a spontaneous formation like an ant-colony or a beehive, a loose and haphazard collection of single men and heterogeneous groups (1964:254).

As such, *La Mafia* is a decentralized and unregimented congeries of semialigned groups having no bearing on and little in common with the óperations of organized crime in the United States.[45]

2. The Black Hand. Comment on the *Black Hand* and its role in the chrysalis of an *American Mafia* received initial currency during the early 1890s (see Illinois Association for Criminal Justice, 1929:935–47; Nelli, 1969). Crime within the Italian communities at that time was seemingly unorganized and the term *Mafia* received little

---

45. This conclusion would tend to support the commonly referenced notion of the "myth of the *Mafia*." It should be noted here that the "myth," as such, does not deny the existence of organized crime per se. Rather, it suggests that crime as an organized "syndicate" in America has not designated itself as *La Mafia*, nor does it represent a branch of the old-world Sicilian *Mafia*. For a full account of the "myth of the *Mafia*," see Bell (1965:138–48). Also pertinent here are Barzini's (1964:270–72) comments on the "myth," and his account of how the Sicilian *società* viewed the deported Lucky Luciano as a gullible American who could be readily manipulated.

recognition. This situation abruptly changed, however, following the murder of New Orleans Superintendent of Police Peter Hennesscy on October 20, 1890. Hennessey had been engaged in a strenuous effort against Italian criminals, and his death was believed to have been engineered by these illicit practitioners. Hundreds of Italians and Sicilians were subsequently arrested, but when repeated attempts to secure convictions had thoroughly failed, rumors of bribery and intimidation of witnesses incited an angry populace to the vengeance of lynch law (Coxe, 1937; Kendall, 1939; Nelli, 1969:374). The emotional hysteria that characterized the entire incident left Italians the objects of open fear. "*Mafia*," believed responsible for Hennessey's murder, suddenly appeared with growing frequency in press reports; tabloids implied a criminal inclination among all Italians; and conspiratorial memberships were deemed widespread among Sicilians (Nelli, 1969:374–75). Yet for reasons of ethnic pride combined with attempts to achieve American acceptance, the Italian communities throughout the nation vigorously denied the existence of a *Mafia*. But with the turn of a new century, *Black Hand* became the explanation for crimes committed by Italians against one another.

Black-handing was extortion communicated through letters containing threats. They were framed in gentle terms, but spoke of rape and murder, and were anonymously signed "*The Black Hand*" or "*La Mano Nera*." The press rapidly seized upon the new concept, propelled notions of a "*Black Hand* organization," and suggested that all crimes within the Italian community were of this common genesis. The *Black Hand* was neither of Sicilian nor *Mafia* ancestry, nor an organized criminal structure, yet *Black Hand* extortion was somewhat reminiscent of the demands for tribute characteristic of the Sicilian *Società onorata*. Recollections of the *Mafia* reprisals in the immigrants' homeland, therefore, instilled fear and cooperation with regard to their new American menace. But the focus of *black-handing* was limited and was never active on Sicilian soil (Barzini, 1964, 1971; Smith, 1969). Testimony indicated no organizational ties among individual *Black Hand* operators in the United States (Illinois Association for Criminal Justice, 1929:943–44). This was evident also in the differential intensity of this field of extortion from one city to another. In areas where law enforcement was effective, extortion might endure only if supported by a communitywide integrated structure which could maintain and extend the fears and superstitions of the old country. In New York and Chicago, where official institutions were corrupt and inefficient, *black-handing* did indeed survive. Yet Milwaukee, New Orleans, and Boston had strict enforcement procedures which permitted Sicilians to shed more rapidly their fears of "individual" criminals, and to adjust to the new American culture. In these cities, the *Black Hand* enjoyed only a brief existence (Woods, 1902:207–9; Illinois Association for Criminal Justice, 1929:947–48, 953–54; Kendall, 1939:504). Finally, when Italian crime began to reflect qualities of organization at the onset of the Prohibition Era, *black-handing* began to dwindle. Those extortionists who had operated individually or perhaps within the limited structure of local neighborhood gangs joined the ranks of the new and emerging liquor syndicates (Illinois Association for Criminal Justice, 1929:946–47; Zorbaugh, 1929:170–74; Nelli, 1969:380).

3. *L'Unione siciliana*. An overview of both historical and contemporary perspectives on organized crime in America would suggest that *L'Unione siciliana* was an outgrowth of the Sicilian or American *Mafia*, or that *Mafia* and *L'Unione* were synonymous embodiments of Italian syndicated crime (see, for example, Thompson & Raymond, 1940; Asbury, 1950; Special Committee of the Senate, 1951; Special Crime Study Commission, 1953; Allsop, 1968; Kefauver, 1968). Yet a more discreet analysis of the historical frame and structure of organized crime yields a contrasting view. *L'Unione siciliana* emerged in late nineteenth-century New York as a lawful fraternal society designed to advance the interests of Sicilian immigrants. The *Unione* provided its members with life insurance and additional social benefits, and was energetic in successive maneuvers aimed at the eradication of crime within the Sicilian-American communities. In this behalf, its prominent role in opposing the festering evil of the *Black Hand* was designed to improve the unfavorable images shared by those immigrants from the southernmost portions of Italy and from Sicily (Nelli, 1969:376–77; Kobler, 1971:32–33). As the early years of the twentieth century witnessed increased emigration from southern Europe, with some 3.2 million from greater *Italia* during the first two decades (Social Science Research Council, 1965:56), additional branches of *L'Unione siciliana* were chartered wherever new colonies of Sicilians expanded into significant population clusters. The Chicago area, for example, contained *L'Unione*'s largest chapter, which was composed of thirty-eight lodges and more than 40,000 members by the 1920s (Kobler, 1971:34).

The respectability and benevolence of the *Unione* became jaded as Prohibition approached. First in New York and later in distant city branches, cadres of gangsters began to infiltrate and pervert the association. *L'Unione siciliana* acquired a dual character: within one frame it was open and meshed in good works among needy Sicilians, yet within another it was hidden and malevolent, dealing in theft, murder, and vice (Turkus & Feder, 1951; Kobler, 1971:34). And on an expanding criminal front, leadership of this "society" emerged as a natural catalyst for any racketeers seeking to multiply their spheres of influence and widen their profit potentials. *Unione* membership included the old and clannish *Mafia* types who stressed the maintenance of the cultural traditions akin to those of the Sicilian *Società onorata*. To these were added the younger Americanized factions that were anxious to compound operations through cooperative agreements with a more expansive variety of criminal groups, even with those not of their own blood. The *Unione* of the 1920s became the object of unyielding power struggles, with delegates from both criminal orientations contending at local, regional, and national levels for the more advantageous post positions (Turkus & Feder, 1951; Kobler, 1971; Sann, 1971b). The tenure of this conflict moved toward termination in 1931 via the Castellammaresi war.

4. La Camorra. *Camorra* was a Neapolitan term ostensibly derived from Arabic and Spanish linguistic items. In Arabic, *kumar* designated a particular game of chance (Lombroso, 1911:212). In the Latin languages, a similar gambling game was noted as *morra*, one generally characterized by heavy wagering as well as a level of argumentation that typically generated crude and brutish fights (Motta, 1967b:933). The Spanish *camorra* referred to a quarrel, dispute, or brawl, and *camorrista* signified a bad character (Lombroso, 1911:212). Descending from the abusive nature of *morra*, *camorra*, and *camorrista*, *La Camorra* was descriptive of a secret society of Neapolitan *malviventi*. Parallel to the loosely structured Sicilian *Società onorata*, these *malviventi* were operative perhaps as early as sixteenth-century Spain. The edicts of Spanish viceroys, for example, threatened galley servitude for those eliciting tribute from gamblers or gambling houses. Similarly, the writings of Cervantes reflect upon an association parallel to the *Camorra* that existed in Seville (Lombroso, 1911:212–15). *La Camorra* became apparent in Naples during the early decades of the nineteenth century. *Camorristi* exercised control over clandestine lotteries and prostitution, levied tribute within a variable context of extortion, engaged in thefts and robberies, and exacted gains from the net proceeds of the *bossi fondi* (underworld) of Naples (Lombroso, 1911:214; Motta, 1967a:284; Smith, 1969:238).

In controlling the daily activity of Naples, members of *La Camorra* generally adhered to the fundamental tenets of *La Mafia*. Similar to the Sicilian *l'omerta*, a sense of honor supported their patterns of intimidation. Yet *Mafia* and *Camorra* differed in many ways. *"Camorrista"* was bestowed upon anyone who demonstrated cleverness and strength in exploiting the weak, and as such, the *Camorra* was even more loosely knit than its southern counterpart. In addition, *Camorra* activity was based on criminal practices while the *Mafia* had its foundations in *ideals* of lawlessness; *Camorristi* knew that they violated the law, yet *Mafiosi* had arrogated to themselves the right to serve a more legitimate law (Serao, 1911a, 1911b; Train, 1912; Allen, 1962:5–10, 14–19; Smith, 1969:238). While the *Mafia* has persisted in western Sicily, the *Camorra* manifested decisive signs of disintegration by the end of the nineteenth century, and its final dissolution was secured in 1911 by the action of the citizens of Naples (Thompson, 1911; Train, 1911, 1912; Symons, 1966:220).

In retrospect, what history offers relative to the origins, growth, and general nature of *La Mafia*, *La Camorra*, *L'Unione siciliana*, and *La Mano Nera* suggests a framework within which organized crime in America may be conceptualized as a structural phenomenon. Each of these "societies" reflected a particular social context and range of cultural traditions and events that served to shape the development of the Italian-American underworld; each occupied specific and functional roles in a process that spanned five decades on portions of two continents. As such, the longitudinal analysis of these Italian/Sicilian social and cultural systems provides base-line data for some understanding of the scope and complexity of organized lawbreaking within this distinct nationalistic orientation, as well as within that of a wider and more diverse ethnic spectrum.

Initially, *Mafia* and *Camorra* were indeed highly manifest forms of criminal enterprise within sectors of southern Italy and western Sicily. Yet it must be emphasized that each had been textured by the arrangement of social, economic, and political conditions that persisted in the given areas. Also, each remained effective without the support of an integrated internal organization for as long as the conditions which evoked them endured. At the turn of the twentieth century, the *Mafia* was an exclusive Sicilian group bound together by blood lines, and structurally similar to ancient feudalism. It was dominant and monopolistic, maintaining the managerial and administrative dictatorship of its agricultural setting through a forceful manipulation of prevailing cultural traditions. The *Camorra* was a vast organization of thieves, less united, and without the rigid discipline of the *Mafia*. *Camorra* activities were of a political-criminal tenor, involving force and violence and supported by contractual alliances with local tenders of law and policy. The *Mafia* and *Camorra*, as distinct and spacially separate bodies, stimulated the design and structuring of Italian-American organized crime within the sociopolitical setting of the late nineteenth- and early twentieth-century United States.

The five decades following 1870 witnessed more than four million Italian and Sicilian immigrants arriving at American ports of call (Social Science Research Council, 1965:56–57). The vast majority were peasants or small craftsmen, poorly equipped for competing in the new urban labor markets. Language barriers were compounded by their lack of formal education, and hence, all but the lowest paying jobs were closed to them. They were clannish and wary of outsiders. Centuries of exploitation had already taught them to mistrust authority, and the hardships and prejudices of urban life further confirmed them in their ancestral tribalism. Among numerous cohorts of these immigrant populations were members of the old-world *Mafia* and *Camorra*. Yet as the political, social, and economic conditions of Naples and western Sicily had previously defined the effective parameters of their extortion and predation, such activities were not readily adaptable to circumstances in the new environments. Urban centers were heterogeneous, and only limited segments of the population were literate in terms of *Mafia* and *Camorra* tradition; criminal districts were already well established, and corps of German, Irish, and Jewish lawbreakers had long since entered into contractual alliances with tenders of the political and juridical structures. Finally, local "organized gangsterdoms" had been operative for years, and sometimes decades, prior to the appearance of *Mafiosi* and *Camorristi* on American soil (Asbury, 1927, 1936, 1940, 1950; Thompson & Raymond, 1940; Smith, 1954; Pierce, 1957).

Nevertheless, the *conspiracy of silence* in these Italian social relationships, the fierce loyalty to group rituals, and the sacredness of clan tradition were old-world traits transplanted, useful in the new environment of the emigrating *amici*. The amoral familism of Sicilian society, compounded by new and expanded perceptions of patriotic allegiance, facilitated the spread and persistence of extortion by violence. Thus, the new opportunities to coerce money from fellow Sicilians came forth in the new industrial state as *La Mano Nera* (The Black Hand). It was patterned from the world left behind, and became manifest among relocated *Mafiosi* and other *first-generation* Italian and Sicilian criminals. As a phenomenon of local sociocultural counterbalances, however, it was lacking in support from any comprehensive network, and was limited to individual or locally grouped endeavors.

By contrast, *second-generation* offenders manifested an alternative behavior system in crime. It was a pattern not unlike that experienced by the immigrant groups who came before them. They inhabited the slum areas where parental tradition and constraint became weak, and where numerous opportunities for crime existed (Park & Miller, 1921:238–58; Shaw & McKay, 1929; Jones, 1960). For the young Italians, an inspirational Algerism defined criminal activity as a means for rapid and substantial monetary gain and success. They were socialized into a field of illegality more inclusive than that of their elders, especially with the coming of Prohibition. In the quest for economic betterment, they transcended the narrowness of the lingering old-country prejudices and embraced illicit networks with diversity and cooperation. Their operations included *Black Hand* extortion, as well as theft, robbery, and providing forbidden goods and services. Northern and southern Italians, and Sicilians, joined together for mutual aid and profit, and activities were often coordinated with those of reigning Jewish and Irish gangs, sometimes resulting in alignments of a polyglot character (Bell, 1950; Maas, 1968; Nelli, 1969; McPhaul, 1970).

Yet the cooperation and coexistence sought by the younger and more Americanized segments of the Italian underworld became firm only after a series of long and bitter skirmishes. Initially, the power and influence of *L'Unione siciliana* were viewed by criminals as a medium for increasing status and opportunities, so its administration was infiltrated by aspiring Italian and Sicilian gangsters of both generational cohorts. At local and regional levels, attempts to gain full control of the *Unione* led to numerous battles and frequent changes of branch leadership. In addition, Italian lawbreakers of the older Sicilian *Mafioso* tradition and the alternatively younger and more progressive criminal entrepreneurs had become further polarized in their ideological perspectives. The resulting Castellammaresi war during 1930 and 1931 secured a purging of the *Mafiosi* delegates from *L'Unione siciliana* rendering powerless any remnants of *Mafia* tradition and influence. The subsequent structural arrangement represented the initiation of an organized coordination of efforts among Italian criminals. The new entity, alternatively called *La Cosa Nostra*, was composed of a series of local units or "families," linked together by a "commission" that supervised the general movements of the entire united body. And elements of bureaucratic design were apparent, for the division of labor, the organization of positions into a hierarchy, the consistent system of rules, and the achievement orientation were constraining members to act in ways that furthered the rational pursuit of *Cosa Nostra* objectives.

Many of the *Cosa Nostra* structural characteristics resembled those of the ancient Sicilian *Mafia:* the code of silence and positional hierarchy. But these were not necessarily remnants of the older brotherhood transported to a newer setting: such traits have been typically present within deviant subcultures whenever organization was a functional prerequisite for efficient and persistent operation. Beyond these generalized attributes, *La Mafia* and *La Cosa Nostra* differed: the new phenomenon found its effectiveness more often through rational economics than through fear, and it dispelled the position of "boss of bosses." *Hence, the ancient Mafia as an organization and society of criminal expertise never existed in the United States. La Cosa Nostra* was the initial formulation of united process within the Italian underworld, with a structure designed to be functionally productive in a specifically American sociocultural context. Today *La Cosa Nostra* and *La Mafia* continue to operate on different continents; they have remained divergent in structure, activity, and leadership (Barzini, 1964, 1971; Dolci, 1968; Albini, 1971).

In addition to *La Cosa Nostra* being a new-world phenomenon, the longitudinal perspective also suggests that this underworld complex represents but one segment of the wider spectrum of organized crime. Both historical and modern sources have documented the activities of numerous non-Italian syndicate bosses and line personnel. Indeed, testimony on the multiethnic character of organized crime is suggestive of supplementary insights relative to the nature and differential scope of racketeering as an integrated network and nationwide alliance.

The earliest reports of "syndicated" gangsterism among non-Italian minority populations were framed in terms of urbanization and trans-Atlantic migration phenomena. More specifically, historical data suggest that graduates from the central city's delinquent gangs and delegates from the second-generation immigrant populace had been instrumental in the growth of the corrupt urban machines which had engineered the organization of gambling and the commercialization of vice (see, for example, Steffens, 1904; Zink, 1939; Strauss, 1968). Significant in this context was the career of Michael Cassius McDonald, a bounty broker, saloon owner, and gambling-house keeper. McDonald controlled urban politics in Chicago from 1879 through the mid-1890s, and is credited with having designed and constructed the city's first "syndicate." He provided political protection within Chicago vice areas through a mechanism that elicited tribute from confidence men, gamblers, bunco steerers, and brothel owners for subsequent division and payoff among corrupt police, city officials, and members of his own organization (Asbury, 1938, 1940; Smith, 1954; Pierce, 1957). The structure of gambling and commercialized vice in New York's Tenderloin and Satan's Circus areas descended from similar contrivances involving Irish immigrants and corrupt Tammany leaders (New York Daily Times, 1871; Werner, 1928; Mandelbaum, 1965). And in parallel circumstances, machine politics in other urban centers generated an underworld organization and structure years before Italian immigration reached significant proportions: Philadelphia, Pittsburgh, Cincinnati, St. Louis, Minneapolis, San Francisco, and New Orleans were controlled similarly by greedy industrialists, venal police, labor demagogues, and elements at the bottom of the social pyramid who constructed and drew support from an underworld coalition of gamblers, prostitutes, professional criminals, and operators of illicit resorts and unlicensed liquor establishments (Steffens, 1904, 1931; Mandelbaum, 1965; Green,

1967). Beyond the framework of city bossism, gangsterism of the polyglot variety received its structure and directionality from personalities already socialized within the isolated regions of vice and criminal habitation. Lou Blonger, for example, a professional gambler and *fixer*, of French-Canadian descent, became perhaps the most powerful figure in the criminal and political playgrounds of late nineteenth-century Denver. He readily manipulated city administrators and police chiefs, dictated the limits of criminal sanction, and determined the nature and extent of the professional predation "allowable" in "his town" (Van Cise, 1936).

Non-Italian as well as the emerging Italian/Sicilian involvement in organized underworld operations at the turn of the century tended to deviate somewhat from the pattern of previous decades. Public disapproval of vice and corruption initiated a series of moral crusades during the 1890s that generated sporadic suppression of criminal districts and their alliances with unwholesome government machines. In consequence, criminal "sanctuaries" became more vulnerable in the general ecology of risk, forcing segments of the deviant counterculture into a variety of alternative courses (see New York State Senate, 1895; Vice Commission of Chicago, 1911; Reckless, 1933; Hofstadter, 1955). Related to this process was the more significant appearance of gangsterism in the form of extortion, predatory offenses, gambling, and vice operations within local neighborhoods. Within this arena, Italian and Sicilian criminals began to achieve stabilization and advancement in their illicit endeavors, but the Prohibition Era stimulated the construction and proliferation of their criminal syndication on a more comprehensive scale. During these "dry years," the power and wealth of both non-Italian and Italian/Sicilian gangland organizations reached unprecedented levels. The early 1930s, for example, found "Dutch" Schultz directing a $20 million numbers lottery enterprise; "Lepke" Buchalter had become the major power in New York's garment industry as well as the benefactor in an extortion scheme that secured one penny for every loaf of bread sold there and within dozens of other urban centers throughout the east and midwest. Irish, Jewish, and Polish syndicate leaders were maintaining the secure and lucrative direction of locally organized gangsterdoms (Messick, 1968, 1969b; McPhaul, 1970; Sann, 1971a). Along parallel trails, Italian and Sicilian mobs often captured even greater heights of economic prosperity, as exemplified by Al Capone and *Mafioso*-remnant Joe Masseria.

Ironically, the reported success of the legendary "Mafia" and the "Capone syndicate" in dominating Prohibition gangsterism ultimately served to relegate the Italian underworld to no more than a secondary role in the wider spectrum of organized crime. Initially, old-world loyalties to the spirit of honor, the limits of tribalism, and the tradition of violence had designated aggression and bloodshed as typical vehicles on which Italian racketeers might ride to power. This was indeed the case, for example, regarding early *Black Hand* operations, the struggles within *L'Unione siciliana*, and Capone's Chicago offensive, which generated an untold score of executions throughout the nation. Yet the futility of succession by assassination and civil war demonstrated an urgent need for rationality in the long-term pursuit of lucrative criminal activity. Alternatively, cooperation, alliance, and joint investment appeared as methods for reducing competition, diminishing risks, and enhancing profits. As such, the tradition of violence was designated as unsound and a cooperative alliance was initiated among local and regional syndicates. With the inclusion of organizations having homogeneous ethnicity, the Italian underworld became one segment of something more comprehensive. This secondary role received additional confirmation through the highly visible character of Italian/Sicilian criminals. Nineteenth-century reports of *Black Hand* extortion by *Mafiosi* and *Camorristi* had given this sector of the

underworld its initial notoriety, and continued publicity was generated by the re-
splendent and richly colored pattern of Italian gangland warfare. This ability of the
Mafia, and later, of the *Cosa Nostra,* to maintain headline publicity enabled the more
comprehensive syndicate to organize, stabilize, and persist in a state of only limited
recognition.

The smuggling and manufacture of illicit alcohol during Prohibition provided
the economic basis for regional cooperation among racketeers, and following the
numerous underworld battles, "combinations" were formed in such cities as New
York, Boston, Chicago, Philadelphia, Cleveland, Detroit, Kansas City, Minneapolis-
St. Paul, Denver, and San Francisco (see Messick, 1969b). It was from this series of
cooperative arrangements that a "national syndicate" evolved. Evidence coherently
suggests, furthermore, that the again-powerful Johnny Torrio masterminded the
formation of this "crime cartel" in 1934 through a gathering of racketeers from across
the country into the fold of a loose but lasting alliance (see Prall & Mockridge, 1951;
Special Committee of the Senate, 1951; Messick, 1969a, 1971; McPhaul, 1970).
Torrio's founding notions had been well conceived, and they were backed by his scroll
of accomplishments and long-standing reputation for logic and rational decision-
making. He suggested, for example, that racketeer-owned businesses cooperate with
one another in the distribution and provision of goods and services. In this respect, Joey
Adonis's 15,000 cigarette vending machines could be appropriately placed in bars,
cafes, and poolrooms owned by syndicate members; or similarly, scotch whiskey might
be provided by Frank Costello while linens could be secured from Willie Morretti's
supply houses. Furthermore, in the distribution of any goods and services, Torrio's
blueprint offered arrangements for avoiding competition among organization members.
This went beyond legitimate business operation to include cooperation in a multiplicity
of rackets. Gangs invited to membership retained their regional or local independence,
and leaders were not subject to the dictates of any "boss" or "bosses." Yet in spite of
this loosely tied confederation, syndicate heads could convene a decision-making body
for recommending sanctions against individuals or groups found in violation of
binding organizational rules and agreements. Significant here was the national syndicate's assassination squad. Popularly known as "Murder, Inc." and under the leadership
of Abe Reles ("Kid Twist"), this mob-generated "hit squad" executed precision murder
on contract (Turkus & Feder, 1951; Berger, 1962).

Contemporary findings suggest that organized crime continues to mirror its
original model. Discoveries of the 1960s and 1970s, when compared with those of
earlier periods, indicate that second-generation arrangements appear as general reflections of the same basic designs as Torrio's artful best.

The Future of Organized Crime

In a more current perspective, available data suggest that organized crime remains
firmly established in the contemporary social structure. Syndicate operations are
extensive and exercise concerted efforts and involvement in illicit gambling, loan-
sharking, narcotics distribution, labor racketeering, and the infiltration of legitimate
businesses.[46] And while there is no accurate strategy for ascertaining organized crime's

---

46. The nature and scope of these operations have been described at length. For both historical
and contemporary materials examining these topics, see Anslinger and Tompkins (1953), Kennedy
(1960), Anslinger and Oursler (1962), President's Commission (1967d), King (1969), and Roberts
(1969).

gross revenues, periodic indicators affirm the highly lucrative nature of its endeavors. Estimates of the annual intake from gambling operations, for example, have varied from $7 billion to $50 billion; $21 million allegedly represents syndicate earnings from narcotics (President's Commission, 1967d:3–4). In addition, organized crime earns a significant share of the estimated national income of $350 million from loan-sharking, $225 million from prostitution, and $150 million from illicit alcohol (President's Commission, 1967b:32–33). Alternatively, the basic parameters of syndicate revenues can be highlighted through analysis of more individualized operations:

> . . . In one Eastern town, for example, the local racket figure combined with out-side organized criminal groups to establish horse and numbers gambling grossing $1.3 million annually, an organized dice game drawing customers from four states, and having an employee payroll of $350,000 annually, and a still capable of producing $4 million worth of alcohol each year. The town's population was less than 100,000 (President's Commission, 1967d:5).

These figures, furthermore, are perhaps only minimal, for they fail to reflect earnings derived from the infiltration of legitimate businesses at both local and national levels. Meyer Lansky, for example, with investments in countless real estate, entertainment, and industrial enterprises in several parts of the world, was reported in 1971 as having a personal fortune of $300 million (Messick, 1971).

Yet, by contrast, there exists an extensive list of indicators which suggests that the future may fail to reward organized crime with the security, power, and wealth that it has known for so many decades:

1. Initially, portions of syndicate earnings were drawn from illicit activities which increasingly reflect reduced profit or greater risk potentials as the current century matures. The production of illegal alcohol, for example, has played a declining role since the repeal of Prohibition. Investment costs are high while the destruction of supplies and equipment by enforcement officers remains likely. In fact, the futility of such an enterprise led New York *Cosa Nostra* leader Carlo Gambino to order perhaps the last known syndicate still shut down in 1965 (Volz & Bridge, 1969:114–16). Prostitution is equally risky since it is difficult to organize and discipline. Furthermore, the convictions of Lucky Luciano and other syndicate figures in prostitution cases during the 1930s and 1940s have made criminal executives wary of such activities (*Luciano* v. *New York*, 305 U.S. 620 [1938]; Sondern, 1959; Tyler, 1962).

2. Traffic in hard narcotics also represents an endeavor with shrinking appeal. For example, Anthony "Little Pussy" Russo, a *Cosa Nostra* underboss in Long Branch, New Jersey, reported in 1964 that a *Cosa Nostra* law had prohibited such activity (Volz & Bridge, 1969:104). At a more significant level, a variety of empirical studies and field observations suggest that changes in the patterns and styles of drug-taking may indeed curtail the value and role of heroin as the drug of preference among addicts. Data indicate that multiple- or *polydrug use* more appropriately characterizes the drug scene as time advances; barbiturates, non-barbiturate sedatives, tranquilizers, amphetamines, narcotic analgesics, and other legally manufactured and distributed pharmaceuticals have become drugs of substitution and drugs of simultaneous abuse among major segments of the addict population (Inciardi, 1971). Furthermore, the growing proliferation of methadone maintenance programs has had a significant impact on the illegal drug-taking activities of thousands of the nation's drug-dependent citizens (Chambers & Brill, 1973).

3. Illicit gambling, which provides organized crime with billions of dollars an-

nually, faces a diminishing sphere of influence with the sanctioning of lotteries and off-track betting by state and local governments.

4. There are numerous instances which suggest that the use of fear, force, and the threat of violence in extortion practices may be losing their former level of effectiveness. A *Cosa Nostra* "soldier," for example, in attempting to "organize" bakeries in an East Coast city, was arrested, prosecuted, and convicted of extortion when more than a dozen victims made official reports to police.[47] Within the same Eastern city, syndicate attempts to infiltrate a number of light-manufacturing concerns in a predominantly Italian district were similarly thwarted. Although a number of older businessmen did respond to gangster threats, syndicate maneuvers were effectively blocked by second- and third-generation Italians and Sicilians who were further removed from the old-world fears of the vendetta by violence.[48] And within a similar framework, New Jersey *Cosa Nostra* boss Simone Rizzo "Sam, the Plumber" DeCavalcante reported that honest realty contractors and developers who refused to cooperate with syndicate offerings of cheap nonunion laborers were usually ignored thereafter (Volz & Bridge, 1969).[49]

5. More and more data relative to organized criminal operations continue to emerge. Efforts and strategies directed against racket activity increasingly reflect legislative measures that place a greater emphasis on controlling an "organization" rather than on convicting "individuals." In addition, recent statutes have focused on frustrating certain legal rights which have heretofore served to block conventional enforcement tactics (see President's Commission, 1967d; Hills, 1969; Salerno & Tompkins, 1969; Lacey, 1970). Title III of the Omnibus Crime Control and Safe Streets Act of 1968, for example, in representing a compromise of civil liberties, authorized a new court-supervised system of electronic eavesdropping.[50]

There is evidence which suggests that sectors of the organized criminal network may have already experienced varying degrees of disorganization. Within *La Cosa Nostra*, for example, a lack of cooperative organization has again given life to the violence and civil war that characterized the era of Capone and the Castellammaresi— the Gallo-Profaci war and the Bonnano war of the 1960s, and the Gallo-Colombo war of the 1970s (see Cressey, 1969; Salerno & Tompkins, 1969; Volz & Bridge, 1969; Buckley, 1971). These highly visible interactions, furthermore, tend to spirit law-enforcement interests for renewed and more intensive investigation and surveillance. In an alternative set, New Jersey *Cosa Nostra* boss Sam DeCavalcante seemingly could not find means to combat the problems of unemployment suffered by numerous "family" members and "friends." Conversations heard through electronic "bugs" indicated that many mob members had been forced to peddle narcotics, engage in armed robberies, or work gambling games in order to subsist (Volz & Bridge, 1969).

Despite the inroads law-enforcement agencies may engineer during the approaching decades, and regardless of any local racket disintegration, organized crime will continue to prosper as long as public apathy and attitudes offer hospitality to gangsterism. The covert tolerance of vice, which is characteristic of Americans, and the moral hypocrisy, which refuses to approve of "evil" through a legalization of the "victimless crimes," combine to support the posture of organized crime. This peculiar atrophy will inevitably continue to construct and perpetuate ideal situations for under-

---

47. Confidential communication from a state government agency.

48. Confidential personal communication from a representative of the victims.

49. For a description of citizen mobilization against organized crime, see Hill, 1970.

50. For a description and comment on this legislation, see Clark (1970) and Harris (1969, 1970).

world exploitation through networks that specialize in providing prohibited pleasures for a price. Prerequisite to the success of any such illicit enterprise is corruption in law enforcement and the polity—similarly, a consequence of the contorted moral ambivalence which pervades law and politics.

EPILOGUE

Professional crime, professional "heavy" crime, and organized crime can be considered as "vocational" in nature since the participants view their respective offense behaviors as their "calling." It is this degree of commitment that differentiates the vocational pattern from non-career-oriented varieties of criminality.

The *professional thief* has the most highly developed of criminal careers. His skill at engaging successfully in specialized crimes has accorded him great prestige among other criminals. His longevity in crime results not just from ability, but also from his motivations by a set of justifications which make his activities and way of life seem reasonable to him. The ensuing philosophy of life reflects a criminal self-image, one which confers a degree of worth upon any illegal movements and functions pursued. The *professional "heavy" criminal* also has a career and self-concept of a criminal nature. His vocation in crime typically begins with involvement in a culture that is either neutral or opposed to the law of the wider society. A career, identified with crime, and criminal self-conception emerge as a result of repeated offenses and of arrests and convictions which create a stigma that prevents entry into more law-abiding social outlets. Finally, while members of the *organized underworld* also have a criminal self-conception and commitment like that of other career offenders, in contrast to the *professional* offenders, they often live a segmented life, seeking the seclusion of respectability within the prestige system initialed by the larger society.

The segmented types of vocational crime, while sharing concepts and commitments within life-styles essentially isolated from the wider society, differ in their approaches to offense behavior. The professional thief is a passive property offender, the professional "heavy" offender is a more violent predator, and the gangster is an entrepreneur of illicit goods and services. Yet these differences often reflect only an "ideal typical" set, for in a variety of circumstances each type may pursue the stylistic activities of the others. This is especially characteristic of the organized underworld. As an entity of hierarchical design, the leaders atop the power pyramid reign firm over a somewhat middle echelon of management personnel (lieutenants) who, in turn, control a tertiary level of members (soldiers, prostitutes, runners). A structure descriptive of such variable order makes any generalizations difficult, since authority, responsibility, and activity tend to change from one rank to another. Those in minor positions, for example, reflect careers similar to those of professional "heavy" criminals. In addition, variations would occur in the size of organizations. Since the structure of the organized underworld seemingly reflects a continuum of operational groups varying in membership from an isolated few to perhaps hundreds, and varying in interdependence from complete autonomy to rigid control, the divisions of labor and systems of role specialization would necessarily engender an equally diverse spectrum.

As a final note, some theoretical comment seems warranted as to the persistence of vocational offense patterns. This chapter has indicated that both professional and organized crime have demonstrated many enduring qualities and structural features. Yet "heavy" crime has generated immunities so limited that the development of a comprehensive social network has been thoroughly precluded. Chambliss and Seidman (1971:484–501) have approached this issue in terms of the political power base occupied by various levels of the underworld. They suggest that symbiotic relationships exist between some criminals and representatives of the criminal justice system which guarantee immunity from sanction in return for various types of service. Yet going beyond this framework, immunity from sanction can be perceived in terms of the degree of *social visibility* of divergent criminal acts which shape the nature and strength of societal reaction to crime.[51] Social visibility, furthermore, can be observed from the perspectives of the victim, the social control system, and the society at large.

Initially, the victim-offender complex contributes significantly to the visibility of a deviant act. In "heavy" crime, *personal* and *property* predation are typically present. In the former case, there is physical contact between the victim and the offender. Such contacts are violations of the moral precepts of the "sanctity of the human body" and "thou shalt not kill." Violations of these precepts are direct assaults upon middle-class morality and are looked upon as "heinous." The offender is then defined as someone different, or sick, a killer, a fiend, someone cruel and diabolically wicked. The visibility of violent personal crime is enhanced by the fact that the offense is readily detected. Even where the assaulted victim is hidden, the mere absence of the victim enhances visibility. Regarding the property aspect, however, the victim-offender relationship is less personal, especially when the victim may be a business organization, although offenses of this type are inconsistent with the sanctity of private property. It is violence against persons that elicits the strongest societal outcry, with demands for compensation and justice to victims calling attention to the offenders. Repeated transgressions by "heavy" criminals have resulted in repeated castigation, thus enhancing their social visibility.

Professional crime of other types occupies a unique position in the complex of victim-offender relationships, one which inhibits the victim from calling attention to the deviant act. For example, the *shakedown* and confidence game offer little risk since the offenders are violators of the law or actors in collusion with the thieves. Similarly, shoplifting offers limited danger since businessmen are reluctant to make accusations of theft against persons who appear to be legitimate customers. Furthermore, when the victim is not himself a deviant, the thief's ability to manipulate people permits him to arrange payment of restitution in lieu of complaint and prosecution. In either case, the overt act is neither intrinsically visible nor made visible by the victim. Organized crime as a restraint on free enterprise or as a purveyor of illicit goods and services is essentially "victimless" at the participant's level, and elicits only minimal individual reaction. Nevertheless, as indicated at the close of the preceding section, its visibility appears to be increasing.

Social visibility can be observed or ascribed by the social control system, yet as Chambliss and Seidman (1971:484–501) have argued, the adequate political power base maintained by professional and organized criminals tends to reduce risk potentials. This, in turn, combined with victim reluctance in exposing such offenders, serves as a shield from public observation that might arouse the collective social ethic. The maintenance of shields and immunities, then, enables professional and organized criminals to construct further defenses from coercion and control.

This process, finally, appears most crystallized relative to professional thieves. Their immunity perpetuates contact among members of the profession. The lack of molestation permits the development of a subculture and social organization aimed at maintaining that status quo—the lack of visibility. An intricate network of relation-

---

51. For a complete discussion of this issue, see Inciardi, 1972.

ships and linguistic constructions develops for the purpose of keeping out "outsiders" —amateur criminals. Codes of ethics develop for the purpose of maintaining the status quo from within. A dissemination of information regarding the *fix, fences,* and untrustworthy members of the profession develops in order to maintain a defense system against the infiltration of outsiders. As Becker stated:

> Where people who engage in deviant activities have the opportunity to interact with one another they are likely to develop a culture built around the problems rising out of the differences between their definition of what they do and the definition held by other members of the society (1963:81).

Codes of ethics, argot, self-segregation, isolation, and the dissemination of information represent the functional aspects of professional theft. It is essential to the group members that low visibility be maintained, and deviants from the "way of life" are looked upon as a threat. Since deviance is "the other side" of conformity, the professional who violates group norms is no longer accepted and protected, and he, too, becomes an outsider or "deviant" deviant.

Essential to the continuance of low visibility are self-segregation and isolation. The size and complexity of the city offers such advantages to the professional criminal. Not only does it provide a highly mobile wealth upon which the thief may prey, but the city also gives anonymity, and has areas in which people may remain unseen. These are the crime and vice areas within which the professionals segregate themselves. In these sections of the city, the social network of thieves and fences maintains itself, and remains isolated from the rest of society. The hangouts, meeting places, residential hotels, and rooming houses provide an arena in which the thief can maintain his social contacts. Indeed, the vice area stands as a defined cultural territory for the total social system of *grifting.* Its geographical location, traditions, occupational specialties, and common language boundaries define the contours of the niche they occupy in social space.

REFERENCES

Adams, Ramon F.
    1948   The Old Time Cowhand. New York: Macmillan.
    1969   Six Guns and Saddle Leather. Norman: University of Oklahoma Press.
Albini, Joseph L.
    1971   The American Mafia: Genesis of a Legend. New York: Appleton-Century-Crofts.
Alexander, Alfred, and Val Moolman.
    1969   Stealing. New York: Cornerstone.
Allen, Edward J.
    1962   Merchants of Menace: The Mafia; A Study of Organized Crime. Springfield, Ill.: Thomas.
Allen, Trevor.
    n.d.   Underworld: The Biography of Charles Brooks, Criminal. London: Newnes.
Allsop, Kenneth.
    1968   The Bootleggers: The Story of Chicago's Prohibition Era. New Rochelle: Arlington House.

Anderson, Nels.
  1923   The Hobo: The Sociology of the Homeless Man. Chicago: University of Chicago Press.

Anonymous.
  1922   In the Clutch of Circumstance: My Own Story. New York: D. Appleton.

Anslinger, Harry J., and Will Oursler.
  1962   The Murderers—The Story of The Narcotics Gangs. New York: Farrar, Strauss & Cudahy.

Anslinger, Harry J., and William F. Tompkins.
  1953   The Traffic in Narcotics. New York: Funk & Wagnalls.

Asbury, Herbert.
  1927   The Gangs of New York. Garden City: Garden City Pub.
  1934   All Around the Town. New York: Knopf.
  1936   The French Quarter. New York: Knopf.
  1938   Sucker's Progress: An Informal History of Gambling in America from the Colonies to Canfield. New York: Dodd, Mead.
  1940   Gem of the Prairie: An Informal History of the Chicago Underworld. New York: Knopf.
  1942   The Golden Flood. New York: Knopf.
  1950   The Great Illusion: An Informal History of Prohibition. New York: Doubleday.

Audett, Blackie.
  1954   Rap Sheet: My Life Story. New York: William Sloane.

Axthelm, Pete.
  1971   "An inscrutable passion for gambling." New York Magazine 4(September 27):55–57.

Aydelotte, Frank.
  1913   Elizabethan Rogues and Vagabonds. Oxford: Clarendon.

Babcock, Charles A.
  1919   Venango County, Pennsylvania, Her Pioneers and Her People. Chicago: J. H. Beers.

Baker, George C.
  1950   Pachuco: An American-Spanish and its Functions in Tucson, Arizona. Tucson: University of Arizona Social Science Bulletins.

Ballou, Robert O., and Roger Benton.
  1936   Where Do I Go From Here? The Life Story of a Forger. New York: Lee Furman.

Barker, John T.
  1949   Missouri Lawyer. Philadelphia: Dorrance.

Barnes, Harry Elmer, and Negley K. Teeters.
  1959   New Horizons in Criminology. Englewood Cliffs, N.J.: Prentice-Hall.

Bartram, F. S.
  1888   Retrographs: New York City Prior to the Revolution. New York: Bartram.

Barzini, Luigi.
  1964   The Italians: A Full-Length Portrait Featuring Their Manners and Morals. New York: Atheneum.

1971   From Caesar to the Mafia: Sketches of Italian Life. New York: Library Press.

Battle, Brendan, and Paul B. Weston.
1954   Arson. New York: Greenberg.

Bean, Walton.
1968   California: An Interpretive History. New York: McGraw-Hill.

Becker, Howard S.
1963   Outsiders: Studies in the Sociology of Deviance. New York: Free Press of Glencoe.

Bell, Daniel.
1965   The End of Ideology. New York: Free Press.

Bell, James A.
1950   "Frank Costello: statesman of the underworld." The American Mercury 71 (August) :131–139.

Berger, Meyer.
1962   "Murder, Inc." Pp. 373–379 in Marvin E. Wolfgang, Leonard Savitz, and Norman Johnston (eds.), The Sociology of Crime and Delinquency. New York: Wiley.

Best, Harry.
1930   Crime and the Criminal Law in the United States. New York: Macmillan.

Black, Jack.
1927   You Can't Win. New York: Macmillan.

Bloch, Herbert A., and Gilbert Geis.
1970   Man, Crime, and Society. Second Edition. New York: Random House.

Block, Eugene B.
1959   Great Train Robberies of the West. New York: Avon.

Bode, William.
1896   Lights and Shadows of Chinatown. San Francisco: H. S. Crocker.

Booth, Ernest.
1929   Stealing Through Life. New York: Knopf.

Brace, Charles Loring.
1880   The Dangerous Classes of New York, and Twenty Years' Work Among Them. New York: Wynkoop & Hallenbeck.

Brannon, W. T.
1948   "Yellow Kid" Weil. Chicago: Ziff-Davis.

Breslin, Jimmy.
1970   "How Marvin the torch fights the recession." New York Magazine 3 (September 21) :27–28.

Bridenbaugh, Carl.
1955   Cities in the Wilderness. New York: Knopf.
1965   Cities in Revolt. New York: Knopf.

Browne, Douglas G., and Alan Brock.
1953   Fingerprints. London: G. G. Harrap.

Buckley, Tom.
1971   "The Mafia tries a new tune." Harper's Magazine 243 (August) :46–56.

Buel, J. W.
1891   Sunlight and Shadow of America's Great Cities. Philadelphia: West Philadelphia Pub. Co.

Bunn, Alfred.
1853   Old England and New England. Philadelphia: Hart, Carey & Hart.

Byrnes, Thomas.
1895   Professional Criminals of America. New York: G. W. Dillingham.

Caldwell, Robert G.
1965   Criminology. New York: Ronald.

Callahan, Jack.
1928   Man's Grim Justice. New York: Sears.

Cameron, Mary Owen.
1964   The Booster and The Snitch. New York: Free Press of Glencoe.

Camp, George N.
1967   "Nothing to lose: a study of bank robbery in America." Ph.D. dissertation, Yale University.

Campbell, Helen, Thomas W. Knox, and Thomas Byrnes.
1892   Darkness and Daylight; or, Lights and Shadows of New York Life. Hartford: A. D. Worthington.

Campion, Daniel.
1957   Crooks are Human Too. Englewood Cliffs, N.J.: Prentice-Hall.

Carlin, Jerome E.
1966   Lawyers' Ethics: A Survey of The New York City Bar. New York: Russell Sage.

Casey, Patrick, and Terence Casey.
1921   The Gay-Cat: The Story of a Road-Kid and his Dog. New York: H. K. Fly.

Castleman, Harvey N.
1944   The Texas Rangers. Girard, Kan.: Haldeman-Julius.

Cavan, Ruth Shonle.
1962   Criminology. New York: Crowell.

Chambers, Carl D., and Leon Brill.
1973   Methadone: Experience and Issues. New York: Behavioral Publications.

Chambliss, William J., and Robert B. Seidman.
1971   Law, Order, and Power. Reading: Addison-Wesley.

Chandler, Frank Wadleigh.
1907   The Literature of Roguery. Boston: Houghton Mifflin.

Child, Maria.
1843   Letters From New York. New York: Charles S. Francis.

Clark, Charles L., and Earle E. Eubank.
1927   Lockstep and Corridor: Thirty-five Years of Prison Life. Cincinnati: University of Cincinnati Press.

Clark, Ramsey.
1970   Crime in America. New York: Simon & Schuster.

Clemmer, Donald.
1958   The Prison Community. New York: Rinehart.

Clinard, Marshall B., and Richard Quinney.
    1973   Criminal Behavior Systems: A Typology. Second Edition. New York: Holt,
            Rinehart & Winston.
Clough, Shepard B.
    1959   The Economic Development of Western Civilization. New York: McGraw-
            Hill.
Coates, Robert M.
    1930   The Outlaw Years. New York: Literary Guild.
Colburn, J. G. W.
    1880   The Life of Sile Doty. Toledo: Blade.
Congregational Churches of Connecticut.
    1875   Report on Temperance. Hartford: Religious Herald.
Cook, D. J.
    1882   Hands Up. Norman: University of Oklahoma Press (1958 edition).
Cook, Fred
    1964   The F.B.I. Nobody Knows. New York: Macmillan.
Cooper, C. R.
    1936   Ten Thousand Public Enemies. Boston: Little, Brown.
    1937   Here's to Crime. Boston: Little, Brown.
Corey, Herbert.
    1936   Farewell Mr. Gangster: America's War on Crime. New York: Appleton-
            Century.
Cory, Donald C., and John P. LeRoy.
    1963   The Homosexual and His Society: A View From Within. New York:
            Citadel.
Costello, A. E.
    1884   Our Police Protectors. New York: Author's Edition.
Coxe, John E.
    1937   "The New Orleans Mafia incident." Louisiana Historical Quarterly 20(Oc-
            tober):1067–1110.
Crapsey, Edward.
    1872   The Nether Side of New York. New York: Sheldon.
Crawford, T. E.
    1962   The West of the Texas Kid. Norman: University of Oklahoma Press.
Cressey, Donald R.
    1969   Theft of the Nation. New York: Harper & Row.
    1970   "Bet taking, Cosa Nostra, and negotiated social order." Emory University
            Journal of Public Law 19(1):13–22.
Crookston, Peter.
    1967   Villain. London: Jonathan Cape.
DaAleppo, Gabriele Maria, and G. H. Calvaruso.
    1910   Le Fonte Arabiche Nel Dialetto Sicilano. Roma: Etmanno Loescher.
Dearden, R. L.
    1925   The Autobiography of a Crook. New York: Dial Press.
DeBaun, Everett.
    1950   "The heist: the theory and practice of armed robbery." Harper's Magazine
            200(February):69–77.

Dimsdale, Thomas Josiah.
  1866   The Vigilantes of Montana. Virginia City: Montana Post Press.

Dolci, Danilo.
  1959   Report from Palermo. New York: Orion.
  1968   The Man Who Plays Alone. New York: Pantheon Books.

Drago, Harry Sinclair.
  1964   Outlaws on Horseback. New York: Dodd, Mead.
  1965   Great American Cattle Trails. New York: Dodd, Mead.
  1968   Roads to Empire: The Dramatic Conquest of the American West. New York: Dodd, Mead.
  1969   Notorious Ladies of the Frontier. New York: Dodd, Mead.

Dressler, David.
  1951   Parole Chief. New York: Viking Press.

Dunham, Dick, and Vivian Dunham.
  1947   Our Strip of Land. Manila, Utah: Daggett County Lions Club.

Earle, Alice Morse.
  1915   Colonial Days in Old New York. New York: Scribner's.

Egan, Pierce.
  1821   Real Life in London, vol. 2. London: Jones.
  1905a   Real Life in London, vol. 1. London: Metheun (reprint of 1821 edition).
  1905b   Real Life in London, vol. 2. London: Metheun (reprint of 1821 edition).

Einstadter, Werner J.
  1969   "The social organization of armed robbery." Social Problems 17(Summer): 64–83.

Elliot, David Stewart.
  1892   Last Raid of the Daltons. Coffeyville, Kan.: Coffeyville Journal.

Ellis, Edward Robb.
  1966   The Epic of New York City. New York: Coward-McCann.

Emery, H. G., and K. G. Brewster (eds.)
  1938   The New Century Dictionary of the English Language. New York: Appleton-Century.

Fabian, Robert.
  1950   Fabian of the Yard. London: Naldrett Press.
  1954   London After Dark. New York: British Book Centre.

Farley, Phil.
  1876   Criminals of America. New York: Author's Edition.

Farmer, J. S., and W. E. Henley.
  1970   Slang and Its Analogues. New York: Arno Press (reprint of original 1890–1904 editions, 7 volumes).

Federal Bureau of Investigation (F.B.I.)
  1967   Crime in the United States: Uniform Crime Reports—1966. Washington, D.C.: U.S. Government Printing Office.
  1968   Crime in the United States: Uniform Crime Reports—1967. Washington, D.C.: U.S. Government Printing Office.
  1969   Crime in the United States: Uniform Crime Reports—1968. Washington, D.C.: U.S. Government Printing Office.

1970a   The Identification Division of the FBI. Washington, D.C.: U.S. Government Printing Office.

1970b   Crime in the United States: Uniform Crime Reports—1969. Washington, D.C.: U.S. Government Printing Office.

1970c   "Profile of a bank robber," in Herbert H. Bloch and Gilbert Geis, Man, Crime, and Society. Second Edition. New York: Random House.

1971   Crime in the United States: Uniform Crime Reports—1970. Washington, D.C.: U.S. Government Printing Office.

Felstead, Sidney T.
1923   The Underworld of London. New York: Dutton.

Ferri, Enrico.
1896   Criminal Sociology. New York: D. Appleton.

Flinn, John J., and John E. Wilkie.
1887   History of the Chicago Police. New York: Arno Press (1971 edition).

Flynt, Josiah.
1899   Tramping with Tramps. Clifton, N.J.: Augustus M. Kelley (1971 edition).
1900   Notes of an Itinerant Policeman. Boston: L. C. Page.
1901   The World of Graft. New York: McClure, Phillips.

Franchetti, L., and S. Sonnino.
1877   La Sicilia nel 1876. Florence: Barbera.

Frank, Bruce
1965   Personal communication, May 7.

Froude, James Anthony.
1864   History of England. London: Longmans, Green.

Furnas, J. C.
1969   The Americans: A Social History of the United States, 1587–1914. New York: Putnam.

Gard, Wayne.
1954   The Chisholm Trail. Norman: University of Oklahoma Press.

Gartner, Michael (ed.)
1968   Crime and Business. Princeton: Dow Jones.

Gates, Paul Wallace.
1966   Fifty Million Acres: Conflicts Over Kansas Land Policy, 1854–1890. New York: Atherton.

Genêt, Jean.
1964   The Thief's Journal. New York: Grove Press.

Gentry, Curt.
1966   The Vulnerable Americans. Garden City, N.Y.: Doubleday.

George, M. Dorothy.
1965   London Life in the Eighteenth Century. New York: Capricorn.

Gibbons, Don C.
1965   Changing the Lawbreaker: The Treatment of Delinquents and Criminals. Englewood Cliffs, N.J.: Prentice-Hall.

Gibbons, Don C., and Donald L. Garrity.
1959   "Some suggestions for the definition of etiological and treatment theory in criminology." Social Forces 38(October):51–57.

Glaab, Charles N., and A. Theodore Brown.
    1967   A History of Urban America. New York: Macmillan.
Goffman, Erving.
    1963   Stigma: Notes on the Management of Spoiled Identity. Englewood Cliffs, N.J.: Prentice-Hall.
Goldin, Hyman E., Frank O'Leary, and Morris Lipsius (eds.)
    1950   Dictionary of American Underworld Lingo. New York: Twayne.
Gong, Eng Ying, and Bruce Grant.
    1930   Tong War. New York: N. L. Brown.
Gosse, Philip.
    1924   The Pirates' Who's Who. Boston: Lauriat.
    1932   The History of Piracy. New York: Tudor.
Green, Constance McLaughlin.
    1967   The Rise of Urban America. New York: Harper & Row.
Greene, Robert.
    1592   A Notable Discovery of Cozenage. London: Thomas Nelson.
Greiner, A. J.
    1904   Swindles and Bunco Games, in City and Country. St. Louis: Sun.
Grose, Francis.
    1811   Dictionary of the Vulgar Tongue. Northfield Ill.: Digest Books (1971 edition).
    1963   A Classical Dictionary of the Vulgar Tongue. Third Edition. New York: Barnes & Noble.
Guerin, Eddie.
    1928   Crime: The Autobiography of a Crook. London: John Murray.
Haggart, David.
    1821   The Life of David Haggart. Edinburgh: Tait.
Hall, Jerome.
    1952   Theft, Law, and Society. Revised Edition. Indianapolis: Bobbs-Merrill.
Hamilton, Charles.
    1952   Men of the Underworld: The Professional Criminals' Own Story. New York: Macmillan.
Handlin, Oscar.
    1951   The Uprooted. New York: Grosset & Dunlap.
Hansen, Marcus Lee.
    1961   The Atlantic Migration 1607–1860. New York: Harper & Row.
Hapgood, Hutchins.
    1903   The Autobiography of a Thief. New York: Fox, Duffield.
Harlow, Alvin F.
    1934   Old Waybills. New York: Appleton-Century.
Harris, Alexander.
    1847   Settlers and Convicts; or, Recollections of 16 Years' Labour in the Australian Backwoods. London: C. Cox.
Harris, Richard.
    1969   The Fear of Crime. New York: Praeger.
    1970   Justice: The Crisis of Law, Order and Freedom in America. New York: Dutton.

Hawgood, John A.
   1969   America's Western Frontiers. New York: Knopf.
Hayward, A. L.
   1735   Lives of the Most Remarkable Criminals. New York: Dodd, Mead (1927 edition).
Hellman, Peter.
   1970   "One in ten shoppers is a shoplifter." New York Times Magazine March 15: 34–35, 39, 42, 44, 46, 49, 52, 54.
Hibbert, Christopher.
   1963   The Roots of Evil: A Social History of Crime and Punishment. Boston: Little, Brown.
Hill, Albert Fay.
   1970   The North Avenue Irregulars: A Suburb Battles the Mafia. New York: Pocket Books.
Hills, Stuart L.
   1969   "Combating organized crime in America." Federal Probation 33(1):23–28.
Hofstadter, Richard.
   1955   The Age of Reform. New York: Random House.
Holbrook, Stewart H.
   1962   The Story of American Railroads. New York: Bonanza Books.
Homsher, Lola M. (ed.)
   1960   South Pass, 1868. Lincoln: University of Nebraska Press.
Hoover, J. Edgar.
   1938   Persons in Hiding. Boston: Little, Brown.
   1971   Personal communication, October 21.
Horan, James D.
   1949   Desperate Men. New York: Bonanza Books.
   1969   The Pinkertons: The Detective Dynasty That Made History. New York: Crown.
Horan, James D., and Howard Swiggett.
   1951   The Pinkerton Story. New York: Putnam.
Horsley, J. W.
   1887   Jottings from Jail. London: T. F. Unwin.
Hough, Emerson.
   1918   The Passing of the Frontier. New Haven: Yale University Press.
Hungerford, Edward.
   1949   Wells Fargo. New York: Bonanza Books.
Huntington, William.
   1959   Bill Huntington's Both Feet in the Stirrups. Billings, Mont.: Western Livestock Reporter.
Hynd, Alan.
   1963   Professors of Perfidy. New York: A. S. Barnes.
Illinois Association for Criminal Justice.
   1929   The Illinois Crime Survey. Chicago: Illinois Association for Criminal Justice.
Inciardi, James A.
   1970   "The adult firesetter: a typology." Criminology 8(August):145–155.

1971   "The poly-drug user: a new situational offender." Paper presented at the annual meeting of the American Society of Criminology, San Juan, Puerto Rico, November 3–7.

1972   "Visibility, societal reaction, and criminal behavior." Criminology 10(August):217–233.

1973   "The history and sociology of professional crime." Ph.D. dissertation, New York University.

Inciardi, James A., and Carl D. Chambers.
1972   "Criminal involvement of narcotic addicts." Journal of Drug Issues 2 (Spring):57–64.

Inciardi, James A., and David M. Petersen.
1973   "Gaff joints and shell games . . . a century of circus grift." Journal of Popular Culture 6(Spring):592–606.

Ingram, George.
1930   Hell's Kitchen. London: Herbert Jenkins.

Irwin, Godfrey (ed.)
1931   American Tramp and Underworld Slang. New York: Sears.

Irwin, Will.
1908   Pictures of Old Chinatown. New York: Moffat, Yard.
1909   The Confessions of a Con Man. New York: B. W. Huebsch.

Ives, George.
1914   A History of Penal Methods. Montclair: Patterson Smith (1972 edition).

Jackson, Bruce.
1969   A Thief's Primer. London: Macmillan.

Jones, Maldwyn Allen.
1960   American Immigration. Chicago: University of Chicago Press.

Judges, Arthur V.
1930   The Elizabethan Underworld. London: George Routledge.

Judson, Z. C.
1848   The Mysteries and Miseries of New York. New York: Berford.

Jue, George K.
1951   Chinatown, Its History, Its People, Its Importance. San Francisco: Chamber of Commerce.

Jusserand, J. J.
1929   English Wayfaring Life in the Middle Ages. London: Ernest Benn.

Katcher, Leo.
1959   The Big Bankroll: The Life and Times of Arnold Rothstein. New York: Harper.

Kefauver, Estes.
1968   Crime In America. New York: Greenwood.

Kelly, Charles.
1958   The Outlaw Trail. New York: Bonanza Books.

Kemp, Harry.
1922   Tramping on Life. New York: Boni & Liveright.

Kendall, John S.
1939   "Who killa de chief?" Louisiana Historical Quarterly 22(April):492–530.

Kennedy, Robert F.
  1960   The Enemy Within. New York: Harper.
King, Rufus.
  1969   Gambling and Organized Crime. Washington, D.C.: Public Affairs Press.
Kirkpatrick, E. E.
  1934   Crime's Paradise. San Antonio: Naylor.
Kobler, John.
  1971   Capone: The Life and World of Al Capone. New York: Putnam.
Lacey, Frederick B.
  1970   Recommendations to the 1970 Session of the New Jersey Legislature Con-
          cerning Legislation Which Might be Enacted to Curb the Power and Influ-
          ence of Organized Crime in New Jersey. Trenton: New Jersey Legislature.
Lake, Carolyn (ed.)
  1969   Under Cover for Wells Fargo: The Unvarnished Recollections of Fred
          Dodge. Boston: Houghton Mifflin.
LeFors, Joe.
  1953   Wyoming Peace Officer. Laramie: Laramie Ptg. Co.
Lemert, Edwin M.
  1958   "The behavior of the systematic check forger." Social Problems 6(Fall):
          141–148.
  1967   Human Deviance, Social Problems, and Social Control. Englewood Cliffs,
          N.J.: Prentice-Hall.
Lening, Gustav.
  1893   The Dark Side of New York Life and Its Criminal Classes. New York:
          Fred'k Gerhard.
Levin, Yale, and Alfred Lindesmith.
  1937   "English ecology and criminology of the past century." Journal of Criminal
          Law and Criminology 27(March):801–816.
Levinson, William A.
  1971   "The tour operator who took doctors for a ride." Medical Economics 48
          (June 21):172–184.
Lewis, Alfred Henry.
  1901   Richard Croker. New York: Life.
  1912   The Apaches of New York. Chicago: M. A. Donohue.
Lewis, Arthur H.
  1970   Carnival. New York: Trident Press.
Lewis, Nolan D. C., and Helen Yarnell.
  1951   Pathological Firesetting. New York: Nervous & Mental Disease Mono-
          graphs.
Lindesmith, Alfred R., and Warren Dunham.
  1941   "Some principles of criminal typology." Social Forces 19(March): 307–
          314.
Lindesmith, Alfred R., and Yale Levin.
  1937   "The Lombrosian myth in criminology." American Journal of Sociology 42
          (March):653–671.
Lombroso, Cesare.
  1911   Crime—Its Causes and Remedies. Boston: Little, Brown.

London, Jack.
    1907   The Road. London: Arco (1967 edition).

Loomis, Noel M.
    1968   Wells Fargo. New York: Bramhall House.

Lord, Fred.
    1957   Fire Alarm. London: Longmans, Green.

Lowrie, Donald.
    1912   My Life in Prison. New York: Mitchell Kennerly.
    1915   My Life Out of Prison. New York: Mitchell Kennerly.

Lyle, John H.
    1960   The Dry and Lawless Years. Englewood Cliffs, N.J.: Prentice-Hall.

Maas, Peter.
    1968   The Valachi Papers. New York: Putnam.

McAdoo, William.
    1928   The Challenge: Liquor and Lawlessness Versus Constitutional Government. New York: Century.

McClellan, John L.
    1962   Crime Without Punishment. New York: Duell, Sloan & Pearce.

McCullough, Edo.
    1957   Good Old Coney Island. New York: Scribner's.

MacDonald, J. C. R.
    1938   Crime Is a Business: Buncos, Rackets, Confidence Schemes. Stanford: Stanford University Press.

MacKenzie, Donald.
    1955   Occupation: Thief. Indianapolis: Bobbs-Merrill.
    1956   Gentlemen at Crime: An Autobiography. London: Elek Books.

McPhaul, Jack.
    1970   Johnny Torrio: First of the Gang Lords. New Rochelle, N.Y.: Arlington House.

Mandelbaum, Seymour.
    1965   Boss Tweed's New York. New York: Wiley.

Manion, Jack.
    1924   "New style highbinder fights tong wars today." New York Times October 19:4.

Martin, Edward Winslow.
    1868   Secrets of the Great City. Philadelphia: National.

Martin, John Bartlow.
    1952   My Life in Crime: The Autobiography of a Professional Criminal. New York: Harper.

Matsell, George W.
    1859   Vocabulum; or, The Rogue's Lexicon. New York: George W. Matsell.

Maurer, D. W.
    1936   "The argot of the underworld narcotic addict: Part I." American Speech 11(April):116–127.
    1938   "The argot of the underworld narcotic addict: Part II." American Speech 13(October):179–192.

1939   "Prostitutes and criminal argots." American Journal of Sociology 44 (January) :346–550.

1940   The Big Con. Indianapolis: Bobbs-Merrill.

1941   "The argot of forgery." American Speech 16 (December) :243–250.

1943   "The argot of the faro bank." American Speech 18 (February) :3–11.

1944   " 'Australian' rhyming argot in the American underworld." American Speech 19 (October) :183–195.

1947   "The argot of the three-shell game." American Speech 22 (October) :161–170.

1964   Whiz Mob: A Correlation of the Technical Argot of Pickpockets with Their Behavior Pattern. New Haven: College and University Press.

1967   "Linguistic hostility as a factor in intra-cultural conflict." Actes Du Xe Congres International Des Linguistes, Bucarest, August 28–September 2.

Mayhew, Henry.
1861   London Labour and the London Poor. 4 volumes. New York: Dover (1968
–62   edition).

Means, P. A.
1935   The Spanish Main. New York: Scribner's.

Mercer, A. S.
1954   The Banditti of the Plains, or, The Cattlemen's Invasion of Wyoming in 1892. Norman: University of Oklahoma Press.

Mercer, Blaine.
1958   The Study of Society. New York: Harcourt, Brace.

Messick, Hank.
1968   Syndicate in the Sun. New York: Macmillan.
1969a   Secret File. New York: Putnam.
1969b   Syndicate Abroad. London: Macmillan.
1971   Lansky. New York: Berkley.

Missouri Joint Committee of the General Assembly.
1868   Report of the Joint Committee of the General Assembly Appointed to Investigate the Police Department of the City of St. Louis. New York: Arno Press (1971 edition).

Moolman, Val.
1970   Practical Ways to Prevent Burglary. New York: Cornerstone Library.

Mooney, Martin.
1935   Crime Incorporated. New York: Whittlesey House.

Moore, Langdon W.
1893   His Own Story of His Eventful Life. Boston: L. W. Moore.

Morehead, Albert H., Richard L. Frey, and Geoffrey Mott-Smith.
1964   The New Complete Hoyle. Garden City: Garden City Books.

Morison, Samuel Eliot.
1965   The Oxford History of the American People. New York: Oxford University Press.

Moritz, C. P.
1965   Journeys of a German in England in 1782. New York: Holt, Rinehart & Winston.

Morris, Lloyd.
    1951   Incredible New York: High Life and Low Life of the Last Hundred Years.
            New York: Bonanza Books.

Morris, Norval, and Gordon Hawkins.
    1970   The Honest Politician's Guide to Crime Control. Chicago: University of
            Chicago Press.

Morris, William, and Mary Morris.
    1962   Dictionary of Word and Phrase Origins, Volume I. New York: Harper &
            Row.

Motta, Federico (ed.)
    1967a   Dizionario Motta della Lingua Italiana, Volume I. Milano: Federico Motta.
    1967b   Dizionario Motta della Lingua Italiana, Volume II. Milano: Federico Motta.

Nahrendorf, Richard O.
    1967   "Typologies of crime and delinquency: classification or methodology?" So-
            ciologica Internationalis, Heft I:15–33.

National Commission on Law Observance and Enforcement.
    1931a   Enforcement of the Prohibition Laws. Washington, D.C.: U.S. Government
            Printing Office.
    1931b   Preliminary Report on Probation. Washington, D.C.: U.S. Government
            Printing Office.

National Police Convention.
    1871   Official Proceedings of the National Police Convention, St. Louis, Missouri.

Nelli, Humbert S.
    1969   "Italians and crime in Chicago: the formative years, 1890–1920." American
            Journal of Sociology 74(4):373–391.

New York Daily Times
    1871   How New York is Governed: Frauds of the Tammany Democrats. New
            York: New York Daily Times.

New York State Senate.
    1895   Report and Proceedings of the Senate Committee Appointed to Investigate
            the Police Department of the City of New York (The Lexow Committee Re-
            port). New York: Arno Press (1971 edition).

New York State Temporary Commission of Investigation.
    1970   Racketeer Infiltration into Legitimate Business. Albany: New York State
            Temporary Commission of Investigation.

Norfleet, J. Frank.
    1927   Norfleet: The Amazing Experiences of an Intrepid Texas Rancher with an
            International Swindling Ring. Sugar Land, Tex.: Imperial Press.

Number 1500.
    1904   Life in Sing Sing. Indianapolis: Bobbs-Merrill.

O'Connor, John.
    1928   Broadway Racketeers. New York: Horace Liveright.

O'Connor, Richard.
    1958   Hell's Kitchen. New York: Lippincott.

Park, Robert E., and Herbert A. Miller.
    1921   Old World Traits Transplanted. New York: Harper.

Parsons, Philip Archibald.
    1926   Crime and the Criminal. New York: Knopf.
Partridge, Eric.
    n.d.   Slang: Today and Yesterday. New York: Bonanza Books.
    1959   Origins: A Short Etymological Dictionary of Modern English. New York:
            Macmillan.
    1961a   A Dictionary of Slang and Unconventional English. New York: Macmillan.
    1961b   A Dictionary of the Underworld. New York: Bonanza Books.
Pasley, Fred D.
    1930   Al Capone: The Biography of a Self-Made Man. Garden City: Garden City
            Pub.
Peterson, Virgil.
    1952   The Barbarians in Our Midst. Boston: Little, Brown.
    1969   A Report on Chicago Crime for 1968. Chicago: Chicago Crime Commission.
Peterson, William.
    1958   "A general typology of migration." American Sociological Review 23
            (June):256–266.
Phelan, Jim.
    1953   The Underworld. London: George G. Harrap.
Phillips, Alan.
    1954   The Living Legend: The Story of the Royal Canadian Mounted Police. Bos-
            ton: Little, Brown.
Pierce, B. L.
    1957   A History of Chicago. New York: Knopf.
Pilat, Oliver, and Jo Ranson.
    1943   Sodom by the Sea. Garden City: Garden City Pub.
Pinkerton, Allan.
    1880   Professional Thieves and the Detectives. New York: G. W. Dillingham.
    1886   Thirty Years a Detective. New York: G. W. Dillingham.
Pitre, Giuseppe.
    1884   Le tradizioni caval leresche popolari in Sicilia. Parigi: F. Vieweg.
    1894   "La Mafia." In L. Capirana, L'isola del Sole. Catania: N. Giannotta.
    1898   "La Sicilia, nei canti popolari e nella novellistica contemporanea." Con-
            ferenza letta il 12 maggio nella sala del Liceo Musicale di Bologna a bene-
            ficio del Comitato Bolognese della Societa Dante Alighieri.
    1902   . . . Curiosita di usi popolari. Catania: N. Giannotta.
Pottle, Frederick A. (ed.)
    1950   Boswell's London Journal: 1762–1763. New York: McGraw-Hill.
Prall, Robert H., and Norton Mockridge.
    1951   This Is Costello. New York: Gold Medal.
President's Commission on Law Enforcement and Administration of Justice.
    1967a   Task Force Report: Crime and its Impact: An Assessment. Washington,
            D.C.: U.S. Government Printing Office.
    1967b   The Challenge of Crime in a Free Society. Washington, D.C.: U.S. Govern-
            ment Printing Office.
    1967c   Task Force Report: Crime as a Profession (unpublished).
    1967d   Task Force Report: Organized Crime. Washington, D.C.: U.S. Government
            Printing Office.

Pringle, Patrick.
    1958   The Thief Takers. London: Museum Press.
    1963   Highwaymen. New York: Roy.

Quennell, Peter (ed.)
    n.d.   London's Underworld. London: Spring Books.

Quinney, Richard.
    1970   The Social Reality of Crime. Boston: Little, Brown.

Radzinowicz, Leon.
    1966   Ideology and Crime. New York: Columbia University Press.

Raine, William Macleod.
    1929   Famous Sheriffs and Western Outlaws. Garden City, N.Y.: Doubleday,
            Doran.

Rascoe, Burton.
    1941   Belle Starr, "The Bandit Queen." New York: Random House.

Reckless, Walter C.
    1933   Vice in Chicago. Chicago: University of Chicago Press.
    1967   The Crime Problem. New York: Appleton-Century-Crofts.

Reid, Ed.
    1969   The Grim Reapers: The Anatomy of Organized Crime in America. Chicago:
            Henry Regnery.

Reiss, Albert J., Jr.
    1964   "The social integration of queers and peers." Pp. 181–210 in Howard S.
            Becker, The Other Side. New York: Free Press of Glencoe.

Reitman, Ben L.
    1937   Sister of the Road: The Autobiography of Box-Car Bertha. New York:
            Macaulay.

Reynolds, Quentin.
    1953   I, Willie Sutton. New York: Farrar, Straus & Young.

Rhodes, Henry T. F.
    1956   Alphonse Bertillon: Father of Scientific Detection. London: George G.
            Harrap.

Richardson, James F.
    1970   The New York Police: Colonial Times to 1901. New York: Oxford Univer-
            sity Press.

Riis, Jacob.
    1902   The Battle With the Slum. New York: Macmillan.

Roberts, Albert R.
    1969   "Reflections on gambling and organized crime." Criminologica 7(1):26–31.

Roebuck, Julian B.
    1967   Criminal Typology. Springfield, Ill.: Thomas.

Roebuck, Julian B., and Mervin L. Cadwallader.
    1961   "The Negro armed robber as a criminal type." Pacific Sociological Review
            4(Spring):21–28.

Rowan, Richard W.
    1931   The Pinkertons, a Detective Dynasty. Boston: Little, Brown.

Rusche, George, and Otto Kirchheimer.
  1939   Punishment and Social Structure. New York: Columbia University Press.
Salerno, Ralph, and John S. Tompkins.
  1969   The Crime Confederation. Garden City: Doubleday.
Sann, Paul.
  1971a   Kill the Dutchman! The Story of Dutch Schultz. New Rochelle: Arlington House.
  1971b   The Lawless Decade. New York: Fawcett.
Sciascia, Leonardo.
  1966   A ciascuno il sud. Torino: Einaudi.
Scott, Wellington.
  1916   Seventeen Years in the Underworld. New York: Abingdon Press.
Sellin, Thorsten.
  1963   "Organized crime: a business enterprise." Annals of the American Academy of Political and Social Science 347(May):12–19.
Semmes, Raphael.
  1938   Crime and Punishment in Early Maryland. Baltimore: Johns Hopkins Press.
Serao, E.
  1911a   "Truth about the Camorra, part 1." Outlook 98(July 29):717–726.
  1911b   "Truth about the Camorra, part 2." Outlook 98(August 5):778–787.
Settle, William A., Jr.
  1966   Jesse James was His Name. Columbia: University of Missouri Press.
Sharpe, May Churchill.
  1928   Chicago May: Her Story. New York: Macaulay.
Shaw, Clifford R., and Henry McKay.
  1929   Juvenile Delinquency and Urban Areas. Chicago: University of Chicago Press.
Shirley, Glenn.
  1957   Law West of Fort Smith. New York: Henry Holt.
  1965   Henry Starr: Last of the Real Badmen. New York: David McKay.
Shover, Neal Elwood.
  1971   "Burglary as an occupation." Ph.D. dissertation, University of Illinois, Urbana.
Simpson, C. H.
  1893   Life in the Far West. Chicago: Rhodes & McClure.
Sinclair, Andrew.
  1964   Era of Excess: A Social History of the Prohibition Movement. New York: Harper & Row.
Smith, Alson J.
  1954   Syndicate City. New York: Henry Regnery.
Smith, Bruce.
  1940   Police Systems in the United States. New York: Harper.
Smith, Denis Mack.
  1969   Italy. Ann Arbor: University of Michigan Press.
Smith, Laurence Dwight.
  1944   Counterfeiting, Crime against the People. New York: Norton.

Smith, Matthew Hale.
   1868   Sunshine and Shadow in New York. Hartford: J. B. Burr.
Smith, P. J.
   1938   Con Man. London: Herbert Jenkins.
Smithson, George.
   1930   Raffles in Real Life; the Confessions of George Smithson, alias "Gentleman
          George." London: Hutchinson.
Social Science Research Council.
   1965   The Statistical History of the United States from Colonial Times to the
          Present. Stamford: Fairfield.
Sondern, Frederic.
   1959   Brotherhood of Evil: The Mafia. New York: Farrar, Straus & Cudahy.
Special Committee of the Senate to Investigate Organized Crime in Interstate Com-
          merce.
   1951   Reports on Crime Investigations. Senate Reports, 82nd Cong., 1st sess.
Special Crime Study Commission on Organized Crime.
   1953   Final Report, California, May 11.
Spenser, James.
   1934   Limey Breaks In. London: Longmans, Green.
   1957   Limey: An Englishman Joins the Gangs. London: Neville Spearman.
Spindrift.
   1932   Yankee Slang. London: Author's Edition.
Sprogle, Howard O.
   1887   The Philadelphia Police, Past and Present. New York: Arno Press (1971
          edition).
Steffens, Lincoln.
   1904   The Shame of the Cities. New York: McClure, Phillips.
   1931   The Autobiography of Lincoln Steffens. New York: Harcourt, Brace.
Stiff, Dean.
   1930   The Milk and Honey Route. New York: Vanguard Press.
Still, Bayrd.
   1956   Mirror for Gotham. New York: New York University Press.
Strauss, Anselm L. (ed.)
   1968   The American City: A Source Book of American Imagery. Chicago: Aldine.
Stringer, A.
   1923   The Diamond Thieves. Indianapolis: Bobbs-Merrill.
Strong, Samuel M.
   1943   "Social types in a minority group." American Journal of Sociology 48
          (March):563–573.
Sullivan, Edward Dean.
   1929   Rattling the Cop on Chicago Crime. New York: Vanguard Press.
   1932   The Snatch Racket. New York: Vanguard Press.
Surface, Bill.
   1968   "The big business of hijacking." Reader's Digest 92 (January):115–119.
Sutherland, Edwin H.
   1937   The Professional Thief. Chicago: University of Chicago Press.
   1947   Principles of Criminology. Fourth Edition: Chicago: Lippincott.

Sutherland, Edwin H., and Donald R. Cressey.
  1970   Criminology. Eighth Edition. Philadelphia: Lippincott.
Symons, Julian.
  1966   Crime. New York: Bonanza Books.
Taeuber, Conrad, and Irene B. Taeuber.
  1958   The Changing Population of the United States. New York: Wiley.
Taft, Donald R.
  1956   Criminology. New York: Macmillan.
Talese, Gay.
  1971   Honor Thy Father. New York: World.
Thomas, Brinley.
  1954   Migration and Economic Growth. Cambridge, England: Cambridge Univer-
          sity Press.
Thompson, Craig, and Allen Raymond.
  1940   Gang Rule in New York: The Story of a Lawless Era. New York: Dial Press.
Thompson, V.
  1911   "Caged men of Viterbo." Collier's 17(August) : 13–14.
Thorwald, Jurgen.
  1967   Crime and Science. New York: Harcourt, Brace & World.
Thrasher, Frederic M.
  1927   The Gang. Chicago: University of Chicago Press.
Time Magazine.
  1971   "Rogue's gallery." 78(August 9) :23.
Toland, John.
  1963   The Dillinger Days. New York: Random House.
Train, A.
  1911   "American lawyer at the Camorra trial." McClure's 38(November) :71–83.
  1912   Courts, Criminals and the Camorra. New York: Scribner's.
Trotter, Robert J.
  1972   "Psyching the skyjacker." Science News 101(February 12) :108–110.
Turkus, Burton B., and Sid Feder.
  1951   Murder, Inc.: The Story of "The Syndicate." New York: Permabooks.
Turner, William W.
  1970   Hoover's F.B.I.—The Men and The Myth. Los Angeles: Sherbourne.
Tyler, Gus (ed.)
  1962   Organized Crime in America. Ann Arbor: University of Michigan Press.
U.S. Bureau of the Census.
  1960   Historical Statistics of the U.S., Colonial Times to 1957. Washington, D.C.:
          U.S. Government Printing Office.
Van Cise, Philip S.
  1936   Fighting the Underworld. Boston: Houghton Mifflin.
Varna, Andrew.
  1957   World Underworld. London: Museum Press.
Vice Commission of Chicago.
  1911   The Social Evil in Chicago. Chicago: Gunthorp-Warren.

Viles, Edward, and F. J. Furnivall (eds.)
  1880   The Rogues and Vagabonds of Shakespeare's Youth. London: N. Truber.
Volz, Joseph, and Peter J. Bridge (eds.)
  1969   The Mafia Talks. Greenwich: Fawcett.
Waldman, Milton M.
  1969   "The swindler in your waiting room." Medical Economics 46(August 4):
         79–85.
Wallace, Samuel E.
  1968   Skid Row as a Way of Life. New York: Harper & Row.
Walling, George W.
  1887   Recollections of a New York Chief of Police. New York: Caxton.
Warner, Matt, and Murray E. King.
  1940   The Last of the Bandit Riders. New York: Bonanza Books.
Webb, Walter Prescott.
  1935   The Texas Rangers: A Century of Frontier Defense. Boston: Houghton
         Mifflin.
Wellman, Paul I.
  1961   A Dynasty of Western Outlaws. Garden City, N.Y.: Doubleday.
Wensley, Frederick Porter.
  1930   Forty Years of Scotland Yard. Garden City. Garden City Pub.
Wentworth, Harold, and Stuart Berg Flexner (eds.)
  1960   Dictionary of American Slang. New York: Cromwell.
Werner, M. R.
  1928   Tammany Hall. Garden City, N.Y.: Doubleday, Doran.
Wertenbaker, Thomas Jefferson.
  1948   Father Knickerbocker Rebels: New York City during the Revolution. New
         York: Scribner's.
White, George M.
  1907   From Boniface to Bank Burglar; or, The Price of Persecution. New York:
         Seaboard.
Willard, Frances E.
  1883   Woman and Temperance: or, The Work and Workers of the Women's
         Christian Temperance Union. Hartford: Park.
Williams, Jack Kenny.
  1959   Vogues in Villainy. Columbia: University of South Carolina Press.
Williams, John D.
  1970   "Highway robbery." Wall Street Journal March 24:1.
Williams, Mary Floyd.
  1921   History of the San Francisco Committee of Vigilance (of 1851). Berkeley:
         University of California Press.
Williamson, Henry.
  1962   Hustler! Garden City, N.Y.: Doubleday.
Williamson, Jefferson.
  1930   The American Hotel. New York: Knopf.
Winick, Charles, and Paul M. Kinsie.
  1971   The Lively Commerce: Prostitution in the United States. Chicago: Quad-
         rangle.

Wood, Stuart.
  1932   Shades of the Prison House. A Personal Memoir. London: Williams & Norgate.
Woodbury, George.
  1951   The Great Days of Piracy in the West Indies. New York: Norton.
Woods, Robert A. (ed.)
  1902   Americans in Process. Boston: Houghton Mifflin.
Wooldridge, Clifton R.
  1901   Hands Up! In the World of Crime, or 12 Years a Detective. Chicago: Thompson.
Wright, Thomas.
  1838   Queen Elizabeth and Her Times, vol. 2. London: Henry Colburn.
Young, Kimball, and Raymond Mack.
  1959   Sociology and Social Life. New York: American.
Zink, Harold.
  1939   City Bosses in the United States. Durham: Duke University Press.
Zorbaugh, Harvey W.
  1929   The Gold Coast and the Slum. Chicago: University of Chicago Press.

CHAPTER **10**

Collective Behavior, Crime, and Delinquency

James F. Short, Jr.

Washington State University

"Collective behavior is the field of sociology that focuses on the sequences and patterns of interaction that emerge in problematic situations" (Lang & Lang, 1968:556). Since virtually all human behavior—certainly all of crime and juvenile delinquency—involves elements that are in some sense problematic, one might expect to find a well-developed literature specifying the nature of these sequences and patterns of interaction, discussed here specifically with respect to matters of concern to criminologists. That such is not the case says much about both criminology and collective behavior as subfields of sociology.

Collective behavior, in fact, has taken as a major point of departure a rather special class of "problematic situations"—those in which participants "lack adequate guides to conduct":

> Whenever imagery that is conventionally accepted or officially sanctioned fails to take account of, or runs counter to, deeply felt sentiments or common perceptions of reality, people create currents of agitation by their actions. They are stirred from the planes along which they normally move and remain agitated until they settle back again into a pattern resistant to further change. What takes place during the interlude is *elementary* collective problem solving rather than structured social action (Lang & Lang, 1968:556).

While acknowledging that "some elementary aspect is actually present in every social encounter, since the behavior of the participants is never completely determined by prior expectations associated with the positions they occupy in stable social structures" (p. 566), writers in this field have focused on special types of social encounters: those which involve large numbers of people, e.g., crowds and social movements. Such phenomena, while often involving crime—e.g., lynchings, property destruction, and assault upon persons—have been considered marginal to the province of criminology. Their neglect by criminologists has been a major lacuna, attributable in part to specialization within the social and behavioral sciences and in part to the social accounting

I am grateful to Armand Mauss and Stuart Hadden for their critical reading of an earlier draft of this paper and to the Social Research Center of Washington State University and the National Institute of Mental Health (Research Grant MH 20721) for partial support for its writing. They are, of course, not responsible for the product.

system by which the phenomena of crime have been both identified and measured. The theoretical flowering within criminology which extended roughly from Shaw and McKay (1929, 1931), through Sutherland (1924), A. Cohen (1955), Cloward and Ohlin (1960), and others to the present has borrowed primarily from the literature on socialization and social structure, and from research of its own spawning, to the neglect of the special theoretical and empirical concerns of collective behavior. The latter, despite the obvious importance of its subject matter, and heroic efforts to rescue it from preoccupation with the novel and bizarre, also has been something of a social science stepchild.

PROBLEMS OF IDENTIFICATION AND MEASUREMENT

Both criminology and collective behavior have suffered special data problems which have hampered their mutual enrichment. Crime has been identified primarily with the acts of individuals, in terms both of the legal focus on individual guilt or innocence and the methods devised to identify and measure phenomena so labeled.[1] The law finds the establishment of guilt other than as an individual responsibility very difficult. When it addresses group (*read* gang, corporation, crowd, social movement, or family) responsibility, it does so in terms of leaders or other functionaries who may be liable as individuals. The problem has been particularly difficult with respect to "white-collar crime" and the types of behavior of special interest to students of collective behavior, e.g., gang activity, riots, protest demonstrations, and other large gatherings in which laws are violated. "White-collar crime" typically takes place within highly structured contexts, such as banks and other businesses, large and small, and, therefore, is not treated in this chapter. Our focus, and that of most of the relevant literature, is on the behavior of more "elementary" collectivities—juvenile gangs and participants in other subcultural groups, crowds of demonstrators, and mobs.

The involvement of special interest groups in lawmaking, lawbreaking, and lawenforcing, and their relationship to agencies of law enforcement in crime, adds further social and political dimensions to the problem. In a society which prides itself on equality of all citizens before the law, but in which "some are more equal than others," those who occupy positions of power conferred by law bear special responsibilities for the strength of the social fabric.

Law-enforcement and judicial agencies experience great difficulty when faced with large numbers of people acting en masse, or in conflicting groups, whether those people are protesting or celebrating (Walker, 1968; Campbell et al., 1969; Hector & Helliwell, 1969; Sahid, 1969; Skolnick, 1969; Marx, 1970; Nieburg, 1970). The response of the public at large, as well as of public officials, to mass demonstrations and civil disobedience contrasts with general public and official acceptance of crowds of celebrants —e.g., a city's exuberance following a World Series victory, or an organization of "respectable" people in convention. This contrast places in bold relief the relevance of public definition and official response to our understanding of collective behavior and crime (see Stark, 1972; Short, 1974).

Both knowledge and official action on crime are affected by the types of records— the official "bookkeeping"—which are kept by police and courts. These records are especially uninformative concerning phenomena of collective behavior, aside from

---

1. By social scientists, as well as others, despite admonishment by many of our colleagues (see, e.g., Blumer, 1971).

general problems of reliability and validity (which are discussed elsewhere in this volume). They note only *individual acts* defined as criminal, or *individuals* involved in such acts, as reported to or judged by the police or the judiciary. Such enumerations are inadequate and misleading both descriptively and analytically. They tell us little about the behavior of collectivities, or concerning the influence of collectivities on the behavior of individuals.

The use of arrest data for measurement of social correlates of crime has long been objected to on the grounds that the guilt of persons arrested has not been established. This is an especially serious problem in episodes of collective behavior in which police tactics of "clearing the streets" often lead to wholesale arrests of persons without respect to criminal behavior. The widespread failure of such arrests to result in convictions, and the dismissal of arrestees which so often has followed them, is testimony to the inadequacy of arrest data for purposes of objective inquiry into the relation between collective behavior and crime.

The legal focus on individual participation in criminal acts and the lack of adequate data concerning such acts when the context is an episode of collective behavior (whether a riot, an "acting crowd," or a gang) have contributed to the neglect by both criminology and collective behavior of the other field. In addition, both fields have suffered from lack of knowledge concerning on-going behavioral processes.

LEVELS OF EXPLANATION

The study of collective behavior has been concerned principally with the *emergence* of such behavior, with defining and classifying the types and processes of interaction and organization that it takes, and with explanatory models for it. Several "classic" and recent writings treat these matters: Turner and Killian (1957), Lang and Lang (1961, 1968), Smelser (1962, 1970), Killian (1964), Turner (1964), Gusfield (1968), Heberle (1968), Blumer (1969), Currie and Skolnick (1970), and Quarantelli (1970).

The theoretical literature is controversial, in part because of gaps in empirical knowledge, which in turn relate to severe problems of research design, data gathering, and analysis. A recent discussion of controversies concerning study of collective violence is instructive. Berk (1972a:113) points out that "it is relatively easy to gather information about conditions *preceding* crowd behavior" and after it, but that "mob process is extremely difficult to study." Acquisition of *process* data, *in situ,* and its analysis have been major methodological problems for most behavioral sciences. These problems become acute when the motivations of participants in the behavior under study are of interest to the investigator. The situation is further complicated when, as so often appears to be the case with respect to the study of crime and collective behavior, both *investigators* and *participants* are motivated by personal and political concerns. Berk describes a number of problems complicating the collection of in-process data on crowds, most of which apply more generally to the study of episodes of collective behavior and, very often, of crime. (In the following, substitute "episodes of collective behavior"—in most cases "criminal behavior" may be also substituted—for "crowd" and "mob.")

1. Events during crowd behavior usually occur rather quickly.
2. Many events occur at once.
3. Actions are often taking place over a relatively wide geographical area.
4. The occurrence of collective behavior is difficult to anticipate, so that investigators interested in the phenomenon usually miss the activities.

5. Mob processes (as compared to the results of mob processes) leave few traces, and frequently the best one can do is gather retrospective accounts.

6. Crowd participants are unlikely to take time out from what they are doing to cooperate with an investigator. And even if they would, the suspicion that a researcher might be a police officer or informant would mitigate against a sincere interaction.

7. Crowd participants or persons who happen to be present during collective violence frequently have very salient vested interests in the interpretation of the phenomenon. Their accounts are thus especially vulnerable to conscious and unconscious distortions.

8. The high risk of personal injury persuades many researchers to study crowds from a distance (Berk, 1972a:113–14).

Berk's discussion of "interpretive pitfalls" resulting from the differential accessibility of data concerning before, after, and in-process behavior and system states warns against the imputation of motives (especially the assumption that all participants are similarly motivated) and of crowd (collective) processes. Instead, he suggests, data must be collected on what happens in crowds by means of direct and systematic observation.

A similar suggestion has been put forth with regard to levels of explanation of crime and delinquency. Cohen and Short (1971) note that "three kinds of questions can be asked about the 'causation' of crime." (Here, looking at the other side of the coin, as it were, it is possible to substitute "episodes of collective behavior" for "crime" and other terms common to criminology.) In abbreviated form these are:

1. Why did *this* individual commit *this* crime? How is his involvement related to his personal characteristics, his background, or the roles he plays? . . . These are "psychological" questions.

2. What is it about the social systems in which events occur that helps to explain their occurrence? This "macrosociological" perspective studies crime and delinquency in terms of their relations to the organization and culture of the community of which they are a part.

3. How did this event occur? What was the interaction situation . . . of which the criminal event was a product, and how did it evolve? This is a question in the "microsociology" of crime. *This question has been the least asked and the least is known about it* (Cohen & Short, 1971:115–16).

All three of these levels of explanation have drawn the attention of scholars concerned with both collective behavior and crime. Lack of systematic data at the microsociological level, however, has hampered theoretical development in both fields, as it has their integration. Such data as are available serve primarily to warn against generalization to this level and to the motivational (psychological) level on the basis of macrosociological theories or data. Perspectives from each level are necessary if holistic explanations based on too limited information are to be avoided.

It is well, at the outset, to stress the fact that the most recent thinking—and the best evidence—emphasizes the *continuity* of collective behavior and conventional behavior rather than their differences (Turner, 1964; Lang & Lang, 1968; McPhail, 1969; Quarantelli, 1970). The differences clearly are matters of degree, rather than of kind. This chapter's emphasis is upon *relationships* of collective and conventional behavior in the special sense designated by "collective behavior," and on the processes involved in their explanation. We begin by inquiring into the role of fads and fashions in juvenile delinquency. We then focus on gangs and other forms of collective behavior among juveniles. The chapter concludes with brief observations concerning contagion and the role of processes of social control and of collective behavior in the politicization of delinquent and criminal behavior.

FADS AND FASHIONS

Fads and fashion "signify a continuing pattern of change in which certain social forms enjoy temporary acceptance and respectability only to be replaced by others more abreast of the times" (Blumer, 1968:342). They deal with matters of sensitivity and taste rather than utility or merit. Fashion is characteristic of societies and groups caught up in continuous social change. It "is scarcely to be found in settled societies, such as primitive tribes, peasant societies, or caste societies, which cling to what is established and has been sanctioned through long usage" (p. 342). Blumer notes that fashion brings order and continuity to certain areas of social life in rapidly changing societies, much as does custom in settled societies. And, "the fashion process nurtures and shapes a common sensitivity and taste . . . analogous on the subjective side to a 'universe of discourse.' Like the latter, it provides a basis for a common approach to the world and for handling and digesting the experience the world yields" (p. 344).

Fads, superficially similar to fashions, are in reality quite different:

> The most notable difference is that fads have no line of historical continuity; each springs up independent of a predecessor and gives rise to no successor. This separate, detached, and free-floating character signifies that fads, unlike fashion, are not part of a regulating social process that gives shape and structure to group life (Blumer, 1968:344).

Fashion is the more important of these phenomena with respect to crime and delinquency as with respect to social life in general. Smelser's (1962) discussion of characteristics of contemporary status systems in the United States and Western Europe suggests why these systems are so "very conducive to fashion cycles" (1962:184). For our purposes the following characteristics are most salient: (1) status symbolization is highly differentiated, thus allowing a high degree of innovation within particular groups; (2) "a distinctive rationality of status symbolization" characterizes large segments of the population; and (3) "prestige" becomes the most common "generalized medium of exchange . . . in status symbolization" (p. 186).

These general conditions of Western society are augmented by special conditions of particular groups, e.g., adolescents. American society, compared with most other societies, is characterized by a lack of *rites de passage*, those ceremonies and symbols marking the transition from one age grade to another. As a result, adolescence in our society has become a period of experimentation in life-styles, including much concern with fads of the moment and what is fashionable. For their own part, adolescents are highly differentiated with respect to these matters. Youth subcultures and status systems, "generation gaps," the youth market, and related matters have been subjects of much comment in popular media and scientific journals (cf. Johnstone & Katz, 1957; England, 1960; Monod, 1967; Schwartz & Merton, 1967).

Similarly, a variety of "status universes" relevant to delinquency have been hypothesized (Finestone, 1957; Short et al., 1962; Short, 1963; Schwendinger & Schwendinger, 1967). Systematic treatment of fads and fashions within these contexts is conspicuously absent but several suggestive accounts are in the literature. From these, it is clear that fads and fashions among these youngsters are closely related to the norms and values, resources, and organizational forms characteristic of the social systems in which they spend their lives.

STREET-CORNER SOCIETY

The nature of the most important social system in the lives of many young people in the slum sections of large cities is captured in the term "street-corner society." Association of street-corner society with delinquent gangs is in some respects erroneous and unfortunate. For while groups classified as delinquent gangs are participants in street-corner society and in some locales they may constitute its central organizational focus, the gang form of organization is neither a necessary nor a sufficient description of street-corner society.[2] The chief connotation of the term is simply that its participants share in varying degrees attitudes and values which set them apart from other "societies," e.g., "middle-class society" or "cafe society."

Kobrin and Finestone's (1968) discussion of street-corner society in relation to "Drug Addiction Among Young Persons in Chicago" during the years 1947–53 is apposite:

> This society flourishes in those communities where the traditional influences and controls over the conduct of the youth group tend to be weak and uncertain. In such communities all young persons either participate in or are exposed to the activities of street groups and share in some measure the attitudes of this society. In the face of counteracting pressures for conformity to the norms of the wider society, of varying degrees of effectiveness, some youngsters merely dabble in street society, taking on only some of its superficial traits; others participate fully but for relatively short periods; and still others become full-fledged members and ultimately the bearers and agents of its code and its culture.
>
> The central feature of this society and its body of practices, or "culture," is the support it gives to behavior which is generally inconsistent with the norms of its expectations. This orientation on the part of street boys is expressed in a variety of ways, but is most clearly and dramatically manifested in delinquency and in the search for the exploitation of the "kick" (Kobrin & Finestone, 1968:118–19).

The following interview excerpts from the Kobrin-Finestone study capture the essence of these relationships.

> Well, I was living on L-Street. . . . There wasn't too much to do. We'd just sit around and go to dances, things like that, go to the park. Didn't have nothing to do. There was a place over here on Madison Street where you used to get some wine. . . . We used to get drunk off that, get crazy, stack chicken coops up on the street car tracks about ten high, set them on fire, watch them burn, watch them street cars line up. We'd do such as all that. Just nothing to do, just roam around, and go looking, or go over to South Water market, take fruit, help somebody on a truck, just something to be doing. Wasn't nothing happening at school so we just decided we wouldn't go to school on some days; we'd go out and have fun. We'd go over there on Madison and get some wine and get drunk and go swimming and just do everything. . . . We used to hang on the corner, wouldn't work. We were going to high school and didn't want to do that so we wanted to loaf around. So we stood on the corner all day and waited for the man to come by, vegetable truck or something come by and we'd take a watermelon and sit down and eat that and wait for the pop man to come by. Hardly ever went home. We just stayed up all night. We'd sit on the corner. We'd talk all night long. . . . Sometimes we didn't go home for two days maybe. . . .

---

2. Whyte's (1955) use of the term had as its primary referent neither gangs nor delinquents —nor indeed adolescents—but the social system of a group of young adult males˙which revolved around "the corner" in their working-class Boston neighborhood.

. . . Some of the older boys was smoking reefers [marijuana cigarettes]. "What's that, what's that?" "Oh, that ain't for you. You're square, you don't know what's happening. You're too young. I'll get put in jail messing with you." . . . Well, then you get to smoking. . . . You say, "You high?" "Yeah, I'm high." You start smoking it and then you really get crazy. Then you wonder, "Well, this ain't like wine. I ain't going to mess with no wine. I'm going to smoke reefers. I want to be a reefer-head. All the big boys is reefer-heads." They just do what the big boys do. Now he smokes reefers, now he's hep, now he goes for himself. Now he'll begin to talk to girls. . . . Then you mess around and you go on, well then you meet with some guy, you see him stand up scratching on the corner, nodding, he looks crazy, you know, and you wonder what it is. . . . Then some guys are talking about, well if I tried this [marijuana] I'll try anything. Yeah, I'll try anything to get high on. I'm game, he's game. . . . Then some guy, he'll come along and turn one fellow on [induce him to use a drug]. He'll come back and he'll say, "I had some stuff to put in your arm, made you feel real nice, you know, you get real high. Never felt nothing like this, you know." . . . "What is it, a needle? No, I don't put no needle in my arm." You're scared. They say, "Well, you're square, you don't know what's happening." . . . I say, "No, I don't want to mess around." They say, "Oh, I'm going to stop running with you, you don't know what's happening." . . . I say, "Well, I'll try it one time. One time and that's it. I ain't trying no more." He go and he probably give you a half of a cap. I got a half a cap and I couldn't even see (Kobrin & Finestone, 1968:119–21).

These and other case materials strongly suggest that the introduction of heroin in street-corner society was facilitated by the fact that use of drugs was "in fashion," and that the search for "newer, stronger, and more status-giving intoxicants" was part of the fashion process.

Kobrin and Finestone go on to attribute the rapid diffusion of heroin in certain areas of Chicago to "a species of social contagion" related to a combination of circumstances: (1) minority (black) status; (2) objective community conditions commonly associated with slum areas in large cities; and (3) the fact that most of the new users were adolescents. They suggest that:

the urban adolescent is exceptionally vulnerable to epidemics of bizarre and unconventional behavior. Briefly, this susceptibility arises from the fact that being neither child nor adult, with the certainties either status might provide, the adolescent tends to be restless in his activity and unstable in his emotional states. Moreover, in periods following social upheavals like wars, this restlessness, often apparent in the entire population, becomes intensified in the adolescent group, usually leading to a greater frequency and persistence of bizarre behavior. Such behavior tends to sweep through the entire youthful population in the form of fads, typically around modes of dress or speech, and sometimes affecting manners and morals (Kobrin & Finestone, 1968:126–27).

But heroin was not adopted by the majority of young black males, even in the communities with the highest rates of addiction. And it became fashionable (as distinguished from faddish) among a relatively small segment of even that restricted population at risk. Finestone (1957) has discussed that segment in terms of the emergence of "the cat" as a social type, representing "the personal counterpart of an expressive social movement." Diffusion of heroin among participants in street-corner society clearly was and is selective among populations studied by Kobrin and Finestone and by others, even among groups with high incidence of alcohol and other drugs (see, e.g., Short et al., 1963; Short & Strodtbeck, 1965; Sutter, 1969). We know much more about patterns of drug use and other behavior which become established among groups, and about roles and social types which emerge among populations and specific groups, than we do about how and why these patterns, roles, and types become established. On the basis of what we know, however, it seems unnecessary to invoke the notion of contagion as a special type of interaction to explain such phenomena (see Brown, 1954: 843; Smelser, 1962:155; Turner, 1964).[3] Both the emergence and maintenance of patterns of behavior and values characterizing subcultures, and of particular groups, roles, and social types, are explainable on the basis of normal processes of social interaction, organization, and learning (Bandura, 1971, 1973).

THE EMERGENCE OF NORMS AND SOCIAL ORGANIZATION

The nature of these processes is suggested in such formulations as Smelser's (1962) "value added" and Turner's (1964) "emergent norm" theories of collective behavior. In both, the categories of social action and the processes of interaction are seen as extensions of characteristics generally applicable to human behavior rather than as ad hoc or otherwise special characteristics of collective behavior. These formulations differ greatly in terms of the specific problems addressed and the types of determinants of collective behavior emphasized. We have noted above, for example, some of the structural conditions of Western society, with special attention to adolescence, that are conducive to a particular type of collective behavior with special importance to delinquency, viz., fashion. It will be suggested later that these same structural characteristics conduce to the phenomenon of ganging among youngsters, and to even more organizationally diffuse patterns of association, such as social movements.

First, we note Turner's emphasis on processes by which norms specific to a given situation emerge to regulate collective behavior:

> Emergent norm theory defines the key problem not as explaining why an unnatural unanimity develops, but as explaining the imposition of a pattern of differential expression which is perceived as unanimity by crowd members and observers. Taking the cue from the work of Sherif . . . and Asch . . . , one can explain differential expression as the consequence of a social norm. The shared conviction of right, which constitutes a norm, sanctions behavior consistent with the norm, inhibits behavior contrary to it, justifies proselyting and requires restraining action against those who dissent. Because the behavior in the crowd is different either in degree or kind from that in noncrowd situations, the norm must be specific to the situation to some degree—hence emergent norm. Specific further problems that take pre-eminence when these assumptions are made include accounting for the neutralization or inapplicability of existing norms, specifying the process by which a collectivity comes to acknowledge a norm as the rule of that body, and accounting for the character of the norm (Turner, 1964: 390–91).

The above analysis is applicable to more than crowd behavior. In terms of our discussion of heroin use among lower-class ghetto males, for example, the problem becomes one of determining how and why the "kick" and the "hustle" emerged as such intense and dominating themes in the lives of the "cats," and why this social type involved particular individuals and not others. Emergence of the social type is explained,

---

3. More generally, the "match-up" of types of interaction, social organization, and normative behavior seems suspect. Responses to the stimulation of interaction with others vary greatly on a continuum from direct and immediate to interpretive, as suggested by Blumer (1969), but are very imperfectly correlated with types of social organization and forms of collective behavior, even more so in specific instances of behavior (see, e.g., Berk, 1972a).

in part, as Finestone notes, as one mode of adaptation to the problems of young black males in the ghettos of large cities. It is an adaptation whereby

a segment of the population turns in upon itself and attempts to develop within itself criteria for the achievement of social status and the rudiments of a satisfactory social life. . . .

The themes of the "hustle" and "kick" in the social orientation of the cat are facts which appear to be overdetermined. For example, to grasp the meaning of the "hustle" to the cat one must understand it as a rejection of the obligation of the adult male to work. When asked for the reasons underlying his rejection of work the cat did not refer to the uncongenial and relatively unskilled and low-paid jobs which, in large part, were the sole types of employment available to him. He emphasized rather that the routine of a job and the demand that he should apply himself continuously to his work task were the features that made work intolerable for him. The self-restraint required by work was construed as an unwarranted damper upon his love of spontaneity. The other undesirable element from his point of view was the authoritarian setting of most types of work with which he was familiar.

There are undoubtedly many reasons for the cat's rejection of work but the reasons he actually verbalized are particularly significant when interpreted as devices for sustaining his self-conception. The cat's feeling of superiority would be openly challenged were he to confront certain of the social realities of his situation, such as the discrimination exercised against colored persons looking for work and the fact that only the lowest status jobs are available to him. He avoided any mention of these factors which would have forced him to confront his true position in society and thus posed a threat to his carefully cherished sense of superiority.

In emphasizing as he does the importance of the "kick" the cat is attacking the value our society places upon planning for the future and the responsibility of the individual for such planning. Planning always requires some subordination and disciplining of present behavior in the interest of future rewards. The individual plans to go to college, plans for his career, plans for his family and children, etc. Such an orientation on the part of the individual is merely the personal and subjective counterpart of a stable social order and of stable social institutions, which not only permit but sanction an orderly progression of expectations with reference to others and to one's self. Where such stable institutions are absent or in the inchoate stages of development, there is little social sanction for such planning in the experience of the individual. Whatever studies are available strongly suggest that such are the conditions which tend to prevail in the lower socio-economic levels of the Negro urban community. Stable family and community organization is lacking in those areas of the city where drug use is concentrated. A social milieu which does not encourage the subordination and disciplining of present conduct in the interests of future rewards tends by default to enhance the present. The "kick" appears to be a logical culmination of this emphasis (Finestone, 1957:6–7).

Other social types and forms of collective behavior—with appropriate norms and values—emerge in response to the structural conditions and strains of ghetto living. Gang leaders studied by Krisberg (1971) in Philadelphia cultivated "bad nigger" and "hustler" images among their peers and with others. Krisberg notes that these images recur in black folklore (Brown, 1965; Malcolm X, 1965; Grier & Cobbs, 1968; Abrahams, 1970). In contrast with Finestone's "cats," the "bad nigger" presents an image of rebellion against white society. "The impulsive resort to violence is antithetical to white demands that the black male be docile and yielding" (Krisberg, 1971:126). The Philadelphia gang leaders "often used the term 'bad nigger' to describe revered members of the training group and other members of their gangs" (p. 127). In the street world, violence and manhood were intimately related, and "acting crazy"—violently and with abandon—often was rewarded.

Krisberg describes the interactional system in manhood testing as having the properties of a zero-sum game.

> One manifested his manhood at the expense of the other's claims of dominance. . . .
>   We observed in these interpersonal contests little effort on the part of the actors to allow the opponent an escape route—a way of backing down without overt capitulation to the other. Note, for example, an "apology" offered by one gang leader to another student after the two were physically restrained by others from engaging in a fist fight:
>   "I apologize for almost killing you. We both was wrong, but you're a jive mother-fucker who ought to be hurt, but I apologize, and if you ever mess with me again, I'll show you who's the man here" (1971:128).

Elsewhere, we have noted that *gang encounters* often are non-zero-sum, in the sense that neither side to a conflict need be defeated (Short & Strodtbeck, 1965:200–2). Points won by one party are not necessarily lost by the other in the context of group rivalry. This is because, in contrast to one-on-one situations involving individuals, status is conferred primarily *within* each group. Defeat—even fleeing the battlefield—offers status rewards if the group has performed with bravery, perhaps against over-whelming odds; or the lack of clear-cut victory may be "explained" by the interven-tion of the police or a detached worker. The dynamics of individual and within-group status games thus press for collective solution, suggesting yet another way in which episodes of collective behavior may be related to group process and social structure.

The relation between the bad nigger and hustler roles doubtless is extremely com-plex. The life style of Finestone's (1957) "ideal type" hustler is incompatible with violence. And Krisberg observes that "the hustler breaks the white man's laws, but does not flaunt them in the same manner as the 'bad nigger' " (1971:134). Yet each of the Philadelphia gang leaders had his hustle:

> A few pursue persistent patterns of thefts and burglaries. One fellow's hustle involves robbing the participants of illegal dice games. His specialty, a dangerous one, always involves the carrying of a gun and often its use. His enemies are not only the police, but also those organized criminal interests in the neighborhood who share in the profits from illegal gambling. "The Mafia has a permanent contract out on me, man." Other students are petty loan sharks or continuous gamblers. Many of the students have sold marijuana and other drugs in limited quantities. Three gang leaders are procurers for prostitutes. They are, for the most part, "small-time" operators in the sense that they are not connected with organized criminal interests, their "take" is relatively small, and they run afoul of law enforcement officials regularly. The victims of their activities are almost always fellow residents of Mantua (Krisberg, 1971:132).

Among these gang leaders, violence was often a part of the hustle:

> Catch a man or woman coming down the street and they've been counting a little money, and I'd run up and take it from them, knock them down and go in their pocket and get all their money. You know, this kind of thing. And burglarize people's houses, you know, and it was a thing whereas, like, I mean, I had to survive and had to get to that money, and this is what I did to get to it (p. 132).

One of these young men told Krisberg he would "look for men in the neighbor-hood who would pay ten dollars to have somebody beat up" (p. 133).

Thus, what appears to be "impulsive behavior"—or pathological—may in fact be collectively cultivated, part of a group's complex adjustment to a hostile and demand-ing environment. Youth in the urban slum, lacking the skills necessary for successfully moving out of this environment or restricted in vision by prior experience in it, have supported each other in norms conducive to a variety of life styles that involve crime and delinquency. These life styles, and the social roles which incorporate them, are both a response and a contribution to the less-structured, less-formalized, and more-problematic situations which give rise to collective behavior in the special sense reserved for that term.

The Langs speak of elementary collective behavior episodes as involving "a partial derailment of social interaction from its normatively structured or expected course" (Lang & Lang, 1968:556). While much social life in virtually all segments of all societies is characterized by spontaneity and lack of formal structure, the extent to which this is the case appears to vary inversely with socioeconomic position. While much order exists in lower-class areas of "Black Metropolis"—structure, relatively stable status relationships, and norms which provide guidelines for behavior—such areas are characterized by a high degree of informality and lack of formal structure (Drake & Cayton, 1945; Short, 1966). These qualities of community life contribute to the viability of social roles such as the "bad nigger" and the "hustler," which in turn contribute to the quality of life in such communities.

Such roles are not always successful, in the sense of being rewarded by one's associates. Both the "bad nigger" and the "cat," for example, pose great problems to group solidarity, since both are so oriented toward personal expression and gratification. From our Chicago study (Short & Strodtbeck, 1965), two examples come to mind. The Vice Kings had a sometime leader who (upon reflection) played the "bad nigger" role to the hilt. His was a "crazy bag," fearless to the point of foolishness in relations with other conflict-oriented gangs and with the police. This behavior was admired as manly but it often ran counter to other group values and supporting norms, especially those having to do with group survival (not bringing too much "heat" down on the gang, or involving them in impossible odds against rival gangs). This boy was an undependable leader, regarded more as "crazy" than manly. At the close of our field research, he was serving a long prison term for homicide.

A second case involved a member of the Chiefs (a conflict gang) who adopted the life-style of the "cat." This boy had been extremely popular among the Chiefs. He was affable and highly skilled verbally, adept at "signifying." His use of drugs at first posed no problem, for nearly all the Chiefs smoked marijuana and experimentation with heroin was not uncommon. As he became caught up in a heavy heroin addiction cycle, however, he spent less time with the Chiefs and more hustling for his habit. Over a period of three years, his status in the gang deteriorated, though it would rise temporarily each time he came out "clean" after a period of involuntary incarceration in jail or in the Federal Narcotics Hospital in Lexington, Kentucky. While the life-style of the "cat" contributed to his loss of status among the Chiefs because it took him away from group activities, his addiction was far more damaging. When in the "frantic junkie" stage, he became an object of pity or disdain. Even when he was clean or in the "honeymoon" stage—and therefore his old self—the boys viewed him with suspicion for they knew this to be temporary. As with the "bad nigger" among the Vice Kings, the Chiefs knew that the presence of the "cat" in their midst was certain to result in closer police surveillance, thus posing danger to the group.

GANGS AND GANGING AS COLLECTIVE BEHAVIOR

The group forms of delinquency and crime have received a great deal of attention over the past half century and more. In his classic treatment of the subject, Fredric M.

Thrasher described gangland as an "interstitial area" and the gang as "an interstitial element in the framework of society. . . . The gang is almost invariably characteristic of regions that are interstitial to the more settled, more stable, and better organized portions of the city . . . the gang develops as one manifestation of the economic, moral, and cultural frontier which marks the interstice" (Thrasher, 1963:20–21).

The relationships here implied between urban ecology and social organization characterized the "social disorganization" interpretation of juvenile delinquency, crime, and many other social ills. The slum—located in areas surrounding the central business districts of large cities—was described as a zone in transition from one stable state (residential) to another (commercial and industrial). A variety of factors—largely economic in nature—led to deterioration of such areas in terms of residential desirability, population turnover was rapid, and conventional institutions were in disarray. Existing social rules of behavior lost their hold on individuals, leading to "a general decay of all institutions of the group" and to the "disintegration of the community as a unit of social control" (Thomas & Znaniecki, 1927:1128).

> Traditional norms and standards of the conventional community weaken and disappear. Resistance on the part of the community to delinquent and criminal behavior is low, and such behavior is tolerated and may even become accepted and approved (Shaw & McKay, 1929:205).

Further:

> Many of the boys' groups that are indigenous to these disorganized areas are unconventional or delinquent in their traditions and norms. It is probably significant that most of the boys appearing in the Juvenile Court are members of delinquent gangs (p. 205).

In the quarter of a century following the painstaking investigations of Thrasher, Shaw and McKay, and others, peer group influence and "the gang" became virtually a "given" in sociological theories of juvenile delinquency. This, despite the realization by these scholars that their work was only the beginning of needed knowledge. Recent theoretical and empirical work permits extension of the findings and interpretations of these classic investigations.

Popular conceptions of social phenomena tend both to simplify and to romanticize. Gangs became tightly knit groups, "all for one and one for all," bound together against adversity by friendship, loyalty, and the free spirit of adventure. That image has an important element of truth in it, based as it is, in part, on the research and interpretations of a generation of sociologists who discovered the crucial importance of peer relationships and community conditions for understanding juvenile delinquency. It has often been fostered in the classrooms and writings of sociologists and others, I suppose because it is attractive to our generally "liberal" political persuasion. We admire the "coping ability" of youngsters faced with overwhelming problems of "making it" in a world they never made, and friendship and loyalty are elusive and much-admired qualities in a society dominated by bureaucratic and impersonal institutions and universalistic criteria of personal worth. In the final analysis, the image is largely fictional, however, and it has contributed to much misunderstanding of the nature of juvenile delinquency.

Many questions remain, including the basic question of just how extensive and important group involvement is to crime and delinquency (Erickson, 1965, 1972). While all available accounts of street groups indicate their extensive participation in

Orientation of Relationship	Type of Norms and Social Relationships	
	Traditional	Emergent
Adolescent	a	b
Adult or Larger Society	c	d

FIGURE 1.   A typology of adolescent social relations.

delinquent activities (Cohen, 1955; Cohen & Short, 1958; Miller, 1958; Short et al., 1963; Thrasher, 1963; Short & Strodtbeck, 1965; B. Cohen, 1969a; Klein, 1971) and peer involvement is shown in both "official" and "unofficial" reports of most delinquencies (Shaw & McKay, 1931; Erickson, 1965, 1972), there is much disagreement concerning such fundamental questions as the extent of gang membership in communities and the relationship of gang membership to delinquency (cf. references cited above and Lerman, 1967b; Short, 1968; Klein, 1969; Miller, 1969). Recent research suggests the nature of status relationships within and between groups, and mechanisms related specifically to delinquency, but we do not know how general these findings may be or how important to delinquency (see, in addition to the above, Jansyn, 1966; Klein & Crawford, 1967; Kobrin et al., 1967; Lerman, 1967a; Mattick & Caplan, 1967). Implications for treatment and prevention of delinquency are even more problematic.

Out of these and other investigations has come a sense of the extreme variability in forms of association and in quality of relationships among adolescents, and between them and the larger society. It is instructive to view these matters in terms of the extent to which they are oriented toward the world of adolescents or toward the world of adults—the larger society—and by the extent to which they occur in traditional institutional forms or in more "emergent" social relationships outside of these forms.[4] This perspective is represented in Figure 1 which adds to social relationships the types of norms guiding these relationships. While these orientations, norms, and social relationships often differ only in degree or in momentary focus, they are treated separately here for purposes of discussion.

In Figure 1, cell *a* has to do with such matters as boy-girl and other peer relationships in traditional contexts (school, church, family), and cell *c* refers to parent-child, other kin, teacher-pupil, employer-employee, and a variety of additional relationships between "gatekeepers" and youth in traditional settings. While these relationships and the norms influencing them are not static—being to some extent "emergent"—they are relatively structured, stable, and traditional in character.

Gangs also vary both in the extent to which they are traditional or emergent and in the extent to which they are oriented toward more strictly adolescent or adult and larger society concerns. The extent to which gangs become traditional apparently varies greatly among and within cities. The factors and processes that account for such variation are not known precisely, but the literature contains many provocative suggestions, e.g., ethnic homogeneity, length and strength of identification with a neighborhood, the relations between criminal and conventional values or institutions, other aspects of

---

4. The latter distinction is similar to Turner's (1964) "emergent norms" in that norms prescribe the nature of social relationships. The match up between norms and social relationships is not always clear-cut, however.

adult-youth relationships, the influence of class-related subcultures, and developments within youth cultures (Kobrin, 1951; Miller, 1958; Cloward & Ohlin, 1960; Sherif & Sherif, 1963; Short & Strodtbeck, 1965; Kobrin et al., 1967; Rivera & Short, 1967).

Even among groups in traditional areas, there is much leeway in the stability and the binding power of norms regulating relationships among adolescents (cell *a* in Figure 1). Youth culture and its many variants tend not to be rigidly structured. Much of the behavior of adolescents, particularly outside traditional institutional contexts, is characterized by emergent norms and relationships.[5] Most gangs in most cities probably are located in cell *b* of Figure 1; their structure, continuity, and normatively guided behavior—despite historical continuity—include much that is properly classified as emergent.[6]

This supplementation of the traditional by the emergent in gang activity is suggested by the "reaction to status threat" phenomenon discussed by Short and Strodtbeck (1965) and Short (1968). Shifting group membership and identity, limited interpersonal skills of gang members, and limited group and community resources combine to reduce gang members' latitude in dealing with status threats. We were led to examine this phenomenon by a series of incidents reported by detached workers which involved delinquent, and usually violent, behavior on the part of gang leaders who were noted otherwise for being "cool." A common thread which ran through these incidents was the fact that each involved provocative circumstances which were threatening to the status of a leader. The delinquent episodes appeared to be a reaction to these status threats. Further analysis of field reports suggested that the reaction of leaders to status threats was a special case of the more general phenomenon of "status management," defined as "behavior oriented toward the achievement of desired social positions or states of being, or the protection of desired social positions or states of being already achieved" (Short, 1964:120).

Brymer's (1967) observations of adolescent street life in San Antonio suggests that similar processes are involved in *creating* gangs. He reports that a large portion of the daily round of activities among boys in that city typically is spent in small, relatively stable, friendship groups. Gangs, comprised of a number of such cliques, emerge as important identities in response to a variety of situational and larger community processes, such as police pressure and newspaper coverage. The shift from clique to gang identity is "dependent upon the number of clique contacts which are defined as threatening." The following case is illustrative:

> . . . one evening a clique group was riding around with their gang worker and the author. Upon passing a neighborhood drive-in restaurant with around 200–300 teenagers in front, the clique group identified the crowd in terms of membership in various neighborhood cliques, e.g., Joe's group, Henry and them, etc. A short time later, we again passed the drive-in, and something in the situation had changed so as to provoke an identification of the crowd in front of the restaurant as "El Circle" gang. The characteristics of the situation which apparently induced this change in designation were that all of the persons in the crowd were facing the street in a tense, quiet atmosphere; this contrasted

---

5. Recent developments, in fact, suggest that such a "being-in-becoming" orientation is especially attractive to some variants of youth culture (Kluckhohn & Strodtbeck, 1961; Spiegel, 1972).

6. Miller (1969) provides a good review of these matters. We concur in most essential respects with Miller's definition of the gang as "a basic associational form": "A gang is a group of urban adolescents who congregate recurrently at one or more nonresidential locales, with continued affiliation based on self-defined criteria of inclusion and exclusion" (p. 26). Our chief quibble has to do with Miller's insistence on the "urban" character of the gang. This seems unnecessary, though documentation of similar rural forms is largely anecdotal.

with an earlier loud, boisterous situation with all persons talking in their respective clique groups, with some "clique-hopping." Upon investigation, it was learned that a rival "gang" passed by in a car and shouted certain epithets about the mothers of the "Circle" boys, as well as challenges. Objectively, it was probably a clique that had passed by, but it had been identified by the persons in the crowd as a "gang." Another type of incident occurred when a boy was shot at in a rival neighborhood. His story upon returning to the area was that a rival "gang" had shot at him, and the ensuing clique discussion revolved around what to do (Brymer, 1967).

Brymer suggests that the more frequently threatening clique contacts occur, the more likely it is that the gang will develop a formalized structure.

The emergence of group structure and group norms, their change, and the patterning of group behavior, which we identify as subcultural, occur by means of such "elementary collective behavior" processes. Change may be induced by events external to the group, e.g., the challenge (real or imagined) of a rival group or agency, or by internal changes, as when a member seeks to change his status in the group. In the case cited by Brymer new relationships among those gathered at the drive-in were required by an event external to that situation. The resulting groupings were not "spontaneous," and certainly they were not random. Rather, they reflected previous relationships among youngsters in the area and the definitions provided by the external event.

The quality of these types of developments among a white group of "pill poppers" in Chicago is captured in the following field observer report. These boys were a segment of a rather diffuse and much larger gang—recognized as such among themselves and among members of the larger gang—distinguished by their common interest in drugs. "Use of pills and other drugs seemed virtually a way of life with these boys, interspersed with other kicks such as sex, alcohol, and 'way out' experiences which distinguished them, individually and collectively" (Short & Strodtbeck, 1965:207). After approximately six months with the group on the street, our observer reported on a hanging session with the boys during which tales about some of the experiences of gang members were related, to the accompaniment of laughter and camaraderie among all:

(1) The time Willie was so high he walked off a roof and fell a story or two and broke his nose. Worker thought he had been on a roof, while Butch maintained he fell from a boxcar. Butch said it was over a week before he went to the doctor. . . . Harry said he walked around the hospital in a crazy looking green coat whenever the guys went to visit him.

(2) The time Snooks, Baby, and Jerry climbed on a roof to wake Elizabeth. One of the guys reached through the window and grabbed what he thought was Elizabeth's leg, and shook it to wake her up. It turned out to be her old man's leg and it woke him up.

(3) The more recent incident in which Sonny leaped over the counter to rob a Chinaman, who proceeded to beat him badly. When the police came, Sonny asked that they arrest this man for having beaten him up. He was doped out of his mind and didn't know what was happening.

(4) Walter got into an argument with a woman over whose car it was they were standing by. He insisted they call the police, and waited confidently until the police showed and took him away.

(5) Sonny tried to break into a building and was ripping off a door when the police found him.

(6) Some of the guys slept out in a car and woke the next morning to find the car was being pulled away. They asked the tower to stop just long enough so they could get out.

(7) One of the guys broke into a car and just about tore the door off doing so—this was a car with all the windows broken out—he was too high to notice.

(8) One of the boys tried to start a car but just could not manage it. The car had no motor (Short & Strodtbeck, 1965:208–9).

The observer expressed the belief that these tales might be "in the process of becoming legendary within the group. They are so characteristic of this group and describe it so well" (p. 209). These boys were differentiated from their peers in other ways, as well. Despite strong urging, and taunts of "chicken" by the members of the gang, they declined to take part in violent opposition to the racial integration of one of Chicago's public beaches (Short & Strodtbeck, 1965:193–94) or in a violent confrontation with young men in the area in which several of the gang members were badly beaten (pp. 209–11). These behaviors by the pill poppers, and by the rest of the gang, were effective in differentiating the two groups, normatively and structurally. The pill poppers moved away from the larger group and became instead participants in the drug subculture.

This case illustrates the interaction of social relationships, other behavioral elements, and related attitudes and values in differentiating subcultures. Once formed, subcultures and their carrier groups continue to change, though change is likely to be constrained increasingly by norms, roles, and structure. Many youth groups, particularly street groups, do not become so "institutionalized," however, and retain a very largely emergent character. Jansyn (1966) has described the development of one Chicago gang as fluctuating between "gang" and "club" phases. Leadership varied between these phases. The latter was characterized by more formal and conventional structure and activities; the former, by the more fluid activities and structure of the street.

Rivera and Short (1967) found that contact with adults varied systematically for their Chicago gang and nongang youngsters. Nongang boys in this study had been contacted through adult-sponsored organizations such as the Boys Club and the YMCA—they were members of clubs. Not unexpectedly, adults nominated by gang boys as those with whom they had the most contact were less often in "caretaker" roles with respect to adolescents:

> Compared to other respondents, the typical gang-nominated adult is simply less concerned with the whole problem of offering opportunities to youngsters. For gang communities, the generations do not interact in a fashion that makes this problem explicit. Adults are seldom reminded that they may have an important role to play in affecting the life chances of a younger generation (Rivera & Short, 1967:97).

There is a good deal of evidence—though not systematically assessed or presented—of important social class and ethnic variations in these matters. Our "pill poppers" were white; Finestone's "cats" were black. These differences doubtless were important in terms of relationships between the groups and their communities. Both were lower class, though the "cats" were nearer the bottom of the socioeconomic ladder than were the "pill poppers."

For lower-class youngsters' experiences, even traditional adult institutional contexts (cell *d* in Figure 1) are likely to be less highly structured and routinized; more of their relationships with adults occur on the streets or in other public, nontraditional, or nonconventional contexts. The tradition of one-sex street groups—and of boy-girl relationships within the context of street life—is more often found in lower-class communities, and is more likely to provide direct links between young people and adults.

Drake and Cayton emphasize the *public* nature of much lower-class life in "Black Metropolis":

> Lower-class people will *publicly* drink and play cards in places where people of higher status would lose their "reputations"—in the rear of poolrooms, in the backrooms of taverns, in "buffet-flats," and sometimes on street corners and in alleys. They will "dance on the dime" and "grind" around the juke-box in taverns and joints, or "cut a rug" at the larger public dance halls. They will "clown" on a street corner or in public parks (1945:610).

In earlier work we have emphasized the fact that a variety of hustles take place in such quasi-public settings and so provide illegitimate role models for the young (Short, 1965:175–77, 1966:436–39; Short & Strodtbeck, 1965:chap. 5). Compared, for example, with the privacy of a middle-class home or club, such settings are likely to be less controlled as to numbers and types of interactants (i.e., whether friends, antagonists, or strangers) and types of interaction. Consider the following, brief descriptions of two common lower-class "institutions," a pool hall and a "quarter party," from two of Chicago's black communities:

> That poolroom down there is nothing but hustlers—the worst type of people in the area. These were known prostitutes . . . dressed in shorts and kind of flashy, and their pimps. . . . There was one guy, he is a dope addict, wears his shades. . . . He is one of the regulars in the other pool hall. He was shooting pool, and he recognized me and spoke to me and to the fellows. . . .
> The three of us started shooting a game of bank on the back table. . . . There was a conversation that the older fellows were having on one of the front tables about some kind of robbery that they had just pulled. . . . They had been busted. It was funny, because they were all teasing one of the guys that was shooting about the fact that he was caught. The police had him chained with another guy around a lamp post. And some kind of way he got his hand out of one of the cuffs, but he still had one of the cuffs on. He couldn't get it off, and they were teasing him about this. . . . Everyone in the poolroom was well aware of what was going on.
> Another thing that was funny—all of them didn't get away. . . . They were laughing about this one guy that didn't get away—he wasn't supposed to go [on the robbery] anyway. He was just there. . . . The guy that had thought up the whole scheme was the guy with the handcuff on his hand. There were two games going on where they were shooting and talking back and forth to the man ringing the cash register. And these guys around the side were commenting, laughing! (Short & Strodtbeck, 1965:108)

> This woman who is called "Ma" was giving the party. . . . There was a lot of drinking—inside, outside, in the cars, in the alleys, everywhere. There were Rattlers and a bunch of boys from the [housing] projects. They had two rooms, neither of them very large. There was some friction going on when I got there—boys bumping each other, and stuff like this.
> There were a lot of girls there. Must have been about 50 to 75 people in these two rooms, plus another 20 or 25 outside. There were some older fellows there, too— mainly to try and grab one of these younger girls. The girls were doing a lot of drinking—young girls, 12- and 13-year-olds. This one girl, shortly after I got there, had passed out. I took her home. Nobody there, but two of the other girls stayed with her.
> The age group in this party amazed me—must have been from about 11 to the 30's. There were girls there as young as 11, but no boys younger than about 15. The girls are there as a sex attraction, and with the older boys and men around, you know the younger boys aren't going to do any good.

We had one real fight. One of David's sisters was talking to one of these boys from the projects—a good-sized boy, bigger than me. I guess she promised to go out to the car with him. . . . To get outside you had to go out this door and down this hall, and then out on the porch and down the stairs. She went as far as the porch. As she got out there, I guess she changed her mind. By this time the boy wasn't standing for any "changing the mind" business, and he started to pull on her—to try and get her in the car. She yelled for David, and he came running out. All he could see was his sister and a guy he didn't know was pulling on her. David plowed right into the guy. I guess he hit him about 15 times and knocked him down and across the street, and by the time I got there the guy was lying in the gutter. David was just about to level a foot at him. I yelled at David to stop and he did. I took him off to the side and told Gary to get the guy out of there (Short & Strodtbeck, 1965:110-11).

A number of characteristics of such settings contribute to their potential for behavior governed less by conventional roles and rules than by emergent properties of situations, and of socially disruptive and often criminal behavior, e.g., the presence of strangers, competition among and between males and females, heavy drinking, a high incidence of guns and knives, and the willingness to respond violently to threats—real or imagined—such as occurs among many youth gangs and is presumed to be indicative of subcultures of violence (Wolfgang & Ferracuti, 1967). It might be well to reexamine the subculture of violence theory in terms of the social disabilities of gang youngsters (Short & Strodtbeck, 1965; Gordon, 1966; Klein & Crawford, 1967), and of processes, such as the response to status threats previously discussed. The emphasis of subcultural theories on normative prescriptions has obscured the microsociological processes which are the heart of the collective behavior perspective.

GANGS AS SOCIAL MOVEMENTS

Gangs thus occupy a position approximately midway between elementary collectivities, such as crowds and mobs, and formally structured and institutionalized aspects of social organizations, such as corporations, schools, and churches. In this respect, they are similar to social movements as a type of collectivity. Killian (1964:429) notes that study of "groups in the process of being organized" has been an important focus of scholarly attention to social movements.

Blumer describes social movements as "collective enterprises to establish a new order of life," and notes that "general social movements take the form of groping and uncoordinated efforts" (1969:99–100). Pfautz (1961) has suggested that the violent adolescent gang is a type of expressive social movement, following Blumer who distinguishes as the "characteristic feature of expressive social movements":

. . . they do not seek to change the institutions of the social order or its objective character. The tension and unrest out of which they emerge are not focused upon some objective of social change which the movement seeks collectively to achieve. Instead, they are released in some type of expressive behavior which, however, in becoming crystallized, may have profound effects on the personalities of individuals and on the character of the social order (Blumer, 1969:114).

Pfautz's discussion centers on descriptions of violent gangs observed by Yablonsky (1959, 1962) and on the theory of delinquent subcultures developed by Cloward and Ohlin (1960). Yablonsky described his gangs as "near groups," characterized by "(1) diffuse role definition, (2) limited cohesion, (3) impermanence,

(4) minimal consensus of norms, (5) shifting membership expectations" (1959:109). These characteristics, of course, vary greatly among and within gangs, as noted in the extensive gang literature. Yablonsky attributes these characteristics primarily to the limited social and psychological abilities of his gang members and particularly of the gang leaders. While there is evidence of such disabilities (in addition to Yablonsky, see Short & Strodtbeck, 1965; Gordon, 1966; Cartwright et al., 1970), there is also a large overlap in abilities among gang and nongang juveniles. Indeed, Yablonsky places a heavy burden on his limited psychological data to explain the highly diverse collective aspects of gang violence.

The expressive nature of much delinquency has been a cornerstone of several delinquency theories (Grosser, 1952; Cohen, 1955; Bloch & Neiderhoffer, 1958; Cloward & Ohlin, 1960; Short & Strodtbeck, 1965). In his quarrel with Yablonsky, Pfautz argues (citing Cloward & Ohlin, 1960) that in areas where both criminal and conventional avenues to success are absent, both stealing and violence are essentially expressive acts in defiance of conventional values.

> The violent behavior is *expressive* rather than symbolic; it is not simply or even primarily the way to "rep" and the badge of "guts" and "heart." Rather, it is the only and the most elementary way in which these youths can act together in the face of the social unrest which is indigenous to their social environment (Pfautz, 1961:171).

Other features of conflict gangs and "garden variety" delinquent subculture gangs (Cohen & Short, 1958) may be similarly interpreted. Pfautz and Yablonsky focus on "violent gangs" but the central features are, in most respects, applicable to a broader class of phenomena. Thus, Yablonsky (1959, 1962) speaks of decreasing cohesiveness as one moves from core to marginal gang members, lack of consensus concerning group norms, definition of membership, and role definitions, all of which have been reported in other gang studies. These characteristics relate to the expressive nature of gangs: "expressive movements are not goal oriented; they are not going anywhere; they do not seek specific reforms" (Pfautz, 1961:172). There is great variation within, as well as between, gangs in these respects, however. Membership definition may depend upon the task at hand, whether a gang fight or a planned dance, for example (Jansyn, 1966). Group norms and roles develop and shift as a result of processes both internal and external to the group (Short & Strodtbeck, 1965:esp. chaps. 9–12). And violence may come to serve instrumental as well as expressive goals among participants in "subcultures of violence" (Wolfgang & Ferracuti, 1967).

There is evidence, in addition, that some gangs previously noted for their violent depredations upon one another and for criminal victimization of their communities, have "gone conservative," organizing themselves for social, economic, and political goals. In the process, group structure undergoes drastic change, moving toward the social organization end of the "collective behavior–social organization continuum." Some of these developments—and their pitfalls—have received widespread national publicity, as when federal grants to Chicago's Blackstone Rangers were investigated by the Permanent Subcommittee on Investigations of the Senate Committee on Government Operations in 1969.

While little systematic evidence concerning these developments is available, it is apparent they have taken a variety of forms and met with varying degrees of "success." Publicity given notable "failures" has obscured both the nature and significance of processes involved in such changes and has rendered assessment difficult.

Some insight into these changes in gangs is provided by Keiser's (1969) ethnographic account of Chicago's Vice Lords. He observed the Vice Lords over a period of years during which they developed an elaborate system of branches, clubs, age grades, and leadership structures with which to accommodate a large and widely dispersed membership.[7] Throughout their early years (1958 to the mid-1960s) their primary orientation was the adolescent street world of clubs and fighting gangs, terms that bifurcate most groups of this world by their emphasis on "social" or "conflict" status-related activities (see Jansyn, 1960, 1966). Toward the close of his field observations in the summer of 1966, however, Keiser reports a "new development" brought on by a combination of circumstances, chiefly we believe, the emergence of the Blackstone Rangers as the most prominent of Chicago's fighting gangs. One of the city's major newspapers had published a week-long series on the Rangers, characterizing them as the best organized and toughest gang in Chicago. This must have hurt and challenged the Vice Lords who regarded themselves as superior in these respects.[8] Keiser (1969:8) observes that in reaction to the series he "heard comments from Vice Lords about how the group was falling apart; how they used to have an organization, but it was going downhill." Out of these circumstances came renewed efforts at formal organization:

> . . . The most important element in the new organizational scheme . . . was the creation of an administrative body called the "board" to deal with matters affecting the entire Vice Lord Nation. Further, regular weekly meetings were instituted with representatives from all the sub-groups present. Finally membership cards were printed with the Vice Lords' insignia—a top hat, cane, and white gloves. Every Lord in the Nation was required to pay an initial membership fee of 1 dollar, have his nickname written on the club's rolls, and carry his card with him at all times (Keiser, 1969:8).

Reorganization of the Vice Lords was followed by a radically different posture of the gang concerning economic, political, and service activities, similar to that which was in process among the Blackstone Rangers (later the Black P. Stone Nation) and the Devil's Disciples, another South Side gang complex, chief rivals of the "Stones." Keiser's discussion of these changes is limited to a brief paragraph:

> In the fall of 1968 I visited the Lords in their new business office on 16th Street, a few doors west of 16th and Lawndale. There had been numerous changes since I had done my first field work. The club was now legally incorporated, and had received a substantial grant from government sources to undertake self-help projects. The group had started a restaurant called "Teen Town," begun an employment service, and opened a recreation center named "House of Lords." They had entered into agreements

---

7. Keiser's (1969) account of the myths of creation and development of the Vice Lords is consistent with ours (acquired during an earlier period of observation, 1960–62) and it is more elaborate. His detailing of the complex and shifting relationships among street gangs, and of events and processes which shape these into particular configurations illustrates the emergent nature of norms and social relationships in street-corner society.

8. I have noted elsewhere that members of conflict gangs often take great pride in media accounts of their activities. A prominent member of the Vice Lords compiled a scrapbook filled with newspaper articles, cartoons, and pictures featuring the Vice Lords. The scrapbook was embellished with sketches of guns, dynamite, "brass knuckles," money, a skull and crossed pool cues, and the motto—"Lords of Lovers." Names of individual Vice Lords were underlined by the compiler of this scrapbook. On the basis of three years' intensive field observations, I noted that "gang boys at first are suspicious and ambivalent about having newsmen [and others] follow them around in search of a story . . . [but] reporters never experience prolonged difficulty and willing informants are usually at hand" (Short, 1968:20).

with both the Cobras and the Roman Saints, and all three of the clubs had cooperated in community help projects. The Vice Lords were strongly involved in Black pride and Black consciousness programs. A staff of both Whites and Blacks was working in the Vice Lord office on legal problems faced by members of the Lawndale community. In the short time I was there, however, it was impossible for me to get more than a few hints as to the basic changes the club had undergone. There were still various Vice Lord branches, but sections no longer functioned within the Vice Lord City. Everyone I talked with, including friends who no longer took part in any of the club's activities, said that gang fighting had completely stopped. If this is true, then it is clear to me that the Vice Lord social and cultural systems must have undergone basic and radical changes. The inflow of a large amount of money from government sources coupled with the complete termination of gang fighting must have had a profound impact on the group (Keiser, 1969:11).

Transitions in organization and group focus of this order of magnitude are not accomplished without considerable turmoil. Old gang conflicts, entrenched status systems, public (and particularly police) skepticism (understandable, but nonetheless an important impediment), and lack of requisite skills to accomplish complex new group tasks foredoom most such efforts. Testimony before the Permanent Subcommittee on Investigations of the U.S. Senate Committee on Government Operations (Government Operations Committee, 1969) has documented some of these problems with respect to the Blackstone Rangers' attempt to provide manpower training for black youth on Chicago's South Side by means of a large grant from the Office of Economic Opportunity. The subcommittee hearings tend toward the sensational, e.g., criminal involvement of program participants and alleged fraud in administration of programs, but they provide dramatic illustration of some of the pitfalls of the transition from adolescent to adult roles, from gang to corporate organization, from the jungles of street-corner society to those of politics.[9]

Peterson's (1969) *Report on Chicago Crime* outlined the program as it concerned the Blackstone Rangers and its newsworthy results:

> Efforts of church groups and even the Federal Government to channel the activities of the Blackstone Rangers, the Disciples and similar groups into legitimate endeavors and to cut down violence as a way of life have been largely ineffective.
>
> The First Presbyterian Church at 6400 Kimbark Avenue headed by Reverend John R. Fry, has provided social workers to act as informal advisers to the Blackstone Rangers, has furnished lodging for needy youths and has retained lawyers to handle court cases involving members of the gang. It also made available to Jeff Fort, second in command of the Blackstone Rangers, a $3,500 Ford Mustang purchased with funds from its Teen Education program. Such funds stem from private gifts from the board of missions of the United Presbyterian Church.
>
> The Federal Government, through the Office of Economic Opportunity (OEO), funded a $927,341 program that sought to train and place in jobs youths from the Woodlawn area. Students in the program were paid $45 a week to attend classes and instructors received $5,200 to $6,500 a year. Four job training centers were located at

---

9. These transitions were enormously complicated by well-meaning adults who sought to encourage the legitimate strivings of the Stones and the Disciples as indigenous community organizations, by complex political struggles within the Democratic party, nationally and locally, and by the glare of publicity of the Senate Subcommittee hearings which would not allow "mistakes" to be covered up and gains consolidated—and legitimized. One wonders whether other ethnic groups would have fared any better had their early social, economic, and political efforts been subject to the scrutiny of legislative investigation and national publicity.

866 East 63rd Street, 1018 East 63rd Street, 6750 Stony Island Avenue and the First Presbyterian Church at 6400 Kimbark Avenue.

The principal beneficiaries of the $927,341 Federal grant were members of the Blackstone Rangers gang and its principal rival, the Disciples. Administering the program was The Woodlawn Organization (T.W.O.) which is made up of 102 community groups on the South Side.

As assistant project director of the T.W.O. program, Eugene (Bull) Hairston, leader of the Blackstone Rangers received a salary of $6,500 a year. Jeff Fort was on the payroll at a salary of $6,000 a year. David Barksdale, president of the East Side Disciples gang, was paid $6,000 a year as an assistant basic education supervisor. Nicholas Dorenzo, vice president of the Disciples, was listed as an assistant project director at an annual salary of $6,500.

The Federally funded anti-poverty training program began on June 1, 1967 and ended in May, 1968. Public hearings held in Washington, D.C., conducted by the U.S. Senate Permanent Subcommittee on Investigations, headed by Senator John L. Mc-Clellan, exposed the prevalence of widespread abuses. A high percentage of signatures on attendance rosters were forged. Some of the students who received $45 a week to attend classes as well as some of the instructors were required to make kickbacks to gang leaders. Some of the instruction programs were in the hands of persons with low I.Q.'s and of doubtful capacity to train.

Under a Federal contract, the University of Chicago was retained to evaluate the project. According to Senator McClellan, "University specialists determined in January, 1968 that the project's classes were poorly attended" and were accomplishing little. Yet, the University's first report was not submitted to the Office of Economic Opportunity until June, 1968, the month after the O.E.O. admitted the experiment had failed and cut off its funds.

Bertrand M. Harding, O.E.O. director, stated that The Woodlawn Organization (T.W.O.) was supposed to report problems to Washington as they developed so they could be corrected immediately. However, this was not done. Harding pointed out that although he had "grave doubts" about the project in January, 1968, he was not then the director of O.E.O. and was not empowered to terminate it. Subsequently, when other reports of the project's deficiencies were received and T.W.O. failed to correct them, it was decided to close down the entire program. Harding told the Senate committee, "In retrospect, Mr. Chairman, it should have been shut down in January, but we can't relive history and make that decision."

Defenders of the project insisted that it was accomplishing good and referred to leaders of the Blackstone Rangers as "geniuses" of organization. And some of these leaders, who have substantial histories of engaging in brutal and violent acts, were described as "lovable" individuals who are highly respected in their community. On the other hand, police officials denounced the project as giving aid, strength, and power to the Blackstone Rangers gang which has been the source of much violent crime on the city's South Side (Peterson, 1969:134–35).

Elsewhere in the report, the strong arm tactics—extending to homicide—of the Blackstone Rangers, and the participation of various Ranger leaders in efforts to promote black capitalism and other black community self-help enterprises are discussed (Peterson, 1969:22–23, 26–30).

If the report and the Senate subcommittee hearings document some of the problems accompanying this transition from the point of view of the larger society, Keiser (1969) captures the essence of these problems from the perspective of street-corner society. Among the factors involved in reorganization of the Vice Lords in 1966, he notes the influence of black nationalist groups which urged against internecine conflict among black gangs in the interest of unity against whites. The attraction of black nationalism for the Vice Lords was marred, however, by "promises . ,. not kept" and by pressure from within the street world. At a meeting called "to discuss the future of the club," Keiser informants reported that:

> . . . Bull who was a member of a militant Black Nationalist organization, had spoken out against a resumption of gang fighting. He felt that all the clubs on the West Side should stop fighting among themselves and unite against the Whites. Others thought that the club's first responsibility was to protect its own members. I was told that, in answer to Bull, another Vice Lord said, "The Cobras may be my 'brothers,' but if one of them fuckers jump on me I'll bust a cap in his ass (shoot him)." The overwhelming number of Vice Lords felt that the group should reorganize to protect themselves and their neighborhoods from hostile clubs, and to re-establish the reputation lost to the Blackstone Rangers. According to my informant, Bull might have been jumped on for his views if he had not left the meeting early (Keiser, 1969:27).

Two years later, however, the extensive changes referred to by Keiser were under way. Institutionalization of efforts to make street gangs a force for community betterment have, in fact, extended to the national level. Youth Organization United, for example, seeks to establish a "coalition of minority youth," according to its president, Warren V. Gilmore, now 40 years old, but still claiming membership in the Vice Lords (Blackman, 1971). Gilmore told reporter Ann Blackman that YOU has established 381 chapters in 95 cities, with a total membership of "between 3,500 and 4,000." These chapters include approximately 350 street gangs which have "gone conservative." In 1970, YOU received a large grant from the U.S. Department of Health, Education and Welfare, plus smaller grants from private foundations. YOU promotes and coordinates self-help programs among minority youth. The appeal to gangs, according to Gilmore, is strong: "Eighty per cent of the time, the gangs are hungry for it. There's action. Dignity. Self-respect, a chance to feel important without ending up in jail" (Blackman, 1971:35). Programs in four cities were cited by Gilmore as examples of YOU efforts:

> —The Conservative Vice Lords have converted some old, rundown buildings into youth centers which include a poolroom, art studio and library.

> —In New Orleans, Thugs United, Inc., operates a record shop, paperback bookstore, an Afro-American clothing store and variety shop, and a recreation program for youngsters.

> —In Philadelphia, The Young Great Society runs a half-way house for boys from problem homes, a tutoring program, a day-care center and, in cooperation with hospitals, a narcotics and alcoholic-rehabilitation center.

> —In San Francisco's Chinatown, LeWays (legitimate ways) operates a recreation center and tutoring service to help Chinese-American youths with school problems (Blackman, 1971:35).

Reporter Blackman's story concerning YOU and Gilmore ends on a hopeful note. The goal is to *"encourage young people in the slums to try and change the system from within, rather than challenge it with violence"* (emphasis added).

But violence remains an important part of the picture. Spergel concludes his study of the Blackstone Rangers' manpower training program with the observation that:

> Some youth gangs today have become—or are becoming again—a political force in the urban ghetto. This is so because of their potential for violence, their new interest in community affairs, and the political interests of other community groups. A number of

gangs sensitized to the power they possess as a threat to the community, are learning to extract benefits from established and official groups. Gangs are becoming, in some cases, a corporate entity concerned with the economic, political, ideological, and social development of its membership to slum residents generally. New opportunities, roles, and access to success status are being provided, at least to gang leaders. It is possible that the gang structure is coming to be a kind of transitional institution permitting the delinquent adolescent to move more directly into—or at least to make an impact on—adult society (Spergel, 1969:1).

Political scientist H. L. Nieburg, noting that the labor movement, crime, and politics were the instruments of upward mobility for various nationality groups in this country, suggests that:

> The role of the Black Panthers as the "muscle" of the latter stages of the Civil Rights Movement brings to the Black Community a stage of development for which sociologists have been searching in vain—that is, para-police enforcement which provides a base not only for organized criminal activities, but also for organized political influence. Earlier waves of immigrants who took up residence at the bottom of the pecking order in American cities eventually formed criminal syndicates and gangs which aided the fight of the group into the social, economic, and political systems, into the suburbs, and into a loss of group identity and an end to the need for para-military muscle (Nieburg, 1970:69).

The Black Panthers apparently have been aware of the political potential of street gang organizations. According to testimony before the Senate Subcommittee on Investigations, however, efforts in the spring of 1969 to merge with the Stones were unsuccessful. This same testimony links the Panthers with the Disciples (rivals of the Stones), with SDS (Students for a Democratic Society), the Young Lords (a Latin American gang) and the Young Patriots (an Appalachian white youth group from the Uptown area of Chicago) (Government Operations Committee, 1969:442–46).

The goals of groups such as these, and of specific programs, remain diverse and often diffuse, and organization at times seems forced and tenuous. Individual gangs, such as the Vice Lords and the Stones, sometimes have given the appearance of moving from largely expressive to more instrumental goals; but the extent to which such changes are in fact real is far from clear (Short, 1974). To the extent that they are real, and as such efforts move from the streets to the community, the city, or the nation, they may take on the characteristics of specific social movements: better-defined goals and objectives, more stable and formal structure, new roles, including leadership, and the development of ideology appropriate to the movement (McPhail, 1969). More importantly, for some gang participants, this process has brought a consciousness of identity with others in common cause, first to the black community, then to other minority groups (Puerto Rican, Mexican-Americans, and poor whites), and to even broader concern with the "liberation" of "oppressed peoples" the world over. Competing ideologies for such identification are well developed and are actively promulgated by a variety of groups, e.g., between "black capitalism" and efforts to more radically change the "system." History records that merging of movements involving discontented people of very different persuasions and identities has many pitfalls. The participation of ghetto youth in movements directed toward radical political and economic change remains more possible than probable. Such "movement" as has occurred is more evolutionary than revolutionary in character; its significance in terms of "black power," or other matters related to fundamental transformation of institutions is clouded. But a beginning has been made and some gangs will never be the same. How these changes will affect long established patterns of gang behavior remains to be seen.

CRIME, SOCIAL MOVEMENTS,
AND THE STRUCTURE OF POWER

A large area of social movements in relation to crime remains unexamined in this discussion and can be treated only briefly. Our focus has been on juvenile delinquency. A large body of literature discusses the violence and crime of adults (chiefly young adults) in relation to a variety of social movements designed to achieve political and economic change, and of those who resist such change, including law enforcement agents and agencies (see Graham & Gurr, 1969; Tilly, 1969; Gurr, 1970; Leites & Wolff, 1970; Short & Wolfgang, 1972). Tilly (1969:5) remarks that "men seeking to seize, hold, or realign the levers of power have continually engaged in collective violence as part of their struggles." The history of relationships between "haves" and "have nots," among groups possessing different degrees and types of power—as in social movements related to labor, peace, or other causes, and in ethnic and race relations—is replete with examples. Skolnick notes that:

> The idea of "militancy" suggests the activities of blacks, students, anti-war demonstrators, and others who feel themselves aggrieved by the perpetuation of old, outworn, or malignant social institutions. The historical record, however, indicates that considerably more disorder and violence have come from groups whose aim has been the preservation of an existing or remembered order of social arrangements, and in whose ideology the concept of "law and order" has played a primary role. There is no adequate term to cover all of the diverse groups who have fought to preserve their neighborhoods, communities, or their country from forces considered alien or threatening. The lack of a common term for Ku Klux Klansmen, Vigilantes, Minutemen, Know-Nothing activists, and anti-Negro or anti-Catholic mobs reflects the fact that these and other similar groups have different origins, different goals, and different compositions, and arise in response to specific historical situations which repeat themselves, if at all, only in gross outline (Skolnick, 1969:161).

In seeking a common threat which runs through collectivities such as these, Tilly (1969) suggests that, historically, the organization base of collective violence has tended to move from communal to associational. We note, for example, that despite their territorial claims to a given "turf," delinquent gangs are associational, i.e., based on group rather than communitywide claims. Recently attempted programs of community service by black youth groups may be reaching out toward broader community identification, but in the still broader context of identification with the plight of all blacks, or of oppressed people, the referrent again is associational. Perhaps the clearest example of modern community organization which involves crime and collective behavior is the efforts of white communities to resist integration, e.g., through residential encroachment or school bussing. Much property destruction and violence against persons—often of a criminal nature—has accompanied such efforts. White gangs often have participated, acting as a line of defense against the invaders. An example may be cited from our Chicago research.

In the late 1950s and early 1960s the south-side community of Grand Crossing experienced an invasion of blacks from contiguous communities. We studied two large gang complexes in this and a nearby area during a period of great tension related to this situation. Numerous incidents involving these gangs and the "invaders" were reported by detached workers assigned to these gangs, and by our graduate student observers. These included the burning of an automobile left by two black men on a public street (apparently as a result of mechanical difficulties), participation in massive white resistance to the integration of public beaches, and chasing black youngsters from the local hangouts when they were found alone or in insufficient numbers to defend themselves. The detached worker assigned to one of these gangs reported the following incident on a September evening in 1959:

> At approximately 12:30 at night, the worker was loitering with a group of teenage white kids at the corner of the park which is immediately across the street from the church. The group was a mixed one of boys and girls ranging in age from 16 to 20. There were approximately 15–20 teenagers, and for the most part, they were sitting or reclining in the park, talking, drinking beer, boys wrestling playfully with girls. I had parked my car adjacent to where the group was gathered and was leaning on the fender of my auto talking to two youths about the remainder of the softball season. The group consisted of members of the Amboys, Bengels, Sharks, and a few Mafia. They were not unusually loud or boisterous this particular hot and humid evening because a police-man on a three-wheeler had been by a half-hour earlier and had warned them of the lateness of the hour.
>
> I noticed a solitary teenage figure ambling along on the sidewalk, heading toward the Avenue. I paid no particular heed, thinking it was just another teenager walking over to join the park group. However, as the figure neared the group, he made no effort to swerve over and join the group but continued by with no sign of recognition. This was an oddity, so I watched the youth as he passed the gathered teenagers and neared the curb where I was sitting on my car fender. At this point, I suddenly realized that the teenager was black and in danger if detected. I did not dare do or say anything for fear of alerting the teenagers sitting in the park, and for a few minutes I thought the youth could pass by without detection. However, a Bengal who had been drinking beer spotted the youth and immediately asked some of the other teenagers, "Am I drunk or is that a Nigger on the corner?" The attention of the entire group was then focused on the black youth, who by this time had stepped off the curb and was walking in the center of the street toward the opposite curb. The youth was oblivious to everything and was just strolling along as if without a care in the world. Behind him, however, consternation and anger arose spontaneously. Muttered threats of "Let's kill the bastard." "Get the mother-fucker." "Come on, let's get going," were heard. Even the girls in the crowd readily and verbally agreed.
>
> Within seconds, approximately a dozen youths arose and began running in the direction of the black youngster. I realized that I was unable to stem the tide of en-raged teenagers, so I yelled out to the youth something to the effect of "Hey man, look alive." The boy heard as he paused in mid-stride, but did not turn around. Again I shouted a warning as the white teenagers were rapidly overtaking him. At my second outcry, the black youth turned and saw the white teenagers closing in on him. Without hesitation, he took off at full speed with the white mob at his heels yelling shouts of "Kill the black bastard—don't let him get away."
>
> I remained standing by my car and was joined by three Amboys who did not par-ticipate in the chase. The president of the Amboys sadly shook his head, stating that his guys reacted like a bunch of kids whenever they saw a colored guy and openly expressed his wish that the boy would get away. Another, in an alibi tone of voice excused his non-participation in the chase by explaining that he couldn't run fast enough to catch anybody. He merely stated that the black youth didn't bother him, so why should he be tossed in jail for the assault of a stranger.

As we stood by the car, we could hear the actual progress of the chase from the next block. There were shouts and outcries as the pursued ran, his whereabouts echoed by the bedlam created by his pursuers. Finally, there was silence and in approximately fifteen minutes the guys began to straggle back from the chase. As they returned to my car and to the girls sitting nearby, each recited his share of the chase. Barney laughingly related that Guy had hurdled a parked car in an effort to tackle the black, who had swerved out into the street. He said that he himself had entered a coal yard, looking around in an effort to find where the boy had hidden, when an adult from a second floor back porch warned that he had better get out of there as the coal yard was protected by a large and vicious Great Dane.

The black youth apparently had decided that he couldn't outrun his tormenters and had begun to go in and out of back yards until he was able to find a hiding place, at which point he disappeared. His pursuers then began to make a systematic search of the alleys, garages, back yards, corridors, etc. The boys were spurred on to greater efforts by the adults of the area who offered advice and encouragement. One youth laughingly related that a woman, from her bedroom window, kept pointing out probable hiding places in her back yard so that the youth below would not overlook any sanctuary. This advice included looking behind tall shrubbery by the fence, on top of a tool crib by the alley and underneath the back porch. Other youths related similar experiences as the adults along the Avenue entered gleefully in the "hide and seek." Glen related that as the youths turned onto the Avenue, he began to shout to the people ahead in the block that "a Nigger was coming" so that someone ahead might catch or at least head off the black youth. The other pursuers also took up the hue and cry (LaMotte, 1959).

The "crowdlike" behavior of the gang members in this incident is not atypical. The Langs observed that "the character of crowd behavior as collective defense is most evident when an aggrieved population acts directly and coercively to assert its own norms against established authority or to impose its own conception of justice against deviants defined as a threat" (Lang & Lang, 1968:563). Here the gang, with considerable support from the adult community, acted against a symbol (the black youngster) of a perceived threat to the community. The action was not a reflection simply of group norms and structure—the major gang leaders present did not participate. Nor was it a product solely of the social unrest and tension which characterized the community at this time, or of the collective excitement of the moment. Both those who participated in chasing the black teenager and those who did not recognized a gamelike quality in this event and in their relations with blacks generally. The boy had crossed into their territory. He had it coming. They would expect the same treatment or worse should they dare to cross into black territory. On another occasion one of these boys remarked of black youngsters generally, "Next year they'll be chasing us," in recognition of the rapidly changing ethnic character of the community. Earlier in the summer of 1959, many of these same boys had chased a black teenager from the park, when he was spotted as the boys were changing field positions on a softball diamond. At this very time, adult blacks were playing tennis with no challenge— and apparently little concern, if observer reports are to be trusted—on the part of the white youngsters. Thus, while their concerns over black invasion of the community were shared by adults, the "game" had distinct youth culture overtones, as well.

The analysis of crowd behavior has been a major source of our generalizations concerning collective behavior. "Crowd episodes are strategic research sites in which to observe collective problem-solving activity in its natural setting" (Lang & Lang, 1968:561). The gang incidents cited above are reminiscent of lynch mobs, and of vigilante movements in which "respectable elements" of society have often taken the law into their own hands (Brown, 1969).[10] In the process, laws have been freely violated, and the most horrendous crimes committed. Yet this criminal behavior rarely has been a major focus of scholarly analysis. Neglect of crime in such contexts by criminologists—with a few notable exceptions—is due in part to the independent development of criminology and collective behavior as fields of study, but it is also attributable to the individualistic focus of the criminal law, reflected in our system of categorizing and measuring crime in terms of individual acts abstracted from social context. Assaults, killings, and offenses against property committed in the course of gang conflict, a riot, or a lynching, for example, are not differentiated in official statistics from these same offenses committed by lone offenders.

Whatever the reasons for the neglect of crime in such contexts, a major lacuna in theoretical development of the field has resulted. Renewed interest in criminal typologies (Clinard & Quinney, 1973), the recent history of violent confrontations between authorities and participants in the civil rights and peace movements (Skolnick, 1969), and the activities of groups such as homosexuals, pressing for social and especially political equality (Humphreys, 1971) have led to the politicization of groups and behavior previously considered simply deviant. The orientation of criminology which takes as a major point of departure the political character of the making and the enforcement of criminal law—and to some extent its breaking—while not new, has been pursued with special vigor by several criminologists in recent years (Turk, 1966; Douglass, 1970; Quinney, 1970). The phenomena of collective behavior provide crucial data for all of this theoretical ferment and we may hope for greater attention to their systematic study in the future.

ELEMENTARY COLLECTIVE BEHAVIOR AND CRIME IN HIGHLY STRUCTURED INSTITUTIONAL CONTEXTS

Some institutional settings are structured so as to encourage elementary expressive behavior, as, for example, "revival meetings" or meetings of some religious sects. Such behavior is rarely directed outside the group, however, and is not likely to be criminal. Ritualistic behavior in some settings may involve commission of crime—or more often delinquency, as, for example, among youth groups which require shoplifting, sex acts, or even assault for "initiation" into the group.

Occasionally, episodes of collective violence erupt in highly structured institutional contexts, so atypical of such settings as to warrant special comment. Such an instance is "A Middle-Class Riot" which occurred in the midst of a solemn church rite, as reported by the then-minister of the church.

> "Old Central," as it is affectionately known to many San Franciscans, is one of the city's oldest surviving church structures. It predates the 1906 earthquake by over twenty years and elderly members like to repeat that "Old Central" rode out the jolt with the loss of just one tower. Bronze and brass plaques remind visitors that President Harding, assorted Governors, and numerous, lesser dignitaries spoke there.
>
> The congregation of nearly 1,000 includes twenty-two distinct ethnic representatives, as one might expect to find in a cosmopolitan seaport like San Francisco. They

---

10. The resurgence of gang activity in New York City during the late 1960s—which continues to this writing—has been accompanied by some vigilante action against dope pushers (Weingarten, 1972). The irony in the situation lies in the fact that heroin addiction apparently was an important factor in the decline of gang activity in that city during the early 1960s.

are generally well assimilated into the dominant American culture that prevails in the church. The membership falls, in general, into that popular, catch-all category of "middle-class." At the time of the survey of church records, virtually all (99 per cent) of the men were employed or retired. Most members were married, owned their own homes in well-kept suburbs, with over half (58 per cent) of their children attending a private, church-sponsored parochial school. The church membership contained large numbers of professionals—engineers, teachers, physicians, and so forth. Education and income among members of the congregation are higher than the average in San Francisco.

An exception to this middle-class pattern is found in a fairly large group of about forty Samoans who attend Central Church—a consequence of the migration to the United States of some of the converts to the church's mission program in American Samoa. This close-knit group maintains many customs and mores of their island culture. The Samoan man is absolute head of his family. When walking down the street, it is common to see him walking several paces in front of his wife and children. Their native language, music, and costumes are preserved in their homes.

In church, the Samoan men sit together, a bit apart from their women and children, who cluster together in back pews of the sanctuary. The Samoans practice the "Chief system" in which one dominant male is the acknowledged leader for all those Samoans grouped together in a social institution, such as a church. Extremely loyal to the church, these men are capable of rage or hilarity, at slight provocation, according to our standards.

Through some peculiar quirk of fate, I became the pastor of San Francisco Central Church when I was just 33 years old, a position I enjoyed for five years, before launching a second career in sociology. I was a witness to the violence and near-riot that occurred in "Old Central" on Easter Sunday of 1967.

It was Easter, a "high day" in the Christian calendar of ceremonies and rituals. The congregation at San Francisco Central was larger than usual—swollen by the addition of many nominal members and visitors—stirred by that rare religious impulse that urges them to church at Easter and Christmas. They sat in neat little family groups: father with his fresh haircut, and well-polished shoes, mother in her new Easter hat, and two or three well-scrubbed children.

During this particular church service, I was conducting a baptism. The scene was beautifully set. The pipe organ filled the sanctuary with its melodious swells. The choir, in their loft, and facing the congregation, were resplendently robed and effective (translation: loud). I had twelve deacons seated in a row on the front pew, directly below me, where they could take up offerings, handle ushering, and other organizational duties.

We were well into the baptismal service, when the real drama began to unfold. Two young men, bearded and wearing customary hippie garb, entered the main door at the rear of the sanctuary and crowded into a back pew. They were talking loudly and one was carrying an open beer can. They were behind most of the congregation, and since the organ and choir music was so voluminous, and the attention of the audience was fixed on the baptism, most of those present were oblivious to the initial antics of the two young men. However, the choir and I, from our vantage point, had spectacular, ringside positions.

As misfortune would have it, the two young men had naively blundered into the midst of the Samoan women and their children. I could see that trouble was inevitable. I could almost hear the beat of Samoan war drums in the distance. However, caught as I was in the midst of a religious ritual, there was little I could do to thwart the rapidly deteriorating situation in the rear of the church.

I saw one hippie place his arm around a surprised Samoan teenager, and bring his bearded face close to hers, as he sought to "make friends." Quicker than I can write these words, the Samoan chief, from his vantage point in the balcony, dispatched four of his "warriors" to where their women were sitting. It was an uneven match from the very start. Most Samoan men are built like members of the Green Bay Packers while the hippies were somewhat gaunt, and seemed eager to "make love, not war."

The choir was rendering, "Blest Be the Tie That Binds Our Hearts in Christian Love," when the first blow landed. They faltered and continued, somewhat off-key. I almost drowned the person I was baptizing at that moment, so entranced was I at the rough and tumble fracas on the back pew. As a beer can rolled down the center aisle, I kept saying to myself, "I'll wake up any moment. This can't happen here; not in good old Central Church!" But it was happening, and with apocalyptical suddenness.

Somehow we continued. The choir kept singing; and I kept baptizing. And surprisingly enough, in such a large building, three-fourths of the congregation—those well forward of the action—were still unaware of any disorder.

Meanwhile, it was a short and bloody bout with the Samoans the clear winners. As quickly as possible, I dispatched my deacons into the fray with explicit instructions to "separate the combatants and restore order" while I continued on with the church service. It was at this point that the situation got out of hand and the battle escalated into a near riot.

As the deacons' flying wedge shot down the aisle and into the fray, the choir director, a bellicose musician even under normal conditions, brought his shuddering choir into a rousing rendition of "Onward Christian Soldiers, Marching as to War." Meanwhile, I continued on with the church service. The last sight I saw of "Old Central's Easter Riot" was of my sophisticated, well-educated, urbane, affable, middle-class deacons, pulling the yelling, bloodied, hippies by their beards, out the doors. What transpired in the foyer of the church was reported by witnesses and participants in a subsequent investigation to a committee that I appointed for that purpose.

The Samoans withdrew almost immediately from the fight, but thirty to forty men continued to struggle with the two young hippies in the foyer and stairwell of the church. These church men were highly aggressive and were supported actively by several women who joined the mob from the "Mother's Room" where they had been caring for their small children. Overwhelming evidence, including personal admissions, indicate that those Christian ladies and gentlemen completely lost control of themselves. While only a dozen persons were in physical contact with the victims, the others were shouting encouragement to the aggressors and threats to the victims. The two hippies were severely beaten and forcibly ejected—literally thrown out into the street. One physician's wife who had hit one of the hippies in the head with a folding chair justified her action on the grounds that he "swore in the Lord's house!"

By the time I got to the scene the people had calmed down and a search outside revealed no presence of the two young men. When I telephoned the police to report the incident, and to ask if any young men as I described to them had been treated for injuries, the police officer replied to me: "Don't worry about them. If they show up any more, just let me know. We'll take care of them!" He seemed totally unconcerned for the welfare of the victims of the riot (Bynum, 1972:1–7).

This incident has many of the classic "stages" of crowd behavior. First, there was social unrest; fear and resentment among straight people concerning the threat to cherished values of hip culture had developed as Haight-Ashbury became a national cause celebre, reinforced by sensational news media accounts of outrages by "hippies" against "straight" society. Second, a precipitating incident occurred. Third, this triggered a violent reaction on the part of some people, which institutional constraints were insufficient to prevent. Legally constituted authorities were either unable or unwilling to intervene. Indeed, one may speculate that, had the initially offending young men been found by the police, it is likely that they would have been prosecuted—or admonished—rather than any of those who had beaten them. The situation is not unlike the vigilante movements which have dotted our history, involving respectable people in defense of their standards of conduct (Brown, 1969; Marx & Archer, 1973).

THE ROLE OF LAW ENFORCEMENT

The customary focus of both collective behavior and criminology has been upon the participants in episodes of collective behavior and, largely, upon their internal dynamics. More recently, however, several studies, including those prepared for national commissions, have stressed the role of police in riot situations, and of political decisions in producing these situations. A report prepared for the National Commission on the Causes and Prevention of Violence (Walker, 1968), in fact, referred to the behavior of the police in collective disturbances associated with the National Democratic Convention as a "police riot." A summary of that report begins:

> During the week of the Democratic National Convention, the Chicago police were the targets of mounting provocation by both word and act. It took the form of obscene epithets, and of rocks, sticks, bathroom tiles and even human feces hurled at police by demonstrators. Some of these acts had been planned; others were spontaneous or were themselves provoked by police action. Furthermore, the police had been put on edge by widely published threats of attempts to disrupt both the city and the Convention.
>
> That was the nature of the provocation. The nature of the response was unrestrained and indiscriminate police violence on many occasions, particularly at night.
>
> That violence was made all the more shocking by the fact that it was often inflicted upon persons who had broken no law, disobeyed no order, made no threat. These included peaceful demonstrators, onlookers, and large numbers of residents who were simply passing through, or happened to live in, the areas where confrontations were occurring.
>
> Newsmen and photographers were singled out for assault, and their equipment deliberately damaged. Fundamental police training was ignored; and officers, when on the scene, were often unable to control their men. As one police officer put it: "What happened didn't have anything to do with police work" (Walker, 1968:1).

Violence thus was escalated on both sides, and the ultimate character of the confrontation was shaped as much police reaction as by the demonstrators. These events were far from unique, or attributable primarily to aroused persons associated with a national political convention. Four months earlier, a peace demonstration in Chicago was met with similar violence. An investigation conducted by a "blue-ribbon" independent committee stressed the importance of high-level political decisions:

> On April 27, at the peace parade of the Chicago Peace Council, the police badly mishandled their task. Brutalizing demonstrators without provocation, they failed to live up to that difficult professionalism which we demand.
>
> Yet to place primary blame on the police would, in our view, be inappropriate. The April 27 stage had been prepared by the Mayor's designated officials weeks before. Administrative actions concerning the April 27 parade were designed by City Officials to communicate that "these people have no right to demonstrate or express their views." Many acts of brutal police treatment on April 27 were directly observed (if not commanded) by the Superintendent of Police or his deputies (as quoted in Skolnick, 1969: 187).

The Walker report (1968) also notes the likely influence on the police of the mayor's public rebuke of the police superintendent, after the police had shown restraint in earlier rioting in Chicago, and his order to "shoot to kill arsonists and shoot to maim looters." Later modified, that order reflected the frustration and lack of understanding of urban officialdom in the face of racial tensions and rioting during the 1960s, and the inadequacies of municipal law-enforcement efforts to keep the peace.

A good summary of the role of the police in "Violent Aspects of Protest and Confrontation" is found in Skolnick (1969:especially chap. 7). This report stresses the importance of hostility felt by "the majority of rank and file policemen" toward blacks, particularly militant blacks, toward student dissent, and toward opponents of our Indochina warfare. These, in turn, are related to the fact, as another report to the Violence Commission indicates, that "police in the United States are for the most part white, upwardly mobile lower middle-class, conservative in ideology and resistant to change. . . . They tend to share the attitudes, biases and prejudices of the larger community, among which is likely to be a fear and distrust of Negroes and other minority groups" (Campbell et al., 1969:291; see also Misner, 1972; *Civil Liberties*, 1973). In addition, as Stark (1972) and others have noted, the police are themselves becoming increasingly politicized. The most important consequence of this process is the fact that many "police reject their historic role as the enforcers of established political and social policies. They now seek the power to determine these policies" (Stark, 1972:178; for a contrary view see Hormachea & Hormachea, 1971).

While these background characteristics, attitudes, and values of policemen are helpful in understanding the role played by police in episodes of collective violence, they provide only a partial explanation—and they oversimplify, for there is much variation among police, individually and collectively, in background and performance. Misner notes:

> The small number of instances in which the police have fulfilled truly impartial roles in mass demonstrations is so significant as to deserve special comment in the press. In these instances, care has been exercised by police leaders to identify the ideological biases of rank-and-file policemen and to take steps to neutralize these biases. Special recognition has been made by police leaders themselves, of the typical policeman's tendency to reject non-conformist behavior. Recognition has also been made of the fact that policemen are beset not only with "commonplace" anxieties, but also that their peculiar occupational setting is likely to give rise to a unique set of psychological strains. Unless these conditions are realized and addressed, policemen are inadequately prepared to cope with certain types of emergency situations (Misner, 1972:349–50; see also Hector & Helliwell, 1969; Sahid, 1969; Berk, 1972b).

The police role, like that of the policed, e.g., demonstrators or rioters, can be fully understood only in the context of ongoing action among participants in a situation. As an example, Berk's "almost race riot" describes the changing role of the police in the course of the crowd action he observed:

> With the crowd now at over 100 on the White side and a small group of 15 or so Black youths gathering on the west side of the avenue, two police cars pulled over near the median strip. Two policemen from one car walked toward the Blacks and two toward the Whites; all four carried riot clubs. The Blacks ran, but the Whites at first stood their ground. The policemen calmly but firmly told the people to "break it up," and the crowd pulled back about 50 yards. The policemen did not pursue the crowd past the corner, but stood resolutely on the corner swinging their clubs. After about five minutes they returned to their cars, and both crowds moved back to the corners (Berk, 1972b: 321).
>
> Around 2 P.M., five Blacks in their early teens feigned a break across the avenue toward the Whites. They acted as if they were going to pick up the white gauntlet, but stopped several yards short of going half-way across the street. In response to this, the group of 20 Whites in the front of the crowd charged toward the Blacks. Although the rest of the crowd moved out partially into the street, they did not follow.

Seeing the Whites approaching the Blacks turned and ran. Several were not fast enough, and a brief fight involving about 15 Whites and 5 Blacks took place on the Black side of the avenue. The police, who at that moment were not standing in a position to intercept the White attackers, hurried over, and the conflict immediately ceased. Several of the Blacks, but no Whites, who participated in the brief skirmish were arrested.

Within a few minutes, three more police cars pulled up; the policemen jumped out and pursued the entire Black mob (50 or so) for about a block back into the ghetto along the side street. At that point they were met with a barrage of bricks and bottles, and the chase ended. Nevertheless, about ten more Blacks were caught and arrested. The police largely ignored the White side of the street, and the crowd stood watching, cheering them on (p. 323).

. . . although the police cars were driving up and down the street trying to break up the crowds, not a bottle or brick was directed toward the police. With hundreds of objects being thrown, the patrol cars were never struck. If there was any intent toward the police, it was to *avoid* hitting the cars. In this neighborhood, as in any slum, there had always been a great amount of distrust and dislike for the police, but this hostility was not in evidence. Considering the limited presence of only four policemen in two patrol cars, the crowd could have chosen to force them to retreat rather than try to stay out of their way (as has frequently happened during civil disorders). Yet, this did not happen. The atmosphere of the "riot" was like a big football game in a neighborhood park, where the police appeared to be needed to keep the game within the rules (pp. 324–25).

Many examples of police participation in crowd situations suggest enormous variation and great importance to potential or actual violence (see especially, Stark, 1972). To a greater extent than the roles of other crowd participants, however, the police role is subject to control by official command procedures, by higher policy decisions, and by attitudes of restraint or anger, judiciousness or excess. Commenting on the contrast between the violence attending the 1968 Democratic Convention and the relatively peaceful counter-inaugural demonstration a few months later, a peace movement leader remarked:

The difference between Chicago and Washington was a permit and a tent. The police react as the officials react. In Washington, the officials reacted well and the police reacted well. As a result, the demonstrators acted well toward the police and the officials (Campbell et al., 1969:351).

The attitudes of Washington, D.C. officials were summarized by the deputy mayor's statement:

It was our intention to minimize the trouble for the weekend. We felt they were entitled to a permit. There didn't seem to be any legal reason to prevent their coming. Therefore the best thing to do was to restrict it within legal bounds. We made clear the boundaries beyond which we would not allow them to cross (Sahid, 1969:115).

The care with which both officials and leaders of the planned demonstration proceeded to insure a peaceful confrontation is documented in the Violence Commission report, "Rights in Concord" (Sahid, 1969). The character of police-demonstrator relationships which resulted is reflected in the following excerpt:

The Smithsonian

The afternoon was rapidly fading and the cold became more intense. The dispersing crowds, moving back towards the tent area up Independence Avenue, began gathering at the Smithsonian Institution Museum of History and Technology Building . . . where a reception for Vice-President-Elect Spiro Agnew was about to take place. Although a group calling themselves "Fat Japs and Polacks for Peace" had announced earlier that they would appear outside the reception, the few police deployed to the area were not prepared for the crowd numbering 5,000 which swelled at the entrance.

Twenty Park Police, eight of whom were mounted, moved into position in front of the History and Technology Building. Forty additional Park Policemen were bussed to the scene. A strong percentage of the group were higher ranking officers.

The entrance to the building is bounded by a large, grassy area, with a few scattered trees. Roads wide enough for two cars criss-cross the grassy area, dividing it into blocks.

The Park Police entered the roadway leading to the entrance and moved the demonstrators onto the grassy areas. . . . No attempt was made to disperse them. The crowd was restrained, but occasionally a clod of dirt and a few firecrackers were thrown at the mounted police. No more than 15 objects were thrown in as many minutes.

Someone threw a firecracker which exploded near one of the horses. Some of the horses, which were being used for the first time in crowd control, became excited and reared. Their riders managed to keep them under control. There was scattered shouting and a few obscenities, but a general calm pervaded the crowd. At 5:00 P.M., Vice-President-Elect Agnew entered the History and Technology Building from another entrance.

The few foot patrolmen made no attempt to line the curbs. They stayed towards the center of the street and occasionally asked demonstrators who had wandered into the street to return to the curb. A few cries of "the streets belong to the people" were heard and many demonstrators had a good time crossing back and forth across the street. The police ignored this obvious provocation and some of them smiled.

Finally, guests began to arrive. Two mounted officers cleared the street by moving their horses forward and sideways at a quick pace. The crowd moved easily.

Several guests began walking down the 13th Street corridor from Washington Drive, where they had been discharged from their automobiles, to the History and Technology Building entrance. They were the first to arrive and did not exhibit much fear. Dressed in mink and formal clothes, they contrasted sharply with the demonstrators. Shouts of "fascist pig," "imperialists," etc. greeted them. Three or four demonstrators out of the crowd of 5,000 threw objects at them. No one was hit but this provided the setting for what was to follow.

The police still made no move against the crowd. It was impossible to identify those few demonstrators who had thrown objects. Instead, the police attempted to protect the arriving guests by ushering them through the corridor.

With each successive arrival, the shouting from the crowd increased. Approximately 10 to 15 objects, including sticks, rocks and mud, were thrown at the next few couples. Finally, the seventh couple started down the corridor. The man smiled happily in an apparent attempt to look unconcerned. Five to ten objects were soon thrown and a firecracker exploded a few inches from his wife's arm. She became extremely frightened and grasped her husband's arm tightly as they hurried down the corridor.

Immediately, one policeman darted into the crowd and seized the arm of a young male. A police lieutenant a few feet away also entered the crowd and seized another young man by the arm. At 5:20 P.M., six mounted policemen moved their horses into the crowd gathered on the grassy area to the right of the entrance from which most of the objects had been thrown.

Interviews have convinced us that most of the demonstrators moved voluntarily once the police indicated that they wanted the area cleared. Those in the crowd sensed that the police could not tolerate the actions of the few people who were throwing objects and were therefore required to disperse the crowd from the area. The mood seemed to be that this was a necessary and legitimate action taken by the police.

After the area in front of the History and Technology Building had been cleared, a MOBE attorney, accompanied by representatives of the Mayor's office, spotted a man in a police slicker and riot helmet beating a young demonstrator with a 3-foot riot club. The demonstrator had remained in a tree during the charge to avoid the crush of people trying to disperse. They rushed to the scene where the city official asked the man, "Why are you beating a kid coming out of a tree?" He replied, "That's what's supposed to happen to them. How would you like to have your wife go through this." The city official replied, "But the one you're hitting wasn't doing anything." The other retorted, "Whoever in the hell you are, you get out of here." The official asked for the man's name, since he wore no name plate. He refused to identify himself. Later, he was identified as a part-time, police surgeon, not a member of the police force, who had no authority to wear a police uniform.

At 5:45 P.M., a police undercover agent reported that a group was planning to forcefully enter the rear door of the History and Technology Building. The reported break never occurred.

A young man in the crowd lost consciousness and fell to the ground, apparently from exhaustion. A city official asked the police to call an ambulance. When no ambulance appeared after about ten minutes, demonstrators began demanding that one be sent. Finally, the city official that had initially requested the ambulance called the command center. He discovered that no ambulance had been requested. He demanded that one be sent immediately. The ambulance which had been parked less than two blocks from the entrance to the Smithsonian, arrived 25 minutes after the city official first notified the police. By the time the ambulance arrived the demonstrator had recovered and the ambulance was used to transport an injured policeman.

The main crowd reassembled further from the entrance but by now its size had decreased. The cold and dark contributed to the exodus which was taking place. Approximately 10 to 20 patrolmen formed a loose line to keep the demonstrators on the curb. Some taunting was directed at them, but not a significant amount. The policemen themselves were quiet and reserved.

One mounted policeman, however, began yelling to his fellow policeman in a voice obviously intended to be heard by the demonstrators, calling them names and suggesting that they needed to be "beat over the head to teach them a lesson." The other policemen ignored him. Restlessly he moved his horse into a corridor between the demonstrators where no other policeman was positioned. A police lieutenant quickly spotted him and ordered him to return.

Several small fires had been started in the crowd. They were extinguished by policemen and no arrests were made. The mood was calm on both sides.

A Deputy Chief of Police, accompanied by a MOBE attorney, went to inspect one of the fires. As they moved through the crowd someone threw or swung a leg support of a wooden police barricade which grazed the attorney's head and hit the policeman behind the ear. The policeman went to his knees and the crowd quickly moved back. The policeman got to his feet, and, apparently dazed, drew a can of mace and rushed forward. The aerosol can failed to work. Two policemen assisted him to a police cruiser where he was examined and treated for his injury.

The Vice-President-Elect left the Smithsonian from a rear entrance at 6:45 P.M. Soon thereafter, the bulk of the crowd wandered away.

During all this activity, which lasted about two hours, no recognizable leaders of any of the groups that had assembled for the march were identified. Less than 10 arrests were made. Few injuries resulted. Several heavy objects, including a fire hydrant cap, had been thrown. Sixteen police officers reported being assaulted. Two were hospitalized that evening, one with a head injury and the other from having been kicked in the stomach. The remaining assaults were minor. Yet the police responded in a measured and restrained manner, maintaining an objective outward composure. Several incidents captured this mood.

A petite female demonstrator moved into the street, pleading with a giant of a policeman who was stationed there to allow her to cross the street so she could be with her friends. He grinned at her size and finally said, in a mockingly gruff voice, "Get back where you belong." She darted back onto the sidewalk apologetically. He broke into a laugh, and the crowd in the immediate area laughed too.

At another point, at the height of the missile throwing, several young demonstrators approached one policeman and asked him how they could leave without confronting policemen at some other point. He pointed down one street and suggested that they take that route since they were probably hungry and there were some inexpensive restaurants along the way.

The suggestion about eating places was not necessary. He could have gruffly pointed the way. But the exchange, overheard by many demonstrators in the area. sharply reduced the tension that had been mounting (Sahid, 1969:99–103).

Despite constitutional guarantees and the hard-earned evidence of *Rights in Conflict* (Walker, 1968) versus *Rights in Concord* (Sahid, 1969), officials apparently find it difficult to grant properly made requests for mass demonstration of grievances. Less than a year after the publication of *Rights in Concord* and the clear affirmation of these rights by the National Commission on the Causes and Prevention of Violence (1969), the request by peace groups for permission to parade past the White House in protest against the war in Indochina was denied by the Justice Department. Permission was later granted, after extensive media publicity concerning the inconsistency of the Justice Department's action and the Violence Commission's evidence. The march, held in November, 1969, took place without incident—further evidence of *Rights in Concord.*

The National Advisory Commission on Civil Disorders concluded that the police were "not merely a 'spark' factor" in the ghetto riots of the 1960s, though police actions were importantly involved as background to "prior" and "final" incidents in most riot cities (National Advisory Commission, 1968). The Commission also concluded that the riots were not the result of conspiratorial activity by militant black leaders or organizations. There can be little doubt, however, that as symbols of white power, as well as by specific actions, the police have played an important role in the polarization which has accompanied the rise of militancy among blacks and other minorities. Two concomitants of recent militancy involve crimes and are enlightened by a collective behavior perspective: (1) prison rioting, and (2) bizarre incidents of sniping in which police and other officials have been targets.

PRISON RIOTING AS "EXPRESSIVE MUTINY"

Outbreaks of escape, collective disobedience, and violence have occurred throughout the history of prisons. Martinson's (1972) discussion of two historical types of such episodes and his characterization of an emerging third type is instructive. All three doubtless have involved the basic principles of collective behavior, but the third is of special interest in the present context.

(1) *Mass escape as a mode of prisoner behavior was associated with a prebureaucratic society and in America with the frontier.* To escape from a dungeon is a dangerous enterprise. Mass escape required shared ingenuity and motivation, some common hope of taking up a new life, concealing one's past, even leaving one's home territory. In this early epoch, the prison was unashamedly brutal and was designed for incapacitation and severe punishment. Prison revolt was commonly put down with deadly fury by officials and guards backed up by deputized locals since every disturbance implied the real probability of a mass breakout followed by spoilation of areas adjacent to the prison.

(2) Prison riot—which dominated the 19th and early 20th centuries—involved a struggle to improve conditions *within* the prison rather than an attempt to escape from

it. Within the armed perimeter, power struggles occurred over the meager privileges prison had to offer. Such riots were often nicely timed to provoke the intervention of the prison reform movement and sometimes led to changes in paroling practices, better food, less punishment for breaking prison rules or fewer rules.

In the 20th century riots increasingly tended to run in cycles. *The riot cycle implied swift communication and contagion reflecting the creation of state systems of corrections, standard penological practices, and a nationwide convict subculture.*

The most recent cycle of riots (1952–1953) began in the disciplinary cellblock of the world's largest prison in Jackson, Michigan, and spread to dozens of prisons in the United States and abroad. One hypothesis maintained that these riots were sparked by inner-prison struggles for control between the "custodial" and "treatment" points of view among the staff. These struggles threatened to change the inmate status quo and led to a preventive counterrevolution led by a corrupt inmate priesthood which preached the inmate code as a means of retaining privileges.

(3) Unlike the riot, the expressive mutiny is not primarily focused on winning power, maintaining privileges or improving conditions within the prison. *It aims to communicate the inmate's plight to the public so far as he understands it.* It is a new form of disturbance not merely a temporary reflection of new left influence among a group of politicized black convicts. The prison is used as an arena in which to stage dramatic renditions of inhumanity and rebellious gestures of inchoate despair and apocalypse. Demands for improvements in prison conditions appear side by side with borrowings from the Black Power movement, the student movement, and the revolutionary sect (Martinson, 1972:3–4, italics added).

The prison, prototypical symbol of the determination of the larger society to maintain "law and order," has become both an arena and an important focal point for those who protest the injustice of the system which it represents (see Jacobs, 1974). "Expressive mutinies," such as occurred at Attica in the fall of 1971, and protests of militant groups charging "political imprisonment" of their numbers, or more broadly of all black prisoners (or brown or red), are part of this volatile situation. So, too, are such events as the bizarre slayings of police, firemen, and others which have occurred in several of our major cities, beginning with Cleveland in 1967 (Masotti & Corsi, 1969), and extending even to the deep South (New Orleans in January, 1973). While these events have never been reliably traced to conspiratorial activity of militant groups, most objective inquiries indicate that they represent a highly individualistic manifestation of the same forces which have produced militant movements. Once publicized, such bizarre episodes tend to be repeated, and collective behavior theory has tried to understand why.

BIZARRE CRIMES: A NOTE ON CONTAGION

Turner notes that "some form of contagion, whereby unanimous, intense feeling and behavior at variance with usual predispositions are induced among the members of a collectivity, has been the focal point for most sociological study of collective behavior" (1964:384). A variety of psychological mechanisms and characteristics of crowds and other collectivities at issue have been posited to explain contagion, e.g., suggestion, imitation, circular reaction (as opposed to interpretive interaction), emotional excitement, leadership roles, and relationships between leaders and collectivities. None have proven completely convincing, for both empirical and theoretical reasons (see Turner, 1964).

Recent attempts to measure "contagion effects" and to explain their operation have revived interest in the concept. Berkowitz and Macaulay (1971) note that

Gabriel Tarde, the French sociologist who invoked imitation as the basic learning process involved in crime, described crimes following and similar to sensational violent crimes as "suggesto-imitative" in nature. Tarde's examples included the famous "Jack the Ripper" murders in London, in 1888, following which:

> . . . in less than a year, as many as eight absolutely identical crimes were committed in the great city . . . there followed a repetition of these same deeds outside of the capitol (and abroad . . .). Infectious epidemics spread with the air on the wind; epidemics of crime follow the line of the telegraph (Tarde, 1912:340–41).

While Tarde's notions concerning imitation have been replaced by more sophisticated learning models, Berkowitz and Macaulay suggest that "contagion" in criminal violence may account for increases in violent crimes that appear to occur following sensational events of this type widely covered in the mass media. They note speculation by law-enforcement officials (and public speculation generally) that two sensational incidents during the summer of 1966 (Richard Speck's murder of eight nurses in Chicago in July, and shortly thereafter Charles Whitman's shooting of forty-five people from the University of Texas tower) may have influenced an 18-year-old Arizona high-school student who entered a beauty school and killed four women and a child. The boy told police he had gotten the idea to kill several people after reading the news accounts of the Speck and Whitman incidents, and that he had begun planning his own incident as soon as his parents gave him a target pistol as a present. It seems likely that "ideas," techniques, and appropriate behavior in otherwise unfamiliar situations often become widely diffused by means of the mass media (Hadden, 1972). A strong element of suggestion to emotionally unstable persons is also widely believed to be associated with the frequency of assassinations of political and other prominent persons, though this has never been empirically established.

Berkowitz and Macaulay's (1971) careful examination of FBI *Uniform Crime Reports* data for the seven-year period, 1960–66, reveals substantial increases in aggravated assaults and robberies (and, to a lesser extent, homicides) following the assassination of President Kennedy in November, 1963, and again following the killing of the eight Chicago nurses in July, 1966. Rape, property crimes, and manslaughter (largely deaths involved in automobile accidents) did not reflect these same patterns. Berkowitz and Macaulay cite a variety of evidence in support of their interpretation that mass media reports of the two spectacular violent crimes (and a third shortly after the Chicago killings) may have been responsible for the increases observed in the three types of violent crime throughout the country.

They conclude that highly publicized violent crimes may create a chain of "contagion influences" that operate in addition to and probably in conjunction with other determinants of such crime. They sketch the following sequence of reactions as a possible explanation of the influence of mass media depictions of violence:

> One, aggressive ideas and images arise. Most of these thoughts are probably quite similar to the observed event, but generalization processes also lead to other kinds of violent ideas and images as well. Two, if inhibitions against aggression are not evoked by the witnessed violence or by the observers' anticipation of negative consequences of aggressive behavior, and if the observers are ready to act violently, the event can also evoke open aggression. And again, these aggressive responses need not resemble the instigating violence too closely. Three, these aggressive reactions probably subside fairly quickly but may reappear if the observers encounter other environmental stimuli associated with aggression—and especially stimuli associated with the depicted violence. The

violent story might then have a relatively long-lasting influence, as was apparently the case in the Arizona murders (Berkowitz & Macaulay, 1971:239).

Bandura's "Social Learning Theory of Aggression" also relies heavily upon *symbolic modeling* by mass media to explain "the shaping and spread of collective aggression" (1973:215). Citing examples of tactics employed in civil rights and peace movements in campus protest and the protests of disadvantaged groups, Bandura notes that

> social contagion of new styles and tactics of aggression conforms to a pattern that characterizes the transitory changes of most other types of collective activities: new behavior is initiated by a salient example; it spreads rapidly in a contagious fashion, after it has been widely adopted it is discarded, often in favor of a new form that follows a similar course (Bandura, 1973:216).

Airline highjackings and consular abductions as a form of "political collective bargaining" also appear to follow such a cyclical pattern. The pattern thus described differs from that examined by Berkowitz and Macaulay (1971) in that violent crimes experienced no abrupt decline after rising in the aftermath of their widely publicized precursors. A fundamental difference in the two studies lies in the different phenomena for which explanation is sought. Berkowitz and Macaulay studied relatively common violent crimes as effects, while Bandura focuses on the occurrence of types of behavior which by comparison are relatively rare.

Bandura suggests three "possible explanations" for the abrupt decline of these types of contagious aggression: (1) development of effective countermeasures by the targets of aggression (e.g., police, university officials, airlines); (2) "discrepancy between anticipated and experienced consequences" on the part of participants, e.g., failure to achieve goals of participation (personal as well as collective) leading to dragging out or changing tactics; (3) "a new style of behavior rapidly loses its positive value through overuse" (Bandura, 1973:218). Thus, learning by observation, symbolic modeling, and direct experience are all involved in shaping the future course of collective behavior, including that which involves crime and delinquency.

CONCLUSION

Drawing together the variety of materials and perspectives discussed in this chapter is a difficult task. A more extensive essay would consider still other problems relating crime and collective behavior. Our attempt in this brief sketch has been to suggest some of the ways in which the perspectives of collective behavior might be brought to bear in enriching our understanding of crime and delinquency, and to add to the perspectives of collective behavior insights and data drawn from the empirical materials of crime and delinquency. Both areas have much to gain from such an exchange. Hopefully, more systematic data and theory will be forthcoming.

REFERENCES

Abrahams, R. D.
1970   Deep Down in the Jungle. Chicago: Aldine.
Bandura, A.
1971   Social Learning Theory. New York: McCaleb-Seiler.

1973   "Social learning theory of aggression," in J. Knutsen (ed.), The Control of Aggression: Implications from Basic Research. Chicago: Aldine-Atherton.

Berk, R. A.
1972a   "The controversy concerning collective violence." Chapter 8 in J. F. Short, Jr. and M. E. Wolfgang (eds.), Collective Violence. Chicago: Aldine-Atherton.
1972b   "The emergence of muted violence in crowd behavior: a case study of an almost race riot." Chapter 23 in J. F. Short, Jr. and M. E. Wolfgang (eds.), Collective Violence. Chicago: Aldine-Atherton.

Berkowitz, L., and J. Macaulay.
1971   "The contagion of criminal violence." Sociometry 34(June):238–260.

Blackman, A.
1971   "Street gangs go conservative." Spokane Daily Chronicle, November 22:35.

Bloch, H. A., and A. Neiderhoffer.
1958   The Gang: A Study of Adolescent Behavior. New York: Philosophical Library.

Blumer, H.
1968   "Fashion." Pp. 341–345 in David L. Sills (ed.), International Encyclopedia of the Social Sciences, vol. 5. New York: Macmillan.
1969   "Collective behavior," in A. M. Lee (ed.), New Outline of Principles of Sociology. Third Edition. New York: Barnes & Noble.
1971   "Social problems as collective behavior." Social Problems 18(Winter):298–305.

Brown, C.
1965   Manchild in the Promised Land. New York: Signet.

Brown, R. M.
1969   "The American vigilante tradition." Pp. 121–180 in H. D. Graham and T. R. Gurr (eds.), Violence in America: Historical and Comparative Perspectives. Washington, D.C.: U.S. Government Printing Office.

Brown, R. W.
1954   "Mass phenomena." Pp. 833–876 in G. Lindzey (ed.), Handbook of Social Psychology, vol. 2. Cambridge: Addison-Wesley.

Brymer, R. A.
1967   "Toward a definition and theory of conflict gangs." Paper presented at annual meeting of Society for the Study of Social Problems, August 26 (mimeographed).

Bynum, J.
1972   "A middle-class riot." Unpublished paper.

Campbell, J. S., J. R. Sahid, and D. P. Stang.
1969   Law and Order Reconsidered. Staff report to National Commission on the Causes and Prevention of Violence (Staff report 10). Washington, D.C.: U.S. Government Printing Office.

Cartwright, D. S., K. J. Howard, and N. A. Reuterman.
1970   "Multivariate analysis of gang delinquency: II. Structural and dynamic properties of gangs." Multivariate Behavioral Research 5(July):303–324.

Civil Liberties.
1973   "On the roads: cops and hippies." 292(January):3–6.

Clinard, M., and R. Quinney.
  1973   Criminal Behavior Systems: A Typology. Second Edition. New York: Holt,
          Rinehart & Winston.
Cloward, R. A., and L. E. Ohlin.
  1960   Delinquency and Opportunity: A Theory of Delinquent Gangs. New York:
          Free Press of Glencoe.
Cohen, A. K.
  1955   Delinquent Boys. Glencoe, Ill.: Free Press.
Cohen, A. K., and J. F. Short, Jr.
  1958   "Research in delinquent subcultures." Journal of Sociological Issues 14(3):
          20–27.
  1971   "Crime and juvenile delinquency." Chapter 2 in R. K. Merton and R. Nisbet
          (eds.), Contemporary Social Problems. Third Edition. New York: Harcourt
          Brace Jovanovich.
Cohen, B.
  1969a   "The delinquency of gangs and spontaneous groups." Chapter 4 in T. Sellin
          and M. Wolfgang (eds.), Delinquency Studies. New York: Wiley.
  1969b   "Internecine conflict: the offender." Chapter 5 in T. Sellin and M. Wolf-
          gang (eds.), Delinquency Studies. New York: Wiley.
Currie, E., and J. H. Skolnick.
  1970   "A critical note on conceptions of collective behavior." Annals of the Amer-
          ican Academy of Political and Social Science 391(September):34–45.
Douglass, J. D.
  1970   Crime and Justice in America. Indianapolis: Bobbs-Merrill.
Drake, St. C., and H. Cayton.
  1945   Black Metropolis: A Study of Negro Life in a Northern City. New York:
          Harcourt, Brace.
England, R. W., Jr.
  1960   "A theory of middle class juvenile delinquency." Journal of Criminal Law,
          Criminology and Police Science 50:535–540.
Erickson, M. L.
  1965   "Class position, peers and delinquency." Sociology and Social Research 3
          (April):268–282.
  1972   "Group violations. Socio-economic status and official delinquency." Unpub-
          lished manuscript.
Finestone, H.
  1957   "Cats, kicks, and color." Social Problems 5(July):3–13.
Gordon, R. A.
  1966   "Social class, social disability, and gang interaction." American Journal of
          Sociology 73:42–62.
Government Operations Committee, Senate.
  1969   Riots, Civil and Criminal Disorders, 1969. Hearings before the Permanent
          Subcommittee on Investigations of the Committee on Government Opera-
          tions, United States Senate, part 20. Washington, D.C.: U.S. Government
          Printing Office.
Graham, H. D., and T. R. Gurr (eds.)
  1969   Violence in America, Historical and Comparative Perspectives. Staff reports

to National Commission on the Causes and Prevention of Violence. Washington, D.C.: U.S. Government Printing Office.

Grier, W. H., and P. M. Cobbs.
1968   Black Rage. New York: Bantam Books.

Grosser, G.
1952   "Juvenile delinquency and contemporary American sex roles." Ph.D. dissertation, Harvard University.

Gurr, T. R.
1970   Why Men Rebel. Princeton: Princeton University Press.

Gusfield, Joseph.
1968   "The study of social movements." Pp. 445–452 in David L. Sills (ed.), International Encyclopedia of the Social Sciences, vol. 14. New York: Macmillan.

Hadden, Stuart.
1972   "Collective behavior; a re-evaluation." Unpublished paper.

Heberle, Rudolf.
1968   "Types and functions of social movements." Pp. 438–444 in David L. Sills (ed.), International Encyclopedia of the Social Sciences, vol. 14. New York: Macmillan.

Hector, L. J., and P. E. Helliwell.
1969   Miami Report. Washington, D.C.: U.S. Government Printing Office.

Hormachea, C. R., and M. Hormachea.
1971   Confrontation: Violence and the Police. Boston: Holbrook Press.

Humphreys, L.
1971   Private correspondence.

Jacobs, James B.
1974   "Street gangs behind bars." Social Problems 21(3):395–409.

Jansyn, L. R.
1960   "Solidarity and delinquency in a street corner group: a study of the relationship between changes in specified aspects of group structure and variations in the frequency of delinquent activity." Master's thesis, University of Chicago.
1966   "Solidarity and delinquency in a street corner group." American Sociological Review 31(October): 600–614.

Johnstone, J., and E. Katz.
1957   "Youth and popular music." American Journal of Sociology 62(May):563–568.

Keiser, R. L.
1969   The Vice Lords: Warriors of the Streets. New York: Holt, Rinehart & Winston.

Killian, L. M.
1964   "Social movements." Chapter 12 in Robert E. L. Faris (ed.), Handbook of Modern Sociology. Chicago: Rand McNally.

Klein, M. W.
1969   "Violence in American juvenile gangs," in D. J. Mulvihill, M. M. Tumin, and L. A. Curtis, Crimes of Violence, vol. 13. Staff report to National Com-

mission on the Causes and Prevention of Violence. Washington, D.C.: U.S. Government Printing Office.

1971   Street Gangs and Street Workers. Englewood Cliffs, N.J.: Prentice-Hall.

Klein, M. W., and L. Y. Crawford.
1967   "Groups, gangs and cohesiveness." Journal of Research in Crime and Delinquency 4(January) :63–75.

Kluckhohn, F. R., and F. L. Strodtbeck.
1961   Variations in Value Orientations. Evanston, Ill.: Row, Peterson.

Kobrin, Solomon.
1951   "The conflict of values in delinquency areas." American Sociological Review 16(October) :657–662.

Kobrin, S., and H. Finestone.
1968   "Drug addiction among young persons in Chicago," in James F. Short, Jr. (ed.), Gang Delinquency and Delinquent Subcultures. New York: Harper & Row.

Kobrin, S., J. Puntil, and E. Peluso.
1967   "Criteria of status among street gangs." Journal of Research in Crime and Delinquency 4(January) :98–118.

Krisberg, B.
1971   "Urban leadership training: an ethnographic study of 22 gang leaders." Ph.D. dissertation, University of Pennsylvania.

LaMotte, John.
1959   Field Report. University of Chicago, Youth Studies Program (unpublished).

Lang, K., and Gladys E. Lang.
1961   Collective Dynamics. New York: Crowell.
1968   "Collective behavior." Pp. 556–565 in David L. Sills (ed.), International Encyclopedia of the Social Sciences, vol. 2. New York: Macmillan.

Leites, N., and N. Wolff.
1970   Rebellion and Authority: An Analytical Essay on Insurgent Conflicts. Chicago: Markham.

Lerman, P.
1967a   "Argot, symbolic deviance and subcultural delinquency." American Sociological Review 32(April) :209–224.
1967b   "Gangs, networks, and subcultural delinquency." American Journal of Sociology 73(July) :63–72.

Lofland, John.
1969   Deviance and Identity. Englewood Cliffs, N.J.: Prentice-Hall.

McPhail, Clark.
1969   "Student walkout: a fortuitous examination of elementary collective behavior." Social Problems 6(Spring) :441–455.

Malcolm X.
1965   Autobiography of Malcolm X. New York: Grove Press.

Martinson, Robert.
1972   "Collective behavior at Attica." Federal Probation 36(September) :3–7.

Marx, G. T.
1970   "Issueless riots." Annals of the American Academy of Political and Social Science 391(September) :21–33.

Marx, G. T., and D. Archer.
   1973   "The urban vigilante." Psychology Today 6(January):44–50.

Masotti, L., and J. R. Corsi.
   1969   Shoot-Out in Cleveland, Black Militants and Police. Staff report to National
           Commission on the Causes and Prevention of Violence (Staff report 5).
           Washington, D.C.: U.S. Government Printing Office.

Mattick, H. W., and N. S. Caplan.
   1967   "Stake animals, loud talking, and leadership in do-nothing and do-some-
           thing situations." Pp. 106–119 in M. W. Klein and B. Meyerhoff (eds.),
           Juvenile Gangs in Context. New York: Prentice-Hall.

Miller, W. B.
   1958   "Lower-class culture as a generating milieu of gang delinquency." Journal
           of Social Issues 14(3):5–19.
   1969   "White gangs." Trans-action 6(September):11–26.

Misner, G. E.
   1972   "The police and collective violence in contemporary America." Chapter 25
           in J. F. Short, Jr. and M. E. Wolfgang (eds.), Collective Violence. Chicago:
           Aldine-Atherton.

Monod, J.
   1967   "Juvenile gangs in Paris: toward a structural analysis." Journal of Research
           in Crime and Delinquency 4(January):142–165.

National Advisory Commission on Civil Disorders.
   1968   Report. Washington, D.C.: U.S. Government Printing Office.

National Commission on the Causes and Prevention of Violence.
   1969   To Establish Justice, To Insure Domestic Tranquility. Final report. Wash-
           ington, D.C.: U.S. Government Printing Office.

Nieburg, H. L.
   1970   "Agonistics—rituals of conflict." Annals of the American Academy of Po-
           litical and Social Science 391(September):56–73.

Peterson, V. W.
   1969   A Report on Chicago Crime for 1968. Chicago: Chicago Crime Commission.

Pfautz, H. W.
   1961   "Near-group theory and collective behavior." Social Problems 9(Fall):167–
           174.

Quarantelli, E. L.
   1970   "Emergent accommodation groups: beyond current collective behavior ty-
           pologies." Pp. 111–123 in Tomatsu Shibutani (ed.), Human Nature and
           Collective Behavior: Papers in Honor of Herbert Blumer. Englewood Cliffs,
           N.J.: Prentice-Hall.

Quinney, R.
   1970   The Social Reality of Crime. Boston: Little, Brown.

Rivera, R. J., and James F. Short, Jr.
   1967   "Significant adults, caretakers, and structures of opportunity: an explora-
           tory study." Journal of Research in Crime and Delinquency 4(January):
           76–97.

Sahid, J. R.
   1969   Rights in Concord: The Response to the Counter-inaugural Protest Activi-

ties in Washington, D.C., January 18–20, 1969. Staff report to National Commission on the Causes and Prevention of Violence (Staff report 4). Washington, D.C.: U.S. Government Printing Office.

Schwartz, G., and D. Merton.
1967   "The language of adolescence: an anthropological approach to the youth culture." American Journal of Sociology 72(March):453–468.

Schwendinger, H., and J. Schwendinger.
1967   "Delinquent stereotypes of probable victims." Pp. 92–105 in M. W. Klein and B. Meyerhoff (eds.), Juvenile Gangs in Context. Englewood Cliffs, N.J.: Prentice-Hall.

Shaw, C. R., and H. D. McKay.
1929   Delinquency Areas. Chicago: University of Chicago Press.
1931   Male Juvenile Delinquency as Group Behavior. Report to National Commission on Law Observance and Enforcement. Washington, D.C.: U.S. Government Printing Office.

Sherif, M., and C. Sherif.
1963   Reference Groups. New York: Harper & Row.

Short, James F., Jr.
1963   "Street corner groups and patterns of delinquency: a progress report." American Catholic Sociological Review 28(Spring):411–428.
1964   "Gang delinquency and anomie." Pp. 98–127 in M. B. Clinard (ed.), Anomie and Deviant Behavior. New York: Free Press of Glencoe.
1965   "Social structure and group process in explanations of gang delinquency." Pp. 155–189 in M. Sherif and C. W. Sherif, Problems of Youth: Transition to Adulthood in a Changing World. Chicago: Aldine.
1966   "Juvenile delinquency: the sociological context." Pp. 423–468 in Lois W. Hoffman and Martin L. Hoffman (eds.), Review of Child Development Research. New York: Russell Sage Foundation.
1968   "Comments on Lerman's gangs, networks and subcultural delinquency." American Journal of Sociology 73(January):513–515.
1974   "Youth, gangs and society: micro- and macrosociological process." Sociological Quarterly 15(Winter):3–19.

Short, James F., Jr., and F. L. Strodtbeck.
1964   "Why gangs fight." Trans-action 1(September/October):25–29.
1965   Group Process and Gang Delinquency. Chicago: University of Chicago Press.

Short, James F., Jr., F. L. Strodtbeck, and D. S. Cartwright.
1962   "A strategy for utilizing research dilemmas." Sociological Inquiry 32 (Spring):185–202.

Short, James F., Jr., R. Tennyson, and K. I. Howard.
1963   "Behavior dimensions of gang delinquency." American Sociological Review 28(June):411–428.

Short, James F., Jr., and Marvin E. Wolfgang (eds.)
1972   Collective Violence. Chicago: Aldine-Atherton.

Skolnick, J.
1969   The Politics of Protest, Violent Aspects of Protest and Confrontation. Staff report to National Commission on the Causes and Prevention of Violence (Staff report 3). Washington, D.C.: U.S. Government Printing Office.

Smelser, N. J.
  1962   Theory of Collective Behavior. New York: Free Press of Glencoe.
  1970   "Two critics in search of a bias: a response to Currie and Skolnick." Annals of the American Academy of Political and Social Science 391 (September): 46–56.

Spergel, I. A.
  1969   Politics, Policies and the Youth Gang. Chicago: University of Chicago, School of Social Science Administration (mimeographed).

Spiegel, J. P.
  1972   "Cultural value orientations and student protest." Chapter 19 in James F. Short, Jr. and Marvin E. Wolfgang (eds.), Collective Violence. Chicago: Aldine-Atherton.

Stark, R.
  1972   Police Riots: Collective Violence and Law Enforcement. Belmont, Cal.: Wadsworth.

Sutherland, E. H.
  1924   Principles of Criminology. Philadelphia: Lippincott.

Sutter, A. G.
  1969   "Worlds of drug use on the street scene." Pp. 802–829 in D. R. Cressey and D. A. Ward (eds.), Delinquency, Crime and Social Process. New York: Harper & Row.

Tarde, Gabriel.
  1912   Penal Philosophy. Translated by R. Howell. Boston: Little, Brown.

Thomas, W. I., and F. Znaniecki.
  1927   The Polish Peasant in Europe and America. New York: Knopf.

Thrasher, F. M.
  1963   The Gang: A Study of 1,313 Gangs in Chicago. Abridged Edition. Chicago: University of Chicago Press (originally published in 1927).

Tilly, C.
  1969   "Collective violence in European perspective." Chapter 1 in H. D. Graham and T. R. Gurr (eds.), Violence in America, Historical and Comparative Perspectives. Washington, D.C.: U.S. Government Printing Office.

Turk, A. T.
  1966   "Conflict and criminality." American Sociological Review 31 (June): 338–352.

Turner, R. H.
  1964   "Collective behavior." Pp. 382–425 in Robert E. L. Faris (ed.), Handbook of Modern Sociology. Chicago: Rand McNally.

Turner, R. H., and L. M. Killian.
  1957   Collective Behavior. Englewood Cliffs, N.J.: Prentice-Hall.

Walker, D.
  1968   Rights in Conflict. New York: Bantam Books.

Weingarten, Gene.
  1972   "East Bronx story—return of the street gangs." New York Magazine 5 (March 27): 31–37.

Whyte, W. F.
    1955   Street Corner Society: The Social Structure of an Italian Slum. Revised Edition. Chicago: University of Chicago Press.

Wolfgang, M. E., and F. Ferracuti.
    1967   The Subculture of Violence: Towards an Integrated Theory in Criminology. London: Tavistock.

Yablonsky, L.
    1959   "The delinquent gang as a near-group." Social Problems 7(Fall):108–117.
    1962   The Violent Gang. New York: Macmillan.

PART II

LAW ENFORCEMENT
AND ADJUDICATION

Introduction—Part II

The state's first reaction to crime is to try to identify the offense and the offender. Two types of state agencies have evolved for this purpose, the police and the courts. Each has many variations, all are highly imperfect in accomplishing their tasks, and all engage frequently in practices that contrast sharply with their official precepts. To describe and explain these practices is the common concern of the chapters in this part of the *Handbook*.

In Chapter 11, sociologists John P. Clark and Richard E. Sykes analyze police organizations and practices in advanced societies primarily on the basis of rigorous research, by themselves and others, in which representative samples of police officers were systematically observed throughout typical duty shifts. Their interpretation of the findings from such research points up the functions of policing, the distinctive characteristics of police organizations, and the social psychology of encounters between the police and the public.

William H. Hewitt draws on his experience as an innovative police administrator as well as a trainer of police officers at colleges and universities to discuss, in Chapter 12, major problems in the performance of tasks that he shows have been expected of police since the beginning of "the police idea." Particular attention is given to methods by which the police can best handle personnel administration, prevent corruption, improve their relationships with the community, and cope with citizen complaints.

Forensic scientist Brian Parker, educated in both biology and the law before becoming a professor of criminology and a police and court consultant on criminalistics, surveys the problems of assessing physical evidence from criminal conduct in Chapter 13. He traces the history of the forensic science professions, instructs us on the tremendous variety of physical evidence and of techniques for assessing it, then points out political, economic, and other barriers to utilization of this evidence.

A striking feature of all criminal justice systems is their insularity, and hence, their inability to learn as much as possible from each other. A major contribution to reduction of such insularity is the monumental world survey of such systems provided in Chapter 14 by M. Cherif Bassiouni, whose comparative legal studies traverse Europe, Africa, Asia, and the Americas, from ancient to modern times. He shows how differently the elusive goal of justice has been pursued, and yet how each civilization and era has had some advantages as well as some deficiencies in this pursuit.

Professor of criminal justice Donald J. Newman, in Chapter 15, demonstrates that even within United States criminal trial courts there is much diversity of role and process to be described and explained. This includes, on the one hand, great specialization in the officially prescribed functions of different offices and stages in the trial process, and on the other, the unofficial merging of these distinct functions and stages in customary decision-making practice.

The greatest influence of informal negotiation on court decisions probably occurs in the separate system of adjudication that has been developed for juveniles. The dynamics of negotiation in this system are distinctively illuminated in Chapter 16 by the "naturalistic" research reported by sociologist Robert M. Emerson. Decision determinants are thereby revealed as uniquely local organizational pressures and initiatives, which are often greatly affected by the perceived attributes and history of individual juveniles brought before the court.

In Chapter 17, lawyer Robert Seidman and sociologist of law William J. Chambliss collaborate in an analysis of the appeal processes available following criminal conviction in our judicial system. They show how the selective input to appellate courts, the socialization of judges, and the organizational characteristics of the courts influence the creation of law by the judiciary. They also analyze separately the U.S. Supreme Court and the use of executive clemency by appellants.

In the last chapter in this part, sociologist Albert J. Reiss, Jr. describes the participation of police, defendants, prosecutors, trial courts, and appellate courts, and probation, correctional institutions, and parole in the United States as separate and largely autonomous systems for the negotiation of justice. He also indicates major determinants of variation in their negotiations, analyzes the relationship of discretion to justice, and raises the ultimate question of how agencies of discretion should be held accountable.

CHAPTER **11**

Some Determinants of Police Organization and Practice In A Modern Industrial Democracy

John P. Clark and Richard E. Sykes

University of Minnesota

The social nature of crime and criminals cannot be well understood without an appreciation of the roles played by informal and formal reactions to the behavior known as crime. One of the most visible, noteworthy, controversial, and interesting instruments of social response is the police. This chapter addresses itself to some preliminary analysis of (1) the *social functions* of policing, (2) the character of police *organization,* and (3) the quality of *social interaction* between the police and the policed.

It should be pointed out that police response, however generated, represents only a fraction of the total response by society to potentially criminal behavior. Overwhelming evidence indicates that the vast majority of social reactions to behavior that could be defined as crime (by popular conception, substantive law, or legal practice) comes from family members, friends, neighbors, school personnel, social workers, clergy, employers, and other nonpolice parties. Most potentially criminal behavior is not "known to the police" (although this varies widely by type of offense). Additionally, most of what is ultimately labeled "criminal," which eventually does come to police attention, has been filtered through the reaction of others before them, frequently for extended periods of time.

It must also be pointed out that most of what the police do is not related (at least in any direct sense) to criminal behavior. Police operations are largely concerned with vehicular traffic and a wide variety of services of a noncriminal content (Reiss, 1971).

The importance of police functioning to the understanding of crime has sometimes been lost with the growth of vociferous public attention to some very limited aspects of police work, e.g., crowd or riot control and drug control, but such a focus may yield a distorted view. Obviously, the vast majority of police actions involving criminal behavior do not stir public attention but are nonetheless significant to the configuration of the "crime picture" in advanced societies. Less passionate observations of the police have noted their critical "gatekeeping" or "front-line" role in the criminal justice system. Others have opined about the enormous impact that police

The authors wish specifically to acknowledge the greatly appreciated assistance of Peggy Giordano, Daniel Glaser, Richard Hall, Richard Lundman, and Phil Patrick.

contact may have upon clientele, especially juveniles. There is abundant speculation about the deterrence of crime and the presence of police personnel. The quality of relations those being policed have with the police has been examined as important to the content of police policy and operation. Policing styles have been categorized, described, and analyzed as to their origins and consequences (Wilson, 1968). Thus, a preliminary basis is being developed for understanding the relevance of policing to the systematic analysis of criminality.

It is particularly true in complex, changing democracies that public institutions are provided extensive opportunities through organization, expertise, and power to affect both their own destinies and that of those they serve. Internal forces demand that they be responsive to their own social milieu in order to survive and to accomplish their own ends. The exchanges made between the policing institution and its social surroundings help assure both its change and its stability, for the functioning of police organizations is kept somewhat in tune with the social environment in which it operates. As the societies police serve have changed in character, the functions of policing have tended to shift in specific content if not in their ultimate abstraction. We shall try to identify both the major current functions served by police organizations and operations, and how those functions reflect their sociocultural milieu.

SOCIAL FUNCTIONS

Among the multitude of functions attributed to police organizations, probably no one is mutually exclusive of another and none is wholly unique to police activities. Nor should one conclude that a listing of these several functions reflects a well-integrated set of organizational operations. It will become clear that, like few other public bureaucracies, the police organization has always operated within a tangle of strong social currents and issues that have prohibited its carving out a secure haven in the social fabric. In hindsight, it might be concluded that creating organizations whose major functions are essentially limited to a collection of volatile and vaguely specified areas of social functioning in democratic societies is basically untenable and unwise. At any rate, four of the most obvious social functions served by modern urban police are: (1) coercion, (2) team member in the criminal justice system, (3) omnibus public-service agency, and (4) symbolic representative of government.

Police as Primary Dispenser of Immediate and Direct Coercion

Perhaps the predominant image of policing focuses upon their potential or actual coercive power in a very broad range of situations (Bittner, 1970). The use of coercion is obviously not limited to a society's urban police departments. In addition to military organizations and a myriad of other police agencies, the power to coerce some to conform to the will of others is distributed in various forms throughout the social fabric, e.g., in parents, schools, housing inspectors, welfare agencies, courts, correctional and treatment institutions of various kinds, and offices of the courts, as well as in citizens generally, under prescribed conditions. The broad nature of the distribution of coercive power undoubtedly lies behind the tendency of those populations that are unusually vulnerable to its use not to distinguish between the coerciveness of the police, courts, schools, welfare, and so forth; all may be labeled "the agency," "the establishment," "the man," or simply "the government" or "they." Nonetheless, the coercive power of domestic police is much more mobile and immediately available throughout a community, is used with more latitude, and dominates the host organization more completely than the coercive powers of other organizations.

The *sources* of coercion exercised by the police are as unexplicated as they are diverse. Historically (and, undoubtedly, currently) much of the impetus for the coercion of others came from those who had something to gain thereby, and who were in circumstances where their desires could be converted into public policy. Therefore, propertied persons, governmental officials, and those with strong moral convictions were particularly instrumental in arming police with coercive power.

Simultaneously, the legitimate resort to the direct use of coercive power (especially through the use of physical force) has gradually been withdrawn from the general public. Partially as a reflection of the centralization of power in municipal, state, and national governments, the concomitant rise of specialized (and frequently professionalized) public agencies, and the gradual shift of societal values to a nonviolent social existence, the police have been endowed with relatively broad authority to coerce citizens directly and forcefully toward or away from certain behaviors.

Coercive power does not derive from the potential of physical force alone, although the actual or potential use of it is an important component of some police work. Certainly much of the police aura, suggested by their being called a police "force," their weapons, their military presence, their standards of physical prowess, and their shows of overwhelming power, is reflective of their capability of coercion by physical force. The roots of most police coercion, however, probably lie in their pre-legitimized, informed, immediate, and authoritative access to the various alternative social regulatory agencies in the community. The threat (in varying degrees of subtlety) of entanglement with the criminal and juvenile justice systems, school authorities, mental-health officials, detoxification centers, parents, or others, which the presence of the police may imply, obviates any real need for physical coercion in most police work. "Armed" with confidence that, if necessary, alternative regulatory forces will follow up on actions they initiate, police are provided great coercive power that falls short of physical force. Informal data indicate that lack of police and public confidence in supportive alternative control services is related to the more liberal use of physical coercion by both the police and the public. Therefore, in a very broad and direct way coercive power is derived not from the sheer physical coercive potentials of the police alone, but from their institutionalized ability to initiate proceedings that may later involve a range of disagreeable circumstances for those affected.

A third significant source of police coercive power, in addition to their physical force and their backup by other agencies, is the assertiveness (albeit largely complaint activated) that, relative to most public-service organizations, distinguishes urban police activities. The combination of a great variety of situations in which police become involved and their inordinately high availability is converted (purposely or not) into coercive power for the police. Their around-the-clock deployment, high mobility, efficient communication system, and ideological bent toward rapid response accrue to their relative advantage as participants in the regulation of others' behavior. Additionally, the largely undefined limits to which police may involve themselves in the lives of citizens, especially when specifically invited into their lives and frequently at times of high vulnerability of at least some of the participants, is conducive to giving a coercive advantage to the police should they care to exercise it.

Yet another foundation of police coercive power (as with any specialized service agency) is its relatively exclusive access to the special knowledge and expertise associated with police work. Organizational intelligence of various sorts, specialized skills, laboratory facilities, and exclusive access to the special services of functionally related agencies place the police in a position of potential coercion relative to others in a police situation.

Contrary to the intemperate observations of some, there are limits and constraints associated with the use of coercion by the police. This is not to imply that, by some explicit standard, police coercion is neither insufficiently constrained nor used unwisely. Given the circumstances in which police might conceivably use their coercive power, however, one must explain why its actual application is selective.

Perhaps most influential are the general normative expectations of the society being policed. These define the extent to which it is appropriate for police to coerce citizens. Although specific empirical verification is lacking, it might be fair to observe that the popular norms support a minimum of police coercion; in the absence of a specific rationale for use of coercive power, police feel that coercion should be avoided. Response to this public expectation probably explains much of the avoidance of coercion by the police.

Police are aware not only of some broad expectations of the total society (after all they were recruited from it, work daily in it, and still live very much in it), but they are perhaps more aware than most people of the variations in the general norms to which segments of the population are committed. They tailor their actions to these more specific expectations. This loose association between cultural prescriptions and police orientations helps to explain variation in police use of coercion over time and across cultural settings.

Another important limiting factor on the use of coercion by police is the police organization's norms and specific policy concerning its use. The relative invisibility of much coercive police activity to official monitoring by their organization does *not* necessarily mean that organizational constraints on its use are absent. Police personnel and the organization in which they serve are unavoidably responsive to the accumulation of past work-related experiences. As they have been given only very general operational guidance by society and frequently find themselves at variance with significant community sentiment, the police are strongly influenced by ingroup traditions and commitments. Organizational boundaries are stoutly maintained, not as much administratively as through the exclusivity of their collective identity. Those who are considered to be "one of us" or "on our side" circumscribe, as with few other large bureaucracies, a very primary referent group for police behavior.

Situational or "relational" norms may represent an immediate and frequent guide to the application of coercion. In fact, in police organizations to which member commitment is very strong, the impact of other restraints on the use of coercion may be only nominally effective until they are legitimized through acceptance into the organizational cultural milieu. This "gatekeeper" function of group norms is not unique to police departments (it applies somewhat in all formal organizations). It has been attributed to the police due to an image of their having military control over their members and a high standard of individual loyalty. (Some contrary evidence will be presented in discussing police "de-bureaucratization.")

Perhaps one of the most potent structural constraints on the use of coercion by police is the fact that their activity is shaped primarily by the nature of the requests they receive (Reiss, 1971). Not only are the vast majority of their contacts with the public initiated by citizen complainants (with whom, it can be assumed, some consensus exists in regard to appropriate police action), but additionally, from whatever the source of initiation, much police activity can be characterized as noncoercive or "service-oriented" in nature. Police activities (particularly patrol) are traditionally configured to preclude their application of coercion to persons other than (1) those who request their assistance (which, as has been noted above, is probably noncoercive to most participants but may be to some), (2) those who may be deterred from activity by "police presence," and (3) those involved in "on-scene" intervention by the police. Of course, because of past experience with a client, police may give more-than-ordinary attention to some members of the public, a phenomenon that will be dealt with later.

Although not well illuminated intellectually, another restraint upon the capability of police to use coercion is the legal milieu within which they work. Apparently, there is no direct and perfect relationship between requirements of legal institutions and actual police practice. While some of this reflects problems of legal statutes and practice, it also seems to reflect to a very significant extent the strength of police norms and of individual officer orientations in the pursuit of police work. While the exceptions of police work to the requirement of the law may be dramatic, actions of the courts, human-relations commissions, review boards, citizen investigations, and the instruction and policy guidance provided the police as a result of legal action accrue to constrain police use of coercion. Particularly, if legal proscriptions and prescriptions are legitimized by the police command itself, legislation and its explicit translations into police terms are one guide to police use of coercion, especially in the areas of its less subtle use. (It should be pointed out here that there is also the possibility that restrictive legislation may stimulate the police to observe legal restrictions on the use of the specific coercive means in question, yet initiate another coercive technique to replace it.)

Not easily distinguished from the previous constraints are the practical limits of coercion as a technique of police work. For obvious reasons police are "problem-solution" oriented. Most police contacts are limited to several minutes, carried out with a strong undertone of dispatch, and closed when the central characters have adopted a course of action not immediately at variance with the broad bounds of acceptability by the police. In such situations, prudence advises against resort to coercion if it is inimicable to early problem resolution. Further, even when coercion is judged to be necessary (and this can be grossly misjudged or poorly managed), the careful orchestration of coercion in order to guide the situation toward some vaguely predetermined end (i.e., "keeping it cool") is an art form that is part of most police officers' modus operandi. To apply more or less coercion may be counterproductive and result in prolonged situations, unsatisfactory solutions, and the flow of events getting out of hand. Therefore, strong influence is exerted by the objectives and methods that officers judge are practical, given the situations with which they are confronted.

Closely related to the above constraint is the last one to be mentioned here, i.e., the limitations on the use of coercion that result from the character of interaction between the police and those whom they police. In this sense, the use of coercion by the police is negotiable. The dynamics of the interaction between the police and the violator (and sometimes others) contribute to the manner and extent to which coercion is utilized. Nonpolice parties frequently provide important input into this interaction process. To the extent that police action is a reflection of the situation and the situation can be partially defined by those other than the police, they are restrained in their use of coercion.

What appears above may have overtones of apologia for police. Such is not meant to be the case. There is no doubt that in the modern American context and when judged by standards by which most individuals would like to be personally treated, police departments sometimes utilize coercion (both physical and nonphysical) illegally, unjustly, unnecessarily, unwisely, and unknowingly. The police in modern democratic societies obviate the "need" of other segments of society to apply coercion, and therefore, the police are specialists acting for the collective in a structurally and functionally differentiated society. Since we consider the police as part of criminal and juvenile justice systems, it must be evident that most of what police do is not characterized by coercion.

Police as Front-Line and Key Team Members in the Justice Systems

In a very major way, the courts, jails, prosecutors, and correctional organizations are heavily dependent upon police activity not only for their clients, but also for preliminary specification of the cases they may eventually handle. Yet, the police are seldom at the very leading edge of the criminal justice system for they largely enter the scene after initial action by other reaction structures, e.g., individual complainants, victims, or schools. Much police action is limited to officially transferring data from various sources to the next step in the legal process. This "report-taking" is frequently the extent of the police response possible or feasible for the spectrum of agencies that constitute the justice systems. The limits on further response are set both by the nature of the data available and by the judgment of the police who make an early determination of the appropriateness of further response.

It should be pointed out here that only in a portion of the situations into which police are invited or insert themselves are they provided with any realistic latitude for arrest discretion. Most police situations do not involve criminal offenses, and thus, provide little basis for arrest. Furthermore, most situations with an offense include only misdemeanors and, therefore, severely limit arrest action by the police unless they have observed the offense. Conversely, little discretion is available to police officers who are serving arrest warrants or in situations where felonies have probably been committed and a violator is reasonably well identified and present. Only beyond these circumstances of "no-arrest" and "sure-arrest" may the police employ their discretionary powers.

Citizen-initiated police actions are termed *reactive* and police-initiated actions *proactive*. As with most components of the social regulatory system in modern industrial societies, the police have adopted a predominantly reactive, rather than a proactive, stance in regard to client recruitment and monitoring of social behavior. The great profusion of patrol activity is apparently largely a holding operation while awaiting assignments from complainants received via radio. Systems of intelligence-gathering and initiative in locating crimes are relatively undeveloped in police departments, even where most efforts of this type have been placed, e.g., vice and morals. This, in part, reflects the qualities of criminality police have focused upon, i.e., unorganized, unsophisticated, and socially disruptive behavior with immediate and evident victims. The exact occurrence of such criminality is not easily predicted, and therefore, it makes more economic sense to respond to criminal situations *ex post facto* than to invest heavily in preventing such behavior. Emphasis has tended to be placed upon rapid response to such violations and speedy handling of the offenders, aspects of the criminal justice syndrome that are thought to be manageable without major investments. Although this perspective may be penny-wise and pound-foolish, it is still, for several reasons, their primary orientation in democratic societies.

Though police operations are essentially reactive, they are heavily influenced by the "crime-fighter" or "crime-stopper" philosophy, which has as its central tenet: the faster one gets on the case, the higher the probabilities of solving the crime, making an arrest, and convicting the criminal. Such a line of thought is appropriate only for limited types of crime, e.g., "burglary in progress." Not only are police organizations dominated by such conceptions but so is the public (particularly the parties just offended). Often quick response or even personal contact by officers is probably not necessary to satisfactory police investigation. For example, many reports could be taken via telephone from the complainant, but the public would not care for this procedure, since the police have traditionally responded in person to a wide range of public requests.

For whatever reasons and however wise, police personnel are the most widely deployed and available representatives of the justice establishment. With few exceptions, a patrol unit is available in cities on a 24-hour, seven-day basis within minutes from the time requested. As a result, police are largely limited tactically to playing most situations "by the seat of their pants." They remain essentially unattached to the population they serve and to other elements of the justice systems.

In a very real way, the appearance of the police signals to participants and onlookers that they are involved in a more-than-casual event. Whether pursuing criminals, responding to an emergency, or merely providing some less dramatic service, police present a commonly understood symbol of official concern that separates those to whom they respond from most others. Their visibility contributes to community awareness of such events and to the interpretation that the events receive. Finding themselves on stage, actors must deal with each other and situations must be "disposed of." The mere fact of finding themselves on stage, however, is in itself an impressive fact with consequences for all parties.

When responding to calls, patrol officers most frequently occupy the management-control role partly because all understand that this is why the police were called, partly because taking the initiative is a police technique of situation control, and partly because police work depends on the imposition of outside influence on a situation that one or more parties find otherwise unacceptable. As front-line representatives of the justice systems, police may make decisions as to the appropriateness of calls for police assistance, but an extremely wide variety of calls are "accepted" that result in police abdicating to the definitions and information provided by complainants. Therefore, the actual implementation of legal statutes depends heavily upon the manner in which police personnel pursue their activities. Their decisions not to respond or not to arrest, or to select an offense to focus reaction upon, may not readily be revised by others later in the system. At this point, too, protection of legal rights is in the hands of the police, and they are undoubtedly involved more frequently than any other agency in the protection of legal rights of clients. In addition, police play a legal-interpretation or legal-education role second to no other agency in the community. Their response to questions and their practice of law are instructive to those who ask and observe.

The front-line character of the police input into the justice systems is drawn upon again when officers are used by the prosecution (and sometimes by the defense) in the judicial phase of the legal process. Beyond this, the arrest and offense reports filed by police officers contribute in various ways to the processing provided the "case" at subsequent points in the juvenile and criminal justice systems.

In summary, then, a second major social function served by the police is as a very visible, available, yet generally reactive, front-line community extension of the juvenile and criminal justice system. As such they make critical screening decisions for society, they provide the majority of the legal service and awareness received by most people from official agencies, and their knowledge of events surrounding a case in the legal system often shapes its subsequent processing through the system.

Police as an Omnibus Service Agency

Perceived through time-and-motion studies, the vast majority of what police personnel do must be categorized as omnibus service that, on the surface at least, *could* be provided by a nonpolice organization. In our opinion, intellectual discourse on the appropriate division of public services among various governmental agencies has tended to be quite sterile, however; for knowledge about how to configure and operate organizations to deliver human services appropriately is extremely limited.

The operations of public-service agencies are heavily influenced by the accumulation of "residues" from past field operations, and from the impact of organizational leaders, governing laws, policy decisions, and cultural and economic conditions. It would be literally impossible to predict much about the activities of police (or for any public human-service agency) only by examining relevant state and local enabling legislation. This condition of relative indeterminacy has permitted agency operations of great diversity and flexibility, and the possibility that current activities diverge from initial intent or traditional organizational philosophies. It appears that urban police departments, responding to a wide variety of community-service needs, have fostered a "natural" growth of organization function in response to their milieu. Although departments vary significantly in their stress on community services, all indulge greatly in activities not directly related to the maintenance of order within law. Yet, this does not mean that police agencies are unselective in the services they perform, whether on their initiative or in response to requests from the community.

One of the first explanations for police investment in provision of services only peripherally related to law enforcement is that this gives them knowledge and control in situations that have been previously associated with disruption of law and order. Intervention in domestic disorders, in milling and ganging behavior of teenagers, in the investigation of unusual noises and events, in helping an array of "vulnerable" persons to the safety of their homes, and so forth, probably represents attempts to forestall events that have more-than-ordinary probability of requiring direct police intervention at a later time, if allowed to pursue their natural course. Thus, provision of a broad range of community services may constitute a low-yield crime-prevention effort where more efficient crime-prevention programs are not easily discernible.

Since police organizations were established, one of their activities as they circulate among the population and respond to their superiors has been to help those who request their assistance. Today's police personnel feel the pressure similarly to indulge society merely on historical grounds. To change (particularly to withdraw service) raises the risk of public and official attention at a time when much is being said about the "isolation" of the police (Clark, 1965) and their "overemphasis" on punitive contacts with the public. Whether these conditions are, in fact, the case may be irrelevant; if a vocal part of the public believe it to be the case, to withdraw or otherwise greatly modify the existing service stance of a police department could bring unwanted attention. Whatever these dynamics, current departments of police (as with any longstanding organization) operate under the influence of their historical legacy. (Parenthetically, it might be noted that as the relationship between police activities and the diffuse character of criminal behavior becomes clearer, police departments may assume the image of a broad public-service agency more securely.)

Yet a third support for the omnibus service function of modern police departments is the very real pressure (beyond its historical component) from the population it serves. Examination of calls received by the police, contacts made with police on the street and through their investigative effort, and correspondence received by the department reveal a very high expectancy of non-law-enforcement services. It is a widely held public belief that it is appropriate to contact the police for non-law-enforcement services since they are a public agency, generally available, widely deployed and quick to respond, generalists by profession, mobile, cloaked with an image of authority ("just in case"), decisive, "nonentangling" in bureaucratic processing, and close to city hall. No doubt, however, many would-be requests for service do not reach the police because others in the public see them as inappropriate, perhaps because they do not perceive the police as having these or other characteristics.

Conceptions of the police as an omnibus general-service agency give them the problem of selecting those requests to which to respond. As mentioned, the possible relevance of the call content to the police role as a front-line team member of the criminal justice system is one criterion upon which judgments are made. The social importance of the source might occasionally be another. But probably among the most important is the time available to respond to such calls. Direct observation of police operations confirms the expectation that relative priorities are given to requests for police services, and those with obvious crime relevance rank high. It also reveals that police organizations assign a high value to "activity"; this seems to be the case in the entire U.S. society, and probably in most complex, industrialized societies (Williams, 1970). The fact appears to be that if police-patrol personnel only handled calls specifically pertaining to criminal incidents, most patrol time would be "wasted." Even accepting a wide range and large number of service calls permits a large proportion of deployed patrol-car time to be spent awaiting the next call. (There seems to be considerable variation in this "waste" phenomenon by city, patrol area, time of day, day of week, etc.) It is rare, for whatever reason, for police personnel responding to calls to be in continuous service. Without attempting to evaluate the consequences of police behavior in this regard, the facts at least indicate considerable discretion on the part of police as to the volume and quality of non-law-enforcement calls in which they will become involved.

Another pressure toward involvement and a criterion of request selection is the constant organizational need (perhaps somewhat greater for police organizations than for other public-service bureaucracies) to maintain good relations with the public. Service to other public agencies (e.g., street and fire departments, schools) and to influential individuals and organizations (particularly business organizations) in the community contributes to smooth day-to-day operations and to the support of police at times of critical need. Also, the police have a constant need for the management of resentment aroused over their more restrictive actions (e.g., traffic tickets, protest control) and to overcome images of poor police practices currently and in the past. Response to requests for service is considered to be one way of counteracting events that have resulted in hostility toward police.

Police officers also provide non-law-enforcement services individually on either their own or on other's initiative because they observe a need, see its being otherwise unmet, believe they can help meet the need, and find satisfaction in doing so. One might expect that the personnel of any other public-service agency, if not occupied by its more exclusive tasks and if in similar interaction with the public in its own environment, would respond in like manner. Some officers and even some departments permit discretion in this area to the point that other officers or other departments characterize the former as "social workers"—a term used somewhat disdainfully by traditional police officers. Labels notwithstanding, police personnel frequently engage in helping behavior simply because they are there and personally wish to assist.

In summary, the omnibus service function of the police has grown from early origins and is perpetuated by forces from both inside and outside the police organization. Services are myriad in type, but range from those closely associated with the criminal justice function to those initiated purely out of the personal interests of individual officers.

Police as a Symbol of Government

Perhaps the most controversial social function served by police in modern democratic societies (and perhaps in others as well) is that of being a symbol of government. The uncomfortable imagery of a democratic government being most visibly represented by military forces and police personnel reflects inversely the problem faced by the police in representing local government to the public. Such social ambivalence accrues to both the police and the public in making the former the recipient of much of the concern (both negative and positive) evidenced by the public for their local government.

Police activities are greatly influenced by state government, since most statutory law under which they operate emanates from state legislatures, but the tradition of local control of police services is far-reaching in the minds of both the police and the public whom they serve. In a very real and pervasive sense police organizations and activities represent the interests of local government. Controversies that have swirled around this police function reflect two main sources: (1) those who challenge the representativeness and sensitivity of local government, and, therefore, of its police services; and (2) those who perceive the quality of police activities being determined by police personnel themselves rather than by the local political process (representative or not), and, therefore, being inappropriate to some community orientations and needs.

Most analyses have pointed out the essentially conservative (or status quo) and singularly moralistic image that police portray. Some have labeled police and their services as the embodiment of the conservative values of the society. Almost all such observations, however, reflect only casual measurement of the values police practice and their possible divergence from those residing throughout the policed population. Illustrations of conservative values frequently dwell on police efforts to thwart public protests, to enforce laws concerning morality, and to provide guidance on topics related to juvenile delinquency. Implications are strong in these analyses that such conservatism results from an inordinately high proportion of police personalities that, largely through the occupational selection process, are politically conservative, morally straight, and personally inflexible. Most such analyses are based upon personal rather than empirically demonstrated values of the total community.

The recent development of knowledge in the areas of occupational and organizational socialization, however, and increased systematic observations of police officers at work suggest that the individual officer's work experiences and the accumulated effect of such experiences on his organization may provide a more adequate explanation for police "traditionalism." (This is in addition to the obvious fact that because of their charge by the government and the public they serve, police have a vested interest in maintaining a predictable and rule-observing community.) It should hardly be surprising that an organization whose personnel deal daily with persons' encroachments upon others, immoral conduct, and property offenses would develop an intense interest in this phenomenon in their society, just as educators and the organizations in which they serve are known for their keen interest in educational matters.

Governmental powers are not expended only on behalf of the status quo; indeed, democratic governments are devoting more and more time and energy to planned community change. Consequently, police may simultaneously play symbolic roles of maintainers of the status quo (e.g., controlling protests, conducting drug raids, and making law-and-order speeches) and advocates of social change (pollution regulation, race relations, and housing codes) (Wenninger & Clark, 1967). Perhaps a shift in police functioning toward increased provision of non-law-enforcement services, combined with their representing governments more involved in community change, will shift the symbolism surrounding local police agencies a little from one of conservatism to a less status-quo orientation. The dynamics of these shifts in the functions served by the police might also provide a significant opening for the development of professionalism among police personnel, since it would seem to require less strict adherence to the "official line" and relatively simple organizational requirements, and more to diverse decision-making and complex program participation by the individual officers. Such a change would place emphasis on both increased general education and specialized training and certification for police officers, on merit promotions, and on interchange of ideas across departments, all attributes of a more professionalized occupation.

In any foreseeable future, police organizations probably will not become "swinging" agencies with the ability to make major goal replacements, serve openly as advocates for underdog segments of the population, or carry their case for a program directly to the public. A major restraint against such dramatic changes is the significant conservatizing effect of being functionally relegated to community-wide enforcement of behavioral standards that have stood the tests of time and the political process. Further, being continually immersed in responding to situations that violate these standards appears to result in an even higher commitment on the part of the responding agency to the rules themselves, thus enhancing the organization's symbolic representation of the standard makers (even beyond the initial intent or after it deserves modification).

One could catalog and elucidate the several functions of police services in a variety of ways. We have listed what seem to be the four major social functions they serve. From this brief description and documentation it becomes obvious that police activities are extremely diverse, that policing is contoured for both high availability and a variety of services, that the police are capable of handling most of the situations they meet, and that they do this with a minimum of prior and subsequent entanglements. The four functions we have chosen to focus upon are characterized by considerable interdependence that probably reflects the high interaction effect among them as police operate in the field. We have also attempted to indicate that in none of these four basic social functions are the police singularly involved. No large, urban, broad-based, and semi-professional agencies, such as the human-service agencies in modern industrial societies, can draw exact hard-and-fast functional boundaries. The configuration of the several functions of police departments, however, is unique and provides the foundation for police organization and the manner in which the organization and its personnel interact with their environments.

THE CHARACTER OF POLICE ORGANIZATION

As with formal organizations generally, police organizations reflect the activities in which they are engaged. Though specific form and content differ somewhat, much similarity exists among various types of police organizations and between police departments and other organizations that have emerged in the public sector. Therefore, the character of police organizations is neither mysterious nor unique. It is shaped by both internal and external conditions and by some basic prerequisites of formal organizations per se.

The External Environment

The need for rule enforcement, order maintenance, and services to a society has probably existed since the dawn of civilization (Wilson, 1968). However, the organizational forms that enact responses to such needs are strongly correlated with the societal host's broader developmental patterns of industrialization, population growth, urbanization, political ideology, and structural differentiation. Early reliance on the policing effort by families, clans, and tribes was modified to include the more specific tasks of citizen organizations and militia. Differentiation of policing tasks grew when special sections of a professional military or other designated agents of central government were assigned policing duties, and courts were served by sheriffs, bailiffs, and others with policing functions. Apparently these forms of policing were not adequate when population centers began to grow rapidly as a result of the push of excessive population in rural areas and the pull of jobs and alternative life-styles associated with manufacturing and commerce. The development of occupational specialization, community heterogeneity, and rapid demographic shifts thwarted support for spontaneous voluntary police service. The increasingly abundant needs and demands for maintenance of order, criminal apprehension, and for a dependable community watchman around the clock dictated a more formal societal response. Police services were gradually more formally organized to reflect the political power structure, the patterns of perceived needs for service, the accumulated traditions of policing, and other factors.

Societies with strong centralized political identities (e.g., Japan, France, U.S.S.R.) organized their police under strong central government control. Societies that placed high value on local autonomy tended to emphasize local (i.e., city, county) police organizations (e.g., the United States and Great Britain). Whatever the formal organizing authority, the need for full-time policing was clearly evident and was met in one way or another. Results were clearly expected in terms of increased order, less offensive public behavior, cleaner cities, and the provision of general services. As the general "interdependency" of the world develops, international policing structures and operations appear to be gaining ascendancy.

As in other public bureaucracies, despite the addition of new organizational forms and operations, much of the old structure and procedures have been retained. Although some police organizations (such as the township or village constable, or even the county sheriff) are slowly being abolished or combined with urban or other regional departments, the organizational map of policing in many modern, industrial societies is complex. This is not to suggest prematurely that a streamlined and technically efficient organizational substitute is indicated, for, as we shall see, many important expectations other than technical efficiency influence the form and substance of policing in all societies. But it does alert us to a characteristic of this public bureaucracy that, although probably not unique, may be an extreme case of organizational segmentation, at least in the United States.

Evidently, legislative bodies at all levels have found it undesirable, unnecessary, or impossible to specify the exact goals, objectives, or tasks of police departments. In the United States policing responsibilities have been largely left to the states. Through city charters and associated legislation, responsibilities have been further granted to local authorities, usually with the most general legal mandate. Not surprisingly, then, major influences on police-department operations in the United States have emanated from various sources within the local community. Backup, emergency, or specialized police services have been retained by federal and state jurisdictions. In other industrialized societies with more centralized governments, the goals or major tasks of local police departments are likely to be more explicit and similar across departments under the same governing jurisdiction. But, regardless of their sponsorship, all urban departments are visibly influenced by local policing needs, physical and cultural configurations of the area to be policed, and local police officials themselves. The fact is that in spite of the heavy overlay in urban policing of pseudomilitarism, responsiveness to the state (or province, prefecture, oblast, etc.) or even national government directives plus police occupational inclination toward universal standards of behavior, local police departments in modern industrial societies exist with sufficient latitude to reflect local exigencies in a wide variety of police activities. This may also characterize other local public bureaucracies with similar relationships to higher authorities. Indeed, it illustrates the degree to which local police organizations are "open systems," responsive to external influences in their determination of major tasks, organization, and operations.

Police department organization and operations have been rationalized toward the bureaucratic mode. Line and staff tasks have emerged, divisions occasion subdivisions, specialties have developed, tables of organization and equipment are evident. In addition to the requisites of any sizeable complex organization to function internally, major influences for this organizational differentiation have come from the police department's environment. These external influences may be categorized as: (1) cultural, (2) legal, (3) organizational ecology, (4) population demography, (5) political, (6) economic, and (7) technological (Hall, 1972).

Cultural Influences. As briefly described above, the dominant influence of the cultural setting pervades the origins of, current existence of, and changes in police departments. A dramatic test of this assertion could be demonstrated through the consequences of taking a city police department from the U.S. and placing it into operation intact in the Soviet Union, France, or Scotland. Obviously, part of the ensuing confusion would result from the discrepancies in the mutual expectations of the police and those policed. Other illustrations of the cultural input are available from the experiences of military-occupation forces (e.g., the United States in Japan), where reforms instituted by outsiders have gradually dissolved upon the withdrawal of the externally applied authority. Less dramatic, but still revealing, would be the results of a transplantation of police departments within the United States between a large university campus and a working-class urban area, or between a New England and a Deep South town. Again, the noticeable effects would partially stem from the more-than-usual lack of consensus on the broad cultural rules in community policing. Cultural meanings and forms of community policing have long and deep roots; the continuous presence of these influences affects current police operations, albeit usually subtly.

In a culturally pluralistic society, the influence of the cultural setting can present diverse and frequently conflicting expectations for police services. The ability of police departments to orchestrate their operations between the universalisms of social justice and the particularisms of cultural differences is a common test of police effectiveness. Their task is made even more difficult as a result of the obscure directives given police departments by their host societies. Indeed, one major source of direction from outside the organization comes from reading the general cultural expectations of police work.

Police practice in the areas of victimless crimes, domestic disturbances, white-collar crime, and offenses by juveniles, for example, reflect cultural expectations and realities and only rarely can be attributed to the specific force of law. While such latitude may be seen as helpful to police in a culturally heterogeneous situation in that it permits differentiated response, it tends to exclude police from the protective cover of higher authority in conflict situations. Therefore, vagueness of directives from host jurisdictions may be both a blessing and a curse from the police point of view.

Police organization itself (e.g., the existence of morals squads, community-relations divisions, juvenile divisions, re-formation of foot patrols, or school-patrol divisions) reflects the obvious impact of cultural influences upon police departments. One of the concrete manifestations of cultural influence on policing in democracies is the occasional "national debate" or "national commission" that is born of a perceived disjuncture between cultural perspectives on policing and actual police practices. Although the results of such debates are difficult to assess, they undoubtedly sensitize the police to public sentiment toward a range of police affairs. In this way they serve to clarify the interface between societal norms and values and the appropriate tasks of police departments. Though much has been written about the extent to which police departments have grown out-of-step with modern society, recent concerns about law and order suggest that this may be the judgment of only one segment (perhaps a minority) of the population in the United States.

Legal Influences. More specific aspects of the general cultural setting may be identified as having direct consequences for the police department. Perhaps the most explicit is the law. Though the correlation is only approximate, the character of the law shapes much police training, the subdivision of investigative forces into specialties (such as "burglary," "homicide," "auto theft," "narcotics," "juvenile," etc.), and the recent introduction of the staff position of "legal advisor" into the major departments.

Within the sphere of legal influence one must also include the impact of court findings and interpretations. Although direct communication between the courts and police in the United States is notoriously meager, landmark cases and impressionistic information about local, state, and national court orientations directly modify police work. Specification of search-and-seizure procedures, protection of citizens' rights, acceptance of evidence, or "won-lost" records of certain types of cases before particular judges are informational inputs into training, police decisions concerning the expenditures of organizational resources, and quality of police response to calls for assistance. Although most police activity is not directly related to the administration of criminal law but to the provision of services and information, the dominant aura of police organizations is traditionally one of law enforcement. Yet, within the written law and its practice, there remains a great range of possible adaptations.

Organizational Ecology. A reality of most organizational life is that each organization is dependent in many ways upon other organizations in its immediate environment (Scott, 1964). Police departments are classic examples of this principle. As one member of the criminal and juvenile justice "system" or network of agencies, police operations and organizational structures must mesh tolerably with the "inputs" and "outputs," even though these are somewhat controlled by the police. Perhaps the strongest influence here is the weight of citizen complaints received by departments and the referrals received from schools, private protection agencies, and other law-enforcement and correctional agencies. Though the police are undoubtedly partially responsible for community understanding about what is and is not appropriate to bring to police attention, much of this phenomenon is beyond their immediate control (Quinney, 1970). This "input" produces the need to accept or reject involvement, negotiate organizational boundaries, engage in conflict and power struggles, coordinate efforts with other organizations, create new programs or expand current ones, etc., with the resultant impact on the department's functioning.

Equally important in the typical police organization's "set" are those to whom cases handled by the police are referred, sent, returned, or otherwise disposed of. For example, the acceptance of police cases by the relevant prosecuting attorney is an extremely important influence on police decisions concerning expenditure of resources, content of training, and field supervision of evidence collection. Detention-home and juvenile-court policies and practices directly impinge upon street decisions about actions to take with alleged juvenile offenders. Since much police activity deals with non-law-enforcement matters, organizations, such as hospitals, detoxification centers, city engineers and firemen, social-service agencies, emergency-help services, towing services, and a host of others exercise influence on the range of options in departmental objectives and means for their accomplishment. Sometimes formal joint programs exist between police departments and selected other agencies, especially in the area of juvenile work, e.g., youth service bureaus, police-school liaison programs, and police-recreation programs.

Probably more than in many other public-service organizations, contacts between police and other related agencies flow laterally between an individual officer and an individual worker in the other organization. The demands and operational procedures of patrol work frequently cast the relationship between these agencies into an "individualized" mold. So does the police investigative style. Frequently, officers are left to their own motivations and devices in direct interaction with other agencies. Where such contact is required by law or by explicit traditions, relations tend to be characterized more by impersonality (and probably conflict) than are those in which both parties are more voluntarily engaged.

Conflict sometimes persists in "required" interorganizational relations because of the diminished opportunities for avoidance and exchange behavior to resolve it. Often relations between police departments and other organizations from the policy levels down to the individual workers are based upon mutual benefit to both parties, e.g., the exchange of information, the provision of service in exchange for the demonstration of respect or status, or the exchange of leniency for intensified efforts to divert clients from further problem behavior in the community.

In addition to these routine exchange relations between the police and other significant organized influences in their environment, many relations are in conflict and problematic in regard to the role of police vis-à-vis other agencies in the network of human-services organizations. One basis for the interorganization conflict is the real and perceived difference between the police and some other agencies (frequently the more treatment-oriented ones) on operating philosophies in regard to services provided to clients and the community (Miller, 1958). Police organizations are often perceived accurately by other agency personnel as placing more emphasis than they do on social control, community protection, and direct and explicit services to complainants. Typical means of conflict resolution are "policy meetings" (sometimes institutionalized, sometimes not) among policy-level administrators (the results of which are frequently vague and not always effectively transmitted to lower-level workers), standing consultative committees, special negotiating sessions among concerned parties, appeal to higher common authority, avoidance of potentially conflicting cases, shifting of organizational boundaries or the domain of operation, and the development of jointly sponsored activities that transcend the issues of conflict.

Police organizations have been seen at a disadvantage in direct negotiations with related organizational personnel because of the former's lower level of formal education and professional status, and their less developed skills of organizational leadership. Furthermore, given the conditions that surround both the "input" and "output" of police cases, the organization must frequently negotiate under considerable time pressure and, therefore, may be put at a disadvantage relative to the position of other organizations. This is not to imply that the police have no negotiating power, for through their critical front-line position among service agencies and their latitude in accepting or avoiding cases, their negotiating power is potentially great.

Conversely, a less well elucidated adjustment of the police (and of organizations generally) to external conflict is to expand the organizational domain to include within police operations the activities that are the occasion for the current conflict with those outside the organization. Though this may confuse past understandings of the functional differentiation of a public-service system (e.g., criminal justice) and may create duplication of services and less expert service, such an adjustment may provide service when it would not otherwise be provided and perhaps in a more holistic manner (Lefton & Rosengren, 1966). An example of this phenomenon is the consistent pressure felt by police juvenile officers not only to detect and apprehend juvenile offenders but also to provide judicial and treatment services, partially in response to a conflict in operating philosophies with the juvenile court and its related services. Another example is the comprehensive or exclusive police response to prostitutes, homosexuals, alcoholics, and tramps. Persistently seen by police as properly somebody else's business after apprehension, conflict over satisfactory solutions to these cases has provided part of the rationale for alternative (sometimes extralegal or illegal) police response that involves expansion of the organizational domain to include adjudication and correction.

Population Ecology and Demography. Another environmental influence on police-department operations and structure emanates from the shifting demographic characteristics of the population being policed. To the extent that the characteristics of the population and their relationships to the physical environment contribute to the generation of police contact, changes in these phenomena directly impinge upon police work itself. Perhaps the most dramatic examples of this factor have been the overrunning of small village suburbs by the rapid population expansion from urban centers and changes in the core-city population characteristics (e.g., age, race, and socioeconomic class structure). Changes in such things as organization size, racial composition, training programs, patrol styles, and specialized units can sometimes be traced directly to demographic shifts within the organizational jurisdiction, although policing has been noticeably slow to respond to some dramatic demographic shifts. The advent of high-rise dwellings has practically gone unnoticed by most police departments. Likewise, minority representation among police personnel has seriously lagged behind population shifts in many central cities. Concentration of student population has generally not been reflected in police operations. Police organizations have generally not gone beyond the long-standing adult-juvenile division in police operations in responding to special segments of the population (e.g., perhaps a "Black Squad," "Indian Squad," "Senior-Citizen Squad," "High-Rise Squad," or "Student Squad" would be appropriate in some jurisdictions). Some departments, however, have created specialized divisions in "landlord-tenant relations" and "domestic relations" that may signal more sensitive internal differentiation of police response to external complexity.

Political Influences. Obviously a creature of complex political processes, the police force cannot be conceived of as completely detached from its origins and means of direction and subsistence. Budgets, major program changes, general operational procedures, and hiring and firing policies have traditionally been responsive to diverse political influences for various reasons, not the least of which is to assure basic agreement between the polity and police on policing practices. Anything else would probably be untenable in democratic government.

Controversies that surround this situation reflect the more pervasive issue of the responsiveness of dominant political organizations to the diverse orientations of a pluralistic community. The visibility, simplicity, emotionality, and drama associated with some police work provides the substance of broader political struggles within communities. Thus, a "police incident" of racial discrimination may quickly become the symbol of dominant and subordinate ethnic relations throughout a city.

The often-heard desire of police officials to be "completely neutral" is probably a wistful (perhaps undesirable) illusion. Equally unrealistic is the call from some segments of the community for the police not to be involved in politics. The mere presence of a police organization, which deftly orchestrates its operations across its jurisdiction, means that it cannot avoid the exercise of influence upon political expression. Particularly with the growth of both "unionism" and "professionalism" among police personnel, they command influence in political affairs, at least as related to their own interests and in the political affairs of their politico-organizational superiors and associates. Thus, police departments may become increasingly active (less sub rosa and passive) participants in community-political interaction. But such political expression is less likely to be manifest in open support for major party candidates than to be exerted indirectly via economic and professional avenues within governmental bureaucracies. Obviously, political involvement is a two-way street. If police organizations (or other bureaucracies) increase their efforts (directly or indirectly) to influence others, they will probably be increasingly exposed to influence by others.

Economic Influences. The direct and indirect effects of economic support for personnel, program operations, equipment, housing, etc. are as pervasive as they are critical. Funds are usually mandated by major expenditure categories through the budget-development procedure (or the granting procedure, if received from special sources such as a state's "crime commission") that restricts the police organization's ability to allocate its resources. To the extent that economic support is tenuous, long-range planning and development of new programs may be suppressed in deference to "those already working successfully" and "those that are basic." Again, this conservatizing effect is not unique to police organizations but is one process of influence between a department's economic environment and its internal organization and operations.

In addition, the nature of the demand for police services may reflect local economic conditions. Economic "booms" or "busts" have clear relevance to police operations via their responsiveness to the type of case being "input" into the organization's response system. Low order but consistent relationships between business conditions and crime and delinquency rates have been documented, although the exact causal linkages are unclear (Glaser & Rice, 1959).

Obviously, too, the basic wealth and traditional share of public funds allocated to the police function is a major underlying determinant of police organization and operations.

Technological Influences. The technology of police organization and operations is as diverse as the sources of relevant technology. Its continual change and development has consequences upon how police efforts are organized and pursued. The rapid adoption of some technology (e.g., radio communication and patrol cars) has had dramatic impact upon the availability of police for service and the quality and quantity of relations with the public; close contact with the public has been sacrificed in the quest for mobility and fast response time, which keeps officers chained to their radio-equipped vehicles. One can only speculate what police work would be like without the omnipresence of the telephone and radio. Yet, police have been laggard in use of some available technology, such as screening procedures for prospective personnel, sensitivity-training techniques, centralized and computerized records systems, program budgeting, and integrated communications networks. There has also been slowness in development of some police technology, e.g., non-harmful riot-control procedures, methods of protecting individual civil rights in regard to centralized intelligence files, and detection techniques for white-collar crimes.

Great differences appear to exist among departments in technological development. The vast majority of departments are small and, generally, these are least technologically competent. Interdepartment cooperation (sometimes statewide) in training, communications, information storage, etc. helps to overcome some disadvantages of organizational scale. Growth of strong support for law-enforcement improvement at state and national levels has been focused upon the diffusion of available technology, particularly of the mechanical sort, and police organizations are responsive to new technologies. Each new technology, however, may occasion new organizational configurations, training procedures, field operations, staff functions, and policing "styles."

It is apparent that policing is performed under the influence of various aspects of its environment, and harmony with its environment is particularly critical to police departments. In their sensitivity to both "input" and "output" conditions of their operations, police practices are guided by something similar to a perishable-market principle; the products being accepted must be examined to assess their being moved effectively and expeditiously on a chancy market. Police organizations are disposed toward sufficient control and predictability at both ends of the process to minimize their "loss of inventory." Awareness and sensitivity to environmental influences are necessary concerns for individual officers on the street as well as for those at supervisory and policy levels.

Intraorganizational Features

Police departments are often described in terms of their divisions and subdivisions and the distribution of activities among them. Though typologies of organizational structures and processes are in their infancy, police departments might variously be categorized as "integrative," "political," or "service" organizations (Hall, 1972: 12–14). More descriptively, police departments have been referred to as paramilitaristic, highly bureaucratized, centralized, slow changing, monolithic in their structure and activities, and relatively "closed." Some available data help us understand to what extent police organizations reflect these vaguely defined characteristics.

It is common to note offhandedly the "paramilitary" nature of the police. Though the meaning of militarism is seldom, if ever, set forth, it presumably refers primarily to the wide use of uniforms, military argot, and the police capability of using organized physical force to defend or achieve a prespecified geographical objective. Some would also attribute a military "mentality" and operational "style" or "presence" to police organizations.

It is an open question as to whether the rank structure and its accompanying discriminations are any more meaningful within police departments than they are in a wide range of other formal organizations. Also, one might observe the practice of many goal-oriented organizations to operate with notions of being on the "offensive" or "defensive," solving problems with "task forces," fighting "battles" with adversaries, and creating "teams" for special action. All of this suggests that "paramilitarism" may not be a useful typological dimension on which to differentiate police from other urban agencies or on which to rank departments. Not only are the police (along with other public-service agencies) attempting to divest themselves of the public image of being rigidly centralized, bureaucratized, and "militaristic," but there seems to be strong evidence that the police in English-speaking countries, not born of military parents, never really measured up to their public image in this regard.

The obvious practice of urban police departments of hiring tradition-oriented, young males who (because of "veterans preference") are likely to have had military experience has undoubtedly resulted in an overrepresentation of military veterans in the organization. In fact, the awareness of military ranks, courtesies, planning, and operations probably contributes to the department's ability to function. It may be that the notions of military operations are critical inputs into department operations (particularly the patrol divisions) since they may offset very strong de-bureaucratizing forces at work within police departments and a rather weak and non-innovative police organizational management.

Those who have systematically observed police operations first hand, however, cannot help but be impressed with their nonmilitary and nonbureaucratic nature. In actual practice, in the critical aspects of responsiveness to top command, identity with a chain of command culminating in the ranking officer, and adherence to notions of centralized communications, control, and supervision, police departments are profoundly nonmilitary. Put in alternative rhetoric, much of the potential militarizing and bureaucratizing effects of selective recruiting from the military, in-house training, standardized dress, formal organizational structure and procedures, and so forth is neutralized by the de-bureaucratizing effects of relatively isolated and atomized police operations in detached individual or two-man patrol or investigation teams, under weak or nonexistent supervision, operating within an organizational ethos of the individualization of each case and each officer's solution to it.

The conversion of external power influences into internal power manifestations is not well understood in an organization with strong de-bureaucratizing influences. That such a conversion process is likely to be very inefficient is evidenced by the startling lack of impact of the policy and power posturing of top management on the lower ranks of large city departments. For example, attempts to change large departments may require that simultaneous change-inducing influences be applied at all levels of the organization (perhaps with the strongest influences being applied at the bottom of the bureaucratic hierarchy), or it may require bringing the organization closer to the highly rational bureaucratic model. Of course (and this is just one instance of organizational variety), small or more specialized police departments might respond to efforts to change in a very different manner.

Seen in the above general perspective, the development of police-department policy has occurred in relatively rarified surroundings. Not that department policy is totally detached from reality, but it has tended to be status quo rather than change-oriented, sketchy at best and nonexistent at worst, frequently uninterpreted or uninterpretable in terms of field operations and sometimes not reflective of the current realities of police work, which includes a maze of organizational tasks.

While such a situation may be dysfunctional to those endeavors that depend upon greater vertical unification or organizational efforts, it provides the opportunity for a fantastic range of responses to situations that come to the department's attention. Not unlike the individualized justice orientations of the juvenile court or the professional latitude specifically provided school social workers, the thwarting of power and policy application by police organizations allows them the luxury (which sometimes runs amuck) of differential organizational response where it might not otherwise be. This suggests that, unless carefully provided for, a more highly integrated or professionalized department might well inadvertently sacrifice some of its response flexibility.

The opportunity for the police to practice the widest possible range of field operations in behalf of their department, however, does not assure their doing so. Just as individual officers develop a loosely integrated "style" of operations in investigations, police-citizen encounters, courtroom testimony, etc., departments and their divisions have developed a restricted number of responses to reoccurring police situations, which impose limits on the possible range of organizational actions. The extent and nature of this informal organizational policy undoubtedly reflects long-range inputs of individual and organizational experience, conditions of official policy, and relevant laws (Gardiner, 1969). It appears to play a major role in the socialization of new members of the department, the decision-making process at all levels, and the presentation of the department to those in its environment.

Occasionally, and sometimes dramatically, the organization's official and unofficial policy may be in conflict. The resolution of such situations depends upon a host of factors, but since official policy is notoriously vulnerable to distortion in actual practice, one might presume it more likely in the usual department for a compromise resolution to be more heavily influenced by its informal policy.

In these situations, organizational-control structure and processes are difficult to maintain. Socialization at the time of entry into the department, if not effectively reinforced, is prey to existing perspectives and standards of behavior. Bifurcation of attitudes and activities into the "official" and "practical" institutionalizes the lack of integration of policy. The realities of police work may thus thwart efforts to control, change, supervise, or otherwise manipulate the behavior of individual officers or of the police collectively. Dramatic cases in point are those of gross ineffectiveness, brutality, racial prejudice, and corruption in spite of repeated "shake-ups" and "reforms." Although it would be inaccurate to conclude that change, sometimes rapid change, does not occur within departments on these matters, successful instances are more likely to be cited where departments are small, well integrated and supervised, with strong personal leadership. Otherwise, efforts to change are likely to be absorbed into the "official" rhetoric and interaction of top police personnel and relevant outsiders but not deeply into the "practical" behavior patterns of organizational life. Although this phenomenon is undoubtedly present within all formal organizations, particularly in public bureaucracies staffed with career personnel, it is probably strongest in police organizations with their unusual exposure to collective public concern but relative immunity from both collective public scrutiny and internal supervision of daily operations. Unless specifically supportive of the realities of daily routine, directives from the organizational hierarchy are not very competitive with the experientially derived procedures already practiced.

Perhaps the most critical unsolved problem confronting organizations dealing in human services is the resolution of the conflict between the need for specialized personnel and the need to deal holistically with clients. Configuring organizational response to provide a wide spectrum of services in complex situations and yet insuring their expertise through specialization is a continual source of organizational strain. Recent emphasis on the development of "team policing" and on different "levels" of police personnel (e.g., community-service officers, police officer, police agent) are attempts to benefit from both perspectives.

SOCIAL INTERACTION BETWEEN THE POLICE AND THE POLICED

While social psychologists may use the term *interaction* with various technical meanings, students of police have seldom used it with other than a common-sense connotation.[1] Generally, they have meant behavior of either a verbal or nonverbal kind directed by police and policed toward each other in a face-to-face situation (hereafter referred to simply as "interaction"). A situation in which such interaction occurs is frequently termed a police-citizen encounter (hereafter referred to simply as an "encounter").[2]

Earlier concerns were with qualities of interaction that led to police violence (Westley, 1953, 1956; Dodd, 1967; Derbyshire, 1968; Hahn, 1971), good or bad police-public relations (Gourley, 1954; Misner, 1967), or decisions by officers to take juveniles into custody (Piliavin & Briar, 1964; Black & Reiss, 1970); and more generally, with such exercises of police discretion as the decision to arrest (J. Goldstein, 1960; LaFave, 1962a, 1962b; Banton, 1964; H. Goldstein, 1967; Black, 1968; Reiss, 1971), or the decision to make out an offense report (Black, 1970). The nature of interaction that led to violations of civil liberties (Hall, 1953; Sowle, 1966; Chevigny, 1969), as well as strategies of interaction in handling specific categories of the policed (Cumming et al., 1965; Skolnick, 1966; Bittner, 1967a, 1967b; Parnas, 1967; Bard, 1969; Bayley & Mendelsohn, 1969; Rubenstein, 1973), has also been considered. Some attention has been given to interaction and collective violence (Skolnick, 1969; Feld, 1971). In addition to interaction between the police and the policed, there are isolated references in the literature to interaction between the police and other functionaries in the correctional system and allied professions (Remington, 1965; Skolnick, 1966).

---

1. Social psychologists differ in their emphasis on the importance of data of subjective self-reports on the meaning of visible acts as opposed to objective "other" reports of outer visible acts, verbal or nonverbal, which persons direct toward one another. Blumer states: "Symbolic interaction involves *interpretation*, or ascertaining the meaning of the actions or remarks of the other person, and *definition*, or conveying indications to another person as to how he is to act" (1970: 285). Such a definition might be contrasted with Thibaut and Kelley: "By interaction it is meant that they emit behavior in each other's presence, they create products for each other, or they communicate with each other. In every case we would identify as an instance of interaction, there is at least the possibility that the actions of each person affect the other" (1959:10). Observational studies of interactions cited herein necessarily are limited to coding or rating the external aspect of interaction, or alternately, interpreting it from the perspective of the observer, since there is little opportunity to assess the inner states of actors in an ongoing encounter. For other discussions, see McCall and Simmons (1966), Argyle (1969), Chapple (1970), Douglas (1970), Cardwell (1971), and Shaw (1971).

2. The term *encounter* probably first appears in the literature on police in Piliavin and Briar (1964). The term probably comes from Goffman (1961) in which it is defined as a "focused gathering" or "situated activity system." "Focused interaction occurs when people effectively agree to sustain for a time a single focus of cognitive and visual attention . . . " (Goffman, 1961:7). He, in turn, refers to Borgatta and Cottrell (1955), but the term does not appear in their article.

Because of relative inattention to interaction from one or another systematic, theoretical, or social-psychological perspective, interaction between police and the policed has been attributed much more uniqueness than it possesses (but see Tauber, 1967; Hartjen, 1972). This has been compounded by lack of a comparative perspective in much of the literature, and by the focus on violence and violations of civil liberties. Possibly this focus is as much a product of the stereotyping of the police by the academic community and other social groupings as it is descriptive of the police themselves, and it allows much police violence to be interpreted as secondary deviance (for example, see Dodd, 1967).

The Bare Bones of Interaction[3]

The great majority of encounters possess the following abstract composition: One actor in the encounter (the officer) occupies a position of high status and power. Not only are other actors typically of lower status but they either need the assistance of the officer, or stand to incur costs from his action. The assistance may be official recognition of a complaint, protection from harm, legal information, medical aid, advice, or psychological support. Costs may range from receipt of a tongue lashing, to a ticket (and, thus, literally a financial cost), to a beating, or loss of freedom. Police possess an even more ultimate power, the right to use deadly force. The circumstances under which they may use their powers are frequently emergency and crisis situations in which the bargaining position of other actors is weakened, or cases in which citizens are caught committing a violation and are thus on the defensive, or even defenseless.

Both common-sense observation and small-group research indicate that several effects are likely to follow from a position of high status and power in a small group. More communications are directed to that position. More of these communications are likely to be positive. The occupant of the higher-status position is not likely to conform willingly to the expectations of those with less status unless he already possesses similar expectations himself. Typically, he is also treated with deference. Some studies indicate the persons higher in status and power are less apt to be perceived as either likable or as desirable social partners.

In an encounter an officer is likely to act and to be treated as any person of high status and power. Indeed, he comes to expect this. In this he is not unlike many others who because of their position expect others to acknowledge their authority by directing communication to them, treating them with deference, and following their directions. An encounter, considered as a human group, is not unlike many other groups: teacher and students, foreman and workers, physician and patient, nurse and patient, father and traditional family, boss and secretary. All expect their suggestions or orders to be followed. All expect to be centers of communication in the group, at least insofar as group tasks are concerned. All take for granted a certain deference from those of lesser status within the group. While punishment in these groups may not be quite so drastic if orders are not obeyed or deference is not displayed as in an encounter, it may be painful, nonetheless.

Persons of high status and power keep themselves at a certain social distance

---

3. The schematic orientation that follows draws selectively from much of the small-groups literature. While ours is not an exchange perspective, we do utilize the concept of *comparison level*. For an excellent introduction to leadership in small groups, power in small groups, communication networks in small groups, and the like, see Shaw (1971). An annotated bibliography of the police literature may be found in Gupta et al. (1972).

from those of lower status within the group. Such is the nature of much interaction between officers and citizens. Through a cool, impersonal demeanor the officer usually maintains distance between himself and his clients. In this he embodies the very canons of most professions: medicine, social work, or law. He cannot become too personally involved as this would constrain the use of his power and limit his discretion to use the alternatives he has at his disposal.

Officers learn to expect others to acknowledge their status and power, for most citizens extend them compliance and deference. They develop a standard from experience by which they judge the interaction that takes place in each encounter (Thibaut & Kelley, 1959). When citizen interaction falls below their standard, they utilize corrective sanctions. In this they are no different from others with high status and power. On the other hand, if their status and power are recognized through compliance and deference, they will give assistance and possibly withhold punishment.

The Function and Contents of Interaction

When an officer is called to an encounter, or when he initiates one himself, he is faced with three basic problems: establishing his authority, collecting sufficient information to structure the situation relative to his job, and accomplishing an outcome satisfying the requirements of his job.[4] Policing is work, and consequently is task-oriented. Yet both the officer's position and role as well as the initial definition of the situation are often ambiguous, either because circumstances have changed since the request for assistance was first received, because not enough information was initially available, or because citizens do not fully understand the rules and norms governing the officer's authority.

The Problem of Authority

Studies of groups have distinguished between authority relations in informal and formal groups. In informal groups authority may derive from custom or from special abilities that an individual may bring to the group and that make him more effective in influencing group decisions. On the other hand, in formal groups, authority, at least in part, is associated with position and, for that reason, is impersonal. In informal groups the process of interaction may gradually result in differentiation of individuals in terms of power and the growth of a set of group norms governing its exercise. Formal groups are hierarchical in form, with authority delegated and delimited, though informal power relationships also develop.

Encounters constitute an especially complex problem. While policemen are specifically "authorized" by law as well as custom to exercise specific powers, they do so across the boundaries of the formal police organization and over citizens in other formal or informal groups (Scott et al., 1967; Scott, 1970). These encounters have certain special characteristics that make citizen endorsement of authority problematic:

1. Citizens and officers in the encounter are usually unknown to one another.
2. Certain of the citizens participate in the group involuntarily.
3. The encounter may take place under conditions of extraordinary emotional stress.

---

4. An excellent discussion of many of these factors may be found in McNamara (1967). An intriguing method of studying police decision processes may be found in Sullivan and Siegel (1972) ; also see Sykes and Clark (1972). For a different approach, see Sacks (1972).

4. The encounter exists, i.e., citizens and officers interact with one another for a very brief period of time (probably about 13 minutes on the average).

5. Citizens do not have experience interacting with officers, so both parties feel uncertain about the expectations of the other.

Briefly stated, encounters have the characteristics of anonymity, coercion, stress, brevity, and little rehearsal.

Authority may pertain to three aspects of the encounter: presence, process, and disposition. While citizens may recognize the authority of officers to be present, they may not recognize the officers' authority to demand certain behavior during the encounter or even the possibility of certain outcomes. For instance, a citizen may insist that he has a "right" to swear in his own home, and that the officer has no "right" to enforce decorum there. Or a citizen may insist that an officer has no right to make an arrest. It follows that from the officer's perspective authority remains problematic throughout the encounter. Not only does he need to establish his right to be present, but once that is granted, his right to control the process and outcome may be questioned.

The problem of authority is even more complicated by the fact that officers are frequently called to intervene in situations over which they do *not* have authorized power, but in which they appear to have substantial endorsed power. This occurs when they regulate private disturbances at the request of citizens. Were they to refuse to do so, they would be viewed by the citizenry as shirking their job, so they must improvise authority as the interaction proceeds. In this sense an encounter is much different from a trial, for the rights of the actors are formed in the process of interaction rather than governed by formal rule or ceremony. In an encounter the self-confidence and bearing of the officer plays an important part.

When the patrolman arrives, his status and power are communicated by a variety of symbolic paraphernalia. Not the least of these is the uniform together with his weapons, which are denied most other citizens. Officers often announce their presence by calling out the name of their position: "Police!" In well over 90 percent of situations these are enough to lead citizens to legitimate their presence, and even when some do not, they are on the defensive. Symbolically, it might even be argued that an officer brings with him some connotation of the "sacred"; that is, his role symbolizes the legal basis of society, embodies, as it were, the foundations of the moral order. He must be treated with deference and as a person apart from others.

There seem to be three distinct and different reasons for the small but significant percentage of encounters where the legitimacy of the officer's presence is not accepted:

1. Citizens are emotionally caught up in their own conflict or mundane affairs and fail to attend to his presence.

2. A citizen may have self-consciously and deliberately violated the legal order and, therefore, recognizes that the officer will impose costs upon him that he is unwilling to pay voluntarily. By lying or escaping he may seek to defer or evade his debt.

3. A citizen of a special group may not recognize that any violation of the legal order has occurred, and, therefore, deny the legitimacy of police intervention. Subcultural or special-interest-group norms may be different from general legal norms and, to the extent these are given precedence over general legal norms, the intervention will be seen as a violation of these norms. In such cases, the officer is not only not granted legitimacy, but is seen as actually violating norms himself.

Officers *must* establish their authority in all cases where a violation may have occurred since the criminal code must be followed, except insofar as the charge that may ultimately be made against the citizen may be modified (for instance, intent, or premeditation). In other cases they must "create" their authority where it does not exist.

Citizen Failure to Attend. Officers most frequently establish authority by displaying either forceful verbal or physical behavior. Two citizens caught up in a fight will be ordered in a loud voice to "Break it up!" If they do not comply, physical restraint will be used, but generally the citizens will not be further attacked unless they turn their blows against the officer. After they are separated, they are forced to attend to the officer's questions or rebuke and in this manner their preoccupation with the original dispute is gradually overcome. They may be taken to separate spaces —different rooms or corners of a large room—and interrogated. In these cases the officer's authority is not usually in question after its initial assertion, even by the combatants.

A second and usually less difficult instance of failure to attend involves a citizen caught up in doing what he may consider to be lawful. Many drunks disturbing others probably do not consider their behavior illegal, nor do they self-consciously lie down in the streets to break the law. Persons holding parties do not ask their guests to be noisy or turn up the stereo just to be objectionable. Lights burn out and mufflers rust without drivers' awareness. Couples may enjoy fighting (or loving), not realizing that they are keeping their neighbors up. In these cases citizens are not caught up in their passions so much as in their own mundane affairs. It is usually only necessary to relay the neighbor's complaint or explain the law for legitimacy to be granted.

Deliberate Violation. The case of the citizen who has deliberately violated the law is quite different. He may even agree, for instance, that there should be laws against theft. In fact, attitude studies show that criminals are in many ways very conservative, but have decided to violate the law. When officers intervene in this pursuit, the violator must decide what strategy to adopt. He may seek to resist and/or escape, but this may involve costs over and above the costs of the original violation. Less serious costs are incurred by trying to talk his way out of it with the officers, or retaining an attorney to talk his way out of it with a judge or jury. In such cases the officers' authority is not as much at issue as is their power. Both the violators and the officers know this, and the "game" is essentially which can overcome the other or at least lose with minimized cost. Where officers define the situation as a contest of power rather than authority, they will generally seek to minimize costs to themselves by the use of overwhelming force. By the threat of such force they seek to intimidate the others into surrender with no loss to themselves. Officers seldom seriously consider such combat in terms of either sportsmanship or a fair fight any more than do the violators. The possible costs are far too serious. They understand that an opponent who stands to lose four or five years of his life in prison for the commission of a felony is willing to use whatever power he has at his disposal to avoid that outcome, even if this involves injury or death to the officer. It is for this reason that officers confronted by such an opponent seek to maximize the likelihood that he will suffer costs even greater than several years' imprisonment unless he surrenders and goes peaceably.

Subcultural Differences. It is the third instance that is most baffling to the officer, partly because, phenomenologically, the situations that arise from differences between subcultural or interest-group norms and general legal norms appear on the surface like instances of one of the two previous cases. For instance, the law distinguishes between public and private space, yet citizens who know the distinction will behave inappropriately. An officer has difficulty, however, in distinguishing those temporarily aberrant from those acting on entirely different norms. Ghetto youth, for instance, may treat a street corner as a private place and behave accordingly (Werthman & Piliavin, 1967; Suttles, 1968). When they and the police come into conflict, both may feel with entire justification that the other is behaving without legitimacy. Such conflicts may be handled in the short run in two ways: (1) one or the other, or both, view it as a simple contest of power; or (2) some temporary compromise of norms may be negotiated in which, for instance, strangers will be allowed to pass through the youths' private (public) space without molestation in return for quasi-official recognition by the officers of the rights of the youth to that space. Some experienced officers recognize the differing norms of subcultures, and come to terms with them even, on occasion, enforcing those norms when intragroup conflict occurs, while other officers wage a continuous contest of power against the members of such subcultures. It is this latter contest that festers continually within subcultural territories of our cities. Here a basic issue of public policy is involved: to what extent and how quickly should subcultures be required to conform to general legal norms? Unfortunately, officers are frequently forced to answer this question in practice without much guidance from other sectors of society.

Task-Relevant Situation Structuring

Control of Communication. Since officers seldom know ahead of time the exact circumstances of the request for police service, or in an "on-scene," whether their interpretation of the situation is correct, they must quickly structure the situation in regard to their own participation. To do so they must control the communication network within the encounter so as to elicit pertinent information immediately. For this reason, officers often appear abrupt and imperative. In circumstances in which there is often either much disorder or in which the expectations of all concerned are unclear, they must create order, at least for themselves. In addition, their control of communication helps insure their status and authority in the encounter. The brief time they have to collect information is in contrast to almost all other helping or controlling professions. Citizens present often do not appreciate the time constraints under which the officer is working or the nature of the information he must collect.

Information Required. The information the officer must elicit is specific to his authority and customary goals. He must gather it following criteria from the law on what information is relevant and on the procedures of collection that are permissible. The law lays down the conditions under which an act is illegal and what aspects are legal. For instance, if a couple is married and has a fight, there is no immediate way in which an officer can force one of them to leave because both have legal access to the private property they rent or own.

The law almost always pertains to particular identities, always so when a case comes to court. Therefore, officers must seek information not only about precipitating events, but on the identities of the participants, and on the actions of each one specifically, presuming that the later uses to which the information will be put are governed by very explicit evidentiary constraints. Few other helping or controlling professions are faced with such a problem. A social-worker's decision of eligibility seldom faces such strict review, and it is seldom that a physician's decision to recommend surgery is reviewed by other physicians. In what court is a television-repairman's judgment of the "problem" of a set tried?

Any Civil Libertarian would heartily endorse the right of citizens to order the police to leave, but the "service" or "advice" that an officer may render cannot be given unless he has a legitimate right to be present. Where citizens are in conflict, it is unlikely that both will take an officer's advice if he is not authorized to be present and to give it. Suppose, by analogy, the legislature authorized a physician to enter homes wherever he had reason to believe a serious illness might exist, or to detain citizens on the street if upon inspection they appeared to be suffering from some illness, or if a dentist were to stop a citizen and give him a ticket for tooth decay. Would not the relationship between physician and patient change radically? It is the legal context, then, that not only shapes the relationships between officers and citizens but even shapes the information-seeking process during an encounter.

In structuring the situation the officer seeks information relative to the criteria on which the authorization for his presence is based:

1. Has a violation of the law occurred?
2. If it has, is the violator identifiable?
3. If it has, is it within the discretionary power of the officer?
4. If it is not within his discretionary powers, should he take extralegal action? If so, what?
5. If it is within his discretionary powers, what action should he take?

He will also be attentive to clues indicative of the citizen's willingness to abide by the rules of the social order after he has left, or whether the situation is likely to become more serious if he does not take decisive action now.

The request for police intervention (or the officer's decision to intervene pro-actively), as well as the precipitating event itself, are exceptional and often intensely personal to the citizen, whereas they are generally routine to the officer (Bordua & Reiss, 1967). What might be a major catastrophe in a citizen's life an officer may soon forget. In this regard, his attitude is not unlike that of the surgeon to whom a major operation is routine, when compared with that of his patient.

Officers are also rather sophisticated about the "stories" with which citizens make sense out of events and justify their actions. People suffering a crisis narrow the boundaries of their perception and view the event in an even more subjective manner than their usual life experiences. But the police are usually involved, and unavoidably so, in "somebody else's troubles." They see or suspect that there are other definitions of the situation quite as legitimate as the complainant's.

Since officers are not advocates of any of the theoretical faiths that pervade the social sciences, they believe that events have knowable causes, and that among these causes are human agents who act with intent (Heider, 1958; Wilson, 1970). They also believe that these actors possess positive and negative sentiments that may motivate their action. With such common-sense constructs they seek to structure the situation as quickly as possible and place it in an appropriate category of their experience; they do not use constructs for explaining human action that a Freudian, cognitive theorist, or Skinnerian might use.

Finally, the officer's perspective is unlike the citizen's in that he is both more self-conscious of the limitations as well as the extent of his authority. In many jurisdictions, an officer has no authority to arrest, even if an offense has occurred, if the offense was a misdemeanor that he did not personally witness. Many citizens, meanwhile, have a naive idea of justice, informed primarily by the heart and a sense of personal outrage. The officer on the other hand has a sophisticated view of justice, often turned to cynicism as he learns further technicalities of the law (Skolnick, 1966; Niederhoffer, 1967).

Task Accomplishment as Negotiated and Coerced Compliance

Observers who have limited their attention to deference and authority have failed to appreciate the extent to which most police work involves the negotiation of compliance rather than arrest for a legal violation. In this regard police work involves judicious use of "the carrot and the stick." If the police arrested every violator they could arrest, the correctional system would break down under the load. If the bookkeeping and drunkometer tests did not take so long, the officers in any major city could make several thousand arrests on any Friday or Saturday night.

Strategies of Negotiated Compliance.

Strategies of Negotiated Compliance. Etzioni (1961) has proposed a general typology of compliance in which he distinguishes three ideal types: coercive, utilitarian, and normative.[5] Coercive compliance is achieved through the use or threat of naked power. Utilitarian compliance is gained through negotiation of advantages that will accrue to the person who complies, most frequently, material advantages. Normative compliance is gained by convincing the subject that he "should" comply, that it is morally right that he should do so. Etzioni also proposes certain ideal types of involvement: alienative, calculative, and moral. When one actor is in a subordinate status to another, his relationship to the superordinate power is alienative if proceeding from compulsion; calculative if from the expectation of material or symbolic gain; and moral if proceeding from the conviction of the moral right of the superordinate to exercise authority and his moral imperative to comply. While these are ideal types and not empirical categories, they may provide a convenient framework in which to examine strategies of negotiated compliance.

Contrary to stereotype, it appears that officers usually seek either utilitarian or normative compliance. Once they decide that action is necessary, whether in a legal or extralegal framework, they seek to persuade the citizen(s) involved to accept an alternative that will constitute a temporary resolution of the situation. They do this even when, technically, they could take a citizen into custody. Proposed alternatives cannot be described exhaustively, but they appear to be of at least four kinds: (1) discontinuance or abatement of activity, (2) change of locale of activity, (3) different means of activity, and (4) structuring an interruption.

Where misdemeanors have or are taking place or where no legal violation has occurred, officers often will not arrest unless the activity continues after a verbal warning has been given. Most minor disturbances are settled in this manner. Loud arguing, parties, and other nuisances will be handled routinely by warning the parties to discontinue the activity, or to "keep it down." Sometimes, but not often, such warnings will be given on two or three different occasions before an arrest is made.

Certain activities are the object of police concern not because they *occur*, but because of *where* they occur. Citizens are encouraged to drink, make love, and dance in certain places but not in others. Police routinely advise them when their activity is occurring in an inappropriate location and sometimes even suggest an alternate locale.

---

5. Although we have not discussed his dynamic hypothesis concerning the shift of compliance structures from incongruent to congruent types, it might be intriguing to examine many problems of the police from such a perspective.

Citizens frequently use legally inappropriate means to settle disputes or to obtain certain satisfactions. Where neighbors or marriage partners come to blows, for instance, officers will advise them of the inappropriateness of the means, and then outline socially approved means. They will advise a wife to go to the city attorney and file a complaint, or if disputes recur over time, even ask bluntly why the couple doesn't get a divorce if they cannot get along together.

On the common-sense view that passions cool and persons become more thoughtful with time, officers often use what might be called the "intermission" strategy of handling disputes. If a couple are fighting, despite the fact that they have no legal authority in the matter, they will seek to get one of the couple to go to a hotel for the night so that both disputants can cool off. If space is more of an issue than time, they may order an obnoxious customer not to come to an establishment any more, although they have no legal basis for the order.

In persuading citizens to comply with their alternate strategies, they may use all three kinds of power. In most extralegal encounters and encounters involving misdemeanor-type violations, while there is the connotation of coercive power in the presence of the uniform, the officer's appeal is to the moral sensibilities or self-interest of the violator. The statement of the law in itself is a moral appeal in that it carries the implication that it "should" be obeyed. Deliberate disobedience after warning places the violator in a different moral category from one who violated the law unintentionally. Officers assume first that "a word to the wise is sufficient."

If a moral appeal is ineffective, then officers will combine the threat of coercion with an appeal to self-interest. Not only "should" the citizen obey, but it is in his interest to do so, because if he doesn't he will incur other costs, not the least of which will be loss of freedom, bail, and possible fine or imprisonment.

It should be noted that the use of arrest is not so much a means of obtaining compliance as of halting noncompliance. Arrest prevents the citizen from continuing to do whatever the officer has judged is contrary to law. There are many activities from which citizens can choose alternatives all of which are within the law. Arrest is exceptional, but it is a means of enforced discontinuance.

Failure of Negotiation. Arrests that do take place appear to result from four sets of circumstances:

1. Citizens have failed to acknowledge the legitimacy of the officer's intervention.

2. While they may have acknowledged the legitimacy, they have refused to accept alternatives to arrest offered by the officer in the process of negotiation.

3. Their commission of an illegal act may have been so blatant or threatening to the safety of others (though not necessarily serious in a statutory sense) as to constitute a good "symbolic" arrest.

4. The act committed is a felony of such seriousness as to be unnegotiable so far as arrest is concerned. The violator must be apprehended and transported to jail as expeditiously as possible and in such a manner as to insure the greatest probability of conviction.[6]

If the officer determines that there is a legal basis for his presence, then arrest will be the fate of the uncooperative. If he can find no legal basis, then he must leave. Since officers are unwilling to have citizens think they can safely ignore their presence,

---

6. While Black (1968) discusses cases in which officers have not made arrests or completed offense reports concerning felonies, in our own experience this would be highly unusual. Perhaps these are departmental differences.

chances are great that if there is no legal basis one will be fabricated, or seldom-used laws will be invoked. Citizens who have used profanity against the officer will be so charged. If a drunk and disputatious husband cannot be arrested in his own home, he may be invited outside on the pretext of a private talk, where he will be arrested for public drunkenness. Such cases may not ever be tried, but the inconvenience of arrest is enough to make the citizen think twice. Officers do not wish their authority to be questioned because it is only by being present at least for a time that they can gain enough information to make a decision. In most instances where officers seek to be present, they are doing so in good faith—that is, they have reason to believe that someone needs their assistance or that a violation is occurring. While they do abuse this authority on occasion, they do not do so routinely, and, in fact, in most cases they are there at the request of a citizen rather than on their own initiative.

Once an alternative is refused, officers frequently feel they have no choice but to arrest if there is a legal basis for the complaint. Arrest in such situations is often a sign of the failure rather than the success of an officer, and a department as well as fellow officers will not judge a colleague favorably who must constantly resort to arrest in routine encounters. Arrests are expensive in terms of time, manpower, and money, not to speak of human relations. A capable officer should be competent in the strategy of negotiation to secure compliance short of arrest in most cases.

Certain offenses, while minor in themselves, may be so blatant or such a threat to the public safety that an arrest is much more likely. Officers will often ignore a driver who, while perhaps drunk, appears to be in control of his car. On the other hand, if he weaves erratically, violates the speeding law, or makes himself obvious by putting on his brakes suddenly or backing into the car behind when trying to get out of his parking place, then his chance of arrest will be greater. Many violations will be tolerated unless they have the appearance of a challenge to the officers or are so obvious as to draw the attention of other citizens.

Finally, where a felony has occurred, such as murder, forcible rape, aggravated assault, robbery, felonious theft, or burglary, arrest is nonnegotiable. Such arrests are "good" from the officer's point of view, ones about which he can feel a degree of satisfaction. In encounters in which an arrest for a felony is the officer's intent, he will seek to control the behavior of the suspect as quickly and effectively as possible so as to minimize danger to officers and other citizens, and to prevent escape. He is authorized to use deadly force if necessary. Interaction in these instances has nothing to do with the decision to arrest and is frequently mutually impolite and hostile.

Extralegal Use of Violence. Officers are not authorized to punish suspects. While cases in which they use unreasonable force in administering "street justice" constitute a small percentage of police-citizen contacts, they are important not only because extralegal use of violence is itself against the law, but also because such incidents are more apt to become newsworthy. Thus, these events give a false impression of the nature of most policemen and of police work.

Extralegal violence, or the threat of its use, appears to have two sources insofar as these pertain to social interaction: (1) the targets of such violence are usually thought by officers to be low-status persons who should express more deference to officers than they do; and (2) such persons usually have committed minor offenses, but in the course of interacting with the officer refuse to openly acknowledge his authority or openly insult him. Extralegal beatings have been observed where a citizen has spit in the officer's face while being booked, fought back and cursed the officer in the course of apprehension for drunkenness, or appeared to disregard the officer's authority (from the officer's perspective) before others. Such extralegal violence is quite different from that displayed by groups of officers at mass demonstrations, since demonstrations are a collective phenomenon, not a phenomenon of relatively small, person-to-person groups.

Extralegal violence may also occur at the end of activities that have occasioned officers much stress and danger, as at the end of a high-speed chase. It may be a form of tension release, or an expression of frustration against the person or persons who created the danger. It may also occur in cases in which officers feel no punishment will be forthcoming.

In a very few cases, extralegal violence may be used against an alleged violator who has committed an especially outrageous crime, but who has "gotten off" because of legal technicalities even though officers are personally certain of his guilt. In such cases violence or its threat is used with premeditation and intent. Thus, a suspect who was freed, but whom officers were personally certain had tortured a woman's baby with boiling water in order to force her into prostitution, was taken to a lonely place and told that he would be killed if he remained in the city. In many ways officers show less moral outrage than the average citizen and for this reason they are often more tolerant of deviance than many of their neighbors might be, but in exceptional cases, they take punishment into their own hands. Trends that accentuate the importance of technical as opposed to actual guilt are likely to increase utilization of such extralegal means.

In describing the phases of interaction in an encounter, we have concentrated on the most problematic cases, that is, those cases in which a suspect or a suspect and a complainant are present, and in which the officer must make a decision related to disposition. In most patrol work these constitute only a small proportion of encounters (routine motor-vehicle stops excepted).

THE BROADER CONTEXT OF ENCOUNTERS

Location of Police Activities

The existence of private places in political democracies, which police may not enter without invitation or probable cause, limits their opportunity to gain knowledge of both serious and petty violations, especially in large cities. Unless they have reason to believe that a felony is being committed, they may not enter without either permission or a warrant. This restricts their knowledge of so-called crimes without victims, as well as of many serious crimes against both persons and property. Even in public places police are dependent upon citizen cooperation for information. Most uniformed police activity results from citizen "demand" (Stinchcombe, 1963; Black, 1968).

Initiation of Activities

The distinction between citizen-initiated activities (termed *reactive*) and officer-initiated activities (termed *proactive*) is not idle, for the likelihood that police authority will be acknowledged in an encounter is greater when the citizen has initiated it than when the officer has (Black, 1968; Reiss, 1971).[7] That the source of initiation may have practical effects is evident from examination of many encounters described

---

7. These terms are adopted from Black and Reiss who indicate that original usage pertained to "analysis of the origins of individual action." Also see Murray (1951).

by those concerned with police brutality and civil liberties. Almost all encounters resulting in complaints against the police were police-initiated (Chevigny, 1969).

Studies of police work based on scientific sampling and systematic observation have shown that the origin of interaction differs according to the division of labor within police departments.[8] Proactive police work is carried out by special squads: traffic, morals, vice, narcotics (Stinchcombe, 1963; Skolnick, 1966). Such work is police-initiated because the relevant laws pertain to conduct about which citizens seldom initiate complaints, though police are charged with control of such conduct— gambling, prostitution, homosexuality, sexually oriented entertainment, and the illegal possession or sale of alcohol, drugs, and other controlled substances—violations sometimes termed "crimes without victims."

Reactive encounters are not by any means confined to violations of the criminal code.[9] While citizens define nearly 60 percent of their calls as criminal, police consider only about one-third of the criminally defined citizen calls as such (Reiss, 1971). Both technical and legal considerations, as well as the orientation of police to resolve an encounter by some means short of arrest or an official offense report, result in this dramatic reduction (Black, 1970). No doubt it is due to police awareness that they normally do not arrest in many cases where they could do so that leads to resentment against the courts for disallowing the actual arrests they do make.

Studies of the distribution and flow of police activities indicate them to be of approximately the following ranks:

1. Between one-third and one-fourth of police activity involves no citizen contact. False alarms, arrival after citizens have dispersed, and calls to investigate silent alarms in commercial establishments, as well as a wide range of other suspicious circumstances, account for most of these.

2. The next largest proportion of encounters involves contact with a complainant. They seldom involve conflict but require the officer to decide whether or not to make an official report of a crime. Here police are called upon to collect information, make social acknowledgment of the existence of a violation, satisfy insurance-company requirements, calm and reassure the citizen, and in some cases call in other public services or other units of the police department.[10]

---

8. In addition to Black (1968) and Lundman (1972), there are a number of other dissertations that include observational data on uniformed patrol. The only study that seems to approach the extent of quantitative data of Reiss and his colleagues (Black & Reiss, 1970; Reiss, 1971) is that of Sykes and Clark (1972). The Reiss data were gathered during the summer of 1966 utilizing thirty-six observers in three major cities, oversampling high crime rate areas, and including about 5,000 police-citizen incidents. The Sykes and Clark data were gathered in two major cities and three suburbs and include a sample of more than 4,000 incidents. Data on 3,300 incidents were collected during 1970–71 (and additional data were compiled in another city during the summer of 1973). An excess of 15,000 citizens will be involved when the study is completed. While the Reiss studies involved observer schedules or booklets filled out after each incident, the Sykes and Clark study utilized special coding equipment by means of which the interaction process is coded as it occurs.

9. Because the Reiss (1971) and Sykes and Clark (1972) studies are not exactly comparable, it is not possible to provide exactly similar category counts. The percentages for reactive and proactive contacts are about the same. Somewhat more than one-sixth of the calls in which there was an alleged violator present did not seem to involve any offense within the purview of the police. About half of such calls involved the use of discretion since a technical, if minor, violation had occurred. The great majority of these were handled short of arrest.

10. Black (1968) reports 49 percent, Sykes and Clark (1972) less than 45 percent of encounters in which a citizen was present.

3. The third largest proportion of encounters involves only violators, but almost all of these are routine traffic stops. Such infractions constitute about 20 percent of all uniformed police–citizen contacts in large cities and a greater proportion in most suburbs. The greatest likelihood of officer-citizen conflict appears to be in situations in which police confront the suspect without any complainant being present.[11]

Responses in which no citizen is present and encounters involving complainants, traffic violators, or simple participants or bystanders constitute over 80 percent of police activities. Confrontations with other violators, or violators together with complainants, account for between 10 and 20 percent of encounters.[12]

Even so, evidence indicates that while only 6 percent of all uniformed patrol encounters result in arrest, these encounters account for more than half of all arrests in every major category of crime, except fraud and so-called crimes without victims.[13] While figures for jurisdictions vary, probably about 10 percent of incidents police define as criminal result in arrest. Legal scholars have been concerned with so-called low visibility decisions by police, decisions *not* to invoke the formal criminal process, that constitute more than 90 percent of uniformed police decisions (Goldstein, 1960; LaFave, 1962a, 1962b; American Bar Association, 1973).

Sex Roles in Encounters

Evidence available indicates that contacts between male officers and women most commonly occur with the woman in the role of the complainant or as party to a dispute between intimates: marriage partners, "boyfriend trouble," and the like. Normally officers are more reluctant to arrest a woman than a man, and inhibitions against using force against a woman somewhat deprive them of their normal means of coercion. In most departments they must also report to the radio dispatcher when they begin to transport a woman to detention, as well as keep a record of their mileage.

Police are often called to mediate disputes involving women. The nature of the rules of evidence, the often secretly masochistic or stereotypical opinions officers have of women, and the generally private nature of such disputes mean that in many cases women have special difficulty in bringing their troubles before the courts. Police often advise them of the necessity of their filling out a formal complaint with the city attorney in order to initiate action, since the police lack authority to take direct action. It would seem that sexual stereotypes militate both for and against women, depending on the circumstances.

Age Roles in Encounters

Because of the influence of an article by Piliavin and Briar (1964), scholars commonly believe that the differences between adult and juvenile violators in the courts

---

11. Almost by definition, a traffic stop involves a suspect or alleged violator. In the Sykes and Clark study (1972), while about 55 percent of the encounters in which there was a citizen present involved a violator, about half of these were routine traffic violations. Black (1968) reports 45 percent.

12. In the Sykes and Clark study (1972) about 600 encounters over a base of 3,300.

13. Arrest percentages vary considerably depending on the base. For offenses cleared by uniformed patrol officers as a percentage of all such offenses, see Reiss (1971). Sykes and Clark (1972) found that about 17 percent of proactive encounters and 14 percent of reactive encounters in which the decision was at the discretion of the officer resulted in arrest. Unlike Reiss (1971) and Black (1968), felonies are not considered discretionary.

result from differences in the nature of adult and juvenile encounters. They found that differences in the disposition of juveniles were related to "cues which emerged from the interaction between the officer and the youth, cues from which the officer inferred the youth's character" (Piliavin & Briar, 1964:210). Among important cues affecting the outcome were deference and dress. However, the particular subjects of their study were *not* ordinary policemen, but juvenile officers. Subsequent references to this study have generalized the findings without recognizing this, in most cases.

Subsequent research does not confirm most of the findings (Black, 1970; Clark et al., 1972). As already indicated, officers have discretion in a wide range of encounters with adults as well as juveniles. Acknowledgment of authority, provision of information, and acceptance of alternatives apply to both adults and juveniles. Replicated studies indicate that the disposition of juvenile offenders is about the same as adult offenders. They also indicate, if anything, that police keep down the official juvenile delinquency rate by not making arrests in situations where they might. On the whole both police and juveniles are about as civil towards one another as police and adults. If anything, juveniles are more respectful to officers than their elders, which might be expected given the lower status of their age grouping, but not expected given the stereotype of youth in rebellion against authority. Evidence indicates that disrespect may increase the chances of arrest somewhat, but it is a much less powerful predictor than type of offense.

Insofar as age leads to stereotyping in American society, another grouping that should be considered is the senior citizen. Impressionistic evidence indicates that police contacts with senior citizens are primarily either with alcoholics in the skid-row areas of large cities, or else are service activities, such as checking on the well-being of someone not seen for several days, responding to the victims of street robberies and muggings, and providing advice about and sometimes transportation to other community agencies.

Minority Citizens in Encounters

Until the pioneering studies of Reiss and his associates (Black & Reiss, 1970; Reiss, 1971), most data on contacts between police and minority citizens were either essentially anecdotal or based on surveys of recollections and interview material rather than systematic observation (Wilson, 1968; Alex, 1969; Bayley & Mendelsohn, 1969; Chevigny, 1969; Skolnick, 1969). The urban riots, many of them sparked by specific incidents between patrolmen and minority citizens, led to a reexamination of relationships, including possible differences in encounters. While there is some information on Puerto Ricans, American Indians, and Chicanos, we shall consider only that which relates to blacks.

Data that have been gathered systematically, in many cases oversampling police-minority encounters, demonstrate that there are differences in interaction when police–white citizen and police–black citizen encounters are compared, though these differences relate primarily to encounters in which a suspect is present (Black, 1968; Sykes & Clark, 1972). These studies indicate that such police–black citizen encounters are more apt to involve disrespect, hostility, and antagonism by both officers and black suspects. In some encounters officers are unilaterally antagonistic, while in others, blacks are unilaterally antagonistic. Unilateral antagonism does not automatically lead to arrest, but when antagonism is mutual, arrest becomes highly probable. It also appears that officers are somewhat more likely to initiate hostility. When only a complainant is present, about 90 percent of encounters involving both blacks and whites are entirely civil.

There is no doubt that the arrest rate of blacks is much higher than that of whites and that a partial reason for the difference is discrimination. But there are several other reasons that account for the differences and that are not a function of color. Blacks appear to commit more serious crimes. Complainants (themselves blacks) are more likely to insist that the suspect be arrested. Since encounters involving blacks tend to be in crowded areas, they tend to involve more participants and bystanders, and officers are less apt to tolerate disrespect displayed before onlookers. Finally, arrest rates are generally higher among blue-collar citizens, and since there is a disproportionately large number of blacks in this grouping, there is an additional effect. Insofar as it has been possible to control all these factors, a differential arrest rate remains that must be attributed to discriminative reaction to color.

It should be noted that most of the systematic data pertains to major American cities outside of the South. Few data are available for smaller cities, rural areas, or large southern cities. There is no reason to believe there is less discrimination in these areas, and some reason to believe there is more.

The reason for the greater hostility of both officers and minority citizens in encounters does not seem to be a function of prejudice or hate alone. Officers are in part symbolic targets and representatives of white domination. In addition, both parties seem much less sure of what to expect of the other, and less able to empathize or understand one another than do white officers and citizens in interaction. For this reason, each appears less predictable and more threatening, with the result that a defensiveness develops, which becomes self-perpetuating (Bayley & Mendelsohn, 1969).

FINAL NOTE

The last decade has been witness to great advances in police research. Before 1965, there were few data available, and what there were came primarily from the perspective of the police profession itself, civic reformers, or scholars whose work, however otherwise valuable, tended to be interpreted in terms of a stereotype of the police as kind of a public, blue-shirted Mafia, given to arbitrary violence and secretiveness. More recent and extensive research has shown:

1. that formal police organization is not unlike other organizations in many ways;
2. that many of its special characteristics are due to the complex of environmental forces with which it must contend, including cultural values of citizens, the framework of law, political pressures, and limitations of economic and human resources;
3. that uniformed police respond to citizen-initiated definitions of situations as requiring police interference much more than they do to police-initiated definitions;
4. that in many ways police are as much a service organization as one utilizing coercion—in fact, they are almost the only organization providing 24-hour service at the citizen's request wherever the citizens are located;
5. that police-citizen interaction may be explained by the same concepts as other interaction is explained;
6. that arrest and violence are both exceptional in police work, that most police-citizen contact involves outcomes other than arrest, and that, in fact, in most cases (other than traffic) a violator is not even present; and finally,
7. that most police decisions to take an alleged violator into custody are not arbitrary, but are most strongly affected by the requirements of the law.

Police organization and interaction can be accounted for by general explanations of social organization, formal organization, and social psychology. Recent police research may have also made a methodological contribution by showing the promise of large-scale, quantitative, observational research.

Many areas of police work need further investigation. Nonuniformed and proactive activity needs further research, and many aspects of police-citizen interaction, as well as decision norms for outcome alternatives, need further specification. Perhaps the greatest scholarly need is to place already completed research in the framework of general sociological and social-psychological theory. There is also a need for scientists to acknowledge that social control occurs by means other than socialization, that external social control takes place in all complex societies, and that present theoretical frameworks need expansion to take these realities into account.

REFERENCES

Alex, Nicholas.
    1969   Black in Blue: A Study of the Negro Policeman. New York: Appleton-Century-Crofts.

American Bar Association.
    1973   The Urban Police Function. Report of an Advisory Committee on the Police Function, Frank J. Remington, Chairman. Chicago: American Bar Association.

Argyle, Michael.
    1969   Social Interaction. Chicago: Aldine.

Banton, Michael.
    1964   The Policeman in the Community. New York: Basic Books.

Bard, M.
    1969   "Family intervention police teams as a community mental health resource." Journal of Criminal Law, Criminology and Police Science 60(June):247–250.

Bayley, David H., and Harold Mendelsohn.
    1969   Minorities and the Police: Confrontation in America. New York: Free Press.

Bittner, E.
    1967a   "The police on skid row: a study of peace keeping." American Sociological Review 32(October):699–715.
    1967b   "Police discretion in emergency apprehension of mentally ill persons." Social Problems 14(Winter):278–292.
    1970   The Functions of the Police in Modern Society. Public Health Service Publication No. 2059. Washington, D.C.: U.S. Government Printing Office.

Black, D. J.
    1968   "Police encounters and social disorganization: an observation study." Ph.D. dissertation, University of Michigan.
    1970   "Production of crime rates." American Sociological Review 35(August):733–748.

Black, D. J., and A. J. Reiss, Jr.
    1970   "Police control of juveniles." American Sociological Review 35(February):63–77.

Blumer, Herbert.
    1970   "Sociological implications of the thoughts of George Herbert Mead," in G. P. Stone and H. A. Farberman, Social Psychology Through Symbolic Interaction. Waltham, Mass.: Xerox College Publishing.

Bordua, David J., and Albert J. Reiss, Jr.
    1967   "Law enforcement," in Paul Lazarsfeld, William H. Sewell, and Harold L. Wilensky, Uses of Sociology. New York: Basic Books.

Borgatta, Edgar F., and Leonard S. Cottrell.
    1955   "On the classification of groups," in J. L. Moreno (ed.), Sociometry and the Science of Man. New York: Beacon House.

Cardwell, J. D.
    1971   Social Psychology. Philadelphia: F. A. Davis Co.

Chapple, Eliot D.
    1970   Culture and Biological Man. New York: Holt, Rinehart & Winston.

Chevigny, Paul.
    1969   Police Power. New York: Pantheon Books.

Clark, John P.
    1965   "Isolation of the police: a comparison of the British and American situations." Journal of Criminal Law, Criminology and Police Science 56(September):307–319.

Clark, John P., James Whelpley, and Richard E. Sykes.
    1972   "Comparative police-juvenile and police-adult interaction" (unpublished).

Cumming, E., I. Cumming, and L. Edell.
    1965   "Policeman as philosopher, guide and friend." Social Problems 12(Winter):276–286.

Derbyshire, Robert L.
    1968   "Children's perceptions of the police: a comparative study of attitudes and attitude change." Journal of Criminal Law, Criminology and Police Science 59(June):183–190.

Dodd, D. J.
    1967   "Police mentality and behavior." Issues in Criminology 3(Summer):47–67.

Douglas, Jack D. (ed.)
    1970   Understanding Everyday Life. Chicago: Aldine.

Etzioni, Amitai.
    1961   A Comparative Analysis of Complex Organizations. New York: Free Press of Glencoe.

Feld, Barry C.
    1971   "Police violence and protest." Minnesota Law Review 55(March):731–778.

Gardiner, John A.
    1969   Traffic and the Police. Cambridge: Harvard University Press.

Glaser, D., and D. K. Rice.
    1959   "Crime, age and employment." American Sociological Review 24(October):679–686.

Goffman, Erving.
    1961   Encounters: Two Studies in the Sociology of Interaction. Indianapolis: Bobbs-Merrill.

Goldstein, H.
    1967   "Administrative problems in controlling the exercise of police authority."
            Journal of Criminal Law, Criminology and Police Science 58(June):160–
            172.

Goldstein, Joseph.
    1960   "Police discretion not to invoke the criminal process: low visibility deci-
            sions in the administration of justice." Yale Law Journal 69(March):543–
            594.

Gourley, G. Douglas.
    1954   "Police public relations." Annals of the American Academy of Political and
            Social Science 291(January):135–142.

Gupta, V. J., R. E. Sykes, and J. P. Clark.
    1972   The Local Police in the United States—An Annotated Bibliography. Ob-
            servations 4 (December) (mimeographed).

Hahn, Harlan (ed.)
    1971   Police in Urban Society. Beverly Hills, Calif.: Sage Publications.

Hall, Jerome.
    1953   "Police and law in a democratic society." Indiana Law Journal 28(Winter):
            134–177.

Hall, Richard.
    1972   Organizations: Structure and Process. Englewood Cliffs, N.J.: Prentice-Hall.

Hartjen, Clayton A.
    1972   "Police-citizen encounters: social order in interpersonal interaction." Crim-
            inology 10(May):61–84.

Heider, Fritz.
    1958   The Psychology of Interpersonal Relations. New York: Wiley.

LaFave, W. R.
    1962a   "The police and nonenforcement of the law—part 1." Wisconsin Law Re-
            view 1962(January):104–137.
    1962b   "The police and nonenforcement of the law—part 2." Wisconsin Law Re-
            view 1962(March):179–239.

Lefton, Mark, and W. R. Rosengren.
    1966   "Organizations and clients: lateral and longitudinal dimensions." American
            Sociological Review 31(December):802–810.

Lundman, R. J.
    1972   "Police and the maintenance of propriety." Ph.D. dissertation, University
            of Minnesota.

McCall, George J., and J. L. Simmons.
    1966   Identities and Interactions. New York: Free Press.

McNamara, John H.
    1967   "Uncertainties in police work: the relevance of police recruits' backgrounds
            and training," in David J. Bordua (ed.), The Police: Six Sociological Es-
            says. New York: Wiley.

Miller, Walter B.
    1958   "Inter-institutional conflict as a major impediment to delinquency preven-
            tion." Human Organization 17(Fall):20–23.

Misner, G. E.
  1967   "The urban police mission." Issues in Criminology 3(Summer):35–46.

Murray, Henry A.
  1951   "Toward a classification of interaction," in Talcott Parsons and Edward A. Shils (eds.), Toward a General Theory of Action. Cambridge: Harvard University Press.

Niederhoffer, Arthur.
  1967   Behind the Shield: The Police in Urban Society. Garden City, N.Y.: Doubleday.

Parnas, R. I.
  1967   "The police response to the domestic disturbance." Wisconsin Law Review 1967(Fall):914–960.

Piliavin, I., and S. Briar.
  1964   "Police encounters with juveniles." American Journal of Sociology 70(September):206–214.

Quinney, Richard.
  1970   The Social Reality of Crime. Boston: Little, Brown.

Reiss, Albert J., Jr.
  1971   The Police and the Public. New Haven: Yale University Press.

Remington, F. J.
  1965   "The role of police in a democratic society." Journal of Criminal Law, Criminology and Police Science 56(September):361–365.

Rubinstein, Jonathan.
  1973   City Police. New York: Farrar, Straus & Giroux.

Sacks, Harvey.
  1972   "Notes on police assessment of moral character," in David Sudnow (ed.), Studies in Social Interaction. New York: Free Press.

Scott, W. Richard.
  1964   "Theory of organizations." Pp. 485–529 in Robert E. L. Faris (ed.), Handbook of Modern Sociology. Chicago: Rand McNally.
  1970   Social Processes and Social Structures. New York: Holt, Rinehart & Winston.

Scott, W. Richard, Sanford M. Dornbusch, Bruce C. Busching, and James D. Laing.
  1967   "Organizational evaluation and authority." Administrative Science Quarterly 12(June):93–105.

Shaw, Marvin E.
  1971   Group Dynamics, The Psychology of Small Group Behavior. New York: McGraw-Hill.

Skolnick, Jerome.
  1966   Justice Without Trial. New York: Wiley.
  1969   The Politics of Protest. New York: Clarion.

Sowle, C. R.
  1966   Police Power and Individual Freedom. Chicago: Aldine.

Stinchcombe, Arthur L.
  1963   "Institutions of privacy in the determination of police administrative practice." American Journal of Sociology 69(September):150–160.

Sullivan, Dennis C., and Larry J. Siegel.
  1972   "How police use information to make decisions." Crime and Delinquency
          18(July):253–262.
Suttles, Gerald D.
  1968   The Social Order of the Slum. Chicago: University of Chicago Press.
Sykes, R. E., and John P. Clark.
  1972   "Comparative characteristics of routine police-minority and police-majority
          citizen contacts" (December, unpublished).
Tauber, Ronald K.
  1967   "Danger and the police: a theoretical analysis." Issues in Criminology 3(1):
          69–81.
Thibaut, John W., and Harold H. Kelley.
  1959   The Social Psychology of Groups. New York: Wiley.
Wenninger, Eugene P., and John P. Clark.
  1967   "A theoretical orientation for police studies," in Malcolm W. Klein (ed.),
          Juvenile Gangs in Context. Englewood Cliffs, N.J.: Prentice-Hall.
Werthman, Carl, and Irving Piliavin.
  1967   "Gang members and the police." Pp. 56–98 in David J. Bordua (ed.), The
          Police: Six Sociological Essays. New York: Wiley.
Westley, W. A.
  1953   "Violence and the police." American Journal of Sociology 59(July):34–41.
  1956   "Secrecy and the police." Social Forces 34(March):254–257.
Williams, Robin M., Jr.
  1970   The American Society. Third Edition. New York: Knopf.
Wilson, J. Q.
  1968   Varieties of Police Behavior. Cambridge: Harvard University Press.
Wilson, Thomas P.
  1970   "Normative and interpretive paradigms in sociology," in Jack D. Douglas
          (ed.), Understanding Everyday Life. Chicago: Aldine.

CHAPTER **12**

Police Administration

William H. Hewitt

Mansfield State College

THE POLICE IDEA

While scholars, researchers, and police leaders have all attempted to define the role of the American police, each has failed, for there is too little uniformity in American policing. We can only precisely define police department roles within each community served.

John Coatman advises:

> The word 'police' had originally the widest possible connotation in relation to organized society, for it was used as a synonym for organized government, and even for civilization itself. As recently as the midnineteenth century, Disraeli could write in his *Sybil*, "These hovels are . . . not provided with the commonest convenience of the rudest police," meaning by "police," civilization (1959:2).

The term *police* has the roots of its contemporary understanding in eighteenth-century France, England, and Germany. These etymons can further be traced to the Romans.

Historically, the role of the police in a free society has not changed, but the scope, nature, and complexity of the police role has differed. As our technological, affluent, and mobile society becomes more complex, so will the police role. The noted British magistrate and first law-enforcement scholar, Sir Patrick Colquohon, in his classic *On the Police* in 1797, observed:

> . . . the evils arising from the multiplied crimes . . . render a correct and energetic System of Police, with regard to the detection, discovery and apprehension of offenders, indispensably necessary for the safety and well-being of society . . . (Colquohon, 1797: 194).
>
> . . . a vast proportion of those who reside in the capitol, as well as the multitude of strangers who resort to it, have no accurate idea of the principles of organization, . . . establishing those conveniences and accommodations, and preserving that regularity which prevails in the particular branches of Police which may be denominated by Municipal Regulations; such as paving, watching, lighting, cleansing, and removing nuisances; furnishing water; the mode of building houses; extinguishing fires; regulating coaches, carts, and other carriages; and a variety of other useful improvements, tending to the comfort and convenience of the inhabitants . . . (p. 331).

When the Police System was first established in the year 1792, the police mind became impressed with an idea that the chief, if not the only, object of the institution was to prevent robberies, burglaries and other atrocious offenses; and that the suppression of those crimes which bear hardest upon society, and were most dreaded by the public at large, was to be the result. These expectations showed that neither the powers nor authorities granted by the Act of Parliament, nor the other duties imposed upon the Magistracy of the Police, were understood. It is not generally known, and perhaps will scarcely be believed, that the Statute, under which the established Magistrates Act (useful as it certainly is in a very high degree in many other respects), does not contain even a single regulation applicable to the prevention of crimes; except that which relates to the apprehension of suspected characters, found in the avenues to public places, with intent to commit felony; who are liable to be punished as rogues and vagabonds, and even this provision does not extend to the city of London (pp. 336–37).

. . . Foreigners . . . join in one general remark . . . viz.—'That we have some shadow of Police, for apprehending delinquents, after crimes are actually committed; but none for the purpose of preventing them . . .' (pp. 350–51).

With remarkable modern relevance, the novelist Charles Dickens noted in the nineteenth century:

. . . We have seen that an incessant system of communications, day and night, is kept up between every station of the force; we have seen, not only crime speedily detected, but distress quickly relieved; we have seen regard paid to every application, whether it be an enquiry after a gypsy woman, or a black-and-tan spaniel, or a frivolous complaint against a constable, we have seen that everything that occurs is written down, to be forwarded to headquarters, we have seen an extraordinary degree of patience habitually exercised in listening to prolix details, in relieving the kernel of a case from its almost impenetrable husk, we have seen how impossible it is for anything of a serious, of even an unusual, nature to happen without being reported; and that if reported, additional force can be immediately supplied from each station; where from twenty to thirty men are always collected while off duty. We have seen that the whole system is well, intelligently, zealously worked; and we have seen, finally, that the addition of a few extra men will be all-sufficient for any exigencies which may arise from the coming influx of visitors (1969:271–73).

. . . such is the peculiar ability, always sharpening and being improved by practice, and always adapting itself to every variety of circumstances, and opposing itself to every new device that perverted ingenuity can invent, for which this important social branch of the public service is remarkable! Forever on the watch, with their wits stretched to the utmost, these officers have, from day to day and year to year, to set themselves against every novelty of trickery and dexterity that the combined imagination of all the lawless rascals in England can devise, and to keep pace with every such invention that comes out . . . (pp. 459–60).

Although Dickens was an outsider to the criminal justice system, he was a keen observer.

More than anyone else, the police officer is symbolic of the governmental establishment, for he is in constant and daily contact with each of the various segments of the population. Every police-citizen contact necessarily involves a measure of intimacy, for police action can affect a citizen's dignity, self-respect, sense of privacy, or civil rights. The policeman tends to become a target of cross fires between those in the community pressing for stricter law enforcement and those who charge "police brutality" at every turn, between those who demand that he "get tough" and those who admonish him to respect the rights of individuals, between those who insist that he prevent crime and stop riots and those who insist that he be reasonable in the use of force. Not only is the policeman thus called upon to serve incompatible ends, he is often frustrated because he has to deal with ills resulting from the social and economic failures of the community. Thus, the policeman has become the visible symbol of the shame of society. By his actions a police officer brings to the police profession, and to government itself, the commendation or the condemnation of the citizenry he serves.

Theoretically, what the police officer does for one individual, he does for the community collectively. A police officer must be given the opportunity to develop rapport and understanding in the community area that is under his protection. This is best accomplished by a police officer who is charged with an area of the community to protect and who stays there without being constantly drawn away because of unusual occurrences or emergencies elsewhere.

POLICE PERSONNEL ADMINISTRATION

All organizations are made up of people. Approximately 30,000 of our 40,000 police agencies have less than five men. Since it takes five bodies to fill one police position (eight hours per shift, three shifts, seven days per week, allowing for sick time, holidays, court time, grand jury time, vacations, training time, and numerous other tasks which detract from the primary police mission), the small departments clearly do not constitute full-time police agencies.

In the larger departments specialists are in abundance. There are helicopter pilots, chemists, data processors, deep-sea divers, polygraph operators, specialized detectives of all kinds, youth officers, public-information officers, police-community relations officers, emergency squads, photographers, planners, purchasers, personnel specialists, training departments, and layer on layer of supervisors. In the larger departments the specialist is *in* and the generalist is *out*. If the patrolman who responds to a particular call cannot conclude the police business there immediately, the appropriate specialists usually are assigned to it.

In the small- and medium-sized departments (10–100 men), specialists either do not exist or are few. Small towns cannot afford the luxury of many specialists. Everyone must first be a generalist, that is, be able to perform almost all police tasks, and then become a part-time specialist in some function if he possesses distinctive capability for it. The inability to provide specialist positions and more promotional opportunities in the smaller departments tremendously impairs their recruiting efforts. After all, why should a young person join an agency where he or she probably will be a patrolman twenty years later doing essentially the same job as on the day hired?

Personnel Selection. The personnel selection process consists of a series of steps: (1) recruitment, (2) selection, (3) training, (4) probation, and (5) assignment. If any one of these steps is not administered properly, it can cause untold problems in all subsequent steps, and in other police operations.

Police recruiting in America generally has been done on the basis of "local jobs for local boys." There are a few exceptions where recruiting is on either a state or national base, with the objective of securing the best personnel for the money allocated. For such recruitment a town must engage in a widespread effort, certainly no less than statewide, for only a small fraction of the potential candidates will reside within the town limits.

A second problem with recruiting is the writing of job descriptions and qualifications, which in many communities is done so that only white, lower middle-class males can readily qualify. In addition, in many towns the applicant must be a lifelong resident. The latter requirement may not be explicit, but is, nevertheless, in effect, for the written examination is designed to test knowledge of local streets, bridges, library location, the mayor's name, a district councilman's name, and numerous other non-germane questions. Blacks and other minority groups, including all females, are continually excluded in the recruiting process despite some alleviation of this problem in recent years.

It is most appropriate that departments recruit on college campuses, which many have not yet begun, if they are to compete with the nation's leading employers for the best youth available. They must present the job there in a challenging but accurate fashion. Youth frequently are seeking an opportunity to participate in the "system," desire challenges, are attracted to police work as a people-to-people business, and can be sold on the service nature of police work. While these are leading recruiting issues, the quality of personnel recruited and retained by a department will always be in direct proportion to the quality of service rendered by the department.

Peace officers are selected today by procedures varying from merely completing a single, small application form to all of the following eleven steps, or more:

1. Short-form application for initial screening.
2. Long-form application.
3. Civil service examination.
4. Fingerprint check (FBI, state, and local).
5. Background investigation.
6. Medical examination.
7. Physical agility test.
8. Psychological screening.
9. Oral board interview.
10. Training academy (if accepted on the above).
11. Eighteen-month probationary period of initial employment.

Even where all or most of these steps are included in a selection program, however, its accomplishment may be rendered questionable by unwarranted waivers and exceptions. Actually, few police agencies employ all of the above procedures. Apart from the question of what steps to include, there are many issues connected with each step, such as age criteria, medical requirements, amount of education, veteran's preference, residence, emotional maturity, and the optimum testing instrument for measuring the potential to be a good peace officer.

The most critical stages in the selection process are the training academy and the probationary period. In New York City, the Rand Corporation studied the files of approximately 2,000 officers and found that those who received poor efficiency ratings during their probationary period later were disproportionately high in percentage accused of being corrupt, of abusing citizens, and of violating departmental rules. They concluded that those men who do poorly during their first six months on the street and during training should be terminated in much larger numbers than has been customary. The police, however, not only in New York but everywhere, are traditionally loathe to discharge recruits once they pass the initial screening stages and the academy. The report noted, for example, that during the last decade only 1.8 percent of the 20,600 men who entered their probationary period were discharged from the service during it. If many should be discharged, of course, there are drastic deficiencies in the prior stages of the selection process.

Training is provided to some degree for most of America's peace officers, since most function in large cities or state forces where academies exist. Only about half of our states have some form of minimum training standards legislation, but some of these only prescribe voluntary standards, in contrast to the more demanding requirements of New York, Michigan, and California, for example.

Many police departments still do not believe in training, particularly the smaller ones, and this view is shared by many city halls. While they may give it lip service, they regularly fail to assign officers to training on the easy excuse that "we cannot spare him." The truth often is that they do not want the officer "contaminated" with outside philosophy and practice. The costs of malfeasance, misfeasance, and nonfeasance of office, however, may often be so much higher from the untrained than from the trained that departments actually cannot afford not to train their personnel.

It should be noted that training and education are not synonymous terms in police circles. Training refers to teaching the recruit the "how-to-do-it" skills needed to function effectively on the street. Education, on the other hand, implies formal schooling in a college or university setting. Criminal justice education is concerned with teaching the student to conceptualize, to articulate, and to comprehend the philosophical issues in criminal justice; to understand man; to appreciate the social, political, and economic causes of crime; to understand the American political and legal process; to be familiar with the American conception of civil rights; and to be acquainted with the literature and authorities in criminal justice, public administration, and politics. Professionals and academicians are in agreement in endorsing both components of the training-education dichotomy, but requiring initial and continuing formal education has yet to be accepted by many in the police community.

The probationary step in formally passing on a recruit need not imply that once one completes probationary status one is secure against pressures to perform the police job correctly, but such security generally prevails in America. As a result, the civil service system has become a millstone around the professional police chief's neck. It curbs the elite and efficient officers while protecting the inept, the insecure, and the corrupt. The probationary period is crucial to the professional molding, training, counseling, motivating, supervising, correcting, and nurturing of the recruit, and if it is not done rigorously, the "old guard" may quickly undo it by passing on to the new officer every mode of unprofessional service known. Advice such as "forget what they taught you in the academy, I'll teach you how to get along out here" frequently prevails. Therefore, the selection of officers to "break in" new recruits after their academy training is a most sensitive administrative decision. For this reason, probation is an organic part of the selection and training process.

Promotion. Assignment to street duties does not conclude the personnel process. Here, more than anywhere else, the officer must be closely supervised until he reaches a level of competence in all aspects of police service. The young officer will generally find himself working in patrol or traffic duty for a few years. If he demonstrates a degree of proficiency at investigation, he may be appointed a detective. Not all men who do other police tasks well are good investigators, yet the myth prevails that any officer can do investigative work. The pattern of officer assignment, however, varies greatly, depending on: (1) the size of the department; (2) the frequency of promotion examinations; (3) the turnover rate; (4) the individual officer's efficiency rating; (5) local politics; (6) the number of specialist positions available; (7) clauses in contracts; (8) the chief's appointing powers; (9) civil service rules; (10) tenure customs, rules, or laws; (11) the professional ability and skills of the individual officer; and (12) local customs in assignment practice.

The issues of civil service, unions, promotion policy, pay, lateral entry, and APT (administrative, professional, and technical) specialists dominate police personnel discussions. If departments are to secure qualified APT personnel sufficient for their needs and in competition with other employers, lateral entry generally is required. This is the personnel practice of bringing into an agency APT and other staff at other than first-level positions on initial appointment. The present personnel structure, unions, customs, and traditional practice are all formidable barriers to lateral entry. Those who regard tenure as a "sacred cow" vigorously oppose bringing much-needed expertise into a department. It must be noted, however, that almost all of today's leading police executives have held a variety of police posts in more than one city. This alone speaks well for a policy of lateral entry. (For more detailed discussion, see Hewitt, 1967.)

Promotion issues tie closely into the concept of lateral entry. Obviously, if we bring into the department someone from the outside, we have eliminated one promotional opportunity. This upsets morale, creates union grievances, and fosters an unhappy environment for the new police executive. On the other hand, departures create vacancies to which someone else may be promoted, so lateral recruitment increases the competition of employers for outstanding personnel. Thus, a policy of lateral entry, if widespread, would accelerate the best use of performance potential in America's police manpower pool.

Additional issues surrounding promotion practice in police organizations include: (1) the nature, form, and type of questions appropriate for oral and written examinations; (2) the components of an ideal promotion test, keeping in mind differences appropriate to the rank and duties involved; (3) how much weight should be given for years of service; (4) how much weight should be given for efficiency ratings; (5) how frequently should tests be given; (6) who should make up the examinations; (7) should the tests stress academic or "how-to-do-it" material; (8) how should the cutoff score for passing be determined; (9) how long should the list run; (10) what procedures should exist for appeals; (11) must appointments be from the top of the list or from one of two or three; (12) must a detective in plain clothes go back into uniform to accept a promotion to sergeant? This is not a comprehensive list, but suffices to show that the issues are varied and complex.

Unions will have increasing influence on promotion policy as time passes. I was once opposed to police unions in any form, but after a decade of close work with numerous police departments, much research, interviewing, and survey writing, it has become apparent to me that law enforcement will not greatly improve while left in the hands of the politicians and various groups that "speak for the police." Only through union contracts, with very few exceptions, have police working conditions, pay, pensions, health plans, and promotion policies been improved. If not for the unions, many departments would still be working 56 hours per week for about $5,000 per year. Because of low pay, insecurity, and poor fringe benefits, the police cannot attract qualified personnel. If the position of peace officer is made attractive and challenging, it will draw superior candidates.

The last issue to be considered in the personnel area is employment of police legal advisors. Because the police function in a highly legalistic milieu, they require all the legal counsel they can muster. A program of using lawyers as civilian legal advisors to the New York City Police Department was initiated in 1972 and other departments have similar undertakings. The legal advisors conduct training programs on legal procedures, deliver lectures on court decisions, and go into the courts and into the field to give on-the-spot legal advice to police. The American Bar Association has contended that when police employ legal advisors, they make fewer arrests and use the advisors to help mold law-enforcement policy. It has also endorsed collective bargaining by the police, but not the right to strike. Compulsory arbitration is suggested as an alternative to the right to strike, and objection is voiced to national police unions, since law enforcement must be locally controlled.

CORRUPTION

The issue of corruption has been connected with police work since the beginning of time. The early Romans, French, Anglo-Saxons, British, and central European police had to confront this problem. Corruption exists, in some form, in almost all American cities today. Hardly a day goes by in which one does not read about a corrupt policeman somewhere in America, partly because the media tend to sensationalize all exposures of corruption.

Corruption takes many forms. It may mean, for example, taking free coffee at a diner, picking up a free newspaper, getting a free meal, receiving other free services from merchants in the community, taking money from a traffic violator, receiving payoffs for not enforcing the law, pocketing evidence from arrests for later personal use, or even participating as an accomplice in crimes. There is the risk that the relatively petty misdeeds, if unchecked, will evolve into the more serious ones. No gift is really free. If the merchant provides free newspapers or coffee, he soon expects special treatment or extra services. The officer is in a position to return favors, the average citizen is not.

Professor Albert J. Reiss, Jr., reports from systematically sampled observations of police in three cities:

> Within each of the cities, one-third (31 percent) of all businessmen in wholesale or retail trade or business or repair services in the high crime rate areas openly acknowledged favors to policemen. Of those giving favors, 43 percent said they gave free merchandise, food or services to all policemen; the remainder did so at discount. When observers were present with officers during their eight-hour tour of duty, for almost 1 of every 3 of the 841 tours (31 percent) the officers did not pay for their meals. Similarly, many officers reported large discounts on purchases. . . . On most occasions, free goods or discounts are not solicited, largely because officers know well which businesses offer them and which do not. The informal police networks carry such information, obviating in most cases open solicitation (Reiss, 1971:161–2).
>
> . . . The bulk of offenses committed by officers provide income supplements derived from exchange relationships . . . the officer provides something in exchange, generally exemption from the effect of the law. Given the relatively low remuneration of police officers, relative to their prestige and life-style, the pressures to supplement income are considerable. Many police departments in the United States either prohibit moonlighting or severely restrict its practice. . . . In any case, the "easy" money available to the officer with the low risk . . . renders it a highly attractive form of income supplementation. . . . Though claims are easily exaggerated, some officers said they could earn as much from their violations as from their salary (p. 160).
>
> The fact that mobility within police departments occurs almost exclusively by promotion from the line *within* a department makes line and staff officers subject to subversion by the line. They readily overlook practices and violations that are common among patrolmen either because they, themselves, engaged in them when they served as patrolmen or many of their friends did so. Not infrequently, when superior officers investigate or hear charges in disciplinary proceedings for men in the line, their judgment is subverted because they served with them. These facts—the absence of lateral

mobility across police departments and mobility within them resting on promotion from the line—are a structural feature of American police departments that renders them vulnerable to many forms of internal subversion and jeopardizes their disinterest in personnel decisions and discipline (p. 162).

Corruption in some form will probably always be with us, but much can be done to reduce it, including: (1) more careful selection of officers; (2) closer supervision at all levels; (3) frequent transfer of officers; (4) lateral recruitment; (5) severe punishment of those caught, as a deterrent to others; (6) having all commanders, and possibly lower ranks, file with the chief an annual net worth statement and income tax return, or having this filed with an independent auditing agency; (7) having an Internal Investigation Unit conduct spot investigations.

POLICE-COMMUNITY RELATIONS

The term *police-community relations* (PCR) must not be confused with public relations. The two concepts are only partially related. Following the riots and urban turmoil of the 1960s, PCR units mushroomed in police departments throughout the United States, but PCR became a euphemism for police-black relations, although the police serve all publics.

Some department heads have flatly refused to implement a PCR unit, stating that "all my men are public-relations and community-relations officers." Every officer, however, does not fully understand the concepts and philosophy of PCR. Second, most officers, due to their work load, simply do not have the time or energy to become greatly involved or concerned with it. Third, due to attitudinal problems, many officers do not effectively improve the police image.

The objectives of a PCR unit and program are numerous, but the key ones are to: (1) open and maintain avenues of communication between the police and the *entire* community; (2) educate the public about the police function and provide the community an opportunity to air its grievances; (3) improve the police image; (4) aid in recruiting police applicants from minority groups; (5) train fellow officers in PCR; (6) work with ghetto and other urban youth to prevent crime, including seeking employment for them and channeling their energy into acceptable activities; (7) research problems and programs related to PCR for the chief; (8) determine the validity of all rumors and complaints and deal with them before they ignite into major police-public confrontations.

The prevailing mistrust, hatred, prejudice, bigotry, violence, generational and group gaps, and the economic-deprivation issues among our people are tightly woven into the fabric of our society. When these problems are coupled with the police and public too often eyeing each other warily over an invisible wall, fraught with latent (and frequently patent) suspicion, polarization of police and publics into opposing groups will be a recurring phenomenon warranting continuous attention to PCR.

CITIZEN COMPLAINTS

A very real part of PCR and the basis of much citizen distrust of their police are "brutality" complaints. Until the community is satisfied that professional ethics are uniformly practiced, cries for civilian review boards in police departments will echo across this country. Whether one is for or against review boards, and whether or not one believes the allegations to be true or false, those making the complaints will persist

and will feel justified in doing so. As long as they do, the police must respond positively—not defensively. Certainly, many complaints are exaggerated and hyperbolic,
but because complaints are both symptoms and infectious sources of ailments in police-
community relations, complaints should not be ignored.

Complaints take two major forms—psychological and physical brutality. An example of the former is an officer's calling a black man "boy"; an illustration of the
latter is the use of excessive force to effect an arrest. There are numerous variations to
each form.

Many departments face complaints positively. They acknowledge the possibility
of unprofessional police performance and take publicly announced measures to identify and correct it. Others, on the other hand, deny all alleged wrongdoing automatically. The image of a chief who thus implies that his men are all perfect would be
greatly improved in his community were he to state his problems honestly.

Detroit is one major city which has effectively handled citizen complaints. It
established, with my aid, a Citizens Complaint Bureau, while its police department
was under former Commissioner John Spreen. This bureau was given staff-level status,
and put in charge of a full inspector, with both black and white officers assigned to it
as investigators. Most importantly, to gain the unit's complete acceptance by all organizations and agencies concerned with citizen complaints about the police, the commissioner, the bureau's head, and I met regularly with all such groups (e.g., the state
Human Relations Commission, the mayor's office, three police unions, police staff officers, the NAACP). As many meetings were held as were necessary to iron out differences, and only after these meetings did the commissioner hold a press conference on
the problem and the program to resolve it. After years of experience with this model, I
can confidently state that it can be widely accepted.

When cries of brutality are heard, there are concomitant pleas for new police
leadership and new programs. In the passion to "do something" about a complaint
that sounds outrageous, there is a demand for a "clean sweep" to remove all involved
officers from the service. Police reactions, depending upon the type of leadership that
directs the department, will consist of either (1) denying all allegations, (2) ignoring
the complaint and withdrawing further from the public, or (3) announcing, for the
media to verify, a full and prompt investigation. The latter alternative is the only one
that demonstrates a police department's integrity, and that can lead to either appropriate charges and penalties, or the removal of clouds of suspicion, for the officers
involved.

Large numbers of complaints are unfounded. Many are made to harass the police.
Nevertheless, they must all be cleared. Each complaint, however, should not become a
part of the officer's personnel file. It must be understood that many officers working in
high-crime areas understandably make more arrests and have more frequent hostile
encounters with citizens than officers elsewhere. Therefore, officers in these areas
should not be penalized because the odds are greater there for provoking complaints.
Good police work should no more be allowed to penalize the officer than poor police
work should be the basis for rewarding him or her. If handicaps to promotion are a
consequence of appropriate action, the police will merely exercise discretion by looking the other way in situations where they should take action.

CONCLUSION

The majority of contemporary police problems involve cross fires of politics, inadequate resources, insufficient planning, and poor coordination or failure to amalgamate,

as well as the nature of our society itself. A variety of key issues have been indicated that must be resolved if America is to continue to have her police "keep the lid on a boiling social pot."

REFERENCES

Coatman, John.
  1959   Police. Oxford, England: Clarendon Press.

Colquohon, Patrick.
  1797   On the Police. London: C. Dilly, Poultry.

Dickens. Charles.
  1969   Uncollected Writings from "Household Words," 1850–1859. Harry Stone (ed.). Bloomington: Indiana University Press.

Hewitt, William H.
  1967   Lateral Entry and Transferability of Retirement Credits. Consultant's Report to President's Commission on Law Enforcement and Administration of Justice. Washington, D.C.: U.S. Government Printing Office.

Reiss, Albert J., Jr.
  1971   The Police and the Public. New Haven: Yale University Press.

CHAPTER 13

The Scientific Assessment of Physical Evidence from Criminal Conduct

Brian Parker

California State University, Sacramento

"*Every secret crime has its reporter.*"—Ralph Waldo Emerson

From the fictional footprint of Friday on the beach to the literal footprint of Armstrong on the moon, physical changes necessarily accompany each human act. These physical changes provide one means of reviewing the past before deciding on a present course of action. The unique progression of each individual's physical changes produces a trail of events over time and is the signature of the human agent. Amid the confusion of other acts, human and nonhuman, in the same space and time, the trail and the signature exist as an intertwined thread of relationship. The recognition of the relevant physical changes and accurate interpretation of the relationship constitutes an intriguing challenge to human interest in, and concern for, justice.

The entire spectrum of scientific disciplines and fields of study is involved, potentially, in retrieving the breadth of information contained in physical changes. No detailed recitation of their separate contributions is attempted. This chapter considers the development of the science and the scientific groups devoted to retrieving physical evidence for public use. A discussion of what physical evidence is, in a broad sense, and how it relates to human behavior follows. Finally, we take a closer look at how physical evidence is retrieved and utilized in the context of social control.

In the administration of justice, especially criminal justice, there is a need to know precisely what happened and specifically who was involved in a given act. A reduction of uncertainty in this knowledge of the past is required to gain public respect for the rule of law. Human conduct of criminal or antisocial import creates a unique set of physical changes capable of retrieval and explanation. In the explanation of these changes, the understanding gained of the physical act is the physical evidence.

A man's criminal conduct can be reconstructed from examining and interpreting the physical changes he cannot avoid making. The scientific reconstruction is carried out by an individual designated by his profession (legal medicine or criminalistics), by his discipline (forensic pathology or forensic chemistry), or by his subject matter (questioned documents or firearms identification). The scientific methodologies employed in fashioning a glimpse into past behavior are essentially those of the appropriate technology combined with legal safeguards to assure integrity and relevance.

While the physical changes examined vary from a written name on a check, a trace of penicillin in a vitamin tablet, a speech on a videotape, an oil slick in a channel, a snatch of cloth on a window nail, a can of cod labeled halibut, to a glass sliver in a shoe sole, the inquiry concerns how the change occurred and who effected it. The range of physical changes is open ended; limitations on their use in describing human conduct come largely from a failure to recognize the content of nonverbal information or to preserve it in the contextual pattern. A third limitation concerns the organizational routes by which the physical evidence is utilized in social control generally. These flows of information start in nonverbal patterns of physical objects but they are subject to the personal biases as well as the organizational restraints acting upon the investigator. As the physical evidence is adduced from these changes, the transformation from nonverbal to verbal information is affected by scientific assessment. Subsequent communication along various administrative pathways brings about additional interpretations and a blending into decisions where the scientific assessments have from negligible to dominant effects. The problems of the proper utilization of physical evidence are poorly formulated at present, and there is a critical need for research on their solutions.

THE FORENSIC SCIENCE PROFESSIONS

"Every piece of evidence derives its meaning from the prior knowledge of the person who uses it."—Karl Deutsch

The explanatory and the predictive strengths of scientific investigative endeavor have sculptured significant economic, political, psychological, and social features in the world since the beginning of the nineteenth century. This influence has permeated the public consciousness and governance; one major effect was the blending of scientific assessment methods into the fact-finding procedures of the public domain.

Mathieu Orfila, in the early nineteenth century, began the systematic study of identifying poisons in biological tissue and determining the amounts present. His work, *Traité des Poisons, ou Toxicologie générale*, published in 1813, initiated forensic toxicology as a primary tool in solving cases of homicide by poisoning. Extensive studies of inorganic and organic poisons in animals were undertaken in the ensuing decades. With industrial development and the manufacture of synthetic chemicals, the problems expanded from intentional poisoning of another human being to intentional poisoning of one's self by drug abuse; accidental poisoning by available medications, products, and industrial environments; and negligent poisoning by general environmental pollution. Physical evidence demonstrating the presence, the quantity, and the activity of a poison is the service rendered by toxicology (Gettler, 1956; Forgotson, 1964; Brodie et al., 1965; Gangolli, 1969; Commission of Inquiry, 1970; Curry, 1970).

A finding of poisoning as a medical cause of death depends on the physical evidence adduced from the pathological examination. While gross pathology, i.e., the study of the anatomical and physiological abnormalities resulting from disease and trauma, was well developed in Europe by the end of the eighteenth century, the physical clues to alteration by and transmission of disease were not made explicit until the nineteenth century. Rudolf Virchow demonstrated the linkages between diseases and changes in cells or groups of cells, which he collected into a book published in 1858, *Cellular Pathology*. In 1857 Louis Pasteur first advanced his germ theory that was to become the foundation of infectious pathology (Dubos, 1950). The important field that explains human injury and death as influenced by the physical environment was developed by the forensic pathologists (Schultz, 1932; Helpern, 1964).

The revolution engendered by Charles Darwin's *Origin of the Species* in 1859 attracted attention to another dimension of physical evidence—human variability. Francis Galton took an intensive interest in the expanding use of fingerprints during that era and calculated that a fingerprint was a unique feature of individual identity. His conclusions, entitled *Fingerprints*, appeared in 1892. Karl Landsteiner's discovery of blood groups in 1901 marked the beginning of scientific studies that established the uniqueness of blood proteins in all individuals (Wiener, 1946); and in 1902, Archibald Garrod was speculating that the chemical processes of two separate individuals were different (Garrod, 1902).

The genetic inheritance, which establishes the range variations in humans, influences the very distinct physicochemical characteristics of each individual (Cummins & Midlu, 1961; Williams, 1963; Hulse, 1965; Lewis, 1971). In addition to the important use of fingerprints for personal identification, the blood types have been a significant contribution in investigation for forensic purposes (Brownlie, 1965; Outteridge, 1965; Sussman, 1968). The work of Margaret Pereira and Bryan Culliford in England within recent years has greatly advanced the use of blood proteins in connecting dried specimens to the probable shedder (Bargagna & Pereira, 1967; Culliford & Wraxall, 1968; Culliford, 1971).

The procedural methods of scientific fact-finding diffused into public investigative agencies from diverse sources. Alphonse Bertillon, as a clerk in the Paris Prefecture of Police, in 1883 introduced the precise measurements of human body structure, or anthropometry, as a solution to personal identification. To the equally important recording of environmental identification, Bertillon instituted the use of photography (Rhodes, 1968). Galton's theory as to the uniqueness of fingerprints prompted Juan Vucetich, a member of an Argentine police force, to devise a classification scheme in 1891. Vucetich's work prepared him for the solution of a tragic murder the following year when he connected the murderess with the crime by fingerprint evidence. Bertillon contributed to the replacement of anthropometry by fingerprints in personal identification through matching the file prints of a murderer, Scheffer, to the prints recovered from the scene of the crime.

In his book, *System Der Kriminalistik*, published in 1891, Hans Gross formalized the importance of scientific aid to criminal investigation and detailed practical instructions for utilizing scientific methods in fact-finding. The words *criminalistics* and *criminalist* were derived from this book and refer to the use of scientific knowledge in the administration of criminal justice. *System Der Kriminalistik* has been translated into all major languages. Undoubtedly, a most influential source in promoting public recognition and governmental acceptance was the fictional character of Sherlock Holmes created by Arthur Conan Doyle. While birth in print occurred in 1887 with *A Study in Scarlet*, public acclaim began in 1891 with the further publication of more Holmes adventures. The key element of physical evidence was clear from the first story where Watson reads from an article written by Holmes, "So all life is a great chain, the nature of which is known whenever we are shown a single link of it."

The increase in knowledge from the biological sciences not only benefited animal husbandry, crop management, and disease control, but focused attention on scientific potential for regulating human conduct in the public interest. The 1842 report of Edwin Chadwick, *Sanitary Conditions of the Labouring Population of Great Britain*, was instrumental in fomenting public health standards. Physical evidence from analytical procedures in bacteriology proved to be a tool of tremendous importance in public health supervision; Robert Koch demonstrated this importance in his Health Department work beginning in 1880 (Metchnikoff, 1939). With the Food and Drug Act of

1860 in England and the Pure Food and Drug Act of 1906 in America, a wide range of regulatory activities started with the guidance of physical evidence from scientific procedures.

The technical competence of fact-finding in the public domain grew with the mounting exploration of the natural and biological sciences. In certain areas of forensic service, professional groups gradually formed; for example, the Society for Analytical Chemists (1874), the Association of Official Analytical (formerly Agriculture) Chemists (1884), the International Academy of Pathology (1906), the American Society of Questioned Document Examiners (1942), the American Association of Forensic Sciences (1949), the Association of Public Analysts (1953), the California Association of Criminalists (1955), the British Academy of Forensic Sciences (1959), the Forensic Science Society (1959), and the International Association of Forensic Toxicologists (1963). The first two groups listed were composed of chemists with the responsibility for furnishing physical evidence needed in regulation of the pure food and drug acts in Great Britain and the United States. Other groups also represent a broad spectrum of forensic professions.

"The knowledge possessed by any science which is utilized in the administration of justice in any way, either in criminal or civil matters" is taken as the meaning of *forensic* by the American Association of Forensic Sciences (Hall, 1956:1). Its major divisions include criminalistics, psychiatry, odontology, toxicology, questioned documents, pathology and biology, and jurisprudence. The British Academy of Forensic Sciences seeks "to encourage the study, improve the practice and advance the knowledge of the forensic sciences" through the efforts of "anaesthetists, biochemists, biologists, chemists, coroners, members of forensic science laboratories, lawyers, pathologists, police officers, police surgeons, prison medical officers, psychiatrists and zoologists amongst many others" (Camps, 1960:1). The Forensic Science Society wants "to advance the study and application of forensic science and to facilitate co-operation among persons interested in forensic science" by a membership of "scientists, lawyers, pathologists, police surgeons and specialist police officers" with interests "both civil and criminal, research and applied" (Forensic Science Society Journal, 1960).

The growth in professional societies is mirrored in the literature related to forensic interests. An examination of the pertinent classifications in *Chemical Abstracts* reveals a doubling in the number of papers every decade for the last fifty years. This matches the current "estimates [which] range from 5% to 8% annual increase and from 10 to 15 years doubling span" for scientific literature in general (Emrich, 1970). English translations of the *System Der Kriminalistik* by Gross are now in the fifth edition (Gross, 1955). Other texts for the general investigator also cover the use of physical evidence (Soderman & O'Connell, 1962; Svensson & Wendell, 1965; Weston & Wells, 1970; Fong, 1971). The laboratory aspects of physical evidence are dealt with by a number of forensic scientists (O'Hara & Osterburg, 1949; Kirk, 1953; Nickolls, 1956; Lundquist, 1962, 1963; Curry (ed.), 1964, 1965; Kirk & Bradford, 1965; Osterburg, 1968; Walls, 1968). A series of three reports of national symposiums on *Law Enforcement, Science, and Technology* has collections of articles on criminalistics (Yefsky, 1967; Cohn, 1968; Cohn & McMahon, 1970). The current state in forensic science as a professional field has been discussed by a number of workers (Kirk, 1963; Parker, 1963; Curry, 1965, 1969, 1972; Nicol, 1967; Turner, 1967; Kwan et al., 1971). Current problems are a frequent topic in the professional literature (Dubowski, 1961; Borkenstein, 1964; Osterburg, 1967; Bradford & Samuel, 1970; English, 1970; Kingston, 1970). A few bibliographies on the forensic sciences have appeared (Brittain, 1962;

Nemec, 1969; American Academy of Forensic Sciences, 1973). Both interests and trends are found in the professional journals.

THE KALEIDOSCOPE OF PHYSICAL EVIDENCE

"An individual is a history unique in character."—John Dewey

Human beings generate physical change as part of the ceaseless shifting of material substance in the world as a whole. As evidence there is each shift or alteration of individual existence and environment. The conception of a human being requires a physical union of spermatozoon and egg. The growth of a human being necessitates the physical formation of bone, muscle, and nerve. The development of a human being involves the physical establishment of neuron networks. The impact of a human being issues from the physical interaction of self and community. The death of a human being begets a physical dissolution of organ and tissue structures. In every action of a human being, *intended or not,* an invariant aspect is physical change, and the quantity of changes generated is enormous as "human beings and the physical world proliferate variety" (Wilkins, 1970). Man's minimal needs for existence are exhibited, for example, in the assimilation of food stuffs, the fluctuation of physiological processes, the expiration of lung gases, the radiation of infrared energy, and the elimination of metabolic products in urine and feces. The uniqueness of his existence is expressed in part by his fingerprints and the structure of his bodily proteins. The personal nature of his existence is conveyed, among other signals, by visual attention, tactile contact, and verbal sound.

The human identity, described as a "continuous thread of sensation" (Lawden, 1970), is permeated and encompassed by physical change. In a matter of days, cells will replace internal membranes entirely with new molecules of protein and lipid. In the open system of the living cell, physical change is unceasing in the activity of maintaining a high energy state. The specific pattern of the individual cells, no less than the "thread" of the individual organism, is retained, while the molecules come and go. The intestinal wall undergoes a progressive renewal of structure; in the deep layers of the wall, proliferated cells move gradually toward the surface lining of the intestinal tract and are extruded. From reabsorbed cellular molecules and the influx of molecules by food assimilation, new cells and tissues are produced constantly. This dynamic renovation for the human existence is a kinetic interplay of physical changes at cellular, tissue, organ, and organism levels. The housekeeping function of the human body is critically dependent on that rhythmic flow of energy locked in chemical molecules. For the nerve cell, the act of transmission produces physical alterations and realignments with a rapidity measured in millionths of a second. Existence, movement, and thought are grounded in physical changes that furnish evidence for explaining the past and predicting the future.

Moreover, the physiological and psychological state of the human being and the sociological state of the human community are evidenced through physical change. Facial expressions and hand gestures are familiar signals: a wince of cheek muscles suggests a toothache or a cramp; while a flip of the hand, a welcome or a dismissal. To an infant, physical changes in light, sound, and personal contact begin the process of learning. The combination of biochemical influence in the individual and external exposure to social patterns presents a kinetic flux of physical changes affecting human development. Biochemical influences can be noted in the fluctuations of body temperature and in the ability to estimate time lapses with the time of day (Halberg et al., 1969). This biological, or circadian, rhythm also exists in the hormonal regulation of cellular activities. The clinical thermometer is a standard household item used to assess the stage of an illness. These periodicities of physical change are thought to be involved in some psychiatric cases (Richter, 1965), the cadence of a language (Jaffe & Feldstein, 1970), and the process of socialization (Key, 1970). A photograph of a social pattern critical to the viewer "can trigger emotional revelations otherwise withheld, can release psychological explosions and powerful statements of values" (Collier, 1967:62). The patterns of tools and other human extensions are rich leads to human behavior and its variations (Hammond, 1971). Emotional stress will result in changes in hormonal output, in blood pressure, and in speech characteristics in human beings (Levi, 1965; Hecker et al., 1968; Luk'yanov & Frolov, 1970; Shapiro & Schwartz, 1970; Michigan State Police, 1972). Conduct between people is related to physical changes, such as the crowding of an area or the scarcity of a commodity (Forrester, 1961; Ehrlich & Freedman, 1971). The continuation of human life at all levels from cellular to social is based on an unending selection of courses of action influenced by implicit and explicit physical changes.

Observation of physical changes provides an informational report for their sequence in a given course of action. As similar courses of action are observed, some changes are noted as repetitious and successive. One change, as a physical clue, can indicate precedent changes and specify a course of action. Several changes, as physical clues, can increase the likelihood that the inferred course of action is an accurate reading of the past. A commonplace illustration is where a mother scolds her son for spoiling his dinner by eating cookies. His reluctance to start dinner crystallizes in her mind several changes marginally noticed: a faint scuff mark on her freshly waxed kitchen floor, a small clump of mud on the rung of a kitchen chair, and a few crumbs about her son's lips. The "patterned relationship between events" (Deutsch, 1967) is perceived through the combination of remembered physical changes. Another illustration is a fire in a locked warehouse late at night. A number of physical changes are to be seen. Near a broken window of the warehouse, the street surface shows heavy black marks. Broken glass is strewn about the floor of the warehouse beneath the broken window. At the base of the wall opposite the broken window, a strip of burnt cloth and dark glass fragments are found after the fire is extinguished. Part of the wall baseboard is wet with a liquid of oily consistency. One inference from these physical changes is that a fire bomb was tossed through the window by a person in a hurry to leave the area. Closer examination of the physical changes will yield additional information to strengthen or weaken the particular inference.

The variety of physical changes emanating from human conduct is unending. A man's worn shoe can provide many possibilities for speculating about the man. Internal measurements present boundaries as to the maximum length and width of his foot. The wear of the sole and the heel offer suggestive leads to the flexibility in the joints of the foot, to the fit between foot and shoe, to the alignment of shoe and foot in movement, and to some characteristics of his gait. Distortions and creasings of the shoe add information. The imprint of his foot internally in dimensions and depth yields hints as to height and weight. In the wear and stain of the shoe lining, when considered along with the imprint features, reside facts about the size of his foot. The shoe style alludes to the man's life and tastes. Cloth fibers inside the shoe indicate the nature of clothing, while animal hairs can specify a pet's species and coloring. The finish on the shoe surface reports his care in appearance and movement. Materials, which adhere to or are embedded in the surface, tell of environmental exposures.

In addition to the physical changes between an individual and his environment as clues to human action, the physiological process is an enticing and potential lead to reconstructing conduct. As a nonverbal indicator, a physiological change is a functional response related to environmental and psychological conditions and is a likely "leakage channel of communication, less susceptible than verbal behavior to either conscious deception or unconscious censoring" (Ekman & Friesen, 1968:213). Conduct, recollected, actively experienced, or contemplated, produces in the autonomic nervous system changes in blood pressure, heart rate, respiration, skin resistance, muscle tension, brain waves, skin temperature, and salivation among others. The human being, as a participant in or an observer of an event sequence, is a highly individualistic record, which is subject to continuous processing. Retrieval from that record can lead to reconstructing the event sequence. However, the difficulty experienced in retrieval involves at least two aspects: a physiological change may not be in a simple one-to-one correspondence to a specific environmental condition (Johnson, 1970), and the dynamic integration in the individual's sensing and storing will create error in the human record (Rigby, 1970; Welford, 1970).

Since the polygraph ("lie-detector") provides an empirical correlation of physiological variables: heart rate, blood pressure, respiration, and electrodermal activity, within a construct of deception, it is often used as a tool in criminal investigation (Reid & Inbau, 1966). The subject individual is conditioned to accept the infallibility of the examiner in detecting deception. The examiner continuously observes the subject during the test procedure, as well as familiarizing himself with detailed background information on the individual. After reviewing with the subject the questions to be asked, the examiner monitors the noted physiological variables as the questions are posed. The diagnosis or interpretation can lead to the hiding place of stolen property or to the unknown grave of a missing person. Even contemplated behavior can be detected by measuring changes in heart rate (Schwartz & Higgins, 1971). However, the polygraph technique suffers from the limitation expressed clearly by Professor Fred Inbau: "the technique is no better than the man who is making the diagnosis" (House Committee on Governmental Operations, 1964; see also Horvath & Reid, 1971). One approach to proving expertise in such techniques could be a monitoring of physiological variables in the expert as he conducts an examination; the insight gained might well provide criteria for utilizing a man as a "black box." The ethical problem is a social question as to the appropriate employment of scientific knowledge. In criminal cases, Professor Helen Silving would prohibit the polygraph technique absolutely holding that "privacy of the Unconscious is thus a minimum requisite of man's dignity" (Silving, 1964:25; see also Skolnick, 1961). The same scientific problem is faced in validating voice identification methods, i.e., the reliability of the expert or examiner (Bolt et al., 1970). "Lacking explicit knowledge and procedures, can individuals nevertheless acquire such expertise in identification from voice patterns that their opinions could be accepted as reliable? This possibility may exist, for the human eye and brain are superb instruments. But it cannot be assumed without proof" (pp. 601-2).

Future reconstructions of human conduct could employ techniques based on evoked brain potentials which afford the possibility of measuring the human treatment of sensory information (MacKay et al., 1970) and re-forming the visual stimuli (Pinneo, 1970). Although a "unifying theoretical framework" is still to be erected for the interplay of psychology and physiology, "there is now a technology for studying the inherent social-biological nature of man" and tapping individual perception of human conduct (Shapiro & Schwartz, 1970:107).

The extent and the amount of physical change associated with a man's actions have

TABLE 1
CRIMINAL CONDUCT AND PHYSICAL EVIDENCE

Offense	Officially Reported Cases (Set)			Study Cases (Subset)			
	Total	Cleared	Laboratory Review Requests	Total	Possible Physical Evidence	Potential Physical Evidence	Physical Evidence Categories in cases with Physical Evidence (median)
Burglary	875	260	0	547	484	139	3
Auto Theft	328	83	0	85	80	18	3
Theft	1,679[1]	332[1]	0	45	33	10	3
Robbery	101	51	1	26	21	13	2
Rape	26	17	0	6	6	1	4
Assault/ Battery	292[2]	244	1	6	5	2	3
Murder	2	2	2	5[3]	5	3	6
Subtotal	3,303	989	4	720	634	186	3
Forgery	165	101	6	—	—	—	
Narcotics, Drugs	532	532	452	—	—	—	
Drunk Driving	35	35	25	1	1	1	
Other	4,168	3,413	2	28	21	15	4
Total	8,203	5,070	489	749	656	202	3

1. 209 cases of the 1,679 total involved thefts in excess of $50; 36 of these 209 cases were cleared.
2. 60 cases of the 292 total involved battery.
3. Suspected offense on initial investigation.

an effect on the use of evidence. If the extent of physical change from a course of action is minor or the amount of change is minimal, only extraordinary care will prevent loss. One useful concept in considering these two aspects of physical evidence is to view the individual as generating a set of kinetic fields. The boundary of each field represents the limit to which a physical change will carry or within which it will be found. Speech, as an example, will become unintelligible at relatively short distances from the speaker. Obviously, a telephone will enlarge the boundary while reducing the amount of physical change to the band width of frequencies employed. This quantity is still considerable, being on the order of 30,000 bits of information per second of speech (Resnikoff & Sitton, 1968), which can be sufficient to identify the speaker (Hecker, 1971; NAS-NRC Committee, 1971; Michigan State Police, 1972; Tosi et al., 1972). For a second example, a man in the course of twenty-four hours will lose a hundred head hairs (Webb, 1964). These will be spread over the area he covers in that period of time. The bed pillow, a hat, and a comb will collect many of these hairs as field boundaries to the distribution.

Patterns of energy and matter provide a scheme for classifying such physical changes, i.e., position, transfer, impression, break or tear, dispersion, and physicochemical nature. Position, including orientation, of a physical object tells possible histories of prior position: a paper beneath the wheel of a car was (1) there when the car stopped, (2) placed there when the wheel was lifted, (3) blown there by a strong gust of wind, etc. Transfer involves a reallocation between three physical objects after contact is broken: the dirt on a small boy's hands is left on the towel. Impression comes from the pressure imprint of one physical object upon another where movement between the two may occur during the imprinting: on biting into a hunk of cheese, the surface configuration of individual teeth is seen clearly. A break or tear presents the split of a physical object by force: a paper match is ripped from a book. Dispersion is the disintegration and scatter of a physical object by force: the fragments of the dropped glass cover a wide section of the floor. Physicochemical nature is the intrinsic structure and composition of the physical object, i.e., the onion is many layered and eye-watering.

Parker and Peterson (1972) measured the amount of physical change in criminal investigation of a wide range of criminal activities. Over a period of three months, crime scenes in the city of Berkeley (California) were examined at first hand for possible physical evidence. There were few crime scenes where no physical residues were observed, i.e., seven out of eight cases yielded recognizable physical residues. About 10 percent of the cases with no physical residues involved scenes that had been cleaned up by the victim or that were inaccessible to the staff observer. In approximately 40 percent of the cases with no physical residues, the conditions of the scene area suggested negligible contact between scene and criminal, e.g., entry was made through an open door and a television set was taken. Physical residues were found at all crime scenes where the suspected offense was rape or murder.

Thus, the degree of physical activity, i.e., extent of violence, appeared to correlate with the quantity of physical residues from criminal conduct. No distinction was noted as to the availability of physical residues between all crime scenes and those crime scenes involving suspects. Tool marks and fingerprints accounted for one-fourth of all types or categories of physical residues; over one-half was accounted for by adding the four categories: foreign matter, glass fragments, paint fragments, and tracks. Table 1 presents a composite picture of criminal conduct and physical evidence. Clearance data from the official records are given for the various offense categories, and official requests for laboratory review are presented. As a subset, the offenses where an actual crime-scene observation was made are shown. The numbers in the "possible physical evidence" column represent those crime scenes yielding physical residues. The numbers in the "potential physical evidence" column represent those crime scenes with physical residues where a suspect was either known or arrested. The "median" column represents the number of types or categories of physical residues found for each offense.

While the physical changes of human conduct offer a nonverbal record of that conduct, they are immersed in a flux of other changes which comprise the totality of the physical world. In time, the changes effected by a given course of action become physically altered by becoming part of other courses of action. The scuff mark on the waxed kitchen floor is gradually abraded by the movements and activities of family members and, finally, is obliterated by a new waxing. The broken glass fragments in the warehouse are swept together with debris from other sources and dumped into the garbage. Volatile components in the oily liquid evaporate quickly from the wall baseboard. Those physical changes recording human conduct of particular interest will be lost more or less gradually in the complexity of material shifts over time. Of equal importance to this loss is the possibility of error in inferring the antecedent physical changes or the course of action producing the noted physical change. The faint scuff mark on the kitchen floor is from a younger child's toy rather than from the movement of a chair to the cupboard. A near automobile accident on the street left skid marks that might be interpreted as the drag marks from the rapid acceleration of a getaway car.

Since human conduct relies heavily on physical changes as cues to guide decisions, an individual can act on prior experience without considering all possibilities, and reach an unwarranted conclusion. This error is more pronounced at times when the given change is presented in isolation from the site of action. Taken out of the context of the action, a physical change is easily misinterpreted. As an illustration, during a series of incendiary attacks on commercial businesses, the drugstore owned by a professed radical catches fire. While the owner is immediately suspected of manufacturing incendiary devices from stock chemicals, a thorough investigation uncovers the accidental origin of the blaze. The perceptual difficulties that can lead to misinterpretations are avoidable by careful consideration and examination of alternative explanations. However, the time dependency of nonverbal information carried by physical changes and the human fallibility in interpretation of physical changes presents a need for methods which will assure greater reliability in utilizing physical evidence as a report on criminal conduct.

UTILIZATION OF PHYSICAL EVIDENCE

*"A technology requires a counterpart in social organization
before it can be used effectively by a society."*—Jerome S. Bruner

The potential for scientific assessment of physical evidence in the public interest is apparent and, in specific instances, is abundantly realized. As routine utilization, however, these assessments are infrequent. The limitations in use are not from a lack of knowing how to assess but rather from a lack of applying that knowledge. By definition, essential ingredients for scientific assessment include competent personnel, adequate tools, and sufficient facilities. But the fulfillment of this definition is often neglected. A report released in May, 1971, characterized the U.S. Food and Drug Administration as "an almost comprehensive catalogue of possible deficiencies in science management that ranges from its subordination of scientific facts to political and economic consider-ations, to bad morale among scientists, low productivity, antiquated equipment, skimpy record-keeping and even laboratories that are actually unsafe" (Nature, 1971:277; also see Ritts et al., 1971).

Also in 1961, data collected from some seventy U.S. cities and states regarding "crime" laboratories was analyzed. Several indices of utilization were constructed: per-cent of all known offenses processed by the laboratories, expenditures in both city and metropolitan areas, expenditures per case processed, percent of city revenue used on the crime laboratory, and case load per professional laboratory staff member (Parker, 1963). Similar indices were constructed on data gathered in a similar survey in 1965 (L.E.A.A., 1968). Cases received by the laboratories relative to all reported cases, the primary index, was under 2 percent for both years (Parker & Peterson, 1972:6). The desirable average costs per case were estimated as $150, and the desirable average work load per professional staff member as 50 cases. The comparison of the remaining in-dices is shown in Table 2. On the basis of these annual estimates, "the forensic science laboratory in the United States must handle five times the normal work load with but one-third the necessary funds" (Parker, 1963:419).

The critical conditions for utilization of personnel, tools, and facilities involve a recovery of physical changes emanating from human conduct, a scientific interpretation of these physical changes, and an integration of this scientific interpretation into the social procedures for seeking justice. It is this last condition, the translation of an interpretation into a procedure for control, that is the key to realizing the potential in physical evidence for public use. An example is the increasing hazard of adulteration in food accompanying the urbanization of a society (Horwitz & Reynolds, 1967). The evolution of forensic chemistry provided measures of adulteration, first qualitative and then quantitative, that established the means for regulating and reducing this hazard. From this capability came a social structure for translating the scientific assessment into a guide for human behavior.

Regulation of raw materials and processing procedures for food has been estab-lished, but similar standards for procedures and reference materials have not yet been achieved in dealing with the traditional crimes against persons and property. While the benefits in utilizing physical evidence for public purposes can be enormous, the difficulties are often of equal magnitude (Library of Congress, 1969). The political matrix can obscure the contribution that physical evidence can make to regulatory policy and procedures. An instance in current history, one aspect of the concern about "crime in the streets," is the relationship between crime and the physical surroundings.

TABLE 2

COMPARISON OF FOUR INDICES OF CRIME LABORATORY UTILIZATION

Index	1961	1965
Laboratory cost per 100,000 population (median value)	$3,650	$3,100
Expenditure per case (median value)	$45	$12
Support from city revenue (median value)	0.06%	0.06%
Case load per professional staff member (median value)	247	300

Source: Parker and Peterson, 1972:6.

The influence of city design and growth on criminal opportunities is slowly being marked out (Forrester, 1969; Luedtke & Associates, 1970; Batty, 1971; Newman, 1973). Many other influences are also a part of the social flux which political decision seeks to regulate.

The role of physical evidence begins in the investigation of complaints about human conduct. Complaints can occur after the fact of damage or injury, or from monitoring conduct with high potential for damage or injury. The secret nature of some crimes, the public apathy in reporting many crimes, and the absence of definitive victims in certain crimes are but a few of the causes that limit complaints and cause problems for those who are trying to establish a basis for reference that will afford a measure for changes in governmental policies (Biderman, 1967; President's Commission, 1967; Edelhertz, 1970). Even if one excludes the unreported incidents, the actual number of complaints exceeds manyfold the investigative resources of society. For example, the federal Food and Drug Administration "can do no more than spot check the food and drugs entering the market" (Nature, 1971:280) and the Internal Revenue Service receives over one hundred million tax returns with an audit of "only 3 million of them" (Congressional Quarterly, 1971a:1049).

As a further example of resource limitation, in 1970 the crime-index offenses, nationally, amounted to more than five million (Congressional Quarterly, 1971b; F.B.I., 1971). The total number of sworn police officers exceeded 400,000; investigational personnel approached 40,000. The standard 40-hour work week means 2,000 hours annually per person. Since a police department handles many noncriminal matters, departmental time spent for criminal matters is less than 40 percent of the available time (Misner et al., 1970:226; Webster, 1973). The seven felonies included in the crime-index offenses account, in number, for a small proportion of criminal incidents known to the police. If these known incidents amount to fifty million for one year, it would require the investigation of one to two criminal incidents every hour by each police investigator. Additional complications, such as simultaneous reporting of several incidents at the same time and distance between the incident locale and the nearest available officer, quickly multiply the work load. The end result is what Gordon Misner calls

> a system of "selective neglect," a system which is common in all sorts of occupations. Administrators—and rank-in-file personnel—may have a keen desire to do an outstanding job. Pressures, competing demands, lack of resources, lack of leadership or supervision, and countless other factors may manifestly interfere with the "doing of the job" (Misner et al., 1970:278).

Investigation, whether a simple check by a patrol officer or a complex activity of several officers and specialized personnel, must be a *selective* process of information gathering, a process that includes gathering the nonverbal information of physical evidence.

The relative abundance of physical evidence in various instances of criminal conduct is of little help in selection. Scientific professionals in the forensic sciences consider physical evidence to be a common, if not an inevitable, consequence of criminal conduct. Director Duayne Dillon of the Criminalistics Laboratory, Contra Costa County, California, reviewed 200 burglaries, equally divided between residential and commercial locations. Table 3 shows the possibilities for physical evidence, although no investigational use was made of such evidence (Dillon, 1970). Other studies have confirmed this view (Shaw, 1970; Parker & Peterson, 1972).

The probative value in certain individual cases is also clear in view of the types of physical evidence, i.e., tool marks, fingerprints, etc., that are found commonly and that are used in the inferences constructed for investigational and administrational purposes. Equally as important as the ready availability of physical evidence is the multiplicity of types of evidence in criminal violations.

An investigator's rationale that physical evidence is uncommon is not supportable. Behind this rationale, which is used to explain the treatment and frequent neglect of physical evidence, is the behavior of investigators that can be categorized into four modes of action. The first mode is determined by a legal requirement for physical evidence. Illegal possession of a narcotic drug, drunk driving, or placing, knowingly or unknowingly, an adulterant in flour would be examples of criminal conduct where the physical evidence is specified.

The second mode of action is determined by a community requirement, which is expressed as a collective abhorrence of specific conduct. Homicide is a classical example; a particularly interesting feature to note is that initial conclusions by investigators of homicide cases too often are not followed by requests for laboratory review for confirmatory opinions. The scientific aid of a laboratory is *not* part of the decision process as to offense classification. This fact is apparent when a contrast is made between homicide and suicide classifications. In one jurisdiction, an examination of "suicide" case records for a five-year period turned up 64 deaths which involved notes (handwritten, printed, and typed!) in a total of 187 but not one request for laboratory review of a note against exemplars (Grazia, 1967). The offense classification of "suicide" appeared to remove a suspicious death from the necessity of considering physical evidence, indeed, stopped investigation in 176 out of the 187 deaths.

The third mode of action is determined by the availability of investigative personnel who act as paraprofessionals. Forgery is one example of an offense where the investigator makes physical evidence decisions, sometimes based on a more or less rudimentary knowledge of document examination. The value of such action to

TABLE 3

POSSIBILITIES FOR PHYSICAL EVIDENCE IN TWO HUNDRED BURGLARIES

	Residential	Commercial
Total	100	100
Type of entry		
Walk in	55	15
Door forced	25	32
Window forced	20	48
Roof forced	0	5
Suspect		
Total developed	12	12
No case made	7	2
Case made, no prosecution	4	0
Arrest and prosecution	1	10
Physical evidence utilized	1	0
Arrest at scene or eyewitness	0	6
Confession resulting from arrest in subsequent case	0	4

Source: Dillon, 1970.

investigation remains to be measured along with the reliability and accuracy of individual investigators.

The fourth mode of action is determined by the investigator's awareness of prevailing case loads for scientific laboratories and an intuitive evaluation of laboratory results. Burglary is a good example where requests for laboratory review are constricted by an informal analysis of practical limitations referred to as a "system of selective neglect" (Misner et al., 1970). The danger in this method of operation is that a lack of practice in retrieving physical evidence is likely to result in overlooking important evidence when the big case happens.

Investigators and others users of scientific information obtainable from physical evidence have two major needs to be met. Leads to suspects are urgently needed by the investigator. Active information (Willmer, 1968) for this purpose may reside in the physical residues at scenes. Affirmation or negation of a physical connection between a suspect and a scene is needed by users in justice administration. Passive information (Willmer, 1968) to meet this desire may be found in comparing the physical residues at scenes with those found on the suspect or in his possession. To make this request for passive information, the investigators submit collections of physical evidence from precisely those scenes to which the suspects are thought to be related. If arrests are random phenomena (Greenwood, 1970), then collections from all scenes with physical evidence must be made if physical correlations between scenes and all suspects are to be examined. If arrests are not random, the relationship to scenes needs to be made explicit in order to make the necessary collections (Willmer, 1970).

There is a critical need to know how scientific information from physical evidence can contribute optimally to the reduction of criminal conduct. Chief Justice of the Supreme Court Warren E. Burger predicts a reduced crime rate if criminal cases were tried within sixty days after indictment (Burger, 1970). Proper planning for the prevention of crime includes utilization of enhanced detection as a factor influencing certain types of behavior. The part to be played by laboratory review in either circumstance is suffering from ignorance. Wolfgang (1971) suggests that an accounting by the criminal justice system to the public, to the victim, to the offender, and to each subsystem by the subsequent subsystem would benefit society. He wants "this system, and all its subparts, to be accountable, to show me that production is higher this year than last, that more [true] offenders have been arrested, that more are correctly prosecuted, that more are returned to society without further criminality" (1971:90). The prevailing state of knowledge about the utilization of physical evidence is inadequate for even a first approximation in such an accounting (Benson et al., 1970; Kingston, 1970; Rosenthal & Plummer, 1970; Parker & Peterson, 1972; but see Parker & Gurgin, 1972).

Physical evidence must be evaluated against *all* types of investigative information if a rational allocation of resources is desired. In that evaluation inherent features to be considered are "the ways in which people see things, and the ways in which they think when dealing with problems" (Bauer, 1967:122). Users and interpreters of physical evidence are fallible despite the best of intentions. The seasoned investigator will still reach for physical objects at a scene just to confirm that what he thinks he sees is real. The competent scientist, faced by a practical problem, "has a capacity that is nearly infinite for reading the evidence in the light of his own interests and passions" (Price, 1965:140). These and kindred difficulties present a fascinating challenge to engaging scientific assessment of physical evidence in the social control of criminal conduct.

REFERENCES

American Academy of Forensic Sciences.
  1973   What's New in Forensic Sciences. Annual publication. Salt Lake City, Utah:
          American Academy of Forensic Sciences.

Bargagna, M., and M. Pereira.
  1967   "A study of absorption-elution as a method of identification of Rhesus
          antigens in dried bloodstains." Forensic Science Society Journal 7:123–
          130.

Batty, M.
  1971   "Modelling cities as dynamic systems." Nature 231:425–428.

Bauer, R. A.
  1967   "Application of behavioral science," in Applied Science and Technological
          Progress. National Academy of Sciences (June). Washington, D.C.: U.S.
          Government Printing Office.

Benson, W. R., J. E. Stacy, Jr., and J. D. Nicol.
  1970   "Systems analysis and the crime laboratory." Pp. 493–503 in S. I. Cohn and
          W. B. McMahon (eds.), Proceedings of the Third National Symposium
          on Law Enforcement, Science, and Technology. Chicago: IIT Research
          Institute.

Biderman, A. D.
  1967   "Social indicators and goals," in R. A. Bauer (ed.), Social Indicators.
          Cambridge: M.I.T. Press.

Bolt, R. H., F. S. Cooper, E. E. David, Jr., P. B. Denes, J. M. Pickett, and K. N. Stevens.
  1970   "Speaker identification by speech spectrograms: a scientist's view of its
          reliability for legal purposes." Acoustical Society of America Journal 47:
          597–612.

Borkenstein, R. F.
  1964   "The administration of a forensic science laboratory," in A. S. Curry (ed.),
          Methods of Forensic Science, vol. 3. New York: Interscience.

Bradford, L. W., and A. H. Samuel.
  1970   "Research and development needs in criminalistics." Pp. 465–476 in S. I.
          Cohn and W. M. McMahon (eds.), Proceedings of the Third National
          Symposium on Law Enforcement, Science, and Technology. Chicago: IIT
          Research Institute.

Brittain, R. P.
  1962   Bibliography of Medico-Legal Works in English. London: Sweet & Maxwell.
Brodie, B. B., G. J. Cosmides, and P. Rall.
  1965   "Toxicology and the biomedical sciences." Science 148:1547–1554.

Brownlie, A. R.
  1965   "Blood and the blood groups." Forensic Science Society Journal 5:124–174.
Burger, Warren E.
  1970   Address to the American Bar Association, St. Louis, Missouri, August 10.
Camps, F. E.
  1960   "Editorial." Medicine, Science and the Law 1:1–5.
Cohn, S. I.
  1968   "Criminalistics." Pp. 313–431 in S. I. Cohn (ed.), Proceedings of the Sec-

ond National Symposium on Law Enforcement, Science, and Technology. Chicago: IIT Research Institute.

Cohn, S. I., and W. B. McMahon.
1970   "Criminalistics." Pp. 453–533 in S. I. Cohen and W. M. McMahon (eds.), Proceedings of the Third National Symposium on Law Enforcement, Science, and Technology. Chicago: IIT Research Institute.

Collier, J., Jr.
1967   Visual Anthropology: Photography as a Research Method. New York: Holt, Rinehart & Winston.

Commission of Inquiry into the Non-Medical Uses of Drugs.
1970   Interim Report of the Commission of Inquiry into the Non-Medical Uses of Drugs. Ottawa: Queen's Printer for Canada.

Congressional Quarterly.
1971a   "White collar crime: huge economic and moral drain." 24:1047–1049.
1971b   "Crime statistics: improving but still incomplete." 24:1336–1339.

Culliford, B. J.
1971   The Examination and Typing of Bloodstains in the Crime Laboratory. Washington, D.C.: U.S. Government Printing Office.

Culliford, B. J., and B. G. D. Wraxall.
1968   "Adenylate kinase (AK) types in bloodstains." Forensic Science Society Journal 8:79–80.

Cummins, J., and Charles Midlu.
1961   Finger Prints, Palms and Soles. New York: Dover.

Curry, A. S.
1965   "Science against crime." International Science and Technology 47:39–48.
1969   "Chemistry and crime." Chemistry in Britain 5:501–504.
1970   "The changing attitudes in toxicology." Aerospace Medicine 41:754–756.
1972   "Recent developments in forensic science." Nature 235:369–371.

Curry, A. S. (ed.)
1964   Methods of Forensic Science, vol. 3. New York: Interscience.
1965   Methods of Forensic Science, vol. 4. New York: Interscience.

Deutsch, K.
1967   The Nerves of Government. New York: Free Press.

Dillon, D.
1970   Personal communication from Criminalistics Laboratory, Contra Costa County, California.

Dubos, R. J.
1950   Louis Pasteur. Boston: Little, Brown.

Dubowski, K. M.
1961   "Organization of forensic chemical laboratories in non-metropolitan areas." Journal of Criminal Law, Criminology and Police Science 51:575–580.

Edelhertz, H.
1970   The Nature, Impact and Prosecution of White-Collar Crime. Law Enforcement Assistance Administration ICR 70-1 (May). Washington, D.C.: U.S. Government Printing Office.

Ehrlich, P., and J. Freedman.
1971   "Population, crowding, and human behavior." New Scientist and Science Journal 50:10–14.

Ekman, P., and W. V. Friesen.
    1968   "Nonverbal behavior in psychotherapy research," in J. M. Shlien, H. F.
            Hunt, J. O. Matarazzo, and C. Savage (eds.), Research in Psychotherapy,
            vol. 3. Washington, D.C.: American Psychological Association.

Emrich, B. R.
    1970   Scientific and Technical Information Explosion. Air Force Weapons Lab-
            oratory, Wright-Patterson Air Force Base, Ohio (November).

English, J. M.
    1970   "Forensic science in criminal prosecution." Analytical Chemistry 42(No-
            vember):40A–48A.

Federal Bureau of Investigation (F.B.I.)
    1971   Crime in the United States: Uniform Crime Reports—1970. Washington,
            D.C.: U.S. Government Printing Office.

Fong, W.
    1971   "Criminalistics and the prosecutor," in P. F. Healy and J. P. Manak (eds.),
            The Prosecutor's Deskbook. Chicago: National District Attorneys As-
            sociation.

Forensic Science Society Journal.
    1960   "The forensic science society." 1:inside back cover.

Forgotson, E. H.
    1964   "Liability for long-term latent effects of toxic agents." American Bar As-
            sociation Journal 50:142–145.

Forrester, J. W.
    1961   Industrial Dynamics. Cambridge: M.I.T. Press.
    1969   Urban Dynamics. Cambridge: M.I.T. Press.

Gangolli, S. D.
    1969   "Analytical chemistry in toxicity testing." Chemistry in Britain 5:510–513.

Garrod, A. E.
    1902   "The incidence of alkaptonuria: a study in chemical individuality." Lancet
            209(December):1616–1620.

Gettler, A. O.
    1956   "The historical development of toxicology." Journal of Forensic Sciences
            1:3–25.

Grazia, A-dis.
    1967   "Suicide? . . . the investigation of suicides and attempts in a city of over
            400,000 population." Graduate paper, School of Criminology, University of
            California, Berkeley.

Greenwood, P. W.
    1970   An Analysis of the Apprehension Activities of the New York City Police
            Department. New York: The New York City Rand Institute.

Gross, H.
    1955   Criminal Investigation. R. L. Jackson (ed.). Fifth Edition. London: Sweet &
            Maxwell.

Halberg, F., J. Reinhardt, F. C. Bartter, C. Delea, R. Gordon, A. Reinberg, J. Gatha,
            M. Halhuber, H. Hofmann, R. Gunther, E. Knapp, J. C. Pera, and M. Garcia
            Sainz.
    1969   "Agreements in end points from circadian rhythmometry on healthy human
            beings living on different continents." Experientia 25:107–112.

Hall, G. E.
    1956   "Editorial—'forensic' sciences." Journal of Forensic Sciences 1:1–2.
Hammond, A. L.
    1971   "The new archeology: towards a social science." Science 172:1119–1120.
Hecker, M. H. L.
    1971   Speaker Recognition: An Interpretive Survey of the Literature. Washington, D.C.: American Speech & Hearing Association.
Hecker, M. H. L., K. N. Stevens, G. von Bismark, and C. Williams.
    1968   "Manifestations of task-induced stress in the acoustic speech signal." Acoustical Society of America Journal 44:993–1001.
Helpern, M.
    1964   "Forensic pathology and the law," in L. A. Bear (ed.), Law, Medicine, Science and Justice. Springfield, Ill.: Thomas.
Horvath, F. S., and J. E. Reid.
    1971   "The reliability of polygraph examiner diagnosis of truth and deception." Journal of Criminal Law, Criminology and Police Science 62:276–281.
Horwitz, W., and H. L. Reynolds.
    1967   "Developments in adulteration of food and its detection." Journal of the Association of Analytical Chemists 50:1024–1032.
House Committee on Governmental Operations.
    1964   "Use of polygraphs as 'lie detectors' by the federal government," Part 1. 88th Cong., 2d sess., April 7–9.
Hulse, F. S.
    1965   The Human Species. New York: Random House.
Jaffe, J., and S. Feldstein.
    1970   Rhythms of Dialogue. New York: Academic Press.
Johnson, L. C.
    1970   "A psychophysiology for all states." Psychophysiology 6:501–516.
Key, P.
    1970   Explorations in Mathematical Anthropology. Cambridge: M.I.T. Press.
Kingston, C. R.
    1970   "A national criminalistics research program." Pp. 453–460 in S. I. Cohn and W. B. McMahon (eds.), Proceedings of the Third National Symposium on Law Enforcement, Science, and Technology. Chicago: IIT Research Institute.
Kirk, P. L.
    1953   Crime Investigation. New York: Interscience.
    1963   "Criminalistics." Science 140:367–370.
Kirk, P. L., and L. W. Bradford.
    1965   Crime Laboratory. Springfield, Ill.: Thomas.
Kwan, Q. Y., P. Rajeswaran, B. P. Parker, and M. Amir.
    1971   "The role of criminalistics in white-collar crimes." Journal of Criminal Law, Criminology and Police Science 62:437–449.
Law Enforcement Assistance Administration (L.E.A.A.)
    1968   Crime Laboratories—Three Study Reports. Washington, D.C.: Law Enforcement Assistance Administration.
Lawden, D. F.
    1970   "The phenomenon of time dilation." Spaceflight 12:178–183.

Levi, L.
  1965   "The urinary output of adrenalin and noradrenalin during pleasant and un-
          pleasant emotional states." Psychosomatic Medicine 27:80–85.
Lewis, W. H. P.
  1971   "Polymorphism of human enzyme proteins." Nature 230:215–218.
Library of Congress.
  1969   Technical Information for Congress. House Document 91-137 (April 25).
          Washington, D.C.: U.S. Government Printing Office.
Luedtke and Associates.
  1970   Crime and the Physical City. NTIS #PB196-784. Detroit, Mich.: Law En-
          forcement Assistance Administration.
Luk'yanov, A. N., and M. V. Frolov.
  1970   Signals of Human Operator State. NASA TT F-609. Washington, D.C.:
          National Aeronautics and Space Administration.
Lundquist, F. (ed.)
  1962   Methods of Forensic Science, vol. 1. New York: Interscience.
  1963   Methods of Forensic Science, vol. 2. New York: Interscience.
MacKay, D. M., E. F. Evans, P. Hammond, D. A. Jeffreys, and D. Regan.
  1970   "Evoked brain potentials as indicators of sensory information processing,"
          in F. O. Schmitt, T. Melnechuk, G. C. Quarton, and G. Adelman (eds.),
          Neurosciences Research Symposium Summaries, vol. 4. Cambridge: M.I.T.
          Press.
Metchnikoff, E.
  1939   The Founders of Modern Medicine. New York: Walden.
Michigan State Police.
  1972   Voice Identification Research. Washington, D.C.: U.S. Government Printing
          Office.
Misner, G. E., et al.
  1970   Prevention and Deterrence of Robbery and Assaults on Bus Drivers, vol. 2.
          Berkeley: School of Criminology, University of California at Berkeley.
NAS-NRC Committee on Hearing, Bioacoustics and Biomechanics Research on Speaker
          Verification.
  1971   Research on Speaker Verification. Washington, D.C.: National Academy of
          Science–National Research Council.
Nature.
  1971   "FDA called unhealthy for science and scientists." 231:277–280.
Nemec, J.
  1969   International Bibliography of Medicolegal Serials, 1736–1967. Public Health
          Service, U.S. Department of Health, Education and Welfare. Washington,
          D.C.: U.S. Government Printing Office.
Newman, O.
  1973   Architectural Design for Crime Prevention. Washington, D.C.: U.S. Gov-
          ernment Printing Office.
Nickolls, L. C.
  1956   The Scientific Investigation of Crime. London: Butterworth.
Nicol, J. D.
  1967   "Present status of criminalistics." Pp. 245–246 in S. A. Yefsky (ed.), Pro-

ceedings of the First National Symposium on Law Enforcement, Science, and Technology. New York: Thompson.

O'Hara, C. E., and J. W. Osterburg.
1949   Introduction to Criminalistics. New York: Macmillan.

Osterburg, J. W.
1967   "Tutorial: what problems must criminalistics solve?" Pp. 297–303 in S. A. Yefsky (ed.), Proceedings of the First National Symposium on Law Enforcement, Science, and Technology. New York: Thompson.
1968   Crime Laboratory. Bloomington: Indiana University Press.

Outteridge, R. A.
1965   "The biological individuality of dried human bloodstains." Forensic Science Society Journal 5:22–51.

Parker, B. P.
1963   "The status of forensic science in the administration of criminal justice." Revista Juridica de la Universidad de Puerto Rico 32:405–419.

Parker, B. P., and V. A. Gurgin.
1972   The Role of Criminalistics in the World of the Future. Menlo Park, Cal.: Stanford Research Institute.

Parker, B. P., and J. Peterson.
1972   Physical Evidence Utilization in the Administration of Justice. Washington, D.C.: National Institute of Law Enforcement and Criminal Justice.

Pinneo, L. R.
1970   Private communication from Neurophysiology Program, Stanford Research Institute, Menlo Park, California.

President's Commission on Law Enforcement and Administration of Justice.
1967   The Challenge of Crime in a Free Society. Washington, D.C.: U.S. Government Printing Office.

Price, D. K.
1965   The Scientific Estate. London: Oxford University Press.

Reid, J. E., and F. E. Inbau.
1966   Truth and Deception: the Polygraph ("Lie-Detector") Technique. Baltimore: Williams & Wilkins.

Resnikoff, H. L., and G. A. Sitton.
1968   "A new type of hearing aid." Rice University Review 3(2):31–35.

Rhodes, H. T. F.
1968   Alphonse Bertillon. New York: Greenwood Press.

Richter, C. P.
1965   Biological Clocks in Medicine and Psychiatry. Springfield, Ill.: Thomas.

Rigby, L. V.
1970   "The nature of human error." Pp. 457–466 in Transactions, 24th Annual Technical Conference, American Society for Quality Control, Pittsburgh, Pennsylvania, May 11–13.

Ritts, R. E., Jr., M. W. Anders, B. A. Cole, J. R. Crout, W. A. Krehl, and L. A. Wood.
1971   Report to the Commission on Food and Drugs from the FDA *Ad Hoc* Science Advisory Committee.

Rosenthal, P., and D. K. Plummer.
1970   "Evaluation of forensic laboratory practices." Pp. 477–491 in S. I. Cohn

and W. B. McMahon (ed.), Proceedings of the Third National Symposium on Law Enforcement, Science, and Technology. Chicago: IIT Research Institute.

Schultz, O. T.
1932   Possibilities and Need for Development of Legal Medicine in the United States. National Research Council Bulletin No. 87 (October). Washington, D.C.: U.S. Government Printing Office.

Schwartz, G. E., and J. D. Higgins.
1971   "Cardiac activity preparatory to overt and covert behavior." Science 173: 1144–1146.

Shapiro, D., and G. E. Schwartz.
1970   "Psychophysiological contributions to social psychology." Annual Review of Psychology 21:87–112.

Shaw, D. F.
1970   "Enhanced resources at the scene." Forensic Science Society Journal 10: 255–260.

Silving, H.
1964   "Manipulation of the unconscious in criminal cases," in L. A. Bear (ed.), Law, Medicine, Science and Justice. Springfield, Ill.: Thomas.

Skolnick, J. H.
1961   "Scientific theory and scientific evidence: an analysis of lie detection." Yale Law Journal 70:694–728.

Soderman, H., and J. J. O'Connell.
1962   Modern Criminal Investigation. Fifth Edition. New York: Funk & Wagnalls.

Sussman, L. N.
1968   Blood Grouping Tests—Medicolegal Uses. Springfield, Ill.: Thomas.

Svensson, A., and O. Wendell.
1965   Techniques of Crime Scene Investigation. J. D. Nicol (ed.). Second Edition. New York: American Elsevier.

Tosi, O., H. Oyer, W. Lashbrook, C. Pedrey, J. Nicol, and E. Nash.
1972   "Experiment on voice identification." Acoustical Society of America Journal 51:2030–2043.

Turner, R. F.
1967   "Technical evidence—its availability in the justice process." Pp. 247–249 in S. A. Yefsky (ed.), Proceedings of the First National Symposium on Law Enforcement, Science, and Technology. New York: Thompson.

Walls, H. J.
1968   Forensic Science. New York: Praeger.

Webb, P.
1964   Bioastronautics Data Book. NASA SP-3006. Washington, D.C.: National Aeronautics and Space Administration.

Webster, J. A.
1973   The Realities of Police Work. Dubuque, Ia.: Kendall/Hunt.

Welford, A. T.
1970   "Perceptual selection and integration." Ergonomics 13:5–23.

Weston, P. B., and K. M. Wells.
1970   Criminal Investigation. New York: Prentice-Hall.

Wiener, A. S.
   1946   Blood Groups and Transfusion. Third Edition. Springfield, Ill.: Thomas.
Wilkins, Leslie.
   1970   "Crime in the world of 1990." Futures 2:203–214.
Williams, R. J.
   1963   Biochemical Individuality. New York: Wiley.
Willmer, M. A. P.
   1968   "Criminal investigation from the small town to the large urban conurbation." British Journal of Criminology 8:259–274.
   1970   Crime and Information Theory. Edinburgh: Edinburgh University Press.
Wolfgang, M. E.
   1971   "Systems must be made accountable to public, offender, victim and its subparts." Criminal Justice Newsletter 2:90–94.
Yefsky, S. A.
   1967   "Criminalistics." Pp. 245–442 in S. A. Yefsky (ed.), Proceedings of the First National Symposium on Law Enforcement, Science, and Technology. New York: Thompson.

CHAPTER **14**

A Survey of the Major
Criminal Justice Systems in the World

M. Cherif Bassiouni

DePaul University

INTRODUCTION

"Justice" is the measure of a society's civilization; but that measure is relative to the perception of values embodied in every society's conception of "justice."

Law, unlike generally held belief, has not always been the difference between tyranny and freedom or barbarism and civilization. All too often it has been the instrument of abuse. It may be a tribute to "law" that even when its processes have been abused, those who wielded the powers of coercion felt the constriction of rationalizing their abuses by relying on some legal arguments.

Law is a means to an end—that is, to justice—but if "law" must lead to justice, then it can be said that there can be no "law" without "justice." As is well illustrated in the various processes of criminal justice administration, however, diverse methods, devices, and practices, legal or extra-legal, so startlingly affect outcomes as to reveal gaps between "law" and "justice." In this area processes have been more significant in effectuating justice or denial thereof than have substantive laws. A person's guilt or innocence, and all that it comports of consequences, has been more often determined by administrative practices than by substantive laws relating to a social interest sought to be protected by legislation.

Throughout the history of humankind's twenty-one recorded civilizations a common thread has emerged: an ever-evolving quest for "justice" is found in all. But human violence is yet to be tamed. Whether wielding the power of authority or defying it, man's use of violence confirms that our civilization is but a thin veneer.

The values and drives that actuate human conduct seem to have preserved their basic character, which neither evolution nor scientific progress has affected greatly. The protection of life and limb, the preservation of economic means and products, the

I would like to acknowledge the assistance of Professor Ellen Thomas in the area of ancient Hebrew criminal justice. The section on the Islamic system is largely excerpted from Bassiouni, 1969b:163–201; the section on the accusatorial system was written in collaboration with John Decker, Associate Professor of Law, DePaul University College of Law; and the section on the criminal justice systems of the U.S.S.R. and the People's Republic of China is based largely on Bassiouni, 1972.

health and safety of citizens are objectives which have seldom changed. Emphasis on their "worth," however, as measured by the sanctions for their transgression, is what has differentiated societies. Definitions of individual and collective deviance with respect to these objectives have been essentially the product of value judgments made by those who control the levers of coercion.

The three most alarming features of societal outlook as to what constitutes deviance from established or accepted norms that have remained constant throughout the times are fear, ignorance, and economic interests. Even scientific advances made in the twentieth century, which have altered the relationship between the socially deviant and the collectivity, have not changed it enough. Ingrained prejudices are loosening up as a result of newly acquired and better-propagated knowledge, but these have yet to be eradicated. To that extent an element of commonality can be seen throughout the history of criminal justice systems, namely, the retributive approach. That one still speaks of "an eye for an eye" in this decade shows that from the early days of the Hebrew criminal justice system, the vindictive approach in dealing with deviant behavior has changed, at best, in degree but not in substance.

The most significant changes have occurred in the field of criminal procedure. The emergence of local and world public opinion as sanctioning forces is to be reckoned with. An arrest or trial in Moscow, Los Angeles, or Athens rings echoes in distant places. Indeed, it takes seven seconds for a news item to be flashed around the globe by satellite. This technological fact has contributed more than anything else to a better understanding of cultural differences. Surely, if law is the embodiment of social values, the greater the gap among such values, the more significant is the distinction between legal systems; conversely, as the gap between basic social values is reduced by communication and understanding, the contrasts between legal systems will be lessened. Time and space limitations preclude a more thorough and broader study of criminal justice systems here; those systems which have had the most far-reaching impact were chosen for coverage. Only the most salient features of these systems are presented, and emphasis is on conceptual framework rather than on specific differences—the latter are used illustratively.

An examination of the ancient systems reveals their historic relevance, as Hebrew concepts have seeped into Christianity and both found their way to Rome and all of Europe. Greece influenced the world, and its philosophy affected the Roman system as well. The Roman system remains the foundation of the majority of contemporary legal systems in the world, including those that have been permeated with Marxist philosophy. The Islamic system still carries its influence over some six hundred million people, even though it was established some fourteen centuries ago. Russia and even China differ in criminal justice systems remarkably little from the eastern European countries; these systems are mainly distinguished from those in the Western countries by the lack of guarantees against politically motivated abuse of process.

Roman law remains the foundation for most world systems, but still, when speaking of justice, one recalls and quotes Aristotle. Modern naturalists look to his writings and those of St. Thomas Aquinas, who followed him, for the methodological as well as the value content of legal philosophy. The common-law countries cherish the Magna Charta, granted in 1215, a document whose protections still find application in most countries of the world.

Monarchies, tyrannies, oligarchies, theocracies, and democracies have succeeded each other, and so to a large extent have the issues of criminal justice, but while the means used in administration of criminal justice have changed, its ideals have remained almost constant—although not yet attained.

Even a cursory examination of some of the major world systems of criminal justice gives a sense of historic continuity to the purpose of "justice" as pursued by humankind, irrespective of time and contrasting cultural values. Probably the most startling overall impression to be gained is the existence of more similarities among those various systems than generally conceived.

The discriminating observer will see that whenever undue impositions on personal freedom have flowed from some form of political ideology, the quest for personal freedom and justice has always resurfaced in one form or another. The theme has yet to be changed by any ruler or system. To that extent, at least, the similarities in basic human drives and natural impulses manifest in all societies are made apparent in some way through the various criminal justice systems of the world. The historic evidence leading to these conclusions may be disputed and the very conclusions doubted, but the idea of a singular and interactive history of humankind has been vindicated and so will that of the evolution of human aspirations.

THE ANCIENT SYSTEMS OF CRIMINAL JUSTICE

THE EGYPTIAN SYSTEM

The Egyptian system goes back beyond 4000 B.C. and was quite elaborate, as shown by the archeological remnants of the palaces of justice. Kings and their supreme judges administered justice. The king's chief minister was also the "chief judge." Justice and general administration were commingled because they were believed to be achieving identical ends. Politics were not of great significance, as in Rome or Greece, since democracy was not practiced. Administrators of provinces were also local judges. There were several provincial courts from which decisions were appealable to a central court presided over by the chief justice. Appeals to the Pharaoh were always possible, since he was constitutionally the supreme ruler, divinely endowed, but even so he was bound to conform to the law. He was the source of law, but was bound to follow it.

Egypt also developed codes, which were placed in the courts before the judges, and scribes recorded the decisions. A peculiar feature of their system was the practiced equality of all parties before the law, and that included equality of sexes. This differed from Greece and Rome where women were not equal to men in legal relations. There was no profession of advocates and procedures were simple because the quest was for truth. To emphasize that aspect judges hearing cases conspicuously wore a medal made of precious stone called "truth." Judges were the fact-finders and parties were limited to expressing their grievances and defenses. There was, however, a preference for written complaint and pleadings, which was in keeping with the great civilization of ancient Egypt with its high level of literacy. Speeches were thus de-emphasized and sophistry and oratory were not recognized arts. Facts were the basis of a judgment, not hypotheses or moving speeches. Administrative officials assisted judges as process servers, clerks, and bailiffs. This eliminated the need for private investigation and personal vengeance. Justice was a matter of state, not of personal, interest because justice was part of the proper administration of the kingdom.

THE MESOPOTAMIAN SYSTEM

The Mesopotamian system coexisted with the Egyptian system for some four thousand years B.C. and endured through successive waves of conquests. Mesopotamia's highly developed civilization helped shape a written legal system. The legal documents discovered were not on papyrus, as in Egypt, but were chiseled on stone. The most famous is the Code of Hammurabi (2100 B.C.). Other archeological findings show that an elaborate judicial system existed with professional judges, clerks, and notaries, using writs and other legal forms. As in Egypt, the king was the source of law and justice, but secular judges carried out the daily activities of criminal courts. The king's ministers and local governors were also judges, and an aggrieved party could always appeal to the chief judge, who was also the prime minister. An appeal from the prime minister to the king was permissible. Plaintiff-victims pleaded first, followed by defendant-accused, then the judges called on both parties to produce their witnesses and show their evidence. Their judgment was then entered. The judgment was certified by a clerk and sealed. Hebrew law grew out of the system developed in Mesopotamia, but it is a distinct system and is discussed later in this chapter.

THE GREEK SYSTEM

The Greek legal system starts with the Homeric or Trojan period, circa 1200 B.C., and continues until its absorption in the Roman legal system, circa A.D. 300. The Greek legal system is the product of its culture and evolved throughout its history. Like other great legacies, it was not the product of a closed or limited society, but rather one of cross-fertilization with other peoples and their cultures. It emerged from indigenous primitive customs and was influenced over a millennium and a half by the Minoan, Mycenaean, Mesopotamian, and Egyptian cultures and their systems. Greece introduced in the history of mankind a system of institutionalized individual justice which lasted from its Homeric days, when it was composed of numerous independent clans and tribes, throughout the formation of the "Polis," the city-state, and even after the unification of Greece.

Unlike Rome, Greece had no real juridical system in the legalistic sense (forms and procedural devices), but it had a solidly embedded sense of justice and, of course, it had laws. Criminal justice in Greece was not administered by the political ruler or a divinely inspired clergy, although at times there have been some manifestations of both, but by the general assembly of the clan, the people. The oracles played their greater role in the political arena, but there was neither trial by battle nor by ordeal, as in other systems, particularly in the earlier days of the Anglo-Saxon system.

The parties to any dispute, civil or criminal, pleaded their cause before the assembly of freemen, presided over by the temporal ruler or by someone elected by the assembly, who acted more like an umpire than a fact-finder. After the case was presented by the parties or their lawyers, the wise men, or elders, skilled in the law of precedent, proferred various possible outcomes. Thereafter the freemen acclaimed the best proposed judgment and thus decided the case.

The spirit of justice was not theocratic, but secular; civil officials administered justice, not priests. Themis, the Goddess of Justice, played a great role in Greek mythology, which was common to all of Greece (even when politically fragmented), but she was the symbol of justice which was, nevertheless, administered by men. Themis still stands today, in modern times, as a symbol of justice throughout most of the world.

The organization of justice in Greece changed according to political fluctuations between democracy, tyranny, and oligarchy. Athens witnessed many upheavals, but the concept of democracy was always well established in the Athenian's mind, even though the reality was often different. Great reformers, such as Solon and Demosthenes, restored procedural fairness to criminal trials as well as to many other areas of the law and social justice. One of these, the jury system for all serious criminal cases, was restored by Solon. In Athens every year a jury list of 6,000 or more names was made up and the ordinary panel of 201 names was drawn by lot. In some important cases, panels of up to 2,500 jurymen were recorded. Socrates, for example, had a jury of 501 men. The juries were made up of men, because women were not admitted to juries nor to councils of wise men either in Athens or in Sparta.

Solon's criminal justice reforms bore on the jury system as well as the substantive law. The presiding magistrate was selected by lot, the jurors were selected from the entire body of male citizens, and any male citizen could be a prosecutor. The defendant conducted his own defense and had the right to be heard or to have someone be heard in his behalf. If there were any preliminary proceedings to establish the validity of the claim or suit to be presented for trial, they were conducted through a fact-finding magistrate aided in some cases by a small jury guided and presided over by the fact-finding magistrate. This procedure was very informal, in contrast to the subsequent proceedings conducted by public assembly; there the presiding chairman was usually elected from the public and could not promulgate the law as the fact-finding magistrate could in the preliminary hearing, but could only direct the proceedings.

There was seldom an appeal once a decision was rendered, but once the accused was found guilty by the first assembly, a second hearing could be held to determine the penalty. The accused could plead for a reduced sentence, which would actually be pleading mitigating circumstances, as in contemporary practice in many countries, particularly the common-law countries. Interestingly, the question of the division of the trial into two phases—adjudication and disposition—is still debated and its application is considered to reflect enlightened policy.

The Athenean system essentially revolved around the jury, which was part of its social and political framework and represented the popular standard of achievement of its people. Acclamation was only one of the means of rendering a verdict, since jurymen could also receive two marked ballots indicating plaintiff and defendant—one ballot was cast in the voting urn and the other in the discard urn. The ballots were then counted in the presence of the assembly and the verdict announced.

Where written laws existed, the jurymen had to interpret them, but if they could not find appropriate laws, they reverted to general principles of laws and customs. As such, they acted not only as triers of the facts, but also as interpreters of the laws, and eventually as legislators. This device was the original form of equity-justice, later developing into the bifurcated concept of law and equity, only to merge in modern procedural reforms in the United States—even though through separate channels.

The Greek system of popular justice may have been highly democratic, but it prevented the development of an enduring and lasting system of law. There was no emphasis on strict rules of law, procedures, or formalities, and this led to the tradition of oratory for which Greece was so famous. When the assembly met at the top of the Pnyx (a hill outside Athens), famous statesmen like Pericles moved the assemblies to the height of delirium. Such great political oratory became confused with forensic oratory which, without the restraining procedural rules and benefit of formalities, gave rise to sophistry rather than to the attainment of truth and achievement of justice.

Ultimately, emotional appeal swayed the popular courts and led critics to argue against a jury system in which emotionally affected jurors were conditioned to respond to the advocate's eloquence and not to the justness of the cause presented. Today's critics of the jury system present these same views, but one observes that a system of law interpreted by men is bound to maintain the same characteristics throughout the times. As Lysias (450–380 B.C.), an eminent advocate, stated: "The laws will be no better than the law-makers." This led Aristotle to record critically in 325 B.C.: "The democracy has made itself master of everything by its vote in the assembly and in the law courts in which it holds the supreme power." It is interesting to note that similarly conceived popular courts can be found in Marxist conceptions, and exist in Cuba and the U.S.S.R., for example. Many advocates of radical democracy in the Western world also advocate a system based on popular judgment.

The weakness of the Greek legal system rested on its social structure—only the free and usually the wealthy wound up as jurors and wise men. They decided the fate of the accused, thereby perpetuating the caste structure, preserving the oligarchy, and protecting the interests of the ruling class to which they either belonged or to which they owed their freedom or wealth. The jury was not the instrument of an accusatorial process but rather of an inquisitorial one, and even then, as today, the key to justice was in the hands of those who initiated prosecutions and administered the process. Professional bureaucracy was at the command of the ruler and ruling class and confined or released the accused and scheduled their trials with little control. Yet, the safeguard of popular redress for possible injustice was both a general deterrent and a form of ultimate protection against abuse of justice.

Solon (638–559 B.C.) remains forever associated with criminal law and the administration of justice in Athens, even though his most substantial reform was in inheritance law. His approach to justice was to look behind the purposes of laws and the functions of procedure, a view of criminal law as a tool of social engineering that now receives considerable attention.

Solon, however, was the exception. Greece, because of its culture, usually approached law more as an intellectual exercise than as a means to achieve social order. In comparison with other civilizations, Greece had a system of justice but not a system of law. It constructed no codes, reported no reasoned decisions, and left no doctrinal treaties. The main juridical contribution of Greece remains the popular jury, but its greatest contribution to civilization is the profound sense of justice which its people had and which went beyond the positivism that marks most of history's twenty-one known civilizations.

This legacy was carried in the teachings of Aristotle (384–322 B.C.) for whom "justice is the summary of all virtues." He called upon reason as a human being's greatest attribute to guide us in all human endeavors. In his *Nicomachean Ethics* (McKeon, 1941), he states that the end toward which men strive in life is happiness. Happiness for each creature is found in the best possible performance of the function for which he is peculiarly adapted. Man then finds his highest and most lasting happiness in the active life of his soul in accordance with virtue. Virtue may be either (1) intellectual, the excellence of the reasoning power, that is, prudence and wisdom; or (2) moral, the control of emotions and desires in obedience to reason, that is, liberality and temperance. Aristotle appealed not only to reason, but to the higher reason and the right reason. To him, as to Cicero centuries later, "law is the right reason." The legacy of Aristotelean natural law found its way to Nürnberg in 1945, where men were judged for not yielding to the same higher reason. The search of its significance has continued throughout history and law reformers seek the "right reason," reminiscent of Diogenes who once went through the streets of Athens in broad daylight with a lighted lamp "searching for an honest man."

St. Thomas Aquinas (1225–1274) carried Aristotle's thoughts to Western Christian philosophy and law. The "naturalists," as they are called, are those whose philosophical interpretation of the law derives from these Aristotelean-Thomistic conceptions of man, morality, and law.

THE ROMAN SYSTEM

In Rome, primitive customs were supplemented by a continuous flow of legislation influenced by the Greek legal system and by the laws of the many peoples who became part of the Roman Empire. As in Greece, and in most legal systems up to modern times, the distinction between torts and crimes was not always clear because both were wrongs. Concern for safety and protection of property was paramount. The word *injury*, most common to contemporary criminal law, derives its origin from Rome's *iniuria*. The Hebrew concept of an eye for an eye was followed closely in Rome as was the legal distinction between intent and negligence *improvidentia*. Both depended on the nuances given the notion of *culpa* or fault. A crime could rise to an *iniuria*, but other acts which are purely civil in nature today were delicts and criminally punishable because of the social significance attributed to them. One such example of an act deemed a quasi-criminal violation was unjust enrichment.

Rome emphasized legislation and legal precedent. A notable characteristic of its system is that presumptions of guilt or innocence did not exist. Victim and accused stood at parity and each enjoyed the neutrality of the law in the proof of their respective contentions. Roman procedure was invariably elaborate and justice was a formal process which added a public dimension to the private interest prosecuted. Rome was the first to introduce an institutionalized public prosecutional process in personal wrongs by establishing jurisdiction over such cases in the *Praetor*. Emphasis on forms and formalities marked the later developments of the Roman system, which can be divided into three phases:

1. The Republic was marked by the enactment of the Twelve Tables (45 B.C.) and the building of criminal courthouses. A court of justice was called a *basilica*, a Greek term for royalty. Unlike Greece, these courts were separate buildings close to the Forum, but not confused with the political arena. In those days, the entire popular assembly could sit in judgment and vote as a popular jury.

2. The early Empire period inaugurated the professional judge and jurist. Later, juries disappeared under the emperors. Under Augustus, the system acquired characteristics of lasting worldwide influence. Judges wrote opinions, and were compelled to follow precedents. Roman law progressed to a science, particularly in the second and third centuries A.D.

3. During the later Empire period, from the third to the sixth century, particularly under Justinian (483–565), the great codifications were made. By A.D. 550, Rome could look to the Pandects (digest), the Code, and the institute to find its laws and procedures. Having reached this apex, however, it was burdened by the diversity of systems and values encompassed in its vast empire. Gradually, it fell into a morass of formalism and legalism which produced more confusion than justice.

Roman law institutionalized the prerogatives of the *pater familias*. The patriarch had power of life and death in the days of the republic and dispensed justice as an absolute ruler. With the advent of the Empire, the *pater familias* lost many of his prerogatives as the sole source of justice in the family. These prerogatives, which extended significantly to civil law, are the basis of contemporary European legal structures, founded on the unity of the family.

Another peculiar aspect of Roman procedure which seems to have affected English law was that of debtors' prison. The debtor could be imprisoned by the creditor until he paid his debt, but the family of the debtor had the right periodically to see that he was treated well and was in good condition. The family of the debtor, therefore, could ask the creditor who detained him to produce him in person in a public place to be viewed by his family. This may be the antecedent to the writ of *habeas corpus* that requires the appearance in open court of the person detained.

The presumption of innocence as understood in the common law also finds its origin in Roman law. It also existed in Sparta and Athens, but its application was different in these systems. An accusation was not enough to prove guilt; denial of a charge by an accused without its being proved by the accuser was enough to warrant acquittal. This did not mean proof beyond a reasonable doubt, but that quantum of proof which is sufficient to convince the judge. This gave rise in the European system to the standard of proof that guilt must convince the judge beyond a moral certainty. Thus, the Roman system and the European system adhere to a presumption of innocence, but are distinguished from the common-law system in that proof of guilt beyond reasonable doubt is not a corollary to the presumption of innocence.

THE HEBREW SYSTEM—A COMPARISON WITH THE GREEK AND ROMAN SYSTEMS OF CRIMINAL JUSTICE[1]

Introduction

The contemporary distinction between a tort and a crime was almost unknown until the Middle Ages. Wrongs were almost always considered crimes, rather than subjects for civil action. The change to civilly actionable torts was due in large measure to proprietary interests and developing commerce and industry (Wormser, 1962:14). Ancient Greece and Rome, as well as the even older Babylonian civilization, were urban groupings whose primary activity was in commerce and industry (Hertz, 1950:405). The ancient Hebrew civilization, on the other hand, was overwhelmingly agrarian. The social interests which each of these countries sought to protect were consequently different and led to the various systems and procedures devised for the protection of their interests.

Seriousness of offenses, which was determined by prevailing social values, often influenced the establishment of special courts and peculiar procedures. Under Mosaic law, for example, no offense against property was listed among the various types of capital offenses, and all offenses punishable by death were either crimes against nature, against public morality, or against God (Mendelsohn, 1968:44–46). Under Roman law, several offenses against property were listed as capital offenses, but the first permanent or standing courts which the Romans had were for extortion, bribing election officials, degrading the dignity of the state, and embezzlement (Gruen, 1968:184), thereby showing the significance they attached to the preservation of their political system. Criminal processes sprung out of each society's need to vindicate its transgressed values, and this varied substantially.

Conceptually, the following distinctions can be made:

1. The Greek legal system was essentially concerned with the preservation of popular justice, even at the cost of allowing sophistry to prevail over truth, and popular attitudes (through the popular jury) over individual justice.

2. The Roman system at first centered around the unlimited power of the *pater familias*. With the growth of the Roman Empire, a most complex system of law and procedure was instituted, but with the Empire's decline, this system became laden with forms and formalities. Justice was sacrificed to procedure, which became the art of the few patricians who made the law their reserved domain. The Greeks left history

---

1. For general sources, see Wigmore, 1936; Nice, 1964; Lawson, 1969; Bassiouni, 1971a.

a sense of popular justice, while the Romans left a legacy of legal principles still the basis of most contemporary European and European-inspired legal systems.

3. The Hebrews, strongly anchored in their religious beliefs, were more community-protection oriented than individual-justice conscious, but they also put more emphasis on due process than the Greeks or Romans.

Enforcement and Prosecution

Private enforcement and personal vindication of a victim by active participation in the public process were the mainstays of all three systems. Under Mosaic law, a person accused of a crime was not brought in by police or other special persons whose job it was to ferret out offenders and convict them. Rather, the offense had to be witnessed by *two* regular citizens who then had to bring the person before the authorities (Mendelsohn, 1968:110). Rome started the practice of having paid public officials to seek offenders and indict them (Smith, 1850:§828). An ordinary citizen of either Greece or Rome could, however, still prosecute another for a crime; it was part of the responsibility of the citizenry to do so. These two systems recognized that the strength of their governments depended on acceptance by the people of this type of responsibility, particularly because of their colonial policy toward other peoples that they conquered (Wormser, 1962:49). This participation by the victim in the process insured that the feeling of individual vengeance was assuaged, thereby permitting public justice to replace the private justice which had prevailed in tribal societies.

The Courts

The authority of the accuser is only one element necessary for a criminal trial. The other one is the tribunal before which the accused is brought. In the Greek and Roman systems, trials were by jury. The selection of the jury in Greece was essentially popular, while in Rome it was a caste privilege where lists of jurors were often made up of either senators or equities or both (Gruen, 1968:201, 208). The laws stated that trials by the people were to be had for all criminal offenses; however, a tribune had to bring the charge before the people and there was no standing criminal court of a popular nature before at least 81 B.C. (p. 8). Prior to that time, the only permanent courts were staffed from the nobility. Under the Mosaic law, however, there was no trial by a jury. An accused was brought before the elders by the very witnesses who accused him.

The Greeks and Romans had many types of courts. In the Greek system they were differentiated by type of jury, and in Rome by type of offense. Under the Mosaic system, the division was administrative, with an inferior and a superior court, as well as a Supreme Court called the Sanhedrin, which was equal in authority to the full Roman Senate. Criminal cases in the lowest court were heard by a panel of three judges and every village had such a court, while the larger cities had lesser Sanhedrins composed of twenty-three members. There was a jurisdictional difference between these two courts: the court of three judges could only try criminal cases where the punishment was either a fine or flagellation, whereas the lesser Sanhedrin had additional jurisdiction in cases involving capital punishment. The Great Sanhedrin was the court of final judgment and the supreme authority in all matters. The Greek courts, being essentially popular in form, had no really comparable way to appeal a decision. The Romans, however, had an elaborate appellate system. Interestingly, the common grounds for appeal in all of these systems was the ignorance or injustice of those who had to decide (Smith, 1850:§74a). Consider, particularly, that the Romans and Hebrews had a well-defined body of law and ample precedents, while the Greeks had only a few laws and seldom relied on precedents as the popular trier of the facts was subject to constant change. While Roman and Hebrew judges relied on law and precedent, Greek popular triers chose among several verdicts proposed by their elders after hearing the advocates of each side.

The Trial

Not only did the types of courts differ greatly in these three systems, but so did the trials themselves. In Greece and in Rome, criminal trials were held outside rather than in a building, whereas the Great Sanhedrin met inside the Temple in Jerusalem. One author reasons that the Greeks and Romans felt that crimes and criminals contaminated a place and they did not wish to be tainted (Smith, 1850:§89a). Romans and Greeks used open public forums for all their social activities and trials were considered another form thereof, although Rome separated its courts from its public political and social forums.

Under Mosaic law, a trial could not be heard after sundown, but the Greeks and Romans held their trials at night when the people could meet after their regular activities. Unlike the Greeks and Romans, the Jewish courts met on a regular basis to hear cases.

In Rome, the legal professions flourished; jurors and judges were part of the same class, chosen from the senators or the patricians, though not excluding equities or learned Romans who were not of the nobility. The Jews, however, had no separate legal profession. The judges were the most respected elders of the community, who were not compensated for their work with the courts. The sages prescribed the minimum age for sitting on the Sanhedrin as 40 years. The Greeks, on the other hand, felt that old age would incapacitate a man's judgment, and relied almost exclusively on the people. Only after the unification of Greece did they develop a group of professional jurors, which was due more to circumstances than to deliberate choice.

Under Mosaic law, judges were assisted by two servitors and two secretaries. The servitors had much the same task as the Roman viatores and lictores combined in that they were responsible for summoning people to testify and for executing the sentences of the court, with the exception of capital offenses. The Jews found it an anathema to have special persons whose jobs were to take the lives of other human beings. The secretaries fulfilled the role of modern court reporters by reporting the opinions of the judges. Where a judge voted for conviction in a particular case, his reasons had to be stated and recorded, but he did not have to give reasons for acquittal. There was no recording in Greece as there was in Rome and to that extent it is very difficult to determine what actually occurred at criminal trials, other than to depend on the works of commentators. The secretaries in Jewish courts not only recorded the judges' decisions, but also took down all testimony given. Hence, there are complete records of trials which are still in existence (Mendelsohn, 1968:91).

Evidence

One of the first and most striking differences in the procedures is the way testimony is given and received. The Romans required that the quaestor prosecute the case and the witnesses who reported the incident only present testimony. The Jews, on the other hand, required the witnesses to act as prosecutors as well. There were strict requirements as to who could or could not be a witness against another. The Greeks, Romans, and Jews all agreed that women, slaves, and minors were incompetent to testify. So also were people suffering from deafness, blindness, idiocy, lunacy, and persons convicted of irreligion and immorality. The Jews, however, went even further in their list of prohibited persons. They also included farmers, tax collectors, illiterate persons, relatives of the parties involved, accomplices, and anyone else with a direct interest in the outcome of the case (Mendelsohn, 1968:115–19). Illiterates were excluded on the theory that one had an obligation to know the law and its consequences. Refusal to allow accomplices to testify against a co-felon comes from the idea that both individuals were involved in a single criminal transaction, and, since no man is required to incriminate himself nor may be convicted on his own uncorroborated confession, to allow the testimony of an accomplice would be the same as a man making a confession about himself (see Jung, 1967:7).

Subject to specific exceptions, the only basic requirements for being a witness among the Greeks, Romans, and Jews was to be a free legal person, but, depending upon the times, the number of free legal Romans and Greeks fluctuated. Considering that for a long period of time debtors could lose their freedom to their creditors and farmers were liable to their landlords for their share of the crop or their person, the wealthy prevailed in number and influenced the quality of justice.

The Romans required testimony to be written, while the Jews did just the opposite: their testimony had to be oral. In Athens a witness could testify as to what he saw but not to what he heard. An exception to this rule was a deposition of a deceased witness. The requirement that testimony be in writing was based on the Greek and Roman fear of mistakes of fact and also to guard against subterfuges and lying (Smith, 1850:§15b, 626b; Mendelsohn, 1968:25, 26). This requirement of testimony in writing allowed the Romans to subpoena records of the accused, a provision found as early as 115 B.C. in the trial of Rutilius (Gruen, 1968:122). Many of these rules of evidence can be found in contemporary systems.

Under Mosaic law, the witness appeared before the full court, including the accused, was required to testify as to the entire case, and was then questioned by the judges. There were two types of questions a witness had to answer—main questions and test questions. Main questions were directly related to the event under investigation and covered four major areas: (1) the defendant as a person (certainty of identification and certainty as to whether or not the witness gave the defendant the necessary warning); (2) the time the crime was alleged to have occurred (the exact year, month, week of the month, day of the week and hour of the day); (3) the place the crime occurred (the exact location and a description of the immediate surroundings in great detail); and (4) the manner in which the crime was committed (circumstances of the event, in detail).

Test questions were used to determine whether a witness was telling the truth. There was nothing akin to either redirect or re-cross examination. The judges questioned until they were satisfied, and when a witness was dismissed he could not be called back, nor was there any other way in which he could change his testimony. Under Roman law, however, there was an opportunity for redirect and re-cross examination since both the prosecution and the defense had legal counsel. No counsel was available to either side under Mosaic law, but a defendant could speak for himself and was encouraged to do so. If he chose not to do so, a probationer or new member of the judicial staff was chosen to speak in his behalf. This did not occur, however, until the closing arguments in the case (Mendelsohn, 1968:132, 133). If, on the other hand, the defendant did speak in his own behalf and decided to confess, his confession would not be accepted as evidence against him unless it was corroborated by the testimony of two witnesses (Jung, 1967:7; Mendelsohn, 1968:133). Under both Greek and Roman law, however, such an admission would be admissible without any corroboration (Smith, 1850:§66).

Under such systems as these, the proving or disproving of a witness's testimony takes on a special importance. Under Mosaic law, a witness who perjured himself was liable to receive the same punishment which the defendant-victim would have received (Mendelsohn, 1968:136). The Greeks had anyone convicted of such an action punished by execution (Smith, 1850:§21b), but there was a difference between having one's testimony merely disproved and having it confuted. Disproof of testimony meant only that the witness was inaccurate, while confutation implied an intent to lie on the witness stand. Under Mosaic law, witnesses who were disproved were not barred from testifying at other proceedings, but were prohibited from joining with another disproved witness and testifying on the same side. The rationale behind this was that if such inaccurate persons were allowed to combine as witnesses their negligence might be so gross as even to imply malice and subject the witnesses to punishment for confutation. A confuted witness, as opposed to one who had merely been disproved, was barred from ever testifying in any judicial proceeding again. The Greeks had a similar practice in that a prosecutor whose case was defeated by more than four-fifths of the votes of the court was said to have been confuted and was thereafter prohibited from prosecuting a case of the same nature again (Smith, 1850:§21b, 537a).

At the end of all testimony both the prosecution and the defense were allowed to make arguments for their side. This practice was common to all three cultures, and exists in all contemporary systems.

Verdicts and Judgments

Under Greek law, certain types of cases had specific penalties fixed by law, such as those involving theft, murder, ill-use of parents, or where the defendant had made a confession or was proved guilty. In such situations, a case heard by a magistrate allowed the use of a summary process with immediate execution and no recourse to appeal to any jury court (Smith, 1850:§66). This is vastly different from Mosaic law where no criminal case is ever heard by a single judge, or in addition, no summary process was ever allowed.

Under both Greek and Roman law only a simple majority was necessary to convict. Under Mosaic law, the number of votes necessary to convict had to equal the number of witnesses necessary for conviction of the offense charged. In other words, the majority had to be at least two votes. One vote, however, was the majority necessary for acquittal. Under Mosaic law the judges were required to give reasons for their decisions, while Greek and Roman judges were not. All three adhered to the assumption that an accused is innocent until guilt is proven. This did not mean, however, "proof of guilt beyond a reasonable doubt" as it is understood in an accusatorial, common-law setting, but merely reflected an adversary equality.

THE ISLAMIC SYSTEM

Introduction

Over six hundred million Muslims inhabit the earth. They constitute a majority in thirty nations, seventeen of which adhere officially to Islam. The emergence of Muslim states in the world community of sovereign nations emphasizes the importance of perceiving the values and attributes of Islamic law. Unlike any other legal system, Islam is an integrated concept of all aspects of human conduct and thought. Islamic criminal justice has existed as long as the Islamic nation, and is preserved, in whole or in part, in the many countries where Muslims are numerous.

Islam is a monotheistic, universal faith relying on an eternal concept of life and a global cosmos outlook. The word *Islam* in Arabic means *submission* or *surrender* to God. "Mohammedanism" is often used as a misnomer for Islam (see Gibb, 1961). Islamic morality is not a narrow concept connected exclusively to what are referred to as "Islamic revelations" (von Grunebaum, 1955), but rather what Islam considers as the terminal and all-encompassing divine revelations of the Koran (*Qur'ān*).

The Concept of the State

Allah, or God, is the principal unifying factor of the Islamic state, for it, as well as the hereafter, is His creation, and man and things respond to Him. Ramadan (1961:42) distinguished Islam from theocracy, however, for theocracies still rely on rules (man-made in interpretation and application) vaguely governed by divine command or devised by a sacerdotal class that lead to the struggle and division of church and state. Islam does not authorize a human institutional source of lawmaking, which results in the Islamic negation of the anthropomorphic implications of theocracy in the realm of faith. This can be verified from a classification of Islamic sources of law.

A Summary Classification of Islamic Sources of Law

Ramadan gives the sources of Islamic law as:
    (1) Chief Sources:
        (a) The *Qur'ān*, or the Holy Book of Islam.
        (b) The *Sunnah*, or the authentic traditions of Mohammed.
        (c) The *Ijma*, or the consensus of opinion.
        (d) The *Qiyas*, or judgment upon juristic analogy which could also include *Al Ijtihad*.
    (2) Supplementary Sources:
        (a) *Al-Istishsan*, or the deviation from certain rules based on precedents derived from other rules based on relevant legal reasoning.
        (b) *Al-Istislah*, which is an unprecedented judgment explicitly covered by the *Qur'ān* or the *Sunnah* and necessitated by public interest.
        (c) *Al-Urf*, or the custom and usage (1961:23).

According to Hamidullah, the roots and sources of Islamic Law, or the *Ousoul*, are as follows:
        (a) The *Qur'ān*.
        (b) The *Sunnah*, or Tradition of the Prophet.
        (c) The orthodox practice of the early Califs.
        (d) The practice of other Muslim rulers not repudiated by the jurisconsults.
        (e) The opinions of celebrated Muslim jurists:
            [1] consensus of opinion, or *Igmah;* or
            [2] individual opinions, or *Qiyas*.
        (f) The arbitral awards.
        (g) The treaties, pacts and other conventions.

(h) The official instructions to commanders, admirals, ambassadors and other state officials.

(i) The internal legislation for conduct regarding foreign relations and foreigners.

(j) The customs and usage (1961:18).

The characteristics of the Islamic philosophy of legislation can be summarized as follows:

(a) An inclination toward establishing general rules, indulging in great detail.

(b) Precepts based on actual events and not hypothetical suppositions, thus strengthening case law as an expression of human behavior and judicial experience, which result in a deliberate and not coincidental determination.

(c) The permissiveness of all that which is not prohibited, thus illustrating the flexibility which is needed to prevent human paralysis and intellectual stagnation.

(d) The wording of specific prohibitions in such terms as to allow implementations by reason of necessity, social and public.

(e) The use of language allowing, the tempering of specific prohibitions by legal excuse or justification arising from necessity in its broadest form and granting judicial power to adapt as the requirements of society and circumstances justify.

(f) The permissiveness and liberality in adapting useful and necessary guidelines not incompatible with the *Qur'ān* or *Sunnah*.

These characteristics are important if we are to find authority in the Islamic legislative process and sources of law for adherence to the World Habeas Corpus Treaty-Statute, to be administered by an "Islamic circuit."

Sovereignty

The sovereignty of God as the source of law and legality leaves to man the prerogative of earthly application, development, and exercise of His commands, mandates, and the fulfillment of mankind's purposeful creation. The trusteeship of vicegerency of man is stated in these terms: "Allah has promised such of you as have become believers and done good deeds that he will most surely make them his *vicegerents* in the earth."[2] Thus, a divine rather than social contract is offered by the Creator-Sovereign to man, its beneficiary, for the enjoyment and use of all other creations in consideration of man's submission to God, man's Islam.[3] The vicegerency of man should not be thought of as a de facto sovereignty versus God's de jure sovereignty, nor should it be likened to the "divine right of kings" or papal authority. It is a concordat between free man, choosing to believe, accept, and submit for the privilege of trusteeship or vicegerency. During the course of man's exercise of his derived powers over other created matter, he will be judged according to the law laid down by the Sovereign in His relevations. Thus, free will, which is indispensable to the attainment of this delicate and precise balance, is not man-made but divinely endowed. Its operation is manifested by the obvious need to choose, but the criterion of choice lies in the purpose for the choice

---

2. Koran 24:55 (emphasis added). Note the similarity of God's sovereignty in Christianity: Matthew 6:10; 11:2–30; 15:3–9; Mark 7:5–13; Luke 19:38–46.

3. A frequent failure among Orientalists is failure to comprehend God's sovereignty and man's vicegerency. Even the great Islamic scholar Coulson states: "While Mohammed's position gradually developed into one of political and *legal sovereignty*, the will of God was transmitted to the community by him in the *Qur'ānic* revelations" (Coulson, 1964:11, emphasis added). Mohammed is not the legal sovereign.

and not its empirical existence. Islamic polity is a "theo-democracy" (Maudoodi, 1967:198). It is, therefore, distinguishable from the democracy in which constitutional principles provide sovereignty to the people. Western political thought imparts the precept that sovereignty is in the "people" and is absolute (Laski, 1917; Miliukov, 1934; Sait, 1949). The conduct of the affairs of state by its own people is original, unbridled, absolute, underived, independent, permanent, and exclusive (see, e.g., Bryce, 1901; Maritain, 1951), even when self-imposed limitations are included in certain constitutions to indicate the need for a higher order of legality.

God is the lawgiver, his trustees or vicegerents compose the *Ummah* (nation) and are empowered to make complementary laws, but their validity will depend upon their compliance with the *Shariah*; i.e., Islamic law. The *Ummah* enjoys a derivative rule-making power and not an absolute law-creating prerogative (MacDonald, 1903; and for a Western constitutional conception, Rostow, 1962).

The interrelationship of the *Shariah*, the source of law and legality for, and with, the rule-making of the *Ummah*, and the *Imam* or Calif are a trilogy of legislative authority of unequal value and standing. The logical continuity of Islamic thought rejects a doctrine of separation of temporal and spiritual—church and state—just as it must reject presently understood secularistic forms of state (Smith, 1957; on the artificiality of secularism, see Toynbee, 1957).

Islamic Law and Source

Law in Islam may be said to be the expression of controlled limitations over the liberty of creatures with the characteristics of absolutism. Regulated by divine and human prescriptions, the knowledge of ultimate accountability to the Lord subordinates all man-made laws to the laws of God in letter and spirit. To balance the interrelationship of individual accountability and the limitation of freedom of conduct by law necessitates the following presuppositions.

Freedom of will and conduct is susceptible of absolutism but is not so intended because absolute freedom negates social responsibility and results in self-destruction (see, e.g., Tritton, 1947; Watt, 1962). Limitations on such freedom are not, per se, arbitrary, because they are dictated by a rule of law conforming to "morality." Morality is the sense of the entire divine purpose and human objectives, having divine judgment as its finality; this morality is the foundation of social and religious order, which constitutes part of the human purpose of creation. Those limitations on freedom are then laws which emanate from "knowledge," in the broadest sense, which, when combined with the revealed source of law, destroys the dichotomy of man-made and divine-made law to become finally *ilm-ul fiqh*. This science of knowledge can be likened to the science of epistemology or the knowledge of things human and divine.

Man is simultaneously ruler and ruled. The Prophet stated: "Every one of you is a ruler and every one of you is answerable to his subjects." Von Grunebaum likens this to the Roman theory of *Jurisprudencia or "Rerum divinarum atque humanarum notitia,* or the knowledge of truth, human and divine" (1955:144; see also Ion, 1907). This knowledge is intended to cover all civil and religious functions of man to man, man to state, man to God, and vice versa. While certain Western scholars consider it as deriving essentially from Stoicism, the source is really to be examined in the context of the classification of Islamic law, which is more likely to reflect a different philosophical characterization (cf., e.g., von Grunebaum, 1955; Ramadan, 1961). Unfortunately, studies of Islamic law, its source and origin, have been undertaken mainly by Western scholars who have always tried to view Islam from the Western point of view and understanding. Islam is a radically different concept from that of the secular West and cannot be seen through the eyes and translations of other Westerners.

The Koranic principle of *"Hudud-Allah,"* the divine limits, constitutes the checks and balances placed upon man in his human endeavors to afford maximum personal freedom and to tolerate only those limited restrictions which distinguish anarchism from organized society. *Hudud-Allah* are the limitations placed on freedom to secure "a scheme of ordered liberty" and to prevent arbitrary and despotic limitations on human freedom (see Watt, 1948; Maudoodi, 1967:151).

The State and the Individual

Unlike other sources of law, the Koran emphasizes duties rather than rights. It insists that individuals must fulfill obligations before they can claim privileges. The individual's rights are neither different from nor conflicting with those of the community, and the fulfillment of obligations by him and by other members of the society provides the reservoir of social rights which are shared by all (Arnold, 1913; Roberts, 1925). The individual enjoys as many privileges as society can afford, but society affords as much as it receives from individuals (Azzam, 1954).

While some authors deplore the lack of specific individual guarantees in Islamic law and impute this to be a weakness of the *Shariah* itself, the basis of the *Shariah* is the principle of *original freedom,* that only free men can be free to choose Islam.

The Growth of the Law

The basis of accountability is strictly personal and primarily subjective; administrative and executive power is left to the *Immam,* or leader. An electoral system granting the consent of the people enables him to rule, and he is required to consult with the people. Furthermore, the process of *Ijtihad,* legal reasoning, is not based solely on the leader, but is the sum total of the jurisconsuls of the nation operating collectively to develop legal theories. Therefore, *siyasat-al-shariah* (the policy of *Shariah*) is not made exclusively by the *Immam,* as some writers have inferred from attaching exclusive significance to medieval practices (e.g., von Grunebaum, 1955).

The maxim that the king can do no wrong is rejected by Islamic law. What is adopted is the maxim of the "just judge." Justice in Islam is not subjective but rests on the *Shariah,* from which comes the guarantee that individual rights shall not be subjected to the whims of any intemperate judge, but to the due process of law.

The Individual and Human Rights

1. The Individual

The "dignity" of mankind has acquired a glorified position in Islam. The Koran abounds with references to its attributes. The duty of "justice" is mentioned twenty times. Admonishments and warnings against "persecution" are referred to two hundred and ninety-nine times. Denunciations of "aggression" and its aims are stated eight times. Warnings against "violations" are made twenty times (Mussa, 1966:236).

The individual is viewed by Islam both as a single and unique unit and also as part of a composite unit, i.e., mankind. ". . . Islamic Law generally aims at the public good [which] does not detract from its fundamental and individualistic character" (Abdel-Wahab, 1962:122). The assertion is made, however, that:

> Because [the state is the] properly constituted political authority representing the rule of divine wisdom, [and the state has] guarantee[d] the welfare of the subject in this world and in the world to come, it follows that the interests of the State and not those of the individual will constitute the supreme criteria for law (Coulson, 1957:51).

Such an approach, unfortunately, "fails to appreciate the [unique] relationship between strict legal doctrine and the practice of *siyâsa shar iyya* which has always prevailed in that field" (Schacht, 1950:138, n.12). Another author confirms this latter point in the following terms:

> Islamic Law is exclusively individualistic insofar as the right of every single member of the community to share public responsibility with the Calif is recognized. Any individual has the right to correct the Calif and to attack his decisions if he commits an error. Moreover, positive Islamic Law on the whole is a system of subjective rights and personal privileges of all individuals as demonstrated by the texts dealing with the principle of "original freedom" and the inviolability of life, liberty, property and honor (Abdel-Wahab, 1962:133).

The individual is regarded in Islam as born free with a right to choose; he is offered Islam: The Right Path. The maintenance of freedom, therefore, cannot be discriminatory, for anyone outside of Islam must be given the prerogative of free choice to become a Muslim and embrace the faith.

2. Human Rights

Classic Islamic law distinguishes between *Zimmi,* non-Muslims residing under the protective covenant of the Islamic state, because they are the people of the Book and recipients of divine revelations (i.e., Christians and Jews), and *non-Zimmi,* who are not people of the Book and have no protective covenant with the state, although they live in the Islamic state. The relationship of Muslim, *Zimmi,* and *non-Zimmi* falls within the purview of internal law, while relations and human rights with people who are not living within the Islamic territory are covered by the *Siyyar,* or external laws or Law of Nations.

The intrastate human rights are said to be unequal as between Muslims and non-Muslims, because of the political structure of the state. The state is under the sovereignty of God; its laws depend for their validity on the *Shariah;* and the Book is the primary source of law. Muslim citizens as a whole constitute the *Ummah,* or Islamic nation. Therefore, non-Muslims are not politically a part of that nation. In no way does this affect equality before the law or equal justice. All who live under the protective covenant of the *Shariah* are entitled to all privileges and immunities without distinction of race, religion, or national origin. The only real difference is one of authority, administration, and jurisdiction. This concept of separate political administration, yet with equal justice for all, is likened to the Roman concept of jurisdiction in the *jus civile.* The analogy is misleading, because the distinction in Islam is not one concerning the rights of the people, but one concerning the administration of the political and legislative process of the state. Non-Muslims are not outside the "jurisdiction" as understood by the *jus civile, orbis Romanus* simply because Muslims are not *princeps orbis terrarum* (lords of the population of the globe) (see Ion, 1907). Neither, for that matter, are the protective covenants between Muslims and non-Muslims a *pax Romana*, because the *Zimmi* are equal before the law in every respect (Hamidullah, 1961:150). The distinction remains one of political administration and not of human rights.[4] Translated in terms of the modern sociopolitical context, the Muslims constituting the majority govern and legislate but cannot affect matters specifically left to the minorities by the Koranic mandate or by covenant. Islam foresaw the possibility of the majority repressing the minority and specified certain rights for the non-Muslim minorities which cannot be tampered with even by the ruling majority (Ahmad, 1956:1).

Freedom of religious practice, personal-status matters, citizenship, and protection of life, liberty, and property are only some examples of specific guarantees that have to be afforded to the minorities who live under the protective covenant of the Islamic state. Islamic law is most benevolent in that it guarantees the rights of the minorities, even if they conflict with the rights of the majority.[5]

The concept of *Jizya*, which is a tax levied on non-Muslims, has often been cited as the main discriminatory feature in Islamic human rights. It is unfortunate that the nature of this tax is not well understood, since the tax is not discriminatory, but different from similar taxes levied upon Muslims—unless the mere fact that the tax is different constitutes inherent discrimination. Traditionally, the *Jizya* constituted a 10 percent tax on income to non-Muslims, while other taxes, including the duty of the *Zakat*, were only imposed upon Muslims. Furthermore, non-Muslims were not required to serve in the military or perform any public service duty as Muslims were (Cragg, 1956:339).

It is often said that while the enjoyment of life, liberty, and property is an absolute right for Muslims, subject only to the limitations of the rights of the community as a whole for the maintenance of a scheme of ordered liberty, which, by its very nature, requires certain self-imposed restrictions, the same right to life, liberty, and property is qualified for non-Muslims. While the statement correctly reflects medieval practices in the context of the relationship of Islam and Christendom, it is theoretically incorrect insofar as the ideal Islamic state is concerned in its relationship with other treaty states or minorities living under its protection (see Ahmad, 1956:16–21). For example, Article 7 of the Egyptian Constitution of 1958 provides: "All citizens are equal before the law. They are equal in their rights and obligations, without distinction of race, origin, language, religion or creed." Article 8, Paragraph 1, of the Malayan Constitution of 1957 states: "All persons are equal before the law and entitled to equal protection of the law." Paragraph 2 provides:

> Except as expressly authorized by this constitution, there shall be no discrimination against citizens on the grounds of only religion, race, descent or the place of birth in any law or in the appointment to any office or any employment under a public authority or in the administration of any law relating to the acquisition, holding or disposition of property or the establishing or carrying on of any trade, business or profession, vocation or employment.

---

4. For example, the Constitution of Pakistan, Article 10a, requires that the president be a Muslim.

5. Ramadan (1961:110–12) discusses preferential treatment for Christianity in some constitutions. Hamidullah (1961:132) states: "The ethical basis of Islam repudiates any distinction as to justice between Muslims and non-Muslims."

The Criminal Process

The criminal process requires a valid accusation made in the presence of the defendant, who will confront his accusers and have the right to interrogate them, cross-examine them, and ask them to take the oath (Baroody, 1967). The burden of proving the charge is always on the accusers, and an accusation itself is inconclusive proof. Imam Khattabbi explained that there are only two kinds of detention under law: (1) detention under the order of the court, mainly when a person has been sentenced by a court; and (2) a detention prior to sentencing during the court's investigation of a criminal violation. He concludes that there can be no other ground for deprivation of a person's freedom (Maudoodi, 1967:267, citing M'Alim Al Sunnah). It must be noted here that this in no way contemplates deprivation of freedom for what may be loosely termed political crimes, but only for specific common crimes validly prohibited by law (see, e.g., Auda, 1959). Statutory criminal violations that are not part of the Koranic precepts, but which are validly legislated, will depend for their constitutionality on their adherence to the Koranic precepts and their guarantee of the individual rights stated therein. The practice of the Prophet and tradition require that mere accusation, in the absence of tangible proof, is insufficient and that an accuser who is an interested party cannot be the sole evidence sufficient to sustain a criminal conviction. The moving plaintiff must appear personally and be accompanied by two witnesses who shall testify to the commission of the crime (see Anderson, 1959).

At an early stage of the Islamic nation, in the days of Aly the Fourth Calif, a group often labeled anarchists revolted against his regime, denying the need for the state's existence. It is reported that Aly sent them a message: "You may live wherever you like, the only condition between us being that you will not indulge in bloodshed and you will not practice cruel methods." Maudoodi (1967:268) draws from such instances the conclusion that even an organized group, opposed to the form of government, may entertain its political opposition provided it is not done in a disorderly fashion and provided it does not call for the destruction of the state by violence.

To insure the individual against abuses by the executive branch, Maudoodi asserts:

> The Executive should in no circumstances be allowed to possess the power of suspending either the fundamental rights or the writ of *Habeas Corpus*. The maximum allowance that can be made in this respect is that in case of actual war, rebellious persons who are charged with high treason, conspiracy against the State or armed revolt may be tried *in camera*. But the power of detention without judicial trial or of suspension of fundamental rights or of the writ of *Habeas Corpus*, should in no case be granted to the Executive (1967:341).

Maudoodi, a great Muslim scholar, was not alone in professing those thoughts. In 1953, a special convention of Ulemas, representing all schools of Islamic thought, gathered to discuss the 1952 proposed Constitution of Pakistan, and submitted a unanimous report that called for an immediate amendment of the Constitution: "Except in the case of an external or internal threat to the security of the state or other grave emergency," the right to *habeas corpus* cannot be suspended by executive decree. The committee reports that Islamic *Shariah* does not, in any circumstances, permit any Muslim or non-Muslim citizen to be deprived of his right to move the highest court for redress against unwarranted detention. The remedy of *habeas corpus* was singled out as the most important safeguard and became the counterpart of the tenth century *Mazalim* tribunal, which also allowed for an extraordinary remedy by petitioning for immediate redress of wrongs.

Criminal Justice Characteristics of the Islamic System

1. Function of the Trial

Procedures in today's courtrooms differ vastly from the early days when the Prophet Mohammed dispensed justice with the advice of the *Sahaba* (the first followers of Islam). Theoretically, the difference should have only been in the setting, but the departure is quite radical in Muslim states that do not abide exclusively by *Shariah* (Islamic law).

A criminal trial in the orthodox Islamic tradition, which is still followed in some countries (with varying degrees of compliance to the letter and spirit of Islam), is not a process designed to pit the state against a defendant. The state's function is to see justice done, not to exact vengeance from an individual—that is the remedy of the victim. The word *vengeance* means individual-to-individual vindication of a wrong within the bounds of the law.

2. The Trial: Public and Private Interest Intertwined

Islam is the most victim-oriented system of criminal justice history has known. The victim-plaintiff-accuser brings forth the charges before the judge. He prosecutes or aids in the prosecution of his case and, as such, the victim-accuser is directly involved in the process. This insures a direct human relationship at the trial between the wrong committed by the accused and the harm suffered by the victim. The accused is not confronted by a dispassionate, disinterested public official, but by the victim, either directly or indirectly, and is, therefore, vividly reminded of his wrongdoing.

In personal wrongs, which range from assault (including insult) to involuntary manslaughter, the wrongdoer must compensate the victim or his heirs. Economic compensation of the victim is, therefore, the essential remedy sought in this type of criminal trial. No further criminal charges will be brought against the wrongdoer if he satisfies the judgment, and the state will no longer be deemed to have an interest when the victim is compensated. However, the judge must find guilt and then decree the remedy. An insolvent wrongdoer can compensate his victim with his work and future earnings. The court will enforce its decision by penal sanctions. The state's interest, therefore, is contingent upon the victim's compensation. Certain personal wrongs, such as murder, also affect the public interest and the state is deemed also to be a victim. The approach of the prosecution is that the state, as a victim, must have satisfaction just as a person who suffered a private wrong, but the state can only exact punishment, which can be corporal as well as death or imprisonment. Penalties are essentially designed to be deterring.

3. The Role of the Judge and the Right to Appeal

The judge combines the roles of arbitrator, mediator, finder of facts, and trier of the law. His prime concern in personal wrongs is for the rights of the victim.

The judge may avail himself of a consultative lay jury of wise men or experts to determine the merits of a given contention. He decides the case on the basis of law and equity and proffers a judgment which takes into account the rights of the victim and the rights of God (the social interest).

Appeals have always historically been permissible to higher courts that could: (a) hold a trial *de novo;* (b) examine any question of law or facts; (c) consider application of the law by the judge; (d) assess the correctness of the judge's reasoning and logic; and (e) reconsider the penalty. An appeal for clemency or pardon to the chief executive has also always been available.

4. Evidence and Proof of Guilt

The parties appear before the judge as equals. A prosecutor, who can also be a private person appointed to represent the public interest, is the accused's counterpart. A presumption of truthfulness, however, arises when a party takes the oath. That presumption is rebuttable by the oath-taking of the opponent. The judge then determines the truthfulness of the oath taken. If one has perjured himself, the penalty is quite severe and, of course, includes loss of the case. If both parties are equally truthful, considering that honest and reasonable perception of facts may differ, the case proceeds because one truthful oath cancels the other. If one party offers to take the oath or asks his opponent to do so and his opponent refuses, then a presumption of truthfulness arises in favor of the one who asked for it. The totality of the evidence presented at a trial must convince the judge beyond a moral doubt. There is much reliance on: (a) logic as an instrument of proof; (b) oral testimony; and (c) oath-taking.

5. Punishment

Penalties are the right of society and are not to be confused with the compensation of the victim, which is a combination of actual and punitive damages. Penalties in Islam have been considered by Western observers as cruel and harsh. Consider the severance of the left hand of a thief for his first theft offense and the right hand for his second offense. The last reported theft in Saudi Arabia, which imposes this penalty, was in the fifties, when the operation was done surgically. Since then, there has been no proven theft case in that country. This is particularly significant during pilgrimages at Mecca, when over one million persons from all over the world congregate and their property (including money) is left in open view and often unguarded. In 1972, Libya announced its return to the Islamic system of justice.

6. The Relationship of the Penalty to Proof of the Crime and the Purposes of Criminal Law

Penalty is often intricately linked to an evidentiary question, which, in turn, is dictated by public-policy considerations. Adultery, for example, is punishable by stoning to death, but proof of adultery requires four eyewitnesses who can testify that if a hypothetical thread were passed between the bodies of the alleged adulterers, the thread's passage would be impeded by an obstacle. In other words, proof of adultery requires sexual penetration witnessed by four credible witnesses. From a practical point of view, this renders proof of the crime very difficult, if not impossible. The conclusion is that not adulterous sexual intercourse, but its public consummation, is the punishable crime. The harshness of the penalty, coupled with its difficult proof, is intended to operate as a deterrent. The crime of adultery could be proven also by the confession of a person corroborated beyond a moral certainty by other evidence. Only the person confessing would be convicted in this case and not the alleged correspondent. This is intended to discourage spiteful or fraudulent confessions. The married person is punished for the crime of adultery, not the unmarried one, whose penalty is corporal punishment (whipping).

7. Contemporary Nonorthodox Systems

Contemporary procedure in those countries that adhere to Islam as a faith and have codified their criminal laws and procedures (practically all countries which declare themselves Islamic in their constitution) has been influenced by Western European conceptions of criminal justice. They are, therefore, essentially inquisitorial systems in the European model, except for countries that have an English common-law influence, such as Pakistan, Nigeria, and the Sudan.

African states with a large Muslim population have been influenced by Islamic precepts (Seidman, 1966; Anderson, 1970), but these have been assimilated with tribal laws, and are now supplanted or incorporated in the codification movement. African states have been codifying their laws since their independence and the influence of England and France is observable in their developing criminal justice systems. The influence of the orthodox Islamic criminal process is practically nonexistent in contemporary criminal processes, even though its presence is noteworthy in substantive laws. One reason is that Islamic states have been under colonial rule for an extensive period of time and have absorbed the legacy of European systems. The other reason is that the Islamic criminal justice system is more a method of rendering justice than an institutionalized process. The former sociological basis of the Islamic nation exists no longer and, therefore, the emerging systems in those states that once were part of the nation reflect new sociological conditions.

4. CRIMINAL PROCESSES IN ACTION: A BASIC COMPARISON OF PROCEDURES IN THE ADVERSARY-ACCUSATORIAL AND INQUISITORIAL MODELS

Introduction

The procedural schemes utilized in adversary-accusatorial and inquisitorial models differ in scope and purpose; so the processes and devices utilized in these two systems are also different (Bassiouni, 1969a).

The judiciary and police are, in that order, the principal legal actors in the systems that have adopted the inquisitorial model. These actors investigate, collect evidence, examine the accused, and determine if guilt attaches. The roles of the accused and the defense are relatively passive. Even if an accused chooses to admit guilt, the state is not relieved of establishing its case against him. The philosophy of this system is that the people of the state, represented by its public institutions, are the only group competent to search for truth and find guilt or innocence.

This philosophy assumes that the best method for the determination of truth is relentless search by all participants in the system. The search is goal-oriented, and theoretically that goal is truth. Contrary to the adversary-accusatorial model, partisan legal actors are warranted only to the extent that they share in the pursuit of that goal. The means of goal achievement in the inquisitorial system is harmony among all its actors in the search for the true facts. In this approach there exists little room for adversary participants because the finding of truth by role-playing is deemed a matter of chance, and lacking the dignity ascribed to the quest for justice.

The adversary-accusatorial model recognizes a more significant role for the accused and the defense in criminal justice administration, for this system is based on an adversary ideology. Its rationale is that if two parties assume contrary and opposite positions on the issues (prosecution and defense) and carry on competitive debate, complemented by the introduction of supporting evidence, the court as an impartial third party is thereby placed in a better position to analyze and evaluate the respective contentions and arrive at a correct finding about the issues in dispute. It prefers means to results and emphasizes processes over goals.

The form, manner, and degree of constitutional review of criminal justice administration practices may well be the major actual difference between the inquisitorial and adversary-accusatorial legal systems. The latter system, vigilant for individual rights, is likely to impose greater restriction on its public agents because it holds the integrity of the process and its means at a higher value than effective results. In the Anglo-American legal system, this is the emphasis (Bassiouni, 1969a:313–24).

The distinction between the two models, however, goes beyond the principles of judicial limitation of administrative practice and constitutional control of judicial standards to the relationship between the individual and the public agencies of the state, the relationship between state agencies, and the practical question of sanctions and enforcement.

Until 1215 criminal proceedings in England and on the European continent were more or less the same. Victims were the movers of the accusation and conducted prosecutions. Several forms of trial existed; the oath *ex officio*, the trial by ordeal, and the trial by battle were known to both systems. During 1215 two events occurred that caused a divergence in the systems of England and Europe. One was the signing of the Magna Charta in England. It guaranteed among other safeguards the right to trial by one's peers. The other, in Rome, was the Fourth Lateran Council, which prohibited clergy from officiating at trials by ordeal. As a result of these two events, England developed the jury system, as well as what has now evolved into the adversary-accusatorial system, while Europe developed a system of official inquiry.

On the European continent an official magistrate was introduced to investigate crimes and to initiate prosecutions. Such investigations and prosecutions were conducted in the form of an official inquiry, from which *inquisitorial* was derived. Under this system there were virtually no rights or procedural safeguards for the accused until the seventeenth century, when public prosecutors started conducting open trials against defendants who were entitled to representation by counsel. The writings of the philosophers, social activists, and revolutionists of that time, among whom we can note Beccaria, Montesquieu, Voltaire, Rousseau, and Diderot, brought about the reform of European criminal justice. The results appeared in the French Codification of Criminal Procedure in 1810, which is still at the base of the 1958 French Code of Criminal Procedure, and the German Code of Criminal Procedure of 1877, which is at the base of their 1965 Code of Criminal Procedure. Almost all European procedures derived from Roman law and these major codifications.

This can be traced to the reception of Roman law throughout the Holy Roman Empire, particularly after the penal code of Charles V in the *Carolinae Constitutio Criminalis*. The contacts of colonial Europe with the Middle East, Africa, and Asia resulted in the exportation of their concepts to these areas of the world.

Throughout the history of what is now called the "inquisitorial" model, there has been little change in the conceptual framework. The changes have been in the area of constitutional and procedural safeguards for the accused and guarantees for the integrity of the process. These have advanced substantially since the end of World War II and are still progressing through the influence of constitutionalism and human rights.

The Police Phase

In the United States, which utilizes the adversary-accusatorial scheme, when an offense is committed, the police have the power to initiate the investigation, but, theoretically at least, they are limited in carrying out their investigation by restrictions in the Fourth Amendment of the Constitution. Searches and seizures for evidence are only permitted when there is a reasonable probability of the discovery of criminal objects (Bassiouni, 1969a:336–410). This includes reasonable searches of individuals who are considered as having some relationship to the crime [*Chimel* v. *California,* 395 U.S. 752 (1969)]. Only in situations where the police have reasonable grounds to believe an individual is armed and dangerous can they search him at the investigatory stage without "probable cause," and then such search is conditional upon fear for the life of the policeman himself or for the lives of others, and is limited to a mere search for weapons [*Terry* v. *Ohio,* 392 U.S. 1 (1968)]. Whenever an investigation goes beyond "investigation" and begins "to focus on a particular suspect" [*Escobedo* v. *Illinois,* 378 U.S. 478, 488–9 (1964)], or a suspect is subjected to "custodial investigation," he is to be warned of his right to remain silent, that anything he says will be used against him, and of his right to counsel, appointed or retained [*Miranda* v. *Arizona,* 384 U.S. 436, 444 (1966)].

An arrest can only be made upon "probable cause" to believe that the arrestee has committed an offense.[6] Thereafter he must be brought before a magistrate without unnecessary delay.[7] A search incident to lawful arrest can also be made but the search must be contemporaneous in time and place to the arrest [*Preston* v. *U.S.,* 376 U.S. 364 (1964)]. Its rationale is predicated on the arrestee's potential use of weapons against the arresting officer or the danger of destruction of the evidence. It is, therefore, limited to the person of the arrestee and the area under his immediate control, which is to be determined by the nature of the crime. Beyond these limitations any other search must be authorized by a search warrant issued by a judicial officer and stating specifically what is to be searched for and seized.

An accused may waive his right to remain silent and make statements or even a confession of guilt to the police. But, in the United States, any admissions obtained by improper police methods are deemed involuntary and not admissible as evidence [*Weeks* v. *U.S.,* 232 U.S. 383 (1914); *Mapp* v. *Ohio,* 367 U.S. 643 (1961)]. Evidence secured in violation of standards set by judicial interpretations of the Constitution will automatically be excluded in the U.S., while it will be excludable at the discretion of the judge in England, India, and Ghana (the latter two having adopted the English model). The Constitutional Court of the Federal Republic of Germany and that of Italy tend to set interpretative standards, which would recognize a given right and reverse a conviction secured on the basis of the violation. This is also the trend of the European Court of Human Rights, which exercises its jurisdiction over fifteen European countries (less Greece, for the time being, since its violations of the European Human Rights Convention) (Bassiouni, 1971b; Linke, 1971).

---

6. Probable cause was defined by the U.S. Supreme Court in *Brinnegar* v. *U.S.* [338 U.S. 160, 180 (1949)]: "Probable means more than a mere suspicion and exists where the facts and circumstances in knowledge of the officers and within which they had reasonable trustworthy information are sufficient in themselves to warrant a man of reasonable caution in the belief that an offense has been or is being committed."

7. *McNabb* v. *U.S.* [318 U.S. 332 (1943)]; *Mallory* v. *U.S.* [354 U.S. 449 (1957)]. This requirement has been held applicable to federal courts only and not to state courts; it was limited by the 1968 Omnibus Crime Bill 18 U.S.C. § 3501(c).

When an offense occurs in Germany, which employs the inquisitorial model, the power of the police depends largely upon their evaluation of the situation.

> . . . Police suspicion alone does not entitle the police to stop a person on the street and question him as to his identity and reason for being where he is, unless he consents to his being questioned. On the contrary, such repressive measures are permitted only in the event of a preliminary arrest based upon "strong suspicion . . ." (Sowle, 1962:56).

Theoretically at least, this criterion of restricting the exercise of police power "is a tougher requirement than the American probable cause" (Mueller & LePoole-Griffiths, 1969:15). This power of arrest by the police is exercised whenever a person is caught in the act or on pursuit "if he is suspected of escape or his identity cannot be established on the spot," *and* if "imminent danger" prevails (German Code of Criminal Procedure, §127). Imminent danger "exists if obtaining a judicial warrant entails a loss of time which would give rise to concern that the arrest of the suspected person might thereby become impossible" (Sowle, 1962:53). If these elements are nonexistent, then "issuance of a warrant of arrest . . . can only be granted by a judge" (p. 53). Where these elements are present and the police make an arrest, such arrest is called a "preliminary arrest" (German Code, §127). This "preliminarily arrested person must be taken before a judge who shall decide whether or not to issue a warrant of arrest" (Sowle, 1962:53).

Frisking "can only be ordered by a judge" but "in the case of imminent danger" the police can initiate a search if "reasonable suspicion" (as opposed to strong suspicion, which is required for arrest) exists (p. 55).

General searches for evidence are permissible upon similar grounds.

> Basically only a judge may order a search, law enforcement officers may search without warrant only in cases of danger in delay. Restrictions have been placed on nighttime searches, and elaborate provisions protect the secrecy or confidentiality of documents, business records, correspondence, etc. The officer conducting the search without a warrant, and not in the presence of a judge, is obligated to call in, as witnesses, a municipal official or two citizens of the municipality (but not police officers). Moreover, the occupant of the rooms or objects to be searched is entitled to be present at the search. If he is absent his representative or an adult relative, fellow-lodger or neighbor shall be called in if possible. This is a commendable protective device (Mueller & LePoole-Griffiths, 1969:19).

In Germany, the police "may question suspects who are at large, or volunteer to an interrogation, or are in legal custody." In the absence of a legal basis, they cannot force "a suspect at large" to submit to an interrogation unless they preliminarily arrest him. "Apart from this, the suspect can always obstruct his interrogation by using his privilege of silence" (Sowle, 1962:54), for prior to his first interrogation, any accused must be made aware that he is legally free to remain silent and that he may request an attorney of his choice at any time (Jescheck, 1970:245–46). Yet, unfortunately, in actual practice he is sometimes tricked into confessing by prosecuting and investigating officials (Pieck, 1962).

During interrogation the defendant is "protected from improper methods of interrogation such as mishandling, exhaustion, bodily harm, the administration of drugs, torture, deceit or hypnosis" (Jescheck, 1970:246). In addition, "the right of the police to interrogate the suspect subsequent to his preliminary arrest is subject to certain time limits" (Sowle, 1962:197). For the purposes of interrogation they

> may detain a suspect arrested by them at the latest until the expiration of the day following his apprehension, whereupon he shall be brought before the appropriate judge. In the event his interrogation (or the collection of other evidence) has already been finished prior to that time, he shall be brought before the judge even earlier, that is, immediately upon completion of the inquiries. The infraction of these rules will constitute an illegal deprivation of liberty. . . .
>
> Going beyond the time limit laid down in the law is not permitted, not even with the consent of the arrestee (Sowle, 1962:198).

Where a warrant for arrest has been issued, police are not entitled to detain the defendant but must take him before a magistrate "without delay" (p. 198). A violation of these rules in Germany, unlike in the United States, does not necessarily result in exclusion of evidence stemming therefrom. It has been said that those "admissions obtained by improper methods may, of course, not be considered during the trial without the consent of the accused" (Jescheck, 1970:246). However, the prohibition extends only to the illegally obtained statement and not to evidence discovered with its aid. Moreover, the German law of procedure known as "the rule of free evaluation of evidence" permits the judge unlimited evaluation of evidence. Thus, illegally obtained evidence is generally admissible in principle (Sowle, 1962:111), while only such evidence procured through "serious" violations is subject to exclusion (Jescheck, 1970). This rule derives from the French penal law, better known in the U.S. as the Napoleonic Codifications. It is based on the notion that the judge must reach within himself a level of personal conviction of the guilt of the accused. The concept originated in Roman law, and is embodied in all European systems and in others influenced by Roman law and by the later Napoleonic Codifications. The Italian Code of Criminal Procedure refers to it as the concept of *"libero Convincimento del Giudice."*

In France, criminal procedure is also inquisitorial in nature. After a crime has been reported, the approach that the police employ is relatively dependent upon whether the offense is *"en flagrant delit."* It is deemed *en flagrant delit* if "within a very short period after the commission of the act, the suspected person is pursued by public clamor, is found in possession of objects, or presents traces or indications which lead to the belief that he has participated in crime" (French Code of Criminal Procedure, Art. 53). If the offense is so considered, the police go directly to the scene of the offense, where they seize all evidence of any utility (Arts. 54, 56). Their powers of search and seizure at this point are quite broad (Art. 56). Any person "whose identity it appears necessary to establish or confirm" must submit to whatever police measures are necessary (Art. 8). The police can prohibit any or all persons from leaving the scene of the crime (Art. 61) and can likewise "require anyone believed to have useful information to come to police headquarters and make a statement" (Harvard Law Review, 1966:1115). These individuals cannot be detained more than 24 hours unless the police substantiate charges against someone and receive authority from a magistrate or the prosecuting attorney to retain him or her for a second 24-hour period (French Code, Art. 63).

Where the offense is not flagrant, police power depends on the circumstances. When a complaint is made to the police "a preliminary investigation by the police is usually held" (Pugh, 1962:13; see also French Code, Arts. 75–78). This preliminary investigation is conducted by the police "either at the request of the District Attorney or on their own initiative" (French Code, Arts. 75–78), although a private individual directly injured by the criminal act may commence the criminal action by bringing a complaint against the perpetrator of the wrong (Pugh, 1962; Sowle, 1962:48). During this investigation the police may conduct searches with the consent of the person on whose property the search takes place (French Code, Art. 76), and can detain persons who may have useful information about the crime for up to 24 hours for interrogation purposes (Art. 77). In any case, on learning of an offense, the police must "report the crime to the prosecuting attorney, who will petition a magistrate to assume the investigation" (Harvard Law Review, 1966:1115; see also French Code, Art. 54). The police are then commissioned by the magistrate to undertake investigation of the offense, and may obtain broad authorization to question witnesses and take their depositions wherever they may be. This authorization is called the *commission rogatoire* (see French Code, Arts. 151–153). It allows detention of witnesses (which, in fact, might include the accused), searches, and other incidental powers of investigation.

Regardless of method of initiation, "once suspicion focuses on a particular person . . . he is entitled to be warned of his right to remain silent and to be questioned only by the magistrate in the presence of counsel" (Harvard Law Review, 1966:1115). However, "protection for the accused is in practice even less than this limited safeguard would indicate since the police can simply ask a suspect to waive his right to be brought before the magistrate, and frequently the suspect will consent in order not to seem guilty" (p. 1115). So, too, there is evidence that the investigation does not cease when the police foresee a pending confession and are thereby tempted to forego the rights of the accused (Hrones, 1969).

Theoretically any proof illegally obtained must be dismissed from the proceedings in court (Sowle, 1962:111). But as a matter of fact, the French do not utilize any semblance of an "exclusionary rule" as is known in the United States. Thus, "a coerced confession is not rejected *per se*" (Hrones, 1969:77).[8]

In Italy crimes are divided between those requiring a *"mandato di cattura"* or warrant and those that do not require it. It is in the case of *"flagrante delitto"* that arrest, search, and seizure require no warrants. In 1968 the Italian Constitutional Court ruled that all police interrogations must be made in the presence of the defendant's counsel, if he has one. There is no requirement for court-appointed counsel, as in the United States. Prior to that ruling the right to counsel at the police interrogation stage depended on the nature of the investigation, which in its turn depended on the charge. There is, however, no decision bearing on the exclusion of evidence be it tangible or intangible, or seized in an unreasonable manner from an accused. Involuntary confessions and improperly seized evidence are submitted to the court, which can exclude either. As a matter of law, however, a conviction secured solely on such evidence is reversible as legally insufficient evidence to support the judge's reasonable conviction beyond a moral certainty of the accused's guilt.

Formal accusation of most crimes is made by a magistrate after presentation of the accused before him and a perusal of the evidence against the suspect.

In France and Italy the investigative aspects of the police process are theoretically under judicial supervision and control; in actuality, the magistrate grants the judicial police broad latitude and discretion in conducting criminal investigations. In these nations, a magistrate usually makes the formal accusation only after *he* interrogates the accused and studies the evidence against him.

---

8. One writer even proclaimed that in France "if the accused is in fact guilty, there the use of all means to gain a conviction is justified" (Hauser, 1959:808).

The Commencement of Prosecution and Pretrial Phase

1. Commencement of Prosecution

As a matter of policy, a nation could adopt any one of three possible methods of prosecution for crime. It could permit the person directly injured by the commission of the crime or his relatives, in the case of death, to prosecute the wrongdoer. It could designate a public official to exercise exclusive right to represent the state in bringing the wrongdoer to justice. Or it could designate a public official to represent the state in the prosecution of criminals, but also allow the victim of the crime, or his survivors, to join with the public official in the prosecution, or to conduct the prosecution alone, in the event that the public official refuses to exercise his right to prosecute.

The choice of method will be determined to a great extent by the philosophy of the nation with respect to the fundamental purpose of criminal prosecution. If a country should focus on the vindication of public rights through the prosecution and punishment of criminals, a system of public prosecution would be established to implement this policy. If, however, a nation believes that the rights of the victim are, if not the primary consideration, at least equally important with those of the state as a whole, it is reasonable to suppose that at least a share in the prosecution will be delegated to the individual. Among other factors which might lead to the establishment of a system of private, as opposed to public, prosecution are the history of the system over the years, considerations of cost and efficiency, and a desire to combine, insofar as possible, both civil and criminal remedies into one proceeding.

In early times all criminal prosecutions were commenced by private individuals due to the lack of a governmental organization qualified to perform the task. Possibly the feeling existed that the victim was the proper person to invoke the power of the state to punish the wrongdoer, so long as the particular crime did not directly injure the state.

In England today, private prosecution, as distinguished from an integrated system of public prosecution, is the rule. Although the office of the Director of Public Prosecutions does exist, it will commence a prosecution only in those rare cases where the offense is one of great public importance or is a matter of particular concern to the government itself. In practice, most prosecutions are initiated by the police. If the offense is a summary one, the appropriate police inspector will prosecute the accused before the local Magistrates' Court. If the offense is more serious—one which will require indictment—the police will retain a solicitor to commence the prosecution, and a barrister in private practice will be briefed to conduct the actual trial. A private individual who considers that he has been wronged by the criminal action of another may also commence a prosecution through private counsel of his choice.

This English system has one very desirable advantage over most other systems of public prosecution. The quality of prosecution is high because well-qualified barristers, successful in private practice, bring to the trial of criminal cases their accumulated knowledge and experience. For the most part, public prosecutors in the United States are elected and, at least at the lower level, their staff are political appointees in the process of gaining trial experience. Indeed, the prosecutor's office in the United States is often considered a stepping stone to other political office or to a lucrative private practice (Sullivan, 1961).

2. Indictment and Information in the Adversary-Accusatorial Model

In the United States there are two methods by which a criminal prosecution is instituted: (1) by information, or (2) by grand jury indictment. The distinction is usually based on the type of crime, i.e., misdemeanor and felony. In an information prosecution, the prosecutor presents a sworn statement to the court, which does not require concurrence by any other party or body. The accused will stand trial on the allegations sustained in that instrument. Federal courts and most state courts utilize the grand jury system to prosecute persons charged with a felony. The grand jury is generally composed of twenty-three jurors who investigate an alleged offense, and, if an offense has occurred, determine who should be brought to trial and how they should be charged.

> The grand jury plays a passive role in most proceedings, the prosecuting attorney presenting *selected* witnesses and evidence to the grand jurors. . . . Usually, the accused has been arrested and is either in jail or on bail at the time the grand jury considers his case, though the prosecutor may seek action by the grand jury before arrest is made. At least twelve members of the . . . grand jury must concur that sufficient evidence has been presented to justify subjecting a person to public trial (Scigliano, 1962:223, emphasis added).

However, the grand jury

> has the right to act independently of the court and the state, enabling it to act fearlessly and conscientiously in discharging its duties and fulfilling its obligations to the public. Neither the court nor the state may limit grand jury investigations. The grand jury has a right to subpoena witnesses and documents and to proceed in independent criminal investigations.
> . . . The grand jury may bring to trial those whom it feels the state has been derelict in not prosecuting (Bassiouni, 1969a:455).

In the great majority of cases, however, the prosecuting attorney assumes the onus in the inquiry, utilizing whatever evidence and witnesses he chooses. Moreover, there are no rules of evidence that a prosecutor must follow in presentation of his allegations to the grand jury. Hence, for example, a grand jury's findings against an accused, which are based almost exclusively on hearsay testimony, do not render the proceeding irregular [*Costello* v. *U.S.*, 350 U.S. 359 (1956)].

The proceedings of the grand jury are not open to the public and only the jurors, representatives of the state, and witnesses are admitted. The individual who is being accused, as well as his attorney, is *not* admitted into the proceedings to rebut the evidence or witnesses being presented by the prosecutor. If it so desired, the grand jury could require an accused to appear before it to give his version, but this is not normal.

If, after viewing the evidence before it, the grand jury concludes that an offense has been committed and that it has been committed by a certain individual, it issues an indictment against him. The indictment is a formal charge indicating that a particular individual is believed to have violated a law and is, thereby, ordered to stand trial on the matter.

The grand jury has been legitimized on the grounds that it stands between the state and the accused, protecting the latter from pernicious or malicious charges [*Wood* v. *Ga.*, 370 U.S. 375, 390 (1962)]. Whether it does or not is highly questionable. The grand jury can be looked upon as a carry-over of the inquisitional system, because of its secrecy and one-sided examination of the facts. The United States Supreme Court has indicated that where a state chooses to use an information system in the prosecution of an infamous crime and not a grand jury, there is no infringement of the constitutional rights of an accused. The Fifth Amendment mandate that "no person shall be held to answer for a capital, or otherwise infamous crime, unless on a presentment or indictment of a Grand Jury" has not been deemed so essential to the rights of an accused as to be required in state prosecutions because of the Fourteenth Amendment's due process guarantee [*Hurtado* v. *Calif.*, 110 U.S. 516 (1884)], even though it is required in the federal courts.

In the various American jurisdictions, where the offense is a misdemeanor, a summons is issued that orders the accused to appear before the court and answer the charges against him.

3. Preliminary Hearing in the Adversary-Accusatorial Model

Although there is no constitutional requirement for grand jury indictments, almost all the states require by statute a preliminary examination subsequent to an arrest for a felony. In this hearing, a magistrate or judge determines if the state has enough evidence against an accused to warrant holding him for further proceedings. If it is determined that there is no chance for a conviction, the charges are dismissed. Usually this hearing precedes the formal charge, i.e., indictment or information, but there is no constitutional requirement that it should be so.

> The purpose of the preliminary hearing is essentially to advise a person of his right to remain silent and of his right, if indigent, to have the assistance of counsel at trial. In addition to these functions, which are now rendered by the arresting officer at the time of arrest, it also serves the following purposes:
> 1. To determine the existence of probable cause for which a warrant was issued for his arrest.
> 2. To inquire into the reasonableness of the arrest and search, and the compliance of the executing officer with the command of the warrant.
> 3. To afford the magistrate who issued the warrant or U.S. Commissioner the opportunity to hear the accused and determine whether probable cause still exists after the hearing of witnesses or examining evidence presented by the accused.
> 4. To release the accused on bail.
> A preliminary hearing is something of an informal trial for probable cause. It does not determine the guilt or innocence of the accused by merely the existence and validity of the probable cause. Thus, it gives the judge the opportunity to discharge the accused and dismiss the charges against him if probable cause is not found to exist. . . .
>   Because preliminary hearings are conducted on an inquiry basis, they are not limited by the rules of evidence which apply to trials. The preliminary hearing assures an individual that he will not be detained in prison without the existence of valid probable cause and gives an accused the opportunity to be released on bail. A release by a magistrate on a preliminary hearing or dismissal of the charges is not, however, binding upon the prosecution in its determination to prosecute the accused. At a preliminary hearing the judge will also determine the jurisdiction of the court trying the case and the validity of the warrants and charges brought against the person and their compliance with the statutes and laws of the state. Persons arrested in another jurisdiction or arrested in the jurisdiction of the court to be transferred to another jurisdiction, also appear before a magistrate for a preliminary hearing (Bassiouni, 1969a:438–39).

In the federal courts and all state courts, an accused can waive the preliminary hearing.

4. The Prosecution in the Accusatorial Model

No discussion of the decision to prosecute criminally in the United States is complete without specifically mentioning the role of the prosecutor. The American prosecutor has great discretion in determining the fate of the accused. It is within his province to decide what type of charge to attach to the accused, to refrain from instituting charges even if he knows grounds exist, and in some cases he even has the power to enter into "plea bargains." This practice allows an accused to exchange a plea of guilt for a lighter sentence or a reduction in the charge (see Alschuler, 1968; Gentile, 1969).

The scope of his investigation of the offense is likewise unpredictable. "In [the] States, in the investigation of a particular crime, the prosecutor may rely entirely on the police, merely accepting the evidence which they turn over to him; he may entirely disregard the police, and any evidence they may have gathered, and make his own investigation; or he may supplement the police investigation by his own" (Berman, 1958:156–57).

In America it is essentially the grand jury, the magistrate at the preliminary hearing, and the prosecutor who make the decision to prosecute after the police have made their investigation and/or arrest. In the continental nations it is basically the investigation (or examining) magistrate and the prosecutor who make that decision. We will discuss the investigating magistrate first.

5. Pretrial Hearing, Judicial Investigations, and Commencement of Prosecution in the Inquisitorial Model

In the continental system of criminal justice, the chief legal actor is the investigating magistrate, *juge d'instruction*. If there is no emergency situation at the time the police become cognizant of an offense, the investigating magistrate initiates the investigation. If he does not take an active role initially in the investigation of the offense—perhaps because it was "flagrant" (as in France), or because it happened in the presence of the officer and there was "imminent danger" (as in Germany)—the examining magistrate comes into the scene subsequent to the initial police inquiry.

Continental law has turned the magistrate into an investigation expert. He is a professional judge, sworn to uphold the functions of the judicial office, yet he is also a skilled investigator with command power over segments of the police. It is to him that the continental police loses its custody of the arrestee. Being a judge, he enjoys the confidence of the community regarding fairness, which it is unwilling to repose in the police. But realizing that the investigation of a suspicion of crime must continue after arrest so as to lead either to a criminal trial or a dismissal of the charges, this investigating magistrate has the duty of judicially and judiciously investigating every angle of a case before him (usually only serious felonies) until he is ready to make a recommendation to prosecute, to dismiss, or to nol-pros. Additionally, the continental investigating magistrate commands the subpoena power of our grand jury, as well as the power to receive the testimony of witnesses under oath. Thus, this unique institution combines the absolute integrity and impartiality of the judicial office, the power of the prosecution, the investigative skill and expertise of the police, and the powerful reach of the grand jury.

Whether the result of the combination brings out the worst or the best of these several institutions wrapped in one really is left up to the society that creates and retains the institution. Unquestionably, as a judge, the continental investigating magistrate has suffered the loss of some of the prestige that ordinarily inheres in the trial or appellate judge. As a super-policeman he is not as mobile, elastic, and efficient as the detective force. Compared with our grand jury he lacks the representativeness of the morals and feelings of society that inhere in that body. Nevertheless, as Mueller says, if in this country we insist on promptly bringing every suspect before a judge, and if we are unwilling to sacrifice the helpful investigative contribution of the police, and Supreme Court decisions would seem to drive us in that direction, we may well have to take another look at the European institution of the investigating magistrate (Mueller & LePoole-Griffiths, 1969).

The investigating magistrate in France, in addition to the powers of the U.S. judge at the preliminary proceedings, "has the right, more, a duty to discover facts for himself" (Hauser, 1959:809). In the case of felonies the magistrate must conduct additional hearings regardless of whether a confession has been obtained, and he, rather than the prosecutor, has the primary responsibility for making all the investigation that he deems useful to the manifestation of the truth (French Code, Arts. 79, 81). Similar hearings are usually held in cases involving lesser crimes.

Briefly, to summarize the function of these hearings and the role of the investigating magistrate in them:

> The hearings are conducted in secrecy, apparently in order to protect the accused from publicity; each witness is heard out of the presence both of the accused and of other witnesses. A major step in this investigation process is the examination of the accused by the magistrate. Counsel must be present when the accused appears unless the right has been expressly waived, and counsel must be allowed to examine the dossier, which contains all the prosecution's evidence, at least twenty-four hours before the hearing. However, counsel for the accused may question his client or other witnesses only with the permission of the examining magistrate, and the accused may not confer with his lawyer prior to answering any particular question. In theory, the accused may refuse to answer all questions, but apparently such a refusal is rare since the magistrate would be certain to draw adverse inferences from it. Indeed, the suspect's opportunity to participate in the inquiry and to advance his version of the facts seems to be regarded as an important right, rather than as an interference with liberty or privacy.
>
> When conflicts appear in the testimony received, the magistrate will frequently resort to confrontation. A witness whose testimony conflicts with that of the accused will be asked to repeat his statement in the presence of the accused, and the accused will then be asked to reconcile his version of the facts with that just given. This technique is undoubtedly of great help to the magistrate in presenting him with demeanor and other clues to the reliability of testimony. In addition, crucial admissions will often be made by the accused, and these become a part of the record along with other testimony. Another device often used to verify testimony is the reconstitution: The accused and the witnesses, along with the magistrate, prosecutor and defense counsel, visit the scene of the crime, where each party re-enacts his role in the incident under investigation. Frequently, this procedure will provide a strong indication of the reliability of testimony, and again a record of the proceedings is included in the dossier.
>
> Thus, the accused occupies a central position in the investigation process from beginning to end, and usually a confession is eventually obtained. Moreover, the investigation will produce an elaborate dossier, providing "a complete record of the events leading up to and constituting the crime, a portrait of the personalities involved in it, and a record of the judicial procedure which has followed upon it." It should be noted, however, that the record of a given proceeding can be included in the dossier only if the required safeguards have been provided. Failure to notify the accused of his right to remain silent and to have counsel, and failure to allow the accused's lawyer to examine the dossier prior to an examination, will render all subsequent proceedings void, and the record of proceedings thus nullified must be stricken from the dossier.
>
> On the basis of the material in the dossier, the magistrate must determine whether to refer the case to an appropriate court for trial. Apparently much more than "probable cause" is required—the magistrate must conclude on the basis of the facts developed that the accused committed the crime, and this criterion seems to be interpreted to

mean that doubts must be resolved in favor of the accused. Moreover, in the case of felonies, the magistrate's order alone is not sufficient. The case is automatically referred to an "indicting chamber" (chambre d'accusation), composed of three magistrates who review the dossier, hear argument by prosecution and defense attorneys and determine whether the facts developed justify trial on a felony charge (Harvard Law Review, 1966:1117-18).

Although it seems the purely investigatory function of the *juge d'instruction* could be taken over by the police, the French do not view the police as "free from the suspicion of being too anxious to secure convictions, and it is felt that investigation by a person of judicial status may shield innocent persons from the risk of being exposed to overzealous police investigation" (Anton, 1960:441). Thus, even if an accused chooses to admit guilt, the continental investigating magistrate must obtain independent supplemental evidence to substantiate the charges. Guilty pleas are never accepted. This is based on "the principle that the court must ascertain the full truth for *itself*" (Jescheck, 1970:248). (This approach is contrasted with the American, where if an accused admits guilt by way of confession or guilty plea, the investigation of the offense is relatively complete.) Moreover, an accused cannot waive the preliminary examination. Hence, the immensely careful preliminary investigation by the investigating magistrate makes it unlikely that persons who are sent to trial in these nations are guiltless (Anton, 1960:456).

Although he generally assumes an independent capacity, "the juge d'instruction does not act on his own motion. Usually he begins an investigation only when authorized by the prosecutor" (Ploscowe, 1935:1012). For example, "if during a particular investigation the juge d'instruction comes upon the traces of other crimes he must ask the prosecuting attorney for an authorization if he wishes to act in these offenses also" (p. 1012). The German investigation magistrate is even more restricted:

> The prosecutor's authorization which opens formal investigation must indicate not only the specific offense but also the individual accused. The juge d'instruction may not proceed against all the individuals concerned in the offense unless the prosecutor has included them all in his demand. The juge d'instruction cannot act in a case if the probable author is unknown (p. 1013).

It would seem that such a relationship certainly detracts from the necessary independence of the judiciary.

The powers of the continental prosecutor are somewhat analogous to those of the American. For offenses which are not petty in nature, the German prosecutor has virtually unlimited discretion in determining whether to prosecute. However, for serious offenses, the prosecutor is bound by the *legalitatsprinzip* or "legality principle" under which he is obligated to prosecute whenever he is able to prove his case in court (Jescheck, 1970:245). In theory it seems the German prosecutor is obliged to prosecute all crimes, yet in practice, if this principle were to be strictly applied without discretion, the structure of criminal procedure in Germany would soon crumble from the weight of a myriad of pending criminal prosecutions. To obviate this potential difficulty, the German prosecutor has been given the option of moving for a penal order which the judge may impose without a trial. The penal order is somewhat analogous to the American guilty plea. The order may include a fine, confiscation of property, withdrawal of a license, or incarceration of up to three months. Often it is quite agreeable to a defendant who is guilty to accept the penal order rather than suffer the expense of an open trial. More than 70 percent of all criminal matters that progress to a point where formal charges are filed are closed via penal order. Therefore, the German prosecutor, while he does not have the discretionary leeway available to his American, and to some extent his French, counterpart, does have a limited ability to dispose of a great majority of the criminal matters in an expeditious manner.

The German prosecutor assumes an impartial posture in his dealings with the accused. He ascertains all mitigating circumstances and even makes appeals for the defendant (Sowle, 1962:199).

In France the role of the prosecutor is analogous to that of the German in that he assumes an active role in the investigation. After the French police learn of a crime they are "required to report the crime to the prosecuting attorney (procureur)" (Harvard Law Review, 1966:1115). At this point "the District Attorney shall take, or cause to be taken, all steps necessary to discover and to prosecute infractions of the penal law. . . . To this end, he shall direct the activities of the judicial police agents and officers within the jurisdiction of the court" (French Code, Art. 41). Subsequently, he reports the offense to the examining magistrate who in turn assumes the investigation (Art. 51).

Similar to the U.S. prosecutor, in France commencing the prosecution "is a completely discretionary matter, and fairly often the prosecutor declines to prosecute upon receiving a promise from the suspect to submit himself to a sort of probation system, thus sparing him the ordeal of a public trial" (Hauser, 1959:808).

There are certain advantages in a system that reaches a real decision as to guilt or innocence during a preliminary judicial investigation. It substitutes a full-time, law-trained, experienced investigator for the butcher, the baker, the candlestick-maker, and their wives. It avoids not only the overemphasis on drama and emotional appeal of many common-law trials but also the necessity of compressing and simplifying the presentation. It eliminates the necessity, and the inefficiency, of thorough, perceptive, advance preparation; if during the investigation a point that the investigator has overlooked or has considered not worth looking into becomes crucial, it is simply a matter of extending the investigation. In short, a civil-law judicial investigation resembles the way most of us would make a serious inquiry anywhere except in a courtroom.

It is probably too much to assume that the so-powerful investigating judge will invariably be disinterested, conscientious, humane, and wise. A biased, lazy, or not-overly-bright judge is powerfully countered by counsel and jury in the common-law system.

There is good common sense behind the adversary system. To many law-abiding people a mere accusation of crime carries a certain prima facie validity. A fortiori, it seems that when the law-abiding person is a civil servant who spends his working hours dealing with criminals and in close association with the police, it is all too easy for him to satisfy himself that the accusation is correct; all his natural human laziness and "reasonableness" encourage such a conclusion. All investigating judges are not always easily satisfied. A system of adjudication that puts so much reliance on the investigating authorities will occasionally convict innocent men. The contrasting merit of the adversary system is that somebody has the sole responsibility and interest to "think otherwise"—somebody who can exert substantial influence on the final decision. Every experienced defense lawyer has obtained acquittals of defendants that the police and prosecuting authorities honestly and reasonably believed were guilty, and presumably not all of these acquittals were wrong.

Even assuming that all of these acquittals were wrong, it may be that protection of individual liberty demands a certain inefficiency in the administration of criminal justice. The choice of that system is dependent upon the stability of legal and social institutions that have been able to afford a system which not only scrupulously acquits the innocent but gives the state a hard time in convicting the guilty. The inquisitorial model suggests a different basic attitude. Where one model regards an acquittal as a vindication of personal freedom and proof of the ascendancy of the individual over the state, the other sees it as a threat to the security of organized society.

Bail and Preventive Detention

After one is arrested in the United States, he can normally be "released on bail" by executing a personal bond or, together with other persons as sureties, naming the sheriff or constable as obligee in a sum generally proportional to the crime charged and the likelihood of his appearance at the trial to answer the charges against him.

> Typically an arrested person is brought by the police before a committing magistrate or judge who fixes an amount of money as security for his appearance at trial. In some courts bail schedules set an amount for each offense, and if the defendant can post that amount, the judge seldom considers the case individually. Under either method if the defendant can post the required amount or can pay a bondsman to post it for him, he is released until trial. If he cannot, he remains in jail. If the defendant fails to appear for trial, the bond may be forfeited (President's Commission, 1967:37).

The only legitimate purpose of this device is to secure the presence of the accused at trial.

The Eighth Amendment to the United States Constitution provides that "excessive bail shall not be required." Requiring bail "at a figure higher than an amount reasonably calculated" to secure the presence of the defendant at trial is considered excessive [*Stack* v. *Boyle*, 342 U.S. 1 (1951); Bassiouni, 1969a:440–48]. Although federal and many state laws require that anyone arrested for non-capital offenses who provides the necessary bail bond shall be released, there has been no declaration by the courts that one accused of crime should be able to put up a bond as a matter of "right."

In practice, the bail system smacks of iniquity. The principal fault is its reliance on the ability to pay. As former President Johnson pointed out:

> The defendant with means can afford to pay bail. He can afford to buy his freedom. But the poorer defendant cannot pay the price. He languishes in jail weeks, months and perhaps even years before trial.
>
> He does not stay in jail because he is guilty.
>
> He does not stay in jail because any sentence has been passed.
>
> He does not stay in jail because he is any more likely to flee before trial.
>
> He stays in jail for one reason only—because he is poor (President's Commission, 1967:37).

There are other concomitant problems associated with unnecessary detentions.

> Defendants presumed innocent are subjected to the psychological and physical deprivations of jail life, usually under more onerous conditions than are imposed on convicted defendants. The jailed defendant loses his job if he has one and is prevented from contributing to the preparation of his defense. Equally important, the burden of his detention frequently falls heavily on the innocent members of his family. Moreover, there is strong evidence that a defendant's failure to secure pretrial release has an adverse effect on the outcome of his case. Studies in Philadelphia, the District of

Columbia and New York all indicate that the conviction rate for jailed defendants materially exceeds that of bailed defendants (American Bar Association, 1968a:2–3).

In the nations which utilize the inquisitorial scheme of criminal justice, there exists the device of preventive detention (Mueller & LePoole-Griffiths, 1969:95). Where there exists strong suspicion that an individual has committed a criminal offense, serious in nature, he may be detained prior to trial if there is "(a) danger of flight, (b) a danger of collusion, *or* (c) a danger of him committing another offense" (p. 94). There has been a call for wholesale adoption of this scheme in the American system (e.g., Hruska, 1969).

A judge in Germany is restricted in his utilization of this device by regulations that list specific criteria which have to be met before preventive detention can be imposed. In addition:

> pretrial detention may not be imposed if it is disproportionate to the significance of the case or to the punishment or measure of prevention and reform likely to be imposed." Besides, if the act is punishable only by imprisonment up to six months by confinement in a jail (which is the form of imprisonment to be imposed for less serious offenses) or by fine, pre-trial detention may not be imposed merely for danger of collusion. In such cases, it may be imposed for danger of flight only if the accused has previously avoided the proceedings against him, has made preparations for flight, has no fixed place of residence or abode, or cannot identify himself. In short, if the accused presents a special risk of possible flight his detention may be ordered (Mueller & LePoole-Griffiths, 1969:97).

Also a German defendant must be released if "less incisive measures" will substitute for the harsh element of commitment. Examples of such measures are:

> —an order to report at designated times at the offices of the judge, the prosecution or a specific office to be designated by it.
> —an order not to leave the place of residence or abode, or a certain area, without permission of the judge or the prosecution.
> —an order not to leave the residence except under the supervision of a designated person (p. 99).

In France, the judge ordering preventive detention "is basically free to order detention when he sees fit" (p. 94). Preventive detention of a suspect generally is requested immediately after the investigation of the offense is initiated. If permission is granted, he or she will be detained pending the outcome of the investigation (Hauser, 1959:810).

> The judge more often than not grants this request when the crime is a serious one, rather than give the suspect bail. For an often considerable period, then, the suspect is in jail without benefit of counsel, for he has not yet been brought before the examining judge. If the latter commits him to trial, he will remain in jail until the conclusion of the trial (p. 810).

The use of pretrial detention in France is very strictly limited when the accused is charged with a misdemeanor. Moreover, it cannot be utilized "when there are no *substantial grounds* for the belief that the accused may flee, exert pressure on witnesses, destroy evidence, commit new offenses, or disturb public order, [whereupon] provisional release is a matter of right" (French Code, Art. 274; emphasis added).

There are certain time limits established as to the duration of pretrial detention. Generally, the Germans utilize a six-month maximum (German Code, §121), while the French restrict such detention to two months (Patey, 1960). In Italy certain crimes are bailable while others are not; the judge has discretion in granting release on bail only for the categories of crimes for which the code permits bail.

Right to Counsel

When one has been charged with a crime in the United States, the retention of legal counsel is deemed a necessity and, as such, a right [*Gideon* v. *Wainwright*, 372 U.S. 335, 344 (1963); Bassiouni, 1969a]. The Sixth Amendment of the Constitution specifically prescribes that "in all criminal prosecutions, the accused shall . . . have the assistance of Counsel for his defense."

As indicated earlier, this provision has been construed to include not only a right to retention of counsel but also a right to appointment of counsel by the court if the accused is indigent. The proceedings for which the assistance of counsel is guaranteed include pretrial, posttrial, and other collateral proceedings,[9] as well as the regular trial. However, it is uncertain as to what type of offense the right to have counsel, appointed or retained, refers.[10] The interpretations of the scope of this right in the various state and federal jurisdictions of the United States have been many (Leu, 1969). However, they fall into three general categories: the right extending to (1) only individuals charged with felonies; (2) all individuals charged in any criminal proceeding and (3) those defendants accused of a misdemeanor where the punishment might be serious, as well as felonies (Leu, 1969).

In the continental nations, the accused likewise has the right to the assistance of counsel. In this respect their system of justice is not without its adversary features. The defendant has some role in actively defending himself and the assistance of counsel is deemed important to this role, but not indispensable. The difference in the importance attributed to the assistance of counsel stems from the type of proceedings, the significance of objective evidence, limited or not by rules of evidence, and the burden of proof. The active role of the judge in the inquisitorial system reduces the need for an adversary advocate, and the proof of guilt needed to convict under this system makes it less necessary.

The German defendant "has the right to avail himself at every stage of the criminal process of a defense counsel of his choice" (Jescheck, 1970:248), but the utility of counsel is somewhat questionable because (1) counsel do not usually have the right to attend interrogation of their clients by the police or prosecutor, and (2) no presentation of proof or cross-examination of witnesses comparable to American practice exists in German trials.

---

9. At arraignment: *Hamilton* v. *Alabama*, 368 U.S. 52 (1961); *White* v. *Maryland*, 373 U.S. 59 (1963); *Coleman* v. *Alabama*, 399 U.S. 1 (1970); during lineup identification: *U.S.* v. *Wade*, 388 U.S. 218 (1967). At habeas corpus: *Carafas* v. *LaVallee*, 391 U.S. 234 (1968); on appeal: *Douglas* v. *California*, 372 U.S. 353 (1963); *Anders* v. *California*, 386 U.S. 738 (1969); at sentencing: *McConnell* v. *Rhay*, 393 U.S. 2 (1968). At probation revocation: *Mempa* v. *Rhay*, 389 U.S. 128 (1967); in *habeas corpus* proceedings: People ex rel., *Harris* v. *Ogilvia*, 35 Ill. App. 2d 512, 221 N.E. 2d 265 (1966); in juvenile delinquency proceedings: *In re Gault*, 387 U.S. 1 (1967). See also, for a description of juvenile proceedings, Bassiouni, 1969a:519–41.

10. The U.S. Supreme Court in *Gideon* v. *Wainright* [372 U.S. 335 (1963)] held that the right to counsel, appointed or retained, is a "fundamental right, essential to a fair trial" for anyone "charged with crime" in a state court. It did not clarify what "crime" encompassed, e.g., whether only felonies, or all offenses classified as crimes in the various jurisdictions, or some other standard.

In France, the defendant generally has no right to counsel, appointed or retained, until he is formally charged (Ploscowe, 1935:1016; Harvard Law Review, 1966:1114; French Code, Arts. 114, 116).

Legal assistance in France is limited in scope. "In the lowest criminal court, the police tribunal, which can impose minor fines and jail sentences of up to two months, there is no statutory authority for the appointment of counsel" (Pelletier, 1967:643), although there does exist the power to retain counsel at these proceedings (Snee & Pye, 1960). At all superior court proceedings the accused has the right to counsel but upon appeal such right to appointment "is a matter within the court's discretion" (Pelletier, 1967:644).

Hence, in the nations using the inquisitorial scheme of administration of criminal justice, counsel is not deemed as necessary to the defense of the accused as seems to be the case in the United States.

Discovery of Prosecutor's Files

In the continental nations—France and Germany—the defendants have relatively open access to the files of the prosecutor. The German defense counsel:

> has access to the prosecutor's entire file, including the material to be introduced into evidence upon completion of the preliminary investigation. The defense counsel may even take the files to his office for study and preparation of his counter-argument. The defendant, after the conclusion of the investigation, may also demand a "final interview" with the prosecuting attorney during which he may, in the presence of his counsel, state his position. But he does not have to reveal to the prosecutor the counter-proof which he plans to introduce at trial other than the names and addresses of his witnesses and experts (Jescheck, 1970:246).

In France, the entire file compiled against the accused "must be placed at the disposal of counsel for the accused no later than twenty-four hours before each interrogation" (French Code, Art. 118). This approach is consistent with the inquisitorial system's insistence on finding truth by any manner, even if it detracts from whatever adversary concept is inherent in the system.

In the United States the defense counsel has lesser access to the prosecutor's files. Although Rule 16 and 17.1 of the federal Rules of Criminal Procedure "are steps in the continental direction" of allowing the defendant full access to all evidence the prosecution has against the accused, most jurisdictions still employ a relatively greater "combat theory of trial procedure" which gives an "unjustified advantage to the side with the cleverer lawyer or the wider facilities of investigation (Berman, 1958:131). Without a doubt the defendant is usually the party who suffers most from this disadvantage. Allowing the defense full access to the prosecutor's files diminishes the possibility of a prosecutor "bluffing" defendants into pleading guilty to lesser charges when they have little or no evidence against them, which one expert maintains occurs more often than most prosecutors would be willing to admit (Alschuler, 1968:65–70 discusses prosecutor bluffing, with examples and techniques).

The Trial Phase

There exist major philosophical differences between trials in nations utilizing the inquisitorial system of criminal justice and those utilizing an accusatorial approach. "The civil system carries the officiality and investigation maxims forward into the trial. In contrast, the Anglo-American trial is almost purely adversary" (Mueller & LePoole-Griffiths, 1969:24; see also Bassiouni, 1969a:476–504). The continental judge investigates

> all aspects of the case before him in a zealously impartial manner.
> It was the prosecuting attorney's or investigating magistrate's burden to collect all the facts before trial, a task for which they are much better equipped than defense counsel. There is an absolute duty of disclosure of facts and data, for the benefit of the defense. This makes for a trial which is virtually without surprises, with little partisanship, before extremely inquisitive judges, sitting jointly with a few jurors (Mueller & LePoole-Griffiths, 1969:25).

The U.S. judge, on the other hand, assumes a passive role. He merely "presides" while the prosecuting and defense attorneys present their respective witnesses and evidence, cross-examine each other's witnesses or otherwise attempt to contradict each other's evidence so as to bolster the "proof" of their respective positions before the court. The judge restricts the introduction of evidence to only those items which are relevant and pertinent to the case in question and otherwise maintains a relatively calm atmosphere in the courtroom. If there is a jury, he instructs them as to relevant rules of law to be applied to the facts as *they* find them. If there is no jury, then he decides the outcome of the case. Essentially, the American judge's role in a trial could be classified as one of a passive reactor. As one famous American judge has said, "the judge should hesitate to fill the gap by becoming himself a participant in the interrogation or to indicate any view of the evidence. For the criminal trial is as much a ceremony as an investigation. Dignity and forbearance are almost the chief desiderata" (Wyzanski, 1952:1291).

The trial in Germany is substantially distinguished from that of the United States. There is "no cross-examination in the Anglo-American sense" and the defendant has no "right to take the witness stand and make a statement under oath" (Jescheck, 1970: 247).

> As opposed to the American trial, in which the taking of proof is split into direct examination and cross-examination, in Germany proof is received according to the "Instruktionsmaxime" and is the responsibility of the presiding judge. The judge interrogates the defendant, the lay witnesses and expert witnesses, and bears the responsibility for the completeness and correctness of the proof. An examination of the witnesses or experts by the parties is certainly possible under German law and is expressly permitted in the statute. This procedure presupposes, however, a common request by prosecutor and defense counsel, and such a request is never made because cross-examination has not yet become popular in Germany (pp. 248–49).

As can be imagined, this "exceedingly small participation" of the parties in the trial itself leads to unfortunate consequences:

> The prosecutor who had conducted the investigation often does not appear but is represented by any colleague who happens by chance to have the time free, and who is therefore much less familiar with the files. Experience shows that some defense attorneys occasionally appear without having adequately studied their own files. So accustomed are they to the taking of evidence by the judge, that they rely completely upon him and often fail to direct the taking of proof in the manner most favorable to their client (Jescheck, 1970:249).

In its quest for truth the German criminal justice proceeding has overplayed the inquisitorial approach. It might be said that this scheme, in its attempt to find the facts, is too willing to set aside a systematic methodology which will, if properly implemented, assist and not hinder the objective of learning the truth. The breakdown in a strict inquisitorial approach (as exemplified by the German's trial proceedings) might be attributed to its attempted efforts to make all agents of the criminal justice system searchers for the truth. In such a framework the legal actors, in effect, push their responsibilities off onto one another. The ultimate consequence is that only one legal actor, the trial judge, makes any meaningful effort at searching for the true facts at issue in a criminal case. And even he is

> put into a psychologically impossible situation, since he is supposed on one hand, to maintain the presumption of innocence and to weigh disinterestedly the results of the interrogations. Moreover, he is expected to discharge these burdens even though he is thoroughly familiar with the facts of the case beforehand (Jescheck, 1970:249–50).

The French trial (Anton, 1960; Kock, 1960; Pugh, 1962) is very similar to the German trial:

> The French trial also seems to have a purpose different from the one generally recognized in common law countries. Apparently the general feeling is that "the immensely careful preliminary investigations of the juge d'instruction make it unlikely that persons who in France are sent for trial are guiltless." It is of course recognized that consideration of the question of guilt in the trial court is desirable as "yet another device to minimize the risk of prejudice and error," and acquittals do occasionally occur. Nevertheless, it seems relatively rare even for the question of guilt to be disputed at trial, since often the defendant will have confessed on several occasions by that time. Although there have been a few celebrated cases of false confessions, usually the confession will also find full corroboration in other facts in the dossier.
> . . . The major issue before the court is the . . . sentence—a decision made by judge and jury voting together (Harvard Law Review, 1966:1118–19).

In the inquisitorial model there is no right of confrontation and cross-examination. In fact, it is the judge who directs questions to the witnesses who are deemed the witnesses of the court. The accused is also the court's witness as he enjoys no privilege against self-incrimination. Witnesses do not have to take an oath, which would subject them to perjury charges if violated. However, false testimony is a crime. There are no limitations on the admissibility of evidence, such as rules barring hearsay or irrelevant and immaterial testimony. Prejudicial and inflammatory statements are not reversible error. The absence of these rules stems from the lack of a lay jury.

In contrast, the adversary-accusatorial model stresses the rules of evidence and their violation is reversible error. The right of confrontation is held to be fundamental to this system. Without it no conviction can be secured.

1. The Jury

The Sixth Amendment to the U.S. Constitution grants the right to a jury trial "in all criminal prosecutions." While there is some question what that right encompasses— the number of jurors required, the necessity of a unanimous vote, and the necessity of extension to nonserious offenses (Bassiouni, 1969a:479–90), essentially a jury is composed of twelve adult persons, randomly picked, having no interest or prejudice in the outcome of a case, who hear the evidence introduced in a trial and then determine the outcome of the dispute. It is generally required that they reach their decisions unanimously and on the basis of the relevant facts as introduced at the trial. They resolve only disputes of fact and are generally guided regarding the relevant law on the subject by instructions provided by the judge.

It is said that American juries

> often do not find the facts in accordance with the evidence, but distort—or "fudge"—the facts, and find them in such a manner that (by applying the legal rules laid down by the judge to the facts thus deliberately misfound) the jury is able to produce the result which it desires, in favor of one party or the other. The facts, we are told, are found in order to reach the result (Frank, 1958:240).

Whether it is true that often jury members "are neither able to, nor do they attempt to, apply the instructions of the court" (p. 241) is an issue that has never been conclusively resolved.

In Germany, instead of a jury analogous to the American institution, there is "the 'Schwurgericht,' in which three professional judges, holding lifetime office as tenured public officials, deliberate and decide the questions of guilt and penalty in common with six lay judges chosen at random" (Jescheck, 1970:243). The professional judges provide guidance to the lay judges in the problems of a legal nature.

> Some commentators believe that the collaboration of laymen in matters of criminal law lends a greater popular support to the administration of justice. Trust in justice is strengthened and the human aspects of the criminal trial are emphasized when ordinary citizens, not just professional judges, participate in the decision. Supporters believe further that onesided "legal" decisions are better avoided, and that cooperation with laymen will give professional judges a fuller appreciation of popular attitudes about crime, criminals and the worth of the public institutions. Through such connections, the professional judges are thought to be able to maintain a contact with the general beliefs of the public as a whole (p. 244).

In France:

> There is a jury only in felony cases, and even then the jury deliberates with the three judges in reaching its verdict. The judges, the prosecuting attorney, and—in felony cases—the jurors all may question witnesses and the accused, but neither the accused nor his counsel has a right to question witnesses except through the presiding judge. Normally the trial begins with the presiding judge's questioning of the accused. The entire contents of the dossier are available to the court, and the judges base their questions on the facts revealed in it. Both favorable and unfavorable circumstances are discussed, and the testimony often ranges broadly over factors not directly relevant to the charge, such as the defendant's background and character. Thus, the trial appears to be more a cooperative investigation than an adversary proceeding (Harvard Law Review, 1966:1118).

The jurors "receive no summing up of the applicable law at the end of the trial and so must turn to the judges for assistance when deliberating with them behind closed doors" (Hauser, 1959:876). Thus, notwithstanding contrary assertions, it seems "both jurors and judges decide the ultimate question" of guilt, but the judges exert such influence upon the jurors that "in truth the jurors have but a small role" (p. 876).

Germany, Italy and the Scandinavian countries, among others in Europe, have developed combinations of lay and professional jurors to sit with judges. Their number will vary depending on the country and the type of criminal charge involved. Unlike the adversary-accusatorial model, the judge-jury combination in Europe decides questions of law as well as questions of facts.

2. Civil Party Intervention

In the inquisitorial model the prime mover in the prosecution of an accused criminal is the victim of the crime, for the outcome of the trial affects his civil remedy. The victim, therefore, is active in the criminal trial not only as a witness but as a party with an interest in the case.

A criminal action in continental Europe may be commenced by a governmental official or the private individual injured by the criminal act. The official, subject to the order of his superiors, may institute criminal proceedings. The possibility of private initiation affords protection against arbitrary governmental inaction. The injured party, by bringing a complaint against the perpetrator of the wrong, constitutes himself *partie civile* or civil party, claiming damages for injuries suffered by him personally.

As a result of the criminal act, the victim may interpose a claim for civil relief. Thus civil and criminal liability may be, and frequently are, determined in one proceeding. Although an injured party may always assert his claim for civil relief in a separate civil proceeding, intervention in a pending criminal proceeding may be quite advantageous. By this means, he can take full advantage of the investigatory facilities and prosecuting personnel of the state, the inquisitorial aspects of the proceedings, and the speed, economy, and more liberal rules of evidence characteristic of the criminal action. In addition, he reaps the psychological benefit resulting from his adversary's position as a criminally accused. Most automobile personal injury suits are handled in this manner.

When a party interposes his claim for civil relief in a criminal action already instituted by the government against an individual, he incurs no liability. However, by taking the initiative, a civil claimant may become liable for damages caused the defendant, in the event of unsuccessful prosecution. This is a deterrent to unwarranted criminal prosecution by private individuals.

Appellate Review

Review of criminal conviction is available in all systems based on Roman law and the French and German codifications. The method and means of such review differ in various ways, but all such systems have in common the two-tiered approach of appellate review and a highest court-of-last-resort review.

The appellate process in these systems, unlike the common-law system, can review facts, and in many instances is in effect a trial *de novo*. The highest court of last resort is usually the *cour de cassation* and unlike the highest court in the common-law countries, the *cour de cassation* only reviews the application and interpretation of the law as it pertains to the case at bar. Such an approach excludes review of the constitutionality or legality of the law, which functions are accomplished in some countries by the same highest court. In Eastern and Western Europe, as well as those systems relying on the Western European model, constitutional controls are outside the competence of higher courts, and for that matter beyond the competence of any court except a special court, wherever it exists. Such constitutional courts exist in Italy and Germany, but they are separate structures and access to them differs vastly. In Italy, for example, only a judge and not a defendant can certify a case for hearing by the constitutional court.

It must be noted, however, that with respect to fourteen Western European countries, the European Commission of Human Rights and the European Court of Human Rights are also available means for reviewing criminal convictions if these involve a violation of the provisions of the European Convention on Human Rights. Many of the provisions of the Convention have a direct bearing on criminal proceedings and include certain minimum due process guarantees analogous to those of the United States Bill of Rights. Thus, through this mechanism it can be seen that the European and common-law systems are moving closer to each other.

Conclusion

As the U.S. system of criminal justice becomes more administrative, as demonstrated by the substantial number of guilty pleas, it moves closer to the European model. The European systems have often appeared unfair to most Anglo-Americans. The European systems of criminal justice are not without their shortcomings. For example, as conditions change, the French criminal structure has found itself unable to cope with the unusual. In 1962, when the Algerian Revolution was in full force, a whole system of criminal courts was established to deal with the threatened security of the French state. Thus, in 1963, the French Penal Code was amended to establish the Court for the Security of the State.

By its very nature, the inquisitorial criminal process attempts to determine guilt or innocence in the most expeditious manner possible. Theoretically, the rights of the individual are protected by constitutional and procedural safeguards. However, if the present tendency of administering justice in the U.S. by virtue of a mass-production line of guilty pleas increases, the safeguards available to the accused will be reduced to procedural niceties, which will only serve to gloss over the fact that the defendant has become helpless in the hands of an efficient, state-operated, bargaining machine. Thus, it becomes also an expeditious system concerned with results and not means.

Theoretically, the accusatorial system operates as a safeguard for the rights of the defendant. However, as the U.S. system strives for greater efficiency, the process unmistakably tends to resemble the inquisitorial system in outcome, as manifested by the defendant's counsel huddling with the judge and prosecutor in an attempt to agree on the fate of the accused without the test of an open trial. It is the open trial, with its no-holds-barred contest between the two parties, that is the heart of the accusatorial system. Without such a trial, this system is moving dangerously toward an administrative inquisitorial process for which it was not prepared. The European model preserves an efficient judicial system, while only gradually moving toward adoption of certain procedural safeguards for the accused; thus it looks to the experiences of the Anglo-American system and moves closer to an adversary-accusatorial model.

Shortcomings of the European system are gradually being corrected by the European Human Rights machinery (Bassiouni, 1971b; Linke, 1971). As the application of the inquisitorial system tends to become more protective of the defendant's rights and interjects into its processes more adversary aspects, and the adversary-accusatorial model tends to become more administrative, the original differences between the two models wither away.

THE CRIMINAL JUSTICE SYSTEMS OF
THE UNION OF SOVIET SOCIALIST REPUBLICS AND
THE PEOPLE'S REPUBLIC OF CHINA

THE UNION OF SOVIET SOCIALIST REPUBLICS

The Basic Structure

A starting point for contemporary Soviet criminal justice procedure is the 1936 Constitution. It adopted as a Socialist principle the maxim *nulla poena sine lege* (no penalty without law) and, correspondingly, claimed to eliminate the doctrine of analogy as a method of statutory interpretation. This doctrine had previously permitted classification of numerous acts as crimes on the basis that they were analogous to those officially listed in the criminal code. The Constitution marked the ostensible rejection of nihilistic legal philosophy even though force and violence as a means of attaining social ends were in no way abolished by Soviet criminal procedure, wherein politics and government were seen as superior to the law. The law was deemed a continuation of politics, and thus a vehicle to serve Marxist goals.

Soviet law is calculated to "discipline, guide, train and educate Soviet citizens to be dedicated members of a collectivized and mobilized social order" (Berman, 1963: 68; see also LaFave, 1965; Berman, 1966).

While reforms were instituted subsequent to Stalin's death, no significant changes were made. For example, in 1958, the Fundamental Principles of Criminal Law revised the maximum criminal penalty downward from twenty-five to fifteen years; yet, in the following four years, the death penalty was extended to a multiplicity of other crimes, including counterfeiting and bribery, largely because of government concern over an increase in the crime rate.[11]

Since March, 1953, there has been a discernible pattern of reform (Berman, 1963: 69–70), manifested by the following tendencies:

1. elimination of political terrorism,
2. liberalization of procedures and substantive norms,
3. systematization and rationalization of the legal structure,
4. decentralization and democratization of decision-making,
5. increased popular participation,
6. threats of harsh penalties against those who would not cooperate in building communism,
7. rejection of some of Stalin's theories.

The Supreme Soviet of the Russian Soviet Federated Socialist Republic (R.S.F.S.R.) on October 27, 1960, adopted three new statutes which substantially revamped criminal procedure. These were the Criminal Code, Code of Criminal Procedure, and Law on Court Organization. While the Criminal Code embodied the entire substantive criminal law, statutes previously adopted were never expressly repealed with the exception of those set out in a published list. The presumption was that any remaining laws that were not inconsistent with the new Codes remained in force. Statutes

---

11. According to the 1958 Principles of Criminal Legislation: ". . . crime shall be considered . . . a socially dangerous act . . . attacking the Soviet social or political order, the socialist system of economy, socialist property . . . as well as any other socially dangerous act attacking the socialist legal order, if so specified by a criminal statute" (Berman, 1963:69).

which have since been enacted have not always been included by amendment to the new Codes.[12]

The 1960 Code of Criminal Procedure reversed the Stalinist doctrine of placing the burden of proof in counterrevolutionary crimes on the defendant and strengthened the new policy with additional safeguards of procedural due process, including protection against police terrorism, false charges, and pro forma trials. This "New Code" superseded the 1923 Code (the "Old Code"), which outlined methods of preliminary investigation, indictment, trial, judgment, and appeal, in a manner reasonably similar to Western European procedure.

The Prosecution

The prosecuting functions are carried by the prosecutor's office. Heading the office is the Procurator General of the U.S.S.R., appointed by the Supreme Soviet. He, in turn, appoints prosecutors to the republics and regions. These, in their turn, select area, district, and city procurators. Procurators have a wide variety of functions, administrative as well as prosecutorial. They participate in pretrial administrative sessions of the courts, give opinions during trial, and protest judgments they feel to be illegal. They have a duty to assure the rights of persons being detained and, therefore, are responsible for securing the release of these individuals, if warranted.

Acting in a purely administrative function, the procuracy makes certain that investigations are carried out in accordance with the Soviet Constitution and laws. It is empowered to bring protests against the legislatures of the republics and their members for any "illegal" acts.

The Pretrial Stage

Unlike the common-law model, the European model calls for "investigation of major crimes by an impartial official" whose function is to examine not only the accused, but the witnesses as well, and to prepare the evidence used to indict (Berman, 1966:65). It is known as the "instruction" phase. The Old Code departed from that European model in several respects, most notably for political crimes.

The courts take an active role in pretrial investigation. The Soviet system is to that extent the same as the European model, where preliminary investigation resembles a scaled-down trial, including questioning of the defendant and witnesses, examination of evidence, and a final statement of the charges. It differs, however, from the Western European systems in that only the procurator, rather than the courts, may hear charges of abuse in the criminal process. There is no right to counsel until the court is about to rule on whether or not to indict, and the investigation itself may be extended over a nine-month period, a delay considered unreasonable in Western European countries.

Both the Soviet and European systems combine accusatorial and inquisitorial features, but the judge plays a far more important role in the U.S.S.R. He is principally responsible for interrogating defendants and witnesses, and he also determines who shall be witnesses and their order.

The Code of Criminal Procedure does not deal with so-called administrative offenses, which are not subject to ordinary criminal punishment but are dealt with by

---

12. At least Berman (1963) was not able to find them within the wording of the Codes.

"sanctions." Those charged with administrative offenses are not given the benefits and protections embodied in the Code of Criminal Procedure.

Sanctions are milder than criminal penalties. They include such measures as fines (which are deducted from the offender's wages), confiscation of property, and, in rare cases, arrest and detention. It is interesting that since fines were introduced in 1960, they have been extended to a number of infractions and violations in the U.S.S.R., although Marxism rejects fines as economically discriminating and thus contrary to Socialist concepts of justice.

There are two methods of criminal investigation: (1) inquiry, used in less important cases; and (2) preliminary investigation, for more serious matters (Berman, 1966: 67). The former is carried out primarily by the police and state security agencies; the latter, by the investigative arm of the procuracy or state security agencies. Police investigations were initially supervised by procurators, but the procedure was amended to permit a state security agency, should it decide to try a case, merely to submit the matter to the court and furnish the procuracy with the results of the investigation. This occurred in the purge trials of the 1930s, but the New Code provided that detention and investigation by state security agencies must come within the rules and safeguards contained in the Code (Berman, 1966:67–68).

Prior to the New Code, it was not uncommon for criminal punishments to be imposed by nonjudicial agencies. A "Special Board" of the Commissariat of Internal Affairs, established in 1934, had broad powers to exile or imprison "socially dangerous" individuals. Secret hearings were held, without the defendant being given the right to counsel, and often without the defendant even in attendance. The practice was justified by the government as an administrative proceeding and, therefore, not within the purview of the Code.

In 1955, Soviet citizens learned for the first time that the Special Board had been abolished. While there has since been no indication to the contrary, there has likewise been no official legislative or administrative confirmation of its abolition. However, the 1958 Fundamental Principles of Criminal Procedure, which formed the basis for the New Code, appear implicitly to prohibit further activity of this type, stating in Article 7:

> Justice in criminal cases shall be administered only by courts. No one may be deemed guilty of committing a crime or subjected to criminal punishment except by judgment of a court (Berman, 1966:70).

However, in 1961, when the R.S.F.S.R. anti-parasite laws[13] were enacted and the jurisdiction of the Comrades' Courts was extended, it did appear possible that the state security agencies might exercise the powers once assumed by the Special Board.

The 1960 New Code also sought to cover many prior functions of military courts. In 1934, the Military Division of the Supreme Court of the U.S.S.R. and military courts in the local districts were given jurisdiction to try cases of treason, espionage, terrorism, and sabotage. At the same time, parallel jurisdiction was exercised by the Special Board. Strict procedures were adopted. In cases of terrorism, for example, investigation was to take no more than ten days, the indictment was to be presented to the defendant 24 hours prior to trial, the defendant and his counsel were not allowed to participate in the proceedings, and no appeals were permitted. Death sentences were to be carried

---

13. The anti-parasite laws are the Soviet version of our vagrancy statutes, making it a crime to be without employment.

out immediately (Berman, 1966:71). For wrecking or sabotage, the procedures were similar. These laws were incorporated into the Old Code but were repealed in 1956. Today, all crimes, including military crimes, are governed by the New Code.

The Old Code limited preliminary investigation to two months, but a one-month extension could be granted by the regional prosecutor, and the procurator of the republic was authorized to grant indefinite extension. Meanwhile, the accused remained in custody until the investigation was concluded.

The 1958 Fundamental Principles of Criminal Procedure limited the period of confinement to two months, although it also provided for extensions of up to nine months. Investigations may, however, continue even after the suspect is released.

Inquisitorial agencies, under the Old Code, were permitted to detain a suspect without a warrant for the purpose of preventing his escape from the jurisdiction. After an initial 24-hour detention period, the procuracy had to be notified and, within an additional 48 hours, "confirm or vacate" the arrest (Berman, 1966:73). Confirmation meant that there was sufficient evidence against the individual to place formal charges against him. This meant a total of 72 hours detention prior to being informed of the charges. Then, as now, prisoners are allowed no visitors or communications while in custody (p. 73).

It was further provided in the Old Code that a suspect was subject to additional measures of restraint after the accusation was rendered, but this provision was also easily modified by agencies of the state. Fourteen days may pass before the suspect is even apprised of the charges.

An arrest without a warrant and 72-hour maximum detention without being informed of the charges are retained in the New Code. The arresting agency has 24 hours and the procuracy, 48, to bring charges. Under Article 90, an exceptional case may warrant confinement for up to ten days, provided approval is first obtained from the procuracy or the court, under Article 96 and Article 11. A stricter definition of "arrest" and "detention" is given in Article 178, which sets out penalties for wrongful confinement of prisoners.

The Rights of the Accused

There was no right to counsel under the Old Code until after the indictment had been issued and trial ordered. The 1958 Fundamental Principles, in response to widespread debate, adopted a compromise whereby counsel was permitted at an earlier stage: when the investigator had done all that was necessary to arrive at the "conclusion to indict."

When it is decided to indict the suspect, the entire record of the investigation must be made available to him, he must be informed of his right to counsel, and he and counsel are permitted to meet in private and review the investigation record. Counsel can challenge officials who worked on the case, petition for a supplementary investigation, submit petitions to the procurator, and petition the judicial agency that makes the final decision on indictment. Article 47 of the New Code makes one exception to the above, giving minors and incompetents the right to counsel from the time the accusation is made, i.e., at the start of the preliminary investigation (Berman, 1966:74–75).

Article 46 of the New Code sets out some of the rights of the accused:

> The accused shall have the right: to hear what he is accused of and to give explanations concerning the accusation presented to him; to present evidence; to submit petitions; to become acquainted with all the materials of the case upon completion of the preliminary investigation or inquiry; to have defense counsel from the moment provided for by Article 47 of the present Code (just prior to indictment); to participate in

the judicial examination in the court of first instance; to submit challenges; and to appeal from the actions and decisions of the person conducting the inquiry, the investigator, prosecutor and court.

The prisoner shall have the last word (Berman, 1966:268–69).

In addition, Article 19 guarantees the right to present a defense, and requires that the inquiry be conducted in such a manner as to safeguard the personal property rights of the accused. If abuses should occur, Articles 218–220 provide for institution of a complaint, and Article 58 requires that the individual's rights be explained to him.

Some provisions indicate attempts to correct past abuses. Articles 123 and 150, for instance, prohibit questioning of either the accused or witnesses at night. Article 158 prohibits leading questions; Article 89 (also Article 144 of the Old Code) eliminates house arrest as a preventive measure; Articles 167 and 168 state that the procurator must approve searches and seizures (although his approval may be granted *ex post facto*); Article 49 makes defense counsel mandatory for certain classes of defendants, e.g., minors, incompetents, and persons facing a possible death penalty; and Article 98 provides that a prisoner's minor children and property must be looked after by the court.

While the defendant has the right to remain silent, this does not apply to any other parties, including his own family (Articles 72–77). Confessions are inadmissible unless corroborated by other evidence under Article 77; and various other provisions are set out to establish the value of other evidence.

Many of the rights contained in the R.S.F.S.R. Code will not be found in a U.S. code, because they may be so fundamental as to be taken for granted, or because they are part of case law. While the R.S.F.S.R. Code may appear overly detailed, with its 413 articles on procedure alone, it must be remembered that the system has suffered many abuses, and this background was conducive to inclusion of detail that might otherwise have been considered trivial.

The Trial

Once the indictment has been rendered, the case is brought to trial.

Under the Old Code, cases tried in the people's courts had adequate procedural safeguards, but those in the higher courts did not. Provincial courts, for instance, were permitted to exclude defense counsel and any witnesses who had testified in the preliminary investigation. They could halt questioning of witnesses, use evidence not considered previously, and refuse an opportunity to present oral evidence (Berman, 1966:78).

Subsequently, the 1936 Constitution did provide for the right to counsel and superseded the Old Code in this regard; but no such right attached in terrorism trials or those conducted by military tribunals.

The Evidence

The judgment rendered by the court had to be based on evidence received at the trial, but that provision was not uniformly followed. In 1948 the Soviet Supreme Court recognized the prevalent abuse and handed down a ruling that the Old Code was in conflict with the Fundamental Principles of Criminal Procedure of 1924 and, therefore, invalid. The regional and higher courts, however, continued the practice unaffected by this ruling and have, therefore, been permitted to use extrinsic evidence if its existence was adverted to at the trial.

Uniform trial procedures in all courts are provided for in the New Code, which broadens the rights of the defense at trial: the right to call defense witnesses, a requirement that judgment be based on evidence presented at trial, and a right to unlimited oral argument. Article 77 of the New Code provides that, even if the defendant should acknowledge his guilt, nevertheless, it must be proven. There must be a thorough consideration of all the evidence, against the background of the law and of Socialist legal consciousness, according to Article 71. A witness must be able to show the source of the information he presents, and questions may be excluded on grounds of irrelevancy (Berman, 1966:82).

While the New Code does not explicitly refer to a presumption of innocence, there are provisions indicating that this is the rule:

    a) The accused has no obligation to present evidence.

    b) No inference of guilt may be drawn from the mere fact of the indictment.

    c) Evidence supporting the indictment must be presented at trial, and the judgment of the court must be based on that evidence alone.

    d) The court may not "assume" that the accused is guilty.

    e) If proof of his guilt is not established, he may not be convicted (pp. 86–87).

New provisions in Article 20 allow the defendant to remain silent; and he cannot be convicted on the basis of his silence.

Some similarity appears in the roles of the Soviet and American prosecutors. In both countries, they present arguments demonstrating how the evidence leads to a conclusion of guilt; and in both countries, there must be convincing evidence of guilt. But the concept of what constitutes "persuasion" differs. The Soviet system (and European systems in general) indicates that the judge's decision is based on his evaluation of the evidence, while the American system stresses competition between the two sides to persuade the court.

Review of Conviction and Appeal

Once the case had been heard, the Old Code permitted a single appeal, called cassation, which consisted of a review of the facts and law, as well as any new evidence. A new decision could be handed down by the regional court, changing the sentence of the people's court, even relying on a different law.

A parallel system of "supervisory" review could be implemented by the president of the provincial court and the provincial or district prosecutor, who could remove cases from the people's court during or after trial for "supervision." A case could be removed to the Supreme Court by its president or vice-president, or the R.S.F.S.R. Procurator or Deputy Procurator (Berman, 1966:87–88).

Therefore, while only one appeal could be made at the request of the parties, certain officials were afforded the right to remove the case, possibly to as high a body as the Presidium of the Central Executive Committee of the Communist Party. This dualism has been retained in the New Code, albeit with limitations on supervision:

    a) protests on the grounds of lightness of the sentence, termination of the case, or acquittal, must be brought within a year (Art. 373);

    b) the court considering a case by way of supervision may not itself increase the punishment or apply a law governing a graver crime than the one under which the accused was sentenced (Art. 380);

c) the court considering a case by way of supervision may not alter the findings of fact, the rulings on the weight of evidence, the decision of guilt or innocence, the application of law, or the sentence, but may only remand the case for retrial or a new investigation, or else reduce the sentence or else dismiss the protest (Art. 380) (Berman, 1966:89–90).

The practice of supervisory appeals facilitates the implementation of political and social policy.

Popular Participation in the Criminal Process

1. Public Participation

One of the reforms brought about by the 1958 Fundamental Principles of Criminal Procedure was popular participation in the criminal process. Article 228 provided for a social accuser and a social defense counsel to represent the opinions of their "social organizations" at the trial. Party organizations, youth-league groups, trade unions, workers at a particular job or institution, members of a collective farm, an educational institution, or other voluntary organizations are entitled to representation, providing they submit a petition to and receive approval from the court (Berman, 1966:346). Article 250 gives the representative of a social organization broad powers to intervene:

> A social accuser shall have the right to present evidence, take part in the analysis of the evidence, submit petitions and challenges before the court, and participate in oral argument, setting forth to the court an opinion concerning whether the accusation has been proved, and concerning the social danger of the prisoner and of the act committed by him. The social accuser may express views regarding the application of the criminal law and the measure of punishment with respect to the prisoner and on other questions in the case. The social accuser shall have the right to withdraw from the accusation if the data of the judicial investigation give grounds therefor.
> A social defense counsel shall have the right to present evidence, submit petitions and challenges before the court, and participate in oral argument, setting forth to the court an opinion concerning circumstances tending to mitigate the prisoner's guilt or to acquit him, as well as concerning the possibility of mitigating the punishment of the prisoner, his conditional conviction or relief from punishment and transfer on surety to the social organization or collective of working people in whose name the social defense counsel speaks (Berman, 1966:353–54).

Public participation in criminal trials is further encouraged by provision for notification of the public by the prosecutor when the proceedings are initiated, and the charges are also publicized.

Cases at the trial level are heard by one judge and two "people's assessors," whose function is more to assure that strict penalties are meted out than to protect the accused.

2. Comrades' Courts

In addition to criminal trials, there are several disciplinary offenses that are dealt with on a less formal level. Like administrative offenses, these are excluded from the Code and, therefore, the defendant is not afforded many of the protections that he would otherwise have. These violations are handled by the Comrades' Courts, comprised of local neighborhood residents or co-workers, which may issue warnings and reprimands, recommend eviction from apartments, demotion in one's job, fines ranging up to 15 rubles, and menial work for up to 15 days (Berman, 1966:8). Being quasi-judicial in nature, the Comrades' Courts are not governed by the law on court organization; and the penalties which they assess are referred to as "measures of social pressure."

The statute creating these courts does not accord members the status of judges, nor does it refer to "the accused" as such. Rather, it uses the terminology, "members of the Comrades' Court" and "the person brought before the Comrades' Court." Should the case appear to warrant more severe action, the Criminal Code and the Code of Criminal Procedure provide for transfer to the appropriate agency; but criminal courts have had the right to transfer cases to Comrades' Courts only since 1960 (Berman, 1966:9).

A Comparison of Some Features of the U.S.S.R. and United States Systems

It must be noted at the outset that the differences existing between the U.S.S.R. and the U.S. systems do not stem from the political ideology of each country, but from the differing models followed. The United States follows the adversary-accusatorial model while the U.S.S.R.'s is the inquisitorial one.

In the United States, the content of the criminal law is set down in statutes; only treason is defined in the Constitution. United States criminal procedure is essentially based on common law with statutory modifications and is subject to constitutional limitations arising out of judicial interpretations. The principle *nulla poena sine lege* and *nullum crimen sine lege* prohibits the punishment of individual conduct unless a law makes that conduct punishable and punishment part of and consistent with that law (Bassiouni, 1969a).

A vague standard of guilt will not be upheld by United States courts. Thus, a criminal statute that is so vague as to leave delineation of such standards to the courts must fall. In *United States* v. *Cohen Grocery Co.*, for example, a statute was declared unconstitutional because the wording "any unjust or unreasonable rate or charge" was, in the words of the court, "not adequate to inform persons accused of violation thereof of the nature and cause of the accusation against them" [255 U.S. 81 (1921)]. The court declared that no specific act was dealt with in the statute.

Internal inconsistency is also grounds for invalidating a statute as vague, and the courts of the United States will not attempt to save it by construing one or the other of its provisions as controlling. Failure to specify properly the standard of guilt is also reason to declare a statute unconstitutional, or failure to comply with "due process" requirements. In general, however, the courts presume constitutionality of the statute.

In contrast to the United States striking down vague statutes, the Soviet Union has formulated many of its statutes with such vague wording that it is difficult to ascertain whether particular conduct is a crime or not. Some attempt has been made in the post-Stalin era to remedy this, but even subsequent to the New Code of Criminal Procedure, these efforts have not progressed significantly.

There are in the Soviet Union no concrete principles to serve as an overall binding framework. While their Constitution does say that statutes shall be the main source of law, this is contradicted by the fact that government departments, by passage of their own rules, are permitted to regulate the everyday conduct of the people (American Bar Association, 1968b:115). Even the Criminal Codes are not solely declarative of the law, because additional laws establishing crimes and penalties are promulgated by both the Soviet Union and the republics.

The Supreme Court of the U.S.S.R., under the 1938 Judiciary Act, was given power to issue general directives to the lower courts. This procedure has been continued under the 1957 Judiciary Act, thus permitting official government policy to be injected into the work of the courts. For example, when, at one point, a movement to halt "economic crimes" developed, a series of decrees were issued establishing the death penalty for certain crimes, despite earlier government efforts to abolish it. The Supreme Court of the U.S.S.R. continued to urge that the struggle against economic crimes be intensified in the lower courts.

The laws are framed in such a manner as to facilitate prosecution and secret statutes (not promulgated) help the government expand its control over the individual. Principles of legality, therefore, are negated by such practices.

The Soviet legal system contains an element of dualism: traditional crimes are precisely defined; but a crime against the state is defined only in broad terms, refers to a number of acts, and often is unrelated to the goal that the statute seeks to accomplish. For example:

1. The crime of treason is defined in Article 64 of the Criminal Code as "an act intentionally committed by a citizen of the U.S.S.R. to the detriment of the state independence, the territorial inviolability, or the military might of the U.S.S.R." It then lists the following treasonable acts:

> going over to the side of the enemy, espionage, transmission of a state or military secret to a foreign state, flight abroad or refusal to return from abroad to the U.S.S.R., rendering aid to a foreign state in carrying on hostile activity against the U.S.S.R., or a conspiracy for the purpose of seizing power (American Bar Association, 1968b:125).

2. Article 66 defines a terrorist act as "killing of a state or social figure or representative of authority . . . for the purpose of subverting or weakening the Soviet authority" (p. 125).

3. Under Article 70, a crime is defined as:

> agitation or propaganda carried on for the purpose of subverting or weakening of Soviet authority or of committing particular, especially dangerous, crimes against the state, or circulating for the same purpose slanderous fabrication which defames the Soviet state and social system (p. 126).

4. The "anti-parasite" laws state that "able-bodied citizens leading an anti-social, parasitic way of life, deliberately avoiding socially useful labor, and likewise those living on unearned income" (p. 126) can be banished to outlying areas.

The Soviet Union, prior to 1960, made widespread use of the analogy clause in the Criminal Code, which permitted prosecution for acts not defined therein. At present, while the clause has been removed from the 1960 Code, it is likely that it continues to be applied by the courts. Interpretation by analogy violates the United States Constitution (Bassiouni, 1969a:37–45).

Under the analogy doctrine, it would be possible in the U.S.S.R. to prosecute a woman for prostitution, although prostitution is not mentioned as a crime in the 1960 Code. She could, however, be charged under Article 206 dealing with hooliganism, which is defined as "intentional actions violating public order in a coarse manner and expressing a clear disrespect toward society." It is punishable by imprisonment of up to one year. Aggravated hooliganism, however, may be punished by a term not to exceed five years, and is defined as hooliganism that is "connected with resisting a representative of authority or representative of the public fulfilling duties for the protection of public order, or distinguished by exceptional cynicism or impudence, or committed by a person already sentenced for hooliganism" (American Bar Association, 1968b:130). The concept of social danger, a remnant of the Stalin era, is still an important element of Soviet criminal justice and holds that the degree of social danger represented by a given criminal act determines the severity of the penalty.

In the Soviet Union, prior to the New Code, there were several aspects of criminal procedure that were regulated by secret statutes. Those were the cases where the investigatory aspects were carried out by the secret police. Today, the New Code contains rules governing investigations, which are supervised by the procurator's office. In the United States, a statute that is not properly promulgated is void.

In the United States, arrest without a warrant is permissible only when the arresting officer has reasonable grounds to believe that the suspect has committed or is about to commit a crime. The Fourth Amendment to the U.S. Constitution guarantees against unreasonable searches and seizures; and case law has established the standards of "reasonableness" and "probable cause" for seizures without a warrant. Arrest warrants are issued by the court and must specify the offense allegedly committed by the individual.

In contrast, the Soviet Union does not require a warrant to make an arrest. Furthermore, an individual can be held for 72 hours initially, during which time he is given the procurator's or court's written decision as to whether charges will be brought against him and the nature of the charges. With the special permission of the procurator's office, he can be held for as long as ten days without even being informed of the charges (American Bar Association, 1968b:125–26).

Detention is limited to two months, during which time the preliminary investigation is made; but, again, this may be extended to three months by the regional procurator, six months by the republican procurator, or nine months by the Procurator General of the Soviet Union. Article 133 of the New Code permits extension of the investigation to four months, or even indefinitely, if approved by the appropriate procurator. Arrest is normally for the duration of the investigation. While this length may seem excessive in the United States, it is not so by Western European standards, where pretrial detention for investigation may last months.

Under the Old Code, the investigators in the U.S.S.R. were not bound by the procurator's recommendations regarding indictment, but the New Code makes the procurator the decision-maker of the legality of the proceedings. When the two authorities fail to agree, they may take the matter to a higher procurator, who may vacate the lower procurator's decision or transfer the case to another investigator. It is the procurator's office that has the final word.

Both legal systems require a warrant for searches and seizures. The Soviet Union requires, in addition, that the search be carried out in the presence of witnesses. In the United States, the court rules on what constitutes a legal search and seizure; in the Soviet Union, it is initially decided by the investigator, subject to subsequent approval by the procurator.

Case law in the United States holds that a suspect may be examined for marks on his body and may be subjected to blood tests. The Soviet Union has written into the New Code the right of an investigator to examine the suspect physically for traces of crime, obtain samples of his handwriting, have him examined by an expert, or commit him to a medical institution. The Soviet Union does not use the lineup for identification of suspects as the United States does.

Most trials in the Soviet Union are open, and decisions are publicly announced. This is a departure from the practice in Stalin's day, when important cases were dealt with in secret, including those cases in which government officials were purged, and the public was completely unaware of what was happening. Article 18 of the New Code allows closed hearings only when state secrets are involved, or in juvenile cases (under age 16), sex crimes, or where there is a necessity to protect the personal lives of participants. Pretrial investigation, however, remains closed. American criminal trials are open to the public.

Under the Sixth Amendment to the U.S. Constitution, the defendant is entitled to be represented by counsel: either an attorney of his own choosing or one selected for him by the court. Case law dictates that this right attaches at the moment the investigation focuses upon him as a suspect and prior to police interrogation. A denial of this right is a denial of "due process." The suspect must, furthermore, be informed of his right to counsel and be provided free counsel if he is indigent. He may contact his attorney or any other person of his choosing at the time of his arrest.

In the Soviet Union, the individual in custody is not allowed to have visitors or send or receive communications during the entire time of confinement. This means that he does not have the benefit of counsel during the investigation. The New Code only permits counsel to be present at that final stage in the investigation when the investigator has done all but render his decision to indict.

American criminal procedure dictates that a confession cannot be received into evidence unless freely given. Any physical violence or psychological coercion renders it invalid, as does too long a passage of time from arrest to confession or failure to warn a defendant of his constitutional rights.

While a confession may neither be the sole basis for conviction in the Soviet Union nor be obtained by illegal means, there are other provisions that weaken this protection. For example, should the defendant refuse to testify, this will be used against him, whereas it is reversible error in the United States. While the Soviet defendant is protected against self-incrimination, it is difficult for him to take advantage of this rule because at the time he may be advised of his rights, he is not yet entitled to counsel. Also, under Article 281, his testimony given in pretrial proceedings may be read in open trial if it conflicts with his statements at the trial, despite the fact that, ostensibly at least, only evidence produced in open court may serve as a basis for decision. This can be done in a modified form in the United States as impeachment of a witness making prior inconsistent statements, but the procedure cannot warrant the introduction of other statements otherwise inadmissible.

In the Soviet Union emphasis is also placed on whether the defendant cooperated with the prosecution. If this is the case, it is weighed as a mitigating factor. Plea bargaining in the United States seems to be the counterpart of this aspect.

Interrogation procedures in the Soviet Union, as in most European countries, are unrestricted. In fact, questioning may be carried on at odd hours and for long periods of time, which would be impermissible in the United States.

The rights of an accused in the United States are quite extensive by comparison to those in the U.S.S.R., due to the American adversary-accusatorial system and the U.S.S.R.'s inquisitorial model. Consider, for example, these rights: trial by jury, indictment by a grand jury, confrontation and cross-examination of accusers and witnesses, release on bail pending trial or appeal, free representation for indigents, extensive appellate review, and extraordinary remedies, such as *habeas corpus* (Bassiouni, 1969a:313–518). None of these are available in the U.S.S.R.

Judicial practice is more significant than theory. In the United States, the judiciary exercises control over police and administrative practices seeking to enforce and implement constitutional rights, whereas in the U.S.S.R. there is no control by the judiciary over administrative and law-enforcement practices.

THE PEOPLE'S REPUBLIC OF CHINA

The Basic Structure

Any attempt to discuss China's criminal justice system must be qualified by noting the limited sources of information available. As a general observation, the Chinese system is more administrative than judicial, is designed to serve the aims and purposes of the revolution, and as such, is inquisitorial by Western standards. It has borrowed heavily from the U.S.S.R. model essentially because the Chinese revolution was Marxist and inspired by the example of the U.S.S.R., which predated it. It must not be forgotten, however, that the Chinese imperial system and its patriarchal feudal approach were well ingrained in the minds of the Chinese people. Lack of communication has slowed significant attitudinal changes in the development of an institutionalized system of criminal justice which does not have patriarchal features. For the time being, these features serve the purposes of the revolution and seem to be preserved by the hierarchical administrative and politically controlled system.

Consistent with Communist theory, law is viewed as an instrument of social policy. An example of this concept is the classification device used shortly after the revolution. All adults were grouped by "class origin"—economic status and their position vis-à-vis the defeated Nationalist regime—as "counterrevolutionary," "landlord," "bourgeois," "bureaucrat" (former Nationalists), but mostly "poor peasants," or "workers." Others were simply designated "bad elements" (Lubman, 1969). These classifications were used to check on individual loyalty to the regime.

Law-enforcement agencies are highly structured, down to the neighborhood police stations, but only the most reliable cadres handle assignments concerning political crimes, which are treated separately from other offenses. The work of such special police is supplemented by that of "security defense committees" who report neighbors' suspicious activities to the police.

Confinement in labor reform camps and death sentences are common. Public trials are not held unless necessary for "educational" purposes. "Control" (surveillance without confinement) and "administrative sanctions" are widely employed by the cadres (Lubman, 1969:543). The complete breakdown of the system came with the "cultural revolution" of the late sixties, but institutional order has been returning since then.

It is not always easy for the average citizen to know what constitutes criminal behavior; although some standards are published, others are reserved for government use. The definition of what constitutes criminal conduct is pieced together from the reading of numerous regulatory statutes. Among offenses which are not publicly defined are some of the major common crimes, such as murder, rape, and robbery (Buxbaum, 1962; Cohen, 1966:168).

Party policy often serves to define an act as criminal where there are no other official guidelines, but it must be noted that even those statutes that are published are sufficiently vague to allow the Party broad interpretation. The government has stressed the necessity of punishing "counterrevolutionaries"; punishment of dissenters is a way of life in any totalitarian regime. Periodic statements from Peking give the police no chance to forget that their task is to facilitate the Party's policies.

The legal agencies themselves are hampered by a voluminous body of rules, regulations, and policies, analyses of judicial decisions, and similar materials from which they must attempt to extrapolate definitions of what constitutes a crime. Unpublished handbooks attempt to illustrate to law-enforcement officials the application of given court decisions to hypothetical fact situations. These materials are constantly being revised as the government's programs and goals are reevaluated.

Public access to these definitive sources is extremely limited. Theoretically, the people are to be guided by the customary conceptions of right and wrong as inspired by Mao's thoughts. Crimes that represent a departure from past government policy are discussed in group meetings, which every citizen is expected to attend, to keep the people informed of "what to advocate and what to praise, what to oppose and what to prohibit" (Cohen, 1968:24). These official standards of conduct are not published but are publicized through the mass media.

The lack of a criminal code is compounded by the fact that China does not publish judicial decisions.

The Evolution of China's System

The First Phase: 1945–53

China has gone through several periods. The first, 1949–53, was marked by a notable abuse of the criminal process to terrorize political enemies, put down dissenters, and assure that the Communist public order would prevail. The new regime dismantled the Nationalist legal system, but, at the same time, put nothing in its place. Where there was a judicial system, summary criminal punishment operated outside its bounds. It was not until 1952–53 that Nationalist holdovers were completely removed from the courts, so the Communists could be confident that the system would operate in a manner likely to insure the success of the aims of the revolution.

Initial "reforms" included disregard of the formal legal structure and abolition of existing statutes. Police were given unlimited powers, military control commissions supplemented a good deal of police work, and "mass movements" were initiated to wipe out enemies of the Communist regime. Meanwhile, "people's tribunals" held their own kind of trials.

Courts were mainly regarded as instruments of government policy with cadres replacing most judges, who were criticized for being unwilling to wage war against the people's enemies. Legal procedures were denounced as tools of reaction, and even formerly recognized principles, such as *nulla poena sine lege*, were struck down.

Secret sessions for judicial agencies were common practice at first; later "mass trials," open to the public, were held at which "enemies" were sentenced to death or to "reform through labor." If any characterization can be made, it would be that this period was one of organized dismantling of the preexisting system.

The Second Phase: 1953–57

The second phase, 1953–57, began in the wake of the First Five-Year Plan to develop the national economy, and ended with the "antirightist" movement of June 1957. The Chinese attempted to fashion a legal system patterned after that of the U.S.S.R. A Constitution and statutes were drawn up comparable to those which existed in the U.S.S.R. from 1921 to 1928.

The Constitution guaranteed protection against arbitrary detention, arrest, and search. The functions of public agencies were more clearly defined. Investigations and arrests were brought under the control of the police. The procuracy verified evidence and rendered the formal accusation. Determination of guilt was made by the courts. Cases were to be heard by one judge and two "people's jurors" who paralleled those of the Soviet Union. Appeals courts were established. Trials were to be public, and defendants had the right to present a defense and be represented by a "people's lawyer." The people's lawyers had to be educated in one of the newly reorganized law schools and hold membership in a lawyers' collective.

It was also contemplated that there would be a new criminal code and procedural rules. Soviet legal experts were called in for assistance and advice with a view toward adopting the Soviet legal system. The reform and projected plans were short-lived when, in 1955–56, intensive campaigns were waged against "counterrevolutionaries" as ad hoc teams of cadre members and activists became major organs of enforcement. At the same time, courts were urged to expedite trials of violators of government directives. There was really no question of guilt or innocence at these trials on the assumption that if the police had done a thorough job of investigation, there could be no doubt in the mind of the judge. The "people's accessors" merely gave the illusion of popular participation in the judicial process. Most frequently, the police recommended the penalties, which were routinely confirmed by the procuracy and courts; only in very few of the cases did they vary (Lubman, 1969:547).

The distinction between judiciary and administrative functions was never well established, but at least there were separate structures with different powers. In 1957 the functions of police, procuracy, and courts merged. It was decreed by statute that the police could impose "minor punishments, such as fines, warnings, and short periods of confinement, for a breach of 'public order.'" They were also authorized to assign persons to labor camps who "do not engage in proper employment . . . hooligans . . . (petty criminals) whom repeated education fails to change . . . counter-revolutionaries and anti-socialist reactionaries" (Lubman, 1969:553). Notwithstanding these conditions, judges, procurators, and people's lawyers acted traditionally, and some arrest and prosecution requests were turned down.

The Third Phase: 1957–63

This paved the way for the third phase, 1957–63. Procurators and people's attorneys were reminded that they must act "in the interests of the state and the people" (Cohen, 1968:15). People's attorneys acting as defense counsels were required to inform on defendants who admitted crimes to them which had not even been charged. The defendant was not treated as the equal of the prosecutor but as an enemy of the people, and he was only entitled to defend himself as long as he did not make any reactionary remarks or distort facts, laws, or policies as perceived by the state. The primary purpose of allowing a defense was to assist law-enforcement agencies in evaluating the evidence and in determining whether the defendant had repented. In turn, a defense would permit the prosecutors to "more fiercely, accurately, and firmly . . . attack the enemy" (p. 15). In other words, a person accused of a crime was guilty as charged and his defense was limited to the mitigation of his penalty.

This contrasted with the Soviet system, where complete political control over court decisions has never been the rule, even under Stalin. As a matter of fact, Soviet party secretaries have been chastised by the newspapers for attempting to influence court decisions. In China, however, "the model judge is one who consults the local party apparatus about any important case" (p. 16).

The year 1959 marked the beginning of the "Great Leap Forward." Law-enforcement agencies were encouraged to improve their own performance and soon newspapers were filled with reports of unusually high numbers of arrests, prosecutions, and convictions, obtained in only a fraction of the time that they had previously required.

The "mass line" was thrust into new prominence. Under this system a "work group," made up of police officers, a procurator, and a judge, would travel to a village immediately after a crime was reported, and, after questioning local Party and government officials as well as citizens, ascertain the offender's identity and detain him. A joint interrogation would be held, forms filled out, local officials consulted about the sentence, and an open-air hearing held before the workers in the fields, culminating most often in sentencing. This procedure was used in dealing with relatively minor offenses; the more important trials continued to be handled at a slower pace.

Some Procedural Aspects

1. Jurisdiction

China takes an absolutist approach to jurisdiction and maintains that her criminal law and procedure apply equally to citizens and aliens. No diplomatic or consular immunity is recognized. Criminal jurisdiction has been asserted over crewmen and passengers of foreign ships passing through territorial waters or in Chinese ports (Tao, 1970).

2. Arrest and Detention

Cases are initiated by arrest. An application for a warrant takes the form of a "recommendation to arrest" and is issued when it appears that the suspect has committed the crime. Included in the recommendation are the nature of the crime, the evidence, the harm, and information about the suspect's class status, family, and past record (Cohen, 1968:33).

Consent must be given by the chief of the trial preparation section and the chief of the subbureau, but while the law provides that the procuracy must also agree, this is often ignored. The unpublished law of some cities may provide, however, that approval must be obtained not only from the chief of the basic procuracy but from the president of the basic court, both of whom meet with the other "chiefs" to make their decision, along with the deputy secretary of the local party committee. These five individuals comprise the "political-legal party group" in that district.

When a major crime has been committed, the suspect is booked on suspicion at a subbureau (as opposed to the public security station). He is placed in the detention house there while investigation is made. Detention differs from arrest: it is "emergency apprehension and confinement of a suspect without an arrest warrant for the purpose of investigating whether there is sufficient evidence to justify his arrest" (Cohen, 1968:28). Arrest, on the other hand, is the "apprehension and confinement, or the continuing confinement, of a suspect on the basis of an arrest warrant for the purpose of investigating whether there is sufficient evidence to justify prosecution" (p. 28).

Police are required by law to question the suspect within 24 hours of detention and either release him unconditionally or secure authority from the procuracy to arrest him. Such a request must be ruled upon within 48 hours (p. 28).

These statutory safeguards are, however, often disregarded. Under Article 13 of the Arrest Act, detention for violation of administrative rules is exempted from the above provisions. In other instances, a suspect may be detained until it is determined whether arrest should be made. In some cities, a subbureau chief must be asked for a ten-day extension when the suspect has been held for ten days. This request comes to the trial preparation section.

A suspect may be released under certain circumstances, although these are severely restricted and seldom used. For example, if the individual is physically or mentally ill, an expectant or recent mother, or is suspected of a minor crime, he or she may be released under surveillance.

Visits and correspondence are carefully regulated by the police and generally are not permitted prior to the conclusion of the police investigation. Until such time as the investigation terminates, the prisoner has no right to inform his family of his detention, and he may even be prohibited from mere conversation with others. Posters are often placed in the cells, and other means are used to induce a detainee to confess.

Article 9 of the Arrest Act states:

> In order to find evidence of a crime, when arresting or detaining an offender, the organ executing the arrest or detention may search his person, his articles, his residence, or other relevant places; if it believes that another person concerned may be harboring an offender or concealing evidence of the crime, it may also search his person, his articles, his residence or other relevant places. At the time of the search, except in emergency situations, they (those who search) shall have a search warrant from the organ that executes the arrest or detention (Cohen, 1968:31).

3. Search and Seizure

A search warrant is generally required, but the police often do not follow this requirement even though they issue the search warrants.

The only check on police powers is the internal regulation within the police department providing that a responsible superior must approve the issuance of a warrant. The interrogator of a suspect may determine that additional evidence is needed and a warrant is necessary to acquire it. He requests approval from the chief of the trial preparation section, who, if he concurs, submits the request for approval to the chief of the subbureau. The chief of the subbureau may also delegate this authority to the chief of the trial preparation section.

Under Article 9, the suspect or a member of his family must be present at the search, as well as one additional witness. There are few restrictions on what may be seized and those present at the search must sign the inventory of items seized.

4. Interrogation

Pretrial interrogation is conducted by a member of the trial preparation staff who has reviewed the file. There is no privilege against self-incrimination and the suspect must answer questions. His statements are heavily relied upon as evidence against him. He may presumably make false statements because he is not sworn to truth, but he may find himself embroiled in inconsistent statements, which will be used against him anyhow.

The basic policy of "leniency for those who confess and severity for those who resist" (Cohen, 1968:30) speaks for itself. Should the accused refuse to confess, he may be put in handcuffs and leg irons; and techniques of psychological coercion are permissible. Any oral statements are reduced to writing and the accused must sign them to verify their authenticity.

5. The Charging Process

The recommendation to prosecute is made by the procurator, who summarizes all the relevant facts. The chief of the trial preparation section, if he approves, transmits the file to the procuracy.

When the file is received by the procuracy, it is assigned to an individual procurator who interviews the suspect and questions him about each of the enumerated charges. If the suspect denies any of the facts or the evidence is not sufficient, the principal witnesses are interviewed. If necessary, the case may be returned to the interrogator for further clarification, such as additional evidence, revision of the charges, or even dropping the case.

In the absence of informal agreement, the procurator may recommend to his chief that prosecution be denied; but this determination may be challenged by the police, who have the authority to ask for reconsideration. Should the procurator decide to propose another bill of prosecution, the chief procurator will consider all recommendations and make the final decision, but even his decision may be overruled by the court.

6. The Disposition of the Case

A case may be disposed of by the judge *ex parte* without a formal trial. The judge to whom the case is assigned, after reviewing the file, questions the suspect at the detention house in order to confirm the charges as stated. The interview may be extended to witnesses or additional investigation may be initiated. When the evidence proves insufficient, the judge, procurator, and police interrogator confer, and the case will either be sent back for further investigation or handled by administrative sanctions. In instances where disposition of the case cannot be agreed upon, there may be an informal compromise under which the judge may agree to recommend conviction for a lesser crime carrying a sentence of "control," as opposed to imprisonment. In case of disagreement, the president of the court may arrange a solution pursuant to a conference with the chief procurator and the chief of the subbureau. If there is still disagreement between these officials, the case may have to be submitted to the district party committee, but this is unusual.

Should the judge find the statement of the charges to be adequate, he proposes a sentence. Generally, he will recommend a number of years in prison (Cohen, 1968: 37). There is no rule that he must impose similar sentences for similar crimes, yet there are guidelines he must follow. Robbery, for example, is generally punishable by a two- to five-year sentence, theft by stealth (as opposed to force) by six months to three years. The judge will take into consideration the offender's past record, whether or not he confessed and repented, whether he falsely accused another, whether he caused injury to state property, his social class, and whether there is increased social concern with suppression of this type of crime. The usual maximum penalty may, if indicated by these factors, be exceeded; conversely, however, mitigating circumstances will lower the penalty.

A draft judgment is prepared by the judge, who transmits it to the chief judge for approval, disapproval, or modification. In accordance with his decision, it is either returned to the procuracy and police or sent to interagency consultation and negotiation. A substantial sentence, such as three years or more in prison, must be approved by the president of the court. A major case also requires "approval of the political-legal Party group or of the district Party secretary" (Cohen, 1968:38).

7. Appeal

The judgment in its final form is posted or announced at a public meeting in the offender's neighborhood or where the crime was committed. The accused is informally notified of his right to appeal, generally within a ten-day period or less, and is given a copy of the judgment.

Appeals are infrequent. Due to lack of education, the offender usually is unable to comprehend the full significance of his plight, and he is convinced that he will get no more sympathetic treatment at a higher level.

Should he decide to proceed with an appeal, however, he files his request with the city intermediate court, which then assigns the case to a judge who decides whether or not to grant the appeal. A frivolous appeal will be rejected; if it is accepted, after study of the file, the judge confers with members of the lower court, and sometimes with the procurators, police, party officials, witnesses, and even the offender, to answer any questions he may have regarding the case. He then makes a recommendation to the chief judge in the criminal division of the intermediate court and he may also take up the matter with the relevant section of the city party committee.

An appeal is more in the nature of an administrative inquiry than a hearing. It amounts to a complete redetermination of the case. The alternatives available to the court are:

1) it may void the judgment of conviction and order retrial below, which usually means that reinvestigation by the police will be necessary;

2) more rarely, it may void the judgment of conviction and dismiss the case;

3) it may affirm both the conviction and the sentence; or

4) it may affirm the conviction, but modify the sentence to make it more lenient than harsh (Cohen, 1968:39–40).

A Brief Contrast with the United States

The Chinese employ an administrative rather than a judicial model, which for a system like China's is more likely to achieve the sociopolitical goals identified by its leadership. A judicial model, such as that of the United States, would be too cumbersome and ineffective for the attainment of radical revolutionary objectives (Cohen, 1970). The doctrine of separation of power does not exist in China; no judicial model can be developed in the absence of this divisional structure.

Administrative divisions exist in the Chinese criminal processes (the plural is intended to reflect the multiplicity of processes). These divisions are: law enforcement, prosecution, and judiciary, and they find their counterpart in the common-law and European models. But, unlike either of these models, the line of authority between Chinese divisions is different (see Davis, 1969).

The Chinese police, procuracy, and judiciary are highly integrated in ways that must be distinguished from the type of cooperative relationship that exists in other countries. In the other systems, these divisions retain their separate identities because of the doctrine of separation of powers.

The practice in some systems raises interesting speculation about such distinctions. For example, the high percentage of guilty pleas in metropolitan areas of the United States renders that adversary-accusatorial system questionable and resembles more the administrative model (Bassiouni, 1969a:458–66). In the American system, however, an alternative to that process exists, whereas there are no alternatives in China.

The Chinese system is like any other which encountered abuses of its own rules by administering personnel. A stronger judiciary, which is gradually assuming the semblance of a supervisory role over abuses, resulted.

Administrative sanctioning agencies exist in the adversary-accusatorial and inquisitorial models, but the difference between these models and China's practice rests in the type of sanction meted out by such administrative bodies, that is, criminal or quasi-criminal. A particularly significant difference is the appealability of the decisions of these agencies to the judiciary.

The inquisitorial methods of China, and to some extent of the Soviet Union, give defendants less of an opportunity to present a defense than they would have under the adversary-accusatorial model, such as that of the United States. China and the Soviet Union bestow upon public officials the right to "protect" the suspect's interests and thereby confer upon him a completely different role than in the common-law model, but one which arises out of the nature of the inquisitorial model.

Chinese law does not accept the notion that individual rights may be at odds with those of society and that the rule of law is the mediator between both. The thrust of the Chinese criminal process is to focus on the individual rather than his behavior. To this end, society, as represented by its trusted public officials, uses the law to attain societal goals, which are not to be hampered or limited by abstract rules. The behavior of the accused is only one indicative factor in the investigation. The ultimate objective is the resocialization of the offender in the sense perceived by current sociopolitical ideology.

REFERENCES

Abdel-Wahab, Salah-Eldin.
    1962   "Meaning and structure of law in Islam." Vanderbilt Law Review 16 (December) :115–130.

Ahmad, Mohammed K.
    1956   "Islamic civilization and human rights." Revue Egyptienne de Droit International 12(Tome II) :1–22.

Alschuler, A.
    1968   "The prosecutor's role in plea bargaining." University of Chicago Law Review 36(Fall) :50–112.

American Bar Association.
    1968a   Standards Relating to Pretrial Release. American Bar Association Project on Standards for Criminal Justice. Chicago: American Bar Association.
    1968b   A Contrast Between the Legal Systems in the United States and in the Soviet Union. Chicago: American Bar Association.

Anderson, J. N. D.
    1959   The Malki Law of Homicide. Zaria, Nigeria: Gaskiya.
    1970   Islamic Law in Africa. London: Frank Cass.

Anton, A. E.
    1960   "L'instruction criminelle." American Journal of Comparative Law 9(2): 441–457.

Arnold, T. W.
    1913   The Preaching of Islam. Second Edition. London: Constable.

Auda, Abdel-Kader.
    1959   Al Tashri Al Ginaiy Al Islami (Islamic Criminal Legislation). Cairo: Al Ourouba Press.

Azzam, A.
    1954   Al Risalah Al Khalidah. Second Edition. Cairo.

Baroody, George M.
    1967   "Shariah, the law of Islam." Case and Comment 72(March–April) :3–10.

Bassiouni, M. Cherif.
　1969a　Criminal Law and its Processes. Springfield, Ill.: Thomas.
　1969b　"Islam: concept, law and world habeas corpus." Rutgers-Camden Law Journal 1(Fall):160–201.
　1971a　"The heritage of the Greek legal system: is history still relevant?" The Summons 4(Summer):2–4.
　1971b　"The human rights program: the veneer of civilization thickens." DePaul Law Review 21:271–285.
　1972　"The criminal justice system of the Union of Soviet Socialist Republics and the People's Republic of China." Revista de Derecho Puertoriqueno 11(3): 163.

Berman, Harold J.
　1958　The Nature and Functions of Law. Brooklyn: Foundation Press.
　1963　Justice in the U.S.S.R. Cambridge: Harvard University Press.
　1966　Soviet Criminal Law and Procedure. Cambridge: Harvard University Press.

Bryce, James B.
　1901　"The nature of sovereignty," in Studies in Jurisprudence and History. New York: Oxford University Press.

Buxbaum, David C.
　1962　"Preliminary trends in the development of the legal institutions of Communist China and the nature of the criminal law." International and Comparative Law Quarterly 11(January):1–30.

Cohen, Jerome A.
　1966　"The criminal process in the People's Republic of China: an introduction." Harvard Law Review 79(January):469–533.
　1968　The Criminal Process in the People's Republic of China. Cambridge: Harvard University Press.
　1970　Contemporary Chinese Law. Cambridge: Harvard University Press.

Coulson, N. J.
　1957　"The state and the individual in Islamic law." International and Comparative Law Quarterly 6(January):49–60.
　1964　A History of Islamic Law. Edinburgh: Edinburgh University Press.

Cragg, K.
　1956　The Call of the Minaret. New York: Oxford University Press.

Davis, Kenneth C.
　1969　Discretionary Justice. Baton Rouge: Louisiana State University Press.

Frank, Jerome.
　1958　"Frank on trial by jury," in Harold J. Berman, The Nature and Functions of Law. Brooklyn: Foundation Press.

Gentile, C. L.
　1969　"Fair bargains and guilty pleas." Boston University Law Review 49 (Summer):514–551.

Gibb, H. A. R.
　1961　Mohammedanism. Second Edition. London: Oxford University Press.

Gruen, Erich S.
　1968　Roman Politics and the Criminal Courts: 149–79 B.C. Cambridge: Harvard University Press.

Hamidullah, M.
   1961   Muslim Conduct of State. Fourth Edition. Lahore: M. Ashraf.
Harvard Law Review.
   1966   "Developments in the law: confessions." 79(March):935–1119.
Hauser, R.
   1959   "Comparative law: the criminal law in France." American Bar Association Journal 45(August):807–810.
Hertz, J. H. (ed.)
   1950   The Pentateuch and Haftorahs. London: Sancino Press.
Hrones, S.
   1969   "Interrogation abuses by the police in France—a comparative solution." Criminal Law Quarterly 12(December):68–90.
Hruska, Roman L.
   1969   "Preventive detention: the Constitution and the Congress." Creighton Law Review 3(Fall):36–87.
Ion, Theodore P.
   1907   "Roman law and Mohammedan jurisprudence." Michigan Law Review 6(November):44–52.
Jescheck, H. H.
   1970   "Principles of German criminal procedure in comparison with American law." Virginia Law Review 56(March):239–253.
Jung, Leo.
   1967   Human Relations in Jewish Law. New York: Jewish Education Committee Press.
Kock, G. L.
   1960   "Criminal proceedings in France." American Journal of Comparative Law 9(2):253–262.
LaFave, Wayne R. (ed.)
   1965   Law in the Soviet Society. Urbana: University of Illinois Press.
Laski, H. J.
   1917   Studies in the Problem of Sovereignty. New Haven: Yale University Press.
Lawson, F. H.
   1969   The Roman Law Reader. New York: Oceana Publications.
Leu, C. Dennis.
   1969   "Right to counsel: the impact of Gideon and Wainright in the fifty states." Creighton Law Review 3(Fall):103–157.
Linke, R.
   1971   "The influence of the European Convention on Human Rights on national European criminal proceedings." DePaul Law Review 21:397–421.
Lubman, Stanley.
   1969   "Form and function in the Chinese criminal process." Columbia Law Review 69(April):537–575.
MacDonald, D. B.
   1903   Development of Muslim Theology, Jurisprudence and Constitutional Theory. New York: Scribners.
McKeon, Richard (ed.)
   1941   The Basic Works of Aristotle. New York: Random House.

Maritain, Jacques.
    1951   Man and the State. Chicago: University of Chicago Press.
Maudoodi, S. A.
    1967   Islamic Law and Constitution. Third Edition. Lahore, Pakistan: Islamic
            Publications.
Mendelsohn, A.
    1968   The Criminal Jurisprudence of the Ancient Hebrews. New York: Hermon
            Press.
Miliukov, Paul.
    1934   "Religious institutions, Christian-Russian." Pp. 265–267 in Encyclopedia of
            Social Sciences, vol. 13. London: Macmillan.
Mueller, Gerhard O. W., and Fré LePoole-Griffiths.
    1969   Comparative Criminal Procedure. New York: New York University Press.
Mussa, M.
    1966   Islam and Humanity's Need of It. Cairo: Supreme Council for Islamic
            Affairs, Ministry of Wagfs.
Nice, R. W. (ed.)
    1964   Treasury of Law. New York: Philosophical Library.
Patey, Jacques.
    1960   "Recent reforms in French criminal law and procedure." International and
            Comparative Law Quarterly 9(July):383–395.
Pelletier, G. A.
    1967   "Legal aid in France." Notre Dame Law Review 42(June):627–646.
Pieck, M.
    1962   "The accused's privilege against self-incrimination in the civil law." Amer-
            ican Journal of Comparative Law 11(Autumn):585–601.
Ploscowe, Morris.
    1935   "The investigating magistrate (juge d'instruction) in European criminial
            procedure." Michigan Law Review 33(May):1010–1036.
President's Commission on Law Enforcement and Administration of Justice.
    1967   Task Force Report: The Courts. Washington, D.C.: U.S. Government Print-
            ing Office.
Pugh, G. W.
    1962   "Administration of criminal justice in France: an introductory analysis."
            Louisiana Law Review 23(December):1–28.
Ramadan, Said.
    1961   Islamic Law, Its Scope and Equity. London: Macmillan.
Roberts, R.
    1925   The Social Laws of the Qorân. London: Williams & Norgate.
Rostow, Eugene V.
    1962   The Sovereign Prerogative: The Supreme Court and the Quest for Law. New
            Haven: Yale University Press.
Sait, E. M.
    1949   Masters of Political Thought. Boston: Houghton Mifflin.
Schacht, J.
    1950   The Origins of Mohammedan Jurisprudence. Oxford: Clarendon Press.

Scigliano, Robert.
    1962   The Courts: A Reader in the Judicial Process. Boston: Little, Brown.
Seidman, R. B.
    1966   A Sourcebook of the Criminal Law of Africa. London: Sweet & Maxwell.
Smith, C.
    1957   Islam in Modern History. Princeton: Princeton University Press.
Smith, William.
    1850   A Dictionary of Greek and Roman Antiquities. Third American Edition.
            New York: Harper.
Snee, J. M., and A. K. Pye.
    1960   "Due process in criminal procedure: a comparison of two systems." Ohio
            State Law Journal 21(Autumn):467–502.
Sowle, Claude R.
    1962   Police Power and Individual Freedom. Chicago: Aldine.
Sullivan, F. C.
    1961   "A comparative study of problems in criminal procedure." St. Louis Uni-
            versity Law Journal 6(Autumn):380–399.
Tao, Lung-Sheng.
    1970   "Communist China's criminal jurisdiction over aliens." International and
            Comparative Law Quarterly 19(October):599–625.
Toynbee, A.
    1957   Christianity Among the Religions of the World. London: Oxford University
            Press.
Tritton, A. S.
    1947   Muslim Theology. London: Luzac.
von Grunebaum, G. W.
    1955   Islam: Essays in the Nature and Growth of a Tradition. Menasha, Wis.:
            American Anthropological Association.
Watt, W. M.
    1948   Free Will and Predestination in Early Islam. London: Luzac.
    1962   Islamic Philosophy and Theology. Edinburgh: Edinburgh University Press.
Wigmore, J. H.
    1936   A Panorama of the World Legal Systems. Washington: Washington Law
            Book.
Wormser, Rene A.
    1962   The Story of the Law. New York: Simon & Schuster.
Wyzanski, C. E.
    1952   "A trial judge's freedom and responsibility." Harvard Law Review 65
            (June):1281–1304.

CHAPTER **15**

Role and Process in the Criminal Court

Donald J. Newman

State University of New York at Albany

THE CRIMINAL COURT IN CONTEXT

The Concept, Structure, and Functions of the Criminal Court

The trial court occupies a central and critical place in the criminal justice system and yet, more than other agencies and offices of this system, it is neither simply defined nor easily delimited. Sometimes the term *court* is used as a synonym for *judge,* but at other times it is used to refer to the entire collection of offices and procedures for processing defendants through the middle stages of the criminal justice system, from postarrest to preincarceration. The difference between the narrower judicial view of the court and its conception as a processing agency is more than a matter of definition. It is, rather, a dramatic illustration of contra-perspectives, of a dichotomy in ideology, that characterizes our entire law-enforcement and criminal justice effort. For both definitions of trial courts are valid, both the judicial and the agency functions apply simultaneously, yet they are related in uneasy and controversial fashion, highlighting Packer's (1964) distinctions between the "due process" and the "crime control" models of the criminal justice system.

In the judicial perspective, the court is a finder-of-fact, a tester of evidence, a judgment-rendering body, whether in the person of the judge or in the combined roles of judge and jury. The court is most clearly the province of law and lawyers, and in spite of admitted shortcomings and occasional fallibility, the place where we as people determine guilt or innocence, truth or falseness, in criminal matters. The court's function is to apply to the fullest the constitutional guarantees of due process and procedural regularity in separating the guilty from the innocent, in resolving "beyond all reasonable doubt" disputed questions of fact, and in assuring fair and public trials of those accused of crimes. Indeed, the trial court does have, and does serve, this function.

From the other perspective, the criminal court is simply another criminal justice agency located between the police and the prisons and acting in concert with them, not so much to seek truth by adversary testing but to process the thousands of persons who flow through the system as their status changes from suspect to defendant to convicted offender to inmate and parolee. In this model matters of evidence and proof are of lesser importance than efficiency in moving cases from the street to correctional programs. And, indeed, the trial court does have, and does serve, this function for the vast majority of defendants, whether accused of felonies or misdemeanors, as they move through adjudication to sentencing without trial (Newman, 1966; Skolnick, 1966; President's Commission, 1967a). In this process the jury is absent and the judge, though a central figure, acts primarily to ratify decisions made by the prosecutorial and probation staffs.

Although from an operational point of view the full scale jury trial of a criminal case is comparatively rare, the idealized adversary process has deeper theoretical and symbolic significance. The formal, circumscribed ceremony of the trial, the attention to due process, the separate though presumed balance of legal advantage, the articulation and testing of evidence standards, and even the architecture of the courtroom and the pomp of the proceedings have cultural meanings that cannot be tested simply by measures of efficiency nor denigrated because of infrequent use. Of all the agencies and processes of criminal justice, the court and the trial, in idealized form at least, come closest to what we mean by "justice" in our society. It has been pointed out that the trial model in criminal justice is the one we think we have, or ought to have, but the administrative system for quickly and quietly processing cases is the one we really desire to maintain (Blumberg, 1967:168).

The two models of justice, the different perspectives of the court, have never really been reconciled. Lawyers, legal scholars, sociologists, and appellate courts have long grappled with differences between "law in action" and "law in the books" at various points in criminal processing, but it is only comparatively recently that the nontrial functions of the courts have received sustained scholarly attention and the merger of the prosecutory, adjudicatory, and sentencing functions of the courts were seen and analyzed as a whole, a decision complex of great importance in its own right, not simply a minor alternative to trial (Ohlin & Remington, 1958).

The relationship between the two concepts of court—as trier of fact and as administrative agency—is a subtle and complex one in operational terms as well as in ideology. Aside from its intrinsic importance as a method of adjudication and apart from its symbolic value, the criminal trial, or at least the potential of a trial, has a good deal of administrative significance. In operational terms, it is both a threat and a promise. It is available to all who feel themselves innocent, or at least nonconvictable, and the threat to demand trial is employed by both sides in the plea negotiation process. In the day-to-day processing of thousands of criminal cases, the *avoidance* of trial is of greatest operational significance, the primary objective of both state and accused in the criminal-court process (Newman, 1966).

Officers and Organization of the Criminal Courts

The court stages of the criminal justice process encompass the major decision points of charging, adjudication, and sentencing. Participants in the process include, in addition to defendants, the judge and trial jury, the prosecutor, and in some cases, the grand jury, defense counsel, probation staff, assorted other personnel, such as clerks, bailiffs, stenographers, court administrators, and occasionally others like psychologists or psychiatrists attached to diagnostic clinics, and court-related personnel like jailers and bondsmen. The number and types of personnel involved in court activity vary, not only from one jurisdiction to another but even in a single court, shifting as calendars change, as cases differ, and as the process ebbs and flows between litigation or cooperation—between trial or guilty plea. The relationship among court participants likewise shifts according to activity but even when stable these relationships are amorphous at best, for though the court may be treated analytically as an agency, it is not a line-staff organization of employers and workers in the usual sense. It is much more complex than this, demonstrating internally the complicated structure and role relationships that characterize the entire criminal justice system.

The array of offices and agencies in criminal justice all operate within a delicate balance of authority emanating partly from legislation, partly from appellate-court decree, and partly from agency rule-making power. The system is actually a federation of bureaucracies and professions, interacting in the processing of cases, but structurally independent. The cement that ties the agencies together, the outline of the complex organization, is the flow of its business—the processing of criminal suspects through various decision points from police intake to correctional output (Remington et al., 1969). In the system as a whole, and in the court process as a part, at least four major dimensions of role selection are relevant to both organization and functions: (1) the extent to which personnel occupying any role are required to be professionally trained and educated for their particular function; (2) the method of selection, whether elective, appointive, or the result of competitive examination; (3) the extent of jurisdiction and the basis used for decision reference (whether local or cosmopolitan, whether oriented to a profession or to an agency); and (4) the extent of outside citizen participation and control in both policy formation and decision-making within the functional ambit of the role. Thus, some offices and agencies of the criminal justice system have professional entrance requirements, such as legal training for prosecutors and judges, while others can be staffed by paraprofessionals or by persons without special training. Likewise, some offices are elective, others appointive, and others based on competitive merit, with incumbents drawn from established career lines. Some criminal justice agencies, like correctional services, have broad statewide or even national orientation, whereas others, sheriffs and prosecutors for example, have local authority and regional loyalty. Some agencies, like prisons, are relatively immune from direct citizen control or participation in decision-making, whereas in others "laymen" have, or can have, direct-decision authority, as in the case of the trial jury.

In contrast to national or state agencies, such as corrections and parole, courts are largely local enclaves though not entirely independent from statewide concern and control. By and large, judges, prosecutors, defense counsel, and even probation staff (as well as other court personnel) are indigenous to the area, nontransferable to other locations, and thus heavily responsive to local expectations and demands. However, courts are tied to the larger jurisdiction in a number of ways: by supervision of courts of appeal, by statewide requirements for office or duties fixed by legislation, by loyalty of participants to their profession and professional organizations, by the administrative skills of state-court administrators, and in some ways, by that portion of the court budget that comes from the state or the federal government.

A number of criminal justice agencies, like the police and the custodial staff of prisons, are structured in classic bureaucratic fashion with clear lines of authority and superordinate and subordinate roles. This is not to say that such agencies, organized in paramilitary fashion, are without conflicts and uncertainties; all multifunctional organizations experience power struggles, shifts in authority, competing ideologies, and less-than-stable relationships, as both police and prisons have discovered in times of crisis. Courts, too, have such problems, but they are even more complicated because basic court structure is far different from common administrative bureaucracy, and certainly is not patterned on the military. While the trial judge is the titular head of court activities and may be the actual employer of bailiffs, clerks, and occasionally of probation officers, he is by no means the "boss" of the prosecutor any more than he is of defense counsel who appear before him. While these participants have functional interdependence with the judge and, in the more formalized trial process especially, have some fairly clearly defined reciprocal roles, the primary allegiance of prosecutors, counsel, and probation officers is to their own offices and professions. Such judicial control as exists is indirect and often informal. In short, the overall role structure of the court is more like an affiliation of semiautonomous professionals, closer in a sense to a medical clinic or a university faculty than to an industrial or military bureaucracy. This is so even *within* offices in the court system. Control by the district attorney of his professional staff is generally limited to formulation of general policies and to his powers of persuasion; judgments in legal matters on the part of his lawyer-assistants rest primarily on their own professional competence and ethics. Likewise, in multi-judge jurisdictions, the authority of the chief judge is limited largely to matters of the court calendar. In decisions of substance—within gross limits of propriety—his colleagues are immune from his control. So it is with court administrators, now prominent and important participants in many court organizations. In effect, such administrators are business officers and calendar clerks; they can affect budget and work loads, but not substantial decision-making.

The relationship among courts in any jurisdiction is, likewise, an amorphous one: each court is an island of relative autonomy within its jurisdictional authority, yet related to the whole both by legislation, which sets standards, defines limits, and controls some budget, and by the appellate process, where both substance and procedures of the law are interpreted and honed. All states, and the federal jurisdiction, have lower and intermediate trial courts and higher courts of appeal, eventually including the United States Supreme Court. Yet, variety within and between jurisdictions is the rule, and everywhere the control of lower by higher courts is largely indirect (except in cases of gross malfeasance) and inferential by the slow, case-by-case appellate process.

There is no pattern of criminal-court organization common to all jurisdictions, nor are there uniform standards and procedures for selection of court personnel (President's Commission, 1967a). As a matter of fact, inquiry as to the number of criminal courts cannot be answered without many qualifications, for determining what is a criminal court is a matter of choice among various definitions. In the federal as well as all state jurisdictions, there are courts with authority to try felony matters. These courts are located in most counties in all states (there are some regional courts in rural areas that combine counties into common jurisdictions), but there are often many felony courts or many branches of a felony court in metropolitan areas. Even more widely distributed are the so-called lower courts, with jurisdiction to try misdemeanors, traffic violations, ordinance infractions, and the like. Most of these courts, intermediate and lower alike, are involved only part-time with criminal matters; many have concurrent civil jurisdiction and, in fact, operate most frequently there.

Only in the most congested areas with correspondingly high crime rates are there courts with jurisdiction limited solely to criminal matters. Some states have youth courts to process offender populations who fall somewhere between the upper age of delinquency and the lower age of eligibility for felony trial. In some of the largest cities specialization of courts goes beyond even this to include separate courts for dealing with certain types of offenses and offenders. In some cities there are, for example, vice courts, rackets courts, homicide courts, narcotics courts, and the like. There are multi-judge courts and single-judge courts. There are courts with full-time prosecutors and in some rural areas there are courts with district attorneys who are only part-time. In some counties or jurisdictions there may be a single prosecutor to service one or more courts where in others a prosecutor may have hundreds of lawyer-assistants, some specializing in certain types of crimes or dealing with certain types of offenders.

This variability in court organization, coupled with the complex mixture of autonomy and functional interdependence of roles found in any court, accounts in good part for both the problems currently confronting criminal courts, from over-crowding to sentence disparity, and the difficulties experienced by virtually all court-reform programs. There is no way to simply order greater efficiency, to command better effectiveness, to legislate uniformity in decision-making. Budget and facilities are important but peripheral to the central concerns of role and function in the court process.

COURT PERSONNEL

The Criminal-Court Judge

The trial judge is not only a symbol of justice but a trier of facts, the chief officer of an administrative agency, and in his own right, a critical decision-maker in criminal justice with his influence having consequences both for the earlier agencies of criminal justice and for postconviction correctional programs as well. The President's Commission put it this way:

> The trial judge is at the center of the criminal process, and he exerts a powerful influence on the stages of the process which precede and follow his formal participation. Many decisions of police, prosecutors, and defense counsel are determined by the trial judge's rulings, by his sentencing practices, and even by the speed with which he disposes of cases. His decisions on sentencing and probation revocation affect the policies and procedures of correctional agencies. And to a great degree the public's impression of justice is shaped by the trial judge's demeanor and the dignity he imparts to the proceedings in his courtroom (1967a:65).

Judges are selected for office in a variety of ways. In most states trial judges are elected and, furthermore, in most of these states they run for office on a partisan basis having been nominated by a political party for the judgeship (President's Commission, 1967a). In a number of other states judges stand for popular election as nonpartisans, getting their names on the ballot by circulating petitions to obtain a required number of voter signatures. In nine states judges are appointed by the governor or by local executives, and in the federal system judges are appointed by the president with the consent of the Senate. In five states judges are appointed (or, as in Vermont, elected) by the legislature. In ten states judges are selected by the "Missouri Plan" (it was first adopted in Missouri in 1940) that involves the following procedures: qualified candidates are nominated by a nonpartisan commission, judges are originally ap-pointed by the chief executive (the governor, mayor, or other local authority) and approved at the next election by the voters. After a term of office, the incumbent judge runs for office again, not against another candidate but on the basis of his own record. In effect, he asks a vote of confidence from the voters. Should the vote be negative, the selection process begins over again.

Judicial selection procedures are felt by many to be an important way to strengthen or reform the criminal justice system, and there are many long-standing arguments about the relative value of merit selection (nonpartisan, bar-association approval, Missouri Plan) as against political campaigning. In general those favoring merit selection argue that such screening enables the best-qualified, most honest candidates to obtain office without incurring political debt or obligation. On the other hand, critics of merit selection point out that such procedures are essentially political anyway ("Are there nonpolitical federal judges?") and result in selection of judges who are not representative of a large segment of the community, more particularly that such procedures exclude members of minority groups. In general, the President's Commission on Law Enforcement and Administration of Justice took the position that merit selection is the best alternative (1967a:67–68).

Judges hold office for various lengths of time. The federal judiciary has life tenure, but in some states the terms of office are as short as four years. More commonly terms range from six to ten years, with a possibility of reelection for life or until a mandatory retirement age defined by statute in some states.

At the felony-court level, there is a universal requirement that the judge be minimally qualified by admission to the bar. This does not necessarily mean that he has received a legal education or has graduated from an accredited law school. Though the apprenticeship system is disappearing by both law and custom, in some states persons can still become members of the bar by passing an examination after fulfilling office-practice training requirements. In lower courts (justice-of-the-peace courts, coroner's courts, and other magistrate's courts) incumbents in some jurisdictions are not mandated to be either a member of the bar or a trained lawyer.

By and large, the American trial judge receives no formal training or even any kind of apprenticeship in the judicial function. For example, while most new trial judges have had some prior experience in the private practice of law, a survey by the Institute of Judicial Administration showed that 25 percent of the judges who responded indicated that their practice included *no* criminal cases. No judge who responded had specialized in criminal law practice (President's Commission, 1967a: 68). Except in moot-court competition (a voluntary activity), most law schools provide little educational exposure to trial-court activities. In fact, the typical law graduate is much more familiar with the roles and functions of a Supreme Court justice than those of a trial judge.

There are some attempts today to provide judicial training for new judges in short-course summer institutes, like those conducted by the National College of State Trial Judges (an affiliate of the American Bar Association). But here, as in law-school training, the emphasis is largely on the adjudicatory function, stressing the appropriate conduct and procedures for trial. Until very recently, and still more common than not, that component of legal education devoted to criminal law emphasized substantive law and procedure only up through adjudication, with even this focused largely on the trial and not the guilty plea. Sentencing and all postconviction processes (except appeal of conviction) were, and are, largely foreign to legal education and, for that matter, rarely experienced in the practice of law.

By far the most unfamiliar and most uncomfortable task of the new judge is sentencing. There is currently increasing attention to sentencing and the postconviction processes in law-school curricula, and the federal government and many states are conducting sentencing institutes for judges in an attempt to make the process more rational and to reduce sentence disparity (Remington & Newman, 1962).

The Prosecutor

The prosecutor not only has an intrinsically important role in American criminal justice but the office itself is historically and theoretically important in American jurisprudence. Prosecutors have functioned prominently in both federal and state jurisdictions since colonial times. The origins of both the office and the traditional "prosecutor's discretion" have been traced to both early English and French common law (Baker & DeLong, 1934; Grosman, 1969). Interestingly, the prosecutor as we know him is virtually absent from European criminal justice, which operates largely under systems of private prosecution with public prosecutors acting only in very serious or unusual cases. In the United States, however, public prosecutors (generally called district attorneys) are necessary in all jurisdictions, for private prosecution of crimes is not permissible in our system.

In almost all jurisdictions the prosecutor is a locally elected official. In the federal system prosecutors, like judges, are appointed by the president but, unlike the judiciary, do not have life tenure, serving rather at the pleasure of the incumbent executive. Only four states provide for appointment of prosecutors, but even here political considerations play an important role (Nedrud, 1960; President's Commission, 1967a). The tenure of the prosecutor is normally much shorter than that of the judge with most counties or districts requiring election every two or four years.

By and large, the office of prosecutor is viewed differently from a judgeship by both candidates and incumbents of both offices. Elevation to the bench tends to cap a career of law practice; the typical district attorney is at the beginning or middle of his career, with higher office or a more lucrative practice hoped for in the future. There are comparatively few career prosecutors (Nedrud, 1960) for this office is commonly a stepping-stone into politics or on to the bench (a comparatively high proportion of trial-court judges were at one time or another employed in prosecutor's offices) or, more subtly, candidacy for office (even if unsuccessful) is a way for local attorneys to become known, for the code of professional ethics forbids a lawyer to advertise. In any event, the office of district attorney is highly political, even more so than judges who have achieved office, because of the necessity for the DA to stand more frequently for election. A two-year term for a new DA often means the first year of learning the job, the second of campaigning for reelection. Yet the office is powerful and relatively independent from both the judiciary and from the other criminal justice agencies, including the police.

Like judges, the minimum requirement for prosecutors is membership in the bar; but unlike the situation with most felony-court judges, a number of prosecutors in small rural districts are only part-time office holders, the remainder of their activity being devoted to the private practice of law. In large cities prosecuting attorneys are usually full-time and may have a legal staff numbering in the hundreds, with job security of these assistants protected by civil-service regulations.

In slightly over half of the states, prosecutors share with grand juries the decision of whether to charge a defendant with a crime and, if so, the specific crime and number of counts to be brought. In secret proceedings the prosecutor brings the case to the grand jury, presenting to them such evidence as, in his estimation, is sufficient to convince them to issue an indictment. In the remaining states, where grand juries are not required or may be waived, prosecution is based on a document called an *information* that, like the indictment, lists in formal language the specific criminal charges on which prosecution is based. The information is drafted by the prosecutor without jury screening but is tested for "probable cause" at a preliminary hearing before a judge, unless such hearing is waived by the defendant with consent of the state (Hall et al., 1969).

The value of the grand jury as "shield and sword" of prosecution has been long debated (Hall et al., 1969:788, 791) for, as might be expected, grand juries indict in the vast majority of cases when requested to do so by the prosecutor (Morse, 1931).

But this is also the case with bind-overs following preliminary hearings; in most in-stances the judge finds sufficient evidence to hold the defendant for trial. The relative worth of each procedure cannot fairly be assessed by whether the prosecutor "wins" or "loses" on probable cause for there are many other factors to be considered, includ-ing some that touch basic values in our criminal justice ideology. For example, the grand-jury system represents a method of citizen participation in the charging process, bringing all the pros and cons of judgment by peers to the pretrial stage. Grand-jury deliberations are closed, which has the advantage of preventing detailed and perhaps damaging pretrial publicity, but since they are closed to defense as well as the press, there is no opportunity for the defendant to learn anything of the state's case against him. In contrast the major defense advantage of the preliminary hearing is discovery (Hall et al., 1969; Miller, 1969), but the corresponding disadvantage is public revela-tion of the state's accusations without, in most cases, the defense being revealed.

The Trial Jury

The right to trial by jury in criminal matters is guaranteed in the Constitution (Article 3, Section 2) and, as a matter of fact, because of the particular wording "trial of all crimes . . . shall be by jury," there was a long-standing controversy whether jury trials could be waived, that is, whether all defendants *must* be tried. By and large, court decisions have allowed waiver of jury trial [*Patton* v. *United States*, 281 U.S. 276 (1930)], although waiver is not allowed in some states in certain serious felony mat-ters, particularly where capital crimes are charged (*Cornell Law Quarterly*, 1966:339, 342–43).

The idea of judgment by peers is deeply imbedded in our political philosophy where, as in criminal matters, the state is seen as potentially repressive and the system as basically punitive. Yet, in practice such judgment is frequently waived by defend-ants who opt for bench trials (the judge alone) or who plead guilty. When state inter-vention is defined as beneficent, as in juvenile-delinquency proceedings, the jury ideology weakens [*McKeiver* v. *Penna.* 403 U.S. 528 (1971); Griffiths, 1970]. Criti-cism of the jury system in criminal cases generally does not challenge its ideological significance, but relates rather to the administration of juror selection procedures and to strategies employed by attorneys to manipulate decisions on emotional rather than rational grounds (Broeder, 1954; Hall et al., 1969).

Extensive studies of criminal juries and their use have shown that jury trials are used in about 15 percent of prosecutions for major crimes (Kalven & Zeisel, 1966:18) and much less frequently in minor crimes and misdemeanors. Judges and juries agree on the outcome of cases about 75 percent of the time, with the jury *less* lenient than the judge in 3 percent of the cases, and more lenient 19 percent of the time (p. 59). While these data suggest that it is advantageous for a defendant to seek judgment by jury, the authors warn against such generalization since the initial decision to take a case to jury trial rests in good part in the belief that it is the type of case to elicit pro-defendant sentiment.

The jury studies were concerned with the relative impact of skilled (or unskilled) defense counsel on jury decision-making. In an elaborate analysis of the lawyer factor (the balance of skills between prosecution and defense), Kalven and Zeisel estimate the impact of counsel on the system to be only about 1 percent, but add:

> The figure should not be misread. In 25 per cent of the cases in which defense counsel
> is superior, he will have some share in moving the jury toward disagreement. But more

important, the lawyer's role is not exhausted by consideration of the disagreement cases alone, since in the vast majority of trials, counsel on both sides are evenly matched. And, indeed, it might be well said that the great role of the defense lawyer, as an institution, is to keep the trial process in balance so that the adversary system can function (1966:372).

Selecting a jury of peers, in the common meaning of the term, could perhaps only be realized, if ever, in colonial America when we were a country of small towns and villages. Even then blacks and women were excluded. Today there is a question of the feasibility of even approximating this ideal jury plan, particularly in metropolitan courts and—for a variety of reasons—even in smaller jurisdictions as well. Part of this concern relates to selection procedures, primarily certain exclusion practices that by law or custom keep those without property or permanent residence, particularly members of ethnic and racial minorities, off jury panels. Because criminal defendants are often poor, transient, and members of minority groups, such exclusions are felt to weaken the spirit, if not the letter, of the law in regard to peer judgment. Another part of the concern is with the grossly inadequate facilities and compensation for jurors (and for witnesses as well) that in most jurisdictions make jury duty an unpleasant and unwelcome task for those who are selected. The President's Commission, in recommending improved treatment of both jurors and witnesses, commented:

> Compensation is generally so low that service as a juror or witness is a serious financial burden. . . . The economic impact bears most harshly on people whose wages are usually paid on an hourly or daily basis. Such experiences can only aggravate the feeling of a major segment of the community that the law does them no good (1967a:90).

The trial jury is best known in its adjudicatory capacity. Yet, in a number of jurisdictions, it also has a sentencing function. It is common in those states sanctioning capital punishment for certain crimes to give the jury the final decision as to the death sentence (Virginia Law Review, 1967:968). This is no longer possible because the death penalty was outlawed by the Supreme Court [*Furman* v. *Georgia*, 408 U.S. 238 (1972)]. Twelve states provide for jury sentencing in non-capital cases. Seven of these give sentencing authority to juries in *all* serious crimes, four restrict the jury function to certain types of offenses, and one (Texas) allows the defendant to request jury sentencing if he so desires [LaFont, 1960:38; Texas Code Crim. Proc., Art. 37.07 (1966)].

The Defense Attorney

Though the right to a jury trial is as old as the Constitution (with an even longer historical precedent), the right of the accused to be represented by counsel at trial is a recent development. While the affluent could always retain lawyers privately to conduct their defenses, indigent defendants had no constitutional right to counsel, except in capital cases, until the Supreme Court so decided in 1963 (*Gideon* v. *Wainwright*, 372 U.S. 335). Overturning a prior Supreme Court holding, the *Gideon* decision extended the right of representation to all defendants, indigent or otherwise, at trial on any charge that carries the possibility of a "substantial prison sentence." This was held to include all felonies and serious misdemeanors, and it was subsequently interpreted to include trials involving petty misdemeanors as well [*Argersinger* v. *Hamlin*, 407 U.S. 25 (1972)]. Though the factual situation in *Gideon* limited the right to counsel at trial, it was subsequently extended to apply to guilty-plea proceedings as well (Newman, 1966). Coming as late in history as it did, the *Gideon* decision probably surprised many Americans who had assumed a right to representation all along. Only those most familiar with courts and criminal procedure were fully aware of the limitations of the right prior to this holding. While a number of states had statutory provisions for counsel, a number did not, but as a result of *Gideon*, the right now applies as a constitutional matter to all jurisdictions. Though representation may be waived by the defendant, it is more common today—in fact, almost routine in many jurisdictions—for defendants in serious criminal cases to be represented by lawyers whether they go to trial, plead guilty, or have charges dismissed.

Privately retained counsel always played an important part in the criminal-court process and the *Gideon* decision and subsequent developments entrenched the counsel's role as a major one in criminal matters and, of course, added great importance to the functions of public defenders or court-assigned lawyers. The initial impact of *Gideon* was to put a strain on available resources, particularly because a series of other Supreme Court decisions at about the same time expanded the right to counsel at "critical stages" other than trial—from early police stages [*Miranda* v. *Arizona*, 384 U.S. 436 (1966)] to sentencing and appeal [*Douglas* v. *California*, 372 U.S. 353 (1963); *Mempa* v. *Rhay*, 389 U.S. 128 (1967)], so that the distribution of legal services became a major problem in many places. Various methods of providing counsel for indigents were developed or expanded, the two major forms being court assignment of lawyers from bar association lists and the development of public defender and other legal-aid services (Silverstein, 1956). Some experimental programs, such as "Judicare," allowed defendants to select their own attorneys with the fee (80 percent of standard fees) being paid by the government.

Studies of the comparative merits of different methods of providing legal services, whether such analysis is based on cost or performance, are generally inconclusive (Silverstein, 1956:73). One argument for the public-defender system is that the lawyer in this office is a specialist in criminal defense and, therefore, more equal in skill to the prosecutor than a randomly assigned lawyer, not only in knowledge of criminal law and procedure but in terms of informal court practices, such as plea negotiation. Assigned lawyers may have neither sufficient criminal-law knowledge nor defense skill and may not even be aware of hallway-bargaining practices. On the other hand, it is argued that if an assignment system is widely used so that eventually all lawyers in a jurisdiction rotate through criminal cases, the result will be involvement of the "better" lawyers, now largely concerned with more lucrative civil practice, in criminal matters. Furthermore, bar-wide involvement of attorneys will generate an interest and concern about criminal justice issues among lawyers at large and, given their collective influence in politics and governmental administration, in turn will eventually lead to improvements in the entire system.

With the exception of experienced public defenders and a handful of specializing criminal lawyers, few members of the bar are really familiar with criminal law and procedure, nor do they rely to any great extent on income derived from the defense of criminal cases. A major study of the *criminal lawyer* used as a working definition of this term lawyers who specified that 10 percent or more of their practice was in criminal law (Wood, 1967). There are a few courthouse regulars in larger communities whose practice is limited to criminal defense but almost all attorneys who appear in criminal court receive the major share of their income and have their major professional interest in other types of law practice (Blaustein & Porter, 1954; Wood, 1967).

Generally speaking, admission to the bar requires formal education, the passing of an examination, and certification as to moral fitness. Though bar admission by apprenticeship in a law office is still with us, increasingly American lawyers are the products of law schools (Carlin, 1962; Johnstone & Hopson, 1967). A fairly large segment of the bar who practice regularly in the criminal courts come from lower- and middle-class families, particularly in large cities. Older minority ethnicity (Irish, Polish, Italian) is heavily represented in criminal law practice; racial minorities are not. Blacks, for example, account for only approximately 1 percent of all American lawyers (Johnstone & Hopson, 1967).

Probation Officers

The authority of the trial court extends beyond imposition of sentence to encompass continued control over offenders who are placed on probation. In addition to his adjudication and sentencing functions, the judge has final responsibility for probation revocation hearings. In any given year over half of all adult felony offenders are placed on probation, thus remaining within the jurisdiction and control of the trial court while they serve their sentences (President's Commission, 1967b). In juvenile courts it is common for the judge to be the chief administrator of the probation service, but in adult felony courts the judge less often has such direct responsibilities as hiring, firing, and setting standards for the work of the probation staff. In most jurisdictions adult probation personnel are employees of a state correctional system or of a separate, statewide probation service and, thereby, do not owe job security to any particular judge. In some thirteen states, however, adult probation services are entirely local operations, staffed, funded, and administered by local courts. The reasons for variations in probation organization are many, probably accidents of history in a number of instances, yet it is of some significance that in larger states, particularly those with extensive metropolitan centers, probation is commonly administered on a city or county rather than a statewide basis. In such cases, judicial control and intervention can be much more direct and influential. Attempts to merge probation services into a state organization, whether integrated with parole and other correctional programs or not, have been resisted on various grounds, among them the great cost and administrative complexity that would result if the state attempted to merge myriad local agencies (President's Commission, 1967b:36). It is likely, however, that the basis of resistance to merger is more than economic; efforts in this regard threaten the autonomy, lessen the power, and decrease the functions of trial judges.

Whatever the administrative structure in any jurisdiction, probation agents are officers of the trial court and their clients remain under court jurisdiction. Probation officers service the court in two major ways: first by the collection and preparation of presentencing information for the judge to use in sentence determination, and second by community supervision of those offenders whom the court places on probation. In some places probation officers are also expected to conduct recognizance bail investigations, to collect debts, fines, costs, and damages as ordered by the court, to initiate revocations when circumstances call for it, to return absconders, and generally to perform such other duties as the judge may see as relevant to the court's postconviction function.

Although probation officers are accountable to the judge and in some cases are actual employees of the court, probation services are still relatively autonomous, somewhat comparable to the prosecutor's office but with significant differences. Nowhere are probation officers elected officials and the probation agent is the only major participant in the trial-court process who is not a lawyer. He tends to identify his professional development not with law, or even with courts, but with the field of social work generally or corrections in particular (Miles, 1963).

The probation officer ordinarily has a marked effect on the sentencing process because he controls the kind of information that is presented to the judge. The judge rarely knows much from personal contact about the offender before him for sentencing except from impressions formed if there has been a trial. In most cases, of course, conviction is by plea and there has been no trial. The typical arraignment reveals little of use to sentencing. Though sentencing authority is formally vested only with the judge, it is clear in practice that both the preconviction activities of the prosecutor in charging and the presentence investigation reports of probation officers are significant, if not actually determinant, factors in the sentencing decision (Dawson, 1969).

Other Court Personnel

Besides the major actors of judge, jury, prosecutor, defense counsel, and probation staff, there are a variety of other personnel attached to, involved in, or otherwise affecting the criminal-court process. Clerks, stenographers, bailiffs, bondsmen, and jailers are all daily participants in or near the courtroom. Some courts have diagnostic services, often called "psychopathic clinics," attached directly to them and used to test the competency of defendants or witnesses or for making sentencing recommendations. These clinics are staffed by psychiatrists, psychologists, and social workers who act in part as a diagnostic aid to the probation service, yet are independent from it. In addition, in a number of jurisdictions there are court administrators who supervise the budget and logistics of the court process. Controls on the substantive work of courts, that is, on adjudicatory and sentencing decisions, are accomplished by the appellate process; the court administrator, on the other hand, functions to improve the efficiency of the court calendar, to balance work loads, and to supervise the activities of nonjudicial court personnel. The President's Commission recommended that the office of court administrator also function to conduct research on court processes in order to make recommendations to state judicial conferences for trial-court improvements (President's Commission, 1967a:95–96).

Nonjudicial court personnel, while not directly responsible for major decisions about defendants, nevertheless are important actors in ways both direct and subtle in the operations of the court. Calendar clerks, for example, play an important informal role by cooperating with defense counsel in the practice of "judge shopping." This is common in multi-judge metropolitan courts where attorneys seek to plead their clients guilty or have them sentenced by a particular judge believed to be lenient in the type of case at hand. To anyone unfamiliar with the daily operations of a trial court, the whole process, even the aura of the courthouse, is confused and cluttered. Court personnel have the important task of steering lawyers, defendants, complainants, witnesses, and family and friends of the accused through the maze of forms and procedures of the court bureaucracy. All this takes place in a setting that is typically overcrowded, staffed by stern officials, and with both defendants and witnesses reluctant, if not hostile. To the extent that the court symbolizes as well as dispenses justice, the impact of processing on defendants and others is dependent, in good part, on the activities of supporting personnel. Decorum may be of minor operational significance, yet the sordidness and appalling confusion that is characteristic of many metropolitan lower courts often makes the entire process a literal degradation ceremony, far from the ideal of ordered liberty and justice.

STAGES IN THE CRIMINAL-COURT PROCESS

Different individuals processed through the entire criminal justice system from arrest to sentence may have significantly diverse experiences though they are accused, indeed convicted, of common offenses. One person may be summoned to the process, appearing in court on his own initiative at a time specified in a citation or summons. Another, suspected of the same crime, may be forcibly arrested by the police with or without warrant, interrogated, held in custody, and taken under secure conditions to the court. At initial court contact, one suspect may be immediately released on bail—monetary or recognizance—while his counterpart is held in detention awaiting further proceedings. A defendant may request and receive privately retained or court-assigned counsel; another may opt to waive his right to representation and go it alone. One may have a full-scale jury trial, the other stand convicted by his own plea. The first may be in court for days, weeks, even months, whereas the entire judicial contact of the other may total only a few minutes. One offender may be placed on probation, the other incarcerated in jail or prison. In brief, while the processes of the criminal justice system can be neatly sketched and the flow of cases traced in uniform array from intake to sentencing, the experiences of different defendants, though formally following the same system, may be grossly different. One defendant can go through the criminal justice system without being in physical custody except momentarily, whereas his counterpart can be forcibly held from the moment of his arrest until the completion of his prison sentence. Obviously, though the system is the same, the objective and subjective experiences of the two defendants in alternative processes are worlds apart.

Beyond the question of bail or jail awaiting trial, and prison or probation following it, defendants' experiences in the processes of the court itself can be quite distinct. A person who is represented by counsel from his initial bail-setting appearance may demand and receive the entire panoply of procedural due process up through and including sentencing. He may challenge his continued custody, the charges brought against him, the admissibility of state's evidence, the decision to bind him over for trial, the quantum of evidence sufficient to convict him beyond a reasonable doubt, and the reasons and rationale for his sentence. Utilizing all available pretrial motions, using the adversary process to its fullest, and taking advantage of appeal procedures mean that the court stage of the process will likely extend over a period of months, even years. In a fully litigated case, a defendant's "day in court" may be a long day indeed. In contrast, a defendant with or without the advice of counsel who waives most formal procedures, including trial, and does nothing to challenge the contentions of the state, indeed cooperates by confessing and pleading guilty, may move very rapidly through the court stages of the process with his day in court shrunk to a few minutes. There is, in fact, some concern on the part of judges and others with too rapid processing. Instances have been noted where defendants, arrested in the morning, have arrived at prison in the afternoon to begin serving a sentence. These "quick justice" convictions are the reciprocal to the problem of delay and, like delay, are receiving increased attention by appellate courts (Newman, 1966).

Given the extremes in both the time and substance of court contacts, it is not possible to trace a single, uniform, typical trial-court process. Various stages where critical decisions about defendants are made can be extracted for analysis but, with the possibility of waiver and of other differential experiences and with variations in procedures from one jurisdiction to the next, at most, these stages remain as abstractions rather than as descriptions of operational reality.

Initial Appearance and Bail

The first court appearance of a suspect arrested for a crime is at a proceeding commonly called *initial appearance before a magistrate*. This is perhaps the least generally understood step in the process, often confused with a preliminary hearing (which is a later proceeding to determine whether or not the state has sufficient evidence to hold the defendant for trial) or with arraignment (which is the time at which a defendant is required to plead to the charges against him). The confusion here is compounded in some jurisdictions where the initial appearance is called *arraignment on the warrant.*

The primary purpose of initial appearance is to determine whether the individual will be released on bail or retained in custody awaiting further processing. In minor offenses the initial magistrate may have jurisdiction to try the case, to accept a guilty plea, and perhaps to levy a fine. This is common, for example, in cases involving traffic violations and other minor misdemeanors. But in serious cases, particularly those involving felonies, the substance of the charge is not litigated here; the jurisdiction of the magistrate is limited to fixing or denying bail. The initial appearance does not test the validity of the arrest, nor is the defendant required to plead to any allegations against him. Provision for initial appearance is made in the statutes or by court rule, and its purpose is to provide a check on the power of the police to hold and interrogate suspects for extended periods of time. A common pattern of control in the criminal justice system is the submission of operational decisions to a neutral authority—judge or referee—in order to provide defendants with protection from excessive intervention by the state. The initial appearance is one illustration of this pattern; the full scale trial, another. Statutory language in most jurisdictions requires that the initial appearance be conducted at the "first opportunity" (i.e., when the court is next open) or within a "reasonable time" after arrest. A significant decision in the federal jurisdiction [*Mallory* v. *United States*, 354 U.S. 449 (1957)] requires suspects to be brought *immediately* before a magistrate. Among other consequences, the *"Mallory* rule" resulted in availability of around-the-clock magistrates in federal jurisdictions. Requirements in most state jurisdictions are not this stringent; in fact, a practice noted in some places is the "Friday-night arrest," giving the police opportunity for in-custody interrogation until the court opens on Monday (LaFave, 1965).

The historical purpose of bail was to control unfettered discretion of the police power of the state by providing defendants with an opportunity for freedom from incarceration prior to trial. The monetary basis of bail—the bail bond—was to insure the return of the defendant with forfeiture added to the other costs and consequences of flight. While some offenses, mostly capital crimes, are defined by statute in some jurisdictions as nonbailable, access to reasonable bail is granted as a right in all jurisdictions for all but these few crimes. The amount of bail fixed by the magistrate must not be "excessive" in violation of the Eighth Amendment to the Constitution.

The monetary bail system in the United States has long been subject to criticism and attack (Foote, 1965; Hall et al., 1969), not only because of the obvious discrimination against poor defendants, but also because of its alleged use for purposes, mostly punitive, other than assurance of appearance at trial (Freed & Wald, 1964; Hall et al., 1969). Within the past decade bail practices have been systematically studied and modified in many jurisdictions. Sparked by the research and experimentation of the Vera Foundation, major bail reforms are now operative many places throughout the country. The basis of this reform is primarily ROR (release on recognizance), in which an investigation of the defendant is made for the purpose of determining his likelihood of reappearing for trial without the necessity of monetary bonding.

Experience has shown that defendants with strong local ties, such as permanent residence and employment, are as likely to show up for later processing on their own word as on their bond (Freed & Wald, 1964). Release-on-recognizance was undoubtedly one of the major reforms in criminal justice administration during the 1960s. Research demonstrated rather dramatically that whether a person was released or not had important subsequent consequences on his fate, including the type of sentence imposed by the judge; defendants released on recognizance were much more likely to receive probation than those held in custody until arraignment or trial (Freed & Wald, 1964:61–63).

In 1966 Congress enacted a Bail Reform Act, which incorporates provisions for recognizance release (Hall et al., 1969). Although ROR programs proliferated after the early Manhattan Bail Project, there has also been opposition to pretrial release programs. A number of "preventive detention" proposals (of debated constitutionality) would enable the court to deny pretrial release, not so much because of risk of flight, but to prevent the defendant from committing "new crimes" while awaiting trial (Harvard Law Review, 1966; American Bar Association, 1968b).

Determination of the Charge

A suspect may be arrested on complaint or suspicion, with or without warrant, and searched and interrogated as incident to the arrest and prior to an initial appearance before a magistrate. Supreme Court decisions of recent years have placed more stringent controls on these processes [*Mapp* v. *Ohio*, 367 U.S. 643 (1961); *Miranda* v. *Arizona; United States* v. *Wade*, 388 U.S. 218 (1967)] but, in general, as a case proceeds onward from the initial intake of arrest, evidence of guilt or innocence accumulates. At some point, sometimes as early as the issuance of an arrest warrant but more often later as evidence builds, the prosecuting attorney is called upon to make a decision in regard to the formal charge or charges he will seek in an indictment or will present at a preliminary hearing.

The charging process is complex (Miller, 1969). Generally, although it is within the prosecutor's authority, in practice it involves the interaction of the police, the grand jury (where necessary), and even the judge (McIntyre, 1968). The charging decision involves more than questions of evidence, although these are of central concern, because it also rests on the discretionary authority of the prosecutor. District attorneys in our system of justice have a traditional power of *nolle prosequi* (sometimes provided in statute, but originating in common law) by which they can decide *not* to prosecute for reasons unrelated to evidence sufficiency (Miller, 1969:312–16).

Common practice is for the police, after arresting and booking a suspect (and conducting him through initial appearance), to turn over their files to a district attorney for determination of both the desirability of and necessary "probable cause" for prosecution. In some cases, particularly in major crimes, the prosecutor may be involved earlier in the process, perhaps actually conducting all in-custody interrogation or otherwise participating on-scene in the intake process. In more routine cases, however, the district attorney does not see the defendant this early but receives an up-to-date police file on the case after the defendant is arrested and booked. In reading the file and perhaps questioning the arresting officer or the complainant, he decides whether to initiate a charge at all, and if so, which crime or crimes and how many counts of each will be leveled.

In evaluating the evidence at hand and estimating the likelihood of obtaining further evidence, the prosecutor presumably brings his legal training to bear in applying the evidence standard necessary for charging. This is normally phrased as "probable cause" to believe that a crime was committed and that the person in question was the one who committed it. The words of this test, while identical or similar to the "probable cause" or "reasonable cause" necessary to effect an arrest, have a different reference basis for the district attorney than for the policeman on the street. The interest of the prosecutor is the applicability of the evidence at possible trial. While he can, indeed, charge a defendant on evidence less than the "beyond a reasonable doubt" needed to convict, his orientation must be to this higher test. The policeman needs only to look backward, assuring himself that the evidence is sufficient to prevent his paying damages in a civil suit for false imprisonment (commonly called *false arrest*). But in making the charging determination, the prosecutor must weigh numerous factors of the *quality* of his case, such as credibility of witnesses, any likely or probable defenses, the skill or reputation of defense counsel, and similar tactical variables, all tested against the probability of winning or losing at trial. In short, it is possible for a suspect to be validly arrested on probable cause and yet not be charged with a crime when the evidence is assessed by the prosecutor's operational meaning of the probable cause standard.

Assuming a decision to prosecute, the legal task of the district attorney is to translate the factual basis of the complaint into the technical language of appropriate statutes, making reasonably certain that the evidence is sufficient to prove all required elements of the crime, from the mental state required of the perpetrator to the consequences of his conduct. Arrest for homicide is necessarily translated into some degree of murder, manslaughter, or related offense. In addition to determining the statutory basis of each charge, the prosecutor must also decide the number of different charges to bring or the number of counts of any particular crime, for in many cases the alleged criminal conduct of a defendant violates several different statutes or he has been arrested for not one but a series of crimes. Issues of joinder or severance, both of offenses and of codefendants into single or separate trials, are complex, controlled in part by statutory law and in part by policies of prosecutors (Remington & Joseph, 1961; Hall et al., 1969). The American Bar Association has issued standards covering these matters (1968c).

When decisions on the charge or charges rest solely on questions of evidence and the probability of conviction, they reflect the legal competence, experience, and confidence of the prosecutor. Under these conditions, the decision is more or less a traditional lawyer's task, justifying both the need for law training and for some experience in the prosecutorial role. More complex and controversial than reading and applying statutes, however, is the broader exercise of the prosecutor's discretion. This makes the office much more than a gatekeeper of the courts, for it enables the prosecutor to determine the *desirability* of prosecution in addition to determining the odds of conviction or acquittal.

The exercise of this discretion, as with charge determination, has both qualitative and quantitative aspects. Qualitatively, the question is whether, in the judgment of the district attorney, the accused *ought* to be charged with a crime at all, or if in the interest of equity, individualization of justice, or mitigating circumstances, it would be fairer, more just, or sufficient for the purposes of law and the objectives of his office to refrain from prosecuting at all. The quantitative facet relates to the *vigor* of prosecution once it is determined to be possible and desirable. In some cases the prosecutor may charge a crime as serious as the evidence permits, may multiply charges to their fullest, or may even level "extra-maximum" charges by invoking habitual-criminal statutes or similar provisions. Contrariwise, he may ignore the highest crime and prosecute for a lesser included offense, perhaps reduce a felony charge to a misdemeanor, or otherwise pursue prosecution with less vigor than both his authority and the evidence would permit. In operation, the exercise of this quantitative discretion often rests on the desire of the state to negotiate a guilty plea. But apart from plea bargaining, this discretion is clearly within the prosecutor's authority and is an important facet at the charging stage of the process (Baker, 1933; Breitel, 1960; Packer, 1964; Davis, 1969; Hall et al., 1969).

Once the district attorney has decided to initiate prosecution, the formal charge is prepared in one of two ways depending upon provisions in the particular jurisdiction. In those states that use the grand-jury system, the prosecutor presents to the jury such evidence as he feels will result in a "true bill"—a formal indictment listing the specific criminal charge or charges on which the defendant will be tried. Grand juries are selected in similar fashion to trial juries, though in composition they are larger and in functioning they are not bound to render a unanimous decision. Typically, such juries are selected and impaneled to meet for a given period of time—a month or a term of the court—acting as needed to consider matters brought to them by the prosecuting attorney. Grand-jury proceedings are secret with neither the defendant nor his counsel normally in attendance. Only the state's side of the case is presented; only that amount of the evidence sufficient to result in indictment need be revealed to the grand jury.

In jurisdictions where the grand jury is not necessary or where it may be waived, the prosecutor drafts the formal charge in an information, testing its sufficiency for bind-over before a judge at a preliminary hearing. This hearing may be waived by the defendant (with consent of the state, which may demand it for a number of reasons, most frequently to preserve testimony which might "disappear" by the time of trial), but, unlike grand-jury proceedings, it is attended by the defendant and counsel and, for that matter, it is open to the press. As with indictment, the prosecutor need introduce only that amount of evidence sufficient to convince the magistrate of probable cause. The defense, however, can challenge the state's evidence if it wishes by cross-examination of witnesses and similar procedures. The defendant has no need to introduce evidence in his own behalf, nor to reply in any way to the evidence presented by the prosecutor, but, at the same time, he cannot demand full disclosure of all the state's evidence. Yet, he may learn something of value to his defense and this is really why defendants, especially those represented by counsel, often demand preliminary hearings. Few defendants actually expect the hearing to result in anything but bind-over; discovery is the major operational motive for defense participation (Fletcher, 1960; Goldstein, 1960). One defendant disadvantage to demanding a hearing is the possibility of adverse publicity because, while it is open to press coverage, it is not a full trial. Generally, only damaging evidence against the defendant is introduced, and partially at that, while the other side of the story, the defense, will not be revealed until the trial, perhaps months in the future.

Arraignment

The next step in the court process is arraignment on the indictment or information, a procedure held in a court of competent trial jurisdiction during which the defendant is notified of his rights (including the right to representation and to jury trial), the formal charges are read, and he is asked to plead to them. Pleas available are not guilty, guilty, and in some instances and at the discretion of the court, *nolo contendere* ("not contested"), a plea that has the criminal effect of conviction but prevents the fact of conviction from being used in any civil damage suits arising from the criminal conduct of the defendants. In some jurisdictions special pleas indicative of particular defenses to criminal liability are also available. "Not guilty because insane" is one of these. Some jurisdictions require disclosure of some anticipated defenses—insanity or an alibi, for example—at arraignment, in order to give the state time before trial to examine the defendant's mental condition or to investigate his whereabouts as stated in his alibi. If a defendant stands mute at arraignment, refusing to respond when asked to plead, or otherwise seems confused, hesitant, or incompetent, a not-guilty plea is entered for him.

If the plea is not guilty, the defendant is bound over for trial at a future date. Bail is reconsidered, with court options to continue bail or recognizance, increase or decrease the amount of the bond, or to deny bail altogether.

If the plea is guilty and is accepted by the court, a future date is set for sentencing with the intervening time used to conduct a presentence investigation. Occasionally, defendants are sentenced immediately after pleading guilty, particularly where mandatory sentences are prescribed so that the judge has no discretion and, therefore, no need for a presentence report. This is comparatively rare and even where it occurs, a correctional *admissions investigation,* similar to the presentence investigation, is often ordered. Although a defendant may plead guilty even with advice of counsel, the judge need not accept the plea, instead ordering the defendant held for trial. This is rare, occurring primarily because the judge somehow feels that the defendant is confused, ill advised, or that conviction as charged is somehow inappropriate. Some trial judges even *acquit* certain defendants even though they have indicated a willingness to plead guilty. Reasons for this are mixed and sometimes quite complex although, in general, these situations occur when the judge is convinced, in considering the total circumstances of the case, that a mandatory sentence following conviction is not warranted (Newman, 1966).

Procedures for accepting guilty pleas are generally simple, cursory, and quick, although the simplicity of the arraignment is now undergoing change. Traditionally, the judge was required to warn the defendant of his rights, to ascertain the "voluntary" basis of the plea, and to inform him of the consequences of his plea. This latter requirement is generally interpreted as requiring the judge to inform the defendant of the maximum sentence he *could* receive, not necessarily to inform him of all lesser alternatives or to reveal the actual sentence that will follow. Within the past few years, the federal and various state court systems have modified guilty-plea procedures, requiring much more elaboration than in the past. Until now the major inquiry at arraignment was directed to the consent of the defendant; that is, the judge was required to determine that the plea was freely and understandingly offered. If the plea was voluntary, free from coercion and wrongful inducement, evidence of actual guilt was superfluous. Now, however, court rules or statutes in a number of jurisdictions require the judge to satisfy himself that there is a "factual basis" for the plea. In short, some evidence of guilt is required, though it is not expressed as "beyond a reasonable doubt" as at the trial. Furthermore, there are some proposals under consideration at present to develop procedures for making plea-negotiation agreements part of the arraignment record [*People* v. *West,* 477 P. 2d 409 (1970) ; Fed. Rules Crim. Proc., Proposed Rev. Rule 11].

Pretrial Motions

Because of Supreme Court decisions in the 1960s restricting certain enforcement practices, pretrial hearings increased on the question of exclusion from trial of certain
evidence held by the state. This increase in pretrial motions was sparked by the expansion of right to counsel, given substantial impetus by the decisions extending the
exclusionary rule (the inadmissibility of illegally seized evidence) to all jurisdictions,
and furthered by the *"Miranda warning"* type of control on the admissibility of confessions. Other decisions placed more stringent controls on evidence obtained from
wiretapping, the use of lineup identification, and other police practices; in each instance the major method of control was exclusion of evidence from trial. Motions to
exclude evidence after the trial has started are generally too late and too cumbersome,
hence pretrial hearings involving these practices are common.

Pretrial-motion hearings are frequent enough today to be considered a distinct
step in the judicial process. It should be noted, however, that Supreme Court holdings
alone are insufficient to account for the increment in such hearings. Increase in enforcement intensity in cases involving organized crime and narcotics, where both
eavesdropping and search are common enforcement techniques, also contributed to
bringing these issues more frequently into criminal litigation. In most jurisdictions
denial of pretrial motions to exclude evidence forces the defendant to go to trial if he
wishes to appeal denial of exclusion; this factor alone may account for a significant
number of demands for trial with corresponding delay in the court processes. Only
New York allows appeal of denial of pretrial motions following a guilty plea [N. Y.
Code Crim. Proc., Sec. 813 (C), 1968 Supp.].

The Trial

Defendants who decide to contest the accusations of the state have the option of a bench
trial—conducted before the judge sitting without a jury—or a jury trial. Actual trial
proceedings in either case are formal and rigidly circumscribed, elaborate ceremonies
when serious felony charges are involved, but more casual, even tawdry, in lower courts
hearing lesser charges. The trial process in some well-publicized cases has deviated
markedly from the ceremonial ideal, with disruptions, violence, and contemptuous behavior—on both sides of the bench (Schwartz, 1971)—evidenced in the courtroom.
Professional organizations have issued standards for the control of courtroom disruptions (American College of Trial Lawyers, 1970) and for the lessening of possibly
prejudicial press and media coverage (American Bar Association, 1968d).

The defendant is presumed innocent at the trial—all other stages of the process,
from arrest on, operate on increasing probability of guilt—with the state having the
burden of proving his guilt as charged, beyond a reasonable doubt. The defendant need
not prove his innocence but only raise sufficient doubts of his guilt to win an acquittal.
A verdict of not guilty terminates the case; protection against double jeopardy bars
retrial. While in a few jurisdictions, the state may appeal an acquittal, the appeal is
limited to matters of law—not to the finding of innocence (Kronenberg, 1959). Should
the jury render a verdict of guilty, the judge may, in his discretion, set aside the verdict if, in his opinion, it is not substantiated by the evidence or is otherwise unwarranted. In fact, he may direct the jury to bring in a verdict of not guilty if, in his
opinion, the evidence is insufficient to convict, but he cannot reverse a jury's decision
to acquit even though he may be convinced personally that the defendant is guilty.

Sentencing

It is common practice in felony cases for the judge to order a presentence investigation of the defendant after he stands convicted by trial or plea. This investigation is usually conducted by the probation staff of the court and, depending upon their orientation, skills, case loads, and the time allowed, the report may pull together a wide variety of information about the offender, partly from official records—police, school, and employment—and partly from interviews with the defendant's family, neighbors, friends, and acquaintances. Depending upon custom, the desire of the judge, and the nature of the case, the report may contain diagnostic evaluation of the offender's personality, predictions of his potential for future criminality, and, perhaps, contain a specific sentence recommendation by the probation officer. Traditionally, the presentence report has been considered a confidential document to be read by the judge alone and not disclosed to the defense (Rubin et al., 1963). Increasingly, however, court decisions, rules, and model sentencing proposals are requiring or recommending at least partial disclosure of the report to the defense to enable them to correct mistakes, inaccuracies, or to otherwise challenge its factual content or conclusions [American Law Institute, 1962; Fed. Rules Crim. Proc., Rule 32 (c), 1962].

The defendant has a right to a sentence hearing and a right to be represented by counsel. At this hearing the trial judge (or in some jurisdictions a council of judges) listens to whatever the defendant has to say, then imposes the sentence he believes to be appropriate within whatever limits are set by statute. Sentencing structures vary considerably from one jurisdiction to another (Columbia Law Review, 1960), with legislation in some instances delegating to the judge wide discretion to choose among types, lengths, and conditions of sentence, but in other jurisdictions limiting alternatives by denying the judge authority to use probation in certain cases or by mandating the imposition of specific minimum or maximum sentences for certain crimes.

A judge can effect a probationary sentence in two ways: he can sentence the offender to a term of imprisonment but suspend *execution* of the sentence and place him on probation, or he can suspend *imposition* of sentence in the first place, putting the offender directly on probation for a specified period of time. Where execution is suspended, should the probation be revoked, the previously imposed sentence is applied. Where imposition of sentence has been suspended, however, the offender must be returned to court, not only for a revocation hearing but to be sentenced on the original charge. In some jurisdictions where suspension of execution was the common practice, offenders whose probation was revoked were sometimes moved directly from field supervision to prison without return to court, with the justification that once sentence was imposed the court had no further jurisdiction, with revocation solely the province of the probation field staff. In 1967, the United States Supreme Court declared a constitutional right to a revocation hearing in a case of "deferred sentencing" at which the defendant had the right of representation by counsel (*Mempa* v. *Rhay*). Subsequently, a number of state and federal appellate courts interpreted the procedural requirements of *Mempa* to apply to all forms of probation revocation, whether the grant technically involved suspended execution or deferred imposition.

THE MERGER OF DECISIONS IN THE CRIMINAL-COURT PROCESS: GUILTY-PLEA PRACTICES

In day-by-day routine operations of criminal courts, a substantial majority of felony convictions and the overwhelming percentage of misdemeanor convictions are recorded by a process far less formal and with fewer distinct steps than the procedural flow of contested cases from arrest to sentencing (Newman, 1966). In the guilty-plea process, including as it does various forms of plea bargaining, a number of steps in process are pro forma, with defendant rights waived, so that, in effect, major decision points of charging, adjudication, and sentencing become merged into a single decision complex (Ohlin & Remington, 1958).

Conviction of defendants by their own pleas of guilty is both the norm and *desideratum* of criminal-court processing much as confession is the bread-and-butter of police investigatory activity. Until recently the guilty plea received little attention in legal literature or sociological research. The plea was assumed to be simply a waiver of trial by the obviously guilty, a quick alternative path from detention in jail to sentence in prison or to probation. Within the past few years, however, both the legal dimensions of pleading guilty and the process by which it is done have come to be seen as much more complex—and much more controversial—than traditionally believed. The guilty-plea process, with all of its variations, is understood today to be more than a simple, fast alternative to trial. Rather, it is *the* major form of criminal adjudication in our criminal system. In operational perspective, the full-scale jury trial, in spite of its ideological significance, is the alternative to a guilty plea rather than the reverse.

This alteration in perception of the importance of the plea came about for a variety of reasons, partly the result of sociological research into the pleading process, partly from appellate-court decisions that have more frequently and more frankly confronted issues in pleading, and partly from total systems analysis such as the President's Commission on Law Enforcement and Administration of Justice and the American Bar Foundation studies. All of these have increased general awareness of the shared nature of decision-making in all of criminal justice, including the consequential link among decisions made at one point to others in the process.

The Guilty Plea

There are a number of reasons why most defendants plead guilty rather than go to trial, the first and foremost being the fact that they are guilty of *some* criminal conduct. The checks and screens in the preadjudication stages are designed to prevent totally innocent persons from being subjected to the cost, inconvenience, and reputational damage of trial. Acquittal at the very end of trial is often a hollow victory for the defense for there are real and sometimes lasting negative effects on persons who are arrested, charged, and tried for a crime although they are eventually acquitted. If a defendant avails himself of all pretrial protections, including his right to legal representation, it is unlikely he will stand convicted by his plea if, in fact, he is totally innocent of the crimes charged. The result is less certain, however, if the screens are waived and the defendant pleads without advice of counsel. Much of the present concern about the plea originated with this possibility.

Most suspects who enter the criminal process—who are stopped and questioned or even arrested by the police—are dropped or diverted from the system at some point prior to trial. In some instances, although suspicion is initially proper, brief interrogation or other investigation shows the suspicion to be inaccurate or otherwise unwarranted. In other cases, though the police may have evidence sufficient to arrest, it does not accumulate to standards sufficient for trial or perhaps it is inadmissible, so the suspects are released. In addition to matters of evidence, all participants—police, prosecutors, and judges—exercise discretion, formally recognized or not, by deciding that some individuals do not deserve or do not need full processing to the point of conviction and sentence though technically, based on available evidence, completion of the process is possible (LaFave, 1965; Newman, 1966; Miller, 1969).

All of these matters—the sufficiency of evidence, the propriety of methods used to gather it, and the exercise of discretion—are applicable to the guilty-plea process as well as to trial. But with the plea they have been muted, they are of low intensity and visibility, submerged in a process of maximum efficiency with such advocacy and contest as exist being informal and sub rosa, occurring in offices and hallways, not before the bench.

As a form of adjudication, the guilty plea has a number of advantages over trial for both the state and the accused. The duality of the advantages accounts for its popularity, for, though it is conceded that most defendants who plead guilty are guilty in fact (though the question of convictability is not the same as guilt), the motivation for pleading guilty, in most cases, is not repentance, but sentencing advantage. Likewise, in accepting pleas, even encouraging them, the state acts less because of the uncertainty of outcome if put to trial, than to achieve the ease and efficiency of the pleading itself. No one is challenged, no proof need be put, and conviction is assured. In order for the guilty-plea system to exist, indeed to prevail, mercy must be exchanged for efficiency and, in general, this is the situation. Sometimes, quite often in fact, there is overt preconviction negotiation for this leniency before the plea is offered and accepted. But most guilty pleas contain the seed of a bargain even without overt negotiation. This "implicit bargain," reflected in differential sentencing leniency shown to those who plead guilty over counterparts convicted only after trial, has been common practice but only recently has it been openly discussed and recognized as operationally significant by judges and others (Remington & Newman, 1962; American Bar Association, 1968a).

The guilty-plea process, and each of its overtly negotiated variations, collapses all of the sequentially distinguishable court decisions into one. Charging and sentencing considerations merge with arraignment used merely to seal the agreement. In effect the prosecutor sentences, while the defendant uses his bargaining power to determine the charge to which he is willing to plead. The skills exhibited by both prosecutor and defense counsel in the pleading process are somewhat different, though reasonably related to the knowledge and art necessary for trial. Negotiation, compromise, and out-of-court settlement are, indeed, part of the lawyer's craft though more commonly associated with civil damage suits and labor negotiations than criminal law. Nevertheless, such settlement of criminal cases is common, even in the norm, in many court systems, with criminal trials infrequent and in some places even involving different actors (Polstein, 1962). Some defense lawyers, prosecutors, and even judges specialize (if at all) in trial work, and they often are not the same personnel who routinely enter and process guilty-plea defendants.

The Negotiated Plea

In routine operation the criminal court has come to depend upon a steady and predictable flow of guilty pleas. Courts are staffed, calendars determined, and budget allocated in anticipation of guilty-plea convictions in about 90 percent of all cases. While it is possible to achieve some of this by relying on the implicit-sentencing bargain to encourage pleading, for many defendants—particularly those who have gone the route before—rewards must be more explicitly stated before they surrender their right to put the state to proof (Newman, 1966). Prearraignment assurance of a sentencing break is the primary defendant motivation in plea negotiation, although softening of the conviction label occasionally has significance beyond or in addition to sentence mitigation. A record of conviction for rape is more repugnant than the label attached to a number of other felonies—burglary, for example—and conviction of a misdemeanor is almost always better than a felony record (Newman, 1966).

Negotiation for pleas takes a number of forms and has somewhat different strategic objectives depending in good part on the type of sentencing structure in a particular jurisdiction. The defendant, of course, hopes to avoid the most severe sentence provided by law and to achieve the greatest leniency he can—he wishes to minimize the maximum and maximize the minimum—and where such sentence limits are fixed in legislation, where there are *mandatory* sentences allowing the judge no discretion to modify them, reduction of the charge is the only way this can be achieved. In jurisdictions where the sentencing judge has wide choice among alternative types and lengths of sentences, charge reduction may be to no avail unless accompanied by a preconviction sentence promise.

While the comparative frequency of different types of plea negotiations varies from jurisdiction to jurisdiction depending, in good part, on the type of sentencing structure in each instance, plea negotiation is present in virtually all jurisdictions with major differences only in the sequential location of bargaining and the number of offices and persons involved in actual negotiations.

The major forms of plea negotiation involve one or a combination of: (1) reduction of charges to lesser offenses; (2) promise of a lenient sentence, most often probation, by the prosecutor in exchange for the plea; (3) conviction on only one count of multiple charges with other charges being dropped or prosecution dismissed; and (4) in some cases the dropping of "super" charges, such as habitual criminal actions. Reduction of charges may be solely a prosecutor's function, especially if it is worked out before indictment or before the information is filed. In some jurisdictions, consent by the judge to reduction of charges is required but as a practical matter it is a rubber-stamp process. It is difficult for a judge to force the state to prosecute on maximum charges if the prosecutor is unwilling to do so. Of course, reduction in charge from a felony to a misdemeanor is almost always a major labeling and sentencing break, but if processing remains on the felony level, common negotiations involve sentence promises instead of or in addition to charge reduction. The sentence-promise type of negotiation is interesting, because normally the judge who has the sole authority to sentence is not directly involved in the negotiation proceedings. Instead, the defendant elicits from the prosecutor a promise to "recommend" or "not to oppose" probation (or some other lesser sentence) in exchange for the guilty plea. The contract is technically not absolutely binding for the prosecutor is not a principal; he cannot actually promise a sentence nor does he have direct responsibility or authority for sentencing. However, many judges routinely ask for the prosecutor's recommendation and tend to follow it, whether in frank support and acknowledgment of the negotiation process or not, so that for most defendants, a promise by the prosecutor is tantamount to a binding contract for leniency. Misunderstandings, even claims of dishonesty, about sentence promises have plagued courts of appeal for, until recently, records of such bargains were rarely kept (Newman, 1966).

The advantages to the defendant of the negotiated conviction encompass all those that flow from the guilty plea itself, and in addition, plea negotiation makes possible measures of equity, fairness, and individualization of justice that are not likely if strict adherence to evidence—slot-machine justice—were the only consideration. From the state's point of view not only is the guilty-plea system—with all of its advantages of efficiency and avoidance of controversy—maintained by plea bargaining, but this process enables the conscientious prosecutor and judge to exercise broader sentencing discretion than provided by strict adherence to legislative mandate. It has been pointed out:

> By downgrading charges and/or by granting probation, the conscientious prosecutor and judge may act to individualize justice by making sensible distinctions between defendants who, although technically guilty of the same criminal conduct, do not deserve either the same record or the same mandatory sentence. Furthermore, plea negotiation and sentencing leniency act to support other parts of the criminal justice system. Leniency in charging or sentencing may be an effective reward for police informers or for cooperative state's witnesses without whom more serious cases could not be developed. Charge reduction and plea negotiation *may* select for the probation staff those offenders most likely to respond to treatment in the community. In short the avoidance of rigidity and slot machine justice—in addition to matters of efficiency and the avoidance of challenge to enforcement methods and quantum of evidence—constitute at least one side of the state's case in plea negotiation (Newman & NeMoyer, 1970:371).

Until very recently, common practices of plea negotiation with accompanying significant administrative consequences were virtually unknown outside the coterie of prosecutors, defense counsel, trial judges, and experienced offenders who participate in the process. Plea bargaining was virtually undiscussed in legal or sociological literature and was of low visibility even to scholars of the courts. It was rarely the basis of appellate litigation and virtually totally ignored in legislation. All this has recently changed. Plea negotiation is currently a matter of interest to researchers and to legal scholars, has recently assumed new importance in appellate litigation, and has been recognized and reflected in court rules and in the minimum standards of the American Bar Association (1968a).

From essentially a sub-rosa process of esoteric interest, plea bargaining has become a matter of major concern and controversy. Questions of the propriety of plea bargaining are now confronting courts, scholars, and various actors in the system, with mixed results. Granting all the advantages of a negotiated justice system, including its use to mitigate the harshness of an automatic sentencing system, questions of its impact on our ideology, of its propriety within our constitutional framework of criminal justice, of its fairness for offenders (some of whom have opportunity to bargain and some do not), and of its impact on the way the general public views court justice in our society are all emerging as issues of major dimensions, all of them as yet unresolved. Whatever the specific concern of critics or supporters of plea bargaining, it is clear that this system of criminal adjudication is much different from the idealized criminal trial though, indeed, it may be no less adversary in its own right.

Critics of negotiated justice argue that it is usurpation of legislative sentencing power by prosecutors and judges. Indeed, the avoidance of legislative mandate is one of the purposes and one of the results of plea negotiation. Supporters of the process answer that negotiation practices simply extend and expand prosecutor and court discretion, enabling justice to be tailored more equitably to the thousands of offenders who pass through the criminal court on their way to jails, prisons, or other correctional programs. Critics argue that inducement of guilty pleas by promises of leniency is really no different from coercion—the third degree—which is clearly an improper basis for law enforcement or adjudication in our society. Opponents answer that inducement and coercion are not different sides of the same coin, that it is quite different and inherently proper to promise and to exercise leniency rather than to threaten, force, or otherwise treat severely. Critics argue with Judge Rives that "Justice and liberty are not the subjects of bargaining and barter" [*Shelton* v. *United States*, 242 F.2d 101, 246 F.2d 571 (5th Cir., 1957)]; opponents point out that plea negotiation already exists as an administrative necessity and that the thing to do is to recognize and control its practice. Critics also argue that plea negotiation lends a general aura of disrespect for the law, comparable to a "fix," and that it breeds cynicism, not reform, in those persons so processed; opponents argue that the purpose of sentencing discretion is to individualize justice, to fit consequences to circumstances, and to do this when such discretion is otherwise prohibited by mandatory sentences. Critics contend that plea negotiation conflicts with both the therapeutic and rational basis of sentencing, allowing sentences to be made in an informal relationship rather than by the careful diagnosis of presentence investigation; proponents, though recognizing the merging of charging and sentencing, propose the establishment of new skills and knowledge in this process, so that both prosecutor and defense become aware of sentencing alternatives and consequences and can appropriately fit cases to different sentence possibilities.

Much about plea negotiation is still unknown, including the full implications of these practices, and much is unresolved. Recently, there have been proposals to recognize the process as appropriate within our court system and to exert some controls on it by building more elaborate procedures into the arraignment process itself [*People* v. *West* (1970); American Bar Association, 1968a]. In a United States Supreme Court case, Chief Justice Burger gave explicit approval to the practice of plea bargaining:

> The disposition of criminal charges by agreement between the prosecutor and the accused, sometimes loosely called "plea bargaining," is an essential component of the administration of justice. Properly administered, it is to be encouraged. If every criminal charge were subjected to a full-scale trial, the States and the Federal Government would need to multiply by many times the number of judges and court facilities.
>
> Disposition of charges after plea discussions is not only an essential part of the process but a highly desirable part for many reasons. It leads to prompt and largely final disposition of most criminal cases; it avoids much of the corrosive impact of enforced idleness during pre-trial confinement for those who are denied release pending trial; it protects the public from those accused persons who are prone to continue criminal conduct even while on pre-trial release; and by shortening the time between charge and disposition, it enhances whatever may be the rehabilitative prospects of the guilty when they are ultimately imprisoned [*Santobello* v. *New York*, 404 U.S. 257 (1971)].

Researchers, legal scholars, and appellate courts will undoubtedly remain occupied with attempts to better understand, describe, and control the process of plea bargaining for, after all, it is the major form of adjudication in our system, and the chief method of operation of our criminal courts.

REFERENCES

American Bar Association.
   1968a   Standards Relating to Pleas of Guilty. American Bar Association Project on Standards for Criminal Justice. Chicago: American Bar Association.
   1968b   Standards Relating to Pretrial Release. American Bar Association Project on Standards for Criminal Justice. Chicago: American Bar Association.
   1968c   Standards Relating to Joinder and Severance. American Bar Association Project on Standards for Criminal Justice. Chicago: American Bar Association.

1968d   Standards Relating to Fair Trial and Free Press. American Bar Association Project on Standards for Criminal Justice. Chicago: American Bar Association.

American College of Trial Lawyers.
1970   Disruption of the Judiciary Process. Chicago: American Bar Association.

American Law Institute.
1962   Model Penal Code. Proposed Official Draft. Philadelphia: American Law Institute.

Baker, Newman F.
1933   "The prosecutor—initiation of prosecution." Journal of Criminal Law and Criminology 23(January–February):770–796.

Baker, Newman F., and Earl DeLong.
1934   "The prosecuting attorney—powers and duties in criminal prosecution." Journal of Criminal Law, Criminology and Police Science 24(March–April):1025–1065.

Blaustein, Albert P., and Charles O. Porter.
1954   The American Lawyer. Chicago: University of Chicago Press.

Blumberg, Abraham S.
1967   Criminal Justice. Chicago: Quadrangle Books.

Breitel, Charles D.
1960   "Controls in criminal law enforcement." University of Chicago Law Review 27(Spring):427–437.

Broeder, Dale.
1954   "The function of the jury—facts or fictions?" University of Chicago Law Review 21(Spring):386–394.

Carlin, Jerome E.
1962   Lawyers on Their Own. New Brunswick, N.J.: Rutgers University Press.

Columbia Law Review.
1960   "Statutory structures for sentencing felons to prison." 60(December):1134–1172.

Cornell Law Quarterly.
1966   "Constitutional law: criminal procedure: waiver of jury trial: *Singer v. United States*, 380 U.S. 24(1966)." 51:339–346.

Davis, Kenneth.
1969   Discretionary Justice: A Preliminary Inquiry. Baton Rouge: Louisiana State University Press.

Dawson, Robert O.
1969   Sentencing: The Decision as to Type, Length and Conditions of Sentence. Boston: Little, Brown.

Fletcher, Robert L.
1960   "Pretrial discovery in state criminal cases." Stanford Law Review 12:293–302.

Foote, Caleb B.
1965   "The coming constitutional crisis in bail." University of Pennsylvania Law Review 113(May):959–999.

Freed, Daniel J., and Patricia M. Wald.
  1964   Bail in the United States: 1964. Working paper of the National Conference
          on Bail and Criminal Justice. Washington, D.C.: National Conference on
          Bail and Criminal Justice.

Goldstein, Abraham S.
  1960   "The state and the accused: balance of advantage in criminal procedure."
          Yale Law Journal 69(June):1149–1199.

Griffiths, John.
  1970   "Ideology in criminal procedure or a third model of the criminal process."
          Yale Law Journal 79(January):359–417.

Grosman, Brian A.
  1969   The Prosecutor. Toronto: University of Toronto Press.

Hall, Livingston, Yale Kamisar, Wayne R. LeFave, and Jerold H. Israel.
  1969   Modern Criminal Procedure. St. Paul, Minn.: West Publishing Co.

Harvard Law Review.
  1966   "Preventive detention before trial." 79(May):1489–1510.

Johnstone, Quintin, and Dan Hopson, Jr.
  1967   Lawyers and Their Work. Indianapolis: Bobbs-Merrill.

Kalven, Harry, Jr., and Hans Zeisel.
  1966   The American Jury. Boston: Little, Brown.

Kronenberg, Jerry.
  1959   "A right of a state to appeal in criminal cases." Journal of Criminal Law,
          Criminology and Police Science 49(January–February):473–486.

LaFave, Wayne R.
  1965   Arrest: The Decision to Take a Suspect into Custody. Boston: Little, Brown.

LaFont, H. M.
  1960   "Assessment of punishment—a judge or jury function?" Texas Law Review
          38:835–846.

McIntyre, Donald M.
  1968   "A study of judicial dominance of the charging process." Journal of Crimi-
          nal Law, Criminology and Police Science 59(December): 463–490.

Miles, Arthur P.
  1963   The Self-Image of the Wisconsin Probation and Parole Agent. Madison:
          Division of Correction, Wisconsin State Department of Public Welfare.

Miller, Frank W.
  1969   Prosecution: The Decision to Charge a Suspect with a Crime. Boston: Little,
          Brown.

Morse, Wayne.
  1931   "A survey of the grand jury system." Oregon Law Review 10:101–295.

Nedrud, Duane R.
  1960   "The career prosecutor." Journal of Criminal Law, Criminology and Police
          Science 51(September–October):343–355.

Newman, Donald J.
  1956   "Pleading guilty for considerations: a study of bargain justice." Journal of
          Criminal Law, Criminology and Police Science 46(March–April):780–790.

1966   Conviction: The Determination of Guilt or Innocence Without Trial. Boston: Little, Brown.

Newman, Donald J., and Edgar C. NeMoyer.
1970   "Issues of propriety in negotiated justice." Denver Law Journal 47:367–407.

Oaks, Dallin H., and Warren Lehman.
1968   A Criminal Justice System and the Indigent. Chicago: University of Chicago Press.

Ohlin, Lloyd E., and Frank J. Remington.
1958   "Sentence structure: its effect upon systems for the administration of criminal justice." Law and Contemporary Problems 23(Summer):495–507.

Packer, Herbert L.
1964   "Two models of the criminal process." University of Pennsylvania Law Review 113(November):1–68.

Polstein, Robert.
1962   "How to settle a criminal case." Practical Lawyer 8(January):35–44.

President's Commission on Law Enforcement and Administration of Justice.
1967a   Task Force Report: The Courts. Washington, D.C.: U.S. Government Printing Office.
1967b   Task Force Report: Corrections. Washington, D.C.: U.S. Government Printing Office.

Remington, Frank J., and Allen Joseph.
1961   "Charging, convicting and sentencing." Wisconsin Law Review 1961(July):528–565.

Remington, Frank J., and Donald J. Newman.
1962   "The Highland Park Institute on sentence disparity." Federal Probation 26(March):3–9.

Remington, Frank J., Donald J. Newman, Edward L. Kimball, Marygold Melli, and Herman Goldstein.
1969   Criminal Justice Administration: Material and Cases. Indianapolis: Bobbs-Merrill.

Rubin, Sol, Henry Weihofen, George Edwards, and Simon Rosenweig.
1963   The Law of Criminal Correction. St. Paul, Minn.: West Publishing Co.

Schwartz, Herman.
1971   "Judges as tyrants." Criminal Law Review 7(March):129–138.

Silverstein, Lee.
1956   Defense of the Poor in Criminal Cases in American State Courts. Chicago: American Bar Association.

Skolnick, Jerome H.
1966   Justice Without Trial. New York: Wiley.

Virginia Law Review.
1967   "Jury sentencing in Virginia." 53(May):968–1101.

Wood, Arthur Lewis.
1967   Criminal Lawyer. New Haven: Yale College and University Press.

CHAPTER **16**

Role Determinants in Juvenile Court

Robert M. Emerson

University of California at Los Angeles

Reflecting an optimistic faith in the ideal of individualized justice, humanitarian reformers pushed the creation of juvenile courts throughout the country during the first decades of this century. Following the model of the first juvenile court established in Illinois in 1899, the philosophy of the new courts emphasized treatment and rehabilitation as the appropriate goals of state intervention in the lives of youth, the use of wide-ranging "scientific" diagnostic inquiry to identify the causes of delinquency problems, and informal, flexible procedures for conducting courtroom hearings in pursuit of these goals. The judge was to function as a fatherly clinician, conducting the hearing so as to maximize personal rapport with the child, directing the investigation into the causes of the delinquency, and implementing a detailed treatment plan giving priority to the care, guidance, and protection of the youth. Illegal offense was to be subordinate to social background:

> The problem to be determined by the judge is not, "Has this boy or girl committed a specific wrong?" but "What is he, how has he become what he is, and what would best be done in his interest . . . to save him from a downward career?" (Mack, 1912:198).

Underlying this philosophy was the assumption that the juvenile court, since it dispensed treatment not punishment, had no interest other than that of the child. Rather than facing charge and punishment, the youth "is alleged to have committed an offense and a petition is filed in his behalf" (Young, 1937:182). While under some circumstances counsel might participate, adversary concerns were antithetical to the nature of court proceedings. The protections afforded by the rules of criminal procedure were unnecessary, and strict rules of evidence, cross-examination of witnesses, and the right to remain silent were not guaranteed.

The strong humanitarian concerns of the founders of the juvenile court, however, were inlaid with authoritarian assumptions and practices. An emphasis on "discipline" and control underlay their efforts to "save" youth from the vices, crimes, and sins prevalent on the urban scene. As Platt notes, "The child-savers . . . were most active and successful in extending governmental control over a whole range of youthful activities that had previously been ignored or dealt with informally" (1969:99). Moreover, underlying the early juvenile-court movement were strong, if often tacit, class and ethnic commitments, apparent in the concern with reforming the way of life of the poor and the foreign. "It was not by accident that the behavior selected for penalizing by the child-savers—drinking, begging, roaming the streets, frequenting dance-halls and movies, fighting, sexuality, staying out late at night, and incorrigibility—was primarily attributable to the children of lower-class and immigrant families" (p. 139).

As the crusading fervor of this "child-saving movement" declined and the juvenile court became an established institution, skepticism toward the realities of juvenile-court practice grew. More and more observers noted that punishment and control were frequent, if not dominant, concerns in the court, that despite the growing professionalization of treatment in the court, rehabilitation often existed in name only, and that the interests of the child were routinely subordinated to the organizational requirements of court and probation bureaucracies and to community and law-enforcement pressures for order and punishment. By the 1960s this skepticism and discontent had coalesced into two complementary forces for change, one primarily procedural and the other substantive in focus.

The procedural critique of the juvenile court, in early statements by Edward Lindsey (1914) and somewhat later by Paul Tappan (1949), emphasized the reality of the punishments and sanctions imposed by the court in arguing for the need to reinstitute the protections of due process. As Francis Allen was to note later:

> the business of the juvenile court inevitably consists, to a considerable degree, in dispensing punishment. If this is true, we cannot more avoid the problems of unjust punishment in the juvenile court than in criminal court (1964:18).

During the past decade procedural changes along these lines have transformed the juvenile court. The 1961 California juvenile-court reform, studied in detail by Lemert (1970), ensured many procedural protections, including right to counsel, separate adjudication and dispositional hearings, and stricter standards of evidence. But the major impetus was provided by the 1967 U.S. Supreme Court decision in the *Gault* case (*In re Gault*, 387 U.S. 1). This ruling held that a minor had to be told the specific charges against him, had a right to an attorney, to confront and cross-examine complainants and witnesses, and could not be forced to make self-incriminatory statements. Since the *Gault* decision, the movement toward procedural due process in the juvenile court has made marked, if nonuniform, progress; a number of constitutional protections have been extended to youth, proceedings have taken on a more formal and "legalistic" character, and lawyers have come to play a regular, if uneasy, role in hearings (Lefstein et al., 1969; Platt, 1969; Lemert, 1970).

A second, more substantive discontent with the juvenile court focused on its efforts to prevent delinquency. In intervening to help youths who seem headed toward delinquency, the court could act in self-defeating ways. Too often court actions effectively stigmatized youths as delinquent in ways that tended to establish and perpetuate, rather than cure, their delinquency. In practice, contact with the juvenile court constituted a stigma that "gets translated into effective handicaps by heightened police surveillance, neighborhood isolation, lowered receptivity and tolerance by school officials, and rejections of youths by prospective employers" (Lemert, 1967:92). This observation led to the policy recommendation that the juvenile court explicitly abolish prevention as a goal in favor of a philosophy of "judicious nonintervention":

> [The court] is properly an agency of last resort for children, holding a doctrine analogous to that of appeal courts which require that all remedies be exhausted before a case will be considered. This means that problems accepted for action by the juvenile

court will be demonstrably serious by testable evidence ordinarily distinguished by a history of repeated failures at solutions by parents, relatives, schools, and community agencies (Lemert, 1967:96).

In this way juvenile-court operations would be narrowed and explicitly organized around its control functions.

This chapter will pursue these substantive issues, drawing illustrations and examples mainly from a case study of the operations of "Eastern Juvenile Court" (Emerson, 1969),[1] and discussing a number of the current problems and issues confronting the contemporary juvenile court.

THE LOCAL CONTEXT OF COURT ACTIVITIES

Perhaps one of the strongest themes of recent research on the juvenile court is the need to view the court as it operates within and is affected by its local environment (e.g., Vinter, 1967:84–87; Cicourel, 1968:58–62, 172–79; Emerson, 1969:29–80). The juvenile court does not function as an isolated, largely autonomous institution. Rather, its activities take place in and are shaped by its local institutional and community context and the pressures and demands emanating therefrom.

Local pressures on the juvenile court take two different forms, reflecting distinct orders of local ties and interests in its activities. On the one hand are fairly diffuse pressures and expectations from the local community, frequently mobilized and expressed by the news media and local political figures. On the other hand are the more focused, concrete demands from local institutions specifically concerned with the control and care of youth.

The Community Setting. One striking feature of many juvenile courts is their strong ties with the local political system.[2] Judges are elected in some states and appointed by the state governor in others. In the latter case they frequently have been his close political protégés, especially where appointments by the governor need not be from the nominees of an apolitical board or commission. Juvenile-court probation positions are often regarded as prime patronage appointments, although increasingly subject to civil service requirements in many areas. Thus, when probation openings appeared in Eastern Juvenile Court, the judge routinely expected a variety of political pressures to fill them, noting in one such instance that he had received so many contacts that "no matter who you take, you're going to make someone mad." Furthermore, juvenile courts require more financial support from local governments than local criminal courts, where fines may offset much of their operating costs. In many areas juvenile-court judges, probation officers, and court clerks actively participate in political party affairs.

In general, dependence upon the political system tends to increase court sensitivity to pressures for *controlling and restraining delinquent youths.* Here the demands and interests of politicians, the press, and community seem to complement and reinforce one another: local politicians often use the occurrence of sensational crimes committed by youths or local "crime waves" as occasions to oppose "crime in the streets" and to press

1. Cases and observations presented without citation in this chapter have been taken from the original field notes collected during this research, unless otherwise noted.

2. Ties between the juvenile court and local political bodies in Eastern City are discussed in Emerson, 1969:chap. 1, 33–38. For a description of the differing political contexts of two California juvenile courts, see Cicourel, 1968:172–74.

for a "get tough" policy on the part of the courts. The local press often provides the initial opportunity for such tactics, giving intensive coverage to some crime, identifying and publicizing "crime waves" and prominently displaying "law and order" statements by politicians. Here both politicians and the press tend to organize and shape community concern over these issues, as well as to reflect and express it. As a result of these processes, the juvenile court and "delinquency" typically become live local issues with demands for upholding public order. As Vinter has noted, court treatment goals are rarely the object of such public attention and support (1967:85).

One consequence is that juvenile-court decision-making comes to be pervaded by a sense of *vulnerability* to adverse public reaction for failing to control or restrain delinquent offenders. Such public concern often is focused on cases involving violent, perhaps dramatic, and newsworthy offenses. These cases become publicly visible, and the juvenile-court's decisions may be subject to specific scrutiny and criticism.[3] Under these circumstances the court staff feels strong pressure to impose maximum restraints on the offender—in most instances, incarceration. Anything less risks immediate criticism. But more than this, it also exposes the court to the possibility of even stronger reaction in the future. For given any recurrence of serious illegal activity, former decisions that can be interpreted as "lenient" become difficult to defend. A judge's comments on the problems posed by these most serious offenses reveal these concerns:

> Since I've been on the bench I have heard several attempted murder cases. In one of these a son had tried to kill his father. On the basis of the psychiatric evaluation I decided to take a chance on it and instead of referring the youth upstairs for criminal (adult) trial, kept the case in juvenile court, committing the youth to YCA so he would be released sooner. I just hope I don't read in the paper one day that he went out and killed somebody.

In its routine activities, however, the court's decisions are not directly affected by such pressures. For by and large, the insulating mechanisms of the juvenile-court structure—the exclusion of the public and press from hearings, nondisclosure of names of juveniles—along with the minor nature of most delinquent offenses, give most court decisions extremely low visibility in the community at large (Goldstein, 1960). Thus, these locally generated pressures on the court for control and restriction are not constant and pervasive.

However, even where the current offense is not particularly violent or serious, the court becomes vulnerable should the delinquent commit such a highly visible act in the future. Thus, any particular disposition, no matter how obvious, appropriate, and defensible it was at the time, can subsequently become evidence of the court's "coddling," overleniency in failing to "protect the community," or outright gullibility, if and when the youth involved commits a newsworthy and sensational offense.

The kinds of pressures analyzed above often introduce a fundamental restrictiveness into the court's handling of its cases. Particular decisions have to anticipate possible adverse public and political reaction. Decisions that might open the court to criticism constitute risks and may well be avoided. Indeed, "risk" specifically reflects the court's vulnerability to criticism for having failed to control and restrain. The

---

3. From police contacts the news media may pick up and report on dramatic or otherwise newsworthy delinquencies. Press coverage may include the details of the incident and perhaps the juvenile-court's ultimate disposition of the matter, although not identifying juveniles by name. In these instances, then, juvenile-court proceedings are "secret" only in a relative sense; it is often public knowledge that there is an accused and that the court is trying the matter.

"safe," defensible disposition is the restrictive, protect-the-community one; to make any other disposition thus comes to involve "taking a chance." The chance is the unknown consequence that may "blow the lid right off," opening the court and its personnel to basic attack and criticism. The court's political and communal ties place presumptive value on restraint and control.

Complainant Pressures. More pertinent than these general community and political pressures for the juvenile-court's day-to-day activities are the immediate demands and interests of those initiating delinquency complaints. For while the juvenile court is fairly well shielded "from generalized public pressures," by that very fact it becomes particularly "exposed to the demands of those units with which it has most frequent contact" (Vinter, 1967:86). Moreover, pressures from these sources, including police, schools, social agencies, and parents, are specific and case-focused. Dealing with these immediate complainant demands is a pervasive and recurrent concern for the court, and constitutes a fundamental constraint on how it processes cases.

Some complainant interests involve highly situational and short-run concerns. The police, in particular, often seek court support against visible challenges to their authority; e.g., they may push to have a youth who has been "fresh" with them held in detention pending hearing. The court may accede to such pressure perhaps, in part, to allow the complainant to cool off. The strength of complainant pressures, even on such short-run issues, becomes a critical consideration in the court's disposition of cases. In such instances, the basic sense in which the court comes to attend to and deal with cases as *complaints about trouble* becomes apparent. At an extreme, decisions may be made not so much to control or help a delinquent as to placate or satisfy an irate and/or powerful complainant (for examples, see Emerson, 1969:86, 102–3). In less extreme instances as well, the court is fundamentally oriented to this sense in which it is being asked to "do something" about a trouble by taking some account of the interests and pressures of complainants. Thus, it can be suggested that one problem confronting the juvenile court is exactly that of *showing complainants that they are doing something*.

But there are also complainant pressures for more consequential and long-term action by the court, reflecting a different set of control contingencies. The situation of the police is particularly critical here.

Many delinquency cases are initiated by juvenile officers, police officers assigned to handle all complaints about youths or investigations of offenses felt to involve youths. Rarely, if ever, making on-the-spot apprehensions of delinquents, the work of the juvenile officer centers on investigating and solving the wide variety of complaints about youthful misbehavior and trouble-making (Werthman & Piliavin, 1967:68–75). A school is broken into, a neighbor complains that kids are breaking his windows, a bike is stolen, storekeepers complain about petty shoplifting or gatherings of youths who intimidate customers. These are the routine kinds of matters that juvenile officers handle.[4]

In dealing with and disposing of such cases, police concern often lies in "keeping peace" rather than in "enforcing the law" (Bittner, 1967). The power to arrest and to initiate juvenile-court cases is routinely a tool or threat used to maintain or establish

---

4. With regard to the police, Cicourel notes: "The amount of time devoted to activities having little or nothing to do with popular or sociological conceptions of crime is impressive. The police spend considerable time answering calls that prove to be 'dead ends,' or they are called in to settle family disputes, or the 'counseling' or punishment of children for family problems, and the like" (1968:87).

some kind of order in the local community. Particularly where minor infractions are involved, juvenile officers typically try to deal with the case informally, where this may entail mediating between the youth and the complainant in order to settle the differences between them. Thus, the juvenile-officer's job involves not so much solving crimes committed by youths as *dealing with* and trying to *settle complaints* about legally ambiguous troubles attributed to youth. (This proceeds within the dual constraints of stopping further complaints and keeping the youth from making further trouble.) One juvenile officer emphasized this goal and procedure in the following terms:

> I try to settle as many cases as I can out of court. A broken window or complaints from neighbors can be handled without going up to the court. When a youngster does something like that it can be handled here in the station between the parents and the child and the person who complains.

In dealing informally with community troubles, the power to arrest and to initiate court action becomes a strategic weapon used to cajole and negotiate settlements, often by threatening the youth into better behavior. Official action provides a resource for influencing behavior, and may be invoked only as a "last resort." In these terms court action is often initiated when the police feel that mediation and attempts at informal handling have failed or are inappropriate. In the first instance, attempts to mediate a settlement may fail when a complainant refuses to compromise and insists on official action, or when the accused youth or his parents resist such settlement. Thus, a juvenile officer provided the following account of how one case ended up in court:

> I had a case once with damages to a car running about $75 to $150. I had the kid in here and he admitted it but the parents wouldn't pay. So the owner said, "Well, I'll take the kid to court." So the kid went to court on his complaint, but he didn't get it. He thought if he took the case to court he would force them to pay damages.

Under a variety of circumstances, however, the police come to feel that informal handling is inappropriate. Thus, court action may be initiated when a policeman has his authority assaulted or challenged in what otherwise might be an inconsequential encounter with a youth. Or, when a youth seems to be regularly getting into trouble and has received a number of "breaks" with unofficial handling of prior incidents, even trivial matters may be seized on in order to get him before the court.

In these situations, where unofficial control and settlement procedures have not worked or are inappropriate, the police go to court to get backing for their control efforts (Bohannan & Huckleberry, 1967). Court backing may take either a routine or an extreme form. In the former, the police want and expect the court to use its authority to sanction and intimidate those juvenile troublemakers who have continued to generate complaints and hence disturb the local peace. In this sense, the police bring into court youths they have had difficulty in managing informally and pressure the court to supplement their controlling efforts with its own supervision and authority. In these instances, the police expect the court to find the youth delinquent, give him a stiff lecture, put him on probation or give him a suspended sentence, and supervise and control his activities in such a way as to discourage him from making more trouble.

More extreme "backing up" is sought where both internal control measures and the threat of court sanction fail (or are felt to be too costly). Here pressure is exerted to have the court remove from the community those persistent troublemakers who have come to be regarded as "uncontrollable" and hopeless. Thus, the police pressure the court to incarcerate the delinquent who has committed a large number of offenses or who has committed a particularly vicious and serious one. This kind of concern is reflected in the following informal comments:

> In the probation office a policeman was talking about a boy who had been stealing handbags in his district. He grabbed them from young and old alike—no one was safe on the streets. The policeman bemoaned the trouble this youth was causing the police: "This Taylor kid . . . he's killing us" (Emerson, 1969:43).

In such cases the police want the youth "off the streets," i.e., out of the community where his misconduct is producing a constant stream of complaints from citizens.

Similarly, a number of other community institutions regularly bring cases to court in order to support and reinforce their internal efforts to control youthful troublemakers. In the public school system, one of the most important of these institutions, court complaints may be initiated by vice-principals or deans in charge of school discipline, truant officers assigned to enforce compulsory attendance laws, and administrators of special schools for those youths who have been expelled from the regular school system. As with the police, these school agents generally take court action after initial attempts to correct the problem have failed. Thus, delinquency charges are used after a period of unsuccessful pressuring and bargaining to settle the trouble.

For example, a truancy complaint often represents a request that the court involve itself in an intractable control problem. As a truant officer commented when asked when he would take a youth to court: "Only when it's impossible. You try everything and get nowhere. . . . The only time's where nothing works. Then you have to do something" (Emerson, 1969:53). In this sense, a truant is not simply a child who has refused to attend school, but one who has done so while resisting all efforts to the contrary.

Court cases initiated by other school agents often reflect similar contingencies of institutional control. While school complaints frequently cite a specific incident of trouble, even a clear legal violation, such as assaulting a teacher or another student, formal court action often represents a more general appeal for supportive action in dealing with what is felt to be a long-standing control problem. The court is entreated either to use its authority to get the youth to conform, or to get rid of him. In the first instance, the court is expected to provide a realistic, supplementary threat to a tenuous situation of control; in the second, to remove a disruptive troublemaker.

Similar control problems and pressures often appear in incorrigible or runaway complaints initiated by parents against their children. What emerges in these situations is often a request that the court back up parental authority and control, which are felt to be under attack or ineffectual. Thus, parents may complain that their offspring refuse to obey them, stay out late without permission, hang around with the wrong friends, or date undesirable boys. In all cases they are requesting the court to throw its support behind their efforts to control or put a stop to such behaviors.

Finally, child-care institutions, particularly the child-welfare agencies, may initiate complaints of runaway and incorrigible children for substantively similar reasons. Here it must be emphasized initially that the court's relations with the variety of treatment resources dealing with children tend to be funneled through the public agencies. Private child-welfare agencies have close control over client selection, tending both to avoid undesirable and difficult cases and to shift the most troublesome to public agencies. Thus, as a public agency caseworker commented about the agency's case load:

> All the cases I get are trouble. For the Department receives most of its cases from other agencies who have decided they can no longer do anything for them. . . . The Child

Abuse League and Family Service refer cases they feel "cannot benefit from their work." A great deal of our cases are cases that other people have looked at and decided they can't do anything for. Or they are referred because they are "too complex," involving too many problems and requiring a great deal of work (Emerson, 1969:58).

Dealing with the least desirable and most troublesome children, control becomes the dominant organizational problem for the public child-welfare agencies. Under these circumstances, the court's capacity to apply coercive sanctions provides a necessary and even essential service. On the one hand, cases may be taken to court to reinforce the internal control regime of a public institution. Thus, incorrigibility complaints may be filed against youth who have made little or no effort to adjust to the rules of the institution. On the other hand, where a youth is felt to be unmanageably disruptive, perhaps even with court backing and support, court action may seek his incarceration in reform school. These contingencies are particularly pressing for the older boys who had moved through and been rejected by many of the local residential placements. The juvenile court and reform schools ultimately help public agencies eliminate these "hard-to-place" youths who have exhausted all placement options, including those usually regarded as "last resorts."

In conclusion, agencies in regular contact with the juvenile court typically appeal to it for control purposes. Demands for more effective coercive sanctions, and not directly or immediately for treatment, lie behind many delinquency complaints. More generally, the most sought-after power the court has is exactly its control of access to the state's correctional system. Primary control agents often come to feel that even the court's supplemental control efforts are inadequate and press to have troublemakers regarded as unmanageable, time consuming, or dangerous taken off their hands completely by incarceration. In an important sense, then, the court has the ability to serve these primary control agencies by eliminating from their case loads those youths who have proved persistently difficult or unmanageable. In this way the state youth correctional system comes to serve as an institutionally vital "dumping ground" for youths judged "hopeless" or uncontrollable by routine control methods, including those invoked by the court itself (Emerson, 1969:63–72).

TREATMENT AND INTERINSTITUTIONAL DEPENDENCE

Whether and to what extent the court goes along with or resists complainant pressures depends in large part upon the specific relations and obligations it develops with the complaining organization. Briefly, when the court becomes dependent upon another organization for services or resources, pressures and demands emanating from that organization cannot be easily ignored. And somewhat paradoxically, the court incurs such obligations and enters into more dependent relations with these organizations largely in pursuit of goals central to its own distinctive treatment commitments. Specifically, the juvenile court has two general strategies available for providing services to help or treat delinquents: first, to try to develop autonomous court programs and facilities; second, to develop access to existing community facilities and resources. In either case, however, the juvenile court is drawn into relations with local institutions which often involve obligations at odds with its helping and treatment purposes.

The local political system provides one main avenue for securing and expanding treatment facilities. Judges may draw heavily on their knowledge and connections in local politics to press for court programs and services. For example, through political contacts and pressure, a judge may obtain a court clinic to test and evaluate delinquent youth. Such a result reaffirms and strengthens ties to the political system and to the public pressures emanating from it.

In addition, court treatment goals require routine cooperation with community agents concerned with the control and/or care of children. For example, juvenile-court staff have to rely heavily upon both police and schools in trying to work with delinquents on probation in the community. In the first place, probation officers are often almost totally dependent upon community sources, especially the police and the schools, for information about the day-to-day activities of their probationers (e.g., whether a boy is drinking frequently, taking drugs, hanging around with undesirable peers, or having trouble with his family). Second, the juvenile court is dependent on the police and other local institutions for more active support in its decisions about how to handle cases in the community. This becomes critical when probation officers begin to "work with" a youth, and may have to call upon police and other officials for support and cooperation. Successful probation work often entails both continuing negotiations with police over what is being done with a particular youth and persistent pleadings to put up with a certain amount of trouble during this time.

Similar relations arise with the schools. A probation officer may want to keep a youth in school, and yet find that the school regards the youth as a troublemaker and wants to get rid of him. The commitment to treatment then leads court personnel to urge the school to accept or keep a delinquent who would otherwise be expelled. These problems may be accentuated in dealings with special schools for problem pupils within the public-school system. Juvenile courts frequently develop close ties with such schools and thereby are more able to obtain this kind of tolerance. But in so doing the court incurs obligations to the school, generally to go along with its requests for restrictive court action in other cases involving more "serious problems" (for such an instance, see Emerson, 1969:52–54).

Third, the juvenile court actively seeks to establish close working ties with a variety of local institutions for the specific purpose of influencing the selection and recruitment of court cases. Associated with the court's treatment goals is a commitment to preventing delinquency, leading, in turn, to a concern with *predelinquency* (Lemert, 1967:93–94). Court staff feel they should deal not only with the obviously delinquent, but also with youths moving toward delinquency or having "delinquent tendencies." Yet the court knows that those agencies that regularly initiate delinquency complaints tend to pass over just these cases; their interest centers more on immediate troublemakers than on currently manageable youths. "Predelinquents," then, are just those youths least likely to be brought before the court, and special efforts must be made if this selection process is to be modified.

Relations with the police are considered particularly critical here. The court recognizes that the police, especially when younger (preadolescent) children are involved, are predisposed toward unofficial solutions, such as sending the youth home with a lecture and "a kick in the pants." The court tries to get these cases brought in, but to do so effectively requires some cooperation with, and hence dependence upon, the police.

These issues are vividly illustrated in Eastern City by the court's relations with the downtown department stores, largely mediated through the police, over the handling of shoplifting cases (Emerson, 1969:50–51). For court staff typically regard shoplifting as a minor, even trivial, offense in itself, yet consider it critical in delinquency prevention to see these cases. Thus, the judge noted about shoplifters:

It helps us to get them early. . . . We want them in. Some of the most serious cases are shoplifters. . . . If they break the law two or three times without getting caught, they think they can get away with it. . . . It hurts them in the long run [to be kept out of court]. For the court shoplifting is one way to grab them quick and stop them.

As these remarks reveal, official complaints in shoplifting cases give the court a hold over youths, and hence an opportunity to review their background and character for signs of trouble. But the court could not count on the department stores to bring in all, or even most, of these cases. Enforcement practices in the stores were *known* to lead to the release of exactly those youths who appeared most normal and nondelinquent on the surface. Special efforts had to be made to get such cases into court. One such effort devised by an earlier judge entailed making adjudications of delinquent shoplifting complaints without requiring the testimony (or presence) of the store detective who had made the actual apprehension and arrest. Conviction could thus rest solely on testimony from the policeman called to the store from central headquarters to handle the case at this later point. A new judge discontinued this practice when he took over (feeling it clearly unconstitutional). The number of shoplifting cases then decreased significantly as court action became more time-consuming and costly for store personnel. This judge continued to press the stores to bring these cases to court. Some immediate accommodations, such as promising to minimize the amount of time store detectives would have to spend in court, had to be made to encourage cooperation. Less apparent are the long-term effects of such ties: in particular, a sympathy with the control problems confronting the stores.

Similar tendencies marked relations between the court and the public schools. As noted earlier, schools are primarily interested in the juvenile court for control purposes. Given some court reluctance to go along with these pressures, relations between schools and court frequently become strained. Lemert has pointed to "the lengthy history of conflict between juvenile court workers and school officials, in which the former accuse the school people of foisting off their own failures onto the court, and the latter replying heatedly that the court is unresponsive or does nothing about really mean kids" (1967: 99). Under these circumstances, the court's commitment to detecting and treating the marginally delinquent tends to weaken its position to resist school pressures to incarcerate these "really mean kids." In the Eastern Juvenile Court, "school problems" were viewed as one of the main indicators and causes of future delinquency, and school agents were entreated to bring children who had such "behavior problems" before the court as soon as possible. In doing this, however, the court incurred obligations to school officials that made it difficult to stand against their demands to get rid of school troublemakers (Emerson, 1969:52–55).

Finally, juvenile-court efforts to arrange residential placement, generally as a treatment alternative to reform school for youths in "serious trouble," tend to create similar dependencies. Juvenile courts often consider such placements, usually in group or foster homes, their most desirable treatment option. Yet access to such placements is largely channeled through the state or local agencies that provide the necessary financing. Relations with such agencies, therefore, are particularly critical for the court, and a great deal of time and effort goes into developing and sustaining close working ties. In return for helping make and paying for placements for court cases, these agencies expect backup support from the court to maintain control over youths in their care. These obligations are not always rigid, however, as each agency recognizes the legal and organizational constraints on the other that might prevent granting any particular request. Thus, the court recognizes that its requests for placements for delinquents might not work out in many instances (e.g., with "hard-to-place" delinquents, such as an older boy with a record of violence). Similarly, the agencies expect the court to be open to the possibility of committing their problem wards to the state correctional facilities, but recognize that in many cases the court will not feel this to be justified. Nevertheless, these exchanges create obligations that cannot be easily ignored by either party.

As a result of reciprocal obligations, control over initiating and negotiating placements for delinquents in Eastern Juvenile Court shifted almost inevitably into the hands of the child-welfare department (Emerson, 1969:59–72). This agency, however, was constrained by the strategic considerations of distributing large numbers of children within a set number of placement slots and maintaining access to as many slots as possible. On the one hand, the department could not lightly risk alienating a scarce placement resource by pushing an "unrealistic" candidate likely to act up and cause trouble. Such a placement, if unsuccessful, would threaten any future placement there. On the other hand, the department often could not adopt the strategy of pushing one particularly needy (but hard-to-place) candidate, but put forward the candidate most qualified for the slot to reduce the risk of losing the vacancy entirely. To try to place a likely "troublemaker" meant giving a scarce opening to a child not likely to retain it, and denying that opening to one more qualified who would have succeeded.

The result was to subject the juvenile court to the underlying bias of the child-placement system against "delinquents," where any child who had court contact was perceived as a dangerous troublemaker to be avoided at all costs. In practice, the public agency pushed the court to seek only "realistic" placements, a requirement which effectively undercut court efforts to place "hardcore" cases. With these delinquents, then, it was often impossible to obtain placement as a treatment alternative, even where the court staff was willing to take the risks involved.

In summary, the juvenile-court's quest for treatment services and resources draws it into a network of mutual obligations and dependencies with local organizations. As well as tending to undermine judicial autonomy in ways stressed by Vinter (1967) and others, increased susceptibility to local pressures generally pushes the court in restrictive, even punitive, directions in accord with the recurrent control interests of the organizations involved. But while the court must usually take these demands into account, it does not simply give in to them. While the police may press to have a "troublemaker" taken off the streets, or a welfare agency may want a problem ward sent to reform school, the court employs its own standards for assessing the appropriateness of such actions. In particular, whatever the strength of complainant pressure, the court feels it either premature or inappropriate to incarcerate youths who do not appear to them either "hopelessly" or "seriously" delinquent. In this sense demands for control are filtered through the court's own procedures for judging the seriousness of any particular case and the necessity for any particular response. The following sections will consider these procedures for processing delinquency cases.

TROUBLE, MORAL CHARACTER, AND DELINQUENT CAREERS

Basic to juvenile-court processing of youths charged with delinquency is a distinction between mild and serious cases. This distinction does not rest simply on the delinquent offense. Acts that would constitute felonies if committed by adults comprise a very small percentage of juvenile-court case loads. When such cases do come before the court, the gravity of the offense and the accompanying publicity and controversy set them off as exceptional. Serious offenses are handled as special cases, receiving special care and

procedures that differ fundamentally from the ways of handling more routine delinquencies. Verbally court staff underline this distinction by noting, for example, that
certain procedures are normal "unless it's an extremely vicious act."[5]

Most petitions brought before the juvenile court involve minor offenses in strict
legal terms—"kid's stuff"—including less serious misdemeanors and youth-specific
violations, such as runaway, incorrigible, and curfew infractions. In their routine work
with these cases, concerns with personal, family, and community "problems," "not the
notion of serious crime, seem to orient the probation officer's definition of juvenile
delinquency" (Cicourel, 1968:102). Specifically, the juvenile court routinely attends
less to the legal offense than to the presence of "problems" or "trouble." Thus, a judge
noted that in conducting hearings:

> we look for tip-offs that something is really wrong. We get some tip-offs just from the
> fact-sheet; truancy, school attendance, conduct and effort marks. . . . If you get some-
> thing wrong there, you know there's trouble. When you get truancy and bad conduct
> plus the delinquency, there's definitely something wrong (Emerson, 1969:84).

In practice, court inquiry typically shifts at an early point from the delinquent act
as a legal offense to finding out what the act indicates for the offender, in short, to
"what is the problem here?" The procedure in the following case is not atypical:

> Two white girls, Jean and Mary, both about 15, had been arrested for shoplifting in
> a downtown department store. Store detectives told of apprehending the girls outside the
> store with stolen clothes in the bottom of a shopping bag. Mary's father questioned the
> store detective very closely, then turned to his daugher and demanded to know whether
> she had actually taken the clothes. She admitted she had.
> Two probation officers then gave verbal reports on the girls. Mary had run away
> from home several times, and, in fact, was a runaway when caught for this shoplifting
> incident. She also was frequently absent and truant from school. But in her interview
> "she seems mild, well-behaved." Her mother had tried to keep her away from Jean, but
> without success. Jean, it was then reported, showed a similar record of running away and
> trouble in school. And she had behaved badly in the office interview: "She seems mean.
> She was most disrespectful to her mother in the interview at my desk. She asked me if
> it was any of my business if she was a runaway when she was charged with shoplifting."
> One probation officer then requested separate dispositions, on the ground: "I think the
> other girl [Jean] may need something more drastic, with her attitude." Judge refused,
> and inquired in detail into previous runaways, especially from Jean's mother about why
> she had not reported her daughter missing. Then questioned the girls about where they
> had been for the several days they had been away; they said they spent the night in a
> doorway in a nearby, lower-middle-class suburb. Judge also questioned them very
> closely about a girl they reported they met in a downtown hotel who offered them jobs
> and a place to stay with her.
> Judge then began to concentrate on Jean: . . . "What's the idea of running in the
> first place?" Jean: "I don't know." Judge: "What's the trouble? Huh? Any trouble at

---

5. In the hearings on such serious offenses, the Eastern Juvenile Court insisted on following
strict legal procedure: competent lawyers were assured, and full-blown trial practices, such as
formal admission of evidence and objections to testimony, were followed. In these instances court
staff seemed to view the cases as purely judicial matters, with major restrictions and punishments
at issue, and sought to maximize due process and adversary proceedings. In most other cases, in
contrast, the strains, discomforts, and dilemmas encountered by lawyers practicing in the juvenile
court appear in full force. The relevant literature here includes Platt and Friedman, 1968; Platt
et al., 1968; Emerson, 1969; Lefstein et al., 1969; Lemert, 1970.

home?" Jean denied this, and was generally sullen and uncommunicative. Judge then questioned Mary, particularly about her school work. Then asked probation officers for their recommendations, which were "continued without a finding" for Mary, "probation" for Jean.

Judge thought briefly and then reacted: "Since they're not going to school and not doing well, I want them held in detention for study. Psychiatrics on both. I want physicals on both too. (Both girls are now crying, as they will be held for another two weeks.) . . . There's something going on with them. I'm not worried about the stealing but that brings it to a head . . ." (Emerson, 1969:88–89).

In these proceedings very little effort went into establishing the legally relevant facts of the shoplifting complaint. Rather, the judge probed into (1) the specific details of the runaway episode, particularly how the girls had gotten by "on the streets"; (2) their general behavior and character; and (3) their home situations. In so doing he seized on several reports as indicators that there was "real trouble" involved. These included the facts that there had been prior runaway incidents, some likelihood of sexual activity, perhaps even prostitution, and recurrent problems in both home and school. As the judge noted, "There's something going on with them." Although this assessment is initial and tentative, its possible seriousness is indicated by the judge's severe response to the case: both girls were to be held in detention and given psychiatric evaluation (where girls, with the exception of state wards, were rarely held in detention).

The judge's feeling that there is "real trouble" reflects an assessment that the girls' activities and situations not only entail some marginal delinquency, but more importantly, may lead to full-blown delinquency. That is, in these activities and situations the judge detects certain indicators of "the short-run and long-run courses of action the suspect is likely to pursue" (Cicourel, 1968:68). These indicators suggest "real trouble"—possible movement toward a further *delinquent career*. In so doing the court relies upon typifications of the causes, circumstances, and processes whereby youths may progressively move from innocuous beginnings into "serious delinquency." One such typification was suggested by a probation officer commenting on a girl delinquent: "Incorrigible can be a prelude to runaway, which is a prelude to prostitution" (Emerson, 1969:86–87). Through the use of such typified constructs of delinquent careers, the court interprets what present behavior or "problems" portend for the youth's future behavior.[6] In so doing the court begins to identify what should be done in response to that particular case.

Moreover, assessment of "real trouble" as the possibility of movement toward "serious delinquency" depends in large part on judgments of *what kind of youth* is involved. Thus, the court's use of concepts of typical delinquent careers implies a fundamental concern with the youth's *moral character*.[7] Moral character involves the judg-

---

6. Lemert suggests that this is particularly characteristic of highly bureaucratic, urban courts, noting that in juvenile courts in small towns and rural areas "sharp distinctions are drawn between less consequential moral and legal infractions—'mickey mouse stuff'—and serious delinquencies, with no implications that one conduces to the other." While, in part, he attributes this tendency to the speed with which hearings in urban settings are conducted, a further critical factor involves the fact that "the functional context of child problems . . . easily gets lost" (Lemert, 1967:94).

7. The concept of moral character recurs throughout the writings of Erving Goffman (e.g., 1961) and has close affinity with Garfinkel's concept of "total identity" (1956). Werthman and Piliavin (1967) analyze the role of assessments of moral character in a variety of interactions between police and delinquent gang members. See also Emerson (1969:89–96).

ment of what a person "really is," what his "essential nature" is, as distinct from the role-specific identity implied by any particular behavior or performance. With the partial exception of "serious offenses," mere violation of a law does not make a youth a "real delinquent" in the eyes of the court staff. As a probation officer noted about one youth: "There are delinquents and there are delinquents. . . . All children steal things. She's not a delinquent." Thus, a "real delinquent" is seen as not simply a youth who has committed a delinquent act, but as one whose actions indicate he or she is the kind of person who has or will become regularly and seriously engaged in delinquent activity. Character assessments of this kind thus underlie the court's handling of cases, particularly its identification of cases as "serious problems." In this sense, a "real," "hardcore" delinquent is a youth who comes to be seen as fundamentally criminal in character by court staff. While such a youth may already be heavily involved in serious delinquent activity, he need not be, and may show only minor delinquent conduct. Nonetheless, he may be felt to be "the kind of kid who will go bad," the kind of youth who in time will become a real delinquent, regularly engaged in serious, perhaps violent, delinquent activity.

Different assessments of the offender's moral character may lead the court to make very different interpretations of the meaning and implications of the same delinquent act. On the one hand, the delinquency may be viewed "as a manifestation of criminal (that is, purposely irresponsible) social character" (Cicourel, 1968:142). In this case the delinquent offense tends to be seen as more "serious," and confirms the underlying imputation of criminal character upon which it is based. On the other hand, imputation of "normal character" may serve to insulate a youth from the criminal implications of his behavior. Here the offense may be viewed as the product of a basically "good kid," but "due to circumstances that the juvenile presumably cannot easily control" (p. 142). Under these circumstances, even with involvement in recurring, perhaps increasingly serious, delinquency, court staff continue to feel that the possibility of such a youth becoming a "real delinquent" is unlikely and/or preventable.

Assessments of career stage and moral character are not static and absolute in nature, but rather assume a changing, tentative, emerging character. For moral character is not simply judged at one point, e.g., on first contact, and that judgment perpetuated thereafter. Rather, initial judgments are made and acted upon with consequences that may drastically modify (as well as confirm) these first assessments. The court itself assumes that initial assessments of trouble and moral character are highly tentative and subject to change, and may respond as to allow explicitly for further evidence and reevaluation, e.g., continuing minor offenses, such as shoplifting, without a finding "in order to see if there is a serious problem." Assessments of moral character, then, constantly change, as the court attempts to deal with the trouble, reassesses its judgments in light of the success or failure of these remedies, and tries new ways of dealing with the youthful troublemaker appropriate to one of that now-recognized character.

It should be emphasized that the juvenile-court's concern with trouble, a delinquent career, and moral character is fundamentally *practical* rather than theoretical in nature. For these assessments are made in and as part of the process of deciding what to do about the variety of cases coming before the court. Locating "real trouble," specifying a career stage, or assessing moral character are not ends in themselves, but are used in deciding what should and can be done with specific cases. That is to say, determining what to do with a particular youth does not involve simply assessing what he has done in the past and trying to anticipate what he will or might do in the future. *Rather, such assessments are made in light of and directed toward deciding among the actual courses of action that are available and appropriate in this particular case.*

One way of indicating what is involved here is to suggest that identifying real trouble and making assessments of a delinquent career stage and character are not final decisions but first steps for the juvenile-court's practical task of actually doing something about the cases brought before it. Determining just what a delinquent has done and what he will in all likelihood do and become in the future serves not to dispose of a case, but to identify a range of "realistic" and "appropriate" options for working out a disposition to the case. For example, in deciding that a youth is only marginally involved in delinquency, the court effectively judges that one of a range of mild, routine responses—some variant of routine probationary supervision—is appropriate. Conversely, to identify a youth as at a late stage of delinquency is to narrow the range of possible ways of dealing with his case to those involving major action, perhaps incarceration. In these ways the court's determination of the career stage and moral character serves to specify institutionally proper and reasonable ways of dealing with delinquency cases.

INITIAL ASSESSMENTS AND COURT CAREERS

In distinguishing between minor and serious delinquency and in determining initial lines of response to cases, court staff attend to a variety of possible signs of trouble and of delinquent moral character. These include features of the delinquent offense, the youth's general pattern of behavior, the personal impression he makes on court staff, and his wider social circumstances.

Court conceptions of the typical features of delinquent acts provide a resource for attending to and making sense of cases. Court personnel come to hold certain stereotyped conceptions about the typical situations, motives, and character of perpetrators of a given kind of delinquent offense (Sudnow, 1965; Emerson, 1969). These "stereotypes" embody the court's locally acquired, common-sense knowledge of delinqency situations. By determining that a particular offense falls in such a known class of acts, the court comes to anticipate a particular set of motives, circumstances, and techniques for the act, and a particular kind of delinquent actor. For example, a probation officer will describe most youths in for joyriding in the following way: "[These] kids work out pretty well on probation. . . . Usually aside from this one weakness they're the nicest kids. They're good at home, behave in school—they wouldn't steal a dime. . . . Usually they're pretty nice type kids. Easy to work with" (Emerson, 1969:108). In contrast, stealing handbags is assumed to involve typically a hardened, more criminally inclined, delinquent youth: "These are generally pretty seriously delinquent boys. They're known to other courts or on parole. . . . They're either probationers or parolees. Very aggressive delinquent boys" (p. 107).

In this way, certain typical offenses lead the court to expect delinquent offenders of a particular moral character. Thus, when the court detects (nontypical) elements of preplanning and professional techniques in "use without authority" cases, or their lack in handbag snatches, the usual expectations do not hold and further probing into the offense may seek to establish what kind of youth was committing it (Emerson, 1969: 106–20).

Beyond inferences from the offense, the court turns to a youth's "record" in assessing trouble and moral character. Almost the first step made by a probation officer in processing a new complaint is to find out whether the youth involved has had prior contact with the juvenile court. This "record" plays a fundamental role in the court's subsequent assessment and handling of the case. A youth without a prior record is usually presumed to be normal in character and his case will typically be handled routinely on some form of perfunctory probation. A lengthy record (even of minor offenses) or conviction for one or two serious offenses is taken to imply commitment to or movement toward serious delinquent activity.

Even when there is no official record, the court may identify general patterns of delinquent activity and hence possible criminal moral character. What is critical is tying a current act to prior incidents of the "same kind." In this way, for example, reference to prior unreported incidents of some delinquent behavior may transform a current act from an isolated incident into evidence of a recurrent pattern:[8]

> At the end of the day the judge talked informally with the social worker from the court clinic about a case he had heard yesterday. The boy had been in for stealing a one-dollar wallet from a large department store. It was very minor. "The only reason they brought him in was he gave the wrong name. I didn't think there was anything to it. Then I asked his father if he had anything he wanted to say. He stood up and told me, 'Yes, there is. This boy's a thief!' Apparently he's been stealing things all over the place. So I referred him to you. . . . Boy, it sure changed it around when that father said he's a thief!" Prior to that it had looked like such a very minor thing—a one-dollar wallet!

What had appeared on the surface as a very minor case had, during the course of the hearing, been revealed to be something a lot more serious. Psychiatric referral, reflecting this sense of real trouble, was ordered to try to determine exactly what caused this behavior.

Court staff read and interpret records of delinquent activity in reference to their conceptions of a delinquent career. Thus, just as it is assumed that minor delinquency may lead to serious delinquency, so it is assumed that the occurrence of serious delinquency will have been preceded (and caused) by minor delinquency. Court staff then expect a youth who is currently charged with a fairly serious offense, such as handbag snatching or armed robbery, to have a prior record of less serious delinquent activity building up toward the present offense. These common-sense notions of how delinquent careers develop also allow identification of anomalous patterns. For example, when a serious delinquent offense is committed without any apparent progression through the normal prior delinquent stages, court staff often feel that the delinquent offender may be disturbed rather than criminal in character. Similarly, unevenness in the appearance of delinquent activity, such as a concentration of offenses in a short period of time, is generally felt to indicate some psychological problem rather than developing criminality. In either instance, psychiatric referral may be forthcoming, with the court clinic expected to fill in the missing background in psychological terms.

Court assessments of trouble and moral character depend not only on how past behavior is interpreted, but also upon immediate impressions of the youth. In the shoplifting case presented earlier, for example, the second probation officer's report focused on the girl's "attitude," with mention made of her disrespect to her mother and her challenge to the probation officer's authority. Probation interviews, in fact, regularly serve as means for interpreting a youth's character. Delinquents who behave politely, show respect for both parents and the probation officer, acknowledge the officer's au-

---

8. What is involved here is the use of the "documentary method of interpretation," analyzed in general terms by Garfinkel (1967). For discussion and illustrations of the use of the documentary method in processing juvenile-court cases, see Cicourel (1968) and Emerson (1969).

thority and right to ask questions, and appear convincingly remorseful—in short, who behave in ways reflecting a "good attitude" (Cicourel, 1968:222)—will tend to be judged as normal in character and inspire the probation officer as someone who can be worked with, perhaps even in the face of recurring delinquencies.[9] In contrast, the youth who persists in acting "fresh," defiantly, who refuses to become repentant or who does so with visibly less than full conviction, will become identified as "hardened," criminally inclined, and will quickly lose the protection and support of the probation officer if he gets into much further trouble.[10]

Finally, court staff also expect the problems and misconduct of youths headed toward serious delinquency to surface in behavior in school and at home. One probation officer noted, for example, that she identified "severe cases" by "late hours, stubbornness, resentment to the parents, 'D' in conduct" (Emerson, 1969:126). The school reports routinely obtained by probation and court staff provide detailed records of performance, trouble incidents, psychological and other testings, and less formal teacher and staff evaluations, all of which may be organized to document the developing disruptive and delinquent tendencies of the youth involved.[11]

Of further interest here is the pervasive assumption of court personnel that "something wrong in the home" is both a cause and a sign of possible future delinquency. Court personnel attend very closely to the family situations of the youths coming before them. "Broken homes," including divorced or separated parents, are frequently identified as the probable source of delinquent misconduct. But the court also recognizes a somewhat broader category of "bad home situations" promoting delinquency. Parents may be judged "weak," disinterested, uncaring, or simply immoral in ways that lead to delinquency by lack of control, neglect, or example. Or some more psychological "family problem," such as strain with a stepparent or an objectionable personality trait of one or both of the parents, may be identified as the source of difficulties and tensions. In general, the integrity and morality of the delinquents' family life is reviewed, evaluated, and cited in justification of official intervention by court staff. A "bad home situation" becomes an expected background feature in serious, "hardcore" delinquency, and its apparent absence may even suggest to the court that the youth's problem is psychological, not criminal. Concretely, a "bad home" is often treated as an indicator of "real trouble" and serious delinquency by court personnel, leading to a more severe response to the case, while an apparently "good home" and parents' reports of "good behavior" at home tend at first to minimize court perceptions of serious delinquency.

In conclusion, the regular use of a youth's family situation by court and probation

---

9. What seems critical here is the court's determination of the degree of the youth's *commitment* to conventional activities, life-styles, beliefs, and worlds. In attending to delinquency cases, the court can read the offense, record, and face-to-face conduct for what they say about the youth's relation to such conventional (as opposed to delinquent) worlds. A sense of normal character is maintained as long as the court staff detect at least some commitment to conventional life-styles and norms. In contrast, as it appears that commitment to illegal activity is increasing, progressively more "hopeless" and criminal character comes to be imputed to the youth. In most instances this movement occurs over the course of prolonged contact with court and probation staff.

10. For several revealing instances of how conduct comes to be seen as reflecting a "good attitude," and of the key role of these processes in case outcomes, see Cicourel (1968:124–30, 222–41). For a discussion of the ways in which the courtroom itself may be made into a scene for displaying, establishing, and detecting "attitude" and moral character generally, see Emerson (1969:172–215).

11. For a detailed analysis of one such school report and its use in this way by probation staff in finding and confirming delinquent character on first contact with a juvenile, see Cicourel's description (1968) of the case of "Smithfield," especially pp. 204–10.

staff to identify "real delinquents" has basic implications for sociological research and theories of delinquency. With other things (e.g., the offense) equal, a "broken home" or "bad family situation" increase a youth's risks of being identified and treated as a "real delinquent" at critical points in his contacts with the juvenile court. As opposed to a youth from a "good" family, he is more apt to be brought to court on a formal petition rather than receive informal handling, to be given intensive rather than routine probation, and incarcerated rather than kept in the community. Identification not only of a "broken home," but also of a "bad neighborhood," "trouble in school," and "bad peer associations," may lead to differential court responses to delinquency cases (Emerson, 1969). In this way, "the ideologies and policies of law-enforcement officials selectively assemble juveniles for probation evaluation according to existing theories shared by the community and social scientists" (Cicourel, 1968:38). Theories of delinquency are not an exclusively sociological prerogative: juvenile-court and probation personnel develop and hold similar theories of the causes of delinquency. And it is the court staff, acting upon and responding to cases on the basis of their theories, that produce the data that the sociologist works with, data such as correlations between official rates of delinquency and family instability, poor neighborhoods, school problems, and the like (Kitsuse & Cicourel, 1963).

CHARACTER AND ROUTINE PROBATION

In identifying cases involving "real trouble" and problematic character, the juvenile court begins to allocate its time, effort, and resources differentially between cases. Facing a large number of complaints about delinquency with limited staff and resources, the court comes to deal with most cases in minimal and perfunctory terms, and must distinguish these from the few to which more costly and demanding responses have to or should be undertaken. The great majority of delinquency cases are seen as manageable with only a minimum of staff time and effort devoted to overseeing the activities and situation of the delinquent. A woman probation officer, for example, commented on the expectedly manageable outcome of girl shoplifters in noting: "I don't see them any more" (after their hearing). On the other hand, in cases where "real trouble" is found, the court decides that more active intervention is needed. Closer supervision and efforts to mobilize resources for changing the life circumstances of the delinquent may be seen as necessary.

By and large, probationary supervision provides the juvenile court with its initial and routine alternatives for dealing with cases. Such supervision comes to center around the enforcement of a minimal set of standard rules aimed at forestalling further troublemaking on the part of the youth. These rules generally include: report periodically to the probation officer; attend and behave in school; get a job if out of school; and observe curfew. In addition, the youth may be warned to behave at home and to obey his parents, cautioned to stay out of trouble in school, and encouraged to complete his school work. Association with undesirable friends may be prohibited. Finally, participation in some after-school program, usually for recreation, may be arranged.

Given relatively high case loads making even supervision on these terms impossible on any large scale (see Vinter, 1967), probation officers come to depend heavily on indirect procedures. In particular, they routinely shift responsibility for direct and regular control of delinquents to other agents. Routine probation, in fact, explicitly involves trying to integrate (or reintegrate) the delinquent into those institutions that normally control and regulate youths' activities. The family and the schools are considered crucial here, for as a probation officer noted:

We keep a close look at the most serious. But with the rest, we probably don't see them all year. We rely on the family and the schools to back us up. Though often the family just doesn't, and if the school reports them, then we surrender them (Emerson, 1969:225).

In this way the probation officer both relies upon and seeks to reaffirm the authority of these primary control institutions.

Thus, indirect probationary control regularly seeks to subject the delinquent to as continuous adult supervision and control as possible. The court makes an effort to involve delinquents in YMCA recreation programs, settlement-house activities, summer camps, etc., simply as a means of occupying and organizing their free time, keeping them off the streets and out of trouble. Similarly, out-of-school delinquents are required to work, since jobs occupy their time and place them in an adult-supervised setting.

In addition, these primary community institutions are relied on not only for day-to-day control and supervision, but also for maintaining surveillance over the youth's activities. In effect, the probation officer tries to enlist the aid of parents, teachers, school officials, social workers, and police to report to him any problems or troubles involving the youth. This gives probation an essentially reactive character: the probation officer assumes that a delinquent is staying out of trouble until or unless reports of misconduct reach him from these sources.

From this it should be apparent that the control regime employed in routine probation rests on the assumption that the delinquent involved is of *fundamentally normal character*. It is assumed that this routine, cursory probation will work with youths who are not "really delinquent." Strategic considerations in allocating probation resources over an extremely high case load seem critical here. For *as a practical matter*, there is neither sufficient time nor resources to provide intensive help and supervision to all those youths who appear on the surface to be "good kids." In addition, the payoffs that can be anticipated from such a strategy are small, for most of these youths are expected to be deterred from further delinquency by their court experience. And while the court obviously recognizes that some will get into further, perhaps serious, trouble, this will involve only a very small percentage that can still be identified early enough to be worked with effectively on more intensive probation. Moreover, ordinary probation serves as a test for the normalcy of such character. It is organized on the basis of control practices adequate for preventing further trouble by a normal youth. With no more than minimal supervision, such a delinquent is expected to proceed through the course of probation without incident (e.g., "I never see them again"). Thus routine probationary control assumes that a normal youth will be deterred by the probation officer's direct assertions of authority, intimidated by his lectures and warnings, and motivated to do better (or at least not make trouble) in his contacts with primary control institutions.

"More trouble" tends to threaten and perhaps invalidate these assumptions. More trouble indicates that routine measures are not working. As a result tighter supervision and control may be imposed.

INTENSIVE PROBATION AND MOVEMENT
TOWARD INCARCERATION

As trouble continues, formal controls may be increased (e.g., a suspended sentence imposed), and closer supervision maintained. The probation officer will make frequent checks with parents and school about current behavior and new problems. The youth may be required to report more regularly to the probation officer on his doings and difficulties, and to participate actively in such court-sponsored programs as tutorial sessions and group therapy.

"Trust," relevant to cursory probation only in that the youth is assumed to be normal and hence expected to stay out of trouble, becomes critical if the probation officer wishes to move beyond a formal relationship of authority to establish a basis for helping the youth and changing his behavior. Intensive probation, in fact, hinges upon the development and maintenance of a "trust relationship" between delinquent and probation officer (Cicourel, 1968). Such a relationship presumes a youth of normal moral character, a youth who "can be worked with" and probably "saved" despite his current delinquency. Probation staff will continue to tolerate and support the youth who through continued cooperation and a "good attitude" conveys normal character. Thus assessments of moral character remain critical during this phase of the delinquent's court career, particularly in the face of continuing delinquency. A youth who can maintain a good attitude and show sincerity toward the probation officer's attempts to help and supervise his activities will usually be kept on probation despite new problems. "Good reasons" will be found in his personal circumstances to explain his shortcomings, while "more trouble" from a youth whose character has become suspect will confirm his inherent criminality, providing "documentary evidence of the 'hopelessness' of the case" (Cicourel, 1968:209).

In contrast, a trust relationship and intensive probation are not developed with delinquents judged to be too far "gone" to be effectively helped and treated. For court and probation staff to get involved in such "hopeless cases"—youths well into criminal pursuits or who appear too "hardened" to be "saved" or "rehabilitated"—is a dubious expenditure of time and effort. Instead, a practical policy of "letting it go" may be preferable:

> The judge commented on a 17-year-old white girl, Joyce, in court for prostitution, a girl the clinic had diagnosed as "one hundred per cent sociopath." "This little girl today, she's hopeless. . . . Absolutely no conscience. She couldn't have cared less about being in here. We couldn't do a thing for her. . . . The best you can hope for in a case like this is to put it on probation and let it go" (Emerson, 1969:99).

Here concern with treatment or rehabilitation is clearly set aside, and the girl placed on probation with the minimal hope that she would stay out of trouble until she became the legal responsibility of the adult authorities. As her probation officer remarked:

> I'm not supposed to do much with it, since the girl is 17 and would be beyond juvenile court jurisdiction in a matter of months when she turned 18. She was just trying to get Joyce to keep from being picked up by the police until then.

"Reform" is considered out of the question: for the court staff it is only a matter of time until she is back hustling on the streets, and their response is one of practically "making do" in the meanwhile.

Even in cases not considered "hopeless," however, more active court intervention and involvement are neither automatic nor inevitable because the court routinely attends to and seeks out *alternatives to its own programs and controls* as ways of dealing with delinquents. Psychiatric care is regarded as a particularly desirable form of help or treatment, for example, and the court will frequently withdraw from a case on the condition that the family agree to have the youth begin therapy. But even where the alternative course of action offers little or no treatment advantage, the court may accept it as a practical, feasible way of disposing of the case. For example, volunteering to join the armed services, moving to live with relatives in a new neighborhood, or for black youths, going "down South," are, on occasion, accepted as ways of dealing with youthful troublemakers. Often these kinds of solutions are seen to offer nothing more than a change of scene, and perhaps a chance to start over without the prejudice of an acquired record. Thus, the court hopes that such action *might* end further delinquency problems. But more importantly, where the youth has moved out of its jurisdiction, the court will not be held accountable even in the face of serious and dramatic offenses. In these ways the court is open to a fairly wide variety of "making do" practices for dealing with its cases.[12]

As a case moves through a court and routine remedies are either rendered inappropriate or exhausted, the court staff may begin to consider more serious dispositional alternatives. If the youth does not seem to be adjusting in the community, incarceration becomes an increasingly live issue, and an active search for alternatives to supplement and/or replace intensive probation may be begun. Distinctively "helping" concerns may hasten, or even themselves lead to, the feeling that "something has to be done." For example, a youth's family situation may appear so untenable or pathological that some other arrangement appears imperative to the court staff. The more desirable and/or therapeutic the placement institution, the greater its attractiveness to court personnel as an alternative to keeping the youth at home in the community.

Arranging placement, however, can involve a difficult, complex, and extremely unpredictable set of negotiations. In the first place, the desires of both youth and family may have to be considered, and their support and cooperation obtained. Probation officers' efforts to arrange what they regard as an extremely desirable placement are easily undermined when the delinquent feels coerced and "messes up" a hard-won admission interview. Second, an institution considered appropriate for the youth and his problems with vacancies must be found. Third, institutions must often be convinced to accept the delinquent. Here many placement institutions have formal or informal policies about the specific kinds of cases they will and will not take. Depending on agency idiosyncrasies, delinquents whose records include drug use, overt sexual behavior, violence, or even recurrent runaways may be either turned down directly or looked upon with disfavor. Admission regularly requires a process of negotiation where the court tries to convince the institution of the youth's basically desirable moral character and suitability for their program.

As a result, an underlying tentativeness and reversibility marks the placement process. The court, having decided that a youth has to be taken out of his home or community, begins to search out an appropriate placement. But the preferred placement simply may not be what the youth wants, may not want him, or may have openings only at some uncertain point in the future. What to do about the case, then, must be reevaluated taking these developments into account. Faced with the alternative of placement at the second-best institution, keeping the youth in his home may reemerge as the best available solution. For example, it may be decided that placement in a psychiatric facility is desirable, but for one of the reasons suggested, it cannot be obtained. The court may then reconsider what to do in terms of a choice between leaving the youth in his home and "on the streets" as against trying to work out some less palatable placement, and on balance may decide in favor of the former. Further trouble

---

12. This openness to the possibilities of alternative solutions, including "making do" ones, encourages and facilitates the phenomenon of *sponsorship* in the juvenile court, as noted by Matza (1964) ; also see Emerson (1969:130–31).

may lead to another reevaluation plus pressure to follow up on the previously discounted alternative.

With continued problems of adjusting in the community or in more desirable placements, that "something has to be done" may take on an even stronger and more fixed sense. Court personnel come to see absolutely no alternative but to take the youth out of the community, institutional placement of some form becomes unavoidable, and the issue shifts to what is the best available institution given the circumstances of the case. Especially serious offenses regularly confront the court in just these terms: where a violent crime has been committed, the court operates on the presumption that the youth must be taken off the streets. Immediate return to the community is a remote, if not quite unimaginable, disposition, primarily because of vulnerability to public criticism if something goes wrong.

Complainant and other outside pressures may also play an important role here. Clearly such pressures involve a key dimension in the disposition of serious offenses. Yet community pressures may arise even without the publicity and attendant visibility of a serious offense. As a youth gets into more and more serious troubles, and the usual community and institutional remedies seem ineffective, local pressures that "something be done" may become stronger and more persistent. Some of the resulting contingencies are reflected in the following case from Eastern Juvenile Court:

> An 11-year-old Italian boy from the tightly knit Italian section of the city was a frequent object of Court complaints. Although in constant trouble, he was fairly severely retarded, and his delinquencies had been more or less tolerated while the Court staff tried to get him into the state school for the retarded. But finally things went too far. Joe Manello, the probation officer who worked this district, brought the boy and his mother into Court. The probation officer explained that the boy, while living at home, had been in even more trouble than before, and had now begun breaking into cars. Although the community was upset, "none of the people who have seen it will come forward to make a complaint" (apparently because of their sympathy with the retarded boy). In addition, the mother has no control over the boy, and "she feels it has reached the point now where removal is the answer." After the Judge had talked briefly with the boy, the probation officer questioned the mother about his behavior leading up to the question: "Do you mind telling the Judge, do you think the boy should be placed now?" Mother: "Yes, I think it's the only thing. There's been too many complaints about the cars now." But the Judge objected that he would not commit the boy to the state correctional authority, for if he did that, "I'm writing him off," . . . so he held the boy at the Detention Center while he tried to arrange something with the Child Guidance Clinic. Eventually, the Court was able to get the boy into a school for the retarded.

It is with these pressures that movement toward incarceration in state reformatories begins to consolidate. In Eastern Juvenile Court, the reform schools run by the state were regarded as strictly custodial institutions almost without the pretense of rehabilitative programs. Only the most clearly criminal, hardened, and irretrievable delinquents—only the "hopeless cases" and "lost causes"—were considered legitimately committed to these institutions, and such commitments were rarely made lightly or automatically.[13]

As incarceration appears increasingly imminent and unavoidable, the court staff will frequently make frantic efforts to arrange some alternative institutional placement.

---

13. A similar attitude prevails in California, where Cicourel found: "the Youth Authority is viewed by probation officers as the last resource available because it is known to be a prison for juveniles regardless of what other label is attached" (1968:229–30).

Other agencies will be pressured to find some "closed" residential facility that would accept the youth; although with agency reluctance and the resistance of most such institutions to "hardcore delinquents," there may be very little chance of success. A more viable option frequently involves trying to get the youth admitted to a non-correctional state institution providing some kind of special care or training. Referrals to the court clinic are made regularly, for example, to determine whether the youth is retarded or psychotic, and hence possibly qualified for admission to state schools for the retarded or mental hospitals. Some residential placement is sought almost without regard to the nature of the delinquent's problems, as any program and focus is assumed to be more desirable than commitment to a state correctional facility.

In addition, as incarceration becomes a live issue, the ability of the families of delinquents to provide the court with alternative courses of action becomes increasingly critical. Here class differences become crucially important, as middle-class parents have more resources to mobilize in the effort to keep their child out of a state institution. Intensive psychiatric care or placement in a residential military school may be arranged by family members with the encouragement and advice of court staff in order to avert threatened or impending commitment to reform school (Cicourel, 1968; Emerson, 1969).[14]

In some cases commitment to the state correctional institution is viewed by court personnel as necessary to restrain a delinquent of hopelessly criminal and dangerous character. Here court and probation personnel see "no alternative" to incarceration. In other instances, however, it is not so much the delinquent's moral character as *the lack of any other practical option* that makes such commitment a necessary and unavoidable decision.[15] As a California probation officer outlined the progress of a typical case to this point:

> Take a basic incorrigible, a runaway. She's placed in a foster home. By this time she's involved in dope, so the home doesn't want her. Or maybe petty theft. We give her an open placement, but they ask that she be removed, she's not cooperating. Try a convent or Las Palmas [the county correctional school]. She's not changing her basic behavior. By this time she's a 602 [adjudicated delinquent for felonious offense]. . . . She gets sent to CYA [juvenile correctional system] if we're lucky.[16]

Youths not felt to be "really" hopeless or criminal-like by court staff, nonetheless, may eventually be incarcerated where alternatives become used up and "nothing else can be done."

While the exhausting of all placement options generally occurs over a period of time, the processes involved were very rapid in the following case when the youth refused to cooperate with the court's arrangements to help him:

> Ralph Robinson, a 16-year-old Negro boy, was brought to court by his mother for incorrigibility. Investigation revealed deep conflict between mother and son, and the

----

14. As Cicourel notes, "Such action saves the county and state considerable monies, avoids the assumed negative influence of incarceration in an environment likely to expose the juvenile to the 'worse' elements, and minimizes the stigma presumed to be forthcoming from the 'community' " (1968:327).

15. The California probation subsidy program attempts to influence just these kinds of contingencies, increasing the benefits of some in-the-community alternative by offering monetary incentives for avoiding commitments to the Youth Authority.

16. From an interview conducted as part of an unpublished research project on incorrigible-child complaints in a California probation department, 1971.

probation officer concluded that the mother "is as disturbed as he is." The probation officer described the home situation as intolerable, and felt that the boy had to be separated from his mother and placed in a better environment. During the summer the boy was placed at a camp and arrangements were completed with the Child Welfare Department to send the boy to a private boarding school in the fall.

In early September, Ralph failed to report to the school as required. He was picked up by the police Monday night and brought to court, but quickly ran away. Meanwhile, the Child Welfare Department worker agreed to "cover" for the court, telling the school that Ralph had been mixed up about when he was supposed to come. (The fact that he had refused to come to the school, plus the fact that he had been picked up by the police and held in detention, would have given the school second thoughts about taking him.) On Tuesday afternoon the probation officer went out and found the boy, gave him his "extra-special lecture," which ended with him turning his back and walking back to his car, trusting Ralph to follow him there and thence to school, but the boy again disappeared.

That night he was again picked up by the police, and sent to Detention. Wednesday in court the probation officer got the judge to put the boy on a suspended sentence, and had another probation officer personally take him out to the school that afternoon. But by six that night, Ralph had run away from the school, and was back in the city. Late Thursday the probation officer apprehended him again and again took him out to the Detention Center.

In court on Friday, the probation officer surrendered Ralph for violating his probation and recommended commitment to the Youth Correction Authority, explaining in some detail about the boy's escape from the school. He concluded: "We've gone as far as we can with him." After a lengthy confrontation with the boy, the judge ordered the commitment.

After the hearing the probation officer commented to the observer: "There's no doubt in my mind that the kid is asking for it (i.e., commitment). If he isn't he's giving a good show. . . . [Although he obviously is a bright kid,] with this we just can't let it go" (Emerson, 1969:239–40).

Here, the court's decision that the delinquent's home situation was untenable initiated a series of interventions aimed at providing an alternative. The youth's resistance to these efforts to "help," however, accelerated his movement through the system of institutional placements open to the court. When he "messed up" the placement worked out for him, he foreclosed a whole series of court options. Further efforts at placement were seen as useless given his "attitude" and the disfavor "good placements" show toward youths with records for delinquency and runaway. In this situation the court felt "forced" to incarcerate as a practical matter because all other viable alternatives had been exhausted. Only the state's Youth Correction Authority, always and easily accessible to the juvenile court, remained open. As the probation officer concluded: "There's nothing else we can do."

THE "LAST CHANCE"

In Eastern Juvenile Court, as cases moved toward a point of imminent incarceration, psychiatric referrals to the court clinic were routinely made as a kind of "last chance" for the youth involved. Nearly all serious offenses were handled in this way. Faced with strong community pressure that "something be done," and seeing a serious offense as prima facie evidence of dangerous and criminal character, the court regularly sent such cases to the clinic for expert evaluation. So, too, were those cases where a delinquent faced the prospect of reform school after having exhausted all available court and outside resources.

In part, the psychiatric report arms the court with a weapon for placating police, parole, or school officials, and for justifying decisions that might later become politically controversial. Thus, the judge noted that where he has a psychiatric recommendation not to incarcerate a seriously delinquent youth "at least we have the opinion of an expert that he would not benefit from an institution. Otherwise, if the kid has been in court four or five times, we'd generally say he's had it" (Emerson, 1969:248). Here, the psychiatrist can deflect punitive pressures by presenting evidence that, despite the serious offense or repeated trouble, the youth is not really dangerously or hopelessly delinquent; that "it is not likely to happen again." Furthermore, the clinic can implement this "last chance" by seeking out or developing an alternative disposition to incarceration. Thus, what is involved is the right to redefine moral character, as any such alternative requires countering the "hopeless" and criminal-like labels that identify the delinquent. In such cases, therefore, referral is a kind of final appeal, a provision for a last review.

In practice, this review usually only confirms and legitimates the court's belief in the appropriateness of the impending incarceration. Several factors contribute to this. In the first place, clinic psychiatrists are heavily dependent on the court and its probation staff in deciding on recommendations for those cases referred to them. Lacking any prior involvement in the case, psychiatrists routinely function by first ascertaining the probation officer's views about what "reasonable" courses of action are open. For example:

A new resident psychiatrist commented about his contacts with the probation department: "My approach is to go along with the probation officer unless there's some good reason against it." Usually he tried to find out what the probation officer wants and will generally go along with it: "I let the probation officer handle it" (Emerson, 1969:260).

But, in routinely "going along" with probation preferences, the psychiatrist also comes to take over probation assessments of moral character. Thus, in discovering that the probation officer expects to commit a particular youth, the psychiatrist also learns to anticipate that this is the kind of youth who should be committed. When his evaluation becomes premised on this assessment, psychiatric confirmation of criminal character becomes more likely.

Similarly, the psychiatrist, isolated from the day-to-day operations of the court, has to rely on the probation officer's informal channels of communication for information about the child, his offense, and his background. In this way, for example, discrediting versions of particular incidents, as well as negative judgments of moral character, may be passed on from the police, family, or other enforcement agency through the probation officer to the psychiatrist.

In addition, to make a recommendation that goes against the court's expectation of criminal character and commitment requires a high degree of personal effort and investment by the psychiatrist. As one of the more experienced clinic staff noted:

"You don't want to make a recommendation they are going to think is ridiculous." But if you do want to do something with a case that the court does not want, you have to put special effort into it. "If you want to do something out of the ordinary, you just can't drop it in their laps and let it go at that." Rather you have to start working on those involved before the case went back into court, getting things arranged before the recommendation is formally made. "You have to justify it, work on it, keep after them." Otherwise, the unusual recommendation would not be accepted (Emerson, 1969:262).

Particularly for an overly scheduled psychiatrist, the ensuing requirements of extra time and effort may become prohibitive. Clinic work proceeds more smoothly the more exactly one follows the expected course of events, relying on what the probation officer has worked out previously and leaving primary responsibility in his hands. For example, one option available to a psychiatrist to stave off institutionalization is an offer to take the youth into therapy. Yet, the restricted amount of time that can be devoted to treatment effectively limits the number of cases the psychiatrist can save in this way. If he is unwilling to take a case for therapy, the psychiatrist is under greater pressure to defer to the wishes of the probation officer, who retains the responsibility and liability for the juvenile.

Additional constraints arise from the psychiatrist's need to maintain his standing with court decision-makers, particularly the judge. Further offenses by a youth "saved" by the clinic discredit both the delinquent and the psychiatrist whose judgment it was that he could be successfully kept in the community. In order to avoid a reputation for unreliability and overleniency, a reputation that would undermine the force of his recommendations, the psychiatrist becomes concerned with conserving his credibility with court personnel. Faced with decisions involving great uncertainty, he becomes extremely selective and cautious in using his power to save. He generally holds himself to "realistic" diagnoses and recommendations. In doing this, he tends to assume the court's standards, modeling his recommendations to their expectations. In practice the psychiatrist comes to avoid "taking a chance" on delinquents considered hopeless by court personnel. He takes smaller "gambles," saving delinquents the court sees some hope for, shunting parolees and other confirmed "hardcore" cases into the correctional system.[17]

A further complication arises from the fact that psychiatrists frequently encounter evasiveness, lack of cooperation, and open hostility from delinquent youths sent to them for diagnosis. These reactions discourage the psychiatrist from trying to save the delinquent, by either making the extra commitment needed to work out placement or refusing to take the case for therapy.

Finally, even where the clinic does redefine character and "save" a delinquent, these actions may be extremely precarious. Psychiatric interpretations may collapse and court perceptions quickly be reasserted with any kind of "incident":

> A 16-year-old Youth Authority parolee, charged with auto use without authority and assault on a police officer, was released into the community on the recommendation of a court clinic psychiatrist. The psychiatrist's report emphasized the youth's passive character, attributed the assault to drinking, and concluded: "I could find little to make me suspect that assaultiveness is typical of his usual style and behavior."
>
> Two days later the youth appeared in court for a new offense, again involving a stolen car and a minor assault on the arresting police officer. On learning the details of this incident, the psychiatrist termed his prior diagnosis a "mistake," concluding that the youth did indeed have assaultive tendencies which he had not discerned previously. He declined any further support for the youth, who was then held in Detention and eventually committed to reform school.[18]

---

17. Probation officers, too, have to guard their standing with the judge. The problems of doing so seem exacerbated where probation and court functions are separate. There can be a very fine line between unrealistically lenient recommendations, leading to a reputation as "soft," and too-frequent use of Youth Authority commitments, which may be taken as indicative of professional ineffectiveness.

18. A more complete version of this case is reported in Emerson, 1969:264–65.

Thus, despite possible extenuating circumstances—the boy had been kicked out of his house after an argument with his mother just prior to the offense—the psychiatrist immediately revised his psychiatric diagnosis to incorporate the court-held view of assaultive character.[19]

In summary, the contingencies surrounding the practice of psychiatry in the juvenile-court setting undermine the independence of the clinic. The clinic's ability and inclination to resist the momentum generated by prior court involvement in cases are eroded by dependence on court personnel incurred in carrying out daily clinic operations. The psychiatrist's recommendations are consequently pulled in a conservative direction, coming to conform to prevailing court standards of what is reasonable and to eschew risk-taking. These factors severely restrict psychiatric reassessment and redefinition of criminal-like character, and hence psychiatric "saving" of hardcore delinquents from incarceration. Only occasionally does the clinic perform its "last chance" function.

CONCLUSION

Recent substantive criticism of the juvenile court has challenged the premise that court actions will necessarily benefit and help youth in trouble. Damaging stigma is held to be a more frequent result of court intervention than effective treatment. The negative consequences of official identification as delinquent may far outweigh any benefits of court help and treatment, particularly with the marginal offender or the predelinquent. In extreme instances, such intervention may reinforce and stabilize behaviors that in all likelihood would have been abandoned with time and increasing maturity (Lemert, 1967).

With the shift of the prevailing model of the juvenile court from benevolent parent–therapist to overreaching stigmatizer came a reformulation of the court's proper approach to delinquency. Early intervention easily undertaken in the presumed interest of the youth has given way to a more cautious, restrained stance. Only serious, "last resort" cases in which the advantages of help clearly outweigh the negative consequences of court contact are appropriate objects of official action. Less serious problems of misconduct should be diverted out of the legal system into unofficial agencies for help and service:

> A great deal of juvenile misconduct should be dealt with . . . in accordance with an explicit policy to divert juvenile offenders away from formal adjudication and authoritative disposition and to nonjudicial institutions for guidance and other services. Employment agencies, schools, welfare agencies, and groups with programs for acting-out youth all are examples of the resources that should be used. . . . Such a policy would avoid for many the long-lasting consequences of adjudication: curtailment of employment opportunity, quasi-criminal record, harm to personal reputation in the eyes of family and friends, and public reinforcement of antisocial tendencies (President's Commission, 1967:16).

In addition to reducing official stigma, policies of judicious nonintervention and diversion promise to circumvent at least some of the difficulties of administering treat-

---

19. That new incidents need not be taken as invalidating a psychiatrically justified disposition is shown in a case analyzed by Cicourel (1968:326–27): a private psychiatrist treating a youth on probation offered a clinical interpretation of a subsequent offense, an interpretation that maintained the psychiatric framework and undercut the possible alternative of viewing the offense as evidence of criminality. The youth remained in his home.

ment programs in authoritative settings. Yet, in viewing the primary problem of the juvenile court as one of official stigma, these approaches remain partial and limited. For this view assumes that it is the actions of the juvenile court that most significantly stigmatize and identify youths as delinquents. But the stigma of delinquency and pressures to restrain, control, and get rid of troublesome youths also develop and acquire momentum from the local community and its control institutions. Here any stigmatizing effects of court contact may be secondary and indirect. Moreover, diversion seems aimed at preventing the stigmatization of the marginally delinquent. It leaves untouched the problems of dealing with hardcore, discredited delinquents felt to be irritating and persistent sources of trouble by local community agencies, including many of those to which delinquents might be diverted. Here efforts to curtail unnecessary stigma become largely irrelevant in the face of pressures to take more drastic action in these more serious cases.

In this light, youths become delinquent not simply by acquiring official stigma. In addition, youths come to be treated as delinquents in progressively exhausting response alternatives open to the court and other agencies. While public identification as a delinquent may play a part, delinquent outcomes in juvenile court more fundamentally involve processes whereby the available ways of handling a youth and his problems are increasingly limited until only incarceration remains.

Taking these factors into account, the real advantage of diversion may lie in its impetus toward increasing the number and range of actions available for responding to youths who get into trouble. But diversion deals only with the marginally delinquent, providing alternatives to court intervention at early contact with the juvenile justice system. At later stages, alternatives to incarceration become critical, as the consequences of commitment to a correctional institution are even more fateful and final. Ensuring a range of varied treatment responses for the more seriously delinquent would keep open nondelinquent options and possibilities. Probation subsidy programs, aimed at keeping in the community youths who would otherwise be committed to a correctional institution, seek to move in this direction.

As the preceding materials have suggested, however, a high degree of institutional autonomy among parts of the juvenile justice system is necessary to ensure the quality of these options. Both the inclination to review discredited character evaluations and the willingness to take chances on cases that others have given up on are undermined by institutional exchanges, close cooperation, and vulnerability to outside agency pressure. But the tendency for these institutions to accept unquestioningly the prior judgments and assessments of what is wrong and what can be done about it is even more detrimental. Greater institutional autonomy would increase the possibilities of redefinition and reassessment. And increased institutional resources would allow the necessary commitment to cases that an agency wants to "save."

A concern with staving off pending incarceration thus should be added to the concern with minimizing the stigmatizing tendencies of the juvenile court. The court occupies a pivotal position here between community and treatment or correctional institutions. Autonomy from local community and institutional pressures facilitates existing court tendencies to act as a bulwark against pressures to get rid of local troublemakers. For "the juvenile court not only labels delinquents, but it also resists labeling by refusing to validate complainant's judgments and to follow their proposed course of action" (Emerson, 1969:275). Along with the mitigation of unnecessary stigma, these dispositions toward resisting and redefining delinquents should be encouraged in the juvenile justice system.

REFERENCES

Allen, Francis A.
  1964 The Borderland of Criminal Justice: Essays in Law and Criminology. Chicago: University of Chicago Press.
Bittner, Egon.
  1967 "The police on skid-row: a study of peace keeping." American Sociological Review 32:699–715.
Bohannan, Paul J., and Karan Huckleberry.
  1967 "Institutions of divorce, family and the law." Law and Society Review 1:81–102.
Cicourel, Aaron V.
  1968 The Social Organization of Juvenile Justice. New York: Wiley.
Emerson, Robert M.
  1969 Judging Delinquents: Context and Process in Juvenile Court. Chicago: Aldine.
Garfinkel, Harold.
  1956 "Conditions of successful degradation ceremonies." American Journal of Sociology 61:420–424.
  1967 Studies in Ethnomethodology. Englewood Cliffs, N.J.: Prentice-Hall.
Goffman, Erving.
  1961 Asylums: Essays on the Social Situation of Mental Patients and Other Inmates. Garden City, N.Y.: Doubleday.
Goldstein, Joseph.
  1960 "Police discretion not to invoke the criminal process: low-visibility decisions in the administration of justice." Yale Law Journal 69:543–594.
Kitsuse, John I., and Aaron V. Cicourel.
  1963 "A note on the uses of official statistics." Social Problems 11:131–139.
Lefstein, Norman, Vaughan Stapleton, and Lee Teitelbaum.
  1969 "In search of juvenile justice: *Gault* and its implementation." Law and Society Review 3:491–562.
Lemert, Edwin M.
  1967 "The juvenile court—quest and realities." Appendix D in President's Commission on Law Enforcement and Administration of Justice, Task Force Report: Juvenile Delinquency and Youth Crime. Washington, D.C.: U.S. Government Printing Office.
  1970 Social Action and Legal Change: Revolution within the Juvenile Court. Chicago: Aldine.
Lindsey, Edward.
  1914 "The juvenile court movement from a lawyer's standpoint." Annals of the American Academy of Political and Social Science 52(March):140–148.
Mack, Julian W.
  1912 "Legal problems involved in the establishment of the juvenile court." Pp. 181–201 in Sophonisba P. Breckinridge and Edith Abbott, The Delinquent Child and the Home. New York: Russell Sage Foundation.
Matza, David.
  1964 Delinquency and Drift. New York: Wiley.

Platt, Anthony.
    1969   The Child-Savers: The Invention of Delinquency. Chicago: University of Chicago Press.
Platt, Anthony, and Ruth Friedman.
    1968   "The limits of advocacy: occupational hazards in juvenile court." University of Pennsylvania Law Review 116:1156–1184.
Platt, Anthony, Howard Schechter, and Phyllis Tiffany.
    1968   "In defense of youth: a case study of the public defender in juvenile court." Indiana Law Journal 43:619–640.
President's Commission on Law Enforcement and Administration of Justice.
    1967   Task Force Report: Juvenile Delinquency and Youth Crime. Washington, D.C.: U.S. Government Printing Office.
Sudnow, David.
    1965   "Normal crimes: sociological features of the penal code in a public defender office." Social Problems 12:255–276.
Tappan, Paul W.
    1949   Juvenile Delinquency. New York: McGraw-Hill.
Vinter, Robert D.
    1967   "The juvenile court as an institution." Pp. 84–90 in President's Commission on Law Enforcement and Administration of Justice, Task Force Report: Juvenile Delinquency and Youth Crime. Washington, D.C.: U.S. Government Printing Office.
Werthman, Carl, and Irving Piliavin.
    1967   "Gang members and the police." Pp. 56–98 in David J. Bordua (ed.), The Police: Six Sociological Essays. New York: Wiley.
Young, Pauline V.
    1937   Social Treatment in Probation and Delinquency. New York: McGraw-Hill.

CHAPTER 17

Appeals from Criminal Convictions

Robert B. Seidman and William J. Chambliss

University of Wisconsin and
University of California at Santa Barbara

When a verdict has been rendered by the trial court in a criminal case, both the accused and the state have the right of appeal to a higher court. Frequently, although certainly not always, in the course of deciding the issue of a particular case, the appellate court, in effect, is making a new law. At times the making of a new law is blatant and has great impact. In the last few years the *Miranda, Gideon,* and *Gault* cases are but a few of many cases decided by appellate courts that have had far-reaching consequences and that, in effect, created a whole body of new law (see Hall, 1952; Chambliss & Seidman, 1971). Thus, the role of the appellate courts and the process of criminal appeals are crucial to comprehend if we are to understand the relationship between crime, law, and society. The fact that appellate courts handle but a small portion of the cases does not alter the fact that appellate-court decisions are a critical feature of the criminal law process. Our discussion of the appeal process will concentrate on (1) the *inputs* into the appellate courts' decision-making process, (2) the *conversion process* in the appellate courts within which a decision is rendered on the appeal, and (3) the *outputs* of the appellate courts in the form of final decisions.

THE INPUTS INTO THE APPELLATE COURTS

The Issues that Come to the Appellate Courts

Trial courts are engaged most of the time in trying issues of fact: listening to witnesses, examining documents, or directing juries in their consideration of these matters. In addition, they engage in a host of ancillary activities, the most important of which is sentencing.

The appellate courts, by contrast, deal only with issues of law. Appellate courts do not take up questions of fact. A person convicted of a crime *may not appeal* to a higher court on the ground that he was "not guilty" or that he "did not commit the crime" except in those instances where he can show that new evidence brings into question facts established in the previous trial. Rather, the appeal of a criminal case must always go to an issue of law. Every issue of law arises because the accused (or more accurately the attorney acting in his behalf) or the state (that is, the prosecuting attorney acting on behalf of the state) asked the trial judge to do something and he has acted or refused to act in ways that the attorney or the prosecutor argues were not permissible by law. For example, the attorney may ask that the judge dismiss the complaint because the accused was not warned of his right to have an attorney before giving a confession. In response the judge must either act or refuse to act on the request. If the party the judge ruled against believes the judge acted wrongly, then he may appeal.

Ordinarily, appeals are written covering a whole host of "wrong decisions" on the part of the judge. Indeed, it is not too much of an exaggeration to say that many criminal attorneys engage not in the practice of trying to prove their client innocent but in the practice of trying to get the judge to make an unlawful ruling that, upon appeal, will permit the case to be dismissed. The appellate court must decide whether or not the judge acted wrongly. If the judge did act wrongly, then the decision of the lower court is negated. A new trial may be set but more often than not because the appeal has limited the evidence that could be presented in a new trial, the case is simply dropped; a new trial is not likely to be to the advantage of the party who lost on appeal.

Thus, when we discuss the appellate courts and their work, we are interested in their rule-defining function. In fact, to define a rule that is in dispute is to make a new rule. We are concerned, therefore, with the scope of discretion of the appellate courts in their rule-creating function. A full discussion is impossible in the confines of this chapter (a fuller treatment appears in Chambliss & Seidman, 1971: chaps. 7–9). We shall concentrate on a summary of the most important social forces impinging on the appellate-court process.

It is self-evident that most issues that call for decision by appellate courts are raised as a result of the choices made by individual litigants to bring the cases before the courts. Judges do not determine those choices. The result is that, on the whole, courts have been particularly active in rule-making in those areas of law that affect litigants who are sufficiently wealthy to be able to activate legal processes. For example, law books are full of cases detailing the rules with regard to the law of trusts. Trusts are a device by which wealthy people place money or property in charge of a responsible person (or, more frequently nowadays, a corporation) to be managed for the benefit of children, widows, or for charitable purposes. The corpus of trust laws concerns the norms of conduct for trustees: what investments they may or may not make, what kinds of accounts they must keep, with whom they may deal, and so on. There are hundreds of appellate cases that define these rules with great detail and relative precision. Yet these cases affect numerically only the tiniest fraction of the population.

By contrast, there are many legal problems affecting the poor that never reach the courts, although the number of persons affected may be very large. Perhaps nowhere has the effect of economic constraint on the issues posed to courts for decision been more significant than in the area of criminal law. One example may suffice: the norms controlling the actions of police in the course of making arrests and interrogating criminal suspects. Proportionately, far more poor people than middle-class people are arrested or interrogated by police. Moreover, the police generally feel fewer restraints in their treatment of the poor, for the poor tend to be politically powerless and hence are usually less capable of exerting unpleasant pressures on a policeman.

As a result, most instances of police malpractice occur with respect to the poor. Only in very, very rare instances are these malpractices brought to the attention of the courts by poor people, for they lack the money to hire lawyers. Thus, if the definition of the norms regulating police conduct vis-à-vis persons suspected of crime depended solely on rules articulated by appellate courts in cases initiated and litigated to the appellate stage by poor persons themselves, the norms would remain vague and ill defined.

There is one important ameliorating factor in this matter (in recent years) with respect to civil rights and civil liberties. A few private associations, nationwide in scope, have interested themselves in these areas, with respect to which they have acted as moral entrepreneurs. The National Association for the Advancement of Colored People for many years supported litigation affecting the civil rights of black citizens, no one of whom was likely to have been wealthy enough to finance the litigations. With respect to police practices, the American Civil Liberties Union has been particularly active. Indeed, it is not too much to say that the entire law of police practice has been created through cases supported by the ACLU.

In recent years a large proportion (perhaps most) of the significant cases that have brought innovations in criminal law have been the result of interested groups serving as moral entrepreneurs to bring about changes in the law.

This is not to say that appellate courts are altogether powerless to influence the kind of cases that come before them. One important formal exception is the United States Supreme Court's discretionary appellate jurisdiction, defined by means of the exercise of the ancient writ of certiorari. Since 1926 the Supreme Court has had the power to decide whether or not to accept most appeals. The statute extending this power to the Supreme Court was enacted because the docket of the Court was becoming seriously overloaded. It was believed that the Court's chief function was not to ensure that justice was done in individual disputes, but to resolve issues of law.

As a consequence of certiorari, the U.S. Supreme Court has at least a veto power over the selection of issues for determination. While it still cannot determine which issues will arise, it can prevent itself from deciding issues that, in its opinion, ought not to be heard at the moment.

Appellate courts can also exercise significant influence over the sort of cases brought before them by the content of their opinions—which is a somewhat less formal, but nevertheless important, procedure. The dissenting opinion may play a particularly important function in pointing out a legal path that might win a majority in the court. Such an opinion practically invites new litigation aimed at the point suggested by the dissent.

All Lawyers Are Equal but Some Are More Equal than Others

The arguments of the counsel in a case are a principal source of the policy arguments used by appellate courts.

Not every lawyer, however, carries as much weight with a court as every other. In every court there are counsel who appeal before it time and again, more frequently than not representing substantial clients. Judges come to respect some of these men and not others. It is predictable that the arguments of some well-known counsel will be accorded weight that will not be accorded to the arguments of lesser-known lawyers.

Not only are lawyers more or less well known and more or less persuasive, but the lower courts from which the cases come are more or less well respected. So also are the appellate courts whose decisions may be precedents for the cause at hand. In a classic study, Rodney L. Mott (1936) received ratings of the various state appellate courts from 259 law-school professors. He also determined the relative frequency of cases from the several appellate courts that appeared in law-school casebooks. In addition, indices were constructed of the number of times the opinions of the several state appellate courts were cited by other state courts, by the United States Supreme Court, and with approval by the United States Supreme Court. From these various indices he constructed a rank order of state supreme courts, which ranged from 25.18 for New York down to 2.12 for New Mexico.

The opinions of other lower courts and the arguments of counsel are, of course, the formal inputs of policy arguments. There are a host of informal ones, however, of which the comments of law-school professors are perhaps the most important. The relationship between leading law schools and appellate courts is close. Many justices, both of the federal and state appellate courts, choose their clerks from young members of the graduating class of either their own law school or, if there is only one major law school in the state, from that. Most important of all are the law reviews. These journals constitute a unique institution, being the only major professional journals whose editors are students. In the cases of the major law reviews—those of Harvard, Yale, Columbia, Michigan, Wisconsin, and a few others—faculty control is quite literally nil. These reviews are the major forum for publishing the results of legal research, and their impact on the courts can be very great. For example, the arguments that justified the "one man, one vote" Supreme Court decision in the legislative redistricting case *Baker* v. *Carr* were first put forward in an article in the *Harvard Law Review* (Lewis, 1959).

The policy input deriving from the law schools is unique, for besides the personal attitudes of the judges themselves, it is the only important policy input that is independent both of the institution of the courts themselves and of the economic, moral, or personal interests of the litigants. Moreover, as we have seen, pragmatic decision-making requires empirical studies of the actual effect of the rules. Such studies, to the extent that they are in fact made, appear in the law reviews. The importance of these reviews is attested by the frequency with which they are cited as authority in appellate opinions.

The Personal Characteristics of the Judges

Since, in many cases, the issue turns upon questions of value, it would seem that the personal characteristics of the judges are relevant. To understand properly why judges make the policy choices they do, it is necessary to examine these characteristics in three dimensions: first, their background as individuals; second, their background as lawyers; and third, their situation as appellate judges.

There are judges on many appellate levels in the United States. Our attention here is directed only towards the highest state and federal appellate judges, and first to the characteristics of judges appointed to the Supreme Court of the United States in the period 1933–57. From the data in Table 1 and further data of the same sort on all past Supreme Court justices, Schmidhauser concludes: "throughout American history there has been an overwhelming tendency for presidents to choose nominees for the Supreme Court from the socially advantaged families" (Schmidhauser, 1959:2).

The degree to which these personal attributes condition judicial decision-making is rather more difficult to ascertain than the characteristics themselves. Statistically significant relationships have been established between certain personal characteristics and voting tendencies. For example, Nagel demonstrated that:

Democratic judges . . . were more prone to favor (1) the defense in criminal cases, (2) the administrative agency in business regulation cases, (3) the private party in regulation of non-business entities, (4) the claimant in unemployment compensation cases, (5) the broadening position in free speech cases, (6) the finding of a constitutional violation in criminal-constitutional cases, (7) the government in tax cases, (8) the divorce seeker in divorce cases, (9) the wife in divorce settlement cases, (10) the tenant in landlord-tenant cases, (11) the labor union in labor-management cases, (12) the debtor in creditor-debtor cases, (13) the consumer in sales-of-goods cases, (14) the injured party in motor vehicle accident cases, and (15) the employee in employee injury cases (Nagel, 1961:845).

Nine of the above findings (1, 2, 4, 6, 7, 10, 13, 14, and 15) proved to be statistically significant relationships.

Whether these results can be construed to mean that a judge reaches his conclusions because he is a Democrat is, of course, subject to serious question. Grossman (1966) reports Bowen's (1965) finding that none of the variables most significantly associated with judicial decisions explains more than a fraction of the total variance among judges. Grossman concludes that "mere tests of association are inadequate, though useful, and more powerful measures indicate the presence of other 'intervening variables' between the case and the ultimate decision" (1966:1561–62).

TABLE 1
THE PERSONAL ATTRIBUTES OF THE JUSTICES APPOINTED TO THE UNITED STATES SUPREME COURT, 1933–57

Occupations of fathers	
High social status (proprietors, wealthy farmers, professional men)	13(81%)
Low social status (mechanics and laborers, small farmers)	3(19%)
Setting of birth	
United States	
Urban	6(37.5%)
Small town	8(50%)
Rural	1(6.2%)
Europe (Austria)	1(6.2%)
Ethnic origins	
Western European derivation	15(93.7%)
Central, eastern, or southern European derivation	1(6.3%)
Religious affiliations	
High social status religious affiliations (Episcopalian, Presbyterian, Unitarian)	8(50%)
Intermediate social status affiliations (Roman Catholic, Jewish)	3(19%)
Low social status affiliations (Methodist, Baptist)	3(19%)
"Protestant" (no other information available)	2(13%)
Nonlegal educational background	
College or university of high standing	10(61%)
College or university of average standing	4(26%)
Academy or school of average standing (public or private)	2(13%)
Legal education	
Law school of high standing	10(61%)
Private apprenticeship and study under prominent lawyer or judge	1(6%)
Law school of average standing	5(32%)
Prior legal or professional experience	
Lawyers who were primarily politicians	10(62%)
Lawyers who were primarily state or federal judges	1(6%)
Corporation (primarily) lawyers	2(13%)
Lawyers by education primarily engaged in academic pursuits	3(19%)

Source: Schmidhauser, 1959:7, 17, 22, 23, 24, 33.

The Socialization of Judges

The socialization of appellate judges can best be regarded as involving three stages: that of law student, that of practicing attorney, and that of lower-court judge—the usual steps in a judicial career.

The American law-school education is a classic example of an education in which the subject matter studied formally is ridiculously simple, but the process of socialization into the profession very difficult. Thurman Arnold (1960) once remarked of jurisprudence what is in many respects true as well of the formal part of the study of law: jurisprudence is a tedious subject, tedious not in the way studying a difficult discipline like physics is tedious, but in the way tossing feathers into the air, hour after hour, is tedious. To the extent that the study of law is a study of the universe of norms alone, there is precious little about the law that would challenge a bright junior-high-school student. By their last year in law school, the better students, those on the law reviews, for example, are getting reasonably good grades on the basis of a couple of days' study prior to end-of-term examinations.

The key to an understanding of the socialization of American lawyers in law school is best found through an examination of the outstanding aspect of their educational method, the case method of instruction (Hurst, 1950). Initiated by Professor C. C. Langdell at Harvard in 1871, the case method has long since become the dominant form of instruction in every American law school.

This method, in its classic form, has two aspects that are important for our purposes. First, it purports to teach the norms of law by presenting the students, not with textbooks stating in type what the rules are, but with appellate opinions giving the facts of the cases, the decisions of the court, and the reasons it gave to justify its opinions. Second, the case-study method is, at least in theory, teaching in the Socratic style (Blaustein & Porter, 1954:167).

There can be no doubt that the case method is a thoroughly inefficient way to teach and to learn the rules of substantive law. Its functions are quite different. Two of these functions are especially important in connection with socialization. First, the constant dialogue between professor and students trains most students very rapidly to be tough-minded and independent in thought. At the beginning of the first year, if the professor said that black was white, most law students would carefully make a note of that proposition. By the end of the year, it sometimes seems that if the professor said that "one and one make two," somebody would ask, "Are there no exceptions?" That kind of hard-nosed questioning of everything is an important consequence of the socialization of lawyers in law schools.

The second function of the case method as originally conceived is perhaps more subtle. The use of decided cases as the basic teaching materials and the concomitant exclusion of an examination of the law in action confines the questions asked to those raised in the cases. Questions that challenge the basis of the system as it exists are thus excluded, except insofar as an imaginative professor raises them. In the latter case, the very use of case materials demonstrates that he is raising an academic question, not an issue with which a hard-nosed, practical lawyer need be concerned.

Hard-nosed independence is necessary if the system is to generate lawyers who can advise competently, i.e., independently. More important, perhaps, is the necessity, for the continuance of the system, that lawyers and judges define the problems presented *within the framework* of the existing systems. So long as they so define the problems, whether they take a "liberal" or "conservative" tack is relatively unimportant. The early socialization of judges and lawyers, thus, tends paradoxically to make them intellectually independent, but to restrain them from looking for radical solutions, for throughout their law-school education, they are taught to define problems in the way they have always been defined.

The seeming paradox of intellectual independence combined with acceptance of the existing definition of the situation persists in later practice. The successful lawyer constantly sharpens his wits in situations of conflict. His whole professional career, however, necessarily requires him to take the institution of American society at any moment as given. One advises a client to act in a particular way because he believes that the system as it is now structured requires him to do so.

The successful lawyer tends to adopt conservative solutions for a second reason. If he is to be financially successful, his clients must be able to pay fees. In general, rich people and businessmen pay larger fees than poor people and wage earners. Successful lawyers represent successful clients. Inevitably, the successful lawyer, if not already attuned to the value sets of his clients, tends to adopt them.

The successful lawyer who becomes a judge tends to avoid advocating radical solutions for still a third reason. In America, one becomes a judge, in all except a tiny minority of instances, in part because he has been a political animal. The appointee to judgeship more likely than not has already served a period, as a young lawyer, in the capacity of prosecutor, city councilman, or the like. He probably is a member of the local political club's executive committee, or its analogue. He cannot successfully play the political game by rocking the boat.

The final stage in the socialization of the appellate judge is, in most cases, a period of time as a trial judge. Judges of all sorts, and trial judges even more than appellate judges, tend to be tied to the existing institutional structure by a myriad of strands of interest and interaction. On their favor turn the careers of many lawyers with whom they were schoolmates and have been professional colleagues, fellow soldiers in political wars, and friends, frequently for many years. It is a rare judge who adopts a value-set markedly different from those of his reference group.

Finally, judging is a career. The successful lower-court judge is promoted to higher courts, including always the possibility of a U.S. Supreme Court appointment. Thus, although the appointment of a judge may be de facto or de jure for life, the career possibilities are sufficient to serve as a restraint on most judges' behavior on the bench. Since those groups and classes that determine judicial appointments will look unfavorably on judges whose decisions are out of line with the status quo, there is a built-in mechanism that virtually guarantees a conservative output.

The socialization of lawyers and judges in the past, therefore, has tended to make appellate judges tough-minded and independent people who define situations in ways conforming to the existing institutional structure. In addition, the reference group of most judges can be expected to make him select relatively conservative answers to the issues raised.

Organizational Interests

A salient characteristic of organization behavior is that the ongoing policies and activities of any organization are those designed to maximize rewards to and minimize strains on the organization. The system of courts is an organization, and it acts in accordance with the general principles applicable to all organizations. Leon Green has said:

> the policies which the courts most clearly articulate are those which concern the administration of the courts themselves. They hesitate to modify the law if the decision

will "open the door to a flood of litigation," make it difficult to define definite limits of liability, require an investigation of factual details for which their processes are not well designed, make the reexamination of corollary or subsidiary principles necessary, or threaten to upset an established equilibrium in social conventions, trade practices or property transactions (Green, 1955:16).

We shall discuss two significant organizational pressures to which courts have responded: the large volume of litigation and "crises."

The Volume of Litigation

The principal source of strain on the courts has been the constantly rising volume of litigation. In the early and middle nineteenth century, this tendency reflected the rising commercial activity of the country. Just as the courts were getting this matter under control through a variety of devices, there came a wave of litigation by employees against employers arising out of industrial accidents. Ultimately, this problem was largely taken out of the courts by the development of workmen's compensation commissions in the second decade of the twentieth century, just in time to clear a few dockets for the enormous flood of automobile accident cases that engulfed the courts in the 1920s, and which have remained the most frequent causes of legal action today.

Yet courts cannot increase their personnel or their physical plant easily. A court cannot expand out of "profits," or by adding a subsidiary or two to meet new problems. It does not control its own purse strings, and those who do have been notably slow in responding to its increased work loads (Friedman, 1967:798–99).

The principal response to the increased work load has been that repetitive, routine sorts of cases, for example, are handled in repetitive, routine ways that obviate formal hearings on the trial-court level in most instances, and rarely raise issues for appeal. Most traffic fines are paid by mail without even the formality of a court appearance. Most criminal cases are routinized.

The courts, in fact, approve real sanctions against those litigants who do not desire to take advantage of the routine responses. It is a rare parking or speeding offender who will litigate a case, even if he is convinced that he is not guilty, so time-consuming are the court appearances required to determine the issues. As a result, only a miniscule percentage of the routine summonses issued ever give rise to any event that consumes a court's time.

Appellate courts have been quick to approve techniques that lower the pressure exerted by the volume of business. In most judicial systems, the chief justice is not only the chairman of the appellate bench, but also the chief administrative officer of the courts' system. Frequently, he and his fellow judges have instituted formalized pretrial conferences, which, although nominally designed to identify the issues, obtain agreement on exhibits, etc., prior to the trial, in fact are primarily glorified bargaining sessions between plaintiff and defense attorneys. In Connecticut, for example, pretrial sessions are held formally for one or two weeks twice a year. During this period all other work of the trial courts stops, and the judges engage in a massive effort to settle every lawsuit on the calendar awaiting trial.

In criminal matters appellate courts have been eager to impose devices designed to reduce the load on the court system. They have frequently placed a stamp of approval on the negotiated plea, asserting that because it saves the state time and money (read: lessens the pressure of business on court dockets), it is a wise and useful device. As a consequence of this approval, over 90 percent of the cases handled in criminal courts are settled by negotiated pleas of guilty by the defendant. All parties to the case ultimately become part of an institutionalized force designed to bring about a guilty plea. This is as true of the court appointed public defender (Sudnow, 1965) and the privately engaged criminal attorney (Blumberg, 1967) as it is of the judges and the prosecuting attorney.

The poor defendant is, of course, the most vulnerable to pressure from the court for a guilty plea. The lawyer is likely to be court appointed and to accept as valid the reports of probation departments and police officers. It is also likely to be in his interests to expedite the case as quickly as possible. The guilty plea is thus an efficient solution for everyone concerned.

In addition to these responses to the pressures of litigation, appellate courts have devised (or have been given by legislation) certain discretionary powers to decline to accept certain appeals. As we pointed out earlier, this power is most notable in the Supreme Court of the United States. That Court has the power to decide for itself, on the whole, which appeals to accept for decision by the granting of a writ of certiorari, and which to reject. Only if four justices affirmatively vote to grant the writ will the Court hear an apppeal. In this way, the Court can limit its decision-making to matters calling for significant rule-making: constitutional issues, matters in which there is a conflict between the rules announced by different courts of appeal in the federal system, problems of statutory construction, and the like.

The increasing volume of litigation, therefore, has probably been the single most important variable in determining judicial responses.

Crises Cases

A second significant variable has been the court's recognition of "crises" cases. Some cases present issues that are highly charged with political or moral significance. Like all decision-makers, in such instances courts tend to perceive a potential threat to their own legitimacy, for if their decision is not enforced in fact, their whole structure of authority may be undermined.

Such a situation has been brought about by recent Supreme Court decisions governing police practices. Although the Court decreed that defendants had to be warned of their rights before a confession would be considered valid, that all de-fendants have a right to an attorney, and that juveniles had the same legal protection as adults, there is mounting evidence that police practices have not changed very much despite these court decisions (Medalie et al., 1968; Lefstein et al., 1969).

Crisis cases, as Friedman (1967) has suggested, are of two different kinds. Some are plainly nonrecurrent. Such crisis cases are not nearly so threatening to a court as cases involving deep-seated social conflicts, in which the court must in its decision advantage one side or the other. Courts tend to avoid such cases for as long as they can. When they do face up to the problem, they try to be unanimous (as the Supreme Court was in *Brown* v. *Board of Education*) in order to legitimize the decision as much as possible. The ruling is likely to be one whose administration can be delegated to other agencies. It will be as objective and as quantitative as possible, in an effort to end constant probing by litigants for its outermost boundaries. Since the simplest of all rules to administer is one that rejects the case and others like it completely, there is perhaps some tendency to solve crisis cases by rejecting any form of judicial interference.

CONVERSION PROCESSES IN APPELLATE COURTS

These inputs into the appellate-court decision-making process—the selection of issues for appeal, the differential influence of lawyers, the personal characteristics of the judges, the socialization of the judiciary, and the organizational pressures and characteristics of the court system—all play a major role in determining the content and the thrust of appellate-court decisions. Their inputs are the structure within which appeals are converted into decisions by the appellate courts.

To understand this conversion, we must consider two principal processes. One is the formal reasoning process that judges are supposed to use in justifying their decision. This is expressed in norms defining the judge's role in decision-making, and probably has been the subject of more jurisprudential writing than any other single aspect of the legal process. The other is informal: the effect of small-group interactions taking place within the collegiate body of an appellate bench.

The Formal Reasoning Process

The Scope of Judicial Creativity

In the early history of the United States the demands for legal-rational legitimacy, and the political and ideological requirements of the new entrepreneurial classes, generated an insistence that courts not make law, but merely find and apply it. Therefore, judges take an oath to support the law and the Constitution. In a clear case, where the facts at hand fall unambiguously within the language of a statute or precedent, a judge has little choice in all but the rarest of cases save to apply the law as it exists. In such a case—and such cases include the vast majority of cases in trial courts—courts do indeed follow the existing law. In such cases, no appeal usually lies. The fact that the case unambiguously falls within the language of existing authority makes it unlikely that the losing side will consider the probability of success sufficient to warrant an appeal.

Where the law is ambiguous as applied to the facts at hand, or where the rules are themselves contradictory, however, nobody can state with certainty what the applicable rule is. For example, the Constitution guarantees a right to counsel "in criminal prosecutions." There can be no doubt that an accused person has a right to counsel at least at the formal trial itself. Does the phrase "criminal prosecution," however, include in-custody interrogation in the police station before any formal charges have been filed? On that issue, reasonable men could differ; at least, the fact situation supposed is not unambiguously included in the phrase "criminal prosecution." When such a case arose, the court was *forced* by virtue of its function to decide the case at hand, to make a choice between competing proposed constructions of the authoritative rule. They are forced, in short, to create law. It is such cases that constitute the grist of the appellate-court's mill.

Precisely because of the way in which the problem arises, however, appellate courts are not free to create new law out of whole cloth. The issue as it comes to them is sharply limited by the leading rule that defines their position: *They may not invoke as a rule to govern the case at hand* (and thus to serve as the rule to control all future similar cases) *any rule not at least arguably a permissible construction of existing case or statutory law.* For example, the rule on insanity in New York, following the rules laid down in England in 1843 in *M'Naghten's* case, provided that it was a defense to a criminal charge if the accused could prove that at the time of the crime he was laboring under such a defect of reason that he did not know that the act was wrong. In *People* v. *Schmidt* [216 N.Y. 324, 110 N.E. 945 (1915)] the accused claimed that God had called upon him to kill the victim as a sacrifice and an atonement. He knew, however, that what he was doing was legally wrong. The trial court charged the jury to the effect that the word "wrong" in the phrase "did not know that the act was wrong" meant *"legally wrong."* The jury, therefore, found the accused guilty of first degree murder. On appeal, he urged that the proper construction of the word was "legally or *morally* wrong." The appellate court was faced, therefore, with a narrow choice: to construe the law with respect of the defense of insanity as though it read, "at the time of the crime the accused was laboring under such a defect of reason that he did not know that the act was *legally* wrong," or, on the other hand, as though it read "legally or morally wrong." (Judge Cardozo, in a famous opinion, decided for the accused.)

Now, in fact, the actual difficulty with which the court was faced was the appropriate scope of the defense of insanity. Whether the test of knowledge that an act is wrong—legally, morally, or otherwise—accords with modern notions of the nature of mental illness is a subject on which there is a vast literature, mostly arguing that the test may match the dominant conceptions of phrenology, the prevailing psychiatric theory of 1843, but not more modern models. Cardozo, however, was effectively debarred from considering the wider scope of the problem with which he was faced by the limitations imposed by the leading rule defining his role.

Thus, the role of appellate judges requires them to make law, but at the same time, it places very sharp limitations upon their creativity in making new rules in response to the problems posed. How do they go about making that choice?

Rationality of Decisions and Legitimacy of Law

Secular, pragmatic policy-making—and the creation of new rules of law inevitably involves policy-making—requires a decision-maker to look to the consequences of the alternatives proposed. Appellate-court rule-creating in the common-law system has almost always arisen in the context of a concrete case. Only in rare instances and only in a few jurisdictions is it possible to propound to an appellate court an abstract question of law. The result is that in choosing between the alternative permissible potential rules, which are urged by counsel as the governing rules for a troublesome case, the court has before it a case study. It can see, very concretely, how each of the proposed rules will affect the facts at hand. Insofar as the facts at hand are typical, it can anticipate the probable consequences of the proposed rules, in one way or the other.

Despite the inherently pragmatic context of common-law decision-making, the way in which judges have justified their decisions was only at first pragmatic; it then appeared to be highly legalistic, and has become once again increasingly pragmatic. Why this strange sea change occurred can be understood best by first examining Max Weber's notions of legalism.

Max Weber (1954) believed that legalism of a sort represented the highest development of a legal order. He held that the two basic activities in law are lawmaking and law-finding. The methodology of each may be *rational* or *irrational;* and each can proceed either *rationally* or *irrationally* with respect to either *formal* or *substantive* criteria. Substantive irrationality exists when law-finders or lawmakers make their decision not on the basis of general norms but on the basis of emotional evaluations of each case. This Weber denoted "khadi justice," because he believed that the Muslim judge rendered his decisions on an emotional basis. Substantively rational lawmaking or law-finding occurs when the judge or legislator consciously follows articulated general principles—whether religious, or ethical, or otherwise. Soviet law is an example of substantively rational law in that it is designed to bring about the goals conceived and articulated by Soviet leaders.

Lawmaking and law-finding are formally rational when the legally operative or material facts in any case are determined not from case to case, but by reference to a general rule. These facts may be determined by general rules of two different sorts, depending upon the criteria for determining the operative facts. These facts may be purely extrinsic—the seal that determines whether a contract is enforceable, or the two signatures at the end of the will that control its validity. The facts may, on the other hand, be determined by generic rules, which, in turn, are deduced from generic and abstract concepts, in which case lawmaking and law-finding are both formally and logically rational (Weber, 1954:63; Friedman, 1966).

This typology of ideal types of legal systems has been conveniently summarized:

1. *Irrational*, i.e., not guided by general rules.
   a. *Formal*: guided by means which are beyond the control of reason (ordeal, oracle, etc.).
   b. *Substantive*: guided by reaction to the individual case.
2. *Rational*, i.e., guided by general rules.
   a. *Substantive*: guided by the principles of an ideological system other than that of the law itself (ethics, religion, power politics, etc.).
   b. *Formal*:
      (1) *Extrinsically*, i.e., ascribing significance to external acts observable by the senses;
      (2) *Logically*, i.e., expressing its rules by the use of abstract concepts created by legal thought itself and constituting a complete system (Friedman, 1966:148).

American law has experienced a shift from the "grand style" to the "formal style" of opinion-writing, that is, a shift, in Weberian terms, from substantively rational lawmaking to logically, formally rational lawmaking.

The formal style, in that it purports to justify decisions by the exclusive use of materials drawn from the legal order, masks the patent fact that in such cases judges create law. We know today, both logically and empirically, that judges *do* make the rules, which they then proceed to apply to the facts in hand. Why did the shift occur from the grand style, frankly conceding that the judge was engaged in lawmaking, to the formal style, denying that patent fact?

The shift reflected the great change in economic and political power from the aristocratic government of the eighteenth and early nineteenth centuries, to the admission of the new men of commerce into the corridors of power during the fourth decade of the century. A variety of different currents, carrying the political and economic demands of the new rulers, reached confluence in the demand for law of Weber's logically, formally rational law.

As Weber himself put it, the "bourgeois interests"

had to demand an unambiguous and clear legal system that would be free of irrational administrative arbitrariness as well as of irrational disturbance by concrete privileges, that would also offer firm guarantees of the legally binding nature of contracts, and that, in consequence of all these features, would function in a calculable way (1954:267).

This demand was met by the five postulates that Weber believed to be imminent in formal, logical, rational law:

> First, that every concrete legal decision be the "application" of an abstract legal proposition to a concrete "fact situation"; second, it must be possible in every concrete case to derive the decision from abstract legal propositions by means of legal logic; third, that the law must actually or virtually constitute a "gapless" system of legal propositions, or must, at least, be treated as if it were such a gapless system; fourth, that whatever cannot be "construed" legally in rational terms is also legally irrelevant; and fifth, that every social action of human beings must always be visualized as either an "application" or "execution" of legal propositions, or as an infringement thereof (1954:64).

The demand that the law be made certain implied, therefore, that the law exist in a "cognizable" form *prior* to the dispute which the judge must decide. For judges to legitimatize their decisions, in this view, they were required to demonstrate that such was the case. Hence, they had to demonstrate in their opinions that they did not create the law, but only found it.

Other political and ideological demands of the rising bourgeoisie coincided with this requirement. The new democratic dogma of the separation of power placed the lawmaking function in a democratically elected legislature, and reserved to the far-from-democratically selected judiciary the dispute-settling function. As Dean James Landis (1947) has suggested, "this led to the conception of the judges as impotent agents, impotent to do otherwise than merely 'find' law." Austin's (1875) analytical positivism contributed to this development, for it taught the judges that their task was merely to determine the "command of the sovereign"—i.e., to examine what the law is, not what it ought to be. Dicey's (1959) notion of the rule of law married itself happily to the Blackstonian conception of the common law as "a fully matured system" to inhibit judicial notions of creativity. Finally, in England the judges adopted a position of political neutrality and hence of self-limitation in lawmaking during the two periods of great creativity in social legislation, the Great Depression of the 1930s and the postwar years of the next two decades. Their neutrality with respect to public law inevitably washed over to inhibit their creativity with respect to the common law itself. In addition to these proliferations of democratic political theory, the Benthamite and Utilitarian emphasis on the dispute-settlement function of the courts tended to focus on the desirability of certainty in law, rather than of creativity.

The Realist Critique

The difficulty is that the dogma that the law is a gapless web, and the corresponding norm of judicial lawmaking that judges must solve cases with material drawn only from the legal order, is a prescriptive and not a descriptive rule: that is, it tells what ought to happen, not what takes place in fact.

Following that prescriptive rule, judges sought to demonstrate that every case was a clear case. They tried to solve every case by the use of clear case rules or some variant of them. The results were logically less than satisfying.

One example from the African experience must suffice. In *Rex* v. *Edgal* [4 W.A.C.A. 133 Nigeria (1948)] appellants were convicted of violation of a section of the Nigeria Criminal Code which read, in part, "Any person who unlawfully supplies to . . . any person anything whatever, knowing that it is intended to be unlawfully used to procure a miscarriage of a woman . . . is guilty of a felony. . . ." Upon appeal, they asserted that no place in the Criminal Code was it explained when an abortion was "lawful" or "unlawful." Moreover, the Code (which had been adopted in 1916) stated explicitly that a person could be tried and punished only under an express provision of the Code. Therefore, the appellants claimed, their conviction was illegal, since there was no express provision of the Code describing whether the miscarriage for which they had supplied the abortifacient was "unlawful." The appellate court affirmed the conviction nevertheless. It argued (1) that when the draftsman of the Criminal Code had written the section in question in 1916, he must have meant that the word "unlawful" meant "unlawful" as it was under the then-existing common law; (2) that a case in England in 1939 [*Rex* v. *Bourne*, K.B. 687 (1939)] had established that the common law held lawful only those abortions which were necessary to preserve the life of the mother; (3) that since the common law has always existed, the judges in 1939 were not "creating" law but merely announcing what the common law had always been; (4) that, therefore, the common law as announced in the 1939 English case was the common law which the draftsman of the Nigerian Code had had in mind in 1916 when he used the word "unlawfully" in the relevant section of the Criminal Code; and (5) that, therefore, the appellants were guilty since they had not supplied the abortifacient for the purpose of saving the mother's life, but merely for the purpose of doing away with the unborn child. An equally "logical" line of argument to the contrary might have been: (1) that to find these appellants guilty one had to read the Code section as though it read, "Any person who supplies to . . . any person anything whatever, knowing that it is intended to be used to procure a miscarriage of a woman under such circumstance that the act would have been unlawful at common law, is guilty of a felony"; (2) that the Code itself states plainly that no person may be convicted under the common law of crimes; and (3) that therefore these appellants cannot be convicted of the crimes charged. Why one line of argument and not the other was selected cannot possibly be determined from the arguments themselves. The ambiguity of the Code statute was a function of the ambiguity of the legal order with respect of the crime of abortion. Examination of the legal order itself with the tool of logic alone could not explain why one rather than the other possible "logical" argument held sway.

It is for this reason that Justice Holmes said long ago that "general propositions do not decide concrete cases. The decision will depend on a judgement or intuition more subtle than any articulate major premise" [*Lochner* v. *New York*, 198 U.S. 45, 74 (1905)].

The principal consequence of legalistic reasoning is that the choice of values by the appellate court is hidden behind a facade of logical necessity. By keeping the premises inarticulate, a court tends to place them beyond discussion. Debate is limited to the relatively sterile question of whether the court's argument is "logical." Thus, the decision is legitimatized within the system.

But, as Holmes (1897:457) so aptly put it, the life of the law is not logic, but experience, and therefore, experience should be the test of the rightness of the law. "How well will it work?" then becomes the test, rather than the arid, conceptual quiddities of the logicians and the legalists.

In recent years (since 1937) the Supreme Court of the United States has led the way in establishing the legitimacy of this position. In case after case the court has asked, "What are day-to-day consequences of this decision?" and they have even gone so far as to take into account social-science data to justify their decision, or at least they have cited such data to justify their decision (Hart, 1959:84).

By frankly and openly facing the lawmaking function with which it is confronted, however, the Court necessarily seemed deviant to the layman, accustomed to the myth that courts only apply fixed and determined law to the facts. Most laymen, in short, are still committed to the role-expectations implied by the formal style of opinion-writing. From that posture, of course, a court that seeks to legitimize its decision in the realist mode will appear deviant. But whatever the appearance, the fact is that courts do now and always have "legislated": it is inevitable that in resolving a dispute, new rules will be enunciated.

Appellate Courts as Small Groups

Appellate courts are institutions, and to a degree, judges exhibit the characteristics of persons who work in institutions. That is to say, they interact among themselves, and with the clerks, bailiffs, lawyers, and others who make up the institution. Inevitably, the conversion process is affected by these interpersonal relationships.

Appellate courts are typically collegiate benches. That is, the judges discuss the cases among themselves, and ultimately vote upon the result. One judge or another is then assigned to write the majority opinion; typically it is circulated for comment by the other judges, and, ultimately, amended by the writer. Dissenting or concurring judges then have an opportunity to write their own opinions.

The traditional legal view has always been that the individual justice on an appellate bench individually studies each case, followed by discussion by the body of justices as a whole, so that the result will represent the mature collective thought of the court (Hart, 1959:84). At the other end of the scale are iconoclastic notions, such as that of Thurman Arnold, who insists that there "is no such process" as the "maturing of collective thought." Instead, he argues: "men of positive views are only hardened in those views by [judicial] conferences. . . . I have no doubt that longer periods of argument and deliberation, and more time to dissent, would only result in the pro-liferation of opinions of which we already have too many" (Arnold,1960:1313).

Behind these positions are differing assessments about the role of reason and logical argument in the formulation of institutional opinions by courts. The orthodox view presents judges as reasonable men, entering discussion with hypotheses about the solution to cases, but with open minds to argument by differing colleagues. It suggests that the central operative force in judicial decision-making is, indeed, the force of reason. On the other hand, Arnold's position tends to denigrate the role of discussion. It suggests that the principal force in judicial decision-making is the value-set of the justice involved, rather than the rational arguments adduced. The ortho-dox view tends to make rational argument the principal motivating factor in reaching institutional appellate decisions; the heterodox view would obviously make institu-tional pressures towards conformity and internal politicking the central device.

The orthodox view accords with the conventional norms that measure our role-expectation of judges. These have been adumbrated in opinions without number. Whether in grand style, in formal style, or in the realist mode, all judicial opinions assume that the central persuasive device is the appeal to reason. The heterodox view seems to assert that judges, in fact, do not reach joint decisions on the basis the norms would seem to require.

There is a considerable body of direct evidence that judges indeed do argue with each other in rational terms, and that mainly they are persuaded simply by the force of argument. For example, in March, 1945, the Court at first voted to affirm a convic-tion under the Sherman Act of union officials and employers in the lumber industry for conspiring to raise prices and wages through monopolizing the lumber business in the San Francisco area. Justice Black, voting with the majority, was assigned the case. He later circulated an opinion reversing the case, stating that after study he had become convinced that there was error. After hearing reargument, the Court voted to reverse 5–3.

This evidence is not alone conclusive. It may be true that in some cases, judges are swayed by argument. In many more, however, the vote taken before the writing of an opinion remains the vote after the opinion is written. In such cases, to what extent is the decision based on reason and argument, and to what extent on group and institutional pressures?

One way to examine this question is to inquire into the nature and character of dissent. To the extent that dissent is openly expressed by judges in opinions that seek to legitimize their positions in terms that appeal to reason, one can be sure that non-rational pressures originating in the appellate bench itself have been resisted. On the other hand, the absence of articulated dissent is ambiguous. It may arise because the judges are convinced, in fact, by rational argument, or it may arise because they have been coerced into uniformity by other pressures.

What is surprising is not that in some courts dissent is a rarity. Rather, it is that dissent is as frequent as it is in many courts. In the Supreme Court of the United States, dissents have increased in frequency in recent years. In 1930, 11 percent of the opinions were accompanied by dissents, 28 percent in 1940, 61 percent in 1950, and 76 percent in 1957 (Zobell, 1959). No state Supreme Court approaches this frequency of dissent. The range of dissent in state Supreme Courts is, however, extremely high, as shown in Table 2.

Small-group sociological theory holds that "an individual is more likely to conform to group opinion in the following cases: if the object to be judged is ambiguous; if he must make his opinion public; if the majority holding a contrary opinion is large; and if the group is especially friendly or close-knit" (Hare, 1964:219). It would

TABLE 2

FREQUENCY OF DISSENT IN THE FIFTY-ONE SUPREME COURTS:
WITH ONE OR MORE DISSENTING VOTES IN SAMPLES OF TWENTY-FIVE

No. of cases with dissent	Jurisdiction
0	Alabama, Arizona, Delaware, Maryland, Massachusetts, Nevada, North Carolina, Rhode Island, South Carolina, Tennessee, West Virginia
1	Georgia, Idaho, Illinois, Kentucky, Maine, Minnesota, Mississippi, Missouri, New Mexico, North Dakota, Vermont, Washington
2	Connecticut, Florida, Iowa, Nebraska, New Jersey, South Dakota, Virginia, Wyoming
3	Arkansas, New Hampshire, Ohio, Oregon
4	Colorado, Kansas, Montana
5	Alaska, Oklahoma
6	Hawaii, Indiana, New York, Utah, Wisconsin
7	California, Louisiana
8	Michigan
9	Texas
10	Pennsylvania
17	U. S. Supreme Court

Source: Sickles, 1965:100.

seem that conformity ought to be the rule, rather than the exception, in appellate decision-making. The subject is invariably ambiguous. Dissenting opinion must be made public. Appellate courts have notoriously long-lived members, whose work and past associations tend to make them friendly and close-knit. Moreover, there is a common institutional pressure upon them all to keep dissent at a minimum. As Judge Learned Hand has observed, dissent "is disastrous [to a court] because disunity cancels the impact of monolithic solidarity on which the authority of a bench of judges so largely depends" (Hand, 1958:72–73).

Why are dissents so frequent despite the institutional pressures towards conformity? Why the difference in the range of dissents between the different courts? The reasons can, perhaps, be found in the peculiar nature of the subject matter of the several courts, the character of the persons selected to be judges, and the norms defining the judges' roles.

In the first place, it would seem evident that the tendency to decline to conform would be correlated with the individual judge's attachment to a particular response. This would seem confirmed by the marked increase in Supreme Court dissents over dissents among the judges of the several state courts. Many of the matters coming before the state courts involve rules toward which only a rare judge could have a deep emotional attachment. It is probably hard to perceive a great social issue in many of the technical problems of property law or precise construction of the uniform commercial code. On the other hand, practically all the problems coming before the Supreme Court of the United States involve questions of high policy about which men not only differ, but differ passionately. In such cases, it would seem that group pressures that might be determinative in compelling conformity in lesser cases would be insufficient to achieve that end.

In the second place, judges are not persons such as the relatively inexperienced university student who is typically the subject of experimental small-group research. They are members of a highly articulate subculture, that of the lawyer; they are drawn, in general, from the most successful in that subculture; they have been trained for all their professional lives to take independent positions. No wonder they tend to resist pressures toward group conformity that might be overwhelming to others.

The range of persons chosen for elevation to the United States Supreme Court bench, however, is markedly wider than that from which state court judges tend to be drawn. Geographical representation is far greater. State supreme court judges invariably are local residents, whereas the U.S. Supreme Court has consistently maintained a relatively high degree of geographical diversity. In many states, which have effectively had a single party in power for many years, the bench is apt to be colored in political monochrome. Where judges in state courts are elected, instead of being appointed as they are in the federal system, they are even more active politically than are some Supreme Court judges before elevation. Although the statistics are incomplete, it seems probable that most state court judges are drawn primarily from practicing, successful, "political" lawyers.

In the third place, there seems to be a marked range among the several courts in the norms of conduct expected of fellow judges. The wide range of dissents recorded in Table 2 would seem sufficient evidence, for judges in the different state courts are not so different from each other, nor are the issues presented of so wide a range of controversiality, to explain the range in dissents. Rather, it seems that the several state courts have different norms of conduct for the judges. In some, we have been told, there is an informal understanding that, except for the most urgent reasons, judges are bound by majority vote in conference. In other states, such as Maryland, in some sorts of cases, individual judges write the appeals, and the other judges simply assent without real consideration (Sickles, 1965).

At the end of practically every case, at least a majority of the justices achieve a consensus with respect to a single opinion. How is that consensus achieved, apart from the use of rational argument? This can best be understood by conceiving of the collegiate appellate court as basically a political organization, in terms of the interactions among its several members. We shall examine this with respect to the United States Supreme Court, upon which most research has been done.

In the first place, the leadership role in a small group is crucial. Small-group theory distinguishes between "task" and "social" leadership. The former is concerned with getting the job done; the latter, with maintaining individual self-esteem and group harmony. The role of the chief justice has sometimes been exercised in one way, and sometimes in the other. The role itself gives the chief justice two important leverages: he presides at the crucial conference, and he has the privilege of stating his views first. He is thus in a position to identify in each case the issues that seem to him to be significant, and thus, to shape the entire discussion. Second, if he votes with the majority, he has the privilege of assigning the opinion to a justice for writing. Chief justices have been known to vote with the majority even when in disagreement in order to be able to name the opinion writer. Charles Evans Hughes exercised his role as a task leader, and dominated the conference. Harlon Stone, on the other hand, was basically a social leader, and did not dominate the conference as Hughes had done (Murphy, 1964:397–98).

Small-group theory also holds that in most discussion groups, the person who talks the most generally wins a position as an informal leader, expertise being equal (Hare, 1964:236). In the Supreme Court an institutionalized procedure has been adopted that has the effect of lessening the importance of the dominating speaker, for tradition requires that each justice state his position in turn, beginning with the justice who is junior on the bench. On the other hand, expertise in many areas of law is not equal. Justice Douglas, who served as chairman of the Securities and Exchange Commission, obviously possesses special knowledge in this area, and almost all the decisions concerning the Securities and Exchange Act have been written by him. It is hard to believe that in specialized areas such as this, individual justices do not take leadership when they have an expert knowledge of the field. Thus, the chief justice by virtue of his role, and justices with specific expertise, exert special influence in deciding cases.

In the second place, judges apparently have frequently sought to exert special influence by extending the glad hand to other members. Fulsome compliments on an opinion are not infrequent. Frankfurter noted on the back of Justice Stone's opinion in *United States* v. *Darby* [312 U.S. 100 (1941)], for example, "This is a grand plum pudding. There are so many luscious plums in it that it's invidious to select. . . . It's a superb job" (Murphy, 1964:51).

Compliments would hardly seem to be very effective in influencing men of the experience and stature of most Supreme Court justices. They would seem an important emollient, however, to the crucial process of bargaining over opinions. Stone once wrote to Douglas: "I have gone over your opinion in this case with some care, and I congratulate you on your lucid and penetrating analysis and the great thoroughness with which you have done a difficult job. If Justice Brandeis could read it he would be proud of his successor" (Murphy, 1964:52). He annexed a single-spaced typewritten sheet of suggested revisions.

It is, of course, the bargaining process which most clearly suggests that opinions of the Supreme Court are in fact the product of the entire Court. A justice has only two sanctions that he can use against a colleague to obtain changes in the majority opinion: his vote, and his willingness to express dissent in a written opinon. Except in close cases, the second is probably the more effective. Stone once wrote to Frankfurter: "If you wish to write, placing the case on the ground which I think tenable and desirable, I shall cheerfully join you. If not, I will add a few observations for myself" (p. 59).

In the course of the bargaining process, occasionally pressures that go beyond what might seem the legitimate scope of judicial argument are used. In *Hirabashyi* v. *United States* [320 U.S. 81 (1943)], the majority of the Court voted to uphold the conviction of some nisei for violating a curfew imposed by the military on the West Coast. Justice Frank Murphy was horrified at the racism that he believed to be embodied in the order, and filed a strong dissent. Frankfurter wrote to him:

> Of course, I shan't try to dissuade you from filing a dissent in that case—not because I do not think it highly unwise but because I think you are immovable. But I would like to say two things to you about the dissent: (1) it has internal contradictions which you ought not to allow to stand, and (2) do you really think it is conducive to the things you care about, including the great reputation of this Court, to suggest that everybody is out of step except Johnny, and more particularly that the Chief Justice and seven other Justices of this Court are behaving like the enemy and thereby playing into the hands of the enemy?" (Murphy, 1964:47).

On another occasion during the war, in *Ex Parte Quirin* [317 U.S. 1 (1942)], the justices had difficulty in agreeing why the Constitution permitted the trial of captured Nazi saboteurs in military tribunals rather than in regularly constituted civilian courts. One justice (whom Murphy leaves unnamed) wrote to his colleagues:

> Some of the very best lawyers I know are now in the Solomon Island battle, some are seeing service in Australia, some are sub-chasers in the Atlantic, and some are on the various air fronts. . . . I [can] almost hear their voices were they to read more than a single opinion in this case. They would say something like this . . . : "What in hell do you fellows think you are doing? Haven't we got enough of a job trying to lick the Japs and Nazis without having you fellows on the Court dissipate thoughts and feelings and energies of the folks at home by stirring up a nice row as to who has what power? . . . Just relax and don't be too engrossed in your own interests in verbalistic conflicts because the inroads on energy and national unity that such conflict inevitably produces, is a pastime we had better postpone until peacetime" (Murphy, 1964:48–49).

Ultimately, a unanimous opinion was produced.

OUTPUTS OF APPELLATE COURTS

Having discussed the inputs into the appellate-court decision-making process and the conversion processes, we move now to a discussion of the outputs. That is, we want to know what types of decisions are characteristic of appellate courts.

As we have seen, appellate courts operate within a rather restricted field. This field is limited by the kinds of issues that will be brought to the court, the social background of the judges sitting on the bench, the socialization of lawyers before they become judges, the situational pressures they experience, and the logical limitations of the law itself. All of these forces lead the appellate-court decision toward a conservative tone. That is, the forces impinging on the appellate courts inevitably lead them to make decisions which, at most, bring about incremental changes in the social structure. It is practically an impossibility that any appellate court would ever establish a law which would go to the very heart of the society—it is inconceivable that a court would ever make a law which would fly in the face of the basic premises upon which the society is built.

The examples are legion. The solution to many of our most pressing social problems today requires a radical redistribution of income. Courts can do this, even if so inclined, only marginally. No matter how lenient a court may be when a landlord-tenant dispute between a wealthy landowner and a poverty-stricken inhabitant of the ghetto comes before it, the rule it articulates must assume the fact that, by and large, tenants must pay rent to landlords. Courts have no way of subsidizing the rent, or of constructing public low-rent housing for the poor. Another example can be found in our system of compensation for injuries in automobile accidents. Such accidents are as much a concomitant of a highly mobile society in which automobiles are very widely owned as industrial accidents are in an industrial society. Just as the cost of industrial accidents ultimately was perceived as part of the cost of production, which ought to be borne by the ultimate consumer largely as part of the price of the product, so, at least, we ought to consider whether or not part of the general social cost of a highly mobile society is the cost of an automobile accident. We have no difficulty in seeing that roads are part of the general social cost; the cost of automobile accidents might well be perceived in the same way. By reason of the several constraints we have mentioned, however, courts are incapable of adopting any so radical a position even if they would. Their position, conversion processes, and place in modern society preclude adoption of such a position.

Appellate courts only make rules in response to stresses arising in existing institutions. Conceivably they can make incremental changes, designed to make the existing structures function smoothly once again—i.e., to return to an equilibrium in which the institution can operate without further intervention by governmental agencies. As might be predicted from the model, their rule output reflects the narrow choice available to them.

In the words of Harold Laski:

> . . . Every society is the theatre of a conflict between economic classes for a larger material benefit, for, that is, a larger share in the results to be distributed from the productive process. Since the power to produce within any society is dependent upon peace, the state must maintain law and order to that end. But, in so doing, it is necessarily maintaining the law and order implied in the particular system of class relations of which it is the expression. In a feudal society, that is, the law and order which the state maintains is the law and order necessary to the preservation of feudal principles. In a capitalist society, the state maintains the law and order necessary to maintain capitalist principles" (Laski, 1935:162).

It seems improbable that courts will ever be able to accomplish, save by miniscule changes moving with glacial slowness, the sort of revolutionary shifts in power that would be necessary to change the system entirely. It would seem highly unlikely that any court would be able to accomplish anything more than incremental change.

Incremental Change and the Supreme Court

It could be argued that the record of the Supreme Court in recent years contradicts the thesis that appellate courts can only make incremental changes. For, in case after case, the court has reversed the propositions which we have just stated. In *Miranda* v. *Arizona* [384 U.S. 436 (1966)], for example, the court laid down a whole manual with respect to the scope of police interrogation on arrest. In *Matter of Gault* [387 U.S. 1 (1967)], it outlined the required procedures for juvenile courts. In *Baker* v. *Carr* [369 U.S. 186(1961)] it ordained far-reaching changes in state electoral laws. In *Brown* v. *Board of Education* [347 U.S. 483(1954)] it laid down a broad rule which demands the integration of facilities in a host of basic institutions within the society, which has had profound effects upon large segments of the social fabric.

In none of these cases can it fairly be said that the rules laid down were designed to bring about only "incremental" or "miniscule" changes. It can be argued that these alterations do not go to the very heart of American society—for example, they do not require changes in the capitalist economy or in America's imperialism towards other nations. They do not question the sanctity of private property.

But to argue that any changes short of a virtual revolutionary alteration of the very basic structures of society are necessarily "incremental" is too narrow a perspective. The fact is that these rules are indeed radical and demand radical changes (if they are followed) in the society. The fact is that the Supreme Court occupies a most unique institutional position among appellate courts in the U.S., principally because it must interpret the Constitution. Furthermore, moral entrepreneurs can and do stand a better chance of making their arguments convincingly when the grounds being argued go to the heart of the Constitution (as contrasted with going to statutes and precedent decisions only). Finally, the movement to more pragmatic decision-making criteria, which has characterized the Supreme Court in recent years, increases the likelihood that more radical decisions will be forthcoming.

The Supreme Court and the Constitution

The fact that the Supreme Court is responsible for determining whether or not legislation or the actions of any government body square with the norms enunciated in the Constitution gives the Supreme Court a maximum amount of discretion. This is so principally because the Constitution is both exceedingly vague and abstract. It concerns itself with broad values such as "fairness," "equality," and "justice." When these ambiguities cut across a multitude of government offices and institutions of the state, any change in the interpretation of the prevailing rule necessarily creates profound changes in the society.

Rules of Importance to Moral Entrepreneurs

The peculiar position of the Supreme Court of the United States in constitutional matters makes it the particular target of "test cases." No individual, probably, would litigate the question of prayers by six-year-old children in public schools to the Supreme Court at a cost of many thousands of dollars. Yet, such cases have repeatedly been before the Court in which the litigation may be carried on in the name of particular individuals, but in which the real party at interest was an organization, such as the American Civil Liberties Union. *Brown* v. *Board of Education*, the school desegregation case, whose impact upon American society has probably been more widespread than any other case in American legal history, was conceived, tried, and appealed by the NAACP. Most of our current rules with respect to criminal procedure were litigated by civil liberties groups, as were most of the cases involving freedom of expression, loyalty oaths, and the like. Many, perhaps most, of these cases arose in areas where it was plainly hopeless to even try to persuade the Congress to move. Indeed, in many of these cases there have been congressional efforts to reverse the Court's ruling by statute.

The existence of moral entrepreneurs has been of great significance in alleviating the built-in bias of the appellate-courts' system—and especially the most expensive of them all, the Supreme Court—to select issues for decision that are of primary interest to the well-to-do. But the constitutional position of the Supreme Court, and the fact that there exist moral entrepreneurs to carry the cases to it, would not explain why, in so many cases, the Court has abandoned incremental change as the core of the judicial technique. These factors, at best, supply the opportunity to use a more wide-ranging decision-making technique. This technique, however, the Court has found at hand in the pragmatic realist mode of deciding cases that has dominated its constitutional decisions since the late 1930s.

Pragmatic Decision-Making

In the last fifty years the history of ideas shows a very clear shift away from reliance on "tradition" as the appropriate source for norms. In place of traditional or even presumably inherently "right" values has come a reliance on the pragmatic effects of values. Marijuana is not seen as bad because it is intrinsically so, nor is it seen as bad because it has traditionally been viewed as such. The question of "goodness" or "badness" of marijuana or anything else has increasingly been decided on the basis of what its effects are.

The Supreme Court is not immune to such shifts in public ideologies. It has, as a consequence of this intellectual revolution, created its own revolution to correspond to it. It is safe to say that today no one disputes the legitimacy of the pragmatic test of Supreme Court decisions. Even when justices disagree with the decision (as some did in the *Miranda* decision), the disagreement is on interpretation of effects; all participants in the dispute concurred that it was legitimate for the Court to make new law and to base the decision on pragmatic considerations. In *Miranda*, Justice White, dissenting, argued:

> . . . the Court has not discovered or found the law in making today's decision . . . what it has done is to make new law . . . this is what the Court historically has done. Indeed it is what it must do and will continue to do. . . .
>
> Decisions like these cannot rest alone on syllogism, metaphysics or some ill-defined notions of natural justice . . . in proceeding to such constructions as it now announces, the Court should also duly consider all the factors and interests bearing upon the cases, at least insofar as the relevant materials are available" [*Miranda* v. *Arizona*, 384 U.S. 436, 531–32 (1966)].

This emphasis upon pragmatism in decision-making combined with the flexibility which inheres in interpreting the Constitution increases the chance that decisions will have far-reaching consequences. For the fact is that in a pluralistic society where many groups are competing with one another and where the institutionalized protections of the individual's rights are reserved for those with the money to bring them into play, empirical evidence will consistently reveal great disparities between the espoused values of the Constitution and the realities of everyday events. Thus, if the Supreme Court will take the issues posed by moral entrepreneurs and will look to empirical evidence of what is happening in deciding constitutional issues, then, inevitably, the Court will make decisions that demand substantial changes in the fabric of society.

This is not to say, however, that there are no limitations upon decision-making by the Supreme Court. Its institutional role requires that it make decisions in constitutional cases only insofar as it can base these decisions on some plausible reading of the

Constitution. It can only consider solutions which can be accomplished through formulating a universalistic rule, applicable to all persons similarly situated. Most important of all, it cannot create a new organization to resolve problems, no matter how plainly the solution requires it.

The *Gault* case is an interesting example of this last, and perhaps most important, constraint on the Court. In that case, a juvenile had been committed as a delinquent to the state industrial school by an Arizona juvenile court, on the ground that he had violated a state statute by using lewd language over the telephone to a woman neighbor. The commitment was accomplished without notice of hearing, confrontation of witnesses, counsel, cross-examination, and on the basis of a confession which, under *Miranda*, was inadmissible because it violated the privilege against self-incrimination. The traditional justification for permitting such seeming violations of constitutional standards in juvenile cases was that the state stood *in parens patriae*, and that in the exercise of its fatherly care for juveniles, it quite properly could help them develop into well-adjusted, law-abiding citizens. Since these were the purposes of commitment, rather than "punishment," it was believed that no "rights" were being violated by doing what was believed to be in the child's interest.

The Court swept all these rationalizations aside in large part by undercutting their factual premises: the "delinquent" classification "has come to involve only slightly less stigma than the term 'criminal' applied to adults." The claim of secrecy of records (invoked to justify the denial of procedural protections) "is more rhetoric than reality." The benevolent, fatherly approach in the interests of the child is not in the best interests of the child after all; modern research suggests that "the essentials of due process may be a more impressive and more therapeutic attitude so far as the juvenile is concerned." The very fact of incarceration is enough; "it is of no constitutional importance—and of limited practical meaning—that the institution to which he is committed is called Industrial School. . . ."

The Court articulated major new rules of procedure for juvenile courts across the nation in a far-reaching opinion that went well beyond the demands of the decision in the case before it. But the Court could not authorize or create organizations capable of implementing the decision handed down. Such powers are beyond the Court, and the lack of such powers is clearly a constraint that critically circumscribes the Court's ability to effect social change.

Other Appeals from Convictions

Appellate courts represent the route of appeal for all but a handful of cases. There is, however, the possibility in Anglo-American law for a convicted offender to appeal directly to the "head of state" (in America, either the governor of a state or the president of the United States) for a pardon or a commutation of sentence. A pardon may be either "full" or "partial." Full pardon sets aside the sentence originally rendered and permits the offender to go free. Whether this represents a setting aside of the conviction is the subject of much debate (Weinhofen, 1963). Regardless, the effect of full pardon is to null the sentence passed by the court. Partial pardons are, in effect, only a reduction of sentence and are thus functionally akin to the commutation of sentence, which is a reduction of the severity of the sentence passed by the court.

In some states (Alabama, Georgia, Idaho, Nebraska, and Utah) the right to issue pardons has been taken from the governor and given to the parole boards. In other states (Connecticut, Florida, Minnesota, North Dakota, and Nevada) a separate board of pardons exists and has the decision-making power over pardons and commutation independent of the governor or the parole board. In Arizona, Oklahoma, South Dakota, and Texas, the governor can grant pardons only on the recommendation of the parole board. The more common relationship is for parole boards to serve as advisory boards with the governor retaining the ultimate decision-making authority.

Little research has been done on the pardon and commutation of sentence process (exceptions are Foote, 1959; Wolfgang, 1959a, 1959b; Lunden, 1963). We do not know, for example, the extent to which formally removing the authority to pardon from the governor to parole or pardon boards changes the character of decisions. Nor do we know whether the governor is able to exert control without responsibility when the pardoning process is shifted to another government agency.

One of the more important functions of the pardon is to reinstate an offender's civil rights. Depending on the state, a convicted felon may lose all his rights to citizenship (he is sometimes referred to as being "civilly dead") or only some of them, such as the right to vote or to hold certain jobs. In California, for example, such occupations as nursing and barbering may be denied a convicted felon after his or her release from prison. In some states a person given a life sentence loses his right to make contracts, to hold legal title to property, and to a marriage contract exactly as if he were dead. A pardon will legally reincarnate the offender and reinstate his civil rights. Probably most pardons are, in fact, the offender's attempt to have his civil rights reinstated.

The political nature of pardons sometimes makes them one of the more dramatic events in the appeal process. In recent years, the governors of Ohio, California, Washington, and Pennsylvania have all been under attack and pressure to grant pardons to notorious offenders who were ardently supported by some politically influential groups and vehemently opposed by others. Generally, the pardoning process takes place outside the public's view but upon occasion (for example, in cases like Caryl Chessman, Jimmy Hoffa, Lt. Calley, and leading organized-crime figures), the notoriety of the offender may bring a particular appeal for executive clemency to the public's attention and create a political and moral dilemma for the executive.

Except insofar as they may create public interest in particular cases, appeals to the executive for a pardon or commutation of sentence do not greatly affect the criminal-law process nor have they, in the past, represented a very important branch of criminal appeals. Rather, this appeal process is a seldom-used mechanism for either alleviating injustices or, more importantly, for making the criminal law responsive to political considerations at the executive level of government.

CONCLUSION

For a whole parcel of reasons, the decisions of appellate courts are among the most important events that take place in the criminal law process. The appellate courts are the "court of last resort" for the defendant or the prosecution. Except for executive clemency, which is rarely used, the appellate-court decisions are final. More important is the fact that statutes passed by legislatures, whether they be concerned with substantive issues or procedural rules, are inevitably vague; their meaning as guidelines to action will invariably depend upon the decisions of courts rather than the language of the statute. Since appellate-court decisions are binding on lower courts, it is the appellate courts generally, and the Supreme Court particularly, that make far-reaching decisions that determine the shape and content of the law. Finally, appellate courts make new laws almost by definition in the process of deciding ambiguities in the law. They are, therefore, an important source of law as well as a crucial part of the criminal-law process.

As we have shown, the entire structure of the appellate-court process in criminal cases is one that systematically limits the issues raised and the decisions rendered in such a way that the criminal law inevitably reflects the assumptions, values, and interests of the more powerful social classes. Only when organizations with financial backing from representatives of the upper classes take on issues relevant to the poor and working classes will their interests be protected. In recent years, the presence of several such groups of moral entrepreneurs, in fact, has been an important source of new law and of innovative interpretation in the old law, especially with respect to laws concerning the legality of police behavior.

The characteristic thrust of appellate-court decisions is going to vary from no change (which is typical) to incremental change. Changes in the most elemental features of the society will simply be an impossibility given the structure of appellate courts. The U.S. Supreme Court, however, does stand in a unique position both structurally and historically. As a result we can expect to see decisions from the Supreme Court that represent a significant departure from the generally miniscule movements that characterize other appellate courts. It is important to realize, however, that this unique position of the Supreme Court does not necessarily lead to "liberal" or "radical" decisions; it can just as well lead to conservative or "reactionary" decisions, depending on the composition of the court at any particular time. Facts being as elusive as they are and as subject to different interpretations, it is quite reasonable to suppose that a Supreme Court stacked with judges of a conservative bent will find no difficulty in construing the facts to fit the interpretations that are consistent with their ideological bias. Nevertheless, far-reaching, major changes in the content and thrust of the law will not be forthcoming, despite the fact that some variations can certainly be expected as we move from liberal to conservative perspectives dominating the nine men who comprise the justices of the Supreme Court.

Thus the appellate-court process is best characterized as one that consistently establishes rules and procedures that protect the prevailing interests of the established social order. But, at the same time, it is too facile to depict all appellate-court activities as simply retaining the status quo. Change as a reflection of historical processes as well as of differences in the structural characteristics of society also is reflected in differences in the degree to which legal innovations emerge from the appeal process in the criminal law.

REFERENCES

Arnold, Thurman.
    1960   "Professor Hart's theology." Harvard Law Review 73(May):1298–1317.
Austin, John.
    1875   Lectures on Jurisprudence. London: J. Murray.
Blaustein, A. P., and C. O. Porter.
    1954   The American Lawyer. Chicago: University of Chicago Press.
Blumberg, Abraham.
    1967   "The practice of law as confidence game: organizational cooptation of a profession." Law and Society Review 1(June):15–39.
Bowen, R.
    1965   "The explanation of judicial voting behavior from sociological characteristics of judges." Ph.D. dissertation, Yale University.

Chambliss, William J., and Robert B. Seidman.
  1971   Law, Order and Power. Reading, Mass.: Addison-Wesley.

Dicey, A. V.
  1959   Introduction to the Study of the Law of the Constitution. London: Macmillan.

Foote, Caleb.
  1959   "Pardon policy in a modern state." Prison Journal 39(April):3–32.

Friedman, Lawrence.
  1966   "On legalistic reasoning—a footnote to Weber." Wisconsin Law Review 1966(Winter):148–171.
  1967   "Legal rules and the process of social change." Stanford Law Review 19 (April):786–799.

Green, Leon.
  1955   "The study and teaching of tort law." Texas Law Review 34(November): 1–27.

Grossman, Joel.
  1966   "Social backgrounds and judicial decision-making." Harvard Law Review 79(June):1551–1563.

Hall, Jerome.
  1952   Theft, Law and Society. Revised Edition. Indianapolis: Bobbs-Merrill.

Hand, Learned.
  1958   The Bill of Rghts. Cambridge: Harvard University Press.

Hare, A. P.
  1964   "Interpersonal relations in the small group." Pp. 217–271 in R. E. L. Faris (ed.), Handbook of Modern Sociology. Chicago: Rand McNally.

Hart, Henry M.
  1959   "The Supreme Court, 1958 term. Forward: the time chart of the justices." Harvard Law Review 73(November):84–125.

Holmes, O. W.
  1897   "The path of the law." Harvard Law Review 10(March):457–478.

Hurst, J. Willard.
  1950   The Growth of American Law: The Law Makers. Boston: Little, Brown.

Landis, James M.
  1947   The Administrative Process. New Haven: Yale University Press.

Laski, Harold.
  1935   The State in Theory and Practice. London: Allen & Unwin (Viking Press).

Lefstein, Norman, Vaughn Stapleton, and Lee Teitelbaum.
  1969   "In search of juvenile justice: Gault and its implementation." Law and Society Review 3(May):491–562.

Lewis, A.
  1959   "Legislative apportionment and the federal courts." Harvard Law Review 71(April):1057–1098.

Lunden, Walter A.
  1963   Pardons and Commutations in Iowa, 1915–1962. Des Moines: Iowa Board of Parole.

Medalie, Richard D., Leonard Zeitz, and Paul Alexander.
1968   "Custodial police interrogation in our nation's capital: the attempt to implement Miranda." Michigan Law Review 66(May):1347–1422.

Mott, Rodney L.
1936   "Judicial affairs." American Political Science Review 30(April):295–315.

Murphy, Walter F.
1964   Judicial Strategy. Chicago: University of Chicago Press.

Nagel, Stuart S.
1961   "Political party affiliation and judges' decisions." American Political Science Review 55(December):843–850.

Schmidhauser, J. A.
1959   "The justices of the supreme court: a collective portrait." Midwest Journal of Political Science 3(February):2–37, 40–49.

Sickles, R.
1965   "The illusion of judicial consensus: zoning decisions in the Maryland court of appeals." American Political Science Review 59(March):100–104.

Sudnow, David.
1965   "Normal crimes: sociological features of the penal code in a public defender's office." Social Problems 13(Winter):225–276.

Weber, Max.
1954   Max Weber on Law in Economy and Society. Translated by Edward Shils and Max Rheinstein. Edited by Max Rheinstein. Cambridge: Harvard University Press.

Weinhofen, Henry.
1963   "Pardon and other forms of clemency." Chap. 16 in Sol Rubin et al., The Law of Criminal Correction. St. Paul, Minn.: West Publishing Co.

Wolfgang, Marvin E.
1959a   "Analysis of selected aspects of the board of pardons." The Prison Journal 39(April):8–22.
1959b   "Murder, the pardon board and recommendations by judges and district attorneys." Journal of Criminal Law, Criminology and Police Science 50 (November–December):338–346.

Zobell, K. M.
1959   "Division of opinion in the Supreme Court: a history of judicial disintegration." Cornell Law Quarterly 44(Winter):186–205.

CHAPTER **18**

Discretionary Justice

Albert J. Reiss, Jr.

Yale University

Criminal justice in the United States is organized to make decisions about information and persons that are legally defined as criminal matters in the body of criminal law. Organizations with legal authority to make these decisions derive it from legislative authority, but operationally they often are administratively responsible to some other authority, and may depend on yet others for their operating resources. A police department, for example, may be responsible to a mayor or city manager, the common council, and a civil service commission, while a county prosecutor may be responsible only to the electorate and a county board of government. Each organization is relatively autonomous administratively from others, though the law links them in a loose network of exchanges that is commonly called a criminal justice system.

Criminal matters necessarily involve decisions. Where alternative courses of action exist, choice is possible. The alternatives and the freedom to exercise choice may be authorized and limited by legitimate authority, and by laws or administrative rules, but they may also arise as unauthorized options and rules within operating organizations. Where an agent is free to choose among alternatives in making a decision, we shall speak of his *exercising* choice. When that choice is not open to review, either de jure or de facto, we shall speak of the choice as *discretionary*. Discretion exists, then, whenever an organization and its agents make choices that are not generally open to reexamination by others. The major goal of the criminal justice system is to decide matters in the interest that justice be done. We shall speak of discretionary justice whenever decisions made in criminal cases are not legally or practically open to reexamination.

THE U.S. CRIMINAL JUSTICE NETWORK

The legally organized system of criminal justice in the United States is a loosely articulated operating network of input-output relationships among seven major systems. Decisions are made within each system about whether and how people and information are processed as inputs to the system and as outputs to others in the network. The organizations are arranged in a hierarchy by legal relationships based on the final authority to review decisions made by others in the network and to make decisions about particular matters, but the flow of people and information in the system does not correspond altogether with these hierarchical arrangements. The seven major systems in the loosely articulated hierarchical network are:

1. The *citizen law-enforcement system* is made up of private citizens and their corporate bodies in their role as enforcers of the law. Citizens control much of the input into the criminal justice system by making discretionary decisions to mobilize the police or to seek warrants from the prosecutor. Citizens also crucially control the information that is input for processing in the system by being the main source of evidence for criminal events. Their oral testimony often is the sole evidence for deciding criminal matters.

2. The *public law-enforcement or police system* controls decisions about the discovery of crimes, investigation of criminal complaints, making arrests or pressing for warrants, and booking offenders. Although the police have legal authority to decide how their resources shall be allocated to law enforcement and when probable cause has been satisfied to justify an arrest, they also exercise considerable unauthorized discretion in deciding what laws shall be enforced and if an arrest shall be made when probable cause for arrest has been satisfied. Their decisions crucially control evidence for the decisions others make about criminal matters. Often the oral testimony of police officers is the only evidence on which the decisions of others are based.

3. The *defendant system* is made up of citizens alleged to have violated the law and their public or private defense counsel. As alleged violators of the law, citizens make important discretionary decisions about cooperating with the police in their interrogation, their disclosures to defense counsel, and their responses to prosecutors, judges, and other officials in the network, such as probation or corrections officers. Defense counsel makes important discretionary decisions that affect the fate of the defendant by the advice given to defendants and the strategy of defense employed.

4. The *public prosecution system* controls decisions about filing the information, making the charge, securing evidence, entering into a bargain with the defendant and his counsel, and the strategy of prosecution in any judicial proceeding. Prosecutors exercise enormous discretion in reducing the volume of cases that are processed within the network.

5. The *misdemeanor and felony courts* must determine substantive and procedural questions of law and of adjudication. Judges have substantial discretion to review prior decisions and to determine the fate of defendants.

6. The *correctional system* is comprised of organizations that assume responsibility for the custody and rehabilitation of convicted offenders. They have considerable discretion to control the conduct of offenders within their custody and to determine the form their rehabilitation will take. They, likewise, have some control over the length of time that offenders will serve, although that control usually resides in an auxiliary organization, a board of pardons and parole, or in the prerogative of the chief executive to grant clemency.

7. The *appellate judicial system* has the sole power to grant or deny appeals and to determine their merits. The appellate system decides questions of law, although it also exercises power to stay the actions of others pending review.

These descriptions do not fully recount the decisions and the discretion that each system exercises over inputs and outputs. Rather, they are intended to show that while each organizational level assumes or is granted jurisdiction over particular decisions, each also has considerable discretion over what will be processed as output to others in the network.

ORGANIZATIONAL DISCRETION IN LAW ENFORCEMENT

There is considerable variation in the organization of law-enforcement agencies in the United States that affects the exercise of discretion by their agents. This variation results largely from the jurisdiction of these agencies, i.e., their legal power to administer and interpret the criminal law for a given territory, their policies of law enforcement, their resources, and their internal structure for making decisions and assigning responsibility for them.

There is considerable variation in the legal jurisdiction of the more than 40,000 public law-enforcement organizations in the United States (President's Commission, 1967:7–9). Of these, fifty have federal jurisdiction, including agencies within the Justice, Treasury, Interior, and State Departments, and government units, such as the Post Office and the Smithsonian Institution. These include agencies of general jurisdiction, such as the FBI and the U.S. marshals, and many of more limited jurisdiction, ranging from the Border Patrol and the Internal Revenue Service to the U.S. Park Rangers.

About 200 law-enforcement agencies in the United States have state jurisdiction. These include state police with general jurisdiction and those limited to offenses that occur only on or within the boundaries of state highways or property, the so-called highway police. Some states also have specialized enforcement agencies, such as forest rangers, park police, fish and game wardens, and state college or university police.

Most law-enforcement agencies in the United States, however, have local jurisdiction granted by the states. There are about 3,050 agencies in counties—usually sheriffs' departments—and 3,700 in cities. The modal police agency in the United States—some 33,000—is located in a borough, town, or village. It is small, with the modal size being fewer than five police officers.

Though little is known about it, there also is a sizeable private police industry in the United States (Kakalik & Wildhorn, 1971b). Private agencies are of two types: (1) purchased or contract private security services, and (2) in-house or proprietary police security services. These include guards and watchmen, detectives, investigators, undercover agents, and private patrolmen. The well-known Pinkerton and Burns agencies and Brinks and Wells-Fargo armored car service are examples of contract security services, but there were about 4,000 smaller contract private security agencies in the United States in 1969. Most major industrial corporations, the railroads, and large commercial establishments employ their own guards and watchmen, or detectives and investigators. The large majority of private security forces do not have full legal powers of arrest, yet they exercise enormous discretion over criminal matters that occur on private property.

About one in every 100 persons in the civilian labor force of the United States is employed in public or private law-enforcement or security work. In 1969 there were an estimated 804,900 persons employed in law-enforcement or security work (Kakalik & Wildhorn, 1971a:11). Of these, 64 percent were employees of public organizations, 49 percent employed as policemen or investigators, and 15 percent as guards and watchmen. The remaining 36 percent were in the private sector. In 1969, between one-fourth and one-third of all privately employed guards and investigators worked for contract security firms and the remainder were in-house employees. Almost nothing is known from systematic inquiry about how these private police exercise discretion over criminal matters.

Local law-enforcement agencies in the United States have a broad legal mandate to enforce the criminal law and preserve the public peace. In the everyday life of citizens, however, the discretionary role of the police extends beyond its law-enforcement and peace-keeping functions: in times of crisis or emergency in noncriminal matters, local police in the United States are called upon to exercise discretion in performing a variety of services. These include intervention in conflicts between members of families, landlords and tenants, and employers and employees, as well as assistance in sickness, in tracing missing persons, and in dealing with the plight of animals or hazardous situations. Of citizen calls to the Chicago Police Department one day in 1966, 26 percent involved disputes or breach of the peace, 32 percent potential offenses against the person or property, 34 percent assistance in personal, family, medical, or hazardous situations, and 8 percent information to the police or complaints about police service (Reiss, 1971:71). Local police, in fact, receive many more calls requesting assistance in noncriminal matters or reporting a crime that has already happened than calls requiring immediate intervention to save victims of crimes that are in progress.

Discretion over inquiry into criminal matters depends upon how the police are mobilized for it. The mobilization of police varies considerably by the jurisdiction of police agencies and the types of criminal and noncriminal matters they process (Reiss, 1971:64–72). When police, on their own discretion or initiative, intervene in the lives of citizens or their environment, they engage in *proactive policing*. Police are proactive when they use discretion by investigating, stopping, questioning, and searching citizens, and by preventive patrol. When discretion or initiative for mobilizing the police lies with citizens or organizations, the police respond as a *reactive organization*, reacting to citizen complaints or requests for assistance by dispatching an officer to look into the matter or by face-to-face encounters with citizens in the field.

The ratio of proactive to reactive police activity varies considerably among law-enforcement organizations, and, within police organizations, some units are more proactive than others. Some federal agencies, such as the Customs Bureau and the Internal Revenue Service, seem organized largely for proactive police work. Others, such as the FBI, appear to be mobilized by a substantial volume of complaints from citizens as well as by their own initiative. Local law enforcement within the United States is more likely to be reactive than proactive. Citizen complaints or mobilization of the police account for a substantial proportion of all contacts with citizens, other than for infractions of the motor-vehicle code, and the bulk of arrests (Reiss, 1971: 96–98). Within police departments, some units, such as traffic, vice, and organized crime, involve more proactive than reactive police work. Generally, the patrol division is organized for both proactive police work, by preventive patrol and techniques of field interrogation, and reaction to citizen mobilizations for assistance. Even though preventive patrol work accounts for a substantial proportion of the time a patrol officer spends at work, productivity, in terms of arrests, is largely accounted for by response to citizen mobilizations (p. 96).

The kinds of matters that come to the attention of the police and whether they originate in proactive police work or result from reactive activity depend upon several factors that determine how police can learn of crime events. First, in liberal societies police access to places where crimes occur is *limited by institutions of privacy* that protect the private place from encroachment by police initiative (Stinchcombe, 1963). Lawful entry into private places can result only from citizen permission to enter, a warrant issued by a magistrate on probable cause, or some special conditions when the police can enter on their own, being satisfied that a serious offense is in progress. Citizens, thus, have discretionary control over knowledge of crimes committed in private places. Crimes of coercion in private life and of the invasion of private places by criminals come to the attention of the police, therefore, primarily on citizen initiative to mobilize the police.

Second, police knowledge of crimes, whether by proactive or reactive police work, is determined by the *predictability* of the occurrence of a given type of crime. The more predictable an event, the easier it is to detect its occurrence, and the more likely such events will be discovered by proactive police work. Predictability of crime events depends upon properties of the event, particularly the frequency of its occurrence in time and place, its duration, and the degree to which the crime event is an organized activity.

When the frequency of a crime event is relatively low, the likelihood that the police can be present when it occurs is low and, therefore, the more dependent the police are on citizen initiative for knowledge of that event. Since most major crime events are infrequent, the police are organized to respond to citizen reports of their occurrence. On the other hand, an event that occurs with high frequency is open to proactive police work, particularly when it occurs in public places. The policing of moving vehicle violations is largely proactive partly because they occur only in public places but also because they do so with such high frequency that the probability of their occurrence in the presence of the police suffices for a high volume of citation or arrest. Although the police fail to detect most moving violations, a high volume in proactive policing of traffic results from enforcement strategies based on the probability of their occurrence.

The predictability of an event depends also upon its duration in time. Some crime events are of very short duration, some episodic, and others continue for a considerable period of time, usually until action is taken to remove the violation. The longer the duration of the violation in time, the more likely it is to be detected by proactive law enforcement. Expiration of a driver's license, embezzlement, fraudulent reporting of income, and a host of similar offenses that continue until action is taken to alter the state of violation are open to detection by proactive means. Mileski (1971) observes that housing inspectors easily detect violations of the housing code since they continue until the condition is altered. Also open to proactive police work are events that can be detected by surveillance because of their episodic nature, such as acts of solicitation, or buying or selling contraband or a good or service illegally. A prostitute who must solicit customers, whether in a public or private place, engages in crime episodes that increase the probability of her arrest by proactive means.

The predictability of an event is likewise affected by the nature and extent of organization of the activity. The more crime events are socially organized, the more open they are to proactive police work. Proactive police work often uncovers criminal activity organized around an economic market, such as the illegal manufacture and sale of alcohol and narcotics or the service of prostitutes, and around the socially organized exchanges in "victimless" crimes. In addition, any group that is systematically organized for criminal activity is open to detection by proactive police work, such as subversive political groups and organized gangs. It should be noted, however, that detection by proactive police work is affected by the extent to which the organization is structured to counter police penetration. It is more difficult to penetrate the top echelon of a criminal organization than the bottom. Proactive policing can also be controlled by the capacity of the organization to allocate resources to counter police penetration, including payments to police officers to ignore knowledge of criminal activity. The more profitable a criminal activity, the more likely it is to allocate resources to control police penetration of the activity.

Third, knowledge of crimes by the police is affected by the *capacity of the police organization to allocate resources to the detection of crime.* The larger and less densely settled a territory to be policed, the more resources one must allocate to proactive detection of crimes and, therefore, the more the organization is likely to depend upon reactive police work. Much policing in rural areas is reactive because the organization cannot allocate resources to proactive police work. The availability of resources to the department affects policies to allocate those resources. Generally, in response to citizen demands, police departments allocate a disproportionate share of their resources to reactive policing, either for reactive patrol and mobilization for assistance or, despite its low level of productivity, for preventive patrol.

Finally, knowledge of crime is affected by two important elements in the organization and operation of police departments: *the degree to which detection of criminal violations is specialized within the department, and the policies for allocating resources to the detection of a given type of criminal violation.* The more specialized the task organization within a department, the more it is engaged in proactive police work and the more likely it is to produce volume in that activity. Gardiner (1969) notes that differences in the level of traffic enforcement among cities can be largely accounted for by the policies of the department to enforce traffic laws and whether or not traffic enforcement is specialized within the department. When traffic enforcement is a specialized division and there is an explicit policy to enforce the law, such as ticket quotas, there is a much greater volume than when this is not the case.

The exercise of police discretion depends also upon the task organization of law-enforcement agencies. Police agencies may be organized around one or more of four major tasks. First, they may be obligated to enforce all criminal statutes or only some specialized body of criminal law. Second, they may be organized to preserve the public peace and maintain public order. Third, they may be responsible for providing a variety of services to private citizens or other public agencies, such as transporting ill persons or accident victims to medical centers, tracing missing persons, giving information to requests for assistance on private matters, and conducting criminal investigations for other agencies. Fourth, they may have important powers to inspect premises or activities and to grant licenses. The powers to inspect and license were historically a main task of local law-enforcement agencies, but these powers for the most part have been assigned to specialized public agencies.

There is considerable variation among law-enforcement agencies in their task organization. The domestic task of the National Guard, for example, is to preserve public order when mobilized by the president of the United States or the governor of a state and to serve as an auxiliary force to defend the country against invasion. Most of the federal law-enforcement agencies enforce and administer a specialized body of the criminal law. Some state police agencies exist primarily to enforce the law on public highways and administer certain portions of the motor-vehicle code. Local police agencies in the United States are usually organized to perform the first three of the tasks described above, but in major metropolitan centers they frequently inspect and license some activities as well.

Variation in the task organization of local police departments occurs largely because police administrators respond to formal and informal policies adopted by the political authority to which they are responsible and to pressures from powerful interest groups in the communities that they police. James Q. Wilson characterizes local police departments in terms of the administrative emphasis placed on these tasks. Each style of police organization and administration has different consequences for citizens. Some departments are characterized by a *watchman style* (Wilson, 1968:140–71), principally performing the traditional police task of maintaining public order. Officers of the department work as peace officers, emphasizing order over enforcement of the law by arrest. The role of peace-keeping imparts enormous discretion to police officers since it is generally poorly structured at law and by department regulation, leaving the exercise of discretion to informal police routines (Bittner, 1967a, 1967b). In keeping the peace, officers generally ignore or handle informally many minor infractions of the law, paying much greater attention to local variation in the demand for enforcement of the law and the maintenance of order. In some areas of the city, for example, laws are enforced to which no attention is given in other areas.

Some departments display a *service style* (Wilson, 1968:200–26) in which citizens expect more personal attention to their private demands. In these departments much emphasis is placed on providing a variety of services to the public in managing order in the community and in regulating conduct by informal means rather than by the legal powers of arrest.

Other departments display a *legalistic style* of administration (pp. 171–99) in which the enforcement of laws takes precedence over order. Even minor infractions of the law are commonly treated as matters for arrest. In this type of department, the public is most subject to arrest.

The internal structure of command and control within police departments makes it possible for officers to exercise an enormous amount of discretion in making decisions. Although police departments are organized around a centralized command and control where subordinates must follow orders, the bulk of police officers are dispersed in field assignments. A dispersed command makes it difficult to control behavior by direct supervision. Most police officers work most of the time without direct supervision. Their discretionary decisions, thus, are not generally open to review by superiors. Centralized control of officer discretion, therefore, is largely indirect, depending upon the development of information systems that permit the command to determine where the officer is, what he should be doing, and what evidence of activity he must submit for inspection (Bordua & Reiss, 1966:68–70). Even when evidence of activity is submitted, such as in an arrest report, the capacity to review discretion is limited. There is no simple way to determine the facts in police encounters with citizens, the alternatives available to make choices, and their behavior.

EXERCISING DISCRETION
IN THE CRIMINAL JUSTICE NETWORK

Discretionary decisions within each organization of the criminal justice network are limited by legal mandate and by its internal structure and policies. Within these limits, however, agents of each organization exercise considerable unauthorized, as well as authorized, discretion in making decisions.

Citizen Discretion. Violations of the law are generated within the family, corporate, and community systems of citizens, who exercise their control over input to the criminal justice network initially because they control the information on violations and can exercise discretion in calling the police. Studies of victimization from crime show that the discretionary decisions of citizens to call the police when a crime has been committed substantially control input into the criminal justice system. The 1965 surveys for the President's Commission on Law Enforcement and Administration of Justice (sometimes referred to as the "National Crime Commission") and more recent surveys by the Bureau of the Census and the Law Enforcement Assistance Administration (LEAA) show considerable underreporting to the police of victimization from crime. A sample survey of United States households made by the National Opinion Research Center (NORC) in 1965 showed that more than half of all crimes and 38 percent of the FBI's index crimes against residents went unreported to the police (Biderman, 1967). Other surveys for the President's Commission (Reiss, 1967) and the Small Business Administration (Reiss, 1969) reveal that at least one-half of all major crimes against businesses and other organizations go unreported to the police, particularly crimes of burglary, shoplifting, employee theft, and passing bad checks. The willingness of citizens to call the police when they *witness* a crime in which they are not victims also is apparently low. This may seem somewhat surprising, given a commonly held belief that law enforcement is the most effective means for controlling crime. There is strong evidence, then, that citizens both as victims and as witnesses of crimes exercise much discretion in making their knowledge available to police so that the events may become inputs into the criminal justice network.

Several major factors account for the exercise of discretion by citizens in mobilizing the police. The reporting of crimes against property is determined to a great extent by insurance coverage. When a person is not insured against property losses or the losses are not covered by insurance (often the case for the poor), the loss is not reported because the victim sees no personal gain in doing so. Even when there is coverage by insurance, many businesses, and some citizens, fail to report losses because they fear their policy may be cancelled or not renewed or that there will be a future rate increase (Reiss, 1969:131–43). Conversely, insurance coverage is an incentive to report property losses from crime, since some people assume that, to collect on their insurance, the loss must be reported to the police.

Another major factor in citizen discretion to report crimes to the police is the relationship between the victim and the offender. The more personal the relationship, the less likely the victim is to report the crime to the police. As yet unpublished surveys show that citizens are most likely to report crimes when the offender is a stranger, less likely when the offender is known but not a relative, and least likely when the offender is a relative.

A third major cause of citizen discretion to report crimes to the police is the attitude of the citizen toward the police and police work. In the Washington, D.C. study of victimization from crime, one of every three victims said he had not reported the crime against him or his property to the police because he felt that nothing could be done about it by the police. Only a relatively small proportion (3 percent) in the Washington study failed to report a crime to the police because of a fear of reprisal, either from other citizens or from the police (Biderman et al., 1967:153–54).

Citizens have little formal control over input of suspected offenders into their system following their processing by one or more agents in the criminal justice system. Yet citizens and their corporate bodies exercise enormous discretion in their responses to persons who have been processed in the criminal justice network. They substantially control the stigmatization of persons who have been processed and, by responding to them as "guilty" or "innocent," affect their life chances. Nowhere is this more apparent than in the discrimination that corporate bodies exercise in employing released offenders or in denying their reincorporation into the small family system.

Police Discretion. At law, the police have the authority to decide when there is probable or reasonable cause to believe that a crime has been committed, but they must arrest those persons they have reason to believe committed it (Goldstein, 1960). Although their discretion to arrest is legally restricted, in practice, when enforcing the law, the police exercise enormous discretion to arrest. Field observation studies demonstrate this point: in one such study, the police released roughly one-half of the persons they suspected of committing crimes—an arrest occurred in only 58 percent of the felony encounters and 44 percent of the misdemeanor encounters (Black, 1971:1093). The police are more likely to make an arrest when they witness the event than when the sole basis of evidence is citizen testimony, though this appears to be the case for misdemeanor rather than felony arrests (p. 1094).

When exercising discretion to arrest citizens, the police appear to be influenced by the preference a citizen complainant expresses for the arrest of an offender. Black (1971:1095) reports that citizens manifest a preference for an arrest in 48 percent of the misdemeanor encounters and 34 percent of the felony encounters observed. When preference was expressed for no arrest but one could have been made, the police made an arrest in only one-tenth of the cases. When the complainant expressed a preference for arrest, the police made an arrest in three-fourths of the situations. When complainants expressed no preference for the arrest of an alleged offender, the police made an arrest in about two-thirds of the cases. The police, thus, are most likely to make an arrest when the complainant expresses a preference for an arrest, somewhat less likely to do so when no preference is expressed, and highly unlikely when the complainant expresses a preference that the subject be released. The police see little reason to make an arrest if the complainant will not be a viable witness in pursuing the complaint. In addition, just as citizens are less likely to report their victimization to the police when they have a close relationship to the offender, so the police are less likely to arrest a suspect when the adversaries in a situation are related.

Although the police exercise enormous discretion in law enforcement, their discretion over citizens appears to be even greater in their peace-keeping role (Banton, 1964:6–7). Bittner (1967b) points out that this discretion seems inevitable since the peace-keeping concept is vague and ambiguous, encompassing all things policemen do when they maintain order without making arrests. He outlines five major structural demand conditions that produce police peace-keeping activity: (1) regulation of licensing services and of traffic; (2) police decisions not to enforce laws that could be enforced; (3) intervention in noncriminal conflicts between citizens, such as disputes and quarrels; (4) incipient stages of public disorder; (5) control of persons who are not fully accountable for their actions, such as those underage, the mentally ill, the intoxicated, or those who create special problems of keeping the peace (Bittner, 1967b: 702–3). Examining the role of the police in one such demand situation, keeping the peace on skid row, Bittner notes that the discretion of the police is exercised in three major ways that they believe are appropriate to skid row life. First, they develop an aggressively personal approach to their area and its residents. This personal knowledge is used to decide what to do as peace-keeping situations arise, since the officer can trade, in part, on this knowledge of the residents and their trust in him. Second, culpability is ordinarily not a criterion for their action in this situation and arrests typically are not made. Rather, when culpability exists, the question is what means are there for dealing with the person without arrest. Such alternatives are ordinarily preferred to making an arrest. Finally, coercive force is used in situations primarily to gain control of the situation rather than to enforce the law. Thus, it is the exigencies of a situation and not technical violation of the law that determine the police decision to arrest. All in all then, peace-keeping involves discretion to use alternatives to strict enforcement of the law by arrest.

Skolnick suggests that police discretion to enforce the law is determined substantially by the occupational environment. Ordinarily the policeman is evenhanded in dispensing justice when (1) as a warrant officer, he is not required to direct the activities of citizens acting within the law; (2) the nature of the offense is minor and the offender does not threaten the officer; (3) the officer is on friendly terms with a repeated violator; (4) the officer believes that his conception of justice will be served by others in the criminal justice network (Skolnick, 1967:89). Policemen, on the other hand, are most likely to exercise discretion when their claim to authority is questionable or illegal and when they face outright hostility but lack the formal capacity to impose legal sanctions (p. 90).

There is ample evidence that the deference and demeanor of citizens influences police discretion to enforce the law and impose their own sanctions in encounters with citizens. This is apparent in the policing of both juveniles and adults. Deference and compliance with police authority are likely to produce the lowest rate of juvenile arrest (Piliavin & Briar, 1964; Black & Reiss, 1970). Antagonism toward the police produces a higher rate of arrest (Black & Reiss, 1970:75), as well as other aggressive behavior toward the juvenile (Piliavin & Briar, 1964). Surprisingly, highly deferential behavior toward the police also produces a higher arrest rate for juveniles (Black & Reiss, 1970:75).

The police exercise considerable discretion in handling citizens not only by their choices in making arrests, but also by imposing their own sense of justice. Police justice without trial may take a variety of forms, but principally occurs as aggressive, demeaning, threatening, and hostile behavior toward citizens, by the improper or illegal use of force against them, or by harrassing them.

In our field observation studies of police and citizen behavior, we observed that officers are somewhat more likely to be uncivil toward citizens by behaving antagonistically or illegally toward them than citizens are toward officers. While in 83 percent of all encounters between citizens and officers both behave civilly, in 13 percent only one party was civil: the citizen was the civil party in 8 percent of these encounters and the officer in only 5 percent (Reiss, 1971:144). All of the openly hostile behavior of officers or of their behavior that provoked aggression from citizens was directed at offenders. Indeed, uncivil behavior and misconduct of police toward citizens were disproportionally directed against citizens the police defined as offenders and the antagonistic behavior of citizens toward the police is disproportionally accounted for by citizens when they are defined and treated as suspects or offenders by the police and citizen complainants. Chevigny also found that complaints of police misuse of authority commonly are provoked by citizen defiance of authority, often, however, only verbal defiance of authority (Chevigny, 1969:70).

When we examined police use of excessive force against citizens, i.e., behavior of aggravated assault toward them, almost all of the victims were suspects or offenders who were young males from the lower classes. Thirty-nine percent of the victims of police assaults had openly challenged the authority of the police, 9 percent had physically resisted arrest, and 32 percent were persons in such deviant offender roles as drunks, homosexuals, or narcotics addicts (Reiss, 1968:15–16). Although deviance or defiance of authority often was a condition for police assaults on citizens, police assaults must involve other elements as well, since most instances of deviance or defiance of authority do not provoke police assaults.

Police will predictably practice harassment whenever influential citizens press them to control unlawful conduct by arrests, but those arrests are systematically disregarded by other agencies in the network of criminal justice. For keeping unlawful behavior within bounds under these circumstances, harassment becomes unofficially, for the police, both a system of control and a means of achieving justice. The harassment of juveniles, minorities, and those engaged in vice or repeated violation can be predicted whenever this paradoxical situation arises for the police. Prostitutes, for example, are subject to harassment when the police must respond to civic pressures to control prostitution, and arresting prostitutes proves to be an ineffective form of control. Arrest often is ineffective because the other agents of criminal justice return the prostitute to the community within a matter of days, if not hours, and her behavior must again be subject to policing. One of the techniques of peace-keeping on skid row, in fact, is harassment of the intoxicated (Wiseman, 1970).

There are other ways, of course, that the police exercise discretionary control over citizens who violate the law. Skolnick (1967:137) points out that the informer system, which benefits the police, is built up by the police rewarding the offender by some sort of "break" in the criminal process. To secure the services of informers, the police, for example, can use their discretion to withhold arrest or to recommend a reduced charge to the prosecutor for those offenders who agree to serve as informants.

Defendant and Defense Discretion.

To the degree that suspects and violators of the law can alter their behavior in encounters with citizen complainants and the police, they undoubtedly can affect citizen preferences for their arrest and the police discretion to arrest, as already noted. However, most citizens who are arrested, and subsequently either enter pleas of guilty or are found guilty by agencies in the criminal justice network, do not regard the police as impartial, neutral, or detached (Casper, 1972:50). Rather, they see that the police are doing a job they are required to do and that the police are not much different from themselves; for lower-class defendants this means that the police are expected to follow the rules of street life with which they are both familiar (pp. 49–50).

Defendants are expected to cooperate with counsel in their defense. A large proportion of defendants who are processed in the criminal justice network cannot afford private counsel and must rely, therefore, on the legal services of a public defender who is appointed by the court. The fact that they cannot choose their counsel contributes greatly to defendant distrust of the public defender and, as Casper (1972:123) notes, even of the more zealous legal assistance lawyers. Given the lack of trust in an inherently fiducial relationship of counsel and defendant, many defendants do not participate actively in their defense. They have little opportunity to exercise choice in the decisions made about their defense; typically they spend only five to ten minutes with their public defender (p. 106).

Defense counsel has considerable authorized discretion in the preparation of the defense, particularly in the advice offered to defendants and in the strategy to be pursued in plea bargaining or trial proceedings. There is much evidence of different styles of defense among defense counsel, based on whether they are public defenders, appointed by a bar association committee, or retained or appointed as private counsel (Oaks & Lehman, 1973:171). Private counsel are most likely to secure dismissals before trial, and public defenders to have defendants plead guilty (p. 165). Silverstein (1965), moreover, found that the public defender had a probation rate of only 18 percent compared with 39 percent for retained counsel. Although such differences do not prove that public defenders are less effective for their clients or that they exercise their discretion improperly, particularly since the overall conviction rates of defendants vary little by type of counsel (Oaks & Lehman, 1973:170), they raise important questions about the effectiveness of the defense of the poor defendant. Blumberg's (1973:80–81) interviews with 724 defendants who entered pleas of guilty to an offense disclosed that only 6 percent entered guilty pleas prior to indictment, largely in response to pressures from the police or prosecutors. Following indictment, the major source of pressure to plead guilty came from defense counsel, accounting for 57 percent of all guilty pleas. Legal aid and assigned counsel were far more likely to suggest a guilty plea at the first meeting with the defendant than was private counsel (p. 81).

The way defense counsel exercise discretion depends to a degree on whether a particular defendant and his crime are viewed in categorical or particular terms. In the latter case, counsel will use whatever special strategies are most effective for the particular case. There is considerable evidence that public defenders are more likely to regard cases in categorical terms. Sudnow (1965) provides evidence that public defenders view the crimes of their defendants in terms of "normal" crimes rather than legal violations. By normal crimes Sudnow means that the public defender regards occurrences in terms of typical features of the form of occurrence and the characteristics of offenders. He usually presumes that the defendant is guilty and prepares his defense or advises him according to the category of normal crime into which the defendant fits. Sudnow further observes (1965:273) that while the public defender's practices usually are legally proper and correct, they do not challenge the system either procedurally, at trials, or by appealing decisions. Their public-employee role places them in a routine working relationship with prosecutors and judges, and cases are processed routinely to ease the administrative burden of their co-workers.

Prosecutorial Discretion. By legal authority and by practice, prosecutors have the greatest discretion in the formally organized criminal justice network. They exercise their discretion in five major ways: (1) by decisions of whether or not to proceed on the information contained in police reports of arrest or requests for warrants (a warrant screen); (2) by decisions as to the particular information to file (the charging decision); (3) by decisions to drop charges once entered (nolle prosequi); (4) by negotiating reductions of charges in exchange for a plea of guilty by the defendant (plea bargaining); and (5) by decisions on the strategy of prosecution in trial proceedings. When grand juries vote indictments and make presentments, prosecutors also have discretionary control of the presentation. The way that prosecutors exercise discretion over input and output varies considerably among jurisdictions. This variation is due partly to the organized forms of discretion available to a prosecutor in a given jurisdiction and partly to historical practice within that office. The discretionary decisions of prosecutors whether or not to file information can exercise substantial control over input into the system, while the quantity and quality of output are determined mainly by their decisions to nol-pros or to plea bargain.

Some indication of the variation that prosecutorial discretion produces in the input and output of jurisdictions can be gained by comparing statistics on the discretionary decisions of prosecutors in eighteen jurisdictions reporting to a Metropolitan Prosecutors' Conference of the National District Attorneys Association (1971:42) and statistics from annual reports of prosecutors' offices. Some jurisdictions such as Baltimore, Maryland, Cincinnati and Cleveland, Ohio, and those in Connecticut have no formal warrant screen, and file police reports as the information. Others eliminate a substantial proportion of the input by refusing to file the information. St. Paul, Minnesota reported dismissing 66 percent of all cases at the screening stage, and it was almost that high for St. Louis, Missouri (N.D.A.A., 1971:47). When there is a grand jury, normally only a small percentage of the input is eliminated by their discretion to indict —in the order of 5 percent of all cases.

Prosecutors can exercise considerable discretion in which charges to prefer and how many to prefer. Our examination of this discretion in Detroit, Michigan shows that the prosecutor preferred a charge different from that of the police on arrest in 22 percent of the arrests where the information was filed (Reiss & Hikel, 1973).

There is very substantial variation in the way the prosecutor disposes of cases once the information is filed or the indictment voted. Among the eighteen jurisdictions compared by the NDAA (1971:42), the proportion disposed of by pleas of guilty ranged from a high of 96 percent in Bronx, New York and 90 percent of all cases in Buffalo, New York, Atlanta, Georgia, and Sacramento, California to lows of 33 percent in Phoenix, Arizona and 10 percent in Baltimore, Maryland. Dismissal of charges, mainly by nolle prosequi, ranged from a high of 33 percent in Phoenix, Arizona and 25 percent in Miami, Florida to lows of 2 percent in Bronx, New York and 1 percent in Portland, Oregon. The proportion of cases going to trial by jury likewise varied considerably from a high of 22 percent in Phoenix, Arizona and 16 percent in Denver, Colorado to lows of 1 percent in Los Angeles, California and 2 percent in Bronx, New York, Miami, Florida, and Atlanta, Georgia. The existence of nonjury-trial options also varies considerably. In Los Angeles, California, the use of trial by transcript accounted for 44 percent of all cases. Nonjury trials accounted for 70 percent of all cases in Baltimore, Maryland but almost no cases in Bronx, New York. All in all, trial by jury, the traditional common-law protection for the accused, accounted for less than 8 percent of the cases in half of the jurisdictions. The fate of these cases lay largely in discretionary decisions by prosecutor and defense counsel, since, typically, the prosecutor and the judge concur in their respective decisions.

It is no simple matter to assess the effect of this discretion on the several parties to a case in the criminal justice system. The substantial reduction in jury trials operates to reduce the work load for all agents and agencies in the system. Defense counsel and prosecutors can handle more cases if charges are dismissed or the defendant pleads guilty; so can judges, since their decision reduces to disposition of the plea by sanctioning the defendant. It is more difficult to assess the effects of these discretionary decisions for defendants. Simply comparing judicial disposition of cases on pleas of guilt with disposition of a finding of guilt by trial shows that defendants generally are treated less severely when they enter a plea of guilty, and their cases are disposed of in a shorter period of time. This suggests that defendants gain from the discretionary use of plea bargaining. The conclusion is unwarranted, however, partly because cases disposed of by both means are not strictly comparable, but also for other reasons. In trial by jury, some defendants are found "not guilty" and, therefore, escape altogether the stigma and sanctions incurred by a plea of guilty. There is evidence, moreover, that the finding of "not guilty" would be substantially greater for cases where pleas of guilt are entered. Often the evidence is weaker in these cases or there are violations of the defendant's rights that would lead to a not guilty finding or a dismissal of the charges. These very weaknesses in the substance and procedure of the prosecutor's case are a major incentive to accept a plea of guilty to dispose of the case. Finally, were all cases to go to trial, there is no evidence that the penalties imposed would be as high on the average as they now are for those that go to trial. What is clear is that a plea of guilty is a cost to a minority of defendants who would otherwise be found not guilty; for others there remains a question of whether they gain at all by plea bargaining.

It would be a mistake to conclude that evidence of discretionary decisions in criminal prosecution is determined solely by the prosecutor since, both formally and informally, there are other parties involved in these decisions. Many decisions by the prosecutors not to file information or to dismiss charges are based on citizen decisions about the matter. When citizens wish to drop their role of complainant, are uncooperative, or simply are no longer available or within the jurisdiction of the prosecutor, the prosecutor's case is weakened. Though legally he could compel those within his jurisdiction to cooperate, prosecutors usually conclude little is to be gained by compelling an uncooperative witness to testify. When dependent on the oral testimony and other evidence from uncooperative citizens, prosecutors often have little recourse but to dispose of matters by refusing to file or dropping charges. Defense counsel, likewise, may exercise considerable control over what appears to be prosecutorial discretion. One way they do so is to induce the prosecutor to accept a particular bargain or to coerce the dismissal of the charges by manipulating the judicial proceedings. Since the prosecutor often is overloaded with cases and it is difficult to assemble the witnesses to proceed with a case, defense counsel can take advantage of these conditions. When the prosecutor is not ready for trial, defense counsel may force concessions by stating he is ready to go to trial on that date. Rather than risk judicial discretion over continuance of the matter, the prosecutor may settle or dismiss charges.

In many ways, the exercise of discretion in the prosecutor's arena is a complex game in which the strategies of citizen complainants, defense counsel, and prosecutors risk different payoffs. It is to control the use of these strategies, and to minimize their cost to defense counsel and prosecutors, that resort to the discretionary strategies of plea bargaining often occurs.

Judicial Discretion. Formally, judges are granted enormous discretion in the criminal justice system. The main forms of discretion that they exercise are by decisions to: (1) detain defendants, grant bail, or release them on their own recognizance; (2) dismiss matters or bind over defendants at a preliminary hearing; (3) accept pleas of guilty or find defendants guilty or not guilty in bench trials; (4) rule on matters of substance and procedure during trial proceedings; (5) decide the fate of defendants found guilty, whether by fines or by determining the sentence and whether it is to be suspended, spent on probation, or in confinement. Decisions about the standing of defendants for appeal and the fate of appeals rest also with judges.

Although the discretion of judges to detain defendants and grant bail has been restricted by decisions about the constitutional rights of defendants, judges still retain considerable discretion over whether defendants shall be released on their own recognizance, the amount of bail, and their detention while awaiting trial. Judicial discretion to schedule hearings and continue or dispose of cases has also been restricted in recent years by legislation, by constitutional decisions, and by the adoption of jurisdictional rules for judicial proceedings. The extent to which judicial discretion in these matters will be circumscribed further or enhanced is at issue in matters of preventive detention, the right to a speedy trial, and the right to be free to participate in one's own defense.

Perhaps nowhere is the discretion of judges more apparent and more controversial than in their disposition of cases. There is very little review of judicial discretion in the imposition of sanctions in the American network of criminal justice. That there is considerable variability in the sentencing practices of judges has been demonstrated for many years. An early study of sentencing practices among judges rotating in the same court showed much disparity in their imposition of sanctions. Gaudet (1933) found that the range of variation among judges in the percentage of all cases disposed of by four types of penalties was from 33.6 to 57.7 percent sentenced to prison, from 19.5 to 32.4 percent granted probation, 1.6 to 3.1 percent given fines, and 15.7 to 33.8 percent given a suspended sentence. These differences among judges in the imposition of sanctions apparently could be accounted for only by differences in the values and attitudes of the judges since differences among their cases were essentially randomized.

This disparity in sentencing practices among judges has been confirmed repeatedly over the years. A study of variation in sentencing practices among Canadian judges, while noting that individual differences among judges, rather than among cases, accounts for some variation in sentencing practices among them, calls attention to the possibility that differences in the perceptions of judges as to the availability of alternatives (e.g., of imprisonment) also may affect their disposition decisions (Jaffary, 1963:45–51). Some state and federal jurisdictions, particularly within New York state, have experimented with the European practice of review of sentences to adjudicate gross inequities created by judicial discretion. This experimental incursion into their traditional discretion encounters considerable opposition from judges.

The extent to which judicial decisions are discretionary on the part of judges is not entirely clear for a number of reasons. Among them is the fact that before disposing of a case, judges receive a report of an investigation and a recommendation for its disposition from a probation officer. Carter and Wilkins find that there is a strong relationship between officer recommendations for probation and court dispositions of probation. The relationship diminishes slightly when recommendations against probation (or for imprisonment) are contrasted with court dispositions of probation. They conclude that where disagreements exist between probation officers and judges, the judge uses his discretion to decide in favor of probation, a less punitive disposition, perhaps (Carter & Wilkins, 1967:506). They suggest that four factors could affect the agreement between probation officers' recommendations and judicial disposition, only some of which indicate the exercise of judicial discretion: (1) reliance of the judge on the professional expertise of the probation officer; (2) seemingly "obvious" candidacy of many offenders for probation; (3) sensitivity of the probation officer to the predilections and desires of the judge in making a recommendation; and (4) consensus between judges and probation officers on the factors that make for success on probation (p. 508).

DISCRETION AND JUSTICE

Perhaps no concept is more difficult to define in a consideration of criminal justice than the concept of justice. Difficulties in conceptualization are compounded when one attempts to measure whether justice is done in fact, and whether the exercise of discretion has any effect on the doing of justice.

Two related but different ideas inhere in traditional definitions of justice. The first idea grapples with the accuracy, fairness, reasonableness, or "justness" of the application of particular sanctions to particular conduct (or in a particular instance). At issue is the appropriateness of the rewards and costs as standards for and when applied to particular conduct. For example, is capital punishment for an offense just? The second idea refers to the distributive property of justice. Are equals treated equally regardless of the reward or the cost? Unequal treatment is inherently unjust or discriminatory. The exercise of discretion can affect these properties of justice in important ways.

The bureaucratization of the administration of justice in the United States presumably should guarantee the distributive property of justice, since a property of bureaucracies is the universalistic application of standards according to rules. Discretion in the application of rules, however, opens the door to unequal treatment, particularly when the limits of discretionary power are unclear (Davis, 1969:97–141). Paradoxically, however, procedural rules to limit discretion or discretion to set standards of justice within bureaucracies may markedly affect the property of what is just.

The bureaucratic organization and administration of criminal justice in the United States has generally neglected the distributive property of justice by focusing on decision-making in the particular case rather than on the distributive effect of decisions in the aggregate of cases. The existence also of a large number of organizations within a jurisdictional network and the multiplicity of local, state, and national networks that are coordinated only weakly, if at all, have led also to high variability in the definition of justice. Since the system of criminal justice both permits considerable authorized discretion by officials in making decisions and fails generally to monitor the unauthorized use of discretion in making decisions, it has contributed further to a variability in the standards of justice and the equity of their administration.

Officially, questions of the "justness" of standards are largely placed within legislative and appellate bodies in the American system of criminal justice. Within recent years, legislative bodies have begun to consider whether given penalties are just for particular offenses, and appellate bodies have applied constitutional standards of justice to a few matters, such as capital punishment. Legislatures, however, have given little attention to placing limits on the discretion to apply standards. In a few controversial areas, such as police search of the person or property, they have actually legitimated unauthorized discretion by the adoption of "no-knock" and "stop-and-frisk" statutes. Appellate bodies have given more attention to limiting discretion, particularly in the unauthorized use of police interrogation, search of persons, and entry or seizure of property. While some attention, thus, has been given to the exercise of police discretion, far less attention has been given to limiting it for other officials in the criminal justice system (though notable exceptions exist, such as in the control of judicial decisions to grant bail).

A growing body of evidence assembled largely by research on the distributive property of criminal justice in the United States demonstrates that there is much de facto discrimination. The poor and minorities when accused of violating the law are more likely to be sanctioned, to be sanctioned more severely, and to be denied their rights and the full opportunity to defend their interests (Schrag, 1971:176–80).

The perspective one has on the nature and dispensation of justice in the American system depends upon one's investments in it. Citizens who are frequently and fully processed within the system fail to perceive that it dispenses justice, and regard it as unjust. Casper's recent study of convicted offenders discloses that they develop common images for each type of agent in the criminal justice system. Though individual police officers are seen as engaging in unjust acts, such as false arrest or improperly using force against them, they are generally held in contempt, more from a belief that they fail to do their job well than from a belief that they are deliberately unjust (Casper, 1972:49). Convicted offenders believe that prosecutors are the central figures in the system of criminal justice whose discretionary decisions control defense lawyers and judges. Defendants feel particularly betrayed by judges, to whom they attribute the authority to decide matters in their interest but who abdicate that discretionary power to prosecutors (p. 143).

In recent years, citizens in the United States have expressed concern over the "breakdown" of criminal justice in the United States. They are divided in their concerns about the causes of that breakdown with a substantial body, particularly of minority-group citizens and proponents of civil liberties, believing that the discretionary authority of officials, especially that of the police, must be restricted. A growing majority, however, appears to demand more punitive standards of justice for offenses they regard as serious and to legitimate the use of discretion by agents of the system.

Within the operating system, the majority of agents within each organization sharply resists any intrusion upon their discretion. The police legitimate their traditional use of unauthorized discretion, prosecutors legitimate plea bargaining, judges resist review of their sentencing decisions, and corrections officers resist review of their decisions to classify, treat, or sanction inmates.

Several trends appear to characterize the exercise of discretion and its effect on criminal justice in the United States. First, there is increasing bureaucratization of work within each agency but resistance to central bureaucratic coordination and control of the agencies as a single system of justice. The increasing bureaucratization of work within agencies has led, in fact, to the bureaucratic legitimation and formalization of discretion that was exercised informally. This is particularly apparent in the formalization of the plea-bargaining process in public prosecution of offenders.

Second, the bureaucratization of justice increasingly denies citizens their formal roles in the system and relegates them to informal control within the citizen system. Citizens have enormous informal control of the criminal justice system in their discretionary decisions to call the police and to cooperate with officials in the system. They still maintain, and perhaps even to a growing extent, the control over inputs into the police and prosecutorial systems. Nonetheless, the waning use of trial by jury and the growing use of plea bargaining decreases the necessity for actual participation of citizens in dispensing justice. Fewer and fewer citizens enter the role of formal witness or juror; their main status is that of complainant. Since plea bargaining places less reliance on evidence and more on compliant or coerced pleas of guilty from alleged offenders, citizens are of less import to the transactions of prosecutors. This withdrawal of citizens from formal participation in the system of justice may have important consequences since citizens do not acquire direct knowledge of it through participation unless they are processed as offenders. That direct experience is important in shaping citizen views of criminal justice is shown by the fact that, on the average, participants are more negative in their views of it than are those who lack such experience. A Detroit area study (Mayhew & Reiss, 1967) showed that more than one in three citizens who participated in criminal trials for the defense, for the prosecution, or as a juror reported some dissatisfaction with the proceedings. The most common response was a personal reaction to the outcome as unfair or unjust. Two of every three witnesses reacted negatively to some aspect of the proceeding. About one-fifth objected to the conduct of court officials, particularly of lawyers and judges, who were seen as officious or bureaucratic. An additional one-fourth objected to the adversary form of proceeding, particularly in the interrogation. And one in ten was disturbed by his ignorance of the proceeding or frightened by the atmosphere of a criminal-court trial.

Third, there is no effective organizational provision for controlling discretion within any of the agencies in the network except when that agency makes an input into another organization. This, on the one hand, makes each agency vulnerable to the exercise of unauthorized decisions and sanctions by all others and, on the other hand, places the control over discretion exercised by other agencies *within* each organization. Each agency can control others only when they process the *same* people, organizations, or information, but they can do so only when these same matters enter their own organization. Citizens can control the police by their decisions to mobilize them, but the police have almost no control over many criminal matters citizens refuse to bring to their attention. Prosecutors can control the police by refusing to regard an arrest as legal or bona fide, but there is no effective control over police failure to arrest or report arrests. Similarly, judges can control prosecutors and others by refusing to comply with their recommendations on cases before them or by applying rules to their processing, but judges lack control over cases that are not brought before them. To be sure, judges and prosecutors have important powers to command others when matters that were not brought to their attention by officials or citizens become known to them, but in practice, such powers are more latent than real.

Each agency develops counterstrategies of control to limit that exercised by other organizations. Their major strategies are to withhold output or information. The police, for example, need conform only to legal standards for those cases they bring to official attention. Correlatively, they may try to control by overloading another organization with information and cases, recognizing its incapacity to handle it.

The fact that the major means of control over discretion are internal to each organization within the American system of criminal justice has certain other important consequences (Reiss, 1971:120). The first is that procedural rather than substantive issues of justice dominate the processing of people and information. Whether legal procedure was followed rather than whether justice was done becomes the focus of concern and processing within the system. A second consequence is that each organization creates its own system of justice, a system of justice without trial (Skolnick, 1967). The police, as already noted, do justice by illegal arrest, improper use of force, and harassment. The prosecutor institutionalizes falsification by the "justice" of plea bargaining. Defendants are told to plead to matters that falsely state the nature of their violation of the law. The defendant, defense counsel, and the prosecutor deny, in response to a necessary query from the judge, that there has been a prior bargain, and the judge accepts the plea of guilty with full awareness that a bargain that has been denied has been struck. Each judge determines within the broad limits of the law the punitive standards to apply and whether alternative forms of justice shall be used. A third consequence is that each organization protects itself from penetration by the others, particularly by creating barriers to contact and communication. Common problems are dealt with only in processing a particular case. Finally, informal cooptation of agents becomes a major means for controlling the conduct of officials in other agencies. This ranges from cooptation through participation in a common political party to cooptation in practice, such as the case conference.

ACCOUNTABILITY FOR DISCRETIONARY JUSTICE

Theoretically in modern democratic societies, government is accountable to the citizens it serves. Each organization of government, moreover, is to be held accountable to legitimate external authority to carry out its mandate and is responsible for holding its employees accountable to it. The control over accomplishing a mandate and over the exercise of discretion in carrying it out depends upon the development of structures that define and limit that authority and of procedures for insuring that discretion is limited to the proper exercise of authority.

We have tried to show that the system of criminal justice in the United States is not generally accountable to external authority. It also is true that most organizations within the criminal justice system are poorly developed to control the internal exercise of discretion. This is so for a number of reasons: first of all, the organizational system of criminal justice lacks central coordination and control by an organization, such as a ministry of justice. Organizational accountability, therefore, lies principally in holding elected and appointed officials accountable by election or appointment. There are, for the most part, no means for continuously monitoring the organization. Second, the organizations are not responsible to a single authority or jurisdiction. The local police department, for example, is responsible to the executive authority of local government, while the courts of general jurisdiction are accountable to judicial authority, though some accountability may derive from their dependence on legislative bodies for fiscal support. Third, the legal powers to hold other organizations and their agents accountable are generally inoperative because there is no formal provision for their implementation. The prosecutor and judges have very broad powers to compel other agents but very limited resources, if any, to detect the improper use of discretion. Fourth, structures for detecting the improper use of discretion are poorly developed and for the most part internal to an organization. Each organization, in fact, protects itself from external detection. Fifth, many of the organizations are controlled by professionals. Since the core of a professional practice is the exercise of discretion, professionals resist its review. Review when it occurs, moreover, is restricted to review by professional peers. Finally, the bureaucratic form of these organizations insulates them from some forms of accountability. Although bureaucracies by their nature limit discretion, it is difficult to control their discretion to make rules. Bureaucracies, furthermore, are recalcitrant in the face of change to deal with problems that arise, which they are not designed to resolve. Unauthorized discretion often is a ready solution to these problems and, in time, the means become institutionalized and themselves resistant to change. The operating system of criminal justice, in fact, appears to represent more a solution to problems generated within the network by using unauthorized discretion than it does to formal design and control. The unauthorized discretion of the police to arrest, of the prosecutor to bargain pleas, and of the judge to hear most cases on pleas of guilty rather than by trial arose primarily as a solution to problems generated within the criminal justice system, subverting much of the system's original mandate.

Paradoxically, the solution to structuring and monitoring the exercise of discretion lies in some of the same sources that interfere with holding organizations and agents accountable for their exercise of discretion since legal, bureaucratic, and professional organizations are the major means for the control of discretion. All of them neutralize civic power, however, and it seems essential to develop viable civic control, whether by civic review agencies, an ombudsman, or public systems of accountability.

REFERENCES

Banton, Michael.
    1964   The Policeman in the Community. London: Tavistock.

Biderman, Albert D.
    1967   "Surveys of population samples for estimating crime incidence." Annals of the American Academy of Political and Social Science 374(November): 16–33.

Biderman, A. D., L. A. Johnson, J. McIntyre, and A. W. Weir.
    1967   Field Surveys 1: Report on a Pilot Study in the District of Columbia on Victimization and Attitudes toward Law Enforcement. Report of research study submitted to the President's Commission on Law Enforcement and Administration of Justice. Washington, D.C.: U.S. Government Printing Office.

Bittner, Egon.
    1967a   "Police discretion in emergency apprehension of mentally ill persons." Social Problems 14(Winter):278–292.
    1967b   "The police on skid row: a study of peace-keeping." American Sociological Review 32(October):699–715.

Black, Donald J.
1971 "The social organization of arrest." Stanford Law Review 23(June):1087–1111.

Black, Donald J., and Albert J. Reiss, Jr.
1970 "Police control of juveniles." American Sociological Review 35(February): 63–77.

Blumberg, Abraham S.
1973 Law and Order: The Scales of Justice. Revised Second Edition. New Brunswick, N.J.: Transaction Books.

Bordua, David, and Albert J. Reiss, Jr.
1966 "Command, control and charisma." American Journal of Sociology 72 (July):68–76.

Carter, Robert M., and Leslie T. Wilkins.
1967 "Some factors in sentencing policy." Journal of Criminal Law, Criminology and Police Science 584(December):503–514.

Casper, Jonathan D.
1972 American Criminal Justice: The Defendant's Perspective. Englewood Cliffs, N.J.: Prentice-Hall.

Chevigny, Paul.
1969 Police Power: Police Abuses in New York City. New York: Pantheon Books.

Davis, Kenneth Culp.
1969 Discretionary Justice: A Preliminary Inquiry. Baton Rouge: Lousiana State University Press.

Gardiner, John.
1969 Traffic and the Police: Variations in Law Enforcement Policy. Cambridge: Harvard University Press.

Gaudet, Frederick J., G. S. Harris, and C. W. St. John.
1933 "Individual differences in the sentencing tendencies of judges." Journal of Criminal Law, Criminology and Police Science 23(January–February): 811–818.

Goldstein, Joseph.
1960 "Police discretion not to invoke the criminal process: low-visibility decisions in the administration of justice." Yale Law Journal 69(March): 543–594.

Jaffary, Stuart K.
1963 Sentencing of Adults in Canada. Toronto: University of Toronto Press.

Kakalik, James S., and Sorrel Wildhorn.
1971a Private Police in the United States: Findings and Recommendations, vol. 1. Santa Monica: The Rand Corp.
1971b The Private Police Industry: Its Nature and Extent, vol. 2. Englewood Cliffs, N.J.: Prentice-Hall.

Mayhew, Leon H., and Albert J. Reiss, Jr.
1967 In Search of Justice. Ann Arbor: University of Michigan, Detroit Area Study.

Mileski, Maureen.
1971 "Policing slum landlords: an observation study of administrative control." Ph.D. dissertation, Yale University.

National District Attorneys Association (N.D.A.A.)
    1971   Report on Proceedings, Recommendations, and Statistics of the NDAA
            Metropolitan Prosecutors' Conference. Chicago: National District Attorneys
            Association.

Oaks, Dallin H., and Warren Lehman.
    1973   "Lawyers for the poor." Pp. 159–172 in Abraham S. Blumberg, Law and
            Order: The Scales of Justice. Revised Second Edition. New Brunswick,
            N.J.: Transaction Books.

Piliavan, Irving, and Scott Briar.
    1964   "Police encounters with juveniles." American Journal of Sociology 70(Sep-
            tember):206–214.

President's Commission on Law Enforcement and Administration of Justice.
    1967   Task Force Report: The Police. Washington, D.C.: U.S. Government Print-
            ing Office.

Reiss, Albert J., Jr.
    1967   "Measurement of the nature and amount of crime." Section 1 in Field Sur-
            veys 3: Studies in Crime and Law Enforcement in Major Metropolitan
            Areas, vol. 1. Report of research study submitted to President's Commission
            on Law Enforcement and Administration of Justice. Washington, D.C.: U.S.
            Government Printing Office.
    1968   "Police brutality—answers to key questions." Trans-action 5(July–August):
            12–21.
    1969   "Appendix A, field survey," in Crime Against Small Business: A Report of
            the Small Business Administration. Senate Document 91–114, 91st Cong.,
            1st sess., April 3.
    1971   The Police and the Public. New Haven: Yale University Press.

Reiss, Albert J., Jr., and Jerry Hikel.
    1973   "Prosecutorial discretion in selected jurisdictions" (unpublished).

Schrag, Clarence.
    1971   Crime and Justice: American Style, Crime and Delinquency Issues. A
            Monograph Series, Rockville, Maryland, Center for Studies on Crime and
            Delinquency. National Institute of Mental Health Publication No. HSM-
            72-9052.

Silverstein, Lee.
    1965   Defense of the Poor in Criminal Cases. Chicago: American Bar Foundation.

Skolnick, Jerome.
    1967   Justice Without Trial. New York: Wiley.

Stinchcombe, Arthur.
    1963   "Institutions of privacy in the determination of police administrative prac-
            tice." American Journal of Sociology 49(September):150–160.

Sudnow, David.
    1965   "Normal crimes: sociological features of the criminal code." Social Prob-
            lems 12(Winter):255–276.

Wilson, James Q.
    1968   Varieties of Police Behavior. Cambridge: Harvard University Press.

Wiseman, Jacqueline P.
    1970   Stations of the Lost: The Treatment of Skid Row Alcoholics. Englewood
            Cliffs, N.J.: Prentice-Hall.

PART III

CORRECTIONS

Introduction—Part III

Once a person is labeled delinquent or criminal by the judicial system, the state faces the task of reducing or terminating the behavior presumed to have justified such a label. This task is called correction.

Clarence Schrag, author of Chapter 19, is an academic specialist in sociological theory and a veteran of correctional employment at many levels, including state director. His chapter critically reviews theories basic to a sociology of corrections. It also encompasses social psychology, a field shared by sociology and psychology. He summarizes, assesses, and improves three theory groups: (1) labeling theory; (2) what he calls "congruence theory," embracing balance, cognitive dissonance, and anomie formulations; and (3) control theory, viewed as a variant of social systems analysis and highly compatible with psychology's behavior modification approach. Implications of these theories for correctional reform are elucidated, with special attention to diversion of offenders from correctional agencies.

Psychologists Michael A. Milan and John M. McKee set forth the principles of behavior modification, and describe applications of these principles to the promotion of education and of cooperative behavior among inmates of correctional institutions. The methods they endorse contrast markedly in basic perspectives and in effectiveness with such diverse alternatives as those of traditional clinical psychotherapy and those of traditional punishment. Application of behavior modification techniques to changing delinquent and criminal behavior in the community is also discussed, although this is much more difficult and less researched than their application in institutional settings.

By far the most neglected correctional facilities of the United States are its jails. To compensate for this neglect we offer the comprehensive discussion in Chapter 21 by sociologist Hans W. Mattick, formerly associate warden of one of the nation's largest jails, and for many more recent years director of university criminal justice study centers. Mattick presents a thorough analysis of the dimensions of jail problems based on extensive survey research, as well as a critical discussion of the potential solutions for these problems.

During most of the nineteenth and twentieth centuries, felony sentences generally consisted of imprisonment, but in the 1960s and 1970s alternatives to incarceration increasingly predominated, either as substitutes or as supplements for confinement. Therefore, correctional management specialist Billy L. Wayson, assistant to the director of the U.S. Bureau of Prisons, focuses on the problems of change when discussing prison administration. He contrasts managerial styles impeding change with those that facilitate progress, indicating a need not only for more two-way communication within prison bureaucracies, but also for approaches to budgeting and planning that take into account the total criminal justice system rather than just the prisons.

The careers of sociologist Charles W. Dean and psychologist N. Dickon Reppucci have combined university teaching with research in juvenile correctional institutions, two of which Dean has supervised. They present national statistical data on such facilities, plus an account and an analysis of distinctive experimental programs, including some that have shifted most correctional activities from the institution to the community.

Former Deputy Director of the U.S. Bureau of Prisons H. G. Moeller, now in the academic world, provides the chapter on community-based correctional services, which he helped pioneer. He analyzes problems encountered in such pioneering and sets forth guidelines for avoiding or resolving them in the establishment of new centers, as well as in furlough and work release programs.

Vincent O'Leary, who wrote Chapter 25, directed parole administration successively for the states of Washington and Texas, and subsequently became a national leader in training personnel and conducting research on parole, most recently as a professor of criminal justice. Much of this research is evident in his description of the variety of legislation, decision-making, and organization of services prevailing in parole, as well as in his presentation of new conceptualizations of parole.

Social worker John A. Wallace has had a long and innovative career as director of probation in Baltimore and in New York City. He analyzes the components of probation activities in relation to their purposes, reports research and experience on alternative court procedures, and describes trends in the modification of probation services and purposes. Finally, he indicates the implications of these trends for modification of traditional values, personnel, and organization to make court services more effective in alleviating all of society's crime and delinquency prevention problems, as well as in helping probationers.

John Irwin analyzes correction not just as an academic sociologist, but from personal experience as a prisoner, which aided and gave greater depth to his subsequent research on the experiences of other prisoners and parolees. He calls our attention to the historic mixing of punishment and rehabilitative objectives in correctional enterprises, and the tendency for the punitive to dominate even in programs presumed to be most oriented to the rehabilitation ideal. He describes a variety of reactions and adaptations by correctional clientele to the often blatantly hypocritical and unjust individualized treatment and programming imposed on them, explaining how these may make many alleged rehabilitation measures counterproductive. Finally, he suggests a series of alternative ideals for corrections.

Sociologist Lloyd E. Ohlin's extensive studies of correctional reform have been pursued not only as an academician, but also as research director in diverse metropolitan and state correctional agencies and in federal offices and commissions. From this perspective he identifies the major sources of resistance to correctional change, and the strategic importance of research on change efforts. This he illustrates by an analysis of alternative models for juvenile correctional systems, by the dynamics of efforts to change such systems, and by the consequences of these efforts for various roles and relationships within the systems. He concludes by suggesting a new model for action-research collaboration, yet points out the special problems likely to be encountered with this model.

Sociologist Stuart Adams, in his service with four major correctional organizations or study commissions, probably has directed a larger volume and variety of useful correctional research than anyone else in the world. In his chapter on such research, the last chapter in this part, he distinguishes effectiveness and efficiency as separate criteria for the assessment of correctional efforts, then classifies and describes diverse research undertakings, with special emphasis on cost-benefit analysis.

CHAPTER 19

Theoretical Foundations
for a Social Science of Corrections

Clarence Schrag

University of Washington

Correctional systems are established for the purposes of reforming lawbreakers, protecting society, and raising the level of justice in general. These are their manifest functions (Merton, 1957). But the systems also serve latent functions, rarely mentioned by the authorities, having to do with status management and with keeping offenders in subordinate social positions. While reform and justice attract people's attention, the subordination of designated offenders is what the systems accomplish.

Moreover, the treatment of law violators is an incoherent mixture of punishment and toleration. Certain offenders are labeled, given the status of outcasts, and systematically deprived of access to middle-class methods of achieving success or self-respect. The more stigma and deprivation they experience, it seems, the higher their recidivism rates.

Severe punishment is not often applied, however. Many offenders, by far the majority, are protected against the penalties prescribed by law. And those who are thus favored do not appear to be any more likely to repeat their offenses than those who are punished. Quite the reverse may be true (Schrag, 1971:211–20). Yet the toleration of crime, when penalties are called for, may tend to undermine faith in the law and in its means of enforcement. Instead of discouraging law violations, therefore, the procedures of crime control may serve to debilitate the persons who are labeled and to alienate those who are not. In this way criminal justice may often encourage criminality.

The field of corrections is accordingly in turmoil. Never before has there been such an emphasis on correctional reform or such a diversity of opinions as to what constitutes reform. Nor is it clear in which direction the field is moving. New programs, many of them inconsistent with one another, are proposed on the basis of disjointed conjectures and uncontrolled observations. Because of the notorious difficulty involved in carrying out studies of program effectiveness, many investigations dispense with controls entirely or use controls that are insufficient to establish causal relationships. Without the necessary scientific information, changes in the field are dictated primarily by political pressures.

Such conclusions are supported by both empirical evidence and theoretical analysis. In this chapter we first examine some relevant developments in sociological theory and then consider their relationship to several recent changes in correctional procedure. Implicit in this discussion is the need for overhaul of the justice system, including legislation, law enforcement, and the courts, as well as corrections.

CORRECTIONAL THEORY: CONCEPTS AND CONVERGENCES

Perhaps the greatest deficiency in the field of corrections today is the lack of an overall theoretical framework. Although the scientific literature is filled with well-documented findings, the theoretical integration of these findings gets little encouragement from practice-oriented officials, agencies that fund research projects, or editors who publish the results. Correctional theories are, therefore, at a preliminary stage of development and are more appropriately termed research "leads" or "strategies." Probably few, if any, of these leads and strategies can successfully meet the tests of logical, operational, empirical, and pragmatic adequacy (Schrag, 1967). Hence, the question that confronts the researcher is whether a given "lead" is worthy of further investigation.

However, it is difficult to estimate the growth potential of a specific approach unless there is a feedback relationship between theory and evidence. This point is illustrated, for example, by the work of Durkheim (1893, 1897) on anomie, Weber (1947) on bureaucracy, Sutherland (1939) on differential association, Cohen (1965) on subcultures, and Cloward and Ohlin (1960) on opportunity structures. These major sociological contributions have directly or indirectly influenced numerous correctional efforts, including Mobilization for Youth, Model Cities and its neighborhood programs, New Careers for ex-offenders, behavior-modification techniques employed at the National Training School for Boys, and others (cf. Marris & Rein, 1967). Some of the programs were intended as tests of the theories involved. But there is little evidence that experience in the field of action has produced any important feedback effects on these theories. Except for the rapid development of behavior modification, which makes some of Sutherland's notions obsolete, the theoretical formulations remain substantially the same as they were before the programs were implemented. Mature theories, or those so regarded, are not noted for their responsiveness to new information.

Perhaps the efforts at corroboration occurred too soon. The theories were not, and are not, mature. Nor have they been abandoned because of their failures. Instead, they serve as building blocks for newer, more comprehensive, and, hopefully, more useful theories. Bits and pieces from many disciplines are gradually being incorporated into what is recognizable as an embryo theory of corrections.

Whether this theory is, in some absolute sense, true or false may be relatively unimportant, certainly less important than evidence of its capacity for organizing observations, coordinating various facts, and explaining new findings or those that were formerly considered inconsistent. The theory is being formulated and retested in an endless process. Its rate of maturation will depend on the feedback it gets from empirical investigations and on the extent to which its assumptions can be integrated with the results of such investigations. Significant steps are being made in this direction by redefining criminality, by examining society's diverse reactions to crime, and by focusing more attention on the transactions that occur between offenders and the community.

These are the hallmarks of the newer inputs into correctional research, coming mainly from the theories of labeling, congruence, and social control. The result is a reconceptualization of the field of corrections.

Labeling

The basic arguments on labeling were presented nearly a half century ago by Frank Tannenbaum (1938). Recent additions include the distinction between primary and secondary deviance (Lemert, 1951), examination of the role that conflict plays in the labeling process (Quinney, 1970), and elaboration of the main concepts (Becker, 1963; Schur, 1971). Labeling consists of criminalization procedures by which a community seeks out its law violators, stigmatizes them, and assigns them to the position of a pariah. According to the theory, it is not the criminal act so much as it is society's reaction to the act that furthers the development of criminal careers.

The assumptions that best characterize the theory are seemingly the following:

1. No act is intrinsically criminal. For every act treated as a crime there are equivalent forms of behavior that are condoned or rewarded by society—taking a human life may be regarded as murder, justifiable use of force, military heroism, or an act of mercy. What makes an act a crime is the application of criminal law. Nor is the law always in accord with human values. Many acts that are morally indefensible and harmful to the community fall outside the purview of criminal law, while some acts defined as crimes have little social significance. Examples of the latter are the well-known blue laws.

2. Crimes, accordingly, are defined by organized groups having sufficient power to influence the processes of legislation and law enforcement. Definitions of crime are enforced in the interest of these groups by their official representatives, including the police, courts, correctional institutions, and other administrative bodies. Although substantive definitions and rules of procedure may be insensitive to the offender's social standing, the way such definitions and rules are applied depends on local authorities whose decisions commonly reflect the preferences of political officials and community leaders. Thus, the law has many faces. Its meanings and effects vary among its makers, enforcers, observers, and violators.

3. A person does not become a criminal by violating the law. Instead, he is designated a criminal by the reactions of authorities who confer upon him the status of an outcast and divest him of some of his social and political privileges. According to self-report studies and other sources, most of the acts committed by criminals are in conformity with the law, while some of the actions of so-called conformists are in violation of the law (Quinney, 1970:18–23). The criminal label, therefore, indicates a person's legal status, not his behavior.

4. Only a few persons are apprehended for law violations though many may be equally involved in infractions. Those apprehended are singled out for special treatment. Their arrest precipitates a sequence of experiences most others do not share. Suddenly there appear the police, the jail, the criminals and misfits found in the jail, and the court with its retinue of lawyers, investigators, judges, and witnesses. There are tests, examinations, allegations, negotiations, and judgments beyond the offender's control or understanding.

The accused person, even if no different from the rest of his group, becomes the central character in a drama that has one of two endings: acquittal or conviction. If he is acquitted, the curtain is soon raised again with someone else in the major role. If convicted, however, the offender is condemned not only for what he has done but for all the evils attributed to criminals in general. The criminal label makes him a scapegoat. He becomes one of the few that many can blame for the ills of all.

5. Legal definitions of crime are reinforced by the moralistic notion that people, on the whole, can be categorized as good or bad. In this popular view, criminals are

not merely law violators. They are bad persons, permanently and naturally bad. Having no intention or desire to do what is right, they remain bad regardless of any attempts to rehabilitate them. Good people, on the contrary, are seen as natural conformists. They respect the law, resist temptation, and retain a clear conscience. Although they may be capable of making a mistake, they can do no serious wrong, at least not intentionally.

An ironic result of this view is that, in the public's conception of criminality, it is the actor's character, rather than the act committed or its consequences, that differentiates between criminal and noncriminal persons. From such a perspective, not all criminals are law violators, nor are all violators criminals. There are also some violators who may be regarded as normally law-abiding citizens.

The distinction between criminal and noncriminal violators may be clarified by the concepts of primary and secondary deviance as these terms are used in labeling theory (Lemert, 1951). Primary deviance refers to aberrant behavior that the community considers alien to the actor's character, a kind of unorganized and unmotivated nonconformity that may occur on occasion among people generally regarded as playing socially accepted roles. Perceived as more of a nuisance than a threat, these rule infractions are commonly tolerated.

Secondary deviance, by contrast, refers to serious or repetitive violations that are organized and integrated as part of the actor's self-image. Essential to its development is the community's negative evaluation of the actor. When it perceives a threat to its welfare, the community ascribes motives to the offender in terms of its beliefs concerning the causes of his behavior. These ascriptions may subsequently be internalized through a sequence of interactions leading from primary to secondary deviance. First, a deviant act occurs. Society, depending on its evaluation of the act, may react by instituting repressive measures against the offender. The frequent result is a feedback cycle that produces more deviance and more repression. Hostilities and resentments are built up, culminating in official labeling and stigmatization, thereby justifying even greater penalties and restrictions of the offender's opportunities for changing his role. Most persons labeled as criminals are accordingly involved in secondary deviance.

6. Identification of a person as a criminal always justifies his being condemned to a deprived status. Official condemnation is ordinarily achieved through ceremonies of status degradation, such as the criminal trial, that strip the offender of his former identity and commit him to the new and inferior status of an evil person. Further deprivation occurs if the lawbreaker is sent to prison, where he is divested of personal possessions, assigned a number, and cloaked in a uniform symbolizing his outcast position. After discharge from the institution, he is shunned by respectable people, prevented from voting in elections or holding office, handicapped in finding employment or other legitimate pursuits, and deprived in many other ways. He cannot leave the community, change his residence, buy a car, get married, or enter into other contractual agreements without the approval of his parole officer.

Although skills may be developed and attitudes modified by correctional treatment, these are of no great significance unless they are accompanied by changes in the offender's social position and in the public's attitudes toward him. Community attitudes are not likely to change, however, since the system of justice dramatizes evil persons rather than evil practices. The criminal label alerts citizens to the presence of an evil one in their midst, and such a label, once given, is likely to be held regardless of the individual's present or future behavior. If he continues his criminal activities, this merely confirms the community's previous verdict. If he mends his ways, he often encounters doubt and suspicion. His efforts may be viewed as a devious device for concealing his criminalistic inclinations. Hence, the public's reluctance in accepting evidence of the criminal's rehabilitation may be one of the reasons for high recidivism rates and for the failure of correctional programs.

7. The criminal label also makes it difficult for a law violator to maintain a conception of himself as a worthy person. At first he may blame his low status on bad luck, lack of opportunity, discrimination, and other things beyond his control. In this way he can resist people's opinions of him. But the rejection of these opinions tends to result also in rejection of the people holding them, and the offender frequently develops antagonistic attitudes toward the community, especially its officials. By rejecting his rejectors, he finds motivation for continued conflict and further offenses.

Further offenses elicit more strenuous countermeasures on the part of the authorities, escalating the negative actions and reactions in a manner that hardens and crystallizes the antagonistic attitudes of actor and reactor alike. Eventually the offender comes to see himself as a public enemy, one engaged in a war with right more on his side than on society's. He acquires the traits first imputed to him and becomes the antisocial person he was labeled to be. In some cases beginning with an isolated and perhaps innocuous violation, an offender may be propelled by criminalization procedures into a career of crime as a way of life.

8. The treatment of law violators accordingly serves as a self-fulfilling prophecy. It forecloses noncriminal options and coerces offenders into a criminal role. Hence, criminal justice may be seen as a system for defining, detecting, identifying, labeling, segregating, and emphasizing the things officially regarded as evil, finding a scapegoat, and making people sensitive to crime and the consequences thereof. It tends to produce criminals by dramatizing, suggesting, stimulating, and evoking the very kinds of activities it is allegedly designed to alleviate.

There is little evidence that the present system—particularly the labeling rituals and the dramatization of evil—has any deterrent effect (cf. Zimring, 1971). Its function, viewed objectively, is not to impede violations of the law but to establish and to perpetuate the subordinate statuses of persons who are labeled as criminals. This it does with apparent effectiveness.

The labeling framework, outlined above, gets much of its support from reports of offenders, case studies, and informal observations of crime-control agencies. Especially relevant are studies of drug abuse, alcoholism, homosexuality, prostitution, abortion, and other offenses against public conceptions of decency.

An illustration is Becker's explanation (1963:chap. 3) of the relationship between criminality and drug addiction. He argues that crime does not result from the effects of narcotics but from society's reaction against certain users. Society's reaction is much influenced by popular notions about why people want drugs. Users are seen as weak-willed individuals, incapable of resisting illicit pleasures. They are accordingly labeled, punished, and forbidden access to narcotics. Unable to obtain supplies lawfully, they make contacts with illegal peddlers, driving the drug market underground and pushing the price so high that few can afford it on a legitimate income. Then, to finance their drug habit, they often resort to theft and robbery.

Some drug users, therefore, are double deviants. Labeled both for addiction and for conventional crime, they continue to commit numerous law violations over long periods of time. Yet many others, very likely the majority, are not so labeled. Those who are wealthy, for example, can purchase drugs without much likelihood of thievery, while those who are very discreet can use drugs without much likelihood of discovery. In these ways they may avoid one or both of the labels.

What attracts official attention, then, is not the drug habit, but the illegal procurement of supplies and the appearance of conspicuous symptoms of drug use. Indiscreet users or those lacking funds are most likely to be labeled, and they are also most likely to be involved in conventional crime. Thus, it follows from the theory's premises that criminality is more closely associated with the labeling process than with the drug habit.

A more empirical approach to labeling theory is exemplified by Turk's (1969) analysis of American crime rates. In this analysis it is hypothesized that society's reaction to criminal behavior is mainly influenced by several identifiable factors. Most important are the severity of the offense, the degree of agreement between criminal laws and social traditions, the relative amounts of power possessed by law enforcers and law violators, the skill or sophistication employed by enforcers and violators in their conflict with one another, and the extent to which violators are organized.

Examination of arrest data for 1958 and 1965 reveals that the highest rates for most offenses are found among males, persons 18 to 25 years of age, and members of ethnic minorities. Moreover, the discrepancies in arrest rates tend to be greatest for the most serious offenses. Arrests involving homicide, rape, robbery, and use of weapons, for example, are eight or ten times as frequent for nonwhites as for whites, while the differences are less than half that large for most other felonies and nearly all misdemeanors. Some exceptions within the latter category are prostitution and gambling, for which the rates of arrest in the nonwhite population are more than ten times as high as among whites.

To interpret such data, it is assumed that males, young adults, and minority groups are characterized by limited power, little sophistication, a small stake in conformity, and the perception of much conflict between laws and other norms. If these assumptions are accepted, they make the findings consistent with several of the hypotheses mentioned. But it is not clear that their acceptance can always be justified on empirical grounds, since there is little reliable information on the distribution of normative conflicts, power, sophistication, criminal organizations, and the like. Nor is there any certainty about the relationship between arrests and law violations in different segments of the population. Hence, studies making these assumptions may take for granted some things without evidence, and their findings may be interpreted as supporting various other theories as well as the labeling framework.

Another problem with the theory is the tendency of some researchers to make labelers the culprits in crime control. Sometimes their argument suggests that crime would not occur if there were no law enforcers and no criminalization procedures. This is illustrated by the way the researchers conceive of crime and deviance. Instead of defining a deviant act as a norm violation and considering its relationship with labeling an empirical question, they make labeling an essential part of the definition. Deviance, they say, is not a characteristic of the act a person commits, but a consequence of the application of society's rules and sanctions. Thus, deviant behavior is "behavior that people so label," and the deviant individual is one "to whom that label has successfully been applied" (Becker, 1963:9).

Such a definition confuses action and reaction. It implies that labeling is both necessary and sufficient for an act to be classified as deviant. As a consequence, neither act nor label can occur except in combination. If this definition were taken literally, there could be no undetected deviance, no secret deviance, and no toleration of deviance. The statement that some violators receive official protection would be a logical contradiction, devoid of meaning. Organized crime and white-collar offenses, since they do not often result in labeling, would have to be considered nondeviant.

Nor could there be studies of erroneous convictions or unjust applications of sanctions. Indeed, the argument that criminal sanctions are unfairly applied against the lower classes, a common theme among labeling theorists, would be deprived of its logical foundation.

Adherence to the definition would impede the documentation of errors and inadequacies in the justice system. The fact is that few law violations result in official labeling and criminalization; many do not. Furthermore, the criminal label is sometimes assigned to persons who have violated no law. These two kinds of error characterize many of the injustices perpetrated by the system of justice. Their investigation requires that the deviant act be clearly differentiated from the labeling process.

Research on labeling is guided more by a social philosophy than by a coherent and well-formed theory. Many of its arguments are inconsistent, polemic in tone, and without empirical corroboration. There are also some problems related to the lack of any close correspondence between concepts and observations, or between assumptions and evidence.

Notwithstanding these limitations, however, the labeling approach makes significant contributions to the study of social control. It focuses attention on the unanticipated consequences of criminal justice, the relativity of perceptions and judgments, and the importance of interaction between the community and the offender, the labelers and those labeled. More than anything else, it reveals the arbitrariness of social norms and the artificiality of many enforcement programs.

In both its virtues and its defects, labeling has much in common with other leading approaches to crime and corrections.

Congruence

Recognizing the need for coherence in criminology, researchers are attempting to integrate various parts and pieces of several different approaches. A good example of this effort, reflecting ideas from numerous sources, is congruence theory.

This theory, like labeling, is more important for its potentials than for its achievements. The potentials are best illustrated by making a number of revisions in the original formulations. Where such revisions occur, of course, the theory is subject to alternative interpretations, some more useful than others. Selection of alternatives is usually left to individual researchers. What makes the research distinctive, then, is a set of concepts and assumptions that serves as a common theme in otherwise diverse undertakings.

1. Fundamental to congruence theory are a few simple ideas about how the social environment influences people's behavior. Many of these ideas can be traced back to early studies of the way biological organisms maintain balance while adapting to environmental stimuli (Cannon, 1929). To illustrate, the perception of an external event may initiate internal reactions affecting respiration, pulse, hormonal secretions, and the like. Ordinarily this helps the organism make effective responses to changes in the environment. Unless the internal reactions are controlled and kept within limits, however, the organism cannot function properly. Disability or death may be the result. In order to survive, therefore, the organism needs not only to adapt itself to changing external conditions but also to maintain an appropriate internal balance.

2. Similar conceptions of balance have been applied more recently to cognitive phenomena (Brehm & Cohen, 1962). The basic assumption is that people strive to maintain balanced cognitive systems or to achieve balance in systems that are unbalanced. Balance can be achieved, for instance, by assigning desirable traits to one's

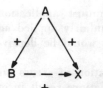

FIGURE 1. Balanced cognitive systems.

friends and undesirable traits to one's enemies. Thus, the characteristics attributed to others are determined, partly at least, by the observer's attitude.

Balanced systems are shown in Figure 1, where A and B represent two persons and X represents some idea, object, characteristic, or event about which A has a strong opinion. A's favorable or unfavorable attitudes are indicated by the plus and minus signs attached to the solid lines directed toward B and X. The broken line at the bottom of each diagram designates A's perception of B's attitude toward X.

A's cognitive system with respect to B and X is balanced whenever the product of the signs attached to the directed lines is positive. In triangular systems, such as those shown, a positive product is obtained under two conditions: either all signs are positive or only one is positive. A negative product occurs if any two signs are positive or if all three are negative, and means that the system is unbalanced. Accordingly, the four possible variations among unbalanced systems can be shown by reversing all of the signs in the balanced diagrams in the figure.

3. Some research findings support the notion that changes in attitude and in other kinds of behavior tend to occur in a manner that facilitates cognitive balance. Consider, for example, the case of a parolee who dislikes his parole officer and is antagonistic toward parole rules. The theory holds that he will perceive his parole officer as favoring the rules. Now, suppose that the parolee observes his officer making critical remarks about the rules. This may create a condition of imbalance for the parolee. If so, he can restore balance in several ways: by developing a more favorable attitude toward the officer, by changing his own view of the rules, or by getting the officer to endorse the rules. Tentative moves in all of these directions are likely to be made, and a distinct shift in any one direction tends to result in a fairly stable cognitive state. It follows that a good way to change a person's attitude is to give him information that throws his cognitive system out of balance.

4. A somewhat analogous argument is employed in Robert Merton's (1957:139–57) famous paradigm of deviant behavior. Here the assumption is that a person's behavior reflects his attitudes toward culturally defined goals and toward the institutionalized means that are prescribed for achieving the goals. The major forms of behavior are conformity, innovation, ritualism, retreatism, and rebellion. Attitudes toward goals and means are characterized as endorsements $(+)$, rejections $(-)$, or substitutions $(\pm)$. These attitudes determine the form of behavior that is most likely to occur in any given situation, as shown in Table 1.

It is easy to see the paradigm's heuristic value. All of the behaviors mentioned can be interpreted in common-sense terms and numerous examples of each are found in everyday experience. Moreover, the actors often seem to have the attitudes indicated. Yet, it is clear that this paradigm is incomplete. If the determinants $+$, $-$, and $\pm$ are taken in pairs, nine combinations are possible. Only five of these are reported. Each of the missing pairs ($+\ \pm$, $-\ \pm$, $\pm\ +$, and $\pm\ -$) involves a substitution for either goals or means.

No reason is given for omitting these combinations. If their omission was deliberate, it suggests that in Merton's view the substitution of both goals and means must occur simultaneously. If, on the contrary, the omission was unintentional, there should be good prospects for identifying modes of behavior that are associated with the missing pairs of determinants. Thus far, however, the search for these behaviors has not been very successful (e.g., Dubin, 1959).

5. Perhaps a better procedure, therefore, is to modify the paradigm, making it more consistent with congruence theory. In the analysis of a social system, congruence theory examines how the main components are interconnected (Schrag, 1971:chap. 3). It investigates two major kinds of normative prescriptions—those identifying legitimate goals and those specifying the alternative means by which goals can be legitimately achieved. The theory also considers the pragmatic relationship between these kinds of norms, separating the means that are effective in achieving goals from those that are ineffective. Finally, the theory makes a sharp distinction between normative prescriptions and individual or group performance.

Further concepts are defined in terms of the observed relationships among the above variables. Performance in agreement with relevant norms is called conformity, for example, while that which disagrees is called deviant behavior. Disagreement among the norms themselves is also a possibility. Thus, the goals a society prescribes for its members may be inconsistent with one another; the means prescribed for achieving goals may be contradictory; or some of the means may be in conflict with some of the goals. To the extent that such discrepancies occur among the goals or the means, or between the two, the social system is disorganized. In addition, the empirical connection between goals and means is symbolized by the concepts of conjunction and disjunction. Conjunction implies that the means are sufficient for the attainment of goals, whereas disjunction refers to connections that are impractical or inefficient.

6. Among these derived concepts, the organization-disorganization continuum seems to be fundamental. Where the norms are inconsistent or there are disjunctions between them, deviance is inevitable because the behavior that conforms with one norm necessarily violates another. Deviance is still possible, of course, in organized systems, but it is not logically necessary. For this reason any systematic analysis of social behavior requires that we consider the linkages between goals and means as well as the actor's endorsements and rejections.

To illustrate, let us assume that in nearly all societies persons can be found for whom there is a conjunction between goals and means (Goals $\longleftarrow^+\longrightarrow$ Means), while other persons can be found for whom a condition of disjunction prevails (Goals $\longleftarrow^-\longrightarrow$ Means). Another assumption is that the prescribed goals and means,

TABLE 1

MERTON'S PARADIGM

Determinants		Resulting Behavior
Goals	Means	
+	+	Conformity
+	−	Innovation
−	+	Ritualism
−	−	Retreatism
±	±	Rebellion

Source: Merton, 1957:140.

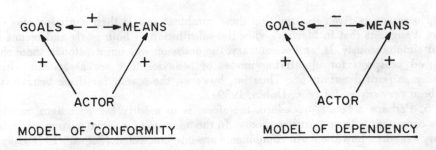

FIGURE 2. Comparison of conformity and dependency models.

whether connected by conjunction or disjunction, may be either endorsed (+) or rejected (−). Then, let us make the further assumption that the behavior associated with any specific combination of endorsements and/or rejections depends upon the condition of conjunction or disjunction that holds true for any given actor.

These assumptions lead to conclusions somewhat different from those stated by Merton (1957). For example, the endorsement of social norms is not exclusive to successful conformists but is also found among persons who are unsuccessful and dependent. Endorsement produces the promised rewards only if there is a conjunction between goals and means, a condition that presumably occurs primarily among members of the middle and upper classes. Disadvantaged individuals and members of the lower classes may face a disjunction between goals and means. Even if they endorse the prescribed norms, these persons are likely to fail in their attempts to attain desired objectives. Confronted by the prospect of failure in spite of their normative attachments, they may tend to exhibit deferential behavior, passive compliance, and dependency. Thus, the essential difference between dependency and conformity is found in the linkages between norms and not in the attitudes or attachments of the actors. This argument is presented diagrammatically in Figure 2.

Note that the conformity model is balanced and that the dependency model is unbalanced. Congruence theory contends that conformity is, therefore, a durable and gratifying model, whereas dependency is relatively uncomfortable and often suggestive of reforms aimed at reducing the imbalance. Balance can be achieved among dependent persons in several ways: by changing their position in the social structure, by changing their attitudes toward the prescribed goals or means, or by changing the disjunctive linkage between norms into a conjunctive one. Of these methods, attitude change is probably the easiest to accomplish. However, it may also be the most inappropriate, since the rejection of goals or means turns the dependents against the system and makes them antagonists. The best way to strengthen the system, then, is by producing a conjunction between goals and means.

Hence, the passive compliance of dependent persons may itself be a threat to the social order. If dependency is an unstable condition, as the theory implies, then the presence of large numbers of dependent persons may serve as a stimulus to social reconstruction. The fact that most societies devise ways of alleviating the symptoms of distress among their dependent members supports this idea. By labeling the treatment of symptoms as reformative measures, they frequently are able to avoid or to delay more basic reforms. Some common examples of symptomatic reforms are the encouragement of philanthropic endeavors, the development of massive welfare programs, and the provision of public subsidies for various groups and individuals. Few of these measures have any influence on the degree of conjunction between goals and means. Their effect is to make imbalance more palatable and in this way to maintain the compliance of dependent people.

7. There are other ways in which unbalanced systems can be perpetuated. Numerous occupations are created to implement the community's norms and to execute sanctions against individuals who fail to conform. Such occupations are found mainly in the institutions of religion, education, welfare, and criminal justice. Their practitioners are the enforcers of the established order. Since these employees are charged with the preservation of peace, the maintenance of moral consensus, and the discouragement of deviant behavior, their loyalty seems crucial to the system's survival. If they were alienated and if they rejected the prescribed norms, it would lend the weight of authority to the arguments of all who favor fundamental social reforms.

Therefore, it might be surprising that the enforcers commonly occupy a subordinate position within the social structure. Much of their reward is in the form of prestige, respect, and other symbolic values voluntarily given by people who approve of their efforts. But the authority invested in the enforcer is largely delegated by higher officials. And the salaries received by many ministers, teachers, social workers, police officers, or correctional agents are only slightly higher than those earned by unskilled laborers, whose status is sometimes considered to be one of marginal dependence.

This makes it difficult to determine if some of the enforcers are full participants in the order they are enforcing or if they are more realistically regarded as marginal dependents. In any event, much social criticism comes from people whose work has to do with order maintenance, and there is evidence that important changes are occurring in their normative attachments as awareness of social injustice grows in modern societies. Many studies have noted that alienation and cynicism are characteristic of workers in this field, especially the older and more experienced ones (Niederhoffer, 1967; Watson & Sterling, 1969). Thus, the marginality of the enforcers may be as much of a problem, potentially at least, as is the dependency of the unemployed or the unemployable.

8. While the disaffection of marginal or dependent persons is always a possibility, the infractions of lawbreakers are generally regarded as a far greater threat to the system. People who have rejected the norms are inclined to endorse and to encourage deviant behavior. Ordinarily, the community reacts to this threat by prescribing punitive sanctions for all serious violations. In practice, however, the transgression of norms is more frequently rewarded than punished.

Congruence theory helps to explain this apparent contradiction. It maintains that society's reaction is not determined by the deviant act but by the way the act is perceived in relation to its social setting. Technically, any act in violation of the community's prescriptions or proscriptions is a deviant act, whether received with approval or disapproval. Its approval by the authorities is more probable if the act is seen as strengthening the conjunction between goals and means. If it weakens or appears to weaken this connection, punishment is the more probable response.

Accordingly, much that is deviant is favorably regarded in official circles. Social inventions, for example, typically involve deviance in the sense that they call for new and hitherto unrealized objectives, new priorities among existing objectives, or new methods of achieving them. The inventions most likely to be absorbed into the normative structure are those that strengthen the perceived linkages between goals and means. Especially important in this connection are the perceptions of people who belong to powerful organizations.

9. Under these conditions, even criminal infractions are likely to be condoned

or rewarded if they benefit the right people. This is evidenced by studies of the transgressions of large corporations, organizations that make important political contributions, wealthy or respected citizens, public officials, and other white-collar agents or agencies (Geis, 1968). Organized crime, no doubt the most profitable of all illegal enterprises, appears to have the lowest probability of a punitive reaction. Such enterprises always involve public officials in the neglect of duty or in other kinds of illicit conduct, and these criminals are often protected by the agencies that are charged with their suppression.

Organized crime takes from nearly everyone and gives mostly to the rich or the powerful. Conventional crime, by contrast, takes mainly from the poor or those of modest means and gives to offenders belonging largely to the same classes. Little of the loot from ordinary crimes remains to be distributed among the more privileged. What attracts most of the attention of the authorities, accordingly, is conventional crime, especially the street variety.

Such a double standard of enforcement, of course, is also found in areas other than criminal behavior. Separate standards for members and nonmembers occur, for example, in the professions, athletic organizations, social clubs, labor unions, political parties, and perhaps most other institutions. Sometimes the discrepant standards can be justified. In the case of medical practitioners, for instance, special privileges and responsibilities may be defended as serving the public interest. But this argument does not seem applicable to crime control, since the sophisticated violations of prominent groups are often as much of a threat to life and property as are the inelegant offenses normally committed by lower-class criminals.

10. When normative standards are in conflict, the actor chooses between them in terms of personal interest. For this reason representatives of an established social order are ordinarily in strong opposition to crimes of the conventional variety while holding a more tolerant attitude—or at least one of greater understanding—toward certain other violations. Meanwhile, the people living in ghettos may be far more antagonistic toward the illegal activities of the privileged than they are toward the kinds of deprivations that occur more frequently in their own environs. In their view the concentration of enforcement effort in the lower classes is registering the corruption of the entire justice system.

11. It is not the threat to life and property, therefore, that differentiates between offenders who are protected and those who are punished. It is rather a question of which normative conjunctions are jeopardized and whose holdings are at stake. This is why efforts at crime control often seem to reflect a fundamental inequality in the values assigned to people and their possessions, depending on whether the individuals involved are rich or poor, young or old, male or female, friends or strangers, insiders or outsiders, and black or white.

Congruence theory, by clarifying how goals and means are connected, adds to our knowledge of labeling, justice, and criminalization. Table 2 lists the cognitive systems, balanced and unbalanced, that produce deviant or conforming behavior, along with the types of societal reaction, whether punishing or rewarding.

The basic assumptions of congruence theory should be kept in mind when reading this table: It seems likely that most societies are well enough organized to maintain a conjunction between goals and means for a majority of their members. Hence, more people are expected to fall in part A of the table (items 1, 2, 3, 4) than in part B (items 5, 6, 7, 8).

Conforming behavior is encouraged whenever the prescribed norms are internalized through the processes of learning and socialization. In this way the individual

TABLE 2

SOME IMPLICATIONS OF CONGRUENCE THEORY: BALANCED AND UNBALANCED SYSTEMS, BEHAVIORAL MODALITIES, AND TYPICAL SOCIETAL REACTIONS

Cognitive Elements		Modes of Behavior	Societal Reactions
Goals	Means		
I. Balanced States:		A. Conjunction between Goals and Means (Goals ← + → Means).	
1. +	+	*Conformity.* Actor works within system to achieve cultural goals by institutionalized means. Generally conservative behavior with limited risk-taking.	Reward and reinforcement.
2. −	−	*Retreatism.* Actor voluntarily withdraws from the established order to pursue specialized goals by uncommon but usually nonthreatening methods. Often found in total institutions (religious, military, etc.).	General toleration. Some public support for total institutions, though this varies in time and place.
II. Unbalanced States:			
3. −	+	*Ritualistic revisionism.* Actor works within the establishment to enhance its integrity. Endorses conventional methods but proposes new priorities among goals, usually minimizing risk and favoring goals that are most readily attained. Less common is advocacy of new and more difficult goals, which entail high risk and the threat of failure.	High rewards if proposed revisions are accepted. Moral crusaders often given respect and prestige. If proposals are rejected, attempt is generally made to resocialize or rehabilitate the deviant insider.
4. +	−	*Innovative revisionism.* Actor works within the establishment to increase its efficiency. Endorses conventional goals but proposes new methods for achieving them. Risk-taking is quite common.	High rewards if proposed revisions are accepted. Emphasis on material rewards. If proposals are rejected, attempt is generally made to resocialize or rehabilitate the deviant insider.

TABLE 2—Continued

B. Disjunction between Goals and Means (Goals ← → Means).

	Cognitive Elements		Modes of Behavior	Societal Reactions
	Goals	Means		
III. Balanced States:				
5.	−	+	*Ritualistic insurgence.* Actor reacts against the established order, rejecting it or working for its reconstruction. Endorses traditional, often outmoded methods but advocates proscribed goals. Moderate risk-taking is common. Examples include vigilantism, racism, extreme patriotism, and the like.	Stigmatization and exclusion from some important activities. Often regarded as an outsider, a moral deviant, and a corrupt influence on society.
6.	+	−	*Innovative insurgence.* Actor reacts against the establishment, rejecting it or working for its reconstruction. Often endorses conventional goals but advocates proscribed methods for their attainment. High risk-taking is a way of life. Examples are street crime, "living by one's wits," and similar forms of antisocial conduct.	Punishment and ostracism. Regarded as a willful wrongdoer. Severe sanctions are often believed necessary to protect the social order.
IV. Unbalanced States:				
7.	+	+	*Dependency.* Actor engages in passive compliance and voluntary subordination. Endorses prescribed goals and means without considering their utility in personal affairs. Often perceives his low status as being the result of fortuitous circumstances.	Toleration and philanthropic aid. Often considered an inevitable burden. More frequently pitied than punished. Welfare measures are nearly universal.
8.	−	−	*Anomie.* Actor exhibits aimless, normless, alienated activity. Found mainly in disadvantaged urban areas where homeless misfits, drunks, dope fiends, and others regarded as "freaks" are segregated. In extreme cases actor tends toward nihilism.	Banishment and isolation. The most severe cases are confined in mental institutions and prisons. Yet many observers deny the existence of true anomie.

Source: Schrag, 1971:62–64.

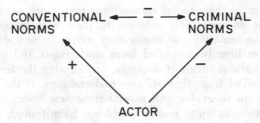

FIGURE 3. Example of relationships among social norms and actor's attitudes.

acquires a social conscience and a sensitivity to the expectations of others. Also important is the application of positive or negative sanctions by the group. Such sanctions may help to make many people productive conformists (item 1), although some of the conformists—because of incompetence, deprivation, discrimination, or bad fortune —may be unproductive dependents (item 7).

Deviant behavior is regarded as one of the products of strain or imbalance in personal and social systems. The main sources of strain are disjunctions between goals and means (items 5, 6, 7, 8), rejection of prescribed goals (items 2, 3, 5, 8), and rejection of means (items 2, 4, 6, 8). It follows that, in terms of this simple model, individuals may experience strain from three sources (item 8), two (items 2, 5, 6), one (items 3, 4, 7), or none (item 1). In the absence of more sensitive measures, the number of sources may perhaps be accepted as a crude index of the amount of strain and the severity of social disorder.

However, it is also assumed that balanced systems are more stable and gratifying than unbalanced ones. The most viable and persistent systems, therefore, are those of conformity, retreatism, and the two forms of insurgence. Anomie, dependency, and revisionism are relatively more labile and distressing. This suggests that conformity is not always an appropriate mode of response and that some forms of deviance are much stronger than others.

Society's reaction to the various forms of deviant behavior depends upon its assessment of their threat to the established order. Of the six kinds of deviance illustrated, three are targets of repressive measures (items 5, 6, 8), while the remainder are tolerated and frequently rewarded (items 2, 3, 4). Punitive reactions are largely directed against deviants for whom there is a disjunction between goals and means. These offenders are commonly regarded as social outsiders, misfits, and potential rebels (Schrag, 1971:61–66).

Merton (1957) makes implicit use of congruence theory in developing his paradigm. None of the unbalanced states in the above table are mentioned. All of Merton's types, with the exception of rebellion, are balanced states (items 1, 2, 5, 6). Rebellion, according to Merton, occurs when conventional goals and means are rejected and alternatives are substituted for them. This kind of deviant behavior may take place in a society having two or more sets of conflicting norms. For example, assume the existence of a subculture, or preferably a contraculture, prescribing criminal behavior as a means of goal attainment. Then the conflict between conventional and criminal norms may be portrayed as shown in Figure 3. In spite of this conflict, however, individuals may maintain a balanced cognitive system by endorsing either the conventional or the criminal norms.

Further research is needed to describe the genesis of criminal and other dissentient norms. But it seems likely that such prescriptions are established in approximately the same manner as the more conventional ones (Cohen, 1965). People who experience severe strain in their social transactions may work with one another in an attempt to arrive at an acceptable solution to their adjustment problems. In this effort, they may make tentative and exploratory moves in new directions, comparing ideas and attitudes ordinarily concealed from conformists and unyielding observers, experimenting with various forms of deviance, and sharing the feedback of experience and information received from their diverse undertakings. If the feedback is encouraging, they may go on to evolve and to elaborate new codes of behavior, thereby producing a collective solution to mutual problems. Even though the codes may be in conflict with conventional norms, they are legitimated in the process of persuasion by which each actor convinces himself of their merits as he reinforces the efforts of his colleagues. In this way there is generated a set of deviant norms and perhaps a criminal subculture (Cohen, 1965:chap. 3).

Where there is conflict between criminal and conventional codes, an actor can maintain a balanced cognitive state by endorsing one set or the other, but not both. Conformists endorse one set, confirmed criminals the other. Moreover, a person can strengthen his balanced state by rejecting any norms that are in opposition to those he endorses.

In any conflict situation, then, it is not sufficient for a person to be merely supportive of his associates. He must also adopt an aggressive posture toward the opposition. Of course, this tends to escalate animosities and sometimes culminates in mutual displays of violence. It follows that the use of extreme measures is not ordinarily restricted to one side in a conflict. The same tactics employed by the "bad guys" in support of their nefarious activities may also be employed by the "good guys" in the interest of law and order.

Yet, it would be naive to assume that crime and convention are always in conflict. In many communities illegal behavior is no less effective than noncriminal activities for attaining goals, such as wealth, power, influence, or high status. When it brings forth the intended objectives, the violation of laws comes to be regarded as an expedient, if not fully legitimate, method of achievement. Especially apt illustrations are the vices, white-collar offenses, shady business practices, and the many varieties of organized crime. Where such deviance is rewarded, the relation between criminal and noncriminal codes is essentially one of congruence, and the sign between these norms in Figure 3 must, therefore, be changed from minus to plus.

One consequence of changing this sign is to make balance possible by either the endorsement or the rejection of both criminal and noncriminal prescriptions. Where both of these formulas are instrumental to the attainment of goals, the endorsement of one set and rejection of the other is indicative of an unbalanced state. This implies that, in communities where there is normative support for illegal conduct, we may expect to find increasing rates of criminal behavior and toleration of deviance, along with various kinds of retreatist reactions against the social order. Conversely, to lessen the amount of crime and retreatism, we need to increase the compensation for legitimate conduct and to reduce or eliminate the earnings of illegitimate enterprises. If the theory is valid, we cannot hope to control crime by merely changing the attitudes of offenders. There must also be a change in the linkages between norms.

So much for the claims of the theory. Unfortunately, the detailed information needed to test these claims is generally lacking. However, some support comes from studies of juvenile gangs, a good example being the work done on opportunity structures (Cloward & Ohlin, 1960). Legitimate and illegitimate methods of achieving social objectives are differentially distributed among the various groups and classes of a society, so that some young people have access primarily to legitimate methods, others to illegitimate methods, and still others to both methods of attaining their goals. Furthermore, the kinds of juvenile gangs that develop in a given social climate depend, at least in part, upon the accessibility of these norms and the relationship between them.

Three main kinds of gangs have been identified: criminal, conflict, and retreatist. Criminal gangs emphasize regimentation, discipline, and rational activity aimed at gaining economic, political, and social rewards. They tend to flourish where big-time criminals have established a symbiotic and mutually tolerated relationship with government authorities and police officials. Such gangs provide, in effect, an apprenticeship training for many young people who later will be involved in organized crime. Conflict gangs are different in that they stress "bopping" and violence. Their attraction is greatest where crime is relatively unsuccessful, where there is little prospect for the achievement of conventional objectives, and where patterns of accommodation have not been worked out between the criminals and the authorities. Retreatist gangs, again, are concerned mainly with drug use and other kinds of "kicks." Their members are recruited chiefly from the ranks of those who are unwilling or unable to ally themselves with either the exemplary or the criminal elements. Oriented around a detached, "cool," "hip," and cynical, though usually nonviolent, style of life, the retreatists place a high value on "doing your own thing."

A person's social position and his normative attachments have a greater influence on his behavior than does his place of residence. Yet, there is a fairly strong relationship between type of gang and type of community, as suggested in Table 3. In neighborhoods where normative support for law violations is lacking, delinquency tends to be infrequent, sporadic, and unorganized. Where crime is highly organized and embedded within the community's social structure, youths tend to endorse or to reject both legitimate and illegitimate norms. Endorsement of both sets of norms encourages involvement in criminal gangs, while the rejection of both often leads to retreatism. Conflict and violence are more prevalent in disadvantaged neighborhoods where criminal behavior ordinarily remains unsophisticated and unlikely to produce social success.

However, violence is not restricted to young people who endorse the illegitimate system. It is also employed in support of established authority, especially in deprived

TABLE 3

TYPES OF JUVENILE GANGS AND THEIR RELATIONSHIP
TO COMMUNITY SOCIAL STRUCTURE

Type of Community	Types of Gangs
I. Illegitimate normative system absent.	No organized gangs. Delinquency is infrequent, sporadic, unorganized.
II. Illegitimate normative system present and congruent with legitimate system.	Two main types of gangs expected: A. Criminal gangs serving as apprenticeship training for adult careers in crime. B. Retreatist gangs for alienated individuals.
III. Illegitimate normative system present, but not congruent with legitimate system.	Two main types of gangs expected: A. Conflict gangs engaging in violence against the establishment. B. Conflict gangs involved in repression of misfits and deviants.

Source: Schrag, 1971:67–71.

areas. Some examples are the beatings administered to "freaks," "queers," "bums," and other kinds of "bad guys." Thus the definition of "bad guys" depends upon the kind of group to which one belongs, and this, in turn, is greatly influenced by the social structure of the community and the normative attachments of its individual members.

While such findings lend some credence to the theory, they also indicate a number of its defects. For instance, the communities that have high delinquency rates are frequently characterized by a diversity of gang organizations, instead of being dominated by one or two types (Spergel, 1964; Downes, 1966). In addition, most gangs do not exhibit the degree of cultural consistency suggested by the theory. They often adopt distinctive titles, special emblems or items of apparel, and other symbols of identity long before they have a stabilized membership or any high degree of organizational autonomy (Klein & Crawford, 1967). Fluid membership, spatial mobility, and considerable versatility with respect to objectives, activities, and internal organization are generally observed among delinquent gangs. More important, the members frequently betray feelings of guilt and in other ways reveal a fairly strong attachment to conventional norms. They are much like nonmembers in their support of basic goals and values, though they differ in their aspirations and in their failure to anticipate success. On all of these points, the empirical data throw some doubt on the validity of certain aspects of the congruence theory, especially the version of it that was adopted by Cloward and Ohlin in their study of opportunity structures (1960).

Theories of labeling and congruence tend to take conformity for granted and to focus on the problem of explaining criminal behavior. They see the human individual, at least the normal one, as internalizing the standards of his society and as having enough social awareness to be responsive to the expectations of other persons. In this view, social order is the normal condition. Deviant behavior is not likely to occur unless the community's standards are rejected for some reason, insight is lacking, or the individual becomes involved in groups whose norms are in conflict with those of the broader society. Although these notions have merit for some purposes, they are receiving a strong challenge from another perspective that takes deviance for granted and tries to clarify the reasons for conformity.

Social Control

This perspective is known as control theory (Hirschi, 1969). It focuses on groups more than individuals, on systems more than their members. It holds that harmony and order are rarer than conflict and disarray.

1. Control theory assumes, for example, that what an individual learns is what the community teaches him, not by its precepts alone, but also, and perhaps more importantly, by its practices. Hence, the child may soon learn that rule violations result in quicker and easier attainment of goals than does conforming behavior. Again, if the reactions of other people are inconsistent enough, the child may learn nothing at all.

Likewise, many an adult belongs to social groups whose standards are so unclear or inconsistent that he can neither comprehend what is expected of him nor anticipate the consequences of his failure to conform. Under these circumstances, one of the virtues of nonconformity is that it may encourage the group to establish boundaries for behaviors that are or are not permitted. In the absence of such boundaries, there can be no social order.

2. Control theory further assumes that the causes of crime are not to be found

within the individual actor but in his community and his relations with it. Especially important are conflicts among the group's behavioral standards, and broken links in the social chains that bind people together. These normative contradictions and disrupted linkages are the chief signs of social disorganization, a condition for which no single person, however powerful, can be held entirely responsible.

Though disorganization is a product of group action, or sometimes inaction, it has significant consequences with respect to individual behavior. The more disorganized the group, for instance, the less an individual member can depend on it for guidance. And the more a person is left to his own resources, the more he is guided by personal, possibly idiosyncratic, interests. It follows that conformity is not likely to occur unless there is some order in the group, and that weak social systems—not weak individuals, necessarily—are the wellsprings of deviant behavior.

3. System, therefore, is a key concept in control theory. The term is abstract, denoting any set of interrelated parts or elements. Physical and biochemical systems are probably the most familiar. The heart, for instance, is a system whose elements are living cells, each of which is a system of molecules, which are systems of atoms. The heart, in turn, may be regarded as part of the circulatory system, which is one of the parts of a living organism (a biological system), which is part of the ecological system. In each of these illustrations the system concept denotes nothing more than a set of elements and their relationships.

Social systems are somewhat more complex. Their fundamental elements are the social transactions that occur among human actors. Such transactions are of an almost infinite variety—physical or verbal, direct or indirect, honest or deceitful, rewarding or punishing, and so on. They are often fleeting, subtle, elusive of measurement, and even resistant to close observation.

Whether obscure or simple, however, transactions tend to take place in pairs, chains, clusters, sequences, and many other patterns. Accordingly, they have many different kinds of relationships with one another. For example, one exchange may stimulate another that stimulates still another, and so on. By means of such conditional relationships among pairs of events, there is established a serial order within the entire set. But even if the pairs are considered alone, their connections may be quite varied. Thus, a preceding event may be the direct cause of a succeeding one, may strengthen the latter, weaken it, or inhibit it entirely. Sometimes the effects flow in the reverse direction, so that the reoccurrence of the initial transaction is contingent upon the occurrence of the later one. Such relationships, and all others that are possible among pairs or sets of transactions, are called patterns of interaction.

Interaction patterns, in general, are influenced by the frequency, duration, and intensity of the transactions involved; by the skills, previous experiences, concerns, and aspirations of the participating actors; and by the rewards, penalties, and trade offs that result. Sometimes the pattern is affected by the presence of a third person, a neutral observer, who may remain unmoved by the transactions between the other participants. A third party is frequently necessary in legal contracts and in dealings that are regarded as morally binding. However, the survival of an interaction pattern is determined by many forces in addition to its legal or moral status.

4. Of particular importance in social systems are feedback relations and pressures toward rationality. Consider feedback first. Some feedback occurs in most forms of social interaction, since the attitudes and activities of the participants are ordinarily modified. A more elaborate example, however, is the free economy. Any change in the supply of a commodity has an indirect influence, through price adjustments, on demand for that commodity, and the resulting change in demand has a feedback effect,

usually somewhat delayed, upon the available supply. In this hypothetical system, price varies inversely with supply and directly with demand. The influences counteract one another, thereby producing a tendency toward stability or equilibrium. But if price were to vary directly with both supply and demand, the influences would be cumulative. The system would then tend to expand without limit and perhaps to disintegrate. Feedback would not keep the system in balance.

5. Feedback seems imperative in rational systems that are used to attain designated goals and objectives. Rational systems are usually constructed to control certain aspects of the environment. Control always calls for the system to perform three interrelated functions: detection, selection, and reaction. Detection means that the conditions to be controlled can be measured with some accuracy. Selection implies that a choice is made from a set of response options, depending upon the conditions detected. Reaction indicates that if the appropriate response option is selected, the desired changes in the environment will follow.

A good illustration is the common household heating system, which is comprised of a furnace, fuel, air ducts, electric current, thermostat, and switching mechanisms. By simply setting the thermostat, a human operator activates equipment that senses the temperature of a room, selects the on or off position of a switch, and starts or shuts off the furnace. In this way room temperature may be kept within a fixed range of variation, whatever may be the weather conditions outside.

Somewhat analogous systems have been constructed for many other purposes— keeping a balance between income and expenditures, maintaining streets and highways for traffic control, providing schools for the education of children, regulating economic activity, controlling crime, and the like. Some of these systems, unfortunately, are incapable of performing even the simplest control functions. The agencies of criminal justice, for instance, are unable to make accurate readings of the amount of crime in the community, and their selection of response options is handicapped by the lack of information regarding the relative merits of fines, probation, imprisonment, parole, and diversionary methods. In addition, there is often some uncertainty about the system's objectives, since the goals of crime control are not always in accord with those of freedom and justice.

Perhaps complete rationality should not be expected. Yet, some degree of control is fairly common. For example, the economy shows growing evidence of at least partial control through the deliberate manipulation of credit, interest, taxes, liquidity, public expenditures, dollar values, and similar devices. To the extent that such devices are able to maintain a desired level of economic activity, we are, perhaps, moving toward rational control in this area.

Whose desires are to be taken into account is, of course, an important question. However, numerous organizations use the concept of rational control as a bench mark in assessing the effectiveness of their operations. The concept serves as an ideal, a hypothetical state of perfection, with which a group's performance can be compared. Thus, the members of a football team, for example, are expected to understand the actions prescribed in every kind of game situation, to learn how certain predicaments can be anticipated before they develop, and to carry out their role assignments despite the disruptive tactics of the opposing players. When a contest is finished, the players are rated by reviewing films of the game and by counting the number of instances in which their performances deviated from the prescribed ideal. Such ratings may be as important to the participants as the final score of the game.

6. Within ratings lies another problem. The criteria used in assessing performance may sometimes have little bearing on the achievement of group objectives. To

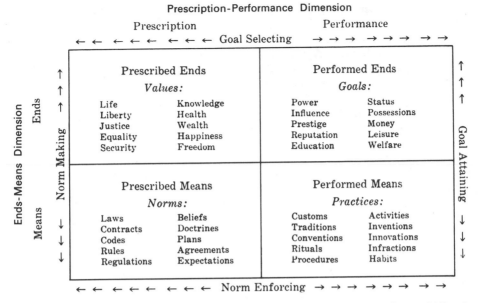

FIGURE 4. Model of a social system in two dimensions: some illustrations from middle-class America. From Schrag, 1971:100.

illustrate, police officers are often rated according to length of service and number of arrests made, including the "big pinch" that resolves a troublesome case or apprehends a notorious criminal. Parole officers are likewise evaluated by the quantity and quality of reports completed. But there is no convincing evidence that the number of arrests or the number of parole reports has any important connection with the amount of crime in a community. If such a connection does not exist, increases in the number of arrests and parole reports are not likely to reduce the crime rate.

7. Because of such complexities, there is need for a simple way of examining social-control systems. One method that seems promising is to classify interactions in two basic but related dimensions: prescriptions-performances and ends-means. Prescriptions include laws, rules, codes, policies, strategies, and any other normative instruments that are designed as guides to human conduct. Performances are comprised of the different activities that actually occur in the group. Ends, of course, designate the group's objectives, while means identify the methods that are employed in the pursuit of these ends.

By cross-classifying the dimensions of interaction, as shown in Figure 4, additional concepts can be formulated for the analysis of social systems. *Values*, for example, are widely supported notions about what is desirable and worthwhile, whereas *norms* specify what ought or ought not be done in any given situation. *Goals*, again, are the objects of human effort and aspiration, while *practices* refer to the forms such effort takes in reality.

These concepts help us to see why rationality is problematic in social systems. There is always the threat of disruptive relationships among the elements. Disruptions are of at least six different kinds: norms may be incapable of preserving the group's values, goals may be beyond the reach of practices, norms may be violated in practice, goals may deny basic values, and there may be contradictions between values and practices or between goals and norms.

When such disruptions occur, people do not necessarily achieve their goals by conforming to the group's norms. Nor does nonconformity always result in social decay or in the destruction of human values. Criminal behavior may have the same goals as noncriminal behavior. And some law violations—abortion, refusal of military service, or victim-precipitated assault are possible illustrations—may be as much in accord with expressed values as are some legal conventions.

Some acts that violate traditional values—fraudulent advertising, profiteering, wanton pollution, neglect of duty—are not proscribed by law. Some that are prohibited —price fixing, monopoly, bribery, conspiracy, violations of safety regulations—meet only sporadic opposition from the authorities. These activities may be as harmful to the community as most conventional crimes. But the systems of justice deal with law violations, and if the preservation of certain values is not written into the law, they cannot be protected by legal means.

8. Another thing Figure 4 suggests is that social systems, in order to operate with even minimum effectiveness, must come to grips with the problems of goal selection, norm formation, norm enforcement, and goal attainment. To date researchers have focused nearly exclusively on matters of enforcement and achievement, perhaps because practices are ordinarily more visible than prescriptions. If some consensus on norms and values is important to justice, however, much more needs to be learned about the ways in which norms are formulated and goals selected.

Even though research findings are limited, it seems clear that official pronouncements, regardless of their merit, cannot by themselves produce coordinated action in the community. Laws and other formal devices remain dead letters unless they are vitalized and validated by personal experiences or informal expectations. While the intent of the law is, perhaps, to be found in the interpretation given by a court, it appears that the effect of the law is more likely to be found in the interpretation given by the people.

9. Much of the time the formal and informal norms have similar or complementary objectives. In the courtroom, for instance, official rules and regulations govern the roles played by judges, attorneys, court aids, defendants, witnesses, and spectators. These formal norms define the conditions and procedures of litigation, spelling out the rights and responsibilities of all the participants. They are supplemented by informal norms covering matters of speech, dress, and general conduct so that, in spite of the contentiousness of many court proceedings, it can be expected that mutual expressions of courtesy and an attitude of dignity will ordinarily prevail.

Judges are officially required to rule on legal questions. It is informally expected that they will learn their subject well, that they will be objective and impartial in their rulings, and that they will maintain the integrity of the judicial process. Attorneys are formally obliged to proceed in a lawful and orderly manner, and it is informally expected that they will present forceful and concise arguments on behalf of their clients. Other participants have their special assignments, each of which is regarded as being essential to legal procedure.

The implicit assumption behind such procedure is that if everyone plays his role properly, the result will be a true and just decision. However, a true decision is not necessarily the same thing as a just decision. A true decision, in most people's view, is one that agrees with the facts in the case; whereas a just decision, from a legal standpoint, is one obtained in accord with the rules of procedure and of evidence. The realms of truth and justice are thus separable.

Judicial performance is commonly evaluated by the number of rulings that are overturned on appeal to higher authorities. Procedural errors are a more frequent cause of reversal than are questions of fact. Court officials may, therefore, face a dilemma demanding a choice between substantive truth and procedural justice. In such cases the legal rituals often seem to place a higher value on procedures than on the factual adequacy of the decisions rendered.

Since procedural errors furnish the chief grounds for appeal, judges tend to be particularly attentive to such matters. Yet, it seems that personal bias and selective perception may be more important than legal procedures in determining the quality of many court decisions. Studies show that judges, notwithstanding their honest efforts to avoid bias, are rather inconsistent in their decisions, especially in the sentencing of convicted offenders (Green, 1961). This should not be surprising when the judgments are evaluated by their legal fitness rather than their empirical consequences. How to make the court share its responsibility for such consequences, therefore, is an unsolved problem.

Attorneys often face the same conflicts and dilemmas. Thus, the prosecutor who goes to court with everyone he believes guilty may be fortunate to get convictions in half of his cases. But if he tries only those whose conviction is almost certain, or if he bargains without restraint for guilty pleas, he can increase the conviction rate to more than 90 percent. While the latter policy may be politically the more expedient, no doubt it reduces the number of empirically correct decisions.

Clients who are believed guilty create a similar problem for the defense attorney. By refusing these cases he forces them to seek another defender, thereby increasing the earnings of a competitor while reducing his own. If, on the contrary, he defends such cases to the best of his ability, he may come to feel responsible for the court's failure to convict those who are in fact guilty.

10. There are no easy solutions to such role conflicts. However, the sense of personal responsibility may be alleviated somewhat by training and experience. Legal ideology encourages lawyers to think in terms of their client's vulnerability under the law, rather than his factual guilt or innocence. Some lawyers argue, for example, that since a person is presumed innocent until proved guilty in court, an attorney cannot be sure of his client's status prior to the verdict. The attorney, of course, may be suspicious of his client's testimony, but his conscience is cleared by the assurance that it is the jury's responsibility to determine the facts (Reichstein, 1970).

This kind of argument is consistent with the norms of criminal justice, especially the adversary procedures and the obligation of confidentiality between lawyer and client. Except for the obvious cases, perhaps, it makes good sense. Moreover, the obvious cases do not often go to trial. Nor does an attorney gain prominence by handling them. He gains more by winning the questionable ones.

Winning a case requires that decisions be made in such a way as to withstand the threat of judicial appeals and reviews. However, the rules and procedures used in settling appeals are, by and large, the same as those used in arriving at the initial decisions. This kind of circularity tends to make the court the final arbiter in questions of truth as well as justice.

But if the courts are to determine what is true, and if their determinations are to be based mainly on procedural criteria, then it must follow that the maintenance of procedural patterns is the major function of the judicial system. Both truth and justice are whatever the judicial authorities declare them to be. Such emphasis on ritualism and pattern maintenance is likely to occur whenever the norms dominate the other elements of a social system.

11. It is not true, however, that all parts of the justice system are dominated by norms. Some agencies are more oriented toward the delivery of services and other

goals. The police, for example, are charged with clearing crimes, while correctional workers have most of the responsibility for reforming the offenders. Unlike the court officials, these workers have to face up to the empirical consequences of their decisions. They do not have exclusive jurisdiction over the information that is used in assessing their effectiveness.

Emphasis on goals that are concrete and visible tends to place mainly pragmatic constraints on those who exercise authority. But there are other dangers inherent in an overemphasis on achievement. Unless it is tempered by commitment to norms and values, the drive for achievement may encourage expedient behavior, disruptive innovations, and exploitation of community resources to the point where normative constraints against the decision-makers are virtually abandoned. In the extreme case the result is anarchy. For most of the community's members this may be no more palatable than the absolutism of an inquisitorial court.

Protection against the hazards of ritualism, on the one hand, and of unbridled innovation, on the other, calls for a delicate balance among the elements of a social system. It requires that the system's goals be clearly defined, that they be consistent with one another, and that objective criteria be developed for measuring their degree of attainment. And since achievement of the goals ordinarily depends upon collaborative effort among people in different social positions, it is also important that norms be provided that facilitate the kinds of practices that are likely to produce the desired results. Unless these norms are in general accord with the community's values, however, it is probable that the system will encounter strong public opposition.

12. Opposition to social systems is always present to some degree. But it can be regulated in various ways. It can often be lessened by arranging the goals in a hierarchy according to their relative values. Then people can choose among them in terms of personal interest or ability. Or the goals may be organized in sequential patterns, so that one must be achieved before another can be pursued. Without such definitions, specializations, sequences, and the like, it is almost impossible for people to profit from experience or to make intelligent modifications in the system's normative framework.

Such ordering of basic elements is often found in the field of corrections. For instance, crime must be defined before the offender can be identified, and identification ordinarily precedes punishment or corrective treatment. Definitions are mainly the result of legislative actions, while the identification of offenders is primarily a judicial function involving the police and the courts. Treatment, in turn, is provided by prisons and other institutions, by probation and parole agencies, or by a variety of related establishments. In addition, most law violations are assigned crude rankings in terms of their perceived severity, and the reactions of officials are more or less in accord with these rankings.

On superficial inspection it may appear that the correctional system's elements are well enough articulated to make the achievement of its objectives quite probable. In fact, however, the system exhibits nearly every kind of disorganization and deviant behavior that is seen in the rest of society. Its goals of punishment, social protection, deterrence, and therapy are often mutually exclusive, lacking a pattern of relative values, and without tangible criteria for measuring any progress toward their achievement. The credence given these goals varies greatly from one part of the system to another. Many police officers, for instance, feel that punishment is insufficient in the modern prison, while the correctional workers counter this argument by complaining that the police harass offenders needlessly and otherwise interfere with effective treatment.

Nor are the system's practices well suited to its goals. Its prisons, allegedly designed for rehabilitation, tend to manage their inmates by the show of force, instilling in them fear and anger instead of respect for the law or compliant attitudes. The police and courts, likewise, rely on a strategy of coercion in selecting a few lawbreakers, castigating them, and making of them exemplars of what the state can do, if it wishes, to those who violate the law.

From the viewpoint of the minority groups against which coercive strategies are mainly directed, it may appear that the authorities are generally interested in preserving their power and privilege. The system's function, in their view, is not to prevent law violations so much as it is to establish and to perpetuate the subordinate statuses of persons who are labeled as criminals. Few options remain for these persons except to attack the system and the society that condones it. Some of the results of correctional processes, therefore, are the criminalization of law violators and the encouragement of criminality.

13. It is a mistake to assume that all crimes are supported by criminal norms. Evidence against this assumption is overwhelming. Numerous studies show that the deliberate and detailed planning of a criminal act, followed by a sequence of responses in accord with the plan, is uncommon. The road to crime does not often have clear markers. It is full of detours, blind alleys, and alternate routes. When the unwary traveler reaches his unexpected destination, he frequently cannot understand how he got there.

In this respect crime resembles wars, riots, rebellions, and many other kinds of deviant behavior. It is often the illogical consequence of a series of logical decisions whose cumulative effect cannot be anticipated. One person seeks an immediate advantage by threatening a destructive course of action. Another responds in kind. Soon the threats and counterthreats reach a point where all options are closed except the one leading to the precise outcome the whole series was intended to avoid.

A common illustration is the gang "rumble." One of the participants displays a weapon. Members of the opposing gang respond with even more threatening gestures. If the first actor retreats, he loses face. If he moves forward and accepts the challenge, someone is likely to get hurt. Yet the intent to injure may have been remote at the beginning (Short & Strodtbeck, 1965:chap. 11).

Most lawbreakers are probably much like most conformists in that they are attuned to conventional norms most of the time. They drift between the world of criminality and the world of conventionality, submitting occasionally to the demands of each, but avoiding the total commitment to either that would sever their connections with the other (Matza, 1964). While there may be differences in relative commitments to these worlds, a person need not join the world of crime to receive normative support for deviant behavior. Such support can readily be obtained in conventional society, where legitimate rationalizations for illegitimate conduct are common.

These rationalizations, or "techniques of neutralization," justify deviance by denying that anyone has been injured, contending that the victim got what he deserved, contending that loyalty to friends is more important than loyalty to an impersonal social system, and so on. Techniques such as these tend to alleviate the sense of guilt that might otherwise discourage violations of the law.

14. Susceptibility to neutralization or to other deviant pressures depends upon a person's linkages with the broader society. These linkages are the bonds that tie people together in groups. Among the more important are the actor's aspirations in relation to the group's goals, his attachments to the group's prescriptions and practices, his participation in procedures of norm formation and norm enforcement, and his en-

FIGURE 5. Bonds linking individuals to social systems.

dorsement of social beliefs and values. If these links are many and strong, deviance is not likely to occur, but if they are few and weak, such behavior is highly probable.

The linkages mentioned are mainly of an attitudinal variety. Considered together they reveal the nature of an actor's commitment to the social system in question, whether the attitudes are positive or negative, weak or strong. In addition to indicating behavioral predispositions, however, these attitudes can also be regarded as products of the actor's previous behavior and of the group's reactions. This means that the attitudes are subject to a considerable amount of group control. Especially significant are the group's policies and practices dealing with member involvement, stakes in conformity, and grounded belief.

15. Theoretical relationships among the aforementioned variables are illustrated in Figure 5. *Involvement* refers to the different ways in which members exert an influence on the social system. For example, there is frequently a division of labor calling for certain members to participate in norm formation, others in norm enforcement, and so on. Some systems, though rare, exclude their members from these activities, while others allow nearly all to participate more or less equally. In most systems, of course, an attempt is made to involve as many members as possible in legislative and judicial functions, or at least to keep up the pretense of their involvement. Otherwise, the norms probably would not be considered legitimate.

It appears that norms must be considered legitimate if they are to elicit voluntary compliance from many actors. The amount of deviant behavior in a community tends to reflect the extent to which people are involved in normative affairs. Where involvement is discouraged or prohibited, violations of norms are likely to be most frequent. An appropriate inference, therefore, is that the correctional system may encourage recidivism by excluding offenders from legitimate activities, especially those related to the enactment or the enforcement of laws.

16. Another way of strengthening social systems is by increasing the members' *stake in conformity*. Here reference is made to rewards or penalties received for conforming to the norms as compared with those received for norm violations. People ordinarily learn to repeat the behaviors that have produced rewards in the past and to inhibit those that have resulted in penalties. However, the effects of such sanctions are influenced by their promptness, frequency, consistency, and magnitude, among other things (Staats, 1968).

If the theory is right, a large volume of crime in certain groups or neighborhoods is evidence that deviance, in these places, has a more desirable rewards-penalties ratio than does conformity. Involvement in illicit activities, such as vice or petty theft, is a major occupation in deteriorated communities where people have a small stake in conformity. Here a change in the rewards-penalties ratio appears to be essential for more effective crime control.

There are two main ways in which the ratio can be changed so as to increase people's stake in conformity. One is by increasing the rewards or reducing the penalties for conformity, and the other is by reducing the rewards or increasing the penalties for deviance. Both methods, but mostly the latter, are employed in corrections.

This raises a question concerning the relative merits of rewards and punishments, one on which the evidence is not yet clear. Rewards seem to have an advantage in that behavior that conforms to the norms often leads to an immediate payoff. Punishments or other negative reinforcers, by contrast, are usually represented as a threat of dire consequences in the event that nonconformity occurs.

Such threats are without doubt a powerful deterrent when they are closely associated with punitive reactions. But they may be of little consequence for people who see no probable association between the word and the deed. The problem is that as long as an actor conforms to the norms, he can get no direct evidence as to the sincerity with which a threat is made. To test the validity of the threat, he must violate the norm. And it is known that criminal violations only rarely elicit the punitive responses that are prescribed by the law.

Punitive threats, therefore, may have their greatest impact on people who endorse the system of justice and have faith in its judgments. These are the people who have the greatest stake in conformity and who enjoy a favorable rewards-penalties ratio. They are willing to accept without proof the notion that there is a close correspondence between the system's norms and its practices. Most lawbreakers, however, are reluctant to credit the system with such a degree of consistency.

The principles of reinforcement, both positive and negative, nevertheless, have been used with some success in the treatment of alcoholics, narcotics addicts, sex offenders, and many other kinds of law violators (Schwitzgebel, 1971). They have also encouraged the development of "token economies" and other reward schemes in several correctional institutions (Cohen & Filipczak, 1971). Yet, their greatest potential is in the free community, where rewards for sustained employment, vocational or academic training, and participation in regulative activities or in the delivery of social services give promise of functioning as effective deterrents against crime, probably far more effectively in the long run than the more conventional methods. Examples of some preliminary efforts in this direction are programs aimed at developing new careers for ex-offenders (Grant & Grant, 1967).

17. The third factor having an important bearing on commitment to social systems is *grounded belief*. Beliefs, on the whole, are valuable in proportion to their empirical support. While factual evidence is not necessary for a belief to gain adherents, there is some risk involved in propagating beliefs that may subsequently be proved false.

To illustrate, young children who believe that crime does not pay are somewhat less delinquent than those who reject this idea. Older children, too sophisticated to endorse the above view, are less delinquent if they feel they can trust their parents and are not deceived by them. While the data are not precisely to the point, it appears that some of the highest delinquency rates are found among those who reject parental and other authorities along with the beliefs they represent (Jensen, 1969). Such findings might be interpreted as indicating that it is perhaps better never to believe at all than to believe and be deceived.

If beliefs are to be well grounded in reality, they should be constructed with care. Yet many of the proverbs pertaining to criminality are of dubious validity. In addition to the adage that crime does not pay, there are others contending that crime and violence are the same thing, that criminals have violated the law while noncriminals have not, or that punishment varies according to the gravity of the offense. These are coun-

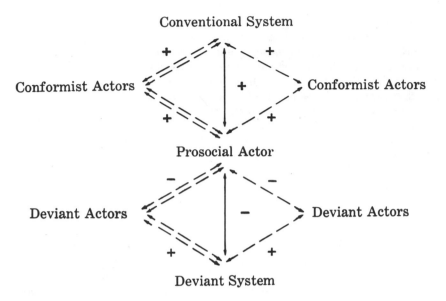

Solid arrows represent positive (+) or negative (−) attachments to conventional and deviant social systems. Arrows on double broken lines represent attachments of conformists and deviants to prosocial actors and to their respective social systems, while single broken arrows represent prosocial actor's perception of conformists' and deviants' attachments to him and to their social systems. Note the system is balanced.

FIGURE 6. The prosocial conformist and his ties to the social system. From Schrag, 1971:112.

tered by the claims of lawbreakers who hold that only suckers work, that everybody has a racket, and that the real criminals never get sent to prison. Confronted by such contradictions, many persons may avoid genuine commitment to any of the beliefs, preferring to choose among them as the occasion demands.

18. In sum, control theory portrays the conformist as a person whose ties to the social system tend to discourage deviant behavior, as illustrated in Figure 6. He gives allegiance to conventional norms, legitimate practices, and other conformist actors, involving himself wherever possible in norm formation and norm enforcement, while at the same time disassociating himself from deviant social forces and deviant actors. He acknowledges both the support received from conventional organizations and the opposition of deviant groups. He shares the system's objectives and its faith in their feasibility. Most of all, his stake in conformity, as he sees it, discourages him from jeopardizing his chances for success. The actor's linkages with the system prevent him from playing a deviant role.

Various types of deviant roles can be shown by changing the signs attached to certain linkages in the figure. For example, many law violators reject the conventional system, while endorsing some kind of deviant subculture. Other offenders, usually regarded as being more sophisticated, affiliate themselves with both systems. Still others, perhaps the least sophisticated, avoid social commitments of all kinds, rejecting both systems and espousing a philosophy of nihilism and immediate gratification. These types of linkages are found to some degree in nearly all studies of criminality (Schrag, 1971:205–13).

Control theory, however, is mainly a heuristic device, incapable of experimental test or corroborative investigation. Basic concepts are too crudely defined and their relationships too often stated with confounding equivocation. Moreover, the feedback model is too complex to be tested by the kinds of data now available. Yet, the theory has important advantages as a strategy of discovery. It sharpens the contrasts among earlier approaches that focused more narrowly on persons or groups, individual actions or societal reactions, conflict or consensus, and so on. It incorporates these approaches in a broader framework that, potentially at least, has a legitimate place for all, depending upon the researcher's interests and objectives. By building on prior efforts, instead of trying to destroy them, control theorists offer some hope for a more comprehensive explanation of crime and corrections.

Another reason for hope is that, in spite of the methodological difficulties mentioned, research patterned after the theory lends credence to many of its assumptions (Hirschi, 1969; Empey & Lubeck, 1971). Perhaps most significant are findings that disagree with common-sense notions. Illustrations include evidence that deviance is less related to differences in personal characteristics than to variations in system linkages, and that stake in conformity may be causally prior to beliefs and attitudes. In fact, the meaning of personal traits—class, race, personality, etc.—seems to be largely derived from system norms and values. And if this is true, the traditional emphasis on individualized treatment of law violators may be badly misdirected. It is the system, not the actor, that needs reform.

Reforming the system is not easy. Efforts thus far have been impeded by conflicts between youths and adults, blacks and whites, rich and poor, rulers and ruled, and many other categories of citizens. Nor have the different branches of government been able to agree on either goals or methods. Under these circumstances, neither corrections nor the broader society can be described as an organized system, and it may well be true, therefore, that the explanation of social conflicts is a more important theoretical problem than the explanation of crime itself.

CORRECTIONAL PROCEDURE: TRENDS AND CONTROVERSIES

Administrative officials, perhaps, should not be judged by what they say but by what they do. They do what they have to do because of their commitments to the dominant groups in the community. What they say is designed mainly to elicit the support of the community's members, especially those whose stake in the established order is greatest. Such support is considered necessary if the authorities are to do what they believe needs to be done. But there is no necessary connection between what is said and what is done. Officials who advocate "tough on crime" policies are hardly distinguishable from those who preach "reform," so far as their concrete programs are concerned.

Conceptions of what needs to be done in the field of corrections, however, are changing. Most important in this connection is the growing evidence that correctional programs have little, if any, impact on the amount of crime in the community. Prisons are ineffective, even those having modern treatment programs. Prisoners who receive treatment appear to have about the same recidivism rates as those who do not (Robison & Smith, 1971). Long sentences, with or without treatment, do not have a better record than short ones. Indeed, if type of offense, prior convictions, and related variables are held constant, the prospects for repeated offenses increase with the length of the sentence (Lamson & Crowther, 1968). And the greater the number of times an offender is incarcerated, the greater the risk he will be incarcerated again.

Failure of prisons to reform has long been suspected. The difference is that we now have theories that explain their failure. Moreover, these theories offer suggestions as to what can be done to improve the correctional system. Control theory, for example, not only identifies the areas where crime rates are highest but it also implies that these rates could be lowered by involving more people in community affairs, modifying the social system to increase everyone's stake in conformity, and developing beliefs that are more in accord with human experience. The most important correctional changes are occurring in precisely these areas. Although details concerning these changes are given elsewhere in this volume, the main trends deserve mention here.

Correctional Reform

Steps are being taken to reduce the social barriers between the prison and the free community. Volunteer workers are entering the institutions to provide social support for the inmates, serving as sympathetic listeners, unofficial counselors, and friends, in this way learning much about the crime problem and the pains of imprisonment. At the same time, inmates get a chance to interact with responsible outsiders, to learn of conditions in the community, and to sense the concern that many people have for their welfare. Social bonds are established with persons and agencies outside the criminal subculture, a new experience for many prisoners. Friendships are built that survive long after the offenders have left the institution.

The modern prison's primary objective is reintegration of offenders in the free community as responsible and productive members. Toward this end labor unions are joining forces with vocational specialists in improving the prison's training programs, holding classes in employment counseling, and helping offenders to find jobs or to keep them. Teachers and graduate students are giving courses, sometimes accredited by universities, on social problems, mental health, community resources, and related subjects. Entertainers and lecturers, commanding high fees in civilian life, are accepting special assignments in prisons, often without pay. The result is a reduction in the isolation and stigma that have long impeded the resocialization of those confined.

However, barriers are also being removed in another direction. Many aspects of prison life are being carried to the world outside. Teams of inmates and staff members tour the countryside, conducting discussions of correctional problems and advocating reforms. Furloughs are given selected inmates, allowing them to leave the institution in order to maintain family relationships, to consult with civilians in preparing their parole plans, or to arrange for housing and employment after release. Work and training releases enable some inmates to attend school or to hold jobs during the daytime while returning to confinement at night. Experience with these programs suggests that instead of increasing the threat of crime in the community, there are relatively few failures or untoward incidents.

Such programs also have an influence on prison management. Many traditional custodial procedures are being discontinued, especially those that stigmatize the offender without having much effect on safety. Elimination of conspicuous uniforms or identification of inmates by number are some examples. Routine censorship of inmate mail is also being abandoned, along with the routine screening of correspondents or visitors. Physical contacts with visitors are more frequently permitted. Need for privacy is more often acknowledged, with some inmates having individual rooms that allow them to keep personal possessions. Steps are being made to pay inmates going wages for institutional employment, from which the cost of maintenance will be deducted. Inroads are in the making toward provision of legal services for inmates and the protection of their constitutional rights. In 1972 the U.S. Supreme Court outlawed capital punishment as then practiced. The trend in executions is now uncertain. Some courts have also demanded drastic reforms in prison administration.

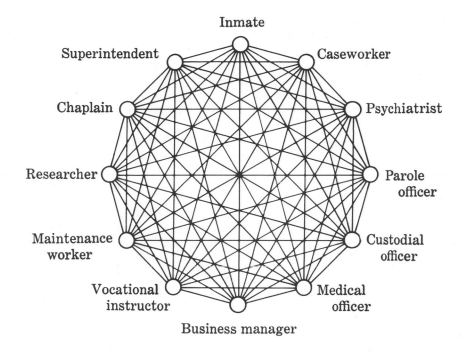

FIGURE 7. Administrative organization of some modern correctional institutions. From Schrag, 1971:200.

Prisoners, in general, are given greater responsibility for their own welfare and are more involved in institutional management. Inmate advisory councils, elected by the prisoners, are commonly engaged with staff members in discussing administrative problems and personal concerns. Sometimes the inmates participate in policy formation and in the evaluation of treatment programs. They are now partners in a participatory management plan in the state of Washington.

The unilateral communication and authority structure, long a bulwark of prison administration, is giving way to a more flexible table of organization that allows feedback of ideas and a two-way flow of information. Instead of trying to write regulations that meet every possible contingency, administrators are encouraging prison workers to exercise discretion and to make decisions on the spot when problems arise. Many kinds of decisions are being decentralized as a result.

When such changes occur in the prison's management style, the superintendent and his top aides can no longer control the institution in an autocratic manner. Their role is not that of ruler but of leader. Their task is to maintain a legitimate social order and to integrate the various components of the institution. In doing this they need to utilize all available skills and resources. Potentially, at least, all staff members and inmates are part of the administration. Moreover, everyone is to be judged by his contributions to prison life, not by his position in some preconceived staffing plan.

The tall, narrow hierarchy of staff positions that characterized prisons until recently is gradually giving way to a relatively flat, flexible, tilting wheel type of organization. Figure 7 illustrates the newer model. In this model problems are examined, policies formulated, and programs assessed by the people most immediately concerned.

When the matter under discussion is mainly in the area of the superintendent's expertise—relations with the legislature, for example—the wheel tilts so that he has the dominant position. On other topics other persons may have more to contribute. Inmates, for instance, may play the dominant role when the topic concerns their attitudes and activities. In this way nearly all members of the prison community have some voice in management affairs. Accordingly, much of the responsibility for prison programs may be delegated to the people, including inmates, who have the greatest familiarity with the problems involved and with each other.

Patterns of communication and influence can be greatly enriched by administrative reorganization. However, the titular heads of an institution cannot abdicate their legal responsibilities. If their policies depart too far from conventional expectations, the response of the community outside is swift and certain. Few administrators are insensitive to this threat.

Difficulties may be anticipated, therefore, whenever an attempt is made to implement programs aimed at reintegrating offenders into the broader society. The reintegration model runs counter to many of the traditions of the prison. It arouses concern among administrators who are fearful of anything that might undermine their power and authority. It is opposed by inmates who receive preferential treatment and have a vested interest in the old order. It is regarded with suspicion by most people in the world outside. One of the main reasons is that reintegration requires a change in the pariah-like status to which law violators are ordinarily assigned. To implement the model, therefore, is to bring about a revolution in correctional administration and in the outside community's conception of crime and corrections.

These difficulties were encountered in a recent attempt to employ the reintegration model in a single housing unit at a large prison (Studt et al., 1968). By involving inmates in the operation of this unit, it was hoped to get them to treat each other with greater dignity, to exhibit respect and concern for the welfare of others, and to rely on social norms and mutual agreements—rather than force and exploitation—in managing their affairs. The inmates apparently responded quite well, showing interest in the program, developing stronger affiliations with staff members, and learning to cooperate more with one another in solving their problems.

But the program had an early demise. Its demise reportedly was brought about by opposition from the other housing units, by decisions issued from the central office, by the resistance of some inmates (not in the program) who were already given favored treatment, and by conflict among the program's employees. Hence, the failure of this effort, it seems, was not due to the lack of impact on the participating inmates. Rather, the program failed because other people, both staff members and inmates, were not able to accept the philosophy of reintegration or to carry out its directives.

Reintegration is still only a model, a prescriptive ideal. Much remains to be learned before the model can be implemented with any fidelity. Until prisons are able to overcome their legacy of outmoded physical facilities, inadequate personnel, totalitarian organization, and repressive policies, the reintegration of law violators must continue to be more of an ideal than a reality. This is why it may be easier to abandon most prisons than to reform them.

Perhaps prisons are already being abandoned. The vast majority of our convicted offenders are on probation and parole, at one-tenth the cost of confinement and with lower recidivism rates than observed among prisoners discharged at the expiration of their sentences. Many others are being diverted from the justice system prior to conviction. Still others escape punishment as a result of administrative policies calling for the toleration of crime or because of statutory revisions providing new definitions of criminality.

Legislative Reform

Much of the cost of crime can probably be avoided without risk to the community by eliminating laws that are passed on the assumption that they will not ordinarily be enforced. Such laws are often enacted because they serve political interests, appeasing one faction of voters by their enactment and another by their nonenforcement. Legislation of this kind is encountering considerable opposition, however, since it encourages political corruption and discourages faith in government.

Among the targets of reform are attempts to legislate morality, especially the laws dealing with prostitution, gambling, narcotics possession, abortion, homosexuality, and other vices. Violations of such laws produce enormous profits for organized crime. Their prosecution is resisted not only by the organized criminals but also by their patrons, and often by public officials as well. When enforcement is attempted, the police frequently find it necessary to use entrapment devices, to pay and protect informants who are themselves engaged in law violations, and to employ other unsavory methods that may sometimes be as offensive, perhaps as illegal, as the crimes they hope to suppress. Although arrests for such offenses number more than a million per year, they make hardly a dent in the amount of such criminal activity. In many communities these laws are openly violated without fear of reprisal.

Because law enforcement against the vices has been unsuccessful, steps are being taken to legalize some of these activities and to regulate them officially. Forms of gambling, for instance, have been legalized in several states, including New York, New Jersey, and Michigan. Here gambling enterprises are designed especially for their appeal to low-income customers. Since the winnings, on the whole, are proportional to the amounts wagered, however, it does not seem likely that legalized gambling will improve the financial status of the poor. What it will accomplish is a marked reduction in the work load of the police and the courts, especially in the field of victimless crime.

Other offenses subject to redefinition are vagrancy, disorderly conduct, and certain forms of juvenile misconduct, such as being ungovernable, a runaway, or a curfew violator. Indiscretions such as these probably are handled better by counseling and informal treatment without court intervention. Alcoholics and drug addicts are likewise given more effective treatment if they do not suffer the stigma of a criminal record. In many cases treatment is purely voluntary, involving the client in the planning, implementation, and evaluation of his own program. The most promising programs, apparently, are those utilizing a variety of approaches—intensive care initially, followed by group therapy, housing with peers, vocational and academic training, employment counseling, legal aid, social welfare, and, finally, aftercare services (Nimmer, 1971). The greatest effects are achieved by strengthening the individual's bonds with the community and by increasing his stake in conformity.

Still other reforms aim at protecting the rights of persons having already received criminal convictions. Such reforms may be needed to prevent the abuse of authority. In several states, for example, recidivists are commonly given the choice of pleading guilty to certain charges or running the risk of long-term commitments as habitual criminals. The pleas are often made under coercion and, therefore, are of questionable legality. Coercion may also occur under technical regulations governing the conduct of probationers or parolees. Regulations ordinarily cover administrative matters, such as keeping appointments with supervisors, staying away from taverns or bars, getting permission for changes in residence or employment, avoiding unauthorized contracts or legal agreements, and refraining from associations with other offenders. Their violation can result in imprisonment even though there is no evidence that a criminal offense was committed.

Perhaps return to prison for technical violations could be justified if it prevented subsequent infractions of a more serious kind. But it is doubtful that crimes are prevented by the enforcement of technical rules (Adams, 1967; Robison & Takagi, 1968). Unless preventive effects can be demonstrated, therefore, it seems wiser to modify the rules than to return parolees to prison for activities that are condoned in the rest of the population. Accordingly, steps are being taken in some jurisdictions to reduce or to eliminate the technical rules.

Much of the rationale for these legislative reforms is based on evidence that resources are insufficient for the enforcement of all laws. Few offenses are reported to the police, perhaps 25 percent or so. About 25 percent of the reports result in arrests, around 5 percent in convictions, and something like 2 percent in prison commitments, though these rates vary widely in time and place. Thus, by eliminating the least serious offenses, it is hoped that greater effort can be devoted to crimes that really threaten the life of the community.

Diversionary Methods

While the law calls for a policy of arrest → conviction → imprisonment, we operate under a policy that diverts most offenders from the justice system before an arrest occurs. And many of those arrested are diverted before trial. The purpose of diversion is to bring into play the community's resources for controlling crime without recourse to the criminal labeling that stigmatizes the offender and makes it more difficult for him to adopt a noncriminal role.

Numerous methods of diversion are employed at all points in the judicial procedure, from the time an offense is reported until the discharge of a convicted offender from supervision. However, four of these methods, all used prior to trial, seem to have the best results thus far. First among these is the deployment of specially trained police officers as agents of crime prevention. A conspicuous illustration is the Family Crisis Intervention Project in New York City (Bard, 1970). Here officers from a high-risk precinct were trained to intervene in family disturbances. Responding in interracial pairs to calls concerning family quarrels, the officers attempted to resolve the conflict on the scene. If unsuccessful, they referred the antagonists to appropriate treatment agencies, trying to avoid making arrests whenever possible.

Not a single homicide occurred in the 926 families handled in this manner. Nor was a single officer injured, though the teams were exposed to an unusually large number of dangerous incidents. Families that had experience with the special officers referred many other families for treatment, and troubled individuals sought the officers out for advice on personal problems. In this way problems were dealt with before they resulted in serious crimes, relations between the police and the community were improved, and a number of incidents were averted that could have led to arrests.

The second major form of diversion is use of summonses or citations in lieu of arrest for law violations. These devices are applied most frequently to white-collar offenders and misdemeanants of all kinds. But they are also employed in felony cases if the offender has ties in the community and represents no serious threat to peace and security. They have the advantage of avoiding criminalization while making the offender available for further investigation or prosecution. There is little doubt that a summons or citation could be substituted for arrest and detention in the vast majority of criminal cases (Vera Institute of Justice, n.d.).

A third method of diversion is the avoidance of jail in favor of bail or the offender's promise to appear for trial. Recent studies have shown that a quick inquiry into the defendant's background can result in the release of about 65 percent of all those charged with felonies. The screening is done by different workers in different programs —probation officers, public defenders, prosecuting attorneys, court staff, law students, ex-offenders, Vista volunteers, or special project employees. This can greatly reduce jail costs, which in New York City, for example, amount to over $10 million per year for holding persons awaiting trial. Experience with these programs shows that very few of the defendants who are released abscond. Moreover, the defendants released are much less likely to be convicted or, if convicted, committed to prison (Goldfarb, 1965).

Some of the differences between defendants who are jailed and those who are released no doubt result from the screening process. The best prospects are released. However, striking differences continue to be found even after researchers hold constant the relevant variables, such as type of offense, previous record, and so on. It is clear that decisions made regarding detention set a pattern that tends to be followed through the rest of the judicial cycle.

However, the fourth method of pretrial diversion is probably the most important. At the time of the first arraignment, ordinarily, selected defendants are recruited for voluntary participation in a treatment program involving job training, employment counseling, group and individual therapy, remedial education, legal aid, and other forms of assistance. If the defendant accepts treatment and performs successfully in the program, the charges are dropped, even in felony cases. In this way the stigma of a criminal conviction is avoided.

Good examples of such programs are Project Crossroads, operated by the Department of Labor, and the Manhattan Court Employment Project (Vera Institute of Justice, 1970; Leiberg, 1971). These give promise of greatly increasing the present level of pretrial intervention, which is about 10 percent of the cases on the arraignment calendar. Such intervention requires skill and patience on the part of the staff, since many of the defendants are alienated, suspicious, incapable of working up the courage needed to apply for a job, and resistant to any kind of social agreement that requires them to make a commitment to others. Ex-offenders and volunteers have been found useful in overcoming the initial reluctance of many defendants to become involved in the programs.

In spite of such difficulties, however, the programs have been remarkably successful to date. The Crossroads Project in Washington, D.C., for instance, found that when a sample of diverted cases was compared with a control group, the diversions had twice the rate of employment and 14 percent fewer cases of recidivism than the controls, the rates after fifteen months being 29.5 and 43.4 percent, respectively (Leiberg, 1971). Unfortunately, cases were not randomly assigned to diversion and control, therefore allowing selection processes to interfere with comparability of statistics. But it does not seem that selection is the whole story. What appears more probable is that many offenders who are subjected to conviction and imprisonment could be handled safely and at less cost in the free community. If this proves to be true, diversionary methods may soon gain greater recognition and visibility. Furthermore, the population of prisoners and ex-prisoners may be sharply curtailed.

Diversion involves informal procedures of crime control. Its rapid development may call for local communities to establish departments of justice or security that will be responsible for integrating all crime-control measures. Ideally, the department should encompass the police, prosecution and defense, courts, correctional agencies, and other organizations dealing either formally or informally with the crime problem. It would establish standards and supervise activities regarding case intake, diagnosis,

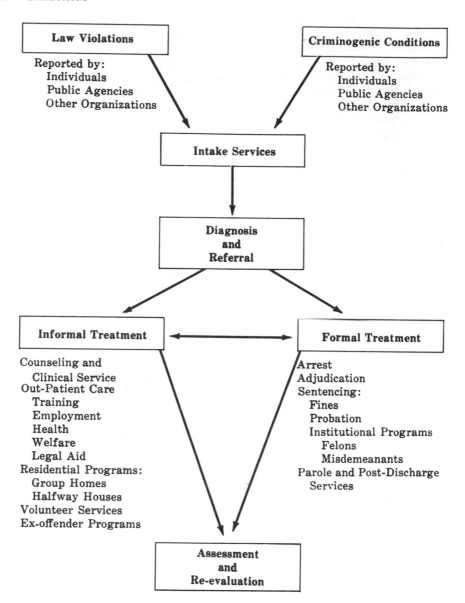

FIGURE 8. Simplified model of a community corrections system. From Schrag, 1971:263.

referral, treatment, prevention, and program evaluation. A general model for such a community program is presented in Figure 8.

According to this model, crime-control programs are organized on a local or regional basis in line with state laws and policies. Each locality operates an intake station around the clock to receive reports of law violations, of criminogenic conditions in the community, and of other situations affecting peace and order. Here the reports are screened and referred to an appropriate agency for action, relieving the informant of making decisions regarding which agency to call. In processing complaints, various agencies may share some of their specialized personnel and facilities. All available information is collated in the preparation of prearrest, pretrial, and presentence investigations that provide the basis for decisions concerning formal as against informal processing of offenders. Since both formal and informal programs are in the same department, cases can be shifted from one to another without delay. Moreover, the department's experience with a variety of treatment alternatives, if carefully documented and analyzed, should enable it to improve the quality of its decisions.

Proficiency in preventing crime and reintegrating offenders should not be expected of all programs. Many will fail because they are not well formulated or fully implemented. Even the more successful ones may be regarded as failures if too much is expected of them. Some may render needed services and have a beneficial impact on life in the community without exerting much influence on the crime rate.

The primary task, if current theories are right, is to promote faith and accountability in government, increase the stake in conformity, and involve more people in community affairs. The most important impact on criminality may be neither direct nor immediate.

REFERENCES

Adams, S.
   1967   "Some findings from correctional caseload research." Federal Probation 31
           (December):48–57.
Bard, M.
   1970   Training Police as Specialists in Family Crisis Intervention. Law Enforcement Assistance Administration. Washington, D.C.:U.S. Government Printing Office.
Becker, H. S.
   1963   Outsiders. New York: Free Press of Glencoe.
Brehm, J. W., and A. R. Cohen.
   1962   Explorations in Cognitive Dissonance. New York: Wiley.
Cannon, W. B.
   1929   Bodily Changes in Pain, Hunger, Fear and Rage. New York: Appleton.
Cloward, R., and L. E. Ohlin.
   1960   Delinquency and Opportunity. New York: Free Press of Glencoe.
Cohen, A. K.
   1965   Delinquent Boys. New York: Free Press.
Cohen, H. L., and J. Filipczak.
   1971   A New Learning Environment. San Francisco: Jossey-Bass.
Downes, D. M.
   1966   The Delinquent Solution: A Study in Subcultural Theory. London: Routledge & Kegan Paul.
Dubin, R.
   1959   "Deviant behavior and social structures: continuities in social theory." American Sociological Review 24(April):147–164.
Durkheim, E.
   1893   The Division of Labor in Society. Translation by George Simpson. Glencoe, Ill.: Free Press (1947 edition).
   1897   Suicide. Translation by John A. Spaulding and George Simpson. Glencoe, Ill.: Free Press (1951 edition).

Empey, LaMar, and Steven Lubeck.
   1971   The Silverlake Experiment. Chicago: Aldine.
Geis, G.
   1968   White-Collar Criminal. New York: Atherton.
Goldfarb, R.
   1965   Ransom. New York: Harper & Row.
Grant, J. D., and J. Grant.
   1967   New Career Development Project. National Institute of Mental Health. Washington, D.C.: U.S. Government Printing Office.
Green, E.
   1961   Judicial Attitudes in Sentencing. New York: Macmillan.
Hirschi, T.
   1969   Causes of Delinquency. Berkeley: University of California Press.
Jensen, G.
   1969   "Crime doesn't pay: correlates of shared misunderstanding." Social Problems 17(Fall):189–201.
Klein, M. W., and L. Y. Crawford.
   1967   "Groups, gangs, and cohesiveness." Journal of Research in Crime and Delinquency 4(January):63–75.
Lamson, R. L., and C. Crowther.
   1968   Crime and Penalties in California. Sacramento: State Assembly Committee on Criminal Procedure.
Leiberg, L.
   1971   Project Crossroads. Washington, D.C.: National Committee for Children and Youth.
Lemert, E.
   1951   Social Pathology. New York: McGraw-Hill.
Marris, P., and M. Rein.
   1967   Dilemmas of Social Reform. New York: Atherton.
Matza, D.
   1964   Delinquency and Drift. New York: Wiley.
Merton, R. K.
   1957   Social Theory and Social Structure. Glencoe, Ill.: Free Press.
Niederhoffer, A.
   1967   Behind the Shield: The Police in Urban Society. Garden City, N.Y.: Doubleday.
Nimmer, R. T.
   1971   Two Million Unnecessary Arrests. Chicago: American Bar Foundation.
Quinney, R.
   1970   The Social Reality of Crime. Boston: Little, Brown.
Reichstein, K.
   1970   "The criminal practitioner's dilemma: what should the lawyer do when his client intends to testify falsely?" Journal of Criminal Law, Criminology and Police Science 61(March):1–10.
Robison, J., and G. Smith.
   1971   "The effectiveness of correctional programs." Crime and Delinquency 17 (January):67–80.

Robison, J., and P. Takagi.
  1968   The Parole Violator as an Organization Reject. Berkeley: University of California School of Criminology.
Schrag, C.
  1967   "Elements of theoretical analysis in sociology," in L. Gross (ed.), Sociological Theory: Inquiries and Paradigms. New York: Harper & Row.
  1971   Crime and Justice: American Style. National Institute of Mental Health. Washington, D.C.: U.S. Government Printing Office.
Schur, E.
  1971   Labeling Deviant Behavior. New York: Harper & Row.
Schwitzgebel, R. K.
  1971   Development and Legal Regulation of Coercive Behavior Modification Techniques with Offenders. National Institute of Mental Health. Washington, D.C.: U.S. Government Printing Office.
Short, J. F., and F. Strodtbeck.
  1965   Group Process and Gang Delinquency. Chicago: University of Chicago Press.
Spergel, I. A.
  1964   Racketville, Slumtown, Haulburg: An Exploratory Study of Delinquent Subcultures. Chicago: University of Chicago Press.
Staats, A. W.
  1968   Learning, Language and Cognition. New York: Holt, Rinehart & Winston.
Studt, E., Sheldon L. Messinger, and Thomas P. Wilson.
  1968   C-Unit: Search for Community in Prison. New York: Russell Sage Foundation.
Sutherland, E. H.
  1939   Principles of Criminology. Third Edition. New York: Lippincott.
Tannenbaum, F.
  1938   Crime and the Community. Boston: Ginn.
Turk, A. T.
  1969   Criminality and the Legal Order. Chicago: Rand McNally.
Vera Institute of Justice.
  n.d.   The Manhattan Summons Project. New York: Vera Foundation.
  1970   The Manhattan Court Employment Project. New York: Vera Foundation.
Watson, N. A., and J. W. Sterling.
  1969   Police and Their Opinions. Washington, D.C.: International Association of Chiefs of Police.
Weber, M.
  1947   The Theory of Social and Economic Organization. Translation by A. M. Henderson and Talcott Parsons. Glencoe, Ill.: Free Press.
Zimring, F. E.
  1971   Perspectives on Deterrence. National Institute of Mental Health. Washington, D.C.: U.S. Government Printing Office.

CHAPTER 20

Behavior Modification:
Principles and Applications in Corrections

Michael A. Milan and John M. McKee

Rehabilitation Research Foundation

The criminal justice system is now in the position the mental-health profession found itself in a half century ago: both professionals and the informed public alike realize the inadequacies of current practices and are actively engaged in a search for more viable alternatives. The criminal justice system can traverse again the arduous and discouraging paths already explored by the mental-health professions, or it can profit by the hard-earned experiences of those in the mental-health field. By examining the successes and failures of the psychologist and psychiatrist, the criminologist can circumvent the tangle of inadequate approaches to the understanding of human behavior that has characterized mental health's recent history and from which that field is only now beginning to free itself. It is appropriate, then, to begin this introduction to behavior modification and its applications in the criminal justice system with a brief overview of the objectives and conclusions of those performing evaluative research in mental health and its allied professions.

Evaluative research in the mental-health field has sought to compare the effectiveness of treatment procedures deduced from two influential models of human behavior, the psychodynamic or "medical" model and the behavioral or "social-learning" model. Essentially, adherents to the psychodynamic model interpret deviant behavior as *symptomatic* of some underlying personality disturbance or "mental illness" in much the same manner as aberrant clinical signs, such as irregularities in pulse and temperature, are taken as symptoms of an underlying physical dysfunction. Following the medical analogy, treatment of the deviant, or "presenting," behavior itself is discouraged as superficial; and, if treatment is apparently successful, it is said to result in only a temporary remission of symptoms. It is assumed that a failure to treat the postulated underlying causes will result in the reappearance of the presenting behavior or, alternatively, symptom substitution will occur wherein previously unseen behavior, perhaps even more deviant than the presenting behavior, emerges. Successful therapy, according to the medical model, calls for diagnosis of the exact nature of an underlying disturbance and subsequent prescription of a proven treatment of choice. The primary objective of treatment is remediation of the underlying disturbance, thereby precluding symptom substitution and insuring a permanent cure (e.g., Harrison & Carek, 1966; Greenson, 1967).

Adherents to the behavioral model, on the other hand, view deviant behavior as *learned*. The principles underlying its acquisition and maintenance are viewed as no different from those governing the acquisition and maintenance of any other behavior. Both deviant and nondeviant behavior are conceptualized as "normal," that is, the same basic laws and principles are assumed to underlie all forms of human behavior. It is the unique experiences of individuals that determine, in large measure, differing patterns of behavior. The implied dichotomy in the psychodynamic model between deviant and nondeviant behavior and, by extension, between those who have and have not been labeled "mentally ill" is, therefore, denied. Diagnosis in the behavioral model requires precise specification of the presenting behavior and the environmental conditions, both social and nonsocial, that control and maintain it. The objective of treatment is elimination of the presenting behavior and, to preclude the uncontrolled learning of additional undesired behavior, replacement of it with adaptive alternatives through instruction and training in concert with the introduction or rearrangement of appropriate environmental contingencies (e.g., Bandura, 1969; Franks, 1969; Yates, 1970).

Behavior modification, then, is the systematic application of proven principles of conditioning and learning in the remediation of human problems. This, the original and proper definition of behavior modification, establishes the boundary conditions of the discipline. It delineates those strategies and techniques that can and those that cannot be legitimately considered within its working domain. A variety of medical techniques, such as psychosurgery, chemotherapy, and electrode implantation, are frequently attributed to the behavior modifier when, in fact, they do not fall within the scope of this discipline. Although these procedures do indeed result in behavior change, they should not be confused with behavior-modification procedures for they are not applications of the principles of conditioning and learning. Techniques such as these involve instead physiological alterations that fall within the domain of the physician, the surgeon, and the psychiatrist—certainly not the behavior modifier.

The results of research comparing outcomes following treatment conducted within the framework of the medical and behavioral models of human behavior have been summarized by Brown (1971). Following his review of the effectiveness of different forms of treatment in a variety of mental-health settings, he concludes that intervention procedures deduced from the behavioral or social-learning model, when compared to treatment conducted within the framework of the psychodynamic or medical model, appear to offer:

> 1. Greater *effectiveness* as a treatment method; i.e., at least for some emotionally disturbed behaviors the results are often clearly superior.
> 2. Greater *efficiency* as a treatment method; i.e., in general it takes less time and fewer sessions to bring about desired changes in the patient's life adjustment.
> 3. Greater *specificity* in establishing goals and outcome of therapy; i.e., the specific end result of therapy is specified at the beginning of therapeutic work.
> 4. Greater *applicability* to a wider segment of the population; i.e., it covers a broad spectrum of maladaptive behaviors rather than, for example, being limited more or less to upper-class neurotic patients with above average intelligence, etc.
> 5. Greater *utilization* as a treatment method by various groups; i.e., they [procedures deduced from the behavioral model] can be used not only by the practitioners of the basic mental health disciplines themselves but by public health and other nurses, caseworkers, counselors, adjunctive therapists, teachers, etc., and even by parents (Brown, 1971:32).

Others have been even more critical of the effectiveness of psychodynamically oriented treatment procedures. Eysenck (1952, 1966), Rachman (1971), and Stuart (1970) document their contention that the traditional forms of psychotherapy have not been demonstrated to be any more effective in the remediation of mental-health problems than is the mere passage of time or everyday life experiences. They also present convincing data indicating that treatment conducted within the framework of the behavioral model regularly results in higher success rates than does the psychodynamic approach. To date, little evaluative research has been directed toward determining the value of these two models in generating successful intervention programs for corrections. The research that has been reported has dealt primarily with psychodynamically oriented programs, and the results of this research have been far from encouraging (e.g., Lerman, 1968; Kassebaum et al., 1971; Beker & Heyman, 1972).

The social-learning model of human behavior, however, presents an alternative conceptualization of the causes of criminal and delinquent behavior (Akers, 1973). It is offered as a more effective vehicle for the understanding, prediction, and modification of human behavior than has heretofore been available. A major thrust of the social-learning model is its emphasis upon overt, measurable behavior as its primary subject matter. Indeed, this aspect of the model is commonly taken as its defining characteristic. This is unfortunate for at least two reasons: first, the subject matter of the behavioral model encompasses considerably more than just the behavior of individuals; and second, the term *behavior* has gained such popularity among nonbehaviorists in both professional and lay circles that its original and appropriate meaning has been all but lost. In many instances, the forced use of "behavior" as an adjective or a suffix appears more a thinly disguised attempt to "update" outmoded formulations and approaches to human behavior than it is the adoption and deployment of a new conceptual system. The term *behavior* refers to activities that are publicly observable. Used in this way, it allows procedures that have been validated in one setting to be applied in a second. Research that attempts to deal with unobservables is not only logically impossible (Ramp & Hopkins, 1971), but tends to employ vaguely defined criteria and procedures, which lessen the chances for replication.

A major contribution of the behaviorists has been the specification of the manner in which environmental phenomena influence or control behavior, combined with a general reluctance to turn to inferred but unobservable "inner" agents or processes to explain phenomena that may be most parsimoniously understood in terms of identifiable relationships between behavior and its antecedents and consequences (Skinner, 1953, 1971). The acquisition and maintenance of behavior are viewed in terms of two distinct arrangements of environmental events. In one, *respondent conditioning*, behavior is elicited by its antecedents. In the other, *operant conditioning*, behavior is maintained by its consequences.

RESPONDENT CONDITIONING

Respondents are relatively fixed responses to specific stimuli, such as orienting in the direction of a sudden, loud noise, tearing in response to an irritant in the eye, and salivating when food is placed in the mouth. The relationship between this class of stimuli and its responses is not dependent upon learning or experience. The respondent is termed the *unconditioned response* and the stimulus that regularly elicits it is termed the *unconditioned stimulus*. Pavlov (1941, 1960) is generally credited with the first systematic investigation of the manner in which reflexlike behavior may be acquired. In the respondent conditioning paradigm (also termed *classical conditioning*), a neutral stimulus (i.e., one which does not elicit the to-be-conditioned response) comes to elicit a response similar to the unconditioned response through its repeated pairing with the unconditioned stimulus that does elicit that response. The neutral stimulus is termed the *conditioned stimulus* while the response it comes to elicit is termed the *conditioned response*. Close examination of the conditioned and unconditioned responses reveals that they are seldom, if ever, identical despite their usual similarity. Although it is sometimes implied that the respondent conditioning paradigm results in "new" reflexes, this does not appear to be the case. Conditioned responses do not follow the same "laws" as do unconditioned responses, indicating that they are distinctly different phenomena (Prokasy, 1965; Black & Prokasy, 1972).

The American criminal justice system has made little systematic use of respondent conditioning procedures. Mental health has, however, employed respondent techniques with a variety of deviancies (Rachman & Teasdale, 1969). Two of these, alcoholism and homosexuality, are also of concern to the criminal justice system. Here, the typical paradigm has involved the pairing of the undesired activity (actually experienced, viewed, or imagined) with some noxious event (e.g., electric shock, vomiting induced by an emetic drug, etc.). The expected outcome is the production of an unpleasant reaction in the individual to alcohol or to homosexual activity. Frequently, some incompatible response is paired with pleasant stimuli in hopes of encouraging more desirable modes of behavior. Behavior therapists now dealing with these problems typically supplement their respondent conditioning procedures with operant procedures by directly teaching skills necessary for the maintenance of these alternatives (Kanfer & Phillips, 1970). The results of these procedures are promising: in one study of the effects of respondent conditioning procedures, approximately 51 percent of 4,096 patients treated for alcoholism maintained their abstinence for two or more years (Lemere & Voegtlin, 1950), while a second study of the effects of traditional psychotherapy indicated that only 5 percent of the population so treated maintained their abstinence for a comparable period of time (Vallance, 1965).

Although the movement to decriminalize offenses attributed to alcoholism and sexual deviancy is gathering momentum, the criminal justice system continues to bear the responsibility of treating many who, either directly or indirectly, come to its attention as a consequence of their alcoholic or sexual activities. Research indicates that respondent procedures have the potential of aiding corrections in meeting this responsibility for so long as it is continued. The nature of these procedures demands, however, that those who would apply them be especially sensitive to the growing number of legal, constitutional, and broad social-policy issues that bear upon their use (Schwitzgebel, 1971). As a general rule, coerced participation must be avoided. There is some question, however, whether a truly "voluntary" program can be conducted within any correctional institution. The voluntary nature of a correctional program can be best guaranteed when participation in no way influences institutional status and time of release. This is not to say that the hoped-for changes in behavior cannot be considered in the correctional decision-making process. To the contrary, such objective changes should provide the basis for these decisions. However, provisions must be made to insure that comparable changes in the behavior of those who have either selected alternative regimens or have chosen not to participate in any of the programs offered are given equal consideration when decisions concerning their status are made.

OPERANT CONDITIONING

The term *operant* is derived from the observation that certain behaviors *operate* upon the environment to produce consequences for the operator. Speaking technically, an operant is a class of such behaviors whose members all operate upon the environment

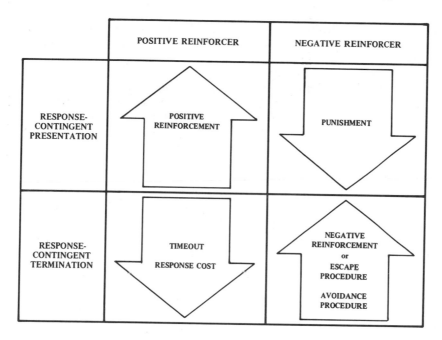

FIGURE 1. The basic paradigms of operant conditioning.

to produce the same consequences for the operator. These behaviors are grouped together because they all change the environment in the same manner rather than because they share one or more physical properties. Indeed, many members of the same operant will not share a single physical property. Their sole similarity is the environmental consequence all produce for the operator. The members of operants are referred to as acts, behaviors, operants, and, most commonly, responses. In the experimental analysis of behavior, an adequate explanation of behavior specifies the environmental conditions that reliably produce the behavior to be explained. This requires an analysis of the conditions that govern the probability that a particular response will occur at a particular time. In this analysis, response probability is typically inferred from the individual subject's rate of responding or, to a lesser degree, from other measures, such as the duration, magnitude, latency, etc., of the responses. Skinner (1938) is credited with the first systematic formulation of this position. Although there are numerous ways in which the basic principles of operant conditioning may be presented, the most straightforward involves a dichotomy between those procedures that increase the probability of a response (the *positive* and *negative reinforcement paradigms*) and those that decrease the probability of a response (the *timeout* and *punishment paradigms*). Figure 1 illustrates the procedures that define these paradigms. The arrows in each cell indicate whether the expected outcome of the procedures is an increase or decrease in the probability of responding.

Positive and Negative Reinforcement

The *positive reinforcement paradigm* is the *response-contingent presentation* of a stimulus or condition that increases the future probability of that response. *Positive reinforcers* are those stimuli or conditions whose *response-contingent presentation* will increase the future probability of that response. The *negative reinforcement paradigm* is the *response-contingent termination* of a stimulus or condition that increases the future probability of that response. *Negative reinforcers* are those stimuli or conditions whose *response-contingent termination* will increase the future probability of that response. The negative reinforcement paradigm is commonly termed the *escape* procedure, implying that an individual may escape from or terminate an undesirable situation by engaging in some activity. A variant of the negative reinforcement paradigm is the *avoidance* procedure. Here, the consequence of the operant is the postponement of a negative reinforcer, rather than its termination as in the escape procedure.

Unconditioned reinforcers* are stimuli or conditions whose reinforcing properties are independent of learning or experience. They are sometimes termed "innate," "primary," or "biological" reinforcers, and they generally hold the same significance for all members of a particular species. *Conditioned reinforcers* are initially neutral stimuli or conditions that acquire their reinforcing properties either by being paired with reinforcers—unconditioned or conditioned—or by being reliable signals that reinforcement is available or forthcoming. Food and sexual contact are typical examples of unconditioned reinforcers, while the smell of cooking and affectionate smiles are common examples of conditioned reinforcers.

Generalized conditioned reinforcers* are the most powerful of the conditioned reinforcers. They gain their power because they have been paired with or signal the availability of a wide range of other reinforcers. "Social" reinforcers, such as praise and the attention of others, are examples of generalized conditioned reinforcers. The child who earns the attention of adults is more likely to have favors bestowed upon him than is the ignored child, and, in like manner, the youth who earns the admiration of his peer group will undoubtedly derive more of the benefits available from that group than will the inconspicuous rank-and-file member. Money as a medium of exchange is perhaps the generalized conditioned reinforcer *par excellence,* for its accumulation in significant amounts signals the availability of an infinite variety of desirable commodities and services.

Timeout and Punishment

Both the timeout and punishment procedures employ stimuli or conditions which either have been, or have the potential of being, identified as positive or negative reinforcers in the positive and negative reinforcement paradigms. *Timeout* (sometimes referred to as "negative punishment") is defined as the response-contingent termination of a positive reinforcer that results in a decrease in the future probability of that response. *Response cost* is a special case of the timeout procedure. In response cost, individuals are required to relinquish tangible conditioned reinforcers, such as money, on a response-contingent basis. Imposing fines for minor traffic infractions is a common example of the response-cost procedure.

Punishment* is the response-contingent presentation of a negative reinforcer that results in a decrease in the future probability of that response. Either conditioned or unconditioned reinforcers may be employed in the timeout and punishment procedures, provided, of course, that care is taken to insure that the conditioned reinforcers are occasionally associated with the unconditioned reinforcers from which they have derived their value.

The punishment and negative reinforcement (avoidance) procedures are commonly confused. This typically results from the understandable tendency to think of these procedures in terms of their common meaning rather than in terms of their technical usage. Although it seems awkward at first, the technical language is to be preferred, for it reduces ambiguity, eliminates uncertainty concerning definitions, and aids communication once it has been mastered. In this instance, the *punishment procedure* specifies that a negative reinforcer be delivered following a response, while the *avoidance procedure* specifies that a negative reinforcer be postponed (not delivered) following a response. Although it is tempting to conclude that an individual who experiences the negative reinforcer in an avoidance procedure is punished for *not* responding, it is obvious that such a statement is technically incorrect when the definition of punishment is reexamined. The delivery of the negative reinforcer in the avoidance paradigm is nothing more than the programmed result of the failure to avoid.

Superstitious Behavior

An analysis of these four basic procedures reveals their reciprocal nature. For example, whenever we employ the timeout paradigm to decrease the probability of a response, we also have set the occasion for positive reinforcement, which, if care is not exercised, might serve instead to increase the probability of either the undesired response or some other, perhaps even less desirable, responses. In the timeout procedure, a positive reinforcer is terminated or removed for a period of time following the occurrence of a to-be-eliminated response. If the timeout operation is to be repeated, the positive reinforcer must first be reintroduced. The reintroduction of the positive reinforcer is the necessary ingredient of the positive reinforcement paradigm, and it would be expected to result in an increase in probability of any response that preceded it. This would, in turn, increase the probability that the response would again precede the reintroduction of the reinforcer following the next timeout operation, etc. Care must be taken to insure that the reintroduction of the positive reinforcer does not follow undesirable behavior. Preferably the reintroduction of the reinforcer is made contingent upon the emission of desirable behavior. If such a procedure is not followed, it is possible that the operation of uncontrolled contingencies will maintain the old, undesired response or result in the accidental conditioning of new forms of undesirable behavior.

Accidental conditioning has been demonstrated by Skinner (1948) and said by him to result in *superstitious behavior*, wherein no contingent relationship exists between the behavior and its maintaining consequences, other than that initially arranged by chance and, later, by the effect of this chance relationship. The development of superstitious behavior clearly demonstrates the *automaticity* of these behavioral principles. Simply stated, reinforcers influence the probabilities of those behaviors that they follow, independent of the intent of those who dispense and those who receive the reinforcers. When one reinforces excuses and promises to change by excusing troublesome behavior, the usual effect is to leave the troublesome behavior unchanged and to increase the likelihood that an individual will again offer excuses and promises to change when the opportunity arises. When one insures that reinforcement is contingent upon actual changes in the undesirable behavior, the usual effect is a change in that behavior.

Functional Definitions

Positive and negative reinforcers have been defined as those stimuli that may be effectively employed to influence behavior in the four preceding behavior-control paradigms. An important characteristic of these definitions is that they not only specify the behavior under examination and its consequences, as is done in the *operational definition,* but they also specify the effect of the consequences upon behavior. Such *functional definitions* emphasize the relativistic and, in many cases, idiosyncratic quality of reinforcers. The reinforcing properties of stimuli must be validated before they may be truly considered reinforcers and deployed as such. It is often tempting to assume on a personal or common-sense basis that certain stimuli or conditions will serve as reinforcers or that stimuli or conditions identified as reinforcers for some members of a group will serve equally as well for others. If the reinforcement paradigms are to be successful, *reinforcement must be individualized.* Praise from a person in a place of authority, for example, might serve as a potent positive reinforcer for one individual, be of no consequence (a *neutral stimulus* or event) for a second, and be a negative reinforcer for a third. Of course, common sense, experience, and the individual subjects themselves aid in the identification of potential reinforcers. Whether or not these potential reinforcers are true reinforcers, however, is dependent upon observed changes in behavior that occur as a function of their utilization in the basic reinforcement paradigms.

Extinction

A fifth procedure, *extinction,* is defined as the breaking of a contingent relationship between a response and its regularly occurring consequence that results in a shift of the probability of that response in the direction of its operant (preconditioning) level. The extinction procedure may either increase or decrease response probability, for its effect depends upon the context in which it is employed. When the extinction procedure is applied to behavior maintained by positive reinforcement, the positive reinforcer that was delivered contingent upon a response is no longer presented or, if presented, is presented on a noncontingent basis—that is, independent of the response that previously produced it. The expected effect of this manipulation is a decrease in the probability of that response until, eventually, it occurs with no greater probability than it did before conditioning (i.e., before the positive reinforcer had initially been made contingent upon its occurrence). Similarly, extinction applied to behavior controlled by the punishment procedure prescribes that the negative reinforcer that had regularly followed some response is no longer so programmed, and that this change is followed by an increase in the probability of the response.

Establishing New Behavior

New behavior may be established in a variety of ways, and the procedure selected to do so should be the most efficient for the specific task at hand. *Direct instruction* and *explanation,* either verbal or written, are probably the easiest and most commonly used techniques of behavior change. When instructions fail, instructors quite often resort to *modeling:* the expected behavior is demonstrated and the client is expected to imitate what he has been shown. Both instruction and modeling have been extensively studied as behavior-change procedures (Bandura, 1969), and there is now a clear understanding of the principles and procedures that must be employed if behavior change is to occur. Basically, the degree to which instructions are followed and modeled behavior is imitated is a function of the consequences of following instructions and imitating a model. Similarly, the degree to which the newly acquired behavior is then exhibited in other situations is a function of its consequences in those situations.

When instructions and modeling fail to instill the desired behavior, typically, too much is expected of the individual—that is, the disparity between the behavior that he now exhibits or is capable of performing and what is expected of him is so large that it is unreasonable to demand that he produce the complete behavior after instruction or modeling. This problem is routinely overcome by use of *shaping*, or the *method of successive approximation.* This approach requires (1) specification of the desired, or terminal, behavior; (2) identification of some bit of current, or initial, behavior that is a portion or precursor of the terminal behavior; and (3) detailing of a number of sequentially ordered and attainable behavioral "steps" (or approximations) that link the two.

The method of successive approximation may be employed to attack a number of behaviors exhibited by "normal" people commonly viewed as "attitudinal" or "motivational" problems. A lack of punctuality or conscientiousness in institutional-training programs, for example, is usually ignored or dealt with by transferring the troublesome individual. Training programs that tolerate such behavioral deficits or view them as causes for dismissal should instead consider them opportunities to shape and insure behavior that will stand the trainee in good stead when he leaves the training situation for the job. Indeed, the mastery of skills such as these may be of equal or greater value than the vocational skills being taught.

If, for example, the method of successive approximation were applied to a problem in punctuality, the distribution of arrival times that describe the individual's performance would be determined and some arrival time that both approximated the desired arrival time and occurred with some frequency would be identified. Arrivals at this time or earlier would be reinforced in some manner, while arrival at all later times would not be reinforced (i.e., would be subject to the extinction procedure). As a result of this operation, called *differential reinforcement,* the probability of occurrence of the earlier response times would increase, while the probability of later arrivals would decrease. This phenomenon, the result of differential reinforcement, is termed *response differentiation.* This procedure would be repeated until the distribution of arrival times came to overlap the desired arrival time. It would then be a simple matter to reinforce that and all earlier times and, once the behavior had stabilized at a satisfactory level, to introduce procedures that would insure the maintenance of the newly established behavior.

Maintaining Established Responses

Generally, the most effective method of increasing the probability of a particular response is to change the environmental circumstances so that a reinforcing consequence immediately follows each occurrence of the response. However, this is neither the most efficient procedure for maintaining a response in the training situation nor of maximizing the probability that a response will be continued once an individual has left the training setting. Reinforcement rarely follows each instance of behavior in the "real world." This involves the scheduling of reinforcement. A schedule of *continuous reinforcement (CRF)* is in effect when each occurrence of a particular response is followed by reinforcement. Between this and the opposite extreme (extinction), where no occurrences are reinforced, there exists a large number of alternative arrangements between responses and consequences, generally referred to as the schedules of *intermittent reinforcement.* The CRF schedule is commonly employed in the development of a response, while the intermittent schedules are introduced when the objective is to insure the maintenance of an already established response.

When reinforcement is contingent upon the number of responses emitted, a *ratio* schedule of reinforcement is in effect. An employer, for example, might foster productivity on the assembly line by paying his employees $5 for every tenth unit completed. A not-so-obvious ratio schedule is that programmed by the slot machine, the "one-armed bandit." One of these machines might average only one $25 jackpot for every 100 silver dollars it consumes, but anyone who has visited Las Vegas can attest to the "addictive" properties of this type of ratio schedule.

There is one important procedural difference between the two examples cited above. The relationship between pieces produced and payoff in piece work is perfectly predictable or fixed, while the relationship between the actual number of silver dollars that must be put into the slot machine and each jackpot is unpredictable or varied from payoff to payoff. A *fixed-ratio (FR) schedule* is in effect when the number of responses required for reinforcement is constant from reinforcement to reinforcement, as in piece work. A *variable-ratio (VR) schedule* is in effect when the number of responses required for reinforcement varies from reinforcement to reinforcement, as with a slot machine.

Each schedule produces typical patterns of responding. The FR schedule produces very high rates of responding, with a brief pause following reinforcement. The VR schedule also produces relatively high rates of responding, but without the post-reinforcement pause seen in the FR schedule. The local rate (i.e., when the subject is responding) in the FR schedule is higher by far than for a comparable VR, but when the FR pauses are taken into account they generate about the same overall rates. Of the two, the variable-ratio schedule has proven to be more resistant to extinction. Both, of course, are considerably more resistant to extinction than is the continuous-reinforcement schedule.

The alternative to the ratio schedule is the interval schedule, wherein reinforcement becomes available after the passage of some specified period of time. The first response emitted after reinforcement becomes available is reinforced. The intervals between one reinforcement and the availability of the next may be constant, or they may vary around some mean value. The *fixed-interval (FI) schedule* is analogous to the FR schedule, with the FI value specifying the interval between the delivery of one reinforcement and the availability of the next. This value is constant from reinforcement to reinforcement. The *variable-interval (VI) schedule* is analogous to the VR schedule, with the VI value specifying the average interval between the delivery of one reinforcement and the availability of the next. The actual values vary around the mean value.

The interval schedules also produce characteristic patterns of responding. Under the FI schedule there is virtually no responding seen immediately following reinforcement. As the interval approaches its termination the individual responds faster and faster, with the highest rate of responding occurring at the end of the interval. When graphed, this constantly accelerating pattern resembles a scallop and, hence, is generally referred to as the "fixed-interval scallop." Unlike the FI schedule, the VI schedule produces very regular, almost paced responding of moderate rates that are easily influenced by a wide variety of environmental events.

As was indicated previously, a primary function of the intermittent schedules is to maintain responding after it has been established. By *thinning reinforcement,* that is, by gradually increasing the number of responses that must be emitted before reinforcement is delivered or by gradually increasing the interval between one reinforcement and the availability of the next, it is possible to decrease drastically the actual amount of reinforcement experienced, while at the same time sustaining or increasing the rate of responding. If appropriate behavior (i.e., appropriate with regard to the individual and the environment in which he will, or does, exist) has been selected for strengthening, the same reinforcers alone or in conjunction with others naturally occurring will be sufficient to maintain the response.

An important product of our knowledge of the effect of the schedules of reinforcement upon behavior is an increased understanding of what are commonly thought of as attributes of *motivation*. "Highly motivated" people are usually identified as those who work diligently for long hours even though reinforcement is either meager, long delayed, or both. Although motivation is commonly thought of as a characteristic of the individual, an alternative explanation of motivated behavior is now possible. This explanation focuses upon the relationship between motivated behavior and its consequences. An analysis of the schedule or schedules of reinforcement in effect appears to offer a better understanding of "motivated" behavior than that derived from a trait inferred from the behavior it is then used to explain.

The Token Economy

Early efforts to employ the operant conditioning model as a vehicle for motivating performance and inducing behavior change typically consisted of one or more treatment personnel working with a single individual. More recently, however, the desirability of employing the principles of behavior modification with individuals in various group settings has been recognized, and increasing effort is being expended in this direction. A technology stemming from work with institutionalized psychiatric patients and formalized by Ayllon and Azrin (1968) now exists that retains the principles of behavior modification and permits their systematic application in the group setting. This technology is generally identified by the name of its key concept, the token economy.

The token economy has three defining characteristics (Krasner, 1970a, 1970b). First, there is the designation by institutional authorities of those behaviors in which individuals should engage. In part based upon a clear value judgment, the activities identified here are also heavily dependent upon the goals of the program and represent those that will earn reinforcement once the token economy is instituted. Second is the medium of exchange: objects (tokens) that individuals obtain when they engage in behaviors deemed desirable and that they may exchange for things they desire, the backup reinforcers. The medium of exchange may be tangible or intangible, and has consisted, among other things, of credit cards, metallic coins, poker chips, green stamps, and bank points. Third are the ways and means utilizing the tokens, the backup reinforcers themselves. These are the things a given individual wants, and can include, among a host of such reinforcers, the opportunity to watch a certain television program, special foods, or extra visiting time.

The token, then, like money, is a generalized conditioned reinforcer. It is employed because it is often not feasible to deliver the backup reinforcers immediately following a desirable behavior, and because it is frequently necessary to arrange the relationship between performance and reinforcement on other than a one-to-one basis. When delivered following a behavior, the token effectively mediates the time interval between that behavior and, when later exchanged, the utilization of the backup reinforcers. Research examining the effectiveness of token economies in a variety of settings has revealed the potential of arranging contingencies relating actions and their consequences in such a fashion. The value of the token economy has been amply demonstrated as both an aid to psychiatric-ward maintenance and as a treatment medium

(Atthowe & Krasner, 1968; Lloyd & Abel, 1970), and as a technique to facilitate learning and maintain order in schoolrooms for both retarded (Birnbrauer et al., 1965) and normal (O'Leary et al., 1969) students.

Behavior Modification and Psychotherapy

Recently, changes in verbal and nonverbal behavior that have been attributed to treatment via psychotherapy have been subjected to an operant analysis, and the results have suggested that the effects of psychotherapy stem from the careful and, in most instances, unwitting application of the principles of behavior modification. Truax (1966), for example, obtained audiotape recordings of a series of Carl Rogers's therapeutic sessions with a long-term patient and categorized the patient's verbal productions on the basis of their content. Nine categories were identified. Truax then examined Rogers's responses to these verbal productions. His analysis revealed that Rogers responded differentially to verbal productions in five of the nine categories, providing responses that communicated understanding, warmth, and affirmation to "healthy" statements while withholding this tacit approval if the productions were "unhealthy." In addition, Truax found that the statements that earned approval (the "healthy" statements) increased in frequency, while the statements that were ignored (the "unhealthy" statements) decreased in frequency. Whaley and Malott, in their review of this study, concluded:

> The therapy process apparently involves differential reinforcement. The patient is reinforced for saying the right things. He receives reinforcement as long as he stays "on the right track," but not when he makes statements which are confused, self-depreciating, pessimistic, or generally unhealthy. As therapy continues, the patient's healthy verbal behavior begins to generalize to areas outside the session. He is more optimistic, relaxed, and clearer than before. Friends and acquaintances see this change and respond to it favorably, thus reinforcing his new personality. Soon it can be maintained by persons other than the therapist, and therapy may be terminated (1971:71).

It appears, then, that even the most nondirect of the nondirect therapists exerts considerable, albeit unintentional, control over the behavior of his clients and that therapists, in general, must come to grips with this possibility and its consequent responsibilities. More important, however, are the implications of these findings for the training of new therapists. If the behavior of successful psychotherapists may be understood as a process involving the careful application of the principles of operant conditioning, it logically follows that the most effective manner of teaching individuals to become effective therapists is to instruct them in these basic principles and how they may be applied to human problems.

Behavioral Assessment

Behavioral assessment refers to an analysis of existent behavior in terms of the interrelationships between four major classes of events: (1) the behavior that is the target of the diagnostic process, (2) the consequences of this behavior, (3) the discriminative stimuli that set the occasion for this behavior, and (4) the setting conditions that further influence the probability of this behavior. The first two classes of events in this fourfold relationship, the behavior and its consequences, as well as some of the possible arrangements between the two, have already been discussed in some detail.

We can summarize the value of concentrating upon the relationship between behavior and its consequences by noting that in so doing we avoid the two major pitfalls of a more traditional diagnosis. First, the description of behavior negates the use of vaguely defined psychological labels that, all too often, become self-fulfilling prophecies (Toch, 1970). Second, attention to the consequences of behavior precludes the possibility that morphologically similar but functionally different forms of behavior will be categorized as the same and treated in an identical manner.

Discriminative Stimuli

The third aspect of behavioral assessment involves a specification of the environmental or stimulus conditions under which behavior is likely or expected to occur. If a particular operant has a high probability of occurrence in the presence of one stimulus and a low probability of occurrence in its absence, the operant is considered to be under the control of that stimulus. Stimuli or conditions that control the probability of operant responses are called *discriminative stimuli*. The controlling power of a stimulus in the operant paradigm is not to be confused with the eliciting power of a stimulus in the respondent paradigm. Discriminative stimuli do not elicit a particular response, but instead "signal" that certain behaviors will be followed by certain consequences. It is in this sense that operants are termed *emitted* rather than *elicited* responses. Whether or not the individual emits a response is more a function of subtle aspects of the past conditioning history of the individual and certain setting conditions (the fourth aspect of behavioral assessment) than of the discriminative stimulus per se.

It is oftentimes impossible to identify discriminative stimuli that set the occasion for operants that people routinely emit, for the stimuli that come to control human behavior are highly complex. They may be as subtle as verbal intonation, as fleeting as a facial expression, and as diffuse as a building's architecture. The only defining characteristic of a discriminative stimulus is that it controls a particular behavior, i.e., a behavior is more probable in its presence than in its absence.

Current law-enforcement and crime-control procedures have focused upon the elimination of discriminative stimuli that set the occasion for crime. The use of high-pressure sodium-vapor lamps to illuminate streets and parks in the evening hours is an attempt to reduce the incidence of holdups, muggings, and rapes through the manipulation of discriminative stimuli. So, too, is the wide-scale deployment of police officers in high-crime areas. Public information campaigns that urge the citizenry to stop the delivery of mail and newspapers when they are away from home for protracted periods of time are also examples of this strategy, as are legal proscriptions against leaving keys in automobile ignitions. Suggesting even further concern for discriminative stimuli by law-enforcement personnel, Jeffery (1971) has argued that the police can play a more effective role in crime prevention by emphasizing prevention and control through the environment rather than by apprehension of individual criminals after the fact. According to Jeffery's concept, the police would establish guidelines for urban planning and building construction and renovation in order to minimize the wide range of environmental opportunities that occasion criminal acts.

Setting Conditions

The fourth component of the behavioral-assessment regimen is the identification of *setting conditions* that actuate members of the response class under examination if and when discriminative stimuli signal that the appropriate contingencies of reinforcement are in effect. Kantor has stressed the importance of these factors in the understanding of both operant and respondent behavior:

> Such setting factors as the hungry or satiated condition of the organism, its age, hygienic or toxic condition, as well as the presence or absence of certain environing objects, clearly influence the occurrence or non-occurrence of interbehavior or facilitate the occurrence of activities . . . (1959:95).

The role of environing objects, as mentioned above, would be subsumed, for our purposes, under the more general classification of discriminative stimuli. Setting conditions, like discriminative stimuli, involve environmental factors that influence behavior. Unlike discriminative stimuli, however, setting conditions are more complex than the mere presence, change, or absence of environmental stimuli. They are best conceptualized as salient characteristics of the individual's past history that, because they exist, affect the probability of occurrence of one or more classes of behavior. They may be events that have occurred in either the recent or distant past, and their effects may be or have been either of brief or long duration. For example, an individual might behave in an offensive manner when under the influence of alcohol. Here, the setting condition for the disapproved behavior is alcoholic intoxication or, in more quantifiable terms, the consumption of alcohol.

A second example of the effect of setting conditions upon behavior is described by social scientists when they point to the close association between certain aspects of disadvantaged people and the incidence of criminal activity. As has become obvious, these setting conditions (e.g., poverty, boredom) are neither necessary nor sufficient conditions for criminal behavior. Many criminals are neither poor nor bored, and far from all those who are poor or bored turn to crime. For some individuals, under particular stimulus conditions, however, setting conditions (e.g., those associated with poverty and boredom) apparently do actuate certain forms of behavior (termed *criminal*) that have a higher probability of producing reinforcing than punishing consequences. For these individuals, one avenue of attack upon their criminal behavior is through the setting conditions. Alternative strategies would involve a concentration upon the stimulus conditions that set the occasion for the act, the consequences of the act, and the act itself. The more of these controlling aspects of behavior that are dealt with in intervention, the more likely intervention strategies are to be effective.

INTERVENTION STRATEGIES

To date, most correctional intervention strategies have dealt with the setting conditions characteristic of disadvantaged persons in general. The current emphasis upon adult basic education and vocational-training programs reflects this conceptualization of the causes of criminal behavior. The question is not whether this view is appropriate, but rather, for how many of those who engage in criminal activity is it appropriate? The objective of behavioral assessment is the identification for each individual of troublesome behavior, maintaining consequences, and controlling stimuli and setting conditions so that appropriate intervention strategies will be formulated. Behavior-change regimens derived from behavioral-assessment procedures will involve the application of the same principles of behavior that have been employed in understanding the phenomena under study.

Although the value of these new behavior-change regimens has been convincingly demonstrated in a wide variety of applied settings (Ulrich et al., 1966, 1970), we are only now experiencing the beginnings of a concerted effort to determine how the principles and procedures of behavior modification may be best translated and applied to the problems confronting workers in the criminal justice .system. The early work of Slack and his associates (Slack, 1960; Schwitzgebel, 1964; Schwitzgebel & Kolb, 1964) explored how procedures deduced from the behavioral model could be employed to encourage "unreachable" delinquents to participate in traditional counseling and psychotherapy. The more recent work of Patterson and his co-workers (Patterson et al., 1972) has focused upon the home life of predelinquent youths and has resulted in a set of standardized social-engineering procedures designed to alter the behavior of highly aggressive youths with the aim of diverting them from a path leading to the juvenile and criminal justice systems. The early research of Staats and Butterfield (1965) demonstrated the potential of employing token economy procedures in the treatment of nonreading in a culturally deprived juvenile delinquent. More recently, comprehensive token reinforcement systems have been demonstrated to facilitate educational performance, control disruptive behavior, and ease management problems with institutionalized delinquents (Burchard & Tyler, 1965; Tyler & Brown, 1968), youthful offenders (Cohen et al., 1967; Cohen & Filipczak, 1971) and adult felons (Ayllon & Roberts, 1973). The following summaries are representative, then, of a growing number of reports dealing with the application of the principles of behavior modification to the understanding and remediation of problems facing the juvenile and criminal justice systems.

Behavior Modification in the Natural Environment

Most would agree that intervention should be carried out in the individual's natural environment (the job, the home, the school, etc.) whenever possible. It is often argued, however, that there are not enough trained and competent professionals available to do this. In response to this personnel shortage, Tharp and Wetzel (Thorne et al., 1967; Tharp & Wetzel, 1969) have trained paraprofessionals in the Tucson, Arizona, area to supervise implementation of behavior-modification strategies. The paraprofessionals were selected specifically for their lack of previous training in any of the helping professions. Their requisite characteristics included only intelligence, energy, flexibility, and qualities of personal attractiveness. These supervisors have included sociology majors, an ex-football player, an ex-stevedore, a carpenter, a returned Peace Corps volunteer, a housewife, a cocktail waitress, and the like. As a consequence of the selection criteria, the supervisors came into the project with little if any personal bias concerning the "treatment of choice" for the problems with which they were to deal. Training for the tasks they were to assume consisted of an intensive three-week course in the principles of behavior modification and their utilization in the applied setting, followed by equally as intense on-the-job training.

All treatment procedures were within the "triadic model," consisting of the supervisor, various mediators, and the target individual. Although the supervisors exercised considerable freedom, they were not completely autonomous with respect to the treatment procedures constructed for the varying problem behaviors dealt with. In addition to the three-week course and the on-the-job training these individuals received during the beginning of the project, the supervisors met with the professional staff on a regular basis to discuss strategies, explore new approaches, and review data pertinent to the course of treatment.

The mediators consisted of "significant others" in the lives of the target individuals—parents, teachers, neighbors, social workers, etc. They were identified on the basis of two criteria: first, the mediator had to possess high-ranked reinforcers for the target individual; second, the mediator had to be able to dispense those reinforcers on the basis of an established contingency. All other information was considered irrelevant. The use of the mediator concept answers the question of "Who is the client in a treatment program?" In the traditional psychotherapeutic approach, the target individual is depicted as the client, and the therapist works directly with him in an attempt to modify his behavior. Meanwhile, the environmental circumstances that set the occasion for his behavior and reinforce it when it occurs continue unchanged. The mediator, then, was the client of the paraprofessional staff. By working with the mediators, it was possible to establish new contingencies in which the target individual's old undesirable forms of behavior were no longer reinforced, and the environment came to occasion and reinforce alternative, desirable forms of behavior.

The target individuals in the Tharp and Wetzel studies were youths referred to treatment. During the course of the program, a total of seventy-seven such persons were seen. Of these, approximately one-third had police records of one sort or another. These records ranged from one to thirteen offenses, consisting of virtually everything from minor curfew violations to armed assault. The effect of the intervention strategies upon the behavior of the target individuals, as indexed by a six-month follow-up, was to reduce the number of youths who were committing offenses by 81 percent and the number of offenses committed by 68 percent. It appears that these procedures have the potential of breaking the chain of activities that eventually lead to incarceration in a juvenile correctional facility and, all too often, to a life of adult crime.

Achievement Place

The behavior modification approach has also been employed with considerable success at Achievement Place in Lawrence, Kansas. Achievement Place is a residential, community-based, home-style living center for predelinquent boys who are (or are about to be) suspended from school, who are in trouble in the community, or who are thought to be uncontrollable by their parents (Phillips, 1968; Bailey et al., 1970; Phillips et al., 1971). Its program is designed to modify undesirable and antisocial behavior while developing new and appropriate behavior patterns within the community and its various social institutions. To accomplish this, Achievement Place employs the token economy as the most efficient medium of treatment.

In the Achievement Place token economy, a youth earns tokens for appropriate behavior and loses tokens for inappropriate behavior. In addition, the token system provides the boy immediate and concrete feedback when he first enters the program. As the boy's skills and self-control develop, the boy may earn his way out of the highly structured token system. As this system is gradually withdrawn, it is replaced by more natural (teacher-parent, peer, and academic) feedback conditions. If a youth's behavior indicates that he needs more experience within the structure of the token system, he can lose his new status and return to the token system. Once a boy has demonstrated his ability to exercise self-control, to take responsibility for his own behavior, and to work productively in the home and school, he is ready to be returned to his own home or to a foster family. To maintain the gains made at Achievement Place, each family receives training in behavioral-management techniques. The boy's progress with his family is closely monitored for several months following his release, and the boy may be returned to Achievement Place if it is deemed beneficial.

Achievement Place differs from the vast majority of other "foster homes" in that its emphasis is upon behavior and upon a technology that enables the practitioner to change behavior. Both desirable and undesirable behaviors are specified, and their frequency of occurrence is determined. Individual and group treatment procedures are implemented, focusing upon the relationship between the behaviors in question and their consequences. Identification of these behaviors and monitoring of the boys' performance allow constant assessment of the effects of treatment and provide the basis for determining treatment success or failure. By so doing, it is possible to develop alternative programs and to progress to further stages of treatment when initial objectives are met. Finally, the extrinsic reinforcers provided by the token economy are gradually faded out, and new behaviors, now occurring at a relatively high frequency, come to be maintained by their natural consequences—those that the individual will encounter in the "real world." The training of individuals in the natural environment (real or foster parents) in behavior-modification techniques and the appropriate use of social and other reinforcers maximize the probability that the behaviors will indeed be maintained once the youth leaves the treatment facility. Outcome research indicates the Achievement Place model is a success. Once the boys enter Achievement Place they have virtually no unpleasant contacts with the law, their public-school attendance improves markedly, and their academic grades rise (Phillips et al., 1973).

More recently, research has examined the feasibility of applying these procedures to adult offenders. This work has been conducted primarily with delinquent soldiers at the Walter Reed Army Institute of Research and with adult male felons at the Experimental Manpower Laboratory for Corrections.

The Walter Reed Project

The Walter Reed ward for delinquent soldiers was established at Walter Reed Army Hospital, Washington, D. C., to treat soldiers who had been diagnosed as having character or behavior disorders (Colman & Baker, 1969; Colman & Boren, 1969; Boren & Colman, 1970). Most had records of repeated absences without leave (AWOL), with past histories that often included dropping out of high school, convictions of minor crimes, suicidal gestures, and difficulty with parents, school officials, police, and Army officers. Homosexuals, drug addicts, and alcoholics were excluded from the program. The design of the treatment program was based on the assumption that these men failed in the military and, previously, in civilian life because of deficiencies in their behavioral repertoire. Specifically, they were viewed as lacking important education or recreation skills, personal habit patterns, such as planning and performing consistently, and interpersonal skills that would make their presence and performance important, in this instance, to other members of their military unit.

The token economy approach was adopted as that best suited to the needs of both treatment staff and soldier. It provided the staff with an extrinsic motivational system that was both capable of overcoming the strong resistance to treatment and change characteristic of these men and amenable to precise control and manipulation. It also allowed individualized treatment and consequent attenuation from the more synthetic tokens to the more natural social reinforcers available for acceptable competent performances in both military and civilian life.

In the token economy itself the soldiers earned points by attending educational classes, dressing neatly, carrying out work projects, and delivering verbal reports (i.e., by engaging in most activities "required" by soldiers in an Army field unit). These points could then be exchanged for a variety of privileges, such as semiprivate rooms, coffee, access to a television set, poolroom privileges, weekend passes, etc. The men planned day-to-day and week-to-week earning strategies. They made decisions that influenced rewards available to them in the future with the reward interval increasingly delayed as they progressed in treatment.

A follow-up comparison was made between forty-six men released from the Walter Reed project and forty-eight comparable soldiers who received either routine disciplinary action or general psychiatric treatment. Of the soldiers in the Walter Reed group, seven had completed their tour and twenty-five were functioning in a unit (69.5 percent "success"), while fourteen had either been administratively discharged from duty, were AWOL, or were in a stockade (30.5 percent "failure"). Of the comparison group, one had completed his tour and twelve were on active duty (28.3 percent "success"), while thirty-three were administratively discharged or in a stockade (71.7 percent "failure").

The Experimental Manpower Laboratory for Corrections

The early work of the Experimental Manpower Laboratory for Corrections (EMLC), operated by the Rehabilitation Research Foundation and located then at Draper Correctional Center at Elmore, Alabama, consisted of explorations into the utilization of behavior-modification and contingency-management procedures in the areas of remedial education and vocational skill training (Rehabilitation Research Foundation, 1968). Draper is a maximum security institution housing approximately 900 adult felons of all custody grades. Adult offenders are, more often than not, the products of the juvenile justice system. They are, in short, its failures, typifying a cross section of the disadvantaged of our land. It is a population group that has been genuinely "turned off" by public education, which has always dealt them constant failure and rebuff, resulting in a mutual hostility and an avoidance of contact. To remedy these deficiencies, the focus of the EMLC was on providing immediate and continuing success in basic education through the use of programmed instruction (PI). In PI the to-be-mastered material is broken down into small units and ordered so that each successive unit is a "natural" extension of the preceding one. The student actively participates in the instruction, for he is constantly required to make responses—usually in the form of filling in blanks or choosing from alternative answers—and given immediate feedback concerning the correctness of his responses. Errors are minimal or nonexistent if the material is properly prepared. If errors do occur with some frequency, they are first explored as signals that the material, rather than the student, is in need of correction.

The Self-Instructional School

A self-instructional school was established in which PI material comprised 95 percent of the curriculum. The operation of the self-instructional school resulted in the development of an Individually Prescribed Instructional (IPI) system, which begins by establishing learning objectives for each student. After the student's learning objectives have been established, the IPI system provides a diagnosis of his educational deficiencies. Based on this diagnosis, the system then allows the teacher or learning manager to prescribe selected PI materials that will remedy the diagnosed deficiencies and move the student in the direction of meeting his learning objectives. As many instructional units are listed on the prescription as are required to bring the student up to a desired grade average in all areas shown on a standardized achievement test.

Each segment of work consists of the amount a student can be expected to accomplish in a given period of time. This unit of work is put into the form of a "contingency contract," which the student is expected to complete before the end of the week. If he finishes sooner than the estimated number of hours, he can accept another contract. Students in such programmed instruction are always required to pass examinations on the material they cover before they are allowed to start new work. The contingency contract requires a progress test for each module, and the student must score 85 percent or better on all module tests. Scores below 85 percent necessitate the student being assigned an alternate module and its corresponding test.

For some, the immediate feedback and verification of responses were sufficiently reinforcing to maintain performance. For others, *synthetic reinforcers,* such as money, free time, the opportunity to work on another portion of the curriculum, etc., were employed to supplement the built-in reinforcers and get the individual started. These synthetic reinforcers were then gradually removed, or attenuated, while the *natural reinforcers*—being correct, praise from others, etc.—were systematically employed to maintain the newly developed behavior. The term *contingency management (CM)* has been applied to the technology of arranging reinforcing consequences for *educational* behavior where the objective is to achieve increased student performance (Homme et al., 1968).

Studies have repeatedly shown that use of programmed instruction with such contingency management can accelerate academic and vocational learning by adult prisoners. In some experiments (Clements & McKee, 1968), reinforcement consisted only of contracts in which volunteer subjects agreed that their daily output after an initial base-line period of a few weeks would be 20 percent greater each week than the preceding, for four weeks. This was followed by two weeks in which the subjects each set their own daily work objectives. These experiments achieved approximately the 20 percent increase per week projected, and the increase was sustained when their studying shifted to a self-management basis. There are many variations on this model, including use of daily performance charts and monetary incentives for accomplishment (Enslen, 1969; Jenkins et al., 1969).

Correctional-Officer Training

The more recent work of the EMLC has explored the feasibility of deploying the principles of behavior modification on a broader scale within the correctional institution itself. The EMLC's correctional-officer training project (Smith et al., 1972) sought to assess the correctional-officers' potential to serve first as a behavioral technician and then as a behavioral engineer. Within this context, the behavioral technician is viewed as one who grasps the basic principles of this new technology and possesses the requisite skills, such as objectivity, consistency, and reliability, necessary for the performance of the routine tasks required in the day-to-day operation of a systematic behavior-modification program. The behavioral engineer is one who not only possesses the knowledge and skills of the behavioral technician, but can also contribute these and his intimate knowledge of the institution as a participating member of a professional team charged with the responsibility of monitoring, troubleshooting, and upgrading such a systematic program.

The training program consisted of classroom instruction in the principles of behavior modification followed by a supervised practicum. The officers were taught how to define, systematically observe, record, and graph behavior. They were also taught the use of positive and negative reinforcement, timeout, punishment, and extinction, as well as shaping, the scheduling of reinforcers, and how to thin reinforcement. In the practicum phase, the officers were given the opportunity to demonstrate both their mastery of the skills taught in the classroom as well as their potential as either behavioral technicians or behavioral engineers. The training-project staff worked closely with each officer; staff members encouraged the officers to identify problems that they faced in the institution, collect base-line data, devise correctional strategies, and then implement these strategies and determine their effectiveness.

Each officer was provided with the minimal supervision necessary to complete his practicum assignment. The results of the practicum phase reflected the wide range of abilities represented in the correctional-officer corps. Some officers could not identify any behavior they deemed in need of remediation. Others defined problem behaviors but could not muster the objectivity and consistency necessary to record baseline data reliably or to manage contingencies in an intervention program. Still others could define and record troublesome behavior and then carry out an intervention program designed by the training-project staff, but could not themselves devise an intervention program. Finally, some officers demonstrated that they could, with minimal supervision, implement and evaluate an intervention program of their own design. This group possessed the skills required of the behavioral engineer and, hopefully, it is officers such as these who would rise to positions of responsibility in an institution that deployed the principles of behavior modification in its day-to-day operation. The preceding group demonstrated the skills required of the behavioral technician, and it is officers such as these who would be expected to perform the routine tasks involved in the on-line operation of the institutional program.

As has been indicated, the primary purpose of the practicum phase of the training project was to establish a means by which the officers' potentials as behavioral technicians and engineers could be assessed in a real-life situation. In this purpose it was a success. In addition, the practicum phase added credence to the contention that whatever potential the correctional officer does possess as an agent of change will not be fulfilled until the operating procedures of the modern correctional institution are subjected to a drastic restructuring. The projects initiated by the officers reflected their general concerns and employed, of necessity, only those contingencies they could arrange and manage in the institution with no alterations of general policy. The problems identified by the officers included such things as inmate punctuality, work performance, leaving work without permission, cursing, making requests that could not be fulfilled by officers, etc. None of the procedures developed by the officers were deemed "cruel and unusual" by the project staff. Indeed, they often appeared less so than the ones typically outlined in rule books. Consequently, the training staff did not have to invoke its previous resolve that projects would be terminated if, in the opinion of the training staff, the behavior dealt with was contrary to the best interest of targeted inmates and/or the procedures exerted an undue hardship upon those inmates. As Ayllon and Roberts (1972) have pointed out, the empirical nature of the behavioral approach to the solution of human problems facilitates such decisions. In this, they protect the individual from the capriciousness of those whose job it is to care for, train, or rehabilitate him.

Virtually all the projects designed and implemented by officers in this project employed either negative reinforcement or timeout. None used positive reinforcement, despite a heavy emphasis upon it, its effectiveness, and its desirable aspects during the initial presentation of the material in the classroom and throughout the practicum phase. Although this may reflect the biases of some of the correctional officers, it is more likely the result of the existent operating procedures of the institution. An analysis of institutional-management procedures reveals that virtually all the potential positive reinforcers are bestowed upon or scheduled for each inmate when he enters the correctional system, and virtually all formalized behavior-control strategies involve their withdrawal or postponement contingent upon evidence of disapproved behavior. The use of these procedures has been labeled the "punishment model," and its continuance will effectively block the deployment of positive reinforcement-oriented procedures in the criminal justice field.

Examination of the Punishment Model

Propagation of a punishment model is the natural outcome of the administrative policies practiced in virtually all American correctional institutions. When each inmate is allowed a specifiable number of telephone calls, mailed letters, visitors, etc., as well as commissary, television, movie, and recreational privileges, as a matter of course, restriction is the only control procedure available for institutional management. Even "good time," which is supposedly earned as a man serves his sentence, is typically computed and awarded early in his stay in the institution. Its loss is then made contingent upon prohibited acts. When systematically applied, as they are in most correctional settings, the tactics of the punishment model permit the efficient management of inmate behavior during confinement. The immediacy with which such procedures take effect, and the cultural endorsement of these procedures when applied to the offender population, have insured their refinement and reification in modern corrections.

There is reason to believe, however, that these procedures have numerous side effects that argue for their elimination in any program emphasizing rehabilitation rather than custody of offenders. Experimental evidence (Azrin & Holz, 1966) suggests that the institution that relies upon the punishment model diminishes in varying degrees whatever potential its agents (educators, counselors, and correctional officers) possess as rehabilitation agents. These procedures would be predicted to engender in the inmate both the active avoidance of those who carry them out and, in the extreme, aggression directed toward agents of the institution and inmate peers, regardless of their relationship to the punishers. To test these hypotheses, a detailed analysis of the effects of routine institutional-control procedures upon inmate behavior was performed.

The EMLC assumed responsibility for the management of one of the dormitory-type cellblocks of Draper Correctional Center. The cellblock, which housed a maximum of forty inmates, had previously been the site of an inmate-training project and had, for that purpose, been subdivided into several rooms of varying size. These rooms were retained and employed variously as dormitories, reinforcing-event areas, and office space. Three measures were employed to determine the effects of the punishment model as practiced in corrections upon inmate behavior. The first was the percentage of morning activities completed each day. These activities included making the bed, maintaining the area around the bunk in an orderly condition, and presenting a neat and clean personal appearance. The second measure was the percent of volunteered-for maintenance tasks completed. These tasks were not directly related to the care of the inmates' immediate living area but consisted instead of tasks necessary for the general upkeep of the cellblock (mopping corridors, cleaning commodes, etc.). The third measure, behavioral incidents, indexed acts, such as insubordination, fighting, destruction of property, etc., that reflect hostility and aggression. An incident rate (acts/census/hours) was computed on a daily basis to control for variations in population and observation time (e.g., the inmates' job and school assignments precluded their presence on the cellblock for half of each weekday but not on the weekends or holidays).

Initially, a laissez-faire approach was applied to the inmates' performance of the morning activities and volunteered-for tasks. Under this condition the inmates were reminded of the duties they were expected to perform, but no attempt was made to force compliance. The levels of performance were low. A median of 32 percent of the morning activities were completed, and 35 percent of volunteered-for maintenance tasks were completed during this seventeen-day base-line phase. Following the base-line period an "Officer Corrects" condition was implemented. During this phase the correctional officer assigned to the cellblock was permitted to employ whatever institutional control procedures—including disciplinary actions, such as the loss of good time and placement in punitive isolation—he deemed necessary and appropriate to insure the performance of the morning activities. The officer was not, however, allowed to employ these techniques to encourage the completion of the volunteered-for maintenance tasks. Instead, the laissez-faire approach of the base-line condition was continued.

The traditional methods of inmate control were highly effective in motivating the performance of the targeted morning activities. The median number of activities rose to 62 percent during the Officer Corrects phase of the study. In addition, the bulk of the days during which performance was lowest were weekends when the correctional officer was off duty and the common practice of sleeping late interfered with meeting the criterion for acceptable performance of the activities. The application of institutional-management procedures to the morning activities had no positive effect upon the completion of the volunteered-for maintenance tasks. Indeed, there appeared to be a slight decrease in the percent of tasks completed during the Officer Corrects condition, but the difference between the levels of performance during the two phases did not reach significance.

To further validate the effect of the Officer Corrects procedure upon the performance of morning activities, the laissez-faire approach in force during the initial base-line condition was reinstated on the fortieth day of the study. There was a general decline in the percent of these activities exhibited during the second base-line condition. The percent of volunteered-for tasks completed was again unaffected by the change in contingency associated with the morning activities. In this study, the application of correction's traditional punishment-oriented methods of institutional control was shown to be highly effective in managing inmate behavior. The effects of these procedures were, however, highly specific; that is, they motivated the performance of only those behaviors to which they were directly applied with little generalization to even closely related activities. These findings support the previous contention that the all-pervasive deployment of the punishment model in the American correctional system provides a self-reinforcing cycle. Since the consequences of the punishment are specific and since its effects are sudden and dramatic, it continuously provides its own justification for being continued.

It was suggested, however, that corrections reconsider the desirability of the wide-scale utilization of punishment-oriented control procedures on the grounds that their demonstrated effectiveness is negated because they are expected to induce undesirable behavioral reactions, such as resistance, counteraggression, and inaction, and their emotional or attitudinal components: anger, hostility, and resentment. This contention was also supported by the present study. The daily rate of behavioral incidents (acts of insubordination, fighting, etc., reflecting these general behavioral and emotional reactions) exceeded zero only twice during the seventeen days of the first base-line condition. There was a sharp increase in behavioral incidents when punitively oriented procedures were brought to bear upon the inmates of the cellblock. Incidents occurred on nearly half (eleven) of the twenty-three days during which the Officer Corrects condition was in effect. Following introduction of the second base-line condition (the reinstatement of the laissez-faire procedure), there was an obvious decrease in the occurrence of behavioral incidents. The incident rate exceeded zero on only six of the twenty-one days of this period, with no incidents recorded during the last ten days of the study.

The increase and decrease in behavioral incidents coincident with the introduction and termination, respectively, of the full range of traditional control procedures available to correctional personnel lend additional credence to the observation that the philosophies and practices of correctional institutions serve to exacerbate rather than remediate the tension and strife growing there.

The EMLC Token Economies

The EMLC's exploration of the feasibility of developing an alternative correctional-management regimen for adult offenders grew from the realization of the serious shortcomings of the existent model of institution management and the demonstrated effectiveness of the proposed alternative in related fields of correctional work. This exploration took the form of two token economies. The first EMLC token economy project (Milan et al., 1972), which was in operation for approximately 420 days, was limited to the inmates' off hours from work (predominantly agricultural field labor) between 6 and 8 A.M. and between 4:30 and 9:30 P.M. weekdays and between 6 A.M. and 9:30 P.M. weekends and holidays. Activities that earned tokens were restricted to those that occurred in the cellblock, and those activities for which the tokens could be exchanged were only those that could be controlled there. The token economy focused primarily upon those aspects of inmate performance of the morning activities of concern to custody personnel: arising at the appointed hour, making the bed, cleaning the area adjacent to the bed, and maintaining a presentable personal appearance. A secondary objective was to motivate participation and performance in a voluntary remedial-education program in operation evenings and weekends.

Tokens earned were exchangeable for: (1) access to the various reinforcing-event areas on the cellblock (the TV room, poolroom, lounge, etc.); (2) time away from the cellblock (and, as a function of this, access to events, such as weekend movies, athletics, etc., which were available in the remainder of the institution); and (3) items, such as soft drinks, snacks, and cigarettes, available from the token economy canteen operated by the project. The token economy itself was modeled after a checkbook banking system. Tokens in the form of "EMLC points" were credited to an inmate's account contingent upon performance of to-be-reinforced activities. In order to obtain a backup reinforcer, he was required to write and relinquish a check in the amount of the point cost of that activity or commodity. At the end of each day a new balance was derived for each participant based upon the balance he carried forward from the previous day and his earnings and expenditures on the current day.

Most outcome data were collected by a correctional officer assigned to the cellblock during the morning shift. He toured the cellblock as the inmates arose, recorded for each inmate the performance of the self-management skills and, during the token economy phase, informed the inmates whether or not their performance was acceptable and, if acceptable, told them the number of points he was crediting to their point account. Frequent reliability checks were made between the officer on duty and members of the EMLC staff; they typically agreed upon more than 90 percent of the joint observations. The effect of the token economy upon the targeted behaviors was dramatic. The daily percent of morning activities completed rose from less than 60 percent to 90 percent or better. Leisure-time participation in the remedial-education program was virtually nonexistent prior to the introduction of the token economy;

introduction of the token economy raised this to about 20 percent of the inmates each day. Supplementary procedures increased this figure to about 50 percent each day, with 80 percent of all inmates spending ten or more of their free-time hours in the education program each week. Based upon the success of this exploratory project, the scope of the token economy project was expanded during the second EMLC token economy to virtually all activities in which these inmates engaged, 24 hours a day, seven days a week.

The second EMLC token economy project, which lasted for 390 days, differed from the first EMLC token economy in two major ways. The most obvious difference was its expanded scope. The second token economy project called for a comprehensive regimen encompassing all aspects of inmate life, including time spent in the cellblock, as during the first project, plus performance on a half-day institutional work assignment and in a half-day education program. Second, the checkbook system of the first token economy was replaced by a punch-card system in the second token economy. A new card was issued to each inmate each day. As an inmate performed to-be-reinforced tasks, holes were punched in the card, and as points were expended, the area surrounding each punched hole was marked with a pen. Points unexpended at the end of the day were transferred as savings to the next day's card. The punch-card system had several advantages. It provided more tangible reinforcement than the checkbook system it replaced; it simplified book- and record-keeping; and it enabled the immediate determination of each inmate's balance, thereby reducing the likelihood that an inmate's expenditures would accidentally exceed his earnings.

The backup reinforcers were basically the same as those of the first EMLC token economy, with the relationship between the expected behaviors and the backup reinforcers also approximately the same. During the latter stages of the second token economy, a policy of "performance-contingent letters of recommendation" was instituted wherein inmates' requests for recommendations to various correctional and parole agents produced letters detailing the specifics of the areas under study and the inmates' levels of performance therein. The results of the second EMLC token economy were as promising as those of the first. Inmate performance improved in each of the three areas under study and was maintained at high levels throughout the duration of the token economy. In addition, these changes in performance occurred without the concomitant increase in behavioral incidents witnessed during the examination of the punishment model. It appears, then, that the principles of behavior modification in general, and the token economy in particular, are particularly appropriate for dealing with the management and motivation problems facing corrections. Moreover, they provide an alternative model by means of which correctional institutions unite the traditionally opposed goals of their custody and treatment personnel while avoiding the regressive side effects of the punishment model.

Validating Intervention Strategies

The efficacy of treatment procedures is a continuing concern of adherents to the behavior-modification approach. Care is taken to insure that the procedures developed and employed do, in fact, induce change in the behavior of target individuals. To do this, it must be demonstrated that (1) the expected change in behavior does occur and (2) the procedures employed are responsible for that change. The first of these two objectives is met by specifying or defining the behavior under study in objective terms to permit public (reliable) verification of its occurrence or nonoccurrence. Its frequency of occurrence is then recorded prior to and throughout the intervention period.

This "on-line" monitoring provides continuous feedback on the effects of treatment, thereby allowing the professional to determine, at any time, the status of the target individual. If progress is not as has been hoped for, it signals the necessity to intensify, change, or alter in some way the intervention procedures. This continuous monitoring of treatment effects in terms of each target-individual's progress toward objectively defined goals is unique to this particular approach to human behavior. Indeed, it may be its single most important advantage over alternative approaches, for it demands accountability *during* intervention as well as *after* intervention, the latter being the characteristic strategy of its alternatives.

If there is a change in behavior *during* the intervention period, it cannot yet be claimed with certainty that the observed change was a *result of* intervention. Individuals in general, and those who have been earmarked as troublesome in particular, are subject to a multitude of pressures and changes in general life conditions. It is always possible that changes occurring during intervention are a product of these happenings rather than the intervention procedures themselves. If this possibility is not ruled out, it is quite possible that ineffective or perhaps detrimental procedures will be advocated as effective and implemented on a broad scale solely because they have been accidentally associated with a change in behavior that itself was induced by some unobserved change in the target-individual's life condition. A variety of research strategies are available to those who wish to rule out this possibility (Sidman, 1960). All stem from the basic behavior-modification premise that behavior is *under the control* of its antecedents (setting conditions and discriminative stimuli) and consequences (the presentation or termination of positive and negative reinforcers).

The behavior of the target individual prior to intervention is attributed to the conditions in effect then. Similarly, the behavior observed during an intervention period is attributed to the conditions in effect then. It follows that a return to the conditions in effect prior to intervention (a discontinuation of the intervention conditions) will result in a return to the behavior seen prior to intervention. This is the rationale of the *ABA* or *reversal design* wherein the first A typically connotes the conditions in effect prior to intervention (the base-line period); the B connotes the intervention or treatment conditions; and the second A signifies a return to the conditions of the base-line period. The reversal design was employed to determine whether or not the improvement in the performance of the self-management skills seen in the first EMLC token economy was a result of the contingent relationship between EMLC points and behavior rather than other variables, such as the availability of small items from the token economy canteen or unknown changes in the institution itself. In this study, the EMLC points were first given on a noncontingent basis for a period of time (the first A condition); then awarded only when the to-be-reinforced behavior was performed (the B condition); and then again given on a noncontingent basis (the second A condition). Performance increased during the B condition and returned to its original level during the second A condition, convincing evidence that it was the contingent relationship between the behavior and the payoff that controlled the observed increase in performance. The B condition was reinstated following this demonstration and, as would be predicted, the high level of performance seen during the original B condition was recaptured. Additional alternations of the A and B conditions and related increases and decreases in levels of performance could be employed to add credence to this conclusion, for it is doubtful that uncontrolled changes in the institution would coincide with each planned change in the variables under study.

The reversal design is often impractical for one or more of three reasons: (1) the behavior under examination is critical (e.g., violent assault), and its reinstatement is undesirable; (2) once established, the behavior under study will be supported by the contingencies of reinforcement operative in the natural environment, thereby rendering the behavior irreversible; or (3) the object of the research itself is to develop strategies whereby the behavior under examination will come to be maintained by the contingencies of the natural environment when such was not the case prior to intervention. When one or more of these conditions is in effect, the *ABB/AAB* or *multiple base-line* procedure is used to validate intervention strategies. This procedure typically indicates that either the same behavior is being monitored in two similar settings or two similar behaviors are being monitored in the same setting. The value of the multiple base-line procedure is that it allows a direct comparison of the effects of intervention on a given behavior without having to return to the initial (base-line) condition at the end of the intervention. The B condition at the end of both the ABB and AAB sequences signifies that the conditions of intervention are continued in each following their introduction.

An expanded multiple base-line procedure was employed to validate the effects of the second EMLC token economy on behavior on the institutional farm, in the experimental cellblock, and in the half-day education program. After the initial levels of performance in these three areas were determined, the tokens were awarded on a contingent basis first on the institutional farm, then, after a period of time, in the experimental cellblock, and finally, after still another period of time, in the education program. The levels of performance increased first on the farm, coincident with the introduction of the performance-contingent payoff there; then in the cellblock, also coincident with the introduction of the contingency there; and finally in the education program, again also coincident with the change in contingency there. This improvement in performance and its subsequent maintenance in the three areas under examination as the intervention procedure was instituted and continued in each constitutes a more-than-adequate demonstration of the effectiveness of the EMLC's token economy procedures.

The programs of the criminal justice system may be subjected to three forms of analysis. The first involves an on-line determination of the effectiveness of operating procedures and their constant refinement, such as the development of more effective vocational-training procedures. The second consists of an analysis of the degree to which the operating procedures achieve specified terminal objectives, such as the placement of trainees in adequately paid training-related positions, and how this compares with the accomplishments of other programs. Finally, the enduring contributions of programs may be assessed via long-term follow-up studies, such as those that seek to determine rates of recidivism following different types of treatment. The research strategies that have been described in this section are the essence of the first level of analysis, and as such are logical precursors of the second and third levels of analysis. They allow the development of programs that most effectively meet their terminal objectives. The long-term evaluation of programs within this model is appropriate only when programs are meeting these objectives. Indeed, a program that cannot meet its terminal objectives is more appropriately discontinued than subjected to a costly follow-up evaluation. If, however, a program is meeting its terminal objectives but has failed to influence the long-term indicators of program success, it should not be considered a "failure." It is, after all, meeting those objectives that it was designed to meet. When a program successfully attains its terminal objectives but has no impact upon long-term indicators, such as recidivism, it is more appropriate to question the validity of the philosophy from which those terminal objectives were deduced than to brand the program itself a failure. Indeed, how can these guiding philosophies be better tested?

CONCLUSIONS

The objectives of this chapter have been to provide an introduction to the basic principles of behavior modification and to give an overview of how these principles may be applied in the solution of human problems of general concern to those in the criminal justice fields. The principles of behavior modification have yielded much more than a "bag of tricks," much more than a variety of procedures or strategies that one may call upon when faced with relatively simple problems of motivation and the like. Those who depict and employ behavior modification in such a manner have not yet grasped the significance of its origins in the continuously developing science of human behavior. The applicability of the principles of this science are broad, allowing the study of the full spectrum of human activity. As has been seen in this chapter, the basic principles of this science provide a common basis for analyzing and understanding such diverse phenomena as progress and outcome in psychotherapy and the manner in which current correctional practices contribute to the hostility and aggression of the inmate population. Once phenomena have been so analyzed, it becomes possible to employ our understanding of these principles to deal more effectively with the problems at hand. Additionally, the mastery of the principles and the techniques of their application by those in corrections will not only upgrade the quality of service they provide, but will also contribute to their flexibility, increasing both the variety of strategies interventionists can bring to bear upon a problem and the range of problems with which they may deal.

The principles that have been discussed in this chapter are "neutral"; that is, they can be as effective in instilling and maintaining antisocial tendencies and maladaptive behavior as they can be in instilling and maintaining prosocial tendencies and adaptive behavior. For this reason, every effort must be made to minimize or overcome the chance or accidental arrangement of environmental contingencies, for unplanned environments appear as likely to generate undesirable behavior as desirable behavior. In this sense, the ghetto environment may be viewed as "well designed," for it effectively instructs, models, shapes, prompts, and reinforces activities that the larger society wishes to discourage and has stigmatized as delinquent or criminal. Equally important, the short-term objectives and long-term effects of planned environments must also be compared, especially in the criminal justice field where the immediate needs of the system often are at odds with the long-range needs of the offender. Too many correctional institutions, with their emphasis upon obedience, passivity, and the punishment model, appear "well designed" to condition dependence, lack of initiative, and resentment, traits all would agree are maladaptive when viewed within the broader context of the offenders' eventual return to a competitive and demanding society. The proper application of the principles of behavior modification can guarantee the "success" of correctional programs. It is those who design such programs who must determine whether the program that has succeeded serves the correctional agency or the offender. For too long correctional programs have served the administrative ends of the system at the expense of the offender's readjustment in the community. Placed in the wrong hands, behavior modification could compound this disservice rather than remediate it.

As has been illustrated in this chapter, the application of the principles of behavior modification to the problems facing the criminal justice system has great potential. It is now clear that institutional programs can be devised that both reduce inmate-management problems and motivate performance in academic and vocational programs, while at the same time fostering individuality and encouraging planning and self-control. It is also apparent that community-based residential programs of the "halfway-house" variety can be more than the charade that most now are. They can teach the skills necessary for successful and productive living, and they can insure that the skills which are taught are practiced, refined, and reinforced *in vivo*. Finally, it has been demonstrated that changes can be made in the environment in which the offender lives or to which he will eventually return that either directly or indirectly strengthen pro-social behavior at the expense of the old antisocial behavior.

It is unreasonable to expect that the skills taught an inmate in the correctional institution will generalize to the community unless there is a programmed transitional phase to both insure that this will occur and to teach community skills that cannot be approximated in the institution. Institutions, through intensified training, can remediate deficiencies and expand skill repertoires, thereby providing the offender with additional options or choices. There is little, if anything, institutions themselves can do to guarantee that the offender will exercise these options once released. Similarly, it is too much to expect that a community program, which can capitalize upon these options, can succeed unless it is backed up by a complementary institutional program that provides the control necessary for intensive, short-duration training.

The ideal program would be one which included (1) supervision and training in the home or natural environment of the offender; (2) a community-based residential facility that provided both an alternative to an unacceptable home situation as well as a site in which a more structured behavior-change program could be operated and from which the full range of community activities of the offender could be monitored; and (3) an institutional program housed in a regional correctional center that provided intensive, short-term, remedial education, vocational instruction, and socialization training. The program would be fluid and dynamic. Offenders could move rapidly from component to component as predetermined criteria were met. Each offender would be under the care of a single supervisor from the time he first encountered the criminal justice system until the time he left it, thereby allowing the development of individualized, comprehensive, and continuous programming. The supervisor, in turn, would be responsible for case management, presiding over the movement of the offender to and from the various components of the system, and directing the activities of the specialists within each component. Such a program is, of course, far from becoming a reality. If such an ideal is to become an actuality, it will require that the criminal justice system embrace this new science of human behavior as the basis of its program operations and embark upon a restructuring of the correctional bureaucracy so continuity of treatment is truly feasible. It appears it is now time to begin approximating these ends.

REFERENCES

Akers, R. L.
    1973   Deviant Behavior: A Social Learning Approach. Belmont, Calif.: Wadsworth Publishing Co.
Atthowe, J., and L. Krasner.
    1968   "Preliminary report on the application of contingent reinforcement procedures (token economy) on a chronic psychiatric ward." Journal of Abnormal Psychology 73(February):37–43.
Ayllon, T., and N. H. Azrin.
    1968   The Token Economy: A Motivational System for Therapy and Rehabilitation. New York: Appleton-Century-Crofts.
Ayllon, T., and M. D. Roberts.
    1972   "The token economy: now," in W. S. Agras (ed.), Behavior Modification: Principles and Clinical Application. Boston: Little, Brown.

1973   The M.O.R.E. Project: First Year of Research and Operation. Atlanta: Georgia Department of Offender Rehabilitation.

Azrin, N. H., and W. C. Holz.
1966   "Punishment," in W. K. Honig (ed.), Operant Behavior: Areas of Research and Application. New York: Appleton-Century-Crofts.

Bailey, J. S., M. M. Wolf, and E. L. Phillips.
1970   "Home-based reinforcement and the modification of pre-delinquents' classroom behavior." Journal of Applied Behavior Analysis 3(Fall):223–233.

Bandura, A.
1969   Principles of Behavior Modification. New York: Holt, Rinehart & Winston.

Beker, J., and D. S. Heyman.
1972   "A critical appraisal of the California differential treatment typology of adolescent offenders." Criminology 10(May):3–59.

Birnbrauer, J. S., M. M. Wolf, J. D. Kidder, and C. Tague.
1965   "Classroom behavior of retarded pupils with token reinforcement." Journal of Experimental Child Psychology 2(June):103–107.

Black, A. H., and W. F. Prokasy (eds.)
1972   Classical Conditioning II: Current Theory and Research. New York: Appleton-Century-Crofts.

Boren, J. J., and A. D. Colman.
1970   "Some experiments on reinforcement principles within a psychiatric ward for delinquent soldiers." Journal of Applied Behavior Analysis 3(Spring): 29–38.

Brown, D. G.
1971   "Behavior analysis and intervention in counseling and psychotherapy," in H. C. Rickard (ed.), Behavioral Intervention in Human Problems. New York: Pergamon Press.

Burchard, J., and V. Tyler.
1965   "The modification of delinquent behavior through operant conditioning." Behavior Research and Therapy 2(April):245–250.

Clements, C. B., and J. M. McKee.
1968   "Programmed instruction for institutionalized offenders: contingency management and performance contracts." Psychological Reports 22(June):957– 964.

Cohen, H. L., and J. Filipczak.
1971   A New Learning Environment. San Francisco: Jossey-Bass.

Cohen, H. L., J. Filipczak, and J. Bis.
1967   CASE I: An Initial Study of Contingencies Applicable to Special Education. Silver Spring, Md.: Educational Facility Press-IBR.

Colman, A. D., and S. L. Baker.
1969   "Utilization of an operant conditioning model for the treatment of character and behavior disorders in a military setting." American Journal of Psychiatry 125(April):1395–1403.

Colman, A. D., and J. J. Boren.
1969   "An information system for measuring patient behavior and its use by staff." Journal of Applied Behavior Analysis 2(Fall):207–214.

Enslen, J. E.
1969   Contingency Management: Monetary Rewards for Progress Charts as Moti-

vators for Inmates Using Programmed Instruction. Elmore, Ala.: Rehabilitation Foundation (unpublished).

Eysenck, H. J.
1952   "The effects of psychotherapy: an evaluation." Journal of Consulting Psychology 16(February):319–324.
1966   The Effects of Psychotherapy. New York: International Science Press.

Franks, C. M.
1969   Behavior Therapy: Appraisal and Status. New York: McGraw-Hill.

Greenson, R. R.
1967   The Techniques and Practice of Psychoanalysis, vol. 1. New York: International Universities Press.

Harrison, S. I., and D. J. Carek.
1966   A Guide to Psychotherapy. Boston: Little, Brown.

Homme, L., P. C'de Baca, and L. Cottingham.
1968   "What behavioral engineering is." Psychological Record 18(Summer): 425–434.

Jeffery, C. R.
1971   Crime Prevention Through Environmental Design. Beverly Hills, Calif.: Sage Publications.

Jenkins, W. O., J. M. McKee, S. Jordan, and Z. M. Newmark.
1969   Contingent Monies and Learning Performances. Elmore, Ala.: Rehabilitation Research Foundation (unpublished).

Kanfer, F. H., and J. S. Phillips.
1970   Learning Foundations of Behavior Therapy. New York: Wiley.

Kantor, J. R.
1959   Interbehavioral Psychology. Revised Edition. Bloomington, Ind.: Principia Press.

Kassebaum, G., D. Ward, and D. Wilner.
1971   Prison Treatment and Parole Survival: An Empirical Assessment. New York: Wiley.

Krasner, L.
1970a   "Token economy as an illustration of operant conditioning procedures with the aged, with youth, and with society," in D. J. Lewis (ed.), Learning Approaches to Therapeutic Behavior Change. Chicago: Aldine.
1970b   "Behavior modification, token economies, and training in clinical psychology," in C. Neuringer and J. L. Michael (eds.), Behavior Modification in Clinical Psychology. New York: Appleton-Century-Crofts.

Lemere, F., and W. Voegtlin.
1950   "An evaluation of the aversion treatment of alcoholics." Quarterly Journal of Studies on Alcohol 11(June):199–204.

Lerman, P.
1968   "Evaluative studies of institutions for delinquents: implications for research and social policy." Social Work 13(July):55–64.

Lloyd, K. E., and L. Abel.
1970   "Performance on a token economy psychiatric ward: a two-year summary." Behavior Research and Therapy 8(February):1–9.

Milan, M. A., L. R. Hampton, M. C. Murphy, J. G. Rogers, R. L. Williams, and L. F. Wood.

1972   "The token economy as an alternative to 'traditional' adult correctional institutional control procedures." Paper presented at the eighteenth annual meeting of the Southeastern Psychological Association, Atlanta, Ga.

O'Leary, K. D., W. C. Becker, M. B. Evans, and R. A. Saudargas.
1969   "A token reinforcement program in a public school: a replication and systematic analysis." Journal of Applied Behavior Analysis 2(Spring):2–13.

Patterson, G. R., J. A. Cobb, and R. S. Ray.
1972   "A social engineering technology for retraining the families of aggressive boys," in H. E. Adams and I. P. Unikel (eds.), Issues and Trends in Behavior Therapy. Springfield, Ill.: Thomas.

Pavlov, I. P.
1941   Conditioned Reflexes and Psychiatry: Volume Two of Lectures on Conditioned Reflexes. Translated and edited by W. H. Gantt. New York: International Publishers.
1960   Conditioned Reflexes: An Investigation of the Psychological Activity of the Cerebral Cortex. Translated and edited by G. V. Anrep. New York: Dover Publications.

Phillips, E. L.
1968   "Achievement place: token reinforcement procedures in a home-style rehabilitation setting for pre-delinquent boys." Journal of Applied Behavior Analysis 1(Fall):213–223.

Phillips, E. L., E. A. Phillips, D. L. Fixsen, and M. M. Wolf.
1971   "Achievement place: modification of the behaviors of pre-delinquent boys within a token economy." Journal of Applied Behavior Analysis 4(Spring): 45–59.
1973   "Behavior shaping for delinquents." Psychology Today 7(June):74–79.

Prokasy, W. F. (ed.)
1965   Classical Conditioning: A Symposium. New York: Appleton-Century-Crofts.

Rachman, S.
1971   The Effects of Psychotherapy. New York: Pergamon Press.

Rachman, S., and J. Teasdale.
1969   Aversion Therapy and Behaviour Disorders: An Analysis. Coral Gables, Fla.: University of Miami Press.

Ramp, E. A., and B. L. Hopkins.
1971   "Foreword," in E. A. Ramp and B. L. Hopkins (eds.), A New Direction for Education: Behavior Analysis, vol. 1. Lawrence, Kan.: Department of Human Development.

Rehabilitation Research Foundation.
1968   Draper Projects Final Reports. Elmore, Ala.: Rehabilitation Research Foundation.

Schwitzgebel, R. K.
1964   Street Corner Research. Cambridge: Harvard University Press.
1971   Development and Legal Regulation of Coercive Behavior Modification Techniques with Offenders. Washington, D.C.: U.S. Government Printing Office.

Schwitzgebel, R. L., and D. A. Kolb.
1964   "Inducing behavior change in adolescent delinquents." Behavior Research and Therapy 1(February):297–304.

Sidman, M.
1960   Tactics of Scientific Research. New York: Basic Books.

Skinner, B. F.
  1938   The Behavior of Organisms: An Experimental Analysis. New York: Apple-
          ton-Century.
  1948   "Superstition in the pigeon." Journal of Experimental Psychology 38
          (April):168–172.
  1953   Science and Human Behavior. New York: Macmillan.
  1971   Beyond Freedom and Dignity. New York: Knopf.
Slack, C. W.
  1960   "Experimenter-subject psychotherapy; a new method of introducing inten-
          sive office treatment for unreachable cases." Mental Hygiene 44(April):238–
          256.
Smith, R. R., L. A. Hart, and M. A. Milan.
  1972   "Correctional officer training in behavior modification: an interim report."
          Proceedings of the One Hundred and First Annual Congress of Correction
          of the American Correctional Association. College Park, Md.: American
          Correctional Association.
Staats, A. W., and W. H. Butterfield.
  1965   "Treatment of nonreading in a culturally deprived juvenile delinquent: an
          application of reinforcement principles." Child Development 36(December):
          925–942.
Stuart, R. B.
  1970   Trick or Treatment: How and When Psychotherapy Fails. Champaign, Ill.:
          Research Press.
Tharp, R. G., and R. J. Wetzel.
  1969   Behavior Modification in the Natural Environment. New York: Academic
          Press.
Thorne, G. H., R. G. Tharp, and R. J. Wetzel.
  1967   "Behavior modification techniques: new tools for probation officers." Fed-
          eral Probation 31(June):21–27.
Toch, H.
  1970   "The care and feeding of typologies." Federal Probation 34(September):
          15–19.
Truax, C. B.
  1966   "Reinforcement and non-reinforcement in Rogerian psychotherapy." Jour-
          nal of Abnormal and Social Psychology 71(February):1–9.
Tyler, V. O., and G. D. Brown.
  1968   "Token reinforcement of academic performance with institutionalized de-
          linquents." Journal of Educational Psychology 59(June):164–168.
Ulrich, R., T. Stachnik, and J. Mabry (eds.)
  1966   Control of Human Behavior. Glenview, Ill.: Scott, Foresman.
  1970   Control of Human Behavior, vol. 2. Glenview, Ill.: Scott, Foresman.
Vallance, M.
  1965   "Alcoholism: a two-year follow-up study." British Journal of Psychiatry 111
          (June):348–356.
Whaley, D. L., and R. W. Malott.
  1971   Elementary Principles of Behavior. New York: Appleton-Century-Crofts.
Yates, A. J.
  1970   Behavior Therapy. New York: Wiley.

CHAPTER **21**

The Contemporary Jails
of the United States: An Unknown
and Neglected Area of Justice

Hans W. Mattick

University of Illinois at Chicago Circle

DEFINING THE PROBLEM

Everyone knows what a jail is until one begins to inquire into its definition. Almost any definition will include those custodial institutions found in most counties and cities that are usually known as "jails," which detain various classes of unconvicted persons, and where short sentences, usually less than a year, are served.[1]

But how much more might be included in a comprehensive study of the institutions that lie beneath, prior to, and feed into the state and federal felony correctional system? The fact that many cities do not have a "jail" as such, but rather a "House of Correction" (e.g., Chicago and Detroit) or "House of Detention" (e.g., New York City and Miami) shows the inadequacy of relying on nomenclature alone. The above description of the traditional jail suggests a functional approach. Specifically, we could define a jail as an institution for (1) general detention, and (2) the serving of short-term sentences.

This approach yields a broad continuum of institutions; at the lower end we have the police lockups, which may have only one cell and hold prisoners for only a few hours. In 1931, Hastings Hart estimated that there were 10,860 such "police jails and village lock-ups" in the United States (National Commission on Law Observance and Enforcement, 1931:327–29). At the other end of the spectrum there are various state-run facilities for short-term offenders, such as state farms, road camps, and women's

---

The contribution of Richard S. Frase, Research Assistant, Center for Studies in Criminal Justice, the Law School, The University of Chicago, is gratefully acknowledged.

1. Webster's *Third New International Dictionary* defines a *jail* as "a building for the confinement of persons held in lawful custody (as for minor offenses or some future judicial proceeding)." More interesting, however, is the etymology supplied: the Latin root is *cavea*, which means cavity, cage, or coop. The earliest references to jails in the United States that have come to our attention come from pre-Revolutionary colonial history: (1) in 1632, Boston ordered "a people pen to be constructed with all convenient speed"; and (2) the first Philadelphia jail, built late in 1682 or early in 1683, "was a cage some seven feet long and five feet wide" (Jordan, 1970:140–41). As we shall see, this is all too apt a description historically, and still exists in many locations today. Were we to define our subject as "public cages or coops," it is unlikely that we would leave out many jails.

reformatories. While the number of the latter is not great, they would add considerable diversity to the phenomenon.

Both of these extremes will be excluded, however, as well as a few specialized areas such as juvenile homes, which have traditionally been dealt with separately. State facilities will be excluded from this functional analysis, in part because they will be covered elsewhere in this book, but primarily because the central evil of the "jail problem," and, therefore, the natural focus for study and reform, is the fact of local administration. Once a penal institution becomes part of a state correctional system, it is more likely to receive the attention of professional administrators who may be concerned with the possibility of instituting corrections functions; it is less likely to be a patronage dumping ground; uniform standards may be formulated and enforced; specialization of institutions and initial and in-service training of personnel can be undertaken; economies of scale become possible; transfers of prisoners and personnel between institutions become easier; civil service and merit promotions can be introduced; and, in general, more financial, human, and other resources become available.

By stipulating that the jails in our definition be locally administered (i.e., by some political entity smaller than the state—usually the county or municipality), we not only put an upper limit on the subject matter, but also, we exclude the entire "jail" system of those states in which jails are state-run, namely, Vermont, Connecticut, Rhode Island, Delaware, and Alaska. All of these facilities, jails, farms, etc. will, however, occasionally provide useful comparisons to the locally run institutions under study.

Most jail studies agree in drawing the line where the state takes control (a notable exception is Robinson, 1944). There also appears to be substantial agreement that all juvenile facilities, whether for detention or correction, should be excluded, as well as hospital "security" wards and specialized treatment centers for alcoholics and drug addicts. At the lower extreme of the functional continuum, however, there is considerable definitional variation. In a study of Illinois jails (Mattick & Sweet, 1969:327), the lower limit for city jails was set by requiring either (1) that inmates be held for 48 hours or more at least once a month, or (2) that inmates be held 24 hours or more at least once a week. This resulted in 59 city "jails," and a total of 160 for the state (all 101 county jails were automatically included). Extrapolating on the basis of Illinois's proportion of the total number of counties in the United States yields a national figure of 4,748.[2]

Contrast the numbers obtained by applying other definitions. The National Council on Crime and Delinquency (NCCD) defined "local adult correctional institutions and jails" as facilities "where a convicted offender may serve thirty days or longer," and in 1966 estimated a national total of 3,473 such institutions (N.C.C.D., 1966:137–39). By this standard only about one-third of the Illinois jails surveyed would be covered. When the Law Enforcement Assistance Administration took its *National Jail Census* in the spring of 1970, it confined itself to "jails with 48-hour retention authority," and found a national total of 4,037, with only 108 in Illinois (L.E.A.A., 1971:1–9).

Considering Hart's figure of 10,860 "police jails and village lock-ups" (which did *not* include county jails) it seems clear that all the above investigators are excluding many if not most "lockups" from their definition, and differ only as to where they draw the line between "lockups" and "jails." There is good reason for continuing to exclude these lowest-level facilities. No doubt the lockup is an important element in the criminal justice system, both in terms of numbers and impact; it is often the offender's

---

2. Illinois has 102 counties, but one county used a neighboring county's jail.

first impression of a custodial institution, as well as the institution containing the highest percentages of innocent and inoffensive persons. It may include "drunk tanks" and police court "bull pens," both of which are far from ideal and greatly in need of reform. "A lasting impression may be created of law enforcement, the police, and correctional institutions in general; the person may become cooperative or antagonistic according to the facilities of the lock-up and the treatment received" (John Howard Association, 1963:5).

But already the diversity and magnitude of this phenomenon are overwhelming, and the available data on these facilities are almost nonexistent.[3] Furthermore, police lockups should probably be dealt with as a problem of police administration and reform. There will always be a need for temporary holding facilities prior to "booking," so much of what will be suggested here by way of jail reform would be impracticable at these levels (e.g., consolidation and regionalization; termination of control by law-enforcement personnel). The same is true for police court "bullpens."

It is not intended to sweep the problem of lockups under the rug in the way jails were systematically ignored when reform swept the state correctional systems. Much of what will be said about jail conditions, however, applies to lockups as well; indeed, considering their small size and high degree of transiency, they are likely to be far worse. The basic standards for detention facilities, at least in terms of separation and segregation of prisoner types, sanitation, and supervision, should apply equally to jails and lockups.

But for present purposes we will adopt the LEAA definition: facilities with "48-hour retention authority." Since the LEAA also used state control as the upper limit, their census of 4,037 jails gives the best current estimate of the total number of institutions we shall be considering. It is probably an underestimate, however, since the LEAA did not survey municipalities reporting less than 1,000 population in 1970. Since all 3,022 counties in the United States were automatically included, and there are probably at least 1,000 cities with jails meeting our definition,[4] it is clear that, after all, we are going to be talking primarily about county and city jails and, like most previous studies, excluding police lockups. So much for definitions.

According to the LEAA census, there were 160,863 inmates in American jails on March 15, 1970 (L.E.A.A., 1971:1).[5] But the significant thing about jails is their

---

3. Attempts to estimate the number of jail-like facilities in the United States by extrapolation are treacherous. In the text above, I conservatively estimated that there are 4,748 "jails" in the United States meeting the definition used in my Illinois survey (Mattick & Sweet, 1969). This figure results when we divide the 160 jails I found in Illinois by Illinois's percentage of the nation's total number of counties (102/3,022, or 3.37 percent). This method can be justified only if we also assume that Illinois is representative of the nation as a whole, and that assumption has some severe limitations.

Just how crude these estimates are is apparent when we compare two other methods of extrapolation, both based on the assumption that the ratio between Illinois and national totals by one jail definition is proportional to the ratio by another. According to the Illinois jails survey, there are 160 jails in Illinois. According to the LEAA, there are only 108 in Illinois, and 4,037 nationally; according to the NCCD, there are only 53, and 3,473 nationally. If the LEAA and the NCCD found 160 jails in Illinois, then, by their definitions and methods of extrapolation, they would find 5,974 and 10,419 jails nationally, respectively (108:160 as 4,037:5,974, and 53:160 as 3,473:10,419). Thus, three different methods of estimating the total number of American jails and lockups produce three completely different figures: 4,748, 5,974, and 10,400! Not very encouraging.

4. The NCCD (1966:139) reported 762 city jails holding sentenced prisoners for 30 days or more.

5. Compare the numbers in state and federal facilities: on December 31, 1967, there were 175,317 prisoners in state prisons, and 19,579 in federal prisons (U.S. Bureau of Prisons, 1969:8).

extremely high turnover rate, due to short detentions and sentences, transfers, releases on bail, etc. On the other hand, in urban jurisdictions where there may be a multiplicity of complex cases, some persons may be held in jails for long periods of time pending the resolution of complicated legal proceedings. So, what we really want to know is, how many human beings pass through these institutions, say, in a year? Or, to put it in convenient statistical terms, how many jail commitments are there every year, and about how many represent the same individuals going through the jail system more than once?

The proportion of jail commitments representing persons committed before in the same year is probably at least one-sixth, and may be as high as one-third. The actual number of persons passing through American jails in a year is at least one million, and may be four million, men, women, and children. This is the population equivalent of a very large city, or a medium-sized state, and is at least four times the number who annually pass through state and federal prisons combined.

The vast majority of jail inmates have either been charged with or convicted of minor crimes.[6] They may, however, also be charged with or convicted of the most serious kinds of offenses, for the jail is the entry point and way station for all kinds of persons being processed by the criminal justice system. The most common legal distinctions among offenses divide them into ordinance violations, misdemeanors, and felonies. Such a simple classification of offenses, however, should not be mistaken for a classification of offenders, nor does it tell us very much about the actual criminal behavior of most jail inmates. The offense with which a person may be charged and the offense for which a person may be tried are complex functions of many factors. It may depend upon the discretion of the charging authorities (the police or the prosecutor) who may, for example, use the charge of drunkenness and that of disorderly conduct arbitrarily and interchangeably. It may depend upon the anticipation or actual outcome of negotiation in the system of plea bargaining. It may depend upon the availability of evidence or witnesses to sustain a conviction. If the authorities anticipate that a more serious charge supported by weak evidence may be bargained down to a lesser charge in exchange for a plea of guilty, the charge to be lodged against an offender will be determined tactically. Moreover, a criminal who is pursuing an active criminal career may commit a felony one week and a misdemeanor the next; what he will be charged with is a function of the time at which his career was interrupted by the fact of his arrest. For these reasons, a classification of offenses should never be confused with a classification of offenders.

The jail population is the most heterogeneous in any residential institution. It may be classified and stratified in many ways:

1. Demographically, it includes males and females, adults and juveniles.

2. Jurisdictionally, it may include city, county, state, and federal prisoners.

3. Legally, it may include both civil and criminal offenders, as well as persons held as material witnesses.

4. Among the criminal cases there will be ordinance violators, misdemeanants, and felons.

5. In terms of the judicial process, it includes both the unsentenced and the sentenced; persons awaiting trial, serving out fines or sentences, or awaiting some postconviction procedure.

---

6. There are at least three major types of offenders who are more likely to be found in jail than in state and federal prisons: the first offender, the chronic petty offender (especially the "revolving-door drunk," who may have been in jail dozens of times before), and the occasional petty offender with one or two prior arrests.

6. It will include persons sentenced to a few days for drunkenness, ordinance violators serving out a small fine for a traffic offense, misdemeanants serving up to one year, felons serving up to life sentences who are being held in jail during a postconviction hearing, and persons sentenced to death awaiting transfer to the place of execution.

7. From the standpoint of criminal sophistication, it will include first offenders, situational offenders, occasional offenders, professional criminals, and hard-core, multiple recidivists.

8. It will include the essentially healthy as well as those who are physically and mentally ill.

9. Finally, it will include a miscellaneous collection of individuals being held for a variety of authorities: probation and parole violators, persons wanted in other jurisdictions, and even simple lodgers or transients who have no place else to spend the night.

In short, the jail is a major intake center not only for the entire criminal justice system, but also a place of first or last resort for a host of disguised health, welfare, and social problem cases. The latter consist, for the most part, of a large number of highly vulnerable or treatable cases for whose protection and improvement society may have expressed a deep concern, but for whom no other treatment facilities have been provided: drunks, drug abusers, the mentally disturbed, and the homeless indigent.

While poverty alone may not be a cause of crime, it contributes directly to the number of persons who are held in jail. Beginning with arrest, the person who is poor, homeless, and friendless is more likely to be arrested than the person of social and economic means. After arrest, it is again the person without resources who remains in jail awaiting trial while those who can pay either forfeit collateral or post bail, and those with connections in the community may be released on their own recognizance. Indeed, the latter offender may not even be arrested, but rather may be given a summons to appear in court, although this is rare.

When it comes to the trial, the poor man is more likely to receive no legal counsel at all, or else be assigned counsel (often young and inexperienced) or the public defender (often remote and overworked). Some studies (e.g., Silverstein, 1965:20–33, 53–57) have shown that public defenders and assigned counsel tend to plead their clients guilty more often, and that in all cases, these clients tend to be convicted more often and receive longer prison sentences. Whether this is due to the ineffectiveness of counsel or to the indigency factors leading to appointment in the first place, it is clear that the poor are getting the worst of it, and, once again, are more likely to be confined in jail. Often, the sentencing judge has no alternative resource at his disposal, there being no reliable friends, employer, or other treatment facility to handle cases that really do not belong in jail. And, of course, if a fine is assessed, the poor man is more likely to "lay out" his fine in jail.[7]

Thus, the jail, in addition to housing persons accused and convicted of crime, also serves as the modern equivalent of the poorhouse and charity ward. The vast majority of its inmates are poor, minority groups are overrepresented, and often the inmates are people in need of special attention or temporary care, for society's protection as well as their own. The legal charges lodged against these latter cases serve to mask the essential social and economic character of a large part of the jail problem. Many jail inmates are really disguised health and welfare cases that require some other mode of help or treatment. Moreover, within a few weeks or months, the overwhelming majority

---

7. But in *Tate* v. *Short* [401 U.S. 395, 398(1971)] the Supreme Court found the practice of jailing for *involuntary* nonpayment of fines to be an unconstitutional denial of equal protection to the poor (see p. 827).

of persons confined in jail will be released to return to the community. What happens then? As we shall see, educational, vocational, and prerelease counseling resources and follow-up measures are almost nonexistent for jail inmates, so it is not surprising that many return to jail before too long. The recidivism rate for jail inmates is, perhaps, as high as 75 percent, as compared to the overall rate of about 60 percent for all correctional institutions combined.[8] Thus, the overall impact of jail confinement is largely negative.

It is possible to speak knowledgeably of the "American jail" because what information we have is so consistent: the jails everywhere are inadequate. Perhaps a few local variations have escaped our notice. But the student of jails quickly discovers that, historically, the "jail problem" has not been a subject of professional disagreement over the basic details of jail conditions, nor even of what to do about them; on the contrary, there has been remarkable agreement (Queen, 1920; Fishman, 1923; Robinson, 1944; Alexander, 1957). Modern survey techniques may make it possible to begin to objectify and quantify the conclusions reached long ago by personal experience and anecdotal evidence. It remains to be seen whether figures speak louder than rhetoric.

A HISTORICAL NOTE ON JAILS

The jail as a multipurpose penal institution, housing both detention populations awaiting trial or some other disposition, and convicted prisoners serving out sentences as punishment, is a relatively recent historical development. Indeed, insofar as the historical record serves to instruct us—and the record is vague or silent on much that pertains to jails—jail-like facilities served primarily as places of detention until the late eighteenth century, when the sentence-serving function was added for reasons that are difficult to determine. At a still later time, there was some tendency toward specialization in the local penal institutions: some served the detention function and others served the sentence function. But this development was fully realized in only a few of the larger jurisdictions, as cities or metropolitan areas came to require more than one jail to house their local penal populations. In general, the vast majority of jails in the United States today house both detention and sentenced populations and, insofar as there are active currents of social change that affect the historical character of jails, the change is in the direction of avoiding jailing altogether through such alternative dispositions as probation or work-release programs.

The jail as a place of detention traces its origins to the earliest forms of civilization and government. Wherever the chief or other effective governmental authority was able to exercise the power or right to impose punishment, a concomitant necessity was to provide or build holding places until the punishment could be imposed or carried out. Unscalable pits, dungeons, suspended cages, and sturdy trees to which prisoners

---

8. The determination of recidivism rates is complex. If we want to know how many released prisoners subsequently commit crimes, we need a prospective study, but very few are available. Instead, we have many studies of the "failure population" already in prison or police custody. Such studies tend to overestimate recidivism. Furthermore, even subsequent arrest or conviction statistics do not measure the actual amount of crime, since not all those arrested are guilty, and not all the guilty are arrested, let alone convicted. Finally, most studies are done with state and federal prisoners, whereas we are presently concerned with the jail population for which recidivism rates are probably higher, due to the nature of the offenses typically involved.

Despite the methodological problems, the data we have are fairly consistent: the overall recidivism rate at the arrest level is about 60 percent (cf. Glueck & Glueck, 1937:11; F.B.I., 1951: 112, 1970:39; President's Commission, 1967a:1).

were chained pending trial are some of the predecessors of the jail. The prototype of the modern jail, as a local governmental institution in the English-speaking countries, has been traced to the year 1166 when Henry II ordered the construction of jails (Barnes & Teeters, 1951:460). At an early date the common-law sheriff, as chief executive officer of the county or shire, became the ex officio jailer and had the right to the custody and control of the county jail (Corpus Juris Secundum, Prisons, §8). The early American settlers brought this English system of county government to the New World with them, and established the earliest American jails under the control of the sheriff or a marshal. The historical tenacity of this early import is evident in the fact that this is still the prevailing practice in most states today.

City jails in the United States, and in England as well, were a later development, were less uniform in function and manner of governmental control, and tended to fall, almost by default, under the jurisdiction of law-enforcement agencies. As a logical implication of the power to arrest, the police needed a place of temporary detention where the accused could await trial, and later, upon conviction, transportation to the county jail or state prison. As cities grew in size, however, these places of temporary detention, through crescive processes of their own accretion of functions, grew into full-fledged city jails holding both detention and sentenced populations. Since this development took place at different times and in varying degrees, but mainly in the larger cities, it is, in some places, still an emergent historical process.

The changing function of the county jail from a place of general detention only to the mixed function of detention and incarceration of sentenced prisoners, who, for the most part, are misdemeanants, is also a crescive process of accretion with a clouded history. To begin with, the practice of imprisonment as punishment is fairly recent. Until the end of the eighteenth century, nearly all punishment was corporal in nature. For serious offenses the punishments were whipping, branding, mutilation, and death; for lesser offenses the punishment was some form of public humiliation like the ducking stool, the stocks, and the pillory (Barnes & Teeters, 1951:343–47; 371–80). Prisoners were sometimes sentenced to confinement in irons, but imprisonment for debt and for religious or political crimes was more common. In sixteenth century England, incident to the Enclosure Acts, which drove many people off the land and into the cities, local governments developed a new kind of penal institution variously called the workhouse, house of correction, or reformatory. These institutions were used as an alternative to corporal punishment for such common offenses as vagrancy, drunkenness, prostitution, and juvenile delinquency. Since similar social upheavals with similar consequences were taking place on the continent, these new forms of penal institutions spread to Europe in the seventeenth and eighteenth centuries and were carried to America by the English and others. In the history of American penology, however, these institutions are more accurately regarded as the forerunners of the American penitentiary movement of the late eighteenth and early nineteenth centuries, rather than as the direct ancestor of the county jails (Encyclopedia of the Social Sciences, 1934:58; Barnes & Teeters, 1951:381–98; Burns, 1971:10).

The Quaker colonies of Pennsylvania and West Jersey were the earliest American experimenters in penology. During the period 1681 to 1718 they had already attempted to substitute imprisonment for corporal punishment. But once the colonists had won independence, the process of penal reform was greatly accelerated. In part, as a reaction to their earlier English and European experience, combined with the influence of Enlightenment thinkers and the leadership of the Quakers, the newly independent Americans began to formulate more humane criminal codes (Barnes & Teeters, 1951:380). The number of crimes punishable by death was sharply reduced, and the penalty for the vast majority of crimes, large and small, was a fine or imprisonment. As a corollary to these law reforms, the separate states soon built their own state-operated penal facilities for the more serious offenders, and thus the modern "prison" was born. The minor offenders continued to be sent to the preexisting county and city jails that had, for the most part, lost their more serious offenders to the new prisons. Thus, the jails of the United States preceded the prison system, but received their unique, and largely contemporary, character as a residual function of a larger movement of legal and penal reform.

It is interesting to speculate, however, just why the states chose to take responsibility only for the more serious offenders, the "felons," whose crimes were previously punishable by death, while the minor offenders, previously punished by whipping, mutilation, and humiliation, were incarcerated with debtors and arrestees in the local jails. No historian of penology has, to our knowledge, addressed this question. Perhaps the reasons were too obvious to require historical documentation. First, it should be noted that jails, although they were as dirty and wretched then as now, were not yet generally overcrowded (Burns, 1971:16). Since they were there, they were available to receive the new subclass of minor offenders.

Second, the local jailing of debtors, drunks, vagrants, and prostitutes served as a precedent. (Indeed, the houses of correction in England had merged with the jails by the middle of the eighteenth century [Barnes & Teeters, 1951:460–61; Corpus Juris Secundum, Prisons, §8], and these combined institutions *may* have provided the actual model for the development of the modern American jail, although such direct cultural transmission of institutions is rare in history.) On the other hand, no one had ever tried to hold large numbers of serious offenders for any length of time, let alone put them to work, so a new, sturdily built and socially isolated structure may have seemed in order for them.

Third, the theory of reform through solitary confinement and penitence, from which the term *penitentiary* derives, may have seemed a little unrealistic in the case of minor criminals. Their sentences were too short to effect repentance, or their crimes were so petty that hard labor and solitude were deemed unnecessary to produce reformation. In those days no one (except, perhaps, the Quakers) thought in terms of rehabilitation for minor offenders; imprisonment for them was probably seen as direct retribution or deterrence, for which it was unnecessary to provide more than simple custody in the most convenient facility, the existing local jail.

Finally, it is possible that, outside of the former Quaker colonies of Pennsylvania and New Jersey, the attempt to rehabilitate felons under state control was secondary to the exploitation of inmate labor, so that they could earn their own keep, or even show a profit (Barnes & Teeters, 1951:376, 384, 412, 413).[9] The greater transiency and shorter sentences of minor offenders would jeopardize the economic efficiency of the new state prison systems. The local officials were simply saddled with the economically least attractive part of the penal system. By the time of the early twentieth century, however, through the reforms of the prison contract-labor laws, the opportunities for profiteering on inmate labor all but disappeared.

After American jails had evolved into combination detention and correction institutions, early in the nineteenth century, they changed very little except that a few categories of prisoners were removed to other facilities from time to time. In the 1820s the

---

9. It is said that the eventual triumph in America of the "Auburn System" of separate confinement and congregate labor over the "Pennsylvania System" of separate confinement *and* labor was due in large part to the economic advantages of the former (Tyler, 1944:280).

juvenile reformatory movement began (Robinson, 1944:3), though it was not widely adopted for some time (Tyler, 1944:287–90). The practice of jailing for debt also began to wane at this time; yet in some states it continued to be legal into the twentieth century (Tyler, 1944:283–85; Barnes & Teeters, 1951:463–64). Later in the nineteenth and early twentieth centuries, hospitals for the criminally insane began to appear, and state farms and adult reformatories began to receive a few of the misdemeanants previously sentenced to jail (Robinson, 1944:3). The developing practice of probation also began to divert a sizable number of misdemeanants from the jails to community supervision. But, as we shall see, the vast majority of sentenced misdemeanants continued to be sent to local city and county jails, along with detainees of all kinds.

CONTEMPORARY JAIL CONDITIONS

Despite the individual differences between them, we shall attempt to describe the "typical" American jail or jails, as well as the major variations from the norm, in terms of who controls them, who works in them, what kinds of prisoners are held, how the prisoners are treated, and how much all this costs. As previously noted, major methodological problems exist in attempting to do this owing to the small number of comprehensive jail surveys, and to the poor record-keeping practices followed in the jails surveyed. Indeed, a diligent search of the literature has revealed only one state in the entire nation whose jails have been individually visited, rated, and comprehensively studied, namely, Illinois (Mattick & Sweet, 1969).[10]

It would not be unfair to utilize Illinois as a fairly representative state: it has a very large metropolitan area, Chicago; it has extensive downstate rural areas; and its jails are neither very new nor very old, relative to the national average. Moreover, what data we have on the jails of other states tend to confirm this argument. Finally, it is fair to assume that "the unknown" in this field may be worse than the known; state and local authorities with something to boast about usually do, and this inherent bias tends to balance the muckraking bias of yellow journalists, pseudoreformers, and political opportunists who exploit poor jail conditions for personal advantage.

In what follows, the reader must be constantly mindful of the paucity of reliable data about jails. One caveat: much of what we do *know* to be true about specific jails and states will probably test the credibility of an uninformed public that usually assumes conditions are much better than those empirically found by specific investigations.

Variations in Organization and Control of Jails

The "typical" jail is a relatively small institution with less than twenty-five cells, built between 1880 and 1920, located in a small town, frequently the county seat of a rural

---

10. The study by the California Board of Corrections (1970) is nearly as comprehensive as the Illinois study, with the following differences: (1) city jails were not included, and the selection of which county institutions to include was apparently left up to the sheriffs, chiefs of police, and superintendents to whom the questionnaires were mailed (p. 8); (2) not all institutions included were personally visited and rated by the surveyors (pp. 8–9); (3) many details of everyday jail operation and treatment of prisoners (such as record-keeping, sanitary facilities, segregation and supervision, food services, and visiting arrangements) were not covered. On the other hand, the California study provides useful information on local and regional administrative variations, and evaluates the available work programs in somewhat greater detail than the Illinois survey. The Illinois study found few work programs to evaluate.

county. There are, of course, some huge urban jails, like the Tombs in New York City and the Cook County Jail and House of Correction complex in Chicago. The large urban jails are disproportionately significant because they represent less than 10 percent of all physical jail buildings but handle more than half of all jail prisoners and tend to be chronically overcrowded. The 90 percent or more of smaller jails are frequently under-utilized and suffer the neglects of disuse and disinterest. The inmates of the "typical" jail consist mainly of three classes of prisoners: (1) detainees awaiting trial, (2) misdemeanants sentenced for a year or less, and (3) a variety of transients awaiting transfers or actions by some authority, including lodgers. The typical jail is operated by a county sheriff or his designated deputy, or a city chief of police or his designee. It is financed by a county board or a city council, and is occasionally inspected by a local grand jury, a judge, health and fire officials, or a visiting committee. Some local jails are used by federal authorities to hold federal prisoners in special sections that meet federal standards of detention. The federal inspection of such jails does not extend to the conditions under which local prisoners are held, but it may have some influence on general conditions. It is already clear that there are wide variations from any artificially derived norm used to describe the "typical" jail, and these variations are also typical both within and between states.

To begin with, not all jails are used to hold detainees and sentenced misdemeanants. In North Carolina, for example, most misdemeanants with sentences over 30 days are sent to state-run prison camps (North Carolina Jail Study Commission, 1969:4).[11] Thus the local jails in North Carolina serve primarily as detention facilities. In Illinois, except for Cook County, the division is made at 60 days, with most misdemeanants sentenced for longer periods being sent to the state farm at Vandalia (Ill. Rev. Stat., ch. 118).[12] A number of other states also use state farms or road camps for misdemeanants, sometimes sending convicted felons to the same facility.[13]

Second, states without centralized misdemeanant institutions sometimes have separate, locally run institutions for sentenced misdemeanants. In Massachusetts, sentenced prisoners are sent to the houses of correction, although in all but one case these facilities are combined with the local jail and separation of prisoners is not always maintained (Massachusetts Governor's Committee, 1965:10). In New York state there are five upstate counties with separate "county penitentiaries." Except in the case of jail overflow, these facilities are used exclusively for sentenced prisoners; apparently there is no minimum sentence for these "penitentiaries." The Unified Department of Correction for the five counties comprising New York City also maintains separate institutions for sentenced and detained prisoners (New York State Commission, 1966:11–19, 51). A few other states and cities also operate separate, locally run institutions for sentenced prisoners.

---

11. The rationale for the 30-day division is that the state rehabilitative programs require at least a month to have some constructive effect (North Carolina Jail Study Commission, 1969:10).

12. The state farm was not included in our Illinois jails' survey because it is state-run (Mattick & Sweet, 1969:271). The average daily population at Vandalia was almost 1,000, while the average daily population of the 160 jails included in the survey was 4,996; thus, the state farm has a major impact on the jail situation in Illinois.

13. In 1970 the Georgia Legislature provided that "misdemeanors of a high and aggravated nature" may only be punished by fine or confinement in a *county* institution [Ga. Code Ann., §27–2506.1 (Cum. Supp. 1970)]. This may be a rare instance of public recognition that a jail sentence is harsher than commitment to a state prison!

A third major variation in sentencing practices and correctional organization is that not all sentenced prisoners in local institutions are short-term misdemeanants. Pennsylvania is probably unique in sending large numbers of long-term felons to local county "prisons" and jails,[14] but there are several other states and local jurisdictions that routinely use jails and other county facilities for prisoners with sentences over one year. Furthermore, insofar as there is any significance left to the felony-misdemeanor distinction, it should be noted that many felonies, which usually result in a sentence of over 1 year in a state prison, are *alternatively* punishable by a sentence of 1 year or less in the local jail [e.g., Ill. Rev. Stat., ch. 38, §9.3(c)(2)(1967), reckless homicide; Cal. Penal Code, §489, grand theft]. But in the vast majority of states and localities, the jails hold both detainees and sentenced prisoners, and the latter are almost always misdemeanants serving terms of one year or less.

When it comes to control, there is much greater uniformity. In the "typical" county the jail is run by the sheriff or his appointed jailer; all deputy sheriffs, guards, and other subordinate personnel are appointed by the sheriff and serve at his pleasure; and all funds for the operation of the jail must be approved by the county board or other governing body.

The consequences of such a system are not surprising. Jail personnel are patronage workers, and a large proportion change office as often as the sheriff, who is usually an elected official. The operation of the jail tends toward its detention function rather than any correction function, since it is operated and staffed almost exclusively by law-enforcement officers, most of whom have major outside police duties, which they prefer. When it comes time for the sheriff to submit his budget to the county board, he is more likely to allocate scarce dollars to his law-enforcement activities than to the jail, since the former are politically more valuable for career advancement. Similarly, when it comes time for the board to vote the money to run the jail, there is a tendency to favor more politically attractive institutions, such as schools and hospitals; as one sheriff, consistently frustrated in his efforts to obtain a modest budget increase, put it, "There are no votes in jail" (New York State Commission, 1966:43).[15] Finally, the division of responsibility for the jail among a variety of executive, legislative, and judicial officials, though justified by the usual considerations of "checks and balances," lends itself to incredible buck-passing; frequently no one can be found who is personally responsible for jail conditions, especially when the sheriff delegates his custodial functions to a jailer or warden.

An excellent example of this, though placed in an analogous city context, occurred in Gary, Indiana. When Gary jail conditions were once again deplored by the city council, the health commissioner, and a local judge, the chief of police pleaded that he was not the custodian: "I'm a tenant there myself." (!) The public safety director

---

14. On February 20, 1964, there were 4,410 sentenced prisoners in the county prisons and jails of Pennsylvania. Of these, 44 percent were sentenced for 1 year or less; 24 percent were sentenced for more than 1 but less than 2 years; and 32 percent were sentenced for 2 years or more (Pennsylvania Commission, 1965:10). Most of these long-term prisoners were held in thirteen county facilities that had been given special statutory authorization. This authorization was repealed in 1966, and thereafter, prisoners with sentences of from 6 months to 5 years were only to be sent to county jails approved by the state Bureau of Corrections, or to a state facility [Pa. Stat. Ann., title 61, §460.4, 460.5 (Cum. Supp. 1970)]. The same law gave the governor the power to require that all prisoners with sentences over 5 years be sent to state-run institutions, and he has exercised the power.

15. The possibility of permitting the jail population to register and vote in local elections is discussed on p. 840.

claimed that the "head custodian" of the jail (paid $7,800 a year) was autonomous, and had "all the rights of a department head." But no one could find the new head custodian. Politically ambitious city councilmen tried to lay the blame on the mayor, an option unavailable to board members in counties and cities without an executive officer. Finally, the public safety director succeeded in handing future responsibility to the reluctant police chief (Robinson, 1971). The only common interest of such officials is to keep things quiet, divert public attention, and maintain political advantage.

There are a few variations on this theme. Some counties have civil-service merit systems for sheriff's personnel, which may be the only advantage to using what are essentially law-enforcement personnel in the jail. In Kentucky, the county jailer is a separate elected official in all counties (except those containing a city over 100,000), and has exclusive custody and control of the jail [Ky. Rev. Stat. Ann., ch. 71 (1969)]. In those states and localities that operate separate institutions for detained and sentenced prisoners, the sheriff sometimes controls only the former.[16] In a few counties, mostly those including large cities, the jails and workhouses are under a unified department of correction, or the board of welfare.[17]

The organization and control of the "typical" city's jail probably displays much less uniformity, considering the wide variety of forms of municipal government, e.g., mayor-council, commission, council-manager, and all the hybrid forms of these basic types (Maddox & Fuquay, 1966:469–88). We must say "probably" because, at present, the possible numbers and types of city jail control are unknown, short of a comprehensive survey on the subject. Since municipalities are commonly given broad powers to legislate and organize their police functions (Stason & Kauper, 1959:105–11), there is no limit to the possible variations. The most common arrangement, especially in smaller cities, gives the chief of police custody and responsibility for the jail and its inmates, most of whom are usually detainees awaiting trial or transfer to the county jail.

In the five counties comprising New York City there are five detention institutions, two sentenced institutions, and one combination institution, all under the commissioner of correction, who is appointed by the mayor. The department also has responsibility for three hospital security wards, and for all criminal court "bullpens," while the police department retains responsibility for temporary and overnight detention (New York State Commission, 1966:50–52). In Chicago, the House of Correction has been merged with the Cook County Jail into the Cook County Department of Corrections, which is "under the direction" of the county sheriff. A five-man board, appointed by the sheriff, with the mayor and president of the county board each nominating two members, may "recommend the policy of the Department," but is not

---

16. In five upstate New York counties the separate penitentiaries are controlled by a superintendent or corrections commissioner, appointed by "county officials" (New York State Commission, 1966:47). In California, four counties operate institutions for sentenced inmates that are not under the sheriff. San Diego has a separate department of honor camps for all sentenced inmates, while the sheriff runs a jail for all presentenced inmates and a few trusties. In Riverside and Kern counties, the road department administers road camps and the sheriff handles presentenced and maximum-security facilities. In Tulare County, the sheriff runs the county jail and the chief probation officer administers an industrial road camp (California Board of Corrections, 1970:15–16). County "penitentiaries" in Essex and Hudson counties, New Jersey are controlled by the county board (Robinson, 1944).

17. St. Louis County's new charter, passed in 1968, places the responsibility for the county jail in the county department of welfare (Mann & Taedter, 1968:3).

to have "administrative or executive duties."[18] An executive director, "to act as the chief executive and administrative officer of the Department," is nominated by the county board, appointed by the sheriff, and must be approved by the judges of the circuit court of the county. A measure of financial independence is suggested by the provision that "the County Board must appropriate and provide funds for the necessary ordinary and contingent cost incurred by the office of the Sheriff in the performance of its powers, duties and functions under this Act." In short, Chicago is now almost completely relieved of responsibility for sentenced and most detained prisoners, though it still operates its own police lockups and court bullpens [Ill. Rev. Stat., ch. 125, §201–215 (Cum. Supp. 1970)].

Before leaving the subject of local control and organization of jails, we must take note of one other arrangement: cooperation between adjoining counties. Many states have laws enabling such cooperation but, since they are not mandatory, they are seldom implemented. Nevertheless, there are basically two forms of cooperation: contracting for the keeping of prisoners in the existing jails of another county, and joint operation of camps or jails by two or more counties, sharing expenses and control.

The contract arrangement is an old one, and is sometimes used for certain classes of prisoners, such as women, children, and mental cases, for whom adequately segregated facilities are frequently not available in smaller jails.[19] Counties having special institutions for sentenced prisoners sometimes receive prisoners from surrounding counties, for example, the Allegheny County Workhouse (Pennsylvania Commission, 1965:9).

Joint county camps and jails are much less common than contract arrangements, since they usually require special statutory authorization, and the loss of some control over jail administration, staffing, and inmate labor. Most statutes usually provide for a governing board of directors, with representatives appointed by or composed of members of the constituent county boards, and with all expenses to be apportioned among the participating counties.[20] A few statutes are worded more broadly, giving the counties involved considerable freedom to decide how to administer their combined efforts.[21] There is reason to believe that the latter arrangement is even less conducive to cooperation, since it leaves the local officials involved free to argue and worry about

---

18. The beginnings of this "policy" are spelled out in the statute: the sheriff is to establish "diagnostic, classification and rehabilitation services and programs," and "whenever feasible, separate detention and commitment facilities" [Ill. Rev. Stat., ch. 125, §203 (c) (d) (Cum. Supp. 1970)]. It took thirteen years of political negotiation to achieve a unified department of corrections for Cook County (cf. Mattick, 1957, 1960).

19. In California, as of April, 1970, twenty-one of the fifty-eight counties were participating in formal intercounty agreements; eight counties were receiving prisoners, and thirteen were sending. Another six counties had informal arrangements for the transportation and confinement of certain classes of prisoners, mainly women and juveniles (California Board of Corrections, 1970:29–31). Ashman (1969:17) reports that out of fifteen "representative" states surveyed, only two, Florida and Virginia, used the contract arrangement.

20. E.g., Cal. Penal Code, §4050–4054 (joint county jails), §4200–4204 (joint county road camps); Minn. Stat. Ann., §641.261–641.263 (Cum. Supp. 1970); Wash. Rev. Code Ann., §26.63.–280.

21. E.g., N.C. Gen. Stat., §153–57.7 gives unlimited authority to establish "district confinement facilities"; Ore. Rev. Stat., §190.003–190.004 gives general authorization for intergovernmental cooperation, which may be accomplished by "consolidation" of departments, joint provision of administrative personnel, joint facilities, operation of facilities by one county for others, or any combination of these.

who will have greater control (University of North Carolina Institute of Government, 1967:23 cites this as a major reason for not using the 1933 authorization for district jails). Yet, to my knowledge, none of the more restrictive authorizing statutes has ever been used, either.

"Inspection, Supervision, and Standards"

A second major aspect of local administration and control of jails is so-called inspection. Traditionally, and even today in almost every state, the county grand jury is supposed to have the primary responsibility for reporting on jail practices and maintaining decent jail conditions (Spain, 1964). In some states this duty is mandatory (e.g., Alabama, Illinois, Kansas, Washington); in others, the grand jury is merely authorized to visit the jail (e.g., Alaska, Arkansas, Maryland, New York). In either case, visits are very infrequent and perfunctory and indictments for improper jail practices are even rarer, since the grand jury's primary function, from the point of view of the prosecutors who usually dominate the proceedings, is to indict common criminals, not to reform the jail. The problem is similar to that regarding law-enforcement workers staffing the jail: chasing, catching, and convicting criminals is politically more glamorous than preventing recidivism through proper jails.

But the inspection problem goes deeper; in general, there are two main issues. The first is the almost complete absence of explicit standards for the grand jury to enforce. California published its minimum standards in 1963, Illinois in 1971. The other issue goes to the heart of the entire jail problem: reliance on local initiative and the unwillingness of local officials to undertake long-neglected reforms for the sake of achieving a rehabilitative ideal that they regard with deep skepticism. As we shall see, this issue exists even where the state has taken a hand in standard-setting and inspection, for it often happens that the actual enforcement machinery—namely, the condemnation power—is lodged in the local courts.

The issue of local indifference is illustrated by the general ineffectiveness of other devices for the maintenance of jail conditions. In some states, the local courts are required to inspect the jail, and are empowered to issue appropriate orders against the sheriff or warden [e.g., Ill. Rev. Stat., ch. 75, §28 (1966)]; other states give the local judiciary complete discretion as to what rules and standards should apply to the jails in their districts [e.g., Neb. Rev. Stat., §47–101, §47–201 (1966)]. What evidence we have suggests that such inspections are almost nonexistent;[22] the extent and effectiveness of the judge's rules are unknown. Other local officials who are sometimes charged with the duty of inspecting the jail are county health officials, fire and building inspectors, and local elected officials. Again, the evidence is that inspections are very rare.[23] It is ironic that the man deprived of his liberty can expect less protection from fire, disease, poor construction, etc. than the average citizen free

---

22. In my study of Illinois jails, I found that 98 percent of county jails and 98.3 percent of city jails had never been inspected by representatives of the local courts, according to the jailers in 1967–68 (Mattick & Sweet, 1969:104).

23. In Illinois, various elected officials occasionally inspected some jails. However, they failed to inspect 78 percent of city and 76 percent of all county jails. Fire inspection officials did not inspect 86 percent of city and 93 percent of county jails. All other kinds of officials, including several state agencies, neglected 88 percent of city jails and 92 percent of county jails (Mattick & Sweet, 1969:104). In the state of Washington health and fire inspections are somewhat more common; over three-fourths of that state's jails are inspected for fire safety once a year or oftener (Washington Department of Institutions, 1968:9).

to come and go in public buildings. The jailers, sheriffs, prosecutors, county boards, and judges apparently feel they have more important tasks than protecting the community through decent and constructive jails. Such reforms require political compromise. What is needed is outside authority, either state or federal.

Most states have some statutory provisions dealing with jail standards, but often they do little more than specify who shall be responsible for the jail, and perhaps provide for minimal segregation of prisoner types [e.g., California Penal Code, §4000–9 (1970)]. Even states with fairly detailed statutory provisions frequently fail to keep them up-to-date. For example, in 1874 Illinois required that buckets "with a cover made to shut tight" be provided as toilet facilities. This may have been less offensive in the days of the outhouse, but it should be unacceptable today. Finally, many statutes covering jails only apply to counties, leaving municipalities almost complete freedom to regulate their own jails. Illinois has a statute covering only county jails [Ill. Rev. Stat., ch. 75 (1966)], and a separate statute authorizing municipal houses of correction, but the latter does not contain any minimum standards, and does not apply to detention facilities [Ill. Rev. Stat., ch. 24, §11–4–1—§11–4–17 (1961)]. The Illinois Department of Corrections has the power to establish minimum standards for municipal jails and houses of correction, as well as for county jails, but the enforcement powers available are weak [Ill. Rev. Stat., ch. 127, §55a.1(5) (Cum. Supp. 1970)]. While this is consistent with the greater degree of "home rule" available to cities, it fails to take account of the need for outside supervision and enforcement to prod local officials into action.

Where state minimum standards exist, there is often a lack of effective enforcement powers. In some states the board of corrections has the power to inspect local jails and to *recommend* minimum standards, but has absolutely no means to compel compliance (California Board of Corrections, 1970:93–96). For example, the California Penal Code [§4015 (1970)] requires the county board to provide the sheriff with "necessary food, clothing, and bedding"at least equal in quality to that prescribed by the board of corrections. Presumably, the county grand jury has the sole power to investigate and enforce this duty. In other states, the state agency is required to petition the local courts for an order to close a substandard facility [e.g., Ill. Rev. Stat., ch. 127, §55a.1(5) (Cum. Supp. 1970); Mich. Stat. Ann., §28.2322 (1954); N.J. Rev. Stat., §30:1–16], or else the agency's own power of condemnation is subject to immediate, unlimited review in the local courts [e.g., N.C. Gen. Stat., §153–53.1; N.Y. Correction Law, §46(8)]. Either arrangement tends to prevent uniformity of interpretation of the standards; moreover, the same local political resistance that is the reason for state intervention in the first place still exists. A few states grant the state agency or the governor express condemnation power [e.g., Ala. Code, tit. 45, §162; Ind. Ann. Stat., §13–1005 (1956)]; this power cannot be inferred, however, out of concern for the doctrine of separation of powers.[24]

In short, the present extent of state control over local jail conditions is slight, though increasing. As developed more fully later, the optimum role of the state in this area is probably a combination of the carrot and the stick: more grants in aid to

---

24. This was, apparently, the reasoning of the Wisconsin Attorney General who interpreted that state's statute as requiring court action. The statute provided that the state Board of Control (now the Department of Welfare) could "prohibit the use" of a jail not meeting its standards [Wisc. Stat. Ann., §46.17 (3) (1957)]. Administrative agencies have increasingly been granted judicial functions; however, the grant of judicial power would still have to be made more explicit than the present Wisconsin statute.

make compliance with minimum standards both attractive and financially feasible, and more explicit, enforceable standards that give the local authorities ample flexibility in complying, but that leave no doubt as to the ultimate power of the state agency to condemn substandard local jails.

The extent of federal control over local jail conditions is very limited. Yet, local jails ought to be of great concern to federal authorities, because there are no federal "jails"; the vast majority of federal unsentenced prisoners are kept in local institutions. Accordingly, the U.S. Bureau of Prisons has for many years carried out a program of local jail inspection, primarily of the small fraction of the nation's jails that provide regular service to federal courts. There is some difference of opinion, however, as to whether this program has had more than a superficial and incidental effect on local jail administration (cf. Mattick & Sweet, 1969:307 and Robinson, 1944:254–55). The main concern of the federal authorities is that the jail be convenient to the federal court, and this produces reverse leverage: the local jail administrators can threaten to be uncooperative, or refuse the use of the most convenient jail, although some states have statutes requiring the sheriff or warden to accept federal prisoners committed by federal authorities [e.g., Ill. Rev. Stat., ch. 75, §5 (1966)]. Finally, the most serious problem with the federal "inspections" in the past has been the lack of specificity in their standards. The U.S. Bureau of Prisons and the American Correctional Association have for many years published "minimum standards" for community detention facilities, but these have consisted almost entirely of broad statements of values, principles, and ideals rather than highly specific directives. The ten-part *Correspondence Course for Jailers* (U.S. Bureau of Prisons, n.d.) was, largely, of this character. Of course, the ACA goes on to provide extensive interpretation of these principles in its *Manual of Correctional Standards* (A.C.A., 1966a), but the impact is still diluted.

A final source of supervision and control of jails is the visiting committee or prisoner aid society. The former is sometimes given statutory support, such as the Missouri Boards of County Visitors (Mo. Rev. Stat., §221.320–221.350), which the circuit court may appoint (and must, if petitioned by fifteen "reputable" citizens— presumably not jail inmates, even if they are unconvicted and "innocent until proven guilty"), which must be bipartisan and composed equally of men and women, and which must inspect the jails at least once in every three months. The latter is generally entirely private in organization and influence, such as the John Howard Association of Chicago. Because they are not dominated by county officials with other priorities, as is the case with the grand jury, these citizens' groups are useful elements and may have some potential for reform. Their potential, however, is limited in that public information and insight into the causes of and remedies for local jail conditions are hard to come by. Moreover, they are obliged to go to those with vested interests and responsibilities for information and instruction. Under such conditions, an uninformed and naive visiting committee or prison aid society, even with a will to reform, is easily misled, misdirected, and misinformed; their time and energy are wasted and their recommendations for reform are superficial. It takes an unusually independent body with good professional advice and access to the mass media to have a significant impact on recalcitrant jail problems.

Record-Keeping Practices

The average American jail obtains very little information about the prisoners committed to its keeping, retains little of what is obtained in any usable form, and reports almost nothing of what is usable to higher authorities. No doubt, this serves to insulate jail administrators from "outside" scrutiny, but it also handicaps thém in their efforts to document the need for adequate funds and personnel, and insures that individual prisoners will only be "stored," not treated. Further, it makes rational planning for jail reform almost impossible, and deprives other law-enforcement and corrections officials of important information about individuals who will almost certainly reappear in the criminal justice system, if they have not already put in an appearance. Record-keeping and reporting practices are better for prisoners charged with felonies, but the majority of jail inmates are charged with or convicted of lesser offenses for which there are few statutory or customary records.

General statistical information is crucial for planning, both in terms of the short-term budgetary needs of the jail's operations and as preparation for longer-term planning. Certainly, it is crucial if any reorganization is contemplated. Jails must be designed to handle peak loads as well as average population flows, while maintaining adequate segregation of prisoner types, supervision, and security. At present, however, many jails keep no such population records, or keep them in ways that render them useless, e.g., for only short periods, in informal and incomplete ways, and in ways that make them difficult to retrieve and generalize upon. In the Illinois survey, 13 percent of the sample of 160 jails and lockups kept no records at all, or no records except daily legal status (Mattick & Sweet, 1969:32).[25]

California is the only other state for which we have any recent, explicit report on record-keeping in local jails. The picture is even bleaker than in Illinois, despite the detailed population accounting specified in the California Board of Corrections' *Minimum Jail Standards* (1963:11). When the board conducted its survey of county jails in 1969, it found twelve of the largest county systems could not even supply gross total "bookings" for the calendar year 1968, let alone day-to-day population flows. Of course, the 1963 standards were only "recommended" and, as noted earlier, the board of corrections would not be able to enforce them even if they were "mandatory."

When it comes to information on individual prisoners, local records are somewhat better, though the major problem here is lack of uniformity. In Illinois only 3 of the 160 jails surveyed submitted no fingerprint records to the FBI; 20 percent fingerprinted all inmates, and the rest pursued a great variety of different policies, usually concentrating on more serious offenders (Mattick & Sweet, 1969:38–39). The larger jails kept more print records and showed greater uniformity, probably because the printing is done on a large enough scale to justify specialization of personnel within the jail. In general, the greatest failures in record-keeping on individual prisoners occur in smaller, rural jails, where few, if any, full-time jail employees exist, and each prisoner is "processed in" by the arresting officer. The problem is organization, not manpower, because the rural jails actually have *more* staff per inmate. (See the discussion of jail personnel, starting on p. 804.)

Larger jails are also more likely to keep criminal history records on all inmates. In general, jails usually keep criminal history records on those categories of inmates for whom fingerprint records were submitted, because the major, if not only, component of the history file is the FBI "rap sheet" received. In Illinois, over 90 percent of the 160 jails surveyed kept such criminal history files on some inmates, while 35 percent kept them on all inmates (Mattick & Sweet, 1969:43). Very few jails keep

---

25. The practice of sheriffs taking all jail records with them upon leaving office should also be noted. This form of "limited liability" was found in thirty-three Illinois county jails (Mattick & Sweet, 1969:33–34).

social histories or any other background information bearing on treatability, cell assignment, etc.

Records on physical and mental condition, visits, and disciplinary treatment were also rare. Of the Illinois jails surveyed 30 percent kept records of the physical or mental condition of all inmates on admittance, while about 25 percent kept records only if something appeared to be seriously wrong, or the inmate complained (Mattick & Sweet, 1969:45). Thirty-six percent of the jails kept records of visits, although, again, the very large jails were much more likely to keep such records. Record-keeping practices in the area of discipline were nonexistent in most jails. When only the thirty largest jails in the Illinois survey were investigated, it was found that most kept some records and twelve claimed they recorded all incidents (pp. 45–46).

Considering that there are no statutory requirements in the area of individual inmate record-keeping, other than for fingerprinting, the above figures are better than most.[26] It will be interesting to see if the record-keeping standards for jails published in 1971 by the new Bureau of Detention Facilities of the new Illinois Department of Corrections can be enforced, for they are quite thorough. According to these standards, a separate record must be kept on each prisoner admitted to the jail, including name, address, marital status, age and birth date, physical description, occupation, religion, offense charged or convicted, details of commitment, attorney's address and name, prior criminal record, medical condition at all times in the jail, list of valuables taken, expenditures while in custody, record of absences from the jail, mail, visits, telephone calls made and received (with names of the other parties), misconduct and discipline administered, persons to be contacted in emergency, and case disposition.

Inmate Population Estimates and Characteristics

The most recent, comprehensive, and best estimate of the jail population in the United States seems to indicate a total of 160,000 persons confined on a single survey day. They are predominantly male and bimodally distributed by age, with the heavier concentration among the young, a lesser concentration of the old, and fewer in the middle-age range. More than half of all persons confined in jails have not been convicted; they are "innocent until proven guilty" but, for the most part, cannot afford bail. The vast majority of them are charged with drunkenness, disorderly conduct, vagrancy, and petty property crimes, but a few are charged with very serious offenses. Most are poor, and minority group members are disproportionately represented among them. Estimates of total annual turnover of persons or commitments are much cruder and, depending upon various sources of information and methods of counting, the total arrived at ranges between one million and four and a half million.

While the average daily inmate population presents a cross-sectional view of jails in time, a more important population figure to attempt to derive relates to volume over time. Since jails are used to serve all detention functions, in addition to being the locus where sentences of less than one year are served, transiency and rapid turnover are characteristic of jail populations. But, if the attempt to derive a valid statistic for average daily inmate population must be qualified by some reservations about accuracy, the attempt to derive an annual turnover figure gives rise to the widest

---

26. Illinois sheriffs and some chiefs of police are required to furnish the Illinois Department of Public Safety with the fingerprints of all persons charged with a crime, with a few exceptions (such as offenses punishable by only a fine or a sentence of 10 days or less) [Ill. Rev. Stat., ch. 38, §206–5 (1967)]; however, the statute is not enforced.

fluctuations bordering on the crudest kinds of guesswork. The major problem arises from the attempt to separate the number of individuals committed to jails in a year as contrasted with the total number of commitments made to jails in a year. It is clear that in dealing with jail populations, where a common charge is drunkenness, time served in jail by the same individual can be short and repetitive. Individuals charged with such offenses have been known to pass through jails one hundred times in the same year, and thirty commitments are not uncommon.

The available ratios of daily inmate population to total annual commitments show wide variation. As might be expected, the ratios based only on sentenced prisoners are lower, reflecting the lower turnover rate for these inmates: it ranges from 1:7.5 to 1:12.[27] The available ratios for sentenced and unsentenced prisoners combined range from 1:9 to 1:64. During 1955–58, as Assistant Warden of the Cook County Jail in Chicago, I estimated a ratio of 1:9 between average daily population and total annual commitments for *that* jail. Upon completing my survey of the entire state of Illinois, however, I was surprised to find the state ratio to be around 1:34! (Average daily population is about 5,000; total annual commitments to Illinois jails were estimated at 170,000.) Coincidentally, this was also the ratio implied in a 1964 survey of Virginia's local jails and jail farms, which reported 127,953 annual commitments, and an average daily population of 3,738 (Virginia Department of Welfare and Institutions, 1964:1–2). The ratio in California county jails in 1968 was not too different: 24,974/581,876, or 1:23 (California Board of Corrections, 1970:11–12). (Most California city jails are not covered by the definition we have adopted from the LEAA.) The ratios obtained from two other states, however, are completely out of line with these figures: in Pennsylvania in 1965 the ratio was only 1:11 (7,200/80,000) (Pennsylvania Commission, 1965:2), whereas in 1967–68 Washington state recorded a ratio of 1:64 (1,947/125,000) (Washington Department of Institutions, 1968:27).

The national ratio of daily population to total commitments must be at least 1:9, and probably is no greater than 1:34. If we apply these ratios to the March 15, 1970 LEAA figure of 160,863, we arrive at an estimated national total of jail commitments per year of 1.4 to 5.4 million (using the Washington ratio of 1:64, the range would be extended to over 10 million!). Most arrests result in at least one commitment, and many persons pass through the jail without being formally arrested, thus, the jail commitment figure of five million is not unlikely.[28]

Almost all states provide for separation of sexes, and most states prohibit the

27. In 1933 the Census Bureau estimated the total annual commitments of *sentenced* inmates to "county and city jails" at 608,484, which was about 12 times the daily population figure given for *sentenced* inmates, 51,436 (Robinson, 1944:6). In 1966 the NCCD estimated that the number of persons "held in one year for service of a sentence is 1,016,748" (N.C.C.D., 1966:140). This was about 7½ times the estimated average daily population serving sentences (141,303). The latest LEAA census figures cast considerable doubt on the absolute size of these NCCD estimates (the LEAA found 69,096 serving sentences), but the ratio of daily to annual figures is still of interest. Finally, it is reported that in 1959 about 26,000 persons were sentenced to Massachusetts jails and houses of correction, while the average daily sentenced population was around 2,300 (Massachusetts Governor's Committee, 1965:6). This suggests a ratio of about 1:11.

28. The FBI reported a total of 5,773,988 arrests in 1969, based on police agencies covering about three-fourths of the nation's population (over 4,000 arrests per hundred thousand inhabitants) (F.B.I., 1970:108). Applying the 1:34 ratio to the 1970 Census population figure of over 200 million yields an estimate of over eight million arrests per year. However, agencies not reporting to the FBI probably make fewer arrests per population unit than those that do report, since the former are primarily rural or small town, so the true total is probably closer to five million than to eight million arrests.

use of jails for juveniles, at least when there is an alternative facility available (N.C.C.D., 1966:142). Practice does not, however, always live up to principle. North Carolina allows children to be kept in jail if (a) there is need for secure restraint, and (b) if no other adequate facility is available. In 1967, only six urban counties in the state had juvenile homes (North Carolina Jail Study Commission, 1969:26). The LEAA census found 7,800 "juveniles" confined in American jails on March 15, 1970, or about 5 percent of the total population of 160,863 (L.E.A.A., 1971:4). Since legal definitions and age limits of "juveniles" vary by state, the LEAA instructed responding officials to apply the definition applicable in their respective jurisdictions (p. 2).

Our survey of Illinois jails estimated that about 6 percent of the total jail population for 1967 were juveniles (Mattick & Sweet, 1969:67). In 1963–64 about 45 percent of those committed to Virginia jails and jail farms were under 18 (Virginia Department of Welfare and Institutions, 1964:1). However, in California, over a nine-year period from 1960 through 1968, the percentage of juveniles in county jails on a given day in September never rose above 1 percent, and was usually less than 0.5 percent (California Board of Corrections, 1970:175–92). It is perfectly legal to confine juveniles in jail in California, but good administrative practice, apparently, keeps such commitments to a minimum.

Information about the age of non-juveniles, while not of such crucial importance for adequate segregation, nevertheless tells us much about the nature of the jail population. Relative to the population at large, jails, like other prisons, have an over-representation of persons under the age of 45. The 1960 U.S. Census revealed 70 percent of the population to be under 45 (U.S. Bureau of the Census, 1962:28). In the same year 82 percent of the inmates in prisons and jails were under 45, while the figure for jails alone was 77 percent. In 1960, 11 percent of the inmates in local jails were under 20, compared with 8 percent for federal prisons and 8.7 percent for state prisons; 21.9 percent of jail inmates were 45 or over, compared with 13 percent in federal and 16.3 percent in state prisons (U.S. Bureau of the Census, 1961:21–24).

This bimodal distribution is consistent with the fact that jails hold many youthful and first offenders, as well as the chronic petty offenders, who tend to be older. The fact that the more serious crimes are committed more often by younger offenders results in the seemingly paradoxical fact that, at least in terms of offenses charged, the "dangerous" criminals in jail tend to be the younger ones. This does not mean that youth has nothing to learn from the old-timers they meet in jail; the oft-noted criminogenic consequences of the indiscriminate commingling of prisoner types in the average jail result from the combination of youthful daring and ambition with the sophistication, cynicism, and recalcitrance of the old, and have little to do with the specific acts that landed these respective "types" in jail.

The overwhelming majority of jail inmates are male. The LEAA found only 7,739 adult females in American jails on March 15, 1970, which was less than 5 percent of the total population on that day (L.E.A.A., 1971:4). In 1967 an estimated 5.2 percent of the total Illinois jail population were adult women (Mattick & Sweet, 1969:67); in Virginia, in 1963–64, 9.4 percent of commitments to jails and jail farms were women (Virginia Department of Welfare and Institutions, 1964:1). The percentage of female juveniles is not available, but it is very small; for if juveniles tend to be about the same, female juveniles must be the smallest proportion of the total jail population. On a given day in late September from 1960 through 1968, the percentage of female juveniles in California county jails varied from 8 percent to 30 percent of the very low proportion (less than 1 percent of juveniles held in jails) (California Board of Corrections, 1970:170–74).

The legal status of jail inmates has relevance both for the proper segregation of prisoners who should be handled differently and for practical reasons of health and security. If the "presumption of innocence until proven guilty" is to have any practical consequences for the criminal justice system, it ought to assure that unconvicted persons are not forced into association with those who have already been convicted and are serving out sentences in jail. In the first instance, the unconvicted may not be legally considered the proper recipients of punishment, or even treatment intended to rehabilitate. The "innocent" should not yet require "rehabilitation." Moreover, there are very practical reasons why these two main classes of prisoners should be separated from others: for reasons of health, as the possibility of their bearing a communicable disease, and for reasons of proper security handling, since the degree of risk represented by a new prisoner requires some time to determine. The common practice in most jails, however, is indiscriminate commingling. Aside from the general separation of the sexes in jails, other kinds of segregation of prisoners are severely limited by lack of space or advance planning in jail construction. Moreover, in view of the poor record-keeping practices in most jails, few jail authorities have any idea of the proportion of inmates representing the various legal statuses that they receive and handle over time. One serious result is that there can be little rational planning for the proper handling of jail prisoners in the immediate future. Nevertheless, a few estimates of inmate legal status have been collected.

The LEAA found that 52 percent of the persons confined in American jails on March 15, 1970, were there for reasons other than conviction—i.e., they were either held for other authorities (including arraignment) or were awaiting trial (L.E.A.A., 1971:1). The distribution of jail inmates by legal status was: 17 percent were held for other authorities or not yet arraigned; 35 percent were arraigned and awaiting trial; 5 percent were convicted persons awaiting further legal action (presumably, either appeal or transfer to another prison); 36 percent were serving sentences of less than one year; and 6 percent were serving sentences of one year or more (pp. 4–5). Individual states show considerable variation from this national distribution, however. In North Carolina, where most sentenced misdemeanants are sent to state-run camps, the percentage of unconvicted persons in jail is much higher: 73 percent (pp. 4–5). At least one practical implication of these disparate findings is that jail planners, whether state or local, cannot rely on general statistics, but must determine specific jail population distributions over a period of time in the particular locality or region that the jail is intended to serve.

The offenses for which persons are committed or sentenced to jails are as varied as the local, state, and federal statutes that describe them. The vast majority of persons, however, are confined for a relatively small group of relatively minor offenses: drunkenness, disorderly conduct and vagrancy, assault, larceny, and drunk or reckless driving. The proportion of jail inmates charged with a felony approximates 10 percent of the total. McGee (1971) estimated that about three million persons annually pass through American jails, and that only about 7 percent of these are charged with or convicted of felonies. The Virginia Department of Welfare and Institutions (1964:20) reported that 11.6 percent of those committed to Virginia jails and jail farms were charged with felonies in 1963–64. In both of these cases we must consider that many persons serving sentences in jails for "misdemeanor" convictions were actually arrested and charged with a felony that was bargained down in exchange for a guilty plea.

In addition, there is a small but important group of inmates confined in jails who have not been charged with a criminal offense: material witnesses, persons held in civil contempt, persons awaiting transfer to mental hospitals, and transient lodgers.

These categories of inmates comprise perhaps less than 1 percent, but they represent a considerable number of persons in the course of a year across the nation.

The drunk is more likely than other arrestees to spend at least the night in jail (Nimmer, 1971:155). If he is in good enough condition to be bailed out, or has a responsible friend to take custody, he will not be arrested in the first place (Alexander, 1957:311). The drunk is also more likely to be sentenced to jail, or to "lay out" a fine. Since 1965, the *Uniform Crime Reports* show a declining arrest rate for drunkenness—dropping below 25 percent of the total arrests reported—but when we add together drunken driving, disorderly conduct, and vagrancy arrests, which are frequently used as interchangeable charges in making drunkenness arrests, the proportion is still at least one-third of the total arrests reported. Thus the 50 percent estimate for drunks in jail is probably still accurate today, except in New York City and possibly a few other locales where drug-related offenses are cited more often than drunkenness (New York State Commission, 1966:21).

Women are sometimes assumed to be in jail primarily for prostitution and commercialized vice, but the record refutes this. Prostitution may replace traffic offenses as the fifth most common cause of commitment, but the vast majority of women are committed for the same four offenses as men: drunkenness, disorderly conduct and vagrancy, larceny-theft, and assault.

To summarize, most people in jail are the petty offenders we expected to find there. The only "serious crimes" accounting for a substantial proportion of the jail population are grand larceny (which is often not distinguished from petty larceny in the available crime statistics) and certain assaults. However, the aggregate problem represented by jails and their population is far from petty, whether viewed in terms of the number of offenders, the number of victims, or the total social and economic costs to the public at large.

Physical Facilities

The physical plant constituting the jail building is the basic limiting or enabling element that affects all other aspects of jail administration. Rural jails are often empty; urban jails are usually severely overcrowded. Toilet and other sanitary fixtures, if any, are primitive. Facilities for work, recreation, counseling, and treatment are usually nonexistent, even where some proportion of the cell space is consistently unused. In short, jails are probably the most poorly planned, ancient, inefficient, and unsanitary of public buildings, and this fact has far-reaching consequences.

The larger urban jails that are consistently overutilized are aging at a rate not proportional to their years but proportional to their overutilization; the smaller rural jails are aging disproportionately through desuetude and neglect. It sometimes seems that the low-level maintenance contracts let to maintain some jails at their marginal condition of repair also serve to insure the maintenance of that marginal condition to insure future maintenance contracts. Yet, a building program that would merely replace the old with new county and city jails would be an equally poor investment. In the long run, it simply would perpetuate the most basic inefficiency of the present system: planning along outmoded, local jurisdictional lines. If empty and overcrowded jails are to be avoided, new jails must be planned and located in such a way as to effect a rational division of labor and distribution of prisoners according to the realities of present and projected prisoner population flow expectancies.

Jails are among the oldest of public buildings, and age is probably the most important aspect of physical plant. Of course, an old jail may be well maintained and operated, and a new one allowed to suffer the effects of systematic neglect, but, by and large, jails tend to look and act their age. In 1966 the NCCD reported that 35 percent of the estimated 3,473 short-term correctional institutions in the country were over fifty years old, 30 percent were twenty-five to fifty years old, 11 percent were ten to twenty-four years old, and 24 percent were less than ten years old (N.C.C.D., 1966: 146). The NCCD survey did not include jails that hold sentenced prisoners for less than 30 days or unsentenced prisoners, while we are including all local penal institutions with at least 48-hour retention authority, a total of over 4,000 "jails." Our Illinois survey found that nearly 70 percent of county jails were over fifty years old, compared with only about 22 percent for city jails (which included many lockups) (Mattick & Sweet, 1969:80–81). A 1968 inspection of county and most city jails in Washington state found that 33 percent of the county jails were over fifty years old, while less than 10 percent of the city jails surveyed were that old (Washington Department of Institutions, 1968:24). However, in the few states where counties operate large numbers of minimum security camps, farms, or ranches, most of which are less than forty years old, the city jails may be older than the *average* county institution (California Board of Corrections, 1970:114–16).

In general, the jails along the eastern seaboard and in the northeastern quadrant of the United States are the oldest in the nation; the building of jails was among the earliest of the settlers' tasks as the population migrated westward. The oldest jails are not necessarily the worst, although they tend to be, and there are some very old jails in southern and western seaport cities. Many of these older jails have been serially maintained in such a fashion that, like the human body replacing every cell in the process of aging, every brick, bar, and pipe has been patched or replaced at some time or other, but the process has been so gradual and so minimal that the effect has been to maintain the original structure.

The chronological age of the physical plant that constitutes a jail is seriously affected by the extent to which it is utilized. Empty or near-empty jails tend to be neglected and the employees who are assigned to operate them on a part-time basis tend to use arbitrary and haphazard procedures. As a result they are inefficient, wasteful, and negligent. On the other hand, a jail that is overcrowded is aging at more than its chronological rate. It is not only a question of human space, but plumbing, electrical circuits, locks and door hinges, ovens, and laundry facilities are working daily at over their planned capacity, and some element essential to basic human living conditions is always breaking down. Every fundamental unit of jail operations: the kitchen, hospital, chapel, work-educational-recreational space, files, guards' locker room, attorneys' and public visiting room, food storage, armory, and mail delivery suffers from overload, multiplies error, and tends to result in human misery for inmate and employee alike. Inmates cannot be properly classified and segregated because the space that becomes available through today's discharges must be filled by today's commitments, and there is no necessary relationship between the classification of prisoners discharged and received the same day. To maintain even the most elementary segregation among the various classifications of prisoners in an overcrowded jail, requires an extensive daily program of internal transfers of inmates. Under these conditions, and given the quality of staff that can be attracted by the low pay scales offered, it is little wonder that most large, urban jails are in a chronic state of incipient crisis.

Ideally, jails should be planned to have at least 10 percent surplus capacity available to handle periodic peak loads and to insure the degree of flexibility required to enable them to classify and segregate their inmates. Such conditions are likely to obtain only if rational planning results in a redistribution and relocation of jail and detention facilities in such a fashion as to insure that each physical plant houses no more than 250 inmates in a planned capacity of 300. Such jails could be staffed and administered in a constructive manner. The usual combination Bastille-dungeon with a planned capacity in excess of 1,000, and holding twice its capacity, can only be an institution designed to maladjust the persons thus confined, and is like an antisocial weapon pointed at the heart of its environing community. Such jails breed crime, disease, perversion, and filth, which are daily discharged to pollute the community.

In 1966 the NCCD estimated that there were 36 percent more beds in local adult correctional institutions than would be needed to accommodate the estimated average daily population *serving sentences* (N.C.C.D., 1966:145).[29] The NCCD noted that this percentage was not inconsistent with the oft-cited overcrowding of jails, since "some of the empty cells are in places where they are not needed; others are vacant because they are unfit for human occupancy" (pp. 145–46). The NCCD neglected to indicate, however, what proportion of beds were set aside for the large daily population *not* serving sentences; when they are added in, most of the surplus beds disappear. In the jails surveyed by the LEAA, 52 percent of the inmates had not been convicted. However, the percentage of unconvicted prisoners held in the institutions surveyed by the NCCD is probably quite low, since jails holding prisoners for less than thirty days were not included.

The 1967 Illinois survey found that, on the day of the on-site interviews, 57 percent of the total available cells were being used, and 54 percent of the beds were occupied. Although most jail cells are designed for single occupancy, most cells contain double bunks, and some contain more (Mattick & Sweet, 1969:82, 89). Inmate population on these interview days, however, was slightly less than average, because interviews tended to be conducted on week days and jail populations increase slightly on weekends (p. 82). Moreover, about one-third of the jails included in our Illinois survey were excluded by the LEAA definition, and these smaller, usually city-run jails tended to be even more underused than the average (Mattick & Sweet, 1969:86; L.E.A.A., 1971:6). For these reasons, it is likely that the true average utilization figure for the jails we are considering is at least 60 percent. Averages are misleading, however. When the few chronically overcrowded urban jails are excluded, it is clear that the overwhelming majority of Illinois jails normally use less than half their capacity.

Other states show wide variation from this figure, however. Pennsylvania county jail cells were 96 percent full on February 20, 1964; but if Philadelphia's three institutions (50 percent overcrowded) are excluded, the occupancy rate falls to 73 percent (Pennsylvania Commission, 1965:9). A survey of Idaho jails found an average of about 33 percent of the cells in use (Idaho Law Enforcement Planning Commission, 1969:13). This difference is consistent with the generalization that rural jails are usually underutilized, while urban and suburban jails are filled to capacity or beyond.

Another perspective on jail utilization is gained by determining how many jails stand *completely empty* at any one time. Much more than overall occupancy rates, emptiness conveys a dramatic impression of the incredible waste of physical plant inherent in our present system of scattered, locally run jails. The Illinois survey found 14 percent of county jails and 49 percent of city jails had average daily inmate populations of less than one; only 8 percent of city jails, and 55 percent of county jails, were never empty (Mattick & Sweet, 1969:63, 66). In Idaho about 40 percent of that

---

29. At this point, the "estimated daily population" is not labeled as *sentenced* only, but earlier the NCCD seems to indicate that the figure cited is "distinct from the number held under pretrial detention" (N.C.C.D., 1966:140).

state's jails were unoccupied (Idaho Law Enforcement Planning Commission, 1969: 13).[30] On the other hand, on the survey day in September, from 1960 through 1968, only 1 county facility in California (out of 166) was ever empty (California Board of Corrections, 1970:175–92).

A third aspect of jail utilization is the average number of inmates per institution. A small jail with perhaps five or ten cells, which is never empty and which normally uses at least half of its cells, might appear to be operating efficiently, but it is not. Per capita costs for personnel, feeding, laundry, etc. are extremely high, while any sort of rehabilitative program seems prohibitive. The LEAA found 160,863 inmates in 4,037 jails, an average of almost 40 inmates per jail (L.E.A.A., 1971:1). But when the few very large, urban jails in each state are excluded, the average is much less. For example, the Illinois survey found that the average number of inmates per jail for the entire state was 32, but when the Cook County Jail and Chicago's House of Correction are excluded, the average falls to 9.7; less than half the Illinois jails surveyed had average daily populations of six inmates or more (Mattick & Sweet, 1969:63). (When lockups are excluded, these figures are probably somewhat higher.) The LEAA survey also reveals quite a number of predominantly rural states with far less than ten inmates per institution, e.g., Idaho, Iowa, Kansas, North and South Dakota, and Vermont (L.E.A.A., 1971:4–6). Thus, the "average" jail is either uneconomically small or underutilized, and most probably both.

The other side of the coin is the overcrowded jail. Almost every major urban center I know has overcrowded jails, or simultaneous disparities of over- and underutilization as between county and city jails within the same metropolitan area. Some urban jails are operating at close to 200 percent capacity. At the same time, "rated capacity" is not necessarily what a rational jail planner would prescribe, or even what the original design of a jail intended. When extra beds are added to cells built for one inmate, or even put in the corridors, "rated capacity" is often increased, but actual conditions deteriorate in every way, especially security and sanitation. Moreover, a simple numerical total for overall capacity and population can be misleading. A complex, multipurpose, urban jail may be severely overcrowded in a particular section— usually the one reserved for adult males—and yet be rated as being utilized "under capacity" because its female and juvenile sections are relatively empty.

Large urban centers do not have a monopoly on overcrowded jails, however; suburban and even rural jails may be chronically or situationally overcrowded. For example, 21 percent of the Pennsylvania counties surveyed in 1964 had overcrowded institutions, and only a few of these counties contained large urban areas (Pennsylvania Commission, 1965:12). In Washington state the most serious overcrowding occurs in certain farming districts during the harvest season, when large numbers of migratory farm workers are arrested for drunkenness (Washington Department of Institutions, 1968:11–12).

But the vast majority of jails are underused, and should be consolidated into regional facilities, which could also absorb the excess from the few jails that are overcrowded. A final observation should be made on the subject of matching jail capacity to prisoner population flows: much of the wasteful underutilization of our current jail system is probably the result of purposive planning designed to insure that each small

---

30. However, since the Idaho study covered 81 county and city jails, while the LEAA included only 61 "jails" by its definition, it is likely that somewhat less than 40 percent of the jails in Idaho are usually empty (assuming, again, that the most transient lockups, excluded by the LEAA, are among the least used of all jails).

jail had sufficient excess capacity to handle peak loads that may result once or twice a year. Thus, some states surveyed reported that their smaller counties had *more* bunks per county population unit than larger counties—to anticipate a wider range in prisoner fluctuations (American Foundation, 1966:31–32; Ashman, 1969:55–56). In general, the answer to the problems of age and underutilization are best addressed through larger, regional facilities. (This topic is discussed further beginning on p. 833.)

Perhaps the most pervasive characteristic of jails and a direct consequence of their general physical condition is their state of sanitation and cleanliness. Some old jails can be kept tolerably clean and some relatively new jails are filthy to the point of human degradation but, in general, the sanitary condition of jails leaves much to be desired. The general low level of cleanliness in jails has an immediate impact on the health and morale of the inmates and staff who are confined together in the jail, and also most serious and widespread effects on the surrounding community. Insofar as jails do not provide adequate facilities for personal hygiene and general sanitation, they expose their inmates and staffs to the dangers of infectious disease and general physical debility. Jail populations have notoriously high rates of venereal disease, tuberculosis, and infectious hepatitis, which are readily passed from inmate to inmate under unsanitary jail conditions, and then into the free community through jail population turnover. The uninformed public tends to assume that cleanliness is a matter of personal habits and training, and sanitation is merely a matter of good management and supervision; thus, any prisoner who is properly motivated has the opportunity to keep clean. The empirical facts tend to be otherwise: such elementary commodities as soap, towels, toothbrushes, safety razors, clean bedding, and even toilet paper are frequently in short supply or totally absent from the jail environment. Sanitation depends on hardware and plumbing, cleanliness depends upon adequate supplies, responsible manpower, and supervision. If cleanliness is next to godliness, most jails lie securely in the province of hell.

To begin with fundamentals, many jail cells have neither toilets nor washbasins. Moreover, many inmates confined in such cells do not have access to any sanitary facilities (including toilets) for long periods of time; the infamous bucket system still survives in many jails. This not only poses a *public* health problem, it creates an unnecessary internal security hazard every time an inmate must be released from his cell to use a common facility or to empty his bucket.

In the Illinois survey, showers were rated inadequate if access was not allowed at least once a day, or if the ratio of inmate capacity to shower heads exceeded 10:1. Fully 70 percent of county jails had inadequate adult male shower facilities, and in this respect, city jails were worse (Mattick & Sweet, 1969:95–96). Females and juveniles (when held separately) tend to have better toilet and washing facilities than adult males, due to less use and more frequent location of such plumbing *inside* the cells. Even where sanitary fixtures are present, however, all of these figures reflect only *potential* facilities; the number of toilets, washbasins, and showers in need of repair is considerable.

Extensive cleaning is *not* possible in some old jails because the ironwork is rusted, the cement floors are broken, and the walls would disintegrate. Such jails are havens for rodents, body lice, and other vermin that can successfully survive sporadic attempts at extermination. Where jails can be cleaned, this is usually done by the inmates themselves.

One problem in using inmates for this purpose is the legal question whether unconvicted persons can be required to work, even to clean their own cells; it would seem to be "involuntary servitude" prior to being "duly convicted" (Thirteenth Amendment, U.S. Constitution). Several of the states surveyed seemed to be concerned about this problem, to the extent of assigning convicts to institutions normally used exclusively for detention (New York State Commission, 1966:70–74; North Carolina Jail Study Commission, 1969:10). The Illinois survey revealed a much higher percentage of city jails not requiring any cleaning by inmates, possibly because many are used largely or exclusively for pretrial detention (Mattick & Sweet, 1969:102). Of course, detainees can and do "volunteer" for various chores, but the jail conditions and administrative methods necessary to encourage this are sometimes undesirable. Perhaps some ambitious jailer should bring a test case to clear up this legal uncertainty in order to fix responsibility for jail cleaning. Under current conditions, jailers are reluctant to spend money to hire free labor for housekeeping tasks and tend to take the attitude that if detainees will not clean the jail, they can just "stew in their own juice."

As for the frequency of cleaning, 70 percent of the Illinois county jailers claimed their jails were swept at least once a day; 59 percent claimed daily mopping (Mattick & Sweet, 1969:100). However, in spite of the exceptional cleaning made possible by advance notice of the interviewer's visit, conditions in many jails belied these assertions. Reports from other states, again not quantitative, are similar; clean, sanitary jails are rare, though some exist in every state and not always in the newest facilities.

Only the largest jails have such luxuries as classrooms, an adequate infirmary, a laundry, separate dining areas, recreation space, and chapels. The 1970 LEAA survey revealed that 86.4 percent of jails had no recreational facilities; the percentage without educational facilities was 89.2. There were no medical facilities *of any type* in 49 percent of the jails surveyed (L.E.A.A., 1971:18–19). The LEAA reported that only 26 percent of the 4,037 jails surveyed were without separate rooms for visiting— especially with attorneys (p. 19). Receiving rooms for newly arrived prisoners are also common, perhaps because any unused space can more easily be adapted to these purposes. It is surprising, however, how rarely unused cell space is converted for other uses, even in jails that are more than half empty. Funding is probably the major problem, considering that in some states funding is not provided even to repair and maintain the existing cell areas (e.g., Washington Department of Institutions, 1968:7). And, of course, there is no substitute for adequate planning and design; a converted cell block or office tends to be unsuited for any alternative purpose. If the original building design does not provide for work, educational, or visiting facilities, conversions tend to build stress and awkwardness into what should be constructive space and functions. They create the illusion of constructive purposes while, at the same time, actually defeating them.

A final aspect of physical plant is current planning for improvement and building. Over 85 percent of Illinois jails had no plans for improvement or replacement, and more than 70 percent were not even *considering* the matter. Of those with active and realistic plans, about one-third were building a new jail (Mattick & Sweet, 1969: 107–8). Yet, simply to replace old jails with new ones, without a systematic appreciation of what a state or metropolitan area may require in the way of jail facilities over the next 25 to 50 years, would be to pour the same old sour wine into new bottles. The first logical decision to be made by any authorities contemplating a rational program of jail reform would be to hold all building decisions in abeyance until the requirements can be determined systematically. It is certain that far fewer jails are required than a piecemeal building-replacement program would seem to indicate.

Characteristics of Jail Personnel

Although the physical presence of a building tends to dominate the impression made by a jail, a far more important factor for the performance quality of a jail is the nature and number of its personnel. If a jail's staff is inadequate in its initial qualifications for the job, in screening, in training, in numbers, and in motivation and morale, even the most modern, well-designed, and fully equipped penal plant will be defeated in its every function and purpose. An understaffed jail with untrained and demoralized personnel tends to perpetuate its own condition, because its present condition is used as an argument against all efforts at reform. Legislative bodies, such as county boards or city councils, ask themselves, in effect, why should good money be thrown after bad, since most jails are evaluated as malfunctioning institutions. Yet, it is precisely this impasse that must be broken if there is to be some improvement in the jail situation of the United States. It serves little purpose to replace old jails with new physical plants if there is no concomitant change in personnel practices.

In the vast majority of American jails, with the exception of the few largest urban jails, an overwhelming number of personnel are either primarily law-enforcement officers, whose main duties and interests are concerned with matters outside the jail, or underpaid jail custodians, whose qualifications for jail work are accurately reflected in their wage scale. Usually, in terms of socioeconomic status and education, such personnel are hardly distinguishable from the prisoners in their keep.

Historically, the sheriff, and later the municipal chief of police, had the responsibility for the jail thrust upon them almost by default, as discussed previously. There has been some tendency, in recent years, for busy urban police departments to relinquish their responsibility for jails and to transfer that function to other city or county departments. At the same time, with increasing urbanization, there has been a tendency for city police departments to perform the major law-enforcement functions for the surrounding metropolitan areas. The net effect of these shifts in functional responsibilities is that the county sheriff, an office that has been declining in importance over the last hundred years, finds himself divested of all the politically glamorous law-enforcement functions, but still saddled with county traffic problems and the jail.

In current practice, one of the few advantages in using policemen as jail officers is that they are likely to be somewhat higher quality personnel by virtue of their police role rather than their jail role. Law-enforcement personnel, as compared with jail employees, more frequently have civil service status, higher qualifications, and higher pay. But when a sheriff's deputy or city patrolman is assigned to work in the jail, he is not likely to undergo a role reversal and become interested in rehabilitative techniques or even the provision of humane conditions for prisoners whom his fellow officers have recently arrested. The law-enforcement psychology of a policeman is to arrest offenders and see to it that they get *into* jail, while the rehabilitative psychology of a correctional worker is to prepare an inmate to get *out* of jail and take his place in the free community as a law-abiding citizen. There is an understandable antagonism between the police and those whom they arrest that seriously limits the prospects of policemen rehabilitating prisoners in jail. Moreover, there is a tendency on the part of some law-enforcement personnel assigned to jail work to misuse the jail as an extension of police work, to achieve "justice without trial" by making the jail a more punitive experience than it ought to be, especially for prisoners who are still awaiting trial.

Even when jail personnel are not primarily policemen, as in the larger urban jails, many of them, in fact, are those who could not qualify for a policeman's job, and many are would-be policemen who view their jail work as a stepping stone to the status they hope to achieve. Such persons are usually unfit for any kind of jail work, for they are unduly preoccupied with the trappings and symbols of authority: the uniform, the badge, and the possibility of carrying and using weapons. Correctional work is seen by such jail personnel as having a lower priority than police work; it is uninteresting to them and unconnected to their self-image and their unrealistic career aspirations.

Many of the larger police departments and sheriff's offices rotate their personnel from division to division; this prevents stability and commitment to jail work, and discourages the establishment of training programs in correctional techniques. Indeed, some law-enforcement administrators are reluctant to engage in such specialized training because they fear that it would reduce the flexibility of assignment of their men (see, e.g., California Board of Corrections, 1970:100). Many of the law-enforcement personnel listed as jail "employees" are, in fact, regular sheriff's deputies and patrolmen, who only occasionally perform jail duties, such as "processing in" their own arrestees or "looking in" on the jail at night. In addition to all the other problems involved in law-enforcement staffing of jails, the fact that these men are frequently only *transient* or *part-time* workers, officially or in practice, means that they will be unfamiliar with the jail as a continuing enterprise that has an important function to serve in protecting the community from crime through the prevention of recidivism.

In March, 1970, there were 28,053 "full-time jail employees" and 5,676 "part-time jail employees" in the 4,037 jails surveyed by the LEAA (1971:14). The LEAA did not define their terms, so it is impossible to say how many respondents interpreted "full time" to mean full time *in the jail,* as opposed to full time working for the sheriff or police department. We believe the former interpretation was used most often and full-time law-enforcement personnel with occasional jail duties were not generally included in the "full-time" figures.[31] But the extent to which jails are dependent on these uncounted "outside" personnel, as well as other part-time workers, can be illustrated by inquiring how many "full-time jail employees" are available on any one shift. Remember that a jail is a 365-day, 24-hour-a-day institution, usually operating three shifts. This yields a national total of only 9,351 "full-time jail employees" per shift. However, even jail employees normally work only a five-day week, so we must adjust this figure to provide coverage for seven days, which yields about 6,680 employees per shift, or about $1\frac{2}{3}$ full-time workers *per jail shift per jail,* not counting vacations, illness, and other absences (the LEAA reported an "average" of about 40 inmates per jail).

However, most of these full-time employees are in the larger urban jails. In small towns and rural counties jail "coverage" is almost nonexistent. When the above analy-

---

31. The Illinois jails survey included many "full-time" city or county employees with substantial duties *outside* the jail, and we arrived at a grand total of 3,280 "full-time" employees (Mattick & Sweet, 1969:258–59). Even allowing for the larger number of Illinois jails covered (160 versus 108 in the LEAA survey), this is far more than the 1,231 "full-time" jail employees reported by the LEAA for Illinois, suggesting that many Illinois jailers interpreted the LEAA questionnaire to mean only full time in the jail. Our Illinois survey found only 660 full-time, jail only, custodial employees.

Similarly, the LEAA reported 4,399 "full-time" jail employees for the state of California, but in 1969 there were at least 3,882 employees assigned full time to detention or correctional facilities, counting only sheriffs' department personnel (both studies covered the same number of California jails, 166) (California Board of Corrections, 1970:103).

Nor does it seem likely that many full-time law-enforcement personnel with only occasional jail duties were reported under "part-time jail personnel" in the LEAA report. If they were, the relative proportion of employees in this category would be much higher, judging by the proportion found in our Illinois survey (Mattick & Sweet, 1969:258).

sis is applied to "cities with population under 25,000," for which the LEAA lists separate figures, we find about 105 full-time workers per shift for 718 jails. In other words, many, if not most, small jurisdictions do not even employ one full-time jailer per shift. Instead, police or sheriff's employees occasionally "look in" on the jail (see, e.g., Washington Department of Institutions, 1968:10; Idaho Law Enforcement Planning Commission, 1969:9). Even where a full-time jailer is employed, he may not be on duty at night, or may spend all of his time at the front desk away from the cell area, answering phones, serving as radio dispatcher, and performing a variety of other police functions.

It is also instructive to inquire into the relative number of custodial employees, medical personnel, counselors, teachers, and other positions included in these 28,053 full-time and 5,676 part-time totals, which the LEAA did not classify further. The NCCD attempted to obtain this information for the "local correctional institutions and jails" it surveyed in 1966, producing the optimum *estimates* of numbers and ratios of *sentenced inmates* to staff for each position shown in Table 1. The NCCD noted that "other employees" include "administrative, clerical, supervisory, vocational, medical, and culinary" workers, and that "custodial officers" constituted 78 percent of all employees, while the "professional staff" categories made up less than 3 percent. It should also be pointed out, however, that many of these so-called professional employees were probably also part-time workers—especially the medical staff and psychiatrists; that, at least for custodial officers, the inmate-to-staff ratios should be more than tripled to take account of the need to cover three shifts a day, seven days a week; that when *unsentenced* prisoners are added, the inmate-to-staff ratios are far higher; and that most of the 501 "professional staff" are concentrated in a handful of large urban jails.

The 600 smaller, more transient jails meeting our definition were not included in the NCCD survey. The LEAA found 33,729 full- or part-time jail employees in the nation, making the overall inmate-to-staff ratio only about 5:1 (L.E.A.A., 1971:14). It is clear that jails are staffed primarily for their custodial function, normally performed either by full-time guards, or law-enforcement personnel. Jails actually ought to employ relatively *more* custodial staff per inmate than felony prisons. The frequent turnover of inmates in jails, as well as the constant movement of prisoners to and from courts, would justify many more personnel for processing prisoners in and out of the institution. Since this processing and transportation normally take priority in

TABLE 1

POSITIONS IN JAILS AND LOCAL ADULT INSTITUTIONS, BY NUMBER

Positions	Numbers	Inmate-to-Staff Ratio
Professional Staff	501	282:1
Psychologists	33	4,282:1
Psychiatrists	58	2,436:1
Academic teachers	106	1,333:1
Vocational teachers	137	1,031:1
Social workers	167	846:1
Non-Professional Staff	18,694	8:1
Custodial officers	14,993	9:1
Other employees	3,701	38:1
Grand Total	19,195	7:1

Source: N.C.C.D., 1966:142.

terms of staff assignments, the pinch is felt elsewhere. As we shall see, both internal security and program flexibility suffer; prisoners can be kept in their cells most of the time to protect staff, but little can be done to protect cell-mates from each other, or to help them occupy their time constructively. Both the jail and the prison inmate-to-staff ratios are seriously overstated on the custodial side, for they take no account of the fact that the custodial staff must be deployed over three shifts, every day of the year. Moreover, insofar as nearly one-half of the daily manpower works on the day shift, the other shifts suffer staff shortages proportionately.

There are considerable variations in the extent of reliance on law-enforcement personnel. In Illinois county jails there are approximately equal numbers of guards and sheriff's deputies assigned to custodial duties, while in city jails 3 times as many patrolmen as guards are used (Mattick & Sweet, 1969:258). In California county jails, however, 8 times as many sworn personnel as non-sworn personnel are assigned to custodial duties, and outside of Los Angeles County sworn personnel are used almost exclusively for custodial functions (California Board of Corrections, 1970:103–4). On the other hand, those jurisdictions discussed earlier that have put control of the jail under "civilian" authority *presumably* use law-enforcement officers less, if at all.

The general inadequacy of jail custodial personnel, whether sworn or not, is apparent when one inquires into the requirements for hiring, salaries paid, and availability of in-service training. The NCCD reported that 53 percent of the estimated 3,473 jails holding sentenced prisoners for at least 30 days had no minimum educational qualifications for custodial officers, and 56 percent of all personnel in these institutions were not covered by any form of civil service or merit system. These percentages may be inflated, since, as the NCCD noted, such requirements often apply only to "regular" personnel, and the large numbers of "temporary" employees are not actually covered. Even more disturbing was the fact that the personal qualifications and educational requirements for "superintendents" were almost identical to those for regular employees (N.C.C.D., 1966:143–44). There could be no clearer indication that patronage interests will not be limited by educational or other qualifications for these positions. The Illinois survey revealed that 5 percent of cities and 62 percent of counties had no educational requirements for their employees; in 3 percent of city jails and 89 percent of county jails, *no one* worked under a merit system. Where minimum requirements were present, they were most often confined to all or some law-enforcement officers (Mattick & Sweet, 1969:272–75).

The NCCD found that the median starting salary for custodial officers in 1966 was $4,000–$5,000, with a range from under $1,500 to $9,000 a year; for superintendents and jailers the median was $7,000–$8,000, with a range of $1,500 to $18,000 (N.C.C.D., 1966:144). It is unlikely that salaries are significantly different in the 600 additional jails we are considering; the average earnings of *full-time* employees in the 4,037 jails surveyed by the LEAA was $617 per month (L.E.A.A., 1971:14). The Illinois survey revealed that city patrolmen doing some jail work are better paid (median starting salary $6,001–$7,500) than county deputies (median, $5,001–$6,000), and both are slightly better paid than non-sworn custodial personnel. The various service personnel—cooks, clerks, janitors—are paid even less, often under $400 per month (Mattick & Sweet, 1969:279–80). It is small wonder that the jail does not attract high quality personnel and that those who remain often seek outside employment to supplement their incomes.

A third determinant of personnel quality is the availability of in-service training. This is crucial, since so few custodial personnel in jails have *any* sort of prior training, and the training that law-enforcement officers receive has little or nothing to do with correctional work. The NCCD reported that only 38 percent of the jails it surveyed had any sort of in-service training, and of those programs found, many were little more than staff meetings or training in such skills as the use of firearms and "supervision of correspondence" (presumably that of inmates) (N.C.C.D., 1966:145). In Illinois, training programs were found to be almost nonexistent in small jails, and only ten of the thirty large and very large jails had what could be considered a minimal training program—usually a single preemployment orientation conference (Mattick & Sweet, 1969:276).

The result of these minimal or nonexistent standards for jail personnel is not surprising: poor staff and rapid turnover. There is a vicious circle here too: low salaries and patronage appointments increase the turnover rate, thus making any sort of training program appear uneconomical and insuring continuing low quality of performance, which further discourage county boards from granting salary increases and tenure. Moreover, the dual problems of low quality and high turnover have a profound effect on the jail milieu: the inmates represent continuity, especially where large numbers have previously been in the same jail, while the staff represents inexperience and transiency. Such a staff tends to be insecure and exhibits both over- *and* underconcern for security, and occasionally, resorts to brutality for lack of training and experience. It is one of the ironies of jail work in the United States that those who may be most in need of having respect for law and order, to wit, the inmates, are placed into the hands of those who are least likely to teach or exhibit it, to wit, the least-qualified and poorest-paid employees in the criminal justice system, the jail guards.

The Operating Costs of Jails

How much do jails cost to operate? Where does the money come from and how is it spent? This information is crucial to an assessment of the function of jails in the criminal justice system, yet it is, for the most part, unavailable. Furthermore, we are usually without the *qualitative* information necessary to put the dollars and cents figures into proper perspective. Low operating costs may or may not be a sign of efficiency; at the lower levels of the correctional system, they more often indicate scrimping on basic jail necessities, such as food, clothing, sanitation, and supervision, not to mention educative and rehabilitative programs. Since we already know that many of these aspects of the typical jail are deficient, however, we can draw at least one conclusion from the overall cost figures: jailing is expensive, and there is little to show for the investment. Alternate, noninstitutional modes of disposition have been found to be far cheaper in both money and human costs.

The LEAA reported that total operating costs for the fiscal year 1969 in the 4,037 jails surveyed were $324,278,000, or $80,326 per jail; $2,027 per inmate per year (assuming a constant inmate population of 160,000); and $6.00 per inmate per day (L.E.A.A., 1971:7–9).[32] The only other operating cost information supplied by the LEAA was payroll: the total payroll for March, 1970, was $18,094,578 (p. 14). When this figure is extrapolated to a full year, the total 1970 payroll cost becomes $217,134,936. Subtracting from total operating costs for fiscal 1969 (although costs for 1970 were undoubtedly higher), we arrive at a figure of $107,143,064 for all other operating expenses. It seems likely, however, that most of this money goes to pay for food. There are extremely wide state-to-state and within-state variations in the cost of

---

32. The LEAA excluded all "capital expenditures," such as "purchase of land and equipment and construction" from "operating expenditures."

jail food—in the state of Washington, for example, it varies from $0.13 to $1.75 per meal (Washington Department of Institutions, 1968:13). An average food cost of $1.50 per day per inmate is based on two facts: (1) for all states supplying a range of food costs, this figure was roughly intermediate; and (2) in about 50 percent of the Illinois county jails supplying this information, food costs per day were over $1.50 (Mattick & Sweet, 1969:145). Assuming this average cost per day and a constant prisoner population of 160,000, American jails would pay $87,600,000 a year for this item alone. As with the personnel statistics, these overall cost figures dramatically confirm the poverty of programs and resources available to most jails.

Local jails tend to have one of three kinds of budgets: (1) separate jail budgets reflecting all costs of jail operations; (2) mixed budgets, a part of which is available from the more general sheriff's or police department's budget and the remainder available from allocations made exclusively for certain jail functions; and (3) budgets that are inseparable from the more general sheriff's or police department's budget. The larger the jail, the more likely it is to have a separate budget, and the smaller the jail the more likely that its budget will be consolidated into a larger budget. In the case of the mixed budget, the most frequently separable item is the cost of food. Considering the record-keeping practices and quality of personnel available to jails, it is doubtful that most jailers have any idea of their operating costs. Moreover, even the annual budgets of jails, sheriffs, or police departments are apt to be misleading unless one makes a very careful search of the records for deficiency appropriations. A sheriff's office may have a budget allocation for jail operations based on estimates that the process of time reveals to have been too low. When that happens, the sheriff makes a special application for deficiency funds to the county board, but that amount is not reflected in the budget that was published some months earlier. The same thing is true of unexpended funds that revert to a general fund at the end of a fiscal year. There is very little cost accounting or cost-benefit analysis in jail operations.

As noted earlier, in terms of *capital* costs, small jails are less efficient because they must be designed with proportionately more surplus cell space to cover the wider percentage of fluctuations in prisoner population. There is some evidence to suggest that the same is true for operating costs; this follows, in part, for the same reasons (e.g., proportionately more staff must be hired, or at least kept on call, to anticipate peak loads), and also because of economies of scale in the purchase of supplies, preparation of food, laundry, etc. In the Illinois jail survey, thirty-two county jails had budgets sufficiently complete to permit analysis of cost factors and to justify comparisons: the average cost per inmate per day in the seventeen small jails was $8.00; in the ten large jails it was $7.50; and in the five very large jails it was only $3.50 (Mattick & Sweet, 1969:249).

Two caveats must be imposed, however. First, the lower costs in the very large jails may only reflect their somewhat lower salary costs per inmate, which is a result of their higher overall inmate-to-staff ratios. This is not necessarily a sign of efficiency; fewer staff per inmate means less supervision, poorer discipline, and fewer programs. However, the fact that relatively more of the staff in larger jails are full-time employees devoting all of their time to jail work does indicate an efficiency factor. Again, this may be the result of less fluctuation in prisoner population, which would justify more full-time help.

The second caveat has to do with how representative Illinois is of the nation. The only other information we have on the relationship between operating costs and jail size comes from North Carolina, and it is contrary to the Illinois figures: no significant differences appear between per capita costs for operating small, medium, and large jails (Ashman, 1969:56). One explanation for this difference may be that North Carolina has relatively fewer sentenced prisoners in its jails, and these are the men whose well-organized labor in the larger jails may contribute substantially to economies of scale. In the absence of data from other states, however, we would not be justified in asserting broadly that small jails are more expensive per capita, though it seems a very likely hypothesis.

A third aspect of jail costs, capital as well as operating, concerns the sources of funds for running the jail. Traditionally, and with few exceptions, jail financing has been the sole responsibility of the county, which means it must be borne by the over-burdened property tax, and must compete with schools, roads, sanitation, and other, more popular projects. Some states also levy jail fees on convicted prisoners; North Carolina charges convicted inmates $2.00 for each day of confinement, and from $2.00 to $15.00 is charged as a "facilities fee" in the court costs, part of which may be used for jails (University of North Carolina Institute of Government, 1967:19). Finally, some funds may be raised through inmate labor, although the jails, like all other prisons, are severely hemmed in by state and federal prison-industry legislation. However, the broader use of work-release programs is producing substantial funds for financing the costs of those few jails that have them. In such jails, the inmate's private-enterprise-scaled salary is first handed over to the jailer for deduction of costs of jailing and administration of the program, which thus pays for itself.

One more aspect of jail budgeting merits attention: the extent to which jails seem to derive some benefit, financially, from law-enforcement control and staffing. As already noted, law-enforcement officers make up a substantial proportion of jail personnel—sometimes 100 percent—and this creates the impression that jails have more funds for payroll than would be the case if jails were under civilian control. Of course, both law enforcement and jail administration suffer, but we must be prepared to admit that, in some communities at least, the public will more readily support the police force than it will a professional corrections program, and that it will vote money *indirectly* for jails that it would never vote directly. The current contribution to jails of budget money actually allocated to law enforcement is considerable; whether it is also wise is problematic.

The law-enforcement and correctional functions represent contradictory orientations toward the offender in different stages of his career. It would be a far better policy position to let the policeman get on with his law-enforcement functions and to operate jails with correctional personnel who are concerned with the successful reintegration of the offender into the law-abiding, free community.

Jail Administration

At the most basic level, the enormous gap between principles that are asserted at times of reasoned reflection and the daily practices that impinge on human lives in jails is the direct and predictable result of the fact that society has no clear sense of purpose about the functions jails should be serving for the community. Instead, there is a contradictory conglomerate of means and ends, including incapacitation, isolation, retribution, punishment, deterrence, and rehabilitation, that are supposed to be served simultaneously and with constructive results. This basic confusion of motives expresses itself in the inadequate provision of money, staff, physical plant, and program for jails that, in turn, perpetuates the vicious cycle of irrationality and waste comprising the jail problem. In such a "system," full of contradictions, dilemmas, and lack of human and material resources, a single overriding principle tends to assert itself as the controlling standard and guide for the relationship between jailers and prisoners: *custodial convenience.* Everyone who can takes the easy way out and makes only the minimal effort. It is a human response and readily understandable, but given the power distribution between jailers and prisoners, it is not surprising that jailers consult their own convenience and neglect that of the prisoners. What appears to be a conspiracy to achieve inefficiency, waste, and human degradation is more simply and accurately interpreted as the principle of custodial convenience asserting itself in the midst of a poverty of resources and imagination.

Prisoner Handling. The receiving of new prisoners and processing them into the jail is the first and most critical stage of prisoner handling. The effort expended at this stage has lasting consequences for every other aspect of jail administration, particularly the areas of record-keeping, health, security, and appropriate future treatment. It is axiomatic that all new prisoners should be thoroughly searched and examined, not only for the sake of security and the discovery of contraband but for the sake of health, i.e., the discovery of contagious disease and vermin. Appropriate identification and treatment records should be initiated. The prisoner's personal property should be inventoried and safely stored, and he should receive a written receipt so that he can reclaim it. There should be a clear and uniform policy on which prisoners are to be fingerprinted and photographed (usually those charged with the more serious crimes included in the FBI index). Each prisoner should receive a written copy of the jail rules and procedures, supplemented by an orientation talk for the sake of the functionally illiterate. Finally, based on the information gained through the foregoing procedures, the prisoner should be classified into the appropriate categories covering degree of security required and treatment method to be adopted in his future jail career. Depending upon his length of stay in the jail, his classification should be reviewed periodically in order to make adjustments based on experience. This is the minimal ideal.

In practice, in the vast majority of jails, few of these procedures, except those relating to security precautions, are followed. There is, of course, some variability in practice in jails of all sizes, with the larger urban jails approaching this minimal ideal more closely. But even there the emphasis is on security measures, with a lesser and decreasing concern for health and treatment. In many cases even the security precautions are superficial and perfunctory. Much of the lack in uniformity of receiving procedures and the inadequacy of record-keeping practices is due to the poor quality of jail personnel or to the use of arresting officers to process their own arrestees. In general, only the more seriously regarded prisoners, or the transient stranger, are likely to be searched and fingerprinted. Female prisoners are least likely to be searched or examined due to the lack of matrons. Only in the largest jails are prisoners given a routine medical examination on the day of admission. Such examinations are usually conducted at a rate of one minute per prisoner, but are better than nothing. In some of the medium-sized and smaller jails, medical examinations are conducted at intervals of every three days, once a week, or twice a month, rather than on the day of admission, and thus miss many prisoners and lose most of their preventive medical functions. Delousing procedures are rare, even in the larger jails, despite the large number of skid-row types received, and extermination measures against bedbugs, cockroaches, mice, and rats are highly sporadic. The vast majority of jails have no written rules for prisoners; the "rules" are arbitrary, improvised, or lie implicit in the realm of discretion. Inmates learn the rules by rumor, trial and error, and the risk of punishment. In the more primitive jails rules are established by the inmates themselves through kangaroo courts or barn-boss systems of control. Some jails post the rules where they can be seen by the inmates, but the jail that issues a set of written rules to every newly arrived prisoner is the rare exception.

The classification of prisoners for purposes of training or carrying out treatment programs is practically nonexistent, as are the programs themselves. Such classification of prisoners as is conducted is done for the sake of segregating prisoners into crude classes for separate celling and security handling. Such segregation seldom goes beyond the separation of the sexes, and the separation of juveniles from adults in the case of male prisoners. In a few of the larger urban jurisdictions, there are separate institutions for prisoners awaiting trial and those already sentenced, and in some of the larger jails containing both types of prisoners, there is effective internal separation of the sentenced and unsentenced. In the vast majority of jails, however, the more usual practice is the almost indiscriminate mixing of all classes of prisoners except males and females.

There is a ready explanation for this failure in elementary penological practice in most jails. When the main classifications of offenders (adult/juvenile, male/female, civil/criminal, sentenced/unsentenced, first/multiple offender, sick/healthy) are all considered, sixty-four categories of prisoners result, all of which should, theoretically, be housed separately. The average jail has about twenty cells, with an average of two beds per cell. It is thus possible for a jail with twenty cells and thirty prisoner types to be simultaneously two-thirds unsegregated and one-fourth empty; "perfect" segregation *and* utilization for such a jail could only be achieved if there were forty prisoners, two of each type. In practice, of course, neither of these hypothetical cases are likely to occur; usually there is adequate segregation and unused space in the cell areas allocated to women and juveniles, while the adult male quarters are overcrowded and commingled. At present jailers often *intentionally* fail to separate prisoner types for lack of staff to supervise them; drunks and suicide risks are placed with others "for their protection," and juveniles may be mixed with adults so the latter can "straighten them out."

The supervision of prisoners, or even simple surveillance, is largely a question of staff. The staffing of jails, generally, is inadequate, especially at night. Simply "looking in" on prisoners in their cells at night to make sure they are still there, have not died, or do not assault each other is frequently neglected. This much is necessary even with adequate segregation of prisoner types; the less segregation, the more supervision is required. The problems of supervising inmates during the daytime, or outside their cells, are avoided in most jails by the simple expedient of keeping them locked up almost all the time. In most of the larger urban jails with full-time guard staffs, there is what might be called adequate surveillance, but there is little supervision because, outside of a few housekeeping tasks, there is nothing to supervise. Except for the few jails with electronic or audiovisual devices (which are sometimes not even manned), inmates are usually left to their own devices for long periods of time, including all night. Prisoners soon learn that they tend to be checked at the change of shift, or at some other predictable time. Such supervision is ineffectual as a *preventive* measure. Reliance on "trusties" to report on inmate activities, usually after the fact, is not only unreliable, but frequently serves the purposes of the informer more than the administration.

Another important aspect of prisoner handling is the manner in which disciplinary problems are managed. Punishment that is consistent, commensurate, and subject to impartial review can be accepted as fair and help maintain morale. It will also tend to preserve a potential rehabilitative relationship between staff and inmates. It is, however, a highly exceptional jail that has any formal procedure for hearing, imposing, and reviewing disciplinary measures taken by the custodial staff. Most jails do not even keep a written record of the event, even though it may indirectly affect later assignment, disciplinary, or release decisions. Some disciplinary measures resorted to are open to question, both on humanitarian and utilitarian grounds. Corporal punishment, humiliation, and group punishment for the infractions of one or a few are far more frequent than an uninformed public may suspect. The various forms of "the hole," or isolation cell, simply serve to compound the behavior problems with which they purport to deal. Depriving inmates of privileges (assuming there are any) is always more effective than psychologically maladjusting or physically assaultive forms of punishment. Finally, it is absurd to punish or reward prisoners without first explaining what conduct is expected; yet, most jails do not even post or hand out written jail rules.

The final aspect of general prisoner handling and one of the most important in terms of preventing recidivism is the procedure leading up to and constituting release. Having spent some period in almost complete idleness, the prisoner has not been taught any useful skill, or even maintained his physical condition; he has not received any counseling or encouragement in finding and keeping employment. If he has been in jail for more than a few days, his economic situation and family ties have deteriorated and his job, if he had one, is gone. In short, in the absence of some concrete help, he is statistically more likely than ever to commit a crime. Yet, seldom is any attempt made to notify local welfare agencies of his release, to investigate job and housing possibilities, or to refer the inmate to a public or private welfare or employment service. Instead, the inmate is usually shown the door, driven to the center of town (or the county or city limits) and "dumped," or at best, given bus fare and a hot meal. Parole supervision is practically nonexistent for misdemeanants. Private prisoner-aid societies do their best to ease the transition, but their resources are meager and extended to very few ex-prisoners. Jails and parole authorities must take responsibility for every sentenced prisoner released. The same resources should be available to nonsentenced releasees on request.

Jail Security. There are two major aspects of jail security: the external or peripheral for the protection of the community by preventing escapes and the smuggling of contraband; and the internal for the protection of inmates and staff from riots, assaults, and suicides. Every aspect of jail administration bears on these problems, considering the serious problems of understaffing and the limitations of physical plant. Jails are much more successful in their task of safely "warehousing" their charges than in any other function (e.g., rehabilitation, or at least the prevention of criminal and moral contagion). But the incentives are high. The law is perfectly clear that prisoners are to be held securely, but is ambiguous or silent on the necessity for jails to have a constructive effect on their inmates. Journalists and political opportunists are quick to exploit any security breaches, but are relatively inarticulate about their underlying causes. Moreover, "success" in security is easy to measure and, for many, philosophically more congenial, especially when it comes to applying strict measures to accused or convicted criminals.

The major security factors have already been discussed under prisoner handling: proper search procedures for prisoners (and for visitors and staff as well); classification and segregation according to internal and external security needs; prisoner counts and identification; adequate, round-the-clock supervision; and swift but fair disciplinary measures. While some jail administrators seem to be unduly lax about security measures and others seem to be overly strict, it is not uncommon to find both tendencies simultaneously in the same jail. Such contradictory tendencies usually reflect "pet theories" about security rather than sound jail administration. Jail administrators who are not overly concerned with maintaining security could often tighten up considerably in some areas. Dangerous staff practices, such as wearing firearms into cell areas where they might be seized, could be eliminated readily from many jails, and detailed plans for emergencies (fire, escapes, riots) should be formulated in advance, but usually are not. Some factors are clearly beyond the control of the local jail administrator, however: inadequate staff coverage, especially on the night shift; jail structures with locks that don't work and walls that are literally crumbling; cells and dormitories designed with large "blind spots"; common toilet facilities, requiring the constant locking and unlocking of cells; insufficient cell space to allow segregation of prisoners dangerous to each other; and generally, the dank, depressive atmosphere so conducive to riots or suicides.

On the other hand, some jail administrators go overboard when it comes to the smaller details of jail security. Instead of relying on good peripheral security and the rational internal deployment of staff, they deplete the time and energies of their limited staffs by harassing the inmates in the details of daily living by frequent head counts, strip searches, cell "shakedowns," and the censorship of prisoner mail. In general, this is a wasteful use of scarce personnel. There is also a general tendency to treat *all* prisoners, except "trusties," as maximum security cases, while "trusties" are given too much freedom and responsibility because they are the de facto operators of the jail. Jailers probably realize that all of human nature cannot be forced into these two categories, but they often have little choice in the matter. In the absence of any substantial work, recreation, or rehabilitative programs, there is no justification for anything less than maximum security, and without sufficient staff, the temptation to rely on trusties to perform essential tasks of jail administration is almost irresistible.

Food Services. Good food is not only essential to the maintenance of health, which is a basic right even of inmates, but also, it is an important factor in maintaining discipline, morale, and reasonable conduct among prisoners. There will always be grumblings about institutional food—especially when the institutionalization is involuntary, and the facility poorly financed—but much can be done to improve the quality and quantity of jail food and the way it is served.

Jail prisoners should be fed three times a day, but frequently are not. The documentary evidence is scarce but the practice is more frequent than most people think. In some states, e.g., Washington, the *majority* of jails serve only two meals a day to all inmates, while "trusties" may receive a noon snack (Washington Department of Institutions, 1968:13). Another problem is the time of feeding; some jails serve meals when the staff has time, or worse, when someone remembers to stop in at the jail and attend to it. The elapsed time between the dinner meal and breakfast is the most persistent problem. If inmates are fed dinner at 3:00 P.M., and breakfast at 9:00 A.M., it is clear that eighteen hours have elapsed between meals. A third aspect of jail feeding is where it takes place; most jails feed in the cells or corridors, though larger jails may have separate dining rooms. As a result, more staff must be assigned to supervise feedings (or inmates must be used to pass out food, with consequent problems of controlling diversion of food or favoritism), and the food cannot be kept hot while serving.

Smaller rural jails frequently use the sheriff's wife as the cook, and the sheriff's family may eat the same food. But, while they may eat the same food, they also eat more of it and supplement it with items that do not appear on the jail menu. For small city jails, increasing reliance is being placed on nearby restaurants for "take-out" orders, or frozen TV dinners. In both cases, food costs are high, but the quality of the food is generally good. Larger jails usually have kitchen facilities of some sort, though they may be unsanitary, poorly maintained, and lack the basic equipment necessary to achieve economies of scale (such as ample storage and refrigeration space for large-scale buying). The food is generally prepared by inmates under the supervision of custodial employees and/or the sheriff's wife, since only the very largest urban jails can afford to pay professional chefs to supervise the kitchen help. Food service in jails has been a chronic problem. In recent years, some of the larger jails have experimented with catering contracts but the results have not been evaluated.

Medical Care. The most significant fact about medical care in jails has already been mentioned: 49 percent of the jails surveyed by the LEAA were without medical facilities "of any type" (L.E.A.A., 1971:7–19). Comparing the LEAA figure for Illinois (51.5 percent "without") with the results of the Illinois jail survey, which included "first aid" as a separate category and found only about 32 percent of Illinois jails with "no medical facilities"—64 percent had "first aid only" (Mattick & Sweet, 1969:164)—suggests that first-aid capacity of some sort was not included in the LEAA figures. Even so, it is shocking to find so many public institutions with such scant regard for public health. Most jail inmates are physically substandard and jails include a disproportionate number of persons with heart problems, diabetes, epilepsy, venereal disease, infectious hepatitis, tuberculosis, and a wide variety of physical injuries. A jail without even a simple infirmary will fail to address these health problems and, worse, will send the disease carrier back out into society to infect the general public. Most jails are simply unequipped and unstaffed even to provide emergency treatment.

The unavoidable implication of systematic medical neglect is confirmed when we examine the availability of trained medical personnel. Only the very largest urban jails employ a doctor, and he usually works on a part-time basis. Instead, when provided by law, reliance is placed on county health officers or physicians who have many other duties. The more usual medical procedure, if that is what it can be called, is to rely on "on-call" doctors or to escort inmates to local hospitals or doctors' offices. Similarly, the availability of nursing personnel, registered or practical, male or female, is no better, and in some states is worse. For example, in all of Illinois's 160 jails, only 2 outside of Chicago had any nurses; 21 had on-call doctors, and 3 had part-time doctors (Mattick & Sweet, 1969:166).

With such a poverty of resources, it is clear that most jails either ignore the medical problems of their inmates, rely on "on-call" doctors, or take inmates out of the jail to local doctors or hospitals. There are serious problems associated with medical care outside of the jail, however. First of all, inmates must display sufficiently obvious and serious symptoms for untrained jail personnel to detect them *and* to be motivated to take the rather drastic step of escorting the inmate out of the jail. Second, there are necessarily considerable delays involved. Finally, most hospitals are not equipped with security wards. This, combined with understaffing, makes jails reluctant to send inmates to hospitals, for guards must be assigned to the sick inmate around the clock, which make some hospitals reluctant to accept prisoners or the mentally ill.[33]

There are similar problems involved in the use of "on-call" doctors: the initial "examination" and the decision to call in professional medical personnel is based on

---

33. The North Carolina Jail Study Commission (1969:16–17) also cited the fear on the part of hospital administrators that they would not be reimbursed for their services. Apparently, neither admission nor temporary county reimbursement is required by law in North Carolina, although it is in some states.

the judgment of untrained jailers, considerable delays are unavoidable, and many doctors are reluctant to visit the jail. Under such circumstances, an inmate's condition must be fairly desperate before the jailer can prevail upon the doctor to come to the jail, generally some distance from the doctor's home or office.

Given the high cost of medical care, however, and the shortage of doctors and nurses, it is not clear what alternatives are available to small jails. A regular doctor's sick call, once a day if possible, is all that can be expected. This is another argument in favor of larger regional jails, of course; a jail which normally admits 25 prisoners a day and normally holds about 300, could afford to hire a full-time nurse and arrange for daily sick calls and admission physicals by a full-time or several part-time doctors. As for dental care, it is usually nonexistent in the jail. In serious emergencies, inmates are occasionally taken out of the jail to private dentists, where the care provided usually consists of extraction. Problems related to eyeglasses, crutches, and prostheses are simply ignored. Here again, there are few economically feasible alternatives for small jails.

The care of the mentally ill, who are still routinely confined in jails in some states, is similarly absent. They may be separated from other inmates if violent, and perhaps physically restrained; nonviolent mentally ill inmates often receive no special handling. The latter are usually viewed as "good prisoners" by untrained jail personnel. Neither type should be held in jails at all, of course. But when no other immediate alternative exists, they should only be held long enough to arrange transfer to the appropriate mental-health facility; while in the jail they should be separated from other inmates and carefully supervised. The lack of medical personnel, however, as well as the lack of properly trained nonmedical personnel, combined with the usual lack of facilities for proper segregation of prisoners, results in the commingling of the mentally ill with all other kinds of prisoners. Under such circumstances, the mentally ill tend to be exploited and victimized, and their condition is aggravated.

Prisoner Hygiene. Considering the inadequacy of medical care in jail, even for contagious diseases, serious illness, or injury, and the general dirtiness of the average physical plant, it is not too surprising to find that prisoners themselves usually go dirty. Between security restrictions on inmate movements, lack of staff, and poor plumbing, personal cleanliness is problematic. The absence of laundry facilities and supplies in many jails is also a factor; even the jails that issue blankets, bed linen, and towels often fail to launder them between uses. The facilities for inmates to wash their own clothes are often lacking. Paradoxically, it is the medium-sized jails that are most often deficient in this respect; large jails usually have some kind of a laundry, and in the smallest jails the jailer's wife may do jail laundry along with her own.

The optimum statement that can be made on behalf of jails regarding personal hygiene is that most jails issue toilet paper, soap, and dirty blankets to incoming inmates. Very few jails provide sheets, toothbrushes, shaving equipment, or any kind of clothing. Haircuts may be available to those who can pay for them, as are some personal-hygiene articles, if the jail has a store. In general, city jails provide less of the personal amenities than county jails, and the inmate without money, or friends to bring him these supplies, stays dirty. Poor prisoner hygiene and general lack of sanitation contribute directly to poor prisoner morale. These are a constant threat to the inmates, the staff, and the community at large. The principle of custodial convenience in this area is the equivalent of maintaining a public nuisance, but there is little interest in prosecution. The negative effect on court appearances by dirty defendants is considerable, especially for the indigent inmate who goes to trial before a judge who values cleanliness.

Jailers argue that it is uneconomical to provide clean clothing, bedding, and personal hygiene articles to their "transient" population awaiting trial, and that some articles pose security risks. The answer to the first point, once again, is that larger, regional jails could readily exploit economies of scale in buying, laundering, and mending. Such jails might even engage in the manufacturing of personal hygiene articles. Moreover, a little use of the imagination in this area could have considerable impact. The use of plastic-covered mattresses, washable mattress covers, paper towels, and disposable cups is not all that novel. Similarly, the temporary issue of electric razors and hair-clippers would not be a threat to security. The repair of toilets, sinks, and shower heads should have the same priority as lock repair. Jails are supposed to be an agency of criminal justice, not the poorly disguised instrument of class and cultural warfare.

Inmate Rights and Privileges. In the absence of enforceable statutory laws or controlling administrative rules, rights for inmates are without practical effect and privileges are easily denied. There is entirely too much left to discretion with a resulting arbitrariness and a lack of equity that works to everyone's disadvantage. Jailers do not know what they can or should do and inmates do not know what to expect.

The first thing that needs to be said about inmate "privileges," such as visits, the sending and receiving of correspondence, and recreation, is that they should be the right of all inmates who observe jail rules. All too often, however, these basic rights are restricted or granted on an arbitrary or discriminatory basis. The fact that some prisoners may require a greater degree of security than others may be a legitimate reason for restricting the movement of some inmates inside the jail, but even here jailers should make finer distinctions than only "maximum security" and "trusty." Other privileges, such as extra food, access to radio or TV, and the occasional distribution of tobacco or cigarettes, which by their nature often cannot be granted to all, should be rotated on an equitable basis. In some situations, it may be possible to allow inmates to earn scarce extra privileges by rotating the opportunity to volunteer for extra work. In any case, the rights of inmates should be published and enforceable and privileges should be earnable equally.

In discussing visiting arrangements, it is necessary to distinguish between attorneys and other visitors. The Sixth Amendment's provision for the right to counsel requires that attorneys be allowed to visit in privacy at all reasonable times. Similarly, it seems clear that the Eighth Amendment's right to reasonable bail is denied if visitors who come to arrange bail are not also admitted at all reasonable hours, but the courts have not yet ruled on this point. As a practical matter, jails that hold large numbers of persons awaiting trial tend to be more liberal about visiting, especially when visitors come to bail out inmates, because they are happy to be relieved of the responsibility for feeding and supervising prisoners. Jails holding a larger proportion of sentenced prisoners tend to be more restrictive about visiting privileges. The visiting policies of jails are largely determined by custodial convenience.

In most jails, members of the clergy are allowed more liberal access to inmates than other visitors, although separate rooms for counseling are rarely available. Not only is there the First Amendment's right to consult with one's minister, but the same right extends to refusing to see a minister not of one's choosing. The latter is worth mentioning because many jailers admit itinerant evangelists into the jail on Sundays to engage in "soul saving." Nevertheless, ministers may provide most or all of the social services available to inmates. They may write letters and furnish stamps, provide reading material, seek assistance and employment, and intercede in family problems. If properly trained and ordained, they may also provide personal guidance and spiritual support.

Visiting rules for other persons should attempt to strike a reasonable balance between the security and administrative needs of the jail, on the one hand, and the goal of encouraging visits to improve prisoner morale and maintain stabilizing ties with the family and community, on the other. It is reasonable for jail administrators to put time limits on individual visits, and establish daily visiting hours, but when visits are as short as fifteen minutes, and scheduled for weekdays during working hours, as is not infrequent, then visiting is discouraged. Moreover, most jails have no suitable place where the constructive purposes of visiting can be served under secure conditions. Instead, visitors usually stand outside the cell area, within earshot of both guards and inmates, where nothing friendly or endearing can pass between them without exposure to the idle curiosity of others.

Finally, considering the paucity of amenities in most jails, a list of acceptable items that visitors may bring to inmates should be published or presented to visitors in advance. As with jail rules generally, however, very few jails follow this practice, and most jails are very restrictive about what inmates may be allowed to receive or keep in their cells. On the other hand, some jails allow visitors to bring in all kinds of food, clothing, and supplies. While such seeming liberality may reduce costs, it is a poor policy for jail administrators to rely on visitors to supply necessities. Too many inmates have no one but the jailer to rely on, so a balance must be struck in this regard.

Mail is a source of considerable friction between inmates and staff due to the common practice of censoring correspondence to and from prisoners. Considering the fact that the content of face-to-face communication is not censored, it seems a little ridiculous for jails to spend so much time reading and editing prisoner's mail when such manpower would more effectively serve jail security if it were employed in supervision and maintenance. Jailers have a profound concern for allegations of brutality, deprivation, and mismanagement often contained in outgoing mail, but censorship does not deal with such problems. Some courts have held that, for this reason, censorship of mail must be justified by "compelling" reasons of jail security. Arbitrary or frivolous censorship has been held to jeopardize the First Amendment's right to petition for redress of grievances. Some jails also limit the number of letters that may be sent or received, and many jails refuse to contribute to the cost of postage. Since many inmates are without funds or local relations, the denial of mail privileges means total isolation.

From the standpoint of physical and mental health as well as general morale, perhaps the most important jail "privilege" is recreation. In many jails the constant playing of a radio, or to a lesser extent, of a television set, which one modern jail study described as "without equal as a pacifying agent in the context of institutional life" (California Board of Corrections, 1970:84), has been the major mode of passive diversion. But there have been few opportunities for exercise offered to jail inmates. The LEAA reported that 86.4 percent of the 4,037 jails it surveyed were without recreational facilities or programs *of any kind* (L.E.A.A., 1971:18). Presumably this percentage refers to exercise yards, gyms, and other physical activities. Generally speaking, playing cards and board games, reading matter, and radio or TV, when they are available, are considered sufficient to meet the recreational needs of jail inmates. The result is predictable: demoralization combined with pent-up energies that are dissipated in constant discussion of planned or previous criminal escapades, alleged sexual encounters, and the possibilities of escape. It is this interminable gossip, daydreaming, and verbal rehearsal of a deviant fantasy life that fills the vacuum left by a lack of constructive recreation activities, which is the major reason why jails are frequently "schools of crime."

The objective conditions that tend to limit recreational activities in most jails are lack of staff, absence of supervision and physical facilities, and budgetary restrictions. Observations of the few jails that do provide active and diverse recreational programs, however, indicate that the attitudes, motivations, and ingenuity of the jail administrator are just as important. Jailers who actively seek donations of books, games, clothes, and other equipment are usually successful; nondeliverable magazines and periodicals can be obtained from the U.S. Post Office at no charge; volunteers can be encouraged to come and engage the inmates in artistic and expressive ventures. Law books should be made available to inmates so that they can learn something about the law. Many functional illiterates have taught themselves to read while in jail pursuing appeals of indeterminate merit. To the extent that these activities lead to broader community awareness and involvement in the jail or the personal development of inmates, they yield additional dividends, both for rehabilitation and finances. Again, it is a question of whether custodial convenience or purposeful effort will be the dominant principle in jail administration.

Work and Treatment Programs. The "curse of idleness" in most jails is reflected not only in the lack of active recreation, but also in the almost complete absence of meaningful work and rehabilitative programs. "Janitorial and institutional maintenance tasks" constitute the entire "rehabilitation program" in most jails, at least for sentenced inmates. There is a constitutional question about "compelling" unconvicted prisoners to do anything more than to clean their own cells, although such prisoners often volunteer for work out of sheer boredom. A court must determine, through conviction, that a person is a fit object for punishment or for "rehabilitation" by mopping the cellblock floors or picking up paper in the yard. In a few of the larger and medium-sized jails, trusties may be used extensively to perform janitorial, maintenance, laundry, and culinary work. To a lesser extent a more carefully screened and supervised group of prisoners may be used to do outside work in the public parks, on highways, and in public buildings and grounds. In some jurisdictions sentenced jail prisoners engage in farming activities to supply food for their own jail and other tax-supported institutions. Nearly all this work is manual and unskilled; it is pursued in such a fashion that it could never lead to efficient and productive work habits. Training prisoners in new and salable skills is invariably subordinated to work or production that benefits the city, county, or state. Such jail prisoner work as there is usually occupies only a few hours a day; three men are assigned to do work that could not keep one man busy, and sometimes it is done only to occupy time:

> a very bright shine of the cement floor was noted. Inmate minors are assigned to polish and buff these floors three times a day, producing a mirror-like finish. So meticulous is the superintendent about the condition of these floors that other prisoners are assigned to follow each buffing machine on their hands and knees and flick the dust out of the cracks between the blocks of cement (New York State Commission, 1966:36).

Despite the general inefficiency and low productivity of the few organized work programs for jail inmates, where they exist they are viewed as valuable by jail administrators and officials concerned with local budgets. Since such labor is usually unpaid, it is viewed as being without cost to the local jurisdiction. It is, therefore, not surprising that jailers and local officials have remarked that they would resist the wider use of rehabilitative programs, such as work-release measures and proposals for regional jails (e.g., North Carolina Jail Study Commission, 1969:10; California Board of Corrections, 1970:50–52, 129–30). Apparently the "something for nothing" psychology that brings many men to jails also infects their keepers. This source of resistance is, however, a minor problem; in most jails the problem is idleness rather than who shall benefit from inmate labor.

Much of the idleness in American jails, particularly in the case of sentenced prisoners, could be mitigated through wider adoption and implemention of work-release statutes, typified by Wisconsin's pioneer Huber Law [Wisc. Stat. Ann., §56.08(1971 Cum. Ann.)]. Under this system, the prisoner is allowed to keep his job in the community or is encouraged to find a job; each weekday morning he is released from jail to go to work, returning in the evening. The inmate's salary is collected directly by the jail administrator, and after costs of administering the program, housing and feeding the inmate, and supporting his dependents are subtracted, the rest is credited to his account to be used for personal expenses while in jail and paid out to him upon release.

Of course, such a program requires a more professional classification system than usually exists to decide which prisoners merit this treatment. Care must be taken that, on the one hand, the risk of runaways does not threaten the advantages of the program and, on the other, that persons are not committed to jail under the work-release program who might better be placed on probation. Ideally, work-releasees should also be segregated from other inmates to avoid the problem of smuggling contraband and to facilitate group movements in the jail. The question of carrying contagious diseases out of, or into, the jail is also a consideration. Employers may also be reluctant to hire or retain convicted misdemeanants without an adequate bonding procedure. For all these reasons, which cause administrative inconvenience, and out of a desire to maintain control over the marginal benefits of inefficiently utilized cost-free inmate labor, many sheriffs and county boards have been reluctant to implement existing enabling statutes. In California, for example, only 36 percent of the counties were using work-release in 1969 (California Board of Corrections, 1970:53). California law requires the board of supervisors to pass an ordinance implementing the statute in the county; after that, however, the "work furlough administrator" (who may be the sheriff, probation officer, or farm or camp supervisor) may assign *any* prisoner to work furlough unless the sentencing court has forbidden it (Cal. Penal Code, §1208). Similarly, Illinois jails may organize work-release programs [Ill. Rev. Stat., ch. 75, §35 (1967)], yet our survey found only 6 jails out of 160 that had embryonic work-release programs. Moreover, of the remaining 154 jails, only 3 anticipated organizing such programs upon the building of new facilities (Mattick & Sweet, 1969:235).

Yet the advantages are considerable; not only does the inmate's salary save the county the expense of both his upkeep *and* that of his dependents (who might otherwise be on relief), but from a rehabilitative point of view, work-release also limits the criminogenic impact of isolation in the demoralizing environment of the jail. It also tends to insure that the inmate will continue to work once his sentence is completed. Furthermore, it avoids the resentment caused by "busy work" or the exploitation of inmate labor for "public" benefit. Work-release also tends to prevent the conversion of all inmate skills to manual labor, regardless of their previous training or experience. Indeed, even the largest jails could not manage to provide the range of work offered in the private sector to match the skills of all inmates. In any case, since the overwhelming majority of jail inmates are unskilled and unemployed, local authorities would have little to fear in lost public-works manpower if work-release were implemented.

Only the largest jails offer any sort of academic training; usually high-school courses are offered to a few of the younger sentenced inmates. Jails of all sizes tend to experiment with volunteer teachers in this area from time to time, but the programs seldom get established. Some work-release statutes provide for daytime release to local education programs, but this option, as well as the possibilities of broader cooperation with local school districts, is largely unexploited. Considering the high illiteracy rate that still prevails among jail inmates, much more needs to be done in this area and is feasible, despite the problems posed by short jail sentences and custodial convenience.

Vocational training programs are even fewer, and, similarly, are limited to a few sentenced inmates. Many of these programs are pursued blindly, with little or no regard for the current demand for the skills being taught. The California Board of Corrections (1970:51–66) compared the skills taught in California county jails with the current and projected demand for those skills, using data from the California Department of Human Resources Development and found that most of the skills being taught were in low demand, limited to a few geographic locations, or were otherwise unsalable due to union membership, or high-school equivalency and bonding requirements. A major reason for failure of these vocational training programs is that they are often institutional work programs in disguise, designed to meet the production needs of the county, not the future vocational needs of inmates or the employment market.

The only other rehabilitative program found in any number of jails is for alcoholics, and it usually consists of permitting outside groups, such as Alcoholics Anonymous, to hold meetings within the jail. Since jails normally have no medical programs for alcoholics, despite the fact that about half the jail population has a severe drinking problem, this is a poor showing; but the answer is probably not more treatment in the jail, but rather confinement in separate detoxification centers (as discussed later, starting on p. 827). It is doubtful whether jails will ever have the medical and counseling resources to handle their alcoholics properly.

There has been increasing agreement that alcoholism should be treated as a public-health problem not simply as a crime, as is implied in arresting and jailing drunks. It would also be cheaper to design and build separate facilities expressly for voluntary housing of alcoholics (and perhaps certain drug users), rather than to try to adapt existing, expensive, maximum-security cell structures to what is, essentially, a minimum-security population. Moreover, jails are neither staffed nor equipped to deal with delirium tremens or other narcotic-withdrawal symptoms. On the other hand, some jail administrators will even resist the removal of alcoholics from their domain:

> experienced jail supervisors know that many of the older alcoholics are docile, amiable, and obedient workers when sober, as well as experienced in the ways of an institution. Some of these same supervisors are reluctant to change the system which provides such workers when no alternative sources of labor are apparent (California Board of Corrections, 1970:130).

RECOMMENDATIONS FOR REFORM

Conditions in contemporary jails of the United States and the problems that plague them are neither new nor uncommon. They are sufficiently general to be considered the "norm" of the nation and have repeatedly been brought to public attention over the past hundred years. There is, of course, some variability among jails: a few have a newer or better physical plant, some are better staffed and administered than others, and some manage to perform constructively despite severe limitations. On the whole, however, the few exceptions only test the rule; they do not break it. The rule is that the vast majority of jails are bad institutions from every point of view.

Only a systematic, fundamental, sustained, and cooperative effort on the part of the legislative, judicial, and executive branches of government at all levels, together with an interested and informed public, will enable the jails of the United States to play a constructive role in a rational system of criminal justice. The problems that beset jails will not be "solved" by improvising a piecemeal political patchwork of minor ameliorations. They will not yield to the political opportunism of scapegoating a few jail administrators who are the prisoners of conditions over which they have little control. If we are serious about jail reform, more basic methods and changes are required.

We have seen what is wrong with contemporary American jails. Implicit in the details of our indictment were many suggestions for change. There have been several serious efforts to formulate specific standards, applicable to individual jails (e.g., Alexander, 1957; California Board of Corrections, 1963; A.C.A., 1966a; Illinois Department of Corrections, 1971a, 1971b), but, for the most part, these "standards" are addressed to the amelioration of existing jails. That is not what we mean by reform in the present discussion. If jail reform is to be effective, it must transcend the individual jail and must be conceived in a broader, more systemic manner, which sees the jail problem as an integral part of the entire criminal justice system. The failure of local reformers, well-motivated jail administrators, and interested politicians to come to grips with the specific jail problems already enumerated is due, in large part, to their inability to adopt this wider perspective.

This broader conception of jail reform can be set forth at three levels of attack, each more fundamental and more likely to be effective in the long run than the last. First, as indicated in the chapters on alcoholic, narcotic, and sex offenders in this book, some forms of behavior, presently defined as criminal, can be decriminalized, and some parts of the present jail population can be diverted to other facilities through noncriminal procedures. Decriminalization does not imply social approval of conduct previously defined as criminal. It simply asserts what has become historically evident: that criminal law is not equally effective in dealing with all forms of individual and social deviance, and that it is time to deal with such conduct, insofar as it remains problematic after the criminal stigma has been removed, by more appropriate agencies, e.g., medicine, public health, welfare, and family counseling. Similarly, the diversion of some portions of the present jail population is not simply a proposal for a wholesale jail delivery; it is, rather, a set of proposals for more individualization of treatment, more adequate screening methods, and other safeguards, so that diversion from jail is consistent with public safety and greater efficiency and economy. This is, perhaps, the least radical approach to jail reform for two reasons: (1) many of these changes could be effected at the state or local level, if there were some disposition to do so, and, hence, do not present themselves as attempts at "outside interference," which is usually resented by local government; and (2) the basic assumption of this level of attack is that local jail conditions, at individual jails, are likely to remain the same for the foreseeable future, but it may be possible to avoid these conditions by either preventing people from entering jails or minimizing their impact on those people who are exposed to them.

The second level of systemic reforms consists of the variety of ways it may be possible to increase state and federal participation in local jail administration, short of outright control. This development is already taking place in some states, but it is hesitant and uneven, and the states have a long way to go in providing effective supervision, control, and financial support. Such cautious state intervention, however, may be a necessary intermediate stage toward the total integration of jails into the state criminal justice system, or the achievement of some lesser restructuring of jail control.

The most radical level of jail reform is to attempt to achieve it through either a reorganization of local government or the restructuring of local control. There are many forms such reorganization can take, although experience with even some of the milder forms casts doubt on their viability. They range all the way from the abolition of county government (or at least some of its criminal justice functions) to the mere upgrading of the sheriff's office. While the latter alternative runs counter to earlier proposals, it may be better than doing nothing except merely maintaining the status quo.

In general, the reform measures presented thus far and elaborated in the following sections are intended as a list, not a strategy; any one or more of these recommended measures, if adopted, would improve jail conditions to some degree.

Diversion

Persons accused of crime, or convicted and sentenced, may be diverted from the traditional criminal legal process at any of several points from arrest to, and after, sentencing.

Arrest. Much jailing could be avoided by more adequate prearrest screening procedures. For example, most nonsupport and other essentially domestic cases could be settled without the need to resort to arrest (see discussion of prescreening procedures, N.C.C.D., 1966:130–31). More careful judicial review for the issuance of warrants, and of decisions by law-enforcement officers to arrest without a warrant, would tend to reduce unnecessary arrests and subsequent jailings. Finally, the policeman's "citation" or "notice to appear," and the court-issued "summons," as a substitute for physical arrest and custody, should be more widely authorized and utilized for the relatively minor offenses that usually result in jailing [A.B.A., 1968b: §2.1, §3.1; Ill. Rev. Stat., ch. 38, §107–1(b) (c)]. Where such procedures have been tried, the proportion of defendants failing to appear for trial has been very low (see, e.g., Robinson, 1944:87; President's Commission, 1967c:40–44; Vera Institute of Justice, 1968). With the increasing combination of radio communications and centralized computer information to help the police in making quick identifications and verifications, the necessity of making physical arrests should be sharply reduced.

Detention, Bail, and Speedy Trial. When an arrest is necessary or unavoidable: to terminate an illegal activity, to permit a more secure identification, or to obtain further assurance of appearance at trial, it does not follow necessarily that the defendant must remain in jail until acquitted, sentenced, or otherwise discharged. Considering the deleterious consequences of jailing, every effort consistent with public safety should be made to divert prisoners from the jail at the earliest possible time. The ordinary procedures that should be available by law to effect such diversion are release on personal recognizance, percentage-deposit bail, or the traditional bail. Despite the Eighth Amendment's prohibition against requiring "excessive" bail, the perennial concern for bail reform, proposals for increased use of release on recognizance, and even a few lawsuits seeking equal protection for the rich and the poor, the fact remains that the poor stay in jail while the similarly accused, but rich, are able to buy their release. For the prisoners who cannot be released through these measures, every effort should be made to guarantee a speedy trial.

The pretrial defendant who is lodged in jail cannot contribute to his own defense. He has difficulty hiring a competent attorney, locating witnesses, and rallying general support. Moreover, through enforced unemployment and reduced income, he cannot pay the cost of his defense. The physical conditions usually imposed on him by his jailing, including idleness, demoralization, and lack of sanitation, result in a dirty and dissolute appearance in court. A defendant who conveys such an impression to the sentencing authorities is readily stereotyped as unreliable, and may be denied the opportunity to demonstrate his trustworthiness and capacity to adhere to some condition of release. The vicious circle is completed: he cannot now be released because he was not previously released. Even if a jailed defendant were clearly guilty and would be convicted in any case, he ought to have the same chance in court as his equally guilty brother who has been free on some form of pretrial release. Studies of comparable bailed and jailed defendants have shown a disproportionate conviction rate for those who were held in jail (Foote, 1954, 1958; University of Pennsylvania Law Review, 1958; Kamin, 1965; O'Reilly & Flanagan, 1967). For all of these reasons, every defendant who can be released from jail, consistent with public safety, should be released pending trial (A.B.A., 1968b).

Among the measures mentioned, the favored method of release should be on personal recognizance, that is, upon the promise of the accused to appear for trial, with explicit penalties for willful failure to appear. If that is deemed inadequate assurance, periodic check-ins or restrictions on movement can be imposed. The defendant may also be released into the custody of a responsible person. If that is insufficient assurance, then the posting of cash bail may be required, but the discriminatory character of cash bail can be mitigated by requiring only a percentage of the total to be deposited in the form of money or other security [A.B.A., 1968b:§1.2(c); Ill. Rev. Stat., ch. 38, §110 (1963); U.S. Bail Reform Act, tit. 18, §3146(3) (1966)]. To force the poor to rely on bail bondsmen is to expose them to an exploitive as well as a discriminatory release procedure as an alternative to jail.

In a number of jurisdictions where release on recognizance is accompanied by adequate screening procedures, the court-appearance rate of persons so released has been more than 90 percent. Moreover, if there is a minimal effort to contact the strays and to remind the absentminded, the actual "jump rate" is about 2 percent (e.g., Ares et al., 1963; Molleur, 1966; Levin, 1969; Hawthorne & McCully, 1970; O'Rourke & Carter, 1970). This performance level is equal to or better than the "jump rate" under traditional bail procedures. The crux of the matter lies in adequate screening and quick verification of information. If the judges who conduct release and bail hearings had a professional staff to interview defendants, verify the information received, and make recommendations about release, perhaps they would feel less vulnerable. The most logical location for this function would be in the probation service. The traditional role of probation officers, who have made presentence investigations and supervised probationers, could be expanded to include prerelease investigations to advise the judge. At present, the resources available to most county probation authorities are meager, and they are already overwhelmed by the case loads they must try to handle. In a more adequate criminal justice system, however, probation departments would not only make presentence investigations and supervise probationers, they would also be the screening staff for pretrial release, they would collect fines on the installment plan so that fine payment could be converted into a counseling and supervision opportunity, and they would supervise all kinds of postinstitutional releasees.

For the accused population not eligible for some form of pretrial release, speedy trials are the quickest way to get them out of inadequate jails. As Senator Sam J. Ervin,

Jr. (1971:291–99) noted, speedy trials are the constitutional alternative to preventive detention. Since most of the crime committed by persons released on bail occurs *after* the first sixty days on release, the problem of crime by bailees could be largely resolved by simply speeding up judicial processes. But, more important, speedy trial could shorten the de facto "preventive detention" of prisoners who cannot afford bail. As the senator also noted, however, the right to a speedy trial is a forgotten guarantee of the Constitution. While some of the present pretrial delays are attributable to defense maneuvers, particularly by those defendants who can afford both bail and knowledgeable attorneys, much of this kind of delay could be eliminated by a closer inquiry into motions for continuances (President's Commission, 1967b:84–88; A.B.A., 1967:§1.3, §2.1). In particular, the "green continuance" some lawyers use to help collect their fees before a trial is resolved should be discontinued and made grounds for disbarment and impeachment. Even when, as at present, urban court dockets are overloaded, rural courts sit too infrequently; if it is impossible to grant an absolute right to trial within a short period, every effort should be made to schedule criminal cases ahead of civil cases, and to give priority to trials for defendants sitting in jail (A.B.A., 1967:§1.1). The implementation of speedy trials by existing judges depends, in large part, on the degree of supervision exercised by the superior courts.

Even at the detention level, the negative impact of inadequate jails could be mitigated for certain particularly vulnerable classes of prisoners who are ineligible for pretrial release, if alternate and more appropriate detention facilities were provided for them. The catchall detention jail with a heterogeneous population can serve none of them well, and does a disservice to the community. Specialized detention facilities should be provided for female and juvenile prisoners awaiting trial. Similarly, the criminally accused, who are mentally or physically ill, the alcoholic, and the drug addict should be routed to more appropriate facilities under secure conditions until their cases are resolved or they recover. The contemporary jails of the United States, for the most part, can only aggravate the vulnerable condition of such defendants.

Sentencing Alternatives. The simplest sentencing alternatives for reducing jail populations are suspended sentence, summary probation, and probation without verdict (N.C.C.D., 1966:119–21). The first alternative is recommended "where apprehension and conviction have so thorough a corrective impact on the offender that supervision by probation is unnecessary" (Council of Judges, 1957:24;A.B.A., 1968a:68). It should be emphasized that the suspended sentence is an alternative to formal probation, and that it should be based on a presentence report from the probation service indicating that supervision is unnecessary. In practice, however, judges tend to base suspended sentences on their own intuition, due to the practical necessity of disposing of minor cases, and the lack of adequate probation services. It is not suggested that a full report is required for *every* offender, but only that investigatory services be available when judges need them. Considering the numerous and far-ranging collateral consequences of criminal conviction and jailing, the increased use of the suspended sentence alternative in every appropriate case is strongly recommended. Such a judicial disposition has the advantages of retaining a deterrent impact, avoiding further criminalizing contacts in jail, limiting the strain on already overloaded probation staffs, and avoiding the economic discrimination inherent in the only other sentencing alternative with all of these benefits, the use of fines.

At an intermediate stage between suspended sentence and probation, in terms of degree of supervision required, are summary probation and probation without verdict. Under the latter sentencing alternative, defendants are afforded the opportunity to nullify their conviction if they avoid further criminal activity within a specified period. Under both alternatives the court may impose certain conditions, provide for contingent jail sentences if those conditions are violated, and rely on varying degrees of supervision by the probation authorities. These practices provide needed flexibility in sentencing; however, as with the suspended sentence, there is a tendency to rely on these alternatives for reasons of expediency and necessity. The general use of "summary probation," without either presentence investigation or supervision, is undesirable (N.C.C.D., 1966:120; A.B.A., 1968a:69).

We come now to the heart of the matter: the current state of probation services for misdemeanants. In general, the degree of state participation in probation is greater than for local detention and corrections as a whole. According to the NCCD survey, twenty states have a state system of probation services for misdemeanants, and seven states have a combined state and local system. In practice, however, many of these "systems" receive very few referrals from lower courts, and the survey of 250 representative counties throughout the United States found about one-third to be without any probation services. Furthermore, even where probation was both available and in use, investigation and supervision were inadequate: of the 277,185 persons placed on misdemeanant probation in 75 sample counties in 1965, only 19 percent had had the benefits of a presentence investigation; the average case load for misdemeanant probation was 114. Thus, it is not surprising that in 1965 at least 4 times as many persons were locked up in jail as were placed on probation; the existing, local probation "systems" were already severely overloaded (N.C.C.D., 1966:121–34).

Adequate probation services for misdemeanants would be one of the wisest investments of scarce criminal justice dollars. First, the investigatory services best provided by these officers would be useful at all the postarrest stages of criminal proceedings: at the prerelease screening stage, at the bail hearing, and at the sentencing stage. Second, the cost of placing prisoners on probation instead of in jail is much lower; even if salaries and staff were upgraded so that more professional probation services could be provided, the savings would still be substantial.[34] Finally, investment in better probation services at the lower levels of the criminal justice system yields dividends throughout the system. The NCCD has indicated that "the national experience with probation demonstrates that, properly financed and staffed, it is an effective method of maintaining social order" (N.C.C.D., 1966:161), but Vincent O'Leary, formerly with that organization, points out that 60 percent of first-time felons have had

---

34. The NCCD did not provide relative cost figures for misdemeanant probation and incarceration, although the cost per probation case can be derived by dividing the estimated total costs ($28,682,914) by the estimated number of persons placed on probation in a year (300,440 in 1965) (N.C.C.D., 1966:126, 129). However, the result, about $95 per case, cannot be compared with any known figure for jailing, since we know neither the total number of persons *sentenced* to jail each year nor the proportion of total jail costs properly allocated to these prisoners.

The NCCD did, however, compare probation and incarceration costs for *felons*, and found that the annual cost per probation case ($280) was about one-seventh of the per inmate cost per year (about $2,000) (p. 175). It might be argued that the per capita cost of misdemeanant probation would be higher than for felony probation, owing to the shorter terms involved, and that jail costs may be lower than penitentiary and reformatory costs, due to the wider range of services and programs offered by the latter. On the other hand, jails ought to be *more* expensive, due to the shorter terms involved, and it should not be an argument in their favor that they are cheaper because they scrimp on essential services. What data we have indicate that, at present, annual per capita jail costs are about the same as for state prisons ($2,026) (L.E.A.A., 1971:9). In the absence of a fuller investigation of misdemeanant probation, the felony figures remain the best estimate.

previous misdemeanant convictions (A.C.A., 1966b:253). Most of those "previous mis-demeanant convictions" probably resulted in a jail sentence; the few that may have been placed on probation were under a probation service that was *not* "properly financed and staffed." By the time these persons "graduate" from jail to major crime, although it may not be too late to sentence *them* to a professional probation service, it is certainly too late for their victims.

The next noninstitutional sentencing alternative is the use of fines, in particular, installment fines. The general disadvantage to fines is that they are discriminatory and judges normally have no idea of the financial resources of defendants. Moreover, unlike some of the European countries, American judges, ordinarily, do not employ a "pro-gressive" rate structure. Such "equal protection" is particularly discriminatory when the poorer man, unable to pay the fine, lands in jail. For this reason, the Supreme Court, in two cases, held that there are constitutional limitations on the use of jailing in lieu of payment of fines. In the first case, *Williams* v. *Illinois* [399 U.S. 235, 242(1970)], the Court held that, where both a fine and jailing are authorized and imposed, a state may not imprison defendants beyond the statutory maximum jail sentence for the crime solely because they are too poor to pay the fine imposed. In the second case, *Tate* v. *Short* [401 U.S. 395, 398(1971)], the Court went further and held that any routine incarceration for failure to pay a fine immediately was a denial of equal pro-tection to the poor. In both cases, however, the Court noted that it saw no constitu-tional difficulties in jailing for *intentional* nonpayment of fines by defendants with resources, and that the states could resort to jailing if other means of collecting the fine were attempted and proved unsuccessful.

A major reason for the holdings in these cases was the availability of alternative methods for satisfying fines, in particular, the payment of fines in installments. The Court noted that several states authorize this procedure, that it has been widely endorsed as an effective collection device, and that it is an excellent means of avoiding the expense of maintaining both the prisoner and his family (see A.B.A., 1968a:§2.7 and commentary). To this may be added the additional advantage that such periodic pay-ments are a continuing reminder of the corrective process, and could easily be com-bined with supervision and counseling in appropriate cases.

Judges confronted with statutes that permit either fines or jailing, or both, may simply resort to jailing in the absence of the necessary staffing to collect fines in install-ments. The defendants who could demonstrate their ability to pay fines immediately and in full could continue to buy their way out under these circumstances, while the defendants who are indigent or suspected of indigency would be sentenced to jail. Since local governments have already demonstrated considerable reluctance to organize and staff noninstitutional methods of handling the accused or convicted offender, such a nullification of the Supreme Court's attempt at "reform" through the application of the equal protection clause of the Constitution is not out of the realm of the possible. None of this pessimistic speculation, however, detracts from the essential justification for the increased use of fines, including fines paid in installments, as an alternative to unnecessary jailing.

The final method for diverting certain prisoners from inadequate jails at the sen-tencing level is the use of specialized treatment facilities for the more vulnerable parts of the sentenced population: females, juveniles, the mentally or physically ill, alcoholics, and drug addicts. The general arguments in favor of such a recourse have already been presented, where the same kind of diversion was recommended at the detention level. The question of specialized treatment facilities is, however, a part of the larger problem of a better division of labor among penal institutions and a more rational distribution of prisoners among them. Changes in local control that foster regionalization, as discussed later, are more likely to lead to such developments.

Release During Sentence and Early Release. Even when prisoners are sentenced to jail, the negative impact of incarceration can be moderated through several available options. The periodic or partial release of sentenced prisoners so they may work or find work, attend vocational or academic schools for training, or simply maintain their family and community ties presents a number of advantages to the prisoner, the jail administration, and the community at large: (1) money earned during the course of sentence is properly subject to attachment to pay the costs of room and board, administration, and other jail services, thus providing a supervised work program at little or no cost to the public; (2) training, counseling, or specialized medical services may be paid for by either the prisoner or the local authorities, and such experiences can make a positive contribution to his future adjustment in the community; (3) temporary or partial release into the community enables the prisoner to encounter potential adjustment difficulties that can be the proper subject of counseling and supervision by the jail authorities before full release so they may be dealt with or avoided in the future; and (4) such release procedures ease or avoid the abrupt transition from jail to freedom in the community, too often experienced as a period of personal disorganization leading to early recidivism. In addition, these midsentence release programs have a hidden benefit that is, ordinarily, not made explicit: they afford the prisoner the opportunity to lead a normal sex life. Considering the problems associated with sexual repression or inversion in the traditional jail, this benefit transcends the private sphere and is not simply a permissive indulgence.

In contrast to a demoralizing and maladjusting sentence in an inadequate jail without either programs or treatment, the periodic and partial release procedures have much to recommend them. To the degree that they are used at all, the most widely employed procedures are "work-release" and "weekender" sentences. The former has been discussed above (starting on p. 819). Most statutes authorizing such sentences provide only daytime release for work, to attend school, or seek medical treatment, but a few also allow release to seek employment [e.g., Ill. Rev. Stat., ch. 75, §35 (Cum. Supp. 1971)]. Ordinarily, prisoners must return to jail during nonworking hours, but in some states (North Carolina, for example) work-release prisoners are permitted an occasional weekend at home with their families (Hepler, 1966:351, 357).

For maximum effectiveness work-release programs should really be located at the pretrial stage of the criminal process so that the offender's employment, if any, is not too seriously interrupted or lost altogether. Work release should also be as responsive as possible to employment-market conditions, including night-shift and part-time work if that is all that is available for prisoners. At the postsentence stage, the major problems with work release are finding jobs and holding the temporary kinds of jobs that tend to be offered to jail inmates. There is also some danger to criminal justice when work-release sentences are "too successful." As local officials become increasingly aware of the cost-offsetting income that can reduce the county or city jail budget, there may be a tendency to substitute work-release sentences for cases that properly merit probation. At present, however, work release is still only a much discussed but vastly underutilized sentencing alternative. Wisconsin passed the first work-release law, the so-called Huber Law, in 1905, and it is still regarded as a daring innovation by most local authorities, so the "dangers of success" are a long way off.

Weekender programs, as the name implies, enable prisoners to remain in the free community during the work week but they must return to jail on Friday night and remain for the weekend. Thus, the sentenced man is able to lead an essentially normal life at work, with his family, and in the community during the week, but he is punished by confinement over the weekend. Apparently the weekender sentence does not need to be authorized by statute, but where it is practiced it functions as a satisfactory intermediate sentencing alternative between the lesser freedom of work release and the greater freedom of probation.

As with all discretionary or informal procedures, however, there may be disadvantages as well as advantages. One disadvantage is that, without statutory authority, jail administrators cannot collect the prisoner's salary for the payment of costs and fines or to insure the support of his family and the payment of his debts, should these be deemed desirable. Such authorization, or a graduated range of such alternatives, could be written into state work-release statutes (A.B.A., 1968a:§2.4 and commentary). Similarly, authorization for family visits could be added to, or authorized independently of, regular work release, so that deserving inmates who cannot work for some reason could better maintain family ties and prepare for ultimate release to the community. Such a "pass" system is already in use on an informal basis, particularly in the smaller jails, where trustics are given extended privileges. But, as noted previously, the extension of privileges at the complete discretion of jailers is subject to abuse. The history of jails in the United States, more by default than design, reflects the results of too much unbridled discretion on the part of jailers in too many areas of jail administration. When a long train of abuses pursuing the same object evinces a design, it is time to throw off such discretion and to provide new laws for future equality.

Prisoners sentenced to jails for misdemeanors and ordinance violations are, for most purposes, regarded as lesser or minor offenders, but when it comes to the provision of early release procedures, they are denied the opportunity for freedom that is routinely extended to felons. As prisoners in state and federal prisons complete the part of their sentences that is specified by law, they become eligible for parole or some other form of conditional release. About two-thirds of all releases from state prison systems are on parole or on conditional release (N.C.C.D., 1966:214). The availability of such early release mechanisms provides an incentive for good behavior during imprisonment, and provides flexibility in correctional administration so the length of imprisonment can be related to the prisoner's progress in adjustment. Also, it can limit the undesirable aspects of institutionalization and, in appropriate cases, hasten the process of reintegration into the community. Parole or conditional release to the supervision of a parole officer (or to a "halfway" house near employment opportunities for offenders without families or homes) are far cheaper than continued incarceration.

Early release procedures are generally not available for local jail administrators or inmates, however. The NCCD reported that 62 percent of the 212 jails it sampled, where prisoners were sentenced for more than 30 days, had no parole procedure; the jails that did have this option used it to release only 8 percent of their inmates. Moreover, where local parole exists, its implementation is discouraged by complicated administrative procedures, by the requirement that application must be made to those least likely to grant it, and by unfettered areas of discretion. In some instances, jail inmates must apply to the sentencing judge for "bench parole," or to both a parole board and the sentencing judge, or simply to the sheriff (N.C.C.D., 1966:209, n. 1). In other jurisdictions the county board, which has many other tasks to do, also makes parole decisions for prisoners serving less than one year (Massachusetts Governor's

Committee, 1965:22). Early release for good behavior and without further supervision, with or without statutory provisions for earning "good time," is believed to be more common [e.g., Ill. Rev. Stat., ch. 75, §30–§34 (Cum. Supp. 1971)], but the extent of its use in jails is unknown.

The statutory provision of the opportunity to earn "good time" is a general feature of the felony prisons. Local authorities have tended to resist the enactment of such statutes because they regard jail sentences as being too short to justify them; besides, they feel they can achieve the same objectives in deserving cases through informal procedures. Past experience with the exercise of local discretion, however, favors a formal parole system. The parole of misdemeanants with shorter sentences will, no doubt, require different methods for arriving at parole decisions and an expanded team of parole supervisors. Local parole boards would have to hold more frequent hearings and make more decisions due to both the shorter sentences and greater numbers of jail inmates, but the problems are not insuperable. The variety of options provided by release procedures before and during sentence, including more extended use of "good time" provisions, should be available to limit the negative impact of inadequate jails, to minimize isolation from the community, to afford supervision as necessary, and to remove prisoners from jail as soon as possible.

Increasing State and Federal Participation

The problem of American jails, put most concisely, is the problem of local control. Almost every aspect of local jailing that has been described as problematic would be better handled if jails were simply to become part of the state correctional system. It is doubtful, however, whether either state or local authorities are ready to adopt such a "radical" approach. For this reason, it is necessary to explore alternative and interim measures that might help jails under local control evolve into more rational, humane, and effective institutions. When, after long neglect, higher authorities threaten to intervene in local affairs, local authorities can become remarkably creative in disguising as forward steps of progress their desperate, rearguard actions to maintain, essentially, the status quo. Although this form of "progress" is mainly designed to gain time, it is not to be despised for the amount of time gained can be considerable and interim improvements are better than no improvements. As early as 1933 the state of North Carolina took control of prisoners sentenced for more than thirty days (N.C. Pub. Laws, ch. 39; see also Ashman, 1969:6–10), and in 1960 the state of Connecticut abolished all county government, and with it, the local control of jails (Ashman, 1969: 80). Both measures had far-ranging effects on local jails, so radical solutions are possible.

Dilemmas in Local Jail Reform. In most states it is politically preferable to begin with minimal state or federal intervention in local jail administration. Among the earliest steps to be taken are the formulation and adoption of state standards, combined with inspection to assess the conditions of local jails. The state standards can be written in such a way as to constitute a phased reform program over a period of years, and inspection can be used to maintain a check on the stages of compliance. As the more advanced stages of compliance approach, local jails will either survive as improved and modernized institutions or they will become too burdensome for local governments to support.

If the enactment and enforcement of strict jail standards are to be more than an indirect attempt to force local government out of the jail business, however, and are seriously intended to upgrade the quality of jail custody and treatment, it will be necessary to combine the pressure of compliance with state standards and the power of condemning substandard jails with the incentives of substantial grants-in-aid to make compliance both attractive and feasible for local governments that are already hard pressed for financial resources. Every grant made to local police, courts, or corrections by the state planning agencies that distribute federal funds has a direct or indirect impact on jails. If those federal funds are mainly invested in the police end of the criminal justice system without a concurrent and proportionate investment in courts and corrections, what is manifestly intended to be an improvement in criminal justice will have the latent effect of continuing to overload the courts and jails. One of the major problems of urban courts and jails is that they cannot handle the work load delivered to them by the police without compromising justice and rational penal treatment. On the other hand, if the state planning agencies would use their fund-granting powers to achieve a better balance in the criminal justice system and, in particular, make compliance with minimum state standards a condition of any grant made to local jail authorities, a great incentive for jail reform would be created.

The detailed content of state standards for jails will vary, necessarily, according to preexisting local conditions, but they are implicit in most of what has gone before. In general, and at the minimum, these standards should include: (1) merit selection, plus preservice and in-service training, for jail personnel; (2) requirements for frequent health, safety, and maintenance inspections by officials from state rather than local agencies; (3) provisions for adequate and uniform record-keeping practices and the obligation to render a comprehensive public report on the work of the jail at least once a year; and (4) state power of full or partial condemnation procedures against jails that fail to comply with minimum standards within a reasonable time. Appeals by local authorities against such condemnation procedures should be taken out of the jurisdiction of the local courts because sheriffs, mayors, and judges at the local level tend to give jail reform a low priority in the political scheme of things. Ample due process could be assured by providing for judicial review at an intermediate court level, as is frequently specified in statutes providing for the review of administrative agencies.

At least two kinds of investment should be *postponed* in any statewide jail reform program based on phased-stage implementation of state standards: the building of new jails and the hiring of more personnel. Investment in new jails, or the major refurbishing of old ones, would merely harden the old problems under somewhat more decent conditions. Why add more cells or living space to large urban jails when most of them are already too large for efficient management? Similarly, why replace or rebuild a small rural jail that is going to stand empty half the time? Increasing the number of personnel in existing jails would only have the effect of giving more persons a vested interest in maintaining the status quo and contribute to greater resistance to future change. By and large, new buildings and more staff should come only after the potential effects of criminal law reform and diversion alternatives have been fully considered. Such collateral reforms, combined with an increasing tendency toward regionalization of jails, would require fewer jails and fewer, but better-qualified and better-trained jail personnel.

Jail reforms that are made at the local level are occasionally logically and practically inconsistent with more basic reforms that could be made at a higher or wider level; sometimes they are mutually exclusive. Only the largest urban jurisdictions can afford to build the number and variety of local penal institutions required to effect a better division of labor and a more rational distribution of prisoners among them. The indefinite multiplication of such institutions is clearly uneconomic if it is undertaken for every county or city that now operates an inadequate, all-purpose jail. Separate institutions for detention and sentenced jail populations, and within that general division, separate institutions for males and females, adults and juveniles, and specialized institutions for especially vulnerable parts of the jail population (drunks, drug addicts, the physically and mentally ill) can only be built and administered on a regional basis, and under state authority. Since such a comprehensive program of jail reform takes time, the question is whether a few interim reform measures might be instituted, despite the fact that partial local reforms will serve to justify delays in addressing the fundamental jailing problem?

Improving Local Jail Administration and Control. Even at the local level, the effective separation of persons awaiting trial from those already found guilty and serving sentences should be undertaken. To house both in the same jail is to do an injustice to both. The detention population, under American law, is supposed to have the benefit of the presumption of innocence; their punishment or "treatment" is not supposed to begin until they are proven guilty. The sentenced population, consisting of convicted misdemeanants and ordinance violators, does not require the security arrangements that may be necessary for those who are accused of serious crime, and maximum security arrangements make rehabilitative treatment difficult, if not impossible. Moreover, while there may be some rationale for using law-enforcement officers to staff jails holding highly transient detention populations, sentenced populations should be subject to rehabilitative measures applied by a full-time, treatment-oriented correctional staff. The law-enforcement psychology of a policeman is to put offenders *into* jail; the rehabilitative psychology of a correctional worker should be to prepare an inmate to get *out* of jail as a law-abiding citizen.

Second, insofar as county sheriffs will have control of local jails in the immediate future, some measures should be taken to improve that office and its personnel. With increasing urbanization the law-enforcement functions of sheriffs are rapidly being lost to the state police and the nearest metropolitan police department. As the sheriff's law-enforcement functions dwindle to highway traffic control and the service of process and attachments, the administration of the local jail may increase in importance. For this reason, the career opportunities of sheriffs might be improved if they became appointed rather than elected officers. In some states an elected sheriff may not succeed himself in office, and in others running for sheriff is regarded as the introductory stepping-stone to higher office. In either case, the sheriff who is responsible for the local jail is almost as transient as the inmates of the jail. A career sheriff comes to understand the jail problem and can work with continuity to make improvements. Elected sheriffs who bring in a new complement of patronage employees contribute to the disorganization and neglect of their jails. Many elected sheriffs feel themselves to be so vulnerable in the administration of the jail that they take their records with them when they leave office; at least one state has passed a law to insure the transfer of records from a sheriff to his successor (Ohio Code Ann., §311.13; see also Mattick & Sweet, 1969:33). It is clear that the office of sheriff, as presently constituted, is poorly suited for jail administration.

Even if the sheriff is an elected officer, his staff can be placed under civil service or some merit system for the selection and promotion of qualified personnel. This may make the jail less subject to partisan political manipulation. The training of sheriff's police and jail guards should be encouraged, regardless of their civil service or patronage status. The infusion of state and federal funds for training, demonstration programs, and consultation services for future planning is the most likely method of making jail improvement acceptable to local sheriffs. It is usually not sufficient to make training programs and materials available. Many sheriffs and jailers are on solid ground when they complain that their budget and manpower situations do not permit them to take advantage of training opportunities. A system of extending grants-in-aid, including pay for the staff who are undergoing training and substitute personnel for those who are absent from duty, would tend to meet these obstacles. However, such strategies of upgrading the sheriff's office must be seen as an alternative method of jail improvement that tends to perpetuate local control of jails. It is a limited, but may be the only possible, method of jail reform at a given time in history.

The Abolition of Local Jail Control. Every serious and comprehensive study of jails conducted during the past fifty years has recommended some form of regionalization, i.e., the abolition of exclusive county or city organization and control of detention and corrections functions (Queen, 1920:128–42; Fishman, 1923:278; Robinson, 1944:274; Barnes & Teeters, 1951:479; Alexander, 1957:312; Bennett, 1964:31, 36; Ashman, 1969:17–25; Mattick & Sweet, 1969:8, 292–93). Even an intensive study of a particular jail in a single jurisdiction inevitably suggests that a better division of labor and a more rational distribution of prisoners would be possible, if the appropriate institutions were available to enable such a distribution (Mattick, 1957, 1960; Mattick & Aikman, 1969), and this leads to a consideration of the possibilities inherent in regionalization. As soon as attention shifts from a single jail to the jailing function in the state's criminal justice system, the inference to regionalize is irresistible.

The tasks to be performed by local penal institutions are directly deducible from the legal status, demographic characteristics, and criminal histories of the populations they are required to handle. Those awaiting trial cannot be treated in the same way as those who have been sentenced. The juveniles must be separated from the adults. The males and the females require separate facilities. The essentially normal and healthy should be separated from the abnormal and the sick. The criminally naive and first offenders should not be exposed to the criminally sophisticated and recidivists. It does not follow that each of these subclasses requires a separate building, although that is the best solution in the case of the sentenced and unsentenced, providing there is sufficient internal space and control to insure the necessary separation of different subclasses of prisoners. Usually, this is only possible in the largest urban jails and then it is inevitably defeated by overcrowding, transiency, and the pressure of numbers. In the smaller, more rural, jails, the objective possibility for adequate separation does not even exist, despite the lesser number of prisoners such jails handle. Smaller jails are invariably built to hold male adults awaiting trial or serving short sentences; when other classes of prisoners are held there, the facilities are inappropriate and inadequate.[35] The regional reorganization of jails would address all these problems.

In any regional reorganization of local detention and correctional institutions, it would be natural that the major metropolitan areas in a state would constitute regions in their own right, although their jurisdictional areas might be considerably expanded. This would tend to minimize the problems that arise from geographic distances within regions, which could pose some problems in the less urban areas of the state. The main benefit to be derived from regionalizing the jails in the metropolitan areas is elimination of the duplication of functions among city and county penal institutions. It can also lead to an immediate redistribution of prisoners among existing institutions

---

35. E.g., females do not use urinals or open toilets; the bunks and sinks are too high for some juveniles; and, generally, there is nothing to occupy the time of sentenced prisoners constructively.

with a better division of labor between them. It may still be necessary, even in a metropolitan region, to build or provide additional facilities to achieve an optimum division of labor and distribution of prisoners, but the preexisting institutions will be utilized in the most rational way and the need for additional buildings will be minimized.

In the more rural regions, a systematic plan of relocation and building of physical plants will be required, complemented by a systematic program of razing the older jails that will lose their prisoners to the new regional institutions. Not only are there considerable economies to be achieved in building and administering larger and more adequate jails in the rural areas, but it is generally agreed that the quality of administration is likely to be improved after jails are removed from the local political milieu where patronage interests dominate what should be technical penal functions.

The arguments that may be adduced against regionalization have some substance, particularly in the case of rural areas, but they are not insuperable. Moreover, they apply with equal force to felons in state prisons, but they are seldom raised in that context: (1) it requires the transportation of prisoners and creates visiting problems for the family of the prisoners, for attorneys, and others; (2) it increases the isolation of prisoners who are jailed at the regional center, and this sense of isolation is a psychological disadvantage in efforts at treatment or rehabilitation; and (3) removal of prisoners from the local jurisdiction would deprive county and city governments that have work programs of a valuable source of labor. Other arguments against regionalization are far more important to local officials, but they remain implicit, without entering into public discussion, because they are less defensible. These have to do with patronage employment, the letting of contracts for supplies and maintenance, and the differential treatment of prisoners in jails under local control. These aspects of jail administration do not automatically disappear when jails are regionalized, but they are placed under wider scrutiny of a larger number of public officials less intimately related to the problems and thus serve as a check and balance that encourages better administration based on merit.

The assertion that the labor of misdemeanants, under present jail conditions, is worth more to the local government than the cost of their upkeep is extremely dubious. At best, such an argument would have application only in those very few localities that have the best and most extensively organized work-release programs, and then only to that part of the jail population that participates in it. Most extramural jail work programs, as previously noted, are low-level, make-work, clean-up tasks that are overmanned and undersupervised. If local officials are serious about the constructive functions that jails should serve on behalf of the community, they would not subordinate the rehabilitation and correction of offenders to such an uneconomic exploitation of their labor. Moreover, insofar as the labor of misdemeanants may have some value, regionalization is no bar to a local government contracting with the regional jail for the labor of inmates.

The problems of transportation and visits by families and attorneys have more substance. In part, they can be addressed by locating detention institutions as close to the courts as the regionalization scheme permits. This would tend to assure the maximum number of visits for, at least, the pretrial detention prisoner. In some states, regional detention facilities for juveniles exist (N.C.C.D., 1966:24–25), but few attorneys are involved in juvenile cases and parents are more highly motivated to visit their children; so visiting has not been problematic. If transportation of inmates to a regional facility is considered a problem due to the number of vehicles and trips required, visitors to the detention facility might also be transported as room is available.

If the state has a regional system for jails to which it transports prisoners, and if visits are seen as a contribution toward a prisoner's eventual and successful reintegration into the community, then the transportation of visitors in state vehicles is serving a constructive function in the penal program. This latter suggestion would, of course, have similar application in the case of sentenced prisoners who might be located in centralized institutions that would be more remote. In the case of sentenced prisoners, a compromise might be struck on separation of those serving short sentences of 30 days or less who could be assigned to the detention facilities as the work complement, thus solving two problems simultaneously: avoiding the imposition of penal work on the unsentenced population and deriving the marginal benefit of potentially increased visits.

In any reorganization there would also be a tendency for other functions related to detention and sentenced institutions to accommodate themselves to regionalization, and this tendency would increase with the passage of time. As long ago as 1923, Fishman (1923:278–79) suggested the regionalization of the police, courts, prosecution, and detention in a program of jail reform. Under such a system, once an offender had been brought to the central lockup for his judicial district, he would have very little traveling to do and, presumably, criminal lawyers would locate their offices near the courts where they would be employed.

The abolition of local control can, of course, be achieved at a level that stops short of the state. Complete state control of jails was achieved in Connecticut in 1960 when all county government in that state was abolished. In North Carolina, prisoners sentenced for more than 30 days have been state prisoners since 1933. In a number of states enabling legislation has existed for many years authorizing limited contractual or quasi-governmental systems between two or more counties or cities that can serve as the incipient stage toward regionalization. In the past, such authorizations have foundered on problems of sharing power and liabilities, but under the encouragement of possible state and federal financing they may be revived from their dormancy. In the area of corrections and, in particular, in the case of local jails, the economics of regional organization are so apparent, and the maintenance of local jails as viable institutions is so indefensible, that regionalization is being actively encouraged by both the federal and state authorities who are distributing financial aid to local criminal justice agencies. It does not follow that, at long last, the local jail problem has been, or is about to be, overcome. We are witness to a "conflict of interest" from which the public can benefit. Whether the desire for federal money can overcome the desire for local control, or whether some compromise will be achieved, will be revealed in the years ahead.

EPILOGUE:
SOME RECENT USES OF THE LAW
AS A REFLEXIVE METHOD OF PENAL REFORM

It is not the lack of knowledge nor the absence of zeal in reform efforts that have permitted jails to survive essentially unchanged for generations. It is, rather, that knowledge and zeal were seldom combined with political power, organizational skill, and sophistication. The lack of jail reform reflects a failure of organizational nerve, and a certain naiveté on the part of those who sought changes. The reformers could frequently mount an attack on jail conditions, but they could not sustain it; the standpatters would never give more ground than they were forced to give to survive. Under these conditions, the history of jail reform is replete with desperate rearguard actions in response to temporary crises that were represented as voluntary measures of "progress," and later subverted when the zeal for reform had passed. Such half-hearted, compromised, and expedient "reforms" have usually been *counterproductive:* they have either compounded the very problems with which they purported to deal, or served merely to defuse and divert reform efforts before the fundamental problems could be addressed. There is a lesson to be learned from this historical experience, but it may not have been learned. Maybe it is a lesson that few care to learn.

Since neither legislative bodies nor executive agencies at the local level could be made to respond to jail reform efforts and the states were reluctant to interfere with "home rule," relief was sought in the courts. Attorneys with specific cases, the prisoners themselves, and, more recently, jail reform groups began attacking the most blatant and vulnerable aspects of penal conditions through litigation. At first the courts, too, turned aside all efforts to involve them in problems of penal administration; but longstanding and continuing neglect on the part of the other branches of government, and a few of the more spectacular examples of prison and jail abuse, made their participation inevitable. Once this Pandora's box of injustice had been opened, however, rapid developments in litigation began to lend some momentum to penal reform. Most of the cases have dealt with conditions in the state felony prisons because the length of sentences permitted protracted litigation and appeals, and the issues at stake seemed to have more serious consequences; but there is enough in common between prisons and jails that even those suits that did not originate with a jail problem have some application to jail reform. To attack the jails of the United States on a case-by-case and issue-by-issue basis, and to apply felony-prison decisions to detention and misdemeanant institutions, is to achieve jail reform the hard way; but when normal political channels are blocked, litigation is the alternative to violence.

Some Lessons from the History of Jail Reform

The main lesson derived from earlier reform efforts is a negative one: do not build a new physical structure or expand an old one until all other alternatives have been explored for their potential contribution toward a solution. The main solution that should be under primary consideration is the feasibility of converting to some regionalization system with the minimum number of jail buildings required to handle the number and kind of prisoners that would result after the full range of noninstitutional alternatives had reduced the population to the absolute minimum.

For the most part, what has passed for jail reform has been the periodic replacement of old structures by new ones. It does not happen very often—perhaps at intervals of seventy to one hundred years—but by that time the old building has been so neglected and abused that it seems logical to build a new and larger jail that will withstand abuse for a long time to come. Moreover, the political administration that happens to be in power at the time it is necessary to yield to progress will have some interest in the substantial gains to be made from the letting of construction contracts, the purchase of supplies, and the employment of labor, representing all this activity as penal reform. The final result is that the city or county has a new jail, which will soon be filled beyond capacity because it is available, but nothing else is changed. It has been repeatedly demonstrated that major jail-building campaigns and replacement programs have been counterproductive (Klein, 1920:41–42; Robinson, 1944:170; N.C.C.D., 1966:27; Mattick & Sweet, 1969:16–17). They have locked the old methods into new buildings, consumed the financial and staffing resources that could have been utilized in the organization of alternatives, and compounded all the problems inherent in jailing.

There are, of course, many jails in existence today that are so inadequate and unfit for human habitation that their continued use must be condemned immediately. Where this is necessary, however, local and state officials should first investigate the conditions, needs, and future workload of jails in the surrounding jurisdictions. It may be possible to use nearby facilities temporarily while a more comprehensive plan is worked out for a new division of labor and redistribution of prisoners among old buildings and new in a common, multicounty, regional facility. If early building is necessary, it should concentrate on the replacement of local detention facilities. Such facilities will always be required for temporary lockup purposes, and they can also be used to help ease the transitional strain involved in conversion from inadequate local jails to a developing regional system. In the larger cities and metropolitan counties, early replacement construction is more readily justified because any future regional or state detention and jail system would be obliged to locate itself as economically as possible with reference to existing population centers. Perhaps the main caution that should be urged in connection with urban jail building has to do with size and permanence. Individual jail buildings should not be constructed so large that individualization of treatment is hindered or that they contribute to their own mismanagement. Moreover, the principle of planned obsolescence should have more application to closed institutions in general. This country has had quite enough of jails that seem to last forever.

Somewhat similar arguments are pertinent to the question of additional staffing. To simply add numbers to the old functions in the same old system is to give unnecessary hostages to a hostile fortune. Such additional staff would learn the old ways and defend them in the political arena, complicating the tasks of reform. The number and kind of personnel required to staff regional facilities under a well-planned system of state control can be determined only after planning and reorganization have been undertaken. It is most likely that fewer institutional personnel will be required, but that a greater number and variety of screening, transporting, supervision, and program staff would be employed. In the transition from local jails to regional facilities, staff resistance and political opportunism cannot be avoided, but they can be minimized by "blanketing in" most of the old employees and being systematic about replacements that occur through attrition. The old employees should, insofar as possible, be used to staff the detention institutions, while expansion goes forward in the community-based programs and sentenced institutions, in order to minimize the contamination between old and new staff components. Preservice and in-service training programs that break with the old traditions will be required, training programs that discredit the old methods without discrediting the old personnel.

State fee systems, grants-in-aid, and state subsidies have to be closely scrutinized and planned in such a way that minimum jail standards follow the state dollar. Some state fee systems in the past, while a definite improvement over a per diem turnkey fee paid to local jailers, have served to support local control and prevented the state from intervening in local jails (Robinson, 1944:203). Considering the influx of federal money being channeled through state planning agencies to local jurisdictions, it is clear that the same danger is present today. Federal and state funding do not produce greater state influence on local jails in an automatic fashion; provision must be made for highly selective granting of money to local jurisdictions that agree to meet mini-

mum standards. Moreover, if the state administrative agency is not reasonably independent of local, partisan, political interests, it may be neither willing nor able to exert
any reform influence on jails.

Similarly, past experience with statutory jail standards has indicated that they
are not always what they seem to be. Sometimes enforcement machinery is totally
lacking; sometimes it is provided for by statute, but lacking in fact; and sometimes it
is provided for in such a manner as to create an illusion. Local agencies of jail inspection, in particular the grand jury, are ineffectual, largely because their main function is conceived of as lying in another area, e.g., the voting of indictments, regardless
of statutes directing them to inspect and report on the local jail, as discussed previously. In some states the board of welfare has the responsibility for inspecting and
enforcing standards in local jails. Since the welfare perspective on jails is in sharp
contrast to the law-enforcement ideology of most local jailers, the board of welfare
inspectors have little success in obtaining voluntary compliance. Moreover, since the
welfare inspectors view the enforcement of jail standards as peripheral to their central
welfare functions, they come to de-emphasize this source of friction that generates local
opposition to their more central operations and goals (Mattick & Sweet, 1969:103–5,
306–7; North Carolina Jail Study Commission, 1969:32–33). Providing decent jail
standards is not simply a question of expressing appropriate sentiments in statutory
form; it is a question of effective law enforcement. By and large, statutory jail standards without enforcement machinery are useless; with enforcement machinery that is
useless, they are fraudulent. What such statutes mean, in fact, is a question that can
only be resolved by empirical research at the field level.

Recent Developments in Penal Litigation

The use of litigation to attack jail problems is a relatively new departure in jail reform.
In all but a few cases, the courts had consistently refused to entertain suits by jail or
prison inmates against their keepers. This policy was based on a fear of subverting
penal discipline and the presumed lack of judicial expertise in penal administration. A
similar modesty had never stayed the judicial process in other complex proceedings,
but this posture came to be known as the "hands-off doctrine." With the recent rapid
developments in the procedural rights of defendants *prior* to conviction, however, it
became increasingly difficult to ignore the claims of sentenced inmates.[36] Moreover,
the general trend in administrative law over the last several decades has been to expand
the areas and scope of judicial review of the actions of administrative agencies and
officials where no express statutory provision or inherent difficulty forbids review
(Davis, 1958:§28.07; Goldfarb & Singer, 1970:182). In addition, two of the specific
procedural devices most useful to prisoners—federal habeas corpus and suits under
the 1871 Civil Rights Act—have been broadened considerably in recent years, permitting relief in the form of release, damages, injunctions, and declaratory judgments for

---

36. There is a large body of literature in law reviews on the subject of prisoner suits. For a
historical view of the traditional role of the courts prior to the 1960s, see the *University of Pennsylvania Law Review* (1962) and the *Yale Law Journal* (1963). The specific problem of insuring
adequate medical treatment in prison is covered by Sneidman (1968). For recent discussions of developments in prisoner litigation generally, see Hirschkop and Milleman (1969), *Georgetown Law
Journal* (1969), Bass (1971), Cohen (1971), *University of Chicago Law Review* (1971). Goldfarb
and Singer (1970) present a particularly comprehensive survey; the *Yale Law Journal* (1970) discusses pretrial detention; and Turner (1971) has a useful section devoted to the specific problems of
litigating claims of jail inmates.

violations of almost any federal constitutional right. As a result, the definition of certain basic constitutional rights, in particular the right to be free from the imposition of "cruel and unusual punishments," has been expanded enormously, and continues to grow.

The rights of prisoners can be grouped roughly into three categories: (1) the right to humane treatment and cell conditions; (2) "civil" rights, such as freedom of religion and expression, the right to vote, freedom from racial discrimination, and the right to counsel; and (3) the procedural rights of due process.

The right to humane treatment, usually approached in terms of common law tort liability or the prohibition against cruel and unusual punishments, has been used to redress the following prison conditions: inadequate medical treatment (especially where serious injury or illness is involved) [*Talley* v. *Stephens*, 247 F. Supp. 683 (E.D. Ark. 1965); *McCollum* v. *Mayfield*, 130 F. Supp. 112 (N.D. Cal. 1955); see also Sneidman, 1968]; medical malpractice by doctors employed by the jail [*Whittree* v. *New York*, 290 N.Y. S.2d 486 (Ct. Cl. 1968)]; wrongful death at the hands of prison guards [*Lewis* v. *State*, 176 So. 2d 718 (La. App. 1965)]; unchecked assaults by other prisoners [*Holt* v. *Sarver*, 300 F. Supp. 825 (E.D. Ark. 1969); see also Goldfarb & Singer, 1970:244]; total reliance on trusty guards to supervise and protect inmates [*Holt* v. *Sarver*, 309 F. Supp. 362 (E.D. Ark. 1970), aff'd 442 F.2d 304 (8th Cir., 1971)];[37] use of cold, dark, dirty, and poorly ventilated "strip" isolation cells [*Jordan* v. *Fitzharris*, 257 F. Supp. 674 (N.D. Cal. 1966); *Wright* v. *McMann*, 387 F.2d 519 (2d Cir. 1967);[38] flogging with a leather strap [*Jackson* v. *Bishop*, 404 F.2d 571 (8th Cir. 1968)]; chronic overcrowding [*Holt* v. *Sarver*, 300 F. Supp. 825 (E.D. Ark. 1969); *Curley* v. *Gonzalez*, Civ. No. 8372 (D. New Mex., Feb. 13, 1970); *Hamilton* v. *Love*, 9 Crim. L. Rep. 2293 (E.D. Ark., June 2, 1971)]; failure to provide a matron twenty-four hours a day when females are being confined (*Hamilton* v. *Love*); and general degradation resulting from a combination of some or all of the above conditions [*Holt* v. *Sarver*, 309 F. Supp. 362 (E.D. Ark. 1970), aff'd 442 F.2d 304 (8th Cir. 1971); *Hamilton* v. *Shiro*, Civ. No. 69-2442 (E.D. La., June 25, 1970); *Pennsylvania ex. rel.*, *Bryant* v. *Hendrick*, No. 1567, 7 Crim. L. Rep. 2463 (Phila. Ct. C. P., Aug. 11, 1970); *New York Times*, May 8, 1971]. It should be emphasized, however, that very few of these cases were decided by the federal or state supreme courts, or for that matter, even by intermediate courts of appeal. Thus, the result in a particular and similar case will still depend on where the suit is brought, and how persuasive the court finds these precedents.

The right to health and physical safety is of somewhat longer standing, and hence is more firmly established than some of the other rights listed above. There is no *right* to conjugal visits—or for that matter, any visits at all, other than by clergymen and

---

37. There is some reason to question whether the use of trusty guards, in the absence of other abuses, will be found "cruel and unusual." The opinion in the second *Holt* case relied on the totality of conditions in the Arkansas prison system, including conditions in the isolation cells, general filth, and the inadequacy of prison clothing and medical care. The case is cited here as authority for the unconstitutionality of reliance on inmate trusties only because the more basic right to physical safety is so well established, and obviously cannot be protected by trusties (cf. Murton & Hyams, 1969).

38. But see *Sostre* v. *McGinnis*, 442 F.2d 178 (2d Cir. 1971) and *Beishir* v. *Swenson*, 9 Crim. L. Rep. 2292 (W.D. Mo. June 28, 1971), both holding that the use of solitary confinement for long periods of time (or indefinitely) is not "cruel and unusual punishment" per se, at least in the absence of other aggravating circumstances, such as poor diet, lack of adequate sanitation, or physical abuse by guards.

attorneys (Goldfarb & Singer, 1970:203–4). While Parchman Prison in Mississippi has permitted conjugal visits since 1923 and California instituted them in 1970, they are not a right, but a privilege. Inmates do not have a right to be paid for their work, and there is, apparently, no inherent right to work, to recreation, or to rehabilitative treatment, even for sentenced inmates (pp. 206–15).

The range of "civil" rights available to prisoners is somewhat narrower than that accorded to citizens in general, but it continues to expand. The limit is probably best defined by the oft-quoted judicial declaration that a "prisoner retains all the rights of an ordinary citizen except those expressly, or by necessary implication, taken from him by law" [*Coffin* v. *Reichard*, 143 F.2d 443, 445 (6th Cir. 1944)], with the stipulation that some rights cannot constitutionally be taken away even by statute. The earliest rights to be protected, and by now the most secure, are in the areas of religious freedom and the "right of access" to court. Prisoners have the right to meet for religious purposes, see and correspond with their minister, and receive and keep religious literature, subject to reasonable limitations if these rights are abused (Goldfarb & Singer, 1970:216–25; Turner, 1971:484). Prisons may not screen applications for habeas corpus [*Ex parte Hull*, 312 U.S. 546 (1941)], nor completely forbid the operations of "jailhouse lawyers" (inmates with a greater knowledge of legal remedies and procedures, who offer or sell their services to other inmates), where no other source of legal aid is available [*Johnson* v. *Avery*, 393 U.S. 483 (1969)]. Similarly, inmates have the right to consult privately with their attorneys at all reasonable times (Goldfarb & Singer, 1970:235–36), and the courts are even beginning to hold that correspondence directed to attorneys, judges, and public officials may not be censored, in the absence of abuse of this privilege, though it may, apparently, still be opened, inspected for contraband, and read to check for "abuse" (*Sostre* v. *McGinnis*, and cases cited). When it comes to other correspondents, however, the courts have yet to significantly restrict the widespread practice of keeping "approved lists" of persons who may send and receive mail from each inmate, and the accompanying censorship of the mail allowed, apparently on the theory that these practices are justified by the need to prevent the smuggling of contraband and to thwart escape plans.[39] The range of literature and periodicals that inmates may receive and keep is expanding, probably because the "clear and present dangers" to prison security offered as a counterargument by administrators are less plausible in the case of these forms of expression than for correspondence (Goldfarb & Singer, 1970:221–23; Turner, 1971:485–88).

Prisoners' rights to be free from racial discrimination and prejudice seem fairly secure, at least where such a policy or practice can be proved (Goldfarb & Singer, 1970:223–26). However, prisoners have not yet won the right to challenge discriminatory hiring practices (which usually result in all-white supervisory and treatment personnel), though it seems only a matter of time before this right is recognized. The right of prisoners to register and cast their votes, whether they be unsentenced or sentenced, misdemeanants or felons, is also in process of litigation (Mattick & Aikman, 1969:117).

We come now to the remedies available to inmates to enforce the rights listed above (Goldfarb & Singer, 1970:243–90). Basically, there are three: (1) awards of damages from guards, doctors, administrators, or the government itself; (2) injunctive

---

39. But see *Palmigiano* v. *Travisano*, 317 F. Supp. 776 (D. R.I. 1970), sharply limiting jailers' rights of inspection and censorship. In August, 1971, the governor of Ohio abolished all censorship in that state's prisons.

relief, either forbidding the violation of rights complained of or ordering affirmative action of some more specific nature; and (3) release, either from a particular part of the jail or prison, from one facility to another, or outright release. The difficulties with awarding damages are: first, that the usual defendant is a low-paid guard with little or no funds with which to pay the judgment; second, that the doctrine of sovereign immunity still prevails in the majority of states, blocking direct suit or recovery against the governmental entity involved; and third, that the practical problems of proof are considerable, especially in the absence of a claim for broad equitable relief, which might encourage fellow inmates to risk retaliation by testifying. Thus, the usual relief requested in prisoner litigation is an injunction that, especially when combined with the procedural device of a class action of all present and potential inmates (or a subclass of inmates, e.g., those awaiting trial), can be cast in broad terms to prohibit the complained-of practice indefinitely.

Turning to the particular rights of jail inmates, it is useful to distinguish between prisoners awaiting trial and those serving sentences (Yale Law Journal, 1970; Turner, 1971:475–78). There are two arguments that can be made in favor of unconvicted prisoners that cannot be applied to the sentenced. First, the former enjoy the presumption of innocence, so any imposition of "punishment," whether "cruel and unusual" or not, is a denial of due process. Second, many of those who remain in jail awaiting trial are there because they cannot afford bail, while similarly accused, but wealthier defendants have been able to pay their bail and are in the free community. Thus, any inconvenience or discomfort imposed on one group but not on the other is a violation of equal protection, unless rationally related to valid state interests, namely, maintaining custody and insuring presence at trial. A number of recent cases have adopted the so-called least restrictive alternative test for pretrial detainees [*Jones* v. *Wittenberg*, No. C-70-388 (N.D. Ohio, Feb. 17, 1970); *Davis* v. *Lindsay*, No. 70 Civil 4793 (S.D. N.Y., Nov. 4, 1970); *Hamilton* v. *Love* (1971)], holding that when one has not been convicted of a crime, any deprivation of his liberty by the state must use the least restrictive means. This test was formerly applied only in civil commitment, sequestration, and medical quarantine cases (Yale Law Journal, 1970:949).

On the other hand, sentenced inmates in jails tend to have even fewer rights than felons sentenced to state prisons, since rehabilitation is rarely even claimed to be a goal of jailing. As a practical matter, the shorter length of confinement of jail inmates, both sentenced and unsentenced, tends to discourage litigation. The resort to class actions is frequently of crucial importance, because only by use of this device can cases be heard and determined without becoming moot by the discharge from jail of individual inmates. To the extent that some one or more of the requirements for a federal class action cannot be met—in particular the requirement that representative parties bringing the suit be able to fairly and adequately protect the interests of the class (Goldfarb & Singer, 1970:283–89)—jail inmates may be left without an effective remedy for violations of their constitutional rights.

Federal Participation in Jail Reform

Federal participation in the field of local detention and corrections improvements was reluctant, minimal, and tardy, prior to the development in the 1970s of law-enforcement assistance funds and revenue sharing. While not specifically and directly aimed at jail reform, these two types of federal aid may yet have the long-run effect of helping to improve jails and foster regional systems.

The Department of Justice, through the U.S. Bureau of Prisons, has always had an interest in those jails where federal prisoners were lodged while they were being processed through the federal courts, or transferred in the federal prison system. While that federal interest was directly confined to those particular jails, and sometimes only to the section of a larger jail where federal prisoners were housed, the federal Jail Inspection Service, which was used to insure that federal prisoners were housed under conditions of minimum decency, could not help learning about the appalling conditions of most jails. Accordingly, in the 1930s, the U.S. Bureau of Prisons began preparing and distributing a set of printed training materials in an effort to improve the conditions under which federal prisoners were held in local jails. Eventually, these training materials were organized into a ten-pamphlet *Correspondence Course for Jailers,* and distributed to any jailer who requested them. The original *Correspondence Course for Jailers* was ideally suited to its audience for it never transcended common sense and simple human decency. It was frequently reprinted, distributed in thousands of copies, and did yeoman service for forty years for those jailers and administrators who took the initiative to obtain them and had the motivation to learn. The Bureau of Prisons, with the help of an LEAA grant and the University of Wisconsin, has reorganized, upgraded, and updated these training materials, and is reissuing them in a very attractive form (Blumer, 1970a, 1970b; Pappas, 1971a, 1971b). They are among the best training materials that are generally available, and have a high potential for making a major contribution to the art of jail administration and the practices of jailers.

A Suggested Sequence of Jail Reform Efforts

First: Every effort should be made to devise means of reducing the number of persons who are jailed. This should include criminal law reform, more stringent arrest criteria, pretrial release, posttrial release, and community-based treatment in preference to jailing. While specific information is lacking due to the primitive state of record-keeping, there is general agreement that far too many persons are being jailed. Every case that can be diverted from jail, consistent with public safety, should be handled in the community, with or without supervision.

Second: An empirical study of the population at risk at the levels of arrest, detention, court, and jail should be combined with the institution of more adequate record-keeping practices at all these levels so systematic and comprehensive information is available to guide rational policy decisions. More adequate records on staff and budgets are also required to learn the cost of present operations and to guide choices in future investment policies.

Third: Opportunities for cooperation and cost-sharing should be explored with nearby communities, as between city and county, or a group of adjacent counties, and as between county and state. For each individual city or county to attempt to supply itself with the number and variety of services and facilities required for an optimum division of labor and rational distribution of prisoners would be all but impossible except for metropolitan jurisdictions.

Fourth: State supervision, if not state control, in the form of minimum standards, inspectional services, and compliance procedures should be invited. Local control of detention and correction has exhibited a two hundred year history of failure. If a compromise must be struck, it is preferable that corrections come under state authority, and detention remain under local control.

Fifth: Only after all attempts at terminating or modifying local control of detention and corrections have failed, should efforts be directed at improving the quality of local services and facilities. Local measures for diversion from jail and a study of the population at risk should precede any increase in staff. *New and replacement building should be a last resort.* Community-based treatment should be encouraged, not only for the sake of its own economics, efficiencies, and decencies, but in order to reduce the pressures toward more and more detention and jail buildings.

REFERENCES

Alexander, Myrl E.
  1957   Jail Administration. Springfield, Ill.: Thomas.

American Bar Association (A.B.A.)
  1967   Standards Relating to Speedy Trial. American Bar Association Project on Standards for Criminal Justice. Chicago: American Bar Association.
  1968a   Standards Relating to Sentencing Alternatives and Procedures. American Bar Association Project on Standards for Criminal Justice. Chicago: American Bar Association.
  1968b   Standards Relating to Pretrial Release. American Bar Association Project on Standards for Criminal Justice. Chicago: American Bar Association.

American Correctional Association (A.C.A.)
  1966a   Manual of Correctional Standards. Washington, D.C.: American Correctional Association.
  1966b   "Probation services to the misdemeanant." Panel discussion, Proceedings, American Correctional Association. Washington, D.C.: American Correctional Association.

American Foundation, Institute of Corrections.
  1966   The Correctional Institutions and Services of Connecticut. Philadelphia: American Foundation.

Ares, C., A. Rankin, and H. Sturz.
  1963   "The Manhattan bail project." New York University Law Review 38(January):67–95.

Ashman, A.
  1969   Lockup: North Carolina Looks at its Local Jails. Chapel Hill: University of North Carolina Institute of Government.

Barnes, H. E., and N. K. Teeters.
  1951   New Horizons in Criminology. Second Edition. Englewood Cliffs, N.J.: Prentice-Hall.

Bass, S.
  1971   "Correcting the correctional system; a responsibility of the legal profession." Clearinghouse Review 5(July):125–127, 145–156.

Bennett, J. V.
  1964   "It's a crime to use the jail." Pp. 31–36 in J. V. Bennett, Of Prisons and Justice. Washington, D.C.: U.S. Government Printing Office.

Blumer, A. H. (ed.)
  1970a   Jail Operations (A Programmed Instruction Course in six booklets). Washington, D.C.: U.S. Government Printing Office.

1970b   Jail Management (An Independent Study Instruction Course in six book-lets). Washington, D.C.: U.S. Government Printing Office.

Burns, H.
1971   Origins and Development of Jails in America. Carbondale, Ill.: Southern Illinois University Center for the Study of Crime, Delinquency and Corrections.

California Board of Corrections.
1963   Minimum Jail Standards. Sacramento: California Board of Corrections.
1970   A Study of California County Jails. Sacramento: California Board of Corrections.

Cohen, M.
1971   "The rights of the civilly and criminally incarcerated." Clearinghouse Review 4(January):399–425.

Council of Judges.
1957   Guides for Sentencing. New York: National Council on Crime and Delinquency.

Davis, K. C.
1958   Administrative Law Treatise. St. Paul: West Publishing Co.

Encyclopedia of the Social Sciences.
1934   "Penal institutions." Pp. 57–64 in vol. 12. Edited by Edwin R. A. Seligman. New York: Macmillan.

Ervin, S. J.
1971   "Foreword: preventive detention—a step backward for criminal justice." Harvard Civil Rights/Civil Liberties Law Review 6(March):291–298.

Federal Bureau of Investigation (F.B.I.)
1951   Uniform Crime Reports—1950, vol. 21, no. 2. Washington, D.C.: U.S. Government Printing Office.
1970   Crime in the United States: Uniform Crime Reports—1969. Washington, D.C.: U.S. Government Printing Office.

Fishman, J.
1923   Crucibles of Crime. New York: Cosmopolis Press.

Foote, C.
1954   "Compelling appearance in court: administration of bail in Philadelphia." University of Pennsylvania Law Review 102(June):1031–1079.
1958   "Foreword: comment on the New York bail study." University of Pennsylvania Law Review 106(March):685–692.

Georgetown Law Journal
1969   "Prisoner's rights under Section 1983." 57(June):1270–1298.

Glueck, S., and E. Glueck.
1937   Later Criminal Careers. New York: Oxford.

Goldfarb, R., and L. R. Singer.
1970   "Redressing prisoners' grievances." George Washington Law Review 39 (December):175–320.

Hawthorne, J., and M. McCully.
1970   "Release on recognizance in Kalamazoo County." Michigan State Bar Journal 49(July):23–28.

Hepler, H.
  1966   "Paroling authorities and work release procedures." Proceedings, American
          Correctional Association. Washington, D.C.: American Correctional Asso-
          ciation.

Hirschkop, P. J., and M. A. Milleman.
  1969   "The unconstitutionality of prison life." Virginia Law Review 55(June):
          795–839.

Idaho Law Enforcement Planning Commission.
  1969   State of Idaho Jail Survey. Boise: Idaho Law Enforcement Planning Com-
          mission.

Illinois Department of Corrections.
  1971a   Illinois County Jail Standards. Springfield: Illinois Department of Correc-
          tions.
  1971b   Municipal Jail and Lockup Standards. Springfield: Illinois Department of
          Corrections.

John Howard Association.
  1963   Chicago Police Lock-ups. Chicago: John Howard Association.

Jordan, P. D.
  1970   "The close and stinking jail," in Frontier Law and Order: Ten Essays.
          Lincoln: University of Nebraska Press.

Kamin, A.
  1965   "Bail administration in Illinois." Illinois Bar Journal 53(April):674–686.

Klein, P.
  1920   Prison Methods in New York State. New York: Columbia University Press.

Law Enforcement Assistance Administration (L.E.A.A.)
  1971   National Jail Census—1970. Washington, D.C.: U.S. Government Printing
          Office.

Levin, G. S.
  1969   "The San Francisco bail project." American Bar Association Journal 55
          (February):135–137.

McGee, R.
  1971   "Our sick jails." Federal Probation 35(March):3–8.

Maddox, R. W., and R. F. Fuquay.
  1966   State and Local Government. Princeton, N.J.: Van Nostrand.

Mann, C., and C. Taedter.
  1968   The Jails of Missouri. Report for the Governor's Citizens Committee on De-
          linquency and Crime. Jefferson City: State Printing Office.

Massachusetts Governor's Committee on Jails and Houses of Correction.
  1965   Report. Boston: State Printing Office.

Mattick, H. W.
  1957   The Cook County Jail. Chicago: Office of the Sheriff of Cook County.
  1960   A Unified City-County Department of Corrections for Chicago and Cook
          County. Chicago: John Howard Association.

Mattick, H. W., and A. B. Aikman.
  1969   "The cloacal region of American corrections." Annals of the American
          Academy of Political and Social Science 381(January):109–118.

Mattick, H. W., and R. Sweet.
  1969   Illinois Jails: Challenge and Opportunity for the 1970s. Chicago: Univer-
          sity of Chicago Law School. Reprinted in 1970 by Illinois Law Enforcement
          Commission.

Molleur, R. R.
  1966   Bail Reform in the Nation's Capital. Washington, D.C.: Georgetown Uni-
          versity Law Center.

Murton, T., and J. Hyams.
  1969   Accomplices to the Crime. New York: Grove Press.

National Commission on Law Observance and Enforcement.
  1931   Report on Penal Institutions, Probation and Parole. Washington, D.C.: U.S.
          Government Printing Office.

National Council on Crime and Delinquency (N.C.C.D.)
  1966   Corrections in the United States. New York: National Council on Crime and
          Delinquency. Reprinted in 1967 in Crime and Delinquency 13(January):
          whole; and President's Commission on Law Enforcement and Administra-
          tion of Justice, Task Force Report: Corrections, Appendix A.

New York State Commission of Investigation.
  1966   County Jails and Penitentiaries in New York State. Albany: State Printing
          Office.

Nimmer, R. T.
  1971   Two Million Unnecessary Arrests. Chicago: American Bar Foundation.

North Carolina Jail Study Commission.
  1969   A Challenge to Excellence: Local Jails in North Carolina. Raleigh: State
          Printing Office.

O'Reilly, C., and J. Flanagan.
  1967   Men in Detention: A Study of Criteria for the Release on Recognizance of
          Persons in Detention. Chicago: Citizen's Committee for Employment.

O'Rourke, T. P., and R. F. Carter.
  1970   "The Connecticut Bail Commission." Yale Law Journal 79(January):513–
          530.

Pappas, Nick (ed.)
  1971a   The Jail: Its Operation and Management. Washington, D.C.: U.S. Govern-
          ment Printing Office.
  1971b   Instructor's Guide to The Jail: Its Operation and Management. Washing-
          ton, D.C.: U.S. Government Printing Office.

Pennsylvania General Assembly Joint State Government Commission.
  1965   The County Prisons and Jails of Pennsylvania. Philadelphia: American
          Foundation, Institute of Corrections.

President's Commission on Law Enforcement and Administration of Justice.
  1967a   Task Force Report: Corrections. Washington, D.C.: U.S. Government Print-
          ing Office.
  1967b   Task Force Report: Drunkenness. Washington, D.C.: U.S. Government
          Printing Office.
  1967c   Task Force Report: The Courts. Washington, D.C.: U.S. Government Print-
          ing Office.

Queen, S.
  1920   The Passing of the County Jail. Menasha, Wis.: Banta.

Robinson, David S.
  1971   "Annual event; Gary jail is deplored—again." Chicago Sun-Times Feb.
          28:76.

Robinson, L.
  1944   Jails: Care and Treatment of Misdemeanant Prisoners in the United States.
          New York: Winston.

Silverstein, L.
  1965   Defense of the Poor in Criminal Cases in American State Courts. Chicago:
          American Bar Association.

Sneidman, B.
  1968   "Prisoners and medical treatment: their rights and remedies." Criminal Law
          Bulletin 4(October):450–466.

Spain, J.
  1964   "The grand jury, past and present." American Criminal Law Quarterly
          2(Spring):119–142.

Stason, E. B., and P. G. Kauper.
  1959   Municipal Corporations. St. Paul: West Publishing Co.

Turner, W. B.
  1971   "Establishing the rule of law in prisons: a manual for prisoner's rights liti-
          gation." Stanford Law Review 23(February):475–518.

Tyler, Alice.
  1944   Freedom's Ferment: Phases of American Social History from the Colonial
          Period to the Outbreak of the Civil War. Minneapolis: University of Minne-
          sota Press.

U. S. Bureau of Prisons.
  n.d.   Correspondence Course for Jailers. Washington, D.C.: U.S. Department of
          Justice.
  1969   National Prisoner Statistics. Washington, D.C.: U.S. Government Printing
          Office.

U.S. Bureau of the Census.
  1961   "Inmates of institutions." 1960 Census of Population, vol. 2, pt. 8-A. Wash-
          ington, D.C.: U.S. Government Printing Office.
  1962   Statistical Abstract of the United States, 1961. Washington, D.C.: U.S. Gov-
          ernment Printing Office.

University of Chicago Law Review.
  1971   "The role of the Eighth Amendment in prison reform." 38(Spring):647–
          664.

University of North Carolina Institute of Government.
  1967   A Preliminary Study on Jails in North Carolina. Chapel Hill: Institute of
          Government.

University of Pennsylvania Law Review.
  1958   "A study of the administration of bail in New York City." 106(March):
          693–730.
  1962   "Constitutional rights of prisoners: the developing law." 110(May):985–
          1008.

Vera Institute of Justice.
 1968   Memorandum from Police Liaison Office to the Police Commissioner of the
         City of New York: "Manhattan Summons Project." New York: Vera Foun-
         dation.

Virginia Department of Welfare and Institutions.
 1964   Commitments to County and City Jails and City Jail Farms. Richmond:
         Virginia Department of Welfare and Institutions.

Washington Department of Institutions.
 1968   Jail Inspection Report—1968. Olympia: Washington Department of Institu-
         tions.

Yale Law Journal.
 1963   "Beyond the ken of the courts: a critique of judicial refusal to review the
         complaints of convicts." 72(January):506–558.
 1970   "Constitutional limitations on the conditions of pretrial detention." 79
         (April):941–960.

CHAPTER **22**

Prison Administration in a Time of Change

Billy L. Wayson

U.S. Bureau of Prisons

Because correctional organizations work with human material and their product is behavior, their design and management differ from other organizations. Unlike manufacturing establishments, their "production process" operates on intangibles, primarily on the relationships between clients and staff. For such human resource organizations, many traditional management tools are not directly applicable. Data describing effects of the correctional process on behavioral or attitudinal phenomena are frequently interpreted in conflicting subjective ways. The feedback loops necessary for judging the consequences of policies are difficult to create and suffer from incomplete and inaccurate information. All of this is further complicated by the fact that both the correctional organizations and their relationships with other organizations are in a period of much more rapid and extensive change than they have previously experienced in this country.

CORRECTIONAL ORGANIZATION

It has long been customary to refer to "systems" when considering the corrections process. The reference was formerly to "penal systems" or "prison systems," and now "correction systems" or even "criminal justice systems" is favored. Such traditional and widespread use of the word "systems" obscures the fact that most jurisdictions are neither designed nor managed as organizational systems.

Correctional services can be described only as nonorganized. In all larger correction agencies there exist organization charts that presume to depict the flow of authority and accountability among the diverse elements that comprise them. There also are policy manuals, job descriptions or position profiles for staff, job specifications, and other organizational and personnel documents and standard operating procedures that reinforce the notion of organization. But the salient characteristic of virtually all correction organizations today is their high degree of interorganizational and intraorganization separatism for legal, political, and bureaucratic reasons.

I wish to thank Norman A. Carlson, Director of the Bureau of Prisons, for providing me the opportunity to observe firsthand a management style that led me to endorse the principles advocated in this chapter. Portions of this chapter were drawn from my work for the National Advisory Commission on Criminal Justice, Standards and Goals.

In substantial part this organizational fragmentation is the heritage of the legal background from which all contemporary correction organizations have evolved. In prisons, especially, this legal heritage limited the operational boundaries or "correctional" responsibility to the time span between sentencing to institutional custody and release from institutional custody. What may occur earlier is perceived as the responsibility of legislative bodies, police, courts, and probation. Whatever may occur subsequent to conditional release from institutional custody is perceived as the responsibility of parole.

Among the negative consequences occurring directly or indirectly from the acceptance by most correction managers of the legal frame of reference are:

1. Managerial thinking has tended to become constricted and reactive to the emergence of problems, rather than innovative and anticipatory.

2. The boundaries of the corrections field have been accepted largely as statutorily and bureaucratically defined, rather than creatively probed and, where appropriate, professionally challenged. For example, definition and prevention of crime tend to be seen as the responsibility of others. Relatively few correctional administrators have been concerned professionally with the existence of wide disparities in the law and court practice regarding sentences.

3. Input of clients into correctional organizations tends to be accepted without demurring, the attitude of correctional managers too often being, "We take what they send us and do the best we can." This acquiescence frequently has resulted in juveniles being sentenced to adult institutions, imprisoning offenders needing psychiatric or other mental health care in institutions lacking competent staff and adequate facilities, and accepting from the criminal justice process inordinately large numbers of the black and the poor.

4. The focus of correctional organizations tends to be institutional, reflecting the emphasis in the criminal justice process on whatever facility it perceived as the "appropriate" extension of the court of jurisdiction: the training school for the juvenile offender, the prison for the convicted adult violator.

Traditionally, the institutional focus has been custodial, regardless of the philosophic rhetoric of the correction jurisdiction. This orientation stems from historic perception of the institution as the "holding" extension of the courts.

In addition to the fragmentation of corrections, nonorganization also results from political arrangements. The federal government, through the U.S. Department of Justice and the judiciary, operates three distinct correctional agencies: the Bureau of Prisons, the Board of Parole, and the United States Probation Service. Each of the fifty states operates a corrections "agency," and, through bureaucratic subdivision, many operate several agencies (for example, juvenile corrections, adult corrections, and probation and parole). Local governments present varied organizational patterns, ranging from a relatively complex correctional organization in New York City to simple detention facilities in small city police stations or rural county courthouses.

Further separatism is the product of bureaucracy. Even within those states with administratively grouped correctional responsibility, bureaucratic subjurisdictions are established. Administratively these may be divided into probation and parole, juvenile corrections, and adult corrections. Bureaucratic fragmentation also affects the criminally insane offender through administratively discrete departments of mental health and corrections.

These major categories sometimes are further subdivided on the basis of the individual's offense, age, and sex. Hence, the "organization" of corrections in each political jurisdiction tends to emphasize separate institutions for the adult offender, subdivided in turn into separate minimum, medium, and maximum security facilities for men and women. Until recently, many correctional agencies also segregated each category of offender on the basis of race, often in separate institutions for each offender category.

Within correctional agencies and specific institutions of such agencies, a philosophic and operational segmentation often exists between those staff members whose duties are principally custodial and those whose responsibilities concern offender rehabilitation. Also, as in all large-scale organizations, informal social organizations of staff and of inmates exist, frequently working at cross-purposes to the formal organization's goals.

Fragmentation hampers the ability of an organization or a group of organizations to respond to new environmental forces and stress. An organization's ability to achieve specified objectives is contingent on its detection of and responsiveness to changing environmental factors. First, it must recognize and accurately assess changes that affect its operation (for example, public attitudes toward alcoholism) and, then, develop a response consistent with overall objectives (for example, treat alcoholism as a medical problem). Similarly, as the general population's educational level increased, correctional agencies were required to provide college-level programs for their clients.

There have been perceptible shifts in public opinion regarding correctional operations and their effects on offenders. This has been reflected in growing legislative criticism and demands for reform. The judiciary has extended the application of civil and constitutional rights to almost all aspects of corrections. Professional groups, such as the American Bar Association, have assumed an active role in advocating reform and direct services to offenders.

The field of corrections faces a period of rapid and dramatic change with a highly fragmented organization and a substantially inappropriate management orientation. The organizational arrangements and managerial approaches that largely characterize the corrections field today did not serve well the relatively stable situation of the past. There is every reason to believe that they will serve even less well in the dynamic and fluid environment of tomorrow.

MANAGEMENT STYLE AND ORGANIZATION CLIMATE

Any organizational system has an administrative climate substantially influenced by the style of its top managers.[1] If these managers are autocrats, the system below them reflects this. If, on the other hand, they are democratic and participative, if they share in decision-making and in distribution of the rewards of organizational accomplishment, the organization is likely to be relatively democratic and participative.

Inertia, of course, characterizes organizations. The attitudes and modes of organizational behavior favored by previous administrations influence staff-conduct patterns in subsequent administrations. Nevertheless, new management at the top can significantly alter an organization's climate.

Since the managerial style of key decision-makers largely determines the climate of an organization or its subparts, it is appropriate to consider management style and organizational climate simultaneously. For this purpose, four quite different management styles and organizational climates may be identified: bureaucratic, technocratic, idiosyncratic, and participative.

Bureaucratic management or organizational climate is rule-oriented, position-

---

1. See Henning, 1972, prepared for the U.S. Bureau of Prisons in connection with its work for the National Advisory Commission on Criminal Justice, Standards and Goals.

focused, and downward-directed in communication flow (Bennis, 1966:5). This is exemplified by military organizations and by paramilitary systems, such as many correctional agencies. Dedicated bureaucratic managers perceive their jobs as requiring loyal, unswerving, unquestioning execution of organization policy.

This bureaucrat tends to avoid developing personal relationships with subordinates in the belief it weakens his "authority." Therefore, organizational input in the form of suggestions, ideas, innovations, and danger signals usually is restricted to those few persons in high office. Consequently, reality feedback to the top from operating organizational levels is slow, at best, and occurs with considerable difficulty or perhaps not at all. Identification of problems and performance monitoring are gained by the top decision group almost exclusively through statistical reports and compilations. These reports may be incomplete, inaccurate, or even deliberately misrepresentative of facts to show lower echelons in a favorable light.

The reasonably efficient bureaucracy is an adequate and sometimes excellent action system for the areas to which it is geared; it is almost universally a poor system for analyzing the need for change, however, and for gaining and holding member commitment or organization goals under conditions demanding rapid alteration or modification of these goals (Bennis, 1966:9–10).

A second managerial style is the *technocratic,* in which the manager views himself as the principal expert in his organization. The technocratic manager largely discounts the importance of hierarchical position or rank, which he associates with "administration" (i.e., paper work), preferring rather to define his role as interpreting technical matters and modifying organizational programs to fit the changing needs of the technological situation.

The technocrat performs the management role as the senior in expertise, relating personally with colleagues but striving to remain dominant through his perceived superior technical knowledge and ability to give specific directions on jobs. Within the corrections field, psychologists and social workers frequently are technocratic in their managerial application.

Within the larger technical organization that employs a number of specialities simultaneously (e.g., many large modern prisons, and most mental hospitals), a "pecking-order" of expertise customarily develops, certain types of experts ranking higher in status than other types of experts. Within each speciality, other personnel arrange themselves in descending order of expertise or seniority in accordance with the status model. When certain higher hierarchical positions in the organization are occupied by individuals with lower expert status, functional and communications bypasses develop, significantly altering the designed or intended structural relationships.

The *idiosyncratic* or "big daddy" manager views his role as administering organizational rules and regulations flexibly to orient them to specific individuals. In the best sense, he manages by attempting to stimulate, guide, and develop individual subordinates to carry out their responsibilities to the best of their abilities. However, he may also manage by personal manipulation. The idiosyncratic manager is likely to reserve a substantial amount of decision-making to himself, and frequently bypasses subordinates in his efforts to influence the behavior of individuals several echelons below in the hierarchy.

This manager's need for information to motivate, influence, or manipulate individuals effectively may cause him to become preoccupied with direct personal contact or minute organizational detail. He usually supposes himself to be adept at the practice of psychology and often believes that control over the organization's affairs and its effectiveness as a system are substantially dependent upon his capacity to deal with differing kinds of personalities, or even upon his charm.

Application of this style is likely to result in certain problems, especially in larger organizations. First, like the bureaucratic and technocratic manager, he reserves most decisions for himself, except in those areas of little or no personal interest to him—he relegates rather than delegates. Decision-making is delayed while subordinates wait for his decisions. Second, the idiosyncratic manager makes his choices more on the basis of personal interest or the personalities involved than on information or the organizational significance of the decision. Third, in the more manipulative applications of this style, the organizational consequences are likely to be either that the organization will lose its more interpersonally skillful subordinates or will tend to deteriorate in a pathology of intrigue.

For example, custodial and treatment staff, under the watchful eye of an efficiency-minded administrative officer, begin to vie for position by playing to the manager's idiosyncracies. Rather than assembling and organizing data for a rational argument, they try to shade the issues so their preferred outcome appears to be a natural consequence of the decision-maker's predispositions. If these stress custody, for example, a request for more caseworkers is justified in terms of the contribution of counseling to institutional security and order by providing an outlet for inmate grievances.

A fourth management style or organizational climate is *participative*. This calls for a group-oriented manager who perceives his role as involving the integration of the work group and its development into an effective team. Toward this end, the participative manager believes he should maintain an informal, friendly relationship with all employees separately or, in the larger organization, with groups. Besides sharing information with them, he solicits and respects their opinions about the work situation. Sometimes this manager becomes too concerned, even sentimental, about his organization. Since he dislikes conflict and lack of harmony, he may tend on occasion to sacrifice the organization's work requirements in his efforts to gain or hold member acceptance and cooperation.

The two management styles most frequently applied in the corrections field historically, and particularly in institutional management, are the bureaucratic and idiosyncratic. But, as specialized intensive treatment institutions more characteristic of juvenile corrections spread to the adult field, the technocratic style may become more prevalent, particularly if the rigid hierarchical features of the bureaucracy are retained. While the idiosyncratic style may result in an effective managerial application in organizations of limited size, and both the idiosyncratic and bureaucratic may be successful under conditions of substantial stability, neither is ideally suited to the administration of large, complex systems under conditions of rapid change.

The idiosyncratic correctional manager is less insistent on lines of authority than the bureaucrat but retains much of the decision-making authority by co-opting subordinates informally. He likes to "tour" the institution casually, not for a grand inspection, but so he can keep in close touch with operations. The general is sacrificed for the specific. He devotes too much time to cases and neglects overall population characteristics and organization progress. His decisions, consequently, are based on anecdotal experiences rather than on aggregate data. His "recidivism statistics" are Christmas cards from ex-offenders.

The idiosyncratic manager prides himself on knowing each inmate and has an index with names and pictures readily available in his office. The bureaucrat's zeal for reports and statistics is replaced by the idiosyncratic manager's errors of omission.

Frequently, some subordinates indulge the manager's unwillingness to abandon his career speciality. Thus, the former food-service administrator may have the best kitchen, but neglects postrelease job placement of graduates from the bakers' training program.

The control function traditionally assigned to corrections may account in large measure for the prevalence of a bureaucratic organizational climate. When coercion is the prime objective, it is efficiently administered by codifying prohibited behavior and making routine the application of sanctions. A more noble objective of "equality" is cited frequently for uniformly following disciplinary procedures that may, for a particular case, be inappropriate. Even a "treatment" purpose implies a limited degree of coercion, because the individual has been sent to a corrections unit to endure his "illness." If a deviation from routine is passed to the bureaucrat for decision, he self-assuredly asserts, "Rules are rules, and if we make one exception, everyone will want to do it."

A significant part of corrections' fragmentation can be explained by the pervasiveness of a bureaucratic mentality. Postrelease adjustment is considered the parole board's problem, probation is a court function, halfway houses are run by a community services unit.

A bureaucratic management style is particularly inappropriate for a "human services" organization, because it focuses on organizational processes rather than on what is being processed—people. The manager's intentional aloofness from his subordinates is reflected by the sort of inmate-staff relations that view programs as done *for* the client, not *with* him. The organization has established certain activities to which individuals are assigned regardless of appropriateness.

However, adding behavioral change to the traditional control focus of prisons requires an organizational structure change to permit integration of more functional specialities. This is almost impossible in an organizational climate that insists on a rigid categorization of functions and the undesirability of shared responsibility. A treatment team composed of different specialists is an attempt to superimpose an interdepartmental procedural arrangement on a functional categorization. Even taking officers out of uniform or allowing the teacher to participate in disciplinary decisions does not obscure the fact that critical judgments regarding their job performance, promotions, etc. are made by their functional supervisors. Under these conditions, the individual's frame of reference probably will be his speciality, which may or may not be consistent with what are perceived as the team's objectives.

The above managerial styles seldom appear in their pure form. As pointed out in *Leadership and Exchange in Formal Organizations* (Jacobs, 1970), the effective manager and his subordinates recognize their role differentiation at the same time that they share in the decision-making process.

IDEAL MANAGERIAL CLIMATE

A well-managed organization is one in which the attitudes and values of the individual members are in substantial agreement with the objectives that the organization's management wishes to foster, and in which jobs are matched properly with the personalities and skills of the occupants of such jobs. Adequate satisfactions for the needs of its members are provided. Organizational members, voluntarily and willingly, undertake to do what is organizationally necessary. As Douglas McGregor (1960:68) emphasizes, "The acceptance of responsibility [for self-direction and self-control] is correlated with commitments to objectives."

This is, of course, an ideal state of affairs. More commonly, the organization's authority system and informal social system drift or are driven apart. The strains between the two finally become so severe, an "emotional" separation of these two components occurs. Following such division, the lower echelons usually organize, as in the case of a union, and formally represent themselves to the authorities as an opposing organization. Their goals are to redress grievances and bring about a more equitable balance between the burdens the organization imposes and the rewards and satisfaction it offers.

MANAGERIAL REQUIREMENTS OF THE FUTURE

To function effectively in today's dynamic and fluid environment, correction organizations must be flexible. If a system knows exactly what it needs to accomplish and how best to accomplish it, and is administered with benevolence and an esprit de corps, a bureaucratically managed organization probably is the most efficient delivery system.

Under conditions of rapid environmental change, however, organizations cannot know exactly what needs to be done or how best to proceed. The urgent requirement confronting modern corrections organizations, therefore, is to structure themselves so they are adaptable, their participants voluntarily embrace the organization's goals as their own, and they have a capability for determining and interpreting forces impacting upon them (see Bennis, 1966:52–55). This requires effective problem-solving processes, employee participation in setting organizational objectives, and access to the decision-making process and mechanisms for testing reality (e.g., avoiding stereotyping).

Employee participation by increasing the sources of information will give management a fuller understanding of the altering environment and a better indication of the organizational consequences of such changes. Management receives environmental assessments from a wider range of perspectives in a form allowing personal interaction and discussion. Full commitment by an organization's membership also will help develop those strategies that are most appropriate for accomplishment of the organization's goals under rapidly changing conditions.

To meet these requirements, corrections must abandon a management orientation and organization structure predicated on assumptions identified by Douglas McGregor as Theory X (1960:33–34) and draw upon contemporary management science.

It was a common belief at one time that individuals inherently dislike work, must be coerced to perform, and want to avoid responsibility and risk. McGregor's (1960: 47–48) Theory Y challenged the validity of these assumptions and hypothesized that work is as natural as leisure, individuals can be self-directed toward organizational objectives, personal commitment is a function of financial and nonfinancial rewards, and imaginative problem-solving is not limited to a few individuals at the top.

Research during the intervening years has added new insights into human behavior in formal organizations. Edgar Schein (1965:60) has articulated a set of assumptions which underlie his "complex man" idea: persons have a preferentially ordered hierarchy of motivations which vary; new motives can be *learned* through experiences in formal organizations, but this may be insufficient to meet other (e.g., social or status) needs; job satisfaction and organizational effectiveness depend on both the total work environment and the individual's motivation; and, finally, managerial strategies or philosophies must take into account these complexities and adapt to highly variable situations.

The history of recent organizational experience clearly reveals that only those managements that recognize the direction, magnitude, and rapidity of change and that can marshal the fullest employee commitment and effort will be able to design and direct the anticipatory, adaptive, and effective organizational systems required. This organizational climate will be conducive to assessing change, deciding where to go, and selecting a method to get there.

MANAGEMENT BY OBJECTIVES

Management by objectives emphasizes a goal-oriented philosophy and attitude. Goal-oriented management focuses on results with less concern for method, as long as it is within acceptable legal and moral limits. Traditional management, on the other hand, tends to be task-oriented, with emphasis on the task performance without adequate regard for results.

The purpose of management by objectives is to: (1) develop a mutually understood statement regarding the organization's direction and (2) provide criteria for measuring organizational and individual performance. The statement is a hierarchical set of interrelated and measurable goals, objectives, and subobjectives. If properly conducted, the process may be as important as the objectives themselves, because it improves vertical and horizontal communication and emphasizes interdepartmental integration.

For a management-by-objectives system to be implemented successfully, it must be based on the participative management philosophy discussed above and fulfill several specific conditions (Schreiber & Sloan, 1970).

First, the full support of top management is essential. Indeed, at each level of management, the superior's degree of acceptance of this managerial approach will determine substantially whether or not subordinates accept and try to make the system work.

A second necessary condition is a goal-oriented management philosophy. The motivational value of a management-by-objectives approach depends in great part upon giving each manager and employee responsibility to carry out a job without constant supervision, and then assessing him on his degree of accomplishment.

Third, each superior-subordinate relationship should be characterized by the highest degree of cooperation and mutual respect possible.

Fourth, managerial focus should be on deviations from agreed-upon levels of goal attainment, not on personalities, and the evaluation system should report any such deviations to the manager or employee establishing the goal, not to his superior.

The fifth condition is feedback. If managers are to be evaluated on the results they obtain, they require timely and accurate readings of their progress to take corrective action when necessary. Further, they need substantially accurate projections and interpretations of demographic, technical, social, legal, and other developments likely to affect their progress and performance.

Finally, to be successful, an intensive training program must precede organizational implementation. A follow-up consultative service should be available to organizational members or units requiring assistance in implementing this system.

THE CORRECTIONAL MANAGEMENT PLANNING ROLE

It is an unfortunate reality that most correction agencies do not engage in planning in the fullest sense. While many have a global notion of where they are going and some engage in specific aspects of planning, such as facilities construction, few are engaged in the full planning process. This involves development of integrated long-range, inter-mediate-range, and short-range plans for the complete spectrum of their administrative and operational functions.

A number of rationalizations are offered as to why comprehensive planning is not being done, the most common among these being "We cannot tell what the legislature is going to do," and "There simply is not enough time—our organization already is overworked and understaffed." These explanations ignore the fact that what the legis-lature does or does not do often is determined precisely because no viable, planned, documented alternative has been proposed by corrections management. Yet corrections management somehow always finds the time and staff resources to deal with system crises.

Too frequently, planning has been left to an isolated office staffed with technicians, and the organization has received their product with reluctance. Failure to differentiate types of planning (e.g., strategic and tactical) has led to two extremes: either the plan-ning function is considered the total purview of top management or it is seen as the aggregation of individual plans from many organizational subunits. In fact, it is neither. The planning process should involve input (information, objectives, progress, etc.) from all organizational units, but the major decisions regarding goals and re-source allocation are the responsibility of top management.

The effective planner is not an ivory-tower technician, but some unique features of his role should be recognized and supported. His effectiveness depends in part on a sensitivity to the changing conditions under which the organization must operate. Therefore, he is frequently seen as an "outsider" by the rest of the organization because he continually raises questions not immediately impinging on daily operations. The planner is a "devil's advocate" and questions the basic assumptions and operating practices of the organization. In examining alternatives to the status quo for their pos-sible application to the organization, he is placed in the role of an unwanted change agent.

The planner sometimes contributes to his own alienation by not recognizing that large organizations always contain conflicting opinions that must be reconciled by the chief executive. There are pragmatic restrictions on what, ideally, should be a rational process. Even though management decisions may be at odds with the "compelling evi-dence," the planning function should, at least, make the reasons for the decisions explicit.

The planner should be a participant-observer in the short-term decision-making of top management. Only in this way can he be in a position to point out the relation-ships between daily action and long-range intentions. Planning can be called a manager's technique to forecast the future, or a systematic examination of future oppor-tunities and risks and the strategies to exploit the opportunities and avoid the risks. It would appear, however, that planning more clearly is the rational process of directing today's decisions toward the accomplishment of a set of predetermined short- and long-range goals. This process depends upon how problems are identified, broken down into manageable dimensions, related to one another, and resolved through the choice of a number of alternatives.

PLANNING AND THE BUDGET

The budget is the correctional manager's plans or goals expressed in financial terms. Budgeting is an administrative mechanism for making choices among alternative and

competitive resource uses, presumably balancing public needs and organizational requirements against available and requested funds. When the choices are coordinated
with the correctional organization's goals, the budget becomes a plan.

Like planning, budgeting is something everyone does. We budget our time,
money, food, entertainment, and other requirements with a general view to meeting
our personal and family goals. The correctional manager is charged with budgeting his
resources to meet organization, staff, and offender goals.

Operating, annual, capital, or facilities budgets are common differentiations in
types of budget. The distinction largely is related to differences in timing (annual
versus long-range), degree of uniqueness (ongoing requirements versus one-time expenditures), and different financing arrangements (annual tax collection versus
bonded indebtedness).

The distinction between line-item and program budgets is of substantial managerial significance. The line-item budget is input oriented, focusing on specific, discrete
items of expenditure required to perform a service, and categorized by organizational
units. A program budget is output oriented, focusing on the function or service performed.

The line-item budget tends to focus and fixate the attention of decision-makers,
including legislators, on specifics such as food, supplies, clothing, books, etc. The program approach tends to elevate the decision-making focus to the level of programmatic
concern and consideration of alternative courses of action.

The "planning, programming and budgeting system" (PPBS) approach, popular
in the 1960s, was a system-oriented effort to link planning, budgeting, and management-
by-objectives processes through programs. Under this system an agency or organization first would ask itself: "What is our purpose, and what goals are we attempting to
realize?" Once purposes or objectives had been determined, action programs to
achieve these objectives would be identified or, if nonexistent, designed. Next, each
existing program would be analyzed in terms of the extent to which it was oriented
toward the organization's objectives, and its level of effectiveness. Newly formulated
programs would be analyzed in terms of their anticipated costs and expected contribution to the accomplishment of organizational objectives.

Finally, existing and new alternative programs would be analytically compared in
terms of their respective costs and anticipated benefits. Should an alternative, on the
basis of such a cost-benefit analysis, be deemed preferable to an existing program, the
latter would be discarded and the alternative adopted.

Implicit in this management system is a longer-range programming perspective
coupled with a continuous reevaluation of objectives, programs, and budgetary
amounts as circumstances change.

Regardless of how organized and formal an organization's planning, there are
six criteria by which managers may judge the comprehensiveness and adequacy of the
planning process. These criteria are stated in terms of questions that should be asked
repeatedly with reference to any specific planning approach (Payne, 1957:111–12):

1. Has the system's planning process adequately identified the key influences in
development and trends of American society, the region, and the state, and properly
evaluated the impact of each such influence on the field of corrections, its functional
components, and on the specific correction system itself?

2. Have the strengths and weaknesses of the system been assessed accurately?

3. Have the capacities and capabilities of different system functions to support
the plan been projected far enough ahead?

4. Have alternatives been considered and evaluated adequately?

5. Is there a realistic timetable or schedule for implementation?

6. What provisions have been made for possible future reverses?

The basis of correctional planning must shift from simple personal accounts to a group framework, and the perspective of the correctional manager and his planners must become broader. "One of the great challenges facing the [planner] is the necessity of coordinating knowledge, influence, and resources on a scale commensurate with the human problems he is addressing. [These] problems are inter-related, complex and resistant to piecemeal efforts" (Perlman & Gurin, 1972:238).

The objective of community corrections, for example, is to maximize offenders' access to local resources, not as an alternative to incarceration, but as a solution in itself. This goal requires more integration of criminal justice components (statewide and within each local area) and coordination with other social-service delivery systems.

TOTAL SYSTEM PLANNING

The process used to apply the general planning concepts previously discussed and their relation to correctional management will use the model recommended by Fred D. Moyer and his associates (1971). Although the end product in this model is a facility, the methodology is applicable with modifications to the solution of any defined problem or to developing a comprehensive plan.

In this section *system* is defined as a group of related and interdependent activities, actions, or events organized to achieve a common purpose. The range of these items necessary to explain the phenomena under examination determines the system's *scope*. For some purposes, the scope may be limited to a state *corrections* system; for others, to the state *criminal justice* system. Throughout this discussion, corrections will be considered a subsystem of the criminal justice system. *Component* will be used as a generic term to refer to activities, actions, events, and subsystems.

"Total system planning" is a process that defines, analyzes, and develops responses to a specific set of problems. While examples from corrections will be used throughout, application of this process is not restricted to a specific subject.

The process is "open-ended" or "open," that is, it describes the interactions between activities or components of one system and those of another. Changes in any single component of an open system or a related system will affect all other components. For example, arraignment scheduling directly affects the number awaiting trial and, consequently, the required detention capacity. Similarly, jail population may be reduced by diverting alcoholics from the criminal justice system. The system resulting from the planning process must be open to link offender needs with definitive solutions.

Results from one step in the planning process may be affected subsequently by feedback from the outcome of another step. In the foregoing example, creating detoxification programs may change judicial practices that previously were considered a constraint on reducing jail populations. Feedback emphasizes that planning is a process, not a discrete event.

Functional integration, at least within a geographic area, is required to implement the results of the planning process. Part of solving a *corrections* problem (e.g., overcrowding) may involve changing a *court* procedure (e.g., rescheduling arraignments). A crime-prevention program operated by a criminal justice system component may involve certain activities of the education, housing, and employment systems. Different systems and subsystems often must work together to attain a solution to a common problem. Thus, their functions will overlap or be complementary.

Insofar as total system planning is not limited to a political subdivision, interjurisdictional cooperation (for example, city-county, multicounty, and state-local) is required. (*Cooperation* is used intentionally to reflect a somewhat less structured working relationship than that implied by "integration.") The openness quality simply implies that the planning process should account for interactions between systems and their components in different political jurisdictions. Similar practices in different jurisdictions should be examined for their effects on offender flows through the system. For example, one jurisdiction may decide to defer prosecution of narcotics-related offenses, but a contiguous jurisdiction continues to prosecute them aggressively. The addict simply has to change residence to decrease the probability of conviction, and the drug-treatment programs may quickly become overloaded. The planning process should consider the consistency of related practices between jurisdictions, even though changing them may be unlikely. This aspect of an open system adds an intergovernmental complication to an intragovernmental operation. While it significantly complicates the planning process, the "service-area" concept requires such interjurisdictional consideration.

The service-area concept is basic to total system planning. Service areas are demarcated by the scope of the particular problem that frequently crosses jurisdictions. Underlying the concept is the realization that social problems and their solutions do not confine themselves to geopolitical boundaries. Each service area may have distinct problems and resources, but there is sufficient commonality to warrant subsystem coordination.

In the 1940s and 1950s, for example, small, inefficient country schools were consolidated into larger "service areas" within counties. In the 1960s, when consolidated schools in small towns no longer could support the range of education services required, further regionalization occurred. The service-area concept involves a similar process for corrections.

In the simplest case, an agricultural economy and low population density may be factors conducive to regionalized correctional services. The multistate Standard Metropolitan Statistical Area (SMSA) represents the other extreme. The SMSA is an integrated economic and social unit containing several distinct, but interdependent, communities or cities. Total system planning for an SMSA may be impossible, but "local" criminal justice problems can be related conceptually and some degree of cooperation or coordination developed. The difficulty of interjurisdictional planning is added to the difficulty of functional integration (police, courts, corrections, health, welfare). Interestingly, many of the arguments opposing consolidated and regional school systems (for example, transportation costs, loss of local control, community identification, and paying for someone else's problems) are being repeated to support fragmentation of correctional programs.

The process of total system planning for a corrections service area involves six phases: problem definition, survey, analysis, program linkage, system concept, and physical translation. Each phase involves a definition of the context (e.g., the service area), an end product (e.g., statement of the problem), and a course of action (e.g., how to allocate planning funds). Each end product and course of action determine what is to be done in the next phase. Subsequent phases may affect prior ones through the feedback mechanism; for example, an initial service-area demarcation (phase 1) may be modified by an analysis (phase 3) of survey data (phase 2).

Identifying the service area to be covered is the initial step of the planning process. This step will determine the scope of the overall effort and result in a preliminary statement of the correctional problem being addressed.

Given the diversity, quantity, and quality of data, the survey and structured analysis of its results are critical steps. Subsequent decisions regarding planning, program development, and construction are dependent on these steps. Lack of objectives and use of obsolete planning standards will perpetuate ineffective programs. There are always information deficiencies (reliability, coverage, inconsistency) that force "best guesses" based on professional judgments.

Four products should result from phases two and three: an inventory of existing correctional programs in the service area; an assessment of current law enforcement, judicial, and detention practices as represented by types of offenders flowing through the system; an inventory of treatment programs and resources not part of the criminal justice system; and a projection of criminal justice system population. These four items are used to assess the community's ability to meet specific program needs.

The "program linkage" phase should include examination of alternative correctional service networks. For example, the population of local institutions can be reduced by diverting certain classes of offenders from the criminal justice system. For offenders not diverted, the potential for community alternatives to incarceration may be examined, including deferred prosecution, summons in lieu of arrest, release on recognizance, and release to a third party volunteer.

If the underlying objective is to divert as many offenders as possible (either from the criminal justice system entirely or from incarceration), representatives of public and private social-service agencies, community groups, and professional organizations should be involved in developing alternatives. Public interest and support are important elements in a planning process that contemplates extensive use of community-based programs.

Definitive treatment programs are developed following an analysis of program interrelationships. While the details of these programs or "delivery systems" vary depending on the service-area's requirements, they will follow either a "regional" or a "network" approach.

Where resources and offenders are not sufficient to justify separate rehabilitation programs, localities may pool on a *regional* basis. Regionalization consolidates existing facilities through cooperative interjurisdictional planning and operation of a new institutional complex. To encompass the planning required in such an approach and to provide the resources it implies may require a redistribution of governmental responsibilities. The two extremes, the underutilized rural facility and the crowded urban facility, clearly are incapable of furnishing the services required. Regionalization is not, however, without complications.

In some respects, a regional community correctional center is a contradiction in terms. In regions comprised of scattered medium-sized cities, it will be difficult to keep individuals involved in their home community. To facilitate reintegration, the inmate must interact continually with his community and must be allowed trips to find employment and postrelease housing. The distribution of jobs over a large territory makes work-release programs more difficult.

A frequent objection to regionalization is the time and cost of moving people to and from facilities. A systematic analysis of cost factors should be part of the planning process and should be included in the overall cost projections for any delivery system—regional or network.

In major metropolitan areas, the corrections program can be developed on the basis of a *network* of dispersed facilities and services geographically located to perform their functions best. The traditional correctional institution, with its inclusion of all functions in a single facility, creates an unnatural environment, physically and psychologically. In the community, boarding schools, for example, are not used for adult education, and individuals rarely work in the same building in which they live. These arrangements may be convenient for the inmate, but they are unrealistic.

Following the survey of program needs, inventory of diverse area resources, and development of detailed program linkages, the planning process must translate this information into physical resource requirements, if any.

CONCLUSION

The processes necessary for any serious attempt to reform corrections refuse to honor jurisdictional boundaries. If total system planning is to be put into operation, the state and federal governments must increase funding for and improve guidance to local jurisdictions. While most accept this point, specifying the respective roles engenders questions of jurisdictional prerogatives, vested interests, and political rivalries. By early 1972, however, Alaska, Connecticut, Rhode Island, and Vermont had assumed responsibility for operating locally based correctional institutions. The potential results are encouraging, though applying this body of experience to larger, more urbanized states undoubtedly will encounter difficulties.

Coordination among all components of the local criminal justice system and between various levels of government is a crucial, though often elusive key to improving the nation's correctional programs.

The rate of change in corrections has not reached a pace that makes planning impossible. Many of today's problems are related directly to the failure to anticipate the operational impact of general social and environmental changes. The extension of the range of offenders' rights, for example, was a natural outgrowth of a similar movement involving racial minorities and students.

The need for a more coherent approach to correctional programs long has been recognized. Historically, correctional reform has been limited to minor variations on a discordant theme. Reform can and should be a continuing process, not a reaction to periodic public criticism. The planner's role as a skeptic or devil's advocate regarding underlying concepts and basic assumptions can keep the corrections field from a state of future complacency.

Even the best plan, however, is of little value if the organization's climate, structure, and employee resistance obstruct its implementation. Employees react negatively to changes imposed from above, so their access to decision-making is important even though the chief executive's leadership responsibilities require that innovations cannot always be vetoed by subordinates.

As human resource agencies, corrections must make a special effort to integrate various functional specialities into an organization team that holds mutual objectives vis-à-vis the client, not only among its members but also between members and the organization. Accomplishing this organization climate will require a participatory and nonthreatening leadership style in which employee, offender, and organizational needs are met in a compatible way.

REFERENCES

Bennis, Warren G.
  1966   Changing Organizations. New York: McGraw-Hill.
Henning, Kenneth.
  1972   "Organization and administration." Washington, D.C.: U.S. Bureau of Prisons (mimeographed).

Jacobs, J. O.
   1970   Leadership and Exchange in Formal Organizations. Alexandria, Va.: Human Resources Research Organization.
McGregor, Douglas.
   1960   The Human Side of Enterprise. New York: McGraw-Hill.
Moyer, Fred D., Edith E. Flynn, Fred A. Powers, and Michael J. Plautz.
   1971   Guidelines for Planning and Design of Regional and Community Correctional Centers for Adults. Urbana, Ill.: University of Illinois Department of Architecture.
Payne, Bruce.
   1957   "Steps in long-range planning." Harvard Business Review 36(March–April) : 95–106.
Perlman, Robert, and Arnold Gurin.
   1972   Community Organizations and Social Planning. New York: Wiley.
Schein, Edgar.
   1965   Organizational Psychology. New York: Prentice-Hall.
Schreiber, David F., and Stanley Sloan.
   1970   "Management by objectives." Personnel Administrator 15(May–June) : 20–26.

CHAPTER **23**

Juvenile Correctional Institutions

Charles W. Dean and N. Dickon Reppucci

University of Hartford and *Yale University*

Although there are over 300 state and local juvenile correctional institutions (training schools) for adjudicated delinquents in this country, there are relatively few written documents pertaining to them. Sociologists have spent large amounts of time, energy, and thought investigating the adult prison system but little trying to understand the juvenile situation. In fact, *Criminology* by Sutherland and Cressey (1970), one of the most used and highly regarded textbooks in the field, devotes less than 2 of its over 650 pages to the topic. Psychologists have also neglected youth corrections. Although they have studied and extensively researched delinquency, seeking causes and developing rehabilitation programs, few, if any, have investigated the relationship between the adjudicated delinquent and the training-school environment, or the development of treatment procedures that can be used within these institutions. An ostensibly comprehensive volume (Cortes & Gatti, 1972) makes no mention of youth institutions, yet offers numerous treatment approaches, many of which either would be impossible to implement within the current institutional structures or would generate conflict when joined with already existing practices.

While social scientists and others have neglected our juvenile corrections system to a large degree, a body of literature has accumulated, nevertheless. The present chapter discusses available knowledge, summarizing the most salient characteristics of juvenile institutions, their staffs, and their treatment programs. A brief historical account is included as well as a concise declaration of the stated goals and objectives of juvenile correctional facilities. In discussing treatment programs, the three major approaches of recent decades—guided group interaction, community treatment, and behavior modification—are summarized. Emphasis is given to rehabilitation programs for entire large institutions (e.g., The Minnesota Training School for Boys and the Connecticut School for Boys) rather than to demonstration projects concentrating on single units within larger institutions (e.g., Cohen & Filipczak, 1971) or smaller, self-contained, newly created settings (e.g., Goldenberg, 1971). Problems of change are discussed in the final section.

In preparing this chapter we encountered a dilemma not easily resolved. On the

We wish to thank Seymour B. Sarason and Brian P. V. Sarata for commenting on an early draft of this chapter.

one hand, we wished to give the reader some idea of what juvenile correctional institutions are like, of the earlier types of institutions from which they grew, and of the resurgence of interest in making them more effective instruments of societal protection and personal rehabilitation. On the other hand, we also wished to spotlight recent developments (by no means widespread) that clearly indict these institutions on three grounds: they are or become evil, they are not necessary, and there are viable alternatives. When one of our states (Massachusetts) is in the process of eliminating its juvenile correctional institutions (Bakal, 1973), and one hears approval of this from sources heretofore convinced that those institutions were absolutely necessary, it may be that we are at the beginning of a new chapter in the story of juvenile delinquency treatment and management. The dilemma inheres in the possibility that the descriptive part of this chapter may become rapidly obsolete as a guide to the future scene. We did not resolve the dilemma. The relatively large amount of space we give to describing juvenile correctional institutions should not be viewed as reflecting a judgment of their value, but as a description of what they are, what they have been, and what many people hope to see them become. The small amount of space devoted to policies directed to the elimination of juvenile correctional institutions should not be viewed unreflectively as an indication of the place of such thinking in the *zeitgeist*. We may well be in that "in-between period" when predicting the future is hazardous.

THE HISTORICAL DEVELOPMENT

The movement in the United States to provide institutions for the care and training of delinquent boys and girls began over 150 years ago. The prison reform efforts of the English Society of Friends provided a stirring example for the New York Society, which met in 1817 for the purpose of considering "a practical measure for the cure of pauperism and the diminution of crime." This meeting led to formation of the "Society for the Prevention of Pauperism," which immediately began to inquire into conditions in the city penal institutions. Members were shocked to find "children housed and associating with thieves, prostitutes and 'lunatics'; no proper classification of offenders; crowded and unsanitary quarters." In the Society's report of 1819, the city penitentiary at Bellevue, "three miles from city hall," was described as "one great school of vice and desperation housing confirmed and unrepentant criminals." The Society protested placing "novices in guilt, those unfortunate children from ten to eighteen years of age, who from neglect of parents, from idleness and misfortune, have never had a sense of morality," in a penitentiary with convicted adults. Finally, the report recommended the erection of a special building within the grounds of the penitentiary for the younger offenders (Pierce, 1869:33).

The Society took one more forward step in 1822 by pointing out the great need for providing separate institutions for juvenile offenders, with the aim of effecting their reformation. A paper issued by the Society that year reads:

> These prisons should be rather schools for instruction than places for punishment like our present state prisons, where the young and old are confined indiscriminately. Youth confined there should be placed under a course of discipline severe and unchanging but alike calculated to subdue and conciliate. The wretchedness and misery of the offender should not be the object of the punishment inflicted; the end should be his reformation and future usefulness (Pierce, 1869:41–42).

The Society for the Prevention of Pauperism was reorganized into the Society for the Reformation of Juvenile Delinquents, and in 1825, the New York House of

Refuge was opened (Reeves, 1929). This was the first public institution in the United States for delinquent boys and girls. The population was comprised of "six unhappy wretched girls and boys clothed in rags and with squalid countenances" (Pierce, 1869: 78). In 1826 the House of Reformation in Boston was established, and the Philadelphia House of Refuge was opened in 1828 (Reeves, 1929).

These early institutions developed many principles of management that helped to revolutionize the treatment of young offenders. Commitment was for no definite term but during minority; this was the beginning of the indeterminate sentence in the United States. The institutions stood *in loco parentis* to the child and could place him in a family or bind him without relinquishing control over him whenever this method of treatment seemed preferable to keeping him in the institution. Moreover, each of these institutions maintained an academic school. Although five to eight hours of workshop labor was exacted from the children, they spent four hours each day in intellectual pursuits. The children were graded according to their age and "morality" and new arrivals were placed in a "good" grade at the start. In the Boston institution, play and recreation were a regular part of the day's routine, and in this establishment and the New York House of Refuge, a limited kind of self-government was practiced involving the use of a jury system and the machinery of a popular election (Robinson, 1923).

In 1847 the State Reform School in Westboro, Massachusetts, later called the Lyman School for Boys,[1] was established with a far greater population capacity than the earlier schools, thereby setting a precedent for similar institutions that were to follow (Teeters & Reinemann, 1950). Massachusetts also founded the first state industrial school for girls in 1854 (Reeves, 1929). By 1900, 105 facilities had been opened (Sutherland & Cressey, 1970) in thirty-six states. They appear now in every state.

During the 150 years of their development, institutions for juvenile delinquents have been known by many names. Initially the House of Refuge was a haven for the child who otherwise would have gone to jail. The idea of reformation was emphasized next and they became reform schools. This name in turn became objectionable so the school idea was given prominence and they were called industrial or training schools. Later, it was thought the best place for a child was in a home and some schools were named accordingly. These changes in names do not represent a chronological evolutionary pattern but rather a collage of ideas, each superimposed on the other with little regard for compatibility of form or philosophy. The present complex system of schools, homes, and institutions for delinquents developed from this background, and their common historical and philosophical antecedents are still easily observed. (For a detailed history, see Mennel, 1973.)

CHARACTERISTICS OF JUVENILE INSTITUTIONS

Presently the field of juvenile corrections is in a period of rapid change due to general public dissatisfaction, the intervention of federal agencies through allocation of substantial funds, and some innovations in treatment. Any description of the field, while becoming inaccurate rapidly due to the rate of change, is useful, nevertheless, as a means of providing perspective.

---

1. In 1971, the commissioner of the Massachusetts Department of Children and Youth Services, which administers the state's training schools, closed the Lyman School in what may prove to be the forerunner of the most extensive reordering of priorities since the first youth institutions opened in the early 1800s.

Capacity

The President's Commission on Law Enforcement and Administration of Justice conducted a comprehensive survey indicating that there are 220 state-operated juvenile institutional facilities in all fifty states, Puerto Rico, and the District of Columbia. There are an additional 83 locally operated programs in sixteen states, although half are in California, where they are partially state subsidized. The state-operated facilities, constituting 86 percent of the juvenile-training capacity in the United States, could house 42,423 in 1965 and had a total average daily population of 42,389 (President's Commission, 1967:143).

In many jurisdictions the capacity of locally and state-run training facilities is extended through use of private facilities. In some instances these are publicly subsidized, but control of the program remains in private hands. At the time of the Commission's survey, forty-two states had plans for new construction, which would increase the capacity by 42 percent by 1975, or to a total of over 60,000. This does not include the numerous community residential centers that are increasingly utilized in lieu of institutionalization or as a step back into the community after institutionalization.

Diversification

While there is general agreement that the heterogeneous population sent to juvenile institutions by juvenile courts requires a diversified program, the juvenile training facilities in most states cannot provide a wide range of programs. It is interesting to note that of the 220 state-supported institutions, 166 were in twenty-four states, leaving 54 institutions for both males and females to be distributed throughout the other twenty-eight jurisdictions (Gibbons, 1968). Six of the larger jurisdictions now have nine or more facilities, but eight states have only one facility serving all juveniles and fourteen states have only two facilities—one for boys and one for girls. Thus, twenty-two states have only one institution that houses the full range of adjudicated delinquents. This range includes everything from truancy, running away from home and incorrigibility, to murder. The program and staff that can serve a juvenile on his first commitment for truancy cannot be expected to serve equally well a juvenile whose criminal activities and institutional experiences are of long duration. This absence of diversified facilities has characterized state juvenile institutional systems for many years.

In states that have expanded their residential facilities to provide greater diversity, the most numerous separate new facilities are small camps for boys and reception-diagnostic centers. Of the 220 institutions surveyed, 138 were classified as either regular boys' or girls' institutions and 13 were coeducational institutions. Of the remaining 69, there were 49 camps and 14 reception-diagnostic centers. The rapid growth of camp programs has been attributed to low cost of operation and to the need for dealing with the less difficult child in such a way as to prevent his being confined with juveniles having longer and more serious delinquency records. Most of the camps have a capacity of 50 or less (Gibbons, 1968); the cost of their operation is often less than half that of a training school in the same state. More importantly, the success rate is generally higher, i.e., recidivism is lower. This result is somewhat deceiving, however, since the populations of these camps are usually highly selective of the low risk cases.

Reception-diagnostic centers are increasingly considered to be a necessary part of juvenile correctional systems. These centers usually serve two purposes. First, they provide the juvenile with a gradual introduction into the institutional system. While in the reception center, only newly committed boys or girls are housed together and the center staff usually has more professionals than the staff of regular institutions. Thus, although a stay in the reception center does not fully prepare the juvenile for the institutional life he will experience during the remainder of his commitment, the shock of being away from home and in an institution may be lessened. Second, these centers usually perform some kind of diagnostic function. In some jurisdictions a child may be committed for a diagnostic summary and then returned to the court for final disposition of the case. In all cases the diagnostic study is considered essential to effective planning for the child, and a classification committee usually attempts to achieve maximum goodness of fit between the committee's perception of the child's needs and the availability of program resources in the system. However, perusal of records suggests that reception centers sometimes recommend services that are not available; coordination between an individual's diagnosis and his subsequent program participation varies considerably, but is often minimal; and the rhetoric of classification, even by seriousness and length of delinquency record, often is not reflected in programs. Thus, the limitations of institutional resources are readily apparent.

Another serious problem relevant to the absence of adequately diverse resources is the practice of transferring juvenile security risks and management problems to adult penal institutions. One of the most important objectives of the juvenile-court movement was the removal of juveniles from the criminal justice system. This was based on concern for protecting juveniles from physical assault by adults and from the attitudes of hardened criminals, as well as for providing them with facilities and programs especially adapted to their needs. Yet postadjudication transfer of children to penal institutions continues in many jurisdictions, although it has been argued that transferred juveniles have not been afforded the constitutional protection of those convicted of crimes, and, thus, are denied due process of law. It is asserted that this procedure is as much a denial of due process as sentencing an adult to a penitentiary without a trial.

Length of Stay

The average length of stay for children committed to state training facilities ranges from four to twenty-four months, with nine months the median. The number of children at the extremes of the range is relatively small. Five state systems, housing 3 percent of the total, report an average length of stay of six months or less. Eight state systems, housing 8 percent of the total, report average lengths of stay of more than twelve months. The remaining three-fourths of the state systems, housing nine-tenths of the institutional populations, have an average stay of six months to a year. This does not include reception centers serving primarily placement or diagnostic purposes that report a surprisingly uniform average length of stay ranging from twenty-eight to forty-five days (President's Commission, 1967:144).

Costs

Estimating the cost of operating a correctional facility is a difficult task. Per capita cost figures are usually misleading because they include only operating costs and do not include special grants, capital expenditures, or depreciation of property and buildings. Neither do they include the property-tax income lost. The President's Commission on Law Enforcement and Administration of Justice (1967:144) reported a total operating cost of $144,596,618, an average per capita expenditure of $3,411.

This figure seems highly questionable. For the year 1970, discussions with administrators indicate there are several institutions with per capita costs above $15,000. While some discrepancy between this and the Commission's figure is due to inflation between 1965 and 1970, most of the discrepancy can be accounted for in administrative techniques of estimating per capita costs. For example, sometimes parole staff are included as part of the institution and parolees are included in the base figure; sometimes they are not. Institution size, type of living unit, length of work week, age of residents, type of programs, and other factors affect per capita costs, and these usually have not been accounted for in the statistics. Therefore, there are no reliable data concerning the actual per capita costs of juvenile institutions, and available figures appear to be grossly underestimated.

Physical Plants

Many of the nation's training facilities are quite old. In several states, patched-onto use of the first reform school is evident. Sharp increases in the population of these facilities have produced some benefits and some problems. The benefits come mainly from the development of new, smaller living units.

The President's Commission on Law Enforcement and Administration of Justice appointed a Special Committee on Correctional Standards who selected from the standards already published by authoritative bodies those that would be useful to the Commission and were amenable to measurement (Special Committee, 1967:205–12). Their *Standards* recommends that a juvenile institution be no larger than 150 children. This is based on experience indicating that smaller facilities enhance the impact of a program. The treatment atmosphere tends to break down more rapidly in institutions where the population is above 150 because of such therapeutic dangers as regimentation and formality. Despite the advantages cited for the smaller institution, the trend has been in the other direction. The bulk of the juvenile institution population is now housed in facilities considerably larger than the prescribed standard. The principal concession to their *Standards* is an occasional attempt to break down large institutions into several small administrative units in the hope that each will take on the climate of a small separate entity (President's Commission, 1967:147).

Living Unit Size

The earliest institutions were based on two principles of moral education: (1) there must be separation of the sexes, and (2) children should be classified by some criteria. This classification was made possible by the development of a cottage system, which originated in Hamburg, Germany, in 1833 as a scheme for giving the child a more normal life while in the institution. This plan was followed for the first time in America in the building of the School for Boys in Lancaster, Ohio, in 1856. Reference to the housing unit as a cottage and the caretaker as a cottage father or cottage mother, instead of as a guard or officer, has become a common part of the organization and rhetoric of the youth corrections movement.

The *Standards* generally calls for the living unit to have a maximum of twenty residents where groupings are homogeneous and from twelve to sixteen where the grouping is heterogeneous or where the children are severely disturbed. Of the 1,344 live-in units in state-run juvenile institutions, only 24 percent have a capacity of twenty or less. In 68 percent, the capacity is from twenty-one to fifty and in 8 percent, it is fifty or more. In general, living unit size is related to period of construction, with the smaller units being relatively new. The importance of the small living unit is generally agreed upon and this is reflected by the fact that in 55 percent of all present construction, the living unit has a capacity of twenty or less. This holds true for 63 percent of all authorized construction and 45 percent of projected construction.

Summary

The above description of youth institutions is based largely on information collected by the President's Commission on Law Enforcement and Administration of Justice for the year 1965. Since that time some new facilities have been completed and others planned. Court rulings are requiring changes that administrative personnel might support but could never initiate. Costs, as with all business and government agencies, have climbed rapidly. The influx of money under Law Enforcement Assistance Acts, administered by the U.S. Department of Justice, has had some impact. There have been some improvements and gains but the demands have increased also. The increased demands have been partially reflected by changes in the institutions and, to a lesser extent, in the personnel.

CHARACTERISTICS OF THE STAFF

The quantity and quality of staff set the parameters within which the effectiveness of programs for children lie. Generally speaking, the staff-client ratios and the quality of staff in juvenile institutions are more favorable than in adult correctional agencies, but this does not imply that a positive situation exists. In many areas there are rather wide discrepancies between the quantity and quality of staff recommended and actually provided.

Staff Size and Ratio to Juveniles

In 1965, state-run juvenile facilities employed 21,247 staff in institutions with a total average daily population of 42,389. Overall, in the 220 institutions surveyed, there was one staff person for every two juveniles. Relative to personnel, the *Standards* suggests:

1. All positions in the juvenile institution, including that of superintendent, should be covered by an adequate merit or civil service system. The 40 hour week should prevail for all employees.

2. The institution administrator should have training in social work, clinical or social psychology, psychiatry, education, or a related field of child development.

3. The following staff ratios should be met:

(a) A minimum of 1 full-time psychiatrist for each 150 children.

(b) A minimum of 1 full-time psychologist for each 150 children.

(c) A minimum of 1 social caseworker for every 30 children.

(d) One trained recreation person for each 50 children.

(e) A minimum of 1 supervisor for 8 or 10 cottage staff, or 1 supervisor for 2 or 3 living units.

(f) A minimum of 1 registered nurse during the working hours.

(g) A minimum of 1 teacher to 15 youngsters with sixth-grade reading ability.

(h) A minimum of 1 teacher to 10 youngsters with third- to fifth-grade reading ability.

(i) Individual teaching staff for each youngster with less than third-grade reading ability.

(j) A full-time librarian for each institution.

4. Major religious faiths represented in a training school population should be served by chaplains on the training school staff (Special Committee, 1967:212).

The Commission's study showed that most jurisdictions fail to meet the standards.[2] Data from this survey are presented below.

Psychiatrists. The *Standards* calls for a minimum of one full-time psychiatrist for 150 children. On the basis of the average population of 42,389 in 1965, the number of psychiatrists required was 282. However, the equivalent of only 46 psychiatrists were serving in the 220 state-operated facilities, and the majority of these were found in only five states. One state alone had over 20 percent of all available psychiatric time and only four states had enough psychiatric services available to satisfy the required 1:150 ratio.

Psychologists. The *Standards* calls also for one full-time psychologist for each 150 children.[3] Thus 282 psychologists would be required, but only the equivalent of 182 psychologists worked in the surveyed juvenile facilities. As with psychiatrists, psychologists were unequally distributed among the states, with 106 found in nine states. Only twelve states came up to the recommended ratio.

Case Workers. The *Standards* holds that under ordinary conditions, a full-time case worker in a juvenile institution should be assigned not more than thirty children. On the basis of the average daily population, the number of case workers required is 1,413. The survey data showed a total of 962 case workers, or 66 percent of the number required.

Teachers. The *Standards* calls for teacher-pupil ratios not exceeding 1:15. Standards bearing on teacher ratios in training facilities are difficult to apply, since public-school systems sometimes assume a portion of the training system's academic burden. Excluding these teachers, there were 2,495 teachers in the 220 institutions for an overall teacher-pupil ratio of 1:17. In twenty-four states, the teacher-pupil ratio was better than the 1:15 cited and in thirty-six states it was less than 1:22. The fact that teacher-client ratios are more favorable than those of other professional personnel probably reflects the historical pattern of academic teaching served as the traditional mainstay of programming. Furthermore, the teacher has a dual function in terms of both treatment and custody, since the teacher is responsible for containment. Finally, there is a more adequate suppy of trained teachers than other professionals.

Chaplain Services. The *Standards* calls for chaplains on each staff in a number sufficient to serve the major religious faiths represented in the institution. The 220 state institutions are served by 158 chaplains and the overall chaplain-client ratio is 1:268.

---

2. It should be noted that staff size alone is an inadequate measure of staff adequacy. Quality of staff and organizational structure that contributes to optimizing the effectiveness of staff efforts are at least equally important. Also, the patterns recommended by the *Standards* are based on a "traditional" institutional program approach, which is being increasingly questioned.

3. The label *psychologist* is not reserved for individuals with the Ph.D.

Medical Services. No area of reported services is more difficult to evaluate than those of the medical-dental-optical fields. While 96 percent of the facilities contacted by the President's Commission reported medical services and 94 percent reported dental services, closer examination of operating practices shows major differences in the *quality* of these services. Where medical, dental, and optical services represent an especially expensive drain on hard-pressed budgets, the decision that treatment is "needed" is reached less quickly than where services are routinely available and already paid for by contract. Close examination would frequently find the quality of services far below minimum standards. Even in many of the more well-financed systems, it is common to observe medicine being administered by nonmedical personnel. Also, great latitude is exercised in interpreting procedures considered standard in almost any other type of setting. Fortunately, the age range served by these institutions is one where medical needs usually are neither frequent nor serious. However, with the increase of narcotics abuse by minors, and the related and more frequent occurrence of serious disorders, such as hepatitis, medical services are becoming more crucial.

Educational Qualifications of Staff

The *Standards* calls for the superintendent to have completed graduate training in the behavioral sciences or related fields of child development. The survey found substantial variations among systems in educational requirements for this position. Twelve jurisdictions require the superintendent to have a graduate degree, twenty-eight require a college background, and ten have no formal educational requirements. This does not mean that trained persons are not sought and recruited, but rather, that reality determines staff selection. For all practical purposes, there are few training programs for correctional personnel. Although psychologists, sociologists, and educators sometimes find themselves in administrative positions in juvenile correctional facilities, this is more often accidental than planned.

The cottage staff in charge of the living unit where most of the minors' time is spent is considered to be the backbone of a training facility program. It is necessary for these people to be able to relate to children, to be emotionally mature, and to be flexible in adapting to new situations. No standard for this position has been offered but the traditional standard has been a high-school education. In a more sophisticated system, graduation from college might be preferable; however, under present salary schedules, college graduates are frequently unobtainable. Salaries are so low that establishing educational requirements is not feasible. One state reported that some of its cottage staff were on public welfare. Even if salary schedules were such that college graduates could be attracted, good training programs for current staff would probably be a more productive alternative, as there is nothing in a college degree that implies competence for dealing with delinquent youth. In fact, since most of these youth come from impoverished backgrounds, it is very unlikely that they will be able to identify with caretakers who are models of unobtainable roles. There is experience to suggest that the most effective child-care workers are from the same socioeconomic stratum as the youth they serve.

Summary

The staff of an institution is the most significant factor in determining the kind and quality of program provided. The verbiage of great concern for treating juvenile delinquents has not resulted in allocating the staff resources this rhetoric would lead one to expect. While a few institutions have staffs that are adequate in terms of quantity and training, many others fall short of the recommended standards. Even those institutions that have the most staff resources often allocate them along traditional lines, a practice increasingly questionable as it becomes clearer that the characteristics of the clients require changes in philosophies, methods, and staff capabilities.

GOALS OF JUVENILE INSTITUTIONS

The goal of the training school is to provide a specialized program for children whose behavior is such that the court rules they cannot be retained in the community. Thus, youth institutions normally house hardened and more unstable youngsters than those placed on probation. The central goal of all juvenile institutional programs is to prepare the youth for the ultimate test of return to the community. The programs planned must be directed toward a population that is not considered responsible for their behavior. The *parens patriae* and *in loco parentis* concepts strongly imply a deterministic philosophy. However, upon reaching legal maturity the youth becomes a free moral agent and is responsible for his acts. This includes being subject to criminal proceedings if he violates the law.

The terms "school of industry" or "reformatory" often designated early juvenile training facilities and reflected their goals. They sought chiefly to teach the difference between right and wrong. Teaching methods were primarily on a precept level, tending to emphasize correct behavior, formal education, and, if possible, learning a trade. To a large extent, these elements continue to bulwark most programs, but their efficacy has been increasingly questioned for two reasons. First, although statistics vary and can be interpreted differently, there is general agreement that over half the persons released from juvenile training facilities will be reincarcerated. Second, there is agreement that if treatment is to produce lasting change, it must touch upon the personal and environmental reasons for delinquency. Delinquent behavior may be a satisfying experience to a youngster, especially if it meets his emotional and social needs. Further, it may be a symptom rather than a cause, and programs must be directed toward the latter if they are to be effective.

The development of a consistent philosophy, even within a single institution, is complicated by the fact that institutions must serve a wide range of purposes.[4] To establish a single goal for the heterogeneous groups they house is next to impossible. There is some question whether the multiplicity of services that must be provided is not a self-defeating situation for a training school. Here is a partial list of functions which the juvenile training school is required to serve:

1. House relatively hardened delinquents in a secure setting so as to protect the community and bring about change in the client.

2. Detain youth awaiting completion of other plans or court hearings.

3. Provide housing for youngsters whose primary need is a foster or residential home.

---

4. A comparative study by Street et al. (1966) delineated sets of beliefs and goals in juvenile institutions under five categories: (1) incarceration and deprivation; (2) authority and obedience; (3) learning; (4) socialization; and (5) therapy. The authors concluded that the first philosophy, incarceration and deprivation, no longer exists and that the other four philosophies were seldom found in a pure form. Moreover, they found that the six institutions they investigated, regardless of goals, all suffered from "the tendency toward routinization, the deficit of information on organizational processes and outcomes, and the inability to integrate all staff, particularly the teachers, into the total program" (p. 281).

4. House large numbers of youngsters whose involvement in delinquency is more situational than patterned and who could be handled more efficiently in a community-based program.

5. Care for mentally retarded youngsters committed to the training school because there is either no room in a retardation facility or no such facility, or because their delinquencies are so serious that the institutions for the retarded are reluctant to accept them.

6. Provide for youth with serious psychological and psychiatric problems because of the unavailability of alternate residential treatment programs.

7. Treat drug-dependent youth whose delinquency is related to drug use.

8. Provide maternity services for pregnant girls.

The possibility of single institutions fulfilling all of these functions staggers the imagination, yet most training schools are expected to do just that.

The President's Commission (1967) found variations in training schools among states as a whole, as well as among counties of a single state, and further showed that many objectives other than "change" are the determiners of practice. If juvenile institutions were actually working toward a single goal, statistics that reflect practice would have some meaning. Length-of-stay statistics do not reflect differences in time needed to effect "change." If they did, one system's length of stay could be compared to another's as the guideline for the effectiveness of a program. Rather, length of stay seems to reflect extraneous factors, such as overcrowding or the availability of other services for children who, though suited for probation programs, must be "held long enough" to avoid court or community problems. Each juvenile court has its own philosophy about the purposes that the youth facility should serve and assigns children to it accordingly.

TREATMENT APPROACHES

Since the early days when the founding fathers of the juvenile corrections movement fought the first battles to provide separate housing for children, there have been relatively few comprehensive "treatment" programs established. The "standard fare" of juvenile institutions has been placement of youth into "cottage" living situations (usually twenty to fifty residents in a cottage) and the provision of some educational and recreational opportunities (see Amos & Manella, 1965). As new practices, such as casework, psychotherapy, remedial education, and group counseling, have been developed, they have generally been added piecemeal to existing programs, and instead of replacing older philosophies, have simply supplemented them. As Empey points out:

> Individual practices, which by themselves might have been helpful, often seem to generate conflict when joined irrationally with other practices. For example, the tendency for custody and treatment people to conflict with each other in correctional institutions often contributes to the cynicism, rather than the reformation of inmates. Inmates are encouraged to concentrate on means for exploiting the rift among staff members, rather than working with staff people to resolve common problems (1967:7).

Moreover, in most cases, psychotherapy of the Freudian view—the most frequently used clinical model—is inappropriate for dealing with the problems of the delinquent, even in those rare instances when adequately trained therapists are available.

Although this "standard fare" is still the "normative" program in most juvenile institutions, there have been a series of experimental programs in this country since the Highfields project was opened in New Jersey in 1950 (McCorkle et al., 1958; Weeks,

1958). These programs can be viewed roughly as falling into three major categories: (1) the guided group interaction tradition as exemplified in the Highfields project (Weeks, 1958), the Provo experiment (Empey & Erickson, 1972) and the Comprehensive Treatment program at Red Wing, Minnesota (Vorrath, n.d.); (2) the community approach as seen in the correctional halfway-house movement (Keller & Alper, 1970) and the California Youth Authority Community Treatment Project (e.g., Warren, 1969); and (3) a social-learning or behavior-modification approach as exemplified by the Robert F. Kennedy Youth Center (KYC) in Morgantown, West Virginia (U.S. Bureau of Prisons, 1970), the National Training School project (Cohen & Filipczak, 1971), and the Connecticut School for Boys (CSB) Project (e.g., Reppucci, 1973; Sarason, 1974:194–215).[5]

These categories are not meant to be mutually exclusive, since many of the projects have integrated concepts from the other approaches, but they indicate the most salient features of the particular projects. Since it is beyond the scope of this chapter to review in depth all of these projects, only brief summaries will be provided of most. To highlight the problems encountered in establishing a program at an old facility with an existent personnel base, as compared to the creation of a completely new facility, a more detailed description will be presented of the Connecticut School for Boys and Kennedy Youth Center projects. These two projects are derived from the same theoretical basis, but one organizes the boys into homogeneous groups for treatment while the other does not. Moreover, both of these projects, to varying degrees, incorporate aspects of the other treatment categories and represent modern ways of organizing a treatment program within a relatively large institution.

The Guided Group Interaction Approach

Since the development of the Highfields project in 1950 (McCorkle et al., 1958), the number of correctional treatment programs that have adopted some form of the guided group interaction (GGI) techniques pioneered there have been phenomenal. Most juvenile institutions that make any claim at all to providing "therapeutic" treatment have some sort of GGI program. Moreover, many community-based programs have also adopted some form of GGI as part of their program. Because of the widespread acceptance of this technique, it is important to examine the meaning of this concept and to present a few examples of programs which have made major use of it. GGI programs:

> are primarily concerned with peer group dynamics and the operation of the peer group in restructuring the youth "subculture" around more socially acceptable norms and values. . . . GGI programs involve the delinquent in frequent and intensive group discussions of their own and other members' current problems and experiences. Based on the theory that antisocial youth behavior receives the support and approval of the delinquent peer group, and that substituting acceptable norms for delinquent values and attitudes also requires the support of the peer group, these programs encourage the development of a group culture and the acceptance by members of responsibility for helping and controlling one another. As the group culture develops and the group

---

5. Almost all experimental rehabilitation programs have been conducted with male delinquents. Only two sources even mention programs for females: the California Youth Authority Project (Warren, 1969) included a sample of females, and a chapter in Glasser (1965) describes the implementation at a training school for girls of a rehabilitation project based on the principles of reality therapy.

begins to accept greater responsibility, the staff group leader allows the group a greater degree of decision-making power. Over time, the group's responsibility may extend to decisions involving disciplinary measures imposed on a member or determination of a member's readiness for release (Center for Studies of Crime and Delinquency, n.d.:16).

These programs are unique in that the group process itself is expected to determine the culture of the entire program. That this is the case more often in theory than in fact has done nothing to diminish the popularity of GGI. In comparison to traditional group therapy, the decision-making authority permitted the group is considerably greater, and may be a crucial factor in the rehabilitation of youth through group support and influence.

The Highfields Project

Highfields is a minimum security residential group center in New Jersey serving around twenty short-term committed first offenders 16 and 17 years of age, who are assigned directly from the juvenile court. The goal was to organize an intensive short-term (three to four months) treatment facility utilizing GGI sessions to encourage the participants to recognize their problems in terms of their behavior, attitudes, and values and allow them to explore alternative solutions to their problems (Weeks, 1958).

In order to test the effectiveness of the program, Highfields' graduates during a three-year period in the early 1950s were compared to a group of committed boys at the New Jersey State Reformatory for Males at Annandale. Using at least a six-month follow-up after release, 63 in every 100 Highfields boys, as contrasted to 47 of every 100 Annandale boys, completed treatment and did not get into enough trouble to be reinstitutionalized. Interestingly, there was little difference in the relative number of white boys from the two facilities with successful outcomes, but 59 in every 100 Highfields blacks, as compared to only 33 in every 100 Annandale blacks, completed their stay and did not get into further difficulty. There was no evidence of any attitudinal or personality change for any of the Highfields boys (Weeks, 1958).

The validity of the results of the comparison between Highfields and Annandale is debatable. Random assignment by the judiciary did not occur, e.g., the Annandale boys tended to be a little older, from poorer social backgrounds, and perhaps more experienced in delinquency than the Highfields boys. However, the Highfields method was at least as successful as the reformatory and it accomplished its success in a much shorter time period and at considerably less expense. Moreover, in 1967, a Rutgers University investigation of more than 1,000 delinquents gave credence to the original Highfields success claims (Stephenson & Scarpitti, 1967).

The Provo Experiment

The basic principles of GGI as developed at Highfields have been applied to nonresidential as well as residential settings with apparent success, e.g., Essexfields (Pilnick et al., 1966; Stephenson & Scarpitti, 1969), Collegefields (Pilnick et al., 1967), and Provo (Empey & Rabow, 1961; Empey, 1967; Empey & Erickson, 1972). The best known of these is the Provo Experiment, initiated in 1959 in Provo, Utah. A maximum of twenty 15- to 17-year-old boys were treated in an intensive daily program including school or work and GGI sessions. Each day, following school or work, the boys went to the center for group sessions, but they returned to their own homes at night.

Delinquents assigned to the experiment initially consisted of youths randomly selected from those adjudicated to regular probation supervision and youths randomly selected from the few who were committed to the state training school from Provo. Soon, however, the county judge decided to send to the experimental program all boys whom he adjudicated for training school, so their control group was completed by selection of similar youth committed to the state training school from other Utah counties. In both the regular probation and the training-school comparisons there were fewer postrelease arrests of those in the experimental program than of their controls. The contrast was greatest in the first postrelease year for the probationers and almost disappeared by the fourth year, but for the training-school cases the contrast was small in the first postrelease year and increased in each of the four postrelease follow-up years. Such year-by-year improvement in benefit from noninstitutional rather than institutional treatment, suggesting long-run criminalizing effects of a training-school experience, was even more pronounced when each case was used as its own control by comparing arrest rates in pre- and posttreatment periods of various durations (Empey & Erickson, 1972).

Positive Peer Culture at the Minnesota Training School for Boys

Minnesota's pioneering application of the GGI technique to a large established juvenile institution (about 650 admissions per year) is important even though there is less clear evidence than in the Provo project as to whether increased success resulted from implementation of the program, as there was no experimental design using control groups. This GGI program was initiated as a reaction to a major crisis at the institution rather than as a positive action by the appropriate authorities in a period of relative calm. Unfortunately, this is the way change in correctional policy is usually brought about.

Demonstration projects that are implemented in new settings or in a particular unit of a more established setting, utilizing especially trained staff, are significantly different as challenges from the conversion of an established institution with an existent personnel base. This is seldom recognized! Yet, if large-scale change is to develop in our juvenile institutions, the special problems of conversion must be confronted. As will be seen when the CSB project is discussed, principles are being developed and data accumulated to help understand this process.

In the fall of 1968, the Minnesota Training School at Red Wing burst into mass media prominence when, in a three-day period, 50 to 100 boys left the grounds for varying lengths of time without permission. This was variously referred to as a "mass walkout," a "riot," or a "disturbance." The reasons given for the incident included weather, racial conflicts, internal staff problems, outside influences, staff incompetence, poor program, or combinations of these.

Such crises are common in youth corrections, and the reactions they arouse are familiar to any experienced youth corrections administrator. Petitions were circulated demanding investigations, erection of a fence, or simply "that something be done." It was urged that there be a "crackdown," a return to a "no nonsense approach," and the end of "mollycoddling." The governor's office called an open meeting to hear the views of the townspeople directly. The local citizens had formed a committee five years earlier that now promised the public they would investigate the entire matter. Generally, the school fared quite well in the investigation, and the decision was made to build the institution's program around the GGI methodology. Traditional programs, such as academic and vocational education, volunteer services, and parental visiting, also were provided, but GGI was the basic treatment tool.

Youth institutions generally are characterized by a resident subculture that militates against the effectiveness of rehabilitative efforts. It was hoped that establishing "positive peer culture" by means of groups would neutralize the delinquent subculture at the Red Wing institution (Vorrath, n.d.). The goal was to redirect peer pressures, and to diminish the we-they battle between boys and staff. Situations that previously would have necessitated disciplinary action by the staff were considered as "problem areas," which the boys would have to work out within the group before they could be released. The assumption underlying the approach of the positive peer culture is that peer influences are the most effective vehicle of change. Following the Highfields example, a list of terms was compiled that everyone in the institution used so as to eliminate semantic confusion. The groups met five nights a week for ninety minutes.

As with all GGI models, the level of therapy in the groups is not geared to uncover deep-seated psychological problems but rather to help the boys acquire better modes of handling immediate needs and to enable them to function successfully in a non-delinquent community. In their very definite format, a youth entering a group has the responsibility for telling his life history. After this, the group members decide at each meeting which boy is going to be discussed and why. The youth selected is referred to as "having the meeting." Generally, the boys consider "having the meeting" to be a privilege. The member reports on the way he has handled particular problems throughout the day and the group points out areas where additional work is needed, problems on which there has been progress, and new problem areas that need attention. This process forces the boy to verbalize the events of the day and, thus, with the group's assistance, to gain insight. Also, this process helps him develop trust as he learns that his misdeeds do not result in punishment but are "problems" that require understanding and attention in order to avoid further problems. The members are with each other all day, so it is difficult for a person to deceive the group in any consistent manner.

The Red Wing approach is worthy of attention because it is an application of the Highfields technique to a relatively large, state-supported institution serving a less-selective, heterogeneous population. Moreover, the program was introduced at a time of serious institutional disorganization and it seems to have ameliorated to a large degree those conditions that had been explosive. The approach provided a framework to organize available resources more effectively and to utilize existing staff resources. The ritual of getting rid of the "bad" staff and thus "solving" the problem was avoided.

The program received enthusiastic support from staff and visitors, and the administration claims that the runaway and recidivism rates have been reduced considerably, behavior problems requiring staff intervention have nearly disappeared, staff morale has increased by their working together for a common goal, and all levels of staff are actively participating in the program. Empirical data to support these claims, however, have not yet been published.

The Community Approach

Halfway Houses

With the rising recognition that responsibility both for preventing and correcting criminal behavior must originate in the community, and in light of the spiraling crime rate and the ineffectiveness of traditional correctional facilities, the need for some action to help reintegrate the delinquent into the community became apparent. The halfway-house movement represents the major positive response thus far.

Halfway houses for released adult prisoners began in the U.S. as early as 1845, when a group of Quakers in New York City, despite hostility and indifference, opened such an establishment, which has survived to this day as the Isaac T. Hopper Home (Keller & Alper, 1970). There were other early, sporadic instances of halfway houses for released prisoners, but it was not until the late 1890s and early 1900s, with the spread of Hope Halls, that any sizeable number of prisoners was helped. These disappeared, however, partially as a result of parole authorities arguing against them on the grounds that such associations between former prisoners were forbidden by regulations. Halfway houses for adult offenders did not reappear in any number until the 1950s. Even more recent are such places for juvenile delinquents. Although an example of a halfway house for delinquents is found in the Philanthropic Society of London in the eighteenth century, such instances are rare indeed. What we know today as the community treatment idea, residential and nonresidential, is largely the product of the last twenty years (Keller & Alper, 1970).

The term *halfway house* generally refers to any relatively small facility, either residential or nonresidential, usually located in or close to a city or town. Individuals involved in the halfway-house's programs participate in the daily life of the larger community, either working, recreating, or going to school "outside" of the house. Halfway houses may serve various types of offenders and are basically of two distinct kinds: "halfway-in" and "halfway-out." The halfway-in house generally serves younger offenders who are under court order of probation, and offers an alternative to incarceration in a larger juvenile institution. The halfway-out house is designed to aid individuals who are ready to leave an institution but need more assistance in readjusting to society. There are no set patterns for either of these types of halfway house and considerable variety is found in their treatment goals, locations, staffing patterns, and residents.

Keller and Alper describe the core of basic elements characteristic of the halfway-house concept as follows:

> First, halfway houses are organizationally related to corrections, either as a result of a court order or the administrative action of some public agency. Second, the halfway house idea connotes a group situation. Third, it is usually small in size, both absolutely as well as relative to the size of our overlarge penal stations. Fourth, contact with the free community is both its hallmark and its essence. Fifth, the trappings of the correctional institution—walls, fences, locked doors, uniformed guards, and weapons close at hand—are absent. Sixth, some rules and regulations, however minimal, assure order and give structure to the living situation. Last, despite varying lengths of time spent in a halfway house, the basic aim is to provide a short, intensive and transitional experience (1970:15).

Treatment methods in halfway houses vary with individual directors and there is little agreement as to the manner in which treatment goals should be accomplished. Halfway houses with small budgets make few formal efforts at treatment, relying instead on the creation of a familylike situation and the establishment of healthy relationships between adult and child. However, as Keller and Alper point out, houses with more financial resources may have a clearly formulated notion of treatment and a large number of staff. Such a "professional" approach may actually prevent the creation of a family living situation. The one common treatment approach in most houses is that group sessions of some form are employed. These group sessions are conducted by individuals from a wide variety of backgrounds, e.g., psychologists, social workers, teachers, custodial officers, and ex-offenders, and their goals may range from easing tension between staff and residents and reducing administrative problems to more intensive therapy aimed at changing basic attitudes, beliefs, and self-concepts. GGI sessions are the most frequently used technique at halfway houses for the juvenile offender. One further treatment method which is frequently used is that parents are encouraged to become involved in group sessions or in private consultation.

One of the more innovative of halfway houses is the Residential Youth Center (RYC) staffed by individuals indigenous to the inner city and serving "incorrigible" 16- to 21-year-old youths (Goldenberg, 1971). Although the purpose of the RYC is to provide an alternative to incarceration for these youths, the top priority of concern is the organization's social structure. This priority was based on the assumption that if people, regardless of their backgrounds or levels of formal preparation, were involved in what for them were meaningful, intrinsically gratifying, and growth-producing activities, the results could not help but be beneficial to the clients with whom they were engaged. Thus the concept of "horizontal structure" was implemented. On a clinical level, this meant that each staff member, regardless of his position in the organization (i.e., director, cook, or RYC worker), would carry a case load and assume total responsibility for all decisions and interventions involving a particular resident and his family; on an administrative level, it meant that the actual administrative functions and duties of the RYC were taken out of the hands of its director and deputy director and distributed among the staff in terms of individual interests, abilities, and past experiences; on a daily work level, it meant a sharing by all staff members of the specific duties usually associated with different jobs, e.g., everyone was expected to "live-in" to relieve the regular live-in counselor and to prepare the meals during the cook's day off. Ongoing staff sensitivity training was used to insure open communication.

The advantageous nature of such a setting can perhaps be best illustrated by the positive results obtained for the "incorrigible" youths serviced at the first RYC. Utilizing a matched control group of youths not serviced, it was demonstrated that RYC youths showed better work attendance records, higher average weekly income, fewer arrests, and fewer days spent in jail than the control group. Moreover, after the RYC experience, this group felt less alienated from the world of social, institutional, and interpersonal relations than did the control group.

The California Community Treatment Project

The best-known project utilizing a predominantly community approach is the California Community Treatment Program (Warren, 1969; Palmer, 1971), an essentially nonresidential endeavor, although it places approximately 25 percent of its clients in foster homes. Beginning in 1961, with joint state and federal sponsorship, its basic assumption has been that there are different types of delinquent youth and they will not all respond satisfactorily to a single treatment formula. Therefore, the first step was to divide the target population into treatment-relevant categories by the Interpersonal Maturity Classification System (Warren, 1969). Youth are differentiated into seven successive stages or levels of interpersonal maturity based upon how they perceive themselves and others around them. The range is from the least mature, which resembles the interpersonal reactions of an infant, to the most socially mature, which is seldom achieved by anyone in our society. Individuals may become fixed at a particular level, and most delinquents fall into levels 2, 3, or 4. Level 2 is characteristic of the completely self-centered, impulsive person; level 3 consists of individuals concerned only with others to the extent that they can manipulate them to serve their own aims; and level 4 consists of persons with guilt feelings, whose discomfort over failure to meet the standards of persons they respect is expressed in antisocial or neurotic behavior. Nine delinquent subtypes fall within these levels: Level 2—(1) asocial, aggressive, (2) asocial, passive; Level 3—(3) immature conformist, (4) cultural conformist, (5) manipulator; Level 4—(6) neurotic, acting-out, (7) neurotic, anxious, (8) situational emotional reaction, (9) cultural identifier.

Boys and girls aged 14 to 18, who are first commitments to the California Youth Authority from Stockton, Sacramento, and San Francisco are eligible for the community treatment program unless they have been adjudicated for a serious assault or other act that has aroused the larger community. About 75 percent of the boys and 90 percent of the girls are admissible to the program, but are assigned randomly either to a correctional institution or to the community programs. Interviews and observation at a diagnostic center determine the subtype, and those in the program are each assigned to a community agent who has been selected for his presumed ability to treat and control specific subtypes. Case loads of twelve to fifteen children are usually assigned to one agent.

The experimental programs are housed in nonresidential halfway houses. The buildings contain class and conference rooms, large indoor and outdoor recreational and play areas, and offices for the agents. In accordance with his appropriate subtype, an individual's use of the building depends upon the program designed for him. For example, if a child is believed to be most likely to benefit from peer interaction, he is involved in group discussions several times a week at the center. If, on the other hand, individual counseling with the child and his family is prescribed, the child might come to the center less often but the community agent might call at his home frequently. The building is open several evenings a week for counseling, instruction, dances, and parties.

About eighty children of various ages are served by one nonresidential center. Those in their early teens are expected to attend school; those who do not wish to continue their education and are beyond compulsory school age are expected to work. If poor academic performance contributed to their delinquency, attendance at small classes held at the center may be compulsory. If a child's home seems to be a directly causative factor, he may be placed in a foster or group home.

The researchers report demonstrably greater success for the community-based program than for the controls (Warren, 1969; Palmer, 1971). After fifteen months in the community only 28 percent of the experimental group had failed on parole as contrasted to 52 percent of the controls who had been at the state training school.[6] After two years in the community, 38 percent of the experimentals and 61 percent of the controls had been returned to institutions. Improved success for girls was particularly noticeable, only 13 percent of the experimentals failing in contrast to 57 percent of the controls; for boys there was a 30 percent failure rate for the community programs and 51 percent for the training schools.

In terms of subtypes of delinquents, eight out of the nine categories responded more favorably to the community program. Only the cultural identifier group did better following incarceration. Warren (1969) has argued that such information would be lost if only the total experimental and control groups were compared. Experimental

---

6. It should be noted that the fifteen-month period for the experimental group began as soon as they left the diagnostic center; whereas for controls it did not begin until they had been released from the training school to which they had been assigned from the reception center.

cases who were well matched with their workers on a priori grounds had a parole failure rate of 23 percent after fifteen months, while another group of experimental cases who were not well matched had a failure rate of 49 percent; after twenty-four months, the differences were 34 and 57 percent, respectively (Palmer, 1973). Warren has suggested that treatment should be conceptualized as a product of at least four major, coexisting interactions—interaction between types of program, type of client, type of worker, and type of treatment environment.

Although methodologically the most sophisticated series of studies on treatment programs that has been produced thus far, it has been noted that there was at least one difference between experimentals and controls with respect to parole suspensions, i.e., temporary rather than permanent revocations of parole usually resulting in a short period of detention (Empey, 1967). The experimental group had an average of 2.6 suspensions per child, while the control group had an average of only 1.4 suspensions. Moreover, 61 percent of all experimental group suspensions were the direct result of arrest action taken by experimental staff as contrasted to only 25 percent of the suspensions for the control group. Although the reason for suspension among the experimental group was frequently the commission of a minor offense, such as placement failure, poor home or school adjustment, truancy, or runaway, it is possible that some agents used suspension on occasions, which, strictly speaking, may have warranted revocation of parole.

The Behavior-Modification Approach

Within the past decade there has been a rapid growth in the experimental study and application of behavior-modification techniques derived from principles of learning theory, especially operant conditioning theory (Skinner, 1956). These techniques, particularly the concept of the token economy (Ayllon & Azrin, 1969), create the potential for significant change in the area of corrections. A major characteristic of behavior-modification programs is their emphasis upon overt behaviors and the systematic manipulation of the environment to change these behaviors. Because of this emphasis on observable behavior, behavior-modification objectives, unlike treatment orientations that focus on such goals as "good mental health," are readily measurable. Thus, a central advantage is that questions about the effectiveness of the approach and its influence on a correctional institution can be answered by empirical study rather than by speculation unsupported by data (Schwitzgebel, 1971).

General guidelines for developing programs for the youthful offender (Saunders & Reppucci, 1972) emphasize six basic principles: (1) *behavior is learned* and, consequently, can be changed; (2) there are three methods of reinforcement that can be used to change behavior: *reward* desirable behavior and, thereby, increase that behavior, *ignore* or *punish* undesirable behavior and thereby decrease it (of the three methods, reward tends to be the most effective and long lasting); (3) the reinforcement contingencies (rules) should be *clearly defined*; (4) reinforcement must be administered *consistently*, (5) *immediately*, and (6) for *specific* behaviors. (For more detailed reviews of this field, see Chapter 20 of this book, and Bandura, 1969.) A few applications of this approach in juvenile correctional institutions will be described.

CASE II Project and the Kennedy Youth Center

The CASE (Contingencies Applicable to Special Education) II project was a well-financed, one-year, demonstration program conducted at the National Training School for Boys (NTS) in Washington, D.C., a modification of a less-structured, CASE I project at the same facility. The forty-one participating juvenile offenders ranged in age from 14 to 18 years and all were school failures. The main objective was the positive expansion of the academic and social repertoires of the boys through the use of operantly formulated contingency systems and the design of a special environment. This special environment was physically located in a completely converted dormitory building on the grounds of NTS and incorporated a set of specified academic content performances with a schedule of reinforcement programs for individual success. An incentive plan or token economy was established in which the boys were rewarded with points for academic competence that could be traded for money and the things money can buy. For example, a boy could use points to pay for snacks, office study space, telephone calls, magazines, and articles from a mail-order catalogue. Conversely, if a boy did not successfully complete his educational tasks, he was known as a "relief" student and would lose his private room and have his meals served on a metal tray after the others had eaten.

The results of this study indicated that there was an average increase of two grade levels as measured by scores on the Stanford Achievement Test for thirty-two boys who had both pre- and posttesting and who had participated in the program for at least ninety days. Moreover, twenty-four students who had I.Q. testing upon entry into the program demonstrated a mean increase of 12.5 points after ten months in the program. Although these results are impressive to a degree, it should be noted that the boys were rewarded by a "generous points payoff" in proportion to their scores when they were administered the examinations for the second time, i.e., had they been motivated to perform at their optimum level during the first testing, the differences between the pre- and posttesting might have been much less.

Recidivism data were also collected. The results indicated that during the first year the CASE students had a recidivism rate two-thirds less than a similar normative group processed by NTS. By the end of the third year there were no differences in recidivism between CASE boys and the control group. The authors concluded, "The CASE program evidently delayed the delinquent's return to incarceration, but his behavior would require additional maintenance in the real world for the CASE experience to remain effective after the first year in preventing recidivism" (Cohen & Filipczak, 1971:134). These results indicate the importance of long-term follow-up in determining success or failure of treatment programs, rather than the usual six months to a year.

An outgrowth of the CASE project was the program begun in January, 1969, at the Robert F. Kennedy Youth Center (KYC) in Morgantown, West Virginia, an institution constructed by the U.S. Bureau of Prisons to replace the National Training School in Washington, D.C. The physical plant was designed to support the planned treatment program. Staff members were carefully selected and no inmates were transferred from other institutions, thus avoiding the danger of transplanting an established staff or inmate subculture.

A classification system was initiated at KYC using a behavior typology developed by Quay and his colleagues (e.g., Peterson et al., 1959; Quay, 1964a, 1964b). It divides boys into four main behavioral categories or BC-types: BC-1, inadequate-immature; BC-2, neurotic-conflicted; BC-3, psychopathic-aggressive; BC-4, socialized or subcultural delinquent; plus some residual cases in an untitled BC-5. Each individual is classified from a checklist of behavior problems completed by a correction officer who observes the subject's interaction in the institution, from a self-report questionnaire filled out by the subject himself, and from a life history checklist completed by the caseworker using available records. Thus, information is utilized that accounts for the subject's present behavior, his own view of himself, and his past history. Difficult to categorize youth are seen by psychiatrists or psychologists for the purpose of rating on the BC dimensions and placing them in the various groups. Reclassification is permitted where there is evidence that a misclassification has occurred. Once classified, the student is assigned to various parts of a program, which are based on operant conditioning principles of behavior modification.

The basic treatment program is centered in the cottage living unit, which is designed to handle up to fifty-five students and is staffed by individuals whose interests and abilities are believed to be best suited to the particular BC-type assigned to that cottage. In each cottage there is an interdisciplinary treatment team, the cottage committee, which consists of the cottage supervisor (a caseworker), the student's counselor (a correctional officer/counselor), and a member of the teaching staff. This committee has the responsibility for developing and implementing appropriate treatment strategies relevant to the particular needs of the student. Since the program at KYC consists primarily of academic and vocational training during the day and an evening cottage program, the main task of the cottage committee is to involve the student meaningfully in these areas. The cottage committee supervisor coordinates the work of the other committee members, gives overall direction to the activities of the treatment team, and serves as liaison with the rest of the institution.

The institution operates on a token economy by which students are rewarded for appropriate behavior. The students earn points for good behavior, and the points have a monetary value that can be used for purchase of various goods and services. Points are earned by a regular paycheck system and by a bonus system in which immediate rewards can be given youths for certain positive kinds of behavior. Points earned are nontransferable from student to student. Each student has two accounts, a savings and a spending account.

All programs are integrated into the token economy that, instead of being rigidly applied to all boys for the same general behavior, is flexibly applied to each boy according to his treatment program. For example, one student may be rewarded mainly in terms of how he conforms to institutional rules and regulations while another may be evaluated primarily on the basis of progress toward obtaining a high-school degree or on his behavior in cottage group sessions. Thus, staff are able to direct the reinforcement contingencies of the token economy system toward what appears to be a particular treatment and training need of a boy and to shift focus as circumstances warrant.

The original treatment and research design had to be made much less rigorous than planned because, after the program was initiated, the federal judiciary decided to stop sending to the center violators of the Dyer Act, which makes crossing state borders in a stolen vehicle a federal offense. Since this category accounted for a majority of the inmate population, the per capita cost rose dramatically. Therefore, the age limits were expanded to admit boys up to the age of 23 years, and when the institution still was underused, two cottages were set aside to deal with youthful female offenders. These changes caused problems for research as the diagnostic system, programs, and staff were designed and validated on male offenders between the ages of 14 and 18 years.

The Connecticut School for Boys Project

The 120-year-old Connecticut School for Boys (CSB) in Meriden was the only training school for boys in the state in June, 1970, when we became involved with changing it from a custody-oriented institution to a rehabilitation-oriented one. The full-time staff consisted of approximately 190 to 200 employees, and CSB had a resident population of between 170 and 200 12- to 16-year-old adjudicated delinquents. Since the 1930s, CSB had been organized on a cottage system, there being one maximum- and seven minimum-security cottages. Each cottage housed about 25 boys and had a distinctive character of its own, reflecting the outlook and behavior of the cottage staff. The main life of the institution went on within these cottages, and the bulk of the employees were "cottage parents." In addition to the cottages, there were a large, unaccredited school, an administration building, a complex of staff housing, a large swimming pool, a small infirmary, and a "treatment unit" of individual cells that was used exclusively for disciplinary purposes.

As with the Minnesota Training School project, the impetus for changing CSB was a much publicized crisis involving a shooting incident by one of the residents and subsequent allegations of brutality by various staff factions. Shortly thereafter, Dr. Dean accepted the superintendency under the condition that a team of consultants from the Yale Psycho-Educational Clinic, under the direction of Professor Reppucci, be actively involved and supported. At the time, staff morale was extremely low. Resident programs other than disciplinary actions for "bad behavior" were nonexistent, the runaway rate was over 365 per year, incidents of brutality were commonplace, cooperation between the professional and line staff was nonexistent, state police were regularly on duty there, and a staff "goon squad" patrolled the grounds to protect the employees. The goal of the intervention obviously had to be massive change aimed at developing a positive social climate or subculture for both staff and residents in which a rehabilitation program could be implemented and successful.

Six general principles for changing an established institution guided the endeavor: (1) a guiding idea or philosophy, which is understandable to, and provides hope for, all members of the institution, must be developed in conjunction with those members; (2) an organizational structure, which will encourage consistency, communication, and cooperation between various staff members and between staff and residents is a necessity; (3) decision-making must involve all levels of staff in a meaningful fashion; (4) employees must be utilized in whatever manner plays to their strengths and fills program needs, regardless of paper qualifications or job specifications; (5) active community involvement, i.e., an external orientation, is a necessity not a luxury, if there is to be any likelihood of long-term behavior change once a resident returns to his home community; (6) a reasonable time perspective, which takes accurate account of both manpower and financial resources, must be adopted regardless of external pressures. (See Reppucci, 1973, for a more complete discussion of these principles.)

The first three months of Dean's superintendency were used as an assessment period in spite of the external pressure for rapid change. The task was to become acquainted with the culture of the setting in a manner that would lead to a clear understanding of the conflicts, personalities, organizational structure, formal and informal power bases, and operative policies and procedures, so that a comprehensive change plan could be formulated. Moreover, this port of entry period was of extreme importance in that acceptance by the majority of the line staff was crucial for the future success of any plan. As a result of a series of group meetings with a majority of the employees, there was agreement on the need for a program that would (1) *improve communication* among various staff and between staff and boys; (2) *increase consistency* in regard to treatment of the boys, and (3) *provide hope*—hope that there was something positive to work toward in the future.

The rehabilitation program that was developed in conjunction with the staff and boys required a structural reorganization to bring staff members closer together and the development of a motivational system to stress the positive rather than the negative. The locus of control for the new program is the cottage, each of which houses twenty to twenty-five boys assigned on a random basis. The academic classroom was moved to the cottage so that the school program would be more fully integrated into the total treatment program. Responsibility for the operation of the rehabilitation program resides with a cottage counseling committee composed of all staff regularly working with the boys in that cottage, including cottage parents, teachers, clinical and recreational staff, aftercare workers, members of the consultant team, and any other relevant persons. This committee meets at least once a week to air problems and discuss general program policy, individualized treatment programs for residents, and cottage operation. Decisions in these areas are reached through a majority vote of the committee members present, except the consultants are not voting members. Each cottage has a coordinator to oversee daily operations and a chairman of the counseling committee to conduct the meetings. These individuals are selected on the basis of ability, not job titles, e.g., in some cottages both of these positions are filled by line staff, whereas in others a cottage parent is the coordinator and a social worker, the chairman.

Residents are encouraged to participate in planning their own programs with the counseling committee and to use the committee as a sounding board for complaints and suggestions. In addition, two boys from each cottage are elected by their peers as voting members of their respective committees whenever any general program issues arise. The same two boys from each cottage also meet weekly with the superintendent so that the boys can bring their complaints and suggestions to him directly.

The 24-hour per day rehabilitation program is based on social-learning principles, specifically on a token economy employing points as tender for the purchase of all goods and privileges available to boys at CSB.[7] The principle of positive reinforcement is stressed. Treatment, particularly as reflected in reinforcement contingencies, is increasingly individualized as boys progress through three levels of achievement.

The first level of achievement is campus-based, excluding any activities in the outside community, and emphasizes cottage living skills. Boys receive "work points" for performing cottage maintenance chores and "conduct points" for acceptable social behavior. The cumulative number of earned points set as the criterion for movement from Level I to Level II is relatively small; it usually takes a boy about six weeks to earn them.

The second level is a transition from living at CSB to successful functioning in the community. Toward this end, residents in Level II are allowed certain weekends at home, which they must earn. School-related activities, both academic and vocational, and specific behavioral problems for each resident are emphasized. Boys continue performing cottage maintenance functions, but for verbal reward only. "Work points" are awarded for acceptable performance in school and trade areas, while the field of relevant social behaviors for "conduct points" is expanded to include those believed to be related to a boy's delinquency. Assuming the greater importance of these behaviors, the cumulative point criterion for advancement is higher than it had been in Level I. Violations of cottage rules in both Level I and Level II result in either a twenty-minute "time out" from positive reinforcement, an increase in a boy's cumulative point criterion for admission to the next level, and/or a brief stay in the treatment unit.

The third level, in most cases, is a period of living in the community on a prere-

---

7. In developing the token economy, the number of points earned for behaviors performed and the number of points necessary for the purchase of rewards were determined by ratings obtained from both residents and staff.

lease basis. Involvement of school systems, employers, and families is actively sought and an intensive effort is made to extend the most relevant contingencies for behavior change to the boy's home life, using parents, teachers, and relevant others as agents. Serious community violations in Level III are an indication that individual goals set in Level II or III were not sufficient to change the delinquent behaviors, and readmission to Level II or III is considered. For residents in all levels, parents are encouraged to visit.

A change strategy was adapted calling for staff training and organization of two "experimental" cottages first, with the others opened successively at about half-year intervals. This strategy, although dictated to a large degree by limited personnel resources, had the advantage of allowing the empirical measurement of social-climate change and program effectiveness with appropriate control groups, i.e., those cottages that were operating with an equivalent juvenile population in the same institution but not on the social-learning rehabilitation system.

Prior to the opening of the fourth cottage, it was apparent that the first three cottages, although functioning with the same guidelines, had each developed very separate identities and in many instances separate rules. A number of problems resulted, e.g., one cottage decided to alter its rules regarding home visits for the Thanksgiving holiday and allowed its Level I boys to go home while the other two cottages did not. The boys in the two cottages who were not allowed to go home gave the staff a great deal of grief, arguing that the boys in the third cottage had gone.

In order to cope with the need for consistency across cottages, as well as within a cottage, a four-page constitution was written that spelled out the general purposes of CSB, principles of operation, general structure of the rehabilitation system, the rights and obligations of staff and residents, and procedures for amending the constitution by a democratic voting process. A staff senate, composed of coordinators, counseling team chairmen, and consultants, was established to develop proposals for CSB. Any policy that staff or boys think is important enough to be followed by all cottages is formulated by the staff senate and brought to a secret ballot vote in all of the cottage committees. These proposals become general policies if accepted by two-thirds of the voting staff. The right of review is left to the superintendent but unless he vetoes an approved proposal, it becomes the law of the school and he is bound by it also. To date, there has been no proposal vetoed.

What has changed? Gross changes have included: (1) a decrease in the number of cottages to six, each with a population of between 20 and 25 boys; (2) a decrease in the total number of staff to about 165; (3) a reduction of incidents of brutality to the point of virtual nonexistence; (4) the closing of the maximum-security cottage; (5) the elimination of the staff "goon squad" and the state-police patrol; (6) the reduction of amounts of time spent in the "treatment unit" to three days or less except in the most extreme cases (in the past an average stay was ten days); and (7) the development of a cottage-based school. More specific changes have included the following: for the staff in the first two social-learning cottages, absenteeism based on the number of sick days in 1971 was 4.75; for staff in the cottages not on the social-learning system, absenteeism was 11.97. There were no significant differences between these same staff members' absenteeism in either 1969 or 1970. In conjunction with this, it should be noted that employees in the social-learning cottages have frequently worked overtime without pay, and a few employees have had either upgrading or other than regular annual salary increases (a number of individuals earned upgrading but a budget freeze in all state agencies in the early 1970s prevented this). Moreover, various questionnaire measures of job satisfaction administered in 1971 and late 1972 indicate extremely high morale. Finally, a modified version of the Moos Social Climate Scale for correctional institutions (Moos, 1968) was administered to the staff of the two social-learning cottages in January, 1971, just after the program began, and again eight months later before the staff of the third cottage had been announced. This scale is intended as a measure of the psychological environment or social climate of an institution and consists of eight subscales—spontaneity, affiliation, order, insight, variety, clarity, autonomy, and responsibility—and an overall value factor which may be interpreted as a general liking variable (Wilkinson & Reppucci, 1973). There were no differences between the measures taken in January and August, which mitigates the possibility of a "halo effect." However, in August the social climates of the social-learning cottages as compared to those of cottages not on the system were significantly higher on the variables of spontaneity, affiliation, clarity, autonomy, responsibility, and the overall liking factor.

Data available on the residents at this time are equally impressive. There was a significant decrease in runaways by the boys in the social-learning cottages. During the first eight months of 1971 there were 296 runaways from CSB. Sixteen percent of these were from the two social-learning cottages, but these cottages contained 33 percent of the resident population. Perhaps more revealing is the following incident that occurred in March, 1972. A boy on runaway status returned to CSB with a gun and forced the men in charge of the disciplinary treatment unit to let all of the boys out. Of the ten boys in the unit at the time, six were from social-learning cottages and four from other cottages. Three of the four boys from the non-social-learning cottages chose to run while only one of the six boys from the social-learning cottages did.

The Social Climate Scale was administered to all residents at CSB in February, 1972. When residents' responses in the two original social-learning cottages were compared to those of residents in the two remaining non-social-learning cottages, there were statistically significant differences on the variables of spontaneity, insight, clarity, autonomy, and the overall value factor (Wilkinson & Reppucci, 1973). When these results are viewed in conjunction with those of staff, the conclusion that success in changing the culture of an existing institution has been achieved seems hard to deny. Clinical observation supports this view. Preliminary analyses of available data indicate reduction in recidivism also.

In conclusion, it should be noted that in the early months of 1973, CSB was physically combined with the Long Lane School for Delinquent Girls in Middletown, Connecticut, with Dr. Dean serving as superintendent of the coeducational facility. The social-learning system has remained intact during this transition and the girls' cottages have converted to it. The governing constitution has proved flexible enough to incorporate necessary modifications and increased emphasis has been placed on community involvement and alternative placement. Perhaps the best indication of the success is that in 1973 the combined institution had in residence no more than 150 boys and girls at any given time, a total that is less than the average number housed in either CSB or Long Lane in 1970.

CONCLUSIONS

The rate of failure from our fixed institutions for young and old offenders has remained more constant through the years than any other index upon which we rely—cost of living, Dow Jones, or the annual precipitation of rain. An average of the recidivism rates reported by the most reliable researchers runs consistently in a range from one-half to two-thirds. No other facility created by our society for dealing with any other area of social pathology which showed such a consistently high rate of failure could so long endure (Keller & Alper, 1970:xi).

Such a statement emphasizes the desperate need for change in our correctional institutions. Models for change in this century have been based mainly on equating humanitarianism with rehabilitation, unfortunately failing to recognize that the humane care of offenders is not necessarily the same thing as changing their behavior. Yet, even if these two goals, humane care and rehabilitation, were combined, as they have been in a few isolated instances, we are unlikely to make major changes in our institutions until we recognize that the key problem is lack of knowledge and of comprehensive correctional theory upon which to base treatment models. Until this conceptual deficiency is overcome, more personnel, smaller case loads, higher salaries and better training can never solve the problem regardless of what the *Standards* implies. As Empey states:

> Until improvements are made in the theories which underlie treatment, changes in correctional structures, by themselves, will be unlikely to produce dramatic reductions in delinquency and criminality. Instead, we will have more refined failure! (Empey, 1967:6)

The concept of "refined failure" is not an acceptable goal to most of us. Yet the criminal justice system continues to act in a fashion that can only result in exactly this. The most extensively planned and well-financed project in the entire field of youth correction is the Kennedy Youth Center, but as we have seen, the lack of coordination and cooperation between courts and corrections—both parts of the larger criminal justice system—apparently increases the likelihood of refined failure there. This example illustrates the fact that changes in one of the major parts of the correctional process— police, courts, penal institutions—have organizational consequences at other points. These correctional units have seldom been considered on any comprehensive basis as constituting a single system. Such an overview is imperative, however, since independent decision-making in any of these units has effects for the other units of which the decision-makers are frequently unaware.

In regard to youth institutions as separate units, little attention is given to the differences in the process of change and innovation at newly created settings as compared to established facilities. Although it is generally acknowledged that these differences exist, this knowledge seems to be forgotten or considered irrelevant when treatment techniques or other innovations are introduced. For example, the introduction of a comprehensive behavioral system at the Kennedy Youth Center was a very different affair from the introduction of a similar system at the Connecticut School for Boys. At KYC there were no existing inmate or staff cultures that had to be altered as there were at CSB. That such an issue was not only recognized at CSB, but also that an attempt was made to deal with it, is by far the exception rather than the rule. What needs recognition is that a general theory of change is necessary even when dealing with a single institution and that the problems may be different when the object of change is an established institution rather than the creating of a new setting.

Another salient feature regarding institutional change is the fact that most attempts at such change are a reaction to crisis rather than positive, planned action. Seldom is an adequate time perspective adopted and in most cases these attempts fail even though piecemeal innovations (e.g., some psychotherapy or recreational features) are made. As Sarason (1971) has pointed out, "the more things change, the more they stay the same." Perhaps the most poignant example of this phenomenon is to be found in Burton Blatt's book, *Exodus from Pandemonium* (1970). This contains two speeches given before the Massachusetts legislature, each pleading for change in our institutions for deviants, and each specifying the same evils. The irony is that the first speech was given by Dorothea Dix in 1866 and the second by Blatt in 1966. The problems were still the same although 100 years had elapsed between the time of Dix's speech and that of Blatt.

On a less lofty level than general theories of innovation and change, it should be noted that there is a move toward an increase in community involvement. This is evident not only from the increasing numbers of halfway houses and group homes, but also from the increased emphasis given to community involvement by the correctional institutions themselves. It is becoming more and more difficult to maintain the "internally focused hypothesis," i.e., that offenders will be reformed and changed within the walls of the correctional facility, and this change will carry over to the outside upon their release. That this focus still prevails in most institutions can hardly be argued, but it is equally true that lip service is now being given by top administrators and planners, and some action is being taken with regard to the dual purpose of reformation and reintegration. One need only look to the quotation at the beginning of this section for evidence that internally oriented correctional facilities have failed, or to more empirical evidence, e.g., the CASE II project (Cohen & Filipczak, 1971), that even carefully planned and well-financed rehabilitation programs, which do not take into account the communities into which the offender is returning, will fail in the long run.

The approach presently being taken in Massachusetts may set the pace for the largest upheaval in juvenile youth institutions since they were first established in the 1800s, i.e., their *dismantlement*. If this should turn out to be the case, it is fitting that Massachusetts—the state which opened both the first boys' and girls' training schools in this country—should become the first state to close these schools. In order to care for the state's youthful offenders, alternatives to incarceration, such as halfway houses, residential youth centers, group homes, and foster placements, are being established at a rapid rate. This may well be the most rational approach to our large training schools; however, it is hard to imagine that this move will fully solve the problems of delinquency, recidivism, or rehabilitation. It, like most changes in correctional programs, seems without adequate theoretical definitions of the causes of delinquency or the development of logical strategies to deal with them, but it may be the preferred route to follow given the long history of failure by juvenile correctional facilities.

REFERENCES

Amos, W. F., and R. L. Manella.
    1965   Readings in the Administration of Institutions for Delinquent Youth. Springfield, Ill.: Thomas.

Ayllon, T., and N. H. Azrin.
    1969   The Token Economy: A Motivational System for Therapy and Rehabilitation. New York: Appleton-Century-Crofts.

Bakal, Y.
    1973   Closing Correctional Institutions. Lexington, Mass.: D. C. Heath.

Bandura, A.
    1969   Principles of Behavior Modification. New York: Holt, Rinehart & Winston.

Blatt, B.
    1970   Exodus from Pandemonium. Boston: Allyn & Bacon.

Center for Studies of Crime and Delinquency.
    n.d.   Community Based Correctional Programs: Models and Practices. Public
            Health Service Publication No. 2130. Washington, D.C.: U.S. Government
            Printing Office.

Cohen, H. L., and J. Filipczak.
    1971   A New Learning Environment. San Francisco: Jossey-Bass.

Cortes, J., and F. Gatti.
    1972   Delinquency and Crime: A Biopsychosocial Approach. New York: Seminar
            Press.

Empey, L.
    1967   Alternatives to Incarceration. Washington, D.C.: U.S. Government Printing
            Office.

Empey, L., and M. Erickson.
    1972   The Provo Experiment. Lexington, Mass.: D. C. Heath.

Empey, L., and J. Rabow.
    1961   "The Provo experiment in delinquency rehabilitation." American Sociolog-
            ical Review 26(October):679–695.

Gibbons, D.
    1968   Delinquent Behavior. Englewood Cliffs, N.J.: Prentice-Hall.

Glasser, W.
    1965   Reality Therapy. New York: Harper & Row.

Goldenberg, I. I.
    1971   Build Me a Mountain: Youth, Poverty and the Creation of a New Setting.
            Cambridge: M.I.T. Press.

Keller, O., and B. Alper.
    1970   Halfway Houses: Community-Centered Correction and Treatment. Lexing-
            ton, Mass.: D. C. Heath.

McCorkle, L., A. Elias, and F. Bixby.
    1958   The Highfields Story: A Unique Experiment in the Treatment of Juvenile
            Delinquency. New York: Henry Holt.

Mennel, R. M.
    1973   Thorns and Thistles: Juvenile Delinquents in the United States, 1825–1940.
            Hanover, N.H.: University Press of New England.

Moos, R.
    1968   "The assessment of the social climates of correctional institutions." Journal
            of Research in Crime and Delinquency 5(July):174–188.

Palmer, T.
    1971   "California's community treatment program for delinquent adolescents."
            Journal of Research in Crime and Delinquency 8(January):74–92.
    1973   "Matching worker and client in corrections." Social Work 18(March):95–
            103.

Peterson, H., H. Quay, and G. Cameron.
    1959   "Personality and background factors in juvenile delinquency as inferred
            from questionnaire responses." Journal of Consulting Psychology 23(Octo-
            ber):395–399.

Pierce, B.
  1869   A Half Century with Juvenile Delinquents. New York: D. Appleton.

Pilnick, S., R. Allen, and N. Clapp.
  1967   Collegefields: From Delinquency to Freedom. Report to the Juvenile Delinquency and Youth Development Office. Newark, N.J.: Newark State College.

Pilnick, S., A. Elias, and N. Clapp.
  1966   "The Essexfield concept: a new approach to the social treatment of juvenile delinquents." Journal of Applied Behavioral Science 2(January–March): 109–124.

President's Commission on Law Enforcement and Administration of Justice.
  1967   Task Force Report: Corrections. Washington, D.C.: U.S. Government Printing Office.

Quay, H.
  1964a   "Personality dimensions in delinquent males as inferred from factor analysis of behavior ratings." Journal of Research in Crime and Delinquency 1(January):33–37.
  1964b   "Dimensions of personality in delinquent boys as inferred from the factor analysis of case history data." Child Development 35(June):479–484.

Reeves, M.
  1929   Training Schools for Delinquent Girls. New York: Russell Sage Foundation.

Reppucci, N. D.
  1973   "The social psychology of institutional change: general principles for intervention." American Journal of Community Psychology 1(October–December):330–341.

Robinson, L.
  1923   Penology in the United States. Philadelphia: John C. Winston.

Sarason, S. B.
  1971   The Culture of the School and the Problem of Change. Boston: Allyn & Bacon.
  1974   The Psychological Sense of Community: Prospects for a Community Psychology. San Francisco: Jossey-Bass.

Saunders, J. T., and N. D. Reppucci.
  1972   "Reward and punishment: guidelines for effective application in correctional programs for youthful offenders." Crime and Delinquency 18(July):284–290.

Schwitzgebel, R. K.
  1971   Development and Legal Regulations of Coercive Behavior Modification Techniques with Offenders. Center for Studies of Crime and Delinquency. Public Service Publication No. 2067. Washington, D.C.: U.S. Government Printing Office.

Skinner, B. F.
  1956   Science and Human Behavior. New York: Macmillan.

Special Committee on Correctional Standards.
  1967   "Correctional standards." Pp. 205–212 in President's Commission on Law Enforcement and Administration of Justice, Task Force Report: Corrections. Washington, D.C.: U.S. Government Printing Office.

Stephenson, R., and F. Scarpitti.
  1967   The Rehabilitation of Delinquent Boys. A Final Report Submitted to the
          Ford Foundation. New Brunswick, N.J.: Rutgers, the State University.
  1969   "Essexfields: a nonresidential experiment in group-centered rehabilitation
          of delinquents." American Journal of Corrections 31(January–February):
          12–18.
Street, D., R. Vinter, and C. Perrow.
  1966   Organization for Treatment: A Comparative Study of Institutions for De-
          linquents. New York: Free Press.
Sutherland, E., and D. R. Cressey.
  1970   Criminology. Eighth Edition. Philadelphia: Lippincott.
Teeters, N., and J. Reinemann.
  1950   The Challenge of Delinquency. Englewood Cliffs, N.J.: Prentice-Hall.
U.S. Bureau of Prisons.
  1970   Differential Treatment . . . A Way to Begin. Washington, D.C.: U.S. Depart-
          ment of Justice.
Vorrath, H.
  n.d.   Positive Peer Culture: Content, Structure and Process. Report from Minne-
          sota State Training School for Boys.
Warren, M.
  1969   "The case for differential treatment of delinquents." Annals of the American
          Academy of Political and Social Science 381(January):47–59.
Weeks, H.
  1958   Youthful Offenders at Highfields. Ann Arbor: University of Michigan Press.
Wilkinson, L., and N. D. Reppucci.
  1973   "Perceptions of social climate among participants in token economy and
          non-token economy cottages in a juvenile correctional institution." American
          Journal of Community Psychology 1(January–March):36–43.

CHAPTER **24**

Community-Based Correctional Services

H. G. Moeller

East Carolina University

Shortly after World War II, a few correctional systems in the United States began, for the first time, to concern themselves with institutional prerelease programs. These were designed to better prepare the offender for his return to community life. They were inspired largely by the experience of many correctional workers who had recently passed through separation centers during the demobilization of the armed forces. It was recognized that, although institutions had long maintained orientation programs that were intended to prepare the newly admitted inmate for life in the institution, no similar programs had been created to facilitate the transition from institutional life to the free society.

The institutional prerelease programs were varied in character. For the most part, inmates were admitted to them during the ninety-day period immediately prior to release. In many instances, separate housing units were provided in which offenders enjoyed somewhat greater privileges than those afforded by the regular program of the institution. An important feature of most of the new programs was the involvement of a broad spectrum of representatives of the community, who functioned as resources in attempting to interpret to the offender the problems that might confront him upon release. Parole officers, law-enforcement personnel, representatives of business and industry, professional workers from human-services agencies, members of Alcoholics Anonymous, other service groups, and many concerned citizens were enlisted in the effort. Regular meetings were held with prerelease groups and various techniques were employed in the effort to assist the inmate in facing the realities of the life to which he would return in the community.

Although there were few efforts to evaluate the effectiveness of the newly organized prerelease programs, it was evident that there were some tangible benefits. Not the least of the advantages arose from the fact that many citizens were, for the first time, made aware of some of the fundamental problems of the correctional system. There were benefits for the inmate participants as well. These accrued from the recognition that members of the "free world" had not totally rejected them but were, indeed, concerned, interested, and supportive.

It was also clear to those who were involved in the planning and management of the programs that the activities, however well designed, had their limitations. The programs tended largely to be academic and didactic in character, and for obvious reasons could not deal effectively with the constellations of problems that the individual would face after release. Nor could the programs deal effectively with the unrealistic expectations that many offenders had for their reception in the community. Consequently, there was an artificiality about the programs—a kind of play-acting that provided a poor substitute for the problem-solving which would become an essential part of the offender's reentry and reintegration into the community.

By the late 1950s, it was increasingly apparent that there was a need to move the process of prerelease preparation into the community. But there were resistances to the idea. Earlier in the history of American corrections, there had been some effort under private auspices to establish halfway houses for offenders. As early as 1896, the Volunteers of America established Hope Hall, a residence in New York for men released from Sing Sing Prison in New York (National Institute of Mental Health, 1971). Other groups in other communities established similar shelters, primarily for homeless, male ex-offenders. In the late 1950s, there were at least three such centers that were well known: Dismas House in St. Louis, Missouri, directed by Father Dismas Clark; Crenshaw House in Los Angeles, sponsored by the Society of Friends; and St. Leonard's House in Chicago, Illinois, which was supported largely by the Episcopalian Church.

Public agencies, by and large, had avoided involvement in such programs. They lacked statutory authority to proceed; there were questions whether the responsibility for their management should properly be assigned to probation or parole agencies, or to state agencies responsible for the management of correctional institutions; and there were concerns about the availability of competent professional personnel to operate units in the community. Beyond these concerns, there were serious apprehensions about the consequences of housing groups of ex-offenders in the community. Traditionally, paroling authorities had insisted that individuals under supervision not associate with other ex-offenders. Indeed, this was a condition of parole that was imposed upon persons under supervision in nearly all jurisdictions.

In 1961, the U.S. Bureau of Prisons was asked by the new national administration to outline its priorities for new programs—especially for youthful offenders. Three high-priority proposals moved to head the list. It was recommended that Congress be requested to fund demonstration projects to:

1. evaluate the effectiveness of the use of correctional officers as individual and group counselors in a youth institution;
2. assess new methods of motivating youthful offenders toward participation in institutional educational programs; and
3. evaluate the effectiveness of professionally staffed prerelease guidance centers for juveniles and youth in three major metropolitan centers.

The proposals were adopted by Attorney General Robert F. Kennedy, who personally testified in their defense before the appropriations subcommittees of the House and Senate. Funds were appropriated for the fiscal year 1962 and the programs were under way.

The decision to establish the first community-based centers for youthful offenders was influenced by several factors. Perhaps the most important was that the provisions of both the federal Juvenile Delinquency Act and the federal Youth Corrections Act provided broad authority to individualize the treatment of offenders. The statutes relating to adult offenders provided the administration much less latitude, and it was not until the enactment of the federal Offender Rehabilitation Act of 1965 that adults could be considered for transfer to community treatment centers.

The design of the prerelease guidance centers, the first three of which were located at Chicago, Los Angeles, and New York, included a number of significant considerations:

1. It was decided early that the units would be housed in property rented for the purposes, and in areas that had ready access to employment and to services supportive of employment stability.

2. The numbers of residents housed would be limited to twenty, and their stay from 90 to 120 days prior to release under supervision.

3. Residents would be carefully selected, and the group would be limited to youths who had demonstrated a need for the services to be provided.

4. The staff would be small, under professional direction, and include one member whose primary responsibility would be to develop employment, educational, and skill-training resources.

5. The program of the unit would focus upon assisting the resident in solving the day-to-day, "here and now" problems that arose in connection with his reentry into the community.

6. The resident would remain in constructive custody, and he and the staff would be accountable for his whereabouts during the period in which he remained in the community.

What the designers had in mind was a program oriented toward the community that would facilitate the offender's access to the resources and services in the community and aid the resident in his efforts to maintain himself both during and subsequent to the period of supervision.

The planners anticipated the proposals of the President's Commission on Law Enforcement and Administration of Justice. They foresaw that a 1969 ecumenical forum on the released offender, in an unpublished paper, described as:

> The development of an entirely new kind of a correctional institution located close to a population center, maintaining close relations with schools, employers, and universities, housing as few as fifty in each; serving as a center for various kinds of community programs and as a port of entry to the community for those offenders who have been exiled for a time to a penitentiary.

Probably one of the most difficult problems experienced during the early history of the prerelease guidance centers was the prevention of their becoming correctional institutions in a traditional sense. There was a tendency to rely heavily upon rules and regulations designed to control the activities of residents. These served to frustrate efforts to make the resident progressively more responsible for his own actions and behavior. There was also a strong tendency to focus attention upon the treatment needs of the offender, which had not been met in the institution from which he was transferred, rather than upon the skills that he required to cope with the problems confronting him in the community. It required sustained efforts on the part of all of those responsible for, and participating in, the program to maintain a clear sense of direction.

As experience was accumulated, it also became clear that the criteria for the selection of residents had been too narrowly drawn. After several months, these criteria were expanded to the point that the centers commenced to receive nearly all offenders who, in the opinion of the institution staffs, were in need of the services offered.

As important as the insights concerning the potentiality of the use of the centers for a broader range of residents transferred from institutions was the discovery that the centers might also provide direct services to courts. From the outset, the U.S. district courts and their probation staffs were involved both in the planning and execution of center programs. It was almost inevitable, therefore, that some judges began to consider the centers as potential resources. In growing numbers, selected residents were admitted to centers for presentence evaluation. The centers were also used, with greater frequency, for offenders committed under so-called split sentences. Under these provisions, offenders were admitted to centers for short periods of commitment, to be followed by more protracted periods of probation supervision. Admissions of the two categories of offenders mentioned were made possible by existing statutory provisions. It was not until 1965, however, that Congress enacted legislation which made the centers available to both probationers and parolees, a step that made the centers available for use at each stage in the correctional process.

Finally, the initial experience began to suggest that for an integrated system of correctional services, the centers offered unusual opportunities for the center director to obtain broad management experience of a character and quality which prepared him for promotional opportunities in management positions of greater responsibility. Similarly, the counseling staff gained significant insights that could be applied in the improvement of institutional programs. Through the interchange of personnel between the centers and the other institutional services of the system, the persistent threat of a dichotomy between institutional and community-based services was held to a minimum.

Thus, in the first five years of the program, the groundwork was established within the Bureau of Prisons for a broadly expanded system of community-based services. Shortly thereafter, the bureau organized programs of work and study release, inmate furloughs, and community treatment centers for all offenders. Concurrently, state legislatures in more than half of the states enacted laws comparable to those adopted by the Congress of the United States, and the foundations for the broad expansion of community-based correctional services were laid.

The thrust of corrections toward the community has been reinforced by the activities of many private agencies and groups. Both the Salvation Army and the Volunteers of America have committed substantial resources to the establishment of professionally staffed community treatment centers. Other citizens' groups and religious organizations have assumed responsibility for development of similar units. The International Halfway House Association, an affiliate of the American Correctional Association, has been organized to provide for the exchange of ideas on community correctional programs and methods.

COMMUNITY-BASED CORRECTIONS: A BROADER PERSPECTIVE

One may be confident that a generation or two from now, thoughtful social analysts in the United States will seize the opportunity to examine the phenomenon of change in the 1960s with insights and perspectives that are denied those who are caught up in its currents. But there is no doubt that one of the most significant benchmarks from which change in the correctional field will be measured is the work of the Joint Commission on Mental Illness and Health, which began in 1955 and concluded five years later with its recommendations:

> The objective of modern treatment of persons with major mental illness is to enable the patient to maintain himself in the community in a normal manner. To do so, it is necessary (1) to save the patient from the debilitating effects of institutionalization as much as possible; (2) if the patient requires hospitalization, to return him to the home and community life as soon as possible; and (3) thereafter to maintain him in the community as long as possible. Therefore, aftercare and rehabilitation are essential parts of all services to mental patients, and the various methods of achieving rehabilitation should be integrated in all forms of services, among them day hospitals, night hospitals, after-

care clinics, public health nursing services, foster family care, rehabilitation centers, work services, and ex-patient groups (Joint Commission on Mental Illness and Health, 1961:xvii).

Reintegration of the Offender the Focal Task

If the influence of the work in the field of mental health does not appear to be readily apparent, consider these comments of the Task Force Report on Corrections of the President's Commission on Law Enforcement and Administration of Justice nearly ten years later:

> The general underlying premise for the new directions in corrections is that crime and delinquency are symptoms of failures and disorganization of the community as well as of individual offenders. In particular these failures are seen as depriving offenders of contact with the [social] institutions that are basically responsible for assuring the development of law abiding conduct . . . (President's Commission, 1967:7).

The fact that one finds reflections of the work of the Joint Commission on Mental Illness and Health in that of the President's Commission should not be particularly surprising. In a very real sense, both the prison and the mental hospital were products of the spirit of reform and were stimulated by the period in Western history called the Enlightenment, which was "part of the great wave of social and moral reforms stimulated by the human squalor produced by the industrial revolution in the late eighteenth and nineteenth centuries" (Joint Commission on Mental Illness and Health, 1961:61).

It is not at all farfetched to believe that a survey of the literature of that period of reform and revolution would reveal that there were those who saw the creation of the new institutions, the penitentiary and the mental hospital, as a turning point in the direction of more rational approaches to the treatment of the offender and the mentally ill. But, over time, and almost imperceptibly, what had been innovations were perverted. Indeed, both became substitutes for the system of banishment that had been part of the criminal sanctions in earlier societies. Not only was the offender banished from the community, but all too frequently so were the institutions to which he was sent. It is not surprising, then, that the prison or penitentiary became increasingly insulated and isolated from the community, and that it became surrounded both by its visible walls and the invisible wall of suspicion, by which the public was kept out.

Those who designed the new systems of rejection, however, overlooked a most important fact. The new system of banishment was not, in most cases, permanent. The earlier systems of ostracism had reasonably assured that the offender would be removed from the offended society for life. The prison, however, usually returned the rejected man or woman to the society, but returned him stigmatized and labeled and strengthened in his feelings of rejection.

> By the beginning of the twentieth century, the profile of the state asylum for the incurably insane was stereotyped both professionally and socially—it was an institution where hopeless cases were put away for the good of society. . . .
>
> Mental hospital superintendents who saw patients accumulate and continue to live their lives out in locked wards, became steeped in this negative outlook. Far from feeling that they had failed in a medical and social responsibility, these first psychiatrists apparently were satisfied that they were fulfilling the mission the state assigned to them. This was to take custody of all persons committed to their institutions by the Courts and thenceforth guard the patients and the public against the latter's irrational acts, if any (Joint Commission on Mental Illness and Health, 1961:65).

It was the mounting evidence of the futility of adding to the ever-expanding capacity of warehouses of human despair that prompted the organization of the Joint Commission, which, in turn, urged a much greater investment of public funds in finding new solutions to the problems of the mentally ill. Out of this effort there have come two significant changes: first, there have been very important modifications in public attitudes and a lower level of anxiety about the potential danger of persons who suffer from mental illness; and second, there has been a greatly increased effort to treat the patient in the community.

In the United States, as correctional workers follow the path that has been marked by the efforts of those concerned with mental health and seek to find meaningful linkages to the community, they will find that other recent developments in our society can probably be exploited to great advantage. During the past several years, funds have been provided for a broad range of new programs, most of which are focused upon the needs of the socially, economically, and culturally deprived members of our society. As new and more vigorous efforts have been mounted to provide the poor and the disadvantaged with new handholds upon the opportunity structure, there has emerged a new appreciation that the task of corrections—the reintegration of the offender into the society—intersects and interfaces with that of other agencies involved in the solution of human problems.

There are, as a result, growing indications of the need for a thoroughgoing reassessment and realignment of correctional services in the United States. For more than fifty years, there have been continuing efforts to build, strengthen, and develop the three principal components of the correctional system. Probation, institutional services, and parole, typically, have grown side by side, and frequently have been actively in competition for the scarce resources of money and manpower. In some few instances, the interdependence of these services has been recognized in the creation of organizational structures for the coordination of services. But, again, as the President's Commission on Law Enforcement and Administration of Justice has emphasized, the criminal justice system in the United States is badly fragmented. The extent of the fragmentation is reflected in our inability to accumulate even the most rudimentary base-line statistical information on the work load of the correctional agencies and services of the country.

Impact of Studies by the President's Commission on Law Enforcement and Administration of Justice

The President's Commission has focused attention upon the application of systems analysis to the study of corrections within the broader framework of the administration of justice. Out of the work of the Commission came the Omnibus Crime Control and Safe Streets Act of 1968, which made funds available to states and to local governments for comprehensive law-enforcement plans. In the development of such plans, an opportunity is present to examine the kinds of correctional services needed at each important decision point in the criminal justice process. Such planning must achieve a more rational approach to the allocation of resources, both of manpower and materials, to make certain that services are integrated and that the various options, or alternatives, available to the decision-maker are appropriately used. Correctional planning encompasses every activity impinging on the offender, from his introduction into the system at arrest until his discharge from supervision. It attempts to create a coordinated system of services related to his needs during this entire time.

Those who do the planning take into account the fact that there have been many significant developments in correctional practice that have blurred the sharp lines of responsibility which have grown up in the past between probation, institutional services, and parole. These developments, in themselves, clearly suggest the possibility of a new alignment of services. The introduction of institutional work-release programs, the experimentation with community treatment centers, the emergence of community-based institutions, and the increasing use of institutional furloughs, singly and in combination, have introduced new dimensions to correctional practice, and strongly suggest a need for organizational change.

Involvement of Noncorrectional Agencies

While work in the field of mental health has provided important suggestions concerning the directions to be taken by corrections in the United States, there have been other important developments that have made the adoption of new programs more possible. Of especial importance has been the recognition by noncorrectional human-service agencies that they, too, must be concerned about the offender and his problems.

Before 1960, corrections had developed few strong aftercare services, and the offender had limited access to community resources supportive to his needs when on probation or parole. In many instances, such care was difficult to obtain because of restrictive intake policies or practices of human-service agencies, or because these agencies assigned a higher priority to helping nonoffenders. During the 1960s and 1970s many agency policies were broadened and the standards of eligibility for services were modified to expand very greatly the range of services available to the offender group. For example, the Rehabilitation Services Agency of the Department of Health, Education and Welfare has increasingly made training services available to offenders. The Manpower Administration of the Department of Labor mounted programs of occupational and vocational training for offenders who are among the hardcore unemployed, as well as employment placement assistance specially designed for the offender group. Community mental-health services also showed special interest in the organization of programs supporting the needs of persons under probation and parole supervision.

The availability of new public services to the offender, of which those cited represent only a few, has been matched by other developments in the private sector of the economy. Work opportunities for the probationer and the parolee in private industry are increasingly available. The National Association of Manufacturers publicized the importance of work-release programs. Industry has cooperated with correctional authorities in introducing into institutions training programs specifically designed to provide the offender with skills scarce in the labor market. An ever-widening range of training opportunities in the community are being opened to offenders.

Community-Based Programs

These developments, very hastily sketched, provide the background within which community-based correctional services are being developed. The introduction of the community treatment center, or halfway house, as a government correctional facility, dates only from 1961, and the possible uses of such centers have still not been fully explored. The conceptual framework for the centers was clearly expressed by the Task Force Report on Corrections:

> The task of corrections therefore includes building or rebuilding solid ties between the offender and the community, integrating or reintegrating the offender into community

life—restoring family ties, obtaining employment and education, securing in the larger sense a place for the offender in the routine functioning of society. This requires not only efforts toward changing the individual offender, which has been the almost exclusive focus of rehabilitation, but also the mobilization and change of the community and its institutions (President's Commission, 1967:7).

If the offender can be positively motivated to learn new skills and to develop new and positive social relationships, the task that remains is to provide a linkage with a noncriminal environment. This is a task that he usually cannot handle by himself. The new assignment for corrections is to open doors to services that, in the past, have been denied to offenders or that they may not have known about. Such an undertaking is more than the creation of formal working relationships between the correctional service and business, industry, organized labor, civic groups, churches, schools, and other community agencies. It requires the correctional service to develop the knowledge and skill to assist the offender in using an array of services to gain the continuing support he needs to maintain himself in the society. In other words, many offenders need help, which they have previously lacked or have been denied, in finding access to the opportunity structure.

A major function of the community center, as now designed, is to provide a residential setting to which offenders may be referred after release from the correctional institution. The center mediates those services needed by the offender restored to society. The resident of such a center also receives from the staff day-to-day assistance in facing the crises arising during his effort to make adjustments to his job, his responsibilities to his family, and his duties as a citizen. The main thrust of the center must be outward. It is not a sanctuary providing the isolation from the community of the traditional institution. Rather, it provides planned access to situations in which the resident can test his skills and measure his expectations against reality.

CENTER PROGRAM DESIGN

Operation

The operation of a typical community treatment center is illustrated by the following program summary (U.S. Bureau of Prisons, 1968) :

Policy. The community treatment center is established to provide a programmed and supervised transition to productive community living for selected offenders who are to live within a twenty-five mile radius of the center. The program is as flexible as possible, geared specifically to case-management needs and directed toward the achievement of each resident's progressive self-sufficiency in the community. The center provides multiple services (both from its own resources and through the use of existing community resources) to a maximum daily resident population of twenty-five individuals. Postrelease and precommitment study and observation and short-term commitment services are provided, as needed, within the limits of the center's capabilities. The center also has the capability of managing a work-release program of significant proportions.

Case Selection. Offenders who are to live within the center's service area upon release are given priority. Others are considered, as sound case management may dictate, and with prior approval of participating agencies.

1. *Types of offenders:* Center intake is limited to adult and youthful male offenders within the general age limits of 20 to 35, who can be expected to benefit from center programs and services. While juvenile delinquents, generally, are excluded from centers for youth and young adults, those who are in their 19th year may be considered on the basis of their need for center services and their relative maturity.

2. *Status of residents:* Intake is limited to sentenced prisoners, persons committed by the courts for study and observation prior to final disposition, probationers, and parolees. All release categories are appropriate for transfer to the center from a regular correctional institution. Usually, parole board action is taken prior to transfer. Any resident who absconds shall be reported as an escapee.

3. *Identification of needs:* Center programs are intended to be problem-oriented. Therefore, admissions are considered on the basis of case-management needs. For purposes of research and program evaluation, full case records and reports for each offender are furnished the center by the institution to identify the precise program and service needs of each offender.

4. *Length of stay:* This is determined by the center staff in accordance with statutory requirements, parole board action, and each resident's response to the program. The necessary length of stay is projected by the referring agency (institution, probation, or parole) at time of referral.

Living Arrangements. Consistent with the mission of the center, the greatest possible amount of each resident's activity will take place in the community. Accordingly:

1. The center does not provide food services. Meals are taken in the community, although residents are permitted to prepare their own snacks, lunches, and occasional hot-plate-type breakfasts and dinners.

2. Except for radio, television, and table games, recreation is found in the outside community.

Use of Community Resources. The center staff makes extensive use of community resources to meet specific needs of individual residents. These include parole officers for residents who are to be released to supervision. Other community agencies and groups, such as Alcoholics Anonymous, family-service agencies, vocational rehabilitation services, public-health clinics, Synanon or other group-therapy programs for narcotics addicts, the adult-education services, and the state employment services, are available to those residents who have particular need for their special services.

Program Outline

The following are the primary program elements of the center:

Employment Placement. Employment for residents has three aspects:

1. *Job development:* High-quality employment opportunities are generated by referral to prospective employers, liaison with community placement services, and development of related supportive resources. Job development is a primary responsibility.

2. *Job placement:* Placement consists of matching prospective jobs to inmate needs. Guidance interviews and simulated job applications, examinations, and job interviews are held using referrals and role-playing to prepare the resident for his actual job contact.

3. *Placement follow-up:* Placement follow-up consists of counseling interviews, job-site visits, and other contacts with employers. The employment specialist has primary responsibility for placement follow-up in the community.

Counseling. Generally, six types of counseling are provided:

1. *Related to employment and training:* Responsibility is shared by all counseling staff.

2. *Related to family problems:* When required, a minimum of two hours per week per resident is provided those who need such help. A combination of group and individual methods are used, as indicated. Referrals to family-service agencies are made when needed, and group sessions may be scheduled to involve all significant members of the family.

3. *Related to drug addiction:* Counseling is provided on an individual basis and referrals made to the proper agency, as indicated.

4. *Related to alcoholism:* Services are provided both on an individual and on a group basis for residents who have had drinking problems in the past and who have demonstrated the need for assistance while at the center. Referrals may be made to an Alcoholics Anonymous group or to community programs that provide psychotherapy and/or a regimen of antabuse.

5. *Related to center and community adjustment:* When inappropriate behavior is observed or reported, whether at the center or in the community, a combination of individual and group techniques will be used.

6. *Related to parole supervision:* Parole preparation is provided both on an individual and group basis, as indicated. The district parole officer will spend about four hours per week at the center to provide residents with information relating to supervision rules and expectations and to discuss anticipated problems incident to the transition to parole supervision.

Residence Placement. If living arrangements appear to present a problem after release from the center, two further phases may be considered:

1. *Development:* A staff member, usually a counselor, is given the responsibility of providing liaison with the family. He also develops and maintains a current listing of suitable residences in the community. The purpose is to help center residents improve their living situation. By helping residents find suitable homes, the high risk areas of the city with their potential contribution to further delinquency may be avoided.

2. *Planning and placement:* The staff caseworker is responsible for formulating and effecting release plans in cooperation with the parole officer. Conferences with family members, if a stable home environment exists, may be conducted at the center or in the home. When independent placements are to be made, residents will be assisted in their search for a suitable residence. There will be close collaboration with the staff member designated for residence liaison in such cases, and with the district parole officer for persons being released under supervision.

Furloughs. By staff committee decision, furloughs may be granted for the following purposes:

1. To visit and assist in family emergencies, such as critical illness or death of a member of the immediate family.

2. To interview prospective employers.

3. To participate in special courses of training of thirty calendar days or less, when commuting is not feasible.

4. To participate in selected community religious, educational, social, civic, and recreational activities, when it is determined that participation will reinforce the achievement of goals set for the resident.

5. To aid the offender in maintaining and strengthening family ties.

All furloughs shall be granted within the general limits of established policy and at no cost to the center. They are not granted as rewards or because a resident may be "technically" eligible. Nonemergency and nontraining furloughs may be granted, not to exceed one week. These are intended, primarily, as opportunities for residents to test their abilities and readiness for broader participation in the life of the community.

Work-Release and Furlough Programs

Work-release or community work programs have also already profoundly affected traditional correctional programs. These programs trace their origin to the 1913 statute in Wisconsin that authorized judges and magistrates, in cooperation with sheriffs in charge of local jails, to impose conditional sentences for specified misdemeanors. The purpose of the law was to enable offenders to work on their jobs in the community while serving short sentences in jail. In 1957, North Carolina adapted the principles of the Wisconsin statute to felony offenders, under limited conditions. Maryland and Michigan subsequently enacted similar laws. In 1965, Congress enacted the Federal Prisoner Rehabilitation Act, which included provisions for work-release, short-term furloughs, and transfer of adult offenders to community treatment centers. Similar actions followed in many states.

In several jurisdictions, the management of the program is the exclusive responsibility of the department of corrections. In others, the affirmative recommendation of the sentencing judge or the concurrence of the paroling authority is required. The most flexible statute enacted was that adopted by the Congress of the United States, and several states have used it as a model. The statute provides:

> The Attorney General may extend the limits of the place of confinement of a prisoner as to whom there is reasonable cause to believe he will honor this trust, by authorizing him, under prescribed conditions, to . . .
>
> (1) visit a specifically designated place or places for a period not to exceed thirty days and return to the same or another institution or facility. An extension of limits may be granted only to permit a visit to a dying relative, attendance at the funeral of a relative, the obtaining of medical services not otherwise available, the contacting of prospective employers, or for any other compelling reason consistent with the public interest; or
>
> (2) work at paid employment or participate in a training program in the community on a voluntary basis while continuing as a prisoner of the institution or facility to which he is committed, ...
>
> The willful failure of a prisoner to remain within the extended limits of his confinement, or to return within the time prescribed, to an institution or facility, designated by the Attorney General, shall be deemed an escape from the custody of the Attorney General (18 U.S. Code, §4082).

The Congress clearly intended that work-release be a correctional tool to be administered on a selective and informed basis by the executive branch of the government. The program is not a substitute for probation or parole. Nor is it designed as a part of an internal system of punishment and reward. While it provides offenders with an opportunity to contribute to the support of dependents, it was not intended as a compulsory means of offsetting the costs of public welfare payments to families. It will succeed to the extent that it is used for specific purposes and as a means to achieve the correction of the offender. Work-release is oriented toward the offender's discharge. It may provide a prerelease transitional experience leading to increasing levels of skill and personal responsibility. It affords an opportunity to test new work skills in the community. It may supplement institutional educational and training programs. The participant may contribute to the costs of institutional care, to the needs of dependents, or to save a nest egg for release. His earnings may also be used to make restitution or to pay debts. His response to the program can provide the paroling authority with a practical measure of his readiness for release. Finally, the program can reduce the risks and fears of both the offender and the community during the critical period of adjustment immediately after imprisonment.

There are a number of side benefits accompanying a well-managed work-release program in a community that has been adequately prepared to participate. The time and care devoted to the preparation of the community is of critical importance, as is the willingness of the correctional service to keep the community fully informed of the program outcome. As he becomes directly involved with offenders on their jobs and in training situations, the informed citizen develops a better understanding of the problems and potentialities of the offender. He also becomes more supportive of correctional efforts. So far as the offender is concerned, work-release provides him with the opportunity to associate with stable fellow workers and to gain their acceptance on his own merits. These associations contribute to an improved climate for the ultimate reintegration of offenders into the community.

Short-term Furloughs

The furlough is another approach to the extension of the limits of confinement. The federal statute enumerates several specific purposes for which unsupervised absences from an institution may be authorized. Serious family emergencies, the search for work, and medical services not provided by the institutions are specified as legitimate purposes for furloughs. But the law recognizes other "compelling reasons consistent with the public interest." So far, the use of the authority by federal institutions has been limited to the functions specifically enumerated in the law. The community centers, however, and as indicated above, take advantage of the provisions of the furlough statute to enable residents who have demonstrated their stability to spend additional time with their families during the period immediately before their discharge. Wider uses of the furlough provisions remain to be explored as correctional managers gain greater experience with them.

PROGRAM EVALUATION

The extent to which these measures have contributed to the correction of the offender and his reintegration into society remains in doubt. Despite the general enthusiasm with which the President's Commission applauded the establishment of new community-based programs and encouraged their extension, there is as yet little concrete evidence that any of the programs have achieved the objectives that have been sought. The lack of such data is related to the serious lack of adequate resources for program evaluation that exists across the entire spectrum of correctional activity. One small fragment of research growing out of the U.S. Bureau of Prisons' community-center experience suggests that among offenders who have been selected for centers in the past, certain identifiable groups of participants appear to achieve much higher levels of success in the program and after return to the community than when paroled directly from prison. The finding is one that, for many reasons, must be accepted as tentative, but it tends to give added importance to development of diagnostic typologies with which the relevance of specific program strategies may be tested. In the federal and other correctional systems, work has been in progress to computerize information about the prison population to provide a more adequate base for the study of the results of program participation. The collection of data on the outcome of community-based programs proceeds concurrently to provide a base for the more critical evaluation of these correctional methods.

At the present time, some 2,000 federal prisoners, or about 10 percent of the average annual population, are reported by the U.S. Bureau of Prisons to participate in work-release programs. Of this total, between 70 and 80 percent complete their programs successfully. The most frequent reasons for failure are leaving the place of work without permission and drinking. Very few of the failures have resulted from involvement in new crimes, and the number of serious offenses has been negligible.

The number of federal participants in the community treatment center program is about 2,500 per year. These are treated in the bureau's centers, or other public or private centers under contract. The center failure rate is about the same as that for work-release. Generally speaking, the older and more mature offenders respond better to community-based programs than the younger and more unstable ones.

Despite the absence of a large body of validated findings, the early experience of community-based programs supports the hope that these programs can contribute to the reduction of recidivism among a substantial proportion of participants. Program managers observe higher levels of job stability among former work-releasees. Center directors, through their informal intelligence systems, report generally high levels of success among offenders who have developed meaningful ties in the community. There is a general feeling of discouragement about the lack of success with rootless, homeless offenders who are referred to centers in the absence of other resources, but they might well be even less successful without the centers. There is a continuing need for data to assist the manager in identifying the groups for whom the community programs have the greatest value.

REFERENCES

Joint Commission on Mental Illness and Health.
   1961   Action for Mental Health. New York: Wiley.

National Institute of Mental Health.
   1971   Graduated Release. Washington, D.C.: U.S. Government Printing Office.

President's Commission on Law Enforcement and Administration of Justice.
   1967   Task Force Report: Corrections. Washington, D.C.: U.S. Government Printing Office.

U.S. Bureau of Prisons.
   1968   The Residential Center. Washington, D.C.: U.S. Government Printing Office.

CHAPTER **25**

Parole Administration

Vincent O'Leary

State University of New York at Albany

When and how he will return to freedom is the inevitable question faced by almost every offender committed to a prison or similar facility. Only a handful of inmates are sentenced for life and, since they are relatively young, few are released from prison by death. Today, for most inmates, reentry into the community from a correctional institution is through parole. Not only is parole the predominant mode of release for prison inmates, but virtually all of those committed to juvenile institutions also are released under a parole type of supervision. It is among those sentenced to jails, workhouses, and local institutions that the most significant gaps and potential for growth in parole services exist. A national survey in 1965 found that almost all misdemeanants were released from local institutions and jails without parole. From a sample of 212 local jails, the survey found that 62 percent did not release by parole and, in the 81 jails that nominally had parole, only 8 percent of the inmates were released through this procedure (President's Commission, 1967b). There is every reason to believe that this is still characteristic of the United States as a whole although a major recommendation of the President's Commission on Law Enforcement and Administration of Justice (1967a) was for greatly expanded parole services at the misdemeanant level, and there has been some growth in this direction during the 1970s.

DEFINITION AND HISTORY

The Attorney General's Survey of Release Procedures (1939:4) defined parole as "the release of an offender from a penal or correctional institution after he has served a portion of his sentence, under the continued custody of the state and under conditions that permit his reincarceration in the event of misbehavior." Though some jurisdictions impose various limitations, generally offenders can be released and returned repeatedly until the term of their original commitment has expired.

In a number of respects, parole resembles probation. In both, information about an offender is gathered and presented to a decision-making authority, the authority has the power to release the offender under specific conditions, and, in the event of his failure to obey those conditions, the offender may be placed in a correctional institution by the authority. Parole, however, differs from probation in two important characteristics. First, it implies that the offender has served a portion of a commitment to a correctional institution before he or she is released (Rubin et al., 1963). For adults, this usually means a state prison system, if convicted of serious offenses, and local jails for those convicted of less serious ones. State training schools are typically the place of confinement for juveniles.

Second, parole is almost always an administrative decision, while the grant of probation is a court function. Under parole the power to determine when an offender may be released, to fix the conditions of his supervision, or to order revocation of such release, passes from the hands of the court to an agency within the executive branch of the state, county, or other political unit. This agency is usually a parole board in the case of adults and an institutional official in the case of juveniles. Although a sentencing judge, as a condition of probation, may require an offender to spend some time in an institution before he is released under probation supervision (since the decision-making authority on release conditions, revocation, and discharge then continues with the court), such a release is almost always called probation rather than parole.

Rubin and his associates argue that "the granting agency is not the distinguishing factor between the two types of release" (1963:180). Recently developed forms of partial institutional confinement, used by both courts and parole boards, however, make the distinction between probation and parole based simply on whether an offender was incarcerated or not increasingly difficult to sustain. Any definitions of probation and parole are subject to exceptions. Their usefulness depends not only on their clarity and consistency, but on the purposes for which they are used. Because of the implications for administration, decision-making procedures, manpower, and correctional programs, the source of decision-making appears to be a very useful basis for distinguishing contemporary probation from parole.

Parole also needs to be distinguished from "mandatory" or "conditional" release from institutions in those jurisdictions for adults—New York, Wisconsin, the federal system—where some long-term offenders are released automatically under supervision for the portion of their term taken off their sentence conditionally for good behavior in prison. The parole authority exercises no discretion in the matter at all (Killinger, 1951). The procedure provides supervision for those offenders who have been denied, who are ineligible, or who have refused parole at an earlier time. Such offenders may be returned to serve the remaining, unexpired portion of their term if they violate any of the conditions of their release. The advantage of mandating release is that supervision is provided those not paroled. Its main disadvantages, according to its opponents, are that time under supervision is usually short and inmates are released simply because they have earned time off for good behavior with little regard for their readiness to cope with the requirements of a law-abiding life in society (Giardini, 1958).

The contingent release of convicted prisoners from correctional institutions has occurred for many years, under various designations, as a reward for good behavior or for compassionate reasons. In France and other Continental countries it is still known as "conditional liberation" (Wines, 1910; Grunhut, 1948:312–27). Today, it is most often called "parole" in the United States and Canada, and also in Britain since the creation of a national parole authority in that country under the Criminal Justice Act of 1967.

Parole, generally, is traced to Australian and Irish origins. In 1840 Captain Alexander Maconochie established a penal program on the Australian island of Norfolk in which prisoners were conceived as not being sentenced to a given amount of time to be served, but as sentenced to complete certain tasks. The rate at which they completed the tasks would determine when they could be released. Each prisoner was credited with ten "marks" per day if his work was satisfactory, with less if his behavior was improper, and he could be fined in marks for misbehavior. For his food he was charged from three to five marks per day, depending upon the quality of food he elected to procure, and he was charged some marks for other services and supplies. Thus, he could save as many as seven marks per day. He had to accumulate various totals for his conditions of confinement to be made less severe than they were initially, and a still higher total to be released. However, release was on a conditional basis, with the prior sentence reimposed if his subsequent behavior was improper. It has been claimed that during Maconochie's administration of Norfolk Island, which was only for four years, over a thousand prisoners were released under the mark system, of whom less than 3 percent were reconvicted. This record was achieved even though a majority of those released, in addition to being convicted in Britain, had been convicted one or more times while prisoners at the Tasmania or New South Wales penal colonies (Barry, 1958, 1960).

After Maconochie's return to England in 1844, he wrote on penal reform and was active in reform organizations that had a considerable impact in the English-speaking world. One of his disciples, Sir Walter Crofton, introduced a modification of the mark system in the Irish prisons, beginning in 1846. The distinctive feature of Crofton's program was that the released prisoners were restricted in the conditions under which they could live, and were required to report periodically to the police. This Irish system was widely publicized in the United States, and Crofton was invited to address the first meeting of the American Prison Association in 1870. His contribution was the addition of supervision to conditional release, but the supervision by the police was quite limited in quantity and frequently was of harmful quality.

The beginning of parole in the United States generally is identified with the Elmira Reformatory in New York, which was opened in 1876 under the supervision of Zebulon R. Brockway (Moran, 1945; Giardini, 1959; Newman, 1968). Brockway had previously established indeterminate sentences for misdemeanants at the Detroit House of Corrections, and had unsuccessfully proposed such sentences for felons in Michigan and New York. Elmira was the first correctional institution to be called a "reformatory." Its sentences were indeterminate, dependent on "marks" earned by good behavior, and release was by way of a 6-months' parole term during which the parolee had to report regularly to a volunteer guardian or sponsor (Wines, 1910).

Elmira inspired wide attention by its new approach to imprisonment, in contrast to the tradition of incarceration for a term fixed when the offender was sentenced. The designation of certain institutions for youthful felons as "reformatories," and the accompanying practice of permitting indeterminate sentences and parole, spread rapidly through the United States in the last quarter of the nineteenth century and the beginning of the twentieth century. This sentencing system and parole were soon extended to prisoners of all ages. Today there exists in each state, the District of Columbia, and at the federal level a single paroling authority (variously labeled Board of Pardons and Parole, Parole Board, Probation and Parole Commission, etc.), which has jurisdiction over the parole of persons convicted of crimes resulting in a prison sentence of over 1 year. In two states, California and Indiana, separate parole boards exist that are exclusively concerned with the parole of women felons (National Parole Institutes, 1972).

This by no means implies uniform development of either parole laws or practices. States still vary markedly in the proportion of inmates who are released under parole supervision as contrasted to those released by discharge. In 1970, for example, among the offenders released in the states of Washington, New Hampshire, and California, over 95 percent were released under parole supervision; during the same period, the percentage of inmates released by parole in Delaware was 8 percent, and in South

Carolina 26 percent. In the United States as a whole, the proportion of those released to parole supervision was approximately 70 percent (U.S. Bureau of Prisons, 1972).

The history of parole for those committed under juvenile-delinquency statutes is different from the history for those sentenced under criminal law. For juveniles, parole is usually traced back to the practices of the houses of refuge for children existing in the late 1800s (Giardini, 1959). In these settings, children were released to work in private homes for several years. Total control of the child was vested in the family to whom he was released. It was their responsibility to determine when he had earned his freedom. The development of child protective programs subsumed many of these activities, and subsequently juvenile programs were closely involved with child-welfare activities (Platt, 1969). However, especially after the *Gault* decision in 1967 (*In re Gault,* 387 U.S. 1), in which the Supreme Court required substantial due process protections for youths found to be delinquent, programs for children tend to be increasingly viewed as "correctional" in nature; not dissimilar, at least conceptually, from those for adults convicted of crimes.

Notwithstanding this trend, juvenile parole authorities are usually anxious to distinguish their programs from those for adults. They typically use the term *aftercare* as a substitute for *parole.* The difference is more than symbolic. The problems presented by the young offender released from a correctional facility (for example, the issues surrounding school attendance) are different in a number of respects from those of the older offender (Arnold, 1970). Juvenile parole services are also organized quite differently from those for adults. Only two states have a board decide on the release of juveniles, although this form of decision-making is by far the most common pattern for adults (President's Commission, 1967b).

PAROLE AND SENTENCING PRACTICES: COMPARISON OF SYSTEMS

While parole has been attacked from time to time as leniency, its proponents argue that it is a correctional procedure that is both humanitarian to the inmate and protective of the public. They advance these arguments on two grounds. First, virtually everyone convicted and sent to a correctional institution is destined to return to live in the community. He can either be turned loose by discharge at the expiration of his sentence with no continuing responsibility on his part or the state's, or he can be released at an optimum time before this expiration, but under state supervision and with state help. From this perspective, parole is simply a form of graduated return to the community, a sensible release procedure. From time to time parole boards, subjected to what they perceive as public pressure to "crack down" on offenders, reduce the proportion of offenders paroled. This causes some inmates to serve a few more months in prison but it is followed by release through discharge from sentence with no supervision or assistance.

The second major argument for parole is that it is better to defer a decision as to the precise time an inmate should be released (Glaser, 1969:197–99). The sentencing judge cannot foretell what new information may be available to a parole board or what circumstances might arise that would indicate one time as being more favorable than another for an inmate's release (Bennett, 1961). A paroling agency also has the advantage of being able to observe the behavior of the offender while he is in confinement. Also, greater objectivity in appraising the offender may be achieved when the passions aroused by his offense have cooled.

Whatever the merits of these views, available evidence indicates that use of parole does not necessarily lead to a lessening of the amount of time that inmates actually serve in prison. As Table 1 shows, those inmates released on parole in the United States in 1967 actually served slightly *more* time than those released through uncon-ditional discharge. Nor does this table show the additional time served by those released on parole who fail to obey parole rules and are returned to prison as violators, something that cannot occur with unconditional dischargees who can be returned only if convicted of a new crime. To account for these data requires much more understand-ing than is allowed by such slogans as "leniency" or "harshness"—they oversimplify what is a complex administrative, legal, and political issue.

As with any criminal justice function, an awareness of the specific characteristics of the jurisdictions in which parole agencies operate is crucial to an understanding of those agencies. And perhaps as important a determinant of actual parole practice in a jurisdiction as any other is the sentencing system under which that parole juris-diction operates, for it is that system that finally fixes the amount and the character of discretion which parole administrators can exercise (Ohlin & Remington, 1958; Daw-son, 1969). Seeking to eliminate the abuses which potentially lurk in any grant of discretion, some persons would eliminate any form of discretionary release from an institution after sentencing by a trial judge (American Friends Service Committee, 1971:chap. 8; Kastenmeier & Eglit, 1973:486–87). However, most authorities dis-agree, arguing that discretion is inevitable; the task is to limit and control it. They point out that to place the entire releasing decision in the hands of the trial judge, or to depend on a system of totally fixed sentences set by the legislature, brings more inconsistency and injustice than if the decision is shared with a parole authority (A.B.A., 1968). The problem is how to allocate decision-making power to produce a fair and effective system.

Sentencing systems are almost everywhere less structured for juveniles than for adults. In a number of states youngsters may be sent to a state training school for a term not to exceed a stipulated time period, as in the state of New York, where it is not more than three years. Many other states place youngsters under jurisdiction of the state up to a certain age, such as 21 years old. In almost all jurisdictions, they may be paroled at any time at the discretion of the releasing authority. There are some exceptions. In five states, the committing judge must approve all release decisions from state training schools and in three states time periods for which a youngster must be confined before he can be released are fixed in advance (N.C.C.D., 1966:103). With these few exceptions, the discretion to release youngsters on parole is quite broad in the juvenile field.

TABLE 1

TIME SERVED BY TYPES OF RELEASE:
U.S. 1967

Type of Release	Number	Median Time Served
Discharge	22,883	20.1 Months
Parole	45,538	21.1 Months

Source: U.S. Bureau of Prisons, 1967.

Among adults, parole boards tend to be more limited in their discretion. The most common method of checking the authority of parole boards is through statutory or judicial fixing of a minimum sentence—the period of time which an inmate must serve before parole can be considered. It is fixed either as a number of years or as a fraction of a maximum term (Columbia Law Review, 1960). In some states statutes require that inmates serve stipulated periods of time if they have a prior criminal history; offenders with a certain number of previous convictions, for example, may not be considered for parole before a given number of years has elapsed. It is also common for certain kinds of offenders, such as murderers on life sentences, to be denied parole before a minimum period of time has elapsed (National Parole Institutes, 1972).

Minimum terms have long been resisted by some parole boards on the grounds that they should be able to decide in a given case when parole is appropriate without being handicapped by arbitrary limitations (National Conference on Parole, 1957: 72). Conversely, the American Law Institute's *Model Penal Code* (1962) proposed a minimum term in each sentence so that an inmate will serve a stipulated period before being considered for parole. The American Bar Association (1968:142) adopted a modified but similar position. On the other hand, the National Council on Crime and Delinquency's second *Model Sentencing Act* (1972a) argues against any minimum sentences and contends that a parole board should have discretion to parole an inmate any time short of the full sentence imposed.

The maximum period of time offenders are subject to state control may be fixed by statute or by a sentencing judge, although in a few instances it may be modified by a parole board. Such maximum sentences are often shortened by so-called "good time" credits, usually awarded by institutional officials for satisfactory conduct by an inmate in the institution (Sutherland & Cressey, 1970:534). The rate at which they are awarded varies widely from one state to the next but it is common for maximum sentences to be reduced by as much as a third through the awarding of such credits. Good time credits may also, directly or indirectly, shorten minimum sentences in some jurisdictions and thus affect the earliest date at which the parole board considers a case.

Policies regarding minimum and maximum sentences, and awarding of good time, create powerful determinants of the actions of parole boards that have profound implications for other parts of the criminal justice system, as well as for prisoners (Glaser et al., 1966). They also confound measures of the effectiveness of a system.

Perhaps this can best be understood by contrasting the systems of two parole boards in the United States, each of which operates in a distinctive but fairly common type of sentencing and correctional situation. One is the state of Washington, which employs the indeterminate sentence (Hayner, 1958a). Basically, the argument for this system is that within very broad limits the time an offender serves should depend largely on the personal and social facts that are peculiar to him, and on his response to correctional programs as assessed by a group of correctional experts. Though the terminology differs, all states provide some degree of indeterminacy; their differences are largely a matter of degree. Washington represents those states that are highly indeterminate—sometimes called indefinite—with long maximum sentences, so the parole board has much power to determine when most inmates are released. Similar boards are found in California, Hawaii, and Utah (Glaser et al., 1966).

In Washington, for example, anyone convicted of forgery receives a sentence of 20 years, and anyone convicted of grand larceny, 15 years. The sentencing judge has no discretion in determining length of sentence once an offender is convicted, except to grant probation or suspend a sentence. Within the maximum sentence, the parole board fixes a minimum term, which is a tentative parole date, and it subsequently decides if the inmate should be paroled at that time or later. Because the parole board has such long-term control over virtually all persons sentenced to prison, 95 percent of the prisoners released in Washington are under parole supervision.

Texas offers a sharply contrasting system, common to many other jurisdictions. Here the sentencing judge fixes a maximum sentence, on the average much shorter than those in Washington, which is reduced by one-third or more through good time awarded by the prison system. A prisoner becomes eligible for parole when he has served one-third of the maximum sentence, less the good time awarded. Though the details vary, this system is generally used in such states as Alabama, Oklahoma, and Wisconsin, and in the federal system (Glaser et al., 1966).

Table 2 indicates the differences in the effects of these two systems. Offenders in the state of Washington spend more time in prison and are also on parole longer than those in Texas. In Washington the average time remaining on a maximum term when paroled is almost 15 years, while in Texas the time remaining is less than 2 years. Actually, many parolees in Washington are discharged from their sentences after being on parole between two and five years because of satisfactory parole performance, but they can be required to serve their entire sentence on parole.

These variations are clearly the result of differences in sentencing systems rather than differences in the characteristics of offenders. Under the Texas system, because of the much shorter time span, many more offenders are released without parole than in Washington. In Texas prisoners may refuse parole, or the board can require that they serve their full sentences; neither would swell the prison population since most prisoners will soon be released by the expiration of their sentence.

In order to forestall this type of release without parole supervision, the American Law Institute's *Model Penal Code* (1962:§6.10) and the National Commission on Reform of Federal Criminal Law (1970:279) proposed a separate term of parole supervision for all prisoners, to be imposed even on those who are not paroled before the expiration of their maximum term in confinement. No jurisdiction has adopted such a proposal, although it is approximated by such measures as the Federal Youth Corrections Act, under which the first parole is mandatory between 60 days and 4 years on a 6-year maximum sentence.

Not only do differences in sentencing systems affect the relationship between the parole boards and inmates in these two states, but they shape many other features of the entire criminal justice systems as well, such as the relationship between the courts and prosecutors. In Texas almost all the rewards necessary for effective plea bargaining are in the hands of local officials (Newman, 1966; Dawson, 1969). Not only do prose-

TABLE 2

COMPARISON OF SENTENCES, TIME SERVED, AND PAROLE USE
IN STATES OF TEXAS AND WASHINGTON, 1967

	State of Washington	State of Texas
Median Maximum Sentence	17.2 years	3.8 years
Median Time Served Before Parole	21.7 months	15.3 months
Percent Released by Parole	95%	52%

Source: U.S. Bureau of Prisons, 1967.

cutors control charge reductions, but they influence judicial decisions as to length of sentence, and thus parole eligibility, a powerful tool for plea negotiation. In the state of Washington the prosecutor can only effectively plea bargain through reducing charges to an offense with a lower but still very long maximum sentence or recommend probation. Since the sentencing judge has no control over the length of sentence, being permitted to impose only the terms stipulated by law for the offense, his direct power in facilitating plea negotiation is generally limited to the grant or denial of probation. The best that can be done to influence the actual time served in prison is a recommendation made by judges and prosecutors to the parole authorities. Thus, communications between the parole board, on one hand, and prosecutors and judges over lengths of time to be served by offenders is much more common in Washington than in Texas. The potential for conflict between court and parole officials is also greater.

The impact of the parole board on the prison system is also obviously quite different in the two states. In Washington, with every inmate serving a long sentence and virtually everyone going out on parole, the board has much greater potential influence on the institution. The board, by its decisions, can quickly and dramatically affect institutional population and the whole reward structure within the institution in terms of program participation and institutional behavior. On the other hand, in Texas, if the board becomes more conservative in its parole practices, there is some impact on the prison, but since most inmates serve relatively short sentences and the prison has power to grant extensive amounts of good time, the board's conservatism can be blunted by a sharp rise in rates of release by discharge.

Another difference between these two states is in the effect of the board on parole supervision. Since everyone is paroled in the state of Washington, it is much more common to find offenders with longer records of prior convictions on parole there than in Texas. In the latter they are more likely to be discharged than paroled. It is also more common in Washington for a person to be paroled a second, third, or fourth time; in Texas a second parole on the same sentence is rare. Accordingly, the alcoholic offender who may represent a fairly minor threat to society but who violates parole regularly by drinking and petty offenses is much more likely to remain within the system for a longer period of time in Washington than in Texas. He can easily get into a series of minor scrapes and have his parole revoked several times before he completes a long sentence. The consequent variations in kinds of offenders on parole pose some differences in work demands on the parole officers in the two states, and they also affect the amount and character of the interaction with police agencies.

The differences revealed by the foregoing brief exploration of the law and policy of just two states point up the problems inherent in trying to assess parole systems by simply comparing the rates of recidivism among them. Texas suspends only about a third of its parolees for violations while Washington suspends nearly half, but Texas selects fewer of its prisoners for parole and supervises them for a briefer period than does Washington. Further, the state of Washington has a well-developed, state-subsidized probation system in all counties, while Texas has a county-based system not much developed in parts of the state. Washington's nonimprisonment of better parole risks because of the greater use of probation must be weighed in evaluating parole revocation levels. For all of these reasons, comparing one parole system with any other requires great care to take into account the wide variety of forces operating on them.

The most ambitious effort yet undertaken to provide parole systems routinely with information by which apt comparisons of effectiveness can be made is that carried out by the Uniform Parole Reports system (Lejins, 1967). The program, which was initiated in 1964, is a cooperative effort by all states in which a standard classification system is employed to describe persons paroled and their behavior on parole. These reports are sent to a national center operated by the National Council on Crime and Delinquency where they are processed and compiled into tables, which are fed back to individual parole agencies. Each agency can compare the outcome of its own practices against similar practices in other jurisdictions for particular types of offenders. Even with this elaborate system of common classifications for parolees, because of the tremendous variations among states, comparisons between systems still must be done with considerable reservation and qualification (Gottfredson et al., 1970:chap. 4).

DECISION-MAKING METHODS

In meeting what parole board members perceive to be their chief responsibility— assessing risk and minimizing the probability of further crime—they are typically dependent on a decision-making method that focuses on the factors within an individual case. Parole board members review a file on an inmate, interview him, and then apply some theory of human behavior or intuitive judgments to the information they have gathered. While such techniques are useful and, for a number of reasons, probably necessary in parole decision-making, the evidence is quite strong that over a large number of cases for the narrow purpose of predicting the likelihood that a specific offender will succeed or fail on parole, they are prone to a fair amount of error.

The National Parole Institutes, an organization jointly sponsored by the National Council on Crime and Delinquency, the United States Parole Board, the Association of Paroling Authorities, and the Association of the Administrators of the Interstate Compact for the Supervision of Probationers and Parolees, has carried out training programs for board members since 1962. In these sessions, case histories are presented routinely to participant parole board members who are asked to estimate the probability that the persons depicted would succeed or fail on parole. A fairly detailed set of instructions regarding the sentencing system and the conditions of release are provided to the parole board members. Table 3 shows the distribution of scores for three

TABLE 3

ESTIMATES OF PAROLE SUCCESS BY
40 PAROLE BOARD MEMBERS
ON THREE HYPOTHETICAL CASES

Probable Success on Parole	Parole Board Member Estimates in Three Cases		
	Case 1	Case 2	Case 3
90—99%	—	1	—
80—89%	3	6	1
70—79%	12	6	2
60—69%	6	7	4
50—59%	6	9	4
40—49%	4	5	11
30—39%	3	2	6
20—29%	4	3	8
10—19%	1	1	3
0— 9%	1	—	1

Source: National Parole Institutes, 1969.

cases presented to parole board members in one session. The results are quite typical and they strikingly parallel those that have been found in similar exercises carried on with judges and probation officers. Not only are there wide differences as to what is an appropriate disposition in a case, but there is also wide disagreement about the estimated probability of success for each case (Remington & Newman, 1962). If this estimate is an important part of the parole decision, it follows that the greater its accuracy, the more likely is an appropriate decision.

Since the 1920s, a number of researchers have concerned themselves with the task of developing statistical techniques for increasing the precision of forecasts of probable recidivism (Bruce et al., 1928:205–49; Ohlin, 1951; Simon, 1971). Though the detailed methods vary, the basic aim of these studies has been to identify factors that can be shown to be statistically related to parole outcome and, by combining them, to develop statements about the probability of recidivism for various classes of parolees (Gottfredson, 1967). These statements have usually been labeled "parole predictions," though in recent years applications other than "predicting" parole outcomes have been made of these probability compilations. One of the more useful purposes to which these estimates may be put is to help assess how well a particular correctional program increases or decreases the chances for success of a group of offenders subjected to it (Mannheim & Wilkins, 1955). Such scores can also be used as base-line data by which case decisions can be monitored to identify variations between expected and actual decisions or outcomes. A large research project sponsored by the United States Parole Board and the National Council on Crime and Delinquency is investigating ways of improving parole decision-making, and one aspect of that project is to provide such feedback to decision-makers (N.C.C.D., 1972b).

Typically, the probability statements produced by statistical techniques are more accurate in estimating likely outcome on parole than traditional case methods. As one example, Ellis Savides, Associate Superintendent of Classification and Treatment at the California Department of Correction Medical Facility at Vacaville, interviewed 283 men when they were about to be released on parole. He studied their files and then rated them from 0 to 10 according to his judgment as to the probability of their success on parole. A similar rating was made by a clinical council consisting of a group of psychiatrists and psychologists. When the actual outcome of these predictions was compared with scores derived from statistical prediction tables, it was quite clear that the statistical prediction method proved superior to either source for distinguishing parole success cases among groups of offenders (Gottfredson, 1961; Savides, 1961). Other comparisons of case studies and statistical prediction procedures have produced similar results (Meehl, 1954; Glaser, 1962); it is a feedback exercise that parole boards and other case assessors should repeat regularly.

Despite the evidence that quantitative prediction methods can be useful, there has been relatively little application of them in the parole field. Part of this may be explained by the lack of resources, skill, and manpower to develop and maintain them, but a major source of resistance to their use is inherent in the nature of the decision itself (Hayner, 1958b). As an illustration, parole board members, in the training session referred to earlier, were asked to indicate, after they had estimated probable success or failure of an offender on parole, whether they would consider parole for the inmate. Table 4 shows how forty parole board members voted in a specific case and their estimates of the offender's probable success on parole.

Parole board members voting to parole the inmate tended to estimate the probability of his success as higher than those who voted to deny parole, but this relationship of estimated outcome to parole decision is highly inconsistent. The two board members who voted for release despite their estimate that the inmate only had a 20 to 29 percent chance of success obviously were focusing on elements in the case different from those stressed by the two members who would deny parole despite their 60 to 69 percent success estimate. Perhaps they disagreed on the value of parole supervision or on the likely reaction of the public to release in this kind of case. Whatever the source of disagreement, it is clear that while the probability of success or failure greatly influences parole decisions, it does not control them.

These results point up other problems with use of parole prediction scores (Evjen, 1962). Parole board members in the training sessions, for example, indicate frequently that they are as much interested in the type of risk as in the violation risk probability. If an offender is more likely to commit a forgery, they may tolerate a higher risk than if an offender is likely to commit a violent crime. Also, most prediction systems depend largely on prior or unmodifiable events, such as criminal record and age, as bases for their forecasts. Thus, a parole resource that was not available earlier, such as a new job, may influence the board's decision but is not built into the prediction score.

This discussion underscores the fact that far from being solely a task of estimating the risk posed by given inmates, the parole decision involves a wide variety of considerations, most of which are common to other criminal justice decision points. There is usually a difference in emphasis on various aspects by diverse decision-makers, which may vary from one jurisdiction to the next, but to one degree or another such concerns as fairness, deterrence, system maintenance, and potential public reaction influence all criminal justice decisions, including parole.

A reflection of some of these concerns is found in the results of a questionnaire which was completed by nearly half of the parole board members in the United States in 1965 (National Parole Institutes, 1966:162). One item asked parole board members what they considered to be the five most important factors in deciding on a parole, and their estimate of the proportion of cases in the past year in which that particular factor

TABLE 4

PAROLE DECISION ON A HYPOTHETICAL CASE
BY 40 PAROLE BOARD MEMBERS

Estimated Probability of Success	Number Voting to Parole	Number Voting to Deny
90—99%		
80—89%	2	
70—79%	2	
60—69%	5	2
50—59%	9	2
40—49%	3	2
30—39%	1	2
20—29%	2	6
10—19%		2
0— 9%		
Average Estimate of Probable Success	56.6%	36.8%

Source: National Parole Institutes, 1969.

influenced their decisions. Table 5 shows the items that were selected by at least 20 percent of the parole board members as being among the five most important.

Clearly, the first three items selected as being the most important were related to the issue of risk. But the next four reflected concerns of another sort. These went to issues of equitable punishment, impact on the system, and the reactions of persons external to correctional organizations. And although the first item was the only one appearing in a high percentage of cases, the other items did appear in a significant number, especially when their cumulative effect is considered. Findings such as these have been reported by several sources, but seldom are these decision factors borne in mind when the propriety of parole decision methods is discussed or when projects are designed to improve decision-making (Gottfredson & Ballard, 1964; Gottfredson et al., 1973).

Technology can make statistical information increasingly valuable to parole board members. Particularly with use of the computer for instant feedback, this kind of assistance should increase over time. But most experts are convinced that the optimum kind of decision system is one that uses both statistical and individual case-history methods. One authority sums up the issue as follows:

> I know of no instance where an established academic criminologist, judge, or correctional administrator has advocated the replacement of case studies and subjective evaluation by statistical tables for sentencing, parole, or other major decisions on the fate of an offender. The many reasons for insisting upon case data may be grouped into three major categories. First, . . . these officials must make moral decisions for the state as a whole in determining what risks justify withholding freedom from a man or grant-

TABLE 5

FACTORS CONSIDERED IN PAROLE DECISION BY BOARD MEMBERS

Factors considered	Percent including item as one of five most important	Average percent of cases item "*consciously* and *significantly*" influenced decision
1. My estimate of the chances that the prisoner would or would not commit a serious crime if paroled.	92.8	79.4
2. My judgment that the prisoner would benefit from further experience in the institution program, or at any rate, would become a better risk if confined longer.	87.1	27.6
3. My judgment that the prisoner would become a worse risk if confined longer.	71.9	13.6
4. My judgment that the prisoner had already been punished enough to "pay" for his crime.	43.2	13.3
5. The probability that the prisoner would be a misdemeanant and a burden to his parole supervisors, even if he did not commit any serious offenses on parole.	35.3	8.9
6. My feelings about how my decision in this case would affect the feelings or welfare of the prisoner's relatives or dependents.	33.8	9.2
7. What I thought the reaction of the judge might be if the prisoner were granted parole.	20.9	7.5

Source: National Parole Institutes, 1966.

ing it to him. For these moral decisions they must try to know each man as a person and know his relationships to other persons who love or fear him. Second, there is always some information on a case too special to be readily taken into account by any conceivable table in estimating the risks involved in a specific official action. Third, besides the prospect of violation, judges and parole boards must consider the type of violation and the consequences of certain types of violation for community treatment of other parolees (Glaser, 1969:204–5).

To the list should be added a growing concern for fairness and the opportunity for a "day in court" that increasingly requires a careful and full hearing of the facts in each individual case.

THE PAROLE HEARING

In most systems the parole hearing is the crucial time in parole administration, for it is then that information about an inmate is studied, he is interviewed, and a tentative or final decision on his freedom or continued imprisonment is made. The President's Commission placed great stress on properly conducted hearings.

> Releasing authorities can also achieve more rational decision-making by improving their hearing procedures. Improvements must promote both fairness and regularity, as well as effective correctional treatment. . . . Hearings commonly give parole boards an opportunity to identify important points on which information is needed in making their decision. For example, a board may well find from interviewing an inmate that he has several contacts in the community not mentioned in any official report, which later investigation by staff may reveal to have considerable bearing on the place to which he might subsequently be paroled.
>
> The other aim of a hearing is to create conditions which enhance the treatment goals for an inmate. This does not mean that the hearing should take on the character of a counseling session. The simple opportunity of being given what he perceives to be a fair hearing can be important in creating those conditions (President's Commission, 1967b:64).

In almost all states, parole hearings for adults are held with the offender present. However, in several states there are no hearings for offenders; decisions, then, are based only on the staff's written reports, occasionally interviews with families, or information provided by the families. For paroling juveniles, formalized hearing procedures are much less common than with adults; reliance instead is on written staff reports or on staff conferences at which the youth may not be present.

The procedures followed in hearings for adult offenders are extremely diverse. In many states, especially those with numerous institutions, the parole board may break up into smaller panels—even into committees of one—each of which conducts hearings on its own. Only in exceptionally important cases is a larger subcommittee or the entire board used for hearings in these states. In some states *hearing officers* or *referees* conduct many of the hearings for the board. Still other boards conduct all hearings with all members in attendance (National Parole Institutes, 1972).

In addition to the board member or members, most boards have a recording secretary and also a clerk in the hearing room. Some states regularly have the warden or one of his senior assistants present during the parole hearing, and in several states, family and representatives for and against the parole may appear. Standards adopted by a 1956 National Conference on Parole (1957:82) call for hearings to be conducted in private with only parole board members, the offender, and an institutional representative present, and these standards usually are observed.

Typically, information available at the time of the hearing is summarized by institutional staff in a "progress report" based on data collected at the prisoner's admission, plus the record of his adjustment and accomplishments while confined, his responses in a preparole interview, and possibly some correspondence or a conference with his relatives or friends. Some parole boards have investigations made of the release plans of the inmate, others prefer to wait until they make at least a tentative decision that parole is indicated. A few states have reports prepared for them by psychiatrists or psychologists for selected cases. The "progress reports" are usually written by caseworkers who, in most institutions, have relatively little opportunity to observe inmates. Major reforms advocated by several correctional authorities and gradually developing include reports from casework teams of guards, vocational trainers, caseworkers, and other personnel who have extensive contact with the offenders (Glaser, 1969:chap. 8).

When a parole board must decide whether an offender who has already been paroled may remain in the community or have his parole revoked for alleged violations of the conditions of his release, the information available to the board almost always is supplied through written reports from the parole officers responsible for supervision of the offender in the community. The nature of this information and its use poses special problems not completely comparable to those encountered at hearings on granting or denying parole.

In few jurisdictions does the offender have any statutory rights in the parole consideration process except, perhaps, for the right to a personal appearance before the parole board. The *Model Penal Code* represented a major break in this tradition. It provided, in part, that an inmate was to be paroled unless the board found he was not ready for release or that certain other conditions militated against parole (American Law Institute, 1962:§305.9). This reversed the usual statutory stipulation that an inmate is *not* to be paroled unless the board finds evidence that he is ready for release. The *Code*'s proposal was resisted strongly by a number of parole authorities who saw it as giving inmates a "right" to parole that, if denied, would tie up the boards in protracted litigation.

The President's Commission sought to bring about change in parole consideration procedures by making the following recommendations:

> The parole decision involves many of the same kinds of factors that are involved in the original sentencing decision. An offender who is eligible for parole should therefore be provided with safeguards similar to those recommended by the Commission for the defendant who is being sentenced. He should, for example, have an opportunity to present to the board facts and arguments regarding his behavior during imprisonment and his readiness to return to the community, as well as an opportunity to challenge any opposing position taken by correctional authorities (President's Commission, 1967b:86).

Since then parole boards have resisted but courts have increasingly, although at a measured pace, encouraged expansion of due process rights at the time of parole hearings (Iowa Law Review, 1968; University of Pennsylvania Law Review, 1971).

The courts have been more willing to correct what they see as abuses of a parole board's powers to fix conditions of parole (Cohen, 1969). Most statutes enumerate some conditions that a parole board may impose, but these are rarely mandatory or exclusive, so boards can waive some rules or can impose others on their own initiative. The traditional view has been that parole is a contract between the parolee and the parole board, and that since the parolee is free not to accept this contract, once he accepts it, he is bound by its conditions (New York University Law Review, 1963). However, the view has had limited influence on the courts that have required over the years that rules must be reasonable and that they not be against public policy (Rubin, 1956). For example, in a case arising in the state of California, the federal court restrained the state from prohibiting parolees from making public speeches [*Hyland* v. *Procunier*, 311 F. Supp. 749, 750 (Cal., 1970)].

In general, court restrictions on parole conditions appear to be likely, if the issue is brought to court, wherever the conditions encompass events that are beyond the parolee's control, are impossible of performance, or are grossly unreasonable. The *Model Penal Code* suggests that parole boards limit their conditions to such matters as requiring a parolee to report to a parole officer and "other conditions especially related to the cause of his offense and not unduly restrictive of his liberty or incompatible with his freedom of conscience" (American Law Institute, 1962:§305.13). In general, however, parole conditions in use in the U.S. today are still fairly lengthy and require such things as obtaining permission to marry, change a job, buy a car, or change residence (Arluke, 1969).

As in the earlier instance of parole consideration, the President's Commission recommended a series of changes in the revocation process:

> The offender threatened with revocation should therefore be entitled to a hearing comparable to the nature and importance of the issue being decided. Where there is some dispute as to whether he violated the conditions of his release, the hearing should contain the basic elements of due process—those elements which are designed to ensure accurate fact finding. It may not be appropriate to require the heavy burden of proof required for criminal conviction, or to provide for jury trials. But the hearing should include such essential rights as reasonable notice of the charges, the right to present evidence and witnesses, the right to representation by counsel—including the right to appointed counsel—and the right to confront and cross-examine opposing witnesses (President's Commission, 1967b:88).

Many parole board members resist such proposals because they would create demands on their time grossly incommensurate with their current personnel and budget. It is also argued that these procedures would make the requirements for revocation of parole so elaborate that parole would lose its crime-prevention functions, since parole agents would be reluctant to act at the first sign of the parolee's deviation from a legitimate, temperate, and self-supporting way of life. It has been claimed that under such circumstances parole boards would declare a parolee a violator only if he or she is convicted of a new offense. Further, parole board members contend that they would be reluctant to release marginal parolees because of the elaborate hearing and evidentiary requirements that would be required to return them to an institution (Kadish, 1961).

The arguments in response to such objections suggest that these fears are exaggerated and that more stringent procedural requirements improve the quality of parole administration and make it more rehabilitative. The essence of the due process requirement, it is contended, is to make the parole agent collect and record objective grounds for suspicions rather than permitting him to report only hearsay. The argument is, further, that the evidence is quite clear that parole boards have not substantially reduced the number of paroles when procedural safeguards have been introduced (Kadish, 1961).

A number of decisions have reversed the earlier "hands off" policy of the courts. Perhaps the most important early case was *Hyser* v. *Reed* [318 2d. 225, 235 (D.C. Cir., 1963)] that, in part, required that the U.S. parole board give parolees charged with a violation an informal hearing at a point as near as reasonably possible to the site of alleged violation. The movement toward expanded court intervention has been especially marked since the U.S. Supreme Court ruled in a probation case that an offender has a right to counsel at the time probation is revoked and the sentence formerly withheld is imposed [*Mempa* v. *Rhay*, 389 U.S. 128 (1967)]. Subsequently, for example, the New York Court of Appeals reversed its former position and required that the New York parole board permit counsel at revocation hearings [*People ex rel.* v. *Warden*, 318 N.Y.S. 2d. 449 (1971)]. A Michigan court a year earlier not only required that the state parole board permit counsel at the time of the revocation hearing but required it to provide counsel to an indigent parolee alleged to have violated his parole [*Warren* v. *Michigan Parole Board*, 179 N.W. 2d. 664, 673 (1970)].

The rationale that most often underlies these and other procedural requirements at the time of revocation was expressed in another federal circuit court case:

> Therefore, while a prisoner does not have a constitutional right to parole, once paroled he cannot be deprived of his freedom by means inconsistent with due process. The minimal right of the parolee to be informed of the charges and the nature of the evidence against him and to appear and to be heard at the revocation hearing is inviolate. Statutory deprivation of this right is manifestly inconsistent with due process and is unconstitutional; nor can such right be lost by the subjective determination of the executive that the case for revocation is "clear" [*Murray* v. *Page*, 429 F. 2d. 1359 (10th Cir., 1970) at 1361].

In 1972 the Supreme Court in the famous *Morrissey* case held that the liberty of a parolee, although indeterminate, includes many of the core values of unqualified liberty and its revocation inflicts a "grievous loss on the parolee. . . . Its termination calls for some orderly process, however informal" [*Morrissey* v. *Brewer*, 92 S.Ct. 2593 (1972)]. While the Court did not decide the question whether parolees facing revocation are entitled to the assistance of counsel whether retained or appointed, it did conclude that due process requires a reasonably prompt informal hearing before someone other than the parole officer involved, near the place of the alleged violation or arrest, to determine if reasonable grounds exist for revocation. It further required that the parolee should be given notice of the hearing and the alleged violations. The parolee may present relevant information, and unless denied by the hearing officer, has the right to question adverse informants. The hearing officer is required to summarize the results of the hearing and on the evidence submitted determine if there exists probable cause to hold the parolee for the final decision of the parole board on revocation. At the subsequent revocation hearing, which must occur within a reasonable time, the parolee is entitled to: (a) written notice of the alleged violations of parole; (b) the disclosure of evidence against him; (c) the opportunity to be heard in person and to present witnesses and evidence; (d) the right to cross-examine adverse witnesses (unless the hearing officer specifically finds good cause for not allowing confrontation); (e) a "neutral and detached" hearing body, such as a traditional parole board; and (f) a written statement as to the evidence relied on and reasons for revoking parole. In 1973 the Court further extended due process protections in parole revocation by providing a limited right to counsel in the proceedings [*Gagnon* v. *Scarpelli*, 93 S.Ct. 1756 (1973)].

Not all procedural innovations are coming about only as a result of direct mandates by the courts (Kimball & Newman, 1968) ; a number of states are now developing their own rules for revocation procedures reflecting the cited decisions and commentaries. The state of Washington's system for handling alleged violators includes the right of the parolee to have a hearing before a parole board member in the community in which the violation is alleged to have occurred; to cross-examine witnesses; to request the board to issue subpoenas; and to be provided a counsel at state expense if he is without personal financial resources. It is clear that parole boards in the 1970s were dealing with a set of concerns about hearings which in the 1960s were virtually absent in most jurisdictions.

THE ORGANIZATION OF PAROLE SERVICES

How a parole board balances concerns for procedural fairness, community protection, rehabilitation, and operational efficiency profoundly influences the effectiveness of a criminal justice system (indeed, it determines the very yardstick by which it will be measured), and also determines how parole services are organized, and the type of personnel needed to carry out the board's tasks.

Most persons concerned with parole release procedures in the juvenile area are full-time correctional staff. The bulk are career employees of juvenile correctional institutions. Relatively few juvenile jurisdictions have part-time or noncorrectional personnel determining parole releases (N.C.C.D., 1966:104).

Contrastingly, parole boards for adults tend to carry many state-level administrative responsibilities. Table 6 shows, for example, that fourteen such boards supervise probation services for the courts of the state. This table also shows the historical link in many states between the parole function and the executive clemency or pardon function of the governor (Rubin et al., 1963:chap. 16). Many boards carry out advisory functions for the governor in executive clemency matters, and in Alabama the same board that grants paroles also has the power to pardon (National Parole Institutes, 1972).

TABLE 6

PAROLING AUTHORITIES' RESPONSIBILITIES, OTHER THAN PAROLE

Additional Responsibility	Number of Boards
Holds clemency hearing	28
Commutes sentences	24
Appoints parole supervision staff	24
Administers parole service	20
Paroles from local institutions	19
Grants or withholds "good time"	17
Supervises probation service	14
Grants pardons, restorations, and remissions	1
Fixes maximum sentence after 6 months	1
May discharge from sentence prior to expiration of sentence	1
Sets standards for "good time"	1
Acts as advisory board on pardons	1
None	5

Source: N.C.C.D., 1966:215.

Although standard-setting bodies call for full-time members, about half of the parole boards for adult offenders in the United States consist of part-time members only or are a mix of full-time and part-time members (National Parole Institutes, 1972). Most part-time parole boards are in the smaller states.

The American Correctional Association in 1966 called for the educational preparation of a parole board member to be sufficient "to provide him with a knowledge of those professions most closely related to parole administration. Specifically, academic training, which has qualified the board member for professional practice in a field such as criminology, education, psychiatry, psychology, law, social work and sociology, is desirable" (A.C.A., 1966:119). As Table 7 shows, 30 percent of parole board members in a 1965 survey had less than a college degree and another 15 percent have no graduate work. There obviously was a considerable gap between that which exists and that which standard-setting bodies deemed desirable.

The various organizational settings in which these parole decision-makers work are reflected in Table 8. Although there is a considerable variety, at least two dominant organizational patterns can be identified—the institutional model, which largely predominates in the juvenile field, and the independent model, most common in the adult field. These two models have provoked considerable controversy.

In general, the institutional model binds parole very closely to institutional programs. It places the decision to release in the hands of the staff of the correctional facility in which the offender is confined. Under this model, parole is simply one more of a series of decisions that have already been made about the offender. The persons who are most familiar with the case make the releasing decision; the development of a rational and consistent set of decisions that affect the inmate is thus afforded. As Table 8 indicates, this form of organization dominates the juvenile field, with thirty-four out of fifty states employing it.

TABLE 7

EDUCATIONAL BACKGROUND OF MEMBERS OF
ADULT PAROLE AUTHORITIES: 1965

Highest Level of Education Attained	Percentage Completing
High School	6.4%
Some College	23.8%
College	15.4%
Some Graduate Work	16.8%
Graduate Degree	37.6%

Graduate Major	Percent Completing Degree
Law	20.8%
Social Work	7.1%
Medicine	1.4%
Sociology	1.4%
Education	2.8%
Religion	2.1%
Other	2.0%

Source: National Parole Institutes, 1966:2–3.

The major argument raised against the institutional model is that too often decisions are influenced by organizational considerations rather than by the needs of the individual case or of the community. Overpopulation and other concerns of institutional management can very easily become the basis of decision-making (President's Commission, 1967b:65). In the adult field, much reform was achieved in the transfer of parole decision-making from institutional control to an independent authority. Undoubtedly, much of the basis for this reform came from the view that paroling authorities had been swayed too easily by institutional considerations or were not objective enough. The reform was so complete that for some time no adult parole releasing authority has been directly controlled by the operating staff of a penal institution.

Whatever its merits in fostering objectivity, the independent parole board, in turn, has been criticized on several counts (President's Commission, 1967b:65). First, the claim is made that such boards tend to be insensitive to institutional programs and fail to give them the support they require. Second, independent boards often base their decisions on what many regard as inappropriate considerations, such as the feelings of a local police chief. Third, their remoteness from the institutional program gives independent boards little appreciation for the dynamics in a given case; their assessments tend to be cursory, often creating the impression that persons who should be paroled are not and that those who should not be paroled are released. Fourth, the argument is made that independent systems most often have parole board members with little training or experience in corrections and this, combined with the distance of the parole board from institutional programs, builds unnecessary conflicts into the system. The rapid growth of partial release programs and halfway houses has increased the probability of those conflicts.

While these arguments and their rebuttals continue, an alternate system has gained considerable support in recent years that is tending to cut the ground away from both of the major models. This alternative system is linked with a general move towards consolidation of all types of correctional services into distinctive departments of correction that subsume both institutional and field programs. In the consolidation model, emerging from the drive toward centralized administration, typically release decisions are made by a central decision-making authority with fairly independent powers but organizationally within the overall department of corrections. The director of corrections may sit on such a releasing authority, or he may designate some of staff to do so, as in the state of Minnesota. At times the releasing authority might even consist of employees of the department of corrections, as in Wisconsin and Michigan. In the youth field, the centralized board may have policy responsibilities for institutions as well as parole decision-making, as is the case with the California Youth Authority.

TABLE 8

ORGANIZATION OF PAROLE AUTHORITIES: 50 STATES

Authority	Adult	Juvenile
Institution staff	0	34
Independent board	41	5
Board in Dept. of Corrections	6	2
Institutions agency	2	6
Other	1	3

Source: Adapted from President's Commission, 1967b:65.

The proponents of the consolidation model argue that where the parole releasing authority becomes part of a centralized system, there is an increased concern for the whole correctional system. They claim that sensitivity to institutional programs, for example, seems more pronounced in these systems than in completely autonomous ones. On the other hand, the removal of parole decision-making from direct institutional control insures fairer decisions based on a broad set of considerations, some of which are external to institutional concerns. Apparently seeking to foster the development of the consolidation model of decision-making, the President's Commission concluded that:

> The principal advantages cited for this system are that it would meet the need in large multi-institution programs for maintenance of consistency in policies among institutions or among field offices which make revocation decisions and would minimize policy conflicts that can arise between releasing authorities and institutions. Properly developed, it also could provide procedural safeguards against capricious or irresponsible decisions.
>
> Such an independent decision-making group within a parent agency seems to be the most effective solution to the problem of coordination within juvenile agencies. It is the one to which the juvenile field is apparently moving and is the alternative to which the adult field also seems to be heading (President's Commission, 1967b:66).

The development of large departments of corrections, with parole decision-making groups as autonomous bodies within them, has resulted in parole field staffs increasingly removed from the administrative control of parole boards and placed under control of the directors of the correctional departments. Although parole board members, especially those operating in an independent agency, tend to resist the removal of such staff from their control, a clear majority of parole officers in the fifty states today work for unified departments of correction.

The impetus for these changes comes not only from the drive for organizational rationality and efficiency, but also from the growth of a wide variety of partial release programs, such as work-release, furloughs, and community-based correction centers, in which parole staff play an increasingly important part in treatment programs. These new programs have implications for the whole concept of parole, which can be seen best against the background of various styles of correctional programs.

CHANGING CONCEPTS OF PAROLE

The evolution of parole practice in the United States has not been limited to legal and organizational developments but has also reflected profound changes in views on sources of criminality, strategies for changing the offender, and desirable relationships between correctional systems and offenders (Glaser, 1966; Empey, 1967; Schrag, 1971: chap. 7). Several writers have found it useful to classify parole officers or total systems by the relative emphasis each places on the community as contrasted to the offender (Hall et al., 1966; Glaser, 1969:291–99). Though such classifications oversimplify a complex set of behaviors and imply a consistency rarely found in human organizations, they do facilitate description and analysis. Employing one such classification scheme, the history of parole can be divided roughly into three eras, each of which embodied a fairly distinctive policy about the goals of parole and the way programs were to be organized to achieve them (O'Leary & Duffee, 1971a).

Although the eras are presented as discrete and as appearing in successive time periods, elements of each were found in an earlier day and variations of them, perhaps somewhat modified in presentation and form, are still very much part of the contemporary parole scene in the United States. In every parole system today policies consistent with different correctional eras function simultaneously. In fact, some of the most serious conflicts in parole administration arise because of the competing sets of goals implied by the various systems that coexist.

The Era of Clemency and Compliance

Although altered in a number of significant ways, the ideas of corrections that flourished in the United States in the nineteenth century were to dominate parole services well into the 1920s and 1930s. The correction model of this era was a reform policy that combined high stress on the community's safety and values with low emphasis on the individual offender's personal goals. In institutions the goal was the instillation of community norms and standards through rigorous discipline and schedules; the development of new habits was the prime correctional task. The inmate had to learn to be a productive citizen, hence there was often a highly moralistic tone to the program and much hard labor, as prisons manufactured much for commercial sale until around 1933 (Glaser, 1969:156–59). The offender's behavior was to be manipulated by a series of punishments and rewards, and change in his behavior was viewed as dependent on his unswerving and continuous supervision by a staff who, ideally, were seen as "firm but fair."

Personnel were not required to be highly educated, except for needed specialists, such as teachers, nor did they need to be specially skilled in behavioral or psychological disciplines. They had to be good administrators—to plan their work and the offender's programs. Under this policy it was highly desirable that staff be dedicated to the ideals and values of the larger society. Offenders had few rights. They had privileges granted by the state in accordance with the conformity of their behavior. These privileges were to be granted and taken away, however, in a unilateral and standardized fashion. The staff had much discretion and was not to be questioned or debated.

The application of this policy to parole is graphically described in the report of the National Commission on Law Observance and Enforcement (Wickersham Commission):

> The parolee will find himself continuously under the eyes of the State. Society need not wait until he is convicted for the commission of another crime in order to lock him up again. The slightest deviation from the straight and narrow path will bring him back within the prison walls. Parole may be a method of punishment, but more than that, it is a method of prevention second to none (1931:130).

It is important, however, to underscore that the emphasis on the community was not simply reflected in a concern for its protection, but clearly for its values as well. It was held that the offender engaged in behavior that must be condemned, and that an appropriate penalty must be paid for the damage that he had done. The all-powerful state could reduce this penalty, provided certain conditions were met. First, contrition for the failure to observe society's values was usually necessary. Second, an indication was needed that the offender would adopt a life-style that showed a willingness to accept the values of the existing social order. Further, the National Commission on Law Observance and Enforcement said parole

> should aim to help the individual find a place in the community, a place which will entitle him to respect himself and to be respected by others, a place which will enable him

to make the most of himself and to discharge his responsibilities to those dependent upon him and to the community as a whole (1931:131).

It was not enough that the offender simply avoid future crime; he was expected to improve himself physically, morally, and spiritually as well.

A contemporary illustration of the persistence of this reform policy is found in an excerpt from one state's conditions of parole. These rules, governing the conduct of the individual parolee in that state, were in effect in 1968:

1. He shall proceed at once to place of employment secured for him, and approved by the Board of Pardons and there remain until he receives a copy of his final discharge properly signed and endorsed.
2. In case he finds it necessary to change his employment or residence, he shall first obtain the written consent of the Board of Pardons.
3. He shall, on the first day of each month, until his final release, report to the Chief State Probation Officer of said Board freely and truthfully in the order suggested, the following report of the previous month:
   a) Whether he has been constantly at work during last month. If not, why not? Number of days lost.
   b) What has been earned? Has it been paid? How spent, and what saved?
   c) Describe first the nature of his work, and second, his surroundings.
   d) What books, magazine articles or subjects have been read and impressed him, if any?
   e) What diversion or amusement taken?
   f) What church or other institution of moral training attended each Sunday?
   Said report must be certified by the person to whom he is paroled.
4. The person paroled shall in all respects conduct himself honestly, avoid evil associations, obey the law, and abstain from gambling and the use of intoxicating liquors. He shall not visit pool halls, or places of bad repute, and shall avoid the company and association of vicious people and shall at least once each Sunday attend some religious service or institution of moral training . . . (Rules of Parole, State of Nebraska, Board of Pardons, 1968).

Although usually not pronounced as emphatically as these, parole systems in the United States continue to demand conformity with community values and styles of life that may actually have little or no relationship to the reason a person originally committed a crime. For example, in 1968, Hawaii, Massachusetts, Missouri, New York, Ohio, and Pennsylvania each had as a condition of parole a prohibition against cohabitation with a woman not one's wife, although nonparolees were rarely, if ever, charged with such an offense in these states. The state of Virginia stipulated in 1968 that parolees must "live a clean, honest and temperate life."

Parole hearings under a classic reform system were often used as much as a device to allow the expression of community sentiment as to judge the fitness of the parolee. The National Commission on Law Observance and Enforcement, for example, described a parole hearing that was open to the public at which the inmate, his family, the prosecutor, and whoever else wished to appear were given an opportunity to make a case before the parole board. Though virtually every state today conducts its hearings in private, a number of states still inquire routinely of police or trial officials about their recommendations concerning inmates being considered for parole.

Consistent with its general emphasis on the community, the ideal parole board member in the era of clemency and control was a person of "good character" who could accurately represent its values and attitudes. Revocation of parole, when it occurred, was usually peremptory and could occur whenever one of the detailed list of rules laid down by the board was violated. Parole staff were expected to expend considerable effort to make certain that parole rules were enforced. It was common during this era to find parole officers located in police stations in close relationship to law-enforcement personnel. Assistance to the offender, if rendered, tended to be directed toward concrete services, such as finding employment, typically provided in a paternal manner, with the parolee's acceptance of the program designed by the parole officer necessary for continuation on parole. Parole officers who employ this style of supervision are still very much part of the present day parole scene (Ohlin et al., 1956; Glaser, 1969:292–99).

The Era of the Clinician

In the 1930s the notion of parole as therapy began to emerge, if not in actual practice, at least as the dominant ideology of the parole field. It is a view that emphasized a professional helping relationship within an authoritarian setting, and it shaped the character of parole systems for the next forty years.

In its idealized form this "rehabilitative policy" apparently placed low emphasis on the community and high stress on the individual's motivations. Much staff behavior and organizational structure were based on a medical model. The offender was often seen as "sick," because he had not been able to adjust to society. Efforts were made to make the prison resemble a hospital—a refuge—isolated from a troublesome environment, where professionals could work with the inmate. Although conformity to society's values was very much a concern, punishment became masked and tended to be presented as an incidental but inevitable control for deviation or an unwillingness to submit to treatment (Duffee & O'Leary, 1971). The therapist became the ideal staff figure. This model more than any other split treatment and custodial staff in the belief that therapy was the sphere of trained professionals. Custodial personnel were charged largely with maintaining a peaceful atmosphere and marshaling inmates between the active phases of programs.

As in the reform policy, there was an objection in the rehabilitation policy to legal interventions. The motivations of staff were beneficent and they were not to be hampered in their rehabilitative work by the sophistry and the legal jargon of lawyers. The harmonious atmosphere necessary for therapeutic change was not compatible with the procedural rights given normal and healthy citizens. It is absurd, argues the therapist in this model, to contest in adversary fashion what is best for offenders. Thus, states most committed to the "treatment" ideal, as measured by the amount of indeterminacy in sentencing or discretion delegated to parole authorities, are clearly more resistant to the appearance of counsel at a parole hearing than those jurisdictions with less full-blown professionalized, correctional establishments (O'Leary & Nuffield, 1972).

From the rehabilitation perspective, the offender is a person possessed of specific traits, usually traceable to early childhood experience, that must be modified through treatment so he can "adjust" more aptly to life in the free community. The public is best protected through the rehabilitation of the offender and that task was precisely defined by the Governor's Special Committee on Criminal Offenders in New York state:

The theory of rehabilitation may be stated as follows:
    1. There are certain personal characteristics that impede an individual's ability to function at a generally acceptable level in one or more basic social areas.

2. The difficulty in performing at a generally acceptable level in such areas significantly contributes to criminal conduct.
3. Treatment should be directed at overcoming the aforesaid personal characteristics.

Thus, the aim of rehabilitation is to treat those characteristics of the offender which are
inconsistent with the basic characteristics needed to function acceptably (1968:87).

The parole board with such an aim resembles a clinical review team in a hospital.
Concomitantly, there is an emphasis on "professionalizing" the board with persons well
versed in correctional and clinical sciences. The type of statutory qualifications increasingly required for parole board membership reflects this trend. The standards of
the American Correctional Association stress behavioral science and correctional
education and training (A.C.A., 1966:119).

Parole board hearings became directed toward determining if an inmate had
"progressed sufficiently" to be released. How this progress was to be measured was
described by a leading national standard-setting group for parole agencies:

Because an inmate's insight into his emotional problems can be very revealing of his
character, it is perhaps the most important element the board is called upon to evaluate.
For this reason, the board must inquire into the inmate's problems as he sees them. If
the prisoner thinks that his only problem is getting out or that his only problem is
alcohol, he has little or no understanding of his situation. On the other hand, if he is
aware of his immaturity, hostility, or insecurity and some of the causes behind them, he
is probably making progress (Advisory Council on Parole, 1963:64).

Parole rules under this system tended to be phrased in a positive vein (e.g., the
parolee shall maintain employment) but were sufficiently inclusive to permit revocation
for a wide variety of behavior if so recommended by a parole officer. Revocation
occurred when a rule was broken, but most of all when the breech was seen as an
indication of an attitude that pointed to the likelihood of further criminality. Return
to prison for parole violation at times was often analogized to return to a hospital
for further treatment after a patient relapsed.

This policy demanded professional skills for parole officers as well as for board
members. National standard-setting organizations declared that the most desirable
training for officers was the Master of Social Work degree (National Probation and
Parole Association, 1949). Great emphasis was placed on helping the offender by
means of a relationship with the parole officer; counseling in a one-to-one relationship became the prime tool of parole supervision. But beginning in the 1950s, increasing emphasis was placed on working with parolees in groups, especially groups
formed in a variety of specialized classifications, such as drug addicts (Yablonsky,
1959; Stafford, 1962).

During the 1960s an even richer array of programs developed that ranged from
partial residential programs to expanding use of behavioral modification techniques
(Keve, 1967). Among the major emergents were systematic criteria for the classification of offenders for assignment to specific kinds of treatment (Grant & Warren, 1963).
While several of these programs foreshadowed the beginnings of another era, their
thrust continued to be directed almost exclusively towards changing the characteristics
of the offender by imposing more or less control, by involving him in groups, by
manipulation of rewards, or by the use of volunteers—but always directed toward the
offender.

Reconciling concern for community protection with emphasis on a personal and benign relationship to the parolee created a sharp dilemma for the parole officer (Cressey, 1959). Some officials argued that parole officers can even be armed and assume policelike tasks without invalidating their casework function (Dressler, 1961: chap. 15). Others asserted that the problems of authority in parole only differ in degree from those in any casework relationship, and that they can be resolved in a similar way (Hardman, 1960). Rather than uneasy integration, another attempt to deal with the "treatment" versus "surveillance" conflict was to have staff who specialize in one of the two functions. Both California and New York thus have special parole-officer units trained for police work who are assigned investigative or surveillance tasks in special cases and are given special responsibility to maintain liaison with police agencies. Though such units may ease the problem, the balance between assistance and control continues to be one of the most difficult problems for parole organizations to resolve.

The System Era

Although its roots can be traced to a number of influences, perhaps the bench mark of this era was the publication of the reports of the President's Commission on Law Enforcement and Administration of Justice in 1967. Their chief idea was that correction had erred in placing too much emphasis on therapy directed toward the offender, and had not placed nearly enough stress on the community as a target for change (President's Commission, 1967b:7). Crime neither results from nor can be treated simply as a trait possessed by an offender; it is an event that arises and is defined in the network of relationships in which an offender lives. The neighborhood, peers, family, school, employment, and the criminal justice system itself are important forces in the life of the offender that must be modified if he is to avoid further criminality. The correctional task becomes one of creating realistic alternatives within the world of the offender through which he can find a life-style that is both satisfying to him and tolerable to the larger community. This view has been labeled a policy of reintegration, and it reflects a high emphasis on both the individual offender and the community (Empey, 1967).

There is no "ideal" staff member in this model. All are valued for the change skills they can bring to the task; the emphasis is on teamwork. Custodial staff is expected to participate as actively in the task of change as professional staff. Indeed, the distinctions between "professional" and "custodial" are blurred, while community workers and resources are sought. Prerelease and partial release programs are near the core of the reintegration program. The attempt is made to minimize all breaks with the community and to keep lines of communication open. The community itself is the center of treatment and the institution, when used, is located in the community of release. This strategy requires a wide range of resources and involves a highly flexible interaction between the offender, the community, and many correctional personnel (President's Commission, 1967b:chap. 1).

From this perspective, the parole authority's attention is directed toward a system of decisions and programs carried out in a variety of locations. It tends to be less involved with case-by-case decisions and directs more of its energy towards policy development and monitoring the decisions of many others. Supporting this development, the Joint Commission on Correctional Manpower and Training recommended that besides a central parole board, there should be a series of local boards made up of representatives from the central board, the community, and the institutions. The function of the central board would be much more that of an overseer than of a maker of decisions.

> Contrary to present practice, the Central Parole Board would not travel from institution to institution to hold routine hearings. Their approval would not be necessary to effectuate the parole of routine cases.
>
> Their primary functions would be:
> a) To establish general policies and develop guidelines for the exercise of judgment by Hearing Boards.
> b) To hear and act on appeals from inmates protesting the action of a Hearing Board in individual cases or directed against policies set by the Central Parole Board.
> c) To hear unusual cases which have major public concern (such as the early release of a person convicted of a heinous crime or the parole of a notorious offender) or other cases at their discretion.
> d) To promulgate guidelines for parole field workers relative to recommendations for parole revocations and to take final action, after a hearing, on such recommendations (Joint Commission on Manpower and Training, 1970:65).

Proposals similar to these also were endorsed by the National Advisory Commission on Criminal Justice, Standards and Goals (1973).

Potentially, the most far-reaching impact of the reintegration policy is in the methods used by the officers responsible for working with offenders. To begin with, changes in the character of institutional programming imply a considerable reallocation of resources. Since the major focus of correctional intervention is the community, the aim becomes to place as many inmates as possible, as soon as possible, into community activities through halfway houses, furloughs, and partial-release programs. Most of these actions require a substantial involvement of parole staff in programs that were traditionally exclusively institutional. Parole officers are expected in most of these programs to work with the offender while he is in custody as well as when he is in the community (Meiners, 1965; Seckel et al., 1973).

Correctional institutions in the community inevitably result in much closer interaction between the parole and institutional functions and there is a great deal of blurring between these two activities that formerly were relatively distinct (Burdman, 1969). One effect of such a change is to make it easier and more common for an offender to be moved from parole status to an institution for a short time period and back to parole again. Such policies have already been attempted in California and their continued use is advocated by some who have tried them. One of the major problems they confront, however, is the growing emphasis on due process, which may well impede the easy movement from parole to institutional programs.

Another way in which the new emphasis reflects itself is in its stress on the organization of community resources and the development of opportunities for parolees. The President's Commission described the task as follows:

> The task of corrections, therefore, includes building or rebuilding solid ties between offender and community, integrating or reintegrating the offender into community life— restoring family ties, obtaining employment and education, securing in the larger sense a place for the offender in the routine functioning of society. This requires not only efforts directed toward changing the individual offender, which has been almost the exclusive focus of rehabilitation, but also mobilization and change of the community and its institutions (1967b:7).

Some have characterized the new role of the parole officer as the advocate rather than the counselor (Martin & Fitzpatrick, 1965). This implies that a high priority should be attached to changing institutions so that resources which were withheld from the offender are made available. For example, removing blocks to employment of adult offenders becomes a major activity. School policies that systematically reject youthful offenders are also targets of change. In some jurisdictions rather than simply case loads of clients, officers are assigned to specific community institutions, such as a school (President's Commission, 1967b:32), and parole agencies are moving their offices into areas of high delinquency to be closer to community forces and activities (Seckel et al., 1973).

Volunteers are also being sought more extensively, not only for the skills they bring in helping individual offenders, but also because of the bridge they represent to the larger community (Joint Commission on Manpower and Training, 1969). The use of the ex-offender on the parole and aftercare staff is also growing. They serve in a variety of roles depending upon their skills and experience but, most importantly, they serve as a model for other offenders; they tend to destigmatize the offender label and thereby increase the pathways for offender reentry into the community (Joint Commission on Manpower and Training, 1968).

Willingness to use a wide variety of skills under a reintegration policy has also meant reduction in the drive by administrators for the employment of staff with specific credentials in the parole field. The influence of these trends on the traditional intimate relationship between social work and parole work will depend in part upon the evolution of the social-work discipline, in part on the effectiveness of new academic programs in criminology and criminal justice, and most important, on what happens to parole itself.

THE FUTURE OF PAROLE

Beginning in the late 1960s and gaining increasing strength in the 1970s were demands for substantial reforms in parole practices in the United States. Hearings of the House Committee on the Judiciary in 1972 (Hearings on HR 13118, Serial No. 15) gave focus to these demands. The emergence of the "political prisoner" and the events associated with that concept—the Attica riot and the Soledad Brothers—gave further impetus to the push for reform (Citizens' Inquiry on Parole and Criminal Justice, 1974). The direction and velocity of this thrust for change is not totally clear but some of its dimensions and the dilemmas they pose can be traced.

Changes in other parts of the criminal justice system produce important changes in parole populations. Research findings have raised severe questions about the extent of corrections' capacity to change individuals, particularly in institutions (Robison & Smith, 1971). One effect of this evidence, although certainly not solely because of it, is the strong trend towards handling offenders through alternatives to prisons and training schools. This increases the extent to which the offenders ultimately institutionalized are those perceived to present the most difficult behavior problems and those with the worst records of criminality. They are seen as needing stronger measures of control than those employed for most of the persons formerly incarcerated. Thus, while the criminal justice system in general becomes more reintegration centered, parole in specific cases comes under increasing pressure to adopt programs with greater measures of control.

Technological advances are rapidly increasing the probabilities that modern variants of the reform policy, with its stress on conformity through surveillance, can be developed. Schwitzgebel (1971), for one, has demonstrated a prototype miniature electronic device which permits an observer to track an offender at all times and to send signals to the offender to prompt certain kinds of conforming behavior. He argues that such a system, in the long run, may be more humanitarian and effective, especially for offenders who pose a high risk and who would remain in confinement unless increased control were available. Presently, the use of this type of device is rejected as abhorrent to the values of a democratic society. Time alone will tell whether such measures would be as abhorrent if employed with a parole population increasingly perceived as difficult or dangerous.

The extent to which a reintegration policy continues will also depend on how much the community will accommodate to change and the degree to which it will permit one of its tax-supported crime-control agencies to foster it. It is quite possible to place offenders in local correctional facilities and carry out essentially the same program of person-directed therapy as was formerly conducted in a distant facility. But a reintegration stance involves more than a simple geographic shift of facilities; it emphasizes social reconstruction as well through a continuing process of community change. As three vigorous proponents of a reintegration strategy put it when speaking of juvenile correctional agencies:

> Will existing agencies dealing with delinquency continue to function to maintain, and to reinforce, the *status quo*—that is will these agencies continue to remain committed to conservatism? Or will these agencies, or many of them at least, come over to the side of domestic reform in the struggle for equality and justice for the nation's poor? (Martin et al., 1970:175)

Whether such an undertaking is really feasible for a parole agency has yet to be demonstrated. Some correctional officials doubt it and are quite conservative in their estimate of the extent to which correctional programs can go in the direction of community change. One head of a juvenile parole program has argued: "because of community opposition, the objectives of a correction system must be modest. . . . Change strategies for community reintegration of offenders should be the responsibility of the community, not of the correctional system. . . . More appropriate for the correctional system is the modest goal of preparing clients for treatment, not performing treatment" (Weber, 1969:128–30).

Few public parole agencies have attempted a vigorous advocacy and conflict model of community change. The history of community-action projects under the Office of Economic Opportunity and its predecessor, the President's Committee on Delinquency and Youth Crime, makes it clear that limits do exist which, if transgressed, can defeat the program (Marris & Rein, 1967; Moynihan, 1969). Probably, the extent to which official parole agencies can openly and actively press for broad-based social change is quite limited. Of necessity they will restrict their efforts to specific tasks, such as job development for their clients and opportunities for them to obtain freely those community health, education, and welfare services which do exist. Beyond this, reform will likely depend on other organizations that can more openly and vigorously press for adequate housing or changes in community educational policies.

In any case it is simplistic to think that any general policy suffices for the wide variety of needs of those on parole. The variations of personal and social problems confronting these offenders are too enormous. They need a number of alternative styles, from no treatment at all to a variety of specific and carefully controlled programs. Perhaps the most discouraging experiments in parole supervision were those that sought to test the thesis that reducing case loads so existing services might be given more intensively to all parolees would reduce recidivism.

One of these efforts, the San Francisco Project, involved an experiment in which federal parolees and probationers were randomly assigned to one of four kinds of case loads: (1) "minimum," in which one officer handled several hundred cases and offenders were required only to submit a monthly written report; (2) "regular," in which officers were responsible for approximately sixty-five cases and for completing a number of probation investigations for the court; (3) "ideal," with forty cases and only a limited number of investigations; and (4) "intensive," in which case loads were comprised of approximately twenty offenders who were contacted at least once weekly (Lohman et al., 1966). At the end of two years, if technical violations of conditions were ignored, there were no significant differences in violation rates among the four types of caseloads (Lohman et al., 1967). The researchers concluded that random assignment to case loads that varied only in intensity of supervision did not produce differences in failure rates.

The San Francisco Project supplemented a ten-year series of controlled experiments undertaken by the California Department of Corrections in its Special Intensive Parole Unit. A number of combinations of case load size at release and length of supervision in such special case loads before transfer to regular case loads were attempted in successive series. The results were almost uniformly negative. Fifteen-man case loads with three months of supervision showed no reduction in parole failures; thirty-man case loads for six months gave similar results; thirty-five-man case loads for one year showed some improvement for the middle-risk parolee, none for the high- or low-risk (Havel & Sulka, 1962); and, fifteen- and thirty-man case loads that matched grossly defined types of agents and parolees produced few important findings. In the last instance, the researcher attributed a large part of the results to the lack of precision in the design of the study (Havel, 1965).

The project that broke most completely from the notion that an increase of standardized services through reduced case loads would reduce recidivism was the Community Treatment Project of the California Youth Authority (Warren, 1969). This involved classification of offenders by an elaborate measure of interpersonal maturity or "I-level," and use of treatment techniques that were specifically designed for each "I-level" type. The treatments ranged from firm, controlling programs for manipulative youths to supportive and relatively permissive approaches for those assigned to an "I-level" category including neurotic and anxious youngsters. With certain exclusions, offenders were randomly assigned to ten-man case loads in the community, each of which was designed to carry out treatments consistent with a particular "I-level" classification, or to a term in a training school followed by regular parole supervision (Grant & Warren, 1962; Warren & Palmer, 1965). The results of the project were impressive. After twenty-four months those assigned to special case loads had a violation level of 39 percent while those who were assigned to a regular program had a 61 percent failure rate. Of interest also was the variation in success rates by "I-level" types (Palmer et al., 1968). Some researchers argue that some of the results of this research should be attributed to differences in official reaction to the behavior of those in special case loads as opposed to those in regular ones (Hood & Sparks, 1970:207), rather than to improvements in the offenders, but the results in the context of other research efforts described by Stuart Adams (1967) make the argument for differential treatment fairly strong.

One source of concern is the growing size and bureaucratization of corrections.

As a case in point, although parole authorities argue they are short of manpower, it is also true that during the 1960s especially, the size of correctional agencies, particularly probation and parole departments, grew sharply. Table 9 shows the number of probation and parole officers in the United States between 1957 and 1970. The number grew more than 2½ times. With the accelerating infusion of federal funds and the stress on community-based programs, the probabilities of continued expansion are quite high. In combination with the movement toward the consolidation of agencies cited earlier, correctional services are now and will be in the future increasingly delivered through large bureaucracies. And one of the oft-noted characteristics of such bureaucracies, as typically constituted, is their inability to adapt readily to change (Bennis & Slater, 1968:53).

Correctional bureaucracies are no exception. Parole organizations are typically organized with a rigid hierarchy of command that tends to push for standardized and routinized behavior in the agency. Such command techniques also tend to be associated with relatively rigid parole-officer behavior highly directed toward the control of parolees and with little capacity for flexibility and adaptability (Piven, 1961). The keystone of a reintegration program is an agency that is responsive to the client and the community. Unless correctional organizations develop structures that are much more flexible and susceptible to influence by those who deal with them, it is doubtful that a reintegration philosophy can prevail (O'Leary & Duffee, 1971b). Nelson and Lovell argue that the development of new forms of correctional organizations is crucial:

> The rationale for dispersion of correctional services, however, goes well beyond a general concern for bureaucratic stagnation and constraint. . . . The successful transition from a predominantly institutional to a predominantly community-based system of corrections will depend upon developing leadership, freedom for innovation, and commitment of human and financial resources close to the locus of action rather than in geographically and hierarchically distant power centers (1969:8).

Another perspective having important implications for changing parole practices sees the parole agency as a social system supporting a specific decision culture that defines the "correct" ways of responding to situations. This culture is manifested, for example, by parole board members tending, over time, to display, with slight individual variations, a consistency in response to case situations of which they may be only marginally aware (Gottfredson & Ballard, 1966). It is as if a decision scale existed for various offenders, offenses, and situations; a scale rarely, if ever, articulated, but which new parole board members quickly learn from the old and by which inmates predict and judge the appropriateness of a board's actions.

TABLE 9
NUMBER OF PROBATION AND PAROLE
OFFICERS IN THE UNITED STATES

Service	1957	1970
Federal	469	608
State	2,233	6,126
Local	6,618	18,024
Total	9,320	24,758

Source: N.C.C.D., 1970.

The process by which a parole organization shapes and maintains its decision culture among parole officers has been described as a complex mix of official rules and unofficial sanctions (Martinson et al., 1964). There is by no means a strict uniformity of norms throughout an organization; considerable variation from one office to the next can occur. But, however they are distributed, these norms have profound and direct meaning for the parolees subjected to them (Studt, 1967). They can determine to a significant degree which parolees remain on the streets and which are returned as parole violators, particularly in parole systems where a sizeable proportion of offenders are returned to prison for reasons other than conviction for new criminal offenses. Robison and Takagi (1970) have clearly demonstrated the power of the decision norms in various parole offices to shape revocation rates independently of the type of parolee supervised. They also point out that such norms have an enormous capacity to withstand changes in official policies.

The resistance to change implicit in present organizational structures and decision cultures makes the rapid infusion of a reintegration philosophy into parole practice problematic. Yet, there are other forces that foster the growth of this philosophy and other characteristics of the system era; for example, the decentralized decision-making style for parole boards is already evident in the use of hearing officers to conduct hearings in several jurisdictions, notably in California and the federal boards. The growth of partial release programs and consolidated correction departments will increasingly require such delegation, as parole decisions require frequent consultation with a wide variety of institutional and community-based personnel. Such decentralized decision-making is also supported by the growing development of base expectancy statistics that, through a statistical reporting system, can quickly cue a central authority when major variations from expected decisions occur. The development of reliable methods of control increases the probabilities of decentralization of decision-making.

Much wider involvement of citizens in the whole parole process is also inevitable. There has been a significant change in the perception of the nature of government since the Great Depression. Then, conventional wisdom decreed that the expert should be freed and resources provided him so that he could perform his tasks efficiently. There has been a growing disenchantment with that view. As Remington (1963) points out, a considerable effort is under way to restrict the power of the government expert and to hold him more accountable for his actions. One symptom of this movement is the stress on due process in parole, which inevitably forces an articulation of the reasons for decisions, and thus sets the stage for tests of the appropriateness of policies now cloaked under the names of expertise and discretion.

A rapid emergent in the 1970s is the "parole contract" procedure. This combines reform and clinical or reintegration objectives with an effort to reduce protests that the powerlessness of prisoners to predict or explain parole board decisions about their confinement makes the indeterminate sentence a cruel and unusual punishment. For example, under "contract programming" pioneered in a Minnesota Department of Corrections' controlled experiment, an "Institutional Performance Agreement" is negotiated with a newly admitted inmate while he is in the initial diagnostic center. This contract stipulates what the prisoner agrees to pursue or to accomplish between specified dates, and it promises that if he does these things he will be paroled on a stated date. If the inmate fails to meet one of the conditions to which he has agreed, or if he requests it, a revised contract can be negotiated. Typical contract clauses include:

I will enroll in high school in December 1971 and graduate in June 1972. To develop positive social relationships and civic responsibility, I will actively participate in

Alcoholics Anonymous activities as evidenced by 80% attendance at general meetings and 90% attendance at squad meetings. A condition of parole will be continued active participation in an AA chapter.

To reduce the number of my vocational interest areas from 7 to those 3 in which successful employment seems best indicated, I will undergo vocational aptitude testing.

I will develop the ability to accept criticism by actively participating in the Gavel Club with 85% attendance from January 1972 to June 1973.

Under a U.S. Department of Labor grant the American Correctional Association in 1973 was establishing controlled experiments in three states involving "Mutual Agreement Programs" of inmates to be paroled to halfway houses, from which they would attend academic or vocational training and receive cost-of-living stipends under personally negotiated contract terms.

These and other trends imply not just the simple narrowing of discretion, but a basic reallocation of authority. Diffusion of governmental power is becoming a common cause for the liberal as well as the conservative (Leonard, 1968:29). Governmental agencies of all kinds, for example, are under increasing pressure for direct participation by citizens in shaping their policies, and parole is not exempt from these pressures. In fact, there are fairly clear indications of the forms of such involvement (O'Leary, 1969). One is the increase in volunteers who work directly with offenders.

Another kind of citizen involvement is aimed more directly toward the development of policy. For example, the President's Commission recommended the formation of advisory groups that would give citizens the opportunity to participate directly in the formulation of correctional programs (1967b:109). The Joint Commission on Correctional Manpower and Training (1970:65) similarly recommended that parole hearing boards number among their membership a representative of the local community as well as professional parole and institutional personnel. The rationale for this kind of community involvement rests not only on the assumption that direct citizen intervention will give parole systems more direct touch with community attitudes, but that it provides an additional and important vehicle for the education of community leaders who can, in turn, develop support for correctional programs and influence the "gate keepers" of opportunities that are so crucial to the success of a reintegration policy.

The infusion of a variety of community representatives into parole programs, to say nothing of the complexities inherent in the use of ex-offenders and paraprofessionals, increases pressures to reorganize the basic mechanisms by which parole supervision services are delivered. The development of team methods of parole supervision to replace the traditional one-to-one, parolee–parole officer relationship is hastened by these changes.

It is increasingly clear that a single parole officer cannot possibly meet the wide variety of needs represented in the case load of parolees for which he is responsible. That requires an array of resources, some of which will be found in the parole agency but most of which will be found in the community. Increasingly, the parole officer's task becomes one of mobilizing those resources and working cooperatively with a variety of persons as well as the offender. The stress on this type of team supervision is supported by similar movements in many types of human-service programs, such as in education, mental health, and welfare. It is also congruent with a general evolution towards more open and accessible organizations.

Increasingly the successful organization is identified as one that has a great capacity for ongoing changes as it responds to the forces that play upon it from its external world. It is this open system that, perhaps more than anything else, may foster the continued growth of a reintegration policy. For of the models of correction, only reintegration is open by nature. Rehabilitation seeks to change the offender so he will adjust to an environment that is unchanging, or in which changes are ignored. Reform seeks to satisfy the environment without concern for the offender. Reintegration alone seeks to shape community forces while simultaneously helping the offender to cope with the realities of those forces.

REFERENCES

Adams, Stuart.
    1967   "Some findings from correctional caseload research." Federal Probation 31(December):48–57.

Advisory Council on Parole.
    1963   Guides for Parole Selection. New York: National Council on Crime and Delinquency.

American Bar Association (A.B.A.)
    1968   Standards Relating to Sentencing Alternatives and Procedures. American Bar Association Project on Standards for Criminal Justice. Chicago: American Bar Association.

American Correctional Association (A.C.A.)
    1966   Manual of Correctional Standards. Washington, D.C.: American Correctional Association.

American Friends Service Committee.
    1971   Struggle for Justice. New York: Hill & Wang.

American Law Institute.
    1962   Model Penal Code (Proposed Official Draft). Philadelphia: American Law Institute.

Arluke, Nat.
    1969   "A summary of parole rules: 13 years later." Crime and Delinquency 15(April):267–274.

Arnold, William.
    1970   Juveniles on Parole. New York: Random House.

Attorney General's Survey of Release Procedures.
    1939   Parole, vol. 4. Washington, D.C.: U.S. Government Printing Office.

Barry, John V.
    1958   Alexander Maconochie of Norfolk Island. London: Oxford University Press.
    1960   "Alexander Maconochie, 1787–1816," in Hermann Mannheim (ed.), Pioneers in Criminology. Chicago: Quadrangle Books.

Bennett, James V.
    1961   "Countdown for judicial sentencing." Federal Probation 25(September): 22–26.

Bennis, Warren, and Phillip Slater.
    1968   The Temporary Society. New York: Harper & Row.

Bruce, A. A., E. W. Burgess, and A. J. Harno.
    1928   The Workings of the Indeterminate Sentence Law and the Parole System in Illinois. Springfield: State of Illinois.

Burdman, Milton.
    1969   "Realism in community-based correctional services." Annals of the American Academy of Political and Social Science 381 (January) :71–80.

Citizens' Inquiry on Parole and Criminal Justice.
    1974   Report on New York Parole. New York: The Citizens' Inquiry.

Cohen, Fred.
    1969   The Legal Challenge to Corrections. Washington, D.C.: Joint Commission on Correctional Manpower and Training.

Columbia Law Review.
    1960   "Statutory structure for sentencing felons to prison." 60 (December) :1134–1172.

Cressey, Donald R.
    1959   "Professional correctional work and professional work in corrections." National Probation and Parole Association Journal 5 (January) :1–15.

Dawson, Robert.
    1969   Sentencing: The Decision as to Type, Length and Conditions of Sentence. Boston: Little, Brown.

Dressler, David.
    1961   Probation and Parole. New York: Columbia University Press.

Duffee, David, and Vincent O'Leary.
    1971   "Models of correction: an entry in the Packer-Griffiths debate." Criminal Law Bulletin 7 (May) :329–352.

Empey, LaMar T.
    1967   Alternatives to Incarceration. Washington, D.C.: U.S. Government Printing Office.

Evjen, Victor.
    1962   "Current thinking on parole prediction tables." Crime and Delinquency 8 (July) :215–238.

Giardini, G. I.
    1958   "Good time—placebo of correction." American Journal of Correction 20 (April) :3–5.
    1959   The Parole Process. Springfield, Ill.: Thomas.

Glaser, Daniel.
    1962   "Prediction tables as accounting devices for judges and parole boards." Crime and Delinquency 8 (July) :239–258.
    1966   "The prospect for corrections," in Charles S. Prigmore (ed.), Manpower and Training for Corrections. New York: Council on Social Work Education.
    1969   The Effectiveness of a Prison and Parole System. Abridged Edition. Indianapolis: Bobbs-Merrill.

Glaser, Daniel, Fred Cohen, and Vincent O'Leary.
    1966   The Sentencing and Parole Process. Washington, D.C.: U.S. Government Printing Office.

Gottfredson, Don.
1961   "Comparing and combining subjective and objective parole predictions."
        Research Newsletter, California Department of Corrections (September–
        December):11–17.
1967   "Assessment and prediction methods in crime and delinquency," in Presi-
        dent's Commission on Law Enforcement and Administration of Justice, Task
        Force Report: Juvenile Delinquency and Youth Crime. Washington, D.C.:
        U.S. Government Printing Office.

Gottfredson, Don, and Kelley Ballard.
1964   The Parole Decision: Some Agreements and Disagreements. Vacaville,
        Calif.: Institute for the Study of Crime and Delinquency.
1966   "Difference in parole decisions associated with decision makers." Journal of
        Research in Crime and Delinquency 3(July):112–119.

Gottfredson, Don, Marcus Neithercutt, Peter Venezia, and Ernst Wenk.
1970   A National Uniform Parole Reporting System. Davis, Calif.: National Pro-
        bation and Parole Institutes.

Gottfredson, Don, Leslie Wilkins, Peter Hoffman, and Susan Singer.
1973   The Utilization of Experience in Parole Decision Making, A Progress Re-
        port. NCCD Research Center. Davis, Calif.: National Council on Crime and
        Delinquency.

Governor's Special Committee on Criminal Offenders.
1968   Preliminary Report. New York: the Committee.

Grant, Marguerite, and Martin Warren.
1962   An Evaluation of Community Treatment for Delinquents. CTP Research
        Report No. 1. Sacramento: California Department of the Youth Authority.
1963   "Alternatives to institutionalization." Children 19(July–August):147–152.

Grunhut, Max.
1948   Penal Reform. London: Oxford University Press.

Hall, Jay, Martha Williams, and Louis Tomaino.
1966   "The challenge of correctional change: the interface of conformity and com-
        mitment." Journal of Criminal Law, Criminology and Police Science 57
        (December):493–503.

Hardman, Dale.
1960   "The function of the probation officer." Federal Probation 24(September):
        3–10.

Havel, Joan.
1965   Special Intensive Parole Unit, Phase IV: The Parole Outcome Study. Re-
        search Report No. 13. Sacramento: California Department of Corrections.

Havel, Joan, and Elaine Sulka.
1962   Special Intensive Parole Unit, Phase III. Research Report No. 3. Sacra-
        mento: California Department of Corrections.

Hayner, Norman S.
1958a   "Sentencing by an administrative board." Law and Contemporary Problems
        23(Summer):477–494.
1958b   "Why do parole board members lag in the use of prediction scores?" Pa-
        cific Sociological Review 1(Fall):73–83.

Hood, Roger, and Richard Sparks.
  1970　Key Issues in Criminology. New York: McGraw-Hill.
Iowa Law Review.
  1968　"Due process: the right to counsel in parole release hearings." 54(December):497–507.
Joint Commission on Correctional Manpower and Training.
  1968　Offenders as a Correctional Manpower Resource. Washington, D.C.: Joint Commission on Correctional Manpower and Training.
  1969　Volunteers Look at Corrections. Washington, D.C.: Joint Commission on Correctional Manpower and Training.
  1970　Perspectives on Correctional Manpower and Training. Washington, D.C.: Joint Commission on Correctional Manpower and Training.
Kadish, Sanford.
  1961　"The advocate and the expert counsel in the peno-correctional process." Minnesota Law Review 45(Fall):803–841.
Kastenmeier, Robert, and Howard Eglit.
  1973　"Parole release decision making: rehabilitation, expertise and the demise of mythology." American University Law Review 22(Spring):477–525.
Keve, Paul.
  1967　Imaginative Programming in Probation and Parole. St. Paul: University of Minnesota Press.
Killinger, George C.
  1951　"Parole and other release procedures." Pp. 361–379 in Paul W. Tappan (ed.), Contemporary Correction. New York: McGraw-Hill.
Kimball, Edward, and Donald J. Newman.
  1968　"Judicial intervention in correctional decisions: threat and response." Crime and Delinquency 14(January):1–13.
Lejins, Peter.
  1967　"National crime data reporting system: proposal for a model." Pp. 197–200 in President's Commission on Law Enforcement and Administration of Justice, Task Force Report: Crime and Its Impact: An Assessment. Washington, D.C.: U.S. Goverment Printing Office.
Leonard, George.
  1968　"A new liberal manifesto." Look 32(May 28):29.
Lohman, Joseph, Albert Wahl, and Robert Carter.
  1966　The San Francisco Project: The Minimum Supervision Caseload. Research Report No. 8. Berkeley: University of California School of Criminology.
  1967　The San Francisco Project: Classification Criteria for Establishing Caseload Models. Research Report No. 12. Berkeley: University of California School of Criminology.
Mannheim, Herman, and Leslie T. Wilkins.
  1955　Prediction Methods in Relation to Borstal Training. London: H. M. Stationery Office.
Marris, Peter, and Martin Rein.
  1967　Dilemmas of Social Reform. New York: Atherton Press.

Martin, John, and Joseph Fitzpatrick.
1965   Delinquent Behavior: A Redefinition of the Problem. New York: Random House.

Martin, John, Joseph Fitzpatrick, and Robert Gould.
1970   The Analysis of Delinquent Behavior: A Structural Approach. New York: Random House.

Martinson, Robert, Gene Kassebaum, and David Ward.
1964   "A critique of research in parole." Federal Probation 28(September):34–38.

Meehl, Paul E.
1954   Clinical versus Statistical Prediction. Minneapolis: University of Minnesota Press.

Meiners, Robert.
1965   "A halfway house for parolees." Federal Probation 29(June):47–52.

Moran, F. A.
1945   "The origins of parole," in Yearbook. New York: National Probation Association.

Moynihan, Patrick.
1969   Maximum Feasible Misunderstanding. New York: Free Press.

National Advisory Commission on Criminal Justice, Standards and Goals.
1973   Task Force Report on Corrections. Washington, D.C.: U.S. Government Printing Office.

National Commission on Law Observance and Enforcement.
1931   Report on Penal Institutions, Probation and Parole. Washington, D.C.: U.S. Government Printing Office.

National Commission on Reform of Federal Criminal Law.
1970   Study Draft of a New Federal Criminal Code. Washington, D.C.: U.S. Government Printing Office.

National Conference on Parole.
1957   Parole in Principle and Practice. New York: National Probation and Parole Association.

National Council on Crime and Delinquency (N.C.C.D.)
1966   Corrections in the United States. New York: National Council on Crime and Delinquency. Reprinted as Appendix A, President's Commission on Law Enforcement and Administration of Justice, Task Force Report: Corrections (Washington, D.C.: U.S. Government Printing Office, 1967).
1970   Probation and Parole Directory. Sixteenth Edition. New York: National Council on Crime and Delinquency.
1972a   "Model sentencing act—second edition." Crime and Delinquency 18(October):340–370.
1972b   Parole Decision-Making. Reports 1–9. Davis, Calif.: National Council on Crime and Delinquency Research Center.

National Parole Institutes.
1966   Selection for Parole. New York: National Council on Crime and Delinquency.
1969   Report on XIV Parole Institute. New York: National Council on Crime and Delinquency.

1972   The Organization of Parole Systems. Second Edition. New York: National
       Council on Crime and Delinquency.

National Probation and Parole Association.
1949   Standards for the Selection of Probation and Parole Personnel. New York:
       National Probation and Parole Association.

Nelson, Elmer K., and Catherine Lovell.
1969   Developing Correctional Administrators. Washington, D.C.: Joint Commis-
       sion on Correctional Manpower and Training.

Newman, Charles.
1968   Sourcebook on Probation, Parole and Pardons. Third Edition. Springfield,
       Ill.: Thomas.

Newman, Donald J.
1966   Conviction: The Determination of Guilt or Innocence Without Trial. Bos-
       ton: Little, Brown.

New York University Law Review.
1963   "Parole: a critique of its legal foundation and conditions." 38(June):702–
       739.

Ohlin, Lloyd E.
1951   Selection for Parole. New York: Russell Sage Foundation.

Ohlin, Lloyd E., Herman Piven, and Donnell Pappenfort.
1956   "Major dilemmas of the social worker in probation and parole." National
       Probation and Parole Journal 2(July):211–225.

Ohlin, Lloyd E., and Frank Remington.
1958   "Sentencing structure: its effect upon systems for the administration of crim-
       inal justice." Law and Contemporary Problems 23(Summer):495–507.

O'Leary, Vincent.
1969   "Some directions for citizen involvement in correction." Annals of the
       American Academy of Political and Social Science 381(January):99–108.

O'Leary, Vincent, and David Duffee.
1971a "Correctional policy: a classification of goals designed for change." Crime
       and Delinquency 17(October):342–386.
1971b "Managerial behavior and correctional policy." Public Administration Re-
       view 31(November–December):603–616.

O'Leary, Vincent, and Joan Nuffield.
1972   "Parole decision making characteristics: report of a national survey." Crim-
       inal Law Bulletin 8(September):651–680.

Palmer, Theodore B., Virginia V. Neto, Dennis A. Johns, James K. Turner, and John
       W. Pearson.
1968   Community Treatment Project: Seventh Progress Report. Sacramento: Cali-
       fornia Department of the Youth Authority.

Piven, Herman.
1961   Professionalism and Organizational Structure. Ph.D. dissertation, Columbia
       University.

Platt, Anthony.
1969   "The rise of the child-saving movement: a study in social policy and correc-
       tional reform." Annals of the American Academy of Political and Social
       Science 381(January):21–38.

President's Commission on Law Enforcement and Administration of Justice.
   1967a   The Challenge of Crime in a Free Society. Washington, D.C.: U.S. Government Printing Office.
   1967b   Task Force Report: Corrections. Washington, D.C.: U.S. Government Printing Office.

Remington, Frank.
   1963   The Jurist Frame of Reference in Parole. New York: National Parole Institutes, N.C.C.D. (mimeographed).

Remington, Frank J., and Donald J. Newman.
   1962   "The Highland Park Institute on sentencing disparity." Federal Probation 26(March):3–7.

Robison, James, and Gerald Smith.
   1971   "The effectiveness of correctional programs." Crime and Delinquency 17 (January):67–80.

Robison, James, and Paul Takagi.
   1970   "The parole violator as an organizational reject." Pp. 233–254 in Robert Carter and Leslie T. Wilkins (eds.), Probation and Parole: Selected Readings. New York: Wiley.

Rubin, Sol.
   1956   "A legal view of probation and parole conditions." National Probation and Parole Association Journal 2(January):33–37.

Rubin, Sol, with Henry Weihofen, George Edwards, and Simon Rosenweig.
   1963   The Law of Criminal Correction. St. Paul, Minn.: West Publishing Co.

Savides, Ellis C.
   1961   "A parole success prediction study." Research Newsletter, California Department of Corrections (September–December):4–10.

Schrag, Clarence.
   1971   Crime and Justice: American Style. Washington, D.C.: U.S. Government Printing Office.

Schwitzgebel, Ralph.
   1971   Development and Legal Regulation of Coercive Modification Techniques with Offenders. Washington, D.C.: U.S. Government Printing Office.

Seckel, Joachim, Esther M. Pond, and Carolyn B. Davis.
   1973   A Comparative Study of the Community Parole Center Program. Research Report No. 63. Sacramento: California Department of the Youth Authority.

Simon, Frances H.
   1971   Prediction Methods in Criminology. London: H.M. Stationery Office.

Stafford, Gordon H.
   1962   "Group counseling with parolees from county honor camps," in Norman Fenton (ed.), Explorations in the Use of Group Counseling in the County Correctional Programs. Palo Alto, Calif.: Pacific Books.

Studt, Elliot.
   1967   The Reentry of the Offender into the Community. Washington, D.C.: U.S. Government Printing Office.

Sutherland, Edwin H., and Donald R. Cressey.
   1970   Criminology. Eighth Edition. Philadelphia: Lippincott.

U.S. Bureau of Prisons.
   1967   State Prisoners: Admissions and Releases, 1964. National Prisoner Statistics. Washington, D.C.: U.S. Government Printing Office.
   1972   Prisoners in State and Federal Institutions for Adult Felony, 1970. National Prisoner Statistics. Washington, D.C.: Federal Bureau of Prisons (April).

University of Pennsylvania Law Review.
   1971   "The parole system." 120(November):284–377.

Warren, Marguerite Q.
   1969   "The case for differential treatment of delinquents." Annals of the American Academy of Political and Social Science 381(January):48–59.

Warren, Marguerite, and Theodore B. Palmer.
   1965   Community Treatment Project: Fourth Progress Report. Sacramento: California Department of the Youth Authority.

Weber, Robert J.
   1969   "Goals of community corrections: a redefinition," in Probation Management Institutes, Problems, Thoughts and Processes in Criminal Justice Administration. New York: National Council on Crime and Delinquency.

Wines, Frederick H.
   1910   Punishment and Reformation. Second Edition. New York: Crowell.

Yablonsky, Lewis.
   1959   "Group psychotherapy and psychodrama for drug addicts." National Probation and Parole Association Journal 5(January):63–70.

CHAPTER **26**

Probation Administration

John A. Wallace

Office of Probation, New York City

Within the field of corrections, probation is the newest program for handling convicted offenders. Essentially a twentieth-century development, probation is the "growth industry" in corrections.

The first probation officer was a volunteer, John Augustus, a Boston shoemaker. In 1841 he offered to assist offenders if the court would release them to his care. At the time of his death in 1859, his activities had gained recognition. The outgrowth was enactment in 1878 of the first probation statute, with provision for appointment of a salaried probation officer.

Before the present century, only six states had recognized in their statutes the word *probation*. Today each state has some form of probation system. In the main, state agencies administer adult probation systems while juvenile probation services are local functions. Within these generalizations, a wide variety of administrative patterns appear. The diversity is probably due to historical accident. Juvenile courts were local and developed their own probation services, while the states added probation to existing statewide parole services (President's Commission, 1967a). The probation services are administered either within the judicial branch of government or the executive branch; again, there is no consistency. Even local probation services are found in the executive branch.

The phenomenal growth of probation is revealed by the directories of the National Probation Association (1937, 1947) (later called National Probation and Parole Association, and still later National Council on Crime and Delinquency). The 1937 directory, covering only probation officers, showed a total of 3,898 for the state and federal governments, of whom 80 percent were regularly salaried probation officers and 20 percent had additional duties, such as sheriff, welfare worker, minister, attendance officer, attorney, or judge. These directories changed in 1947 to include both probation and parole staff. The expansion in probation staff nationally in the last twenty years is shown in Table 1. In 1970, only 2 percent of these personnel had other duties, such as county welfare worker or sheriff.

The *Task Force Report: Corrections* described probation as "the correctional treatment used for most offenders today" and as "likely to be used increasingly in the future" (President's Commission, 1967a:27). Its growth has indeed continued, often at an accelerated pace. The concern of this chapter is with this "growth industry," regardless of where it is administered. The same issues prevail whether the probation agency is administered by the state, county, or city, or whether it is located in the executive or judicial branch.

WHAT IS PROBATION?

In the first legislative enactment, the word *probation* was used without explanation or definition (Attorney General's Survey of Release Procedures, 1939:23). That situation is still found in many statutes. Practically every agency uses the word as a process. The *Standard Probation and Parole Act* of the National Council on Crime and Delinquency says: "Probation is a procedure under which a defendant . . ." (1955:2). The American Bar Association's Project on Standards for Criminal Justice refers to probation as a "sentence not involving confinement which imposes conditions and retains authority in the sentencing court . . ." (1970:9).

However, probation administration refers to more than a process; it connotes an organization, basically a service agency, designed to assist the court and to perform particular functions in the administration of criminal justice (A.C.A., 1966:98). These services traditionally are the investigation of persons convicted and supervision of those placed on probation. Some probation agencies have absorbed other functions, such as operating juvenile detention facilities, foster homes, psychiatric clinics, doing marital counseling, adoption investigations, handling support payments in domestic relations and divorce cases. The inclusion of additional functions is most often seen in local (county or city) probation systems involved in juvenile-court jurisdiction. The courts have undoubtedly urged such functions on the probation system. Administrators in this "growth industry" continually need to reassess the problem of the role and function of their agencies.

Drucker (1954:50–56) has aptly pointed out that answering the question, "What is our business?" is difficult and requires careful thought and study. He contends that "our business" is not determined by the producer but by the consumer, that is, by satisfying the wants of the consumer. That answer naturally evokes a second question: "What will or should our business be?" Answering these two questions should provide a better understanding of the purposes of probation investigation and supervision, and thus provide insight into future probation organization (see also Miller & Rice, 1967).

TABLE 1

EXPANSION OF PROBATION STAFF IN THE UNITED STATES

	1952	1963	1970
State Officers			
Probation only	178	556	750
Probation and parole	483	1,070	3,063
Local Officers			
Juvenile only	1,668	2,701	4,395
Adult only	1,220	1,219	1,807
Juvenile and adult	2,048	5,284	11,822

Sources: National Probation and Parole Association, 1952:xii; N.C.C.D., 1963:xii-xiii, 1970: xii-xiii.

Redefining the Purpose of the Presentence Investigation

To make a recommendation for disposition in a presentence report, a probation officer must make a decision. To pass sentence, a judge must also make a decision. We can predict with a fair degree of success the relationship between the recommendation and the actual disposition. With our present state of knowledge, we cannot predict with certainty the future success or failure of the decision. What is achieved in the presentence report is the presentation of information in the hope that, as a result, a better decision will be made. The model for the presentence report was taken from social work; essentially, it was a life history of the defendant. The information was organized under various captions similar to those a social agency would use, plus two peculiar to probation—offense and prior record.

The literature indicates that presentence reports serve five purposes: to assist the judge at time of disposition, to aid the institution if the defendant is committed, to aid the parole authority if the defendant is committed and is eligible for parole, to aid probation staff if the individual is placed on probation, and for research.

Presentence reports developed without careful thought as to their functions in the decision-making process, although their information is gathered to facilitate decision-making. The *San Francisco Project* (Robison et al., 1969) raised questions about the value for sentencing decisions of all the material presently contained in these reports. Using a "decision game," the project staff classified the material in a set of presentence reports under twenty-four subject headings commonly used by the probation staff. Each piece of information was reproduced on a 4 by 6 inch card, with a caption printed at the lower edge of the card to describe the information it contained. The cards were so arranged that only the lower edge showing the caption was visible, and all twenty-four titles were visible at the same time. Probation staff participating were allowed to collect information in any manner they desired, i.e., they could select any heading they wanted and secure that information. After each card had been used, they were asked if they could make a recommendation and, if not, they were permitted to select another card. When they had decided on their recommendation, they could use other cards and modify or change their decision if they so desired.

The results upset traditional ideas about presentence reports. Some decisions were made after only one card had been selected. The most cards required by any one probation officer was fourteen, but the average number used to make a decision was 4.7 cards. Only one card—the offense—was always selected prior to a decision. Significantly, the initial decision remained unchanged even though probation officers were required to select at least three more cards after their original decision, to see if they confirmed, modified, or rejected that initial decision.

The study suggests that probation staff regard only a few factors (primarily offense and prior record) as essential for their decision. Some factors, such as attitude, employment history, and marital status, were only of moderate importance. However, most of the data traditionally set out in the presentence report are not really used by probation staff to develop their recommendations.

Presentence reports were analyzed by Yona Cohn (1969:20) to determine if the work of the probation officer is actually based on a framework of diagnostically oriented casework. He examined the variables most frequently given in presentence reports and the variables significantly associated with court disposition, and concluded that "differences in the theoretical frameworks of the reporting probation officer and sentencing judge are not revealed" (p. 111).

In 1970 over 120 judges in New York City were questioned by an Interdepartmental Committee on Probation Reports to determine what classifications of information they deemed essential, desirable, or unessential in the presentence report. The judges were from two courts, one from the felony jurisdiction and the other covering misdemeanors. Their responses were strikingly similar, with only eight subjects deemed essential by 55 percent or more of the judges. The topics most selected were offense, mitigating circumstances, prior record, employment history, and drug involvement.

If we accept the premise that only a limited amount of information is used by probation staff and judges for decision-making about the sentence, then information relevant to the purpose of the report should suffice. This implies retraining staff to prepare briefer presentence reports, and consequent redeployment of limited staff resources.

Resistance to this proposal occurs because it upsets the traditional process of report writing done by probation staffs for years. Correctional institutions and parole boards question the brevity of such presentence reports, saying they need information that is now lacking, but users of the reports have a responsibility to demonstrate their informational needs. Each probation officer will gather more information in the course of an investigation than he will include in a report designed for the judge. For those individuals committed to correctional institutions, the probation agency could prepare a supplemental report to fulfill the needs of the institutions and/or parole boards. These reports would not strain clerical services because the presentence reports would be shorter for all cases.

Redeployment of staff resources also can be achieved through more rational standards for investigation work loads. With investigation reduced, more staff should become available for supervision or, more importantly, for other activities in which a probation agency could become involved. The adult probation agencies have often ignored or passed up opportunities to serve defendants and families prior to conviction. Traditionally, probation staff working with juvenile courts have helped to decide whether children should be detained or released pending hearing. Few probation agencies have undertaken a similar function in the adult courts.

Expanding Pretrial Services

One of the long-standing concerns in the administration of criminal justice has been the bail system and its injustices to the poor and the innocent alike. The Manhattan Bail Project was developed by the Vera Institute of Justice to learn what would happen in the fixing of bail if information were provided to the court at arraignment. The results were as predicted; the prospects of release on recognizance or parole are enhanced by added information (Ares & Sturz, 1962). The prototype of the Manhattan Bail Project has been adopted largely by private agencies, rather than by probation agencies.

In developing release on recognizance (ROR) programs, probation administrators must answer two questions: What information is needed by the judge for this type of decision? What staff should be used for the ROR program? The basic information used by most agencies in such "bail" programs is address, length of residence, employment, prior criminal record, and history of drinking or drug abuse. The question of the present offense is set aside because the defendant has not yet pled or been found guilty. Based on the premise that only limited information is collected and limitations are placed on the discretion in decision-making by the staff, the Office of Probation in New York City uses a civil service title of Investigator for their ROR program. The qualifications required are high-school education and two years of interviewing experience, in contrast to the educational requirement of a college degree for a probation officer. The salary of the investigator, of course, differs from that of the probation officer. In 1971, the title of Investigator Aide also was incorporated in this program, utilizing the "New Careers" concept. These investigator aides carry out basically clerical functions now done by investigators, go into the field to verify residence and employment, and to seek individuals who have been released and have missed court appearances. The aides are provided opportunities for education in order to upgrade their skills and qualify them for promotion to investigators.

Redefining the Purpose of Supervision

Supervision is generally discussed as being both a form of treatment for a probationer and, at the same time, providing control over the probationer. Treatment and control may be emphasized equally or only one may predominate. Probation staff working with juveniles are more likely to emphasize the treatment aspect, probably because juvenile courts have always been considered as designed to help the child. The control aspect may be emphasized for probation staff working with adults on the premise that adults arc supposed to know right from wrong and are responsible for their behavior. The emphasis is likely to be a reflection of the attitudes of the probation administrator. The emphasis may even shift as the person at the top changes his attitudes or when a new probation administrator is introduced.

The function of supervision, like that of investigation, has drawn heavily from social work, using the casework model. If supervision is used as a treatment program, the probationer has been defined literally as being sick and needing help or "rehabilitation." Some significant challenges of this concept have come in the last decade from students of social work. Elliot Studt (1967), instead of asking the purpose of supervision, has asked, "What is the parolee's task?" For the word *parolee* we can substitute *probationer*. In answering the question, she has used the concept of "passage of status," i.e., transition from one status to another. For example, engagement is a transition step from the status of a single person to that of a married person, or an employee goes through a transitional probationary period before achieving permanent employee status. An individual placed on probation goes through several transitions. The first is from a citizen to a defined status as a criminal deviant. The next transition is to the status of a person in the community but not completely free, i.e., as a probationer. A third transition comes when the person is no longer on probation. The question is how defendants make these transitions. Studt has proposed that the supervision function should be defined as establishing the general conditions most favorable for task success for a population of clients. The implications of this definition mean realigning some of the traditional assumptions and restructuring some activities traditionally used in probation supervision.

The restructuring follows if we are to develop those conditions deemed particularly favorable for successful status passage. Those conditions include: support at the initial point, plus tolerance for trial-and-error behavior; actively involving the individual in making decisions and acting on his own behalf; having the individual accept responsibility for increasingly difficult tasks; providing support by associates who are also experiencing the transitional status; and use of role models who represent a desired status.

Some conventionally held assumptions may have to be rethought and altered. One is the casework model, including the relationship between the probation officer and the defendant. Casework as a treatment program implies that the probation officer has the expertise to conduct treatment, and that the defendant should rely upon this expertise just as a patient uses the expertise of a physician. (This discussion presumes that case-workers have graduate education in social work, but such an assumption is questionable as only a minority of staff have such professional education. Casework theory asserts the right of the client to self-determination; however, probationers have not always been viewed as having rights.) Developing tolerance for trial-and-error behavior alters criteria for violations of probation. Support by associates also experiencing the transitional role means that probationers must be brought together. This contrasts with the practice of some courts and probation agencies, which insist that probationers refrain from associating with other probationers or ex-offenders. The introduction of role models who represent the desired status implies use of ex-probationers.

The term being used more and more today to describe this new model for corrections is *reintegration*. The emphasis is placed on the defendant and the community, in contrast to *rehabilitation*, where the emphasis is on the defendant alone. (See also Chapter 25 in this book in which Vincent O'Leary compares the rehabilitation and reintegration models.)

"Probation Department" or "Department of Court Services"

Traditionally, the organization with which we are concerned has been called "Probation Department" even after it added new and nonprobation functions. This is particularly true of local probation agencies. A quick look at the functions carried out by local "probation departments" indicates functions within the agency not implied in that title, but related by organizational design and administrative convenience, e.g., operation of juvenile detention facilities, probation camps, adoption investigations, collection of monies in support cases and divorce matters, marital counseling, and psychiatric clinics.

Traditionally, the head of a probation agency is the "Chief Probation Officer." As will be elaborated later, one often could question whether this person was considered as "first" among his peers. Although probation adopted the social-work model, the job of unit supervisor was established only many years after probation systems were launched. It was not until the mid-1950s that the federal probation system introduced the "Deputy Chief Probation Officer" and "Supervisor" positions into their systems.

For those organizations that have added functions beyond that of probation, a more descriptive title would be "Department of Court Services." Hennepin County, Minnesota, made that change of designation in the 1950s, but it has been followed by only a few agencies. More probation systems, however, are being headed today by a "Director of Probation." In 1971, New York state made that change in title for the heads of all local probation agencies by statute.

VALUES AND ADMINISTRATION

The base for all decisions is either facts, values, or a combination of these (Simon, 1957). Facts are used in decisions only as answering objective questions for which answers can be proved right or wrong. Routinized decisions are based essentially on facts, e.g., which finger is best to use in striking a typewriter key, what is the shortest route to go to the store, which form is used to prepare federal income tax reports, etc. As specific knowledge decreases, values play a larger and larger part in decision-making. However, in discussions, people often confuse facts and values, insisting that they are talking from a base of facts when actually they are attaching values to some knowledge. An illustration is the disagreement to be found in a probation staff appraising the same information, such as an arrest or conviction record. The staff is likely to have different views about the magnitude of an offense, which means that they have attached different values to a specific fact.

Administrators essentially deal in the arena of values, particularly as they develop policies. Most policy decisions are a choice of values. Actual knowledge on which to base a policy decision is very limited; untested assumptions may have been presented as though they were facts. However, careful scrutiny of the rationale for policy decisions will reveal that the predominant base in the decision is values. This is especially true in probation, where there is very limited knowledge, since only limited research has been done. An illustration is the policy that the same probation officer should do both investigation and supervision. The argument is based on the alleged "fact" that the same individual investigating and supervising a defendant will be able to do a more thorough job and the defendant does not have new people entering his life. That "fact" has never been validated; some limited studies indicate that most defendants in the course of their probation will encounter two or more probation officers because of staff turnover or the probationers' moving, requiring cases to be reassigned anyway. Values also enter into the preference of many officers for paper work rather than field work, or for inquiry in contacts with clients or others rather than assistance or counsel, as well as the fact that in many offices staff are evaluated primarily by their investigation reports, as that is the portion of their work producing the most tangible product.

The values held by administrators influence the destiny of their organizations. One of the best descriptions of the role of the administrator in corrections, by Street, Vinter, and Perrow in their book *Organization for Treatment* (1966:45–66), portrays executive leadership in three dimensions. First, executive leadership must formulate specific goals and basic policies that give meaning and direction to the organization. Second, the executive is the key link between the organization and its environment, receiving both mandates and resources from the environment and being held accountable by the external units for organizational performance. Third, the executive establishes a structure of roles and responsibilities within the organization that enables it to pursue its goals. This means defining tasks, allocating personnel, and managing the interdependent relations within the organization.

The probation administrator will make policy decisions either deliberately, unconsciously (e.g., by failure to make a decision, which, in fact, sets forth a policy for the agency), or will have them made for him by others even outside his organization. His values are the vital key to policy decisions. If he makes an organizational decision to change an objective or goal, such as moving from a rehabilitation model to a reintegration model, he immediately introduces conflict into his organization. The same thing will happen from the decision to shift from one frame of reference for administration (e.g., the classical approach) to another (e.g., a human relations approach). March and Simon (1958:112–35) suggest that organizations react to conflict by four major processes: problem solving, persuasion, bargaining, and politics. The processes are used, probably too many times, in an unconscious or random fashion. To be effective the probation administrator needs a conscious frame of reference if he is to be consistent in his actions, and to have a chance of gaining adherence to new policies being introduced. Otherwise, the conflict may be resolved only through power struggles and often futile attempts at imposition of decisions on still resistant factions.

Values help shape the role that the probation administrator will play in serving as the key link between the organization and its environment. The activities in which he engages to seek support for the organization may be influenced by personal likes and dislikes. His reactions when held accountable for organizational performance are likely to be selected from several choices; managers know what they like, what seems to work best for them.

Values enter again in designing the structure of roles and responsibilities within the organization to enable it to pursue its goals. Simon has indicated that the actual task of carrying out "an organization's objectives falls to the persons at the lowest level of the administrative hierarchy" (1957:2). In a probation agency, this person is the probation officer, for he is both a worker and a manager. He works in a system in which there are controls above him, but he is also a manager of those probationers for whom he has responsibility. The task of the probation administrator in selecting his objectives and establishing the structure of roles and responsibilities to carry out those objectives involves selecting the means of directing or influencing the probation staff. The choices are either: (1) imposing external constraints on the behavior of the employees, usually by decisions reached at higher levels in the organization; or (2) "establishing in the operative employee *himself* attitudes, habits and a state of mind which lead him to reach that decision which is advantageous to the organization" (Simon, 1957:11).

Orientation training is often discussed in terms of acquainting the new staff with the purposes of the organization and the way in which the organization conducts its business. It is through orientation that the new employee becomes acquainted with the values held by the organization, by the administrator, and by the staff itself. Becoming acquainted with the values of the organization occurs even if there is no formal orientation, because each new employee must learn the "ground rules" if he is to survive. Each new staff member brings to the organization his own set of values, implicit in his concept of how probation supervision is to be done. Those values may be modified by happenstance or by the deliberate actions of an administrator who designs orientation training to modify values. Ongoing staff training may add to the knowledge and skills of staff, but always the question of values must be considered and respected. Staff will not always be in accord as to what "probation" is and what methods they will use to achieve the objectives sought (McEachern, 1961:215). The values staff bring to the agency may change. Although the state of Wisconsin had more staff with a graduate degree in social work (36.2 percent) than most agencies, the basic identification of the staff was shown to be with the field of corrections, not social work (Miles, 1963).

Lessons from the Prison System

Ohlin has aptly pointed out:

> One of the major needs in the field of probation and parole is for evaluative research that would seek to define the effect of the formal and informal structure of the agency and its conflicting work orientations on the cases processed through the agency (1956:47).

This comment is still applicable, and there is probably even greater need today because probation is the "growth industry" of corrections.

Many similarities exist between correctional institutions and probation, and studies of prisons provide some understanding of problems and conflict encountered in probation systems. Cressey (1965) observed that the role of the guard or correctional officer is both that of manager and worker. The way "authority" is organized in prison is similar to probation—either based on rank or based on expertise. In prison, the guard is charged with the control of the inmate and with modifying or influencing the inmate's behavior. Specific criteria exist by which the guard can be judged on his first responsibility, e.g., was there a disturbance in the cell block. No specific criteria have ever been developed for the second task and, consequently, the guard is unable to know whether he is successful or not in influencing the inmate.

Similarly, a probation officer is charged with the control of the probationer, who is supposed to report to him, and with the task of influencing his behavior. If a probationer violates the rules in such a way that his conduct comes dramatically to public attention, the first questions usually asked deal with control, such as: When was the last time the probation officer saw the defendant? How often was the defendant seen? A probation officer's effectiveness theoretically could be examined by looking at the violation rate of the probationers, but this does not tell whether it was the probation officer's influence that successfully affected the probationers so they did not violate the rules.

If probation systems are to add new functions and classes of personnel other than probation officers or clerical staff, the prison systems can serve as an object lesson. Noncustodial personnel were added to prison organizations when education, vocational training, and rehabilitation became prison functions. The place and status of the new functions were determined in part by the amount of formal authority and position status given to the noncustodial personnel. In some systems, the formal authority and high status remained with the custodial staff, which meant the noncustodial personnel had limited influence on the prison organization. When the noncustodial personnel were given formal authority and position equal to those in charge of custody, those prisons were more likely to change from a custodial to a treatment orientation.

What plan and status will probation systems give to new classes of personnel if new functions are added? Will probation administrators be willing to give high status to someone other than a probation officer? Some probation systems have approached the question by encompassing all other functions under some form of probation title, even for those personnel working in probation camps or juvenile detention institutions.

A major lesson for probation administrators is the positive utilization of a crisis. Organizations react to crisis in ways similar to individuals—by anxiety, by withdrawal, by flight, or by attack. Organizations, in addition, may react by moving all decisions upward toward the center of the organization, by closing up communication channels, or by stubbornly holding to some preconceived plan. For a prison system, a major crisis is a riot, and more than one prison administrator has used that riot as a means of gaining increased budgets, new institutions, new personnel, or other added resources. Probation systems also have crises, though not usually as spectacular as a prison riot. The crisis may take the shape of an appointment of a new supervisor, or criticism about too much time in preparing presentence reports, or staff dissension because of excessively high case loads, or budget cutbacks and reduction of staff. The skill of a probation administrator is tested when he faces crisis. As Gross has pointed out, "crisis may provide the best opportunity to get things done that would otherwise be impossible" (1968:592).

GROWTH AND PROFESSIONALISM

When probation agencies were small, they had characteristics common to small organizations. Communication was likely to be face to face. Policies, procedures, and practices were passed on informally. The values of the administrator were known to all staff and probably acceptable to them. Growth brings changes and sometimes people or organizations are not prepared for growth. As the size of the work group increases, communications become more complex and communication channels are more difficult to manage and keep open. Policies, practices, and procedures become formalized by setting them down in writing to insure consistency and continuity. The top administrator is further removed from staff, and speculation exists about his values and priorities. In essence, as probation agencies become large, they tend to adopt the characteristics of a bureaucracy.

Even before probation became the "growth industry" of corrections, an emphasis on professionalism existed. As early as 1923, a Joint Committee of the U.S. Children's Bureau and the National Probation Association proposed as minimum qualifications for probation workers: graduation from college or its equivalent; or graduation from a school of social work and one year of experience in casework under supervision (U.S. Children's Bureau, 1923). This predates today's formal standard, the Master of Social Work degree. The literature about probation abounds with articles and comments about "professionalism."

Growth and professionalism make their own demands on the individual and the organization, and they often conflict. Unintended consequences or dysfunctioning can develop if a lack of congruency exists between the demands of the individual and the organization (Argyris, 1964). It appears that the growth of probation and the emphasis on professionalism has led to incongruencies.

1. *As staff become professional, they increase their knowledge, skills, and expectations; however, as agencies grow in size, the constraints on the activities of probation staff are increased.*

Common to all professionals is their specialized competence, commitment to a career based on that, extensive autonomy in exercising that competence, and influence and responsibility in the use of their special competence. The professional worker has as his reference group the others identified as fellow professionals; they tend to form voluntary associations for the purpose of self-control by the profession, but in the bureaucracy, control is exercised by the hierarchy (Crozier, 1964; Wasserman, 1971).

New graduates of schools of social work are reluctant to enter probation and indicate a belief that they cannot function there easily as professionals. Those probation agencies that have sent newer staff members to graduate schools of social work have seen them leave the agencies early. Administrators may attribute this to offers of better paying jobs. However, these workers often indicate that their reason for change is dissatisfaction with the lack of opportunity to use their knowledge and skills.

A probation agency seeking to professionalize its staff introduces conflict into the organization. The results cannot always be anticipated. Studies of the Wisconsin probation and parole staff indicate dilemmas faced by staff and the choices they selected (Ohlin et al., 1956; Miles, 1963). The accommodation to the conflict faced by another group of professionals (scientists) and the bureaucracy employing them provides some insights probation administrators should acquire (Kornhauser, 1962).

2. *Probation staff derive satisfaction from helping others, which suggests that emphasis in work assignments be given to the probationer; but due to limitations on the time available, priority is likely to be given to the requirements of the judge.*

Only a few studies have been made about how probation officers spend their time. A study in the federal system indicated that 33.7 percent of the time was devoted to presentence investigations and 29.4 percent to probation supervision (Wahl & Glaser, 1963:21). The disturbing part of the study is the limited amount of time available for interviewing (45.5 percent) and the block of time (33.1 percent) spent on paper work (p. 24). Significantly, when the probation officer gets in the field, more time is spent in interviewing and less time on paper work, but the officers studied spent over half their time in the office. A study done ten years earlier in two juvenile probation systems likewise revealed only one-third of the time was available for interviewing (Hengerer, 1953). If probation staff are to have the chance to achieve satisfaction from their work, it becomes important for probation administrators to provide ways and means for protecting and increasing the time the staff have for interviewing their probationers, families, employers, etc.

Probation, as started by John Augustus, involved working with the defendant. As probation became institutionalized, the presentence report for the judge developed. Today, the probation officer can achieve satisfaction and status from service to any one or a combination of the probationer, the judge, and his own agency. The judge has the highest status of the three. It is to be expected, therefore, that a probation officer will seek to meet the requirements of the one with the greatest potential for rewarding him. This priority may also be the result of meeting deadlines for presentence reports, a priority not as clearly defined for most other tasks.

3. *Probation officers are expected to make decisions about their probationers but to be submissive to decisions made by probation administrators.*

One of the characteristics of this field is the high visibility of decision-making by the probation officer, coupled with reviews or appeals from the decisions. His recommendations to a court for sentence of a defendant are likely to be known to the defendant, police, and prosecutor—to name but a few. Appeal can be made to his superior in the agency, to the court or a higher court, or to public opinion. New staff have left probation agencies because, in making decisions that affected the future of defendants and probationers, they had difficulty in avoiding being overruled by their superiors who were, perhaps, more worried about possible criticism by public opinion.

If a probation officer hopes for advancement, either in salary or by promotion, he knows it is his superior who is the "gatekeeper" to success. Consequently, any subordinate wants to know the criteria his superior is going to use to evaluate his work, in addition to evaluating his professional knowledge and skill. A worker quickly learns that the key criterion may be, and often is, "don't be a boat-rocker." Research summarized by Argyris indicates the preference in business for "subordinates who make no trouble, avoid arguments, are somewhat retiring, meek"; but even when aggressive, energetic applicants were sought, the executives personally wanted "tactful" subordinates (1964:105). Probation administrators are probably the same as the other executives.

4. *The emphasis in probation has been on one-to-one relationships; although the supervisor and the administrator should be dealing with their staff as a group, most relationships between supervisors and administrators are likely to continue on a one-to-one basis.*

In using social work as a model, probation drew most heavily on casework. Probation staff working with groups of probationers are the exception. Consequently, very few individuals promoted to supervisory or administrative positions are equipped to lead groups. The tendency is always to use the skills with which one is most familiar, namely one-to-one. Yet, as probation agencies grow, new staff bring their values, which may be in conflict with those already held by staff. This conflict may be handled constructively in group meetings provided there is opportunity for effective participation of all staff. Providing such opportunity for effective participation, in turn, depends upon the understanding and skill of the administrator/supervisor in the group dynamics of staff conferences.

5. Emphasis on training and on a cosmopolitan professionalism has been applied to probation officers; however, probation administrators are "local," not "cosmopolitan," in orientation.

An examination of the literature in probation reveals abundant material about training probation officers, but little about training for administration. As stipends became available for training, the priority, even in probation agencies, has been for training line staff. When agencies sent supervisors and administrators to school as full-time students, the faculty sought to equip them with the knowledge and skills of social casework. More recognition is now being given to the special requirements of people who return to their agencies to function not as caseworkers, but as supervisors and administrators.

The complexities of administration in a growing industry have undoubtedly made some probation administrators uncomfortable. A survey by Louis Harris and Associates for the Joint Commission on Manpower and Training (1968a:10, 28–29) revealed not only a low level of training of administrators in business or public administration, but a feeling by administrators themselves that they need more training in public administration. Piven and Alcabes (1969:20–21) found consensus among key academic, administration, and professional groups on social-work training as appropriate for probation and parole officers, but not for administrators of probation and parole systems. Those advocating public-administration education apparently reflect a primary concern about managerial responsibilities, while supporters of social-work education represent a concern with substantive practice matters.

Administrators can be identified as "local" or "cosmopolitan" (Merton, 1957: 387–420; Blau & Scott, 1962) according to the reference groups to which they turn. "Locals" have primary loyalty to their organization and seek their recognition chiefly from their organizational associates. "Cosmopolitans" are similar to professionals in that their commitment is to specialized professional skills and their loyalty is to a colleague group outside the organization employing them. The study of correctional administrators made by Nelson and Lovell (1969:23–32) indicates that they are "locals" for the most part.

These data regarding probation administrators are especially disturbing. Both age and years in corrections are greater for probation and parole administrators than for administrators of institutions. Social work is the most common field of study in probation and parole, but more second-echelon managers had taken courses in administration than had their superiors. Probation administrators are more likely to belong to a state or regional correctional association (33.1 percent) than to the National Council on Crime and Delinquency (23.5 percent) or the American Correctional Association (8.4 percent) (Nelson & Lovell, 1969:30). Outside corrections, social-work associations drew more memberships (11 percent) than any other professional group. More probation and parole administrators have membership in administrative science organizations than those from institutions or state headquarters, but the percentage is low (3.6 percent). The lack of membership identification outside corrections is reflected in the reading of work-related publications. Very little is read outside the field of corrections. Probation and parole administrators read the least of any correctional administration group in journals of the behavioral sciences and education, and were not much greater readers in management or administrative science (p. 31).

For a field that has doubled, tripled, and quadrupled in size and still has growth possibilities, the quality of administration becomes highly significant. The administrators with professional education have now largely shifted their loyalties from their profession to their organization. The influence of these administrators is likely to retard the development of cosmopolitan administrators from among their subordinates, who now have or may acquire professional education. A shift in priority on training and education is long overdue. Greater attention, emphasis, and funds must be directed to resolving the issues of administration if the impact of any of these incongruencies is to be lessened.

NEEDED: A MODEL FOR ADMINISTRATION

Research has identified the workings of probation systems and the development of administrators for probation systems as the two major needs (Ohlin, 1956; Nelson & Lovell, 1969). The third need is to conceptualize a model of a probation agency that would recognize the needs of line staff, supervisory/administrative staff, and probationers, and the tasks and roles to be assigned to each.

"Most innovations in an organization are the result of borrowing rather than invention" (March & Simon, 1958:181). That statement can be applied to probation, which has already borrowed heavily from the field of social work. What has been lacking is borrowing from such fields as public administration, economics, business administration, behavioral science, and political science. Social work has now begun to do that, as illustrated by the publication of *Social Work Administration: A Resource Book* (Schatz, 1970). A final model cannot be given, but the following indicates some areas worth exploring.

Framework for Decision-Making

The probation administrator usually comes to his position with experience as a probation officer or as a supervisor. There he has had experience in decision-making on separate cases. To be an effective administrator he must make decisions on a system basis, which requires a shift in his thinking and in his mode of operation. An illustration of his responsibility for decisions on a system basis is recruitment and selection of new staff. Is a decision made on the basis of policy, or on a haphazard basis? Is it made with concern for an agency objective, such as increased recruiting from minority groups? The basis for the decision will give some forecast about that probation agency five or ten years from now.

Another aspect of decisions on a system basis is who can make what decision? As probation agencies grow, the staff becomes so large that the administrator must delegate some decisions to others. How large does the staff have to be before the administrator delegates authority to a deputy or a supervisor to approve presentence reports going to the judge? If decentralization in decision-making in a probation agency is limited, the character of the probation agency is more likely to be authoritative (Likert, 1961:229).

Decentralizing decision-making in probation agencies seems indicated for several reasons. If the defendant is to be given greater opportunities for decision-making, using the reintegration correctional model, then, likewise, staff must be given opportunities to participate in decision-making. More important, research indicates a greater potential for organizations where decision-making is distributed throughout the organization (Likert, 1961; Blau & Scott, 1962; Argyris, 1964). Such organizations are found to be more effective, better equipped, and more able to undergo change than authoritative organizations. The term *participative management* is sometimes used to describe the nature of decentralized organizations. Unknown for probation systems are the "decision rules" indicating when participative management decisions are preferable to any other type (Argyris, 1964:212).

Decentralization is not achieved easily. Careful thought and an investment of time, money, and attention must be devoted to it if the results are to have payoff. The types of decisions to be made and the level of staff with sufficient information to make the decisions must be identified (Wallace & McDivitt, 1969). Training should follow because values play such an important part in the decisions. The individual has to make a decision that is rational both to him and to the people in his organization. *Rational* means here that the decision is consistent with the values and the information used for the decision. Training is a means of influencing the values of the individual and the organization (Simon, 1957:241–47).

At present we talk glibly about client participation and self-determination. However, it is questionable how much they actually exist. For defendants to have the right to make decisions about themselves means that the discretion accorded to probation staff must be curtailed, and this probably involves reorienting their values. Probation administrators are a base from which staff acquire values, and not all administrators are certain what "rights" are accorded to defendants placed on probation. A heated discussion in a meeting of the Professional Council of the National Council on Crime and Delinquency ensued from one sentence of a proposed position paper: "This paper is based on the premise that an individual placed on probation has the right to be continued on probation without revocation and enforcement of sentence except where judicial review is held while he is present and justification is given for the revocation." The provocative word was *right*. When the position paper was adopted in 1969, that word did not appear. The premise is stated instead as: "The probation agency has the responsibility to continue probation except where there is justification for revocation," and there is a responsibility on the agency to provide definite proof of any alleged violation.

Supervisory-Subordinate Relationships

A supervisor is the man in the middle. He is at the top of one pyramid composed of himself and his subordinates. He is at the bottom of another pyramid when he meets with his own superior. This is true whether we are discussing the first-level supervisor and a unit of probation officers or the probation administrator and his deputies or assistants.

Supervision of staff in probation agencies is again adopted from the social-work model. A fundamental premise in social work is that of providing the worker with insight, which includes analyzing his behavior to determine what motivates his choices, including his resistance (Blau & Scott, 1962:188–91).

Studies of supervision indicate potentials as yet untapped by probation agencies and probably not clearly taught as a technique of supervision. The "linking pin" concept expressed by Likert (1961:113–15) has relevance to a probation agency that attempts to shift its practices. The ability of the supervisor to influence his subordinates is dependent not only upon the formal status of his office but also on his securing their allegiance because he is able to help them. Helping subordinates may take the form of assisting on a problem related to their probationers. Assisting them by securing favorable response from higher authority to demands lower-level personnel place on the organization is expected of an effective supervisor. The effectiveness of the linking pin concept is dependent upon its presence at all hierarchical levels above the nonsupervisory personnel. This model of supervisory-subordinate relationships is more oriented to the concept of participative management than the social-work model.

Literature on social-work supervision has focused instead on the teaching relationship of the worker to his organization.

Work Load and Deployment of Staff

The work load standard of the probation officer has been set by tradition and never validated (Wallace, 1964). The first appearance of a case load figure of fifty probationers per probation officer was in 1917 as a recommendation from a "Committee on Courts of Domestic Relations" (National Probation Association, 1917:82). That recommendation became the standard, later modified to include investigations. The presentence investigation was calculated to be equivalent to supervising five probationers. This standard was challenged by the President's Commission recommendation of an "average ratio of 35 offenders per officer" (1967b:169).

Reducing case loads does not necessarily result in better probation services. Stuart Adams points out a valid criticism: "We have reduced the caseloads but we haven't told the parole agents what to do with the extra time" (1967:55).

In the *San Francisco Project*, Robison and his associates (1969) established four levels of supervision: the ideal case load, the intensive case load, the normal case load, and minimum supervision. The ideal case load was fifty cases or a combination of supervision and investigation, with one investigation each month counting as five supervision cases. The intensive case load was set at half the fifty-case standard; the normal case load was approximately twice that of the recommended fifty-case standard; and the minimum was two hundred fifty cases. Under minimum supervision, an offender was required to submit a written monthly report but there was no other mandatory contact between the probation officer and the offender. If any contact was made, it was initiated by the probationer. After approximately two years, assessments were made of three of the case loads—minimum, ideal, and intensive. The offenders appeared to be doing equally well and the violation rates were well within those that would be expected from federal offenders under "normal" levels of probation supervision. The data also indicated that the number of contacts between an offender and the probation officer had little relationship to success or failure under supervision. The findings raised questions both as to the value of the fifty-case standard and the effectiveness of probation supervision as presently practiced (Robison et al., 1969:3–8).

Three developments should be considered in restructuring work loads: classification or typology of offenders, the team concept, and use of paraprofessionals. Classification of offenders may permit case loads ranging from twenty-five to two hundred and fifty, depending on the supervision required (Robison et al., 1969:73–75). To do this requires careful attention and research to insure that the efforts provide payoff.

A study done in social work may have relevance to probation administrators interested in exploring the idea of a team. Barker and Briggs (1968) studied the organization and functioning of social-work staff in a mental hospital confronted with a shortage of persons with a Master of Social Work degree and a need for manpower. The structuring was done around three elements. One was a team wherein "several members of the staff work together to achieve the goal for and with the client rather than a single person assessing the need and performing those activities that would serve to fulfill it" (Barker & Briggs, 1968:165). The team leader was responsible for achieving the goal, determining the need to be met by the team, and defining the limits within which choices were made about the most appropriate means. He did not perform the means; that was assigned by him to another member of the team. The second element was the typology of clientele. The team considered everyone who had something to gain by some kind of contact with them as a client. They identified eight client groups: the individual patient, his family, his personal associates, the patient community, the staff community, the service community, the vulnerable public, and the lay public. The episode of service was the third element. This was identified not as a case, the traditional pattern, but as "a cluster of activities that go together to achieve a social work organization's specified goal" (p. 167). The concept was actually used and studied for a one-year period. The goal was to increase quality and quantity of work output, and the conclusion was that it was achieved. There was a reduction in casework therapy for some hospitalized patients. A major gain was that services were provided to client groups never before reached. Movement into the community by social-work staff became a reality.

Sullivan (1972) describes both the temporary problem-solving teams created for specific purposes and three possible models for probation. For the resource-coordinating model, the entire team is given a case load, rather than a case load for each individual probation officer. In the reintegration model, the probation team endeavors to bring about change in the opportunity structure, power groups, and the criminal by defining sources in the community as well as effecting change in the probationer. The new careers model calls for probationers to have an opportunity to assume a major role in their own adjustment, including that of developing a permanent career for themselves in probation or other areas of human service.

The use of paraprofessionals in probation was a natural outgrowth of the shortage of trained personnel in health and welfare. Critical examination of the tasks done by professionals indicated tasks could be broken up and jobs designed for those with less training. Moreover, services could be provided that are not given now and that could be done suitably by the paraprofessional. The idea that offenders and ex-offenders could be employed to the advantage of the corrections agency and the individual himself proved true (Benjamin et al., 1966; Joint Commission on Manpower and Training, 1968b).

A strong argument for the use of paraprofessionals with the probation officer is the application of the principle of redundancy, as set forth by Landau (1969). He indicates that redundancy provides an extraordinary increase in reliability. An illustration is in communication: e.g., when we make an appointment for a time in the future, we are likely to give the day of the week as well as the date, then the hour and indicate whether it is A.M. or P.M. This redundancy insures reliability in the message. Landau observes that efforts are made to reduce the redundancy to a zero degree in public administration. However, if we want to get a message across to probationers, the use of the probation officer and the paraprofessional will provide reinforcement and support for the signals being given the probationer, provide greater safety factors in the sense of evaluating how the probationer is adjusting, permit more flexible responses to problems presented by the probationer, and provide "a creative potential for those who are able to see it" (1969:356).

A note of caution is needed on the frequent objective of providing opportunities for upgrading the paraprofessionals, e.g., promotional opportunities within two or three years and avoidance of dead-end jobs. To secure a college degree for appointment as a probation officer when starting with a high-school education or less poses serious time problems, which need not be insurmountable. Two options are available. One is to change the standard for appointment of probation officers and to drop the requirement of a college degree. The requirement and impetus for graduate education in social work for the probation officer are diminishing. The possibilities for eliminating the civil service requirement of a college degree for appointment as a probation officer is doubtful, but another possibility is to provide promotional opportunities within a probation agency to other titles as intermediate steps on the way to appointment as a probation officer. An example is promotion to the position of investigator, which can be done in agencies using such titles in functions, such as family-support matters or release on recognizance programs.

The use of paraprofessionals on a part-time basis, and not necessarily as a job leading to a career in corrections, is also worth exploring for probation administrators interested in bringing change into their agency.

Social Action

The social values of a society are reflected in legislation, but probation administrators have had little influence on legislative actions, except possibly legislation that would protect or advance the self-interest of their agencies. Some argue simplistically that corrections should be taken out of politics. That argument is very apt with respect to appointment and tenure of staff, but not with politics as defined by Meyerson and Banfield to encompass "the activity (negotiation, argument, discussion, application of force, persuasion, etc.) by which an issue is agitated or settled" (1955:304). To make a complete separation between administration and politics is to ignore the potential strength of the probation administrator in influencing social change.

Probation administrators have had a low degree of visibility, but that is changing. The isolation in which they have operated is dissolving as probation agencies grow in size. The criminal justice system, of which probation is a part, has been receiving greater priority in funding, leading to more accountability being demanded of the system. Probation administrators also are being asked for advice and for their position on various subjects, such as whether incorrigibility and truancy should be removed from the jurisdiction of the juvenile court, how to divert youthful and adult offenders from the criminal justice system, the elimination of crimes without victims, such as drunkenness, and restoration of rights to offenders and ex-offenders. To be effective in utilizing the reintegration correctional policy, an administrator must be both an advocate and an influencer. If the legal and social barriers to offenders and ex-offenders striving for decent housing, medical service, and employment are to be reduced, the probation administrator must be involved in political action.

The role of the probation administrator as an advocate on broad issues of social policy is still unclear. His activities as an influencer appear more clearly. His effectiveness is enhanced by securing and using relevant information, by studying the decision-making structure involved in legislative and executive action on social policy, and by knowing how to maximize his power and authority. It would appear that the first step is to pay more attention to the world outside the correctional system and to secure and use relevant information about that world. Business does just that to chart its future (Aquilar, 1967). Wilensky's (1967) account of how knowledge shapes policy in government and industry is worthy of study by probation administrators.

The skillful use of knowledge provides a base for power; social change does not necessarily develop because of widespread publicity about a given issue. Social change may also be the result of pertinent information supplied to selected individuals. If an administrator looks about for persons who have information that is important to him, he will develop contacts with persons outside his organization. His relationship with them will be enhanced if he is willing to trade information with them.

In short, he has to look for allies or potential supporters. He must remember that someone may be an ally on one issue, neutral on another, and opposed on still another issue. Concerned legislators interested in correctional reform may be seeking issues to advance. The probation administrator, on identifying such legislators, can be an important source of information to them, and an influence in their political decisions and actions. The administrator may be most effective in the background and must be content with such a role.

The risk the probation administrator takes in attempting to influence social action will be dependent upon his knowledge of the political process in establishing social policy, his reading of the political climate, and his awareness that many reforms are compromises. Political decisions are not always the result of knowledge; again, values may override any given set of facts.

REFERENCES

Adams, Stuart.
    1967   "Some findings from correctional caseload research." Federal Probation 31(December):48–57.

American Bar Association.
    1970   Standards Relating to Probation. American Bar Association Project on Standards for Criminal Justice. Chicago: American Bar Association.

American Correctional Association.
    1966   Manual of Correctional Standards. Revised Edition. Washington, D.C.: American Correctional Association.

Aquilar, Francis Joseph.
    1967   Scanning the Business Environment. New York: Macmillan.

Ares, Charles, and Herbert Sturz.
    1962   "Bail and the indigent accused." National Probation and Parole Association Journal 8(January):12–20.

Argyris, Chris.
    1964   Integrating the Individual in the Organization. New York: Wiley.

Attorney General's Survey of Release Procedures.
    1939   Probation, vol. 2. Washington, D.C.: U.S. Government Printing Office.

Barker, Robert L., and Thomas L. Briggs.
    1968   Differential Use of Social Work Manpower. New York: National Association of Social Workers.

Benjamin, Judith G., Marcia K. Freedman, and Edith F. Lynton.
    1966   Pros and Cons: New Roles for Non-Professionals in Corrections. Washington, D.C.: U.S. Government Printing Office.

Blau, Peter M., and W. Richard Scott.
    1962   Formal Organizations. San Francisco: Chandler.

Cohn, Yona.
    1969   "The presentence investigation report in court: a correlation between the probation officers reporting and the court disposition." Ph.D. dissertation, Columbia University.

Cressey, Donald R.
1965   "Prison organizations." Pp. 1023–1070 in James G. March (ed.), Handbook of Organizations. Chicago: Rand McNally.

Crozier, Michael.
1964   The Bureaucratic Phenomenon. Chicago: University of Chicago Press.

Drucker, Peter F.
1954   The Practice of Management. New York: Harper & Row.

Gross, Bertram M.
1968   Organizations and Their Managing. New York: Free Press.

Hengerer, Gertrude.
1953   "Organizing probation services," in Reappraising Crime Treatment. New York: National Probation and Parole Association.

Joint Commission on Correctional Manpower and Training.
1968a   Corrections 1968: A Climate for Change. Report of a survey made by Louis Harris and Associates. Washington, D.C.: Joint Commission on Correctional Manpower and Training.
1968b   Offenders as a Correctional Manpower Resource. Washington, D.C.: Joint Commission on Correctional Manpower and Training.

Kornhauser, William.
1962   Scientists in Industry: Conflict and Accommodation. Berkeley: University of California Press.

Landau, Martin.
1969   "Redundancy, rationality, and the problem of duplication and overlap." Public Administration Review 29(July/August):346–358.

Likert, Rensis.
1961   New Patterns of Management. New York: McGraw-Hill.

McEachern, A. W. (ed.)
1961   View of Authority: Probationers and Probation Officers. Los Angeles: University of Southern California Youth Studies Center.

March, James G., and Herbert A. Simon.
1958   Organizations. New York: Wiley.

Merton, Robert K.
1957   Social Theory and Social Structure. Revised Edition. Glencoe, Ill.: Free Press.

Meyerson, Martin, and Edward C. Banfield.
1955   Politics, Planning and the Public Interest. Glencoe, Ill.: Free Press.

Miles, Arthur P.
1963   The Self-Image of the Wisconsin Probation and Parole Agent. Madison: Wisconsin Department of Public Welfare.

Miller, E. J., and A. K. Rice.
1967   Systems of Organizations. London: Tavistock.

National Council on Crime and Delinquency (N.C.C.D.)
1955   Standard Probation and Parole Act. Second Edition. New York: National Council on Crime and Delinquency.
1963   Probation and Parole Directory. Fourteenth Edition. New York: National Council on Crime and Delinquency.

1970   Probation and Parole Directory. Sixteenth Edition. New York: National Council on Crime and Delinquency.

National Probation Association.
1917   Annual Report and Proceedings. New York: National Probation Association.
1937   Directory of Probation Officers. New York: National Probation Association.
1947   Directory of Probation and Parole Officers, U.S. and Canada. New York: National Probation Association.

National Probation and Parole Association.
1952   Probation and Parole Directory. New York: National Probation and Parole Association.

Nelson, Elmer K., Jr., and Catherine H. Lovell.
1969   Developing Correctional Administrators. Washington, D.C.: Joint Commission on Correctional Manpower and Training.

Ohlin, Lloyd E.
1956   Sociology and the Field of Corrections. New York: Russell Sage Foundation.

Ohlin, Lloyd E., Herman Piven, and Donnell Pappenfort.
1956   "Major dilemmas of the social worker in probation and parole." National Probation and Parole Association Journal 2(July):211–225.

Piven, Herman, and Abraham Alcabes.
1969   The Crisis of Qualified Manpower for Criminal Justice: An Analytic Assessment with Guidelines for New Policy. Vol. 1, Probation/Parole. Washington, D.C.: U.S. Government Printing Office.

President's Commission on Law Enforcement and Administration of Justice.
1967a   Task Force Report: Corrections. Washington, D.C.: U.S. Government Printing Office.
1967b   The Challenge of Crime in a Free Society. Washington, D.C.: U.S. Government Printing Office.

Robison, James, Leslie T. Wilkins, Robert M. Carter, and Albert Wahl.
1969   The San Francisco Project. Research Report No. 14. Berkeley: University of California School of Criminology.

Schatz, Harry A. (ed.)
1970   Social Work Administration: A Resource Book. New York: Council on Social Work Education.

Simon, Herbert.
1957   Administrative Behavior. Second Edition. New York: Macmillan.

Street, David, Robert D. Vinter, and Charles Perrow.
1966   Organization for Treatment. New York: Free Press.

Studt, Elliot.
1967   The Reentry of the Offender into the Community. Washington, D.C.: U.S. Government Printing Office.

Sullivan, Dennis C.
1972   Team Management in Probation: Some Models for Implementation. Hackensack, N.J.: National Council on Crime and Delinquency.

U.S. Children's Bureau.
1923   Juvenile Court Standards. U.S. Children's Bureau Publication No. 121. Washington, D.C.: U.S. Government Printing Office.

Wahl, Albert, and Daniel Glaser.
  1963   "Pilot time study of the federal probation officer's job." Federal Probation
          27(September) :20–25.
Wallace, John A.
  1964   "A fresh look at old probation standards." Crime and Delinquency 10
          (April) :124–129.
Wallace, John A., and C. Boyd McDivitt.
  1969   "Decision-making in probation: two dimensions," in Alvin W. Cohn (ed.),
          Problems, Thoughts and Processes in Criminal Justice Administration. New
          York: National Council on Crime and Delinquency.
Wasserman, Harry.
  1971   "The professional social worker in a bureaucracy." Social Work 16(Janu-
          ary) :89–95.
Wilensky, Harold L.
  1967   Organizational Intelligence. New York: Basic Books.

CHAPTER **27**

Adaptation to Being Corrected:
Corrections from the Convict's Perspective

John Irwin

San Francisco State University

For two hundred years, the purposes and functionings of penal systems have been influenced by a noble ideal. Simply stated, the ideal is that the criminal should not only be punished, but also helped or improved. This ideal has appeared in various forms. First it was "reformation," then "correction," "cure," "treatment," or "rehabilitation." Whatever it is called, the pursuit of this ideal has established the direction for many, perhaps most, penal administrations in the United States. The consequences of this, however, have not been to "help" the prisoner. As in the case of most enterprises in history, outcomes have been quite different from that intended by the planners. When considered from the convict's own point of view, his life has not been made any more tolerable during or after his passage through correctional systems that have been erected to help him. Moreover, he has not been helped from society's viewpoint. It appears that he is no more likely to be changed into a noncriminal than he was before improving him became an important goal.[1]

Our intentions here are not to focus on the effectiveness of penal measures from the perspective of the society or from some body of functionaries within the society. Instead, we will examine the impact of these measures, particularly the more recently introduced measures, on the perspectives and the adaptive strategies of the persons receiving the help. However, to do this we must first review briefly the emergence, the major contours, and the overall impact of the correctional perspective. This digression is necessary because we must have a clear understanding of what prisoners are adapting to in order to make sense out of their adaptations. We will touch mainly on those features of corrections that are particularly relevant to the convict's efforts to cope with the prison and the correctional programs. After this digression, we will turn to our primary concern—the impact of the correctional ideal on the perspective and adaptive strategies of prisoners.

---

1. Many studies and surveys of the criminological literature have indicated that modern correctional techniques have not made any significant difference in the future criminal activities of convicts. Two of the best discussions of this issue are: Wilkins, *Evaluation of Penal Measures* (1968), and Kassebaum, Ward, and Wilner, *Prison Treatment and Parole Survival* (1971).

THE APPEARANCE OF THE PRISON

The prison, the bulwark of American corrections, actually came into existence, in part at least, to help the prisoner. It appears that imprisonment, which had been used mainly in pretrial detention, supplanted corporal and capital punishment because of the influence of a utilitarian philosophy in penal administration. The utilitarians, though they were recommending punishment for the primary purpose of deterring others from transgressions, also introduced a concern for the offender himself. For instance, the social theorist, Sidney Smith, after recommending that the apprehended offender be used as a demonstration to others, also considers the improvement of the "culprit" himself:

> Our primary duty, in such a case, is to treat the culprit that many other persons may be rendered better, or prevented from being worse, by dread of the same treatment; and making this the principal object, *to combine with it as much as possible the improvement of the individual* (Radzinowicz & Turner, 1943:93, emphasis added).

This emphasis eventually led to imprisonment, which was viewed as the only way to punish the offender without permanently damaging him.

Simultaneously with the English concern for the improvement of the felon, a group of Quakers in Philadelphia mounted a reform movement, which eventually led to widespread use of the prison. Again, the concern was improvement of the offender, for whom they designed a system of solitary confinement in which he was held totally isolated from others. This system was never given a thorough trial (mainly because of its extreme costliness), but there is considerable evidence that it produced more insanity than reformation.

The point is, the general practice of imprisonment was firmly established by two slightly different concerns for the "reformation" of the offender, and in the nineteenth century it became the central sanctioning technique.

I do not want to suggest that reformation and deterrence of the convicted person were the only, or even the most important, goals of the emerging penal systems. Other goals, such as punishment and removal from society, were not replaced and were still operative in the construction of prison systems—as they are still important today. The prison, *theoretically*, accomplished all these—the less noble ones of punishment and segregation of criminals, plus deterrence, and the newer, more humane goal of reformation.

DETERMINISM AND THE REHABILITATIVE IDEAL

In the last part of the nineteenth century, the conception of man as a free-willed thinker striving to maximize his pleasures and minimize pain changed to the view of the determined man (for an excellent discussion, see Platt, 1969:chap. 2). The impact on the penal field of the growth of positivism in the social sciences was the implementation of the rehabilitative ideal in the correctional field. In short, the positivistic model holds that man's behavior is caused by forces outside his consciousness and, therefore, outside his control. Primarily, it contradicted the notion of free will. Importantly, it suggested that we would soon be able to identify the forces that propel man, and eventually control them. The implications of these ideas for penal systems are obvious. They led to what has been referred to as the rehabilitative ideal. Francis Allen, one of the early critics of this ideal, spells out its main components:

The rehabilitative ideal is itself a complex of ideas which, perhaps, defies completely precise statement. The essential points, however, can be articulated. It is assumed, first, that human behavior is the product of antecedent causes. These causes can be identified as part of the physical universe, and it is the obligation of the scientist to discover and to describe them with all possible exactitude. Knowledge of the antecedents of human behavior makes possible an approach to the scientific control of human behavior. Finally, and of primary significance for the purposes at hand, it is assumed that measures employed to treat the convicted offender should serve a therapeutic function, that such measures should be designed to effect changes in the behavior of the convicted person in the interests of his own happiness, health, and satisfactions and in the interest of social defense (1959:226–27).

We should add one subsidiary point that is implicit in Allen's description of the premises of the rehabilitative view and is very important in the operation of rehabilitation in corrections, that is, the measures to determine when changes in behavior have occurred in fact must be available to make the rehabilitative enterprise function.

At this time we must point out that none of these premises has been confirmed. Whether they will in some near future seems less likely now than it did, say, at the turn of the century. Rehabilitative concepts entered penology, shaped correctional routines, and supplied the criminal justice system "rationalizations" for other goals. Yet, it is clear that we cannot do the things that are required to make it work. That is, *we cannot with appreciable precision and utility in most individual cases identify the causes of criminal behavior, devise strategies to change this behavior, or, indeed, know accurately when it is changed.*

THE CRIMINAL TYPE

In point of fact, positivism and the deterministic model entered criminology through the development of the concept of a criminal type (for an excellent account of this subject, see Sarbin, 1969). Under former social theories, criminals were not differentiated from other citizens. All persons had the capability of transgressing for their own selfish purposes. The discovery by Lombroso (1911) of a biologically abnormal brain in the corpse of a "criminal," which led to his developing the mistaken notion of a biological throwback, was the first of a series of theories that distinguished criminals from normal people and purported to explain their criminality. Lombroso theorized that atavistic traits were developed in earlier ages of man's history and still occasionally reappeared in some persons. Biological explanations for the criminal type gave way to environmental explanations, such as "emotional disturbance," "personal disorganization," "subculture carrier." Importantly, all these explanations of criminality perceive the "systematic" criminal (most social scientists recognized that many "normal" persons break some laws occasionally, and made exceptions of many types of lawbreakers) as a different biological, personality, and social-cultural type. In actuality, the view of the criminal as a psychological type—that is, as emotionally disturbed, as mentally ill or "psychopathic"—figured most prominently in the emergence of the rehabilitative ideal (Platt, 1969:chap. 2).

In regard to penal measures, after the development of types other than the biological, the social scientists' ideas on reformation of the criminal took a new direction. Instead of teaching the criminal to obey the law through learning the consequences of his acts or through penitence, social scientists proposed that he be "rehabilitated" by first discovering the factors that made him into a criminal, and then introducing techniques that would change him back into a "normal" human being.

THE MIXTURE OF REHABILITATION AND PUNISHMENT

Let it be emphasized that prisons never became hospitals and criminals have never been treated as merely sick persons. Other goals were never forgotten or abandoned. What was remarkable about the emergence of the rehabilitative ideal in the penal world was that it was able to take what appeared to be contradictory ideas and, through intellectual gymnastics and a great deal of hypocrisy, combine these into a system that, for the time being, made everyone but the convicts happy. To demonstrate that there was a serious contradiction in the actual implementation of the rehabilitative ideal, read Principle Five of the "Declaration of Principles" of the American Correctional Association:

> The length of the punitive sentence should properly be commensurate with the seriousness of the offense and the extent of the offender's participation. Inequality of sentences for the same or similar crimes is always interpreted as an injustice both by the offender and the society. On the other hand, the length of the correctional treatment given the offender for purposes of rehabilitation depends on the circumstances and characteristics of the particular offender and may have little relationship to the seriousness of the crime committed. In a correctionally oriented system of crime control, statutes providing maximum flexibility in the determination of the appropriate release date can assure the optimum benefits of correctional treatment (1970:32).

Clearly, there is at least one glaring inconsistency in this statement of correctional principles. If injustice is experienced from inequality of sentences in a punitive system, how could the authors of the principles suppose that unequal "lengths of correctional treatment," which are clearly prison sentences, would not be experienced as injustices.

Given these contradictions in the foundations of most modern penal systems, we must look closely to discover why the "rehabilitative ideal" has been embraced so unanimously by most interested segments (except, as mentioned above, the convicts). This is necessary not only because this question is interesting in itself, but also because we will discover characteristics of the operation of the systems that are essential for understanding the system's impact on convicts.

Humanitarians and the Rehabilitative Ideal

The first group whose motives and purposes we must examine are the "humanitarians," those persons who were repulsed by former means of punishment and who supported, and still support, forcing convicted persons into rehabilitative routines for their own good. To understand their motives and actions, we cannot ignore an important force that led to the growth of the rehabilitative ideal: the mixture of hatred, fear, and revulsion that predominantly white, middle-class, Protestant reformers have felt toward lower-class persons, and particularly foreign-born lower-class persons who have not shared their values, life-style, or the Christian ethic. These sentiments are explicitly revealed in two excerpts from official committee reports in the last century:

> As a surety, we must, as a people, act upon this foreign element, or it will act upon us. Like the vast Atlantic, we must decompose and cleanse the impurities which rush the poison into our whole national system (New York State Assembly, 1857:3).

> As Christian men, we cannot look upon this great multitude of unhappy, deserted, and degraded boys and girls without feeling our responsibility to God for them. The class increases: immigration is pouring in its multitudes of poor foreigners who leave these young outcasts everywhere in our midst. These boys and girls, it should be remembered,

will soon form the great lower class of our society. They will influence elections; they may shape the policy of our city; they will assuredly, if unreclaimed, poison society all around them (Committee on the History of Child-Saving Work, 1893:20).

Their fear, hate, and revulsion, it appears, were expressed as thinly disguised humanitarian concern for the health and well-being of these different subculture members. If our suspicion is warranted, then imprisonment disguised as "treatment" was a particularly suitable response for these reformers' complicated and contradictory feelings. On the surface, they expressed their humanitarian concern for the well-being of the criminals and the society, and simultaneously received satisfaction for their less noble feelings by supporting imprisonment for the persons who threatened them so deeply.

The Punitively Oriented and the Rehabilitative Ideal

District attorneys and police officers see a problem in the system of imprisonment based on utilitarian beliefs. When individuals whom the district attorneys and police perceive as "dangerous criminals" finish their set sentence for a crime, perhaps a minor crime, they have to be released. Those who believe in punishing some people for long periods immediately perceived, and accurately so, that under a rehabilitative system, which focused on the causes of crime in the individual, "dangerous" persons can be kept indefinitely. So many punitively oriented persons have consistently supported the rehabilitative ideal because it is possible to keep many persons for indefinite lengths of time.[2]

Prison Administrators and the Rehabilitative Ideal

Prison administrators with vision or with experience in rehabilitative systems have supported them enthusiastically; not because of any humanitarian concerns, but because they have realized that rehabilitation has offered a highly efficient control mechanism. The control motive glares through Zebulon Brockway's statement, made in 1868, regarding indeterminacy: "To commit these persons to the House of Correction until they are reformed will be a strong inducement for them to enter immediately upon the work of self-improvement!" (McKelvey, 1968:63). The rehabilitative prison system rewards conformity to prison regulations with reductions in sentences. This is not an obvious contradiction to the spirit of the rehabilitative ideal, since in most behavioral theories underpinning therapy, the "healthy," "adjusted," or "cured" person is one who has learned to conform.

From this examination of the actual functions performed by the rehabilitative ideal, we learn that failure to achieve "success" in correctional efforts has not been simply failure to discover the right treatment program and then to implement it fully. In the first place, it is very possible that the original promise was a pipe dream and, second, it is clear that penal systems have not, and will not, abandon some of their other functions and purposes when they implement any penal strategy. It is especially

---

2. Correctional people understood this almost from the outset and used it to argue for the indeterminate sentence system. For instance, Paul Garraud, at the 1910 Proceedings of the Prison Association, said: "Therefore, I conclude that the indeterminate sentence is the best form of prolonged imprisonment for delinquent adolescents up to the age of 25, who are susceptible of reformation, and for incorrigibles and recidivists of every kind" (Garraud, 1910:301).

important to be cognizant of the other functions the rehabilitative ideal has served when we examine its consequences for convicts.

Relevant Dimensions of Rehabilitative Penal Systems

Three key dimensions of the rehabilitative systems are particularly important when we examine its impact on convicts. These are *individualization, indeterminacy,* and *discretionary power.* Individualization was introduced into the system when punishment for the purposes of correction was replaced by the concept of cure. The focus shifted from the law violation to the criminal himself. He was a different type of person and the law infraction was merely a manifestation of this difference. There was *not* one type of criminal, however, and a system was needed that, after discovering particular causes for a given person's type of criminality, would permit an individualized treatment routine.

In order to implement the individualized system in which many decisions had to be tailored to each case, a system with broad margins was needed to make the individualized routine possible. The epitome of this individualization is the indeterminate sentence system, in which the individual is sentenced to prison for an unspecified length of time so that various rehabilitative routines can be introduced and the person can be released when, and only when, he is "cured" of his criminality. In this case, a sentence of up to life imprisonment for all serious crimes is ideal. This ideal has never been realized, however, and the states that have adopted it actually have partially indeterminate systems.

Finally, implementation of the rehabilitative system with its individualization and indeterminacy requires greatly expanded discretionary powers for persons in decision-making positions.

We must again emphasize, although theoretically these dimensions are necessary to implement an ideal rehabilitative system and, in fact, all three dimensions were greatly increased in systems that adopted rehabilitation as one of their goals, the scientific tools to operate such a system effectively are lacking. Individualization, indeterminacy, and discretionary power have been planned and used for other purposes; for instance, to control convicts and to discriminate between the rich and the poor, the powerful and the powerless, and the white and nonwhite.

Besides the expansion of these dimensions, two other attributes seem to have accompanied the rehabilitative systems: the length of sentences increase, and they are delivered to more persons. This has been the case in the California correctional system, which is considered the model of the rehabilitative system, and is probably the case in most states that have moved towards individualization, indeterminacy, and expanded discretionary powers.[3]

---

3. In California, according to the Research Division of the California Department of Corrections, the median time for first-time releases rose from approximately 24 months during the 1950s, when the rehabilitative ideal was introduced in full force, to 36 months in 1969. Also the number of persons in prison rose to 145 per hundred thousand population from 65 in 1944, before the rehabilitative ideal was maximized. This is probably a national, historical high. There are other reports of sentences becoming longer under the indeterminate sentence system. Amos W. Butler, reporting to the 1915 Congress of the American Prison Association, stated, "Under the present system of the indeterminate sentence with parole, accompanied as it is with efforts at reformation, the average length of sentence is markedly longer" (Butler, 1915:169). Nathaniel Cantor, speaking at the 1937 Congress, stated, "There is evidence to show that the average period of imprisonment under the minimum-maximum sentence is decidedly longer than under the determinate sentence. It is extremely probable that under an absolute indeterminate sentence periods of confinement will be longer for the 'hardened' criminals as well as for many *misdemeanants* who receive sentences of 5 or 10 or 30 days four, fourteen or forty times" (1937:36).

Adapting to the Rehabilitative System

Now that we have completed this review of the essential aspects of the rehabilitative system, let us turn to actual programs and the adaptive patterns of convicts in modern correctional systems. In this discussion, we will rely heavily on the California system of corrections, first, because most of my experience has been with this system, and second, the California system is generally considered to be the most innovative, most treatment-oriented, large correctional system in the country, perhaps in the world.[4]

Classification

The prison routine for the convict starts with classification, which is one of the most important facets of the actual implementation of the rehabilitative ideal. This facet of the modern correctional routine is founded on the practice of "typing" criminals according to different background characteristics. The earliest classification was on the basis of sex, and then age. With the growing belief in criminal types or different personality types, and the shift from a focus on the crime to a focus on the individual, there was a steady movement toward greater and greater differentiation of prisoners. This differentiation is not only for segregation, but to a great extent for planning and implementing different rehabilitative strategies to treat the different kinds of problems or sicknesses of individual prisoners.

Ideally, classification has three major steps. The first is diagnosis. In this stage, experts, psychologists, social workers, sociologists, vocational counselors, and psychiatrists study the individual criminal by examining his records, seeking information from various organizations and parties (such as his family), and interviewing and testing the criminal himself.

In the second stage, the initial classification, this information is collected and reviewed by a panel of experts who make decisions on the type of individualized treatment, custody, and training required by this person and make actual decisions as to the implementation of these decisions, e.g., assignment to a particular prison, jobs, and treatment programs.

In the third stage, the classification committee reviews the case at regular intervals to evaluate progress, to check on the implementation of the original recommendations, and to decide on changes in treatment, custody, or training routines.

Theoretically, therefore, classification is the backbone of rehabilitation. Let us turn, however, to the actualities of the classification process, which do not come close to fulfilling its stated purposes. Of course, the rehabilitative function of the classification process to a great extent is not fulfilled simply because the basic tools to make it work are not available. These tools are the scientific knowledge of the "causes" of human behavior, the strategies to change it, and the techniques to measure its change. However, this is not the only source of failure of the classificatory process in its treatment function. The tools that are used—the tests, interviews, and evaluations of experts —are applied in a cursory fashion or under such unpropitious circumstances that even if they were potentially valid techniques, they would not be valid in this setting. For instance, it is typical to give I.Q., aptitude, preference, and personality tests in the first week or two after entering the reception center of the prison, even though the dramatic transition from the outside or from jail to prison, ill health incurred in a long

---

4. For example, Norman S. Hayner, in comparing correctional systems in various countries, says that California "easily ranks at the top from the standpoint of emphasis on treatment with a score of 122 points out of a possible 140" (1962:165).

pretrial jail detention period, or the person's "atypical" life routine prior to imprisonment (such as a period of heroin addiction), may affect him so he is functioning in a
manner that is different from his typical or potential levels. Moreover, diagnosis, evaluation, and conclusions about the individual convict, his character, and his future course
are often made by classification personnel without giving any serious consideration
to the motives and aspirations of the convict himself. The following classification experience was related to me by a convict in San Quentin in August, 1967:

> In about the fourth week in the guidance center, I was directed in to see a vocational
> counselor. I sat down and he was looking over my jacket. He asked me a few questions
> but he did most of the talking. He talked fast and I could hardly get a word in. Well,
> anyway, he looked at my IQ score and my aptitude tests and decided that I would make
> a good electrician. He told me that and I said "wait a minute, I don't want to be no
> electrician. I don't care nothing about being an electrician. I want to go to school."
> But he wouldn't pay no attention to me. He had made up his mind and before I knew it,
> the interview was over.

Failure to use the tools of treatment (if they exist) is not the only, or the most
serious, obstacle on the road to rehabilitation. As mentioned earlier, the modern
rehabilitative prison system has never abandoned other basic penological goals and,
as all other facets of the prison routine, classification actually serves other unstated
goals, such as control and administrative convenience. Sutherland and Cressey suggest
that "treatment" is the least important consideration in the classification process:

> Probably most classification committees base their decisions on considerations of custody,
> convenience, discipline and treatment, in that order. Thus, it may be decided that a par-
> ticular inmate must be handled as a maximum security risk, and if, for example, psy-
> chiatric services are not available to maximum-risk prisoners, then that decision will
> mean that the psychiatric help will not be available to the inmate in question, no matter
> what his treament needs (1970:501–2).

These other functions of classification are not openly communicated, especially to the
convicts who are engaged in the process; in fact, they are usually disguised as treatment. For example, when convicts are transferred from the location of classification to
the prison where they will begin serving their sentence, though the final choice was
made mainly on the basis of custody concerns (i.e., their perceived escape potential) or
convenience (i.e., the availability of space), they are frequently given a justification,
such as the following: "the institution you are being sent to has a training program in
a trade which we feel is especially suited for you." The statements made by convicts in
San Quentin in March, 1968 suggest that they are aware of the primacy of the other
goals:

> Man, don't believe that shit about sending you some place for your own good.
> They'll send you to a joint where they have space and where they think they can hold you.

> When it really comes down to it, bed-space, the time they think you're gonna do,
> and your escape record make the whole difference.

Increasingly, convicts resent the hypocrisy in correctional classification treatment
programs. However, the major response seems to be to try to manipulate the system to
further their own goals. At present, these are somewhat or totally different from those of
the prison administrators. I say "at present," because in the early stages of the full

implementation of the rehabilitative ideal, it seemed that convicts tended to accept the promise of rehabilitation and the deterministic view of themselves, and to place themselves in the hands of the correctionalist to be made over into more effective, adjusted persons.[5] But this period has passed, and after witnessing the failure of rehabilitation, observing that the other penological goals, such as punishment, are still operating, and learning of the disillusionment in the ideal on the part of the experts themselves, the convicts presently tend to view rehabilitation with extreme skepticism. The result is that they see their goals as basically incongruous with those of the prison administration, and believe that the administration is trying to manipulate them toward ends that are detrimental to them.

Prisoners want to be released as soon as possible. During their imprisonment, most want to enjoy a maximum amount of freedom or a maximum number of privileges. Finally, many want to follow some preparatory course for a future life-style that may or may not be acceptable to the prison administration. Some want to prepare themselves to be more sophisticated criminals, political activists, artists, or writers. The result is that most convicts, when passing through the classification process, attempt to discover the variables upon which the decisions are made, and then to devise strategies whereby they can manipulate these variables to their advantage. Of course, this is very difficult to do successfully because the actual criteria, when they exist, are not known and cannot be controlled by them, for example, the bed space available in different prisons. However, some control can be achieved, and the attempts go on. For instance, one common strategy for reducing the length of sentence to a minimum is to manifest rather serious behavior problems in the classification stage, continue these through the first stage of imprisonment, and then, about six months or a year before the estimated minimum release time, reveal a drastic improvement in behavior. Some convicts have confided to me that they purposely scored lower than they were capable of on I.Q. tests, because they think that revealing high intelligence might make them serve more time. Others have reported that they attempted to answer personality tests, such as the Minnesota Multiphasic Personality Inventory, in such a manner as to reveal favorable personality characteristics. Whether or not these efforts are successful is unimportant. The important thing is that both sides of the classification process—the convicts and the administration—enter into the enterprise with separate, conflicting, and to some extent, hidden purposes in mind, and each attempts to manipulate the process for his own ends.

One important characteristic of the classification process must be noted. Information gathered under atypical circumstances in a cursory fashion with tools of questionable validity and without the degree of mutual confidence between classifier and classified necessary to promote sufficient reliability forms the core of the convict's "jacket," the foundation for all judgments that will be made regarding him. All other layers of the convict's prison record are shaped around this core and tend to take on its contours. Future evaluations will be made at regular intervals—such as before each yearly parole board appearance—and will be prepared after another interview, but they tend to follow the major interpretations and recommendations made in the initial classification stage.[6] In other words, a set, an image, and a program for each convict is constructed at the classification stage, and no matter how inaccurate and ill

---

5. I base this conclusion on my experience as a convict in the 1950s as compared with my experiences in a study conducted in the late 1960s.

6. In examining the central files of California convicts, I discovered that many reports contained verbatim statements or close paraphrases from earlier reports, which give added evidence to this conclusion.

conceived it may be, it dominates the official attitudes toward him throughout his prison career. For instance, the convict quoted above, regarding his interview with a vocational counselor, commented further on the effects of the counselor's recommendation:

> Every year when they would reclassify me, I would get called in and asked "why aren't you in the electric shop?" I would tell them "I never wanted to be an electrician; that guy made that recommendation without knowing anything about what I wanted to do, and that would they please take that off my record because I was doing fine in the job I was working at." It didn't work, next year it would happen again.

"Programming"

In California prisons, when referring to the convict's participation in the various treatment programs, both the convicts and the staff use the following kinds of statements: "I'm going to get a program," "you better get yourself a program," "get a program and you'll get a parole next time," or "look at————, he's programming." This use of the terms *program* and *programming* reflect two characteristics in the prisoner's attitudes toward treatment: (1) one must, at least tokenly, participate in treatment programs to be paroled; and (2) treatment programs are "phony," that is, they are hypocritical and ineffective. This is presently the general consensus of the convicts, and to a great extent, the staff. We must ask, then, is this just peculiar to California because of the correctional system's inability to implement sound treatment ideas, or is there something inherently wrong with the programs. I would like to suggest that the latter is true, that is, treatment programs in prison have inherent flaws that insure their failure.

To examine this point, it is useful to divide the programs into two general classes: therapeutic and educational-vocational. In the case of the first, a wide variety of therapeutic programs has been experimented with in California. In about 1955, group counseling was introduced and eventually involved the vast majority of convicts. In fact, for several years it was practically mandatory that prisoners participate in order to receive a parole. Group counseling takes many different forms; some groups have been led by trained personnel (sociologists, psychologists, and psychiatrists), some by untrained personnel (guards and various staff persons). The groups vary greatly in the regularity of their meetings; some meet once a week, some as often as every day.

Many or most convicts participate in these sessions only because they have to. They lack commitment to the therapeutic function of the program, and they are fearful that anything that is truly significant about themselves, revealed in these sessions, would damage their chances of receiving a parole. Moreover, convicts who are mainly lower- or working-class individuals do not share the middle-class's willingness to exchange personal experiences. They are intolerant of "sniveling" or "spilling one's guts." Consequently, the group counseling sessions seldom move beyond the bland and the trivial. As an example of this, the following excerpt from *On The Yard,* a novel by a San Quentin ex-convict, has captured the essence of prison group therapy sessions:

> He found his group already gathered, sitting in the usually symbolic circle. The therapist, a Dr. Erlenmeyer, occupied what was intended as just one more chair, but the group automatically polarized wherever he seated himself. He was dressed entirely in shades of brown, and his shirt was darker than his coat. His glasses were tinted a pale tan, and his head full of hair seemed soft and dusty.
>
> "You're late, Paul," he said, in a tone that didn't admit the obvious quality of his remark. His voice was opaque.
>
> "I lost track of the day," Juleson said.

This hung in the air for a moment like a palpable lie, then settled into the heavy silence. The group had nothing going. No one, as they said, was coming out with anything. Juleson settled around in his chair, careful not to look at Erlenmeyer, who might try to make him feel responsible for this wasteful silence. Once Erlenmeyer had stressed how therapy was working on them even while they sat dumb, as sometimes happened, for the entire hour. But he didn't like their silences. . . . .

Finally, Erlenmeyer cleared his throat to ask, "Why do you suppose Paul is late so often?"

They looked at each other to see if anyone was going to attempt an answer. Bernard only shrugged; he didn't care. After a moment Zekekowski said quietly, "He's got better sense than the rest of us" (Braly, 1967:103–4).

Group counseling is the "weakest" of the therapeutic experiments tried in California. The most powerful have been some of the attempts to initiate "milieu" therapy. For instance, in one of these an entire cell block at one of the new prisons, which houses younger convicts, was turned over to a professional with a doctorate in social welfare and long experience in rehabilitative correctional work. Various "treatment" techniques were implemented in the course of two years of the "C-Unit program" (Studt et al., 1968). There have been many other in-between programs, such as the PICO project in the California prisons, in the last fifteen years (Adams, 1970). Generally, these have not been successful from the administration's point of view—that is, they have not had any measurable effect on recidivism—and most often they have been bothersome or painful from the convicts' point of view.

The record for educational-vocational programs is not so completely dismal. There is, however, still some inherent weakness in this type of treatment in a prison setting, especially for vocational programs. In California, theoretically, a person may learn the following trades, among others: cooking, baking, butchering, dry cleaning, sewing machine repair, auto mechanics, printing, auto body and fender repair, sheet metal, machinist, plumbing, painting, welding, and hospital techniques. In fact, however, few men learn these trades. First, although there has been great expenditure for vocational programs, there are only enough openings in these programs for a small percent of the total convict population.[7] Second, the vocational programs themselves do not equip a man for a position on the outside in the particular trade. There seem to be two main reasons for this. One is that many training routines are actually appendages of the prison housekeeping enterprise, and are not related to outside occupational settings. For instance, every prison has a bakery that supplies the prison bakery products. The men working in the bakery are ostensibly in a vocational bakery program, but actually spend most of their time merely baking the prison products, and even after years of experience in the prison bakery, if they desire to continue the trade, they will have to learn a considerable part of the trade after leaving. Second, in the programs that are designed primarily for vocational training, such as the body and fender repair shop or some machine shops, often the equipment, the techniques, and the knowledge of the instructor are very obsolete. A man leaving one of these training programs, with a few exceptions, will not be ready for a journeyman position on the outside. As evidence that these programs are not effective, an unpublished study conducted by a regional office of the California Parole Agency discovered that only 36 percent of parolees had received any trade training, and that only 34 percent of these were working in a field related to their training.

---

7. For instance, in 1967 in San Quentin, there were only 316 trade-training openings for 3,500 to 4,000 convicts at the prison. Further evaluation of the trade-training programs in California is given in Irwin (1970:chap. 5).

In the case of academic education in California, convicts can complete elementary school, high school, and even some college courses. The emphasis is on elementary and beginning high school. Most convicts are required to complete at least a fifth-grade equivalency test or continue in school. After this, if they desire, many can continue school. In some of the prisons, such as San Quentin and Susanville, there are college courses given by local state or community colleges. Most of the prisons have limited funds for correspondence courses. Generally, however, as we proceed up the grades, the number of educational slots become fewer and fewer.

Gleaning

Perhaps the most significant impact of the expanding educational opportunities is that they have opened up a new style of adaptation to the prison world. I have referred to this mode, in another study, as *gleaning*.

> [In gleaning,] convicts choose to radically change their life styles and follow a sometimes carefully devised plan to "better themselves," "improve their mind," or "find themselves" while in prison. . . .
>
> Gleaning may start on a small scale, perhaps as an attempt to overcome educational or intellectual inferiorities. . . .
>
> . . . The convict may complete grammar school and high school in prison educational facilities. He may enroll in college courses through the University of California (which will be paid for by the Department of Corrections), or through other correspondence schools (which he must pay for himself). More recently, he may take courses in various prison college programs.
>
> He learns trades through the vocational training programs or prison job assignments. Sometimes he augments these by studying trade books, correspondence courses, or journals. He studies painting, writing, music, acting, and other creative arts. There are some facilities for these pursuits sponsored by the prison administration, but these are limited. This type of gleaning is done mostly through correspondence, through reading, or through individual efforts in the cell.
>
> He tries to improve himself in other ways. He works on his social skills and his . . . physical defects, has dental work done, and builds up his body "pushing iron" (Irwin, 1970:76–78).

There is some evidence that the number of "gleaners" is increasing.[8] Exactly what the relationships are between this prison mode and future life-styles, recidivism, or other success criteria is impossible to evaluate at present. One thing is important to note: this adaptation is voluntary and to a great extent self-determined. The convict makes up his mind to follow a course in order to effect changes in his own life. Then, perhaps with a great deal of advice both from the convict and staff world, he decides on a course of action. Very often, unfortunately, the course of action is not encouraged or is actively blocked by the administration.

Getting a Parole

As mentioned earlier, one of the primary goals of every prisoner is to be released. In the rehabilitative system this almost invariably means being granted a parole. So a great deal of the convict's action throughout his prison career is directed expressly toward,

8. An unpublished study of a sample of California convicts using the same instrument to classify "gleaners" discovered 24 percent gleaners rather than the 19 percent in my study conducted in 1967 (Irwin, 1970:77).

or influenced heavily by, this goal. However, "getting a parole" is like a game in which the rules are never known. In the interminable speculation on the subject, different theories are offered. Some of the major ones are: (1) "They'll release you when you get your time done." This theory places greatest importance on the time served for a particular crime and suggests that when the norm for that crime—considering its peculiarities, such as amount of violence or amount of money involved—is served, then a person will be released. Rehabilitative factors, then, are irrelevant. (2) "There's a group of psychologists and sociologists in Sacramento who look over your record and recommend how much time you should serve. The board may vary this three or four months each way, but they usually follow the recommendation." This theory reflects the disbelief by many that their fate could be decided in their short parole board appearance by a group of men who, at best, could make the most superficial examination of their record and progress. (3) "It all depends how you present yourself in the meeting. If you catch the right member, and he believes you are sincere and goes for your plans, then he'll give you a parole, I don't care how much time you got in." This theory suggests that the meeting itself is the most important factor, and that a parole can be won or lost in the hearing. (4) "It's your past record. If you got a lot of priors or if the D.A. is writing bad reports on you or you got a lot of silent beefs, then you are going to do some time. If not, then they are going to let you out in your minimum."[9] This theory suggests that prior criminal involvement is the most important factor in explaining time differentials. (5) "Show them some good progress, man, and you'll get a parole. They want to see some improvement." In this theory, evidence of rehabilitation is the most important decider of release. (6) Finally, "You got to go along with the program. Just do what they say, get some counseling, school, whatever. They just want to have some reason to let you go, then when someone asks them why they let you go, they can tell them that you took this program and that program." This theory, which is becoming the common one, suggests that the outward display of participation in treatment programs is the most important factor in getting a parole.[10] It is inferred that the prison administration and parole board actually do not believe in the efficacy of the programs, but rely on them mainly because some tangible justification for prisoner release can be cited, should justification be required.

The validity of the various theories is unimportant to us. What is important is that the criteria of release are not knowable to convicts and this precipitates the speculation described above. Moreover, it becomes clear that indeterminacy coupled with the vagueness or nonexistence of release criteria encourage manipulativeness and dissembling on the part of convicts.

Being on Parole

The terminating program in the rehabilitative system is parole, and in many ways it epitomizes the contradictions in the rehabilitative correctional system.[11] In parole the

---

9. In cases where a man is held accountable and made to serve extra time for crimes that were not charged against him and/or crimes for which he was not guilty, it is possible for the California Adult Authority to give a person an additional sentence for those crimes because of the leeway that exists in most indeterminate sentences.

10. These "theories" on the determination of sentence were constructed from informal conversations with convicts and ex-convicts of the California correctional system over the last twenty years.

11. The vast majority of convicts in California are released at least once on parole, so parole is an important phase in the career of the felon. In 1970, for example, of the 5,150 first releases, 96 percent were released on parole, while only 3.9 percent were discharged from prison, according to the Research Division of the California Department of Corrections.

contradiction appears as the surveillance-help dimension that underpins the parole routine. Theoretically, the parole agent aids the parolee's transition back into the community by mixing the two functions—help and surveillance. On the one hand, he enforces (with considerable leniency) a set of special rules of parole. In this way he protects the parolee from slipping back into harmful behavior patterns and, likewise, helps the community by keeping the parolee out of trouble. On the other hand, he "works with the parolee," that is, gives him counseling, moral support, and some concrete help, such as help in securing employment and residence.

In practice there is a serious flaw in this helping-surveillance relationship. The parole agent, who is answerable to conservative segments of the society, is required to enforce formally rules of conduct so restrictive that the parolee's chances for success would be seriously reduced if he were forced to live by them even for a short period. For instance, one of these rules in California is that the parolee must not "associate" with other ex-convicts or persons with bad reputations. For a person who lives among other working and lower-class persons, which is the case for most parolees, not associating with ex-convicts or persons with "bad reputations" is clearly unrealistic. Furthermore, the California parolee may not leave the county of residence, drive a car, or change jobs without his agent's permission, and he may not drink "to excess" (California Department of Corrections, n.d.).

In actuality, the agent, in order to prevent having to "violate" the majority of his case load and in order to increase the life chances of the parolee, enforces a much more lenient set of informal rules. However, the formal rules still exist and are invoked when some outside attention is directed towards a particular parolee. When this occurs, the parolee is often required to answer for behavior that the parole agent had known about and had explicitly or implicitly condoned. This usually results in the parolee experiencing a deep sense of injustice.

Moreover, the agent actually has few resources to help the parolee. He is not a professional therapist, even if this would help. And he has few resources to supply concrete help, such as a job, which the parolee often desperately needs. So parole, as with many of the rehabilitative programs that mix treatment and punishment, fails to aid the ex-convict's transition into the community. At best, it is an obstacle he has to contend with among the many other obstacles in his path. At worst, it is a trap that, when sprung, intensifies his feelings of injustice towards the hypocritical, unpredictable rehabilitative system.

The parolee copes with this flawed system by varying three aspects of his performance: (1) the amount and kinds of deviant or criminal behavior he will engage in (the assumption being that all parolees will engage in some deviant or criminal behavior); (2) the degree of deceit he will employ in his interaction with the agent; and (3) the distance he will maintain from his agent. How he balances these, in turn, depends on his perception of his agent's degree of *tolerance* for deviant and criminal behavior, the *intensity* of the agent's supervision, and his agent's "*all-rightness.*" All-rightness is a complex concept related to the parolee's conception of high moral character. It includes the dimensions of being fair, keeping one's word, being dependable, and treating others (the parolee) with respect.

Most parolees, by adjusting their performance to their particular agent's style of parole work, manage to achieve some degree of equilibrium. However, this is an unstable equilibrium and the agent may break through the parolee's screens of deceit and distance, and discover behavior that is intolerable to the agent. Or the police may arrest the parolee. Or the parolee may change agents, which occurs often in the typical parole career. Then, the parolee may find himself having to readjust to another set of expecta-

tions, or he may find himself being charged with acts that the former agent has tolerated. When the system is disrupted and the parolee finds himself being judged and
punished by a different set of standards than were operative in the ongoing relationship with his agent, when he finds himself being charged retroactively for acts that he
feels were condoned by the agent, or when he discovers his agent acting differently
toward him, apparently because of acts that the agent knew about all along, the parolee
almost always emerges with a feeling that he received a "dirty deal."

> They have that parole system set up to make you fail. I guess they have a business going
> in this state and once they get you hooked into the system, they don't want to let you go.
> They release you from the institution with a line on you and after a while they give it a
> jerk and you find yourself back (Field notes, San Quentin, October 1966) (Irwin,
> 1970:173).

THE IMPACT OF REHABILITATION

Suffering

We pointed out earlier that we suspect, because of the growth of the rehabilitative idea,
that sentences have become longer and have been given to a larger number of people.
We would like to argue also that in the "nonpunitive" rehabilitative system, suffering
was not diminished, perhaps it has increased. It is different in kind, but every bit as
painful. Mainly the pain comes from living in a social milieu characterized by indeterminacy and hypocrisy.[12] In the treatment-oriented prison, most of the important decisions that affect the life of the prisoner, particularly the length of sentence, are made by
"experts" with no explicit guidelines. From the perspective of the convict, the decisions
are often whimsical, arbitrary, discriminatory, and unjust. For instance, let us examine
more closely the general procedure for the determination of length of sentence in California prisons, since this decision is absolutely the most important to the prisoner.

California, having one of the most indeterminate forms of the indeterminate sentence system, leaves the final determination of length of sentence and time of parole
release in the hands of a government-appointed nine-man panel—the Adult Authority.[13]

---

12. David A. Ward and Gene G. Kassebaum, in their study of the women's prison in California,
recorded testimony to the increased suffering under the rehabilitative system: "The total waste of
time spent while here and the constant mental torture of never really knowing how long you'll be
here. The indeterminate sentence structure gives you no peace of mind and absolutely nothing to
work for. . . . The total futility of this time is the most maddening thing to bear. You realize nothing
but frustration from the beginning to the end of your confinement. This situation is compounded
by the 'never knowing' system of the indeterminate sentencing law" (1965:20–21).

13. In 1944, when the Adult Authority was formed, the legislature wrote, "One member shall
be an attorney-at-law, one have had practical experience in handling adult prisoners, one a
sociologist in training and experience" (California Penal Code, para. 5075). In 1951, when two
additional members were added, the Code provided that these two new members should have "had
all or any one of these qualifications: Paragraph 5075." During 1945–51, the board had three
members who had extensive police experience. One of these persons had a degree in law, but there
was no sociologist. After 1953, this paragraph was deleted, and exact composition of the board was
not spelled out. Currently, the board has nine members, all appointed by the governor. The current
board is composed only of individuals who have law-enforcement backgrounds, such as a former
chief of detectives of Los Angeles County, a former FBI agent, a former assistant district attorney,
a former correctional sergeant, and similar past experience. This composition leads California
convicts to refer to the Adult Authority euphemistically as being composed of "eight cops" (there
was one vacancy on the board at the time).

This parole board has wide margins in which to work. The statutory limits for second-degree burglary are 1 to 15 years, and for first-degree robbery 5 years to life. Roughly, the average statutory sentence is 1 to 15 years. The general procedure for determining the sentence is for the prisoner to appear annually before a panel that will contain one or two Adult Authority members. Before the parolee makes his annual appearance, one of the members of the panel has read his "jacket"—a compilation of information, such as test results, psychiatric and psychological evaluations, work and disciplinary reports, probation and arresting officer reports, etc. Key information from this file has been summarized in a fifteen- or twenty-page "Cumulative Summary" for the board appearance, and the board member usually confines his examination to his "Cum Sum." Moreover, this five- or ten-minute perusal is being done while another board member questions another prisoner.

During the actual hearing, the discussion led by the panel member who is the chief examiner in a particular case will cover a variety of topics, such as the crime, his prison record, and his future plans. The hearing lasts about fifteen minutes, after which there is a determination of his sentence and either granting of a parole date or a "denial."[14]

It has become obvious to many prisoners that there is no valid or consistent criterion operative in this sentencing hearing. Furthermore, there are occurrences that convince the prisoners that the decisions are arbitrary and unjust. For instance, often one or more members will recommend that a prisoner follow some "program" for the next year, but when he returns to his next annual board appearance he discovers there is an entirely different panel who are ignorant or uninterested in last year's hearing. Until recently, there was no record kept of the yearly recommendations of the panel members.

Moreover, the determination of his sentence and many other facets of the California rehabilitative routine are seen as extremely hypocritical. The prisoner feels that recommendations and justifications in terms of treatment strategies, such as the denial of parole for the stated purpose of pursuing some treatment program, more often hides other reasons for the denial, e.g., not having enough time served for the particular crime, suspicion of other crimes, and outside concern over his type of crime. Prisoners react strongly to being held in prison longer, coerced into various treatment experiments, and given job and prison assignments in the name of "rehabilitation," when they believe that either the rehabilitative programs are not working or that other factors, such as administrative exigencies, hostility, or the desire to punish are actually determining the decision.

The Sense of Injustice

Besides suffering from the indeterminacy and the hypocrisy in the penal situation, the convicts in prisons with rehabilitative systems with their attendant indeterminacy are experiencing a more profound form of suffering. This is the pain of being treated unfairly or unjustly. It has probably always been true that many, perhaps most, prisoners have felt some diffuse sense of injustice about the way they have been treated. But in

---

14. However, the inmate is *not* told at the time of his hearing what the board has actually determined his fate to be. Current Adult Authority practice calls for this information to be withheld from the inmate until the board has left the grounds of the institution. The convicts interpret this as fear by the board members of retaliation from individuals denied parole.

recent years, with changes in the prison routine and growth of the rehabilitative ideal, all for the ostensible purpose of helping the prisoner, and with the determination of sentence and other important administrative decisions made on an individual basis, the sense of injustice has become more intense and specifically focused. Two factors have augmented this sense of injustice: the first is that disillusionment with the rehabilitative ideal has become widespread, not only among prisoners, but among prison administrators also; and the second is the growing sophistication among prisoners regarding constitutional precepts and basic legal rights. In brief, the prisoner has a growing tendency to view procedures based on the rehabilitative ideal as clever strategies for stripping him of his constitutionally guaranteed rights.

There are several legal rights that, from the convict's perspective, are regularly violated. For instance, convicts believe that they are often denied due process in convicting them of crimes. This occurs when crimes or rule infractions that have not been proven against them in a procedure involving full due process are discussed in the parole board appearance and seem to result in their serving a sentence much longer than normal. This is possible with the wide limits of discretion that accompany any indeterminate sentence system and make it the cornerstone of the rehabilitative system. The following case reported to me by a convict is an example in which he felt that he was being denied due process.

> S. was convicted for second-degree burglary and served two years. While on parole, he stated that his relations with his parole agent were not good even though he was working steadily and conforming to parole regulations. After completing eighteen months on parole he was arrested two blocks from his home at 11:00 P.M. He was on his way home from a nearby bar where he had just spent two or three hours. The police were looking for someone who had committed a burglary several blocks away about an hour earlier. When they discovered that S. had a record for burglary, he was taken to jail and charged with this crime. When his alibi was established and there was no evidence to connect him with the crime except for his being in the neighborhood, the judge dismissed the charge and admonished the arresting officers.
>
> S.'s parole was cancelled, however, and he was returned to prison. When he appeared before the A.A. for a parole-violation hearing, he was asked if he knew why he had been returned. He replied that he did not. The A.A. member became irritated with him and told him that just because he "beat the charge" in court did not mean that he was not guilty, and that the best thing he could do was to admit that he was guilty. He refused to do this and tried to explain to the member that the judge clearly believed him to be innocent and that he could prove this from the transcript of the preliminary hearing.
>
> S. was denied parole consideration and postponed for another year. The next year he brought the transcript of his case to the hearing and the member said that he did not want to read it and that it made no difference to him anyway. He was guilty as far as they were concerned. Once again he was denied parole and scheduled for another hearing in a year (Interview, San Quentin, December 1967) (Irwin, 1970:56–57).

In a similar manner, many convicts feel that the parole board violates the legal principle of "just desert." Edmond Cahn makes the following comments on this concept:

> The law is regarded as an implement for giving men what they deserve, balancing awards and punishments in the scale of merit. As *general* merit is so difficult of admeasurement, legal action is usually expected to relate to particular merit: that is, to the right, duty or guilt acquired in a specific circumstance (1949:16).

In particular, many convicts serving time under the indeterminate sentence system feel that the crimes of others aggravate their own crime. In an interview with me a convict reported:

> D., an armed robbery offender, appeared before the Adult Authority after serving 4½ years. He felt that because of his crime, the time served, his past record and his institutional record, he should be paroled at this time. However, approximately two months prior to this board appearance, an armed robbery had occurred which, because of having excessive violence, received considerable news media coverage. Furthermore, many statements by law-enforcement officers and political leaders had followed, which requested harsher treatment of armed robbers. At D.'s board appearance, very little was said about his progress in prison; instead the conversation turned to the recent violent robbery and the attendant publicity given to this crime. D. was not granted a parole at this time and was scheduled to return for another board appearance when he had served 5½ years. Needless to say, D. felt that he was being punished for the acts of other persons (Interview, San Quentin, December 1967) (Irwin, 1970:59–60).

Besides these two types of violation of constitutional and basic legal rights, a growing number of persons living under rehabilitative routines feel that paroling authorities regularly are guilty of punishing them cruelly and unusually by making them serve unduly long sentences and through *ex post facto* enforcement of laws. The latter occurs when parole is denied after a person has been convicted because, in the meantime, more stringent legislation has been passed.

In most rehabilitative prison systems that employ an indeterminate sentence system, the majority of the convicts serve a sentence that is very close to the median sentence. A minority, however, serve longer sentences for reasons they feel are vague, invalid, or not constitutional or legally admissible in the sentencing procedures. For this, they and others around them feel a sense of injustice. This sense of injustice is contagious and its effects are profound. Edmond Cahn describes this contagion as one of the important basic human responses:

> Finally, the sense of injustice is no mere generic label for the concepts already reviewed. It denotes that sympathetic reaction of outrage, horror, shock, resentment, and anger, those affections of the viscera and abnormal secretion of the adrenals that prepare the human animal to resist attack. Nature has thus equipped all men to regard injustice to another as personal aggression. Through a mysterious and magical empathy or imaginative interchange, each projects himself into the shoes of the other, not in pity or compassion merely, but in the vigor of self-defense (1949:24).

Because of this spreading sense of injustice and because of the lengthening of sentences, indeterminacy, and hypocrisy in rehabilitative systems, it is far from the truth that suffering has decreased. The opposite seems to be the case: rehabilitation has introduced a new form of brutality, much more subtle and elusive and, therefore, much less offensive and disturbing to the deliverers who, consequently, have spread it among a much larger number of persons.

The Vitiation of Help

Finally, mixing "treatment" with coercion in the rehabilitative system not only has the effect of lengthening sentences and increasing the suffering and the sense of injustice, it vitiates the treatment programs or strategies that are offered for the purposes of correcting or helping the offender. In the first place, many people have pointed to the difficulties inherent in implementing treatment in prison. For instance, Harvey Powelson and Reinhard Bendix, writing in 1951 about the rapidly expanding California treatment-oriented prison system, identified this basic therapeutic flaw in the prisoner situation, where custody concerns were necessarily primary and the moral depravity of the prisoner must be assumed in order to legitimate custody.

They further warned of the danger that existed in disguising custody concerns as treatment, which inevitably happens. Donald Cressey (1960) and Lloyd Ohlin (1960) recognized potential difficulties in implementing treatment in prison because of organizational obstacles stemming from the multiple, and possibly conflicting, goals of the prison.

But beyond the special problems of effecting "treatment" in a prison, is it possible to coerce people into "treatment" in any setting? There is considerable feeling that the necessary therapeutic relationship between the helper and the helped is irrevocably damaged if the person to be helped is forced into the relationship. Psychiatrists have argued that in order for psychotherapy to be effective, the client must enter the relationship voluntarily. When he is coerced into the relationship, resentment, suspicion of the motives of the therapist, and lack of commitment to the therapeutic goals destroy any chances of success.

SUMMARY AND SUGGESTIONS

After sketching a highly critical picture of the correctional enterprise, it seems appropriate to offer some suggestions for the rectification of the problems described. Before doing this, it is necessary to present what I believe is the fundamental dimension that underpins all the particular criticisms made above: most correctional systems approach and act upon convicted felons as if they were less than worthy or whole human beings. In other words, to a great extent felons are treated as objects.

This has been consistent with interpretations of the Constitution that have justified convicts' treatment as persons with virtually no civil rights. However, recent judicial decisions have departed somewhat from this very narrow interpretation of convicts' legal status, and it is certain that future rulings will extend more of the rights granted the general citizenry to convicts (Hirschkop & Milleman, 1969; Goldfarb & Singer, 1970; Schultz, 1971; Turner, 1971). In the meantime, convicts themselves are challenging whether society can deny them all rights guaranteed others under the Constitution.[15]

In the second place, convicted felons are often denied basic human rights. Of course, the notion of human rights, as that of "civil rights," is something that takes shape in human history and varies from place to place and time to time. Let us agree that presently it involves at least the right to maintain one's physical health and safety, and freedom from physical and mental torture. Needless to say convicts, as well as all humane persons, object to the denial of these rights. But in spite of this, their denial

---

15. In the prison disturbances across the country from 1968 to the present, convicts have presented many "demands" to prison administrators and other selected parties in which the issue of expansion of constitutional rights was central. For instance, at Folsom in November, 1970, the striking convicts produced a "manifesto of demands" that had as the number one item: "We demand the constitutional right of legal representation at the time of all Adult Authority hearings, and protection from the procedures of the Adult Authority whereby they permit no procedural safeguards, such as an attorney for cross-examination of witnesses or witnesses in behalf of the parolee, at parole revocation hearings."

continues, not only as an expression of "punishment" or "control," but of "treatment" as well.[16]

These two aspects of nonhuman ("unconstitutional" and "inhuman") treatment are very important, but we are presently focused on a particular facet of the criminal justice enterprise, that is, "corrections," in which another type of nonhuman treatment exists. This is the "scientific objective" treatment. Since the impingement of the social-scientific rationale upon correctional systems, the convicted felon has been treated as a scientific object to be experimented with and to be converted, as the techniques for conversion are discovered. As stressed earlier, by and large, these efforts have failed. The basic reason for this failure, I argue, is that the attempts do not take into account the convicted felon's humanness, his subjectivity (for a complete discussion of this failure, see Matza, 1970). Instead of responding as an object, he persists in thinking, planning, "manipulating" if you will, and acting in a human manner.

Two aspects of his *human* response are of prime importance to us. First, he examines the particular treatment routine, explores its contours, and then proceeds to devise strategies to cope with it while maximizing progress towards his own personal goals. (The treatment strategies are not necessarily different from his own goals, but they usually are.) Second, he experiences coercion into programs or routines that he does not see as beneficial to him, but as punishment, which invariably angers him. He usually understands that the price of not participating can result in more punishment in the form of longer sentences. Moreover, he perceives, accurately or inaccurately, that instead of his well-being, the implementors of treatment are pursuing other ends, such as control. Therefore, the three together, the coercion, the disguised ulterior motive, and the hypocrisy succeed in producing more rage than rehabilitation.

In other words, the attempts to produce desirable changes in convicted felons fail primarily because the felons have been approached using an inaccurate conception of their nature. The suggestion that should follow from this analysis is *not* that new treatment strategies be devised which take into consideration these augmented dimensions of the individual. Hopefully, the conclusion that most readers will reach is that rehabilitation, as it is practiced—that is, with the essential component of forcing persons into routines designed to change them—be abandoned and in its place a penal routine be substituted that allows convicts to seek dignity and plan their own destiny. For this to become possible, certain penological principles must be followed: first, *punishment and treatment must be separated*. To do this, it must be recognized that whatever we do to others against their wishes is punishment, and any help we offer them must be accepted voluntarily. Of course, this means that the degree of punishment, such as the length of prison sentence, cannot be varied according to participation in treatment programs. Moreover, it follows that the help offered must be defined as help from the convicts' standpoint.

Second, to avoid the gross injustices that have undermined our criminal justice system and embittered the convict, *punishment must be for acts not statuses*, whether the statuses be "delinquent," "criminal sociopath," "member of a dangerous class," or anything else. As viewed from the standpoint of the person receiving the punishment, the only legitimate grounds for punishment are for something he has done, not something that he is or is not. This principle, though it is deeply rooted in the human psyche, is easily forgotten by persons not receiving the punishment, who are benefiting instead

---

16. For instance, at the California Medical Facility at Vacaville, the drug Nectine, which produces a desperate feeling of dying, was used on more than a hundred inmates in behavior-modification experiments.

from its being withheld. (A fuller explication appears in American Friends Service Committee, 1971:chap. 9.) Edmond Cahn (1949) argues that legal structures emerge because man has a capacity to be enraged by certain intrinsically unfair practices.

In the same spirit, *punishment must be uniformly applied.* Again, the person who receives punishment is deeply embittered when he constantly witnesses others receiving much less or no punishment for the same acts, whatever nonsense is spoken when the disparate punishments are delivered.

Finally, we *must use restraint in delivering punishment,* for at least three reasons. First, the general deterrence value of penal sanctions is not increased significantly when punishment becomes excessive (American Friends Service Committee, 1971:chap. 4 discusses the deterrent effects of criminal sanctions). Second, there is some evidence that longer sentences reduce the likelihood that a prisoner can return to a successful outside life (two separate studies in Assembly Committee on Criminal Procedure, 1968: 31–32 support this). Finally, and most important, once we accept that what we do to convicted persons against their will is punishment, the only way to maximize our humanity is to insist upon restraint in administering that punishment.

REFERENCES

Adams, Stuart.
   1970   "The Pico project," in Norman Johnston, Leonard Savitz, and Marvin E. Wolfgang, The Sociology of Punishment and Correction. Second Edition. New York: Wiley.

Allen, Francis A.
   1959   "Criminal justice, legal values and the rehabilitative ideal." Journal of Criminal Law, Criminology and Police Science 50(September–October):226–232.

American Correctional Association (A.C.A.)
   1970   "Declaration of principles." American Journal of Corrections 32(November–December):32–34.

American Friends Service Committee.
   1971   The Struggle for Justice. New York: Hill & Wang.

Assembly Committee on Criminal Procedure.
   1968   The Deterrent Effects of Criminal Sanctions. Progress report of the Assembly Committee on Criminal Procedure, California Legislature.

Braly, Malcolm.
   1967   On the Yard. Boston: Little, Brown.

Butler, Amos W.
   1915   "The operation of the indeterminate sentence and parole law." Proceedings of the Annual Congress of the American Prison Association, Oakland, California, October 9–14.

Cahn, Edmond.
   1949   The Sense of Injustice. Bloomington: Indiana University Press.

California Department of Corrections.
   n.d.   How to Live Like Millions. Publication No. 272. Sacramento: California State Printing Office.

Cantor, Nathaniel.
   1937   "A disposition tribunal." Proceedings of the Sixty-Seventh Annual Congress of the American Prison Association, Philadelphia, October 10–15.

Committee on the History of Child-Saving Work.
    1893   Report of the Committee on the History of Child-Saving Work. Twentieth
            National Conference of Charities and Corrections, Chicago, June.
Cressey, Donald.
    1960   "Limitations on organization and treatment in the modern prison," in Rich-
            ard Cloward et al., Theoretical Studies in Social Organization of the Prison.
            Social Science Research Council Pamphlet 15. New York: Social Science
            Research Council.
Garraud, Paul.
    1910   "The indeterminate sentence and conditional release." Proceedings of the
            Annual Congress of the American Prison Association, Washington, D.C.,
            September 29 to October 8.
Goldfarb, Ronald, and Linda Singer.
    1970   "Redressing prisoners' grievances." George Washington Law Review 39
            (December) :175–320.
Hayner, Norman S.
    1962   "Correctional systems and national values." British Journal of Criminology
            3(October) :163–170.
Hirschkop, Phillip J., and Michael I. Milleman.
    1969   "The unconstitutionality of prison life." Virginia Law Review 55(June) :
            795–839.
Irwin, John.
    1970   The Felon. Englewood Cliffs, N.J.: Prentice-Hall.
Kassebaum, Gene, David Ward, and Daniel Wilner.
    1971   Prison Treatment and Parole Survival. New York: Wiley.
Lombroso, C.
    1911   Crime, its Causes and Remedies. Translated by H. P. Horton. Boston: Little,
            Brown.
McKelvey, Blake.
    1968   American Prisons: A Study in American Social History Prior to 1915.
            Montclair, N.J.: Paterson Smith.
Matza, David.
    1970   Becoming Deviant. Englewood Cliffs, N.J.: Prentice-Hall.
New York State Assembly.
    1857   Report of the Select Committee Appointed to Examine into Conditions of
            Tenant Houses in New York and Brooklyn. New York State Assembly Docu-
            ment No. 205.
Ohlin, Lloyd.
    1960   "Conflicting interests in correctional objectives," in Richard Cloward et al.,
            Theoretical Studies in Social Organization of the Prison. Social Science
            Research Council Pamphlet 15. New York: Social Science Research Council.
Platt, Anthony.
    1969   The Child Savers. Chicago: University of Chicago Press.
Powelson, Harvey, and Reinhard Bendix.
    1951   "Psychiatry in prison." Psychiatry 14(February) :73–86.
Radzinowicz, Leon, and J. W. Turner.
    1943   "A study of punishment." Canadian Bar Review 21(January) :91–101. Re-

printed in Anthony Platt, The Child Savers (Chicago: University of Chicago Press, 1969).

Sarbin, Theodore R.
1969 "The myth of the criminal type." Monday Evening Papers. No. 18. Middletown, Conn.: Center for Advanced Studies, Wesleyan University.

Schultz, Jay L.
1971 "The role of the Eighth Amendment in prison reform." University of Chicago Law Review 38(Spring):647–664.

Studt, Elliot, Sheldon L. Messinger, and Thomas P. Wilson.
1968 C-Unit: Search for Community in Prison. New York: Russell Sage Foundation.

Sutherland, Edwin H., and Donald R. Cressey.
1970 Criminology. Eighth Edition. Philadelphia: Lippincott.

Turner, William.
1971 "Establishing the rule of law in prisons: a manual for prisoners' rights litigation." Stanford Law Review 23(February):473–518.

Ward, David A., and Gene G. Kassebaum.
1965 Women's Prison. Chicago: Aldine.

Wilkins, Leslie.
1968 Evaluation of Penal Measures. New York: Random House.

CHAPTER **28**

Organizational Reform in Correctional Agencies
Lloyd E. Ohlin

Harvard University

The most neglected area of knowledge about criminal justice agencies is the process of organizational reform. We know least about how to change the systems we now have to ones we believe would work better. We lack sophistication about the depth and strength of vested interests, the role of the political process in effecting change, the function of crises, such as exposés and prison riots, the significance of organizationally entrenched ideological conflict, and the means for resolving problems of administrative succession. As pressures increase on criminal justice agencies to make major changes in the basic premises and patterns of their organization and modes of operation, the need for a deeper understanding of the processes and problems of organizational change will correspondingly grow in saliency. This chapter explores these problems especially as they relate to change in correctional organizations.

CRISIS IN CRIMINAL JUSTICE

Over the past decade the nature and dimensions of the crime problem in the United States have been changing rapidly. The criminal justice system has not adapted itself fast enough despite repeated studies, specific recommendations, and substantial new commitment of private and public resources. The prevailing response has simply been to commit more personnel and resources to the traditional patterns of crime control and prevention. There are now more police and patrol cars, better communication equipment, more prosecutors, judges, and courtrooms, more probation and parole agents, larger jails, and even in some states, new prisons.

Occasionally, innovative ideas have been tried out. Generally, these have not dealt with the basic problems of criminal justice. They have rarely been evaluated, nor have they been permanently adopted, although there have been a few significant exceptions, such as the bail reform and police summons program in New York City, correctional halfway houses in some states and in the federal system, and community-based treatment programs and probation subsidy in California. The criminal justice system, perhaps more than other public bureaucracies, is rigid, slow to change, and reluctant even to try useful or promising new ideas. It is increasingly apparent that we cannot hope to cope successfully with the crime problem until we find better ways of renewing our criminal justice agencies and their capacity to respond more sensitively and effectively to the problems confronting them.

Sources of Resistance to Change

Though it may not be possible without a much more detailed study to outline all of the various sources of this resistance to change in the criminal justice system, nevertheless, several of the most serious obstacles can readily be identified.

Fear of Failure. Until fear of crime in the streets became a national public issue in the 1960s, the criminal justice system had operated for years in relative obscurity and neglect. Crime rates were relatively stable during the fifties and early sixties until the large birth cohort of the post–World War II period began to reach the late adolescent, high criminal risk age groups. Crime was not a salient public concern. Criminal justice agencies found themselves customarily at the end of the line when new budget appropriations were being made. The old methods of crime control seemed adequate. Agencies were under no pressure to innovate or reward those who wanted to try out new ideas. Perhaps this was less true of the correctional field than of other criminal justice agencies; yet even there, in most states, promotions were made from within the ranks, traditional ideas were followed with relative safety, and most systems became inbred and resistant to suggestions for change from within or without.

Now, however, the criminal justice system is exposed to the intense spotlight of public scrutiny. Personnel from top to bottom feel justifiably threatened by the demands to produce quick and spectacular results. They are fearful of interference by outsiders whom they regard as inexperienced and uninformed about the real problems they confront daily. Lacking the capacity to innovate successfully from within, they fear the risk of failure that basic innovations imposed from without might entail. Ways must be found to create a climate of mutual trust and respect in which new types of knowledge and skill drawn from other professions can be tested against the crime problems faced by criminal justice agencies.

Protection of Vested Interests. Perhaps the most important source of resistance is the fear that new ideas may call for radical changes in traditional ways of doing things. They may require new definitions of the problems the agency is facing and major changes in the priority of objectives, authority relations, staff roles, use of resources, and the knowledge and skill required to do the job. Many agencies may consent to small experiments, but are much more likely to reject or sabotage large ones. It is not only easier, but there are a wide variety of vested interests in established procedures, which seldom become apparent until efforts are made to change. For example, agency personnel develop strongly held beliefs about the crime problem and how to solve it. They are understandably fearful of losing authority, special privileges, or their position in line for promotional opportunities. Many have invested much energy in learning the established system and developing appropriate work habits. Furthermore, the disruption and uncertainty of the transitional period that invariably attends a major change in the system can create great anxiety. Many persons may feel deeply insecure about their ability to fulfill the new job requirements.

The problem is exacerbated by the fact that usually the means for resistance are readily at hand. Nearly all criminal justice agency personnel are covered by some form of civil service protection that prevents dismissal except for extreme dereliction of responsibilities. This provides a base of resistance to new training demands or policy and program changes that can be met, if necessary, by overt compliance and covert sabotage. In addition, there are potential allies in other criminal justice agencies, related social services, the political system, civic groups, and business interests. Such groups may have an equal stake in shielding the existing system from impending change. When aroused, this combination of internal and external vested interests can create an extraordinarily powerful array of obstacles to major organizational and policy changes in criminal justice agencies. It seems obvious that major changes cannot be carried out successfully until the nature and depth of entrenchment of these interests are clearly perceived and ways are found to accommodate to or oppose them successfully in the change process.

Difficulty in Evaluating Effects of Programs and Policies. No small part of the capacity of criminal justice agencies to resist change is due to the inherent difficulty of demonstrating that a new policy or program is indeed better than the one it seeks to replace. Four of the reasons will be cited here as significant examples.

In the first place, social science methods for evaluating the impact of public programs are in their infancy. The most rigorous research methods that serve as models have been developed under the artificially controlled experimental conditions of the laboratory. There the basic research problems are sharply defined and the variables tightly controlled. Until relatively recently, except perhaps for economists, social scientists have not been actively involved in either the development or the assessment of public policies and programs. They are now beginning to adapt or invent a variety of methods suitable to the study of human behavior in real life situations. To achieve greater advances more rapidly in the criminal justice field, it is imperative that more resources be devoted to the development of a technology of evaluation under field conditions capable of producing the sense of confidence and validity furnished by laboratory studies. In the absence of such an effort, the evaluation of new programs is left to the competing claims of expert opinion, the biases of vested interest, or the numbers game of administrative statistics.

Second, the programs and policies of criminal justice agencies ordinarily serve rather diffuse and often competing objectives. For example, a correctional policy of a prolonged prison term prior to parole is often defended on the ground that it serves the ends of retribution, incapacitation, and deterrence of others from committing similar crimes. Such a policy, however, may do nothing to deter the sentenced offender or to rehabilitate him for the future, though these are also prime objectives of a correctional policy. The task of deciding which of these objectives should be given priority is clearly an extremely complicated one. It is capable of rational solution only if the long-run consequences of pursuing one or the other can be determined. To do this means devising some fairly objective measures of such abstract goals. For example, there is, perhaps, no more fundamental concept in our system of justice than the concept of deterrence. All manner of laws, penalties, policies, and programs of criminal justice agencies are justified on the grounds that they deter potential offenders. However, virtually no work has been done to develop criteria by which we might determine whether such measures deter in fact. The problem is obviously not easily solvable or we would not be as uninformed as we are about the validity of this fundamental premise of the system. Thus, evaluation studies have been impeded not only by a failure to define more clearly the operating objectives of criminal justice agencies, but also by an equal failure to devise criteria by which the attainment of these objectives might be readily evaluated.

Third, evaluation studies are made difficult and complex by the need to account or control for the operation of a large number of variables that influence human conduct in everyday social situations. The evaluation problem is to determine the effect of a particular policy or program in achieving a particular objective, such as, for example, the effect of a new police–community relations program on crime rates in certain demonstration precincts. However, there are a large number of factors that affect the crime rate in a police precinct. The crime rate might have gone down anyway for other reasons. A sharp change for the better may have taken place in employment opportunities. New programs of social service may have been introduced into the area by other agencies, and so forth.

There are, of course, some steps that can be taken to rule out such alternative explanations. One might compare trends in rates in the demonstration districts with control areas and also compare conditions and rates in the same districts before and after the experiment began. Yet, in the current state of evaluation technology, it is extremely difficult to rule out all other plausible explanations that one might think of. Furthermore, the process of trying to do so is costly and complex. The problem, of course, lies as much in the nature of the criterion measures we are forced to use as it does in the number of variables to be considered. The crime rate is a far more complex and unreliable measure to use in a cost-benefit analysis than the economist's dollar. As matters now stand, much more effort is needed to devise more satisfactory measures of the output of criminal justice agency programs. We need much more experimentation with systems analysis procedures and computer operations to handle the range of variables that must be taken into account in evaluation studies. There may also be much promise for criminal justice agencies in the evaluation possibilities of related techniques used in simulation studies. It is probable, however, that before these more sophisticated techniques can be effectively applied, we will need measures of the achievement of criminal justice programs and policies, and methods to quantify or otherwise objectify such indicators.

Finally, in the area of human services there are legal and ethical limitations on the types of demonstrations or experiments that can be tried and the types of controls that can be imposed for evaluation purposes. A few examples may serve to illustrate the problem. There are rights of privacy that cannot be abridged by demonstration and evaluation projects in the field of criminal justice. For instance, in evaluating a drug-control program, the research worker could not employ techniques for gathering information such as those available to a police investigator, i.e., stop and frisk, eavesdropping, surveillance, or wiretapping. There are also constraints against violating legal rights to equal protection or ethical rights to equal treatment. Offenders equally deserving of services are entitled to the best available services. This may make it extremely difficult to set up experimental and control groups with different amounts and types of services. Many studies in criminal justice are constrained by the necessity to avoid any interference with the due process of law, as, for example, in the pretrial or trial stages of a criminal offense. To some extent such problems can be met by securing the voluntary compliance of offenders with the experimental and evaluation program by which they, in effect, waive the exercise of their rights.

Another serious legal constraint for research is the privileged character of certain information, records, or communications. Here again, to some extent the problem can be met by securing the voluntary participation of the privileged persons. However, very often useful research projects have been blocked from going ahead because police, prosecutors, judges, probation and parole officers, or correctional personnel have insisted on restrictions that permit access to their files only to authorized criminal justice personnel. In a number of instances, such restrictions have been circumvented by removing names from records or otherwise insuring their confidentiality, or even sometimes providing the research worker with some type of official status. In most instances, however, such measures severely restrict the scope of the study or involve an undesirable form of subterfuge. Research work in the criminal justice field would be greatly enhanced if it were possible to legislate some type of privileged official status for the professional research worker. Then, the researcher might be held to a professional oath of confidentiality that would permit him to have freer access to restricted official data.

The foregoing three barriers to change in criminal justice systems constitute a major dilemma for the field in the face of mounting pressures for more effective action on the crime problem. The studies of the President's Commission on Law Enforcement and Administration of Justice (1967a) repeatedly revealed the underdeveloped and neglected status of criminal justice agencies throughout the country. The vast majority of them continue to perpetuate nineteenth-century traditions of criminal justice organization and operation. Nearly everywhere the system is showing the strain or actually breaking down under the heavy burden of late-twentieth-century crime problems, especially in large metropolitan centers. These studies suggest that simply providing more money is not enough. There is a need to find ways to renew and reshape the system as a whole to deal with the crimes of the present and future. To do this, however, means finding ways to overcome some of these basic sources of resistance to change in criminal justice systems. The foregoing analysis suggests three primary goals for action-research projects in the immediate future. The first is to identify the major barriers to criminal justice reform and the means for successfully introducing major innovations. The second requires an assessment of the impact of new criminal justice programs and policies. The third involves the development of more effective methods of evaluative research.[1]

STRATEGIC IMPORTANCE OF RESEARCH ON CORRECTIONAL REFORM

Thus far, the discussion has highlighted major barriers to reform that are common to all of the principal agencies of criminal justice. There are, undoubtedly, few jurisdictions in the United States where these agencies constitute an integrated system of criminal justice. They are funded and operated relatively autonomously, though of necessity they cooperate, exchange information, and frequently come into conflict with each other. They also pose somewhat different types of problems for any major reform effort. Adequate research on any one of these agencies is difficult enough, though unquestionably many of the findings may turn out also to be equally applicable to other agencies.

There are strategic advantages to be gained in studying the process of reform in correctional agencies. The field of corrections has become increasingly open to research and demonstration projects over the last twenty years, and correctional institutions are now the most accessible of all criminal justice agencies to new experiments and evaluation studies. Correctional agencies more often employ social workers, psychologists, psychiatrists, and teachers whose professional training has led them to accept the usefulness of research as an aid to program and policy development. Of course, there are still many states where maximum security prisons oppose the testing of new program possibilities. However, on balance, correctional agencies throughout the country are more likely to make use of new knowledge about agency reform, effective programs, and evaluation procedures.

Recent research evidence suggests that correctional programs involving institu-

---

1. These are, in fact, the goals of a study of radical organizational and program changes in the Massachusetts Department of Youth Services being conducted at the Center for Criminal Justice, Harvard Law School. An overview of the phases of this reform movement is found in Ohlin et al., 1974.

tional confinement are not only ineffective but all too often make matters worse.[2] Recidivism or reconviction rates are high, varying from estimates of one-third to three-fourths of released offenders.[3] Case studies of criminal careers show that confinement in juvenile or adult institutions tends to increase alienation and criminalization of the committed offender.[4] On his release it exposes him to invidious labeling at work, in school, in the neighborhood, and often in the home that serves to push him further toward the development of a criminal self-concept. Corrections is an integral part of a community labeling process that crystallizes a delinquent and criminal identity, making the achievement of a more conventional and constructive adjustment exceedingly difficult (Horlick, 1961; Glaser, 1964:487–89). To be able to develop a correctional system capable of breaking through the tightening circle of this labeling process would represent a social innovation of enormous importance to the prevention of future criminality.

In a large number of research studies, the early onset of delinquency has proved to to be a key predictor of an adult career of crime. For example, studies of delinquent careers in Chicago show that those children who are committed earliest to a juvenile training school are most likely to develop careers of adult arrests (President's Commission, 1967b:107–13). It must be concluded that offenders who start early and continue on into adult life account for a major part of the crime problem when they are in the free community, or alternatively cost the state large sums of money each year for prolonged confinement. The research studies also consistently show extremely high rates of recidivism among those who have been confined in juvenile training schools. If these criminal careers could be cut off by effective treatment programs at a much earlier age, a significant reduction might be made in the total crime problem.

It is this last consideration that makes the reform and development of an effective juvenile system of corrections a matter of foremost importance in criminal justice policy. Can a policy of juvenile corrections be devised that will terminate rather than perpetuate criminal careers at this early formative stage? It is not clear now which of several correctional philosophies and programs might do this most effectively. Well-designed evaluation studies closely tied to the evolution of correctional policies are sorely needed to test the relative effectiveness of alternative courses of action.

Alternative Models of Juvenile Correctional Systems

Correctional policies over the past hundred years have been greatly affected by the pervasive humanitarian drift of Western societies in devising public and private solutions to social problems. At various times these policies have drawn on religious, psychological, and sociological precepts of character reformation. The current result is that several different models of juvenile correctional systems now compete for recog-

---

2. This point is repeatedly documented in studies by the research units of the California Department of Corrections and the Youth Authority over the past twenty years especially. Annotated bibliographies of these studies can be found in annual reports of the research division in each of these agencies.

3. Glaser (1964:13–31) provides a review of recidivism studies. See Ward (1967:205) for a more recent reappraisal. The continuing follow-up of criminal careers contained in the survey of federal offenders by the FBI's *Uniform Crime Reports* shows very high rates for subsequent arrest of released offenders. Arrest rates ran as high as 74 percent over a six-year period for persons under age 20 when released to the community by federal authorities in 1963 (F.B.I., 1970:39).

4. Excellent descriptions of this process can be found in the studies carried out by the Institute of Juvenile Research in Chicago (see, for example, Shaw, 1930, 1931; Shaw et al., 1938). For a more general view, see the several studies on prison socialization experiences of inmates in Cressey (1961).

nition and adherents. To some extent they reflect the historical progression in explanations and solutions for juvenile misconduct along a repressive versus expressive dimension. Nevertheless, they now coexist in institutional form throughout the country and often within the same state. The movement from one model to another involves major crises for individuals, agencies, and governments.

Before considering some of these problems of transition, let us contrast the basic organizational characteristics of the three major models of institutional services for juvenile offenders that are now in active contention for the allegiance of youth correctional workers in the United States. Though these are the principal correctional models now in operation throughout the country, there are other emerging models not considered. For example, Massachusetts is now trying to close all of its large institutions for residential care of delinquent youth in favor of a highly decentralized network of small group homes and individualized service arrangements involving basic reliance on the purchase of services from a wide variety of other public and private treatment agencies. It should also be emphasized that the descriptions to follow represent internally consistent ideal types that reflect the dominant characteristics in each model. In any actual situation there is always some borrowing of certain special features of other models.

In Table 1 the organizational characteristics of these three different types of correctional models are compared. This table may clarify the essential differences between the protective-custody, clinical-treatment, and therapeutic-community models in the following discussion. There are, of course, a number of other differences between these three ideal types, but a review of the correctional literature suggests that these differences are essentially consistent with the principal characteristics set forth in the table.[5]

Protective-custody Model.
This model is probably still the most common pattern of correctional training schools for youth in the United States. It, in turn, is an outgrowth and humanization of a far more repressive and punitive form of organization patterned after the adult maximum security prison.

In the protective-custody institution the staff generally shares the view that the delinquent conduct of youth is essentially a result of poor character training resulting from a loss of respect for authority in the home. From this, it follows quite naturally that the basic task is to teach respect for authority and good character through obedience to adults and proper conduct within the institution. In fact, this task of instilling

---

5. The characterization of these three models of juvenile correction draws on a number of different studies to isolate distinctive features. An unpublished comparative study of a protective-custody- and a clinical-treament-oriented training school for boys in the state of New York conducted by Richard Cloward and Lloyd Ohlin from 1957 to 1959 provides a basis for many of the distinctions noted in these brief institutional portraits. Another primary source is the descriptions of six juvenile corrections institutions in Street et al., 1966. This study provides detailed descriptions of three models of juvenile correctional institutions labeled (a) obedience/conformity, (b) reeducation/development, and (c) treatment. The treatment category included two subtypes, i.e., institutions organized to provide individual clinical therapy and those providing group therapy experiences. In Table 1 the category "protective custody" includes as subtypes the "obedience/conformity" and "reeducation/development" categories of the study by Street et al. The movement of the field is such that these are now better viewed as variants of a paternalistic style of institutional management. However, the subtypes of treatment institutions in Street et al. are treated here as independent categories to highlight the emerging conflict in the field between individual and group forms of treatment ideologies and practices. For a recent description of a punitively oriented maximum security institution for juveniles, see Rolde et al. (1970:437–43).

TABLE 1

JUVENILE CORRECTIONAL MODELS

Organizational Characteristics	Protective Custody	Clinical Treatment	Therapeutic Community
Theory of delinquency	Deficient character training and loss of respect for authority.	Emotional deprivation and psychological conflicts, blockage of insight to emotional problems.	Loss of respect for self and others, failure of interpersonal socialization.
Correctional remedy and procedure	Teach respect for authority and good character through obedience to adults and proper conduct in cottage, school, and work.	Encourage insight into sources of emotional disturbance through individual counseling with professional clinicians.	Teach respect for self and others through understanding one's own feelings and those of others in group therapy and discussion sessions with inmates and staff.
Decision-making authority	Centralized in cottage-life staff.	Centralized in clinical staff.	Decentralized to therapy group (subject to staff approval in most situations).
Control techniques	Regimentation, segregation, loss of privileges, physical force, broad discretion to discipline, informal sharing of authority with inmate leaders, use of special privileges, transfer, withholding of parole or home visits.	Additional clinical sessions, special privileges or loss of privileges, segregation or transfer, control of release and home visit decisions by clinical staff, low visibility of criteria of decisions.	Group discussion of rule violations or disruptive conduct, group advice on disciplinary measures subject to staff veto, group advice on release, furloughs, and other special rewards of achievement, high visibility of criteria of decision.
Inmate subcultural roles and norms	Domination by inmate clique of leaders sharing power with staff for special prerogatives despite ideology of equal treatment—stress doing one's own time, no ratting, minimal contact with staff, ritual conformity to rules—subculture closed to staff and resists character training approach.	Inmate role model is "right" guy defending self-integrity against staff intervention—stress conformity to group norms against ratting or discussing behavior of others with staff, and not threatening group privileges by conduct—subculture closed to staff and resists treatment approach.	Subculture open to staff through group discussion with some taboo topics that put others on spot—role model is active participant in group discussion—decisions visible to group more acceptable, norm is to participate but not at expense of others.

TABLE 1—Continued

Organizational Characteristics	Protective Custody	Clinical Treatment	Therapeutic Community
Staff training and desired abilities	No professional training needed except for school teachers. Cottage-life model is authoritative but protective parent. Reliance on previous experience as parent, tradesman, or teacher. Political patronage appointment likely.	Stress specialized professional training for clinicians, teachers, recreational directors, vocational instructors, and special competence as cottage parents to create receptive and understanding climate. Clinicians try to match inmates with appropriate cottage parents. Professional recruitment.	Preference for professional training in group therapy or discussion methods for group leaders. All staff, including maintenance staff, capable of warm and empathic responses to children and especially capable of handling aggressive, hostile, verbal assaults. Professional recruitment.
Relations to central office	Largely autonomous—rely on central office for administrative support and crisis management.	Central office furnishes administrative support, general policy, technical assistance, crisis intervention.	Central office exercises strong planning and development function, backup services, expert supervision and training.
Relation to aftercare services	Little contact—no regular institutional visiting. High parole case loads, nominal supervision, patronage appointment, no professional training required.	Professional training required—low case loads, some institutional prerelease visiting, regular client visiting and counseling expected.	Close integration of institutional and aftercare program. Use of group discussion approach continued in aftercare. Part-time voluntary participation in institutional program by client group of parolees. Professionally trained aftercare workers.

obedience to adult authority and respect for moral values takes precedence over the attainment of academic and work skills. It is not felt that much can be achieved in these latter areas in the period of time the youth are confined. Consequently, school and work programs tend to deteriorate into rather perfunctory time-filling activities except where close rapport develops in some cases between teachers and students. The primary decision-making authority, therefore, becomes centralized in the cottage-life staff. Most of the decisions on cottage placement, work and school assignments, and disciplinary actions, and the pertinent reports on a youth's progress toward release or special privileges become the responsibility of the cottage staff.

The protective-custody institution relies primarily on regimentation to produce a sense of order. Lines are formed to march inmates to their school or work assignments, to recreation, to the mess hall, or other group activities. Silence is often strictly enforced while marching in formation, while eating, and often for long periods in the cottage. Serious infractions are punished by segregation or isolation in a special unit and less serious ones by loss of privileges. It is not improper for a staff member to use physical force when provoked. There is, in general, very broad discretion to exercise discipline. The staff may withhold or delay parole and deny home visits if a youth's behavior and attitude is intransigent or hostile. In some instances the threat of transfer to an even more authoritarian institution is available as a means of inducing conformity to rules. Inmates may also be rewarded by access to special privileges at the discretion of cottage staff.

In response to this official system in protective-custody institutions, there develops an inmate subculture characterized by certain dominant inmate roles and norms. Despite the institutional ideology of equal treatment, an inmate clique of leaders dominates the situation in the cottages while sharing authority with staff in return for special prerogatives. Inmates stress the importance of doing one's own time, and enforce norms requiring no ratting on one another, minimal contact with staff, and a ritualistic conformity to rules. Enforcement of such norms of conduct takes place in the informal relationships that develop among the inmates beyond the reach of staff intervention and reinforces covert inmate resistance to the character training approach of the protective-custody institution.

Except perhaps for school teachers, the staff of the correctional training institution is not required to have had special training. The model for the cottage supervisor is that of the authoritative but protective parent. Therefore, it is possible to place reliance on the previous experience of staff as parents, tradesmen, or teachers. The lack of professional standards for staff makes the system especially vulnerable to the intervention of political patronage in the appointment process.

The superintendent of the protective-custody institution tends to function as the final authority for almost everything that happens within the institution. Where a central office and more than one institution exist in the state, the central office primarily provides administrative support and assistance at times of crisis. There also tends to be little contact with aftercare services. There is no regular institutional visiting by the aftercare staff and they are rarely asked for prerelease reports on home conditions. The aftercare officers carry heavy case loads and, therefore, are able to engage in only nominal supervision of youth on their release. Here, also, the absence of professional training requirements lays the system open to patronage appointments.

The Clinical-treatment Model. A number of protective-custody institutions have been transformed into treatment institutions dominated by the philosophy and insights of the mental-health professions. The delinquent conduct of youth committed to these institutions is perceived as deriving from emotional deprivation and psychological conflicts arising out of family experiences. Delinquency results from a failure of insight into these emotional problems and represents a blind acting out of a powerful but hidden emotional drama. As a consequence of this view, the treatment task becomes one of encouraging insight into the sources of this emotional disturbance through individual counseling with professional clinicians. More recently, experimentation is going on with group therapy under professional guidance but still oriented primarily to the achievement of personal emotional insight. This treatment ideology concentrates the decision-making authority with regard to cottage assignment, discipline, home visits, and release in the clinical staff. School work and recreational activities are also assigned with the advice of the clinical staff. Treatment institutions are often characterized by considerable conflict and tension between the clinical staff and cottage parents. Cottage parents feel they know the inmates better from daily observation of their behavior while clinical staff see the inmates only on periodic office visits. Although the clinical staff solicits reports from cottage parents, who, in fact, often sit in on decision-making committees, they feel they have relatively little influence on the decisions made.

Because of its ideology the clinical-treatment institution tolerates a much higher degree of rule violation, aggressive conduct, and hostility among inmates and between inmates and staff. The assumption is that youth trying to cope with their emotional conflicts will show frustration and hostility in interpersonal relations. Often disciplinary infractions will simply lead to additional clinical sessions. Regimentation is rejected because it represses expression of conflicts and, consequently, an effort is made to create a permissive and receptive homelike environment. Similarly, for clinical reasons, the response to a disciplinary infraction, such as running away, may produce a very different administrative response depending upon what are perceived to be the individual needs of the youth. He may receive a special privilege or lose privileges, be segregated in a special unit, or be transferred to a different cottage or even to another institution that is seen as more suitable to his needs. In other instances, a furlough or a home visit may be indicated. The consequence is that the reasons and criteria for many disciplinary and other types of decisions are often obscure to the inmates and can be said to have low visibility from their point of view.

In the inmate subculture the prestige role model is the "right" guy defending his self-integrity against the intervention of the staff. He is usually the inmate with the clearest sense of self-confidence and personal identity. He plays the arbiter in fights and quarrels among the inmates, and the interpreter of what often seem to be inconsistent staff responses to the behavior of the inmates. Great stress is placed upon conformity to the inmate norms against ratting or discussing the behavior of others with staff. There is also strong pressure to avoid personal conduct that would threaten group privileges. This informal inmate subculture regulating affairs among inmates and their behavior toward staff is kept hidden from the staff as much as possible and tends to encourage resistance to the treatment approach.

In the clinical-treatment institution considerable stress is placed upon the need for specialized professional training on the part of clinicians, teachers, recreation directors, and vocational instructors. The cottage parents also are rather carefully chosen to enlist those able to create a receptive and understanding climate in the cottage for the youth. A diligent effort is made by clinicians to identify the special strengths of cottage parents and to match an inmate with those parents regarded as most suitable to his special emotional needs. Staff recruitment generally is based upon professional qualifications and is relatively well insulated from political patronage.

In a system committed to the development of clinical-treatment institutions, an effort is made to create a number of such institutions, relatively small in size, containing 50 to 150 inmates. In contrast, protective-custody institutions often contain as many as 300 to 500 inmates. Consequently, there is more reliance in clinical-treatment institutions on the central office for furnishing administrative support, general policy guidelines, technical assistance in the development of special programs, and intervention when crises arise. There is also a conscious effort to encourage institutional prerelease visiting by the parole officers in the aftercare services. Parole officers are also required to have professional training, case loads are low, and regular visits and counseling with the parolees are expected.

The Therapeutic-community Model. The staff of a therapeutic-community institution locates the sources of delinquency in a loss of respect for oneself and others that constitutes, essentially, a failure of interpersonal socialization in early childhood, neighborhood, and school experiences. The basic thrust, therefore, in treatment in the therapeutic community is to teach respect for oneself and others through understanding one's own feelings and those of others. This is achieved through group therapy and discussion sessions involving inmates, counselors, and staff of the cottage unit. The prevailing norm is that most anything can be said and understood by others in the context of the group discussion if it honestly expresses one's own feelings. The central purpose of the group discussion is to expose dishonesty about one's feelings to oneself and others and to overcome fear of recognizing and expressing one's true feelings through the reassurance and recognition received from the group. Since the group is perceived to be the central therapeutic unit, most of the decision-making authority is decentralized to individual therapy groups. This is subject to final staff approval in most situations, especially about such matters as final release from the program.

As one might expect in such an institution, major reliance is placed upon group control to handle rule violations or disruptive conduct. Such matters are grist for the mill of group discussion. Offenders are encouraged to explore feelings associated with the acts of violation and to participate in the group discussions on what types of disciplinary measures would be appropriate. The group's advice on an inmate's progress in developing insight is regularly sought in connection with such decisions as release, furlough, and other special rewards for achievement. Thus, the capacity of the group to control misconduct is very strong indeed. The presence of the staff, their participation in the discussion, and their capacity to veto unreasonable decisions serve as protections against group dominance by inmate cliques. Decisions are made in the open during the course of group discussions and the inmate about whom the decision is being made is able to participate, challenge, and express his satisfaction or dissatisfaction with the result of the discussion. Consequently both the criteria and the process for reaching a decision are more readily understood and are characterized by a much higher degree of visibility than those in the protective-custody or clinical-treatment institutions.

In the thoroughly developed therapeutic-community institution, the inmate subculture and its various roles and, controlling norms of conduct are a matter for open discussion with staff and inmates in the group meetings. In less well developed institutions there are undoubtedly taboo topics, such as those that may serve to put others on the spot in the group sessions. The prestige role model is the active participant who verbalizes freely and directly in group discussion, though not at the expense of others. Pressures toward the development of an inmate subculture tend to be markedly reduced in a therapeutic-community setting because hostility toward the staff, the institution, or other inmates and special grievances are supposed to be brought out in the open, shared, and accepted as legitimate if the feelings are honest. Thus, the therapeutic-community institution eliminates one of the main functions of the inmate subculture: to provide an outlet for the expression of hostility and discontent beyond the reach of staff and disciplinary reprisals. In addition, there is less inmate dependency on inmate subculture leaders to interpret what often appear in the protective-custody or clinical-treatment institutions as inconsistent and arbitrary staff decisions.

In recruiting staff, preference is given to those who have acquired professional training in group therapy or discussion methods for group leaders. Since the model therapeutic community is small, numbering no more than twenty-five to thirty staff and inmates, all staff, including the maintenance personnel, are expected to participate in group sessions. As a consequence, two of the primary criteria are that the staff be capable of warm and empathic responses to children and especially capable of handling aggressive conduct or hostile verbal assaults. Since the criteria of recruitment are professional, there is little vulnerability to the influence of political patronage.

Any state creating a set of institutions around the therapeutic-community model would need to envision the development of a large number of small institutions each capable of caring for no more than twenty inmates. Though the group therapy process is regarded as the primary correctional remedy, the various group homes would be organized to provide other specialized treatment resources according to the needs of the inmates. The daily hours not spent in group sessions might be devoted to remedial education, vocational training, work therapy, forestry-camp work, or other types of useful activities. Consequently, the central office is required to exercise a strong planning and development function as new needs are identified and new program ideas emerge. It is also expected to provide backup services, expert supervision, and training for those carrying on the therapy programs, in addition to the necessary administrative arrangements and assistance in times of crisis. Since the therapeutic-community model calls for small community-based institutions, there is expected to be a very close integration of institutional and aftercare programs, with the group discussion approach continued as a supportive device in the aftercare situation. An effort is made to define the therapeutic-community institution as a resourceful home base to which parolees may return on a part-time or full-time basis when confronted with especially difficult problems to solve. This model envisions aftercare workers who have professional training similar to the counselors in the therapeutic-community institutions.

Comparison of the different characteristics of these three correctional models for the treatment of juvenile offenders suggests the radical reorientation that may be involved for many staff members in making the transition from one model to another. In many states today an attempt is being made to move an institutional system organized essentially around the protective-custody model toward the therapeutic-community model as the end in view. It is clear from Table 1 and the descriptions provided for each model that the changes contemplated are pervasive and extraordinarily complex.

THE DYNAMICS OF CORRECTIONAL REFORM

In order to investigate the complexity of correctional reform effectively, it is essential to set forth in advance the general framework of theory, concepts, and assumptions that should guide the research process. The reasons for doing this are to sensitize the research process to key problem areas that need exploration, to insure collection of the type of data that will test the validity of the theoretical framework against reality, and to help identify gaps in the framework of explanation where more intensive inquiry ought to take place. Specification of the theoretical framework insures that the research process builds on previous work in the area and increases the likelihood that it will add to the sum total of our knowledge. It further increases the economy of the research process by concentrating on problems and information likely to pay off in understanding.

Interest Group Networks

Public bureaucracies, including correction agencies, carry on their work in the context of a network of interest groups.[6] Those persons and groups with a general or specialized interest in the way the agency is organized and functions represent a system of influence with coalitions both for support and criticism of agency practices. They restrict the autonomy of the administrator of an agency in many ways. The relative balance of power struck between these coalitions determines whether or not the agency can continue to do business as usual.

A correctional agency must deal with many such groups. The other agencies of criminal justice, the police, the courts, probation, defense, and prosecution obviously have a direct interest in the way the youth agency does its work. They also have the power to bring sanctions on the agency when departures from normal and expected practices occur. The residents of the communities in which the agency institutions are located also develop over a period of time specialized interests as employees, interested civic group members, or as householders threatened with the prospect of runaways and criminal acts.

Where political patronage remains a strong force, political interests in the recruitment and promotion policies of the agency are of considerable importance. A wide variety of professional groups concerned with the welfare of children provide a most significant source of potential support or criticism. The interests of the newspapers and mass media are alerted to the performance of a correctional agency by the constant prospect of crises. There are also business groups interested in the purchasing policies, development, and construction plans of the correctional department.

These interest groups represent different degrees of power and influence on what takes place in the correctional agency. If the balancing and mobilization of support in these networks of interested groups and persons may be termed the "politics of corrections," then this must be a central concern of an administrator bent on introducing major changes in the character of his agency.

The vulnerability of a correctional organization to the influence of interest groups lies in its relative dependence on others for the basic resources in personnel, facilities, and funds to do its job. It must also rely on the cooperation and coordinated activities of other organizations to carry out its programs. For example, in the recruitment and promotion of personnel and in the setting of tenure provisions and personnel qualifications, agency autonomy may be severely restricted by the civil service system, a system of political patronage, or both. Similarly, control of increases in pay, fringe benefits, budget appropriations, and the authorization of new positions is generally lodged in legislative committees and in the state office of the budget or of finance and administration. Usually, the appropriation of resources for the development of new facilities for new programs or the alteration of old ones rests with outside groups rather than

---

6. The concept of interest groups as they relate to the work of correctional organizations is elaborated on in Ohlin (1960:111–29). The primary political science sources are Bentley (1908) and Key (1952:23–182).

within the agency itself. Thus, the capacity to effect change is highly dependent on close cooperation and support of other governmental or legislative units external to the agency.

The dependence of the agency on the support and coordination of its activities with those of private groups is also of considerable importance. For example, in the area of youth corrections, other public or private agencies may refuse to take referrals for supplemental or needed services. They may invoke red tape or outmoded rules making effective coordination of effort impossible. They may engage in constant harassment or disagreement over small matters and magnify them into public issues, thus diverting the efforts of staff from program developments to constant peace-keeping operations.

It seems apparent, therefore, that one of the first tasks in research should be to map the network of interest group relations that constitutes the effective working and decision-making environment of the correctional agency. This network needs to be assessed in three dimensions. In the first place, how attentive are these interested persons or groups to the organizational and policy changes taking place in the agency? Second, how much of a stake do they have in maintaining the existing system or in effecting the proposed changes? Third, what types of positive or negative sanctions can they bring to bear to influence developments within the agency? It is also important to note the method by which these groups are kept informed as to the state of their interest in the agency's activities. For example, is it through routine official contact, through a liaison agent or committee, or through representation in the staff or on advisory boards of the agency? A major hypothesis would be that appropriate shifts in the influence and capacity of different interest groups to promote policies in the correctional agency is an essential precondition to major changes in its practices.

The Process of Agitation

The process of transition from one model of correctional practice to another involves basic changes in the official ideology of the agency, its organizational structure, recruitment sources, and relations with other groups. It can be assumed that such changes do not occur without considerable conflict in a public crisis situation.[7] Ordinarily, public agencies go through alternating periods of relative public anonymity and periods of public crisis and concern. The latter are the periods of change, the former the periods of consolidation and routinization of program activities and agency relationships, internally and externally. Even in periods of relative calm, the agency encounters frequent disagreement and conflict with the interests of other persons and groups with whom it must work. However, there gradually emerges a fairly complicated pattern of accommodation and compromise to minimize this conflict. A public crisis signals the breakdown in this structure of accommodation. Correctional agencies go through such periodic crises, because this structure of compromises is essentially unstable. The power and influence of other groups grow and shift, new alliances are formed, and customary ways of handling problems are called into question.

Public crises that are the focal point for major change in a correctional organization do not occur without warning. A correctional organization can experience serious

---

7. This section, describing the process for achieving major changes in correctional organizations, draws on theoretical views originally stated in Ohlin and Pappenfort (1956), which was based on detailed studies of a major change of correctional philosophy from 1949 to 1955 in the Wisconsin adult system of probation, parole, and institutional treatment.

institutional riots, mass runaways and escapes, and even widespread scandals in its operations without having to make major changes, provided its system of accommodation with influential interest groups is strong and intact. The public crisis that precedes major change involves a considerable period of preparation. The initial sign is a noticeable increase in the communication of discontent within relevant interest groups, both inside and outside the correctional agency. Increased awareness of the shared discontent leads to a testing of dissatisfaction among other possible allies and a search for some common points of criticism.

These groups may differ markedly on what they see as being wrong with the agency operations. Concerning the treatment of youthful offenders, police and juvenile judges may feel that youth committed to the agency's care are not being held long enough. Social-welfare and mental-health advocates may feel that the children are not getting adequate treatment during their stay or that children are being overdisciplined or abused. In the institutions, the clinical staff may feel its recommendations are being ignored or the cottage-life staff may feel its disciplinary authority is being undermined. It is not so much that the reasons for criticism are shared as it is the dissemination of a common sense of discontent and readiness to adopt a critical attitude publicly. This initial mobilization of discontent leads to a gradual definition of the public issues and the emergence of coalitions criticizing and defending the organization. A part of this process tends to link dissenting groups within the organization in informal ways with these outside coalitions.

At this point in the emerging public crisis, the tactics adopted by the correctional administrator are of crucial importance. If the agency moves aggressively to win over and maintain alliances with powerful interest groups, the crisis may be avoided. The administrator may succeed in bringing conflicting demands and criticisms into the open. By exposing the latent conflicts among his critics, he may gain public recognition of the incompatible and impossible demands being made on the agency.

On the other hand, the administrative tactic may be solely to tighten control over the organization by forbidding discussion of agency affairs with outside groups. In the process many potential informal avenues for explanation of the agency's problems and needs may be cut off. A circular process is set in motion in which the increased formalization of internal and external relationships places the agency in an especially vulnerable position for the misinterpretation and exploitation by its critics of every untoward incident that occurs in its everyday affairs.

The net effect of these skirmishings between the agency, its critics, and its defenders is the creation of a public "crisis audience." It is in developing this audience that the news media play such a vital role. The public is slowly alerted by the sensitivity of the press to emerging crises. A gradual buildup of public interest occurs, along with a gradual crystallization of issues in criticism and defense, as critics and allies of the organization are encouraged to express their views publicly. Without preparation and participation by the mass media only a major catastrophe could create this type of public crisis for a correctional organization.

We do not yet have studies of correctional crises in enough detail to do more than outline the dynamics of this developing process in the most general terms.[8] There are many questions unanswered. Why is it that some crises of correctional agencies create

---

8. One of the most graphic and insightful descriptions of the dynamics of a major shift in correctional organization and treatment procedures is reported in McCleery, 1960:49–77. A revised account is provided in McCleery, 1961a, 1961b; and a report on a subsequent crisis in this same prison is covered in McCleery, 1968.

only a minor stir while others lead to wholesale reorganization of the agency? What are the tactics by which administrators successfully defend the position and status of their agency in such situations? What types of relationships between the proponents of correctional reform, the political system, the mass media, and the national standard-setting organizations in the correctional field prove to be effective in winning a public mandate for agency reorganization? The life of a public agency is a series of crises, and there is much to be learned about the way in which the network of interest groups relates to these crises either to maintain the status of the agency or to effect reform.

The Crisis-Precipitating Event

It is a commonplace observation that there are major discrepancies between the ideal public image which agencies of criminal justice project about their operations and what actually goes on in everyday affairs. This discrepancy leaves them constantly vulnerable to criticism and public exposure. Once a public crisis audience has been focused on an agency's activities, almost any form of trouble can precipitate an intensive flood of coverage by the mass media, and a burst of public criticism so widespread that it can no longer be ignored. The precipitating event may be a serious crime by a paroled offender, a mass runaway, acts of brutality in the disciplining of inmates, or corruption among staff. The precipitating event by itself, however, does not seem sufficient to explain what follows. Instead, it is the intense climate of criticism and public awareness that seems to magnify the precipitating event sufficiently to initiate a searching public investigation of the "cause of the trouble."

Crisis Resolution

Once the crisis has reached proportions where something clearly must be done to reflect the responsiveness of government to public concern, a new stage is reached. Relationships among interested groups again become more fluid as they search out allies interested in common proposals for resolving the crisis. Since many of those who join in criticism of the correctional agency do so for disparate and rather diverse reasons, they are likely to favor rather different proposals for resolving the problem. Those critical of the agency's leniency and inconsistency and in favor of more repressive correctional practices now find themselves in conflict with proponents of a more vigorous treatment ideology. A realignment of interest groups takes place as the alternative proposals for resolving the crisis become more clearly defined.

The normal political response in such crisis situations is a promise of action that will get to the bottom of the problem and solve it. The most common device is to form a fact-finding committee. This can be a legislative committee or a citizens' committee appointed by the governor, and may involve a request to a national standard-setting agency in corrections to investigate and make recommendations.[9] A fact-finding committee can perform two alternative functions for those in positions of political responsibility. First, even when there are no major political obstacles to change, time is required to prepare a solution that will appease the contradictory demands of the special interest groups and convince the aroused public audience that responsibilities have been met. Fact-finding takes time and during this period the relative strength of various

---

9. This was the most common response of state governors to the wave of prison riots that swept through some of the country's most progressive prison systems from 1951 to 1953; cf. American Prison Association, 1953, and Ohlin, 1956:22–26.

groups can be explored to determine what might constitute a satisfactory resolution of the crisis. Second, for those who wish no fundamental changes, the fact-finding committee offers a possible way of avoiding change without great political cost. While the investigation is being drawn out over a long period of time, the crisis dies and with it the public crisis audience. Under such conditions, it is possible to publish a report some months later that glosses over the crisis or, if the fact-finding committee recommends changes, its suggestions may be allowed to fade away for lack of any appropriate actions based on them.

However, if the coalitions of interest groups advancing a particular set of reorganization proposals remain highly active during the fact-finding process, addressing questions and presenting evidence to the fact-finding committee, and if these groups are able to invoke successfully the prestige of national standard-setting organizations, such as the National Association of Training Schools and Juvenile Agencies, the National Council of Crime and Delinquency, or national welfare and mental-health groups, along with their local state counterparts, it becomes much more probable that some changes in the direction of their proposals will need to be made. Those groups with model correctional plans and standards and with experts readily available to press their proposals are more likely to succeed in specifying the types of changes needed than less well prepared proponents of alternative positions. The likelihood of success is even greater when these groups also have developed ready access to the mass media and when a base for legislative support among a large body of relatively neutral legislators has been carefully laid.

Here again, though a general description of a sequence of events is possible, the lack of detailed studies makes it impossible to identify the most crucial influences determining the course of crisis resolution. It is not clear just how much realignment of interest groups takes place after the crisis, compared to the situation before it reaches its peak. Recently, in Massachusetts, for example, it appears that the Department of Youth Services weathered several crises before it reached the point where a major reorganization became effective. Study of the circumstances surrounding the public crises confronting this agency will shed much light on the dynamics of the process of change (Ohlin et al., 1974). The development of such a detailed case history will unquestionably yield new understanding of some of the major obstacles to effective reform at times of public crises in correctional agencies, as well as the conditions under which reform can succeed.

The Mandate for Reorganization

A major public crisis of the proportions described above, especially where it leads to new legislative acts designed to reorganize the agency, usually results in the dismissal of the organization's administrator. Earlier criticism of his regime and the need for a fresh start make him expendable. The history of the crisis and the means of its resolution set conditions that affect the subsequent administrative decisions of the successor and the course of organizational development. The solution to the crisis provides the new administrator with a mandate. In effect, the new administrator is put in office to implement changes decided upon by the groups that have been successful in imposing their solution for the crisis. He tends to be selected because his philosophy of corrections and his commitment to a certain type of program are consistent with this type of solution. As the choice of the groups that formed the successful coalition for reorganization, he is committed to them to carry out their program. The circumstances of his choice have alerted him to the significance of "public relations," and, in particular, to the crucial role of groups in the correctional agency's network of interests and the types of administrative failures that excite their criticism. He knows that future crises must be avoided if he is to fulfill the mandate that brought him to office.

PROBLEMS IN THE RADICAL TRANSFORMATION OF CORRECTIONAL INSTITUTIONS

One of the most difficult problems in radical change from one correctional model to another is gaining acceptance for the new treatment ideology as a more realistic, insightful, and workable definition of the problem to be solved than the system of beliefs which it seeks to supplant. It is not only that personnel who have worked in a particular type of correctional system for a long time acquire a shared definition of the causes of delinquency and what needs to be done in the institutional program to correct delinquent tendencies; it is also that a correctional model may have developed and become routinized over a period of years. During this period the model gradually sorts out personnel for whom the agency's definition of the delinquent problem and its remedy is thoroughly consistent with the personal and moral beliefs that the staff have acquired in the course of their own personal development. This double reinforcement of the basic institutional definition of the situation is extraordinarily difficult to dislodge. It means asking personnel to rethink and reevaluate fundamentally held premises about human conduct, or simply to set these personal beliefs aside and play a role based upon a new set of institutionally prescribed definitions of the situation.[10] There may be great resistance to retraining or there may be a disposition to subvert administrative directions. It means asking personnel trained in a protective-custody model, who believe that loss of respect for authority is the root cause of delinquency and teaching respect for authority the cure, to believe that loss of respect for oneself is the true cause and teaching respect for self can only take place in a face-to-face confrontation that permits free display of hostility and disrespect for authority.

Staff Loyalty

The new administrator is likely to find the staff composed of persons recruited under the previous administration and committed to the defeated ideology. In addition to this, his succession to office threatens a denial of access to organizational rewards, such as promotions, salary increases, and so forth, which subordinates feel they have earned. Since the new administrator was not a participant in the former system of loyalties and obligations and brings new criteria for the evaluation of staff competence and output, his arrival creates anxieties and tensions throughout the system. Furthermore, the correctional agency has been through a long period of internal dissension and external criticism, culminating in repudiation of the organization and its practices. The new administrator is likely to encounter a hostile staff with low morale. One strategy the new administrator may pursue is to appoint a cadre of lieutenants whose loyalty is unquestioned and whose philosophy of correctional treatment agrees with his own. Armed with their support, he can effect better administrative authority over existing programs

---

10. McCleery (1960, 1961a, 1961b, 1968) traces the loss of authority by the custodial force in the Hawaiian prison system in considerable part to their inability to adopt the treatment ideology of the new warden.

and begin the process of winning over the loyalty and philosophical commitment of staff members held over from the previous administration.[11]

This strategy may not work, of course, if there are only a very few vacancies, all at a high level and difficult to fill, and if a deeply entrenched civil service system exists. Under such circumstances, personnel may have maintained close links with the political system and over the years may have formed connections with a variety of other external interest groups. Such relationships may constitute a formidable base for opposition to new programs and policies. Information about what is happening within the agency can be spread quickly through established communication channels. Internal crises can be magnified and made visible externally. The dissemination of definitions of disorder, loss of control, and threats to authority can again arouse widespread public concern. There are possibilities for effective sabotage of new programs through nonconformity or overcompliance, the withdrawal of disciplinary controls over inmates, and even the encouragement of runaways, all backed by union protests about the undesirability of the new practices.

There are, of course, a variety of countermeasures that a new administrator may undertake. Among the existing staff he may find persons previously ignored whose philosophy of treatment accords with his own. Through selective promotion of such persons he may build a structure of new loyalties to the model of corrections he wishes to introduce. Through in-service training programs, educational leaves, and constant exposure of the old staff to the newer ideologies of treatment, he may open up the possibility of advancement as an inducement to acceptance and implementation of the new program. Since life for staff and inmates alike in the protective-custody institution tends in time to get highly routinized and boring, he may find it possible to stir new interest by permitting staff to participate in new programs or try out ideas they were not permitted to express or test before. The degree of success in handling these problems of internal staff dissatisfaction and grievance may prove, in the end, to be the key to the relative success or failure of his efforts toward organizational change.

Reallocation of Authority

One of the central problems of a new state correctional administrator is to reallocate decision-making authority. For example, if he is trying to change from a protective-custody to a therapeutic-community model of youth corrections, he must bridge the relative autonomy of the institutions and their superintendents from central office authority, and establish a greater measure of control over program developments and organizational arrangements. He must gradually shift decision-making authority from the cottage-life staff to those professionally trained in group therapy and, ultimately, to the members of the therapy group itself as a communal base for decisions. Initially, a move in this direction will be seen as undermining the authority of the former cottage-life staff members and the institution administration. If this process is carried forward too abruptly, chaos may ensue, since in the period of transition no one will know who has authority to make decisions or what the criteria of decisions ought to be. The location of decision-making authority, the process by which decisions are reached, and the

---

11. This was one of the key strategies pursued by the new administrator in the Wisconsin reorganization reported by Ohlin and Pappenfort (1956). The same organizational problem and its solution are described in great detail in Gouldner's studies (1954a, 1954b) of administrative succession in an industrial setting.

criteria to be employed are radically different in the two systems. The problem of re-distributing authority from that required by the protective-custody model to that required by the therapeutic-community model is an extraordinarily sensitive one and will require great tolerance for misunderstanding and resistance from many quarters.

Redefinition of Role Relationships and Responsibilities

Such a shift from one correctional model to another necessitates a redefinition of the responsibilities and duties of some staff members and inmates as well as a definition of the rights to which they are entitled. In addition, they are being asked to assume very different relationships with each other. This entails a shift from a superior-inferior relationship to one of equals in the group discussion situation, where no member is protected from attack.

Inmate Response to New System

It would seem that the inmate response would be overwhelmingly in favor of a change to a therapeutic-community model. However, there are some other distinct possibilities. The more verbally facile inmates may find it exciting and gain a sense of power from being able to dominate the discussion. However, as the therapeutic community builds relationships in the group discussions, this skill becomes less important than the ca-pacity to feel and express emotion, no matter how inarticulately. The "con man" per-sonality may find an initially favorable terrain rough going later on. Furthermore, the give and take of the encounter session is strong medicine and there are many who would rather avoid the anxiety and the uncontrollable feelings that such sessions often arouse. Other inmates may welcome the opportunity to express openly hostility to staff and the institution, but, as the sessions continue, this satisfaction may be short-lived as they face the necessity of accounting for the sources of their hostility.[12] In addition, there may be a number of inmates who were leaders under the previous system and much prefer an authoritative system in which they are able to exercise their own form of power within the inmate group (Garabedian, 1962).

It is certainly not self-evident what the inmate response will be to such a new pro-gram. This is particularly true if one considers that the period of transition will be a long one, with a great deal of confusion about the sources of authority and the rule system actually in force. Also, confusion about the system of rewards and discipline, and appropriate channels for the correction of grievances may create insecurity, uncer-tainty, anxiety, and threatened loss of power for many staff and inmates alike.

These institutional problems are very formidable ones. Just how they are handled will determine whether the reform program succeeds or fails. The research problem is to keep track of the responses that are made throughout the system to the various changes that are introduced. There is a great deal to be learned from such an analysis about the key leverage points for effecting successful reform, the pace at which inno-vations can be introduced, the order of priority for dealing with different problems, and the type of measures that succeed or fail.

---

12. These various reactions are well documented in McCorkle et al. (1958). One of the most vivid descriptions of the dynamics and subculture of the therapeutic-community institution is pro-vided by Stephenson and Scarpitti (1968).

External Relationships

Attention has been focused thus far on the internal problems confronting a new state correctional administrator during a transition period of major change. There are, of course, at the same time external problems that may well consume a major share of his attention. It is common bureaucratic practice for the top administrator to be concerned with the external relationships of his agency while deputies and other staff members handle matters of internal routine and reorganization. This is why the development of a cadre of trusted lieutenants may become an essential requirement for success. The new administrator cannot afford to neglect the problem of consolidating external support behind the reforms that he proposes to introduce. He must prepare from the outset for inevitable counter-crises that will challenge his authority and the legitimacy of the correctional model he seeks to impose.[13]

For example, in Massachusetts the public departments are extremely dependent on the support of the Department of Finance and Administration in the executive office of the governor for funds, positions, and facilities. All government departments are also dependent on the legislative appropriation committees for approval of the appropriations recommended by the executive branch. In the highly politicized atmosphere of the state legislature in Massachusetts, each department is expected to develop its own system of relationships with the legislature to insure support for the funds and authority it requires to do its job. Those department heads who have grown up in the local system of politics may find this a much easier task than a new commissioner from another state. The support of the governor's office and the development of trustworthy and loyal political counsel can accomplish a great deal, but this, inevitably, is a problem area on which any new state commissioner must focus much energy to ensure the ultimate success of his program.

A NEW MODEL FOR ACTION-RESEARCH COLLABORATION

For the most part two general models for research activity have been pursued in the field of criminal justice. In one model, projects are developed and conducted by a research center located outside the agency and committed solely to the further development of knowledge in the field. Such a research center accepts no obligation for drawing implications for the agency's programs and policies except in the most general way. Ordinarily, these studies have been short term and the research relationship with the operating agency lapses between projects.

It is important to carry out such studies to contribute to the general base of knowledge in the field, but they have been criticized by operating agencies because of the limited character of their contribution to the development of more effective policies and programs in the cooperating agency. The results find their way into textbooks but not into programs. Part of the difficulty here is the failure to work out a mechanism by which joint consideration of program and policy implications of the research findings can be developed by the research center and action agency as a team. Furthermore, the episodic character of the relationship between the research center and the action agency means that individual programs are studied apart from their contribution to the total system of policies and activities.

The second principal model of research participation has been the development

---

13. This process of "counterrevolution" is clearly described by McCleery (1960, 1968) in his observations of change in the Hawaiian prison system.

of an operational research arm within the agency itself. Sometimes, as the need arises, a sharply defined contractual arrangement is made instead with an independent research organization to perform much the same function. The difficulty with relying solely on a research arm within the administration of the agency is that it tends to become subverted, with rare exceptions, into an office for gathering administrative statistics and data for annual reports and speechmaking. The use of contractual arrangements with independent operational research organizations is also unsatisfactory because it tends to be episodic and employed rarely when funds are tight. Furthermore, the research tends to focus on rather narrow operational problems that lend themselves to quick solutions of a technical order. They do not provide the opportunity to address long-range program objectives or to analyze the contribution of particular policies and programs within the total system of the agency's activities.

The field of criminal justice needs to get broadly based feedback on the output of agencies in order to design more effective policies and programs. What may be needed is an action-research arrangement in which an independent research center, preferably university based, agrees to establish a long-term relationship with an agency for two purposes. On the one hand, the relationship should provide the opportunity to engage in extended research projects with long-range payoffs, ones that are designed to contribute to the advancement of the knowledge base of the field rather than to influence day-to-day policy and program decisions of the agency. On the other hand, the research center should serve as an evaluation arm for the agency, feeding back neutral findings on the effects of the agency's programs and policies. At the same time it should accept an obligation to participate with the agency in searching out the implications of those findings for the further development of its program. Though it shares the commitment of the agency to the long-range goals that the agency seeks to achieve in the rehabilitation of offenders, it is not necessarily committed to any particular correctional philosophy nor any particular set of means or procedures for achieving those goals. It plays the role, instead, of a constructive critic.

Problems of Action-Research Collaboration

There are certain problems that must be resolved in this arrangement if the research center is to preserve its objectivity and its ability to secure unbiased responses from its respondents over a number of years. It is essential that its integrity as a research center should not be compromised by its action involvements. A brief comment on two problems that typically arise in action-research programs may serve as illustrations.

Confidentiality. The integrity of the research program can only be maintained if the respondents interviewed during the course of the research have complete confidence that their answers to questions will not cause them personal disadvantage. They must feel free to speak frankly and express their opinions. It is altogether likely that if the norm of confidentiality is carefully pursued, a relationship of trust may, in fact, be built up more successfully in a long-term project than a more limited and episodic research effort.

Generality versus Specificity of Reporting. Some of the data gathered in the project will be politically sensitive to the extent that it might adversely affect the career of individual respondents. For example, a special crisis unit of research interviewers should be available to monitor significant crises, both internal and external to the agency. Gathering data on crises is important for the purpose of understanding how crises develop, how they are resolved, and how they contribute to the process of change. They also offer revealing insights into the dynamics of events in the agency. In times of crises, attitudes and beliefs of staff and emerging problems—which may be taken for granted or concealed during normal circumstances—emerge sharply into view. However, reporting of results from these data would need to be confined for a period of time to the statement of general principles and conclusions without some of the supporting data necessary to document the statements.

CONCLUSION

The foregoing exploration of the need for greater knowledge about the processes of major organizational change has focused on the problems of change in correctional institutions, especially juvenile agencies. However, both the crisis theory of change and the identified problems of change outlined in this chapter are conceived to be generally applicable not just to other criminal justice agencies but to most public service bureaucracies. To gain greater sophistication about the problems of organizational reform, we must undertake detailed studies of such efforts from a comparative perspective over relatively long periods of time. Though much can be learned from retrospective construction of case studies of organizational change, we shall advance our knowledge much more rapidly if research evaluation is undertaken while reforms are in progress. We now have neither the theoretical nor the factual base on which to construct postulates for the management of social and organizational reform. This chapter and the past work by former colleagues and myself on which it is based are contributions toward such an objective.

REFERENCES

American Prison Association.
    1953   Prison Riots and Disturbances. American Prison Association Committee on Riots. New York: American Prison Association.

Bentley, Arthur F.
    1908   The Process of Government. Bloomington, Ind.: Principia Press (republished in 1949).

Cressey, Donald R. (ed.)
    1961   The Prison. New York: Holt, Rinehart & Winston.

Federal Bureau of Investigation (F.B.I.)
    1970   Crime in the United States: Uniform Crime Reports—1969. Washington, D.C.: U.S. Government Printing Office.

Garabedian, Peter G.
    1962   "Legitimate and illegitimate alternatives in the prison community." Sociological Inquiry 32(Spring):172–184.

Glaser, Daniel.
    1964   The Effectiveness of a Prison and Parole System. Indianapolis: Bobbs-Merrill.

Gouldner, Alvin W.
    1954a   Patterns of Industrial Bureaucracy. Glencoe, Ill.: Free Press.
    1954b   Wildcat Strike. Yellow Springs, Ohio: Antioch Press.

Horlick, Reuben S.
1961 "Inmate perception of obstacles to readjustment in the community." Pp. 200–205 in Proceedings of the American Correctional Association. Washington, D.C.: American Correctional Association.

Key, V. O., Jr.
1952 Politics, Parties and Pressure Groups. Third Edition. New York: Crowell.

McCleery, Richard.
1960 "Communication patterns as basis of systems of authority," in Richard Cloward et al., Theoretical Studies in Social Organization of the Prison. Social Science Research Council Pamphlet 15. New York: Social Science Research Council.
1961a "The governmental process and informal social control." Pp. 149–188 in Donald R. Cressey (ed.), The Prison. New York: Holt, Rinehart & Winston.
1961b "Authoritarianism and the belief system of incorrigibles." Pp. 260–306 in Donald R. Cressey (ed.), The Prison. New York: Holt, Rinehart & Winston.
1968 "Correctional administration and political change," in L. Hazelrigg (ed.), Prison Within Society. New York: Doubleday.

McCorkle, Lloyd W., Albert Elias, and F. Lovell Bixby.
1958 The Highfield Story. New York: Holt.

Ohlin, Lloyd E.
1956 Sociology and the Field of Corrections. New York: Russell Sage Foundation.
1960 "Conflicting interests in correctional objectives," in Richard Cloward et al., Theoretical Studies in Social Organization of the Prison. Social Science Research Council Pamphlet 15. New York: Social Science Research Council.

Ohlin, Lloyd E., Robert B. Coates, and Alden D. Miller.
1974 "Radical correctional reform: a case study of the Massachusetts Youth Correctional System." Harvard Educational Review 44(February):74–111.

Ohlin, Lloyd E., and Donnell M. Pappenfort.
1956 "Crisis, succession and organizational change." Paper presented at the annual meeting of the American Sociological Society, September.

President's Commission on Law Enforcement and Administration of Justice.
1967a The Challenge of Crime in a Free Society. Washington, D.C.: U.S. Government Printing Office.
1967b Task Force Report: Juvenile Delinquency. Washington, D.C.: U.S. Government Printing Office.

Rolde, Edward, John Mack, Donald Scherl, and Lee Macht.
1970 "The maximum security institution as a treatment facility for juveniles," in James E. Teele (ed.), Juvenile Delinquency. Itasca, Ill.: F. E. Peacock.

Shaw, Clifford R.
1930 The Jack Roller. Chicago: University of Chicago Press.
1931 The Natural History of a Delinquent Career. Chicago: University of Chicago Press.

Shaw, Clifford R., Henry D. McKay, and James F. McDonald.
1938 Brothers in Crime. Chicago: University of Chicago Press.

Stephenson, Richard M., and Frank R. Scarpitti.
1968 "Argot in a therapeutic correction milieu." Social Problems 15(Winter): 384–395.

Street, David, Robert D. Vinter, and Charles Perrow.
    1966   Organization for Treatment. New York: Free Press.
Ward, David.
    1967   "Evaluation of correctional treatment: some implications of negative find-
            ings," in S. A. Yefsky (ed.), Proceedings of the First National Symposium
            on Law Enforcement, Science, and Technology. New York: Thompson.

CHAPTER **29**

Measurement of Effectiveness and Efficiency in Corrections

Stuart Adams

American University

Few kinds of research are more vital to corrections than measurements of the effectiveness and efficiency of correctional practice. Ironically, such research has been slow to develop. Good descriptive studies of criminal histories, correlates of crime, offender characteristics, treatment processes, program structures, and prediction instruments exist in abundance. Well-designed analyses of correctional outcomes and correctional worth, on the other hand, are all too rare.

The reasons for this lag are undoubtedly numerous. Corrections is a complex process whose results are difficult to sift from the network of personal and social influences that shape human careers. Furthermore, research in corrections has long been a peripheral activity, carried on by academicians as an incidental interest, or by relatively untrained correctional staff marginally supported by their organizations. Such circumstances have not been conducive to rapid advance in precise measurement of correctional results.

One additional reason for the lag may be that there is nothing to measure. Bailey, evaluating one hundred studies of correctional outcomes, found that "evidence supporting the efficacy of correctional treatment is slight, inconsistent, and of questionable reliability" (1966:157). Similarly, Robison and Smith, after a review of scattered studies in five basic areas of correctional programming in California, concluded that "there is no evidence to support any program's claim of superior rehabilitative efficacy" (1971:80). Martinson (1971) made this judgment even more sweeping by examining 231 of the "more rigorous" evaluations of correctional treatment in the nation and concluding that there is very little evidence that any mode of correctional treatment has a decisive effect on recidivism. Conceivably, if there is little or no sign of efficacy to reward the inquiring researcher, motivation to measure will remain low.

Must the correctional administrator conclude at this juncture that his is an inherently ineffective enterprise? Or should he merely assume that correctional research is a young science that has not yet had a chance to discover what is effective and what is not?

In actuality, an optimistic stance seems warranted, on both the effectiveness of new correctional procedures and the potential of correctional evaluation. Adams (1967b), Speer (1972), and Berkowitz (1973), using smaller but more precisely defined samples than Bailey, Robison and Smith, and Martinson came to more hopeful conclusions. Some new correctional programs are clearly more efficacious than the ones they replaced, and some new research and development efforts in corrections bring improved offender behaviors or advances in benefits over costs. Interestingly, the percentage of new projects yielding worthwhile returns in corrections may be as high as in industry, where a former president of du Pont is quoted as saying that not more than 5 percent of that firm's research projects ultimately pay off (Lessing, 1950:115).

These considerations suggest that corrections is not markedly different from other human enterprises in ability to devise and test new procedures for improving its performance. In fact, corrections may be a little ahead of numerous other organizations in this regard. Admittedly inefficient, and in many respects quite irrational, corrections should, for these very reasons, be readily able to conceive new procedures that test out as more effective than the ones they replace.

Given such grounds for optimism about the future efficacy of corrections and about the capability of evaluative research, we still face the problem of specific strategies and techniques. What are the characteristics of productive evaluative research? What are the conditions that underlie good research? How is such research implemented?

BASIC CONSIDERATIONS

Evaluative research in corrections addresses itself to a wide range of tasks. At one extreme is the matter of *program effectiveness*—how well a particular activity achieves its goals or objectives. At the other extreme is *system productivity*, which is concerned with resource utilization as well as goal attainment. Assessment of corrections thus involves questions of both effectiveness and efficiency; it also brings in the concept of "system."

Effectiveness

Rigorous measurement of the effectiveness of corrections requires at least two conditions. First, effectiveness must be defined, unambiguously, and preferably in quantitative terms. Second, the process of measurement must follow the rules of objective, unbiased inquiry, using suitable techniques. If "effectiveness" is the primary focus of measurement, research designs such as the controlled experiment or the quasi-experiment may be specified as the preferred techniques for drawing comparisons. If "efficiency" is the object of measurement, the experimental design alone is not adequate and supplementary procedures will be required.

With respect to effectiveness, we are concerned with the expected outcomes or results of correction. Here some unclarity exists. By definition, corrections has the mission of reforming, correcting, rehabilitating, or, more recently, reintegrating the former offender into lawful, productive, and satisfying community life. These nuances of "correction" pose problems for the definer and quantifier. There are additional problems arising from other objectives or outcomes ascribed to corrections. These include incapacitation and punishment of the offender, protection of the public, and deterrence of both present and future offenders.

I shall assume that "rehabilitation" or "reintegration" is either the primary objective of corrections at the present time or will soon become so. Objectives such as punishment or incapacitation will be regarded as secondary to restoration of offenders to full social functioning. This is consistent with currently visible trends in social valuation that identify the primary function of corrections as rehabilitation (Joint Commission on Manpower and Training, 1966). These trends appear to be redefining the purpose of correctional agencies and presaging a decline in the roles of prisons and reformatories—the primary instruments of punishment and incapacitation—in the total correctional process.

With regard to the applicability of the rules of objective, unbiased inquiry, corrections is an activity in which rigorous evaluation is perhaps more readily possible than in many other social fields, including mental health, welfare, the courts, and law enforcement. The political, legal, and emotional obstacles to experimental investigation of the effectiveness of agencies in these other social fields tend to be higher than they are in corrections.

Efficiency

Since resources are expended in correction, effectiveness must be examined, sooner or later, in relation to costs. In the past this has been left largely to funding agencies, but a new awareness is becoming evident among correctional administrators and researchers. In an era of scarce resources, growing ever scarcer, new programs are being viewed in terms of both improvement in effectiveness and increase in return on investment. The operating frame of reference becomes: "given a new unit of resources, what increase in outcomes can be expected from its utilization?"

The efficient procedure, in one sense, is the worthwhile procedure. This concept is important for researchers because measurement techniques capable of dealing with issues of effectiveness are not necessarily able to manage questions of worth. The controlled experiment, for example, is useful for answering questions about effectiveness; it is less useful when the central issue is efficiency or worth.

Programs and Systems

A final consideration in need of comment is the fact that measurement of correctional effectiveness must be viewed as a series of operations of varying complexity. Simpler levels are concerned with the effectiveness of one program element in relation to another: academic versus vocational training for similar individuals, a new type of counseling versus an older type, inclusion or omission of a particular treatment procedure.

Intermediate levels focus on the effectiveness of correctional configurations: what is the result of a given program mix in an agency as compared with a different mix for the same agency, assuming basically similar populations? Also, how do different agencies compare in overall effectiveness, again given comparable populations?

At complex levels, correctional effectiveness may be examined in relation to the position of corrections in the total criminal justice system. Is a particular system more or less effective because of the manner in which the correctional subsystem interfaces with other elements in the system? Or commands resources in relation to those available to other parts of the system? This level of evaluation becomes important as matters of overall efficiency and the optimal allocation of criminal justice resources emerge as foci of interest.

In the present state of correctional research, the larger frames of reference are difficult to manage, certainly in practice, and even to some extent in concept. It is likely that for some time the field of corrections will concentrate its measurement efforts at the level of program element comparisons, with gradually rising interest in configuration and agency comparisons. System effectiveness measurement at the criminal justice level appears no farther along at present than the early planning and trial stages. Its active implementation remains somewhere off in the future. Still farther into the future is the assessment of system effectiveness at the community or societal level, where the basic conditions of crime causation may be assumed to lie.

MEASUREMENT TECHNIQUES AND STRATEGIES

If we define the immediate task of correctional evaluation as that of ascertaining how "effective" a particular correctional practice is, we can state the basic elements of the measurement problem. It is to describe the differential in results, if any, derived from the application of a given correctional effort. For example, if we add an intensive counseling program to the correctional structure, how much additional rehabilitation is achieved?

Historically, questions of this type have been answered by the use of various procedures for information collection and interpretation, including:

1. subjective impressions of operating staff, during the treatment process and afterward;
2. testimony of the clientele, during and after the treatment experience;
3. test and inventory scores;
4. comparison of preprogram and postprogram test scores, attitudes, and behaviors of the clientele;
5. comparison of the behaviors of program clientele and those of the general correctional population, after treatment only, or both before and after treatment;
6. comparison of the behaviors of program clientele and those of selected members of the correctional population, chosen by procedures other than random (i.e., "comparison groups");
7. comparison of the behaviors of program clientele and those of a "control" population created, like the program clientele, by random assignment from a "pool" of treatment eligibles;
8. comparison of agency reactions to treated and control subjects during equivalent periods of time and, if possible, in equivalent situations;
9. comparison of "return to system" rates of treated and control subjects during equivalent periods of time after release; and also,
10. comparison of time-until-return means and time-in-lockup means.

More recent developments in the search for productive methods of measuring the results of correctional effort are the following:

11. comparison of the behaviors of program clientele and selected members of the correctional population—the latter identified as comparable in characteristics to the program clientele because of similarity in parole success probability scores (base expectancies);
12. comparison of performance-related costs, particularly "new correctional costs," in the first or subsequent years after release;
13. comparison of monetary data relating to both costs and benefits, including correctional costs before and after release and also a variety of benefits that may be assumed to result from treatment, such as new arrests and incarcerations averted, work continuity improved, job status advanced, welfare costs reduced, and social relationships enhanced;

14. development of correctional models or criminal justice models of conceptual or mathematical kinds, and exercising or operating the models to produce hypothetical outcomes for comparison with existing outcomes; and

15. development of indicators of status and movement (system rates) in the agencies of criminal justice to permit evaluation of component and system effectiveness by analysis of the system rates under varying conditions.

The recent history of corrections has witnessed the rise of the controlled experiment (procedures 7, 8, and 9 above) as an especially convincing mode of measurement. More recently, the quasi-experiment (procedure 6) has come into prominence, particularly in the complex setting of pretrial-diversion demonstration projects. Less elegant but more practical than the "true" or controlled experiment (i.e., with cases assigned by randomization), the quasi-experiment seems likely to increase in importance, particularly as skill in the creation of comparison groups develops.

The controlled experimental approach yields definitive information if its techniques are properly applied in favorable settings. The results of some major experimental assessments of correctional programs are among the landmarks of contemporary correctional development. However, controlled experimentation is often expensive, onerous, and slow. Some agency administrators demur at its cost and inconvenience and are unwilling to wait for its results.

There are further problems with this approach: it raises serious ethical questions in some applications, it cannot by itself handle questions about program or system efficiency, and it tends to break down under the elaborate structuring often required for questions other than the most simple.

One historical observation on the controlled experiment is relevant here. Despite its power in uncovering definitive information, it has shown little success thus far in "impacting" correctional policy. A recent review of evaluative studies that have decisively influenced correctional or criminal justice practice shows field surveys, panel interviews, time series studies, and quasi-experiments ranking ahead of the controlled experiment (Adams, 1974).

Whether this apparent underperformance of the controlled experimental approach is a misinterpretation of the data, a temporary phenomenon, or a realistic representation of the policy potential of the approach is not yet clear. In the meantime, the experimental method has produced some of the most definitive information thus far available on correctional effectiveness. It has, therefore, a place of importance in the measuring process and is given full attention in this discussion. Examples of the use of the approach will be presented in a number of case studies to explore not only the substantive results of experimentation but also the strengths and weaknesses of the experimental method in correctional settings.

CRITERIA OF EFFECTIVENESS

Measuring correctional effectiveness requires not only an evaluative design but also meaningful and manageable units of measurement. This is the familiar "criterion problem." How do we quantify precisely the outcomes of results of corrections?

One approach uses psychological test scores: pretest-posttest changes in score are taken as indicators of personality modification or attitudinal change under treatment. Another measures functioning in social contexts: remaining employed, advancing on the job, avoiding adverse agency actions, being a successful spouse or parent, complying with the conditions of parole, relating effectively to the parole agent. Still others use agency reactions to allegedly unsuccessful functioning: parole revocation, arrest, detention, trial, sentencing, and reincarceration. The latter criteria have come to dominate evaluative studies in corrections, partly because of their greater objectivity and accessibility, and partly because they appear legally and logically more appropriate.

The "hard" criteria that are especially useful to evaluators tend to be elaborated in many ways. Arrests may be enumerated, and they may also be recorded by time until occurrence. This tells how long the client remained "clean" after release from his last incarceration. Incarceration may be regarded as a unitary, either-or matter, or it may be handled as a continuous variable—months of lockup, for example.

New offenses also may be graded in terms of seriousness. Recidivism may be viewed in terms of volume, i.e., number of new arrests per year for the average offender. In the case of parolee performance, the focus may be upon parole revocation, and distinctions may be made between technical violations of parole and removals for commission of new offenses.

Usage has brought some of these criteria into prominence. In one highly regarded correctional experiment involving juveniles, parole revocation was the most frequently reported criterion (Grant et al., 1963). In another, the principal criterion was arrest (Klein, 1971). In still another, the major criterion was months of time back in state lockup within a specified time after release from last incarceration (Adams, 1961a).

The last-mentioned criterion—months back in lockup—has the special merit of being translatable into monetary valuation. This is a useful measure that has been introduced into correctional assessment in recent years. It provides a single index that meaningfully assimilates diverse other criteria, including time before rearrest and duration of reconfinement.

The monetary criterion involves both "cost" and "benefit" components. If correctional processes entail expenditures, they also promise returns of various kinds: reduction in future expenditures on crime control and corrections, increased earnings, lower welfare costs.

In its simplest form, the monetary criterion focuses on differences in the costs of processing control and experimental subjects. If postrelease behavior is similar, advantage lies with the program in which the processing costs are lower. If postrelease behaviors differ, a new possibility of advantage arises. There may be differences in new correctional costs incurred by the two groups after release. This may be ascertained by estimating police, court, or correctional costs that may be entailed in dealing with disapproved behaviors. For many purposes, a summary economic index of this kind is more useful than knowledge of the many percentages by which arrests, convictions, and reincarcerations differ between the experimentals and controls.

In more elaborate forms, the monetary criterion examines benefits as well as costs. The corrected offender not only reduces his future correctional costs, he also takes his family off welfare, earns wages or salary in regular employment, is a productive worker, and otherwise augments the economic and social condition of the community.

Since cost-benefit analysis is becoming an important instrument of decision-making in government (Hinrichs & Taylor, 1969), the monetary criterion will probably follow a parallel course in corrections. It is clearly useful in facilitating communication with persons who control funding. More important, from the perspective of measurement, this criterion sharpens comparisons of the desirability of programs at various intervals along the correctional continuum. Recidivism rates alone provide no clear clue to choice between treatment in jails, prisons, or under probation, for example. Expansion of probation at the expense of institutional facilities is often argued in terms of the lower recidivism rates associated with probation. However, the lower rates can be explained in large part by the selectivity of the sentencing process. The better risks get probation, generally speaking, and the poorer risks prison. A more plausible argument for probation is its lower cost per man-year, but these relative costs tell us nothing of relative effectiveness. It is only when costs and monetary benefits, as well as behavioral improvements, are considered that sound judgments about the relative desirability of program alternatives can be made.

MEASUREMENT PROBLEMS

It hardly needs repeating that measurement of correctional effectiveness is a process beset with problems. First of all there are the obvious difficulties of devising and monitoring a controlled experiment in an operational setting, maintaining data-collection procedures, and checking on the comparability of experimentals and controls. In addition, there are other problems that confront the evaluator as he conducts the experiment and interprets his data. These include:

1. *Masking effects.* Subpopulations within the experimental group may interact differentially with the treatment, some favorably, others unfavorably, so that the net effect appears inconsequential.

2. *Regression.* Performance levels of groups drawn from the extremes of a distribution (i.e., the very best and the very worst outcome cases) may move toward the mean of the distribution because their prior locations were chance-determined; this movement may occur independently of any effects of treatment, thus confusing the measurement of actual effects.

3. *Maturation.* A group may show improvement in performance over time as a result of a "growing up" process, independent of treatment, and interference with measurement may result.

4. *Context problems.* Outside of a laboratory, the controlled experiment cannot readily be separated from its environment, with the result that outcomes may be seriously, though indeterminately, affected by uncontrolled influences.

5. *Operating biases.* Despite careful project design and watchful monitoring, operating staff may unwittingly influence the randomization process or otherwise bias project outcomes in favor of the experimental group.

6. *Relevance.* Research models vary in their relevance to the objectives and needs of agencies; the questions that are answered are not the questions that are important.

7. *Efficiency.* Some research designs, such as the controlled experiment, are more useful in handling questions about effectiveness than about efficiency.

8. *Timeliness.* In an age of rapid interaction and close interdependence, continuous flows of information from research are essential to responsive and competent management in corrections. Some research designs and strategies are better adapted than others to providing quick inputs, useful for decision-making.

9. *Erosion of treatment effect.* Significant changes may appear in client perceptions and behavior during treatment and disappear afterward, possibly because of dysfunctional influences in the release environment or lack of reinforcement for induced behaviors. These changes sometimes go unnoticed, either because of delay in measurement or because of the use of insensitive criterion measures. Even if the changes are noticed initially, their disappearance may be interpreted as evidence of the inefficacy of treatment.

10. *Selection bias.* The selection of control and comparison groups by randomization or by group matching is sometimes faulty, so that significant differences in key

characteristics may appear between experimentals and controls, biasing the measurement of possible treatment effects.

11. *Contamination.* Some control subjects may become exposed in various ways to the treatment variable, either in partial or full intensity. On occasion, staff dealing with the control subjects may assimilate aspects of the treatment procedure, and thus impair the integrity of the control experience.

The foregoing problems differ somewhat from the "threats to validity" previously elucidated by Campbell (1969). However, the differences may be less noteworthy than the overlaps. The effects of some of these problems of measurement, together with procedures for coping with them, are taken up in the examples of evaluative research that follow.

MEASUREMENT APPLICATIONS

In these first examples, some form of recidivism is the major criterion of effectiveness. The cases range widely in complexity, however, and illustrate different methods, goals, and problems in the measurement of correctional effectiveness.

Experimental Applications: I—Recidivism Rate Analysis

The seven cases in this section draw heavily from correctional experience in California. They reflect that state's disproportionately large contribution to correctional measurement, both in volume and in quality of effort or product.

Special Intensive Parole Unit, Phase III (SIPU III). The California Department of Corrections between 1953 and 1964 conducted four major experiments to ascertain whether a reduction in parole case load size increased the likelihood of parole success. The first two experiments, SIPU I and II, involved about 10,000 parolees, who were randomly assigned to small (15- and 30-man) and large (90-man) case loads during the early months of parole. After three months (SIPU I) and six months (SIPU II), the experimental cases were transferred to regular case loads on the assumption that intensive supervision was now less needed. In neither SIPU I nor II did the experimentals significantly outperform the controls (California Department of Corrections, 1956, 1958).

SIPU III randomly assigned parolees to 35-man and 72-man case loads and provided for continuous rather than discontinuous stays in the smaller case loads. The total sample consisted of 3,717 parolees, 911 of whom were in the small, and 2,806 in the large case loads. The parolees in the small case loads showed significantly better results at both twelve and twenty-four months out. Returns to prison at twenty-four months were 36 percent for the experimentals and 41 percent for the controls (Havel & Sulka, 1962).

Performance differentials varied by risk class of parolee. For example, the gain was larger for parolees of medium risk (as measured by base expectancy scores) than for the best or poorest risks. It was larger for parolees released to northern regions of the state than for those released to the southern regions.

These findings suggested that the outcome of the experiment was less a function of case load size than of various types of interrelationships between persons, places, and the parole experience.

A fourth phase of SIPU was undertaken in 1959 to examine some of these interactions. After five years, the report on SIPU IV added little of significance to the findings in phase III. It was concluded that some of the failure to show additional results may have been due to lack of precision in the study design and to insufficient knowledge of the parole process (Havel, 1963).

The SIPU Project was a major landmark in the history of measurement of correctional effectiveness. It was a massive and sustained pursuit of definitive information on one approach to improving parole performance. The outcomes of the project were disappointing, in most respects, especially because of the meagerness of the findings. Nevertheless, the project served as an important learning experience and as a spur to further research.

Perhaps the major problem in SIPU was the inability of correctional research technology to provide a study design adequate for the task at hand. Interestingly, the project was made more complex than necessary in the transfer of parolees from small to large case loads after three- or six-month intervals. It was insufficiently complex, however, in relation to a typology of parolees. Masking was probably present in phases I and II of the project; this problem became clearly evident in phase III.

A typology that might help deal with the problem of masking came along in mid-project with the development of base expectancy measures in the California Department of Corrections. These were employed in SIPU III and some methodological gains were made. However, this mode of classification was not wholly adequate for the needs of the situation. Even with some matching of agent and parolee types, the light thrown on interaction between parolee types and the parole supervision experience was apparently too limited to constitute a real breakthrough.

The next two examples show more successful breakthroughs by use of clinical typologies rather than base expectancies, and by a more sustained effort to achieve meaningful ward-agent matching.

Pilot Intensive Counseling Organization (PICO), 1955–61. This project was a controlled experimental study of the effects of intensive individual interview therapy on young adult offenders in Deuel Vocational Institution in California. The SIPU experiments had begun as two-way designs—experimentals versus controls—with some four-way variations in SIPU IV. PICO, benefiting from early discussions about design problems in SIPU I and II, was conceived as a four-way experiment.

In this experiment, 1,600 Youth Authority wards in their late teens and early twenties were clinically adjudged at intake to be either "amenable" or "nonamenable" to the proposed treatment. The two categories of admissions were then assigned randomly to experimental and control statuses. The experimentals received the regular institutional program plus individual interview therapy. The treatment lasted about nine months, on the average. After release to the community, the four categories of subjects were followed up on parole to ascertain levels of performance in the community and also rates of return to the institutional system (Rudoff & Bennett, 1958).

The project was evaluated by both the Department of Corrections and the Youth Authority. The researchers in the Department of Corrections studied psychological score changes and parole outcomes for the entire release cohort and concluded that there were no significant differences in performance between experimentals and controls (Rudoff, 1959). The researchers in the Youth Authority studied outcomes for the first 100 releasees in each of the four subject categories, namely, experimental amenables, control amenables, experimental nonamenables, and control nonamenables. These results showed significantly better performance for the experimental amenable parolees than for either group of controls. They also showed that the experimental nonamenables performed significantly worse than the experimental amenables, and worse than the two groups of controls—whose performances on several criteria were virtually identical. The results are shown in Table 1.

The results obtained by the Youth Authority differed from those obtained by the Department of Corrections because the criteria for judging amenability had shifted partway through the experiment, after the transfer of the chief of the clinical team. There was a lack of awareness in the department of the consequences of the transfer for the typing of the subjects. As a result, the procedure that was adopted to safeguard against masking inadvertently failed and the experiment was nullified for the Corrections researchers.

The Youth Authority researchers, by design, elected to study the first 100 releasees in each of the four subject categories, primarily for the purpose of seeing how each of thirteen outcome criteria would describe the groups' performances. Also, by restricting the subjects to the first one-fourth of the population flow through the project, a longer follow-up time would be insured.

These two decisions by the researchers led to the discovery of (1) a very significant interaction of amenability with treatment, and (2) the fact that time spent back in lockup was the most sensitive of the several criteria available.

The results of the PICO project were noteworthy for at least three reasons. They provided a good demonstration of the masking problems created by a change in the internal conditions of an experiment. They highlighted the importance of knowing the

TABLE 1

COMPARATIVE STANDINGS OF PICO COHORTS ON
SEVERAL CRITERIA OF PAROLE PERFORMANCE

Performance Criterion	Failures or Successes by Cohort (N = 100 per cohort)			
	Treated Amenables	Control Amenables	Control Nonamenables	Treated Nonamenables
Rated "poor" at six months after release	31%	38%	39%	44%
First suspensions at 6 months	15%	27%	26%	32%
First revocations at 6 months	2%	6%	3%	4%
Unfavorable discharges at 6 months	1%	7%	8%	4%
Removals under suspension at 6 months	3%	13%	10%	8%
Removals under suspension at 12 months	14%	25%	23%	29%
Removals under suspension at 24 months	29%	38%	43%	48%
Unfavorable discharges at 33 months	29%	36%	40%	45%
Favorable discharges at 33 months*	30%	22%	17%	21%
Months of return to state custody (at 33 mo.)	206	480	481	550
Months of return to any custody (at 33 mo.)	460	724	767	863
State custody as percent of postrelease time	6.2%	14.5%	14.6%	16.7%
Any custody as percent of postrelease time	13.9%	22.0%	23.2%	26.2%

*A "success" criterion.
Source: Adams, 1961b; Johnston et al., 1970:533.

subtypes within a treatment population by presenting vivid evidence of interaction between the clinically defined population types and the treatment experience. Finally, they pointed up the significance of criterion analysis. The Youth Authority study examined the results of PICO in terms of thirteen criteria, ranging from agent ratings of parolee adjustment to months back in lockup within thirty-three months after release. The criterion analysis had been undertaken in the hope that something useful might be turned up, and something useful did, in fact, turn up. The lockup differentials for the four subject groups were observed to be continuous variables, unusually sensitive, and readily amenable to the application of costing techniques as a measurement device —a procedure that will be explored later.

Community Treatment Project (CTP), 1961–73. The Youth Authority's Community Treatment Project developed from the Preston Impact Study (Adams, 1959), which reported an apparently dysfunctional effect from the Preston School of Industry's rehabilitation program for older juvenile offenders. CTP was designed as a complex controlled experiment to test the efficacy of treatment in the community as an alternative to institutionalization for these juveniles (Adams & Grant, 1961).

CTP was organized around two basic features: (1) the randomizing of subjects into institutional and community treatment, and (2) the use of an "interpersonal maturity" typology for the assignment of wards to different kinds of community treatment. Later in the experiment, community treatment staff also were "typed" and a third feature of ward-staff matching by types was incorporated into the experiment (Grant et al., 1963).

The experiment was structured into phases. Phase I (1961–64) focused on the comparative effects of institutional and community treatment on the nine subtypes in the study populations. These consisted of about 80 percent of the intake of juveniles from two communities, Sacramento and Stockton, assigned randomly to experimental and controls after a determination of eligibility at the reception-center clinic. Excluded from the randomization process were cases that fell into certain unacceptable categories: safety, public relations, or operational risks. The "unacceptable" categories were established in a conceptualization process that involved juvenile-court judges and police chiefs in the communities involved in the experiment.

The experimentals were returned to their communities for intensive treatment in case loads of about twelve. The controls continued on through Youth Authority institutions as the juvenile court had ordered. Assessment of the experiment was accomplished by comparing the experimentals and controls (after subsequent paroling of the latter from CYA training schools) on parole revocations in equivalent periods of exposure time in the community.

The findings, as shown in Table 2, indicated that the experimentals had significantly fewer parole revocations than the controls (Warren, 1967, 1970). The performance differentials varied markedly by I-Level (interpersonal maturity) type, with some categories performing significantly better in the community, some types performing equally well in community and institution, and one type (Cultural Identifier) performing better after institutional experience.

Phase II of the Community Treatment Project (1965–69) was expanded to include a test of differential treatment against guided group interaction and both against institutional treatment. In the guided group interaction units no attempt was made to differentiate the wards into personality types. For the differential treatment subjects, the results were similar to those of Phase I: the experimentals performed considerably better overall than the controls on the criterion of parole revocation. The guided group interaction subjects performed about the same as the control group, and significantly less well than the differentially treated subtypes.

Although the CTP results for the differentially treated wards have been consistently reported since the early 1960s as indicative of superior parole performance by the experimentals, one observer has entered an objection. He interprets the findings to indicate that the parole revocation differential was due in part to more permissive parole-agent decisions relating to offenses of lesser seriousness on the part of the experimentals (Lerman, 1968). Lerman's observations regarding differentials in decision-making appear valid but the implications for final project outcomes seem much less weighty than he has concluded. After accounting for the more permissive decisions by officers in some experimental cases, there remains a wide margin of performance superiority on the part of the experimentals, especially on the harder criteria, and an ultimate benefit/cost ratio that definitely favors the community treatment procedure.

The CTP experiment concluded Phase II with the transformation of the several experimental centers into Community Parole Centers, which incorporated the differential treatment philosophy and procedures as operating principles and standards. If past experience is a guide, these centers will bring lower rates of reported recidivism, and they will also be more efficient in terms of the cost of institutional commitments averted, building needs reduced, and economic and social performance enhanced.

Since 1969, CTP has been operating in Phase III, which is scheduled to terminate in 1974. This phase makes use of a short period of institutionalization in a special treatment center before return to the community for the experimentals. The need for such treatment appeared indicated by some of the findings in phases I and II. It is not clear whether there will be further phases of the project. From the researchers' point of view, the need for further experimentation seems endless, but the motivation to continue is weaker on the part of executive staff and the funding agencies. The main points useful to the policy-makers seem to have been established.

As an example of the use of controlled experimentation in the measurement of correctional effectiveness, CTP is unquestionably outstanding. The design was the most elaborate thus far attempted in any correctional experiment. The duration of the study has been unprecedented in length—illustrating rather well that operating staff

TABLE 2

PAROLE PERFORMANCE OF EXPERIMENTAL
AND CONTROL GROUPS IN CTP

Percentages of Parole Violations and Unfavorable Discharges
during 15 Months Community Exposure
Experimentals: N = 134; Controls: N = 168

Delinquent Subtype	Proportion in Population	Percent Failure in Subtype	
		Control	Experimental
Asocial, Passive	5%	55%	18%
Conformist, Immature	16%	58%	18%
Conformist, Cultural	10%	46%	15%
Manipulator	14%	48%	32%
Neurotic, Acting-out	20%	71%	23%
Neurotic, Anxious	26%	48%	41%
Situational Emotional Reaction	3%	17%	20%
Cultural Identifier	6%	22%	57%
Total	100%	52%	28%

Source: Warren, 1967:8, 1970:678.

must often wait patiently for the final results of controlled experimentation. However, the combined practical and theoretical accomplishments of the project appear unmatched by any other social action study.

In the conceptualization of the project, the possibility of interaction between offender type and the supervision experience was not only anticipated but also prepared for both analytically and operationally. On the other hand, the initial design did not provide for intensive cost-benefit analysis—understandable in view of the project's inauguration date. Recently, CTP has given more emphasis to such analysis.

Reduction of Delinquency through Expansion of Opportunity (RODEO), 1967–71.

RODEO was a controlled experimental study of the efficacy of treatment of juveniles in small probation case loads in lieu of placement in a county probation camp. With the cooperation of juvenile-court judges in Los Angeles County, juveniles who ordinarily would be sent to the county forestry camps were randomly assigned three ways: to the RODEO case loads, to regular probation case loads, and to the camps.

The thirty-boy RODEO case loads were under intensive supervision by a probation officer and two aides indigenous to the residential areas of the probationers, working together as a treatment team. The rehabilitative efforts of the team were extended to the family as well as to the juvenile, and the community also was involved to an unusual degree as a source of assistance (Hunter, 1968).

The original plan for RODEO had called for assignment of camp-ordered cases to camp and to RODEO in a 1-to-3 ratio. However, at the request of the presiding judge of the juvenile court, a third group—regular probation—was created, also as part of the randomizing procedure. The assignment process was designed to insure comparability of the three groups; however, no data were presented to indicate that the groups were indeed comparable.

The outcomes for the three groups, with return to an institution (juvenile hall, camp, or CYA training school) as the criterion of performance, are shown in Table 3. These data indicate that regular probationers perform least well, camp placements next best, and RODEO participants best. The distribution of successes suggests that the county correctional system had initially optimized the rehabilitation process by supplementing regular probation with forestry camps. The addition of RODEO as another alternative apparently increased the level of optimization still further. The validity of this judgment can be clarified by access to relative cost data—which will be discussed later in the chapter.

In size, RODEO is overshadowed by such giants as SIPU and PICO. The project is notable, however, for its accomplishment of a three-way randomization over alternatives as diverse as regular probation, county forestry camps, and RODEO.

TABLE 3

COMPARATIVE PERFORMANCE OF RODEO, COUNTY CAMP
RELEASEE, AND PROBATION SUBJECTS

Group	Number of Subjects	Percent Institutionalized
RODEO	120	25%
Camp	44	32%
Regular Probation	32	50%

Source: Hunter, 1968:13.

Long Beach Experiment, 1964–65. The Long Beach Experiment was a controlled experimental study of the effects of group counseling of juveniles on probation (Adams, 1965). Six probation officers identified about twenty eligibles in each of their case loads, using six predetermined criteria as the basis of identification. The eligibles were randomized into experimentals and controls, and the experimentals were called in for once-weekly counseling sessions with their probation officers. The sessions were "nondirective," following guidelines laid down in a number of training meetings with a CYA group counseling specialist. The group counseling sessions were an addition to the regular probation service provided to the juveniles.

Experimentals and controls were pre- and posttested on the Jesness Inventory, routine performance data were collected periodically during the course of the experiment, and group interviews were held regularly with the probation officers to ascertain trends and incidents in the treatment procedure.

At the end of six months the experimentals and controls were compared on (1) number of police contacts, (2) detentions in juvenile hall, (3) placements in the county probation camps, and (4) commitments to the California Youth Authority. The six-month results disclosed twice as many police contacts and twice as many placements in institutional settings for the controls as for the experimentals.

The psychometric data were inconclusive, showing no improvement for the experimentals but slight improvement for the controls in social adjustment scores. On the other hand, the experimentals improved in scores on predicted delinquency, while the controls worsened on that index.

Police contacts with the experimentals were generally for less serious offenses than for the controls. Consequently, the experimentals not only averaged fewer police contacts over the six-month period but also were contacted for offenses of a less serious nature.

Several features of this evaluative study are of interest. It was a project that was initially proposed by operational staff to improve their functioning. The study was quickly organized, and required little additional staff time either for operational or for research purposes. After the initial organizational and training sessions, research unit staff were required for only a few hours of monitoring and analytical services.

The project used three kinds of data for evaluation: psychometric information, behavioral data, and agency reaction data. The most clear-cut data were those based on agency reactions toward behavior. Cost data also were computed for this experiment, although its "economics" were immediately self-evident. The addition of group counseling, by increasing the volume of desired outcomes at no increase in staff cost, made the probation operation more efficient.

Group Guidance Experiment, 1962–66. During 1962–66 the University of Southern California, the Los Angeles County Probation Department, and the Ford Foundation collaborated on an experimental assessment of the Probation Department's Group Guidance program. The program had been set up in 1945 to deal with juvenile gang depredations in the Los Angeles area. Detached workers (special probation officers) established contact and developed relationships with potentially destructive gangs and attempted to convert them to more conventional goals and activities.

Grant monies permitted intensification of rehabilitative activities in an area designated as "experimental." Nonintense areas of comparable types were identified as controls. Studies of control and experimental area activities and trends in rates of recidivism permitted evaluation of the effects of treatment intensification.

The four-year result was a virtual absence of evidence that the intensified group guidance program brought a reduction in gang delinquency, as measured by arrests. In actuality, one of the major conclusions of the study was that the project design resulted in increased group cohesiveness, which was directly related to deviant activity and to arrests (Klein, 1971).

Simultaneously with the USC study of the Group Guidance Project, research on the same activity, using a quasi-experimental design, was being carried on by the Research Office of the Probation Department. The principal criterion in the Research Office study was new correctional costs incurred by members of the experimental and control gangs after the inception of group guidance service (Adams, 1967a). Results from the use of this criterion are presented later in this chapter. They are of special interest because they contradict the results obtained in the USC study using arrests as the criterion.

Silverlake Experiment, 1967–71. One of the most thoroughly conceptualized attempts to measure correctional effectiveness was the Silverlake Experiment (Empey & Lubeck, 1971). Operationally, this experiment provided a "therapeutic milieu" for a group of twenty-five juvenile delinquents who would ordinarily have been placed in a private residential treatment facility. A randomization process created the experimental and control groups from a moderately screened pool of eligible juvenile delinquents. The controls went to Boys Republic for an average stay of thirteen months; the experimentals spent about six months each in Silverlake House in the community before being released to their homes.

The design of the treatment setting and processes was based on extensive theorizing about the causes of delinquency and the postulation of appropriate strategies for successful intervention. Evaluation of the project involved comparisons of experimentals and controls on (1) relative frequency of arrest for new offenses during the first year out, (2) seriousness of offenses committed, and (3) relationship of arrests in the "before" period to those in the "after" period.

The findings indicated no significant difference between experimentals and controls in relative frequency of arrest in the postrelease phase. Also, there were no differences between experimentals and controls in before-and-after rates of arrest. One difference that did emerge was that experimentals appeared to become involved in slightly less serious offenses in the after period as compared with the controls.

One incidental finding of the Silverlake Experiment, which had not been anticipated in the initial conceptualization of the project, was that the experimentals were processed through their residential facility at about half the cost of the controls.

Several matters of interest are evident in this experiment. One is the fact that despite extensive conceptualization and the formulation of intervention strategies on theoretically relevant bases, the project failed to show a reduction in delinquency. Another is the contrast between returns on a recidivism criterion and those on a cost-benefits criterion. Still another is the contrast between the attention given to guarding against erroneous interpretation because of regression effects and maturation and that given to possible misinterpretation because of a failure to allow for interaction between delinquent types and the treatment experience. The Silverlake Experiment differed markedly from the Community Treatment Experiment in this latter regard.

Discussion. Seven projects have been described as examples of evaluative correctional studies designed on the model of the classic experiment. They attempted to ascertain whether the application of some form of intervention with a group or groups of offenders brought a reduction in deviance, or a related reduction in arrest, detention, or sentence to incarceration. The experiments all made recidivism the principal criterion of outcome.

Not all the experiments showed clear gains for the experimentals in comparison with the controls. One, the USC evaluation of Group Guidance, found delinquency to increase with intervention. Another, the Silverlake Experiment, found little or no difference between experimentals and controls in arrests following release. In both these experiments, however, either a "new correctional costs" or "treatment costs" approach showed the experimentals at an advantage over the controls despite the neutral or negative indications from the recidivism criterion.

In two of the experiments—RODEO and Silverlake—monetary benefits were reported by the project staff. In one case, the gains arose from a reduction in treatment time; in the other case, there were savings because of treatment in less expensive settings and also because of reduction in new correctional costs—a reduction that was associated with a lowered recidivism rate. In two other experiments—PICO and Group Guidance—monetary benefits were reported, but not by the original project staffs, and in the case of Group Guidance, not on the original experiment but on a quasi-experimental replication.

Before discussing the full implications of some of these observations, it will be useful to examine (or reexamine) a second group of studies whose primary focus is the economic consequences of treatment. Recidivism will be present as a criterion, but it will be secondary to the criterion of comparative costs or benefit/cost ratios.

Experimental Applications: II—Cost Comparisons

Of major interest in the five following studies is the fact that economic analysis of correctional outcomes may take several forms. First, a new treatment program may be less costly than another, yet achieve as much in recidivism reduction. Second, a new program may bring additional costs, but it may reduce recidivism enough that the added costs are more than compensated for in one form or another. Third, the results of a new program may be viewed as having economic consequences of several kinds, beginning with savings that might arise from cheaper treatments, going on to possible reductions in new correctional costs, and extending to the various kinds of savings or returns that become evident as released offenders earn wages, support their families, pay taxes, and so on.

In the immediate present, to talk of measuring correctional effectiveness in economic terms requires that attention be restricted to fairly elementary examples of assessment. Correctional research has barely entered the field of cost analysis, cost-benefit studies, and benefit/cost ratios. Such examples as are available are likely to be rough, exploratory, and preliminary approaches to the use of economic measures in the assessment of correctional procedures.

PICO Project, 1955–61. The PICO Project, the second example in the preceding section, focused primarily on agency reactions to disapproved behaviors as criterion measures. The criterion that proved most rewarding was "time spent back in state lockup" within a specified number of months after release from treatment. This criterion is at once sensitive and practical. It is sensitive in that it takes account of longer stays for more serious crimes or more adverse reaction of the criminal justice system to the offender—information that is obscured if arrest or incarceration rates are the sole criterion. It is practical in that it can easily be translated into monetary terms and thus permits several types of analysis that are not possible with recidivism rates.

PICO was a project in which the new treatment program cost more than the old; hence, there was no possibility of showing savings achieved through lower treatment costs. There remained the possibility of showing that treatment costs (1) were lower than the savings in new correctional costs in a specified follow-up period, or (2) were lower than all benefits accruing in a given follow-up period. However, no benefit data were accumulated in the project; hence, the center of interest became the cost of treatment in relation to new correctional costs during a thirty-three month follow-up.

One way of specifying the costs of treatment in PICO was to note that one therapist carried a case load of 25 clients for nine months, on the average. This meant that in one year the therapist could "finish off" 33.3 cases.

Treatment benefits expressed as reduction in lockup time were estimated from the following: average months of lockup in California state prisons during the first 33 months after release from the project were 3.78 months for experimentals and 4.81 months for controls. The more detailed averages for the four subject groups were: experimental amenables, 2.1 months; control amenables, 4.8 months; control non-amenables, 4.8 months; experimental nonamenables, 5.5 months (Adams, 1961b; Johnston et al., 1970:551). Since a therapist-year provided treatment for 33.3 cases, one year of treatment by one therapist brought a saving of 33.3 times 4.81 months minus 3.78 months equalling 32 months of lockup. In monetary terms, this is a total of about $13,000 in systems where lockup costs average $400 per month.

If the treatment had been confined to amenable cases, the treatment year of one therapist would have produced a saving of 33.3 times 4.8 months minus 2.1 months equalling 90 months of lockup. At $400 per month, in one year a prison therapist could have reduced new prison costs over the first 33 months after release by the amount of $33,000. This result is quite rewarding in a narrow monetary sense, let alone in its behavioral implications. It should be even more rewarding in a broad monetary sense, if one could take into account the long-range potentiality of job earnings and welfare reduction, in addition to reductions in future criminal justice and corrections costs.

Evaluation of the Group Guidance Program. As was noted earlier, the Group Guidance Program of the Los Angeles County Probation Department became the subject of an experimental study by the Youth Studies Center of the University of Southern California. Simultaneously, the Research Office of the Probation Department undertook an independent evaluation of the Group Guidance Program by means of a "natural experiment" design. Data were located in the records of the department and in police files on three gangs, one a former recipient of Group Guidance service, another a partial recipient, and the third a nonrecipient. Background data on gang members suggested that the gangs were comparable enough to be considered elements in an experimental design in which the action to be studied had already taken place (Adams et al., 1965).

The three gangs were traced through the records of the two agencies. Gang-member characteristics, offender histories, and criminal justice experiences were documented in great detail. The correctional-cost histories of the gang members were then reconstructed by applying current budgetary estimates of the costs to all the many criminal justice actions and services that appeared in the youths' histories.

These reconstructions were designed to cover six-year periods in the gang members' careers—generally, the years from 15 to 20, inclusive. The time spans provided a three-year "before" and a three-year "after" period. Treatment for the fully serviced and for the partially serviced gangs came in the after period.

The total before and total after costs for each of the three gangs permitted calculation of average before and after costs. This provided measures of the presumed effect of applying full or partial treatment to the two "experimental" gangs, as indicated in Table 4.

A summary interpretation of these data is that delinquency prevention service to Gang C reduced average correctional costs per gang member by $3,241 over a period of about three years. Instead of going up about $1,600 per member, as in Gang A, they declined about $1,600. For the forty-three core members of this gang, this represents a total reduction of $139,263 over three years, or a saving of approximately $45,000 per year (Adams, 1967a).

A major point of interest here is the implication that the services of a half-time delinquency prevention worker for a year were apparently responsible for a direct reduction of about $45,000 in costs during the year. This saving continued for the three-year period under study. It might be predicted with some confidence that this saving would continue, especially after observing the changes that had become evident in the life-styles and daily pursuits of some members of the treated gang who were called in for interviews. In essence, a relatively small investment in prevention had apparently repaid itself in the immediate future, and gave promise of continuing to repay itself many times again in the reoriented careers of numerous of the treated gang members.

An intriguing question arises from comparisons of the results of the Youth Studies Center experiment and the Probation Department quasi-experiment. The former found that the treated gangs had higher arrest rates. The latter inferred a major saving from the application of treatment to one of the gangs in the quasi-experiment. The Youth Studies Center staff, noting the unfavorable arrest data, hypothesized that the gangs under treatment developed additional cohesiveness and that their delinquency rates rose as a result. It might also have been hypothesized, alternatively, that the police were concerned about the experiment and gave the gang members much more attention than they gave untreated gangs in the area. This suggests the intrusion of a context problem roughly analogous to the one that obscured the results of the PICO project for the Corrections Department researchers. The suggestion is admittedly tenuous. It may be noted, nevertheless, that cost analysis provides a powerful technique that may be more effective than recidivism rate analysis alone in uncovering the full effects of some correctional programs. It remains for replicative work to explore the full implications of this proposition.

RODEO. The RODEO project, like the PICO project, focused primarily on agency reactions to recidivism, but also made a cost analysis. It concluded that the management of juvenile delinquents in a community-based intensive treatment pro-

TABLE 4

BEFORE AND AFTER COSTS OF GANG MEMBERS

Treatment Status	Number in Gang	Average Correctional Costs Before	After
A. Untreated	24	$2,934	$4,576
B. Semitreated	33	3,695	2,601
C. Fully Treated	43	3,944	2,354

Source: Adams, 1967a:176.

gram was less costly than the processing of delinquents through the county probation camps. The saving was estimated at $950 per boy over a period that approximated eight months—a monthly reduction of $106 per boy (Rushen & Hunter, 1968).

It appears likely that two other gains have occurred or will occur and may be identified by appropriate analysis. One is the reduction in new correctional costs because of the superior performance of the RODEO cases, which was not fully accounted for in the listed savings. Another will be the long-term benefits arising from work gains and from welfare and criminal justice costs averted during the lifetimes of the subjects.

The present discussion has been restricted to immediate savings from treatment design; it ignores the two broader areas of new correctional costs and work or welfare benefits for lack of data. It is important, nevertheless, to keep in mind the large potential for additional savings in these unanalyzed areas of future performance.

Silverlake Experiment. This experiment was originally conceived as a test of formal theories of delinquency causation and related intervention strategies. After extensive analysis of comparative performance data, Empey and Lubeck (1971) concluded that there was little or no difference in arrest rates of experimentals and controls.

The authors then disclosed that as a result of the lower cost of the experimental program per capita (principally because of the reduction of intervention time from thirteen to six months), the project saved the county $225,281/121 equalling $1,890 per ward. Savings ranged from $2,859 per successful graduate to $881 per unsuccessful releasee. The benefit/cost ratios for graduates and nongraduates were 2.6 to 1 and 2.3 to 1, respectively, over the duration of the residential treatment period (Empey & Lubeck, 1971:309).

These figures were seen by the authors as implying (1) that there is much potential in community-based programs for reducing correctional costs, (2) that such programs may pose little added danger to the public, and (3) that many offenders may be helped in brief time and with less risk of debilitation or degradation from total incarceration (p. 310).

Operationally, these seem to be highly useful conclusions for both the correctional and budget-office staff. The importance of the cost data in the Silverlake Experiment is, thus, markedly in contrast with the unimportance of the recidivism data.

Project Crossroads, 1968–71. This quasi-experimental project examined the effects of diversion after preliminary hearing and before trial on 825 offender participants in Washington, D.C. A comparison group of 240 was identified by a file search for apparent program eligibles who had been processed through the courts during a period of several months immediately prior to the start of the project (Leiberg et al., 1971).

The purpose of the project was to show that a system of pretrial services could provide selected offenders, who had been arrested but not yet tried, superior alternatives to delinquency adjudication or criminal prosecution.

The procedures called for the assignment of a community-worker counselor to each participant. The counselor provided supportive services, ascertained the clients' needs, aided in securing employment (the principal function), aided with financial assistance problems, and with any other personal or family problems that required referral to local social-welfare agencies.

Cumulative enrollment in two phases (juvenile and adult), as of September, 1970, reached 825, of whom 297 were juveniles and 528 were young adults. By September, 1970, charges against 467 of the 825 enrollees had been dropped because of successful program participation, 74 were still active, and 283 were returned to normal court processing, primarily because of unsatisfactory program performance.

The benefit/cost ratio was computed for the project by taking the first 200 individuals enrolled in the project and a control sample of 107 individuals who presumably would have been project eligibles had the project started several months earlier.

The two groups were followed up for fifteen months after the arrest that made them project eligibles. During this time, recidivism (a new arrest) for the experimentals and controls amounted to 26 percent and 36 percent, respectively. For the experimentals, the fifteen-month follow-up included a three-month project experience and a twelve-month postproject follow-up.

To estimate the benefit/cost ratio, the benefits (diversion from criminal justice processing, earnings, reduced recidivism) were calculated and the costs of the project were computed. The total benefit from the program was taken as the present value of the several benefits summed. The diversion benefit was defined as accruing in year zero for foregone court procedures and over the first year or two for foregone sentences. The other benefits (earnings, reduced recidivism) were regarded as accruing over several years. Future benefits were discounted at several interest rates (5%, 10%, and 15%). Benefit/cost ratios for each rate of discount were presented.

The values and the benefit/cost ratio at 5% discount are shown in the following tabulation:

Benefits	Diversion	$109,994.52
	Earnings	190,282.00
	Reduced recidivism	216,963.13
	Total benefits	$517,240.00
Total costs		233,256.00

Benefit/cost ratio = 2.2 to 1.

If the correctional administrator considers any benefit/cost ratio over unity a worthwhile investment, then the benefit/cost ratio for Project Crossroads suggests that this particular project is an unusually good investment and an efficient use of the community's resources (Holahan, 1970b).

Applications: III—Nonexperimental Cost Studies

A number of evaluative researches in corrections that have diverged from the classic experimental tradition are of interest for several reasons. First, they appear to have high validity despite the absence of the kinds of controls that are usually desired in definitive research. Second, they push beyond the methodologies now in vogue, and do this in a manner that suggests much unrealized potential. Four such studies follow.

The Saginaw Project: A Study of the Economic Effects of Probation Expansion, 1957–60. The Saginaw Project was an "experiment" in Saginaw County, Michigan, seeking to disclose whether (1) probation use could be expanded extensively with little additional risk to the community; (2) the success-to-failure ratio under expansion would remain about the same as before; (3) substantial savings in public monies would result; and (4) the quality of probation procedures would be improved (Michigan Crime and Delinquency Council, 1963).

The project ran from July 1, 1957 to June 30, 1960. It involved 477 experimental cases who came before the county circuit judges during the three-year period. Probation staff had been doubled (from three to six persons) to make possible the more intensive services. Assessment of the project was accomplished by researchers from the University of Michigan School of Social Work, Ann Arbor. For purposes of comparison, 491 circuit-court cases drawn from the court calendars between mid-1954 and mid-1957 served as controls (Ball et al., 1963).

In terms of reduction of rates of subsequent incarceration, the results of the Saginaw Project were dramatic. Imprisonment after conviction for a new offense was cut one-half for potential first-termers, one-half for potential second-termers, and two-thirds for potential "many-termers."

In cost-benefit terms, the data were no less dramatic. An estimated eighty-eight fewer persons were sent to prison during the three-year "after" period than would ordinarily be expected. This eliminated about $300,000 in prison costs over and above the increased probation costs. It eliminated another $80,000 in welfare costs and about $50,000 in parole costs (Ball et al., 1963).

The total benefits from the project during the demonstration period were estimated at $524,434. The related costs were about $33,000 per year—expenditures on three probation staff members and some minor administrative costs. In the three years of the study, these costs amounted to about $100,000. Expressed as a benefit/cost ratio, and without regard to discounting rates, the results of the project may be stated tentatively as 5.2 to 1.

Some questions remain about the estimation of benefits and costs in this project. Did some of the reported benefits come from beyond the three-year study period? Were some costs from the poststudy period chargeable to the total cost estimate of $100,000? Should some jail costs be charged against the averted-prison benefits? Why were earnings of the nonincarcerated men not included in the benefits?

These questions suggest that other observers working with the same data might have arrived at different benefit and cost estimates. One's initial judgment, however, is that the final benefit/cost ratio might properly be higher than the one stated here, mainly because at least eighty-eight man-years of earnings appear to have been omitted from the benefit estimates. Consequently, this appears to be a convincing demonstration of the fact that corrections is presently a very uneconomical process, and that only a small effort is required to make it much more efficient in the economic sense. Correlated with this increase in efficiency, of course, is an increase in social benefits in the form of improved adjustment in the community on the part of former offenders and their families.

This type of analysis does not deny the validity of claims that for some prisoners the objective of incapacitation or punishment may override economic considerations. The analysis speaks primarily to those cases, possibly 60 percent to 80 percent of the total presently imprisoned, for whom knowledgeable observers consider imprisonment to be an inappropriate disposition of their case.

Cost Analysis of the District of Columbia Work-Release Program, 1966–69. This study examined the first thirty-nine months of operation of the District of Columbia's work-release program, during which more than 1,000 men were released to the community. Duration of program participation averaged three months for felony offenders and six weeks for misdemeanants.

During Phase I of the project, which operated out of one of the Lorton, Virginia prisons of the D.C. Department of Corrections, with busing of releasees to the District each day, benefits to the community were estimated at $2,315 per felon work-releasee year. The corresponding value for a misdemeanant work-releasee year was $2,023.

During Phase II, which operated out of the D.C. jail and thus did not require commuter busing, the benefits were estimated at $2,363 per program man-year. The benefits of the program consisted mainly of (1) lower maintenance costs in the program because of reduced staff-inmate ratios, and (2) earnings of the work releasees.

Given the fact that during the time the work release program operated out of the Lorton Correctional Complex or the D.C. jail maintenance costs for a prisoner for one year were about $4,500, it is evident that benefits from the program were about one-half the costs of ordinary prisoner maintenance. One way of viewing these results is to consider that the first-year benefit/cost ratio for the work release program was $2,363/$4,500, or about 1 to 2 (McArthur et al., 1970).

It is not clear how this ratio should be interpreted against the benefit/cost ratio for an ordinary prisoner. One possibility is to assume that such a ratio is 0 to 1, indicating no benefits and unit costs. Another is to estimate that the typical prisoner had engaged in at least $4,500 worth of predatory activity during his last year on the streets, so that the ratio is more likely to be 1 to 1, suggesting that imprisonment has some economic value to society.

Accepting this as a largely unexplored area, and assuming that the typical prisoner constitutes a benefit/cost ratio of 1 to 1, then the work releasees under this assumption could be regarded as achieving a somewhat higher ratio, possibly 1.5 to 1. These estimates are, primarily, speculative attempts to begin definition of the parameters of the problem, not to propose particular values. The estimates are illustrative, however, of the directions that inquiry may take as corrections begins to exploit the techniques of cost-benefit analysis.

It is now clear that among the base-line data needed in correctional management are widely ranging estimates of depredation costs, welfare costs, and similar costs associated with both the free and incarcerated statuses of offenders. Data of these kinds would permit the development of provisional values for a number of typical benefit/cost ratios at the probation, community correctional center, prison, parole, work-release, and study-release levels. Correctional planning and management could then proceed from a sounder informational and conceptual base.

Economics of Drug Addiction and Control in the District of Columbia: A Model for the Estimation of the Costs and Benefits of Rehabilitation. During 1969 and 1970, the D.C. Department of Corrections and the District of Columbia administration planned and implemented a community-based treatment program for narcotic offenders and for heroin addicts generally. The program was initially conceptualized as multimodal (Adams et al., 1969), but it soon developed into a program strongly oriented toward methadone maintenance.

Approximately 3,000 addicts out of an estimated 16,800 in the District were involved in the Narcotics Treatment Administration's programs, with an estimated client-year cost of $1,400 for the first year and $250 for each succeeding year. It was assumed that the success rate for the program was 40 percent in the first year—a conservative estimate for methadone maintenance programs (Gearing, 1970).

Given the 40 percent success rate, it was estimated that the benefits to be derived from keeping 1,000 addicts under treatment would be $5,750,770 for the first year, and $21,662,377 at eleven years, discounting present value at 10%. The declining per-year value reflects attrition in the number of addicts remaining in treatment (and thus being able to produce benefits) and also the cost (interest or discount rate) of money. A future return must be discounted to attract present monies. The benefits were defined to include police, court, and corrections costs averted; productivity and earnings restored; health costs reduced; and private crime prevention costs reduced (Holahan, 1970a).

Costs of treatment were estimated at $1,400,000 for one year and $1,676,688 for eleven years. This cost drops sharply as survivors in treatment diminish and the need for treatment by survivors becomes nominal. Included in benefits were assumptions as to gains from successes in treatment and alternative assumptions as to the costs to society had the successes not been achieved through treatment. Cost estimates were based on the expected expenditures of the Narcotics Treatment Administration.

The benefit/cost ratios were computed at two time spans and with two assumptions about rates of heroin purchase and proportion of property crimes committed by addicts. Table 5 shows these ratios.

Assuming that socially worthwhile expenditures are being made when the benefit/cost ratio exceeds unity, it may be concluded that the Narcotics Treatment Administration's program is clearly profitable if the estimates as to heroin cost, addict-nonaddict crime ratios, and other elements in the analysis are realistic.

One noteworthy feature of this analysis is its approach to results in the future. This is a matter that has not been confidently dealt with by older methods of studying outcomes. The use of recidivism rate analysis provides only a tenuous grasp on results at remote dates—except possibly for an estimate of the "ultimate" recidivism rate (Glaser, 1964). Cost-benefit analysis, on the other hand, encourages specification of the worth or profitability of a particular course of action with offenders at some distant time. The use of discounting procedures and the choice of discount rates provide both stimulus and guidance to the conceptualization of the future results of present actions.

Corrections Cost Projections: A Simulation of the California Criminal Justice System. Project Crossroads used a quasi-experimental approach for the estimation of a benefit/cost ratio for a correctional operation on which rather extensive empirical data were available at the time of analysis. The analysis held close to the available experience. On the other hand, the Economics of Drug Addiction and Control Model in D.C. relied heavily on assumption and ventured further into the future to derive both a near and a remote benefit/cost ratio, and to estimate in this manner the efficiency of a new narcotic treatment program. The Corrections Cost Projection project made an even broader conceptual leap. A simulation model was developed to ascertain the efficiency of a criminal justice system. The model provisionally allocated persons convicted in the Superior Courts of California to various correctional programs. It

TABLE 5

HEROIN COSTS, AND CRIME AND
BENEFIT/COST RATIOS

Heroin Cost	Crime Ratio	One-Year B/C Ratio	Eleven-Year B/C Ratio
$25 per day	33%	2.7 to 1	8.5 to 1
$40 per day	50%	4.1 to 1	12.9 to 1

Source: Holahan, 1970a:71.

then proceeded to examine the costs of operating the system under alternative sentencing policies, including the one currently in effect (Kolodney & Daetz, 1969).

The model, mathematical in form, distributed the convicted population to probation, jail, prison, and parole. It then applied hypothetical costs per convicted person to the program populations to ascertain total costs of operating each of the programs. The program costs were then summed to obtain the total criminal justice system costs.

Exercising or running the model to represent each year's operations in a five-year period yielded a series of comparable costs that reflected the outcomes of managing the system under existing sentencing policies and under an alternative policy. The results indicated that implementation of an alternative sentencing policy could bring about major savings.

The alternative policy, which called for a reduction of 20 percent in mean time served under state supervision, was not wholly arbitrary. It had been identified as a commitment policy already in effect in some California counties. The specification of such a policy appeared realistic, and also feasible, particularly when proposed in conjunction with a return to the counties, as a subsidy, the savings that occurred at the state level from the reduced length of time served. The subsidy, which would depend for its magnitude on the performance of the counties as measured against existing sentencing policy, could be used to improve and extend county programs within the larger criminal justice system.

This project was a primarily conceptual means of measuring the effectiveness of a criminal justice system—the formulation of a mathematical model and the exercise of this model under conditions that took into account both realistic possibilities within the current system and the long-range goals of persons responsible for effective operation of the system. The practice of constructing such models for evaluative purposes is now well established, definitely in industry, and to a lesser extent in social-science or social-action fields. With the growing use of computers as aids to research and planning, it appears likely that this mode of evaluation in corrections and criminal justice will soon become much more common.

DISCUSSION

The foregoing reviews provide clear evidence on a number of points. First, there is a definite indication that correctional effectiveness can be measured and that this process has been going on with at least moderate success for some time. Second, it is evident that the measurement process has found some new correctional procedures to be more effective and/or more efficient than the older procedures they were tested against. These discoveries have begun to affect correctional procedures and structures, and it is likely that this effect will accelerate over time. Finally, it is clear that the measurement process is changing. It is evolving toward greater diversity of method, increased complexity of design, broader range of application, and heightened sophistication of both technique and strategy. Some of these changes are exploratory and will probably prove abortive; others are likely to show superior capability in measurement, and will result ultimately in further acceleration of changes in the structure and operations of corrections.

One significant development has been the establishment of the *controlled experiment* as a correctional measurement technique that is noteworthy for several reasons. First, experiments such as SIPU, PICO, and CTP indicate an impressive ability of correctional administrators and researchers to work cooperatively for many years on a joint effort to improve knowledge of the correctional process.

Second, they show the possibility of carrying out not only simple experimental designs but also rather complicated patterns and sequences of designs. A review of accomplishments over the past two decades suggests that corrections has moved ahead of most social agencies in the scope and quality of its experimental studies.

Third, these studies are testimony to the persistence of correctional researchers in recognizing and overcoming obstacles, dealing with obscuring effects, coping with the complexity of correctional operations, and striving to handle conceptually some of the problems of measurement that classic experimental design is poorly equipped to handle. The phased projects, with designs elaborated from one stage to the next, are demonstrations of resourcefulness in the quest for knowledge.

Fourth, the productivity of the experimental studies suggests that these techniques are inherently effective with at least some aspects of the correctional measurement process. However, the various difficulties that remain unresolved in SIPU, PICO, CTP, the Group Guidance Experiment, and the Silverlake Experiment are useful reminders that the controlled experiment, impressive as its contributions have been, is not the final answer to corrections' need for measurement. As has been pointed out by a number of observers (Weiss & Rein, 1969; Guttentag, 1971), evaluative research in the social field requires more than controlled experimentation in the traditional form.

A second development of note in the evolution of measurement processes in corrections is the *emergence of cost-benefit analysis*. This technique has seen a rapid upsurge, particularly in some federal agencies, since around 1960. The initial indications are promising. When applied to the results of the typical controlled experiment in corrections, this technique provides information on efficiency that usefully supplements—and often overshadows—the findings on effectiveness, which formerly were the sole objective of the experiment.

One of the noteworthy characteristics of cost-benefit analysis is its capability of showing important results on some occasions when the traditional experimental procedure has failed to disclose significant differences in outcome; e.g., the Group Guidance and Silverlake experiments.

A third development of note is the *use of parole success probabilities*—often termed "base expectancies"—as a device for evaluating program effectiveness. The rationale of the base expectancy "experiment" is that indicated probability of success on parole and actual performance on parole might be expected to differ if a significant treatment experience were administered after the predictive scores were established. If the strategy of comparing actual with expected success rates can be made to work, the need for expensive and cumbersome experimental designs is obviated.

Thus far in the history of corrections, this method has worked better in concept than in practice. Part of the problem is apparently the low precision of existing prediction instruments. In the past decade, such instruments have been developed primarily by multiple regression analysis and configuration analysis. More recently, use has been made of a method described as "direct search in mathematical space" (Adams et al., 1971). The predictive efficiency of the resulting instrument, measured by the technique of "mean cost rating" (Duncan et al., 1953), appears to be about twice that of prediction instruments currently in use in corrections. If this apparent superiority in predictive ability holds up, the new instrument may revive interest in evaluation against base expectancies.

A fourth promising development in the measurement of correctional effectiveness is the *rise of simulation or modeling*. Such procedures, still rare in corrections, depend upon the availability of computers and specialized staff. The technique should grow in importance as the focus of interest in correctional measurement shifts from program element to system effectiveness. This appears to be a likely development under the present tendency toward solution of the crime problem through the coordinated efforts of various combinations of agencies and political entities.

A fifth development that deserves comment is the *concept of system rates.* The concept of rates as isolated indicators in criminal justice is already familiar; e.g., reported crimes, crimes cleared by arrest, and recidivism. Conceivably, these isolated indicators can eventually be replaced by coherent sets of rates whose successive patterns could convey to the experienced eye significant information about the condition and effectiveness of society's mechanisms for the control of deviant behavior.

A first attempt to state the characteristics of a system-rate approach to planning and evaluation in criminal justice has recently been completed. Klein and his associates (1971) identify six key elements in the rate system and seven determinants that govern the system rates. With appropriate development of record systems and information procedures, the functioning of the criminal justice system can be described in terms of the key rates, and the system can then be operated in a manner that affects the determinants of the rates. Ostensibly, this will maximize some rates and minimize others in relation to broader social values and objectives.

Because they embrace criminal justice in its entirety, including even the deviance processes, these system rates are ambitious in concept. They will require time for development into operational entities. In the process, they may follow the route of base expectancies—a period of disillusionment, succeeded perhaps by a resurgence in more efficient and more functional forms.

REFERENCES

Adams, S.
  1959   "The Preston impact study." Sacramento: California Youth Authority (unpublished).
  1961a   Effectiveness of Interview Therapy with Older Youth Authority Wards: An Interim Evaluation of the PICO Project. Research Report No. 20. Sacramento: California Youth Authority.
  1961b   "Interaction between intensive interview therapy and amenability classification in older Youth Authority wards," in Inquiries Concerning Kinds of Treatment for Kinds of Delinquents: Monograph No. 2. Sacramento: California Board of Corrections. Reprinted in Norman B. Johnston et al. (eds.), The Sociology of Punishment and Correction. Revised Edition (New York: Wiley, 1970).
  1965   "An experimental assessment of group counseling with juvenile probationers." Journal of the California Probation, Parole and Correctional Association 2(Spring):19–25.
  1967a   "A cost approach to the assessment of gang rehabilitation techniques." Journal of Research in Crime and Delinquency 4(January):166–182.
  1967b   "Some findings from correctional caseload research." Federal Probation 31(December):48–57.
  1974   "Evaluative research in corrections: status and prospects." Federal Probation 38(March):14–21.

Adams, S., and M. Q. Grant.
  1961   Evaluation of Community Located Treatment for Delinquents: A Demonstration Project Proposal to the National Institute of Mental Health. Sacramento: California Youth Authority.

Adams, S., D. F. Meadows, and C. Reynolds.
  1969   Narcotic Involved Inmates in the Department of Corrections. Research Report No. 12. Washington, D.C.: District of Columbia Department of Corrections.

Adams, S., W. Plair, and J. D. Spevacek.
  1971   Validation and Implementation of a Scoring Device for Predicting In-Program Success on Work Release. Research Memorandum 71-7. Washington, D.C.: District of Columbia Department of Corrections.

Adams, S., R. E. Rice, and B. Olive.
  1965   A Cost Analysis of the Effectiveness of the Group Guidance Program. Research Memorandum 65-3. Los Angeles: Los Angeles County Probation Department.

Bailey, W. C.
  1966   "Correctional outcome: an evaluation of 100 reports." Journal of Criminal Law, Criminology and Police Science 57(June):153–160.

Ball, A. C., R. C. Fletcher, and E. Cranefield.
  1963   The Saginaw Probation Demonstration Project. Ann Arbor: University of Michigan School of Social Work.

Berkowitz, F.
  1973   Evaluation of Crime Control Programs in California: A Review. Sacramento: California Council on Criminal Justice.

California Department of Corrections.
  1956   Special Intensive Parole Unit: Phase I, Fifteen-Man Caseload Study. Sacramento: California Department of Corrections.
  1958   Special Intensive Parole Unit: Phase II, Thirty-Man Caseload Study. Sacramento: California Department of Corrections.

Campbell, D. F.
  1969   "Reforms as experiments." American Psychologist 24(April):409–429.

Duncan, O. D., A. J. Reiss, Jr., and H. R. Stanton.
  1953   "Formal devices for making selection decisions." American Journal of Sociology 58(May):573–584.

Empey, L. T., and S. G. Lubeck.
  1971   The Silverlake Experiment. Chicago: Aldine.

Gearing, F. R.
  1970   "Successes and failures in methadone maintenance, treatment of heroin addiction in New York City." Paper presented at the Third National Conference on Methadone Treatment sponsored by the National Association for the Prevention of Addiction to Narcotics and the National Institute of Mental Health, New York City.

Glaser, D.
  1964   The Effectiveness of a Prison and Parole System. Indianapolis: Bobbs-Merrill.

Grant, M. Q., M. Warren, and J. K. Turner.
  1963   Community Treatment Project: An Evaluation of Community Treatment for Delinquents. CTP Research Report No. 3. Sacramento: California Youth Authority.

Guttentag, M.
  1971   "Models and methods in evaluation research." Graduate Center, City University of New York (unpublished).

Havel, J.
  1963   Special Intensive Parole Unit, Phase IV: A High Base Expectancy Study. Sacramento: California Department of Corrections.

Havel, J., and E. Sulka.
  1962   Special Intensive Parole Unit, Phase III. Sacramento: California Department of Corrections.

Hinrichs, H. H., and G. M. Taylor.
  1969   Program Budgeting and Benefit-Cost Analysis. Pacific Palisades: Goodyear Publishing Co.

Holahan, J.
  1970a   The Economics of Drug Addiction and Control in Washington, D.C.: A Model for Estimation of Costs and Benefits of Rehabilitation. Washington, D.C.: District of Columbia Department of Corrections.
  1970b   A Benefit-Cost Analysis of Project Crossroads. Washington, D.C.: National Committee for Children and Youth.

Hunter, E. F.
  1968   Reduction of Delinquency through Expansion of Opportunity. Research Report No. 33. Los Angeles: Los Angeles County Probation Department.

Joint Commission on Correctional Manpower and Training.
  1968   The Public Looks at Crime and Corrections. Report of a survey made by Louis Harris & Associates. Washington, D.C.: Joint Commission on Correctional Manpower and Training.

Johnston, Norman B., et al. (eds.)
  1970   The Sociology of Punishment and Correction. Revised Edition. New York: Wiley.

Klein, M. W.
  1971   Street Gangs and Street Workers. Englewood Cliffs, N.J.: Prentice-Hall.

Klein, M. W., S. Kobrin, A. W. McEachern, and H. R. Sigurdson.
  1971   "System rates: an approach to comprehensive criminal justice planning." Crime and Delinquency 17(October):355–372.

Kolodney, S. E., and D. Daetz.
  1969   Corrections Cost Projections: A Simulation of the California Criminal Justice System. Mountain View, Calif.: Sociosystems Laboratory, Sylvania Electric Systems.

Leiberg, L., R. Rovner-Pieczenik, and J. F. Holahan.
  1971   Project Crossroads: Final Report. 3 volumes. Washington, D.C.: National Committee for Children and Youth.

Lerman, P.
  1968   "Evaluating the outcomes of institutions for delinquents." Social Work 13(July):55–64.

Lessing, L. P.
    1950   "The world of du Pont: how to win at research." Fortune 42(October):115–134.

McArthur, V. A., B. Cantor, and S. Glendinning.
    1970   A Cost Analysis of the District of Columbia Work Release Program. Research Report No. 24. Washington, D.C.: District of Columbia Department of Corrections.

Martinson, R.
    1971   The Treatment Evaluation Survey. New York: Office of Crime Control Planning of the State of New York.

Michigan Crime and Delinquency Council.
    1963   Saving People and Money. East Lansing: Michigan Crime and Delinquency Council.

Robison, J., and G. Smith.
    1971   "The effectiveness of correctional programs." Crime and Delinquency 17(January):67–80.

Rudoff, A.
    1959   The Pilot Intensive Counseling Organization Project: Second Technical Report. Sacramento: California Department of Corrections.

Rudoff, A., and L. Bennett.
    1958   The Pilot Intensive Counseling Organization Project: First Technical Report. Sacramento: California Department of Corrections.

Rushen, R., and E. F. Hunter.
    1968   "RODEO: in-community supervision of minors in lieu of probation camp." Paper presented at the annual meetings of the Pacific Sociological Association, San Francisco.

Speer, D. C.
    1972   "The role of the crisis intervention model in the rehabilitation of criminal offenders." Buffalo, N.Y.: Erie County Suicide Prevention and Crisis Service (unpublished).

Warren, M. Q.
    1967   The Community Treatment Project: Five Years After. Sacramento: California Youth Authority.
    1970   "The community treatment project." Pp. 671–683 in Norman B. Johnston et al. (eds.), The Sociology of Punishment and Correction. Revised Edition. New York: Wiley.

Weiss, R. S., and M. Rein.
    1969   "The evaluation of broad-aim programs: a cautionary case and a moral." Annals of the American Academy of Political and Social Science 385 (September):133–142.

PART IV

PREVENTION OF CRIME
AND DELINQUENCY

Introduction—Part IV

The least adequately researched or utilized aspect of applied criminology is prevention. Its underdevelopment is, in part, a consequence of the diversity of delinquency and crime; in part, a result of the variety of their alleged causes; and, in part, a reaction to the magnitude and complexity of these causal conditions. A major first step toward prevention is conceptual clarification. For this we offer two quite different but highly complementary chapters.

Economists Harold L. Votey, Jr. and Llad Phillips are unique in their discipline for the extent of their close collaborative research on the economic aspects of crime control. Their chapter develops abstract models applicable to two approaches to property offense prevention: first, keeping youth in the employed labor force, and second, expending public funds on protection and deterrence. It also addresses the problem of estimating when the social costs of the latter expenditures exceed those of the offenses they prevent.

The unusually creative career of sociologist LaMar T. Empey includes both strictly academic theorizing and intimate interaction with delinquents in community agencies while directing some of history's most rigorous correctional experiments. In our concluding chapter he first points out the basis for the war-on-crime and diversion approaches to crime prevention, but explains their limitations. He then argues for making prevention more effective by changing some of the legal rules and criminal justice practices that are counterproductive. His major stress, however, is on changing socializing institutions and interaction patterns, especially in the schools, so that youth may more readily acquire legitimate identities and anticriminal attitudes.

CHAPTER **30**

The Control of Criminal Activity:
An Economic Analysis

Harold L. Votey, Jr. and Llad Phillips

University of California at Santa Barbara

1. INTRODUCTION

While solutions to the crime problem inevitably require decisions that modify the allocation of economic resources, relatively little analysis of this problem has considered appropriate alternatives in such resource allocation. This chapter applies the economist's tools and methodology not only to aspects of the crime generation problem, but also to the control of criminal behavior.

We begin by attempting to pinpoint and evaluate the economic alternatives available to society in dealing with the high social cost of crime. The analysis reveals two alternatives for policy: to modify the social and economic conditions that provide a strong incentive to criminal behavior, or to influence potential criminal behavior through the deterrent forces of crime control.

While it seems reasonable to believe that much of our law-enforcement policy is based on faith in the existence of a strong deterrence effect, there has been scant recognition of such a force in criminological theory. A notable exception to this is a theoretical study by Gary Becker (1968) who builds a theoretical model in which, through an adaptation of the economic analysis of choice, he links the economic motivations for crime and the deterrence effects of punishment. He shows that the strength of the deterrence effect depends upon the probability of punishment. Thus, the generation of crime, in his model, is not independent of the force with which public authorities respond to crime. Out of his analysis of the costs of crime and crime control, Becker shows that the optimal amount of law enforcement depends on both the nature of punishment and the costs of operating the criminal justice system (a further discussion of the optimal amount of law enforcement may be found in Stigler, 1970).

In our work we have formulated theoretical models for empirically testing the basic conceptual framework of Becker. Our empirical results lend emphatic support to the efficacy of his approach in ultimately formulating optimal policies for crime control. Our technique has been to formulate the analysis within the context of a problem in social control in which we assume there are two interacting processes: the first of these is crime generation, from which emanates a flow of offenses in response to a set of social and economic conditions. The second is the operation of the criminal justice system, which is organized society's response to the costs imposed upon it by criminal behavior. Finally, it is assumed that society's goal is to minimize the social cost of crime.

The fundamental approach is general in nature and appropriate for the analysis of many types of crime. For reasons that become apparent as the details unfold, we concentrate on what we refer to as economic crimes, i.e., the major felonies (larceny, burglary, auto theft, and robbery) for which there is an economic motive. Because of the strongly age- and sex-specific nature of the crimes, we concentrate on 18–19-year-old males. In dealing with the criminal justice process, we narrow our focus to the effects of law enforcement and, hence, to the apprehension aspects of the process, rather than including prosecution, adjudication, and punishment. The consequence of these simplifications, which can be justified on both empirical and pragmatic grounds, is that some important relationships are readily revealed. Success in establishing these relationships suggests that the same techniques may be employed effectively to analyze other components of the criminal justice and crime generation processes.

The research reported here must be regarded as just a beginning. We have not carried analysis of the process of minimizing the social cost of crime to the point that we are able to provide policy-makers with sufficient tools to select the appropriate cost-minimizing allocation of resources to deal with criminal behavior. We have, however, provided strong statistical substantiation of the power of the deterrence effect and of the influence of economic variables on crime generation. We hope this provides an incentive and points the way for further research that will reveal improved techniques for minimizing the social cost of criminal behavior.

2. AN ECONOMIC ANALYSIS OF CRIME

In this section, we examine the costs of criminal behavior within an economic framework and indicate how our objective function logically evolves from our understanding of these costs. We then develop the conception of an equilibrium process of crime generation and control that can be stated in terms of an optimization model for social control. This model links the processes of crime generation and deterrence, and pinpoints clearly the opportunities available to society for control.

2.1 The Social Objective

Society's objective in dealing with the problem of crime cannot be simply the elimination of crime, as desirable as that may seem. This becomes clear when we consider the nature of the various costs of crime and the way they vary with the level of crime. To facilitate an understanding of the relationships involved, it is useful to distinguish between the costs imposed on society as a consequence of criminal behavior and the self-imposed costs to society for protection and the deterrence of crime.

The direct costs of criminal behavior, i.e., the costs imposed on society by a criminal's acts of aggression against persons or property, or acts of expropriation, are difficult to measure directly. As was pointed out by the President's Commission on Law Enforcement and Administration of Justice (1967b:42), the only comprehensive study of the costs of crime in the United States was made by the National Commission on Law Observance and Enforcement (the Wickersham Commission) in 1931. Both of these documents note the difficulties in measuring costs of crime. A major difficulty is the fact that the costs of crime, although very real, are implicit. Only to the extent that people insure against losses do we have any measure of the value individuals place on avoiding a particular form of victimization. In the case of homicide, such losses are seemingly immeasurable. At the opposite extreme are losses from petty theft. Even these are not easily quantifiable in a social accounting sense. Nevertheless, in order to conceptualize the problem properly, these costs must become a meaningful component of the analysis.

Even the costs society pays for protection and deterrence are not adequately documented to give us the total picture. Public costs are fairly well recorded for such activities as police protection, the judicial process, and corrections.[1] On the other hand, private expenditures for protection by individuals and businesses are not well documented. These comprise the costs of guarding personal and real property, including valuables in transit, protection devices, such as alarms, fences, and locks, and even the cost of watchdogs. All of these are a direct or indirect result of criminal behavior.

The appropriate criterion (objective function) for society becomes apparent when we observe the relationship of each of these classes of cost to the incidence of crime. As expenditures for protection and deterrence increase, the losses to victims decrease; yet the overall social costs must increase at some point. This was recognized by the President's Commission (1967b:42), which noted that where the objective is protection of private property, economic losses due to crime must be evaluated in comparison with the costs of improved protection. These relationships are depicted in Figure 1. We indicate a cost of criminal behavior approaching zero only if society is willing to pay infinite sums for prevention and control. At the other extreme, as we approach zero expenditures, we would expect to find crime levels burgeoning out of control. The social optimum falls at L_0 with a tolerable level of crime at a social cost C_0.[2] Picking this point maximizes the amount of resources available to produce other things, thus we can conclude that it is a social optimum.

2.2   The Equilibrium System of Crime Generation and Control

The generation of crime and the social response to crime may be thought of as a pair of simultaneous relationships, i.e., each modified by the other. Socioeconomic conditions contribute impetus to the generation of crime, whereas the deterrent and punitive forces of society impose a measure of control on the volume of crime. In turn, the processes of control operate at a greater intensity as they respond to the acts of criminals.

The schematic diagram of Figure 2 (a modification of Phillips & Votey, 1972:331) is useful in illustrating the foregoing relationships. Here, the crime generation process is represented as being a response function reacting to social and economic conditions and to the deterrent influences of the criminal justice system. Social influences are comprised of the prevailing social attitudes, institutional influences and constraints, and the various other efforts at social control. Economic influences stem from the effects of varying levels of economic well-being and economic growth being transmitted

---

1. Aggregate measures of state, local, and total expenditures for police protection are published in the U.S. Bureau of Census's *Governmental Finances* series, payroll information is in their *Public Employment* series, and information on police employees may be found in some detail both in these publications and in the Federal Bureau of Investigation's *Crime in the United States: Uniform Crime Reports* series.

2. This is a "tolerable" level of crime because the direct costs of criminal behavior are measured in terms of the correct implicit prices society itself places on the total costs of criminal behavior. Thus, there is nothing arbitrary about this point although, as we have noted, it may be difficult to determine empirically.

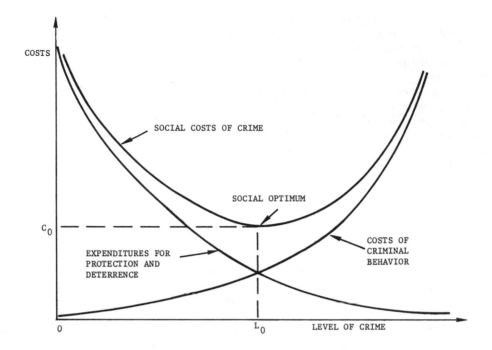

FIGURE 1. The social cost of crime. Note: Social costs of crime ≡ expenditures for protection and deterrence + costs of criminal behavior.

to individuals in the system in the form of real income levels, employment, and other economic opportunities.

Organized society's response to the crime generation process is the criminal justice system. This system is also subject to social influences. Its control is a consequence of public policy decisions exerted directly through allocation of economic resources and indirectly through policies influencing education and scientific research. The raw input into the criminal justice system is the aggregate of crimes committed. The output is a combination of rehabilitation and punishment, both of which impose real costs on offenders. It is the punishment costs that have a deterring influence, both on these persons with respect to the commission of additional crimes, and to potential offenders who might otherwise be tempted to undertake criminal activities.

At this point, it is appropriate to note that this view of the system of crime generation and control is not a universal one. Theories of criminality generally may be classed in two basic categories: situational and historical (Sutherland & Cressey, 1970:74–75; for alternative classifications, see Glaser, 1956). The "situational" class of theories postulates that some set of circumstances and provocations, existing at a moment, leads directly to criminal action. These theories may be useful in the explanation of crimes of passion or unpremeditated crimes. The "historical" class of theories postulates that criminal activity by an individual is a consequence of a large number of factors that have influenced the individual over a period of time. Such theories encompass arguments that are anatomic, physiologic, genetic, psychologic, and socio-economic. These theories provide an explanation for crimes that are premeditated.

The school of criminology denoted as differential association has adopted an

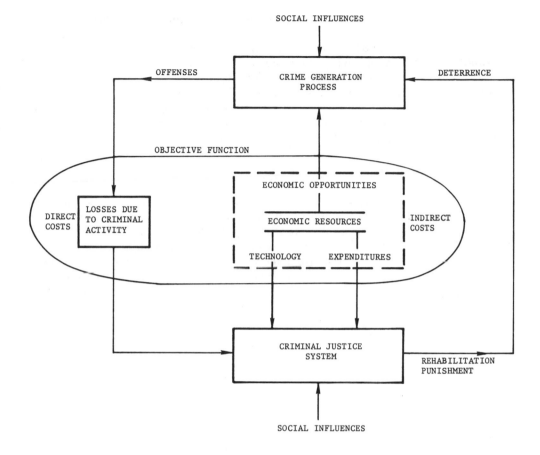

FIGURE 2. The equilibrium system of crime generation and control.

eclectic approach encompassing both situational and historical theories of criminal behavior (Glaser, 1956; Cressey, 1960; Burgess & Akers, 1966). This school postulates that, of the many factors associated with criminal behavior, some undefined and variable subset must be present for crime to take place. This provides the rationale for the more sophisticated statistical studies that use factor analysis to find significant relationships between a host of factors that may be expected to lead to criminal behavior (Schmid, 1960; Schuessler & Slotin, 1964; Wilks, 1967). In most of this research, however, the deterrent effect of the social response to crime is systematically ignored.

It has been pointed out that such a multifactor approach can hardly be regarded as a theory, in the sense that a direct cause and effect relationship is identified (Sutherland & Cressey, 1970:57–61). Cressey (1960:54) makes a distinction between principles or epidemiology, which order *known* facts, and theory, which is detailed sufficiently to permit derivation of testable hypotheses. The lack of a unique set of necessary or sufficient conditions leading to crime renders most of this theorizing inappropriate for the sort of model building that has been used effectively in analyzing the relationships between aggregate social behavior and economic variables.

As Gibbs (1968) points out, it is difficult to find a major theory that emphasizes the effect of the social response to crime on the rates of crime. He further holds that the theoretical argument that a deterrent effect exists has not been effectively tested. A rigorous theoretical model suitable for empirical testing was not formulated prior to the work of Becker (1968). While the formulations tested in our work differ from his in detail, virtually all of the theoretical concepts we utilize may be found in one form or another in his seminal work. A significant statistical confirmation of a substantial deterrent effect would imply the need for a reorientation in the thinking of those concerned with the problem. In the following section, we present a model for the analysis of the problem of minimizing the social cost of crime.

2.3   The Cost Minimization Model

The criterion we formulate is to minimize the sum of the losses to crime and the costs of the criminal justice system, subject to the interaction between crime generation and crime control. One can formalize these relationships by setting up an objective function, which we wish to minimize, subject to a set of constraints. The objective function includes the direct costs emanating from the criminal process and the indirect costs society imposes on itself for control. The constraints include the technical parameters of both the crime generation and criminal justice processes. In functional notation this can be expressed as follows

Minimize:

$$C = C_D + C_I \tag{2.1}$$

Subject to:

$$OF = f(S_1, E_1, CJ) \tag{2.2}$$

$$CJ = g(S_2, E_2, OF) \tag{2.3}$$

where C is the social cost of crime; C_D is the direct cost to society of criminal behavior; C_I is the indirect cost, i.e., the reaction of society; OF is the level of offenses (crime); CJ is the output of the criminal justice system; S_1 and S_2 are indices of state variables representing social conditions; and E_1 and E_2 are indices of state variables representing a given allocation of economic resources between those activities that create greater economic opportunities for society and those that attempt to control criminal behavior directly.

Alternatively, we could think of S and E as simply vectors of the same social and economic variables, respectively, in both the OF and CJ functions, in which the parameters associated with each of the individual S or E variables would differ between the two functions so that both S and E enter differently into the OF and CJ functions.

In relating this representation of the model to Figure 2, we see that the area within the broken lines represents the opportunities for economic policy. Adjustment to the cost minimization process is exerted through changes in the state variables E_1 and E_2. Control of the direct costs of criminal behavior is through the indirect processes of adjusting either the deterrence effect or the economic conditions that individual potential criminals face, whereas the indirect costs, i.e., the responses to crime, are subject to direct determination by public authorities. It is this asymmetry that makes it difficult to evaluate the effectiveness of the system.

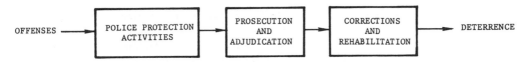

FIGURE 3. A schematic partitioning of the criminal justice system.

2.4 Opportunities for Control

As noted above, we describe the possibilities for solving the crime problem as a single pair of alternatives. That, of course, is only the first stage of the optimization process. For example, even if we are certain the next dollar should be allocated to the criminal justice system, it is still not clear how that dollar should be spent, because the system may be partitioned into its major components, as indicated by Figure 3. Important for our purposes is the fact that even this representation may be further compartmentalized. For example, police protection activities can be divided between responses to felony crime and all other police activities. Felony crimes, in turn, may be classified as crimes against property and crimes against persons. This separation of felony crimes is not only important from the point of view of resource allocation within the sphere of law enforcement, but is also important in distinguishing between the motivating powers of alternative resource allocations with respect to the different felony crimes.

In the analysis which follows we will be postulating that variables measuring police protection activities are a proxy for variables representing the entire criminal justice process in regard to the deterrent effect on crime. Such a simplification is probably reasonable since, as Becker (1968:176) notes, judicial experts appear to believe that a change in the probability of conviction has a greater effect on the level of offenses than a change in the degree of punishment. This view was also held by Becarria (quoted in Vold, 1958:22), who theorized that the certainty and celerity of punishment, rather than the severity, would have the greatest preventative effect.

3. EVALUATION OF THE COMPONENTS OF THE SYSTEM

Let us examine separately the process of property crime generation and the production process that we call law enforcement. In dealing with both of these processes we utilize national data for the U.S. in the 1950s and 1960s.

In dealing with crime generation in Section 3.1, we will formulate a behavioral model implicitly assuming that the impact of law enforcement does not vary over time. Such an assumption is necessary if we wish to take account of the age- and sex-specific nature of the generation of property crimes. In subsection 3.1.2, we move directly into a discussion of economic opportunities for youth. The justification for this is developed more fully in subsection 3.1.3 where we set forth our hypothesis for empirical testing. The fact that we find strong statistical verification for the relationship between economic variables and property crime (in the face of the frequently noted conflicting evidence regarding such a relationship) lends support to our conviction that studying crime by age and sex is a correct approach (Vold, 1958:181 discusses conflicting evidence).

In dealing with the analysis of law enforcement as a production process (Section 3.2), we can be more comprehensive in our approach. Our only problem here, and one that we virtually ignore (regarding it as a theoretical problem in economic analysis rather than a crime-related problem), is that of estimating production relationships on a crime-by-crime basis when there is no cost-accounting information on law-enforcement inputs on such a basis. The only information available, in fact, is on total expenditures and employees. A theoretical justification for using total values is presented in Appendix B.

3.1   Crime Generation

3.1.1. The Economics of Choice. For several centuries criminologists have been suggesting economic motives as one of the possible causes of property crimes (Bonger, 1916, 1943; Vold, 1958). Illegal gains are an alternative to income earned honestly. The critical question is how does one choose between socially acceptable and illegal alternatives for earning income? From an economic point of view, it would be reasonable to assume that a rational individual, implicitly at least, will consider all of the opportunities open to him in terms of a benefit-cost analysis. From normal employment, the benefit is a stream of income. The associated costs include the everyday costs of acquiring and maintaining one's self in a job. In the case of an economic crime, the benefits are any returns from its commission. The direct costs associated with the actual commission of a crime include reconnoitering, transportation, and the cost of disposing of illegally obtained goods. In addition, there may be the costs associated with being apprehended, including the cost of having an arrest or prison term on one's record, the cost for legal defense, the loss of income from being incarcerated, and the psychic cost of being branded a criminal. The expected costs of these latter possibilities will be all of the costs associated with the event multiplied by the probability that the event (arrest, trial, imprisonment) will take place. In summary, given his own implicit evaluation of the expected costs and benefits, the rational individual will naturally select the alternative that yields the greatest net benefits.

Both the alternatives for legal income and those for illegal gain are affected by many factors beyond the control of the individual. When, for any reason, the alternatives faced by the individual are reduced, he must choose from those which remain. In fact, if the schedule of costs and benefits for legal and illegal activities is simply modified, he may choose an altogether different set of alternatives. We must be careful to note that the intent of such a model is not to deny the importance of all other (noneconomic) causal factors. Rather, it is to postulate an essentially classical theory that permits empirical testing on the assumption that, in the aggregate, other contributing factors remain constant. In what follows, we will see that our theory of behavior has implications not only for predicting the way the individual behaves, but also for determining the alternatives society may choose to control that behavior. We will begin by examining the set of alternatives available to youth.

3.1.2. Economic Opportunities for Youth: 1952–67. The problem of economic choice is most crucial for youth who are making the transition from schooling into the job market. As previously noted, we will concentrate on 18–19-year-old males. We concentrate on males because they commit the preponderance of the four crimes against property listed in the FBI crime index: larceny, burglary, robbery, and auto theft. (For example, in 1967, of all arrests for auto theft, burglary, and robbery, males accounted for 94 percent; for larceny, males were more than 75 percent of arrestees [F.B.I., 1968:119].) The 18–19-year age group was selected as satisfying the two

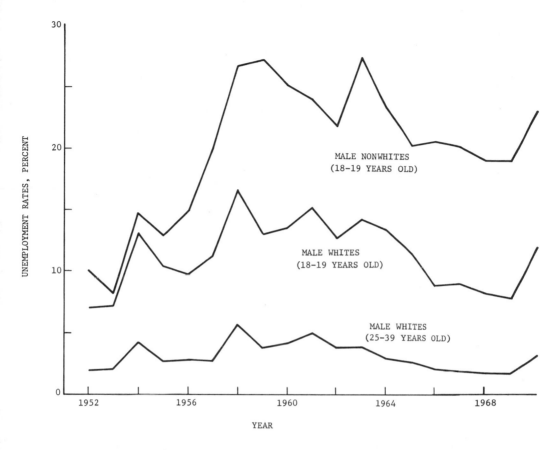

FIGURE 4. Male unemployment rates by race, selected age groups.

criteria of having a high crime rate (characteristic of youth) while being at the threshold of choosing between further education, the labor force, or other alternatives.

What do we know about this set of alternatives faced by youth? If we look at the figures for the years 1952 through 1967, as shown in Figure 4, we find that unemployment rates for white males are at a low of 7.0 percent in 1952, reaching a high of 16.5 percent in 1958, then declining erratically to 9.0 percent in 1967. Over this period, unemployment rates for nonwhites commenced at a low of 10.0 percent in 1952, rising to 27.2 percent in 1959, then falling to 20.1 percent in 1967. In contrast, aggregate unemployment rates for the labor force never exceed 6.8 percent over this entire period (U.S. Department of Labor, 1970:231).

Another measure of the economic status of a population subgroup is that group's labor force participation rate. This variable measures the proportion of the group who are either employed or actively searching for work. Participation rates for youth generally fall for one of two reasons. Youths may be entering school in increased numbers or they may have become so discouraged at the possibilities for employment that they drop out of the labor force. Figure 5 illustrates the decline in participation rates for white and nonwhite youths compared with older white males. We observe that

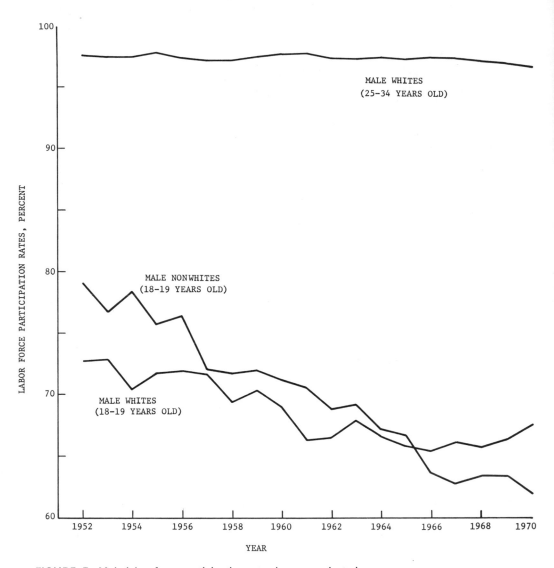

FIGURE 5. Male labor force participation rates by race, selected age groups.

youthful labor participation declined during the period covered, and it fell more precipitously for nonwhites (U.S. Department of Labor, 1970:219).

School enrollments must be regarded as one form of economic opportunity since such activity represents an investment in greater future earning power for the person involved. A rational individual will consider the lifetime opportunities associated with greater schooling relative to those from immediate employment; however, further education may be eliminated from an individual's choice set for reasons beyond his control. In Figure 6, which illustrates the pattern of school enrollments, we find 38 percent of 18–19-year-old white males were enrolled in school in 1952 compared with 35 percent for nonwhites. By 1967, the comparable figures were 62 percent and 55

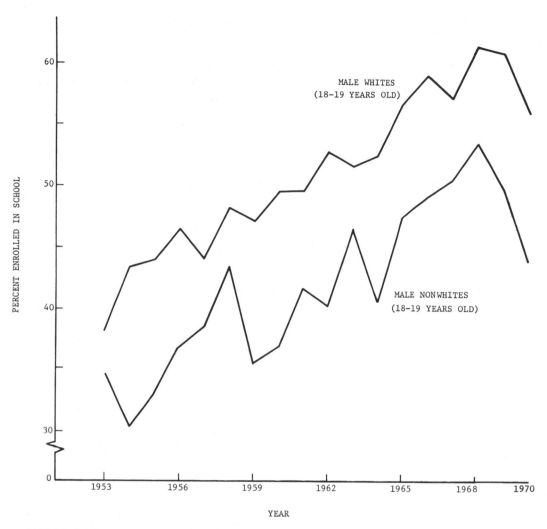

FIGURE 6. Male school enrollment ratios by race.

percent, respectively.[3] Again, we see that nonwhites have become relatively disadvantaged and that the more precipitous decline in labor force participation rates for nonwhites cannot be explained by the rate of increase in school enrollments alone.

3.1.3. A Crime Generation Hypothesis for Youth. Accompanying the upward trend in unemployment rates (Figure 4) and the decline in participation rates (Figure 5) for youth in the period we are studying, we observe that arrest rates (per person) for the four economic felonies grew exponentially at rates between 3.0 percent and 4.7 percent between 1952 and 1960. Youth commit a much more than proportionate

---

3. This information is summarized from "School Enrollments" in the U.S. Bureau of the Census's *Current Population Reports*, Series P-20, for the years indicated.

share of these crimes. Arrest rates for these offenses are two to three times as great for age groups between 14 and 24 as for males a generation older, and nonwhites have substantially higher arrest rates than whites. For example, for youths under 18 in 1967, the urban arrest rate for larceny (per ten thousand population) was 93.1 for whites contrasted with 268.0 for nonwhites. For other FBI index crimes, the differences by race are as great or greater.[4] It would be desirable to study crime rates by race as well as age, but arrest rates by race have only been collected since 1962 and then only for the broad categories of 18-and-over and juveniles. As a consequence, it is only possible to separate the data by race on the causal side.

The striking increase in crime for youth, accompanying the dramatic shift in age distribution toward a more youthful population, since World War II suggests that some of the apparent increase in crime may be simply a consequence of the increasing proportion of young people in the population.

Studies lend support to this hypothesis, indicating that some part (e.g., 15 percent in the case of larceny) of the rise in the aggregate arrest rate during the time period under discussion is a consequence of the increased proportion of youths in the total population (Phillips et al., 1969).[5] Consequently, it is even more important to explain the rise in youthful crime rates.

The nature of the crime and the economic opportunity data suggest a strong link that may be translated into a formal model. We postulate that the labor force status of youth is a representation, in the aggregate, of economic opportunities for youth. The hypothesis that economic opportunities for youth are inversely related to their crime rates has been tested successfully with respect to unemployment rates by Fleisher (1963, 1966) and Glaser and Rice (1959). The advantage of the proportionality formulation we are about to present is that it expressly takes account of all subsets of the population, thus allowing for the fact that, since youths have low participation rates, unemployment rates will have less weight because of the considerable fraction of youths outside the labor force. Hence, if the rational process of choosing between alternatives truly represents the way people behave, we would expect aggregate crime rates for a given age group to vary with the proportion of that age group in each of the population subsets (an earlier study of a similar hypothesis is reported in Phillips et al., 1972b; a more sophisticated study, the basis for the results included here, is presented in Phillips et al., 1972a).

The relationship we might expect is illustrated in Figure 7. In this Venn diagram the population is subdivided between those in the labor force (which can be separated into employed and unemployed) and those not in the labor force. In addition, we have smaller subsets of the population classified as those in the armed services, and institutional population (persons in mental hospitals, prisons, etc.). At a given point in time, a person committing a crime must be in one of these classifications. These persons are included in the shaded area at the center of the diagram. We hypothesize that the number of crimes committed is proportional to the number of persons committing crimes. This, in turn, varies directly with the proportion of the population in each of the subsets representing economic opportunity. This proposition is developed formally in the following section.

---

4. All crime data used in the text or in the empirical work following is derived from the F.B.I.'s *Uniform Crime Reports*. See also Phillips and Votey (1972).

5. This has also been pointed out by others, including the task force on the assessment of crime (President's Commission, 1967b:25, 207–10), in which the effects of these changes from 1960 to 1965 are measured.

W_{nw} = WHITES NOT IN LABOR FORCE

W_{nn} = NONWHITES NOT IN LABOR FORCE

W_{ew} = EMPLOYED WHITES

W_{en} = EMPLOYED NONWHITES

W_{uw} = UNEMPLOYED WHITES

W_{un} = UNEMPLOYED NONWHITES

IP = INSTITUTIONAL POPULATION

AS = ARMED SERVICES

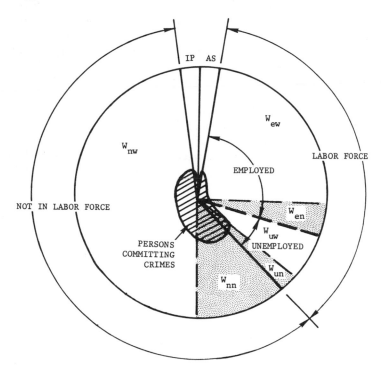

FIGURE 7. Venn diagram of population categories used in model of crime generation. The ratio of the shaded area to the total area represents the offense rate for the population subset represented (18–19-year-old males in the tests reported here). The diagram shows that the proportion of offenses committed by members of each of the subsets adds up to the total (the entire shaded area).

3.1.4. A Model of Crime Generation for Youth.

The age-specific crime rate for a particular crime can be viewed as a weighted average of the arrest rates for each population subset, where the population may be classified in a number of alternative ways. For example, if we use the most detailed breakdown the data would permit, we would have all the population subsets illustrated in Figure 7, each divided by race. If we concentrate on males and distinguish between the more meaningful economic opportunity classifications, we can write the equation

$$Y = r_{ew}W_{ew} + r_{en}W_{en} + r_{uw}W_{uw} + r_{un}W_{un} + r_{nw}W_{nw} + r_{nn}W_{nn} + r_oW_o \quad (3.1)$$

where the first subscripts, e, u, and n represent employed, unemployed, and not in the labor force, respectively, and the second subscripts represent white and nonwhite, respectively. The subscript o represents all others, which includes all females and males of both races in the armed services or in institutions. The r's represent the crime rates for each of the respective population classifications, and the W's represent the proportion of the total population of the age group studied that is in each subgroup. For example, W_{ew} represents the proportion of the population who are white males (18–19 years old) and who are employed. The other W's have similar interpretations. Y represents age-specific crime rates for a given economic crime for youths (again, 18–19 year olds). Ideally, the dependent variable would be offenses committed by a particular age, race, or sex group. Since we cannot obtain age-specific data broken down by race over a sufficiently long period, we can only analyze the data by race on the causal side.[6]

It would be desirable to estimate the values for the r's, knowing the crime rates (Y's) and the population weights (W's). This can be done utilizing standard linear regression techniques once two sets of statistical problems have been dealt with. First, the model must be reformulated in such a manner that the estimated relationship is not an identity. Second, the high degree of collinearity between the W's makes further simplification of the model necessary in order to estimate statistically meaningful results. The details of the derivation of the model are shown in Appendix A.[7]

In surmounting these difficulties, two alternative formulations of the model are tested. The first divides the population between those males working and those not working (W_{nww} and W_{nwn} for whites and nonwhites, respectively), and all others. The equation estimated is of the form

$$Y = r_r + (r_{nww} - r_r) W_{nww} + (r_{nwn} - r_r) W_{nwn}, \qquad (3.2)$$

where r_r represents the coefficient for the residual population that includes all those not in W_{nww} or W_{nwn}.

The second alternative divides the population between those in the labor force and those not in the labor force. In this case the equation estimated was

$$Y = r_r + (r_{lw} - r_{nw}) W_{lw} + (r_{nw} - r_r) W_{cw} + (r_{ln} - r_{nn}) W_{ln}$$
$$+ (r_{nn} - r_r) W_{cn} \qquad (3.3)$$

where r_r is the coefficient for a residual population from which those in the labor force (subscripts lw and ln, for whites and nonwhites, respectively) and those not in the labor force (subscripts nw and nn) are excluded. Subscripts cw and cn represent civilian noninstitutional population.

---

6. To obtain a proxy for offenses by age note that

$$\text{Offenses} = \text{Arrests} / \frac{\text{Arrests}}{\text{Offenses}}.$$

If we assume that arrests/offenses for 18–19 year olds are proportional to that ratio for the total, i.e.,

$$\frac{\text{Arrests}}{\text{Offenses}} \text{ (18–19 year olds)} = k \frac{\text{Arrests}}{\text{Offenses}} \text{ (all ages)},$$

then we can write,

$$\text{Offenses (18–19 year olds)} = \text{Arrests (18–19)} / k \frac{\text{Arrests}}{\text{Offenses}} \text{ (all ages)}.$$

Thus, for our dependent variable (Y) we divide the age-specific arrest rate by the total arrest ratio to obtain a proxy for age-specific offense rates.

7. The technique utilized to reduce the degree of collinearity was to reformulate the model in terms of fewer economically meaningful and, at the same time, less collinear variables. This problem is dealt with in greater detail in Phillips, Votey, and Maxwell (1972a).

3.1.5. Statistical Results and Conclusions. The statistical results support the hypothesis that crimes committed by youth are related to their economic opportunities. For both equations 3.2 and 3.3, it was not possible to distinguish between white and nonwhite coefficients because of the high degree of collinearity between the white and nonwhite weights. Therefore, these equations were also estimated separately for whites and for nonwhites. While the quantitative results are essentially the same in all cases, both the significance of the coefficients and the proportion of variance explained by the equations are increased. The results for equations 3.2 and 3.3 are displayed in Appendix A (Tables A–1 and A–2, respectively). These tables indicate that for both whites and nonwhites those working tend to have lower criminality coefficients than those not working. Equation 3.3 yields more significant results in relating labor force status to crime. Both for whites and nonwhites, those not in the labor force have higher criminality coefficients than those in the labor force. Once more it was not possible to distinguish between white and nonwhite coefficients.

The results in these tables appear to indicate that nonwhites have greater criminality coefficients than whites. As is pointed out both by algebraic and empirical analysis in our work (Phillips et al., 1972a), this would be an incorrect interpretation of the results. The fact that such a close proportionality exists between the independent variables for whites and nonwhites renders a test of the hypothesis that criminality coefficients for a particular economic variable differ by race virtually impossible with the data we had at our disposal.

The results from equation 3.2 that crime rates vary positively with unemployment rates (see Appendix A) tend to confirm the work of Fleisher (1963, 1966) and of Glaser and Rice (1959), who find a positive relationship between unemployment rates and property crime for this age group. Fleisher's results consistently show a positive relationship between unemployment rates for youth and arrest rates for property crimes. Glaser and Rice hypothesized that unemployment rates for youth were inversely related, and for adults positively related, to crime rates. In their model, 18–19 year olds would have to be regarded as adults. Their results with respect to property crimes, for this age group, tend to be consistent with Fleisher's.

In addition, our results draw attention to the importance of the labor force participation rate as a measure of economic opportunity and as an explanatory variable in crime generation. The participation rates' explanatory power may be a consequence of its measuring the cumulative effects of past unemployment. The important distinction, probably, is not simply between working and not working, but between working or temporarily unemployed, and long-term unemployment that would cause an individual to stop seeking employment. The impact of this distinction over the period studied can be seen when one observes that employment rates were rising in the latter 1960s. During this period, participation rates were falling at a greater rate than school enrollments were rising. Thus, *it is the falling participation rate that foretells much of the rise in youthful crime.* The power of this model is further demonstrated by its ability to forecast crime rates for the years 1968, 1969, and 1970 (for details, see Phillips et al., 1972a). The results of this forecast are depicted in Figure 8. For eight of the twelve forecasts, predicted values fall within plus or minus two standard errors of estimate of actual values. Forecasts of robbery for 1968 and 1969 fall within three standard errors. Only in the years 1969 and 1970 does larceny fail to meet the latter test.

These results provide an important implication for the control problem policymakers face. To minimize the cost of crime, they must be able to evaluate the benefits that may be obtained by the creation or improvement of economic opportunities for the youthful population.

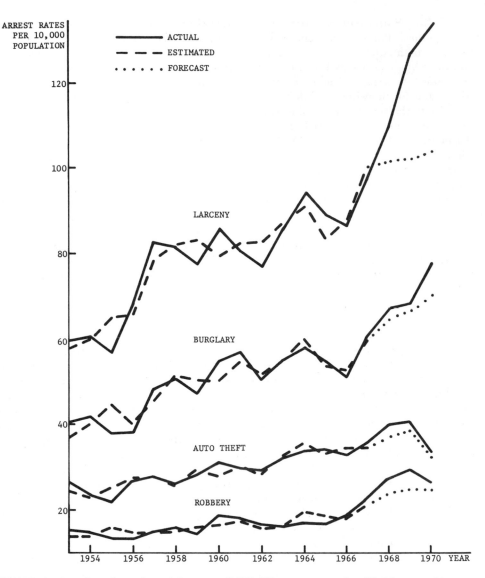

FIGURE 8. Actual, estimated, and forecast (1968–70) arrest rates for 18–19 year olds.

3.2   Law Enforcement as a Production Process

Thus far we have examined the process of crime generation, implicitly assuming that the impact of the criminal justice system on that process is constant. In reality, of course, as we see from our schematic of the system of crime generation and control (Figure 2), the inputs into the law-enforcement process are a major component of the social control of crime. We will now concentrate on law enforcement, the first stage of the criminal justice process.

3.2.1. Conceptualizing the Production Process. To achieve a conceptual understanding of the operation of the process of law enforcement in economic terms,

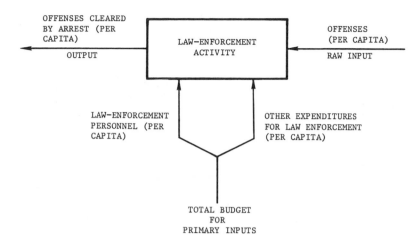

FIGURE 9. Schematic diagram of a law-enforcement production process. Note: For the total budget to be a measure of the real inputs, i.e., law-enforcement personnel and the index of other inputs (other expenditures on law enforcement, deflated), prices and wages must be taken into account. Thus, total budget ≡ number of employees × average wages + other expenditures × price deflator.

refer to Figure 9. In this broad-brush analysis of the law-enforcement production process, we concentrate on the net relationship between inputs and outputs and do not involve ourselves in a detailed examination of the inner workings of the production process. This is an appropriate point of view for an analysis of the general problem of resource allocation, in which case we assume that the process operates with economic efficiency. It would, of course, be appropriate for each individual agency to conduct its own operations analysis to insure that efficiency does prevail, in fact.

Thus, in Figure 9, the law-enforcement process is a black box whose inner workings are known only to those directly concerned with the details of law-enforcement practice. Into this black box, we observe a flow of offenses, which are of the nature of a raw material input. The law-enforcement agency must take these as given. To deal with this flow of offenses, the agency is allocated a budget that is converted into payrolls and expenditures on equipment and supplies. Payrolls may be expended either on a large number of relatively untrained personnel, or on fewer, highly trained officers and technicians. The output of this system is a flow of crimes cleared by arrest. In our analysis we deal with all these measures on a per-capita basis to remove the effects of population growth.

3.2.2. Economic Production Functions.

With any production process, we postulate that a mathematical relationship prevails between inputs and outputs.[8] Corresponding to our diagram (Figure 9), this may be represented by

$$C_i = g(t_i, OF_i, EMP_i, OTE_i), \ (i = 1, 4 \text{ crimes}) \tag{3.4}$$

---

8. For noneconomists interested in obtaining a deeper understanding of the theory and nature of production functions, any good text on microeconomic theory could be consulted. Excellent examples are Ferguson (1969) and Lancaster (1974).

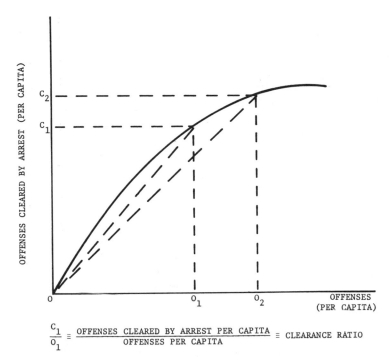

$$\frac{C_1}{O_1} \equiv \frac{\text{OFFENSES CLEARED BY ARREST PER CAPITA}}{\text{OFFENSES PER CAPITA}} \equiv \text{CLEARANCE RATIO}$$

FIGURE 10. The law-enforcement production process: variation in the clearance ratio with the offense rate, given law-enforcement expenditures.

where C represents crimes cleared by arrest,[9] OF represents offenses reported to police, EMP is law-enforcement employees, and OTE is other (nonpayroll) expenditures on law enforcement, measured in real terms (i.e., adjusted for inflationary effects). As is typical of virtually all production processes, we would expect diminishing returns to prevail, i.e., an increase in a single input while the other inputs are held fixed would result in a less than proportional increase in output (crimes cleared by arrest). Thus, if there is no change in other inputs or in law-enforcement technology and offenses increase, offenses cleared by arrest will increase, but not by as much as offenses. As a result the clearance ratio (percent of crimes cleared by arrest) will fall. This is illustrated in Figure 10. Conversely, if the budget for law enforcement is increased and offenses remained unchanged, we would expect clearances to rise and, consequently,

---

9. In our studies we have consistently used clearance rates or the clearance ratio as a dependent variable in preference to conviction rates since the latter do not measure the output of law-enforcement agencies so much as that of the system of criminal prosecution and adjudication, given the effectiveness of law enforcement. This is particularly important in the section that follows since, at least for first offenders, the threat of arrest alone may be a sufficient deterrent in many cases irrespective of the degree of punishment. While the clearance rate is criticized for being subject to bias as a consequence of the plea bargaining process and the desire of police to improve their efficiency ratings (see, for example, President's Commission, 1967b:38; Skolnick, 1967), on the other hand, arrest rates are equally biased by the practice of arresting for a more serious charge than would otherwise be appropriate simply to be able to control a possible offender with greater force at the scene of the crime. The clearance ratio *as conceived*, we feel, is the appropriate variable for our studies.

would find an increase in police effectiveness as measured by the clearance ratio. With both offenses and expenditures for police protection rising, the quantitative nature of the production function will determine the outcome with respect to police effectiveness.

3.2.3. Empirical Results and Conclusions.

The model tested using linear regression techniques is of the form

$$C_i = k_i e^{\tau_i t} \, OF^{\alpha_i} \, EMP^{\beta_{1i}} \, OTE^{\beta_{2i}}, \ (i = 1, 4 \text{ crimes}), \tag{3.5}$$

that was further modified by dividing by the offense rate so that

$$CR_i = k_i e^{\tau_i t} \, OF_i^{\alpha_i - 1} \, EMP^{\beta_{1i}} \, OTE^{\beta_{2i}}, \ (i = 1, 4 \text{ crimes}). \tag{3.6}$$

This equation was estimated in logarithmic form. In the estimation, aggregate values for *EMP* and *OTE* are substituted for the breakdowns of these variables by crime, which are not generally known. (The assumptions and theory that permit us to make these substitutions are explained in Appendix B and treated in greater detail in Votey and Phillips, 1972.)

The regression coefficients (α, β_1, and β_2) may be interpreted as elasticities, i.e., they represent the percentage change in output that will result from a 1 percent change in the respective inputs. The conversion of the dependent variable to the clearance ratio makes no quantitative difference in the estimates. Since the clearance ratio is an untrended variable that actually takes on an inverted-U pattern over the period studied, its use shows more emphatically that the explanatory power of the estimated relationship does not derive simply from regressing one trended variable upon another. Results of the estimation are shown in Appendix B (Table B–1).

An illustration of the explanatory power of the production function formulation is presented in Figure 11. Major turning points, as well as the general overall secular pattern, are matched quite well by the estimated production function. A detailed analysis to determine the cause of the inverted-U pattern for clearance ratios reveals two important factors. Using robbery as an example, we observe that from 1952 to 1959 offense rates were not increasing, whereas expenditures on law enforcement rose. In the later period, from 1963 to 1967, on the other hand, offense levels were rising rapidly, whereas the rate of increase in expenditures (per capita) for law enforcement was slightly lower than in the earlier period. Thus, it should not be surprising that in the earlier period, when expenditures rose more rapidly than offenses, the clearance ratio rose, whereas in the later period, when the converse was true, the relationship between rates of increase in expenditure and offenses had reversed itself. These patterns are illustrated for robbery in Figure 12.

A further test of the empirical relevance of the model is the ability to forecast beyond the estimation period. The last set of estimates reported in Table B–1 (equations from which the insignificant variables had been deleted) were used to forecast the clearance ratios for 1968. The results are shown in Table 1 (robbery is illustrated in Figure 12). Applying the usual statistical standards, we conclude that this production function approach is effective in both the measurement and the prediction of the relationship between inputs and outputs of the law-enforcement system.

We find that the results with respect to individual crimes are intuitively satisfying. For example, solutions to burglaries, which benefit from the analytical techniques of detective bureaus, are affected substantially by increased manpower (*EMP*) and to a

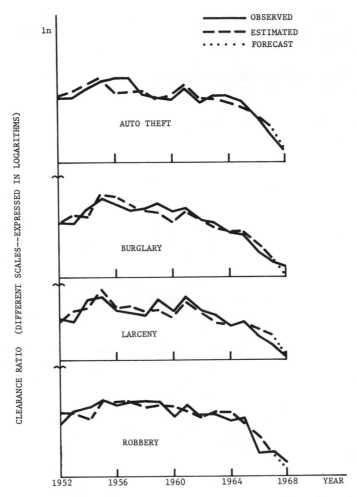

FIGURE 11. Patterns over time for observed clearance ratios and for estimated and forecast values of the ratio based on the law-enforcement production function.

somewhat lesser extent by increases in nonpayroll expenditures (*OTE*). Similarly, employees (*EMP*) have a greater impact on the clearance ratio for larceny than other expenditures (*OTE*). The effect of both inputs is less than that for burglary, perhaps because apprehension of the criminal, in this case, depends upon someone observing

TABLE 1
FORECASTS OF CLEARANCE RATIOS (CR) FOR 1968

Crime	Observed Value	Forecast Value	Forecast Error	Standard Error of Estimate
Larceny	.177	.178	.001	.010
Burglary	.194	.182	−.012	.010
Robbery	.274	.258	−.016	.010
Auto Theft	.187	.185	−.002	.011

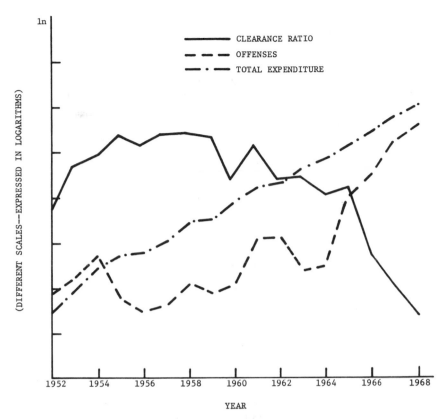

FIGURE 12. Patterns over time of the clearance ratio and offenses for robbery, and local expenditures for law enforcement, 1952–68.

the commission of the crime. In contrast, the solution of robberies depends upon a high degree of mobility of the police force and on effective communications, since, typically, these crimes are committed in areas where continual surveillance is virtually impossible. Consequently, this crime is affected more by other expenditures (OTE) than either of the other two crimes. Likewise, auto theft clearances are affected very little by the number of employees, but substantially by nonpayroll expenditures. Such expenditures may be more important for auto theft than for robbery simply because autos are more easily traced by capital-intensive techniques (e.g., computers) than are people. The finding that time is not a significant variable in these equations suggests that technological change has taken place very slowly in law enforcement. This is probably due, in part, to the fact that relatively little research has been applied to law-enforcement problems as compared with virtually any other rapidly growing private or public enterprise. The President's Commission (1967a:273) pointed out that a small fraction of 1 percent of expenditures for law enforcement are devoted to research, whereas approximately 15 percent of expenditures for national defense are for research.[10]

These results make one point emphatically clear: increased law-enforcement effec-

---

10. Typical examples in industry in terms of percent of sales in 1961 are: aircraft, 24.2 percent; electrical equipment, 10.4 percent; chemicals, 4.6 percent (Mansfield, 1968:56).

tiveness is, in large measure, a resource allocation problem. If we wish to increase clearance ratios in the face of rising offenses, we must increase the allocation of resources to the task.

4. THE DETERRENT EFFECT OF LAW ENFORCEMENT

Now we link the two relationships we have studied in detail in the preceding section, taking note of the empirical results we obtained in formulating our theoretical model incorporating a deterrence effect. Our equation representing crime generation becomes more sophisticated on this account, but, on the other hand, must be simplified in terms of the economic variables to conform to the aggregate nature of the production relationship, since it is not possible within this framework to take account of the age- and sex-specific nature of property crime. The production function is also simplified by combining inputs into a single variable that represents total expenditures allocated to each crime. (The technical details are relegated to Appendix C.)

4.1   Rational Behavior and Deterrence

The benefits from police protection must be measured in terms of the degree to which potential criminal behavior is deterred. While there may be a measure of psychic satisfaction from seeing criminals being punished, for the most part, society is concerned with avoiding victimization. In the postulated model, we see the effect of police protection as raising the probable costs to the criminal of his criminal acts, thus reducing the potential gains, hopefully to the point at which he will decide that a criminal act is no longer profitable.

   In relating this to the two facets of the simultaneous system of crime generation and control, we see that increased law-enforcement activities should have the effect of raising clearance ratios. Clearance ratios may be regarded as measures of the probability of arrest for a given criminal act. The higher this probability, the lower will be the expected net benefits of a particular criminal act.

   Referring back to equation 2.2, which depicts the basis for rational decision-making with respect to economic opportunities, the increasing effectiveness of the criminal justice system has the effect of increasing the expected costs and thus reducing the expected net benefits of those activities associated with crime. Therefore, rational persons may be expected to respond in a socially favorable way to law-enforcement activities.

   We must not ignore the fact that deterrence does not depend solely on the expected cost of an illegal act. There are certainly differing degrees to which rational considerations determine behavior. Homicide leads to severe penalties if detected and the clearance ratio averages close to 90 percent. Nevertheless, a considerable number of homicides per capita are committed each year. If penalties and the clearance ratio are increased, it is not likely that homicide offenses would be completely eliminated. The evidence shows, however, that even for homicide the deterrent effect of law enforcement is very strong in spite of the irrational elements of behavior that are an important element in much of the personal crime committed. Gibbs (1968) found rather strong evidence of a deterrent effect for homicide that was emphatically confirmed in our own work (Phillips et al., 1971). In the case of crimes against property, we should be able to expect the deterrence relationship to work with greater certainty, since these crimes, for the most part, are committed for rational economic reasons. Thus, in these cases the calculation of costs and benefits should weigh more heavily.

4.2 A Model of the Simultaneous System

In dealing with crime generation in the preceding section, we implicitly assumed that the impact of law-enforcement activities on crime generation was constant. In evaluating the input-output relationships of law enforcement, it becomes obvious that law-enforcement effectiveness has varied considerably over recent years, first rising in the fifties, then falling with increasing rapidity in the sixties, as shown by the FBI's *Uniform Crime Reports* (and see Phillips & Votey, 1972:339). While the partial equilibrium approach facilitates analysis of property crime by the age of the offender, simultaneous evaluation is necessary to assess the deterrent effect of the criminal justice system. Again, note that for simplicity we limit our attention to law enforcement, assuming the effects of penalties to be relatively constant. This latter assumption should, of course, be tested empirically to determine the importance of the degree of penalty in deterring crime.

Our model at this stage consists of modifications of equations 2.2 and 2.3, formulated more precisely on the basis of information derived in Section 3. Our law-enforcement production function in simplified notation is

$$CR = g(OF, E_1) \tag{4.1}$$

in which CR represents the clearance ratio, OF is offenses per capita for a given crime, and our control variable, E_1, is expenditures per capita for law enforcement.[11]

Our crime generation function may be expressed as

$$OF = f(CR, E_2) \tag{4.2}$$

where OF and CR are defined above, and E_2 is an economic variable. The latter variable is a proxy for the variables representing labor force participation and unemployment in the crime generation analysis in Section 2. Social conditions (S_1 and S_2) are assumed to remain unchanged over the period studied.

4.3 The Simultaneous Solution of the System

The simultaneous solution of equations 4.1 and 4.2, given the parameters of the two equations and the values of the state variables, E_1 and E_2, will determine the level of offenses (OF) and law-enforcement effectiveness as measured by the clearance ratio (CR). This solution is portrayed graphically in Figure 13.

As depicted, the crime generation function indicates that, for a given level of the state variable (E_2) representing economic conditions, the level of offenses will fall as the level of police effectiveness rises. Thus, this curve must be downward sloping to the right, starting at a maximum clearance ratio of 1.0, at which the level of offenses might be expected to approach zero, and indicating a very high level of offenses as police effectiveness falls toward zero. In similar fashion, the law-enforcement production function has an upper limit for police effectiveness at 1.0. For a given level of the state variable representing expenditures on law enforcement (E_1), this function will also slope downward to the right, indicating that as offense levels rise and police personnel are

---

11. Our empirical studies, at one point, included time as a variable in this model in order to test for technological change. Our results with respect to this variable were insignificant, consistent with the results reported in Section 3.2, hence we have deleted it from the discussion that follows.

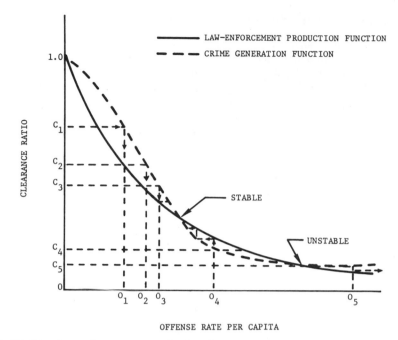

FIGURE 13. The *law-enforcement production function*, illustrated for a given level of law-enforcement expenditures and a given level of technology, interacting with the *crime generation function*, illustrated for a given level of economic conditions and social attitudes toward crime.

spread more thinly in terms of the magnitude of their task, their effectiveness (in terms of the clearance ratio) will fall.

Given the shape of the curves in Figure 13, we can see that there is a stable equilibrium at the point shown. This can be illustrated by postulating a given level for the clearance ratio, C_1, which will produce an offense level at O_1, which in turn will lead to a clearance ratio at C_2, etc., until we reach the stable point. If we had started with a clearance ratio C_4, resulting in an offense level O_4, a reverse process would have occurred, again reaching the stable point.

The system will always have a stable solution at the point depicted as long as the law-enforcement production function cuts the crime generation function from below. There is, however, another, more alarming possibility depicted by the situation around the unstable point. We can envision a society in which, if the clearance ratio is allowed to fall very far, a different kind of equilibrium might occur. Should we find ourselves in equilibrium at the unstable point, we face the possibility that a small shock to the system pushing us to the left of this point will ultimately move us to the stable equilibrium point. This, of course, would be no cause for alarm, the stable point being a position socially preferred to the unstable point. But, should we be moved in the opposite direction, the potential result is disturbing. A clearance ratio such as C_5 would produce an offense level O_5, which would lead to an even lower clearance ratio until the system would literally explode out of control with no power within itself to curb crime generation effectively.

It is interesting to note the possibilities for social control within a system of this nature. Each of our control variables plays a potential role in controlling the equilibrium level of crime. If, for example, we make adjustments to E_2, say, increase legitimate economic opportunities for a potentially criminal segment of society, the crime generation curve will be pivoted downward to the left. Given the resources devoted to law enforcement, the effect would be to shift the unstable point to the right and move the stable point upward and to the left, improving the possibilities from society's point of view. In a like manner, an increase in resources available for law enforcement would swing the law-enforcement production function upward to the right, producing a similar result. The degree of improvement provided by either of these alternatives may not be the same for a given allocation of resources to the problem. The goal must be the selection of policy that moves society to a stable solution, while at the same time minimizing the cost of crime. Achieving this measure of efficiency requires an ability to measure the parameters of this system. Some results to this end are reported in the next section.

4.4 Empirical Evaluation of the Simultaneous System

The empirical results we will discuss in some detail are those for larceny, which were estimated for the years 1953–68. Larceny is probably the most appropriate example because it is the crime that is the most purely economic in the sense that no element of violence is associated with it as would be the case with robbery or, to a lesser extent, burglary and auto theft. Thus, the motivation for it should be purely economic.

The formulation actually tested is as follows

$$CR_L = k_L \, OF_L{}^{\alpha-1} \, EX_L{}^{\beta} \tag{4.3}$$

and

$$OF_L = h_L \, CR_L{}^{\gamma} \, W_n{}^{\delta} \tag{4.4}$$

where CR_L is the larceny clearance ratio, OF_L is larceny offenses reported to the police, EX_L is police protection expenditures for control of larceny, and W_n represents 18–19-year-old nonwhite youth who are not in the labor force, which we use as a proxy measure of the social and economic conditions influencing crimes of this nature. Our theory would predict that α, β, and δ are positive and γ is negative.

The estimates for the structural coefficients for the simultaneous system for larceny are

lnk	lnh	α	$\phi\beta$	γ	δ
5.61	-6.51	.697	.292	-1.57	1.12

Since these coefficients were calculated from reduced form estimates (see Appendix C for the interpretation of $\phi\beta$), we cannot directly conduct significance tests, but we can see from the reduced form estimates (presented in Appendix C) that the two coefficients that determine δ are both highly significant. The deterrence effect is strong, in fact, having the greatest power of the coefficients in the system. The signs of the other coefficients are also as one might expect, and they are consistent with the estimates from the partial equilibrium analysis in Section 3. It is similarly gratifying to note that the system is stable, i.e., the equilibrium is as depicted at the stable point in Figure 13. Hence, the situation remains under control.

We should note that over the period studied the average clearance ratio for larceny was 19.9 percent and the average per capita offense rate was 1,437.38 crimes per hundred thousand population. The average annual rate of growth of the offense rate per capita over the period studied has been 5.7 percent, while that for offenses cleared by arrest per capita has been 5.0 percent. The net effect has been a decline in the clearance ratio at a rate of 0.7 percent per year. But from 1959 to the present, the picture looks more grim, with offenses and clearances rising at 6.1 percent and 4.4 percent, respectively, so the clearance ratio has been falling over this more recent period at the rate of 1.7 percent.

By utilizing the model, it is possible to demonstrate that per capita expenditures to deal with larceny should have risen at 5.9 percent per year to hold the clearance ratio (police effectiveness) constant (Appendix C outlines calculations yielding this percentage and the figures which follow). Larceny offenses would still have been rising at a rate of 4.2 percent in this event. Raising expenditures sufficiently to hold per capita offense levels for larceny constant, given the nature of changing social and economic conditions, would have required an increase in per capita expenditures for law enforcement at the rate of 9.2 percent per year. The actual rate of growth of per capita expenditures on law enforcement for the nation over this period has been 2.9 percent (although our estimates indicate that expenditures to control larceny rose by 3.3 percent). It is interesting to note that the growth of state and local expenditures for all governmental services was rising at the rate of 3.5 percent over this same period.[12]

If we look at the other side of the coin, i.e., the effect of social and economic conditions on crime generation, we can calculate another set of alternatives. Suppose national priorities had been such as to maintain social and economic conditions at stable levels, and per capita expenditures had grown at the observed historical rate of 2.9 percent. This rise in law-enforcement expenditures would then have been sufficient to yield an annual rise in the clearance ratio at the rate of 1.8 percent, with offense levels declining by 2.9 percent per year.

4.5   Comments and Conclusions

The results we obtain from the simultaneous equation model are most gratifying in the degree of consistency evident between these results and those reported in Section 3. We note that the production function coefficient for α estimated in the simultaneous model is within one standard deviation of the single equation estimate discussed previously. From Table B–1, estimate 3 for larceny, the coefficient on α is .628. The standard deviation is .094. Thus, a one standard deviation interval for α is .534 to .722, which includes .697, the estimate for α given in the summary on page 1079. The coefficient on total expenditures, which should be approximately a weighted average of the coefficients on employees and on other expenditures of the single equation estimates, appropriately falls between those two estimates and closer to that for employees. In terms of dollars expended, employee expenditures is the greater part of total expenditures. While the crime generation function results are not strictly comparable with those from the simultaneous equation model (since the former is estimated in a purely linear form,

---

12. These figures are obtained by deflating the observed annual expenditures by the Government Goods and Services Deflator from the U.S. Department of Commerce, *Survey of Current Business*. The figures used in our empirical analysis were broken down between payrolls and other expenditures, which were then deflated by the Consumer Price Index and the Government Purchases of Durable Goods Index, respectively. The rise in real inputs based on these calculations is 4.3 percent. The relevant comparison between expenditures on police protection and other governmental services, however, is still 2.9 percent versus 3.5 percent, since these are both deflated on the same basis. The rise in real inputs figure is not comparable to these latter figures.

while the latter is derived from a log-linear estimate), the signs are consistent and the variable that worked well here was the one that had the greatest explanatory power in the single equation estimation. The most striking feature of the model is the strength and significance of the deterrence effect. The model confirms emphatically that the importance of law-enforcement activity is more than simply the provision of direct physical protection to life and property, and punishment for offenders. The results indicate that there is a multiplier effect from expenditures for police protection, which can be written

$$\% \ \Delta \ \text{Offenses} = \frac{\gamma\beta}{1 - \gamma \, (\alpha - 1)} \ \% \ \Delta \ \text{Expenditures}$$

where α, β, and γ are simply the parameters of the simultaneous system, and offenses and expenditures are those related to a particular crime.

We have shown that the level of crime generation is indeed dependent upon the degree of public financial support for law-enforcement activities. There is also in these results a warning to those who would indiscriminately place all their policy emphasis on law enforcement alone. As has been demonstrated above, those who argue that social and economic conditions are major factors in the creation of crime are equally well supported by this analysis.

5. RESOURCE ALLOCATION AND CRIMINAL JUSTICE: CONCLUSIONS

We began our analysis by pointing out that the appropriate goal for society is minimization of the total cost of crime. In conceptualizing the problem, a pair of alternatives that differ radically is revealed. One is to deal with the causes of crime by attempting to modify social and economic conditions so that economic incentives for crime are reduced or eliminated. The other is to increase the deterrents to crime by strengthening law-enforcement effectiveness. Our research suggests that both of these alternatives will work. For example, our study of crime generation indicates a strong link between economic opportunities and felony crime rates for youth. Our work with law-enforcement production functions demonstrates that law-enforcement agencies can be analyzed with the same tools used to evaluate the performance of an industry. The estimation of these relationships within a simultaneous equation system confirms the effectiveness of law-enforcement activities in reaching beyond the roles of protection and punishment to provide a substantial deterrent force combating criminal activity.

The crucial question is, how do we go about minimizing the costs of crime? One might suspect that society has not been doing this effectively in the immediate past. It is evident that we know very little about either the costs of crime or the effectiveness of the various alternatives to control it. Since the force of the deterrence effect has gone largely unrecognized, it seems unlikely that society has effectively utilized its power.

One conclusion is immediately obvious from our work on law-enforcement production functions. A reduction in crime levels or an increase in clearance ratios will require the allocation of increased economic resources to the task. This does not mean that improvements could not be achieved through better organization or greater technical efficiency. To achieve improvement in technique, we are talking about technological change. Such change requires research in law-enforcement practices. As should be evident from our discussion of the production function, such research has been strikingly lacking in law enforcement. If, on the other hand, we believe funds are not being spent in the right places, improvement implies economic and operations research, which has also been neglected. Both of these are costly.

If we believe society should increase its efforts to create a more favorable social environment to reduce crime, again we lack the essential information on the benefits (in terms of reducing crime) of a dollar spent for social and economic opportunities. So far, we only know that improved economic opportunities will lead to reduced crime rates.

Economists argue that a great potential economic resource, the output lost through unemployment, results from the incorrect establishment of priorities. The likelihood that crime can be reduced in the process of realizing potential output bolsters their argument. However, precise answers require a greater understanding of the costs as well as the benefits of creating improved economic opportunities. In any event, more research is needed here, also.

Given the possibility of instability, such as that illustrated in Figure 13, and given the strength of the deterrence effect, one would be tempted to argue that police effectiveness should not be allowed to deteriorate further. More resources should be directed to the task of law enforcement. At the same time, long-range solutions demand a more fundamental approach to get at causes rather than only treating the symptoms. If we wish to reduce the flow of youth into criminal careers and lessen the potential for future crime, we should also do those things that expand economic opportunities for those who presently have the greatest potential need for the returns from illegal activities. The massive evidence of our inability to reduce recidivism rates lends additional strength to this position. Expanding economic opportunities may, in the long run, be the key to reducing the cost of crime effectively.

APPENDIX A

DERIVATION OF THE CRIME GENERATION MODEL (SECTION 3.1)

The age specific arrest rate (Y_i) for a particular crime may be viewed as a weighted average of the arrest rates (r_{ijk}) in each population class, where the most basic classifications are employed, unemployed, not in the labor force, and other. Thus

$$Y_i = \sum_j \sum_k r_{ijk} W_{jk}, \ (i = 1, 4 \text{ crimes}), \tag{A.1}$$

where the j's are the population classifications and the k's represent race (white or nonwhite). Thus equation A.1 is equivalent to equation 3.1 in the text. (Hereafter, for convenience, we will drop the i subscripts.)

Note that the population may be combined into various combinations of the basic classifications. For example, we can combine other and employed for both races into a single subset, which we will treat as a residual group and label W_r, at the same time combining unemployed and not in the labor force by race to produce two subsets, W_{nww} and W_{nwn}, which represent those not working who are white and nonwhite, respectively. Noting that the population weights, however formulated, sum to 1, we have

$$W_r = 1 - W_{nww} - W_{nwn}, \tag{A.2}$$

which, substituted in equation A.1 defined as above,

$$Y = r_r W_r + r_{nww} W_{nwn} + r_{nwn} W_{nwn}, \tag{A.3}$$

yields

$$Y = r_r + (r_{nww} - r_r) W_{nww} + (r_{nwn} - r_r) W_{nwn}, \tag{A.4}$$

which is simply equation 3.2 in the text. Regression results for this equation are presented in Table A-1.

In a similar fashion, we can combine those in the labor force into a single weight for each race so that the distinction is between in the labor force and not in the labor force. Thus

$$W_r = 1 - W_{lw} - W_{nw} - W_{ln} - W_{nn}, \tag{A.5}$$

which, substituted into equation A.1 defined as noted,

$$Y = r_r W_r + r_{lw} W_{lw} + r_{nw} W_{nw} + r_{ln} W_{ln} + r_{nn} W_{nn}, \tag{A.6}$$

yields

$$Y = r_r + (r_{lw} - r_r) W_{lw} + (r_{nw} - r_r) W_{nw} + (r_{ln} - r_r) W_{ln} + (r_{nn} - r_r) W_{nn}, \tag{A.7}$$

which can be reformulated into

$$Y = r_r + (r_{nw} - r_r) W_{cw} + (r_{lw} - r_{nw}) W_{lw} + (r_{nn} - r_r) W_{cn} + (r_{ln} - r_{nn}) W_{ln}, \tag{A.8}$$

TABLE A–1

REGRESSION ESTIMATES FOR EQUATION 3.2 IN TEXT
OR EQUATION A.4 IN THIS APPENDIX

Crime	Intercept	W_{nww}	W_{nwn}	$\bar{R}^2$	F	D-W
Larceny	.66 (.62)	−4.53 (− .41)	167.66 (3.94)	.67	15.5 (2, 12)	1.02
Burglary	−.57 (−.64)	5.33 (.58)	69.44 (1.96)	.46	6.9 (2, 12)	.60
Robbery	.01 (.05)	.79 (.30)	12.68 (1.24)	.18	2.5 (2, 12)	.60
Auto Theft	−.03 (.05)	1.54 (.30)	39.33 (1.96)	.39	5.6 (2, 12)	.57
Larceny	.32 (.49)		154.47 (5.74)	.70	33.0 (1, 13)	1.06
Burglary	−.16 (−.30)		84.97 (3.78)	.48	14.3 (1, 13)	.52
Robbery	.07 (.47)		14.98 (2.32)	.24	5.4 (1, 13)	.57
Auto Theft	.01 (.30)		43.82 (3.47)	.44	12.0 (1, 13)	.57

The *t*-values of the coefficients are in parentheses.
The R^2 are corrected for degrees of freedom.

which corresponds to equation 3.2 in the text. Regression results for this equation are presented in Table A-2.

The W's Defined

As we have noted, the W's are population weights. These may be determined from readily available population and labor force data as follows:

$$W_u = \frac{U}{POP} = \frac{U}{CLF} \cdot \frac{CLF}{CNIP} \cdot \frac{CNIP}{TNIP} \cdot \frac{TNIP}{POP},$$

where U = number of unemployed for a given population subset (e.g., 18–19-year-old white males), CLF = civilian labor force for that same subset, $CNIP$ = civilian, non-institutional population, $TNIP$ = total noninstitutional population for the subset, and POP = the population of the subset. In every case $TNIP/POP \simeq 1$, and is ignored. We can, as a consequence, define

$$W_u = \mu \cdot \rho \cdot \theta,$$

TABLE A–2

REGRESSION ESTIMATES FOR EQUATION 3.3 IN TEXT
OR EQUATION A.8 IN THIS APPENDIX

Crime	Intercept	W_{cw}	W_{lw}	W_{cn}	W_{ln}	$\bar{R}^2$	F	D-W
Larceny	6.86 (1.66)	−4.74 (−0.44)	−20.22 (−0.93)	257.82 (4.73)	−260.95 (4.09)	.87	24.5 (4, 10)	2.16
Burglary	3.00 (.97)	2.26 (.28)	−9.41 (.58)	122.10 (2.98)	−162.17 (3.38)	.82	17.3 (4, 10)	1.52
Robbery	−.34 (−.29)	−.72 (−.24)	3.22 (.53)	33.25 (2.16)	−41.30 (−2.30)	.55	5.3 (4, 10)	1.19
Auto Theft	−.10 (−.06)	−1.87 (− .39)	7.63 (.80)	76.01 (3.15)	−107.70 (−3.81)	.79	14.0 (4, 10)	2.07
Larceny	14.77 (2.65)	36.06 (3.90)	−95.22 (−4.16)			.61	12.0 (2, 12)	1.51
Burglary	5.79 (1.71)	26.80 (4.78)	−54.61 (−3.93)			.66	14.3 (2, 12)	1.29
Robbery	.49 (.46)	5.58 (3.16)	−8.37 (−1.91)			.38	5.3 (2, 12)	.99
Auto Theft	1.47 (.69)	14.33 (4.09)	−22.20 (−2.56)			.53	9.1 (2, 12)	1.35
Larceny	.04 (.01)			256.29 (5.06)	−259.46 (−7.71)	.84	38.1 (2, 12)	2.06
Burglary	1.62 (.89)			130.56 (4.07)	−178.51 (−8.37)	.84	39.6 (2, 12)	1.84
Robbery	.15 (.22)			30.48 (2.54)	−35.92 (−4.50)	.61	12.1 (2, 12)	.92
Auto Theft	1.00 (.91)			69.16 (3.60)	−94.32 (7.38)	.81	30.8 (2, 12)	1.68

where μ is the unemployment rate for the subset in question, ρ is the labor force participation rate, and θ is the population weight $CNIP/TNIP$. In similar fashion we can define

$$W_e = (1 - \mu)\rho\theta, \ W_n = (1 - \rho)\theta, \text{ and } W_c = \theta.$$

When the race subscripts are included, the μ's, ρ's and θ's are thus defined for a given race.

Thus, $W_{nww} = \mu\rho\theta + (1 - \rho)\theta$, when these variables are defined on the 18–19-year-old white male population. It is this variable and its nonwhite counterpart that are used in equation 3.2.

The Response of Crime Rates to Unemployment and Participation Rates

Based on the definitions of W_{nww} and W_{nwn}, from equation 3.2, we can derive the result that $\partial y/\partial \mu_w = (r_{nww} - r_r)\rho_w\theta_w$. A similar relationship can be determined for $\partial y/\partial \mu_n$. As defined above, ρ and θ are always positive. Noting that from Table A-1 $(r_{nww} - r_r)$ and $(r_{nwn} - r_r)$, except in the case of larceny for whites, are all positive, we can conclude that, in general (exception noted), changes in crime rates with respect to changes in unemployment rates for 18–19 year olds are positive, based on equation 3.2. In like manner we can show that $\partial y/\partial \rho_w$ and $\partial y/\partial \rho_n$ are negative, indicating that crime rates are inversely related to labor force participation rates, based either on equation 3.2 or equation 3.3.

APPENDIX B

DERIVATION OF THE LAW-ENFORCEMENT PRODUCTION FUNCTION (SECTION 3.2)

We assume that law-enforcement agencies have a preference function in which the arguments are the clearance rates (C_i) for the i crimes with which they must cope. Thus we

$$\text{Max} \quad U = u(C_i), \ (i = 1, \cdots, n \text{ crimes}). \tag{B.1}$$

Subject to:

$$C_i = g(t_i, OF_i, X_{ij}) \ (i = 1, n; j = 1, m \text{ primary inputs}), \tag{B.2}$$

which corresponds to the production function equation 3.4. Total expenditures,

$$T = \sum_j r_j X_j, \tag{B.3}$$

where the r_j are the prices of inputs X_j, and

$$X_j = \sum_i X_{ij}, \ (j = 1, m), \tag{B.4}$$

which implies that the inputs utilized for each crime sum to the total utilized by police. It is assumed we know the X_j but not the breakdown by crime, X_{ij}.

Substituting equation B.4 into equation B.3 is equivalent to maximizing the Lagrangian function.

$$L(C_i, X_{ij}, \psi_i, \psi_{n+1}) = u(C_i) + \sum_i \psi_i[C_i - g(t_i, OF_i, X_{ij})]$$
$$+ \psi_{n+1} (T - \sum_i \sum_j r_j X_{ij}). \tag{B.5}$$

Deriving first order conditions yields

$$\frac{\partial L}{\partial C_i} = \frac{\partial u}{\partial C_i} + \psi_i = 0, \; (i = 1, n \text{ conditions}). \tag{B.6}$$

$$\frac{\partial L}{\partial X_{ij}} = -\psi_i \frac{\partial g_i}{\partial X_{ij}} - \psi_{n+1} r_j = 0 \; (nxm \text{ conditions}). \tag{B.7}$$

Conditions B.6 yields $n - 1$ marginal rates of substitution of the form

$$\frac{\partial u/\partial C_r}{\partial u/\partial C_s} = \frac{\psi_r}{\psi_s}, \; (r, s \; \& \; i). \tag{B.8}$$

These may be paired appropriately with the $m(n - 1)$ marginal rates of transformation from Conditions B.7

$$\frac{\partial g_r/\partial X_{rj}}{\partial g_s/\partial X_{sj}} = \frac{\psi_s}{\psi_r} \tag{B.9}$$

to yield $(n - 1) \cdot m$ marginal conditions determining the optimal output combinations

$$\frac{\partial u/\partial C_s}{\partial u/\partial C_r} = \frac{\partial g_r/\partial X_{rj}}{\partial g_s/\partial X_{sj}}. \tag{B.10}$$

Equation B.10 combined with equation B.4 yields a set of $m \cdot n$ equations, which, if Cobb-Douglas forms are assumed for the n production functions and the utility function, can be solved for the X_{ij} in terms of the X_j, yielding typical X_{ij} values (in the $n = 3$ case)

$$X_{11} = \frac{\theta_1 \beta_{11}}{\theta_1 \beta_{11} + \theta_2 \beta_{21} + \theta_3 \beta_{31}} X_1. \tag{B.11}$$

Substituting in a production function of the form

$$C_1 = k_i \, e^{\tau_1 t} \, O_1^{\alpha_1} \, X_{11}^{\beta_{11}}, \tag{B.12}$$

where there is a single primary input, yields

$$C_1 = k_1^* \, e^{\tau_1 t} \, O_1^{\alpha_1} \, X^{\beta_{11}}, \tag{B.13}$$

where the k^* includes the constant coefficients on X_1. Thus the β_{ij} can be estimated using the known values for the totals of each class of inputs utilized in law enforcement.

The result can be generalized to m inputs to produce equations of the form of equation 3.5 in the text.

TABLE B-1

REGRESSION ESTIMATES FOR EQUATION 3.5

Crime		Intercept (ln k)	Time (τ)	Offenses (α)	Employees (β₁)	Other Expenditures (β₂)	R̄²†	F	D-W
Auto Theft	1.	3.03 (0.44)	-0.91 (-.28)	.583 (-1.72)**	.244 (0.29)	.315 (1.86)**	.684	9.10 (4, 11)	1.242
	2.	4.72 (1.64)		.532 (-3.18)*	.058 (0.12)	.280 (2.61)*	.708	13.12 (3, 12)	1.226
	3.	5.05 (18.41)*		.546 (-5.84)*		.2865 (3.27)*	.730	21.29 (2, 13)	1.209
Burglary	1.	-2.80 (-0.41)	0.56 (-0.18)	.152 (-3.88)*	1.141 (1.39)	.284 (1.94)**	.844	21.35 (4, 11)	1.321
	2.	-1.67 (-0.72)		.121 (-6.83)*	1.016 (2.45)*	.265 (2.69)*	.857	30.96 (3, 12)	1.324
	3.			.186 (-9.16)*	.722 (12.79)*	.303 (3.72)*	.862	47.98 (3, 12)	1.253
Larceny	1.	4.470 (1.38)	2.53 (1.47)	.374 (-3.26)*	.046 (0.06)	.077 (1.24)	.712	10.27 (4, 11)	1.863
	2.	-.023 (-0.02)		.626 (-4.09)*	.409 (1.76)**	.143 (3.21)*	.684	11.82 (3, 12)	1.770
	3.			.628 (-6.64)*	.405 (9.27)*	.144 (3.60)*	.709	19.20 (3, 12)	1.771
Robbery	1.	-5.50 (-0.88)	-4.34 (-1.88)**	.641 (-3.93)*	1.159 (1.40)	.367 (2.61)*	.775	15.02 (4, 11)	2.643
	2.	-5.72 (-2.64)**		.563 (-4.86)*	-.273 (-0.76)	.203 (1.68)**	.744	15.54 (3, 12)	2.441
	3.	4.11 (10.22)*		.529 (-6.21)*		.131 (1.77)**	.753	23.81 (2, 13)	2.467

*Significant at the 1% level.
**Significant at the 5% level.
†Corrected for degrees of freedom.
t-statistics are shown in parentheses below coefficient values.
Degrees of freedom are shown in parentheses below F-statistics.

APPENDIX C

DERIVATION OF THE SIMULTANEOUS EQUATION MODEL
(SECTION 4)

We assume the functional relationships take a log-linear form as follows

$$CR_i = k_i \, OF_i{}^{\alpha_i - 1} \, EX_i{}^{\beta_i}, \tag{C.1}$$

and

$$OF_i = h_i \, CR_i{}^{\gamma_i} \, SE^{\delta_i}, \tag{C.2}$$

where the variables are as interpreted previously in the text. EX_i is total expenditures by law-enforcement agencies applied to the solution of crime, i. We assume further that law-enforcement officials, who are given a total budget EX, vary the proportion of EX allocated to the control of a particular crime in proportion to the number of offenses for that crime relative to the total or

$$EX_i = \left(\frac{OF_i}{OF_O} \, EX \right) \phi, \tag{C.3}$$

where OF_O is the level of offenses for the remaining felony offenses (with the exception of rape, whose definition was modified in the period studied). (While we didn't feel that it was necessary to consider the possibility of varying the proportion of EX allocated to each crime in our partial analysis of the law-enforcement production function, since OF_i/OF_O is relatively constant over the period studied, we felt that the possibility of EX_i varying should not be ignored in a simultaneous evaluation.) By substitution we obtain

$$CR_i = k_i \, OF_i{}^{\alpha_i - 1} \left(\frac{OF_i}{OF_O} \, EX \right)^{\phi\beta}. \tag{C.4}$$

Assuming EX/OF_O to be exogenous to this simultaneous equation system, taking logarithms, and writing C.2 and C.4 in matrix notation (deleting subscripts in the interest of simplicity), we have

$$\begin{bmatrix} 1 & -(\alpha - 1 + \phi\beta) \\ -\gamma & 1 \end{bmatrix} \begin{bmatrix} lnCR \\ lnOF \end{bmatrix} = \begin{bmatrix} lnk & \phi\beta & O \\ lnh & O & \delta \end{bmatrix} \begin{bmatrix} 1 \\ ln \, (EX/OF_O) \\ ln \, SE \end{bmatrix}. \tag{C.5}$$

Solving for the reduced form equations yields

$$\begin{bmatrix} ln \, CR \\ ln \, OF \end{bmatrix} = \frac{1}{1 - \gamma(\alpha - 1 + \phi\beta)} \begin{bmatrix} 1 & (\alpha - 1 + \phi\beta) \\ \gamma & 1 \end{bmatrix} \begin{bmatrix} lnk & \phi\beta & O \\ lnh & O & \delta \end{bmatrix} \begin{bmatrix} 1 \\ ln \, (EX/OF_O) \\ ln \, SE \end{bmatrix} \tag{C.6}$$

or equivalently

$$ln \, CR = a_0 + a_1 \, ln(EX/OF_O) + a_2 \, ln \, SE, \tag{C.7}$$

and

$$\ln OF = b_0 + b_1 \ln(EX/OF_0) + b_2 \ln SE, \qquad \text{(C.8)}$$

where $a_0 = [lnk + (\alpha - 1 + \phi\beta)lnh]/|A|$, where $|A| = 1 - \gamma(\alpha - 1 + \phi\beta)$
$a_1 = \phi\beta/|A|$
$a_2 = \delta(\alpha - 1 + \phi\beta)/|A|$
$b_0 = (\delta \, lnk + lnh)/|A|$
$b_1 = \gamma\phi\beta/|A|$
$b_2 = \delta/|A|$.

Solving for the structural parameters yields

$$\gamma = b_1/a_1$$
$$\alpha - 1 + \phi\beta = a_2/b_2$$
$$\delta = b_2(1 - b_1a_2/a_1b_2)$$
$$\phi\beta = a_1(1 - b_1a_2/a_1b_2).$$

Empirical Results for Larceny

Equation Parameter	a_0	a_1	a_2	b_0	b_1	b_2
Coefficient	5.77	0.30	−0.01	2.33	−0.47	1.14
t-statistic	11.12	5.20	−0.28	1.38	−2.50	7.96
R^2	.85				.95	
$F_{2,13}$	37.10				125.25	
D-W	1.87				1.83	

Structural Estimates of Coefficients

lnk	lnh	α	$\phi\beta$	γ	δ
5.61	−6.51	0.70	0.29	−1.57	1.12

Note that ϕ and β are not identified. So long as the ratio of larceny offenses to other felony offenses remains constant, $\phi\beta$ is simply the elasticity of CR with respect to total law-enforcement expenditures.

Calculations of the Values of the State Variable Required to Hold CR Constant

From equation C.1:

$$\% \Delta CR = (\alpha - 1) \% \Delta OF + \beta \% \Delta EX.$$

Substituting equation C.2:

$$\% \Delta CR = (\alpha - 1)[\gamma \% \Delta CR + \delta \% \Delta W_n] + \beta \% \Delta EX.$$

Setting

$$\% \, \Delta \, CR = 0$$
$$0 = (\alpha - 1) \, \delta \, \% \, \Delta \, W_n + \beta \, \% \, \Delta \, EX$$
$$= -.30 \, (1.12) \, (3.77) + .29 \, \% \, \Delta \, EX, \text{ assuming } \phi = 1.$$
$$\% \, \Delta \, EX = .30 \, (1.12) \, (3.77) / .29$$
$$\Delta \, EX = 4.38\%.$$

From equation C.2, this implies for $\% \, \Delta \, OF$

$$\% \, \Delta \, OF = \gamma \, \% \, \Delta \, CR + \delta \, \% \, \Delta \, W_n.$$

Setting $\% \, \Delta \, CR = 0$ and substituting the observed average change in $W_n = 3.77$, which is used to represent SE,

$$\% \, \Delta \, OF = -1.57(0) + 1.12(3.77),$$
$$\Delta \, OF = 4.2\%.$$

Calculation of the Values of the State Variable Required to Hold *OF* Constant

From equation C.2:

$$\% \, \Delta \, OF = -1.57 \, \% \, \Delta \, CR + 1.12 \, \% \, \Delta \, W_n.$$

Setting

$$\% \, \Delta \, OF = 0$$
$$0 = -1.57 \, \% \, \Delta \, CR + 1.12 \, \% \, \Delta \, W_n$$
$$\Delta \, CR = \frac{1}{1.57} \, [1.12 \, (3.77)] = 2.7\%.$$

From equation C.1:

$$\% \, \Delta \, CR = -.30 \, \% \, \Delta \, OF + .29 \, \% \, \Delta \, EX$$
$$\Delta \, EX = \frac{1}{.29} \, [2.69 + .30(0)] = 9.2\%.$$

Calculation of the Values of *CR* and *OF* Holding W_n Constant

Noting that $\% \, \Delta \, EX_{\text{Larceny}} = 3.3$, from equation C.1:

$$\% \, \Delta \, CR = -.30 \, \% \, \Delta \, OF + .29 \, (3.3).$$

From equation C.2:

$$\% \, \Delta \, OF = -1.57 \, \% \, \Delta \, CR + 0.$$

By substitution:

$$\% \Delta CR = -.30 \, (-1.57 \, \% \, \Delta \, CR) + .96$$
$$\Delta CR = 1.8\%.$$

From equation C.1:

$$\% \Delta OF = -1.57(1.8) + 0$$
$$\Delta OF = 2.9\%.$$

REFERENCES

Becker, Gary S.
    1968   "Crime and punishment: an economic approach." Journal of Political Economy 76(March/April):169–217.

Bonger, William A.
    1916   Criminality and Economic Conditions. Boston: Little, Brown.
    1943   Race and Crime. New York: Columbia University Press.

Burgess, Robert L., and Ronald L. Akers.
    1966   "A differential association—reinforcement theory of criminal behavior." Social Problems 14(Fall):128–147.

Cressey, Donald R.
    1960   "Epidemiology and individual conduct." Pacific Sociological Review 3(Fall):47–58.

Federal Bureau of Investigation (F.B.I.)
    1968   Crime in the United States: Uniform Crime Reports—1967. Washington, D.C.: U.S. Government Printing Office.

Ferguson, C. E.
    1969   Microeconomic Theory. Second Edition. Homewood, Ill.: Irwin.

Fleisher, Belton M.
    1963   "The effects of unemployment on juvenile delinquency." Journal of Political Economy 71(December):543–555.
    1966   The Economics of Delinquency. Chicago: Quadrangle Books.

Gibbs, Jack P.
    1968   "Crime, punishment and deterrence." Southwestern Social Science Quarterly 48(March):515–530.

Glaser, Daniel.
    1956   "Criminality theories and behavioral images." American Journal of Sociology 61(March):433–444.

Glaser, Daniel, and Kent Rice.
    1959   "Crime, age and employment." American Sociological Review 24(October): 679–686.

Lancaster, Kelvin.
    1974   Introduction to Modern Microeconomics. Second Edition. Chicago: Rand McNally College Pub.

Mansfield, Edwin.
  1968   The Economics of Technological Change. New York: Norton.

National Commission on Law Observance and Enforcement.
  1931   Report on the Cost of Crime. Washington, D.C.: U.S. Government Printing
          Office.

Phillips, Llad, and Harold L. Votey, Jr.
  1972   "An economic analysis of the deterrent effect of law enforcement on criminal
          activity." Journal of Criminal Law, Criminology and Police Science 63
          (September) :330–342.

Phillips, Llad, Harold L. Votey, Jr., and John Howell.
  1971   "Apprehension, deterrence, guns and violence: the control of homicide."
          Paper presented at the annual meeting of the Western Economic Associa-
          tion, Vancouver, B.C. Abstract in Western Economic Journal 9(September):
          343.

Phillips, Llad, Harold L. Votey, Jr., and Darold Maxwell.
  1969   "Labor market conditions and economic crimes." Paper presented at the
          annual meeting of the Western Economic Association, August (unpub-
          lished).
  1972a   "Crime, youth and the labor market: an econometric study." Journal of
          Political Economy 80(May/June) :491–504.
  1972b   "Economics and jobs, or crime," in Thomas Palm and Harold G. Vatter
          (eds.), The Economics of Black America. New York: Harcourt Brace
          Jovanovich.

President's Commission on Law Enforcement and Administration of Justice.
  1967a   The Challenge of Crime in a Free Society. Washington, D.C.: U.S. Govern-
          ment Printing Office.
  1967b   Task Force Report: Crime and its Impact: An Assessment. Washington,
          D.C.: U.S. Government Printing Office.

Schmid, Calvin F.
  1960   "Urban crime areas." American Sociological Review 25(August) :527–542.

Schuessler, Karl, and Gerald Slotin.
  1964   "Sources of variation in U.S. city crime, 1950 and 1960." Journal of Re-
          search in Crime and Delinquency 1(July) :127–148.

Skolnick, Jerome H.
  1967   Justice Without Trial. New York: Wiley.

Stigler, George J.
  1970   "The optimum enforcement of laws." Journal of Political Economy 78(May/
          June) :526–536.

Sutherland, Edwin H., and Donald R. Cressey.
  1970   Criminology. Eighth Edition. Philadelphia: Lippincott.

U.S. Department of Labor.
  1970   Manpower Report to the President. Washington, D.C.: U.S. Government
          Printing Office.

Vold, George B.
  1958   Theoretical Criminology. New York: Oxford University Press.

Votey, Harold L., Jr., and Llad Phillips.
　1969　Economic Crimes: Their Generation, Deterrence and Control. Springfield,
　　　　Va.: U.S. Clearinghouse for Federal Scientific and Technical Information.
　1972　"The law-enforcement production function." Journal of Legal Studies
　　　　1(June) :423–436.
Wilks, Judith A.
　1967　"Ecological correlates of crime and delinquency," in President's Commission
　　　　on Law Enforcement and Administration of Justice, Task Force Report:
　　　　Crime and Its Impact: An Assessment. Washington, D.C.: U.S. Government
　　　　Printing Office.

CHAPTER 31

Crime Prevention: The Fugitive Utopia

LaMar T. Empey

University of Southern California

For most people, the idea of crime prevention is attractive. To the traditionalist, it bespeaks a kind of fugitive Utopia in which the citizenry is protected from the ravages of human predation by a vigilant and efficient system of social control. To others, the utopian society would be one in which each individual is given a stake in conformity and thereby rendered unlikely to become delinquent or criminal. But there is reason to be leery of utopian hopes because crime, like organic malfunction, seems to be a normal aspect of human life (Durkheim, 1895:chap. 3). The conceit that either can be ultimately vanquished "involves a particularly trivial kind of utopian dreaming. Out of control, malfunction and crime could possibly overcome life, but control could never succeed in more than keeping them to a level appropriate to the prevailing form of human life" (Bittner, 1970:49).

Crime is found in varying degrees in all modern nations, particularly those that are urban and highly industrialized. The particular forms that it takes in any society are related to the ways in which that society is organized (Wheeler et al., 1967:409). A society like America's, for example, that places a high premium on freedom, that fosters a tradition of wanting to get ahead, and that prizes material success is not likely to be able to contain all its members within a conventional mold. Paradoxically, the dominant values that foster a high level of aspiration and striving may also be the very ones that encourage crime as one means of achieving them (cf. Merton, 1957:chaps. 4, 5; Cloward & Ohlin, 1960:chap. 4).

These considerations, then, should act to caution against any easy assumption that the total prevention of all crime is desirable, or even conceivable. "Its historic roots, its familiar occurrence in urban society, and its particular relation to the American value system suggest that we are dealing with a chronic problem which is unlikely to yield easily to preventive efforts" (Wheeler et al., 1967:409–10).

THE WAR ON CRIME

During the turbulent years of the 1960s and early 1970s, concern for better methods of crime prevention and control reached a peak. Evidence from official sources indicated that crime and delinquency were on the rise. Although questions might be raised regarding the complete accuracy of this evidence, a far more important issue has to do with the ways in which it was perceived and interpreted by different groups of Americans. The contrasting ideologies that emerged may portend the future.

One significant segment of the populace responded positively to a body of rhetoric suggesting that the nation is in dire peril. As Bittner described it:

> A figure of speech that has recently gained a good deal of currency is the "war on crime." The intended import of the expression is quite clear. It is supposed to indicate that the community is seriously imperiled by forces bent on its destruction and calls for the mounting of efforts that have claims on all available resources to defeat the peril. The rhetorical shift from "crime control" to "war on crime" signifies the transition from a routine concern to a state of emergency. We no longer face losses of one kind or another from the depredation of criminals; we are in imminent danger of losing everything! (1970:48)

In some cases, the immediate peril seemed to come from deviant acts that were not entirely traditional in character. Rather, these acts were often political in nature, and were perpetrated in response to the problems of a rapidly changing world. Consider Carter and Gitchoff's summary of them:

> [Americans] have observed rebellion against the establishment in forms encompassing freedom riders in the South, to looters in the North. American youth in increasing numbers have withstood tear gas and mace, billy clubs and bullets, insults and assaults, jail and prison in order to lie down in front of troop trains, sit-in at a university administration building, love-in in public parks, wade-in at non-integrated beaches, and lie-in within our legislative buildings. These youths have challenged the establishment on such issues as the legal-oriented entities of the draft, the right of Negroes to use the same restrooms and drinking fountains as whites, the death penalty, and free speech. They have also challenged socially oriented norms with "mod" dress and hair styles, language, rock music, and psychedelic colors, forms and patterns. [The nation has] watched the development of the hippy, and yippy, the youthful drug culture, black, yellow, brown, and red power advocates, and organizations such as the Third World Liberation Front, The Peace and Freedom Party, and Black Studies Departments on the campus. We have been exposed to violence, vandalism, assault, destruction, looting, disruption, and chaos on our streets (1970:52).

Rhetoric favoring a "war on crime" also took strength from the FBI's annual account of traditional crime. During the decade of the 1960s, for example, crimes of violence per hundred thousand population (murder, forcible rape, robbery, and aggravated assault) went up 104 percent, while crimes against property (burglary, larceny, and auto theft) went up 123 percent. Overall, the total number of these seven offenses per hundred thousand went up 120 percent (F.B.I., 1969:4).

Ironically, available data also implied that, if a crime war were to be waged, it would have to be directed against the nation's youth. According to the President's Commission on Law Enforcement and Administration of Justice (1967b:44), more burglaries, larcenies, and auto thefts are committed by young people, ages 15 to 17 years, than by any other group. Fifteen year olds are arrested most often, with 16 year olds a close second. For crimes of violence, those from 18 to 20 are the most responsible, with the second largest group in the 21 to 24 age range. Hence, in projecting the possibility that age-specific arrest probabilities for future years would remain the same as they were in 1965, Christensen (1967:221) estimated that the chances that a male would be arrested sometime during his life for an offense other than a traffic offense were 47 percent, and for a female, 13 percent.

Coupled with the protests and riots of a decade, the increasing incidence of traditional crimes created a climate of fear throughout the nation, especially in our large cities. Taken on a collective level, a vision was evoked that portrayed thousands, if not millions, of Americans sitting crouched behind locked doors, fearful that if they ventured forth they would become additional victims of their own, criminally disposed youth. These are among the reasons, then, why the catchwords for many Americans became, and still remain, "law and order," not "prevention and control." In place of a routine concern for crime, a state of emergency was declared.

Fearful that such a state of emergency, and all that it implied, would be destructive of basic humanitarian and democratic values, other groups of Americans expressed an opposing point of view. Some warned that a climate of fear does not abide patient study (Bittner, 1970:49). The implementation of a "war on crime," for example, projects hopes for victory that cannot possibly be realized. Worse yet, it extends the stamp of legitimacy to methods that would not be acceptable on moral and constitutional grounds. Instead, the organizational posture that is implied is a military one in which ferocity and coldly calculated expediency could or do result—a posture in which the representatives of authority, especially the police, are expected to be as unsparing of themselves as they are of the enemy. Yet, as many scholars have pointed out (Lasswell, 1950:228; Janowitz, 1968:8; Silver, 1968:12–14; Bittner, 1970:50), the trouble with such an approach is not only the danger that it poses for democratic institutions, but for the policemen who are enlisted in the crime war. Unless the police are totally brutalized, it is unlikely that they can ever be as unscrupulously ruthless against criminals as against an alien enemy, especially since the former are comprised largely of the nation's youth. The values and organizations that are needed by a democratic society to win a military victory are not the same as those needed to prevent and control crime.

Seeming to speak to this very issue, the President's Commission (1967a:41) noted that, since our system of justice holds both juveniles and adults responsible for their misconduct, and imposes sanctions upon them accordingly, it also obligates itself to provide potential criminals with educational, social, and economic means to understand and accept responsibility. A "war on crime," by contrast, and the ruthlessness it implies, not only fails to address this societal obligation but probably abides little consideration of it. Yet, the capacity of any citizenry to act in a responsible way depends, in the last analysis, on the viability of its basic socializing institutions—the home, neighborhood, school, and economy—not on the exercise of coercion or repressive military rule.

Because this notion appeals to common sense as well as scientific thinking, it has long been a popular one. In many ways, in fact, it has been the primary antidote to the ideology that favors a militaristic response. Yet, if one traces the development of social thought in recent decades, one is also struck by the emergence of an additional and, in some ways, a more sophisticated rationale for concentrating upon crime prevention rather than coercion and punishment. This is the labeling approach to deviance, with its suggestion that society's customary ways for responding to delinquents and criminals may have done more to incubate the crime problem than to solve it. This approach probably is the most popular rationale today for responding to crime in other ways than making war on criminals.

THE LABELING APPROACH

In 1938, Tannenbaum argued that the final step in the making of the adult criminal occurs when youth become enmeshed in society's institutionalized patterns for dealing with them, in their experiences with police, courts, and correctional institutions. Tannenbaum felt that these experiences often tended to dramatize rather than to eliminate evil. As he put it, "the process of making the criminal is a process of tagging, defining, identifying, segregating, describing, emphasizing, making conscious and self-conscious; it becomes a way of stimulating, suggesting, emphasizing, and evolving the very traits that are complained of" (1938:30). The official process not only tends to isolate an individual from conformist influences, but makes him even more dependent upon the support and encouragement of his deviant peers.

Tannenbaum's comments mesh well with the perspective of symbolic interactionism in sociology (cf. Blumer, 1969), which emphasizes: (1) that social organization and the person are two facets of the same thing; and (2) that a person's self-conception should be seen as the product of an ongoing process of interaction, not as a static and fixed entity. Accordingly, Cressey argues that the criminal, like any other person, should be

> seen as a part of the kinds of social relationships and values in which he participates; he obtains his essence from participation in rituals, values, norms, rules, schedules, customs, and regulations of various kinds which surround him. The person (personality) is not separable from the social relationships in which he lives (1965:90).

Hence, if the person interacts primarily in conventional settings, he will likely perceive himself as a conformist and behave in a conventional way. But, if he is segregated from conventional people and forced to seek his identity among those who are deviant, he will be more likely to acquire a deviant concept of himself.

Lemert (1951:70–78), and later both Kitsuse (1962) and Erikson (1962), suggested that it is not just the deviant act alone to which attention must be directed, but the way in which others respond to it. Erikson, for example, argued that:

> Deviance is not a property *inherent in* certain forms of behavior; it is a property *conferred upon* these forms by the audiences which directly or indirectly witness them. Sociologically, then, the critical variable in the study of deviance is the social *audience* rather than individual *person*, since it is the audience which eventually decides whether or not any given action or actions will become a visible case of deviation (1962:308).

Lemert (1951:71) has also suggested that if deviant behavior is not identified and negatively sanctioned by some audience, its impact on the individual will be minimal. In all likelihood, he will rationalize and deal with it as a function of one of his socially acceptable roles.

Lemert called this kind of unsanctioned deviance, *primary* deviance. Although it may be problematic in the sense that deviant and conformist inclinations are coincidental within the same person, it is unlikely that he will develop a deviant self-identity. Rather, as Davis (1961) suggests, he will be inclined, as most people are, to disavow the implications of his deviant acts. Since his social status has not been changed by the reactions of others to him, he will tend to retain a conformist self-concept and avoid many of the negative consequences of being defined as a deviant person.

If, on the other hand, the person's deviant behavior has high visibility, and if society reacts severely to it, then the results will be markedly different. It is not behavior per se that differentiates deviants from nondeviants, says Kitsuse, "it is the responses of the conventional and conforming members of the society who interpret behavior as deviant which sociologically transforms persons into deviants" (1962:253).

In the case of the young delinquent, for example, this transformation is often subtle and complex. Not only must he deal with the stigma associated with his delinquent status, but he must respond to more subtle cues regarding what is expected of him. Strong negative reactions by officials may disrupt his self-concept and his normal roles, and the reactions of friends and associates will also have a marked impact. Paradoxically, responses from peers, delinquent and nondelinquent, as well as from officials, may tend to affirm his delinquent status. Hence, to the extent that he is sensitive to the expectations and actions of others, his behavior may easily mirror not his normal role, but a deviant one. Even his clothes, his speech, or his mannerisms may be altered, reflecting the appurtenances of his new role.

Lemert (1971:13) also suggests that once a person is labeled, he is expected to adhere to an additional set of rules that apply only to him. But, rather than helping to reduce his problems, they may only increase them. When a delinquent is placed on probation, for example, he is often forbidden to live with an "unfit" parent or to associate with his girl or boy friends, and he is expected to reverse suddenly his pattern of failure at school. Any failure to adhere to these special rules will, in itself, constitute a new act of deviance. Hence, the justice-correction system, in attempting to "treat" the delinquent, can actually escalate the grounds whereby his future behavior may be termed delinquent.

This increase in rules, coupled with the tendency for the delinquent to begin behaving in accordance with the expectations of his deviant status, may result in what Lemert calls *secondary* deviance. This kind of deviance evolves out of the adaptations the labeled person makes to the problems created by official and conformist reactions to his primary deviance. "When a person begins to employ his deviant behavior as a role based upon it as a means of defense, attack or adjustment to the overt and covert problems created by the consequent societal reactions to him, his deviation is secondary" (1951:71). Thus, even though unique historic or situational factors may have contributed to his original acts of deviance, the reactions of society to them may actually escalate the chances that further secondary forms of deviance will be forthcoming.

Lemert (1951:75–78) expresses doubt, however, that secondary deviance will follow hard upon the heels of any single official, even punitive, reaction to an individual. Rather, as Tannenbaum (1938) had suggested earlier, it is the product of a rather long process in which the deviant will have been involved progressively in a series of interactions with the agents of social control. The acquisition of a deviant identity and acts of secondary deviance are the product of a learning experience. Lemert failed to denote the circumstances in which interactions between the deviant and officials do not result in secondary deviance, but his analysis was extremely useful in suggesting that official processing often has the opposite of its intended effect. This occurs because deviance is escalated by official reaction, "entangling the deviant and the persons surrounding him in a web of rigidity and self-fulfilling prophecy which may become increasingly difficult to escape" (Polk & Kobrin, 1972:16).

In his definitive statement, Becker added to the labeling school themes already mentioned a stress on rule-making:

> . . . *social groups create deviance by making the rules whose infractions constitute deviance,* and by applying these rules to particular people and labeling them as outsiders. From this point of view, deviance is *not* a quality of the act the person commits, but rather a consequence of the application by others of rules and sanctions to the "offender." The deviant is one to whom that label has successfully been applied; deviant behavior is behavior that people so label (1963:9).

In conclusion, the labeling perspective suggested that social groups create deviance because of the particular rules they make and enforce, and accordingly,

> acts can be identified as deviant or criminal only by reference to the character of reaction to them by the public or by the official agents of a politically organized society. Put simply, if the reaction is of a certain kind, then and only then is the act deviant (Gibbs, 1966:11).

Implications of the Labeling Perspective

The impact of the labeling perspective on social policy, as well as on social theory, has been great. Emphasis upon the negative effects of labeling helped to provide the rationale for a social movement favoring the diversion of youth and adults from the justice-corrections system, and revision of the rules and processes by which people are defined as criminal. Because this ideology stands in such marked contrast to the ideology favoring a war on crime, its moral and policy implications merit careful scrutiny. The following summary builds upon Schur's (1971:171) statement of its implications.

First, the labeling perspective reemphasizes the assertion long made by criminologists that crime is *relative* and varies according to time and place. It stresses prevention in a most fundamental sense by challenging society to examine its own rules and to determine wherein they may be harmful rather than helpful. The "injurious" quality of some criminal or delinquent acts, as Gibbs (1966:10) notes, is by no means obvious. Far from being harmful, some acts may be defined as criminal because, and only because, they are proscribed legally.

Second, by suggesting the need to scrutinize the rule-making and political processes by which crime is defined and offenders labeled, the labeling perspective highlights a growing division in sociology over two contrasting models for analyzing society, *consensus* and *conflict*.

The consensus model emphasizes the idea that all of the elements of social organization—values, norms, roles, and institutions—are a closely knit whole (cf. Dahrendorf, 1959:2). It suggests that most people share the same objectives, agree on basic definitions of right and wrong, and engage in a mutually supporting set of activities. Therefore, the various elements of social organization are presumed to reflect this consensus, and, by definition, a person who is criminal is one who rejects the basic consensus and threatens the stability of the whole.

Conflict theorists, by contrast, argue that the consensus model implies a set of values that not only favors the status quo and those in power, but also ignores reality. Modern society, they suggest, is characterized by diversity and change, and is held together, not by consensus, but by force and constraint. Although certain values predominate, they do so more by the fact that they are enforced by dominant groups and interests than by the members of society as a whole (Dahrendorf, 1958:127). The turbulence of the 1960s and early 1970s exemplifies such societal conflict over basic practices and beliefs. By stressing conflict elements and rule-making processes, labeling analysis eschews the idea that society is held together by consensus and by a static structure, emphasizing instead the importance of value and political conflict in determining how crime is defined and rules applied.

Third, because of its emphasis upon the negative effects of official processing, the labeling perspective attracts attention to deficiencies in our control and correctional structures. It helped to popularize the important notion that conformist self-concepts are forged *outside* of correctional structures, not within them, and that official processing can actually inhibit this process. Hence, there has been a rapid search for means by which to divert known and potential offenders from the stigmatizing and role-disrupting effects of the justice-correctional system.

The President's Commission (1967a:19–21) popularized the notion of youth service bureaus through which delinquents could be dealt with nonjudicially in their own communities. California instituted a probation subsidy program by which state funds are used to subsidize local counties for retaining in their communities many adults, as well as juveniles, who would otherwise have been confined in state institutions. As a result, some institutions have been closed, and new ones remain unopened (cf. Smith, 1971). In Massachusetts recently, steps were taken to eliminate entirely all of the state's juvenile training schools and to substitute community programs for them. Although cases of primary deviance would not be prevented by the closing of institutions, it was hoped that the incidence of secondary deviance would be prevented.

Such diversions contrast with the implications of the war on crime that deterrence through punishment is the best way to prevent crime. In fact, as early as 1965, the President's Commission (1967c:1) reported that two-thirds of all offenders, many of them felons, were under supervision in the community while only one-third were in institutions. Such evidence indicates that the diversionary philosophy, instigated in part by the labeling perspective, has been a powerful one.

Fourth, the flat rejection by the labeling approach of the idea that the criminal or his deviant acts are characterized by some feature that is intrinsic to them has caused scientists and professionals to question many long-held assumptions regarding the causes for crime. Most people would now agree that distinctive biological features do not characterize criminals. In fact, as Gibbs (1966:10) suggests, the possibility that such characteristics exist even for particular criminal types, such as murderers or bigamists, not only lacks scientific verification but defies logic. "Since legislators are not geneticists, it is difficult to see how they can pass laws in such a way as to create 'born' criminals." But the same kind of thinking has been applied as well to the search for unique psychological characteristics, attitudes, or values. That search for them has not been particularly successful either. As Hathaway et al. put it, personality measures "are much less powerful and apply to fewer cases among total samples than would be expected if one read the literature on the subject" (1960:439). Summaries of other studies suggest (1) that known offenders are more like than different from the general population, and (2) that measures of personality that yield deviancy variations reliably still do not distinguish criminal behavior types (cf. LaGache, 1950; Schuessler & Cressey, 1950; Short & Strodtbeck, 1965:371). It appears that legislators are unable to identify psychological aberration by passing laws any easier than they can identify born criminals.

These kinds of negative findings, as a result, lend support to labeling proponents who argue that the causes for crime cannot be found in the static structural characteristics of the offender or solely in the structural characteristics of society, but in the interaction between the two.

This concern with the dynamics rather than the structures of societal life has reinforced the need to study crime prevention on several different levels: on the societal level where rules are made, in the organizations that process offenders, and on an interpersonal level where the offender interacts with others.

Deficiencies in the Labeling Approach

Despite its contributions, the labeling perspective has some deficiencies, both as a body of theory and in its relevance for social policy. These two deficiencies are interrelated because, as Schrag suggests, the seminal capacity of any theory to produce effective social action, as well as research, depends upon its ability to meet three criteria:

> First, the theory should have sound logical structure. That is, its postulates should be connected in such a manner that a number of claims or assertions can be derived from them by means of logical inference or deduction. Second, the theory should have operational significance. Some of its terms should be related by rule to observable data so that its meaning is clear and its claims can be tested by evidence and experience. Third, the theory should have high congruence with the world of experience. Its major claims should be generally consistent with the preponderance of relevant factual evidence. When these three requirements are met, the theory can be used successfully for pragmatic purposes (1962:167).

According to a number of different observers, the labeling perspective does not meet these criteria. Gibbs (1966:9), for example, argues that it does not yet contain some of the necessary elements of a substantive theory—a careful delineation and definition of concepts, and a logically developed and integrated set of propositions. These elements must be developed before the weaknesses as well as the strengths of the labeling perspective can be fully understood.

Gibbs (1966:11–12) also suggests that one major weakness lies in the failure of proponents of the labeling approach to indicate clearly whether they are seeking an explanation of deviant behavior, of reactions to it, or both. For example, the point is stressed continually that acts can be identified as deviant only by the character of reactions to them. Yet, Becker (1963:20) alludes to the existence of "secret deviance," implying that acts of deviation can be identified by reference to existing norms regardless of societal reaction. Similarly, Kitsuse and Cicourel (1963:138–39) assert that they do not mean to imply that forms of behavior that the sociologist might categorize as deviant have no basis in fact. And Erikson (1962:313) notes that in some societies, deviance is considered a natural pursuit of the young, while in others, license is given to large groups of persons to engage in deviant behavior in celebration of certain holidays or seasons of the year. This license, he suggests, is granted without resultant penalties or negative reactions.

What all these comments imply, of course, is that deviance can be identified, not merely in terms of reactions to it, but in terms of existing social norms. Otherwise, one could not speak of "secret deviance," or distinguish, as Lemert does, between primary (unsanctioned) and secondary (sanctioned) deviance. Moreover, the fact that norms, as well as sanctions, do have a role to play can be illustrated by drawing some fundamental distinctions between different types of deviant acts. Glaser (1971) argues that the failure of labeling proponents to do this has inhibited a clarification of the distinctive contributions they have to make.

Granted that for many acts, such as prostitution, gambling, homosexuality, drug use, drunkenness, or some juvenile-status offenses, societal rules and reactions vary greatly; "crime" in these terms is indeed relative to time and place. But what about such acts as homicide, unprovoked assault, robbery, and burglary? Condemnation of "crime" in these forms is far more common. In all but the simplest of societies, state concern with protecting property rights, and with insuring immunity against physical attack, is virtually universal. Acts such as these, in other words, can be readily identified by allusion to existing norms, as well as by reactions to them.

Finally, the methodological thrust of the labeling approach, as Schur (1971:34) has noted, has been away from the statistical and positivistic biases of contemporary social science, and toward a greater concern with process and the social psychology of the individual. These differences in orientation are reflective, says Glaser, of two types of science—nomothetic and ideographic.

> Nomothetic disciplines seek only general laws, applicable to all phenomena of a specified class, with rules of evidence and inference modelled on those of the so-called "exact sciences." Ideographic studies, on the other hand, are concerned with understanding particular events or sequences of events, using rules of evidence and inference best exemplified in the works of historians, biographers and political commentators (1968:1).

Clearly, the labeling proponents favor a sophisticated version of the ideographic studies. They wish to discover what the processes are by which a person is labeled as deviant, or how he comes to feel and act like one. But in stressing the ideographic, they leave unanswered some basic theoretical and policy questions that nomothetic studies might answer. If, for example, there are some acts that are universally condemned, such as murder or robbery, then it may well be appropriate for social science to study these acts apart from, as well as concurrent with, the processes by which they are labeled as deviant. By the same token, since prevention programs are concerned with societal as well as individual welfare, with the victim of a crime as well as with its perpetrator, it is important to seek nomothetic generalizations about predation, to outline its differential occurrence among different subpopulations, and to seek some knowledge of its causes. Even though predatory acts occur for which no offender is apprehended or reactions applied, it is important to be aware of their incidence. Validated propositions regarding these matters surely are necessary as guides to their prevention.

It seems unlikely that members of the labeling school would be opposed to nomothetic research of this type. There are, in fact, some ways by which it could be viewed as a vital adjunct to labeling research. Studies of self-reported delinquency, for example, reveal that undiscovered illegal acts throughout all elements of the juvenile population are great (cf. Empey, 1967 for a summary). Such findings not only provide a useful means by which to compare and contrast rates of primary deviance with those of official delinquency, but raise serious questions regarding the most appropriate methods for responding to them. Clearly, if acts of primary deviance are common despite the existing control apparatus, then persons concerned with prevention must seek either to change the rules or to find remediation in other forms.

At any rate, this brief review of questions may indicate why, as Schur suggests, it has been difficult to define precisely the operational and pragmatic implications of the labeling approach. "Apart perhaps from promoting a very broad injunction 'to avoid unnecessary labeling,' the orientation does not seem to provide a clear-cut general direction for public policy toward deviating behavior" (1971:171). Hence, like the war on crime, it leaves many questions unanswered. Policy makers and practitioners have had trouble in conceptualizing and implementing successful diversionary, nonlabeling programs.

Consider, for example, the major efforts since 1967 to divert juveniles and thus to prevent delinquency by creation of youth service bureaus. In 1971, a conference to exchange information on these bureaus, held at the University of Chicago, highlighted several difficulties (Seymour, 1971). Delegates were unable to agree on the basic goals and functions of youth service bureaus. Was it to change the stigmatizing effects of existing rules and practices, or to change children—to adapt children to society, or society to children? Put another way, should the bureaus be designed to provide direct services to the individual, or should they seek to alter the community so that it, rather than the bureaus, would do a better job of socializing and diverting children?

These are fundamental and age-old problems and require an explicit directive from theory.

The inability of bureau delegates to agree on basic functions also meant that they could not agree on overall strategy. Some believed that the bureau should become an integral part of existing organizations in the community, while others believed that because current organizations represent the establishment, they only enhance labeling. They wanted youth bureaus entirely independent, providing whatever services are needed for whatever clientele are deemed important.

A third major problem was to decide what "diversion" means. Those who define it in restrictive terms suggest that the sole mandate of the bureaus is to divert juveniles from the justice-correctional system. This means that only those children on the threshold of entry into that system are served. Others who define diversion more broadly believe that youth bureaus should be concerned with all delinquency prevention and youth development, in preventing primary acts of deviance as well as trying to divert those juveniles whose delinquent behavior was actually discovered.

Building on his labeling perspective, Lemert (1971) provides not one but several models for diversion—a school, a welfare, a law-enforcement, and a community organization model. Yet, his analysis of existing programs probably documents more problems than workable solutions. The labeling perspective, like virtually all other conceptions in social science, is still in an embryonic state insofar as setting forth clear and testable guidelines for public policy is concerned. But, if such an elusive concept as crime prevention is to be given better substance, the strengths of the labeling perspective must be added to those of other perspectives.

DEFINITION OF CRIME PREVENTION

In the past, as Polk and Kobrin (1972) point out, the tendency has been to search out those factors that are presumed to cause crime, and then to define prevention in terms of programs that will address those causes. While such an approach has merit, it fails to specify how legitimate pursuits are cultivated. Besides indicating what one seeks to avoid, one should make explicit what is being sought. Therefore, prevention could be defined as an attempt: (1) to identify those institutional characteristics and processes most inclined to produce legitimate identities and nonpredatory behaviors in people; (2) to restructure existing institutions or build new ones so that these desirable features are enhanced; and (3) to discard those features that tend to foster criminal behaviors and identities.

A first step in operationalizing this definition is to identify the major institutional structures to which reference is being made. Ohlin (1970) has suggested that, for the purposes of prevention, they can be organized into four major categories:

1. the legitimate, normative system, which includes the legal rules, policies, and practices by which society attempts to regulate behavior;
2. the primary socializing institutions, such as the family, school, world of work, or church, all of which are expected to produce legitimate identities in young people and to prepare them for adulthood;
3. the illegitimate structures in society that support crime, all the way from organized and professional subcultures to youthful gangs and associations; and
4. the agencies of social control, such as the police, the judiciary, and corrections, whose responsibility it is to react officially to those who violate legal norms.

All of these structures are obviously central to the cultivation of either legitimate or deviant identities, but the ways in which they affect behavior, and thus the ways in which they might be involved in any crime prevention effort, are not the same. For example, one might wish to examine rules and rule-making processes, as the labeling proponents have suggested, and then make alterations in the laws that govern behavior. By contrast, changes of a much different sort might be involved where the basic socializing institutions or the illegitimate structures in society are concerned. As a method of considering the ways in which efforts at prevention might be related to these four structures, let us examine them one by one.

THE SYSTEM OF LEGAL RULES

Given the catch-all character of the legal statutes that define both crime and delinquency, and the fact that they prescribe a legal reaction to such nonpredatory acts as truancy, neglect, gambling, drunkenness, and other kinds of "immoral" behavior that do not involve a victim, there are virtually no noncriminals. It is clear, therefore, that a tremendous amount of law-violating behavior could be "prevented" and, perhaps, the likelihood of secondary deviance reduced simply by making changes in legal statutes and policies. Many such changes are occurring, in fact.

Arguing in favor of them, Morris and Hawkins say that

> we must strip off the moralistic excrescences on our criminal justice system so that it may concentrate on the essential. The prime function of the criminal law is to protect our persons and our property; these purposes are now engulfed in a mass of other distracting, inefficiently performed legislative duties. When the criminal law invades the spheres of private morality and social welfare, it exceeds its proper limits at the cost of neglecting its primary tasks. . . .
>
> For the criminal law at least, man has an inalienable right to go to hell in his own fashion, provided he does not directly injure the person or property of another on the way . . . (1970:2).

Thus, these authors would distinguish between those acts that are predatory, and those that are not, and alter the rules to eliminate many of the latter as crimes.

The same kinds of suggestions have been made with respect to legal rules that apply only to juveniles. A number of different people and organizations (cf. Kvaraceus, 1964; Morris, 1966:643; President's Commission, 1967c:25; Rubin, 1970) all suggest that young people should not be prosecuted and receive penal sanctions for behavior that, if exhibited by adults, would not be prosecuted. Some also suggest that legal rules should not put judges and other authorities in the position of having to decide what is moral or immoral conduct for young people. Such decisions are better left to other institutions and processes.

Morris and Hawkins (1970:4–25) argue that if these kinds of changes were instituted, three major benefits would result. First, the number of people defined as criminal would be reduced by as much as three million annually, a sizeable prevention effort indeed. In numerical terms, this kind of reduction might be far greater than that achieved by more traditional and limited kinds of diversionary programs. Moreover, the pressure on police, courts, and corrections would be greatly reduced, leaving society's agents of control with much greater means for combating serious and predatory crime—violence, burglary, robbery, and professional and organized crime.

Second, prevention through the revision of legal rules would result in much less interference in the private moral conduct of the citizen, leaving the resolution of many juvenile status problems—drunkenness, drug use, sex, and gambling—to other institutions. If the labeling proponents are correct, then many forms of secondary deviance could also be prevented.

Third, since many of the sources of income for organized crime come from the sale of such things as narcotics, gambling, and illicit sex—activities around which there is no normative consensus in the populace—these sources would be dried up. The financial power of organized crime would be seriously hurt.

While these proposed changes have considerable appeal, it is clear that, according to our definition of prevention, they would be devoted more to restructuring legal institutions and eliminating harmful practices than to indicating how legitimate identities are developed. This is not to denigrate the importance of such changes, but to indicate the many dimensions and complexities of prevention as a basic concept. Moreover, it is important to recognize that the removal of such acts as public drunkenness or drug usage as criminal offenses, while it may reduce the effects of legal stigma and the burdens on the criminal justice system, would not really solve the problems of the alcoholic or the addict. Medical detoxification clinics are being set up for the alcoholic and methadone is being administered to many addicts, but neither represents anything approaching a lasting solution for their problems. Each still continues to suffer considerable stigma and each is still costly to society. The point is that rule changes are but one of the kinds of steps needed for the prevention of even secondary deviance. And unless they are accompanied by additional forms of remediation, they may be little more than a sociological sleight-of-hand, a kind of social magic without lasting positive effect.

As a method of trying to insure that alterations in legal rules will have a desirable effect, two suggestions have been made. First, Morris and Hawkins (1970:27) suggest that every legislature should have a Standing Law Revision Committee charged with the task of reviewing constantly the adequacy of existing rules and the impact of any changes that are made. The task of legal reform, in other words, would not be a one-shot thing; rather the committee would act as a monitor over the normative system, and be charged with the responsibility of cleaning out the debris of useless laws and policies and seeing that new ones fulfill the purposes for which they were created.

Second, Rubin (1970) suggests that any alterations, either in basic legal rules or in their administration, be tried on an experimental basis. Whenever radical alterations are made in the services rendered by the justice-correctional system, an experimental design should be set up to see if the new social alternatives are any better. Research would be conducted regularly to determine the actual effects of legal changes.

These two suggestions, while obviously debatable, approach the task of change in a reasonably systematic and rational way. Without such approaches, it will be difficult to build the knowledge necessary to test, revise, and improve existing theory and practice.

THE SOCIALIZING INSTITUTIONS

The incidence of predatory acts, highest among young people, suggests that more than alterations in the legalistic and control-oriented aspects of the criminal justice system are needed to prevent delinquency and crime. These offenses are at a very low ebb before the onset of adolescence, rise sharply after its onset, hit their peak at around 16 or 17, and decline sharply after that point (President's Commission, 1967b:44; Empey & Erickson, 1972:chap. 11). Hence, any serious effort at crime prevention would have to consider ways by which socialization per se might be made more effective.

This conclusion is based upon four assumptions, each of which is central to the definition of prevention set forth above:

1. The primary focus of prevention efforts should be upon the establishment

among young people of a legitimate identity. To seek only the avoidance of a deviant identity by refraining from the use of labels or stigma is, in one sense, to approach prevention negatively. The more difficult and prior task is to insure that young people acquire a productive, satisfying, and legitimate self-concept.

2. A legitimate identity among young people is most likely to occur if they have a stake in conformity (Toby, 1957a); if, in other words, they develop a sense of competence, a sense of usefulness, a sense of belonging, and a sense that they have the power to affect their own destinies through conventional means (Polk & Kobrin, 1972:5).

3. The cultivation in young people of a legitimate identity and a stake in conformity requires that they be provided with socially acceptable, responsible, and personally gratifying roles. Such roles have the effect of creating a firm attachment to the aims, values, and norms of basic institutions and of reducing the probability of criminal involvement (Polk & Kobrin, 1972:5).

4. Since social roles are a function of institutional design and process, ". . . a rational strategy of delinquency reduction and control must address the task of institutional change" (Polk & Kobrin, 1972:2–3). The changes that are sought should be capable of greatly expanding the range of legitimate roles available to young people.

In the most general of terms, these assumptions imply two things. First, if institutional change is the first order of business, a radical alteration of societal priorities is needed. Before the members of society and their elected representatives can prevent crime on any large scale, they will have to eradicate the poverty and ignorance that make life helpless for a significant minority of the American people, and break the bonds that confine many to miserable and unacceptable living conditions in our urban ghettos and rural slums. It is ludicrous to speak of fostering a legitimate identity or a stake in conformity among those for whom crime is one major way of alleviating unacceptable conditions and of realizing the American dream of getting ahead. Unless the necessary resources are forthcoming, such methods of intervention as youth service bureaus can be little more than Band-Aids on a huge and gaping wound.

It would be a mistake, however, to suggest that all crime would be eliminated were poverty removed. That is too convenient a shibboleth. Many predatory law violators are relatively affluent young people who have not acquired a stake in conformity. One reason that many of them are inclined to leave the creature comforts of their homes and to seek escape through drugs or some other means, or to justify their acts of senseless vandalism, theft, and violence, is because they feel they have no power over, or stake in, what is happening to them. The childish self-indulgence that is so common among many reflects a loss of purpose and direction. Lacking institutional constraints of a rewarding kind, some young Americans behave in an immature and destructive way.

A second implication has to do with our lack of knowledge. Even if American priorities were revised and more resources made available, it is difficult to say exactly what should be done to cultivate legitimate identities more effectively, or where and how new social roles for the young might be created. Many social action programs— whether urban renewal, the poverty program, or remedial job training—have ignored the cultural pluralism of America and the tremendous complexities associated with developing modes of intervention that are appropriate to different settings and people. No single grand strategy of prevention, invariably applied, is likely to succeed. The organizational networks in which the young are socialized vary too greatly. These problems must be confronted on both an organizational and an interactional level (cf. Empey & Lubeck, 1971:chap. 11 for a longer formulation of this analysis).

ORGANIZATIONAL LEVELS

Organizationally, there are two kinds of networks to be considered—the legitimate network consisting of home, neighborhood, school, and so on, and the illegitimate network involving the youthful gangs, the sources of drugs and vice, or career-oriented adult groups. Both are instrumental in the cultivation of deviant and legitimate identities.

The Legitimate Network

Research has indicated that family disorganization is greater among known delinquents than among nondelinquents, but how this contributes to illegal behavior is not clear. On one hand, some studies indicate that intrafamily conflicts and tensions are differentially productive of law-violating behavior (Shulman, 1949; Monahan, 1957; Toby, 1957b; Hirschi, 1969; Chilton & Markle, 1972). On the other hand, existing evidence also suggests that intrafamily characteristics cannot be treated in isolation. Influences that may be attributed to the home may actually have their roots in ethnic, class, subcultural, and other networks of which the family is only a part. For example, in their analysis of race differentials in gang behavior, Short and Strodtbeck found that

> . . . Negro gang delinquency tends *not to be clearly differentiated from nondelinquent behavior*—that participation in the "good" aspects of lower-class Negro life (responsibility in domestic chores and organized sports activities) is closely interwoven with "bad" aspects (conflict, illicit sex, drug use and auto theft).
>
> The literature of lower-class Negro life is rich in detail which supports such a conclusion among adults as well as children and adolescents. As compared with lower-class white communities, delinquency among lower-class Negroes is more of a total life pattern in which delinquent behaviors are not likely to create disjunctures with other types of behavior (1965:105-6).

There was much evidence throughout their study that family and community life for both adults and children was held much more in common among blacks than in other racial and neighborhood settings.

By contrast, *white* gang boys have been found to be more openly at odds with adults in their community (Short & Strodtbeck, 1965:105-12). Their activities were often seen by adults as rowdy and delinquent, and they were unwelcome in adult hangouts and groups. Much more than among black boys, their delinquent acts represented a protest against, rather than a component of, conventional family and community obligations. Thus, subcultural variations in adult-child relations and intrafamily disruptions are among a number of interdependent variables that must be taken into account. Even within families of the same social class, important differences along ethnic and other lines exist. Therefore, attempts to explain or prevent *individual* delinquent behavior without taking such differences into account are not likely to be very successful.

In all these examples, the neighborhood as a socializing institution was closely linked with that of the family. Yet, there has long been a disagreement in the literature whether those neighborhoods with the highest rates of law violations are disorganized or organized. On one hand, Thrasher concluded that illegal acts are most likely to occur in "what is often called the 'poverty belt'—a region characterized by deteriorating neighborhoods, shifting populations, and the mobility and disorganization of the slum" (1963:20-21). On the other hand, it was Whyte's (1955:viii) opinion that the slums may be highly organized, but not in the way the white middle class thinks of social organization. Yet, if it is *degree* of organization that is at issue, it is difficult to see how some slum neighborhoods could be much more anonymous and unintegrated than are many white, middle- and upper-class neighborhoods. The point is that the degree and kind of neighborhood organization is likely to vary greatly from place to place, and from time to time.

Into this welter of different families and neighborhoods—white, black, brown, and mixed; lower, middle, and upper class; rural, suburban, and urban—is inserted the one institution in society that is supposed to resolve all differences, and to provide a uniform kind of socialization for all young people. This institution, of course, is the school. People expect it to provide equal opportunity for every child, and since it is the one major link between childhood and adulthood, any failure on its part has serious consequences. Yet, these expectations notwithstanding, the overall structure of the educational system, especially in our urban centers, is often ill adapted to the different localities and subcultural groups to which it must relate. Its local branches, the neighborhood schools, usually operate on centralized policies set up and administered by people whose view of the world is often vastly different from those of the children and their parents whom it is supposed to serve. Operating from a central headquarters, attempts are made to impose uniform policies and practices on widely divergent groups that have little in common. This often results in lack of communication, conflict, and deviant behavior.

The problems that have occurred in the schools illustrate those likely to occur in any other prevention or socialization effort that attempts to maintain uniform practices across different ethnic, familial, and neighborhood lines. Since these vary greatly, institutional programs designed to give the young a stake in conformity will also have to vary, if for no other reason than to foster effective communication. Before pursuing that issue further, it is important to consider the impact of illegitimate structures on socialization of the young.

Illegitimate Structures and Traditions

Often inseparable from familial, neighborhood, and educational networks are illegitimate structures in the community. Many investigators have observed that much illegal behavior results from local traditions of group-supported delinquency, some of it criminally and career-oriented, that are transmitted to juveniles (McKay, 1949; Kobrin, 1951; Thrasher, 1963; Cressey, 1964). This was indicated when Short (1963) asked the staff of a YMCA gang program in Chicago: "What are the most significant institutions for your boys?" The answer from a detached worker was revealing. "I guess," he said, "I'd have to say the gang, the hangouts, drinking, parties in the area, and the police." While these would scarcely be acknowledged as "institutions" in the conventional sense, there was agreement among other workers that the answer of the first worker was correct. One of them would have added the boys' families to the list, but the overall conclusion was that the most viable places for the boys were the street corners, the pool halls, taverns, and the "quarter parties" in which adults as well as juveniles often participated. Relating this back to the system of formal norms, it is easy to see why law violations would be high in such an area. Many of the regular activities of these juveniles, although a normal part of daily life, were officially illegal. Without any deliberate intent to be delinquent, they were law violators by definition. Therefore, both the larger society and the juvenile have problems of social organization and of defining the behaviors that shall and shall not be tolerated. The potential for conflict is high.

Information regarding the network of illegitimate "institutions" for middle- and upper-class juveniles is not so readily available, documenting a serious omission in the literature. But with their drug scene, predatory crimes, and various forms of protest—some violent and some involving vandalism—there undoubtedly are parallel conflicts in these social strata. Illegal structures, as part of the lives of diverse juveniles, undoubtedly contribute to the problems of defining effective prevention programs.

Reactions within these structures are often mixed. In their study of various adolescent groups in a long-established Italian neighborhood, for example, Kobrin and his associates (1967) found that the prestige of sophisticated delinquents was greater than that of respectable boys. There was, they say, a touch of disdain for the respectables as "do-nothing" kids. The sources of this disdain, moreover, stemmed not only from the adolescent perspectives of the boys but from others in the neighborhood as well.

According to Kobrin et al., "there had existed for some time a firmly established integration of the legitimate and illegitimate elements of the community, manifested in a locally acknowledged alliance between the political leadership and that of the city's gambling, vice, and other rackets" (1967:101). Furthermore, the prestige of the respectable group may have suffered because their fathers tended to be civil servants in local government who had moved out of local social circles because they enjoyed some independence from the control of local politicians. Thus, this particular neighborhood seemed to be characterized, at the very least, by an ambivalence toward law-abiding and conventional structures, or, at the very most, by stronger ties to illegitimate than legitimate ones. Without doubt, the perceptions and behaviors of juveniles were influenced by these conflicting elements.

While this may well be an atypical community, much about it is familiar. As Daniel Bell (1959) has noted, Americans generally are characterized by an "extremism" in morality, yet they also have an "extraordinary" talent for compromise in politics and a "brawling" economic history. American culture, as Matza and Sykes (1961) suggest, is not a simple puritanism exemplified by the middle class. It is, instead, a complex and pluralistic culture in which, among other traditions, there is a subterranean tradition of deviance. These contradictory features, as a result, form the basis for an intimate and symbiotic relationship between crime and politics, crime and economic growth, and crime and social change—not an oppositional relationship. The tradition of wanting to get ahead by the shortest possible route, sometimes illegal, is no less an ethic than wanting to observe the law.

Adult crime, not just delinquency, has been a major means by which a variety of people have achieved the American success ideal and obtained respectability, if not for themselves, for their children. Hence, it is likely that this deviant tradition contributes more than we realize to the behavior of younger, as well as older, people—to adolescents from all strata and communities, not only those from the lower status and deprived communities.

The task of indicating how these and the legitimate networks in any locale induce conformity or deviance will occupy scientists for a long time. Yet, research and action can be used collaboratively in the interest of promoting productive roles for the young and giving them a larger stake in conformity. One method for this would be to accompany any attempt to alter basic institutions with the analysis and construction of neighborhood typologies by which the effects of differential organization could first be cataloged, and then empirically related to efforts at change.

For example, a neighborhood typology could specify how neighborhoods are ordered along one or more dimensions, what factors determine this ordering, and how these factors are related. The typology might incorporate racial, subcultural, and institutional variables that heretofore have been analyzed separately, and relate them to legitimate or illegitimate behavior. Such a framework might indicate with greater clarity what it is about institutional operations in some settings that provides young people with a stake in conformity, but in others produces alienation and deviance.

INTERACTIONAL ANALYSIS

Few can say why, even in high delinquency areas, most young people do not become official delinquents, or why, in low delinquency areas, some juveniles violate the law. What are the institutional forces, even in ghetto neighborhoods, that encourage and foster a legitimate identity in most people, or some of the opposite even in affluent neighborhoods? Questions of this type, organizational analyses alone cannot answer. Research and innovation on the interactional, face-to-face level are needed to provide more information on the way existing institutions organize and affect interpersonal behavior: (1) what is there about the individual in a given social context that might motivate him to want to participate in either a deviant or conformist game; and (2) assuming that he is inclined to play such a game, in what position and under what circumstances would he be inclined to play it?

Using a game analogy, Cohen and Short (1971) have suggested that most human life is organized in terms of social games. Each game operates according to a set of rules, some informal, some formal. These rules specify a set of positions or roles—third baseman, teacher, pupil, minister, clerk, or con politician—and indicate what the player of each position is supposed to do in relation to the players of other positions. They also include criteria for evaluating the success of the total enterprise or the contributions of individual players. In order to "fit in," as Cohen puts it,

> you have to know the rules; you have to "have a program," so that you may know what position each man, including yourself, is playing; and you have to know how to keep score. You cannot make sense out of what is going on, either as a participant or as an observer, unless you know the rules that define this particular sort of collective enterprise (1960:2).

The point is that each child's identity is constituted not just of characteristics peculiar to him but of the positions he plays in various games. Others are able to place him and have successful relations with him in terms of the positions he plays and the positions they play. His public reputation, his self-respect, depend upon how well he plays his position and, if he is a part of a team game, how well his team as a whole does. Too little attention has been paid, however, to game phenomena in understanding youthful behavior.

We have not been cognizant enough of the variations in rules operative among juveniles in different kinds of communities within the overall society. Thus, if one's own, or an official and conventional, definition of the situation were imposed upon them, one might not only fail to understand the games being played but would miss much that is significant. The same body of interaction occurring in different settings might have much different meaning. Behavior that might represent a disruption of ties between youth and adults in one setting might be just the opposite in another. For example, "It often shocks the unsophisticated to find that many *professional* criminals . . . are graduates of loving homes, who are successfully identifying with their fathers" (Glaser et al., 1966:20). Thus, we need to take cognizance of the way characteristics of different subcultures, neighborhoods, and communities are translated into action on the interactional level (Cohen & Short, 1971).

In the Italian neighborhood discussed above, the sophisticated delinquents were apparently tuned in to illegitimate as well as legitimate structures as a method of realizing their goals, while the "respectables," the children of civil servants, were oriented to the more conventional expectations of the larger community. There was not a serious disjunction between parents and children in either case, for both groups reflected the conflicting sets of expectations that existed side-by-side in the same neighborhood and were carried not only by juveniles but by parents.

In a black neighborhood, by contrast, Short and Strodtbeck (1965:275) suggest that reasonably common patterns between adults and children have relatively less meaning simply because neither adults nor children were tied very effectively either to legitimate or illegitimate structures.

> We firmly believe that need dispositions which are requited by gang membership arise in the interaction between the lack of preparation for school-type achievement in the home and in the absence of access to alternative adaptions to failure in the schools. . . . By the time boys acquire the identity associated with gang membership, a police record, or dropping out of school, the process of selectivity for failure is established (Short & Strodtbeck, 1965:275).

Thus, understanding and altering individual behavior in either case rests not only upon delineation of differences on an organizational level, but on the way differences are translated into action on the level of the child. Were policy-makers more sensitive to issues of this type, and were ongoing institutional programs better designed to account for them, socialization that was both more effective and yet more rewarding would be likely to occur.

THE INSTITUTIONAL BASE FOR PREVENTION

One problem of most prevention and control programs has been their insular character. Rather than being tied to a strong institutional base, they usually set themselves apart, even if located in the community. In terms of a medical model, they eschew a strong institutional affiliation and operate as an outpatient clinic, a recreation center, or a store-front hangout. Rather than fostering institutional change, therefore, their major targets have been single individuals. While useful functions are performed, little is done to affect the opportunity structures of the institutions themselves.

The problem is not easily solved. Polk and Kobrin (1972), however, make a strong case for using the school as the main institutional base for prevention efforts, especially when prevention is defined in terms of the means needed for young people to acquire a legitimate identity and a stake in conformity. Consider the evidence.

First, a series of studies indicates that poor academic achievement may be related more strongly to official delinquency than any other single variable (Call, 1965; Polk & Halferty, 1966; Empey & Lubeck, 1971). These studies indicate further that, while delinquency is uniformly low among boys from all social classes who are doing well in school, it is uniformly high among those who are doing poorly. Contrary to the usual assumption that it is membership in the lower class that is of crucial importance, these studies indicate that it is the child's achievement in school that is the deciding influence.

Second, in contrast to welfare, the church, or even the family, in some instances, the school is the one legitimate institution that cuts across all neighborhoods, social classes, and ethnic groups. Reflecting its capacity to have a lifelong impact on young people, the school is the one institution upon which employers and governments, as well as parents, rely for the preparation of the young for a legitimate and satisfying adulthood. As a consequence, it is the one setting where resources for the young are concentrated most heavily.

Third, the young have become superfluous in the world of work (Musgrove, 1969). The unskilled, highly routine jobs once reserved for them have disappeared, and child labor laws, designed ironically to prevent their exploitation, now exclude them from satisfying skilled work. Hence, the school has become a place of segregation for the young; if legitimate identities are not acquired there, they may never be acquired.

Finally, many cultural, recreational, and sports activities are funneled through the school. If not a part of the school, the school provides access to them. The consequence is that in many communities the school has become the major focal point for adolescent activity and a sense of belonging. Even dropouts, despite their feelings of alienation, congregate at the school during lunch, recess, or other free periods. It remains a place of considerable salience to them.

These are some of the reasons why the school occupies a position of crucial importance in crime prevention. As the major avenue for legitimate achievement, a sense of belonging, and competence, the school may now be the most important youth institution and source of socialization in society, although its potential is seldom fully realized. Without it, young persons are denied access to the roles that establish them as legitimate, meaningful people, with consequences that can be disastrous both in the short and the long run. Without the school in a major role, crime prevention, as defined here, could be seriously hampered.

Despite the central position of the school, Lemert is pessimistic regarding its ability to contribute to prevention. "There is," he says, "an empty ring to all such thinking, for substantially little seems to have come of it, either in the form of organizational innovation or new philosophy to comprehend youth problems under the aegis of education" (1971:19). Judged according to past performance, one would have to agree with this conclusion. Yet, it may be unfair to suggest that the school has proven any less capable than most other societal institutions in preventing high rates of crime in recent decades. The school is particularly subject to the values and whims of the citizenry at large, and just as they have proven ineffective, so the school has proven ineffective. If, however, the school could do the following kinds of things, its capacity to give the young a greater stake in conformity might be enhanced:

1. It could do more to analyze the peculiar characteristics of any neighborhood in which it is located. Its curriculum, its organization, and its activities could then be tailored to better fit the needs of the clientele it is trying to serve. Coupled with efforts to apply some of the principles of learning theory, the academic capabilities of the school could also be improved.

2. By facilitating its linkage with other legitimate institutions in the neighborhood, other school functions could also be performed more capably. It is often true, for example, that teachers have a difficult time establishing contacts with the parents of those children who are having the greatest difficulty. Yet, only rarely have efforts been made to solicit parents or others indigenous to the neighborhood to help with this problem, either as volunteers or as employed personnel. Rather than participating in some formalistic enterprise, such as PTA, parents could be asked to join with a specific group of their own children and their children's teachers in an endeavor to improve

the quality of the school experience. This would be tapping the direct vested interests of the persons involved, and would be establishing stronger ties between two major institutions.

3. Much attention could be paid to reducing the coercive methods of control upon which the school now relies so heavily, and seeking more effective normative means in their stead. As Polk and Kobrin (1972) suggest, self-study groups could be created whereby students and their families, and perhaps other adults, come together on a regular basis to analyze and deal with problems that are of concern to all. Far too often, however, there is a tendency for some teachers, administrators, and many students to think only of coercive controls. That is nonsense. No organization can exist without norms and some dedication to the collective welfare. In fact, in the Provo Experiment (Empey & Erickson, 1972), the one organizational component from which delinquents said they learned the most and gained the greatest personal benefits was that in which they helped to solve problems, make decisions, and even impose controls. Their participation in these activities seemed to reduce their sense of alienation and to promote the normative power of the organization. Added to the school, therefore, such activities might address a much larger range of childhood and adolescent difficulties than mere academic performance.

4. Traditionally, the school has failed to provide the young with the kinds of experiences that give adults a sense of usefulness and competence. Yet there are any number of constructive roles students do not now play that could be sponsored by the school: (a) in conjunction with school personnel, analyses could be made of the school's tracking, stratification, discipline, and sociometric systems to see if, in some way, these could be changed to enhance involvement rather than alienation; (b) tutorial programs could be organized so that students at all levels help others; (c) drug education programs or programs designed to reduce racial conflict or conflict with the police could be organized, and students given the chance to educate adults as well as the reverse; (d) the school could act as an advocate in behalf of its students so they contribute a youth perspective to the policy decisions made by many community groups and agencies; and (e) the school could make it possible for students to participate in constructive community programs—cleaning up the environment, registering voters, participating in crisis-intervention programs, and so on. To do these things, the school would not have to lower its academic standards; rather, the latter could be enhanced by firsthand experience and a greater sense of self-worth.

It is difficult to conceive of any societal institution in which, if significant changes were made, greater results could be achieved. The school has access to virtually every young person. In many neighborhoods, it may be the only institution in which a majority of the people, young and old, have a vested interest. Hence, the opportunity it has to enlarge the number of responsible and gratifying roles for the young is probably unexcelled. Should it do that, it could have the effect of creating among young people a firmer attachment to the aims and procedures of legitimate institutions, and of reducing the probability of criminal involvement.

It must be recognized, however, that without an enlargement of its mandate, a change in educational philosophy, and greatly increased resources, the educational system could not add to its present burdens those implied here. Ordinarily, the primary institutions in society, such as the school, do not see it as their responsibility to prevent crime and delinquency. This is due probably to two things: (1) the tendency to define prevention in terms of controlling deviance rather than enhancing legitimacy; and (2) the evolution of our institutions in the twentieth century.

For a long period, responsibility for prevention, such as it was, was assigned to the agencies of control—the police, courts, and corrections—not to such agencies as the school. Not only did this free the latter from responsibility for dealing with difficult young people, but it encouraged the agencies of social control to develop a vested interest in receiving them. Their powers, budgets, and bureaucratic structures depended, in part, on maintaining that interest. In recent years, of course, the growing interest in diversion has done much to change this state of affairs. But, while diversion has emphasized a reduction in police roles, it has not really stressed the importance of an increase in the role of the educational establishment. Until that perspective is changed on the part of the citizenry as well as among educators, support for the kinds of changes proposed here may not be forthcoming.

AGENCIES OF SOCIAL CONTROL

Turning now to the agencies of social control, it should be noted that nothing said heretofore should be construed as suggesting that the control agencies should go out of the prevention business. The issue is not whether they have a role to play, but what that role should be.

In terms of preventing cases of secondary deviance or a recurrence of criminal behavior in convicted offenders, they have a central role to play. However, using the definition of prevention we have, their role is in need of clarification. Consider first a revision of legal rules and the possible consequences it might have for the criminal justice system relative to the illegitimate structures in society.

Preventing Organized and Professional Crime

Contrary to the traditional focus on processing the alcoholic, the homosexual, or the dependent juvenile, prevention efforts should address organized criminal and delinquent structures, and devise ways to deal with them. Despite continuing and growing evidence that these structures are related in a symbiotic way to prevailing business and political activities, few inroads have been made upon them. For example, greater concentration on the political and economic methods used by organized crime to purvey harmful drugs to the young could have significant consequences for prevention.

There seems little doubt that large quantities of dangerous drugs are being produced by legitimate firms, fed into illegitimate channels, and then directed to young people. The federal government regulates the amounts of dangerous drugs produced domestically, but evidently not well enough to prevent abuse. The public seems more concerned with controlling surface symptoms of drug problems—the addicted thieves and muggers who prey upon others to maintain their habit—than with finding and convicting the organized professionals who supply dangerous drugs. The most effective prevention in this case would be to shut off the sources of supply. By the same token, a greater focus upon the roots of other kinds of predatory crime—truck hijacking, auto theft rings, etc.—and upon the economic and political bodies that give them sustenance, could do much to allay public fears and to inhibit the recruitment of the young to criminal careers.

Criminal Sanctions and Deterrence

A mistaken assumption often made about those who advocate reforms of the type mentioned throughout this analysis is that they do not view crime as a serious problem. That they advocate a kind of permissiveness in which crime would only be encouraged, not deterred, is not true. But respect for the law and the use of criminal sanctions as a deterrent to the would-be predator has certain prerequisites: (1) there must be consensus on the criminal acts that are disavowed—a set of statutes concerned only with harm to persons or property might help to accomplish this; (2) the response of the criminal justice system to predatory acts must be swift and efficient; and (3) the convicted person must learn from his experience, and procure a set of alternatives to his criminal behavior.

Contrary to much public opinion, there is evidence that the fear of punishment, as well as the anticipation of reward, has a strong influence on human behavior (Bandura & Walters, 1963; Bandura, 1969:118–216; Empey & Erickson, 1972:chaps. 4, 5). Even an abstract belief that the probability of punishment is high may directly affect the likelihood of deviant behavior (Jensen, 1969). These and other studies suggest that punishment may deter, either when it is personalized or when it is believed that punishment is a probability.

On the other hand, available evidence documents a striking contrast between the belief that the criminal justice system can accomplish these ends and the way it actually operates. A clogged and overburdened system permits the most serious offenders to delay or escape prosecution, while the poor and ignorant are most likely to be prosecuted or to be treated unjustly (cf. Wittner, 1970:20–25). Thus, the system at present is not only failing to protect society from serious, criminal predators, but is also unjust and inefficient.

Because current trends and projections for the system are so preposterous, they are labeled by McEachern et al. (1970:24) as a potentially absurd system. In using the term *absurd,* these investigators indicated that if solutions are to be found vast and innovative changes will be required—less concern with nonpredatory acts now labeled as crime, a greater concentration upon the elimination of organized criminal structures, and a more efficient and progressive method for dealing with offenders. Were these steps taken, the chances would be increased that the agents of control could deter, and thus prevent, more crime.

Diversion by the Agencies of Control

With the growing emphasis upon the negative effects of official labeling, there has been an increasing tendency to divert offenders, especially juveniles, from the criminal justice system. Methods of help and control that have been utilized most effectively in middle-class communities—suspended action by the police, referral to parents, or placement in some remedial program—have been promoted in slum and lower-class settings so that diversion can be made more effective for the youth who live there. The basic goal seems to be to inhibit acquisition of a deviant identity and commission of acts of secondary deviance. To accomplish that, youth from all strata and ethnic groups require equal opportunity.

Lemert suggests that the police are in a crucial position to effect diversionary programs. "[They] encounter youth problems more frequently than other community agencies; they meet the problems at the time of their occurrence; and they wield a great deal of coercive and symbolic authority" (1971:68–69).

The available evidence regarding the willingness of police to divert juveniles, however, is mixed. In two different studies of a large number of police departments (Goldman, 1969; Klein, 1970), the proportion of juvenile arrestees who were diverted rather than referred to court varied from a low of 2 percent in one department to a high of 82 percent in another. Such striking evidence indicates that to know why some juveniles become official delinquents while others do not, one should know the determinants of such widely discrepant rates.

Several determinants have been suggested by research—the social-class level or ethnic background of the juvenile (Goldman, 1969), his demeanor at the time of his arrest (Piliavin & Briar, 1964; Black & Reiss, 1970), whether the police were highly professionalized or indigenous to a neighborhood (Wilson, 1970), or whether a complainant was present to insist that the juvenile be officially charged and processed (Black & Reiss, 1970). By no means were the determinants uniform, suggesting the lack of anything approaching a universal police policy toward diversion and its utility.

Significantly, in his study of forty-six police departments in Los Angeles, Klein (1970) found that one crucial and deciding influence was whether the police had an agency, readily available, to which they could divert a juvenile—a counseling program, a capable parent, or an ongoing program of some sort. This finding is central to the underlying assumptions of this chapter because it suggests that, even if police practices were to become more uniform, the arresting officer would still have to look for some neighborhood resource to which a juvenile could be referred. If young people are to be diverted from the justice-correction system, the primary institutions in the community—the family, school, and neighborhood—will have to take up the slack. As with primary prevention, nonjustice agencies are crucial to the success of secondary prevention.

These reasons warrant skepticism about the capacities of large and bureaucratic systems, such as probation departments or large community mental health programs, to perform this service. Instead, programs of diversion, like those of primary prevention, may have to be neighborhood-specific—related to the immediate context in which the individual lives. This is especially true for juveniles, as they often fail to see the relevance of programs that are divorced from the realities that confront them daily.

A number of neighborhood programs now use indigenous people who either work alone or in concert with the police. In some cases, these programs have used ex-felons, ex-addicts, police aides, paraprofessionals, or black and brown power advocates to serve as a resource to whom juveniles could be referred. While such programs have much in their favor, problems of continuity, funding, and lack of a strong institutional base continue to plague them, just as they plague other prevention programs. No less than others, anyone diverted from prosecution requires enduring opportunities for education, work, and even food and shelter. It is for these reasons that strategies of secondary and primary diversion require planning and resources that are immediately relevant to particular kinds of problems in specific kinds of neighborhood and community settings. Grand and bureaucratic strategies that do not take these factors into account are prone to failure.

SUMMARY AND CONCLUSIONS

This chapter has noted that, in response to high crime and delinquency rates, some segments of society are inclined to evoke a war on crime, implying that through a militaristic emphasis upon law and order, law-violating behavior can be controlled. Other segments, relying heavily upon the labeling perspective, have suggested that society's customary ways of responding to delinquents and criminals may have done more to incubate the crime problem than to solve it. Diversion from, rather than involvement in, the criminal justice system is implied as the most appropriate approach to prevention. It was pointed out, however, that both social movements failed to address a series of fundamental issues.

An emphasis upon repression or diversion fails to account for the means by which a person acquires a legitimate identity and a stake in conformity. These factors, rather than fear of punishment or avoidance of a deviant identity, constitute a primary focus on prevention.

As a method of approaching prevention in these terms, certain possibilities were suggested:

1. The system of legal rules should be changed to eliminate nonpredatory, victimless crimes from the list of criminal offenses;

2. the network of legitimate socializing institutions and the illegitimate structures in any particular locale or neighborhood should be analyzed and prevention programs should be adapted to those explicit circumstances, for the success of these efforts depends upon the extent to which changes can be introduced into the specific institutional networks in which young people are socialized; and

3. the agents of social control should be freed to concentrate upon predatory crimes and the illegitimate structures that are at the root of the crime problem, and they should also be encouraged, in collaboration with neighborhood-specific socializing institutions, to divert many more offenders from the justice system as a means of preventing the incidence of secondary deviance.

REFERENCES

Bandura, Albert.
　　1969　　Principles of Behavior Modification. New York: Holt, Rinehart & Winston.

Bandura, Albert, and Richard H. Walters.
　　1963　　Social Learning and Personality Development. New York: Holt, Rinehart & Winston.

Becker, Howard S.
　　1963　　The Outsiders. New York: Free Press of Glencoe.

Bell, Daniel.
　　1959　　The End of Ideology. Glencoe, Ill.: Free Press.

Bittner, Egon.
　　1970　　The Functions of the Police in Modern Society. Publication No. 2059. Washington, D.C.: U.S. Government Printing Office.

Black, Donald J., and Albert J. Reiss, Jr.
　　1970　　"Police control of juveniles." American Sociological Review 35(February): 63–77.

Blumer, Herbert.
　　1969　　"Sociological implications of the thoughts of George Herbert Mead," in Herbert Blumer (ed.), Symbolic Interactionism. Englewood Cliffs, N.J.: Prentice-Hall.

Call, Donald J.
　　1965　　"Frustration and noncommitment." Ph.D. dissertation, University of Oregon.

Carter, Robert M., and G. Thomas Gitchoff.
　　1970　　"An alternative to youthful mass disorder." The Police Chief No. 37(July): 52–56.

Chilton, Ronald J., and Gerald E. Markle.
  1972   "Family disruption, delinquent conduct and the effect of subclassification."
         American Sociological Review 37(February):93–99.

Christensen, Ronald.
  1967   "Projected percentage of U.S. population with criminal arrest and con-
         viction records," in President's Commission on Law Enforcement and
         Administration of Justice, Task Force Report: Science and Technology.
         Washington, D.C.: U.S. Government Printing Office.

Cloward, Richard A., and Lloyd E. Ohlin.
  1960   Delinquency and Opportunity: A Theory of Delinquent Gangs. New York:
         Free Press of Glencoe.

Cohen, Albert K.
  1960   "Delinquency as culturally patterned and group supported behavior." Ad-
         dress to the 12th Annual Training Institute for Probation, Parole and Insti-
         tutional Staff, San Francisco (mimeographed).

Cohen, Albert K., and James F. Short, Jr.
  1971   "Juvenile delinquency," in Robert K. Merton and Robert A. Nisbet (eds.),
         Contemporary Social Problems. New York: Harcourt, Brace & World.

Cressey, Donald R.
  1964   Crime and Differential Association. The Hague: Martinus Nijhoff.
  1965   "Theoretical foundations for using criminals in the rehabilitation of crimi-
         nals," in Hans W. Mattick (ed.), The Future of Imprisonment in a Free
         Society. Chicago: St. Leonards House.

Dahrendorf, Rolf.
  1958   "Out of utopia: toward a reorientation in sociological analysis." American
         Journal of Sociology 67(September):115–127.
  1959   Class and Class Conflict in Industrial Society. Stanford: Stanford University
         Press.

Davis, Fred.
  1961   "Deviance disavowal: the management of strain interaction by the visibly
         handicapped." Social Problems 9(Fall):120–132.

Durkheim, Emile.
  1895   The Rules of Sociological Method. Eighth Edition. Translated by Sarah A.
         Solovay and John H. Mueller. Edited by G. E. G. Catlin. Chicago: University
         of Chicago Press (1938 edition).

Empey, LaMar T.
  1967   "Delinquency theory and recent research." Journal of Research in Crime
         and Delinquency 3(January):28–41.

Empey, LaMar T., and Maynard L. Erickson.
  1972   The Provo Experiment: Evaluating Community Control of Delinquency.
         Lexington, Mass.: D. C. Heath.

Empey, LaMar T., and Steven G. Lubeck.
  1971   Explaining Delinquency: Construction, Test and Reformulation of a Socio-
         logical Theory. Lexington, Mass.: D. C. Heath.

Erikson, Kai T.
  1962   "Notes on the sociology of deviance." Social Problems 9(Spring):307–314.

Federal Bureau of Investigation (F.B.I.)
 1969   Crime in the United States: Uniform Crime Reports—1968. Washington,
        D.C.: U.S. Government Printing Office.

Gibbs, Jack P.
 1966   "Conceptions of deviant behavior: the old and the new." Pacific Sociologi-
        cal Review 9(Spring):9–14.

Glaser, Daniel.
 1968   "Research and theory on deviant behavior: nomothetic or ideographic."
        Paper presented for discussion at roundtable luncheon, American Socio-
        logical Association, August 28.
 1971   Social Deviance. Chicago: Markham.

Glaser, Daniel, Donald Kenefick, and Vincent O'Leary.
 1966   The Violent Offender. Washington, D.C.: U.S. Government Printing Office.

Goldman, Nathan.
 1969   "The differential selection of juvenile offenders for court appearance." Pp.
        264–290 in William Chambliss (ed.), Crime and the Legal Process. New
        York: McGraw-Hill.

Hathaway, Starke R., Elio D. Monachesi, and Laurence A. Young.
 1960   "Delinquency rates and personality." Journal of Criminal Law, Criminology
        and Police Science 50(February):433–440.

Hirschi, Travis.
 1969   Causes of Delinquency. Berkeley: University of California Press.

Janowitz, Morris.
 1968   Social Control of Escalated Riots. Chicago: University of Chicago Center for
        Policy Studies.

Jensen, Gary F.
 1969   " 'Crime doesn't pay': correlates of shared misunderstanding." Social Prob-
        lems 17(Fall):189–201.

Kitsuse, John I.
 1962   "Societal reaction to deviant behavior: problems of theory and method."
        Social Problems 9(Winter):247–256.

Kitsuse, John I., and Aaron V. Cicourel.
 1963   "A note on the uses of official statistics." Social Problems 11(Fall):131–139.

Klein, Malcolm W.
 1970   "Police processing of juvenile offenders: toward the development of juvenile
        system rates." Los Angeles County Sub-Regional Board, California Council
        on Criminal Justice, part III.

Kobrin, Solomon.
 1951   "The conflict of values in delinquency areas." American Sociological Review
        16(October):653–661.

Kobrin, Solomon, Joseph Puntil, and Emil Peluso.
 1967   "Criteria of status among street corner groups." Journal of Research in
        Crime and Delinquency 4(January):98–118.

Kvaraceus, William C.
 1964   "World-wide story." The Unesco Courier 12(May).

LaGache, D.
    1950   Psycho-Criminogenese: Tenth General Report. Paris: 2nd International Congress of Criminology.

Lasswell, H. D.
    1950   World Politics and Personal Insecurity. Glencoe, Ill.: Free Press.

Lemert, Edwin M.
    1951   Social Pathology. New York: McGraw-Hill.
    1971   Instead of Court: Diversion in Juvenile Justice. National Institute of Mental Health, Center for the Study of Crime and Delinquency. Washington, D.C.: U.S. Government Printing Office.

McEachern, A. W., R. M. Carter, H. Adelman, and J. R. Newman.
    1970   Criminal Justice Simulation Study: Some Preliminary Projections. Los Angeles: University of Southern California, Public Systems Research Institute.

McKay, Henry D.
    1949   "The neighborhood and child conduct." Annals of the American Academy of Political and Social Science 261(January):32–41.

Matza, David, and Gresham M. Sykes.
    1961   "Juvenile delinquency and subterranean values." American Sociological Review 26(October):712–719.

Merton, Robert K.
    1957   Social Theory and Social Structure. Glencoe, Ill.: Free Press.

Monahan, Thomas P.
    1957   "Family status and the delinquent child: a reappraisal and some new findings." Social Forces 35(March):250–258.

Morris, Norval.
    1966   "Impediments to penal reform." University of Chicago Law Review 33(Summer):627–656.

Morris, Norval, and Gordon Hawkins.
    1970   The Honest Politician's Guide to Crime Control. Chicago: University of Chicago Press.

Musgrove, Frank.
    1969   "The problems of youth and the structure of society in England." Youth and Society 1(September):38–58.

Ohlin, Lloyd E.
    1970   A Situational Approach to Delinquency Prevention. Washington, D.C.: U.S. Government Printing Office.

Piliavin, Irving, and Scott Briar.
    1964   "Police encounters with juveniles." American Journal of Sociology 70(September):206–214.

Polk, Kenneth, and David S. Halferty.
    1966   "Adolescence, commitment and delinquency." Journal of Research in Crime and Delinquency 4(July):82–96.

Polk, Kenneth, and Solomon Kobrin.
    1972   Delinquency Prevention through Youth Development. Washington, D.C.: U.S. Government Printing Office.

President's Commission on Law Enforcement and Administration of Justice.
    1967a   Task Force Report: Juvenile Delinquency and Youth Crime. Washington, D.C.: U.S. Government Printing Office.
    1967b   The Challenge of Crime in a Free Society. Washington, D.C.: U.S. Government Printing Office.
    1967c   Task Force Report: Corrections. Washington, D.C.: U.S. Government Printing Office.

Rubin, Ted.
    1970   "Law as an agent of delinquency prevention." Paper presented at the California Conference on Prevention Strategy. Sacramento: California Youth Authority.

Schrag, Clarence.
    1962   "Delinquency and opportunity: analysis of a theory." Sociology and Social Research 46(January):167–175.

Schuessler, Karl, and Donald R. Cressey.
    1950   "Personality characteristics of criminals." American Journal of Sociology 55(March):476–484.

Schur, Edwin M.
    1971   Labeling Deviant Behavior: Its Sociological Implications. New York: Harper & Row.

Seymour, John A.
    1971   "The current status of youth service bureaus." Chicago: University of Chicago Center for Studies in Criminal Justice (mimeographed).

Short, James F., Jr.
    1963   "Street corner groups and patterns of delinquency." American Catholic Sociological Review 24(Spring):13–32.
    1965   "Social structure and group processes in explanation of gang delinquency." Pp. 158–188 in Muzafer Sherif and Carolyn Sherif (eds.), Problems of Youth. Chicago: Aldine.

Short, James F., Jr., and Fred L. Strodtbeck.
    1965   Group Process and Gang Delinquency. Chicago: University of Chicago Press.

Shulman, Harry M.
    1949   "The family and juvenile delinquency." Annals of the American Academy of Political and Social Science 26(January):21–31.

Silver, Isidore.
    1968   "The president's crime commission revisited." New York University Law Review 43:916–966.

Smith, Robert L.
    1971   A Quiet Revolution: Probation Subsidy. Social and Rehabilitation Service, Youth Development and Delinquency Prevention Administration, Department of Health, Education and Welfare. Washington, D.C.: U.S. Government Printing Office.

Tannenbaum, Frank.
    1938   Crime and the Community. New York: Columbia University Press.

Thrasher, Frederic M.
    1963   The Gang. Revised Edition. Chicago: University of Chicago Press.

Toby, Jackson.
   1957a   "Social disorganization and a stake in conformity." Journal of Criminal
           Law, Criminology and Police Science 48(May–June):12–17.
   1957b   "The differential impact of family disorganization." American Sociological
           Review 22(October):505–515.
Wheeler, Stanton, Leonard S. Cottrell, and Anne Romasco.
   1967   "Juvenile delinquency: its prevention and control," in President's Commis-
           sion on Law Enforcement and Administration of Justice, Task Force Report:
           Juvenile Delinquency and Youth Crime. Washington, D.C.: U.S. Govern-
           ment Printing Office.
Whyte, William F.
   1955   Street Corner Society. Chicago: University of Chicago Press.
Wilson, James Q.
   1970   "The police and the delinquent in two cities." Pp. 111–117 in Peter G. Gara-
           bedian (ed.), Becoming Delinquent. Chicago: Aldine.
Wittner, Dale.
   1970   "Log jam in our courts." Life 69(August 7):18–26.

Name Index

Clark, Dismas, 896
Clark, G. R., 136, 155, 156
Clark, J., 158
Clark, John P., 453, 455, 462, 465, 477n, 486n,
    487n, 488, 491, 492, 494
Clark, Ramsey, 378n, 384
Clark, W. G., 171
Clarke, Dorris, 32
Clay, Henry, 325n
Cleaver, E., 275, 294
Cleckley, H., 144, 145, 157
Clemente, C. D., 101, 157, 160, 162, 163, 169
Clements, C. B., 763, 773
Clements, S. D., 129, 157
Clemmer, Donald, 328n, 384
Climent, C. E., 154
Clinard, Marshall B., 68, 69, 79, 143, 157, 284,
    294, 295, 299, 345, 361, 385, 430, 443,
    447
Clough, Shepard B., 303, 385
Cloward, Richard A., 7n, 40, 88, 94, 98, 189,
    190, 191, 199, 404, 416, 420, 421, 443,
    706, 720, 722, 741, 992, 1001n, 1019,
    1095, 1119
Coates, Robert B., 1019
Coates, Robert M., 347n, 352, 385
Coatman. John, 495, 504
Cobb, J. A., 775
Cobbs, P. M., 411, 444
Cohen, Albert K., 7n, 40, 88, 94, 98, 189, 197,
    199, 272, 297, 404, 405, 415, 421, 443,
    706, 719, 720, 741, 1111, 1112, 1119
Cohen, A. R., 711, 741
Cohen, B., 415, 443
Cohen, Fred, 922, 942
Cohen, Harold L., 731, 741, 759, 773, 865, 876,
    884, 891, 892
Cohen, J. S., 296
Cohen, Jerome A., 581, 582, 583, 584, 585, 586,
    587, 589
Cohen, L., 289, 294
Cohen, M., 120, 157
Cohen, M., 838n, 844
Cohen, Stanley, 19, 20
Cohn, S. I., 508, 519, 520, 522, 524
Cohn, Yona, 951, 966
Coke, Edward, 23, 46
Colbeck, Dinty, 364
Colburn, J. G. W., 334, 385
Cole, B. A., 524
Coleman, James S., 93, 98
Coles, R., 197, 199
Collier, J., Jr., 510, 520
Colman, A. D., 761, 773
Colombo, Joseph, 378

Colosimo, "Diamond Jim," 363, 364
Colquohon, Patrick, 495, 504
Conger, John J., 75, 79
Conklin, J. E., 297
Conner, R. L., 106, 113, 122, 157
Conners, C. K., 150, 151, 157, 158, 164
Connor, A., 173
Connor, Thomas, 229, 230
Conwell, Chic, 311
Cook, D. J., 348, 351, 352, 385
Cook, Fred, 354, 385
Cooper, A. J., 152, 157
Cooper, C. R., 328, 330, 342, 342n, 353, 355, 385
Cooper, D. B., 361
Cooper, F. S., 519
Coppen, A., 124, 125, 157
Corey, Herbert, 354, 385
Cormier, B. M., 185, 199
Corsi, J. R., 439, 446
Cortes, J. B., 109, 141, 157, 865, 892
Cory, Donald C., 328n, 385
Cosmides, G. J., 519
Costello, A. E., 341, 385
Costello, Frank, 364, 367, 376, 383, 395
Cottingham, L., 774
Cottrell, Leonard S., 475n, 491, 1123
Coulson, N. J., 540n, 543, 589
Court Brown, W. M., 134n, 157, 162
Cowan, Samuel H., 17
Cox, A. E., 290, 294
Coxe, John E., 370, 385
Cragg, K., 544, 589
Cranefield, E., 1047
Crapsey, Edward, 303, 305, 307, 317, 320, 336,
    341, 385
Crawford, L. Y., 415, 420, 445, 722, 742
Crawford, T. E., 351, 385
Cressey, Donald R., 7n, 40, 42, 65, 68, 70, 71,
    72, 74, 79, 80, 82, 83, 92, 94, 99, 101,
    109, 171, 191, 206, 228, 232, 285, 294,
    299, 313, 314, 361, 365, 367, 367n, 378,
    385, 399, 448, 865, 867, 894, 914, 933,
    942, 947, 956, 967, 978, 989, 992, 993,
    1000n, 1018, 1019, 1058, 1091, 1092,
    1098, 1101, 1109, 1119, 1122
Crisafulli, A., 196, 200
Crofton, T. A., 156
Crofton, Walter, 911
Croker, Richard, 324, 391
Cromwell, Oliver, 24
Crookston, Peter, 305n, 385
Crossbiter, Laurence, 317
Crossley, Helen M., 230
Crout, J. R., 524
Crowther, C., 733, 742

Subject Index

Index of Legal Cases

PRINTED IN U.S.A.